Dictionary of Literary Biography

1 *The American Renaissance in New England*, edited by Joel Myerson (1978)

2 *American Novelists Since World War II*, edited by Jeffrey Helterman and Richard Layman (1978)

3 *Antebellum Writers in New York and the South*, edited by Joel Myerson (1979)

4 *American Writers in Paris, 1920-1939*, edited by Karen Lane Rood (1980)

5 *American Poets Since World War II*, 2 parts, edited by Donald J. Greiner (1980)

6 *American Novelists Since World War II, Second Series*, edited by James E. Kibler Jr. (1980)

7 *Twentieth-Century American Dramatists*, 2 parts, edited by John MacNicholas (1981)

8 *Twentieth-Century American Science-Fiction Writers*, 2 parts, edited by David Cowart and Thomas L. Wymer (1981)

9 *American Novelists, 1910-1945*, 3 parts, edited by James J. Martine (1981)

10 *Modern British Dramatists, 1900-1945*, 2 parts, edited by Stanley Weintraub (1982)

11 *American Humorists, 1800-1950*, 2 parts, edited by Stanley Trachtenberg (1982)

12 *American Realists and Naturalists*, edited by Donald Pizer and Earl N. Harbert (1982)

13 *British Dramatists Since World War II*, 2 parts, edited by Stanley Weintraub (1982)

14 *British Novelists Since 1960*, 2 parts, edited by Jay L. Halio (1983)

15 *British Novelists, 1930-1959*, 2 parts, edited by Bernard Oldsey (1983)

16 *The Beats: Literary Bohemians in Postwar America*, 2 parts, edited by Ann Charters (1983)

17 *Twentieth-Century American Historians*, edited by Clyde N. Wilson (1983)

18 *Victorian Novelists After 1885*, edited by Ira B. Nadel and William E. Fredeman (1983)

19 *British Poets, 1880-1914*, edited by Donald E. Stanford (1983)

20 *British Poets, 1914-1945*, edited by Donald E. Stanford (1983)

21 *Victorian Novelists Before 1885*, edited by Ira B. Nadel and William E. Fredeman (1983)

22 *American Writers for Children, 1900-1960*, edited by John Cech (1983)

23 *American Newspaper Journalists, 1873-1900*, edited by Perry J. Ashley (1983)

24 *American Colonial Writers, 1606-1734*, edited by Emory Elliott (1984)

25 *American Newspaper Journalists, 1901-1925*, edited by Perry J. Ashley (1984)

26 *American Screenwriters*, edited by Robert E. Morsberger, Stephen O. Lesser, and Randall Clark (1984)

27 *Poets of Great Britain and Ireland, 1945-1960*, edited by Vincent B. Sherry Jr. (1984)

28 *Twentieth-Century American-Jewish Fiction Writers*, edited by Daniel Walden (1984)

29 *American Newspaper Journalists, 1926-1950*, edited by Perry J. Ashley (1984)

30 *American Historians, 1607-1865*, edited by Clyde N. Wilson (1984)

31 *American Colonial Writers, 1735-1781*, edited by Emory Elliott (1984)

32 *Victorian Poets Before 1850*, edited by William E. Fredeman and Ira B. Nadel (1984)

33 *Afro-American Fiction Writers After 1955*, edited by Thadious M. Davis and Trudier Harris (1984)

34 *British Novelists, 1890-1929: Traditionalists*, edited by Thomas F. Staley (1985)

35 *Victorian Poets After 1850*, edited by William E. Fredeman and Ira B. Nadel (1985)

36 *British Novelists, 1890-1929: Modernists*, edited by Thomas F. Staley (1985)

37 *American Writers of the Early Republic*, edited by Emory Elliott (1985)

38 *Afro-American Writers After 1955: Dramatists and Prose Writers*, edited by Thadious M. Davis and Trudier Harris (1985)

39 *British Novelists, 1660-1800*, 2 parts, edited by Martin C. Battestin (1985)

40 *Poets of Great Britain and Ireland Since 1960*, 2 parts, edited by Vincent B. Sherry Jr. (1985)

41 *Afro-American Poets Since 1955*, edited by Trudier Harris and Thadious M. Davis (1985)

42 *American Writers for Children Before 1900*, edited by Glenn E. Estes (1985)

43 *American Newspaper Journalists, 1690-1872*, edited by Perry J. Ashley (1986)

44 *American Screenwriters, Second Series*, edited by Randall Clark, Robert E. Morsberger, and Stephen O. Lesser (1986)

45 *American Poets, 1880-1945, First Series*, edited by Peter Quartermain (1986)

46 *American Literary Publishing Houses, 1900-1980: Trade and Paperback*, edited by Peter Dzwonkoski (1986)

47 *American Historians, 1866-1912*, edited by Clyde N. Wilson (1986)

48 *American Poets, 1880-1945, Second Series*, edited by Peter Quartermain (1986)

49 *American Literary Publishing Houses, 1638-1899*, 2 parts, edited by Peter Dzwonkoski (1986)

50 *Afro-American Writers Before the Harlem Renaissance*, edited by Trudier Harris (1986)

51 *Afro-American Writers from the Harlem Renaissance to 1940*, edited by Trudier Harris (1987)

52 *American Writers for Children Since 1960: Fiction*, edited by Glenn E. Estes (1986)

53 *Canadian Writers Since 1960, First Series*, edited by W. H. New (1986)

54 *American Poets, 1880-1945, Third Series*, 2 parts, edited by Peter Quartermain (1987)

55 *Victorian Prose Writers Before 1867*, edited by William B. Thesing (1987)

56 *German Fiction Writers, 1914-1945*, edited by James Hardin (1987)

57 *Victorian Prose Writers After 1867*, edited by William B. Thesing (1987)

58 *Jacobean and Caroline Dramatists*, edited by Fredson Bowers (1987)

59 *American Literary Critics and Scholars, 1800-1850*, edited by John W. Rathbun and Monica M. Grecu (1987)

60 *Canadian Writers Since 1960, Second Series*, edited by W. H. New (1987)

61 *American Writers for Children Since 1960: Poets, Illustrators, and Nonfiction Authors*, edited by Glenn E. Estes (1987)

62 *Elizabethan Dramatists*, edited by Fredson Bowers (1987)

63 *Modern American Critics, 1920-1955*, edited by Gregory S. Jay (1988)

64 *American Literary Critics and Scholars, 1850-1880*, edited by John W. Rathbun and Monica M. Grecu (1988)

65 *French Novelists, 1900-1930*, edited by Catharine Savage Brosman (1988)

66 *German Fiction Writers, 1885-1913*, 2 parts, edited by James Hardin (1988)

67 *Modern American Critics Since 1955*, edited by Gregory S. Jay (1988)

68 *Canadian Writers, 1920-1959, First Series*, edited by W. H. New (1988)

69 *Contemporary German Fiction Writers, First Series*, edited by Wolfgang D. Elfe and James Hardin (1988)

70 *British Mystery Writers, 1860-1919*, edited by Bernard Benstock and Thomas F. Staley (1988)

71 *American Literary Critics and Scholars, 1880-1900*, edited by John W. Rathbun and Monica M. Grecu (1988)

72 *French Novelists, 1930-1960*, edited by Catharine Savage Brosman (1988)

73 *American Magazine Journalists, 1741-1850*, edited by Sam G. Riley (1988)

74 *American Short-Story Writers Before 1880*, edited by Bobby Ellen Kimbel, with the assistance of William E. Grant (1988)

75 *Contemporary German Fiction Writers, Second Series*, edited by Wolfgang D. Elfe and James Hardin (1988)

76 *Afro-American Writers, 1940-1955*, edited by Trudier Harris (1988)

77 *British Mystery Writers, 1920-1939*, edited by Bernard Benstock and Thomas F. Staley (1988)

78 *American Short-Story Writers, 1880-1910,* edited by Bobby Ellen Kimbel, with the assistance of William E. Grant (1988)

79 *American Magazine Journalists, 1850-1900,* edited by Sam G. Riley (1988)

80 *Restoration and Eighteenth-Century Dramatists, First Series,* edited by Paula R. Backscheider (1989)

81 *Austrian Fiction Writers, 1875-1913,* edited by James Hardin and Donald G. Daviau (1989)

82 *Chicano Writers, First Series,* edited by Francisco A. Lomelí and Carl R. Shirley (1989)

83 *French Novelists Since 1960,* edited by Catharine Savage Brosman (1989)

84 *Restoration and Eighteenth-Century Dramatists, Second Series,* edited by Paula R. Backscheider (1989)

85 *Austrian Fiction Writers After 1914,* edited by James Hardin and Donald G. Daviau (1989)

86 *American Short-Story Writers, 1910-1945, First Series,* edited by Bobby Ellen Kimbel (1989)

87 *British Mystery and Thriller Writers Since 1940, First Series,* edited by Bernard Benstock and Thomas F. Staley (1989)

88 *Canadian Writers, 1920-1959, Second Series,* edited by W. H. New (1989)

89 *Restoration and Eighteenth-Century Dramatists, Third Series,* edited by Paula R. Backscheider (1989)

90 *German Writers in the Age of Goethe, 1789-1832,* edited by James Hardin and Christoph E. Schweitzer (1989)

91 *American Magazine Journalists, 1900-1960, First Series,* edited by Sam G. Riley (1990)

92 *Canadian Writers, 1890-1920,* edited by W. H. New (1990)

93 *British Romantic Poets, 1789-1832, First Series,* edited by John R. Greenfield (1990)

94 *German Writers in the Age of Goethe: Sturm und Drang to Classicism,* edited by James Hardin and Christoph E. Schweitzer (1990)

95 *Eighteenth-Century British Poets, First Series,* edited by John Sitter (1990)

96 *British Romantic Poets, 1789-1832, Second Series,* edited by John R. Greenfield (1990)

97 *German Writers from the Enlightenment to Sturm und Drang, 1720-1764,* edited by James Hardin and Christoph E. Schweitzer (1990)

98 *Modern British Essayists, First Series,* edited by Robert Beum (1990)

99 *Canadian Writers Before 1890,* edited by W. H. New (1990)

100 *Modern British Essayists, Second Series,* edited by Robert Beum (1990)

101 *British Prose Writers, 1660-1800, First Series,* edited by Donald T. Siebert (1991)

102 *American Short-Story Writers, 1910-1945, Second Series,* edited by Bobby Ellen Kimbel (1991)

103 *American Literary Biographers, First Series,* edited by Steven Serafin (1991)

104 *British Prose Writers, 1660-1800, Second Series,* edited by Donald T. Siebert (1991)

105 *American Poets Since World War II, Second Series,* edited by R. S. Gwynn (1991)

106 *British Literary Publishing Houses, 1820-1880,* edited by Patricia J. Anderson and Jonathan Rose (1991)

107 *British Romantic Prose Writers, 1789-1832, First Series,* edited by John R. Greenfield (1991)

108 *Twentieth-Century Spanish Poets, First Series,* edited by Michael L. Perna (1991)

109 *Eighteenth-Century British Poets, Second Series,* edited by John Sitter (1991)

110 *British Romantic Prose Writers, 1789-1832, Second Series,* edited by John R. Greenfield (1991)

111 *American Literary Biographers, Second Series,* edited by Steven Serafin (1991)

112 *British Literary Publishing Houses, 1881-1965,* edited by Jonathan Rose and Patricia J. Anderson (1991)

113 *Modern Latin-American Fiction Writers, First Series,* edited by William Luis (1992)

114 *Twentieth-Century Italian Poets, First Series,* edited by Giovanna Wedel De Stasio, Glauco Cambon, and Antonio Illiano (1992)

115 *Medieval Philosophers,* edited by Jeremiah Hackett (1992)

116 *British Romantic Novelists, 1789-1832,* edited by Bradford K. Mudge (1992)

117 *Twentieth-Century Caribbean and Black African Writers, First Series,* edited by Bernth Lindfors and Reinhard Sander (1992)

118 *Twentieth-Century German Dramatists, 1889-1918,* edited by Wolfgang D. Elfe and James Hardin (1992)

119 *Nineteenth-Century French Fiction Writers: Romanticism and Realism, 1800-1860,* edited by Catharine Savage Brosman (1992)

120 *American Poets Since World War II, Third Series,* edited by R. S. Gwynn (1992)

121 *Seventeenth-Century British Nondramatic Poets, First Series,* edited by M. Thomas Hester (1992)

122 *Chicano Writers, Second Series,* edited by Francisco A. Lomelí and Carl R. Shirley (1992)

123 *Nineteenth-Century French Fiction Writers: Naturalism and Beyond, 1860-1900,* edited by Catharine Savage Brosman (1992)

124 *Twentieth-Century German Dramatists, 1919-1992,* edited by Wolfgang D. Elfe and James Hardin (1992)

125 *Twentieth-Century Caribbean and Black African Writers, Second Series,* edited by Bernth Lindfors and Reinhard Sander (1993)

126 *Seventeenth-Century British Nondramatic Poets, Second Series,* edited by M. Thomas Hester (1993)

127 *American Newspaper Publishers, 1950-1990,* edited by Perry J. Ashley (1993)

128 *Twentieth-Century Italian Poets, Second Series,* edited by Giovanna Wedel De Stasio, Glauco Cambon, and Antonio Illiano (1993)

129 *Nineteenth-Century German Writers, 1841-1900,* edited by James Hardin and Siegfried Mews (1993)

130 *American Short-Story Writers Since World War II,* edited by Patrick Meanor (1993)

131 *Seventeenth-Century British Nondramatic Poets, Third Series,* edited by M. Thomas Hester (1993)

132 *Sixteenth-Century British Nondramatic Writers, First Series,* edited by David A. Richardson (1993)

133 *Nineteenth-Century German Writers to 1840,* edited by James Hardin and Siegfried Mews (1993)

134 *Twentieth-Century Spanish Poets, Second Series,* edited by Jerry Phillips Winfield (1994)

135 *British Short-Fiction Writers, 1880-1914: The Realist Tradition,* edited by William B. Thesing (1994)

136 *Sixteenth-Century British Nondramatic Writers, Second Series,* edited by David A. Richardson (1994)

137 *American Magazine Journalists, 1900-1960, Second Series,* edited by Sam G. Riley (1994)

138 *German Writers and Works of the High Middle Ages: 1170-1280,* edited by James Hardin and Will Hasty (1994)

139 *British Short-Fiction Writers, 1945-1980,* edited by Dean Baldwin (1994)

140 *American Book-Collectors and Bibliographers, First Series,* edited by Joseph Rosenblum (1994)

141 *British Children's Writers, 1880-1914,* edited by Laura M. Zaidman (1994)

142 *Eighteenth-Century British Literary Biographers,* edited by Steven Serafin (1994)

143 *American Novelists Since World War II, Third Series,* edited by James R. Giles and Wanda H. Giles (1994)

144 *Nineteenth-Century British Literary Biographers,* edited by Steven Serafin (1994)

145 *Modern Latin-American Fiction Writers, Second Series,* edited by William Luis and Ann González (1994)

146 *Old and Middle English Literature,* edited by Jeffrey Helterman and Jerome Mitchell (1994)

147 *South Slavic Writers Before World War II,* edited by Vasa D. Mihailovich (1994)

148 *German Writers and Works of the Early Middle Ages: 800-1170,* edited by Will Hasty and James Hardin (1994)

149 *Late Nineteenth- and Early Twentieth-Century British Literary Biographers,* edited by Steven Serafin (1995)

150 *Early Modern Russian Writers, Late Seventeenth and Eighteenth Centuries,* edited by Marcus C. Levitt (1995)

151 *British Prose Writers of the Early Seventeenth Century,* edited by Clayton D. Lein (1995)

152 *American Novelists Since World War II, Fourth Series,* edited by James R. Giles and Wanda H. Giles (1995)

153 *Late-Victorian and Edwardian British Novelists, First Series,* edited by George M. Johnson (1995)

154 *The British Literary Book Trade, 1700-1820,* edited by James K. Bracken and Joel Silver (1995)

155 *Twentieth-Century British Literary Biographers*, edited by Steven Serafin (1995)

156 *British Short-Fiction Writers, 1880-1914: The Romantic Tradition*, edited by William F. Naufftus (1995)

157 *Twentieth-Century Caribbean and Black African Writers, Third Series*, edited by Bernth Lindfors and Reinhard Sander (1995)

158 *British Reform Writers, 1789-1832*, edited by Gary Kelly and Edd Applegate (1995)

159 *British Short-Fiction Writers, 1800-1880*, edited by John R. Greenfield (1996)

160 *British Children's Writers, 1914-1960*, edited by Donald R. Hettinga and Gary D. Schmidt (1996)

161 *British Children's Writers Since 1960, First Series*, edited by Caroline Hunt (1996)

162 *British Short-Fiction Writers, 1915-1945*, edited by John H. Rogers (1996)

163 *British Children's Writers, 1800-1880*, edited by Meena Khorana (1996)

164 *German Baroque Writers, 1580-1660*, edited by James Hardin (1996)

165 *American Poets Since World War II, Fourth Series*, edited by Joseph Conte (1996)

166 *British Travel Writers, 1837-1875*, edited by Barbara Brothers and Julia Gergits (1996)

167 *Sixteenth-Century British Nondramatic Writers, Third Series*, edited by David A. Richardson (1996)

168 *German Baroque Writers, 1661-1730*, edited by James Hardin (1996)

169 *American Poets Since World War II, Fifth Series*, edited by Joseph Conte (1996)

170 *The British Literary Book Trade, 1475-1700*, edited by James K. Bracken and Joel Silver (1996)

171 *Twentieth-Century American Sportswriters*, edited by Richard Orodenker (1996)

172 *Sixteenth-Century British Nondramatic Writers, Fourth Series*, edited by David A. Richardson (1996)

173 *American Novelists Since World War II, Fifth Series*, edited by James R. Giles and Wanda H. Giles (1996)

174 *British Travel Writers, 1876-1909*, edited by Barbara Brothers and Julia Gergits (1997)

175 *Native American Writers of the United States*, edited by Kenneth M. Roemer (1997)

176 *Ancient Greek Authors*, edited by Ward W. Briggs (1997)

177 *Italian Novelists Since World War II, 1945-1965*, edited by Augustus Pallotta (1997)

178 *British Fantasy and Science-Fiction Writers Before World War I*, edited by Darren Harris-Fain (1997)

179 *German Writers of the Renaissance and Reformation, 1280-1580*, edited by James Hardin and Max Reinhart (1997)

180 *Japanese Fiction Writers, 1868-1945*, edited by Van C. Gessel (1997)

181 *South Slavic Writers Since World War II*, edited by Vasa D. Mihailovich (1997)

182 *Japanese Fiction Writers Since World War II*, edited by Van C. Gessel (1997)

183 *American Travel Writers, 1776-1864*, edited by James J. Schramer and Donald Ross (1997)

184 *Nineteenth-Century British Book-Collectors and Bibliographers*, edited by William Baker and Kenneth Womack (1997)

185 *American Literary Journalists, 1945-1995, First Series*, edited by Arthur J. Kaul (1998)

186 *Nineteenth-Century American Western Writers*, edited by Robert L. Gale (1998)

187 *American Book Collectors and Bibliographers, Second Series*, edited by Joseph Rosenblum (1998)

188 *American Book and Magazine Illustrators to 1920*, edited by Steven E. Smith, Catherine A. Hastedt, and Donald H. Dyal (1998)

189 *American Travel Writers, 1850-1915*, edited by Donald Ross and James J. Schramer (1998)

190 *British Reform Writers, 1832-1914*, edited by Gary Kelly and Edd Applegate (1998)

191 *British Novelists Between the Wars*, edited by George M. Johnson (1998)

192 *French Dramatists, 1789-1914*, edited by Barbara T. Cooper (1998)

193 *American Poets Since World War II, Sixth Series*, edited by Joseph Conte (1998)

194 *British Novelists Since 1960, Second Series*, edited by Merritt Moseley (1998)

195 *British Travel Writers, 1910-1939*, edited by Barbara Brothers and Julia Gergits (1998)

196 *Italian Novelists Since World War II, 1965-1995*, edited by Augustus Pallotta (1999)

197 *Late-Victorian and Edwardian British Novelists, Second Series*, edited by George M. Johnson (1999)

198 *Russian Literature in the Age of Pushkin and Gogol: Prose*, edited by Christine A. Rydel (1999)

199 *Victorian Women Poets*, edited by William B. Thesing (1999)

200 *American Women Prose Writers to 1820*, edited by Carla J. Mulford, with Angela Vietto and Amy E. Winans (1999)

201 *Twentieth-Century British Book Collectors and Bibliographers*, edited by William Baker and Kenneth Womack (1999)

202 *Nineteenth-Century American Fiction Writers*, edited by Kent P. Ljungquist (1999)

203 *Medieval Japanese Writers*, edited by Steven D. Carter (1999)

204 *British Travel Writers, 1940-1997*, edited by Barbara Brothers and Julia M. Gergits (1999)

205 *Russian Literature in the Age of Pushkin and Gogol: Poetry and Drama*, edited by Christine A. Rydel (1999)

206 *Twentieth-Century American Western Writers, First Series*, edited by Richard H. Cracroft (1999)

207 *British Novelists Since 1960, Third Series*, edited by Merritt Moseley (1999)

208 *Literature of the French and Occitan Middle Ages: Eleventh to Fifteenth Centuries*, edited by Deborah Sinnreich-Levi and Ian S. Laurie (1999)

209 *Chicano Writers, Third Series*, edited by Francisco A. Lomelí and Carl R. Shirley (1999)

210 *Ernest Hemingway: A Documentary Volume*, edited by Robert W. Trogdon (1999)

211 *Ancient Roman Writers*, edited by Ward W. Briggs (1999)

212 *Twentieth-Century American Western Writers, Second Series*, edited by Richard H. Cracroft (1999)

213 *Pre-Nineteenth-Century British Book Collectors and Bibliographers*, edited by William Baker and Kenneth Womack (1999)

214 *Twentieth-Century Danish Writers*, edited by Marianne Stecher-Hansen (1999)

215 *Twentieth-Century Eastern European Writers, First Series*, edited by Steven Serafin (1999)

216 *British Poets of the Great War: Brooke, Rosenberg, Thomas. A Documentary Volume*, edited by Patrick Quinn (2000)

217 *Nineteenth-Century French Poets*, edited by Robert Beum (2000)

218 *American Short-Story Writers Since World War II, Second Series*, edited by Patrick Meanor and Gwen Crane (2000)

219 *F. Scott Fitzgerald's* The Great Gatsby: *A Documentary Volume*, edited by Matthew J. Bruccoli (2000)

220 *Twentieth-Century Eastern European Writers, Second Series*, edited by Steven Serafin (2000)

221 *American Women Prose Writers, 1870-1920*, edited by Sharon M. Harris, with the assistance of Heidi L. M. Jacobs and Jennifer Putzi (2000)

222 *H. L. Mencken: A Documentary Volume*, edited by Richard J. Schrader (2000)

223 *The American Renaissance in New England, Second Series*, edited by Wesley T. Mott (2000)

224 *Walt Whitman: A Documentary Volume*, edited by Joel Myerson (2000)

225 *South African Writers*, edited by Paul A. Scanlon (2000)

226 *American Hard-Boiled Crime Writers*, edited by George Parker Anderson and Julie B. Anderson (2000)

227 *American Novelists Since World War II, Sixth Series*, edited by James R. Giles and Wanda H. Giles (2000)

228 *Twentieth-Century American Dramatists, Second Series*, edited by Christopher J. Wheatley (2000)

229 *Thomas Wolfe: A Documentary Volume*, edited by Ted Mitchell (2001)

230 *Australian Writers, 1788-1914*, edited by Selina Samuels (2001)

231 *British Novelists Since 1960, Fourth Series*, edited by Merritt Moseley (2001)

232 *Twentieth-Century Eastern European Writers, Third Series*, edited by Steven Serafin (2001)

233 *British and Irish Dramatists Since World War II, Second Series*, edited by John Bull (2001)

234 *American Short-Story Writers Since World War II, Third Series*, edited by Patrick Meanor and Richard E. Lee (2001)

Documentary Series

1 *Sherwood Anderson, Willa Cather, John Dos Passos, Theodore Dreiser, F. Scott Fitzgerald, Ernest Hemingway, Sinclair Lewis,* edited by Margaret A. Van Antwerp (1982)

2 *James Gould Cozzens, James T. Farrell, William Faulkner, John O'Hara, John Steinbeck, Thomas Wolfe, Richard Wright,* edited by Margaret A. Van Antwerp (1982)

3 *Saul Bellow, Jack Kerouac, Norman Mailer, Vladimir Nabokov, John Updike, Kurt Vonnegut,* edited by Mary Bruccoli (1983)

4 *Tennessee Williams,* edited by Margaret A. Van Antwerp and Sally Johns (1984)

5 *American Transcendentalists,* edited by Joel Myerson (1988)

6 *Hardboiled Mystery Writers: Raymond Chandler, Dashiell Hammett, Ross Macdonald,* edited by Matthew J. Bruccoli and Richard Layman (1989)

7 *Modern American Poets: James Dickey, Robert Frost, Marianne Moore,* edited by Karen L. Rood (1989)

8 *The Black Aesthetic Movement,* edited by Jeffrey Louis Decker (1991)

9 *American Writers of the Vietnam War: W. D. Ehrhart, Larry Heinemann, Tim O'Brien, Walter McDonald, John M. Del Vecchio,* edited by Ronald Baughman (1991)

10 *The Bloomsbury Group,* edited by Edward L. Bishop (1992)

11 *American Proletarian Culture: The Twenties and The Thirties,* edited by Jon Christian Suggs (1993)

12 *Southern Women Writers: Flannery O'Connor, Katherine Anne Porter, Eudora Welty,* edited by Mary Ann Wimsatt and Karen L. Rood (1994)

13 *The House of Scribner, 1846-1904,* edited by John Delaney (1996)

14 *Four Women Writers for Children, 1868-1918,* edited by Caroline C. Hunt (1996)

15 *American Expatriate Writers: Paris in the Twenties,* edited by Matthew J. Bruccoli and Robert W. Trogdon (1997)

16 *The House of Scribner, 1905-1930,* edited by John Delaney (1997)

17 *The House of Scribner, 1931-1984,* edited by John Delaney (1998)

18 *British Poets of The Great War: Sassoon, Graves, Owen,* edited by Patrick Quinn (1999)

19 *James Dickey,* edited by Judith S. Baughman (1999)

See also DLB 210, 216, 219, 222, 224, 229

Yearbooks

1980 edited by Karen L. Rood, Jean W. Ross, and Richard Ziegfeld (1981)

1981 edited by Karen L. Rood, Jean W. Ross, and Richard Ziegfeld (1982)

1982 edited by Richard Ziegfeld; associate editors: Jean W. Ross and Lynne C. Zeigler (1983)

1983 edited by Mary Bruccoli and Jean W. Ross; associate editor Richard Ziegfeld (1984)

1984 edited by Jean W. Ross (1985)

1985 edited by Jean W. Ross (1986)

1986 edited by J. M. Brook (1987)

1987 edited by J. M. Brook (1988)

1988 edited by J. M. Brook (1989)

1989 edited by J. M. Brook (1990)

1990 edited by James W. Hipp (1991)

1991 edited by James W. Hipp (1992)

1992 edited by James W. Hipp (1993)

1993 edited by James W. Hipp, contributing editor George Garrett (1994)

1994 edited by James W. Hipp, contributing editor George Garrett (1995)

1995 edited by James W. Hipp, contributing editor George Garrett (1996)

1996 edited by Samuel W. Bruce and L. Kay Webster, contributing editor George Garrett (1997)

1997 edited by Matthew J. Bruccoli and George Garrett, with the assistance of L. Kay Webster (1998)

1998 edited by Matthew J. Bruccoli, contributing editor George Garrett, with the assistance of D. W. Thomas (1999)

1999 edited by Matthew J. Bruccoli, contributing editor George Garrett, with the assistance of D. W. Thomas (2000)

Concise Series

Concise Dictionary of American Literary Biography, 7 volumes (1988-1999): *The New Consciousness, 1941-1968; Colonization to the American Renaissance, 1640-1865; Realism, Naturalism, and Local Color, 1865-1917; The Twenties, 1917-1929; The Age of Maturity, 1929-1941; Broadening Views, 1968-1988; Supplement: Modern Writers, 1900-1998.*

Concise Dictionary of British Literary Biography, 8 volumes (1991-1992): *Writers of the Middle Ages and Renaissance Before 1660; Writers of the Restoration and Eighteenth Century, 1660-1789; Writers of the Romantic Period, 1789-1832; Victorian Writers, 1832-1890; Late-Victorian and Edwardian Writers, 1890-1914; Modern Writers, 1914-1945; Writers After World War II, 1945-1960; Contemporary Writers, 1960 to Present.*

Concise Dictionary of World Literary Biography, 20 volumes projected (1999-): *Ancient Greek and Roman Writers; German Writers; African, Carribbean, and Latin American Writers.*

Dictionary of Literary Biography® • Volume Two Hundred Thirty-Four

American Short-Story Writers Since World War II
Third Series

American Short-Story Writers Since World War II
Third Series

Edited by
Patrick Meanor
State University of New York College at Oneonta

and

Richard E. Lee
State University of New York College at Oneonta

A Bruccoli Clark Layman Book
The Gale Group
Detroit • San Francisco • London • Boston • Woodbridge, Conn.

Printed in the United States of America

The paper used in this publication meets the minimum requirements
of American National Standard for Information Sciences–Permanence
Paper for Printed Library Materials, ANSI Z39.48-1984. ∞™

ISBN 7876-4651-2

10 9 8 7 6 5 4 3 2 1

In honor of Dr. Jerome Rose,
great pianist, teacher,
and human being

Contents

Plan of the Series xiii
Introduction xv

Alice Adams (1926–1999) 3
    Christine C. Ferguson

Donald Barthelme (1931–1989) 16
    Gwen Crane

Wendell Berry (1934–) 33
    Thom Conroy

Sallie Bingham (1937–) 42
    Frederick Smock

Robert Boswell (1953–) 49
    Alexander McIlvaine Parsons

Larry Brown (1951–) 57
    Robert A. Beuka

Peter Cameron (1959–) 64
    James Coan

Elizabeth Cullinan (1933–) 72
    Amy M. Lilly

Nicholas Delbanco (1942–) 79
    Gregory L. Morris

Gail Godwin (1937–) 87
    Jane Hill

Richard Grayson (1951–) 96
    Tom Whalen

Barry Hannah (1942–) 105
    Richard E. Lee

William Harrison (1933–) 117
    Sharon L. Jones

William Hoffman (1925–) 124
    William L. Frank

Mary Hood (1946–) 135
    Dede Yow

William Humphrey (1924–1997) 142
    Ashby Bland Crowder

Charles Jackson (1903–1968) 153
    Curt Meanor

Shirley Jackson (1916–1965) 161
    Dale Hrebik

Greg Johnson (1953–) 172
    Michael Upchurch

Rachel Maddux (1912–1983) 181
    Nancy A. Walker

Jill McCorkle (1958–) 186
    Robert A. Beuka

Reginald McKnight (1956–) 197
    Karl Zuelke

Lorrie Moore (1957–) 205
    Robin A. Werner

Kent Nelson (1943–) 214
    Teresa Winterhalter

Lewis Nordan (1939–) 227
    Tom Noyes

William Peden (1913–1999) 235
    Meg Watson

C. E. Poverman (1944–) 242
    Victoria Nelson

Padgett Powell (1952–) 250
    Brad Vice

Francine Prose (1947–) 257
    Troy L. Thibodeaux

Mark Richard (1955–) 266
    Adam Sol

Jane Smiley (1949–) 272
    Thom Conroy

Michael Stephens (1946–) 279
    Eamonn Wall

W. D. Wetherell (1948–) 285
    Carol-Lynn Marrazzo

Richard Yates (1926–1992) 295
    Blake Bailey

John Yau (1950–) 305
    Garrett Caples

Books for Further Reading 317
Contributors 321
Cumulative Index 325

Plan of the Series

The advisory board, the editors, and the publisher of the *Dictionary of Literary Biography* are joined in endorsing Mark Twain's declaration. The literature of a nation provides an inexhaustible resource of permanent worth. We intend to make literature and its creators better understood and more accessible to students and the reading public, while satisfying the standards of teachers and scholars.

To meet these requirements, *literary biography* has been construed in terms of the author's achievement. The most important thing about a writer is his writing. Accordingly, the entries in *DLB* are career biographies, tracing the development of the author's canon and the evolution of his reputation.

The purpose of *DLB* is not only to provide reliable information in a convenient format but also to place the figures in the larger perspective of literary history and to offer appraisals of their accomplishments by qualified scholars.

The publication plan for *DLB* resulted from two years of preparation. The project was proposed to Bruccoli Clark by Frederick G. Ruffner, president of the Gale Research Company, in November 1975. After specimen entries were prepared and typeset, an advisory board was formed to refine the entry format and develop the series rationale. In meetings held during 1976, the publisher, series editors, and advisory board approved the scheme for a comprehensive biographical dictionary of persons who contributed to North American literature. Editorial work on the first volume began in January 1977, and it was published in 1978. In order to make *DLB* more than a reference tool and to compile volumes that individually have claim to status as literary history, it was decided to organize volumes by

topic, period, or genre. Each of these freestanding volumes provides a biographical-bibliographical guide and overview for a particular area of literature. We are convinced that this organization—as opposed to a single alphabet method—constitutes a valuable innovation in the presentation of reference material. The volume plan necessarily requires many decisions for the placement and treatment of authors who might properly be included in two or three volumes. In some instances a major figure will be included in separate volumes, but with different entries emphasizing the aspect of his career appropriate to each volume. Ernest Hemingway, for example, is represented in *American Writers in Paris, 1920–1939* by an entry focusing on his expatriate apprenticeship; he is also in *American Novelists, 1910–1945* with an entry surveying his entire career, as well as in *American Short-Story Writers, 1910–1945, Second Series* with an entry concentrating on his short stories. Each volume includes a cumulative index of the subject authors and articles. Comprehensive indexes to the entire series are planned.

Since 1981 the series has been further augmented by the *DLB Yearbooks,* which update published entries and add new entries to keep the *DLB* current with contemporary activity. There have also been *DLB Documentary Series* volumes which provide biographical and critical source materials for figures whose work is judged to have particular interest for students. One of these companion volumes is devoted entirely to Tennessee Williams.

We define literature as the *intellectual commerce of a nation:* not merely as belles lettres but as that ample and complex process by which ideas are generated, shaped, and transmitted. *DLB* entries are not limited to "creative writers" but extend to other figures who in their time and in their way influenced the mind of a people. Thus the series encompasses historians, journalists, publishers, book collectors, and screenwriters. By this means readers of *DLB* may be aided to perceive literature not as cult scripture in the keeping of intellectual high priests but firmly positioned at the center of a nation's life.

DLB includes the major writers appropriate to each volume and those standing in the ranks behind them. Scholarly and critical counsel has been sought in deciding which minor figures to include and how full their entries should be. Wherever possible, useful references are made to figures who do not warrant separate entries.

Each *DLB* volume has an expert volume editor responsible for planning the volume, selecting the figures for inclusion, and assigning the entries. Volume editors are also responsible for preparing, where appropriate, appendices surveying the major periodicals and literary and intellectual movements for their volumes, as well as lists of further readings. Work on the series as a whole is coordinated at the Bruccoli Clark Layman editorial center in Columbia, South Carolina, where the editorial staff is responsible for accuracy and utility of the published volumes.

One feature that distinguishes *DLB* is the illustration policy—its concern with the iconography of literature. Just as an author is influenced by his surroundings, so is the reader's understanding of the author enhanced by a knowledge of his environment. Therefore *DLB* volumes include not only drawings, paintings, and photographs of authors, often depicting them at various stages in their careers, but also illustrations of their families and places where they lived. Title pages are regularly reproduced in facsimile along with dust jackets for modern authors. The dust jackets are a special feature of *DLB* because they often document better than anything else the way in which an author's work was perceived in its own time. Specimens of the writers' manuscripts and letters are included when feasible.

Samuel Johnson rightly decreed that "The chief glory of every people arises from its authors." The purpose of the *Dictionary of Literary Biography* is to compile literary history in the surest way available to us—by accurate and comprehensive treatment of the lives and work of those who contributed to it.

The *DLB* Advisory Board

Introduction

This volume of the *Dictionary of Literary Biography* focuses on short fiction since 1945, and it continues the plan set out in *Dictionary of Literary Biography 130: American Short-Story Writers Since World War II* and expanded upon in *DLB 218: American Short-Story Writers Since World War II, Second Series.* The fact that a third series is necessary (with a fourth planned) indicates the explosion of interest—in both mass and academic markets—in short fiction. In the introduction to the second series of this volume, the editors track the increasing appearance of academic havens for burgeoning writers and assess the role of schools of writing in the development of short-story writers. Two events have occurred more or less simultaneously with these two developments: writers have been forced from the "world" and into a more stratified existence within academia, and the novel slowly has given way to the shorter form. Writers must respond to market forces if they wish to become published, and it is noteworthy that the more-universal truths one often sees expressed in the novel have become replaced with the more-contingent truths of the short story. Rather than publishing novels that celebrate unity of the human experience and deep truths, publishers have increasingly supported texts that celebrate partial and relative truths, ambivalence, and uncertainty. As the editors of *DLB 218* observe, citing critic Gary Krist, those interested in what it means to be alive in late-twentieth-century America need to concern themselves not with the totalizing vision of the novel but with the fragmentary mosaic tiles that are short stories. It is not, then, surprising that so many of the authors in the current volume problematize the relationship of the short-story form to the novel as a form of history and underline the partiality of all truth.

Since World War II, experimentation in the novel has led to texts that call attention to themselves as writing rather than as referential texts concerned with external reality. In this way, at least, the overall cultural tendency to challenge authority has found a vent. Authors such as Thomas Pynchon, Donald Barthelme, John Fowles, and many others have refused to write "traditional" novels. In the current volume many of the authors who are presented have written both novels and short fiction, and each has, inevitably, a sense of

what distinction exists between the two forms. As Austin M. Wright observes in his 1989 essay "On Defining the Short Story: The Genre Question"—one of several seminal articles in Susan Lohafer and Jo Ellyn Clarey's highly regarded collection, *Short Story Theory at a Crossroads* (1989)—there is a general sense that something is, indeed, distinctive about the short story as a form of literary endeavor, but something is little agreement as to what the nature of that distinctiveness is.

After World War II, many cultural developments in the United States were accelerated: for one, nationalism escalated as the United States emerged from the war as the ultimate superpower, leading to the jingoist fervor of the McCarthy era. Simultaneously, a new generation of voices questioned the principles that temporarily lofted Joseph McCarthy to power. Women retreated from munitions factories to spend the reactionary 1950s in their kitchens, experimenting with new labor-saving devices and instant cake mixes, only to burst angrily out of their houses during the women's liberation movement of the following decade. The civil rights and antiwar movements coalesced in the 1960s to produce a generalized re-examination of earlier forms of authority. All of these radical upheavals are reflected in the developments in the short-story genre during these decades; this volume, along with *DLB 130,* charts the representative voices of the debates and revolutions of the last half of the twentieth century.

During the 1920s, 1930s, and 1940s, authors could make a living by writing short stories for the large-circulation magazines. After World War II, weekly magazines such as *The Saturday Evening Post* and *Collier's* declined and eventually ceased publication. Starting in the 1950s, the massive presence of television began to undermine the reading habits of the American public. Widespread television viewing ushered in what George Garrett has called "the new illiteracy." Today, because the popular market for short stories has shrunken, most American short fiction is published by literary journals and university presses. Though there are recent signs that the short-story form is gaining ground with readers and publishers, no more than a dozen magazines currently pay four-figure amounts for a story.

Volumes of stories did not sell well in the 1950s, 1960s, and early 1970s. A market-driven publishing world had made it difficult for more-experimental writers to get their novels published, as well. Many of the remaining magazines that had previously published short fiction began to feature memoirs, which frequently replaced short stories. One of the effects of Truman Capote's "nonfiction novel," *In Cold Blood* (1965) was to blur distinctions between fiction and nonfiction, and writers such as Edward Abbey, Joan Didion, Annie Dillard, John McPhee, and Gay Talese began to publish personal essays that had the appearance of first-person short stories.

Additional influences appeared during these same years: the experimental literary techniques of such avant-garde writers as Samuel Beckett, Franz Kafka, and André Breton became the new models, replacing, in some instances, the earlier influences of Ernest Hemingway, William Faulkner, F. Scott Fitzgerald, and Sherwood Anderson. Creative-writing schools also emerged at universities, beginning with the University of Iowa Writers' Workshop, which stressed originality of method rather than content and thus encouraged a variety of new forms that had already begun to appear in the work of younger experimental authors such as Barthelme, Pynchon, and John Barth—writers additionally influenced by Argentinian Jorge Luis Borges and the so-called literary outlaws, including Charles Bukowski and William Burroughs.

Because of the dwindling commercial market for short stories, writers could no longer make a living in New York, and they began accepting jobs throughout the university systems as writer-professors. Tenured positions in English departments enabled them to support their families and continue writing or stop writing altogether. The University of Iowa, in the late 1940s, began training students in creative writing and then sending out graduates, certified with their Master of Fine Arts degrees, to initiate new creative-writing programs throughout the country.

While the universities became protective environments for many fiction writers, certain risks arose in their sometimes-insular atmospheres. Hortense Calisher, one of the most respected American fiction writers, suggests that "the university has willy-nilly become the café." Writers, who often need a variety of experiences to spark their imaginations, spend a large portion of their academic lives enclosed within the walls of graduate school. Calisher also warns that artists must be careful in talking about their craft too much: "If one teaches and writes there as well, the effect of immersion in talk about 'techniques' may also enter in. Subtlest of all influences or hazards for the silent persona of a writer may be the constant verbalization of energies and

meditations better saved for the page." She points out the appearance in the 1970s and 1980s of more stories set in academia. John Updike, concurring with Calisher regarding the possible negative repercussions of the creative-writing industry, put it another way in 1984:

> for the bright young graduates that pour out of the Iowa Writers' Workshop and its sister institutions, publishing short stories is a kind of accreditation, a certificate of worthiness to teach the so-called art of fiction. The Popular market for fiction has shriveled while the academic importance of "creative writing" has swelled; academic quarterlies, operating under one form of subsidy or another, absorb some of the excess. The suspicion persists that short fiction, like poetry since Kipling and Bridges, has gone from being a popular to a fine art, an art preserved in a kind of floating museum made up of many little superfluous magazines.

Though Calisher and Updike warn against some of the hazards of creative-writing schools, the fact remains that academic quarterlies have become, since the 1950s, a major venue in publishing short fiction in America. The few national magazines that still publish short stories have, however, established much higher literary standards than many of the magazines that folded in the 1950s and 1960s. Until recently many New York trade publishing houses did not publish or promote short-story collections, and, as a result, university presses have become the most important vehicles in publishing short fiction for most of the writers in this *DLB* volume. Frank Conroy, head of the Iowa Writers' Workshop, claims that the success of the university presses in promoting short fiction has "contributed significantly to the forces responsible for the current resurgence of interest of the big houses in serious short fiction."

Whatever long-term effects creative-writing programs may have had on fiction writing since 1945, they play an important role in this *DLB* volume because almost all of writers included have either graduated from creative-writing programs, have worked, or are presently working in creative-writing programs as professors in various universities. Barry Hannah and William Peden have both cautioned against combining the teaching and writing of fiction, but both have clearly benefited from the collegiality of their own academic work because they supported themselves as professors for many years.

Besides the flight of writers to universities and the emergence of academic literary quarterlies, the lack of major publishers' interest in short fiction gave rise to independent associations of writers, who established their own little magazines. They sought no direct connections with either the commercialized New York literary scene or the academic world. Just as the writing programs became new centers, so, too, did the little magazines create their own independent centers, where they were free to create their own aesthetic communities. Many of the editors of and contributors to these magazines strongly objected to the homogenized eclecticism coming out of the more-conservative writing programs and academic journals such as *The Kenyon Review, Sewanee Review,* and *The Southern Review* or a more trendy liberal journal such as *The Partisan Review.* The radical founders of magazines such as *Big Table, Kulchur, The Black Mountain Review, Io, Lillabulero, Caterpillar, The Evergreen Review, The Chelsea Review,* and many other maverick publications claimed that the M.F.A. workshops' emphasis on craft and technique had inadvertently replaced viable aesthetic and cultural traditions that had previously activated innovative fiction writing.

The Black Mountain Review published work by students and teachers at Black Mountain College who had come out of a tradition that revered Ezra Pound, William Carlos Williams, and other objectivist writers such as Charles Olson and Louis Zukofsky, along with the additional influences of both European and American avant-garde artists such as Henri Gaudier-Brzeska, Paul Klee, Pablo Picasso, Clyfford Still, Jackson Pollock, and Franz Kline. Students at Black Mountain College were steeped in European traditions in literature, art, and music through artist-scholars such as Josef Albers and Buckminster Fuller and musical performers and composers Lou Harrison, Stefan Wolpe, John Cage, and Merce Cunningham. Craft, as such, was discussed only in relation to a specific tradition and never became the major focus that it assumed in the workshop approach at Iowa and like-minded schools. As Michael Anania puts it in his comprehensive study of the history of little magazines, published in *TriQuarterly* (Fall 1978): "In the almost totally decentralized literature of the late Sixties and early Seventies, these associations are measures of what was once called influence."

Though there has been since the 1950s a drastic reduction in the number of magazines that publish short fiction, a certain few still maintain their respected positions at the top echelons of the publishing world. *Esquire* has always been one of the most desirable places to publish because it pays well and its readership is literate and sophisticated. Rust Hills is the present fiction editor at *Esquire,* but former editor Gordon Lish, particularly during the late 1960s and early 1970s, published many younger writers who eventually attained major careers, including Joy Williams, who eventually married Hills. But there has been a gradual reduction in the number of short stories published in major magazines in recent years. While *Playboy,* since its inception in the late 1950s, has published stories by established writers

and paid them handsomely, it has published less and less fiction over time. The only weekly mainstream magazine to publish short fiction is *The New Yorker,* which launched and sustained the careers of both Hortense Calisher and Ann Beattie. *Harper's,* edited by Lewis Lapham, and *The Atlantic Monthly,* under fiction editor C. Michael Curtis, continue to publish one story a month. *Redbook,* under editor Lesley Jane Seymour, also continues to publish short stories monthly.

More than half of the remaining writers in this volume, however, established their literary reputations without having appeared in any of the mass-circulation magazines just mentioned. Most of them have appeared in one or more of a group of important, academically connected journals, ones with editors whose aesthetic and political tastes established new literary centers that fostered and promoted writers whose work seemed to express their own viewpoints. Certainly editor Frederick Morgan's conservative tastes helped determine the kinds of stories that *The Hudson Review* would be more likely to accept, just as the liberal political sympathies of *The Partisan Review* editor, William Phillips, might decide the kind of work that would appear there. Other powerful editors include Robert West of *The Carolina Quarterly,* George Plimpton of the nonacademic *Paris Review,* and Reginald Gibbons of *TriQuarterly.* Academic journals based in the South that have traditionally published highly crafted fiction are *The Southern Review,* edited by James Olney; *The Sewanee Review,* edited by George Core; and *The Virginia Quarterly Review,* edited by Staige Blackford. For many years Frederick Turner directed and edited the conservative *Kenyon Review,* later edited by David Lynn. There is little doubt that during the 1960s and 1970s, Theodore Solotaroff's *New American Review,* though not an academic journal, was responsible for the promotion of many major careers, including those of Philip Roth and Stanley Elkin. Solotaroff also edited, while at Harper and Row, the work of Max Apple, along with other young writers. Other journals located in different parts of the country in the decentralized world of the American short story are *The Georgia Review,* edited by Stanley Lindberg; *The Southwest Review,* edited by Willard Spiegelman; *The Missouri Review,* edited by Speer Morgan and Greg Michaelson; and DeWitt Henry's *Ploughshares. The North American Review* from the University of Northern Iowa, edited by Robley Wilson, has been particularly sympathetic to more-experimental fiction writers, as has *The Chicago Review* under the editorship of Andrew Pathmann. And certainly *The Iowa Review,* edited by David Hamilton, has maintained its influence as the journal connected to the mother of all creative-writing programs, the Iowa Writers' Workshop. Editor, short-story writer, and novelist Gordon Weaver edits the excellent *Cimarron Review.*

There are other highly influential journals, not connected to any particular university or school of writing. Their literary venue is usually built around the reputation of a writer-editor who publishes only those writers whom he or she holds in high esteem. Bradford Morrow's journal, *Conjunctions,* which has not been connected to any school until its recent affiliation with Bard College, has been publishing writers with a heavily international/multicultural emphasis and a postmodernist perspective. *The Granta Book of the American Short Story* (1992), edited by Richard Ford, and the *Vintage Book of Contemporary American Short Stories* (1994), edited by Tobias Wolff, together feature twenty-one stories written by authors found in both *DLB 130* and this volume. The former editor of *Granta,* Bill Buford, is now the editor of *The New Yorker.* Another highly respected journal not affiliated with any academic institution is *Witness,* edited by Peter Stine; each issue is devoted to a featured topic, such as "Writings from Prison," "The Holocaust," and "Evangelism and American Politics."

There is, however, life outside the walls of the writing schools and the academic quarterlies. Several of the writers in this volume have rarely, or never, taught in university writing programs, published their works with university presses, or appeared in university-related scholarly journals. Small journals, some of them long gone, in which many of the most influential story writers found a place for their work include: *The Falcon;* Robert Kelly's *Chelsea Review; The Evergreen Review,* edited by Barney Rosset and Donald Allen; and *Caterpillar,* published in the 1960s and 1970s by Clayton Eshleman. A selection of distinguished little magazines includes Richard Grossinger's *Io;* Irving Rosenthal's *Big Table;* Robert Bertholf's *Credences;* Russell Banks's *Lillabulero; Kulchur,* alternately edited by Gilbert Sorrentino, Joel Oppenheimer, and LeRoi Jones; and *Neon,* edited by Sorrentino and Hubert Selby. Other long-defunct magazines of note are the *Floating Bear, Yugen, Wild Dog,* and *Measure.*

So-called small presses have had about the same life expectancy as the little magazines, but several of the survivors have maintained the integrity of their single-minded vision in the face of overwhelming pressures. Many of the authors discussed in this series have published with two of the most distinguished small presses in the United States. John Martin's Black Sparrow Press in Santa Rosa, California, is responsible, to a great extent, for the literary careers of some highly influential short-story masters, such as Charles Bukowski, Paul Goodman, Fielding Dawson, and Paul Bowles. William D. Turnbull's North Point Press of San Francisco—now distributed by Farrar, Straus and Giroux—publishes several of the most respected writers in America, such as Lydia Davis and Deborah Eisenberg.

The most notable surprise is that small presses and university presses have been responsible for the success of so many of the writers featured in this volume. This fact dramatically demonstrates that, until recently, the indifferent attitudes of many of the mass-circulation publishing houses, with the exception of Knopf; Norton; Holt; Putnam; Little, Brown; Scribners; and a few others, have failed to appreciate the rich harvest of short fiction that this country has produced. The level of writing of these artists is, most of the time, highly accomplished, yet they have often gone unnoticed by the market makers in the publishing world.

Other important factors that contribute to the complex world of the contemporary American short story, and substantially promote a writer's career, are the prizes that various organizations award each year and, in most cases, the influential anthologies in which these prizewinning stories appear. There can be little doubt that Shannon Ravenel, whom Updike called "that St. Louis saint of scrutiny," is probably the most influential editor of short stories in the United States today. As a senior editor of Algonquin Books of Chapel Hill, North Carolina, she has served as the co-editor of the anthology *Best American Short Stories* for the past twenty years. She reads between fifteen hundred and two thousand short stories yearly and sends one hundred to her co-editor for the final awarding of the prizes. Her co-editors have included the most respected short-story writers in America. Not only are the prizewinners of the *Best American Short Story* Award given national recognition and a substantial sum of money, but also their stories appear in an annual collection along with other winners. Most of the writers in this volume have been recipients of one or more of the following awards, an achievement that has substantially advanced their careers. Besides that given by *Best American Short Stories,* the major awards honoring short-story writers are the O. Henry Prize, the Iowa Short Fiction Award, the P.E.N./Hemingway Award, the Pushcart Prize series, and the John Simmons Short Fiction Award. Publishers often look to the award winners first when scouting around for fresh talent. A common pattern with prizewinning writers is that such an award leads to more public recognition, which in turn leads to offers of academic positions that allow them to support a family and have the time to devote to new work.

As important to the promotion of the publication of short fiction as the O. Henry Prize and *Best American Short Stories* is the active role that university presses have played during the 1980s in awarding prizes and publishing series of annual short-story collections. In 1980 the University of Pittsburgh Press Drue Heinz Literature Prize, under director Frederick Hetzel, was specifically created to recognize and encourage the writing of short fiction and to address the neglect of short fiction by the national publishing community. The University of Pittsburgh Press awards $5,000 annually to an outstanding young short-fiction writer and publishes his or her first collection. The press also began to publish short-story collections as part of their University of Pittsburgh Short-Story Series. The University of Missouri Press, under editor Clair Wilcox, also initiated a short-fiction series of publications, the University of Missouri Press Breakthrough Series. The University of Illinois Press awards an annual prize and has published more than sixty volumes in its Illinois Short Fiction Series, and the University of Georgia Press has sponsored the Flannery O'Connor Award for Short Fiction for many years. The Iowa Short Fiction Award has been given by the University of Iowa. Some literary journals also award prizes for short fiction, such as the William Goyen Prize for Short Fiction from *TriQuarterly*.

Journals devoted exclusively to short fiction now include *Short Story,* under editor Mary Rohrberger; *The Journal of the Short Story in English; Story,* edited by Lois Rosenthal; Francis Ford Coppola's *Zoetrope: All Story;* and *Studies in Short Fiction,* edited by Michael O'Shea at Newberry College in Newberry, South Carolina.

Defining the genre has been an abiding concern of the scholars participating in the ongoing battles between traditional and experimental literature. In his 1975 study *Form and Meaning in Fiction,* short-story theorist Norman Friedman calls for a critical consensus on rigorously, logically articulated criteria for distinguishing the short story from other kinds of writing. One of the leading American short-story scholars, Mary Rohrberger, has offered a different approach in her many studies of the genre, suggesting that literary developments do not lend themselves to the kind of logical rigor Friedman is looking for, and that a definition of the genre can only be approximated in the form of metaphor. The problem with such subjective criteria is that it does nothing to help define the limits of the genre. Structuralists, poststructuralists, narratologists, and cognitive psychologists have all produced their own definitions, many of them interesting, yet none sufficiently inclusive. It is difficult to find even two critics arriving at the kind of critical consensus Friedman demands. In the decades following World War II, the short stories produced by American writers have defied generalization. Calisher, however, has given one of the more useful metaphorical definitions of the short story as it has evolved since World War II: the short story today, she asserts, "is an apocalypse, served in a very small cup." A survey of the stories considered in this volume discovers a fertile field of vibrantly individualistic writers, many passionately involved in expanding the boundaries of their art. Paradoxically, even while critics worry

about the stifling effects of the academic writing programs where increasing numbers of younger writers sojourn, the work these authors produce continues to evolve in unexpectedly exuberant ways. The short story has flourished since World War II, continually redefining itself and serving as a richly varied chronicle of a tumultuous age. Contemporary writers are using new tools to explore new territory—an historical and intellectual landscape marred by unprecedented violence, illuminated by new knowledge, and shadowed with profound philosophical and religious doubts.

Although there are many competing claims for the honor of having produced the first short story—including those who point to the Bible as a primary source—ultimately, it is less important to pinpoint a date than it is to evaluate what short stories do. The stories discussed in *DLB 234* all speak to a certain subversiveness on the part of the genre. As Charles E. May observes in *The Short Story: The Reality of Artifice* (1995), "The wellsprings of the form are as old as the primitive realm of myth. . . . a myth not only expresses the inner meaning of things . . . but it does so specifically by telling a story." May conceptualizes the short story as a sort of precursor to the novel form; it is easy to agree, but this agreement begs the question, then, of why the shorter form has blossomed at the same time that the novel has held sway as a dominant form. May and many other theorists, including the Russian formalist critic Boris Eichenbaum, see a historical movement from the realm of myth—and the religious tales of morality prevalent in the Middle Ages—to the mundane and the profane. "The short story begins in what Mircea Eliade calls 'the sacred,' which later accumulate and become conceptualized into the organized narrative form we have come to know as the novel." Or, as May quotes Eichenbaum: "The novel is a syncretic form (whether its development be directly from collections of stories or complicated by the incorporation of manners-and-morals material); the short story is a fundamental, elementary (which does not mean primitive) form." Even disregarding the deep origins of tale-telling in the mythic past, the short-story form is identifiable in narratives as ancient as *The Satyricon* by Petronius (first century A.D.) or the tales of Sheherazade. At first glance it is difficult to see what the "plotless marvels" of Donald Barthelme, for example, have in common with such older works, but critic Gwen Crane makes the point in her essay in the current volume that the parodic and ironic view of the world that characterizes Barthelme's writing presents, in a sense, the "world turned upside down"—a carnivalesque escape from the tortuous pressure of a coherent vision of the world. The perfectly postmodern wordplay in Barthelme's stories signals a need to connect with the traditions of the past coupled with a refusal of the static. In much the same manner, the linguistic brilliance of Padgett Powell, according to Brad Vice, allows Powell to claim his own imaginative territory while still paying homage to Faulkner, the "big train" of all Southern writers. Even in the least traditional texts, therefore, there is an insistence that something has gone before.

It is a commonplace that the Italian writer Giovanni Boccaccio probably produced the first collection of short stories in the European literary tradition. Among the similarities shared by Boccaccio's *Decameron* and *The Tales of the Arabian Nights* is this often-overlooked connection: both are recognizably opposed to any easy connection between fiction and history. In fact, each collection occurs in a fictional flight from history, because the characters of the frame tales are, in Boccaccios's case, fleeing the Black Death when they take refuge in an abandoned abbey to tell their ten stories each over ten days: their "decameron."

In the case of *Tales of the Arabian Nights*, first "published" in about 1450, Scheherazade holds death at bay by entertaining a sultan with tales told each night, but with climaxes deferred until the next night. This strategy enables the wily Scheherazade to do what all good writers do: she informatively teases, yet defers gratification so as to hold the reader's attention. Boccaccio's Italian aristocrats are seeking to escape one of the waves of plague that swelled throughout the fourteenth century, and they seek to pass the time away from reality, secluded in their convent in the country, by telling tales grouped around various thematic treatments. In neither case do the collections fulfill their stated design (nor did Geoffrey Chaucer's adoption of several of Boccaccio's stories and overall design achieve fulfillment in the slightly later *Canterbury Tales,* in which the frame narrative also includes a "holiday" from the mundane). In contemporary fiction the distinction between urban "reality" and bucolic escape is often expressed ironically. For example, Ashley Bland Crowder suggests that William Humphrey attempts to escape categorization as a regional Southern writer by questioning the suburbanization of the American New South. As every place starts to look like every other place, distinctions such as country and city become highlighted, not erased. Michael Upchurch makes much the same point in his entry on Greg Johnson, observing that although many characters leave the semirural towns of their births for the glamour and opportunity of the big city, the attempted flight often leads to a heightened awareness of difference, rather than to homogenization.

In terms of characterization, Boccaccio's aristocrats, and the characters in the tales themselves, have no real existence: they are merely functional, having none of the characterization or depth that Renaissance

developments in perspective in the visual arts later lent to increasingly complex literary figures. In fact, one of Boccaccios's central accomplishments in his work is to "mark a shift from the realm of the sacred to the profane world" that came to characterize the growth in modern consciousness associated with the Renaissance in Europe. What matters is that, especially in the case of *The Decameron,* readers are treated to stories of the local and the particular and to tales of lives lived in the interstices of history. In this volume, writers such as Larry Brown and Mark Richard, who focus attention on the lives of the underclass, are working in this rich traditional vein. Brown's so-called trailer-park fiction is not as far from Boccaccio as it at first seems: Robert Beuka's entry sees escape and avoidance as a theme central to Brown's fiction. This volume is subversive of a notion that history matters. Thus, Boccaccio is not as alien to a discussion of contemporary fiction as one might at first think. Interestingly, Boccaccio functions as much, or more, as an editor of traditional tales, lays, and fabliaux as he does as a writer and re-presenter of those tales, lays, and fabliaux. In many ways, those contemporary artists who transfer tales from lives lived beneath the gaze of everyday society—writers such as Brown and Richard—are writing during their own decameron night.

As Miguel Cervantes, Wilhelm Kleist, and E. T. A. Hoffmann continued the narrative tradition in the eighteenth and nineteenth centuries, they utilized clockwork automatons and tales of the fabulous connected purely to the local and not the universal. By the time Edgar Allan Poe began writing short stories in the early nineteenth century, the dominant literary form was the novel. Poe's famous statements about the "requirements" of short fiction—that each story should be digestible in one sitting and that a singularity of effect should mark the composition—established him as one of the first theorists of the genre. Other genre theorists such as Ian Watt and Michael McKeon have linked the development of the recognizably modern world—industrialized, urban, goal-oriented, individualistic, and capitalistic—to the growth of the novel. The short-story form continued to develop in contravention to the dominance of the novel, by an increasing tendency to tell the stories that exist in the gaps between the tectonic plates of the novelistic scope.

All of the authors presented in this volume contribute to the dual tendencies of short fiction located here: they insist upon the fragmentary nature of truth, and they tell tales written from within the gaps of the historical, the normative, American vision. As such, each extends the traditional role of the storyteller even as he or she questions the assumptions that underlie those traditions.

Although there is much to celebrate in the differences between and among the authors discussed in this volume, there is also a great deal of common ground. Christine Ferguson's treatment of Alice Adams's short fiction stresses the autobiographical nature of Adams's work and includes a trenchant analysis of her method of fictional creation. The autobiographical wellspring is a recurrent theme in many of the authors under consideration. Specifically, Ferguson elaborates on Adams's belief that every act of writing involves the "subjective appropriation" of one's own travels and experiences.

Several of the authors in the current volume have notably found inspiration in the natural world. Tom Noyes describes Lewis Nordan's work, and although Nordan is not (primarily) a nature writer, Noyes finds that his wrenching autobiographical portraits often use a particular natural symbol for effect, a metaphor of "lake water as a black mirror," for example. Nordan has said that he likes the image because it allows him to have "each character face the mirrored water, and before the end of the story be beneath its surface to confront all of its joys and all of its terrors." Teresa Winterhalter's entry on Kent Nelson also foregrounds a concern with nature, but Winterhalter sees Nelson as moving beyond naturalistic description in favor of "a poetics of perception through which to rediscover an already inhabited land."

Thom Conroy suggests that the work of Wendell Berry highlights a similar concern with the natural world, particularly Berry's native Kentucky, where the author sets his stories of family, responsibility, and tradition.

In thematic contrast to the regionalism of Berry and the environmentalism of Bass, Frederick Smock observes that Sallie Bingham's fiction reflects the urbanity of a woman who came of age as a writer in New York City in the 1960s. Bingham is a woman of privilege, and her work investigates the status of women in the metropolis. According to Smock, Bingham's fictional women move, in her oeuvre, from a place where they define themselves in relation to the men in their lives to a place where they speak and act as independent and confident players in the world. A slightly more contemporary writer, Jane Smiley, also presents many female characters whose surface passivity often masks a maelstrom of emotional intensity, as Conroy indicates in the present volume.

Another Kentuckian, Robert Lann Boswell, is presented by Alexander McIlvaine Parsons as a writer bound up in the great American debate on race but fascinated as well by personal conflicts between ethics and desire. Karl Zuelke's essay on Reginald McKnight also, inevitably, focuses upon the "vivid voices" McKnight displays in his (usually) first-person narrations of those marginalized within the dominant white reality of America. McKnight varies his settings, sometimes writing not about Africans in America, but about Africa itself and the strange, often poorly understood and mythologized power it exerts on African American intellectuals. Boswell's explorations of race and class, often set in the American Southwest, also explore the dark side of the American dream—and of those pulled into the American orbit regardless of their personal desires.

James Coan, writing about Peter Cameron, also sees a focus on interpersonal struggles and the alienation that comes from being alive at this moment in American cultural history. Cameron's work, like that of so many other contemporary writers, offers a document of the changing attitudes of American youth culture. His studies of marginalization share characteristics with stories more explicitly on similar topics, such as those involving race, class, and gender.

Similarly, Amy Lilly's entry on Elizabeth Cullinan highlights the essential nature of ethnicity in the lives of her female characters, who are "often tenacious rather than strong." A strong sense of the importance of family and tradition in the Irish American urban experience also links Cullinan to Michael Stephens. As Eamonn Wall notes in writing about Stephens's short fiction, the interrelationship of the Irish in America with a myriad of other ethnic groups—especially within the immigrant communities that served as launching pads for multigenerational family growth—allows readers to experience America macroscopically. The tenacity with which the protagonists in Cullinan's and Stephens's stories approach life mirrors the process of writers seeking publication, working through rejection and emendation to finally see their work in print.

In much the same manner, Tom Whalen observes that Richard Grayson is concerned with the interaction of the creative and commercial processes. As Whalen relates, the postmodern and metafictional concerns of Grayson's social criticism and experimentation led him to coordinate a conference titled "Can publishing and literature co-exist?"

Gregory Morris's entry on Nicholas Delbanco presents another highly original writer, one who is vigorously engaged with the "rhythm and resonances of language" rather than with the transmission of content merely. Much like Padgett Powell, another stylist of the highest order, Delbanco exults in the sheer pleasure of language display itself. Likewise, the often-transgressive prose of Barry Hannah, as Richard Lee observes, luxuriates in language usage and the pithy point tellingly told. Hannah is one of those writers, notes Lee, who is often pigeonholed as a Southern writer and then dealt with only within that matrix of understanding. William

Frank points up the same issue in his essay on William Hoffman, writing that reviewers who see Hoffman as a "regional writer" fail to appreciate the universal applicability of his work. Dede Yow notes that Mary Hood embodies this same marriage of the parochial with the universal, detailing Hood's position within the "second Southern Renaissance," one in which strong women protagonists mingle traditional regional concerns with broader demographic shifts. Another leading voice of the New South, Jill McCorkle, is characterized by Robert Beuka as a writer primarily concerned with the common lives of her working-class protagonists.

Hannah's Mississippi, Hoffman's Virginia, Hood's Georgia, Berry and Boswell's Kentucky, the urban, ethnic ghettos of Stephens, and the other particularized settings of many of the authors in this volume speak to each other. They interrogate the processes of exclusivity and belonging that operate simultaneously at all moments in America. They all accentuate the particular with an avian eye cast toward the universal. And they all reflect a demon's bargain: individuals aspire to affiliation with groups for (psychic and other) protection; yet, the nature of American culture forces alienation upon all. The particular is the universal, but people's differences one from another—ephemeral yet powerful—blind them to that fact.

Gale Godwin's fiction, like that of Hannah and many other authors within this volume, vacillates between experimentation and traditional motifs in both novel and short-story form. Godwin's concern with the pressures women face, and the compromises they are forced to make as they waver between family and professional obligations, is a focus well-suited to the multigenre approach. Curt Meanor's essay on Charles Jackson notes that Jackson's short-story work was often overshadowed by the success of his first novel, *The Lost Weekend* (1944). However, Jackson, writing much earlier than Godwin, had the financial freedom to explore the man-centered world of the time; Jackson and Godwin speak to many of the same issues but use different filters to sieve the effects of culture on their protagonists. Writing at roughly the same time as Charles Jackson, Shirley Jackson was overshadowed by the success of a single piece: her story "The Lottery." Dale Hrebik's entry stresses that Shirley Jackson's consistent return to the supernatural and its effects on her (usually female) protagonists provides a psychic roadmap for the status of woman during the middle years of the twentieth century. Because of such connections, these three authors might be profitably viewed together.

Unlike the stories of Shirley Jackson, Rachel Maddux's surreal and magical short fiction went largely unpublished in her own lifetime, as Nancy Walker observes in her entry on Maddux's work. Whether this circumstance was due to Jackson's inclusion within a literary circle, including her husband, critic and author Stanley Edgar Hyman, and her relatively easier access to short-story publishing forums; to the relative dominance of the novel during her lifetime; or to something else—or some combination—is uncertain. Maddux, like Shirley Jackson, also tends toward stories reflecting powerlessness on the part of her protagonists, though she often imbues the powerless with access to occult and mystical compensatory abilities.

Sharon Jones also makes plain the necessity of seeing a writer such as William Harrison in a thematic context rather than merely as a genre writer. Harrison's stories, with their nonconformist protagonists, embody the subversiveness that the editors suggest exists at the heart of short-story creation in the waning years of the twentieth century. Lorrie Moore's quick wit and sure-footed ironies also develop the basic themes of alienation and the struggle for interpersonal connectedness, according to Robin Werner. The ennui that seems to be the spirit of the postwar age often presents its "palpable pain" through satiric representation, and Lorrie Moore is certainly adept at that. Troy Thibodeaux presents another sardonic commentator on human behavior, Francine Prose. In his view, Prose writes along a spectrum that spans from traditional folklore to uncompromising contemporary satire.

Particularly important to this volume is the work of William Peden. Meg Watson's entry shows Peden as one who has worked in the service of establishing the short-story form as the dominant literary genre of the late twentieth century. As Watson details Peden's contributions to the field, including the publication of his groundbreaking survey, *The American Short Story: Front Line in the National Defense of Literature* (1964), she highlights his claim that the short story was "the most suitable genre for capturing the accelerated tempo and fragmented character" of the era. Also of particular relevance to this volume is Victoria Nelson's entry on C. E. Poverman. According to Nelson, Poverman uses the short-story medium to focus on an "outlaw" motif, contrasted to the stifling domestic world of in-laws. Nelson links the development of the normative in culture to novelistic explorations and suggests that short stories work in the spaces between the normative.

Writer Mark Richard's work is also consistent with a vision of the short-story genre as one that tells the tales of those who have fallen below the radar of the novel's scope. Adam Sol locates the work of Richard within the broad field of "trailer-park fiction"—making Richard a kindred spirit with Larry Brown—even while Sol distinguishes Richard from the label by focusing on Richard's interests in the surreal and the fantastic. Lives lived below what is societally expected find a comfortable place within short fiction. Equally unflinching is the fiction of Richard Yates, whose characters tend to lead lives of quiet desperation within the cocoons of bourgeois existence. Blake Bailey describes Yates as a writer who told the truth too truly, and perhaps suffered because of it, reconfirming the conception of the short-story writer as a prophet of the culture's dark secrets. A related, yet different conception of lives lived outside of the normative American cultural portrait is detailed by Garrett Caples in his entry on John Yau. Caples sees Yau as an artist disconnected from both his own Chinese ancestry and from American culture. The status of the "hybrid" is one that seems to be particularly difficult for American culture to embrace, as it prefers that its classifications separate, rather than folded together. Yau's "restlessness with fixed forms" has led to fictional experimentation whereby he erodes the boundary between prose poem and short story.

Carol-Lynn Marrazzo presents W. D. Wetherell as a writer whose characters embody particularly American convictions of social and individual perfectibility. The tendency to disappointment and disillusionment that pervades his characters suggests not a failure of this particular normative American mythology, says Marrazzo, but rather Wetherell's conviction that there is an American character that can be conveyed by fictional methods, particularly that of short fiction.

In sum, though it is reductive to lump together thirty-five writers of any sort, there are commonalities and thematic consistencies between and among many of the writers surveyed within this volume. Rather than viewing individual authors in isolation, readers of short fiction might do well to view authors as integral parts of culture and their works as expressive of the dominant trends within that culture.

Anticipating later scholars, literary theorist George Lukács observed in 1920 the natural suitability of the short story for limning "the strangeness and ambiguity" of modern life, a "strangeness" Charles May has elaborated as "the arbitrary nature of experiences whose workings are always without cause or reason." The author's shaping power is more obviously foregrounded in the short story than it is in the novel. The reader of the short story is compelled to consider the decision-making involved in beginning and ending such brief pieces, to question the author's choices, and, in an extension of Lukács's theory, to go on to question all arbitrary authority—aesthetic, political, or cosmological. This invitation to question the role of the author, and by extension to question the role of all authority figures, makes the short story a valuable political tool. Several of the authors included in this volume do in fact use the short-story form with specifically political intent. Although almost any of the authors in this vol-

ume can be read as ideologically driven, the works of Reginald McKnight and Greg Johnson in particular speak to the necessity of working from marginalized positions.

Since 1978, when the Pulitzer Prize–winning *The Stories of John Cheever* became the first short-story collection in a long time to find a place on the best-seller lists, interest in the short story both as a marketable commodity and a fit subject for academic research has mushroomed, although the market for individual stories lags behind that for book-length story collections. In a recent interview, Frederick Busch observed that "the most excellent short story, the most wonderful soul-stretching short story as a work of gorgeous language and breathtaking event is alive and plentiful, but not *well*, because . . . the selection process, for whatever reason, is not very good." Busch has hopes that the situation will improve, if magazine editors can be kept in their jobs long enough to become more experienced. Other writers have enjoyed better luck with their editors. Lewis Nordan, for example, benefited from the influence of Shannon Ravenel, and Barry Hannah's earlier work was guided by Gordon Lish.

In fact, older editors such as Lish and George Plimpton have been generous in promoting the careers of new writers, and the increasingly well-attended meetings of the Society for the Study of the Short Story attest to a healthy future for the short story in the university classroom, whence a new generation of editors should arise. The hostility many critics expressed toward the short story during the furor over minimalism has abated somewhat in recent years. Critic Gary Krist recently commented on the current importance of the genre: "In the last two decades, it's been the short story that has given us the more nuanced picture of the way we live now—the ironic rhythms of our speech, the casual heartbreak of our small domestic failures, the twisted warp and woof of our daily moral compromises. Future historians trying to determine what it was like to be alive in *fin de millennium* America should read the last two decades of *O. Henry* and *Best American* short-story collections." Granted, novels such as those of Don DeLillo and Russell Banks might provide a broader view of the philosophical and social landscape, but it is the short story that peers directly into readers' houses.

—Patrick Meanor and Richard Lee

References:

Susan Lohafer and Jo Ellyn Clarey, *Short Story Theory at a Crossroads* (Baton Rouge: Louisiana State University Press, 1989);

Charles E. May, *The Short Story: The Reality of Artifice* (New York: Twayne, 1995).

Acknowledgments

This book was produced by Bruccoli Clark Layman, Inc. Karen L. Rood is senior editor. Charles Brower was the in-house editor; he was assisted by Tracy S. Bitonti, R. Bland Lawson, Jan Peter F. van Rosevelt, and Carol Fairman.

Production manager is Philip B. Dematteis.

Administrative support was provided by Ann M. Cheschi, Dawnca T. Williams, and Mary A. Womble.

Accountant is Kathy Weston. Accounting assistant is Amber L. Coker.

Copyediting supervisor is Phyllis A. Avant. The copyediting staff includes Brenda Carol Blanton, Allen E. Friend Jr., Melissa D. Hinton, William Tobias Mathes, Nancy E. Smith, and Elizabeth Jo Ann Sumner. Freelance copyeditor is Rebecca Mayo.

Editorial associates are Andrew Choate and Michael S. Martin.

Layout and graphics supervisor is Janet E. Hill. The graphics staff includes Karla Corley Brown and Zoe R. Cook.

Office manager is Kathy Lawler Merlette.

Photography supervisor is Paul Talbot. Photography editors are Charles Mims and Scott Nemzek.

Permissions editor is Jeff Miller.

Digital photographic copy work was performed by Joseph M. Bruccoli.

SGML supervisor is Cory McNair. The SGML staff includes Frank Graham, Linda Dalton Mullinax, Jason Paddock, and Alex Snead.

Systems manager is Marie L. Parker.

Typesetting supervisor is Kathleen M. Flanagan. The typesetting staff includes Mark J. McEwan, Patricia Flanagan Salisbury, and Alison Smith. Freelance typesetters are Wanda Adams and Vicki Grivetti.

Walter W. Ross did library research. He was assisted by Steven Gross and the following librarians at the Thomas Cooper Library of the University of South Carolina: circulation department head Tucker Taylor; reference department head Virginia W. Weathers; Brette Barclay, Marilee Birchfield, Paul Cammarata, Gary Geer, Michael Macan, Tom Marcil, Rose Marshall, and Sharon Verba; interlibrary loan department head John Brunswick; and Robert Arndt, Hayden Battle, Barry Bull, Jo Cottingham, Marna Hostetler, Marieum McClary, Erika Peake, and Nelson Rivera, interlibrary loan staff.

American Short-Story Writers Since World War II
Third Series

Dictionary of Literary Biography

Alice Adams

(14 August 1926 – 26 May 1999)

Christine C. Ferguson
Tulane University

See also the Adams entry in *DLB Yearbook: 1986.*

BOOKS: *Careless Love* (New York: New American Library, 1966); republished as *The Fall of Daisy Duke* (London: Constable, 1967);

Families and Survivors (New York: Knopf, 1974; London: Constable, 1976);

Listening to Billie (New York: Knopf, 1978; London: Constable, 1978);

Beautiful Girl: Stories (New York: Knopf, 1979);

Rich Rewards (New York: Knopf, 1980);

To See You Again: Stories (New York: Knopf, 1982);

Molly's Dog: A Story (Concord, N.H.: Ewert, 1983);

Superior Women (New York: Knopf, 1984; London: Heinemann, 1985);

Return Trips: Stories (New York: Knopf, 1985; London: Heinemann, 1986);

Second Chances (New York: Knopf, 1988; London: Methuen, 1988);

After You've Gone: Stories (New York: Knopf, 1989);

Mexico: Some Travels and Travelers There (New York & London: Prentice Hall, 1990);

Caroline's Daughters (New York: Knopf, 1991);

Almost Perfect (New York: Knopf, 1993);

A Southern Exposure (New York: Knopf, 1995);

Medicine Men (New York: Knopf, 1997);

The Last Lovely City: Stories (New York: Knopf, 1999);

After the War (New York: Knopf, 2000).

SELECTED PERIODICAL PUBLICATIONS– UNCOLLECTED:

FICTION

"Sea Gulls Are Happier Here," *Cosmopolitan,* 147 (January 1967): 108–111;

Alice Adams (photograph by Sydney Goldstein; from the dust jacket for Return Trips, *1985))*

"Young Couple with Class," *Redbook,* 129 (September 1967): 72ff.;

"Henry and the Pale-Faced Redskin," *Cosmopolitan,* 163 (October 1967): 146ff.;

"A Propitiation of Witches," *Redbook,* 134 (February 1970): 60–85, 150, 152, 158, 170, 172;

"Afternoons at the Beach," *McCall's,* 100 (November 1972): 84–85, 150, 152, 159, 170, 172;

"The Nice Girl," *McCall's,* 101 (August 1974): 94–95, 108–110, 112, 114;

"A Week in Venice," *McCall's,* 102 (November 1974): 112–113, 182, 184, 188;

"Learning to Be Happy," *Redbook,* 147 (September 1976): 100ff;

"The Polar Route," *Mademoiselle,* 84 (March 1978): 92ff;

"The Last Married Man," *Virginia Quarterly Review,* 54 (Spring 1978): 289–296;

"A Change of Season," *Redbook,* 153 (September 1979): 41ff.;

"The Chase," *Cosmopolitan,* 191 (August 1981): 252ff.;

"Lovers and Friends," *McCall's,* 109 (August 1982): 94–95, 127–128, 130, 132, 134;

"A Legendary Lover," *McCall's,* 112 (November 1984): 90;

"Against All Odds," *Redbook,* 165 (August 1985): 52ff.;

"Time Alone," *The New Yorker,* 62 (4 August 1986): 28–36;

"The Drinking Club," *The New Yorker,* 63 (31 August 1987): 28–34;

"Earthquake Damage," *The New Yorker* (7 May 1990): 4–49;

"The Last Lovely City," *The New Yorker,* 67 (11 March 1991): 33–39;

"Up the Coast," *Gentleman's Quarterly,* 62 (May 1992): 113–116;

"Love and Work," *Southwest Review,* 77 (Autumn 1992): 466–479;

"Kind Strangers," *Southwest Review,* 79 (Spring/Summer 1994): 191–198;

"Complicities," *Michigan Quarterly Review,* 34 (Summer 1995): 324–329;

"A Very Nice Dog," *Southwest Review,* 82 (Spring 1997): 199–204;

"The Visit," *Ploughshares,* 23 (Fall 1997): 7–12;

"Arabel's List," *Ploughshares,* 24 (Fall 1998): 76–84;

"Great Sex," *Southwest Review,* 83 (Winter 1998): 512–519.

NONFICTION

"A Talk with Biographers," *New York Times Book Review,* 20 April 1980, pp. 29–31;

"On Turning Fifty," *Vogue,* 173 (December 1983): 230ff.;

"The Wild Coasts of Portugal," *Geo,* 6 (November 1984): 56ff.;

"Dolls," *Life,* 13 (July 1990): 103;

"Balcony Scenes," *American Film,* 16 (March 1991): 76;

"Author's Statements," *Southwest Review,* 79 (Spring/Summer 1994): 540–556.

"The short story," noted Alice Adams in a 1980 interview with Neil Feinneman, is "the form I love best." Spanning thirty years, Adams's career as a short-story writer was one of the most prolific and successful in recent American literature. In addition to nine novels and many uncollected stories, Adams published six short-story collections, the last of which, *The Last Lovely City,* appeared only shortly before her death on 26 May 1999. Adams's starkly realist yet emotionally intense prose and her thematic interest in the quest for self-knowledge has drawn her comparisons with Colette, Ernest Hemingway, and F. Scott Fitzgerald. Critics and popular readers have lauded her depictions of the lives and romantic pursuits of independent female protagonists who, even in the face of loss and suffering, refuse the mantle of victimhood and instead become survivors.

Adams's success, marked both by the size of her audience and the number of prestigious prizes she has won (including the O. Henry Award, which she earned each year from 1971 to 1982 and then again from 1984 to 1996), does not indicate that her work is free from complex and arguably problematic ambiguities. As yet, no book-length critical review of her work exists, a fact attributable to uncertainty on the part of the critical establishment as to the place of her work on the American literary spectrum. Adams has alternately been praised for the craftsmanship and technique of her stories and criticized for what some have perceived as the uniformity of her characters and themes. In a largely positive notice in *The New York Times Book Review* (16 January 1979) of Adams's first story collection, *Beautiful Girl* (1979), Katha Pollitt observed, "Too many of these stories are about a certain type of woman." Although many of Adams's female protagonists share white, middle- to- upper-class background and advanced, often artistic, professions, it would be a mistake, as critics such as Cara Chell have noted, to ignore the variation and diversity of their emotional lives, which exist independent of the characters' external similarities. The variety of reactions and interpretations inspired by Adams's writing represents the richness and complexity of her artistry.

There are many ways to read Adams's short stories, and one of the most frequent and accessible is as autobiography. Adams herself affirmed the connection between her own life and her fictional constructions, lacing her stories with references to the troubled family and Southern childhood of her own experience. Born on 14 August 1926 in Fredericksburg, Virginia, Alice Boyd Adams was the only child of Nicholson Barney Adams and Agatha Erskine Boyd Adams. Shortly after her birth, the family moved to Chapel Hill, where Nicholson Adams taught Spanish at the University of

North Carolina; Alice stayed with them until the age of sixteen, when she left to pursue studies at Radcliffe College.

Her early years were tumultuous ones, marked by encounters with the stifling racial and sexual stereotypes of the Depression-era South, a troubled relationship with her mother, and the breakdown of her parents' miserably unhappy marriage. These experiences later became essential elements in her fictional landscape, echoing with particular resonance in the opening trilogy of her first short-fiction collection, *Beautiful Girl*. The three stories "Verlie I Say Unto You," "Are You in Love?," and "Alternatives" treat the breakdown in relations between various members of the Todd family, focusing particularly on Jessica Todd's growing awareness of her husband's infidelity and her own deep alienation from those around her. Like Agatha Adams, the fictional Jessica dies relatively young, leaving her husband to marry again. Adams notes in an autobiographical article for *Vogue* (December 1983): "My mother suffered . . . and died rather young . . . of sheer misery, I believe. My father endured after that, several years of black debilitating guilt; but later he married a woman with whom he was happy." If Adams's mother came to represent a tragic figure in the young writer's life, however, she was also an inspirational one. In the interview with Feinneman she stated: "I came from the kind of intellectual background that made writing seem like the most praiseworthy thing to do, so there was never anything else. My mother wanted to be a writer and was a failed one; she was depressed, unhappy and peripherally involved with the literary world."

While her success as a writer ultimately was far greater than that of her mother, Adams shared with her the initial discouragement and rejection that so frequently characterized the experience of women writers in the 1940s and 1950s. Even as an adolescent, she was censured for her intellectual precocity, which some considered to be decidedly unladylike. In a 1978 interview with Nancy Faber she wryly recollected that "I was bright in school and ran into trouble because of that Southern thing that women are supposed to be stupid." The gender-biased discouragement of her literary pursuits did not end with her departure from North Carolina. While studying writing at Radcliffe (the only subject she claims ever to have felt a real affinity for), teacher Kenneth Kempton advised her: "Miss Adams, you're a very nice girl. Why don't you forget about this writing and go get married?" Adams's celebrated career has since proved an eloquent retort to this piece of advice.

After her graduation from Radcliffe in 1946, Adams became involved in the literary world of New

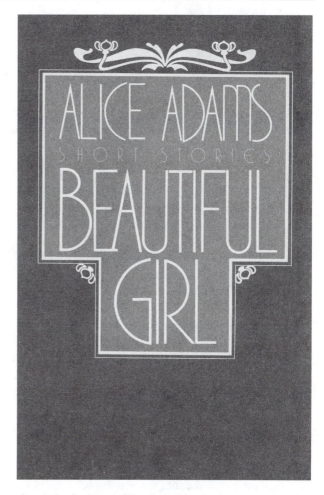

Dust jacket for Adams's first collection of stories, focusing on the diverse inner lives of privileged white women

York City, not as a writer but as an employee of a major publishing house. Not long after her entry into the publishing business, Adams was fired for spending too many weekends away, visiting fiancé Mark Linenthal Jr., whom she married in 1947. Once wed, the couple moved to Paris, where Linenthal spent a year studying at the Sorbonne. Despite already apparent difficulties in her marriage, Adams loved the exhilarating energy of Paris and later used the city as the setting for her first published story, "Winter Rain." Upon their return to the United States, the couple took up residence in San Francisco, where Linenthal taught English at San Francisco State University. The years that followed were, apart from the birth of Adams's beloved son, Peter, in 1951, some of the unhappiest of the writer's life: "When I was thirty, I was miserably married. I had a difficult young child. . . . No money, no profession: I was always writing, but not published."

The misery of these years shows up in many of her fictional treatments of women's search for economic and emotional independence beyond the confines of conventional marriage. A year before selling her first story to *Charm* magazine, an accomplishment that surely helped fuel her search for personal and artistic autonomy, she divorced Linenthal in 1958. The years that followed were occupied by the physical and emotional exhaustion of raising a child, struggling to maintain financial survival through a series of part-time secretarial jobs, and striving to achieve the literary success that had tantalized her since childhood. "It was a depressing period in terms of work," she noted to Feinneman. "I felt bleak, lonely, envious. I kept on writing, but it struck me as an excessively neurotic thing to be doing—to be wasting all that time on something I was not good at. I went to a psychiatrist who told me that I should stop writing and stay married, but I've been a strong rebel, and in some recesses of my mind, I must have thought I was good—and known he was a fool—because I did keep writing."

Various developments in the mid 1960s assured Adams that she was neither neurotic nor delusional in her assessment of her writing talents. She met and befriended prominent editor William Abrahams and interior designer Robert McNie, with whom she later shared her life; both supported and lauded her work. In 1966 Adams's talent, dedication, and endurance were rewarded with the publication of her first novel, *Careless Love,* by New American Library (republished in the United Kingdom a year later as *The Fall of Daisy Duke*). British audiences and critics favored the book far more than their American counterparts, who missed the irony and satire that accompanied Adams's treatment of a divorcée seeking romantic fulfillment in the steamy climate of the sexual revolution. Undaunted by the negative response in the United States, Adams's output in the following years was steady and increasingly drew positive critical attention. The first of Adams's many stories for *The New Yorker,* "Gift of Grass," appeared in the November 1969 issue; two years later the same story took third prize in the *O. Henry Annual.* By the time Adams published her first short-story collection in 1979, she had added two more novels (*Families and Survivors,* 1974; *Listening to Billie,* 1978) and many uncollected stories to her literary repertoire. Given the literary successes and artistic richness that marked Adams's move into middle age, it is hardly surprising that so many of her short stories challenge and disrupt the myths of dependency and asexuality constructed around the mature woman.

Beautiful Girl displays Adams's expert manipulation of the form she loves best, through sixteen stories dealing with loss and the possibility of redemption. They are, for the most part, stories written after the fact, intricate tales of the aftershocks produced by pas-

sion, friendship, and beauty. Tobacco heiress Ardis Bascombe in the title story was beautiful in her youth, "a small and slender black-haired girl, with amazing wide, thickly lashed dark-azure eyes and smooth, pale, almost translucent skin—a classic Southern beauty"; now she is a battered alcoholic slowly drinking herself to death in her San Francisco home. Enslaved by the unfulfilled promise of the past, which she has never really acknowledged, Ardis closes the story by declaring angrily to her would-be lover, Walpole Greene: "I am a beautiful girl." Greene, who has tracked down Ardis, his college crush, after twenty years of separation, suffers from a similar bondage to the past. Confronted with Ardis's decline, he resorts to a kind of denial, promising to take her away to a treatment center where she may be restored to her former beauty and talent. Her final declaration reveals the impossibility of any such restoration while Ardis still clings to an ideal of herself that has long since faded.

The theme of loss permeates many of the other stories in the collection, including "Ripped Off," which describes a young woman's confusion of a burglary with romantic abandonment, and Adams's personal favorite, "A Pale and Perfectly Oval Moon." Written at a time when cancer was still, as Adams later noted, a relatively taboo subject, the latter story details the shifting relationship between a married couple as Penelope Moore dies of the wasting disease. Penelope is no tragic heroine passing mutely into the night, but a strong-willed, often antagonistic, and fiercely independent fighter. "Dying, for a time Penelope Moore behaved atrociously. To her husband Van, who loved her (in his way), both the fact of her dying and her continuous, fiercely whispered accusations were intolerable." Adams's concern is less with the validity of Penelope's accusations of infidelity (which, it turns out, are justified), or indeed with defending Penelope and Van's often tempestuous relationship; rather, she focuses on the lingering love that continues to haunt him, despite the difficulties of their marriage, long after her death.

This focus on the traces that survive violent passion, on the survival of bonds that have weathered many storms, saves Adams's characters from the fate she once ascribed to other female protagonists in contemporary literature. In an interview with Patricia Holt for *Publishers Weekly* (16 January 1978) she complains that "there has really been too much about women and their endless problems with love and sex, and with the kind of addictive love affair that is so all-consuming it makes sex an excuse for delaying the things that matter, like getting down to work." Adams's statement may seem somewhat contradictory; after all, the majority of the stories in *Beautiful Girl* do take the role of romantic love in women's lives as their central subject. Love, and the devastation that it can produce, acts not to define women's experience, but as a vehicle through which to expose their resilience. In "Verlie I Say Unto You," the opening story of the collection, Verlie Jones has suffered years of trial with a violent husband and the indignities routinely proffered to her as a black maid working in the racially divisive climate of the Depression-era South; eventually she loses her lover, Clifton, to a sudden illness that might have been treatable had not the only hospital that would accept African Americans been so far away. Despite the intensity of these sufferings, the closing image of Verlie offered by the narrative is not of a woman overcome and ruined but of a moment in which her capacity for joy and hope is at a peak: "But on that rare spring day months earlier . . . Verlie walks with an exceptional lightness of heart, smiling to herself at all the colors of the bright new flowers, and at the smells of spring, the promises."

Beautiful Girl was well reviewed and won acclaim from critics who celebrated its style and its thematic rejection of some of the more typical clichés about women and love. Susan Wood, in *The Washington Post Book World* (21 January 1979), wrote, "It is refreshing and hopeful to find a writer in this day and age who, although recognizing love's possibilities for destruction, can still write about the ways in which love, both sexual and platonic, is akin to salvation." In *The Christian Science Monitor* (12 February 1979), Janet Domowitz asserted that "Adams concentrates on emotions so poignant that they are almost beyond words of expression."

The period that followed was one of the most productive of Adams's career. In 1980 she published her fourth novel, *Rich Rewards,* the half-satirical, half-earnestly romantic first-person narrative of a divorced woman's attempt to find a place for herself through love and work. The popular reception of this novel, although manifest, was not as strong as that produced by *Superior Women* (1984), Adams's first best-seller. In the midst of this period of constant production, Adams was also able to publish her second volume of short stories. Critics generally agreed that *To See You Again: Stories* (1982) showed an expansion in Adams's narrative scope. These nineteen stories, many of which originally appeared in *The New Yorker,* range in milieu from the high society of San Francisco to the plantation life of the West Mexican coast, and in character from compulsive gamblers to teenage waitresses. Adams displays her trademark thematic concern with the durability of the human spirit and its continual desire for new stimulus and growth.

Nowhere is this focus handled more deftly than in "Greyhound People," the story that many critics

Dust jacket for Adams's 1982 collection, including stories with settings ranging from San Francisco to a Mexican plantation

have described as the finest in the collection. The story derives its premise from the dread people experience when they feel they have taken a wrong turn and lost their way, only to manipulate this sense of displacement into an opportunity for revelation. Its protagonist is a recently divorced commuter in Northern California who spends her days in transit, both literally from Sacramento to San Francisco and psychologically from the cloying dependency urged upon her by her overprotective friend Hortense to the total emotional independence she desires. One night she discovers, to her horror, that she has taken the wrong bus; instead of taking the express to San Francisco, she must take a convoluted route that stops at various small towns. Her distress quickly turns to pleasure as the trip affords her an opportunity to meet and observe people and situations outside her own rather banal class experience. Her exhilaration is so intense that, despite Hortense's dismay at her lateness, she is unable to refrain from repeating the experience, almost compulsively boarding the wrong bus at the end of the workday. Finally, she admits: "Actually, the Greyhound system of departure gates to San Francisco is very simple; I had really been aware all along of how it worked." The wrong bus has been the right bus after all, its true destination inhabiting a psychological rather than a geographical space. At the close of the story she purchases a special pass that allows her to travel limitlessly over all of California and break the ties that have held her firmly to routine and dependency.

"Greyhound People" is not the only story of the collection to transform a mistake or a wrong turn into an unanticipated boon. "By the Sea" works as a sort of modern revision of the Cinderella story. Its protagonist, Dylan Bellentyne, is an eighteen-year-old waitress working in a much-hated job at a seaside holiday resort while her former hippie mother tries to free herself from a controlling boyfriend and build a life for herself. Dylan spends her time fantasizing about being adopted by a respectable older couple or, more plausibly, of being whisked away from her mundane life by a handsome, dark, and rich stranger. With the arrival of the wealthy and young Mr. Iverson at the lodge, the latter fantasy seems about to come true. Adams, with her usual aversion to conventional scripts, is quick to subvert romantic cliché, however. When the emphatic Mr. Iverson does woo Dylan, she views him only with mild distaste: "Instead of being moved, as she might have been, Dylan thought he sounded a little silly . . . and she stepped back a little, away from him." Despite his repeated urgings, Dylan continues to resist his advances; though young, she has been freed from the myth of love as a fairy-tale solution to the banal sufferings of everyday life. Like the deliberately misdirected protagonist in "Greyhound People," she is wary of those emotional paths that seem well-worn and overly familiar.

Not all of the stories in *To See You Again,* according to some of its critics, are so successful in avoiding the conventional. Benjamin DeMott, in *The New York Times Book Review* (11 April 1982), leveled the charge of repetitiveness, a criticism that continued to haunt Adams throughout her career: "By the middle of the book I found myself in need of change, desirous of esthetic (not moral) relief." While DeMott laments the recurring elements of her stories, other critics condemned Adams's departure from them in the story "Teresa." The first of the many collected Mexican stories spawned by Adams's love of that country, "Teresa" details the misfortunes of a woman living in an impoverished area outside of Ixtapanejo. The narrative tone is unusually sentimental, verging on the mawkish, as it describes the murder of Teresa's husband, Ernesto, by the cruel gringo plantation owner, Senor Krupp, and the subsequent imprisonment of her son, Felipe, for his revenge killing of Krupp. In the preface to her 1990 collection of stories exclusively devoted to Mexico, *Mexico: Some Travels and Travelers There,* Adams suggests that the story was drawn from a real-life incident that she and some friends learned of while traveling through the country in the 1960s. This basis in reality perhaps prevents Adams from maintaining an ironic distance from her subject, as she does in other stories. Writes Robert Phillips in *Commonweal* (25 March 1983): "Teresa is the least convincing protagonist in the book. It is as if the author needs the trappings of 'civilization' to fully comprehend her character's motivations." Convincing or not, "Teresa" represented a new movement in Adams's work toward the depiction of nonurban and non-middle-class lifestyles, a movement that testifies to the sometimes criticized diversity of her work and her humanistic, although rarely overtly political, interest in the plight of the oppressed.

Another interesting tendency is apparent in the critical reception of *To See You Again,* one that most female authors encounter at one point or another in their careers. There is an urge in some of her reviewers to place Adams within, or in direct opposition to, a gendered concept of writing. Typifying the first of these responses, William Buchanan states in *Studies in Short Fiction* (1983): "The blurb on the jacket suggests a comparison with Katherine Mansfield. This comparison seems apt. Both use mainly women protagonists, and their stories show a very feminine concern for the quality of relationships and moods. . . . The blurb goes on to suggest a comparison with Flannery O'Connor. This comparison does *not* seem apt. There is nothing feminine about Ms. O'Connor's stories." Buchanan's characterizations of "feminine" and "masculine" writing obviously reveal far more about his preconceived notion of gender difference than they do about Adams's art, but they nonetheless represent a not uncommon mode of interpreting her stories. Carolyn See, in *The Los Angeles Times* (13 April 1983), parodies this tendency to reduce all artistic output to the gender of the producer, asserting that Adams is similar to O'Connor or Mansfield only in that "she is also a woman and writes short stories. It might be more productive to think of Alice Adams as comparable to Walter Cronkite because you can believe what she says. Or to Albert Michelson, Einstein's predecessor, because of her experiments in motion, time and light, or to evangelist Terry-Cole Whittaker, because Adams insists—philosophically and intellectually—on the possibility of happiness for intelligent people. Or to Norman Mailer because she'd knock him out in the first round." See finds in *To See You Again* a strong and accurate representation of the diversity that marks the life of most women as "neither slave nor feminist, but something in between," rather than a trite encapsulation of "feminine" emotional homogeneity.

The title story of the collection is also its most impressionistic one. Based loosely on Thomas Mann's *Death in Venice* (1912), the narrative details the passionate fixation of a female college instructor with her attractive student Seth. Laura's love is played out purely on an internal level; she never confronts Seth or betrays herself in front of him, and indeed the story opens with his departure from her senior-level English class and also ostensibly from her life. Her anguish at his departure becomes a metaphor for the greater losses within her marriage to Gerald, a once handsome young architect who has become crushed under the weight of recurrent and deadening depression. Her desire for Seth, which is never explicitly sexual in nature, becomes a desire for regeneration in general. Imagining what he will look like when he reaches her age, she muses "at that time, your prime and our old age, Gerald's and mine, Gerald will be completely well, the cycle flat, no more sequences of pain. And maybe thin again. And interested, and content. It's almost worth waiting for." A thin shaft of hope, one of the most recurrent motifs in Adams's fiction, pierces the gloom of a relationship dulled by years of depression.

In 1984, Adams was again included in the *O. Henry Prize Stories* collection after a two-year absence; her work then continued to appear regularly in the collection through 1996. Adams's productivity remained consistently high throughout the 1980s, and in 1985 Knopf published her third volume of short stories, *Return Trips*. While *To See You Again* focused on the possibilities for hope and growth offered by its characters' diversions from traditional and familiar routes, this volume speculates upon both the desire for and the impossibility of return to once beloved places and relationships. The common destination of all these fifteen narrative "trips" is a past that is neither fixed, stable, nor accessible. In the title story, Emma plans to pass through the site in Yugoslavia where, many years before, she spent a torturous summer with her much cherished and fatally ill lover, Paul. Her meditations on this revisitation evoke memories of an earlier return trip taken years before to the small, southern university town that she, like Adams, left at the age of sixteen. There, after meeting with Popsie Hooker, the woman who had been her father's lover, Emma realizes with profound disillusionment that not only is the past irretrievable, but it may never have actually meant what she thought it did. Popsie reveals herself to be vitriolic, petty, and mean, where Emma had hoped to find evidence of compassion, understanding, and wisdom. Cautioned by this experience, Emma decides not to visit the precise location of her sojourn with Paul, thinking "that particular

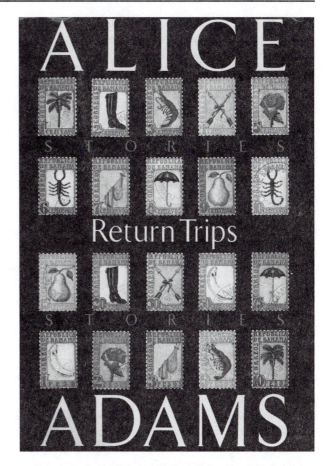

Dust jacket for Adams's 1985 collection of stories, which describe various characters' attempts to recapture a lost past

ugly, poorly built structure has probably been torn down. Still, I very much like the idea of being in its vicinity." If one's idealized visions of times gone by crumble when confronted by the harshness of material reality, then one might still access them through emotional conduits.

"You Are What You Own: A Notebook" depicts a woman quite literally burdened by the oppressive bulk of the past in the form of a collection of heavy furniture inherited from her mother. "My inheritance: it weighs me down as heavily as my feet, a part of me. Like my husband, who is also heavy, to whom I am connected, whom I cannot leave. Where do I end? And he begin?" Just as the furniture acts as a physical deterrent to the character's daily movement, jutting in her way and bruising her thighs, so too does her professor husband, Carl, bind her to the role of staid faculty wife. Unsurprisingly, he is secretly extremely proud of his wife's inheritance and takes great pleasure in polishing it as his wife slides deeper and deeper into a depression. She fantasizes about breaking the furniture or simply leaving Carl and abandoning it to the deterioration that seems to threaten her.

Decay and deterioration also represent liberation for Miriam in the story "Mexican Dust." Small, dark, and artistic, she differs tremendously from the party of three tall, blond, "super-gringo" relatives with whom she is traveling through Mexico. Miriam's husband, Eric; his twin sister, Joan; and her husband, Russell, are skittish and smug travelers, disdaining the dangers of roadside food concessions and the chaos of second-class bus travel while implicitly congratulating themselves over the cultural superiority that, they assume, frees them from the superstition and dirt of rural Mexico. "They think God will get them across highways," snorts Eric upon witnessing two traffic accident victims lying by the side of the Pan-American Highway. Later, when they reach a scenically beautiful yet disorganized and filthy hotel in Escondido, Miriam alone does not share the revulsion that propels the others to seek a more sterile and maintained environment. Indeed, she recognizes it as a symbol of escape and revolt against the middle-class orderliness of her own married life and begs the party to return to it when they face an interminable delay at the Estrella de Oro bus station. Her plea only angers the others and further establishes her difference from them. When the group finally reaches a "nice" hotel in Ixtapa, replete with cleanliness and good service, Miriam is besieged by thoughts of escape and begins to dread the dangers lurking in the adjacent sea.

The last story in *Return Trips*, "My First and Only House," represents the most personal of all Adams's return trips. Echoing "Berkeley House" (1982), from "To See You Again," it describes Adams's dreams of her childhood home in Chapel Hill. Despite her sometimes pronounced aversion to the Southern milieu of her youth, Adams admits to feeling possessed by the house in which she grew up and where her parents' marriage collapsed. She confesses, "I am writing, then, at least in part, about the vagaries of memory and about the house that in dreams I permanently inhabit–or, it might be more accurate to say, the house that inhabits me." Upon revisiting the house in 1983 shortly after her stepmother had put it up for sale ("a serious trauma that: it was made clear that I had never owned the house"), Adams finds it greatly changed and almost unrecognizable due to recent renovations. The experience also provokes an awareness of an ownership quite separate from and, in some ways, more valid than that authorized by inheritance; she writes "that freshly painted, viewless house is non-existent in my mind. It is not where I live. I live in a huge, mad house with the loveliest view. With everything in bloom." Ultimately, it is the house of subjective memory that takes precedence over that which exists in reality.

Reviewers responded warmly to Adams's depiction of the resonance of place and her typically unsentimental treatment of mature love. "Nobody writes better about falling in love than Alice Adams," commented Beverly Lowry in *The New York Times Book Review* (1 September 1985). "The protagonists of her stories, almost always women . . . know exactly what is about to happen: no nitwits, never victims or too gaga, they have been there before. They fall with eyes open." In *After You've Gone* (1989), Adams writes with equal adroitness about the process of falling out of love. The title piece of the collection, called "a wonderfully cultivated revenge story" by Ron Carlson in *The New York Times Book Review* (8 October 1989), takes the form of a letter from a successful female lawyer to her poet husband, who has recently deserted her for a younger woman. Characteristically, Adams's focus is not upon the most violent of the emotional vicissitudes provoked by abandonment but rather upon the stubbornly mundane resilience of the narrator: "The truth is, for a while I managed very well indeed. I coped with the house and its curious breakages, and with the bad nights of remembering you only at your best, and the good days suddenly jolted by your ghost."

The narrator's recovery is jeopardized when she begins to receive letters from her husband's new young lover, Sally Ann, earnest and trite missives begging for forgiveness and asking for personal advice. Her anger eventually turns to sympathy and pity as she realizes that Sally Ann is being subjected to the same kind of abandonment, albeit in an emotional form, that she herself has suffered. Sally Ann writes desperately of being ignored, rejected, and negatively compared to her predecessor. In response the narrator writes to her husband: "It is clear to me that in an emotional sense you are battering this young woman. She is being abused by you. I could prove it to a jury. And, unlike me, she is quite without defenses." She closes by asking him to leave Sally Ann just as he left her so that both women might be free of his emotional tyranny. "All three of us, you, me, and Sally Ann, will be much better off–you without her, and she without you. And me without the crazy burden of these letters, which, if I were *really* fair, I would send on to you." Thus, a scenario that could easily lapse into familiar depictions of jealousy and female rivalry becomes instead a vehicle for feminine solidarity and emancipation. In sympathizing with the sufferings of her young replacement, the narrator is able to free herself from her husband's thrall and ultimately recognize the hollow neediness of his nature.

As a result of such depictions, Adams is frequently classified as a feminist, if not radically political, writer. In her 7 May 1990 *Los Angeles Times* review of *After You've Gone,* Elaine Kendall noted, "There's a per-

The widowers ~~ Secret Gifts

"I'm extremely happy as I am, is the truth, I don't care much about meeting people," says Gloria Seashoales, a recently (acrimoniously) newly divorced graphics artist, more recently arrived in Mill Valley, CA, where she hoped to find a clearer, more peaceful life. Not new men—

the speaks these ungrateful, half-true words to her friend Melissa, a long-time resident. Melissa who found her this tiny house; who now has invited her to a party. To meet someone—

"Besides, I'm too young for widowers, aren't I?" Sensible Melissa laughs, tells her friend, "It's just a party. I'm not a marriage broker."

Hanging up, looking down into the little garden behind her house, Gloria sees that there are there again, a doz. 2 lemons (she thinks). So lovely, with their great dumb eyes, beautiful clumsy legs. Gloria would like to feed them, but doesn't know how, or what they like. They do not seem to like the rhododendron leaves at which they sniff, perhaps hoping for change. And so the rhododendron might not miraculously be roses. Gloria smiles, as she thinks that what she said to Melissa is at least half true— she is actually a little frightened by California, the great sweeps of space, across hills, the depthless churning waters of the Bay. She is also less frantic, less guilty, for confused than in NY she often felt herself to be. What she needs is a job. Today she has a list of people to call—

ceptible feminist undertow to these stories, a slight but noticeable pull that becomes apparent only when you're standing safely on shore. . . . While Adams never actually disparages her male characters, she lets them bare the less agreeable sides of their personalities, while the women glow with courage, understanding and resilience–sometimes that's enough." Rosalind Warren, writing in the *Women's Review of Books* (7 May 1990), agreed: "If there's a war between the sexes, in these stories the women are winning." Adams does not marginalize or ignore male characters, however; indeed, two of the most important stories in *After You've Gone,* "Ocracoke Island" and "A Sixties Romance," feature male protagonists. In the former, an aging male professor is left by his wife for a dashing young poet, Brennan O'Donnahue. While a similar situation provoked reader empathy with the abandoned partner in "After You've Gone," here Adams suggests that the husband's initial neglect led to the departure. Discussing the events with his former wife, Emily, the professor notes, "I did one really dumb thing, though. At some point, I told Cath that she should have an affair. Of course I spoke in jest, but can she have taken me seriously?" Emily replies: "Well, jesting or not, that's really worse than dumb. That's cruel. It's what men say to wives they want to get rid of."

Similarly, Roger Michaels in "A Sixties Romance" shows himself to be ultimately responsible for the loss of a beloved partner. Upon his initial meeting with Julia Bailey, a somewhat plain and unstylish mathematician, Roger reflects that "she's not up to my usual standards" but proceeds to fall in love with her intensity and intelligence anyway. Later, he is dumped by Julia when she learns of his infidelity with a previous lover, Candida. Roger's love for Julia is real and his pain at her absence excruciating, but somehow it fails to move the reader in the same way as Adams's other treatments of female abandonment.

After You've Gone is not solely concerned with the relations between the sexes; it also takes up the topic of female friendship. Recalling "Roses, Rhododendron" and "A Southern Spelling Bee" from earlier collections, "Tide Pools" traces the development of a friendship between Judith Mallory and Jennifer Cartwright from youth to maturity. After sharing a similar Californian childhood marked by the alcoholism of their parents, Judith leaves to become a marine biologist while Jennifer remains in Santa Barbara and gradually becomes an alcoholic herself. Upon renewing their friendship after an interim of many years, Judith takes a sabbatical and moves home to nurse her friend. The situation proves therapeutic for both women, reducing Jennifer's alcohol intake and restoring her to relative health and allowing Judith an escape from the frantic careerism of her profession and an opportunity to address the issues of her past.

In 1990 Adams published her first and only collection of nonfiction stories about the country she had been visiting for decades. *Mexico: Some Travels and Travelers There* also has the distinction of being the author's most controversial work. While it received generally positive reviews, the book was lambasted by some critics for its preoccupation with the mundane details of travel planning rather than Mexico itself. In a review for *The Washington Post Book Review* (21 November 1991) Alan Ryan noted: "There is little of Mexico here. Adams is interested only in her ill-planned plane reservations, changing her room in every hotel, the inadequate size of closets and service that is not up to her own high San Francisco standards, of which she constantly reminds us." Expressing similar concerns, Frank Prial wrote in *The New York Times Book Review* (1 December 1991): "Sometimes Mexico does come through. Here and there–among the logistic details–a bright passage appears, about a flower-filled courtyard or a dramatic sunset. It's just enough to make one wish that Ms. Adams had taken as much care with her narrative as she did with her hotel reservations."

Despite such criticisms, the collection neither is nor claims to be "about" Mexico per se, but rather about the strategies by which travelers attempt to grasp and see it, strategies that, in Adams's view, are almost always doomed to failure. She notes that "Americans in Mexico make whatever they will of the country," constantly blurring the reality of the country with their own preconceived cultural stereotypes. She stresses this point with particular eloquence in the preface to the volume, where she claims that "Mexico has always been invasion-prone. I do not cite this as a fault but rather as a historical fact, a fate. . . . The most recent invaders have been the tourists, and it seems to me that these tourists have the invasive instincts, not only in terms of plunder but also in a curious urge to make Mexico their own, to impose, that is, their own sensibilities on 'Mexico' and to export it as their own product." Adams, while distancing herself from the worst of the American tourists who travel south of the border, recognizes herself as a sort of literary plunderer and realizes that her travel commentary will ultimately reveal more about herself than Mexico. The stories, while ostensibly nonfictional in their origin, in reality are nonetheless colored by the inescapable subjectivity that typically characterizes fiction. She calls the reader's attention to this limitation by highlighting rather than concealing the arbitrary conditions, such as her emotional state and connection to her traveling companions, that have focused the lens through which she views Mexico.

The opening trilogy of travel accounts in *Mexico* describes three different meetings with the same place, Zihuatanejo. The first of these, "Zihuatanejo A," is the most joyful. It describes Adams's initial visit to the area with her then-lover "R," a shadowy figure who appears in various of the travelogues in the collection. Together they swim in the ocean, relax on the beach, and spend time with Celeste and Charles Martin, a dignified elderly couple in the fiftieth year of their marriage. The strength and endurance of the Martins' relationship provides the hopeful perspective through which Adams views her connection with both "R" and the landscape. Subsequent visits are far less idyllic. "Zihuatanejo B" describes the real events that inspired Adams's fictional story "Teresa" in *To See You Again*. On revisiting the town, this time with German friends Helene and Otto, Adams and "R" learn of a young local boy, Ernesto, who has been imprisoned for avenging the murder of his father by a rich plantation owner. Horrified by what they perceive as a miscarriage of justice, the party visits the seventeen-year-old Ernesto in jail and attempts to secure his release or at least a speedy hearing for his case. Their efforts fail, and Adams returns home heavy-hearted over the needless condemnation of a young life to years in prison.

The description of Adams's third trip to Zihuatanejo, "Zihuatanejo C," is the most disheartening of all. Charles Martin has died, and Celeste Martin is now traveling with an alcoholic gigolo named Chuck and her offensive friend Dorothy, who, as Adams notes, was "politically somewhere to the right of Ronald Reagan. She was prepared, it came out, not to like Mexico at all—so full of Mexicans, those shiftless wetbacks." Witnessing the once-dignified Celeste fall prey to such vulgar parasites effects a deep disillusionment in Adams. She returns to San Francisco, where she and "R" break up "after all that time. Most wretchedly. And so I do not go back to Zihuatanejo anymore. I know people who do, however, and they tell me that it is quite unchanged, which is what I would like to think."

In the subsequent travel accounts, Adams devotes almost as much attention to the flawed interpretations of Mexico of arrogant Western tourists as she does to her own impressions. While staying in Baja California, she meets a Texan couple who insists on sharing with her a negative and patronizing story about "the Mexican character (about which nearly all Texans are experts, just as many Southerners used to insist that they were able to tell you what Negroes are 'really like')." The tone of irony is unmistakable here, as it is in all her denunciations of what she terms "the wrong, worst kind of tourist." There are parts of the text, however, where she seems, if only momentarily, to partake of the same culturally superior attitude that she berates.

She refers to the "primitive" beauty of the country's art and complains with some regularity about poor accommodations and unsatisfying food. At the Ballet Folklorica in Guadalajara with her son, Peter, and his companion, Phil, Adams complains of the tedium of the national dances. "There were many dances, one for each region in Mexico, but they all bore strong similarities to each other; they were, in fact, far too much what one would have expected them to be—long skirts and tight long-sleeved tops, with very high heels. Plain suits and white shirts for the men. The women did a lot of skirt swinging." The narrative voice verges here on ridicule. But perhaps Adams is to be excused by virtue of the unforgiving and honest appraisal of her own limitations and hangups that permeates the stories. In the midst of a temporary flight delay, she ruefully recognizes the tendency of "middle-class, middle-aged Americans (of which I am certainly one)" to exaggerate problems and discomforts that are in truth relatively insignificant. Ultimately, Adams's connection to Mexico is similar to the relationships of many of her strong female characters with their romantic partners, a "love-hate relationship" that, by virtue of her constant return, "seems mostly love."

After the appearance of *Mexico,* Adams devoted herself primarily to novel writing. *Caroline's Daughters* (1991), *Almost Perfect* (1993), *A Southern Exposure* (1995), and *Medicine Men* (1997) were all published to critical acclaim, and in 1992 she was awarded the Academy and Institute Award in Literature by the American Academy and Institute of Arts and Letters. While devoting much energy to the production of longer works of fiction, Adams maintained her affection for the short story; and appropriately her final publication during her lifetime came from this genre. *The Last Lovely City* (1999) distills Adams's long-term thematic concerns with love, loss, memory, and women's quests for self-knowledge. Perhaps fitting for the late 1990s milieu in which they were produced, the thirteen stories that appear here also feature a greater preoccupation with sex and its dangers than the author's earlier work. The sexual dangers in which Adams is most interested in this collection are of an emotional rather than physical nature, however. Sex functions in *The Last Lovely City* as a means for individuals to fail themselves and each other. Characters betray each other sexually, struggle with impotence, and engage in desultory affairs and alcoholism to ward off the dull emptiness of their middle-class lives. But throughout all these conflicts and disappointments there persists a sense of hope for the characters who, while pursuing happiness misguidedly, are unwilling to give up the fight.

In "Great Sex" two professionally successful young women muse over lunch upon the difficulties of

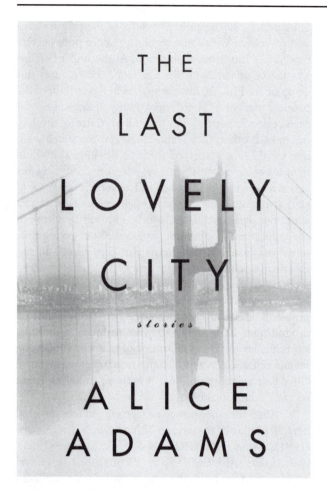

Dust jacket for Adams's 1999 collection of stories, published the month before her death

thing in life." These questions remain unanswered. At the conclusion of the story she accidentally runs into Jack again, and they restart their affair, having "the greatest sex." This resumption is probably not the right thing to do—the typical Adams character is an intelligent woman who nonetheless makes questionable romantic decisions—but the author is less interested in judging her character than in dramatizing the jubilant, however fleeting, happiness she is able to find.

In "Old Love Affairs," a mature woman reviews her sexual career while trying to resolve her current involvement with two men, one whom she is "crazy about (hopelessly, irreversibly, it seems)" and another who is "in his way crazy about her." Like many feminist writers, Adams frequently fights the myth that older women become sexless, and her depiction of the desires of a woman past the age of fifty is refreshing and uplifting. Like Alison in "Great Sex," protagonist Lucretia Baine has gotten into a fair amount of trouble by virtue of her sensuality—"I married the first two times for sex. How dumb can you get?" If privileging sexual attraction in relationships is a folly, however, it is one that Lucretia has heroically refused to outgrow. She replaces the staid and somewhat humorless Burt McElroy, who has been rendered impotent by prostate surgery, with Simon Coyne, a crush of her youth. Burt assumes that this rejection is a result of his physical impediment, but truly Lucretia is reacting to his spiritual impotence, which renders him "no longer subject to much change. Or to passion." She chooses Simon even though she is more attracted to her memory of him as a dashing young man than to his current status as a distinguished elderly gentleman. Lucretia acknowledges that such a basis is perhaps not the best on which to establish a relationship and declares, "I won't even think of falling in love." But as the narrative wryly notes: "of course she did." Adams's tone in this description is, once again, more exuberant than condemnatory. To feel at all, even in a dangerous, foolish manner, is preferable at any age to anesthetized caution and security.

Reviewing *The Last Lovely City: Stories* in *The New York Times Book Review* (14 February 1999), Susan Bolotin stated that Adams is calling attention to the fact that "when we search for love, we are not always lovable." While many characters in the collection certainly become foolish, selfish, and petty in their romantic pursuits, Bolotin's assessment may also be reversed. Adams's characters become supremely human and thus worthy of empathy because they act so erratically despite superior intellect and experience. Their flaws, like those of most humans, are never of spectacularly malignant nature; rather, they are rooted in mundane selfishness and petty hypocrisy. In the title story of the

their past relationships. The first of these women, Sheila Williams, explains her long-term involvement with a man who "in many ways made her unhappy" on the basis of the "great sex" they had together. This statement prompts her companion, Alison Green, to reflect on the tendency of what she terms "holy, earthquake sex" to cloud and distort her ability to properly perceive her relationships. Her most recent lover, Jack, a married environmental lawyer with three children who has broken off their relationship because she refuses to terminate her pregnancy with his child, seems an obvious cad. Alison is never quite sure how to estimate his behavior, however, and the reader is also continually kept off balance. Adams is careful to prevent her readers from quickly and unproblematically adopting conventional moral platitudes toward sexuality. Alison wonders which of the many Jacks she knew represented his true self: the sensual lover; the "loud-voiced angry Jack who insists that she have an abortion"; or "the kind and super-intelligent good friend with whom for hours she discussed almost every-

collection, a respected, recently widowed doctor, Benito Zamorra, accompanies an attractive young woman to a party in California. He has not known the woman, Carla, for long and wonders what she might want of him and whether the possibility of a relationship might arise. "She could brighten my life, he thinks, and lighten my home, all those rooms with their splendid views that seem to have darkened." At the party he encounters a woman from his past, the vulgar, badly aged Dolores Gutierrez, who teases him about their mutual previous involvement in some shady property dealings. He shuns her and indulges in a fantasy of a future with Carla, removed from the ugliness of the past that Dolores symbolizes. He is soon awakened into the realization that Carla's interest has not at all been what he hoped, just as he perhaps has not always epitomized the ideals to which he aspired. His yearning has been as misguided as his compulsion to wholly differentiate himself from Dolores has been unfair and inaccurate, and he resolves to return to Mexico to mourn his wife and nurse his dying mother alone. Perhaps the most tragic figure in these thirteen stories, he compels the reader's respect in the nobility with which he faces failure.

Adams's place in the landscape of late-twentieth-century American literature has been earned not only by the skill and deftness of her prose, but also by her challenge to the hackneyed dismissal of love's redemptive possibilities. She presents a world where the potential for smart and independent women to have their cake and eat it, too, to enjoy professional and romantic success, stubbornly persists even if not often realized. No romanticist, Adams never flinches from describing all the vagaries and disappointments that afflict sexual and platonic relationships, but neither does she ever permit these descriptions to produce a sense of crushing pessimism. Ultimately Alice Adams was that most rare of writers, a staunchly realistic optimist who always retrieved a glimmer of hope from even the most adverse of situations.

Interviews:

Patricia Holt, "PW Interviews: Alice Adams," *Publishers Weekly,* 213 (16 January 1978): 8–9;

Nancy Faber, "Out of the Pages," *People,* 9 (3 April 1978): 48-49;

Sandy Boucher, "Alice Adams–A San Francisco Novelist Who Is into Her Third Book," *San Francisco,* 20 (October 1978): 130–133;

Wayne Warga, "A Sophisticated Author Gets by with Help from Her Friends," *Los Angeles Times Book Review,* 16 November 1980, p. 3;

Neil Feinneman, "An Interview with Alice Adams," *Story Quarterly,* no. 11 (1980): 27–37;

Alix Madrigal, "The Breaking of a Mold," *San Francisco Chronicle Review,* 9 September 1984, p. 11.

References:

Cara Chell, "Succeeding in Their Times: Alice Adams on Women and Work," *Soundings: An Interdisciplinary Journal,* 68 (Spring 1985): 62–71;

Barbara Herman, "Alice Adams," in *Contemporary Fiction Writers of the South: A Bio-Bibliographical Sourcebook,* edited by R. Bain and J. Flora (Westport, Conn.: Greenwood Press, 1993), pp. 11–21.

Donald Barthelme

(7 April 1931 – 23 July 1989)

Gwen Crane
State University of New York at Oneonta

See also the Barthelme entries in *DLB 2: American Novelists Since WWII First Series; DLB Yearbook: 1980; and DLB Yearbook: 1989.*

BOOKS: *Come Back, Dr. Caligari* (Boston: Little, Brown, 1964; London: Eyre & Spottiswoode, 1966);

Snow White (New York: Atheneum, 1967; London: Cape, 1968);

Unspeakable Practices, Unnatural Acts (New York: Farrar, Straus & Giroux, 1968; London: Cape, 1969);

City Life (New York: Farrar, Straus & Giroux, 1970; London: Cape, 1971);

The Slightly Irregular Fire Engine; or, The Hithering Thithering Djinn (New York: Farrar, Straus & Giroux, 1971);

Sadness (New York: Farrar, Straus & Giroux, 1972; London: Cape, 1973);

Guilty Pleasures (New York: Farrar, Straus & Giroux, 1974);

The Dead Father (New York: Farrar, Straus & Giroux, 1975; London: Routledge & Kegan Paul, 1977);

Amateurs (New York: Farrar, Straus & Giroux, 1976; London: Routledge & Kegan Paul, 1977);

Here in the Village (Northridge, Cal.: Lord John Press, 1978);

Great Days (New York: Farrar, Straus & Giroux, 1979; London: Routledge & Kegan Paul, 1979);

The Emerald (Los Angeles: Sylvester & Orphanos, 1980);

Presents (Dallas: Pressworks, 1980);

Sixty Stories (New York: Putnam, 1981; London: Secker & Warburg, 1989);

Overnight to Many Distant Cities (New York: Putnam, 1983);

Paradise (New York: Putnam, 1986; New York & London: Penguin, 1986);

Sam's Bar: An American Landscape (New York: Doubleday, 1987);

Forty Stories (New York: Putnam, 1987; London: Secker & Warburg, 1988);

The King (New York: Harper & Row, 1990; London: Secker & Warburg, 1991);

Donald Barthelme (photograph © 1981 Thomas Victor; from the dust jacket for Sixty Stories, *1981)*

The Teachings of Don B.: Satires, Parodies, Fables, Illustrated Stories, and Plays of Donald Barthelme, edited by Kim Herzinger (New York: Turtle Bay, 1992); *Not-Knowing: The Essays and Interviews of Donald Barthelme,* edited by Herzinger (New York: Random House, 1997).

PLAY PRODUCTIONS: *Snow White,* Rehearsed Reading, American Place Theatre, New York, 10 June 1976;

Great Days, American Place Theatre, New York, 8 June 1983.

RECORDINGS: "The Piano Player," read by Barthelme, on *New Sounds in Fiction*, edited, with an introduction, by Gordon Lish, Cummings 51612, 1969;

Come Back, Dr. Caligari, Everett Edwards Cassette 114, 1970;

Donald Barthelme, Pacifica Tape Library, BC 2720.01, 2720.02, 2720.03, 2720.04, 1976;

"Donald Barthelme," on *Six Interviews*, Washington, D.C., Tapes for Readers, 1978.

OTHER: Introduction to *Architectural Graphics* (Houston: Contemporary Arts Museum, 1960);

The Emerging Figure, edited, with accompanying text, by Barthelme (Houston: Contemporary Arts Museum, 1961);

Ways and Means, edited, with accompanying text, by Barthelme (Houston: Contemporary Arts Museum, 1961);

Introduction to *she: 3 December 1970 to 16 January 1971* (New York: Cordier & Ekstrom, 1970);

Untitled commentary on "Paraguay," by Barthelme, in *Writer's Choice*, edited by Rust Hills (New York: McKay, 1974), pp. 25–26;

"Robert Morris," in *Robert Morris: Feb. 10 – Mar. 6, 1976* (New York: Washburn Gallery, 1976);

"Appreciation," in *Robert Rauschenberg: Work from Four Series, a Sesquicentennial Exhibition* (Houston: Contemporary Arts Museum, 1985);

One + One: Collaborations of Artists and Writers, text by Barthelme and Janet Landay (Houston: Glassell School of Art, Museum of Fine Art, 1988).

SELECTED PERIODICAL PUBLICATIONS–
UNCOLLECTED: "Culture, Etc.," *Texas Observer* (25 March 1960): 7;

"The Case of the Vanishing Product," *Harper's*, 223 (October 1961): 30–32;

"After Joyce," *Location*, 1 (Summer 1964): 13–16;

"The Tired Terror of Graham Greene," *Holiday*, 39 (April 1966): 146, 148–149;

"The Elegance Is under Control," *New York Times Book Review*, 21 April 1968, pp. 4–5;

"A Symposium on Fiction," by Barthelme, William Gass, Grace Paley, and Walker Percy, *Shenandoah*, 27 (1976): 3–31;

"Current Cinema," *New Yorker* (10 September 1979): 120–122; (17 September 1979): 132–134; (24 September 1979): 132–133; (1 October 1979): 103–105; (8 October 1979): 164–166; (15 October 1979): 182–184;

"The Most Wonderful Trick," *New York Times Book Review*, 25 November 1984, p. 3.

Two years after Donald Barthelme's death, his friend Robert Coover observed that his name had achieved a new currency as an adjective: the term "Barthelmesque," Coover wrote, refers not only to a style–"precise, urbane, ironic, rivetingly succinct, and accumulative in its comical and often surreal juxtapositions"–but also to a perspective familiar to Barthelme's readers, a worldview "bleakly comic, paradoxical, and grounded in the beautiful absurdities of language." John Barth, another friend, noted that Barthelme's view changed only slightly over the course of his career as editor, journalist, novelist, and short-story master–that he seemed as an artist "to have been born full-grown." In comments included in the Summer 1991 issue of *Review of Contemporary Fiction*, Barth speaks for most of Barthelme's critics in noting further that his immediately recognizable voice found its most influential forum in the rigorously confined genre of short fiction: "His natural narrative space was the short story, if *story* is the right word for those often plotless marvels of which he published some seven [i.e, nine] volumes over twenty years."

While some critics find Barthelme's "plotless marvels" both depressing and demandingly difficult, other readers find his explorations of postmodern sensibility oddly consoling. As one staffer who had worked with Barthelme at *The New Yorker* commented in a 14 August 1989 tribute to the author: "When he was writing a lot, you had this sense that there was someone else sort of like you, living in your city, and saying things that meant something about your life. It was like having a companion in the world." Some reviewers found his parodies and experiments tedious, repetitious, even trivializing; others found them exhilaratingly irreverent, radically subversive, and entertaining even when most profoundly serious, as the author of a tribute in *The New Yorker* recalled: "Barthelme was erudite and culturally rigorous, but he was always terrifically funny as well, and when his despairing characters and jagged scenes and sudden stops and starts had you tumbling wildly, free-falling through a story, it was laughter that kept you afloat and made you feel there would probably be a safe landing."

His idiosyncratic humor is perhaps the one constant in his work, which coheres around his comic view of a tragically fractured cosmos. His humor made his writing classes a delight for his university students; even while his influence in university circles grew, however, his satirical eye savaged academic presumptions and absurdities throughout his novels and stories. Yet, his humor could be gentled to accommodate young readers, as he demonstrates in his foray into children's literature, *The Slightly Irregular Fire Engine; or, The Hithering Thithering Djinn* (1971), which won the National

Dust jacket for Barthelme's first collection of short stories, which includes parodies of works by James Joyce, T. S. Eliot, and philosopher Henri Bergson

Book Award in 1972. Barthelme wrote this book for, and with the considerable editorial assistance of, his daughter, Anne, born in 1965. His frequently chilling representations of unfeelingly disengaged parenthood in his stories does not reflect his own experience as a parent: he was by all reports a devoted and loving father to his daughter. Similarly, his consistently jaded assessments of the possibilities of marriage are belied by his own experience: after three early divorces, he was more fortunate in his fourth marriage, which lasted until his death twenty-seven years later.

Much of Barthelme's humor grows out of his topical references to recognizable developments on the newspaper front page and style sections–his weirdly warped echoes of currently fashionable ideas and consumer products, his surrealistically skewed sketches of familiar urban locales or banal current events, and his gleeful, albeit revisionary, deployment of current slang.

While some critics in the 1960s predicted that the popularity of Barthelme's adult works would be short-lived, precisely because of the recognizable specificity that appealed to enthusiastic readers of his many *New Yorker* stories in the late 1960s and early 1970s, Barthelme went on to win the PEN/Faulkner Award in 1982 for his retrospective collection *Sixty Stories* (1981). Since his death of cancer on 23 July 1989, at the age of fifty-eight, his oeuvre has become a rich mine for cultural and literary critics, who find his short stories both arid and playful expressions of postmodern anxieties.

One strategy that facilitates Barthelme's construction of short pieces is his use of startlingly, even bizarrely informative opening lines. His readers can often identify one of his stories after reading only the Barthelmesque first sentence, such as the unsettling comment introducing his brief story "On Angels": "The death of God left the angels in a strange position." The readers drawn in by these engaging sentences find themselves (along with Barthelme's characters) in a similarly "strange position"–mysteriously displaced in a universe where incongruity and futility are the only remaining principles of order. If God is dead, what use are the angels? And what uses are men to devise for themselves in God's absence? All knowledge becomes questionable in Barthelme's stories. In "On Angels" the homeless seraphs find new lives as ubiquitous television personalities but remain at the end still mourning the loss of all faith and certitude, inconclusively "searching for a new principle," a new center from which to view the universe.

Barthelme was himself just slightly dislocated throughout his life, never quite a native of any particular place, however much he may have loved his adopted home in New York City. He was born on 7 April 1931 in Philadelphia, where his father, Donald Sr., had met his wife-to-be, Helen Bechtold, at the University of Pennsylvania. The family moved to Houston when Donald Jr. was two years old. There, his father worked both as a practicing architect and as a professor of architecture at the University of Houston. Helen, a former English major, helped her husband create a stimulating oasis of scholarly interests in the midst of what seemed to their son an intellectually barren Texas culture: at home, with his three brothers and his sister, Barthelme dined with his parents' academic and artistic visitors and read widely from his parents' library, moving from Norse myths to art history, from classical literature to joke books. At school, as he began reading and writing imitations of James Joyce and T. S. Eliot in his teens, Barthelme found himself somewhat isolated from his less cosmopolitan classmates at the parochial St. Thomas High School in Houston. He began publishing his imitations while editing his high-school newspaper, *The Eagle*. His juvenile work brought him several awards: honorable mention in a short-story contest sponsored by *Scholastic Magazine* in 1946, when he was fifteen years old; a fourth-place prize in another *Scholastic Magazine* contest in 1948; and the 1948 Poet Laureate of Texas Award for his poem "Inertia." He continued his journalistic work after transferring to Lamar High School, where he was associate editor of the literary magazine *Sequoyha*.

At the University of Houston, Barthelme contributed both fiction and nonfiction pieces to *The Cougar*, the student newspaper. In his mature work in the 1960s, his lasting interest in both kinds of writing were conflated in his contributions to the "Comments" column in *The New Yorker*, where he published short pieces combining objective reportage and subjective impressionism in his own Barthelmesque form of New Journalism.

He was able to indulge both his writing ambitions and his interests in the visual arts–inherited from his parents–while working as a reporter on cultural events for the *Houston Post*, where he was hired after dropping out of his junior year of college in 1951. Even after he was drafted into the army during the Korean War two years later, he was fortunate enough to be assigned editorial work on the army newspaper. Arriving in Korea on the same day a truce was signed afforded him a non-threatening opportunity to observe military life, and his observations of the absurdities of military bureaucracy resurface in his later stories.

Beginning with his somewhat patronizing treatment of the characters he met in the military, Barthelme often invited accusations of elitism. His work demands an intelligent, educated, and engaged reader. Critics have often objected to his "terrifying absence of explanation," as it was referred to in the *New Yorker* tribute, his frequent, unglossed references to academic arcana. He expects the reader to recognize–without footnotes–references to mathematician Kurt Gödel's Uncertainty Principle, Coptic hagiography, Celtic military history, medieval mysticism, seventeenth-century alchemists, eighteenth-century theories of perspective, and nineteenth-century symbolist poetry. Critic Mark C. Krupnick responded to Barthelme's work with charges of "self-congratulatory narcissism." Other critics, however, hold that missing the occasional erudite allusion does not invalidate the pleasure of reading Barthelme's work; still others defend Barthelme by pointing out that throughout his life he maintained contacts with friends and relatives representing a broad range of social classes and educational levels. In addition, his former students and protégés have frequently expressed their gratitude for his patient and generous treatment of youthful, inexperienced, and inept artists. Certainly, Barthelme disparaged himself as often as he patronized his characters and discombobulated his readers. In the story "Me and Miss Mandible" he draws upon humbling experiences from his own military service to show the democratically leveling effects of universal absurdity. He depicts hierarchical rank as meaningless to all but those at the top of the chain of command–elusive, infinitely recessive sources of authority who may or may not exist:

> In the Army, too, I was ever so slightly awry. It took me a fantastically long time to realize what the others grasped almost at once: that much of what we were doing was absolutely pointless, to no purpose. I kept wondering why. Then something happened that proposed a new question. One day we were commanded to whitewash, from the ground to the topmost leaves, all of the trees in our training area. The corporal who relayed the order was nervous and apologetic. Later an off-duty captain sauntered by and watched us, white-splashed and totally weary, strung out among the freakish shapes we had created. He walked away swearing. I understood the principle (orders are orders), but I wondered: Who decides?

Barthelme had lost his religious faith while a student at the University of Houston; he later claimed to find renewed creative energy in blasphemously working on his Sabbath: "Sunday seems to be my best day, probably because I'm a lapsed Catholic." Having discerned the godlessness of the universe, he began to see similar absences at the top of most human hierarchies. Like his television angels, Barthelme finds no guiding principal to impose principles of order. In his military stories the army's ultimate authority perpetually recedes from view, like an increasingly reclusive deity, until determining whether the top brass is absent or insane becomes an irrelevant futility.

After being discharged from the army, Barthelme worked only briefly at the *Houston Post* before taking a position at the University of Houston, where he worked as an editor in the public-relations office and as a speechwriter for the university president. After a decade of artistic fermentation, this experience served as the foundation of his story "See the Moon?" In this story the narrator is offered a position as speechwriter for a university president, a retired admiral who has moved from the top of one hierarchy to another and seems vacuously enigmatic even when visibly present.

While Barthelme's satire of university pomp and incompetence is scathing in this story and in many other pieces he wrote in the following decades, he remained deeply involved in scholarly pursuits all his life. Although he suffered the professional and social demands of his public-relations work at the University of Houston only grudgingly, he found time during this period to work closely with members of the faculty, as he edited *Acta Diurna,* a faculty newsletter, and *Forum,* a journal publishing work by leading local art and literary figures. He simultaneously enrolled in philosophy courses, which shaped his future work as an artist.

During his busy years as a public-relations officer, speechwriter, editor, and student, Barthelme developed an intense interest in phenomenology and existentialism, and particularly in the work of philosopher Henri Bergson. Bergson proposed that the phenomena of the past are not ephemeral, as some might wish them to be, but instead are permanent, even constitutive elements in the subjective experience of the present. This view of history as a formative influence on the future later became a serious philosophical problem for Barthelme and other writers in the 1960s, when modernist writers began to despair of the possibility of originality. When an aspiring writer at Johns Hopkins University asked Barthelme why he wrote the way he did, Barthelme replied, "Because Samuel Beckett already wrote the way he did." In Barthelme's stories the philosophical problems of postmodern aesthetics are translated into the quotidian activities of the late-twentieth-century existentialist Everyman. Gerald Graff, in a 1975 article, identified Barthelme's "special theme" as "the comic impossibility of heroism in a world paralyzed by self-consciousness."

Heroically acknowledging the paradoxical difficulties of postmodern writing, Barthelme proceeded to write works that strike some readers as not coherently exemplifying any literary theory; rather, they are emphatically not participating in received literary tradition. Thomas M. Leitch addresses this aspect of Barthelme's work:

> Perhaps the most striking feature of Donald Barthelme's fiction is the number of things it gets along without. In Barthelme's fictive world, there appear to be no governing or shaping beliefs, no transcendent ideals or intimations, no very significant physical experience . . . no psychology of character, indeed no characters in the usual sense of the term, no guarantee, at the level of incident, of verisimilitude or of rational causality or of plot itself, no thickness of circumstantial detail which might make his world seem more densely realistic, and no considerable exploration of such themes as love, idealism, initiation, or death.

Particularly in his earlier works, Barthelme, more dauntlessly than any of his literary cohorts, ventured into the dangerous realm of innovation. The result was a richly varied body of work. His stylistic experiments defy generalized summary. David Porush suggested in 1991 that academic commentators who would generalize on Barthelme's oeuvre would better spend their time listing repeated themes, and then proceeds to prove that list of themes as impossible to complete as a list of Barthelme's stylistic experiments:

> Like the styles in his individual sentences, those themes are both varied and enticing dances of suggestion and strange attractors: oppressive fathers, intimate lesbians and pairs of stray women, casual and unfulfilling affairs of the heart, the postmodern condition, love of architecture and spaces, infidelity, philosophy and fairy tales, "the pleasure of cutting up and pasting together pictures," collections of *objets* artfully arranged, words as things, the list is long.

Barthelme's concern with "the postmodern condition" and "words as things" produced some strange and difficult narrative excursions: a story consisting of a single sentence ("Sentence"), a story reworking a traditional German fairy tale into a series of numbered sentences ("Glass Mountain"), and a story comprising many sentences joined by their failure to define the single word "nothing" ("Nothing: A Preliminary Account"). Some readers applaud Barthelme's less reader-friendly pieces. Ihab Hassan praises Barthelme for experimenting "with non-linear narratives and absurdist techniques . . . while maintaining his commitment to a world wildly out of joint." But for other readers, Barthelme's early writings stand less as literary achievements than as proofs of the end of literary possibility. Assessing Barthelme's first decade of serious writing in 1974, Albert J. Guerard called him a "cheerful historian of collapse." More recently, Guy Davenport described him as the restorer of an already collapsed genre: "When Donald Barthelme took up the short story he had a sense that it was a form that had proved its eligibility for responding to radical innovation. It was a form that had periodically collapsed under overuse, and just as periodically renovated itself. It answered to style in the hands of a master. Like the poem, it demanded style. All else would follow."

Barthelme expected, and duly received, critical censure for his stylistic risk-taking, but he gave as good as he got. In one of his ahistorical revisions of literary history, "Conversations with Goethe," he makes Johann Wolfgang von Goethe himself intone against reviewers: "Critics, Goethe said, are the cracked mirror in the grand ballroom of the creative spirit."

In 1961 Barthelme became, at the age of thirty, the youngest director ever appointed at the Contemporary Arts Museum in Houston, where he edited several exhibition catalogues before relocating to New York to edit the short-lived literary magazine *Location* the following year. He also began publishing comments and stories in *The New Yorker* in the early 1960s. The first of the 128 stories he eventually published in *The New Yorker* appeared in May 1963, and by 1964 he had produced enough for his first collection, *Come Back, Dr. Caligari.* Two of the more enduringly readable stories included in the collection recapitulate his youthful imitations of Joyce and Eliot, but imitation has given way to parody at this point in Barthelme's career. "For I'm the Boy" recounts a car trip evoking several passages in Joyce's *Ulysses* (1922). A group of Irishmen regale each other with graphic details of their failed romantic relationships. The genuine communication that constitutes genuine relationships can take place in this story only as a response to physical or emotional violence. Josephine Hendin has traced such events as a theme in Barthelme's works and concluded that, for Barthelme, anger is "the only irresistible emotion" left to citizens of the politically cataclysmic twentieth century and that he sees a furious sadism at the center of the twentieth-century soul. Many of the stories included in *Come Back, Dr. Caligari* present a much less bleak view of human potential, however, and most avoid suggestions of sadistic cruelty altogether. In "Will You Tell Me?" Barthelme weaves echoes of Eliot's *The Waste Land* (1922) together with allusions to Bergson's theories of time and Edmund Husserl's phenomenology to create a disturbing but not altogether despairing revision of the family romance. He begins the story with the annunciatory sentence "Hubert gave Charles and Irene a nice baby for Christmas." Baby-swapping rapidly leads to wife-swapping, and the nuclear family seems not to be faring well at all—new characters are barely introduced before they begin sleeping with other characters even less familiar. Traditional values have evaporated, and language itself becomes unmoored from reality. And yet, Barthelme offers the possibility of joy. At the end of the story, his two central characters try to determine a definition of the word *wonderful*: "They thought the answer might be in their eyes, or in their mingled breath, but they couldn't be sure. It might be illusory." Perhaps Anne Tyler was alluding to such moments of possibly illusory epiphany when she wrote that Barthelme's readers may find that they have "undergone a peculiar alteration of vision. Life, for a while, will hold more promise."

    Come Back, Dr. Caligari was enthusiastically received. The year following its publication, Barthelme was awarded a Guggenheim Fellowship, which allowed him to spend a year living in Denmark. That same year, *Come Back, Dr. Caligari* was published in England and established Barthelme's international reputation. This period was a productive one: after returning to the United States in 1967, Barthelme published his first novel, *Snow White;* by the following year, he had produced enough new stories for his second collection.

Dust jacket for Barthelme's 1970 collection of stories, featuring satires on technological progress and patriarchal authority

    Barthelme's second story collection, *Unspeakable Practices, Unnatural Acts* (1968), includes several of his most famous pieces. "The Indian Uprising" has elicited a particularly impressive body of critical commentary. The primary effect of the story, however, would seem to be a denial of the possibility of a single, complete interpretation of any story. Barthelme later articulated this position in his essay "Not Knowing." In that uncharacteristically theoretical piece, Barthelme reprimands the academic critics who would lay claim to a singularly, exclusively correct reading of his work: "In the competing methodologies of contemporary criticism, a sort of tyranny of great expectations obtains, a rage for final explanations, a refusal to allow a work the mystery that is essential to it. . . ." Barthelme proposed a new respect for the artist's product, the "object" presented to the audience. Resurrecting Keats's doctrine of "negative capability," Barthelme remarks that "What is magical about the [artistic] object is that it at once invites and resists interpretation."

    Barthelme consistently resisted any systematizing limitations on aesthetic possibility throughout his career; one of the many themes threading through his novels and stories is the ridicule of those pompously misguided intellectuals who paradoxically employ dauntingly complex systems to oversimplify and delimit human potential in any arena, including the human capacity for artistic creation, ethical responsibility, or gross incompetence. *Unspeakable Practices, Unnatural Acts* includes Swiftian parody of such intellectuals in "Report," in which the pompous intellectuals are scientists who employ flawed philosophical systems to justify genocide. Like literary critics who love their interpretive methods more than the texts they interpret, the scientists in "Report" are more in love with their new weapons than they are with the fellow humans whose deaths prove the value of the scientists' work.

Barthelme does not always unequivocally condemn technological advances. As Porush wrote in 1991, "Report" initiates "a deep-abiding relationship to technology that persists throughout Barthelme's fiction in the subsequent two decades." Porush finds the machine "a robust trope" in Barthelme's work: "On the one hand, the machine is an avatar of an age which has led to a bland pedestrianism, a white-bread culture, and a widespread anomie which he deplores and mocks. The values of the machine and the values of humanity are opposed. At the same time, Barthelme admits that technology is also a form of human expression, however dismal, with which the artist must contend and from which the artist will find it difficult to escape."

Barthelme continues to worry about the rise of the machine in his third collection of stories, *City Life* (1970), which *Time* magazine listed among its "Best Books of the Year." In "The Explanation" two disembodied voices discuss a mysterious "black box," reproduced for the reader as a black rectangle on the first page of the story. One voice describes the box as a machine that will be "helpful in changing the government . . . making it more responsive to the needs of the people." For engineers such as the conventioneers in "Report" and the first voice in "The Explanation," black boxes are devices whose workings cannot or need not be explained, representing in technical diagrams machinery that is detailed on other blueprints or diagrams outside the margins of the illustration in question. Porush argues that the black box in "The Explanation" represents "this elusive story itself, which is similarly mysterious and permits numerous interpretations, an ironic counterpoint to its title." For the first voice in "The Explanation," the black box inspires confidence not only in technology and bureaucracy, but in art, as art, authority, and technology overlap in the black box's opaque, awe-inspiring mysteries. After suggesting that the machine may be an art form suitable for replacing the dead genre of the novel, the first voice

continues: "It has beauties. . . . We construct these machines not because we confidently expect them to do what they are designed to do–change the government in this instance–but because we intuit a machine, out there, glowing like a shopping center."

While the second voice has some reservations, finding the black box too mysterious to be trustworthy, both voices agree in the end that machines and humans share both functions and mysteries, finding the "error" messages of the black box and the facial expressions of clumsily, ineffectively flirtatious humans easily comparable. As in "Report," machinery in "The Explanation" proves both a comforting promise of future governmental stability and an obviously inutile tool for systematizing or controlling human behavior.

The complexities of human disorganization defy systematization elsewhere in *Unspeakable Practices, Unnatural Acts*. "Robert Kennedy Saved from Drowning" (written two months before Kennedy's assassination in 1968) presents a fragmentary portrait of an authority figure exercising his authority. Kennedy cannot control his own family, however, let alone a country of wayward and error-prone citizens. He mulls over the problem of urban transportation and concludes that systems "at once complex and inadequate" have created "seemingly insoluble difficulties and present methods of dealing with these difficulties" that "offer little prospect of relief." Kennedy is the strongest leader portrayed in *Unspeakable Practices, Unnatural Acts,* the nearest approximation Barthelme offers of a traditional hero. Yet, he is mysteriously dressed in a cape, sword, and mask, like an early cinema star rather than a political leader, and his musings on political responsibility lead him to take no "reasoned and intelligent action." On the contrary, he appears in the next narrative fragment flailing about in his own personal catastrophe, drowning in a nameless sea, losing his hero's costume in pieces. When hauled ashore, he gasps his thanks to his nameless savior but offers no further words of guidance or leadership.

It is not only political or military leaders who disappoint in Barthelme's stories; most often, it is fathers–leaders of the nuclear family unit. The typically abrupt opening of "Views of My Father Weeping," included in *City Life,* plunges the reader into a classically Barthelmesque situation: "An aristocrat was riding down the street in his carriage. He ran over my father." The narrator spends the rest of the story investigating the events preceding his father's death. He imagines that the hit-and-run was not an accident, becoming only more determined in his sleuthing as the clues he uncovers become more resistant to coherent organization. His persistent, inconclusive detective work begins to seem slightly

Dust jacket for Barthelme's 1972 collection of stories, set in a variety of claustrophobic environments

paranoid. He seems more concerned with the larger possibility that all events are plotted, planned by a nameless author, than he is by the single instance of a plotted event that he is investigating. This story indicates why Barthelme has been named the literary antecedent to postmodernists such as Thomas Pynchon, who develops a similarly paranoid character, Oedipa Maas, in *The Crying of Lot 49* (1966). Like Oedipa, Barthelme's narrators vacillate between dread of a plotless chaos devoid of competent authorities (gods, presidents, generals, and fathers all being irrevocably absent) and a furious resentment of patriarchal manipulation (when authority figures are present but irremediably demented). In 1991 Lance Olsen traced this persistent focus on patriarchy to Barthelme's own childhood: "Donald Jr. spent his life rewriting and righting his father." Critic Paul Lilly Jr. has also considered this theme in the Barthelme's work: "The ways that the father can be reduced, made impotent, inverted, are myriad." Lilly finds in Barthelme's continual revisions of the classical oedipal situation evidence of his intention not to inflict but to alleviate pain. Josephine Hendin's reading of "For I'm the Boy," where she finds in Barthelme's fiction a perpetuation of the "sadism" at the center of the twentieth-century soul, is countered by

Lilly's reading, where he sees Barthelme using humor to make the experience of a fatherless universe at least more tolerable, if not redemptive.

Teresa L. Ebert reads Barthelme's invalid or defunct fathers in political terms: "The Dead Father also signifies the Law of the Father, unmasking its seemingly universal benevolence and showing how it serves to keep others, particularly sons, in their place and to preserve the authority and power of the All-Father and his surrogates (ordinary fathers)." In the title story of *City Life*, daughters disrupt the Law of the Father when women are somewhat grudgingly admitted into the realm of jurisprudence. Ramona and Elsa enter law school, startling the paternal administrators, who advise them to wear only plain clothes and to avoid shouting "Yoo Hoo" across the quad: "We don't use those words in this school." Elsa soon drops out, returning to the traditional female role of childbearing. Ramona stays the course, however, and finds that male claims to judicial authority are no more justified than those of the Wizard of Oz. At the end of the tale, however, viewing her nameless city from a lofty vantage of splendid, unconquered isolation, Ramona concludes that the human condition, with all the inequities and abuses of power it entails, cannot be transcended in any meaningful way: "I have to admit we are locked in the most exquisite mysterious muck. This muck heaves and palpitates. . . . Our muck is only a part of a much greater muck–the nation state–which is itself the creation of that muck of mucks, human consciousness. Of course all these things also have a touch of sublimity–as when Moonbelly sings, for example."

In this story, redemption is available in two forms. The exquisite, mysterious muck of urban existence is redeemed by art; the muck of urban mating rituals is redeemed by love, which becomes an art form in itself. Ramona finally decides to join in the depressing but aesthetically erotic quadrilles of urban romance: "These dances constitute an invitation of unmistakable import–an invitation which, if accepted, leads one down many muddy roads. I accepted. What was the alternative?"

In 1970, the same year he published *City Life,* Barthelme began contributing unsigned pieces to the "Comment" section of *The New Yorker*. Many of these brief nonfiction essays were later developed into stories, and others appeared interspersed and unchanged among the fictions collected in *Guilty Pleasures* (1974) and *Overnight to Many Distant Cities* (1983). Jerome Klinkowitz, in his essay "Barthelme's Canonical Village" (1991), has argued that publishing anonymously in *The New Yorker* was "Barthelme's way of keeping a journal (and from such a shelter being able to see how the public might react)." Some of these textual flinders record Barthelme's perambulations through the streets of New York City and anticipate the many stories he went on to write about urban life, stories that focus on the sense of community, the feel of the cosmopolitan village, which Barthelme enjoyed in Manhattan for much of his writing career. He noted this sense of community in an interview when he discussed his friendship with fellow author Grace Paley: "With someone like Grace Paley, who is a dear friend and lives across the street from us in New York, there are always lots of things to talk about besides art because first we have the life of our street to worry about. Grace is very concerned with our street, and we have really significant conversations having to do with our street."

In Barthelme's stories the urban village may be presented as a tumultuous, surreal, or claustrophobic space, but it remains for most of his characters the desideratum of contemporary life. Yet, those who gain citizenship in these communities remain perennially unsatisfied. Barthelme's fourth collection of stories, *Sadness* (1972), includes the story "City of Churches," in which Barthelme creates Prester, an earthly City of God composed entirely of church buildings. The citizens of Prester live in communities of apartments within the churches of their chosen denomination, apparently waiting for God to notice the perfection of their utterly static city, where nobody comes, nobody goes, and nothing happens. Even dreams are legislated in Prester.

Barthelme seems to have viewed the community of academia as a too-cliquish, too-airless community like Prester, even while he enjoyed the friendships he made with faculty and students. Barthelme made his first extended stay in academia in 1972: just prior to publishing *Sadness,* he was encouraged by John Barth to take Barth's place as distinguished visiting professor at the State University of New York at Buffalo. He moved to another visiting professorship at Boston University in 1973 and began teaching at the City University of New York in 1974. He received much recognition from the academic community during these years, including the Morton Dauwen Zabel Award from the National Institute of Arts and Letters in 1972 and the Jesse H. Jones Award from the Texas Institute of Letters in 1976. Scholars and critics continued to applaud his work throughout his career: in 1982, after Barthelme had been teaching at the University of Houston for a year, *Sixty Stories* won a nomination for the National Book Critics Circle Award, the PEN/Faulkner Award for Fiction, and the *Los Angeles Times* Book Prize. He received his last award, the Prix de Rome, in 1988, after he had been diagnosed with throat cancer. Barthelme enjoyed teaching, and his colleague Raymond Carver noted in his *Alive and Writing* that Barthelme was tremendously influential as a creative-writing teacher. Barthelme harbored a lifelong suspicion of scholarly pretension, intellectual isolation, and critical bombast, however, perhaps especially when he found himself evidencing symptoms of infection with these academic plagues.

Barthelme's characters similarly seek community, yet enter into social contracts only with the most grievous misgivings. Barthelme delineates a variety of claustrophobic communities in *Sadness,* perhaps most horribly and hilariously in his "Critique de la Vie Quotidienne," which shows the communal constrictions of the individual family group. The story begins with a description of an ending–a stifling, moribund marriage on the rocks: "Our evenings lacked promise. The world in the evening seems fraught with the absence of promise, if you are a married man. There is nothing to do but go home and drink your nine drinks and forget about it."

The addition of children to this bell jar of a marriage has helped not at all. Progeny may suggest the possibility of fulfillment:

> Slumped there in your favorite chair, with your nine drinks lined up on the side table in soldierly array, and your hand never far from them, and your other hand holding on to the plump belly of the overfed child, and perhaps rocking a bit, if the chair is a rocking chair as

mine was in those days, then it is true that a tiny tendril of contempt–strike that, *content*–might curl up from the storehouse where the world's content is kept, and reach into your softened brain and take hold there, persuading you that this, at last, is the fruit of all your labors, which you'd been wondering about in some such terms as, "Where is the fruit?"

But the child breaks that illusion, feeling that its own content cannot be achieved without the addition of a pony to the household. Denied a pony, it wants to sleep in the parents' bed. "Holy Hell," our narrator exclaims, "Is there no end to this *family life?*" There is, as it happens: by the fourth page of the story, the narrator is divorced, living in bachelor digs, and no happier than he was when crowded into a nuclear-family unit. His former wife, Wanda, is studying Marxism in France, the child is being cared for in a Piagetian nursery school, and the narrator is left with the promise of only more Scotch: "The J&B company keeps manufacturing it, case after case, year in and year out, and there is, I am told, no immediate danger of a dearth."

Like Wanda, the narrator of "The Rise of Capitalism" blames economics for his marital problems. He and his wife disagree on this point. She sees their problems as the natural result of his boneheaded masculinity, his Marxist sympathies as superficial excuses for personal shortcomings, and Marxism itself as the negation of everything that makes even their unsatisfactory attempts at happiness possible:

> "Rupert," she says, "you are no better than a damn dawg! A plain dawg has more sensibility than you, when it comes to a woman's heart!" I try to explain that it is not my fault, but capitalism's. She will have none of it. . . . "Rupert," Marta says, "the embourgeoisment of all classes of men has reached a disgusting nadir in your case. A damn hawg has more sense than you. At least a damn hawg doesn't go in for 'the bullet wrapped in sugar,' as the Chinese say." She is right.

Barthelme's female characters are often right, and his male characters are often boneheaded slaves to ignoble, irrational motives.

Sex, class, and economics are again the subject of "The Party," where a carefully planned academic gathering conjoins irresponsibly expensively and somewhat menacingly costumed guests to engage in forced, fashionable conversation. As the guests exchange opinions of Franz Kafka and Heinrich Wilhelm von Kleist, noises outside suggest a possible revolution in the streets, and a television news program in the background reports on the nationalization of emerald mines in some unnamed country. The bibulous faculty ignore all external disruptions, preferring the distance of a critical, theoretical discussion to involvement in the real

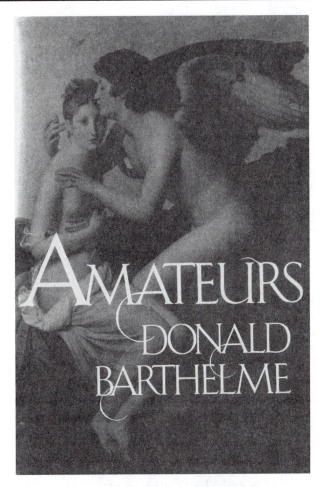

Dust jacket for Barthelme's 1976 collection of stories surveying various permutations of love

events in the streets below. The narrator, however, realizes that cocktail-party theorizing cannot supplant or insulate against real life and that the intellectual community is an illusion: "Can we go home? I mean you to your home, me to my home, all these others to their own homes, cells, cages? . . . What made us think that we could escape things like bankruptcy, alcoholism, being disappointed, having children?" The ivory tower of the academic community fails to comfort or protect its members here.

Barthelme refines his critique of capitalist society in his next collection, *Guilty Pleasures,* where many pieces detail the commodification of everything unique and beautiful, human and divine. In "The Photographs" two scientists decide to suppress evidence of the existence of a human soul (they have photographed a peculiarly gnarled and unattractive soul on its flight to heaven) because of the socio-economic cataclysm they imagine would follow publication of their discovery: "There's our responsibility to science and truth and all that. But aren't we sort of in the position of those chaps who made the atom bomb and then were sorry afterward?" Maintaining the hegemony–a world where people might blithely pursue blandly adulterous affairs while casually shopping at Marks & Spencers–outweighs solving the riddles of the universe for these cogs in the sociopolitical machine of capitalist culture.

Barthelme reaches back into the nineteenth century to examine earlier examples of the rise of capitalist dehumanization in "Eugénie Grandet." Before beginning this story, he provides a helpful summary of Honoré de Balzac's 1833 novel of the same name and then proceeds to offer fragmentary bits of a revision of that work. Rewriting precedent works was one of Barthelme's favorite strategies. "The Indian Uprising" can be read as a reworking of Flann O'Brien's *At-Swim-Two-Birds* (1939), while "Paraguay" in *City Life* comprises in large part an extended, nonsensically revised borrowing from Le Corbusier's *Modular* (a 1968 museum catalogue), blended with resonant quotations from Jorge Luis Borges's short stories. In "Eugénie Grandet" Barthelme shows how women, like slaves and sugarcane, were assessed with monetary values by Eugénie's faithless fiancé, who writes her a baldly mercenary letter ending their engagement:

> Dear Cousin: I have decided to marry a Mlle. D'Aubrion, and not you. . . . A brilliant life awaits me, is what I am trying to say to you, if I don't marry you, and that is why I am marrying this other girl, who is hideously ugly but possessed of a noble, if decayed, position in the aristocracy. Therefore those binding promises we exchanged on the bench, are, to all intents and purposes, mooted.

Barthelme develops the theme of valuation of human beings further in his "A Manual for Sons," excerpted from his novel *The Dead Father* (1975) and reprinted as a short piece in *Sixty Stories*. As Jeannette McVicker notes, the patriarchal order sketched in "Manual for Sons" is paradoxically grounded in female sexuality:

> Of course the patriarchal order–the socio-symbolic contract–cannot function without women. Because she is necessary, woman's sexuality is therefore tolerated or accommodated, but only within the limit of her reproductive capacity. Outside this limit, woman's sexuality poses a threat, and is therefore interdicted. So, in the first passage, fathers . . . sleep with "hired women," i.e., prostitutes: women whose non-reproductive sexuality is totally inscribed within the system. They are hired to provide a service for men, so that their sexuality, while not fulfilling the reproductive imperative, is nonetheless contained within the limits imposed by the patriarchal order.

Accordingly, the manual provides detailed instructions for adventurers who would pay native women for sexual favors (rusty nails and cheap beads work well as sexual wampum, the manual advises).

Barthelme further parodies precise estimates of value in *Guilty Pleasures,* interrogating the practice of assigning specific and universal value to anything, including human beings. In the discursive exercise "Nothing: A Preliminary Account," the narrator precedes any discussion of What Is Anything by assessing What Is Nothing and circularly begins his prolegomenous assessment of What Is Nothing by listing What Nothing Is Not. It is not physical, nor is it metaphysical: "Nothing is not a nightshirt or a ninnyhammer, ninety-two, or Ninevah. It is not a small jungle in which, near a river, a stone table has been covered with fruit. . . . Neither is it *esse est percipi,* nor is it any of the refutations of that proposition. Nor is it snuff. Hurry. There is not much time, and we must complete, or at least attempt to complete, the list. Nothing is not a tongue depressor; splendid, hurry on." Unexpectedly, his obviously futile exercise grows increasingly cheering. "We cannot finish," he admits, "but we can at least begin." The list cannot be completed, but in this story the impossibility of finishing becomes a kind of reason for continuing to live.

Barthelme finds new occasions to rejoice in the impossible in his next collection of stories, *Amateurs* (1976). In an often-quoted passage at the end of the story "Rebecca"–a tale of a lovers' quarrel and reconciliation–the narrator advises the reader that the one subject which cannot be captured, and yet which demands endlessly repeated attempts at definition, is love: "The story ends. It was written for several reasons. Nine of them are secrets. The tenth is that one should never cease considering human love, which remains as grisly and golden as ever, no matter what is tattooed upon the warm tympanic page."

Barthelme surveys various permutations of love in this collection. "At the End of the Mechanical Age" posits the possibility of a new epoch in human history. Tired of waiting, however, two of the characters decide to marry in what has become the tradition in the twentieth-century mechanical age–a travesty of the awful and mysterious rites of preceding centuries. The revised vows make the ceremony seem more a doom than a blessing: "And do you, Thomas, promise to explore all differences thoroughly with patience and inner honesty ignoring no fruitful avenues of discussion and seeking at all times to achieve rapprochement while eschewing advantage in conflict situations?"

Such a vow can result only in catastrophe. Quotes from William Butler Yeats's "The Second Coming" (1925) sprinkled throughout the text add to

Dust jacket for Barthelme's 1979 collection of stories, including several pieces composed entirely of dialogue

the sense of impending disaster. God himself chooses to appear at this ceremony of "hollow pretense and empty sham": "God came to the wedding and stood behind a tree with just a part of His effulgence showing. I wondered whether He was planning to bless this makeshift construct with His grace, or not. . . ." This manifestation may not be the conclusive sign of grace Barthelme's characters seek, but, as is often the case in Barthelme's stories, it is better than nothing.

One of the occupations Barthelme himself found to be much better than nothing was the field of visual arts, an area of study where he seemed to find glimpses of God's effulgence quite frequently. Raised in a household of art books and blueprints, he developed an early fondness for the graphic arts and remained throughout his career entranced with the physical aspect of printed texts, enjoying creative layout and playful typography from his earliest editorial days. Throughout the 1960s and 1970s he experimented with cutting and pasting graphics to accompany his shards of text. "I am fated to deal in mixtures, slumgullions," he once confessed. His illustrations defy interpretation and initially disorient rather than illuminate the reader. As Barthelme noted in an interview the year before he died, art should reflect the interior subjective landscape, rather than an idealized world of coherent order. "Art," he intoned in

an uncharacteristically solemn moment, "is a true account of the activity of mind." For most readers, his disjunctively and fantastically juxtaposed graphics project the disorderly state of a mind shell-shocked by postmodern cultural developments. In her book-length study of Barthelme's short fiction, Barbara L. Roe contrasts Barthelme's use of graphics with the more conventional illuminated manuscripts: "In sixteenth-century emblem poems, the meaning that links motto, picture, and text is implied in the pictorial details and explicitly stated in the poem's moral instruction. But neither systematic orders nor authoritative instructions about the world solace Barthelme's readers. Rather than 'correct' the world's confusion by falsifying it in the still life of artifacts, Barthelme's collages diminish life's vagaries to an 'ongoing low-grade mystery.'" Thus, in the mysterious "At the Tolstoy Museum," included in *City Life,* the reader finds that contemplating the legends Barthelme offers for his graphics leads only to more questions.

Barthelme employs collages in other stories, creating surrealistic pastiches where Victorian crinolines mingle with machine parts, seductively bared breasts loom to nightmarish proportions, and ice cream cones quite inexplicably carom about the page on Michelin tires. These graphics quite entertainingly fail to produce

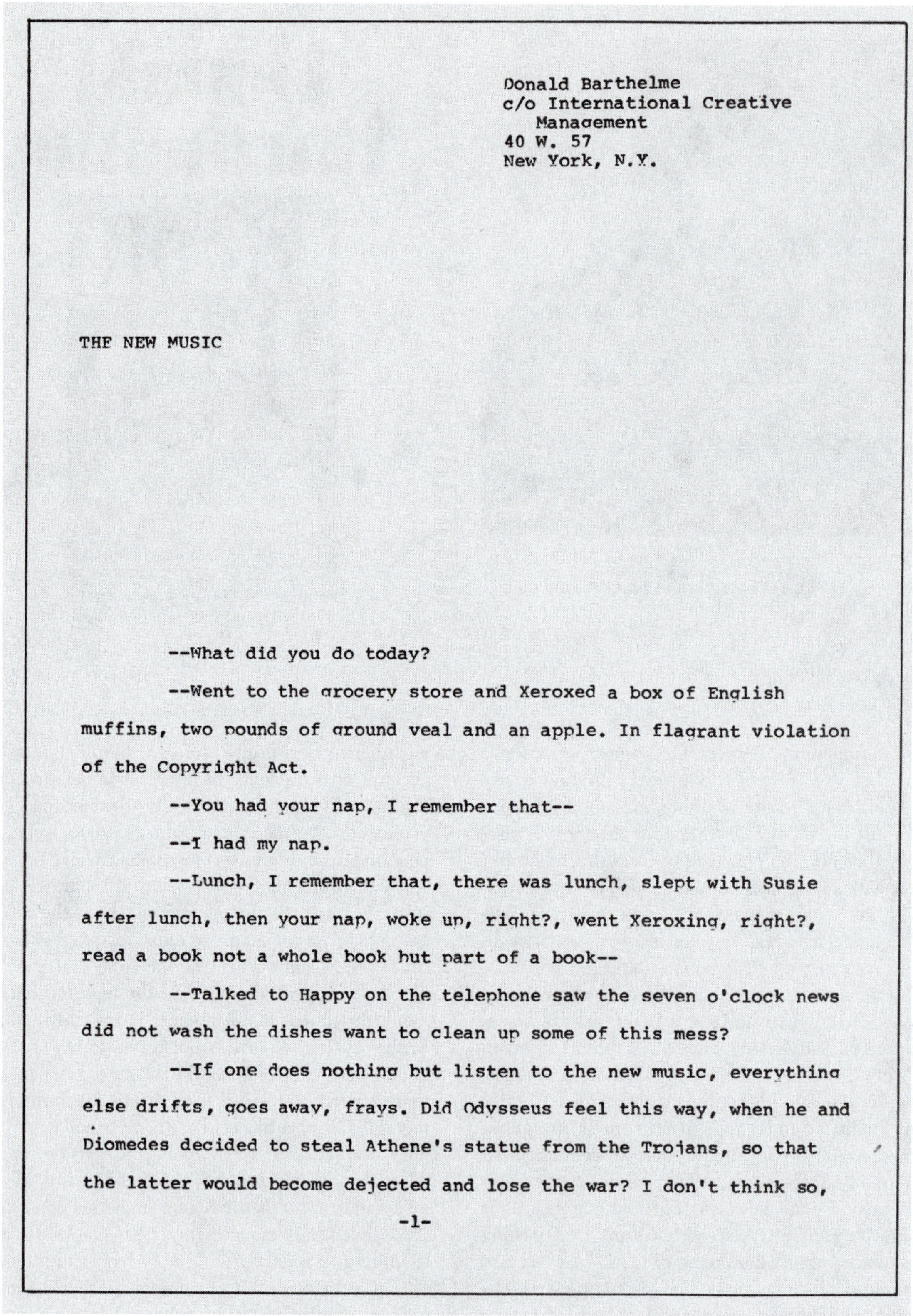

Donald Barthelme
c/o International Creative
    Management
40 W. 57
New York, N.Y.

THE NEW MUSIC

     --What did you do today?

     --Went to the grocery store and Xeroxed a box of English
muffins, two pounds of ground veal and an apple. In flagrant violation
of the Copyright Act.

     --You had your nap, I remember that--

     --I had my nap.

     --Lunch, I remember that, there was lunch, slept with Susie
after lunch, then your nap, woke up, right?, went Xeroxing, right?,
read a book not a whole book but part of a book--

     --Talked to Happy on the telephone saw the seven o'clock news
did not wash the dishes want to clean up some of this mess?

     --If one does nothing but listen to the new music, everything
else drifts, goes away, frays. Did Odysseus feel this way, when he and
Diomedes decided to steal Athene's statue from the Trojans, so that
the latter would become dejected and lose the war? I don't think so,

-1-

Page from the typescript for Barthelme's story "The New Music," included in his 1979 collection, Great Days

an objectively verifiable statement on the nature of reality. Many of his characters are artists; none succeed in producing the kind of traditional art that audiences expect. Lee Upton identifies this inability as an index of genuine artistry: "Failure seems to be one certainty in Donald Barthelme's *Sixty Stories*. His artists inevitably fail, within their work, to meet the full implications of their visions; failure becomes the good artist's lot."

Responsible artists can no longer pretend to oracular truth in Barthelme's stories. As John Leland notes, the best the Barthelmesque artist can hope to achieve is to map out a "play space" where his works can negotiate "between the promise and the lie of signs." Barthelme discussed this kind of inconclusive art with interviewer J. D. O'Hara: "I believe that my every sentence trembles with morality in that each attempts to engage the problematic rather than to present a proposition to which all reasonable men must agree. . . . In this century there's been much stress placed not upon what we know but on knowing that our methods are themselves questionable—our Song of Songs is the Uncertainty Principle."

Barthelme abandoned his playful graphics in his 1979 story collection, *Great Days,* but continued to investigate the art of the absolutely elusive meaning with other kinds of narrative devices. Several stories in *Great Days,* including the title story, "The Crisis," "The Apology," and "The New Music," consist entirely of dialogues utterly devoid of clues that would allow the reader to identify the speakers or place them in any visual context. In "The New Music," the central drama seems to arise from the contrast between the promise and the reality of Pool, a planned community of glowing theaters, sublime monasteries, and sparkling circuses: "The idea was that it be one of those new towns. Where everyone would be happier." The town is well advertised: "Pool projects positive images of itself through the great medium of film. . . . So even if one does not go there, one may assimilate the meaning of Pool." As the disjointed conversation limps forward, the "meaning" of those "positive images" becomes increasingly unstable. The town begins to seem less lovely, less nurturing, and finally alarmingly totalitarian in its very promise of perfection. And yet, while the city may not live up to its promises, there is always the possibility of revolution waiting beyond the horizon.

Barthelme did not publish another short-story collection until 1983, when *Overnight to Many Distant Cities* appeared. Having thoroughly mined the theme of collaboration between artist and audience in his earlier collections, he turned to consider less intellectualized collaborations between human beings, exploring a renewed vision of romantic, or at least lustful, unions between his characters. The narrators and protagonists

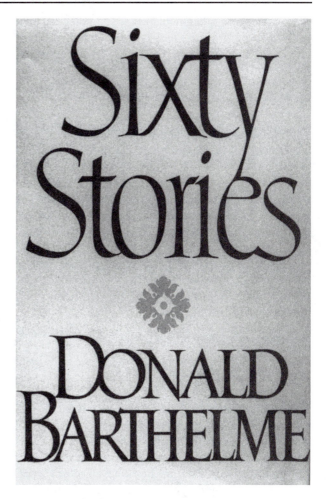

Dust jacket for Barthelme's 1981 retrospective collection, winner of the PEN/Faulkner Award in 1982

of these stories display a remarkably lemming-like tendency to give themselves over to great loves, grand desires, and enormously improvident debauchery. Rebuffed, abandoned, betrayed, they rejoice in their painful but undiminished delight in their own foolhardiness. "Terminus" chronicles an adulterous affair set in a vaguely European hotel. The sense of repetition, combined with the setting, echoes the serial encounters between the lovers in Vladimir Nabokov's story "Spring in Fialta," particularly at moments like this one, almost devoid of Barthelme's habitual ironic distancing: "He looks at the sleeping woman; how beautiful she is! He touches her back, lightly." Elsewhere in the story, Barthelme acknowledges the inadvisability of such self-indulgence: "He has learned nothing from the gray in his hair; the additional lenses in the lenses of his spectacles have not educated him; the merriment of dental assistants has not brought him the news; he behaves as if *something* were possible, still; there's whispering at the Hotel Terminus." The couple experiences a lifetime of repeated encounters in a few months, falling in and out of love with each other, until they seem in the final lines to be offering greetings and farewells simultaneously, interminably, in the Hotel Terminus: "Walking briskly in a warm overcoat toward the Hotel Terminus, he stops to buy flowers, yellow freesias . . . he falls back in love again, forever. She comes toward him fresh from the bath, opens her robe. Goodbye, she says, goodbye."

Their affair, despite the terminal date they have vaguely established, seems here an infinitely renewable source of romantic energies; many of the other characters in this collection have similarly reaffirming experiences of their own humanity at its most reckless and vulnerable. "Now that I am older . . ." is an exceptionally optimistic love story, as Roe notes: "In 'Now that I am older . . . ,' desire transforms ordinary food and furnishings into spiritual accoutrements. . . . The ironic analogy here between mortality's best and worst possibilities is unmistakable. For now, at least, life's coffers are full."

Barthelme's last anthology of fiction, *The Teachings of Don B.: Satires, Parodies, Fables, Illustrated Stories, and Plays of Donald Barthelme,* collects all of his previously uncollected stories and was published in 1992, three years after his death. The tone and effect of these stories varies considerably, but the collection was nonetheless welcomed by Barthelme's readers. As Raymond Carver observed in Larry McCaffery and Sinda Gregory's *Alive and Writing: Interviews with American Authors of the 1980s* (1987), "Barthelme has done a *world* of work, he's a true innovator who's not being devious or stupid or mean spirited or experimenting for experimenting's sake. He's uneven, but then who isn't?" His obituary in *The New Yorker* opined that during years of cultural crisis, when Richard Nixon exemplified the kind of surrealistically fallible authority Barthelme had been writing about for a decade, his writing "seemed more real–saner and more coherent–than anything else going on in the world."

Barthelme begins to sound increasingly disheartened in his later novels. In one of his last interviews, he confirms that he began in the 1980s to despair of the writer's postmodern future: "I think there are lowered expectations, not aesthetic expectations for the work, but lowered expectations in terms of life. My generation, perhaps foolishly, expected, even demanded, that life be wonderful and magical and then tried to make it so by writing in a rather complex way. It seems now quite an eccentric demand." He continues to strive for the wonderful and magical in his late short stories, however. Lee Upton finds the portraits of the postmodern artist in Barthelme's short stories particularly encouraging: "in some of these stories the artists–those whom we most often think of as creative organizers–may briefly align themselves with full tragic dimensions, if

not above the angels and certainly not exactly among the gods, at least in shaky step formation–almost, I think, happily–amid the full richness of an ambiguous and uncertain realm."

Interviews:

"PW Interviews Donald Barthelme," *Publishers Weekly* (11 November 1974): 6–7;

Joe David Bellamy, *The New Fiction: Interviews with Innovative American Writers,* edited by Bellamy (Urbana: University of Illinois Press, 1974), pp. 45–54;

J. D. O'Hara, "Donald Barthelme: The Art of Fiction LXVI." *Paris Review,* 80 (Summer 1981): 181–210;

Jo Brans, "Embracing the World: An Interview with Donald Barthelme," *Southwest Review,* 67, no. 2 (1982): 121–137;

Larry McCaffery, "An Interview with Donald Barthelme," *Partisan Review,* 49, no. 2 (1982): 184–193.

Bibliographies:

Larry McCaffery, "Donald Barthelme, Robert Coover, William H. Gass: Three Checklists," *Bulletin of Bibliography,* 31 (1974): 101–106;

Jerome Klinkowitz, "Donald Barthelme: A Checklist, 1957–1974," *Critique,* 16, no. 3 (1975): 49–58;

Klinkowitz, Asa Pieratt, and Robert Murray Davis, *Donald Barthelme: A Comprehensive Bibliography and Annotated Secondary Checklist* (Hamden, Conn.: Archon, 1977);

Steven Weisenburger, "Donald Barthelme: A Bibliography," *The Review of Contemporary Fiction,* 11 (Summer 1991): 108–113.

References:

Jochen Achilles, "Donald Barthelme's Aesthetic of Inversion: Caligari's Come-Back as Caligari's Leave-Taking," *Journal of Narrative Technique,* 12, no. 2 (1982): 105–120;

John W. Aldridge, "Donald Barthelme and the Doggy Life," in his *The Devil in the Fire: Retrospective Essays on American Literature and Culture, 1951–1971* (New York: Harper's Magazine Press, 1972), pp. 261–266;

Maclin Bocock, "'The Indian Uprising' or Donald Barthelme's Strange Object Covered with Fur," *Fiction International,* no. 4/5 (1975): 134–146;

Paul Bruss, *Victims: Textual Strategies in Recent American Fiction* (Lewisburg, Pa.: Bucknell University Press, 1981), pp. 101–166;

Ewing Campbell, "Dark Matter: Barthelme's Fantastic, Freudian Subtext in 'The Sandman,'" *Studies in Short Fiction,* 27 (Fall 1990): 517–524;

Guy Davenport, "Style as Protagonist in Donald Barthelme," *The Review of Contemporary Fiction,* 11 (Summer 1991): 69–74;

Julian Cowley, "'Weeping Map Intense Activity Din': Reading Donald Barthelme," *University of Toronto Quarterly,* 60, no. 2 (1990–1991): 292–304;

Maurice Couturier and Régis Durand, *Donald Barthelme* (London & New York: Methuen, 1982);

Morris Dickstein, "Fiction Hot and Kool: Dilemmas of the Experimental Writer," *TriQuarterly,* no. 33 (Spring 1975): 257–272;

John M. Ditsky, "'With Ingenuity and Hard Word, Distracted': The Narrative Style of Donald Barthelme," *Style,* 9 (Summer 1975): 388–400;

Régis Durand, "On the Pertinaciousness of the Father, the Son, and the Subject: The Case of Donald Barthelme," in *Critical Angles: European Views of Contemporary American Literature,* edited by Marc Chénetier (Carbondale: Southern Illinois University Press, 1986), pp. 45–52;

Teresa L. Ebert, "Postmodern Politics, Patriarchy, and Donald Barthelme," *The Review of Contemporary Fiction,* 11 (Summer 1991): 75–82;

Walter Evans, "Comanches and Civilization in Donald Barthelme's 'The Indian Uprising,'" *Arizona Quarterly,* 42, no. 1 (1986): 45–52;

William H. Gass, "The Leading Edge of the Trash Phenomenon," in his *Fiction and the Figures of Life* (New York: Knopf, 1970), pp. 97–103;

James R. Giles, "The 'Marivaudian Being' Drowns His Children: Dehumanization in Donald Barthelme's 'Robert Kennedy Saved from Drowning' and Joyce Carol Oates' *Wonderland,*" *Southern Humanities Review,* 7 (1975): 68–75;

Lois G. Gordon, *Donald Barthelme* (Boston: Twayne, 1981);

Gerald Graff, "Babbitt at the Abyss: The Social Context of PostModern American Fiction," *TriQuarterly,* no. 33 (Spring 1975): 305–337;

Graff, "The Myth of the PostModernist Breakthrough," *TriQuarterly,* no. 26 (Winter 1973): 383–417;

Albert J. Guerard, "Notes on the Rhetoric of AntiRealist Fiction," *TriQuarterly,* no. 30 (Spring 1974): 3–50;

Josephine Hendin, "Angries: S-M as a Literary Style," *Harper's,* 248 (February 1974): 87–93;

Cheryl Herr, "Fathers, Daughters, Anxiety, and Fiction," in *Discontented Discourses: Feminism/Textual Intervention/Psychoanalysis,* edited by Marleen S. Barr and Richard Feldstein (Urbana: University of Illinois Press, 1989), pp. 173–207;

R. E. Johnson Jr., "'Bees Barking in the Night': The End and Beginning of Donald Barthelme's Narrative," *Boundary 2,* 5 (1976): 71–92;

Jerome Klinkowitz, "Barthelme's Canonical Village," *The Review of Contemporary Fiction,* 11 (Summer 1991): 94–101;

Klinkowitz, "Donald Barthelme," in *Literary Disruptions: The Making of a Post-Contemporary American Fiction* (Urbana: University of Illinois Press, 1975), pp. 62–81;

Klinkowitz, *Donald Barthelme: An Exhibition* (Durham: Duke University Press, 1991);

Klinkowitz, "Donald Barthelme's SuperFiction," *Critique* 16, no. 3 (1975): 5–18;

Eberhard Kreutzer, "City Spectacles as Artistic Acts: Donald Barthelme's 'The Balloon' and 'The Glass Mountain,'" *Anglistik und Englischunterricht,* 13 (1981): 43–55;

Mark C. Krupnick, "Notes from the Funhouse," *Modern Occasions,* 1 (Fall 1970): 108–112;

John Kuehl, *Alternate Worlds: A Study of Postmodern Antirealistic American Fiction* (New York: New York University Press, 1989), pp. 97–100, 112–116, 162–164;

Thomas M. Leitch, "Donald Barthelme and the End of the End," *Modern Fiction Studies,* 26, no. 1 (1982): 129–143;

John Leland, "Remarks Re-marked: What Curios of Signs!" *Boundary 2,* 5 (1977): 796–811;

Paul Lilly Jr., "Comic Strategies in the Fiction of Barthelme and Kosinski," *Publications of the Missouri Philological Association,* 4 (1979): 25–32;

Carl Malmgren, "Barthes's *S/Z* and Barthelme's 'The Zombies': Cacographic Interruption of a Text," *PTL,* 3 (1978): 209–221;

Carter Martin, "A Fantastic Pairing: Edward Taylor and Donald Barthelme," in *The Scope of the Fantastic: Theory, Technique, Major Authors,* edited by Robert A. Collins and Howard D. Pearce (Westport, Conn.: Greenwood, 1985), pp. 183–190;

Larry McCaffery, *The Metafictional Muse: The Work of Robert Coover, Donald Barthelme, and William H. Gass* (Pittsburgh: University of Pittsburgh Press, 1982), pp. 99–150;

Jeannette McVicker, "Donald Barthelme's *The Dead Father*: 'Girls Talk' and the Displacement of the Logos," *Boundary 2,* 15 (Spring/Fall 1988): 363–390;

Charles Molesworth, *Donald Barthelme's Fiction: The Ironist Saved from Drowning* (Columbia: University of Missouri Press, 1982);

Lance Olsen, "Linguistic Pratfalls," in his *Circus of the Mind in Motion: Postmodernism and the Comic Vision* (Detroit: Wayne State University Press, 1990), pp. 104–114;

Olsen, "Slumgullions, or Some Notes toward Trying to Introduce Donald Barthelme," *The Review of Contemporary Fiction,* 11 (Summer 1991): 7–14;

Olsen, ed., *The Review of Contemporary Fiction,* special issue on Barthelme, 11 (Summer 1991);

Clarke Owens, "Donald Barthelme's Existential Acts of Art," in *Since Flannery O'Connor: Essays on the Contemporary American Short Story,* edited by Loren Logsdon and Charles W. Mayer (Macomb: Western Illinois University Press, 1987), pp. 72–82;

Richard F. Patteson, ed., *Critical Essays on Donald Barthelme* (New York: G. K. Hall, 1992);

David Porush, "Fiction at the End of the Mechanical Age: Barthelme's Art 'which has not yet been invented,'" *The Review of Contemporary Fiction,* 11 (Summer 1991): 83–93;

Porush, "Technology and Postmodernism: Cybernetic Fiction," *Sub-stance,* 27 (1980): 92–100;

Barbara L. Roe, *Donald Barthelme: A Study of the Short Fiction* (Boston: Twayne, 1992);

James Rother, "Parafiction: The Adjacent Universe of Barth, Barthelme, Pynchon, and Nabokov," *Boundary 2,* 5 (Fall 1976): 21–44;

Robert Scholes, "Metafiction," *Iowa Review,* 1 (Fall 1970): 100–115;

Mary Doyle Springer, "Aristotle in Contemporary Literature: Barthelme's 'Views of My Father Weeping,'" in *Narrative Poetics: Innovations, Limits, Challenges,* edited by James Phelan (Columbus: Ohio State University Press, 1987), pp. 93–102;

Wayne B. Stengel, *The Shape of Art in the Short Stories of Donald Barthelme* (Baton Rouge: Louisiana State University Press, 1985);

Stanley Trachtenberg, *Understanding Donald Barthelme* (Columbia: University of South Carolina Press, 1990);

Lee Upton, "Failed Artists in Donald Barthelme's *Sixty Stories,*" *Critique,* 26, no. 1 (1984): 11–17;

William B. Warde, "Barthelme's 'The Piano Player': Surreal and Mock Tragic," *Xavier Review,* 1, no. 1–2 (1985): 58–64;

Warde, "A Collage Approach: Donald Barthelme's Literary Fragments," *Journal of American Culture,* 8, no. 1 (1985): 51–56;

Tom Whalen, "Wonderful Elegance: Barthelme's 'The Party,'" *Critique,* 16, no. 3 (1975): 45–48;

Alan Wilde, "Barthelme Unfair to Kierkegaard: Some Thoughts on Modern and Postmodern Irony," *Boundary 2,* 5 (Fall 1976): 45–70;

Wilde, *Horizons of Assent: Modernism, Postmodernism, and the Ironic Imagination* (Baltimore: Johns Hopkins University Press, 1981), pp. 166–188;

Wilde, *Middle Grounds: Studies in Contemporary American Fiction* (Philadelphia: University of Pennsylvania Press, 1987), pp. 24–42, 161–172.

Wendell Berry
(5 August 1934 –   )

Thom Conroy
Ohio University

BOOKS: *Nathan Coulter* (Boston: Houghton Mifflin, 1960; revised edition, San Francisco: North Point, 1983);

The Broken Ground (New York: Harcourt, Brace & World, 1964; London: Cape, 1966);

November Twenty-Six, Nineteen Hundred Sixty-Three (New York: Braziller, 1964);

A Place on Earth (New York: Harcourt, Brace & World, 1967; revised edition, San Francisco: North Point, 1983);

Openings (New York: Harcourt, Brace & World, 1968);

The Rise (Lexington: University of Kentucky Library Press, 1968);

Findings (Iowa City: Prairie, 1969);

The Long-Legged House (New York: Harcourt, Brace & World, 1969);

Farming: A Hand Book (New York: Harcourt Brace Jovanovich, 1970);

The Hidden Wound (Boston: Houghton Mifflin, 1970);

The Unforeseen Wilderness: An Essay on Kentucky's Red River Gorge, with photographs by Eugene Meatyard (Lexington: University Press of Kentucky, 1971; revised and expanded edition, San Francisco: North Point, 1991);

A Continuous Harmony: Essays Cultural and Agricultural (New York: Harcourt Brace Jovanovich, 1972);

The Country of Marriage (New York: Harcourt Brace Jovanovich, 1973);

An Eastward Look (Berkeley, Cal.: Sand Dollar, 1974);

Falling Asleep (Austin: Cold Mountain, 1974);

The Memory of Old Jack (New York: Harcourt Brace Jovanovich, 1974);

Horses (Monterey, Ky.: Larkspur, 1975);

Sayings and Doings (Frankfort, Ky.: Gnomon, 1975);

To What Listens (Crete, Nebr.: Best Cellar, 1975);

The Kentucky River: Two Poems (Monterey, Ky.: Larkspur, 1976);

There Is Singing around Me (Austin: Cold Mountain, 1976);

The Agricultural Crisis: A Crisis of Culture (New York: Myrin Institute, 1977);

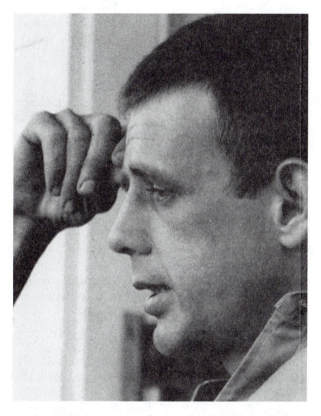

Wendell Berry, circa 1960 (photograph by James Baker Hall)

Clearing (New York: Harcourt Brace Jovanovich, 1977);

Three Memorial Poems (Berkeley, Cal.: Sand Dollar, 1977);

The Unsettling of America: Culture and Agriculture (San Francisco: Sierra Club Books, 1977);

The Gift of Gravity (Deerfield, Mass.: Deerfield Press, 1979);

A Part (San Francisco: North Point, 1980);

The Salad (San Francisco: North Point, 1980);

The Gift of Good Land: Further Essays, Cultural and Agricultural (San Francisco: North Point, 1981);

The Nativity (Great Barrington, Mass.: Penamen, 1981);

Recollected Essays, 1965–1980 (San Francisco: North Point, 1981);

The Wheel (San Francisco: North Point, 1982);

Standing by Words (San Francisco: North Point, 1983);

Collected Poems, 1957–1982 (San Francisco: North Point, 1985);

The Wild Birds: Six Stories of the Port William Membership (San Francisco: North Point, 1986);

The Landscape of Harmony: Two Essays on Wilderness and Community (Madley, Hereford, U.K.: Five Seasons, 1987);

Home Economics: Fourteen Essays (San Francisco: North Point, 1987);

Sabbaths (San Francisco: North Point, 1987);

Some Differences (Lewiston, Idaho: Confluence, 1987);

"Higher Education and Home Defense." From the Heartlands: Photos and Essays from the Midwest, Midwest Writers Series 1, edited by Larry Smith (Huron, Ohio: Bottom Dog, 1988);

Remembering (San Francisco: North Point, 1988);

Traveling at Home (Lewisburg, Pa.: Bucknell University Press, 1988);

Harlan Hubbard: Life and Work (Lexington: University Press of Kentucky, 1990);

What Are People For? (San Francisco: North Point, 1990);

The Discovery of Kentucky (Frankfurt, Ky.: Gnomon, 1991);

Fidelity: Five Stories (New York: Pantheon, 1992);

Sex, Economy, Freedom, and Community: Eight Essays (New York: Pantheon, 1993);

Entries (New York: Pantheon, 1994);

Watch with Me: And Six Other Stories of the Yet-Remembered Ptolemy Proudfoot and His Wife, Miss Minnie, née Quinch (New York: Pantheon, 1994);

Another Turn of the Crank: Essays (Washington, D.C.: Counterpoint, 1995);

A World Lost (Washington, D.C.: Counterpoint, 1996);

Two More Stories of the Port William Membership (Frankfurt, Ky.: Gnomon, 1997);

The Selected Poems of Wendell Berry (Washington, D.C.: Counterpoint, 1998);

A Timbered Choir: The Sabbath Poems, 1979–1997 (Washington, D.C.: Counterpoint, 1998);

Jayber Crow: The Life Story of Jayber Crow, Barber, of the Port William Membership, as Written by Himself (Washington, D.C.: Counterpoint, 2000);

Life Is a Miracle: An Essay against Modern Superstition (Washington, D.C.: Counterpoint, 2000).

OTHER: *Meeting the Expectations of the Land: Essays in Sustainable Agriculture and Stewardship,* edited by Berry, Wes Jackson, and Bruce Colman (San Francisco: North Point, 1984).

A distinguished essayist and accomplished poet, Wendell Berry has also established himself as an impor-

tant novelist and short-story writer. Since the publication of his first novel, *Nathan Coulter* (1960), Berry has earned a place as an important American thinker and artist whose philosophy and aesthetics are grounded in a regional, environmentally sound, agrarian approach to community. Berry's fiction, as well as his essays and poetry, are closely tied to the farming community of Port Royal, a small town near the confluence of the Kentucky and Ohio Rivers. Entrenched in the people and land of this northern Kentucky region, Berry's short fiction focuses on the enduring values of family, moral and environmental responsibility, and tradition.

In Berry's short-fiction collections, *The Wild Birds: Six Stories of the Port William Membership* (1986), *Fidelity: Five Stories* (1992), and *Watch with Me: And Six Other Stories of the Yet-Remembered Ptolemy Proudfoot and His Wife, Miss Minnie, née Quinch* (1994), characters emerge as strong, often defiant individuals, whose struggles and passions are embedded in the history and landscape of Port William, a fictional version of Port Royal. Though some critics contend that Berry advocates the return to an irrecoverable way of life, most agree that Berry's writing does not call for a nostalgic restoration but for an exploration of the ideas, values, and relationships that have informed small, agrarian-based communities. In an article written for *Studies in the Literary Imagination* (Fall 1994), Stephen Whited explains, "Berry's writing places value not on a literal or historical return, but on the restoration of a traditional understanding that measures value by a mutual interdependence and by fidelity to place, community, and family."

The fidelity to place, community, and family that characterizes Berry's short stories is deeply rooted in the author's own life in and around Henry County, Kentucky. Wendell Erdman Berry was born on 5 August 1934 to John M. and Virginia Berry (née Perry), the eldest of four children. John Berry was one of the founding members of the Kentucky Burley Tobacco Growers Cooperative Association and a respected attorney in New Castle, the county seat. According to Andrew J. Angyal in *Wendell Berry* (1995), the Berry and Perry families can trace their local heritage back four and five generations, respectively. Berry's childhood was also influenced by the nearby Kentucky River, on which his family owned a small cabin known as Curran's Camp, after Curran Matthews, a great-uncle of Berry's.

Starting from the time when he was fourteen years old, Berry relied on Curran's Camp as a refuge, a role that it served for many years. In his autobiographical essay "The Long-Legged House" (1965) Berry recalls learning the "ruling idea" of his life during his earliest days at Curran's Camp: "And those days that gave me peace suggested to me the possibility of a greater, more substantial peace—a decent, open, generous relation between a man's life and the world—that I have never achieved; but it must have begun to be then, and it has come more and more consciously to be, the hope and the ruling idea of my life."

From 1948 to 1952 Berry and his brother John Jr. attended the Millersburg Military Institute, a small, all-male preparatory school outside of Paris, Kentucky. Upon graduation Berry attended the University of Kentucky in Lexington, where he co-edited the literary magazine, *Stylus,* and graduated with a B.A. in English in 1956. In that same year Berry won a fiction contest sponsored by *The Carolina Quarterly* and enrolled in the master's program in English at the University of Kentucky. While earning his master's degree, which he received in 1957, Berry met Tanya Amyx, his future wife. When the two of them were married, in May 1957, they moved to Curran's Camp to spend their first summer together. During that summer Berry wrote what he calls "the first poetry that I felt represented by." After teaching at Georgetown College for the academic year of 1957–1958, Berry was awarded a Wallace Stegner Fellowship to study creative writing at Stanford University, where he took a seminar with Ken Kesey and Ernest J. Gaines. During Berry's second year at Stanford he was appointed Edward H. Jones Lecturer in Creative Writing. He also finished his first novel, *Nathan Coulter.*

In *Nathan Coulter* the title character narrates his family's tale of suffering and competition in a small Kentucky farming community before World War II. The novel also introduces many characters whose stories are told in more detail in the author's short fiction, including Jarrat Coulter and his bachelor brother Burley. *Nathan Coulter* foregrounds ideas about environmental stewardship, communal responsibility, and rural hardships, which characterize much of Berry's later fiction, poetry, and essays.

In June 1960 Berry moved from California to the 250-acre farmstead in New Castle that had served as a home to his father and grandfather. The fall of the following year a Guggenheim Foundation Fellowship allowed Berry and his family to move to Italy, where he continued work on a second novel, *A Place on Earth* (1967). In 1962 Berry accepted a position as assistant professor of English and director of freshman English with New York University. New York was the last place Berry lived before returning to Henry County to write and farm for the next three decades. The following year, Berry's *November Twenty-Six, Nineteen Hundred Sixty-Three,* an elegy for President John F. Kennedy, was published in *The Nation,* securing his place as a poet of merit; the poem was published in book form in 1964. Though the department chair of NYU tried to

Dust jacket for Berry's 1992 collection of stories set in the fictional Kentucky community of Port William

persuade Berry to stay on as a professor, the author and his family returned to Kentucky in the summer of 1964, where Berry had a job waiting for him at the University of Kentucky. Berry has said that his return to Kentucky was an inevitable choice for a writer whose work binds him so closely to the land and the community it supports. Though he was living in "the greatest city in the nation," Berry writes of the time in *The Long-Legged House* (1969), "I had not escaped Kentucky, and had never really wanted to. I was still writing about it, and had recognized that I would probably need to write about it for the rest of my life. Kentucky was my fate—not an altogether pleasant fate, though it had much that was pleasing in it, but one that I could not leave behind simply by going to another place, and that I therefore felt more and more obligated to meet directly and understand."

In 1965, Berry moved to Lane's Landing, near the site of Curran's Camp on the Kentucky River. Two years later, Berry won the Bess Hopkin Prize for poetry, and he published *A Place on Earth,* which introduces the name *Port William* for Berry's setting and tells the story of Mat Feltner, a tobacco farmer and an important character in many of Berry's short stories. In addition to Mat, the novel centers around Mat's wife, Margaret; his son, Virgil, who is killed in World War II; and Virgil's widowed wife, Hannah, all of whom figure prominently in other stories. *A Place on Earth* also introduces the elderly Jack Beechum, the main character of Berry's third novel, *The Memory of Old Jack* (1974), and a central character in two of Berry's short-story collections.

In *The Memory of Old Jack* Berry concludes many plotlines that began in the previous two novels and flushes out the complex history of Port William and the surrounding region. As Angyal has noted, the rich heritage of Berry's fictional Port William can be compared to William Faulkner's Yoknapatawpha County. The primary distinction between the two places rests in the fact that Yoknapatawpha County is "romantic and mythic," while Port William is situated within the boundary of realism. From early on in his career, as he recalls in *The Long-Legged House,* Berry recognized that he would have to overcome the "literary tradition" he had inherited: a "corrupt and crippling local colorsim of the 'Kentucky' writers." Indeed, if Port William is less romantic than Yoknapatawpha County, it is because of Berry's desire to write against the background of this sentimental and inauthentic legacy.

In his fiction, poetry, and essays, Berry consciously crafts a vision of agrarian community and culture that is accurate, morally complex, and emotionally poignant. In spite of his effort to resist Romanticism, however, Berry is occasionally accused of oversimplification, even by critics who hail his ideas and craftsmanship. In an article written for *The New York Review of Books* (14 June 1990), Bill McKibben conceded that Berry "minimizes the trouble such small societies can cause—the unnecessary feuds, for instance, that derive from some forgotten insult three generations back, or the mean prejudices and claustrophobia that so many people move to the city to escape."

In the years between writing *The Memory of Old Jack* and the publication of Berry's first short-fiction collection in 1986, the author continued to expand his reputation as a poet and essayist. In 1974, he was appointed Elliston Poet at the University of Cincinnati. The following year, he was awarded first place from the Friends of American Writers for his poetry collection *Sayings and Doings* (1975). Berry was also awarded three honorary doctorates during this period, from Centre College of Kentucky (Danville) in 1978, Transylvania University (Lexington) in 1981, and the University of Kentucky in 1986.

In 1986 Berry published *The Wild Birds: Six Stories of the Port William Membership,* a collection of short stories that continues to explore the lives of characters introduced in his three previous novels. In "Thicker than Liquor (1930)" Wheeler Catlett, a lawyer in the fictional county seat of Hargrave, travels to the Stag Hotel in Louisville to retrieve his besotted Uncle Peach, a bachelor who may be roughly based on Berry's great-uncle Matthew Curran. Though Dorie Catlett, Wheeler's mother, accepts that "blood is thicker than liquor," Wheeler sees Uncle Peach as a burden. On the way home from the Stag Hotel, Uncle Peach vomits beside Wheeler in a crowded train, and Wheeler's low opinion of his elder intensifies. Once Wheeler has managed to get Uncle Peach into a clean bed later that night, he sits by the old man's side, listening to snatches of a horrible nightmare. By the story's end, Wheeler climbs into bed with Uncle Peach to comfort him. In "Thicker than Liquor (1930)" Berry gives the reader insights into the early life of one of the patriarchs of Port William and explores the theme of accepting family responsibility. Though the story lacks character development, it presents an effective sketch of Uncle Peach's alcohol-ravaged life and demonstrates the unflinching generosity of his family's love.

"It Wasn't Me (1953)," the third story in *The Wild Birds,* chronicles the sale of the late Jack Beechum's farm. Although Jack wrote a note that indicates that he wanted to sell his farm to Elton Penn, Jack's daughter, Clara Pettit, returns to Port William to claim her father's property. Wheeler, who promised Jack that he would see the farm passed on to Elton, seeks to persuade Clara and her husband, Glad, to accept her father's wishes. Though Wheeler explains to Clara that passing on the farm to Elton is "not a question of what was owed and what was paid," Clara refuses to sell the farm at anything under a fair market price. Elton must compete for Jack's property at auction, and he wins by bidding three hundred dollars an acre, more than he is capable of paying. Wheeler, who encouraged Elton to bid high, uses his own money to establish a fund to help Elton pay off the land. When Elton protests, Wheeler explains that his action is based on a communal and agrarian conception of economy that cannot be reduced to price and profit.

In "It Wasn't Me (1953)," Wheeler espouses an economic philosophy in which the nurturing relationship that people foster with the land carries over into the relationships that bind a community together. Though the dramatic action of the story fizzles during Wheeler's long monologues, "It Wasn't Me (1953)" presents the ideal of a healthy agrarian community in clear and heartfelt terms. According to Whited, Berry's "healthy community" is one in which people's use of

Dust jacket for Berry's 1994 collection of stories chronicling the courtship and long marriage of a Kentucky farm couple

"practical knowledge of a larger, natural order *necessarily* informs the social order." In this story, Wheeler's "practical knowledge" of "a different line of succession" determines succession in the community to which he and Elton belong.

The next two stories in the collection, "The Boundary (1965)" and "That Distant Land (1965)," narrate the elderly Mat Feltner's possible stroke and his death. In "The Boundary (1965)" Mat wanders into the woods around Shade Branch Creek to check a cow fence that he believes his son-in-law, Nathan Coulter, may have failed to mend. When Mat finds that Nathan had mended the fence after all, he continues downstream, recalling days spent along the creek. Mat continues walking until he realizes that he has come far and the way back is all uphill. Though it takes him many hours, he eventually makes it to the top of a ridge and collapses beside a chestnut tree, where he is eventually discovered and helped to his feet by Wheeler and Nathan. The story ends on a chilling note, however: later that night, Mat's wife, Margaret, discovers him wandering through their home, lost and disoriented. "The Boundary (1965)" stands as the strongest story of

the collection. While Mat's reminiscences in the creek bed provide a glimpse into the history of Port William, they also serve to fully develop his character. Moreover, the understated dramatic action of the final paragraph is one of the most emotionally resonant moments in all of Berry's short fiction.

"That Distant Land (1965)" begins where "The Boundary (1965)" ends. Mat's mind slowly returns from the state of confusion that followed his return from Shade Branch Creek. Though he regains full mental capacities before he dies, he remains bedridden. Margaret and his grandson, Andy Catlett, now thirty-one years old (the same age as Berry in 1965), spend the summer looking after him. On one occasion, Mat wakes up in the middle of the night and recites the Twenty-third Psalm. Andy recounts the impact that his grandfather's sudden recital had on him:

He said the psalm to me. I lay listening to his old, slow voice coming through the dark to me, saying that he walked through the valley of the shadow of death and that he feared no evil. It stood my hair up. I had known that psalm all my life I had heard it and said it a thousand times. But until then I had always felt that it came from a long way off, some place I had not lived. Now, hearing him speak it, it seemed to me for the first time to utter itself in our tongue and to wear our dust. My grandfather slept again after that, but I did not.

One day in September, when Andy, Nathan, Burley, Elton, and Jarrat are harvesting tobacco, Wheeler drives out to where the team is resting to announce that Mat has died. Jarrat, now the oldest man on the farm, stands and says "Let's load 'em up," an indication of his understanding that he is now the patriarch of the community. "That Distant Land (1965)" provides another portrait of tobacco farming and further develops Berry's idea of the "healthy community." As in many of the other stories in *The Wild Birds,* the dramatic action of the ending is significant for its symbolism.

In the title story of the collection, Burley, his wife, Hannah, and his nephew Nathan come to Wheeler's office to ask the lawyer to assist with Burley's will. Burley wants to leave his farm to Danny Branch instead of Nathan. When Wheeler expresses his opposition to this, Burley reveals that Danny is his child from an affair with a woman named Kate Helen. He goes to explain his philosophy of the "wayward," an approach to life at odds with Wheeler's idealistic concern with the way things should be. The rest of the story is comprised of dialogue and Wheeler's memories of hunting at night with Burley. In "The Wild Birds (1967)," Berry again allows philosophy to take precedence over dramatic action. While some critics may attribute Berry's tendency to foreground ideas as an aesthetic weakness, Whited explains that Berry's stories are forthrightly crafted in the didactic tradition. "To illustrate the values of the 'Great Economy,'" Whited writes, "Berry follows the example of the ancients by offering stories that at once exhibit and celebrate the knowledge of community."

Between the publication of *The Wild Birds* and his next collection, Berry continued to further his reputation as a scholar, poet, and essayist. After receiving an honorary doctorate from the University of Kentucky in 1986, Berry returned to his alma mater as a teacher in 1987. That same year, he received the Jean Stein Award from the American Academy and Institute of Arts and Letters, the Milner Award, and a fifth honorary doctorate from Santa Clara University. The following year, Wendell Berry published *Remembering* (1988), a novella composed during his tenure as writer-in-residence at Bucknell University.

Remembering tells the story of Andy Catlett, the first-person narrator in Berry's first and second short-story collections and the character who most closely approximates Berry himself. In this fourth long fictional work by Berry, Andy suffers the loss of his right hand, which symbolically severs him from both himself and his family. Before he leaves for a trip that will eventually take him to San Francisco, Andy squabbles with his wife and children. At a Midwestern agricultural conference, he indulges in an outburst in which he accuses the other members of the conference of hypocrisy and indifference to actual farmers. In San Francisco, he spends a sleepless night in introspection and self-debate about himself, his role as a farmer, and corporate agriculture in general.

In 1992 Berry published *Fidelity: Five Stories,* his most carefully crafted and compelling collection of short fiction. The collection features two long stories, "Pray without Ceasing" (fifty-nine pages) and "Fidelity" (eighty-four pages), which fill in much of the early and late history of the region and serve as an exquisite beginning and ending to the Port William chronicles. The collection received the Victory of Spirit Ethics Award from the Louisville Community Foundation, while "Pray without Ceasing," Berry's most successful short story, was reprinted in the 1993 edition of *Best American Short Stories.*

In "Pray without Ceasing" Andy relates the poignant story of his great-grandfather's murder in 1912. In 1965, while Mat is still alive, Andy visits his grandparents after reading an old newspaper article recounting the death of his great-grandfather, Ben Feltner. Andy's grandmother, Margaret, tells him the whole story of Ben's death. In her version, Thad Coulter, a Port William farmer, is faced with the threat of losing his family farm after financing his son's failed business endeavor. Thad drinks himself into a deep alcoholic stupor and rides to the farm of his best friend, Ben. When Ben asks his friend to come back after he has sobered up, Thad is insulted, and that evening in Port William he finds Ben and shoots him dead. Mat, Ben's son, finds his father lying dead in the road and craves revenge, but Jack Beechum, Mat's uncle, holds onto the young Mat until his visible rage drains out of him. Despondent over killing his best friend, Thad turns himself in at the Hargrave jail, where he ends up taking his own life.

The climax of this complex plot, however, does not occur until a lynch mob, unaware of Thad's suicide, approaches the Feltner farm seeking the family's approval to exact vengeance on Thad for Ben's death. When Mat declines and asks the crowd to come inside and join them for supper, the narrative transforms into a moving story about forgiveness and its impact on the Port William community. In fact, as descendant of a Coulter and a Feltner, Andy realizes that his own identity is bound up in the events that happened more than two decades before his own birth: "My grandfather made a peace here that has joined many who would otherwise have been divided. I am the child of his forgiveness." The terse narration of "Pray without Ceasing" evokes anger, love, and sympathy. In addition to evoking an intense emotional response, the narration explores the complex relationship between Berry's "Great Economy" and an indifferent capitalism. The story also succeeds in demonstrating the place of the individual in Berry's healthy community. Most critics agree that "Pray without Ceasing" represents the pinnacle of Berry's accomplishment as a short-fiction writer. In a review for *The New York Times* (15 November 1992), John Kenny Crane observed that, "In ['Pray without Ceasing'] and the others that accompany it, Mr. Berry's sentences are exquisitely constructed, suggesting the cyclic rhythms of his agrarian world."

In "Making It Home," the third story in *Fidelity,* Art Rowanberry, discharged from World War II after a shrapnel injury, walks from Jefferson, on the other side of the Kentucky River, to his family farm near Port William. As he walks he reflects on the horror of his experiences while fighting on the European front. Seeing the familiar countryside all around him, at first Art can do nothing but imagine the destruction of it. Berry dramatizes the damage war wreaks upon the psyche of those who must participate in it, evoking a feeling that he often explores in his poetry. In "The Morning News" (1970), for instance, the speaker makes a distinction between killing in "hot savagery like a beast" and the cold horror of killing "by design, deliberately, without wrath," which is "the sullen labor that perfects Hell." After spending the night in a church in Ellville, Art bathes in a tiny creek not far from home. His immersion in the water of his childhood renews his connection with the land, reaffirms his place in the agrarian community, and fills him with a new sense of purpose and manhood.

"Fidelity" narrates the last days of Burley Coulter, a familiar character in the Port William chronicles. At the opening of the story, Burley, eighty-two years old, lies unconscious in a hospital bed in Louisville, kept alive by intravenous injection. Unable to accept that his father has been separated from his community and the land that has sustained him, Danny, Burley's son, sneaks into the Louisville hospital, unplugs Burley, and takes him to an abandoned tobacco barn in Stepstone Hollow. Kyle Bode, a one-dimensional detective with no fondness for the countryside, investigates the case, while the Port William community—including Nathan Coulter, Wheeler Catlett, and Wheeler's son Henry, also a lawyer—abets Danny. As Bode questions Henry and Wheeler in their Hargrave office, Burley dies in the tobacco shed, and Danny spends the day digging a grave for his father so that he can return Burley to the land he knew so well when he was alive. The rest of the story is divided between Wheeler's diatribe against a government that has waged war on the agrarian lifestyle of Port William and the quiet burial of Burley in a flagstone grave. As Wheeler lectures Bode, the citizens of Port William gather in his law office to show solidarity, not only to Burley and Danny, but also to their way of life. Despite Bode's accusations, there is no solid evidence against Danny, and the story ends with Wheeler's wishing Burley peace. Though the dramatic action diminishes during Wheeler's monologues, "Fidelity" is notable for the quiet dignity of Burley's burial scene. Moreover, Wheeler's speech in the Hargrave office, with the Port William community gathered, serves as a touching elegy to the rural lifestyle that once defined their community.

"Are You All Right?," the final story of the collection, functions to lighten the quiet, somber mood evoked by "Fidelity." Andy and Elton, a man whose death is alluded to in "Fidelity," venture out to check on Art and Mart Rowanberry, older men whose property has been mostly submerged in a recent flood. They are not especially concerned about the Rowanberrys, and they begin to enjoy walking among flowers in the moonlight. At last, Andy and Elton reach a bank just across from the Rowanberry place. When Elton shouts "Are you all right?", the Rowanberry men reply that they are fine. In the final few paragraphs, the narrator makes an interesting leap forward in time, shifting in point of view to a time after Elton's death. Thus the title is revealed to apply not only to the old Rowanberry men, but also to Elton. The last-minute change in point of view in "Are You All Right?" is an intriguing narrative device, and one that Berry employs with varied success in his third collection.

Berry's third collection of short fiction, *Watch with Me: And Six Other Stories of the Yet-Remembered Ptolemy Proudfoot and His Wife, Miss Minnie, née Quinch,* breaks new ground. Though the six stories are all set in Port William, each of them centers on two characters new to Berry's short fiction: Ptolemy Proudfoot and his wife, Minnie Quinch. The collection also departs from Berry's previous writing by utilizing the oral tradition of storytelling, in which sketches depict place, mood, and character.

In "A Consent (1908)" a first-person narrator takes the reader back into the early days of the Katy's Branch community outside of Port William. After sketching the Proudfoot family, "a large, exuberant clan of large people," the story tells the tale of the early courtship of Tol Proudfoot and Minnie Quinch, teacher of the local Goforth school. Tol, who is capable of "damag[ing] his clothes just by being in them," is not only "overabundant in both size and strength" but also in the tenderness of his unexpressed feelings for Min-

Berry and his wife, Tanya

nie. After a few awkward encounters with her Tol works up the courage to go to the Harvest Festival at the Goforth school. After Minnie's students recite poetry, there is a baked-goods auction, at which Tol pays ten dollars for an angel food cake baked by Minnie. The story ends with Minnie accepting Tol's offer to walk her home. "A Consent (1908)" effectively introduces the Katy's Branch neighborhood and the central characters of the collection. By itself, the story does not offer rich character development, but considered across all the stories in the collection, Tol emerges as a distinct and complex personality.

"A Half Pint of Old Darling (1920)" recounts an episode from the married life of Tol and Minnie during Prohibition. They visit the county seat of Hargrave to buy Christmas presents for one another. While in town, Tol purchases a bottle of Old Darling, a local whiskey, which he uses to revive weak lambs on his farm. On the trip back to Katy's Branch, Minnie, who favors Prohibition, finds the bottle under the seat and proceeds to empty it to save Tol from the temptation of drink. She becomes so intoxicated that she shouts political slogans to passing wagons. In the final paragraphs Berry employs the narrative device he uses at the end of "Are You All Right?", propelling the story forward in time to Minnie's widowhood. The sudden leap in time functions to contrast a lively, lighthearted past with the fact of Tol's death. It also evokes a mood of unsentimental nostalgia that characterizes the tone of the collection.

In the stories that follow, Berry does not weave complex plots, but rather composes sketches in

which the return to an agrarian past both entertains and serves as a moral example for the present. Moreover, the contrast between the past, in which Tol symbolizes material and spiritual abundance, and the present, in which Tol's death indicates the decline of abundance, provides a cohesive thematic structure for the collection.

Perhaps the most poignant tale in the collection, "The Solemn Boy (1934)," is a leisurely, descriptive story that contrasts the fruitful but childless life of Tol with the poverty-stricken lives of a homeless boy and his father. Having spent a November morning harvesting corn, Tol is driving his wagon load of bounty home when he encounters the poorly dressed, solemn boy and his father. Tol gives them a ride to his house and invites them inside for lunch. Minnie plies the boy and his father with food while Tol makes several unsuccessful attempts to bring a smile to the solemn boy's face. Tol finally accomplishes his task by pouring buttermilk down the front of his shirt. After lunch, the father accepts Minnie's offer of a spare coat for the boy, but he refuses one for himself. As the man and the solemn boy walk away, Tol jokes, "You might as well leave the boy with us." When Minnie recalls the story nine years later, less than a year after Tol's death, she reveals that Tol always wanted children. Minnie's closing remark reverberates with the sense of loss underly their childless marriage. It also serves to deepen the reader's understanding of Tol's character.

In another story, "Turn Back the Bed (1941)," the narrator returns to the jubilant and lively past of the Proudfoot clan. This playful story, recounted by Tol himself, centers on the Proudfoot family gatherings that he remembers fondly. The gatherings, always attended by great numbers of adults and children, were officiated over by Tol's grandfather, Old Ant'ny. To a crowd gathered around him in the trees by the Goforth church graveyard, Tol narrates the antics of his cousin Lester, who drops a cat and dog down the chimney, leads a chase through the Proudfoot house, and finally spills a chamber pot onto Old Ant'ny's hat. When Tol finishes telling his story, his laughter resounds with the decency and freedom that unites the community through space and time. Berry writes, "It was a good laugh, broad and free and loud, including all of us as generously as the shade we sat in, and not those of us who were living, but Old Ant'ny and Maw Proudfoot and Uncle O. R. and Uncle Fowler and Aunt Belle and Lester and the rest whose bodies lay in their darkness nearby." Tol emerges as a deeply symbolic character, one who encompasses the abundance of farm and family and links the present community with its own past.

The title story, the longest in the collection, tells of the day Thacker Hample took Tol's shotgun.

Known as "Nightlife" for his poor vision, Hample is a man who suffers from "spells" that render him irrational and unpredictable. Incensed over being barred from preaching the sermon during an evening service and under the powerful influence of one of his "spells," Nightlife wanders off with Tol's loaded gun. Tol leads a growing band of locals who track Nightlife through the Shady Creek countryside for the rest of that day, through the night, and into the next day. At last, the men follow Nightlife right back to Tol's workshop. There they listen to his rejected sermon, a moving allegory about his own benighted existence. His spell is finally broken when Tol's hen flies up at him, and Nightlife settles the bird with a firm punch.

The story's relaxed, highly descriptive passages invoke a serene past in which the threat of harm is held at bay by the influence of a tightly knit community. In a review written for *The New York Times* (13 November 1994), Robert Wilson compared "Watch with Me (1916)" to "Eudora Welty's wonder-filled 'Wide-Net,' in which a decidedly miscellaneous party of neighbors helps a young husband drag a river, looking for his wife, who has threatened to drown herself." "Watch with Me (1916)" expands Berry's vision of the healthy community to include members who may threaten it. When Miss Minnie recalls that the hen Nightlife punched lived to raise her baby chicks, she foregrounds resiliency of the community in the face of internal tensions. As the final story in the collection, "Watch with Me (1916)" solidifies Tol's centrality in the healthy operation of the Shady Branch neighborhood and provides a culminating example of the past that can bind a community together.

Wendell Berry's short fiction may be best understood as one component in a lifelong project to reaffirm the vitality of the connection of human beings to a past in which community, generosity, and attachment to the land foster an environmentally sound moral philosophy. Profoundly aware of the ties that bind him to his own past, Berry's healthy community exists across generations of time. In his poem "The Current" (1970) Berry imagines the intimate relationship that binds a farmer simultaneously to his past and his future by way of the land: "The current flowing to him through the earth / flows past him, and he sees one descended from him, / a young man who has reached into the ground, his hand held in the dark as by a hand." This profoundly universal connection to the earth characterizes Berry's regionalist impulse. He returns to Port William again and again in his stories because he recognizes that his native soil contains the same truths that may be found in any region of the world. "A man can be provincial," Berry writes in *The Long-Legged House,* "only by being blind and deaf to his province." The short fiction of Wendell Berry embodies and enacts that same moral philosophy that compelled him to return to the land that has sustained his family for generations.

References:

Andrew J. Angyal, *Wendell Berry* (New York: Twayne, 1995);

Bill McKibben, "Prophet in Kentucky," *New York Review of Books,* 14 June 1990, pp. 30–34;

Stephen Whited, "On Devotion to the 'Communal Order': Wendell Berry's Record of Fidelity, Interdependence, and Love," *Studies in the Literary Imagination,* 27 (Fall 1994): 9–28.

Sallie Bingham

(22 January 1937 –)

Frederick Smock
Bellarmine College, Louisville

BOOKS: *After Such Knowledge* (Boston: Houghton Mifflin, 1960);

The Touching Hand, and Six Short Stories (Boston: Houghton Mifflin, 1967);

The Way It Is Now (New York: Viking, 1972; London: Constable, 1973);

Passion and Prejudice: A Family Memoir (New York: Knopf, 1989);

Small Victories (Cambridge, Mass.: Zoland Books, 1992);

Upstate (Sag Harbor, N.Y.: Permanent Press, 1993);

Matron of Honor (Cambridge, Mass.: Zoland Books, 1994);

Straight Man (Cambridge, Mass.: Zoland Books, 1996).

OTHER: "Winter Term," in *The Best American Short Stories,* edited by Martha Foley and David Burnett (Boston: Houghton Mifflin, 1959);

"Mending," in *Solo: Women on Women Alone,* edited by Linda Hamalian and Leo Hamalian (New York: Dell, 1977);

"Captain Bud," in *From Mt. San Angelo: Stories, Poems & Essays,* edited by William Smart (Sweet Briar: Virginia Center for the Creative Arts, 1984; London: Associated University Presses, 1984);

"Reunion," in *Here's the Story: Fiction with Heart,* edited by Morty Sklar (Iowa City: The Spirit that Moves Us, 1985);

"A New Life," in *American Wives: Thirty Short Stories by Women,* edited by Barbara H. Solomon (New York: New American Library, 1986);

"Fear" in *New Women and New Fiction,* edited by Susan Cahill, (New York: New American Library, 1986);

"Off-Season," in *The Beach Book: A Literary Companion,* edited by Aleda Shirley (Louisville, Ky.: Sarabande, 1999);

"A Woman's Land," in *Literature and the Environment: A Reader on Nature and Culture,* edited by Lorraine Anderson, Scott Slovic, and John P. O'Grady (New York: Longman, 1999).

SELECTED PERIODICAL PUBLICATIONS–
UNCOLLECTED: "Pleyben," *American Voice,* 6 (1987): 30–37;

Sallie Bingham

"On the *Hercules*," *Louisville Review,* no. 33–34 (Spring 1993): 91–98;

"Speak Now," *American Voice,* 32 (1993): 48–55;

"Sundagger," *Southwest Review,* 81, no. 3 (1996): 423–431;

"Swings," *American Voice,* 41 (1996): 33–45;

"Going Native," *Glimmer Train,* no. 28 (1998): 63–69;

"Little Miss X," *American Voice,* 48 (1999): 29–40.

Sallie Bingham came of age as a writer in New York City in the 1960s, a time of great cultural energy. Having recently graduated from Radcliffe College and married to Arthur Whitney Ellsworth, one of the founders of *The New York Review of Books,* she traveled in the literary circle that included Elizabeth Hardwick, Robert Lowell, Frederick Seidel, and Arthur Kopit. Perhaps not surprisingly, some of her earliest stories are told from a male point of view, and many of her young women characters define themselves in relation to the men in their lives. Often, the women occupy a superior position, either because of their social class or their education, but this inequity does not always work to their benefit. The sexes, drawn together by money, desire, and, sometimes, simple loneliness, are forever negotiating accommodation. As Bingham's career matured, her women characters step from the shadows and begin to assume center stage, though their lives are no less fraught; they move from an almost despairing powerlessness in the early collections to a state that encompasses the possibilities of both conflict and hope.

Feminism and privilege have been the greatest social influences on Bingham's writing. Born of Southern aristocracy, she writes out of the world of the well-to-do; yet, she writes with irony and restraint and with an empathy for the many servants who populate her stories. She also writes out of—and often against—a man's world: her father and brothers dominated her childhood, her teachers were all male, and she has had three marriages and three sons. So it is not surprising that a central theme of her work is the uneasy relation between the sexes. Her tone often achieves a haunting meld of dreaminess and bleakness. At various times in her career she has written poetry, plays, novels, and a memoir, but she has always written and published short stories, in which she has worked out the themes that define her most conclusively as a writer.

Sarah "Sallie" Montague Bingham was born in Louisville, Kentucky, on 22 January 1937, during the great Ohio River flood. Melcombe, the family estate, sits on a bluff overlooking the river, and her parents, Barry and Mary Caperton Bingham, were compelled to negotiate the flooded streets of the city to reach the hospital. The Binghams are a wealthy family whose members have included educators, diplomats, and cultural benefactors. The family traditions of Latin and Greek culture, Presbyterianism, and severity have probably been more influential for Sallie Bingham as a writer than the family's post-1917 accumulation of money and power through their media empire, the center of which was the *Louisville Courier-Journal* newspaper and radio and television stations.

Bingham and her siblings were encouraged in all things cultural. Her father read stories and poems

Bingham, age eight, with her younger brother, Barry, and her older brothers Worth (left) and Jonathan, at the family's "Big House," 1945 (courtesy of Sallie Bingham)

aloud to them in the evenings, and both her mother and father encouraged her as a child writer. There were other published writers in the family, notably her maternal grandmother, Helena Lefroy Caperton, who published two collections of short stories (one with a foreword by Dorothy Parker) and spent many hours telling young Sallie tales of Ireland and Virginia in the nineteenth century, which were highly romantic but carried a bitter undertone that fascinated her. Sallie showed everything she wrote—short stories and poetry—to her parents, who carefully edited them, correcting spelling and making other editorial suggestions. She nursed dramatic ambitions as well, presenting original and adapted plays with her schoolmates at a four-hundred-seat amphitheater on the grounds at Melcombe.

After World War II, when she was a young teenager, her father took a role in implementing the Marshall Plan in Europe, and the family moved to France for a year. She attended Le Convent d'Assumption, where she was introduced to the works of Jean La Fontaine, Victor Hugo, and Jean Racine. Upon returning to the United States, her brothers went away to boarding school while she attended the local Louisville Collegiate School, a clear indication to her that, unlike her brothers, she and her sister, Eleanor, were not being groomed for the family business.

Bingham lost her two older brothers to separate freakish accidents in their early adulthood. Her brother Jonathan was electrocuted while attempting to string an electric line at the family's barn, and her brother Worth was killed in a motoring accident on Nantucket. Her one living brother, Barry Jr., narrowly survived a bout with Hodgkin's disease. These events profoundly affected her, and they certainly speak to the sense of loss and heightened awareness of death that permeates many of her stories.

She graduated magna cum laude from Radcliffe College in 1958. That same year she married Ellsworth, whom she had met in college. They had a son, Barry Bingham Ellsworth, in 1961. That marriage ended in divorce. In 1965 she married Michael Iovenko, a Wall Street lawyer. They had two sons together, Christopher Caperton Iovenko and William Bingham Iovenko. When that marriage ended in divorce, she moved back to Louisville and began writing plays and teaching at the University of Louisville. In 1983 she married Louisville builder Tim Peters. They divorced in 1989. Bingham currently resides in New Mexico.

Her first book, the novel *After Such Knowledge* (1960), is about a privileged young woman–the only daughter of a worldly woman who married beneath herself and regrets it bitterly–who voyages from adolescence into married life and disillusionment. Mona Tate has an unsatisfactory affair with a man she does not love, and later, thinking in error that she is pregnant, she marries a man who has long courted her. From there, the novel details the subtle ways in which Mona's weak husband makes her pay for her youthful indiscretion and in which she withdraws from life; in the process Mona fails her own daughter as her mother failed her. The story ends with Mona making a positive resolution about her life, however. *After Such Knowledge* is also centered on the issue of abortion, still a taboo subject at the time the novel was published.

Bingham wrote *After Such Knowledge* the year after graduating from college. At Radcliffe she had studied under Albert Guerard and Archibald MacLeish, yet she felt at a remove from the all-male pantheon of profes-

sors, acknowledging in her memoir, *Passion and Prejudice* (1989), that they taught her "little more than this: that some people seemed to want to hear what I had to say." One of her early short stories, written when she was still at Radcliffe, "Winter Term," won the Dana Reed Prize for the best piece of undergraduate writing (the first time it was won by a woman) and was included in the 1959 edition of *The Best American Short Stories*. As the author describes it in *Passion and Prejudice,* the story concerns "the dependency of a young college couple trapped in a clandestine, unhappy affair." For its time, it was fairly frank in its depiction of sexual attraction and unusual in portraying the coed, Ellie, as the sexual pursuer–until the end of the story, when her boyfriend suddenly gets rough and sexual aggression becomes violence. The story was first published in the *Harvard Advocate,* with the unforeseen result that students began to call up Bingham for dates. One of the Radcliffe deans, alarmed by the theme of the story, summoned Bingham to her office and informed her that alumni did not want to hear about the sex lives of students and that her story was certain to threaten alumni giving. Bingham accepted the dean's suggestion that all references to Cambridge be deleted from the story before it was reprinted in *Mademoiselle.* "Winter Term" appeared (still without any reference to Radcliffe or Harvard) in her first collection, *The Touching Hand, and Six Short Stories* (1967), as well as in *40 Best Stories from Mademoiselle, 1935–1960* (1960).

The novella-length story "The Touching Hand" tells of the transatlantic crossing of two bright, rather spoiled children in the company of their nanny, to meet up with their parents in Europe. Unlike other writers of her generation and class, Bingham often writes from the point of view of the servants, perhaps reflective of the central importance of servants in her own upbringing. In this case the nanny, Lutie, thinks to herself midway through the voyage: "A nurse sinks so deep into a family she thinks she's there forever, and that's when her foot hits the bottom. It's usually the mother, watching who the child runs to when he's scraped his knee. 'The children seem so happy with you . . . ' Too happy, that was the problem." Lutie has, late in her long life of servitude, devoted herself utterly to these children. She possesses the "touching hand," but the children are now just old enough to begin to resist it. The nanny's gift of love to these children makes them vulnerable and yet is the one gift that can save them from their little pranks, from the dangers that surround them, from their own precocious proclivity to world-weariness. This effect is made most touching when, at the end of the journey, she must hand them over again to their parents with no thought of herself. John Frakes, in an 18 June 1967 review in *The New York Times,* appraises this story as "first-rate," a "skillfully suggestive amalgam of Katherine Mansfield and Eudora Welty, together with a most refreshing de-sentimentalizing of children."

Bingham had early luck placing stories in respectable and influential magazines. "Moving Day," "The Banks of the Ohio," "Neighbors," and "The Ice Party" all appeared in *The Atlantic Monthly*. The final story in this first collection, "Bare Bones," appeared in *Redbook*. Others appeared in *Mademoiselle* and *Ms.* These stories begin to delineate various aspects of the relations between the sexes, which became one of Bingham's continuing artistic interests. In "The Banks of the Ohio" an upper-class girl named Bay takes up with an aimless young man, Shriver, who is "driving a taxi for the time being." He owns an old rowboat, very different from the craft her late father piloted on the river as a member of the local yacht club. Bay struggles with herself, weighing her love for her mother and for the life they have together against the attraction she feels for Shriver—or is it a female protectiveness? A similarly protective relationship is explored in "Moving Day," in which class and affection also get mixed up. A white mistress, Miss Ada, and her black servant Winston negotiate the physical and emotional logistics of moving out of the old family home. Each of them has come to the end of the line, but a tender rapprochement is reached when, as they leave, Miss Ada takes the driver's seat and invites Winston to sit up front with her.

In "The Ice Party" a new father feels himself displaced in his wife's attentions by their first baby. He considers a fling with a former lover at a skating party; yet, he rejects the possibility, realizing that, while consoling on the surface, such an escapade would ultimately be both shallow and futile. At the other end of the spectrum, "Bare Bones" is a sympathetic treatment of a newly divorced woman, Lilly Morrison, who comes to realize that her divorce does not provide the happiness she had expected. Her sense of isolation has only deepened: her days are endless rounds of trivia and her nights are sleepless. Finally she suffers a breakdown during a desperate call to her former husband.

Significantly, Bingham has avoided the trap that her privileged upbringing could have sprung: that is, she is capable of true empathetic insight into characters radically unlike herself. Anne Wolfe, reviewing *The Touching Hand* for the *Chicago Tribune* (25 June 1967), wrote, "There is a wry humor and a measure of existentialist irony in Miss Bingham's view of the human condition, and her insights are generally informed by pity." *The Atlantic Monthly,* which published four of these stories, also noted their existential nature in a July 1967 review: "they all have a com-

Bingham in 1956, at age nineteen (photograph by Hal Phyfe)

mon basic pattern—the interdependence of people and their persistent resentment of it. More bias perhaps than formal theme, this notion is twisted seven ways in seven adroit stories. Miss Bingham is much too clever to suggest a cure for it anywhere." Poet Anne Sexton, quoted on the dust jacket of the collection, observed, "Sallie Bingham writes with precision, irony, and subtle compassion."

The themes that Bingham sounded in *The Touching Hand* are extended, both in complexity of thought and refinement of style, in her second collection, *The Way It Is Now* (1972). These stories are all centered on women and subtle family tensions. The social and psychological observations are acute and conveyed with an austerity of action; almost everything of importance happens offstage or inside someone's head. "Love," writes Jean Spang, in a review for the 15 January 1972 issue of *Library Journal*, "is not a romantic ideal, but a working human interchange, requiring an understanding and awareness unknown in the mannered existence and false expectations depicted in these vignettes of the 1970s." Yet, in truth, many of these stories draw their inspiration, if not their actual circumstances, from the still-lingering 1950s. Thus is the title of the collection subtly ironic, possibly in more ways than one. The characters flirt with change and promise and with the dark side of change and promise: failure.

In "The Facts of His Life" Jake has a well-employed wife, a half-finished novel, and a lover in the former wife of a good friend, and he knows that he has chosen none of it; these facts have come to stand for his life, which now seems strange and unresolvable to him. "To comfort himself," Bingham writes, "he went for long walks every afternoon, searching the faces of passersby for their opinion. They did not seem to notice him as much as they once had when their faces, strangers and friends alike, had reflected some of the magic he had felt in himself. He had been so bright at school; he had stunned his parents and his teachers with his brashness, his certainty of success. . . . But the ladies walking dogs in the park did not see it and were no longer startled by his intense staring eyes." When his lover corners him at a cocktail party and he gently puts her off, she opens her mouth and screams; as his wife goes to comfort her, Jake can only slip out into the cold night, "both doomed and defiant."

The thin line between failure and fulfillment shows itself in several of the stories in *The Way It Is Now*. "The Big Day" concerns a young woman who has grown apart from her soldier husband, away in an unnamed war. As the day of his return nears, she grows edgy out of fear and uncertainty. "She wanted to ask him what good it had done for them to have been, always, so careful. She thought he might agree with her that there had been no use in it at all, that they had been deceived, like children. They could have cried together then, or screamed." Bingham is adept at getting the reader to empathize with her characters through descriptions of their gestures, the small domestic details of their lives, and their fears. One of the most gripping stories in the collection is called "Fear"; it portrays the terror of a young mother who has "plunged" her baby too hard to stop his crying and sees that there seems to be something wrong with his legs. This act has already happened when the story opens. Dread hangs in the air from the first sentence—"Turning the knob so slowly it seemed to glide, greased, under her palm, Jean finally opened the baby's door"—and the author maintains this tense psychological state right up to the end: "John looked away. The gap of their silent understanding widened between them: Jean knew they would never speak of what she had done."

In the title story, a young woman on the day of her divorce comes to a new realization about her lover

and the possible neglect of her son, but the insight does not provide her with any new capability. "I hear the organ bleats which summoned my first husband to our undoing," she says to herself. "I need you, I need you, I need you. Already my relief is gone and I feel the grid bars of consequences across my face." Little touches, like the mewling verb *bleats,* earned Bingham early acclaim as a stylist. She cites as early influences on her work the novels of John Updike, particularly *The Poorhouse Fair* (1959), for their melding of style and serious content. Peter Taylor has been important in showing the way to write about the South with a sharp and complex vision of its charm and its inequities. Among novelists, she lists Virginia Woolf first among her influences, especially *Mrs. Dalloway* (1925) and *To the Lighthouse* (1927), although she adds that the Brontës really taught her how to write, especially Charlotte in *Jane Eyre* (1847), the title character of which was the first recognizable girl she found in fiction.

As the market for short-story collections began to dry up in the late 1970s and early 1980s, Bingham turned her attention to novel writing, further extending themes she had sounded in her short stories. During this time she also found herself mired in issues surrounding the disposition of the Bingham media empire. Her aged parents looked to hand off the companies to their oldest surviving son, but many other members of the large, monied family asserted their right to a share as well. When Bingham sold her share of the family business to an outside buyer, she was portrayed as the villain in this domestic drama. To purge the resulting ill feelings she experienced and also in part to correct the accumulated misinformation, she wrote *Passion and Prejudice.* The family's history is told with a grand sweep yet also with a novelist's eagle eye, from Bingham's grandfather's mercenary romances to her Aunt Henrietta's dalliance with Bloomsbury figure Dora Carrington to her own rebellion and estrangement from the family. Published by Alfred A. Knopf, *Passion and Prejudice* became a much-talked-about book. Bingham made the rounds of the television talk shows, appeared on the cover of *Ms.* magazine, and became celebrated as something of a monied rebel.

At the same time, Bingham was still writing short stories and publishing them with regularity in little magazines. In 1985 she established her own literary journal, *The American Voice,* with Frederick Smock as the editor. Bingham wrote essays for *The American Voice,* such as "Maenads and Satyrs: Some Thoughts on W. M. Spackman's Novels," which appeared in the second issue and reflects the open, inclusive feminism embodied by the journal. In that same spirit, she endowed the Kentucky Foundation for Women both to underwrite the journal and to offer grants to local women artists.

2/6

A Debutante's Smile

For RWB and RWB

My oldest brother has been dead for thirty-seven years, a period of time longer than his life, long enough to extinguish almost every detail. But memory, by good fortune, is selective, and of the many details, dark and bright, of our shared childhood, the ones that remain vivid to me are from the period of his young manhood in the 1950's.

It was a time of great privilege and apparent security (even the Korean War was still the future) for a young man of the top class; perhaps it was the last time privilege would be unquestioned, and certainly leisure gaiety (there is no other word for it) was largely the fruit of that unquestioned privilege. Vietnam, the Civil Rights movement and the Modern Women's movement, while doing little to alter the status of top class men, would raise questions about their right to rule; but that, too, was still in the future, and a handsome young man of good family knew no superior force, even the law was, apparently, disarmed.

One of the curious effect of privilege is the prolongation of a sweetness we usually associate with children. He was sophisticated and cynical, but running alongside that was a sweetness that was deeply appealing, deeply disturbing to his younger

Page from the manuscript for Bingham's uncollected story "A Debutante's Smile" (Collection of Sallie Bingham)

The American Voice won eight Pushcart Prizes, and work from its pages was regularly republished in *Best American Essays, Best American Poetry,* and other prize annuals. In 1998 the University Press of Kentucky published *The American Voice Anthology of Poetry.* The journal published until the fall of 1999, when, with its fiftieth issue, a fiction retrospective, the foundation closed it out and substituted a literature program more finely tuned to emerging Kentucky feminist and activist writers.

Several of Bingham's short stories appeared in *The American Voice.* The earliest, "Pleyben," is set in Brittany and concerns a husband and wife traveling through the countryside. Things have not gone particularly well: "In crippled French, Lovett asked for a meal, and explained why they were so late: the road, the car breakdown, the sudden deluge of rain, which they had come to accept as part of the landscape." Mrs. Lovett is haunted by their accidental visit to an ossuary, and the trip is revealed to be an attempt to get past the recent death of their young daughter. As with many of Bingham's best stories, the central event has already happened; the story describes the survivors as they attempt to deal with the event, and it harks back to the early deaths of her two older brothers.

Her most recent story to appear in *The American Voice* is another sort of evocation of life in a troubled Southern family. "Little Miss X" begins, similarly, with a death offstage–the immolation fifty years previously of a girl at a circus, known only as Little Miss X–and the profound effect the event has on a young woman of limited intelligence who finds herself made pregnant by her stepfather. Intuitively, the girl chooses against abortion. When she takes stock of what little she has to support herself and the child, she concludes, "The main thing I own is the egg, because it's going to be a person. Maybe it'll be a girl, and she'll come out of me pretty, without a mark on her, like the picture they showed on TV of Little Miss X. My girl'll never have a mark on her, if I have any say in the matter."

Bingham is a master of dramatic irony. In many of her stories, the reader is guided to know more than the characters know, and within this discrepancy is the crucial dilemma articulated. Bingham's ear for dialogue and for the unsaid elements in conversation are no doubt informed by her experience as a dramatist, beginning perhaps with the childhood summers in the family amphitheater. Her plays have been performed at theaters around the country, including "Couvade" at the Actors Theatre in Louisville; "Paducah" at Horse Cave Theater in Horse Cave, Kentucky; and "Milk of Paradise" at Julia Miles's The Women's Project and Productions in New York.

During the 1990s Bingham was at the height of her fame, as a memoirist, playwright, and novelist: three novels–*Small Victories* (1992), *Matron of Honor* (1994), and *Straight Man* (1996)–were published by Zoland Books in Cambridge, Massachusetts, and a fourth, *Upstate,* was published by Permanent Press in 1993. Many of her old themes remained, although in new permutations. Erica Abeel, in *The New York Times Book Review* (16 November 1996), wrote of *Straight Man:* "Colby Winn, a middle-aged bad boy, goes all out to seduce an attractive young woman. At the same time, he hopes she'll elude him: he knows he's a nasty piece of work. That's as tender as it gets in this latest dispatch from the war of the sexes. In a bold strategy not much adopted by contemporary women novelists, Sallie Bingham . . . takes up residence in the mind and body of her male antihero. The result is that Colby hangs himself with his own words. But since we get an insider's view of his struggle to tame his devils, he also gains our grudging sympathy."

Since moving to the Southwest, Bingham has found new subjects for her work, especially by connecting women's issues to issues of the land. In "Sundagger," a story published in *Southwest Review* in 1996, she writes from the point of view of a personal assistant to a wealthy woman who has taken it upon herself to reclaim Native American artifacts as legacies for their proper inheritors. That the older woman vanishes raises questions about the danger of such work, particularly when undertaken by a woman. In "Going Native," a story published in *Glimmer Train* in 1998, a woman and a man, both of them easterners transplanted to the Southwest, try to balance their desire for love and their need for solitude; the territory between those two poles of emotion is large and rough, made palpable as the desert dust and heat. The narrator's "outsider" status among the true natives of Taos Pueblo reflects a more personal alienation: "When he kissed me, I felt that vast unjustifiable admiration for male initiative and daring–are we losing it in this age of equality?–because it feels like courage."

Bingham has always demonstrated a feeling for the suffering of women, but the only predictable thing about her career is a certain degree of unpredictability. She once said in an interview: "Children who are born to power and money must learn, and learn well, several fierce lessons. They must give up evidences of independence or originality that conflict with the family's view of itself and ideas that challenge the status quo." She goes on to note, however, such lessons are not always learned as they are intended; as a writer, Bingham has never been content to let the status quo go unchallenged.

Interview:

Bonnie Jean Cox, "Interview with Sallie Bingham," *Kentucky Review,* 8 (Autumn 1988): 5–25.

Robert Boswell
(8 December 1953 –)

Alexander McIlvaine Parsons
New Mexico State University

BOOKS: *Dancing in the Movies* (Iowa City: University of
Iowa Press, 1986);
Crooked Hearts (New York: Knopf, 1987; London: Quartet, 1998);
The Geography of Desire (New York: Knopf, 1989; London: Quartet, 1997);
Mystery Ride (New York: Knopf, 1993; London: Quartet, 1996);
Living to Be a Hundred (New York: Knopf, 1994);
Virtual Death, as Shale Aaron (New York: Harper Prism, 1995);
American Owned Love (New York: Knopf, 1997; London: Quartet, 1997).

PLAY PRODUCTION: *Tongues,* Las Cruces, New
Mexico, Hershel Zohn Theater, 17 March 1999.

OTHER: Introduction, *Ploughshares,* 4, special issue,
edited by Boswell (Winter 1996–1997).

Robert Boswell is a novelist, short-story writer,
and dramatist whose primary thematic preoccupation is
the conflict between desire and ethical demands that
people face in their relationships with others. In his
writing he gives additional scope to this issue of how
one navigates the difficult terrain of emotions and relationships by linking it tightly to larger issues within the
United States–specifically race. As he said of his work
in a 1990 interview with Anne Marie Mackler, "I tend
to write a lot about how men and women get along–
and race, how people of different races get along. I'm
obsessed with these matters because I feel they are
important. They are issues essential to being alive,
being human, in this country." In this preoccupation
Boswell is a quintessentially American writer, continuing in part the ongoing conversation about race that
Mark Twain (one of Boswell's seminal influences)
undertook in *The Adventures of Huckleberry Finn* (1884).
Boswell's volumes of short fiction, which more or less
bookend his career to date, show the genesis of his thematic foci, as well his stylistic maturation. In these col-

*Robert Boswell (photograph by Marion Ettlinger; from the
dust jacket of* American Owned Love, *1997)*

lections Boswell's singular combination of emotional
insight and moral centeredness, which has assured his
place in American letters, is both developed and show-
cased to its best effect.

Born 8 December 1953 to Albert Russell Boswell
and Annelle Eley in Sikeston, Missouri, Robert Lann
Boswell, the second of four children spent his early
childhood on a tobacco farm in Wickliffe, Kentucky.
Their home was near the confluence of the Mississippi
and Ohio Rivers, where, as Boswell noted in a 1993
interview with William Clark, "Huck and Jim miss
their turn," referring to *The Adventures of Huckleberry Finn.*
Boswell's father, an elementary-school principal, over-

saw the integration of his school, and though quite young at the time, Boswell was acutely aware of the complications of such a process. He remembers not only the day the first black child arrived at school, but also returning home to find a group of black teachers in his living room. As he said in a 19 May 1997 interview with Dahleen Glanton, "They were very upset because, though they believed he [my father] was trying to do the right thing, it meant they would lose control over the one part of their lives they felt they had control over: the education of their children. And secondly, they were all going to lose their jobs because they knew there would be no black teachers of white children in rural Kentucky in the early 1960s."

When Boswell was in the sixth grade his family moved to Yuma, Arizona, where César Chavez's migrant-worker labor movement began. Boswell worked alongside migrants for extra money, picking cantaloupe, watermelon, and cotton. His father taught high-school government; his mother worked as a realtor. Boswell attended the University of Arizona in Tucson, where he met his first wife, Janet Bombard, whom he married at age twenty and divorced four years later. He finished at Arizona with a double major in psychology and English and followed with a master's degree in rehabilitation counseling. Writing had always been a dream of his, but at the time he did not believe that it was a possibility as a career. In 1979 he began a job as a counselor in San Diego, guiding the physically disabled, Vietnam veterans, schizophrenics, and the poor into job training programs.

In 1981 Boswell returned to the University of Arizona to enroll in their master of fine arts program in creative writing. In his third year at Arizona, where he studied under Francine Prose and Steve Orlen, he met Antonya Nelson in a workshop and shortly thereafter, in 1984, they married. Boswell's 1984 M.F.A. thesis, a collection of stories, won, in slightly different form, the Iowa School of Letters Award for Short Fiction in 1985 and was published the following year by the University of Iowa Press as *Dancing in the Movies* (1986). Boswell went on to work as an assistant professor of English at Northwestern University in 1986 and began teaching as a professor of English at the low-residence Warren Wilson Master of Fine Arts Program for Writers in Asheville, North Carolina, the same year. In 1987 Boswell won a National Endowment for the Arts Fellowship, and his daughter, Jade, was born. Two years later, Boswell left Northwestern for New Mexico State University in Las Cruces to share a teaching post with his wife, who has since become an established novelist and short-story writer in her own right. This same year, 1989, he was awarded a Guggenheim Fellowship.

Las Cruces proved to be fertile ground for Boswell's writing. New Mexico is one of the poorest states in the nation, and the Mexican border lies only forty miles south of Las Cruces. Mexican immigrants both live in the area and pass through as migrant workers in the chili fields and pecan orchards, and to that extent the town resembles Boswell's childhood home of Yuma, Arizona. Issues of race and poverty are in sharp relief in daily life, and such surroundings have been incorporated into Boswell's novels and short fiction since his move to southern New Mexico, most specifically in his 1997 novel, *American Owned Love.* Boswell and his family—including his son, Noah, who was born in 1991—have remained in Las Cruces.

The stories in *Dancing in the Movies,* while somewhat uneven, clearly predict the tone and subjects that Boswell goes on to explore in his later work. Love and race figure strongly, and the stories are linked by and give expression to a singular pathos—a composite of loss, connection, and stark awareness of the world—that has become a hallmark of Boswell's work.

The hub of the collection is "The Darkness of Love," which addresses and movingly describes Boswell's preoccupation with race and his fascination with love and desire. It is filled with the darkly luminous pathos that makes much of Boswell's later work so striking. In the story a black New York cop, Handle, has retreated to his in-laws' house in rural Tennessee to rest and recuperate, convinced that his job is making him internalize racial prejudice and turn it against his own people. There, he realizes that he is in love not only with his wife, Marilyn, but also with her younger sister, Louise, who is staying at the house. As the story develops, it becomes apparent that self-knowledge and any hope of fulfillment and development come as a result of recognizing and grappling with one's desires, with no guarantee that any sort of harmony will ensue from the struggle. In Handle's case, his heart makes demands that seem contradictory and impossible to fulfill. There is truly a darkness in his love for these two women, but to cut himself off from either is to deny his humanity; also, on some level, his desire to recognize who he is—not whom a racist society would have him be—requires that he confront the painful memories and desires that have shaped him without his conscious knowledge. The story, appropriately, ends with a statement that sums up such struggle: "Neither could say that what they'd done was right or that it was over or that there was any escape."

The title story, "Dancing in the Movies," works with similar themes. Freddie, a college-age white boy, returns to his hometown of Langston to find his black girlfriend, Dee, and take her away from her junkie existence. His love for her is something that both his parents and friends find difficult—his parents because of racial prejudice; his friends because she is a junkie who will only break his heart. Lonnie, one of Freddie's black friends whose brother has been a heroin addict, asks him, "Oh, Freddie, why on earth do you want to love Dee?" Freddie responds, "Didn't say I want to. I just do." In these simple words is the recognition that one's desires are not dictated by reason or convenience—or by the desires of others—but are rather immutable and monumental in the face of such considerations. Eventually, Freddie gets Dee to agree to leave town, but only if he will first try heroin—in this request she is asking for him to show what he is willing to sacrifice given his demand that she quit the drug. The demands of love, as in "The Darkness of Love," are crushing and inescapable, as much a fact of existence as gravity. It bears noting that Boswell's central character is almost always a strong individual, someone who may make the right or wrong decision but always does so as a result of what they alone feel, not what society would have them feel. This sort of characterization is Boswell's strongest argument against racism: by depicting characters that think and act as individuals, he seeks to make discrimination born out of stereotypes provided by others more difficult to sustain.

Though Boswell engages with the subject of race, he is not attempting to proselytize and avoids complacently reiterating what he sees to be self-evident truths. In fact, he is notably aware of this risk both in terms of how it affects his authority as a writer and how it can compromise a work of literature. In his words, delivered in his January 1997 lecture "Writing the Political Novel: The Responsibilities of the Writer in an Inconvenient Time" to the Warren Wilson Master of Fine Arts Program,

> Any novel that merely reiterates or even embodies an existing ideology is not a work of art because a knowledgeable reader, in this case one familiar with the ideology, will not be asked to alter her vision one whit. The novel becomes reduced to a handmaiden of the ideology, a servant to theory that often comes . . . at the expense of the truth. After all, if what the literary novel is asked to do is poke through the illusions a culture clings to, thereby altering how the reader sees the culture, then a novel that merely illustrates an ideology takes as truth that ideology.

"Little Bear" is one of two stories of war in the collection and, given the fact that Boswell was of draftable age during Vietnam, it not surprising that he ruminates on this subject. As he recalls in "Writing the Political Novel,"

Dust jacket for Boswell's 1994 collection, including stories about frustrated desire and failed relationships

the war in Vietnam was no abstract issue. My final year of high school I used to lie awake at nights making a series of plans for what to do if I got a low lottery number in the draft. In my noblest of moods, I pictured myself going to prison rather than join the fray. Shackled but unswayed, my head held high, I marched defiantly and with dignity into the big house, a prisoner of principle. More often and more realistically, I imagined becoming a fry cook in Vancouver.

While peripherally concerned with race, the story centers on the conflict between the desires of the individual and the demands of society. In this case the individual is a young soldier, Joey Malone, who loses his feet while fighting a war that seems to have no relevance to his life.

Set in Korea during the Korean War, "Little Bear" depicts Joey and his friend Owens, a young black soldier. Neither has much of a sense of the threatening tide of Communism or feels particularly invested in the war—it is far more remote than their memories of the lives they have left. Resting up before he will again be sent into the field, Joey spends his time chatting with Owens about baseball, home, the army, and girls.

Owens is a virgin, while Joey made love to a girl before leaving for the war. As he and his girlfriend sat on a field beneath the stars she pointed out the constellation Ursa Minor, the Little Bear. The story ends with Owens carrying his friend, now maimed after a second visit to the front, from a field hospital at night so that they can view the same constellation. The mood captures the marked pathos that fills Boswell's work. Irrevocable loss is juxtaposed with the boys' sense of a deep connection to one another. Boswell's signature prose is shown to good effect in this story. His clear, almost bare language emphasizes and lends resonance to the stark nature of the tale, and the tone of the story captures perfectly the emotional tenor that defines much of his work.

The other war story, "The Right Thing," is the least successful of the collection. Told by Hagget, a Vietnam War veteran suffering flashbacks, the story is a pastiche of moments that involve his experiences in the war, a trip to Mexico, and the progression of a day spent in the house with his young girlfriend, which includes a visit from an old army buddy. The quick cuts in time create a somewhat disjointed narrative (all told in the present tense), which underscores Hagget's disorientation and the immediate presence of his past but is not a wholly effective strategy. Hagget's curious remove from everything around him offsets the stylistic intentions and distances the reader as well. Furthermore, Boswell's cool prose, so effective in "Little Bear," tends to compound the sense of emotional distance.

Like the other stories, "Flipflops" shares in the dark emotional tone that binds the collection, but it lacks the weight of the better pieces. Two lovers, who have yet to sleep with each other, go to Mexico to celebrate Thanksgiving. They have both recently ended prior relationships, and they sit awkwardly on the beach trying to make conversation. A long joke begins, and in the course of it two men venture too far into the water. The narrator leaps to the rescue, but by the time he swims out one man has drowned and the other has saved himself. Returning, the narrator finds that someone has stolen his flip-flops. The story is ironic and the humor black, but it lacks the resonance of the better stories in the collection.

"Kentucky" is notable in that it is more directly autobiographical than the other stories and because, ultimately, it grew into Boswell's next novel, *Crooked Hearts* (1987). Told from the first-person point of view, it is inspired by a dilemma Boswell faced in his childhood, when his father ordered him not to buy any more cigarettes for him and then reversed himself shortly thereafter. As Boswell commented to Mackler, "Finally I bought him the damn cigarettes and felt bad about it. It was a moment I never forgot. . . . Ultimately I came to understand that moment embodied my relationship with my father. That is, I always felt I was in a situation where whatever I did was not quite right."

In "Kentucky" the father of the family cannot go to Hale's Café for cigarettes on his own because he has had an affair with Jenetta, the waitress who works there. Although the affair has been over for a long while, a strong undercurrent of emotion remains. The two young boys, Ask and the narrator, Tom, love hanging out at the café, drinking Cokes and watching Jenetta. One night, after their father tells them he no longer wants them to buy cigarettes for him, they sneak down to the café anyway. There, they see their oldest brother, Charlie, curse Jenetta at a moment when it looks as if they might kiss. When Charlie returns home they pry the story out of him. Though too young to comprehend exactly what has gone on between their father and Jenetta, the revelation is nonetheless a moment of profound loss for the boys, in which their concept of their father irrevocably changes. This change is further stressed when Tom's father asks him to buy cigarettes the following day, after Tom has promised he will not. The story highlights the charged dynamics of the family, where, no matter the intensity of love and hate, people are held together by familial bonds. Loss and disappointment are presented as inevitable experiences that mark one as indelibly as any triumph or joy.

Loss and familial conflict comprise the thematic core of *Crooked Hearts*. Addressing this aspect of his work, Boswell told Mackler: "Much of life has to do with loss. . . . I also try to get at moments that are smaller, more subtle, that also have to do with—I don't like the term 'growth,' but I'll call it growth. . . . I don't like fiction that denies loss, that belittles loss, its importance, by sentimentalizing it or something of that nature. Failure is often tied to loss, and failure is essential for a writer to embrace. If you can't embrace it as a process, you may embrace it as a subject matter." In *Crooked Hearts* Tom has dropped out of his first semester at Berkeley to return home to Yuma, Arizona, a place that "embodied failure as other cities embody light or reason." His family, the Warrens, literally celebrates failure on a regular basis, holding parties to commemorate such occasions, and Tom's departure from school is no exception. The family is modeled after Boswell's own, though the unfolding story is fictional.

In writing about the Warrens, Boswell shows a mastery of multiple points of view not evident in *Dancing in the Movies*. In addition to his use of third-person narration, family members relate stories from their own points of view; yet, the switches in voice are handled so seamlessly as to feel perfectly natural. Such a tactic highlights not only Boswell's understanding of disparate characters, but also the ease with which he orchestrates a large cast. *Crooked Hearts* was followed by the novels *The Geography of Desire* (1989) and *Mystery Ride* (1993), both of which are equally stylistically mature in terms of how they handle point of view and characterization.

Boswell takes the issues of class and race that arise in *Dancing in the Movies* and moves them to Central America in *The Geography of Desire*. The protagonist, Leon Green, escapes his life in the United States to run a small hotel in the coastal village of La Boca in an unnamed country. He avails himself to the pleasures the town has to offer with a singular blindness to the effects of his desires. Reflected in Green's relationship with the townspeople are larger issues of competing visions of the world and differing means of communication—most specifically those of the United States versus those of its southern neighbors. The book is particularly remarkable for its flavor of magical realism revealed in the stories of Ramon Matamoros, the oral historian of La Boca.

Mystery Ride, which moves between the worlds of Southern California and rural Iowa, remains Boswell's most commercially successful work. It was also a great critical success, firmly establishing his literary reputation. Sandra Scofield, in an enthusiastic review for *The New York Times Book Review* (24 January 1993), wrote: "Boswell is an exuberant and enormously talented writer . . . with dazzling technical skill, intelligence and moral seriousness. . . . To read it [*Mystery Ride*] is to enlarge one's own life." Centering around the stories of Stephen and Angela Landis, *Mystery Ride* is remarkable for its scope, encompassing the lives of a variety of characters over a period of more than two decades. The book is a thoughtful examination of the nature of love and familial bonds, much like *Crooked Hearts,* but has a greater maturity and range. Boswell's characters, for example, run the gamut from a deeply troubled teenage girl to a family of born-again Christians to a Los Angeles talent agent, all of whom are realistic and portrayed without condescension.

Living to Be a Hundred (1994), Boswell's second book of short fiction, is a collection of eleven stories written between 1987 and 1994, many of which are set in the Southwest. It is tightly bound by a haunting combination of loss, desire, disillusion, and difficult, painful love that informs virtually every paragraph. In an introduction to the Winter 1996–1997 issue of *Ploughshares,* which he guest edited, Boswell wrote:

> To attempt to fully name one's desires is, I think, one of the primary reasons that people write stories. *This is the story of a man whose heart is breaking,* the author writes. There is no need to add, *And I desperately need you to hear it.* Great stories are measured not only by the elo-

quence and accuracy of desire's expression, but by the magnitude of the desire. It is often this magnitude that separates literature from entertainments, that determines what is serious and what is fluff.

By such standards, *Living to Be a Hundred* is a fine work of literature and perhaps Boswell's best and certainly most representative book to date.

"The Earth's Crown" is one of several stories that define the tone of the collection. It is the story of the lost Alvin Bishop, a sad man whose wife has come unstrung in the wake of the death of their infant daughter. He finds himself having an affair with a pregnant black woman, Cheryl, who often comes to his store for cigarettes. From his affair arises the opportunity to begin anew with his wife, whom he loves; and yet he is unable to end his futureless relationship with Cheryl, though it will mean the end of his marriage. As Boswell writes, "There are ten thousand ways to ruin your life, a million ways to lose the people you love. And this is the way Alvin has chosen. This one is his." As always, it is emotion—complex, contradictory, and irresistible—that triumphs over reason, that forces one, wide-eyed, into the arms of consequence.

"Living to Be a Hundred," "The Products of Love," and "Rain" are all similar in nature to "The Earth's Crown" in that they deal with troubled relationships and people struggling to make sense of their desires. In "Living to Be a Hundred" Boswell plays on the tensions between Castellani and Linda, a married couple, and their friend Harvis. Boswell has said that the situation for this story began in part from an experience he had with his first wife, when they were recarpeting a house together and he was working in construction to support them. They were having trouble at the time, and as the job was arduous and time-consuming, they found it easier to have someone around them to diffuse the tension. Conversely, in this story, as in several in the collection, Boswell uses a third party as a source of sexual tension that creates a more dramatically charged atmosphere. While Harvis and Castellani are good friends who work in construction together, Harvis is lonely and in love with Linda, and she is equally conflicted. Further, Castellani is beginning to realize that, while he does not want to give up Linda, he has traded in his dreams for his marriage: "I tried to pinpoint the moment when my life had turned wrong, and I came to decide that I never should have married Linda, that I should have struggled to pursue my obsessions, that I had been made a coward by love." Given Boswell's preoccupation with pitting desire against ethical considerations, it is hardly surprising that he gravitates to this triangular relationship

Robert Boswell

Guests

Bobby Bell's fingers numbered four to a hand, thumb and pointer identical to God's, but [*His*] [*were*]

those remaining, fleshy stubs, stunted and fused, and only two, on each slender paw. [*the others were*] [*He WAS*]

[*a*] dumb kid, besides, if progress in school is a fair measure. He sized me up my first week in

town, came by my locker to demand a fight, the fall of 1967. [*the*]

We'd moved to New Mexico from Illinois because my father was sick. How the

change was supposed to help, I didn't know. When I asked, he removed his glasses as if

the problem were with the black-rimmed lenses. His head tipped slightly on its thin

scaffold of bone. I felt a corresponding tilt in my senses. "I'm host to a disease," he said.

A smile flickered across his lips.

I began to tremble.

He continued. "You could say it's a landlord and tenant affair." When he focused

on my expression, his attitude shifted. He slipped the glasses on again, which made his

eyes the wrong size for his face. "You're worried." His hand lighted like a butterfly upon

my head. "All right. I'm host but there are no tenants, just uninvited guests, too small to

see." His lips crinkled, a modest grin. "Too small," he assured me, "to even imagine." His

head tilted once more. "You won't worry, all right?" [*Move? to later*]

I promised.

I had inherited my father's slight build, which must have cheered Bobby Bell, to

think he'd found a frame, at last, more flimsy than his own. I colored easily, as well, which

provided him a hope even he knew to leave unsaid: blood that surged so close to the

1

Page from the typescript for Boswell's story "Guests," which was published in the Fall 1998 issue of Ploughshares *(Collection of Robert Boswell)*

model–it provides the perfect construct for exploring such tensions.

"The Products of Love" and "Rain," while told from differing points of view in different settings, both feature troubled trios struggling with the demands of their desires. The more compelling of the two is "Rain." The story opens with Karen; her husband, Lawrence; and their neighbor, Orla, on a search for a boy who has gone missing in the woods. Karen and Orla, paired together, get lost. Though the boy is found, the experience of the search leaves Karen feeling unsettled, unmoored. Suddenly she is unsure of what she wants, of the nature of her relationships with Orla and Lawrence, and of her understanding of herself: "Her closeness to and distance from Lawrence, for example, now fluctuate wildly, although he apparently notices nothing new or unusual. And the same is true even with herself, feeling one moment as she has always felt and the next wanting to shed the skin of her present life through some bold action." As the story continues, Karen struggles to calm her roiling emotions, eventually venturing back into the woods and into a mute–if not understanding–awareness.

All of these works end in moments of comprehension or clarity, though such lucidity does not seem to have any immediate utility nor carry with it the promise that life will somehow improve or become more manageable. Many of the stories, in terms of tone, triangulation of characters, and endings, are similar; while virtually all the reviews praised the book as highly accomplished and compelling, some reviewers were led to comment that the stories sounded the same emotional note a time too often. In the words of the reviewer for *Publishers Weekly* (24 January 1994), "the collection suffers somewhat from a certain sameness of theme, though Boswell's tales are gracefully written and often haunting." The story "Brilliant Mistake" offsets this complaint, defining a moment of sexual awakening that is rife with energy and optimism. The story recounts an evening in which a young boy ends up in a pool with several older girls who, given that it is dark and his body is beneath the surface of the water, mistake him for one of their peers. It affords him the chance to taste the sexual promise of the teen years he is just entering and is, by Boswell's own admission, an only slightly embellished account of an encounter he had. In the words of the narrator looking back on that evening, "It is the one perfect moment in my life."

"Salt Commons" is a story that seems to owe much to Flannery O'Connor, another of Boswell's literary influences. Paul Hosea, a "tall and frail man entering middle age much as he had the car–gracelessly and alone," is kidnapped by a hired killer who is looking for Paul's neighbor. As the story unfolds, the killer, "Jane," begins to elicit the reader's sympathy; she is, in fact, an agent of mercy, juxtaposed with a cowardly man whose life can be distilled into a single, failed courtship and years of passive solitude. Paul's survival of the ordeal takes on a surprisingly tragic note, and the reader is left to ponder Jane's response when Paul announces to her that there is no point in killing him: "Well, I don't see the point in your living."

Perhaps the most accomplished story of the collection is "Glissando," a deeply affecting account of a young boy and his con-artist father that, Boswell says, captures his feelings for his own father and their relationship more than anything else he has written. The three-character geometry Boswell so often employs involves in this case a father and son, Louis and Jim Barley, who both love Louis's young girlfriend, Alida. Alida is highly sexual, a girl whose mother "married her way up the same social scale that Alida, in turn descended" and who has bottomed out with Louis in Gila Bend, Arizona. Jim is fourteen and just beginning to see his father in a new light, as a man blind to the fact that others see through what he pretends to know and whom he pretends to be. His struggles over his desire for Alida, combined with his increasing disillusion with his father, make him angry and jealous in spite of the deep love he has for the man. In "Glissando" Boswell seeks to strip bare the nature and dynamics of love and connection and hold them up to a clear, unsentimental light, such as when Alida says to Jim, "I could never resist the things my mother hated. My whole life has been an answer to that gift."

In his guest introduction for *Ploughshares* Boswell writes: "The ability to comprehend and create complex narratives requires one to conceive of abstractions and sequences, and to connect events in terms of cause and effect. Typically, it requires something like compassion, and often, I would argue, the ability to hold contradictory ideas simultaneously." In "Glissando," as in the other stories of this collection, such compassion and contradiction is not only evident, but also explored and illuminated in a striking and memorable fashion. Boswell's prose, which evokes the cool feel of Raymond Carver's minimalist stories, works to magnify his eloquence and appreciation for the nuances of human emotion. Boswell's writing plays on the stylistic strengths of the minimalist school but avoids the emotional flatness that plagues such writing.

Virtual Death (1995) was a marked departure for Boswell, a science-fiction novel he wrote after *Mystery Ride*, which had proved exhausting, requiring by Boswell's estimation thirty to forty drafts and five hundred pages that ended up on the cutting floor. Though he wrote it under the pen name Shale Aaron, Boswell has said that he would like to see *Virtual Death* republished in his own name, largely because the project, which began as a lark, ultimately became as serious as his other novels. Boswell's eye for social criticism is everywhere apparent in the novel: vending machines dispense disposable guns; death artists–who die and are revived in front of crowds–are the new rock celebrities; and an American dystopia has sprung up in the wake of a technological collapse. *Virtual Death* was shortlisted for the Philip K. Dick Science Fiction Prize, and *Science Fiction Chronicle* selected it as one of their best books of 1995.

American Owned Love takes the concerns of race and class that surface in much of Boswell's work and sets them squarely in New Mexico. One of the topics the book engages is the existence of *colonias,* unincorporated towns often without electricity or running water, in which Mexican workers live within the United States. One of the main characters, an angry teen named Rudy Salazar, hails from the *colonia* of Apuro, which faces the town of Persimmon, New Mexico, the Rio Grande winding between them. While race surfaces as a source of conflict between blacks and whites in *Dancing in the Movies,* in this book it is manifest in how Anglos and Hispanics relate. To this extent *American Owned Love* specifically reveals the world in which Boswell grew up and has made his life and raised his family. Though more superficially political than some of his other works, it is a sensitive and thoughtful portrayal of the Southwest border region with compelling characters.

Boswell's work documents life in the United States in the latter half of the twentieth century: the political and social debates of the time, as well as what it is to love, to be member of a family, to be engaged with the complexities of the self and society and their relation to one another. Particularly in his short fiction, he achieves an extraordinary degree of mimesis, closely recreating and encompassing the richness and scope of the world, a talent that makes him one of the most effective literary portraitists among contemporary American writers. Perhaps he himself has said best what he intends to accomplish: "I'm just trying to be honest and decent, to be true to the people I love and the things I hold dear, which includes literature–the story. Because I believe that storytelling is crucial to humans for existence, that in very complex ways, it helps us to see our own lives with more clarity."

Interviews:

Anne Marie Mackler, "An Interview with Robert Boswell," *Puerto del Sol,* 1 (Summer 1990): 9–27;

William Clark, "Robert Boswell," *Publishers Weekly,* 25 January 1993: 65–66;

Don Lee, "About Robert Boswell," *Ploughshares,* 4 (Winter 1996–1997): 216–221;

Dahleen Glanton, interview with Boswell, *Chicago Tribune,* 19 May 1997, V: 1.

Larry Brown

(9 July 1951 –   )

Robert A. Beuka
Louisiana State University

BOOKS: *Facing the Music* (Chapel Hill, N.C.: Algonquin, 1988);
Dirty Work (Chapel Hill, N.C.: Algonquin, 1989);
Big Bad Love (Chapel Hill, N.C.: Algonquin, 1990);
Joe (Chapel Hill, N.C.: Algonquin, 1991);
On Fire (Chapel Hill, N.C.: Algonquin, 1994);
Father and Son (Chapel Hill, N.C.: Algonquin, 1996);
Fay (Chapel Hill, N.C.: Algonquin, 2000).

Larry Brown's first two volumes of short stories, *Facing the Music* (1988) and *Big Bad Love* (1990), firmly established him as a major new figure in the school of American fiction that has alternately been referred to as "Dirty Realism" or "Trailer-Park Fiction." Like the short fiction of such kindred spirits as Raymond Carver and Richard Ford, Brown's stories chronicle the lives of down-and-out men who are most often addled with drink and facing dead ends in their personal and working lives. While Brown has garnered much attention and critical praise for his novels *Dirty Work* (1989), *Joe* (1991), and *Father and Son* (1996), his short fiction offers the best and most sustained glimpse into his world. Setting his stories in working-class, rural Mississippi–a place Clancy Sigal aptly described in the *Washington Post Book World* (23 December 1990) as "Third World America"–Brown consistently portrays the plights of struggling male characters whose difficulties in life are matched only by their dogged, laconic persistence.

William Larry Brown was born in Oxford, Mississippi, on 9 July 1951 to Knox Brown, a sharecropper, and Leona Barlow, a postmaster and store owner. Much of his youth was spent in Memphis, Tennessee, where his family moved when he was three years old. Brown returned with his family to Oxford at age fourteen, and he has remained in the area ever since. As a young man Brown worked at a variety of jobs, including stints as a carpenter and lumberjack, and he served in the Marines during 1972 and 1973. After returning from his military service Brown joined the Oxford Fire Department. He remained a firefighter for the next seventeen years, serving as captain for the final four years

Larry Brown (photograph by Bruce Newman; from the dust jacket for On Fire, *1994)*

of his service, 1986 to 1990. During his years at the fire department Brown continued to work outside jobs and for a time was the owner and operator of a local grocery store. He married Mary Annie Coleman on 17 August 1974, and the couple has two sons and a daughter.

Always an avid reader–he has cited William Faulkner, Flannery O'Connor, Cormac McCarthy, and

Carver as among his favorite authors and literary influences—Brown decided at age twenty-nine to try his hand at writing and eventually took two writing courses at the University of Mississippi, his only formal higher education. After several false starts and rejections from publishers, Brown saw his first story, "Plant Growin' Problems," published in *Easy Riders* magazine in 1982. Brown's first book, *Facing the Music,* published in 1988, won the Mississippi Institute of Arts and Letters award for literature in 1990.

A bold first step into the world of fiction, *Facing the Music* announced the central themes and concerns that resurfaced in Brown's subsequent story collection, *Big Bad Love.* The stories deal mainly with male characters who are in various states of desperation: alternately drawn to and fleeing from the women in their lives, working in unsatisfactory jobs or not working at all, and usually drunk. Brown's male protagonists are hardly typical heroic figures; yet, they are not antiheroes either, because Brown, for all his acid wit in relaying the foibles of his characters, still handles them with compassion. While it might be an overstatement to say that Brown's short fiction offers a sense of redemption for his troubled characters, certainly one gets the sense that they will persevere. Nevertheless, along the way these protagonists face hard traveling; as Barry Walters noted in *The Village Voice* (22 November 1986), Brown's characters "sleepwalk through his stories, waiting for catastrophe to wake them up."

The title story, which opens the collection, introduces a recurring theme in Brown's short fiction: the dissolution of romantic and sexual intimacy between married partners. The unnamed first-person narrator, who shares Brown's occupation of firefighter, resists the advances of his wife of twenty-three years, who has recently had a mastectomy. Fearing the inevitable advances of his wife and thinking, "She may start rubbing on me. That's what I have to watch out for. That's what she does," the narrator sits on the bed late at night drinking, trying to avoid conversation with his wife, and watching a rerun of Ray Milland in *The Lost Weekend.* As he watches, he recalls a recent one-night stand he had with a woman he met in a bar—his first extramarital affair, he says—and struggles with the guilt brought on by his pleasurable recollections of the night and in particular of the woman's breasts, which he describes as "like something you'd see in a movie." Interspersing the stark prose of his narration with terse, monosyllabic bits of dialogue between the unhappy couple, Brown relates the utter breakdown of communication between them.

The one sense of connection the narrator has is to Milland's character on the television screen, a drunken would-be writer. Brown thus introduces a fig-

ure—the hard-drinking, struggling writer—who becomes a recurring character-type in Brown's fiction, presumably drawn from autobiographical experience. As the story draws to a close, there is a moment of near tenderness as the narrator recalls the couple's honeymoon, twenty-three years earlier: "I'm thinking that your first love is your best love, that you'll never find any better." At the same time, the fatalism of that statement is all too clear, and the closing image of the story depicts what could be a reconciliatory moment in utterly hopeless terms: "She turns the lights off, and we reach to find each other in the darkness like people who are blind." If this closing in a sense recalls the fadeout ending of Carver's "What We Talk About When We Talk About Love" (1981), the comparison is understandable—in both his theme and his handling of dialogue, Brown reveals Carver's influence.

The next story, "Kubuku Rides (This is It)," which was anthologized in *Best American Short Stories of 1989,* is one of the bleakest in the collection and also one of the most accomplished. Written in the third person, the story is focused through the perceptions of the central character, a woman named Angel, who sacrifices her relationships with her husband and son because of her increasing addiction to alcohol. If Brown's typically spare prose and dialogue are at least in part an inheritance from such literary influences as Carver and Tobias Wolff, in this story Brown takes such minimalism in a different direction, relating the narrative itself in the broken language of the lead character, whose mind-numbing dependence on alcohol has lowered her sensibility to a brutish, merely instinctual level. This use of language lends particular resonance to Brown's descriptions of Angel's thoughts, as in a passage in which she regrets the decision to stay out drinking instead of returning home to her family: "She wishing now she'd just gone on home. Wouldn't have been so bad then. . . . Way it is, though. Get started, can't stop. Take that first drink, she ain't gonna stop till she pass out or run out. She don't know what it is. She ain't even understand it herself."

While this focus on alcohol as a destructive factor in relationships is familiar territory for Brown, "Kubuku Rides (This is It)" stands out for two other reasons: first, the story features a female lead character and narrative perspective, something Brown returns to only once more in this collection and not at all in *Big Bad Love.* In addition, "Kubuku Rides (This is It)" is noteworthy for the utter desperation it depicts: once again the final image is of a light being turned off, but in this case Brown leaves little hope for reconciliation and little doubt that this character has been ruined by her alcoholism. At the end of the story Angel, who has been in the habit of deserting her family to feed her craving for alcohol, does so once again, driving off to buy a six-pack of beer at the convenience store. Before she does, she pauses to look at the porch light her husband has left on for her, and Brown closes the story by contrasting this image of comforting domesticity with a reminder of Angel's ultimate isolation:

> She turn the wipers on to see better. The porch light shining out there, yellow light showing rain, it slanting down hard. It shine on the driveway and on Randy's bicycle and on they barbecue grill setting there getting wet. It make her feel good to know this all hers, that she always got this to come back to. This light show her home, this warm place she own that mean everything to her. This light, it always on for her. That what she thinking when it go out.

While these first two stories emphatically announce the prevailing tone and thematic concerns of *Facing the Music,* a trio of stories in the middle of the collection reveals Brown's willingness to experiment and expand his thematic and formal horizons. In one of these, "The Rich," Brown relates the rage his protagonist, a struggling travel agent named Mr. Pellisher, feels toward his wealthy clients. Eschewing linear plot structure and relying instead on an extended interior monologue, Brown distills the rage of the underclass down to its purest form. While Mr. Pellisher is driven by envy of his clients, at one point thinking, "if some way, somehow, he could be rich, too, he knows he would be exactly like them," he understands this fantasy will never be, and his raw anger overtakes him: "he hates the rich. What he'd really like to do is machine-gun the rich. Throttle the rich. . . . He'd like to see the rich suffer everything he ever suffered that all their money could heal."

If "The Rich" offers both formal and thematic contrasts to the bulk of the stories in this collection, so, too, does "Boy and Dog," a darkly comic tale, structured in blank verse, of a child's retribution on the man who ran over his dog. But certainly the most structurally experimental story of the collection is "Julie: A Memory," a disjointed narrative of teenage sex and pregnancy, a rape, an abortion, and a murder, relayed from a variety of perspectives. Recalling in its structure Faulkner's narrative experimentation, "Julie: A Memory" stands as the best case for the often-made comparison between Brown and Faulkner. While these three stories stand in marked counterpoint to the remainder of the collection, they offer evidence of a writer, early in his career, willing to experiment not only with content but also with form. As Harry Crews reflected in the *Los Angeles Times Book Review* (24 October 1990), "Here was a writer who did not know what was not possible, so he would try anything."

While Brown's experimental efforts in this collection may seem inconsistent–"Boy and Dog" comes off as a bit showy, while "Julie: A Memory" challenges interpretation perhaps more than it should–the cumulative effect of the remainder of thematically interrelated stories creates the singular force of *Facing the Music.* These stories map a common ground–the barrooms, desultory homes, and lonesome country highways of rural Mississippi–peopled by characters whose desperation is more often than not measured in bottles of beer, shots of whiskey, and violent outbursts. For his part, Brown ascribes this thematic continuity to personal experience; as he told Jean W. Ross in a 1990 interview (published in 1992), "I guess I write about characters who are from the poor side of town, because that's what I know the best. I just write about what I know." Through Brown's narrative voice–precise, often graphic, yet nevertheless sympathetic–one gets the sense that he does know his characters, and that this personal experience allows him to imbue even the least palatable of his characters with a sense of humanity.

This sense of empathy toward his characters is precisely what allows Brown's stories to transcend the merely banal or brutal. "Old Frank and Jesus," for example, concerns Mr. Parker, an aging farmer who–drunk and despondent over both his financial troubles and having recently put to sleep his squirrel dog, Old Frank–contemplates suicide; while the basic plot may resemble that of a hackneyed country song, the effect of the story is altogether different. As the unhappy protagonist pulls a borrowed gun out from under his couch, Brown ends the story with the blunt observation, "Mr. Parker, fifty-eight, is reclining on his couch." After investing his character with a rounded, idiosyncratic personality through the use of extended interior monologue, Brown leaves his plight unresolved, in the process adding another layer of desperation to the mounting aura of gloom that comes to pervade the entire collection.

Elsewhere in the collection Brown's empathy for his characters helps to temper what otherwise are a series of starkly violent moments. "Night Life," for example, closes with the image of the protagonist, Gary, viciously beating Connie, his would-be lover, after seeing the way she mistreats her children. And "The End of Romance," the final story in the collection, chronicles an absolute bloodbath of a convenience store shoot-out, which Brown plays strictly for laughs, presaging the wry and almost savage humor which more fully informs his next collection of stories, *Big Bad Love.*

While "The End of Romance" predicts the prevailing tone of Brown's subsequent collection, the penultimate story of *Facing the Music,* "Leaving Town," serves as the more appropriate conclusion to this collec-

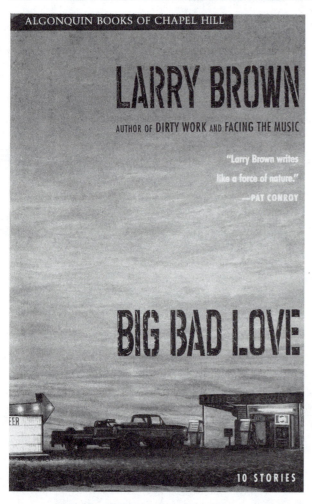

Dust jacket for Brown's 1990 collection of stories, focusing on the failing relationships of desperate male protagonists

tion. Combining the thematic concerns of the majority of the stories—broken relationships characterized by physical and psychological abuse, hard drinking, and isolation—with experimental narrative technique, "Leaving Town" in a sense sums up the collection as a whole. The story concerns Richard, a struggling laborer and part-time independent contractor, and his relationship with Myra, an older, battered wife who is hoping to repair her house (and her life) in the wake of her husband's departure. The story is told through both characters' viewpoints, as Brown shifts the first-person narrative perspective between Richard and Myra throughout the story.

Richard, nearly destitute and supporting a live-in lover whom he despises and her crippled daughter whom he loves and feels responsible for, agrees to replace the doors in Myra's house, which had been destroyed in her estranged husband's final fit of rage. The two kindred spirits nearly come together romantically, but their physical union is short-lived and

incomplete—defeated, as are so many of the relationships in this collection, by the destructive effects of alcohol and by each character's sense of isolation. Nevertheless, there is a glimmer of hope for true communication in this relationship, as Richard thinks to himself, "She knew what I felt like. She was as miserable as I was." Although he considers calling Myra at some point in the future, Richard leaves town and his own troubled relationship at the end of the story, abandoning the work on Myra's house for someone else to finish. Ultimately, the image of the battered doors serves as an apt metaphor for this collection as a whole, which throughout evokes the pain of broken homes and lives in need of repair.

In 1989, one year after the publication of *Facing the Music,* Brown published his first novel, *Dirty Work.* Widely heralded for its strong antiwar sentiment, *Dirty Work* advanced Brown's reputation in the literary world, announcing him as a powerful novelist as well as a short-story writer. The story of two wounded Vietnam veterans who share their experiences in a VA hospital, *Dirty Work* draws on the author's life experience. Brown, a former Marine, dedicated *Dirty Work* to his father, a World War II veteran who "knew what war does to men." While one senses a pronounced thematic break between this novel and the short-story sequences that preceded and followed it, the story of war and what it does to men resurfaces in "Old Soldiers," one of the best stories of *Big Bad Love.*

As a whole, *Big Bad Love,* which is divided into three sections and features nine short stories and a novella, includes many of the same elements that characterized *Facing the Music.* The stories in *Big Bad Love* feature male characters struggling with troubled relationships, marital infidelity, and hard drinking. The rural milieu remains the same in this collection, and fully half of the protagonists spend the bulk of their time driving the Mississippi back roads, coolers of iced beer by their sides, as they shuttle between an inhospitable home life and the bars that beckon them despite the promise of even more trouble to be found there.

Despite these thematic similarities to the first collection, one also notices in *Big Bad Love* new areas of concern for Brown. For the most part, the structural experimentation that had played a prominent role in the previous collection is gone here, replaced by a more straightforward collection of narratives, all told in the first person. Brown is more willing to allow the voices of his narrators to carry the stories, and his strength lies in his ear for the cadence of those working-class speakers. As Stuart Dybek noted in the *Chicago Tribune* (23 September 1990), Brown's "gift is the ability to capture convincing Southern voices and to allow them to tell their stories in their own words." In addition to this development in Brown's use of perspective, there is also new thematic ground in this collection: of particular note is Brown's increasing interest in chronicling the life of the struggling writer, a subject that becomes the focus of two stories as well as the novella.

As the majority of the stories in this volume indicate, Brown's forte remains chronicling the troubled lives of his male protagonists, most of them ne'er-do-wells who seem to attract the troubles that follow them around. Such is the case of the unnamed narrator of "Falling Out of Love," the opening story in the collection, a hilarious variation on the road narrative that captures the difficult love life of the narrator and his beloved, Sheena Baby, through the story of their ill-fated trip to the store to buy beer. After their car develops not one but two flat tires on the trip, Sheena Baby deserts the narrator, giving him occasion to ponder, in darkly humorous fashion, the trouble of their relationship: "Sheena Baby didn't hurt for me like I did for her. I knew it. I'd thought about shooting her first and me second, but that wouldn't have done either one of us any good." With his characteristic eye for detail, Brown reveals the narrator's understanding that his own shortcomings have led to his and Sheena's falling out: "I knew I'd done it to myself, staying up all hours of the night playing *Assorted Golden Hits* and cooking french fries at two a.m., and letting the garbage pile up in the broom closet, not keeping my toenails cut short enough and scratching her legs with them at night in my sleep."

Eventually the narrator starts the car back up and goes after Sheena, drinking beer, smoking a joint, and listening to classic rock on the car stereo as he bumps down the road on two flat tires. When he finds her, the lovers briefly enjoy a passionate reunion before Brown creates yet another stumbling block for the couple: "That was when the cops pulled up, two of them, with hard faces and shiny sunglasses, and I saw with a sick feeling in my heart that our happy ending was about to take a turn for the worse." In a sense, this closing to the story is typical of Brown: as each of the stories in his previous collection indicated, there are no happy endings in his short fiction. But at the same time, the world-weary yet undefeated tone of the narrator's final statement is indicative of a significant change of tenor in this collection as a whole: in contrast to the prevailing sense of desperation in *Facing the Music,* the majority of the stories in *Big Bad Love* cover similar thematic terrain in a more wry manner, as Brown uses humor to explore other aspects of the troubled side of romantic relationships.

"Falling Out of Love" sets the tone for a string of stories in part 1 of the collection that focus, as Bruce Allen succinctly put it in *The New York Times Book Review* (2 September 1990), on "confused men who admit their weakness for cheap liquor and available women." Another such story is "Wild Thing," the story of a man whose dissatisfaction with his life as a husband and father leads him nightly to the bars in search of available women. Brown captures the narrator's lifestyle in a blunt opening paragraph: "She came into a bar I was in one night and she took a stool. I noticed the tight jeans, the long brown hair, the pretty red blouse. A woman like her, you have to notice. That's what you're sitting in there for." The narrator recounts a series of misadventures with this would-be lover, intercut with passages describing his increasingly fractious home life. Eventually he encounters the woman's boyfriend, a "big maniac," in a bar one night and smashes him "straight across the teeth" with his wooden bar stool before escorting the woman from the bar.

This protagonist's reckless, relentless pursuit of cold beer and loose women makes him something of a representative figure in the collection. The narrator of "Gold Nuggets," a man whose misadventures in a third-rate strip club on the Mississippi Gulf Coast ultimately leave him robbed, beaten up, and reeling from alcohol poisoning, seems a similar character type, albeit one with worse luck. Indeed, the narrator of "Gold Nuggets" closes that story with an observation that could apply to the majority of the protagonists in the collection; trying to fight off the brutal effects of last night's alcohol and make it through the day, he longs for nothing more than nightfall itself, "knowing that the sun would always go down, and another night would come, that our forms of salvation were ours to choose, as blessed to the misguided like me as any church."

Though they are enlivened by edgy prose and caustic humor, there is a sameness to stories such as "Falling Out of Love," "Wild Thing," and "Gold Nuggets." But Brown balances the hyper-masculinity of these stories with several stories that reveal vulnerable protagonists, men for whom manly posturing is part of a process of self-affirmation—one that does not always work. The title story falls under this category, revealing the insecurities of the narrator, Leroy, who fears the voracious sexual appetite of his wife, Mildred. To avoid Mildred's impending return home from work, Leroy downs a six-pack of Old Milwaukee beer and drives around in his pickup truck, eventually stopping at a bar to drink more.

The reader learns that the source of Leroy's fear of sex with his wife is what he calls her "over-large organ"; as he sits in the bar drinking, Leroy reflects on his problem, concluding "I would have had to be the Moby Dick of love to adequately satisfy Mildred." In a sense, this story recalls the much bleaker title story of *Facing the Music:* in both cases, the protagonist's fear of his wife's physicality spells an end to their intimacy.

And while in "Big Bad Love" this problem is treated with humor, the end of the tale deflates Leroy's sense of superiority as he comes to discover his own insignificance. Upon returning home, Leroy finds a note from Mildred informing him that she has run off with a man who "has the equipment to take care of my problem." Finding himself alone and drunk, replaced by another man, the narrator closes the story with an observation that recalls the sense of isolation that characterized Brown's earlier stories: "I thought about Mildred in that other man's arms, and how fine she looked in a bathing suit. Right about then I started missing her, and the loneliness I have been speaking of really started to set in."

A similar theme of masculine vulnerability can be found in "Waiting for the Ladies," a tightly crafted story concerning the psychology of male sexuality. In this story, the narrator pursues a man who has been exposing himself to women, most recently the narrator's wife. Enraged at the flasher's "perversion," the narrator tracks him down, eventually pursuing him, loaded shotgun by his side, in a high-speed chase back to the man's house. Brown uses the first-person mode to maximum effect in this story, as the narrator's ruminations during the chase reveal not only his interest in the flasher's motivations, but also his insecurity regarding his own marriage and his fears that his wife is having an affair with her boss. Eventually sensing the connections between his rage at the flasher and a fear of his own emasculation, the narrator changes the nature of his mission. As he opens the door to the flasher's house and walks, gun in hand, into the living room, he encounters the object of his pursuit, sitting next to his weeping mother: "He said one thing, quietly: 'Are you going to kill us?' Their eyes got me. I sat down, asking first if I could. That's when I started telling them what my life was like." In many ways the inverse of the sort of surging masculinity found in stories such as "Wild Thing," "Waiting for the Ladies" demonstrates that Brown's men are far more troubled and complex beings than they might first appear to be.

Brown further develops his portrait of male vulnerability in one of the best stories in the collection, "Old Soldiers." A rumination on the lasting psychological and emotional pain of war, "Old Soldiers" is drawn from Brown's personal experience. As Brown told interviewer Tom Rankin in 1995, war stories were a major part of the conversation at the local store he frequented as a teenager in Tula, Mississippi, where the community—primarily the men and the boys—would congregate. Brown recalled that the old men told stories about World War I, while his father's generation shared stories about another war: "Daddy talked about World War II. All these grown men that I knew around here, they'd all been in World War II, every one of them." Perhaps drawn from recollections of this habitual telling of war stories, "Old Soldiers" is shaped around the sharing of war experiences between the main characters. The story chronicles the relationship between the narrator, Leo, and two older veterans, Squirrel and Mr. Aaron. Notable for both its elegiac tone and its focus on men's relationships with other men, "Old Soldiers" stands in stark contrast to the rest of the stories in the collection, offering the most vivid counterpoint to the figure of the reckless, carousing male.

The story opens with Leo's recollections of times he had spent with Mr. Aaron, a wounded World War II veteran and friend of Leo's deceased father. Mr. Aaron is presented as a quiet man—as Leo observes, "He despised all the needless words that people said"—who stoically bears the continuing pain of the leg wound he received in the war. But Leo knows that, despite his placid front, the wounds go deeper still: "War had hurt him. He never got the bullets and the bombs out of his head." In this sense, Mr. Aaron is akin to Squirrel, a Korean War veteran who appears later in the story. Squirrel, drunk and desperate, approaches Leo in a bar one night and begs him for a ride home. At first Leo is annoyed, but when Squirrel begins to tell him about his experiences on the front line in Korea, Leo has a change of heart: "I listened then, because moments like that are rare, when you get to hear about these things that have shattered men's lives." The resolution of the story finds Leo taking Squirrel back to Mr. Aaron's, as Brown's narrator reflects on the bonds—created by mutually painful experiences—that unite old soldiers: "I just realized something. Squirrel didn't want to go home that night. . . . He wanted to be with somebody who knew him. And if there was anybody that night who knew what he was feeling, and what it meant, Aaron did. Aaron did for sure." A war story that is primarily about the telling of war stories and the need to communicate shared pain, "Old Soldiers" reveals a level of communication absent from most of Brown's stories of romantic relationships.

Another counterpoint to the prevailing theme of love gone wrong can be found in a series of tales about the life of the struggling writer. Strong autobiographical content informs two of these efforts, the short story "The Apprentice" and the novella "92 Days," while the third, a satirical drama titled "Discipline," takes a comic look at the paranoid fears of the plagiarist. "The Apprentice" concerns the relationship troubles between the narrator and his wife, Judy, an aspiring author. Judy's horrific early fiction and the accumulated rejections of her short stories and novels by publishers are handled in comic fashion, presumably a cathartic mode for Brown in dealing with a subject he knew well from his own early years. Brown, as Brandon Griggs reported in a *Salt Lake Tribune* article (2 February 1997), "wrote five novels and more than 100 short stories–and eventually tossed them all" before finding his voice as a writer.

There are several parallels in "The Apprentice" to Brown's own early writing life: much like his character Judy, who ritualistically awaits the mail every day, hoping for an acceptance letter while fearing the manila envelope that signals rejection and the return of the story, Brown told Rankin that his wife, Mary Annie, had to endure the same behavior on his part: "I think she said one time that the worst thing for her was to watch me go down to the mailbox and see if anything had come back. . . . And she said the worst thing was to see me come back up the driveway with those manila envelopes under my armpit." Judy's first failed novel is about Yellowstone Park, also the setting for one of Brown's failed novels. In the end, Judy achieves a measure of success as a writer, but the victory is bittersweet, as the narrator notes that her increasing involvement in her writing has worked to the detriment of their relationship. Still, the narrator and Judy persevere where other couples in Brown's stories fail; after professing his love for Judy, the narrator comes to accept his wife as a writer: "I don't know where this writing thing came from or what caused it, but it's a part of her now, like her arms or her face."

The novella "92 Days" furthers Brown's exploration of the writerly life. Critical reaction to this major effort has been widely mixed: while Sigal referred to it as one of the better stories of the collection, Dybek thought it "the weakest and least funny in the collection," and Allen found it "vitiated by shapelessness, redundancy, and sentimentality." While Brown's chronicle of the pitfalls faced by his clearly autobiographical narrator, Leon Barlow, does lapse into pathos perhaps more than it should, there is something to be said for the presence of repetition in the work and for Brown's choice of the longer novella form. "92 Days" is a metafictional work in the truest sense: concerned with presenting the struggling writer's repeated ordeal of creation, rejection, and dogged perseverance, Brown's narrative calls for a cyclical, repetitive structure.

That this novella ultimately stands as Brown's personal, autobiographical statement on the challenges of the literary life is made clear in the conclusion, which finds Barlow in the act of writing. In the middle of a story about a girl and her parents who are running from an unknown "something beyond bad," Barlow reflects on his difficulty ending his story, in a manner that helps to illuminate a central point of Brown's novella: "They were running, running, the cars going by, and I could see the slippery sidewalks, and the lights in the stores, and I could see my mother and my father looking back over their shoulders at whatever was chasing us, and I ran as fast as I could, terrified, not knowing how it would end, knowing I had to know." Even as Barlow struggles to close his tale, confusing his fictional character and himself, the reader senses that Barlow is in some sense finally getting it right, merging the fictional and the autobiographical to the extent that he is able to identify with his characters. As so much of Brown's short fiction shows, this empathy fostered by autobiographical experience is often essential to the success of a story. Hence Barlow seems at the end to be learning the lesson that Brown concedes he himself learned the hard way. As he told Rankin, "A long time ago. . . . I didn't know that you had to write about what you know. . . . I think you really have to draw on your own experience to create from what you know best. That's just one of the things that you learn if you spend enough time writing."

Since the publication of *Big Bad Love*, Brown has written three additional novels–*Joe, Father and Son,* and *Fay* (2000)–as well as a nonfiction work, *On Fire* (1994). Though his themes and subject matter vary, the hallmarks of Brown's fictional work continue to be his perceptive eye, his keen ear for dialogue, and his ability to evoke a sense of place. Perhaps most significantly, Brown continues to be the voice of an often-overlooked group, the rural working class. As Allen noted, "At his best, he convincingly renders the lives of plain people muddling through as best they can, and he does it as well as any writer around." In the short-story collection Brown has found an apt genre for doing what he does best: allowing a variety of narrative voices to share stories of pain, humor, desperation, and ultimately, perseverance.

Interviews:

Jean W. Ross, "Larry Brown," in *Contemporary Authors,* volume 134, edited by Susan M. Trosky (Detroit: Gale Research, 1992), pp. 88–91;

Susan Ketchin, "An Interview with Larry Brown," *Southern Quarterly: A Journal of the Arts in the South,* 32 (Winter 1994): 94–109;

Kay Bonetti, "An Interview with Larry Brown," *Missouri Review,* 18 (1995): 79–107;

Tom Rankin, "On the Home Front: Larry Brown's Narrative Landscape," *Reckon: The Magazine of Southern Culture* (Fall 1995): 90–101.

Peter Cameron

(29 November 1959 –)

James Coan
State University of New York College at Oneonta

BOOKS: *One Way or Another* (New York: Harper & Row, 1986; London: Viking, 1986);
Leap Year (New York: Harper & Row, 1990; London: Hamilton, 1990);
Far-flung (New York: HarperCollins, 1991);
The Weekend (New York: Farrar, Straus & Giroux, 1994; London: Fourth Estate, 1996);
Andorra (New York: Farrar, Straus & Giroux, 1997; London: Fourth Estate, 1997);
The Half You Don't Know: New and Selected Stories (New York: Plume, 1997).

Peter Cameron established himself as a craftsman of the short-story form with the publication of two short-story collections: *One Way or Another* (1986) and *Far-flung* (1991). Written in the spare, lean prose style sometimes called minimalist and eschewing description and setting in favor of conversation and fragmentary observation, the stories are "as contemporary as an overheard street conversation," according to Victor Kantor Burg in *The New York Times Book Review* (22 June 1986). Several stories have been selected for the *O. Henry Prize Stories* volumes, and a reviewer for *People* magazine (21 July 1986) called him "one of the form's best practitioners."

Cameron's stories for the most part portray average, middle-class people in various situations of family and personal life, dealing with parents and children, teachers, and friends and sometimes coping with tragedies such as death or the ending of a love affair, as well as with pain and loss that springs from no easily determinable source. "Longing, mixed with self-reflexive irony, is Cameron's trademark," remarked Amy Hempel in the *Los Angeles Times* (11 May 1986), discussing the sense of incompleteness and alienation that haunts many of the characters. The stories of the two collections, many written in the first person and present tense, are "appropriate to the age of shortened attention spans, fractured marriages and splintering families," David Leavitt commented in *The New York Times Book Review* (12 May 1985), grouping Cameron with

Peter Cameron (photograph © by Jerry Bauer; from the dust jacket for Andorra, *1997)*

short-story writers Hempel, Marian Thurm, Elizabeth Tallent, and Meg Wolitzer. These writers were identified by Leavitt as "recording through their fiction the changes in the way young people think about family, marriage, love and loyalty."

Cameron was born in Pompton Plains, New Jersey, on 29 November 1959, into a family of four children, including two older sisters and one younger brother. His father, Donald, was an economist employed by Chase Manhattan Bank, and his mother, Sally, was a homemaker. From the middle-class surroundings of this suburban New Jersey community about twenty miles west of New York City, the family relocated to the urban, multicultural environment of London in 1968 and lived there for several years while his father was employed by an English bank. He recalled to Philip Gambone that these years were "a great time to be in London. It was a really wild town. The world was a different place then. I had a lot of freedom. I went from living in this small New Jersey town to London. It was very liberating and exciting." In London he attended the American School, a private school that differed from his previous public schooling in the United States in its nontraditional curriculum and greater emphasis on creativity. As Cameron remembered, "we did a lot of creative writing. We wrote a lot of plays. So that's when I actually started writing creatively."

Returning to the United States, he graduated from high school in Pompton Plains and then attended Hamilton College in Clinton, New York. There he pursued a major in English literature; he studied poetry with David Lehman and "got very excited about writing poetry." At this time he was reading the short stories by Anne Beattie that were being published in *The New Yorker* and realized his affinity with her work. The similarity of the settings and characters in her stories to the daily life and situations he perceived in his surroundings made an impression on Cameron and inspired him as a writer. He began working in the short-story form in creative-writing classes at Hamilton and, according to his own words, "just kind of found this voice." During his final year at Hamilton he began sending stories to *The New Yorker*. None were accepted for publication at the time, but "it was sort of this great apprenticeship, where they would reject a story and tell me why it didn't work and then say, 'Send us something else soon.' And, of course, I would immediately want to write another story and send it back."

Graduating from Hamilton in 1982 with a B.A. in English literature, Cameron moved to New York City and found employment at St. Martin's Press. His story "Memorial Day" was accepted by *The New Yorker* and published in May 1983. The Beattiesque subject matter of people in everyday situations occupied him in his writing at this time, and his treatment of the subject echoed the minimalist style of Beattie, Raymond Carver, Tama Janowitz, and Bobbie Ann Mason. In a survey of then-current fiction for *The Boston Review,* Rosellen Brown found similarities in Cameron's work with writers such as Bret Easton Ellis, Jay McInerney, and Susan Minot. She pointed out that "these writers . . . give the impression that to comment on the lives of their protag-

onists or invite judgment on them, or to prod a story into any shape more complex than a simplest chronology, . . . is to spoil the purity of their observation."

Cameron's first collection of stories, *One Way or Another,* appeared in 1986 when Cameron was twenty-six years old. The title of the collection is not shared by any of the stories within; as with the title of his second collection, *Far-flung,* the author did not wish to highlight any one story over another and instead created titles he thought conveyed the tenor of the collection as a whole. Comprising fourteen stories, most of which originally appeared in *The New Yorker, One Way or Another* was favorably reviewed by many critics and assured a place of some stature for the young author in contemporary American short fiction. Short-story writer Lorrie Moore was quoted on the jacket: "Quiet, human situations made art by Mr. Cameron's unfailing sense of voice and form." Critic Alice H. G. Phillips, in *TLS: The Times Literary Supplement* (5 September 1986), pointed out that in many of the stories "the preoccupations are those of young adults, wrapped up in their own problems, surprised that other people can feel pain." The collection received a special citation for first book of fiction in 1987 from the Ernest Hemingway Foundation/PEN America Award.

In the early stories of *One Way or Another* many of Cameron's protagonists are young, male, middle-class, and at a crisis point in their lives. In "Memorial Day," the first story in the collection, the main character has responded to his family's dissolution by erecting a wall of silence around himself at home. His mother has entered into a relationship with Lonnie, who the young narrator says looks more his age than his father's. As they mill around the house on Memorial Day, the narrator's mother and Lonnie attempt to engage him. The story ends as mother and son stand poised in the middle of a passage of time and emotion, a portrait of two estranged family members on the brink of change and acceptance. Unresolved differences and disappointments hover in the background. The terseness of the author's style is evident when, near the end of the story, the narrator says: "I sit up. I look at my mother's chest, as if I could see her heart beating. She has on a polo shirt with a little blue whale on her left breast. I am afraid to look at her face." At seven and one-half pages "Memorial Day" is long enough to present only a few brief images; yet, the character's pain, emotional confusion, and inner strength are convincingly depicted.

Similarly, "Homework" is narrated by eighteen-year-old Michael Pechetti, who is sinking into a malaise, ostensibly brought on by the death of the family dog. Isolated in his own world, he rejects the people around him—his mother and father, his sister, his guidance counselor—and begins cutting school. He still con-

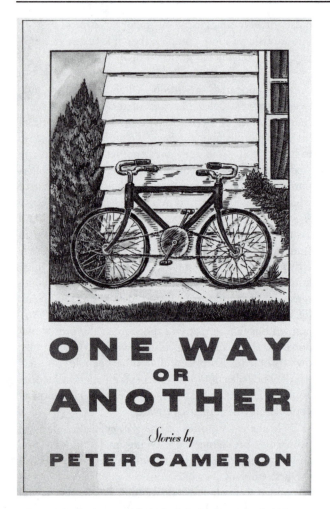

Dust jacket for Cameron's first collection of stories, most of which are about young characters in a a state of crisis

templates algebraic problems, however, a metaphor for the incomprehensible difficulty of coming to terms with life and loss. In the central scene Michael returns to school and is confronted by the guidance counselor about the contents of the note he wrote explaining his absence: "I was unhappy and did not feel able to attend school." In the end Michael has apparently matured, if only incrementally, although he seems to have traded depression for cynicism when he says near the end: "I'm not really listening. It's all nonsense." He continues to try to understand his problem in algebraic terms, with his own feelings and fears, his state of mind, and his future making up the variables.

School subjects also confound the narrator, a little older but not much wiser than Michael, in "Fear of Math." Calculus is presented as an unfathomable foreign language and an almost insurmountable hurdle to the narrator, a young woman, Julie, in her quest for an M.B.A. at Columbia University. Her approach to graduate school and life is summarized in her belief that

"things you are scared of are things you shouldn't dwell on too long." She immediately begins an affair with her calculus teacher, for which she seems unprepared. She also visits her parents, retirement-age people in Upstate New York who seem almost as adrift as she is. Deception within the family emerges as the central theme of the story: Julie lies about her work in school to her mother, who is leaving the father and his migrant life-style. "Lies always reveal something in these stories, but they are never made explicit. Like other improvised actions, deception is neither judged or reduced," noted Burg in his review. In Julie's case the deception becomes a self-fulfilling prophecy: she is able finally to meet her goals and begin her studies in the graduate program. She has been able to free herself, and returning to school becomes a metaphor for reengaging in life and regaining equilibrium. The ending to the comic story is upbeat and realistic.

In "Fast Forward" Alison, a friend of the narrator, Patrick, has been telling her dying mother that they are engaged and invites Patrick up to her mother's house for a probable final visit. Alison's lies are double-edged; she has told her mother that Patrick is in law school, to which he responds: "'Law school! Alison, that's cruel.' I had applied and been denied admission to almost every decent law school in the eastern United States." For Alison, the deceptions are both a form of harmless wishful thinking and an escape route from her unfulfilled life as a movie projectionist. The characters never seem to waste much time pondering the effects of their actions or lies; they are too busy navigating their way through an alien world of fad diets and junk food. The title "Fast Forward" refers to the fact that as Alison and Patrick listen to tapes while on their trip, Patrick picks only a few songs from each tape and fast-forwards the cassette player over the rest. Alison's mother's death has brought the two of them closer together, but this closeness only briefly connects them amid the ongoing confusion and emptiness of their lives.

The alienation and disconnectedness in which Cameron's characters are mired never becomes morbid because of the lively sense of humor that informs most of the stories. In "What Do People Do All Day" Mark, another bored and drifting teenager, lives in a faceless, middle-class suburb surrounded by a father, mother, stepmother, stepbrother, and babysitter. Evidently, the chaotic situation is still unresolved after the breakup of his parents' marriage. Though the story is brief, it manages to invest a fairly large cast of characters with life and soul. The conclusion of the story focuses on Ted, Mark's father, who struggles to understand the forces that are driving him and all the people who depend on him. He attempts to gather himself, realizing his feelings for his second wife, Helen, ending a secret affair, and getting serious about beginning a new career. Touches of slightly screwball comedy crop up occasionally to lighten tense situations: Ted is locked out of the men's room at an office where he is seeking employment; Mark's mother hangs up quickly when her husband's present wife answers the phone, then calls back and offers an unlikely excuse for hanging up. Conversations bounce from external reality to personal relationships and back in humorous non sequiturs, as when Ted and Mark are watching television:

> "Was Mommy here today?"
> "Yes," says Mark.
> "Isn't there a movie on?"

Several of Cameron's stories focus on male homosexual characters. Throughout his writings, from the early stories to the more recent novels, gay relationships are part of the environment he creates, but they do not predominate; many of the short stories have no obvious gay characters. "Being gay is one aspect of who I am," he told Gambone, referring to the relationship of the author's sexual orientation to the creative process. "I don't understand this desire people have to categorize novels according to the sexuality of the authors or characters." Cameron rejects the idea that there is a particularly gay sensibility that a gay author imparts to his work. His stories portray an array of characters, some homosexual, some not, because, he says, "when I got an idea for a story, I got a specific idea about a specific character." He acknowledges that as a gay man he has felt that "my writing should be political or socially conscious in a way, but for some reason I'm not interested in making my writing be like that." The nature of the gay consciousness in his work has been remarked upon by some critics, for instance in Myles Weber's essay "When a Risk Group Is Not a Risk Group: The Absence of AIDS Panic in Peter Cameron's Fiction" in *AIDS–The Literary Response* (1992).

Gay relationships occupy a central position in "Jump or Dive." The narrator, Evan, is "stuck in a pre-adolescent funk, with no clear cause or cure," according to Burg. Like other young narrators of Cameron's stories, Evan is an innocent who views the world around him without prejudice or preconception, gleaning random impressions here and there that rarely add up to any kind of manageable totality. Evan and his parents are visiting Evan's uncle at his condominium in Arizona. Uncle Walter has a gay lover, Jason, whose propensity for eating late-night meals, lying, and swimming nude unnerve Evan. The title of the story refers to a game Jason teaches Evan in the pool, involving one player diving off the board and changing in midair either to a jump or a

dive as the other player calls it out, an obvious metaphor for Evan's troubled feelings about his sexual orientation. Near the story's end, when his parents offer him a chance to remain behind while they take a short trip, Evan begins to understand his fear, confusion, and indecision in terms of this threatening game. As other young, naive characters in these stories watch ostensibly mature people (such as parents) act, they try to pick up hints about how to behave. Most of the time they find only confusion, comedy, and delusion. Leavitt felt that "the child takes on the traditional parent role" in many ways in the stories. Hempel felt that "Jump or Dive" was "the riskiest, most disturbing story in the collection" in its depiction of the vulnerable young Evan at the mercy of forces he can barely comprehend.

A mature gay relationship is at the center of "Excerpts from Swan Lake," integrated into a larger picture of a multigenerational family that includes a senile grandmother who provides both comic relief and a refreshingly different perspective from the cynicism and worldliness of the two young characters Paul and Neal. They seem to be at a crisis point in their relationship as they tend Paul's grandmother. "I think I'm going to move back into the apartment," Neal says. "I feel funny here. I don't feel comfortable," reiterating the unnameable discontent that infects so many in these stories. This particular story probes the nature of gay relationships, particularly covert relationships and the stress they can create. Paul's grandmother has always wanted to see a production of Pyotr Ilich Tchaikovsky's *Swan Lake* (1877), and she and the two men attend a performance but are unable to connect with it because it envisions a world far removed from theirs, which seems to lack all grace and music.

Taken as a whole, *One Way Or Another* presents a vividly humorous vision of a world of isolation, alienation, lack of communication, and inability to express true feeling. Many of the stories seem connected by focusing on young lives out of sync and characters trapped in a vaguely familiar yet alien world. Cameron's subject matter and style communicate a recognizable image of the world of his generation, coming of age in the 1970s and 1980s.

During the 1980s Cameron continued to live in New York City. He left St. Martin's Press after a year or so, deciding he was not cut out to work in the publishing business because, as he told Gambone, "people who work in publishing don't have time to read what you want to read. I valued reading too much to get myself in that kind of situation." He then worked for the Trust for Public Land until 1987, after which he was occupied with writing a novel and reviewing books. He was awarded a grant from the National Endowment of the

Arts in 1987. He also spent fruitful periods at the Yaddo and MacDowell writers' colonies. He tried teaching as well, spending a semester at Oberlin College in Ohio as an assistant professor of creative writing and also returning to Hamilton College as a visiting professor.

Leap Year, Cameron's first published novel, came out in 1990 after appearing in serial form in weekly installments in the New York magazine *Seven Days* throughout 1988. In this work Cameron introduces an expanded set of characters, related by blood or friendship, and juggles the events of their lives as they find new relationships and end old ones. It is written in a fast-paced yet fluid comic style that includes witty observations about life in New York City. The characters are derived from those in an earlier unpublished novel he wrote while in college; he devised a new plot suitable to the serial form, with a significant event happening in every installment. The story "Cafe Hysteria" in *Far-Flung* is also derived from the earlier novel. *Leap Year* moves beyond the sometimes bleak and faceless landscape of the stories and portrays a warmer and less threatening, less existential and angst-ridden universe than the early stories.

After spending 1988 occupied with *Leap Year* Cameron decided that he did not want to devote his time exclusively to writing, and in 1990 he became affiliated with the Lambda Legal Defense and Education Fund, an organization devoted to gay issues and rights. He worked there in the afternoons only and spent mornings writing, an arrangement which he found suitable to his personal and creative temperament. As he told Gambone, "I like my job at Lambda, because even though the work I do there isn't really advocacy work, I feel that I'm contributing to something that I believe in that's helping to change the world in a good way."

A second collection of twelve short stories, *Far-flung,* was published in 1991, comprising stories written from 1985 to 1990. The dust jacket of the first edition depicts images of postcards and canceled stamps, and the stories deal, appropriately, with themes of geographical and personal displacement. The style in *Far-flung* seems more fleshed out; many of the stories are longer and several are interrelated, giving the feeling of a larger, novelistic canvas than *One Way or Another.* His recurring themes are still in evidence, however: disconnectedness, the sense of things falling apart amid familiar surroundings, lack of communication, and deceptiveness.

The collection was generally well received by the critics. The reviewer in *Publishers Weekly* (9 August 1991) characterized the stories as a "series of poised, quiet, mainly first-person narratives concerned with loneliness and abounding with gently reverberant epiphanies." *Library Journal* (15 September 1991)

called the stories "terse, elliptical . . . always stylish and often affecting." In *The New York Times Book Review* (29 September 1991) Roxanna Robinson felt that the characters "find their lives changing around them and are paralyzed, unable to inhabit themselves," and that they "fail to connect. The characters see themselves as impotent, and they see experience as random." She also stated that "the writing . . . is often fine . . . Mr. Cameron achieves an elegant poignancy." The stories are skillfully crafted, with Cameron's trademark clear, flowing prose in the service of a vision colored by bleakness and emptiness but leavened with pungent observations and a sharp wit.

A family responding to tragedy occupies the center stage once again in "Not the Point," which shares themes and character types with stories in the first collection; one of the earlier pieces in *Far-flung,* the story originally published as "Point of View" in *The Mississippi Review* in 1986. Ellery Groener's insistence upon wearing sunglasses in response to his twin brother's suicide–which recalls the young man's silence in "Memorial Day"–worries his mother, Arlene, and the guidance counselor and nurse at his school. Arlene, the narrator, is confused and anxious about her family's status: her husband has relocated to the Philippines in the aftermath of the suicide and is expecting her and Ellery to join him. As Arlene arranges the move, selling the house and their belongings, she discovers that Ellery may be reconsidering his desire to move away, preferring to stay and make a life for himself instead of running away to the Philippines. Like many of the characters in these stories, both Arlene and Ellery find the courage to look at life squarely, but only briefly and fleetingly, in the midst of the ongoing rush of events and the meaningless trivia of small talk with strangers and interviews with school bureaucrats.

In "Just Relax" Elaine arrives in New York City exhausted from a stint in the Peace Corps. In several days her life spins out of control. After a misunderstanding with her mother she is mysteriously evicted from her rented living quarters and refused readmission to the Peace Corps; in the end she finds herself bewildered and working at an amusement park. Robinson pointed out the recurring theme of the defective mother in this and other stories in the collection. Elaine's mother has inexplicably become a performance artist, forgets to pick up Elaine at the airport upon her arrival from Africa, and is evidently divorced or separated from the father. Her mother indirectly goads Elaine into a crisis from which she has not recovered at the conclusion of the story.

In "The Middle of Everything" Jack's mother, who committed suicide years ago, is only a painful memory for him, but his grandmother is still very much alive and part of his life, possibly the only real part left. As the title suggests, Jack is between lives, wives, homes, and realities. His grandmother, Enid Winns Carter, like the grandmother in "Excerpts from Swan Lake," is confused but unconcerned about it, while Jack worries about his upcoming art show, his divorced wife, his twin daughters, and his relationship to his girlfriend, Langley. Some of the situations in this story resemble those in *Leap Year:* the art gallery, the Los Angeles movie scene, the children of a failed marriage, the extended family more fully developed than in some of his earlier stories. In New York for a showing of his paintings—he muses that his paintings "always looked inexplicably different and invariably worse in New York"—he seems to be an artist of some repute, but not much is said about his work except that his grandmother does not like it.

At the end of the story Jack returns to an old family haunt, a beach house, a scene that Cameron sketches with more detail than usual. He goes there to paint a picture for his grandmother, to utilize his art to create a connection to the past instead of wasting it on narcissistic self-expression. In this way he hopes that the painting will help him come to grips with the emotional dislocation of his life, his inability to connect with his former wife, his children, his new girlfriend, or even his art. The characters in "The Middle of Everything" are not middle-class dwellers in suburbia like those in the early stories but wealthy successful people, and adult neurosis has replaced teenage alienation as the central thematic concern. No longer drawing from his childhood in suburban New Jersey, Cameron finds subject matter in New York City—although, as he stated to Gambone, "I don't write autobiographically. I write from my imagination."

Two sets of interrelated stories make up the other sections of *Far-flung*. The emotional relationship between male lovers Tom and Charles is at the core of the first set, composed of the stories "Slowly" and "The Meeting and Greeting Area." Their relationship provides a backdrop for "Slowly," a touching tale of death and dreams. Tom relates a visit to his brother Ethan's widow, Jane. Sleep and dreams are recurring motifs in the story: Tom watches Jane's brother sleep while they sit in a car waiting for a ferry out to Jane's parents' island home, and during the course of the story both Jane and Tom observe each other sleeping. Tom introduced his brother to Jane, and he has come to the island as a surrogate for his departed brother to bid a belated farewell to his wife. Jane's emotional numbness and pain resonate with the feelings Tom is experiencing in his uncertain relationship with Charles.

"The Meeting and Greeting Area" explores more fully the relationship of Tom and Charles. The story is

Dust jacket for Cameron's 1991 collection, which includes two cycles of interrelated stories

set in an unidentified African country, not so much a real place as a state of mind, somewhat like the setting of Cameron's novel *Andorra* (1997). The narcissistic characters barely notice their surroundings because they are so wrapped up in themselves. One of the longer stories in the collection, it takes place at a later stage in the relationship of Charles and Tom, after the separation that was suggested at the conclusion of "Slowly." Tom arrives in Africa to visit Charles and possibly to resurrect their relationship but finds himself at the intersection of two complex triangles: one comprising him, Charles, and Albert; the other, Charles, Albert, and Albert's wife. Charles, the narrator of this story, deceives others and remains a mystery to himself. He tells Albert, his new lover, that he loves him but immediately qualifies the declaration: "I said this partially to disarm Albert and partially to see if it might be true. I couldn't tell."

Tom seems to be the eternal victim in his relationship with Charles, who in "Slowly" called him "wonderfully and pathetically naive." In "The Meeting and

Greeting Area" Tom is described as a virgin: "He is constantly losing some sort of virginity," remarks the jaded Charles. Charles reflects on the nature of love: "that is how you fall in love: by not being yourself, or being too much yourself or by letting go of yourself." In its formulaic delineation, this observation seems to illustrate the emptiness of Charles's heart, even when in love. The loss of feeling in the relationship is first seen from Tom's perspective in "Slowly" as he attempts to come to grips with their lack of connection. In the second story the viewpoint is Charles's, who seems to understand his own motivations as little as Tom does.

The final section of *Far-flung* is a trilogy of inter-related stories set in Indiana, which were part of an unpublished novel Cameron had written before *Leap Year*. Two of the stories were published in different magazines and one, "Everywhere and No Place," was not previously published. There is little overtly Midwestern about the characters in these stories, and little is made of the location specifically, except as a setting someplace in the middle of nowhere. "The Half You Don't Know" is pitch perfect in its depiction of the inner life of a confused, depressed, yet plucky and humorous octagenarian, Miss Alice Paul. The story begins: "Miss Alice Paul was in a quandary." Unsure of where she will live since her housemate, Rose, who owned the house, has died, Miss Alice Paul fears she may end up out on the street. She imposes herself on Rose's family, who have no idea what to do with her. The story is presented in a series of hilarious scenes; yet, the reader is always reminded, usually through Miss Alice Paul's tart, neurotic comments, of the desperation of her situation. She resists doing what she does not want to do, even if she has no choice. Unable to fend for herself, she is forced to rely on others; yet, she struggles for dignity and independence. Cameron transforms vulnerability into strength, making Miss Alice Paul a formidable and memorable woman.

Various younger members of Rose's family comprise the characters in the next two stories, "Everywhere and No Place" and "The Winter Bazaar." In "The Winter Bazaar" Topsy, a grandmother, becomes involved in a love affair with Walter Doyle. Topsy and Walter are ordinary people with deeper selves lurking just beneath the surface, unknown to everyone around them and to themselves. Walter is a bank president who stops by one afternoon to check on an abandoned house owned by his bank and finds himself taking a bath and nap there. When he awakes, he finds Topsy in the house, and they develop an attraction for each other. After a series of comic misunderstandings, they discover a mysterious empathy. They have known each other before, but only vaguely and in a distant past. Topsy, the narrator, remains unsure of herself, unable to

recall having loved her long deceased husband. Later, she muses that "you and all the things that could possibly happen in your life were floating in a pool the size of an ocean." As the reviewer for *Library Journal* noted, the "old, empty house becomes a symbol of the peace and contentment denied to two lovers"; but after the contents of the house have been removed for sale in the bazaar of the title, Topsy no longer has a pretense to come there and decides to end the affair. In the end she begins a long walk from the empty house back to her real life. The numbness and passivity of the characters are recurrent themes in the stories, but in this trilogy Topsy and Miss Alice Paul also show an inner strength and individuality in dealing with their emotionally disorienting situations.

The stories in *Far-flung* pick up where the first collection leaves off and continue to develop the themes of alienation and disconnectedness, most particularly with respect to teenage or young adult characters. The longer stories and sets of stories in *Far-flung* represent a step forward for Cameron in his progression from the short story, with its narrow focus and poetic terseness, into the larger world of the novel. The second collection is more varied in its treatments and themes, and he explores older characters and more complex relationships in more vivid detail.

"Departing" and "Aria" are the only stories in the 1997 collection *The Half You Don't Know* not to appear in either *One Way or Another* or *Far-flung*. "Departing" introduces characters who appear in *The Weekend*, Cameron's second novel, which was published in 1994. The basic kernel of the novel, a visit to John and Marian's estate in Upstate New York by family friend Lyle and his new lover, Robert, is included in the story, which has many of the important dramatic scenes of the novel. The gathering is to mark the anniversary of the passing of Tony, John's half brother and Lyle's former lover, who died of AIDS. Cameron wrote the story first; afterward, as he recalled in an unpublished interview in 1999, he was "intrigued by the characters, they stuck with me, and I decided to employ them in a novelistic way." The characters are wealthy, successful, well educated, and sophisticated, except for Robert, a young aspiring painter, who is unable to fit in. Scenes from the past with the deceased Tony are intermingled with the current narrative in the novel, and a neighbor, Laura (named Rosa in the story), who attends the dinner party at the climax of both the story and the novel is presented more fully, including details of her family life with her daughter. The novel concentrates on emotional relationships, memories, nuances of conversation, and deceptions, all of which culminate in a misunderstanding at the dinner party, and a break in the budding relationship of Lyle and Robert. Joyce Reiser Kornblatt, in *The New York Times Book Review* (29 May 1994), remarked that "human-centered suffering gives way to the larger reality in which it arises and ebbs, that beautiful and indifferent world where our dramas come and go like squalls." Kornblatt also identified echoes in the novel of British novelists such as Virginia Woolf and E. M. Forster. As Cameron acknowledged to Gambone, "I've been reading a lot of British women writers from the thirties and forties. For me the novel reached a pinnacle there. A lot of that influenced *The Weekend*."

The novel *Andorra* was generally hailed by critics as a daring and fascinating study of deception and delusion, representing a major advance for the writer. Ostensibly the story of Alexander Fox and his visit to the country of Andorra, the novel shifts in tone and perspective, until it ends up someplace entirely different from where it began. Critic Margot Livesey, writing in *The New York Times Book Review* (29 December 1996), remarked on Cameron's "carefully calibrated prose" and noted the humor in the novel, "now unmistakably harnessed to a darker purpose." Cameron's earlier short stories are set in a neutral, faceless, one-dimensional world defined by omission and the small details that occasionally crop up in the narrative. In *Andorra* he takes the tiny European country and reimagines its topography and history, only to use it as the setting for a larger deception.

Cameron gave up his position at the Lambda organization in 1998 and began working at Sarah Lawrence College in their graduate writing program. During the 1990s he also taught in the graduate writing program at Columbia University. In the July 1999 issue of the *Yale Review* he published "Accidents," an excerpt from a novel-in-progress. Cameron seems to have left behind the form of the short story for the novel. In 1997 he stated: "I haven't written very many stories in the last five or six years, since I started writing *The Weekend*. I'm not quite sure why I've stopped writing stories." Concerning his novelistic style, he declared that in his stories "the prose is simpler, it's not as lyrical," but that later, "as I started reading more and admiring denser prose, I began wanting to try to do that." The progression in his artistic career seems as much a function of style as a change or deepening in the creative vision.

Interview:

Philip Gambone, *Something Inside: Conversations with Gay Fiction Writers* (Madison: University of Wisconsin Press, 1999), pp. 284–300.

References:

Rosellen Brown, "The Emperor's New Fiction," *Boston Review,* August 1986, pp. 7–8;

David Leavitt, "New Voices and Old Values," *New York Times Book Review,* 12 May 1985, p. 1;

Myles Weber, "When a Risk Group Is Not a Risk Group: The Absence of AIDS Panic in Peter Cameron's Fiction," in *AIDS–The Literary Response,* edited by Emmanuel S. Nelson (New York: Twayne, 1992), pp. 69–75.

Elizabeth Cullinan

(7 June 1933 –)

Amy M. Lilly
University of Iowa

BOOKS: *House of Gold* (Boston: Houghton Mifflin, 1969; London: Faber & Faber, 1971);
The Time of Adam (Boston: Houghton Mifflin, 1971);
Yellow Roses (New York: Viking, 1977);
A Change of Scene (New York: Norton, 1982).

SELECTED PERIODICAL PUBLICATIONS–
UNCOLLECTED: "Idioms," *New Yorker,* 52 (31 January 1977): 31–35;
"A Good Loser," *New Yorker,* 53 (15 August 1977): 32–38;
"Echoes," *New Yorker,* 57 (15 June 1981): 38–45;
"Commuting," *Irish Literary Supplement,* 2, no. 1 (1983): 34–35;
"The Black Diamond," *Threshold,* 34 (Winter 1983–1984): 39–43;
"Pleasure," *Denver Quarterly,* 19 (Winter 1985): 50–57;
"The Promised Land," *Colorado Review,* 20 (Spring 1993): 148–164;
"In Passing," *Colorado Review,* 22 (Spring 1995): 130–142.

Elizabeth Cullinan's two short-story collections and two novels examine in detail the lives of Irish American Catholics in or from the New York City area, the nuances of their family and romantic relationships, and the place and meaning of the Church in their lives. Identifying herself primarily as Irish American, Cullinan has been grouped with Tom McHale, Jimmy Breslin, and Pete Hamill, but, as Eileen Kennedy points out in the *Biographical Dictionary of Contemporary Catholic American Writing* (1989), "no other writer of the Irish-American experience has probed it so closely, so aware of the tenacious network that binds together family and Church." Cullinan's first novel, *House of Gold* (1969), won the Houghton Mifflin Literary Fellowship Award, placing her in company with Elizabeth Bishop and Philip Roth. A second novel, *A Change of Scene* (1982), was funded by grants from the National Endowment of the Arts and the Carnegie Fund. Through her short stories, however,

Elizabeth Cullinan (photograph by Alen MacWeeney; from the dust jacket for The Time of Adam, *1971)*

which appeared regularly in *The New Yorker* magazine from 1960 on, Cullinan gained national acclaim.

Critical attention has centered on Cullinan's narrative style, which is controlled and objective with a fine awareness of and ability to render precisely the emotions experienced by her characters; *Commonweal* reviewer Richard Elman (22 January 1971) called her a "fastidious . . . dramatist of feeling and perception." As frequently noted is her careful attention to the crafting of the structure of a story, leading different critics to draw comparisons between her writing and that of James Joyce, Anton Chekhov, and Henry James. With a few exceptions her stories feature heroines who are tenacious rather than strong, "obstinate people with something to work out," as the author put it in an unpublished 1999 interview. What these small girls, teenagers, and women have to work out often involves negotiating a place for themselves in an environment fraught with expectations and disappointments. "Her first reverence is for the sacredness of individual personality," wrote *Saturday Review* critic Muriel Haynes in the 27 February 1971 issue; a second and comparable reverence is for the ties of devotion so ingrained in the Irish American Catholic middle class and so often a source of private conflict for her independent-minded characters. The ordinariness of their realistically portrayed world—sometimes spiritually drained, typically concerned with property and respectability—serves as the vehicle for extraordinarily nuanced insights into human relationships that transcend their parochial setting.

Cullinan describes her fiction as openly autobiographical, and much of her life can be traced in the development of her heroines, from Winnie Carroll, the quiet but boldly assertive teenager of *House of Gold,* to the fifty-year-old, calmly assured Celia Dorsey, who orchestrates her parents' final move in the 1995 story "In Passing." Born in the Bronx, New York, on 7 June 1933, Cullinan was the third daughter of Irene O'Connell and Cornelius Cullinan, both from Manhattan. Before meeting Irene, Neil Cullinan had studied to be a priest, a vocation common among both their families. He then earned a law degree but never practiced, working instead as an insurance investigator for most of his life; Irene gave piano lessons at her daughters' high school after they had graduated. Like Winnie Carroll's parents in *House of Gold,* Neil's weakness for betting on horses and Irene's close relationship with her mother resulted in the family's living upstairs in the matriarch's house for many years. Cullinan and her sisters, Margaret and Claire, like the sisters Celia and Georgia in "In Passing," "had, from an early age, to be serious, to put the needs of others ahead of their own desires."

Cullinan was soon to leave behind this small, closed world, as she describes her origins, though the move resulted in a conflict of loyalty that she admits was difficult. After graduating from Marymount Manhattan College in 1954, she worked as a typist at *The New Yorker,* where she became the secretary of the fiction editor, novelist William Maxwell. Cullinan learned what makes a short story successful through Maxwell's editorial comments to contributors, as well as through his novels, which she calls "extremely well-made and very complete." Ten of her own stories appeared in *The New Yorker* during the 1960s and were later collected in

The Time of Adam (1971), published two years after her first novel appeared. In a 1981 interview with Kennedy she commented that perhaps she had started to write because all her friends were getting married while she did not; the first collection of stories suggests that the motivation was more a need to assess the closed world of her upbringing from her new position as an independent woman and writer in literary New York.

The title story of *The Time of Adam,* dedicated to Maxwell, depicts the "primordial society" of ten Irish American families, interrelated, clannish, and middle-class, who spend their summers at the beach. This mock-anthropological study of a community of strict mothers and obedient but happy children, all biding their time until the Friday evening arrival of the fathers from the city, is also infused with the striking detail of personal memory: the children's respect for the "tender whiteness of their [the fathers'] hairy bodies"; the mothers' rule forbidding the children to cross the street, forcing them to "stare at each other over those macadam rivers, yelling messages that burst in the air." Halfway through the story humorous generality narrows to a specific memory of six-year-old Skippy Conklin, whose father and uncle arrive together one night with a Charlie McCarthy doll. After delighting Skippy and her older sister with the doll, they put it back in the box: they have neglected to tell the girls that it is meant for their five-year-old cousin Bobby. The point seems obvious to "the fathers," to whom boy dolls are meant for boys, but Skippy is sent to bed confused and upset, wondering, "What words did she miss—words that could have told her the doll was not for her?" In Cullinan's stories it is often not the words but the unspoken, subtle assumptions conveyed between lines of seemingly banal dialogue that finally prompt revelations within her characters and structure this well-mannered world.

The third story in the collection, "The Nightingale," features a similar young girl's relationship to the moral center of her world, her mother. Second-grader Annie Flood and her older sister, Sheila, are invited to Jean Tierney's birthday party, where Annie sings an enthusiastic rendition of "A Nightingale Sang in Berkeley Square." Annie has already noted the differences between the Tierneys' plush apartment and the Floods' own cramped rooms on the top floor of her grandmother's house. She is additionally aware of her own secondary role at the party, which is to keep Jean's younger sister company; consequently, her time in the spotlight infuriates Sheila, who abruptly drags her home before Annie can begin a new song. As she tells her mother what happened, Annie recalls the glint and warmth of the Tierneys' and her cumulative distress dissolves in her mother's comforting attention and

Dust jacket for Cullinan's first collection of stories, about Irish and Irish American family life

interest. Later, she is heard, to Mrs. Flood's surprise, bursting into song in the next room; her mother, in fact, enabled such courageous spontaneity by restoring in her a peaceful order, like the "pieces of that paisley landscape fitted together" on her apron. Cullinan admits that the story, insofar as it is a tribute to her own mother's love for her daughters, is unusual in the larger scope of her work; she describes her mother as "someone who gave herself entirely to her children, and that's a gift that's hard to receive gracefully," as her stories featuring older daughters demonstrate.

In her essay "Elizabeth Cullinan: Yellow and Gold" (1979) Maureen Murphy likens "The Nightingale" to James Joyce's "Clay," in which Maria's song, like Annie's, contrasts ironically with her life. The difference, however, as Murphy notes, is that Maria is unaware of the irony while Annie's choice of song is deliberate. Cullinan admits to a more conscious Joycean influence in "The Reunion," in which Edwina and

Xavier hold their annual dinner for a group of Xavier's old seminary friends, now successful priests. For Edwina it is a formal affair, a chance for her to entertain at a level she deems appropriate to the religious vocation; but for Xavier it is a reminder of his own lack of success, and he retreats to the kitchen by the end of the evening with the awareness that, in his wife's eyes, he is a comparative failure. Murphy points out that "the parallel with Joyce's Little Chandler in 'A Little Cloud' is obvious: for each man, the reunion is a reproach and a reminder of what he might have been . . . each realizes that the woman he changed his life to marry does not really respect him and that she copes while he only struggles." Murphy insists, however, that Cullinan is by no means a derivative writer, as does Kennedy, who identifies Joyce's influence on Cullinan as primarily one of formal experiment.

Roman Catholicism, a theme of at least five of the ten stories, receives a complex, objective treatment. Often, as in "The Reunion," it is seen as a social ladder or a boost to self-importance by characters whom Muriel Haynes dubbed "petit-Catholics" in her 27 February 1971 *Saturday Review* piece on *The Time of Adam*. In one of the most critically acclaimed stories in the collection, however, "The Ablutions," Catholicism is seen through a priest's eyes. Father Fox is blessed with a flair for befriending the wealthy of his parish, but during a routine lunch at the distinguished home of Isabel and Marcus Conroy he learns with horror that the Mass is little more than a spectacle to these lofty and patronizing friends. A few humorous touches at the beginning of the narration, such as Father Fox's "surge of confidence" in his ability to inspire large donations "that was also relief that God's will almost always corresponded to his own," are hints of the innocence he finally recognizes in himself as he silently concludes, outside the Conroys' door, the Ablutions prayer performed during Mass: "But as for me, I have walked in my innocence." Haynes writes incisively that Cullinan's "preoccupation is with the frailties that corrode the virtues of the Catholic truth, the total of those venial sins that betray its grace: self-righteousness, snobbery, passivity, the substitution of ritual and habit for engagement with life."

Two more stories, "The Power of Prayer" and "The Old Priest," address the relationship of a young woman to her Catholic background. In "The Power of Prayer" fourteen-year-old Aileen Driscoll's father has provoked a silent family tension by habitually coming home drunk from the horse races, if he comes home at all. At school on her mother's birthday, Aileen prays for him to return, partly out of obedience to her Latin teacher, a nun who requires her to say a rosary for a minor offense. The inability of the nun to relate to the girls she teaches as individuals is mirrored by Aileen's inability to identify with nuns in general, and their mutual misunderstanding suggests a lack of courage on either side to break roles and engage truthfully with each other. Aileen's prayers are finally answered, but ironically: her father returns sober but too late for a birthday celebration and without remorse for having missed it. Less structurally successful than the other stories and rarely mentioned by critics, "The Power of Prayer" is drawn from Cullinan's own parochial education, administered entirely by nuns from grammar school through her years at Marymount.

Three stories in *The Time of Adam,* "A Sunday Like the Others," "A Swim," and "Maura's Friends," are set in Ireland and based on Cullinan's experiences there. In 1960, after five years at *The New Yorker,* she moved to Dublin for three years. Though her father's parents and mother's grandparents had emigrated from Ireland, her family had not maintained ties with the country and were perplexed at her choice. For Cullinan it was a step of independence, a chance to "establish a context for myself," as she recalled in 1999. While in Ireland, she completed her first novel, an extended study of the church-family network first explored in the story "The Voices of the Dead" (appearing in the second collection), and her second novel, *A Change of Scene,* is set there. Through a letter of introduction from a *New Yorker* editor, she got to know the Irish short-story writer Mary Lavin, to whose writing Cullinan's has been compared. Cullinan describes Lavin as "a wonderful, generous person" whose influence on her own writing came as much from her character as from her art: Lavin inspired Maura in "Maura's Friends," who also evokes Mrs. Ramsay from Virginia Woolf's *To the Lighthouse* (1927), and Oona, the lively and helpful widowed mother in *A Change of Scene.* In general "the Irish are a critical people–which is one of their great virtues," Cullinan said in 1999. The stories set in Ireland tend to reveal criticism on both sides, an awareness of subtle cultural differences raised by the question of Irish American identity in an Irish, rather than New York, context.

In his review of the collection in the 22 January 1971 issue of *Commonweal* Richard Elman concentrated on the characters' frustrated sexuality, an aspect that also prompted Joyce Carol Oates, in *The New York Times Book Review* (7 February 1971), to ask: "What are we to make of such an assemblage of bloodless people?" In "*Le Petit Déjeuner*" the cause of this frustrated sexuality is as much the tension between a mother's expectations and a daughter's wish to find her own place as it is Catholicism: twenty-year-old Nora Barrett watches a suggestive dance number on television on a Sunday morning before Mass, appalling her mother and spurring Nora to defend herself in the name of aestheticism

and objectivity. She finds that the immense burden of loyalty is too much, however: attitude alone "would never get her through all that was expected of her." In one of the three Ireland stories, "A Sunday Like the Others," Frances has to turn off a Mozart recording because the overly structured music reminds her of the "order, balance, discipline, attention to details, devotion to duty" that characterize the monotonous, oppressed life she wants to leave behind but has only found again in her relationship with Irishman Michael Callan. Muriel Haynes named "A Sunday Like the Others" and "A Swim" as studies not simply of repressed sexuality but of "bad faith," where "disappointment, that state of muffled being, a retreat from humility and the courage essential to authentic love," is the real issue.

Many of the themes and some of the characters of *The Time of Adam* are carried over into the twelve stories of *Yellow Roses* (1977), all but two of which were first published in *The New Yorker.* Murphy identifies the chief development between the two collections to lie in Cullinan's "ability to extract greater meaning from experience and in the increased power of her emotionally precise prose." The most consistent theme of the collection is the complex demands of love between men and women, parents and children. The heroines are more self-assured and less elliptical about their desires: Nora Barrett, reappearing here in "The Perfect Crime," comments aphoristically that "the nature of anyone's desire, the image of its satisfaction, was the essence of that person," and surgery patient Ellen MacGuire in "The Sum and Substance" is forced to realize that the fragility of the body overwhelmingly defines a person's existence.

In the opening story, "Estelle," one of three written in the first person, Margaret Fisher quietly assesses the character of her romantic relationships: each was not really love but "a kind of grudging attachment," a description that sums up the nature of the relationships in the stories of the previous collection, particularly "A Sunday Like the Others" and "A Swim." Love, as this narrator defines it, requires something she does not have: confidence in one's authority to lay claim to another person–to, in effect, own them. Like Cullinan herself in the realm of her art, Margaret "invariably see[s] both sides of the situation, which is fatal in love, where to admit the other's doubts is to set that person free."

A trio of stories featuring Louise Gallagher and her affair with a married man, Charlie Davis, further explore the interlocking but incompatible elements of love and ownership and the struggle between devotion and independence that Cullinan's work chronicles in so many different ways. In the title story of the collection yellow roses are Charlie's offering of gratitude to his lover. A momentary sense of the disproportion between the stunning effect of the flowers and the necessarily inconclusive relationship they represent causes Louise to throw them in the garbage, then retrieve them with the realization that the people close to you "weren't really at your disposal, because the truth was they not only belonged to you but you belonged to them." When it dawns on her that yellow roses mean eternal devotion, her laughter expresses both pleasure at having found what she was looking for in love and the pain of recognizing that it has happened under the wrong circumstances: Charlie, with his Anglo-Saxon background, will never divorce his wife to marry a Roman Catholic.

In the next story, "The Accident," the art of loving casually that Louise has learned from her first painful experience with Charlie (who married a woman with a talent for fierce ownership instead) is an equal source of pain for her. The range of their regrets and affections is conveyed in a realistic, intelligent, and often witty running dialogue. The relationship comes to an end in "A Foregone Conclusion" when Louise returns the heirloom ring Charlie gives her over lunch by slipping it into his pocket as they leave the restaurant. Like the yellow roses, the gift is not suitable to the nature of their relationship, but when Charlie finds it and assumes it is her final goodbye, Louise is "surprised to discover that her gesture, like the ring itself, had a meaning of its own, a meaning she now recognized as a foregone conclusion." In another twist, even the breakup is an accident—but one that was inevitable anyway. In all three of these stories circumstance and will become inseparable: while Louise's character points to the immense courage needed to overcome a state of passive acceptance and self-protectiveness, patterns of circumstance (such as the fact of Charlie's marriage) and conventions of behavior (such as Charlie's objection to Louise's religion) seem inevitably to preclude that possibility.

Cullinan occasionally uses paintings as ironic counterpoints in her stories, as in the earlier "*Le Petit Déjeuner*," in which the easy charm of the eponymous painting by Claude Monet stands in Nora Barrett's mind as the impossible Platonic idea of family happiness. In one of the most critically acclaimed stories in *Yellow Roses,* "The Perfect Crime," three instances of incongruity are seen in succession through Nora's painterly eyes. On a ferry from the city to her parents' modest island summer home she spots a mysterious woman in black looking oddly out of place in her environment, reminding Nora of early Renaissance paintings of the Madonna in contemporary settings; later, the woman is revealed to be a cleaning lady for the island community. When Nora learns from her mother that a small boy she befriended last summer

has since died of cancer, her shock comes from another sense of disparity between perception and reality. Little Andrew seemed to Nora to have been almost saintly, the embodiment of a noble future, making his death completely incompatible with her image of him. When her musings ultimately shift to the uncanny resemblance between Mr. Ascappo, who installs the island's gas tanks, and Pablo Picasso, the series of revelations coalesces: these surprises, good and bad, are the clues to the "spirit" at whose mercy humanity lives, the spirit of life itself. The implications of the Louise Gallagher stories are here expanded to a much broader compass: human beings are artists of their own lives up to a point, at which they realize that fate is the more brilliant, and more clever, artist.

"Usually," wrote Jane Larkin Crain in her review of *Yellow Roses* in *The New York Times Book Review* (17 April 1977), "it is family and religion that both sustain and oppress those who struggle with this 'spirit.'" Angela Ganley's relationship with her father in "In the Summerhouse" recalls Aileen Driscoll and her father in "The Power of Prayer." To the serious and self-aware Angela, "love is a discipline" that Mr. Ganley, now in the sanatorium for gambling, has been unable to give his twenty-six-year-old daughter. Having given her savings to make up for his mistakes, Angela reflects that her self-sacrifice was as much a choice as an inescapable obligation—another entwining of will and fate—and a relief as well from the obligation to be happy. Cullinan's reflections on family life are not all as serious as Angela's, however. "The Voices of the Dead" involves another family scene told in a tone more inclined to acknowledge the rare moments of family bonding. The aging matriarch, Mrs. Nugent, has summoned her extended family to her house for Easter Mass, with her son Father Clem as the celebrant and the television set as the altar. Alternately falling asleep and interrupting Father Clem to ask what point has been reached or to assign her meager belongings to different offspring, Mrs. Nugent cuts off the end of the Mass, demanding that all join her in singing an Irish love song. The kind of humorous grace that descends on the family at the end of the story, in spite of all, serves to affirm what Kennedy, in her essay "Bequeathing Tokens: Elizabeth Cullinan's Irish-Americans," identifies as "the real church" of Cullinan's fictional world, more demanding than the institutional one but also more spiritually and morally inflected.

If "The Voices of the Dead" ends on a note of farewell to the spirit of an earlier Catholic generation, "Only Human" addresses the difficulties of adjusting to a Church undergoing radical transformation. The historical changes wrought in the 1960s by the Second Vatican Council on the Catholic Church underpin this

Dust jacket for Cullinan's 1977 collection, featuring a trilogy of stories about an adulterous affair

story of a wake in memory of Father James Murray—a Jesuit version of Father Clem—narrated by his niece, Marjorie Cunningham. Recently divorced and trying to find a way to recover and move on emotionally, Marjorie observes with dissatisfaction how, while she had been absorbed in her three-year marriage to a non-Catholic, the Church had traded in its "mystery" for an ethic of casualness: the nuns at the wake wear hair spray and homemade habits, the priests have become independent-minded, and the whole Cunningham family is invited to eat with the priests in their dining hall, once open to clergy only. Marjorie is aware that she mourns exactly this aspect of the Church—its mystery and discipline, its ideal of absolute sacrifice, that had first attracted her former husband to her and then gradually reduced her, in his eyes, from an individual to an abstract set of traits. Yet, Marjorie herself has an investment in seeing the Church as occupying a separate realm from the human, since it allows her, as one of the Jesuit priests tells her bluntly, to remain indifferent, passive, and alone—the opposite, she comes to realize, of her dead uncle, who, toward the end of his life, accepted the changes in the Church and dedicated himself even more fully to caring for others. Only when she is brought to stand, physically, in the priests' site of

authority—by an enthusiastic Brother Desnoes, eager to show her the place where her uncle's funeral mass will be celebrated—is she able to come to terms with the great shift within the Church and thereby see her way to a new emotional stability. Marjorie follows Brother Desnoes out onto the altar with its room-size Oriental carpet, and the mystery suddenly falls away as it strikes her that "the place where the rows of pews were and the sanctuary where she was standing seemed to be the same size, though when you were down in the pews the altar seemed so small and such a long way off." The leaders of Church are, she realizes, only human.

"Only Human" also implicitly reassesses the role of family through Marjorie's meditative narration. Her mantra—that family is "what the truth about everyone can be traced to"—voices one of Cullinan's central preoccupations: hence her frequent use of extended passages recounting the narrator's or heroine's family background, often sparked by single lines of dialogue. "Only Human" recognizes the possibility of achieving an individuality that is not accounted for by family background, however. Marjorie may be able to explain her uncle's original choice of the priesthood by way of his position as a middle child in a large family and his desire to please a domineeringly religious mother, but by the end of the story she realizes that her uncle's dedication to his vocation had transcended a psychological commitment to family to become something both human and holy. Cullinan finds an image to embody this paradox as striking as Mr. Ascappo's resemblance to Picasso in "The Perfect Crime": the image of Father Jim as Marjorie last saw him before he died, ensconced in an oxygen tent that hooded him like a monk or priestly ascetic, and yet looking "very much a man—a man besieged by the infection in his body."

What Marjorie at first begrudgingly admits as "only human"—an excuse necessitated by her focus on Father Jim's repressed sexuality—she finally acknowledges is "essentially human" because of the "pure and simple" fact of his death. In the story that follows, "Life after Death," the narrator, Constance, sounds the same note of reflective reconciliation: "I'm half convinced that time is on our side, that nothing is ever lost, that we need only have a little more faith, we need only believe a little more and the endings will be happy," she observes about three-quarters of the way through the story. "Life after Death" is Constance's imaginary headline for a spread of mental photographs of the Kennedy sisters after President John Kennedy's death that she takes each time she passes them walking through her New York neighborhood. In its figurative sense the title phrase comes to encompass a philosophy of life for Constance: the story is constructed of a series of her reflections on the difficulties in her own past and on her sense not necessarily of having moved beyond them but of seeing the possibility of their coherence—as one might see the coherence of past history. Indeed, ancient history, Constance's newfound interest, merges with the "Death" of the title, and she sees that the varied human life around her—the young Ethiopian office worker named Yeshi, the Mediterranean flower sellers at the corner of Sixty-eighth and Lexington—recalls and continues the life that has already cohered into a static picture in the history books. Although some readers might question the narrator's readiness to aestheticize history and deem its "labor and sacrifice" as "necessary or at least inevitable," the final passage of the story, inspired perhaps by John Keats's 1819 poem "Ode on a Grecian Urn" (though without his burden of regret), recalls in its cadence Joyce's closing of "The Dead":

Yesterday's headlines told of trouble in the Middle East—Israel of the two kingdoms, Israel and Judah; Iran that was Alexander's Persia; Egypt of the Pharaohs and the Ptolemies. I love those ancient peoples. I know them. They form a frieze, a band of images carved in thought across my mind—emperors, princesses, slaves, scribes, farmers, soldiers, musicians, priests. I see them hunting, harvesting, dancing, embracing, fighting, eating, praying. The attitudes are all familiar. The figures are noble and beautiful and still.

In 1978, a year after the publication of *Yellow Roses,* Cullinan began a career in teaching with a semester at the University of Iowa and two more at the University of Massachusetts. She then taught for eighteen years at Fordham University in Manhattan. When asked what aspect of writing she promoted most in her classes, she responded, simply, "structure." Throughout the 1990s she continued to contribute stories to *The New Yorker* and other magazines and worked on another novel.

Following the publication of *Yellow Roses,* Murphy predicted that Cullinan would probably not oblige those reviewers who looked forward to the author's widening the scope of her fiction: "What she is likely to do is to continue to focus on the clearly defined landscapes in her own life and, in a modest sense, to forge the conscience of a hybrid race." The prediction has been accurate, and Cullinan's uncollected stories address familiar themes, particularly "the stubborn wish to be what you were as well as what you are," in Cullinan's own words, describing both her heroines and herself. Indeed, her achievement is to have been consistently vertical in her vision, to have claimed as her exclusive territory an Irish American Catholic world that strikes chords of recognition in many readers, and to have probed thoroughly its tensions and demands, its ironic humor, and its unexpected redemptions.

References:

Eileen Kennedy, "Bequeathing Tokens: Elizabeth Cullinan's Irish-Americans," *Eire-Ireland,* 16, no. 4 (1981): 94–102;

Maureen Murphy, "Elizabeth Cullinan: Yellow and Gold," in *Irish-American Fiction: Essays in Criticism,* edited by Daniel J. Casey and Robert E. Rhodes (New York: AMS, 1979), pp. 139–151.

Nicholas Delbanco

(27 August 1942 –)

Gregory L. Morris
Pennsylvania State University at Erie, Behrend College

BOOKS: *The Martlet's Tale* (Philadelphia: Lippincott, 1966; London: Gollancz, 1966);

Grasse, 3/23/66 (Philadelphia: Lippincott, 1968);

Consider Sappho Burning (New York: Morrow, 1969);

News (New York: Morrow, 1970);

In the Middle Distance (New York: Morrow, 1971);

Fathering (New York: Morrow, 1973);

Small Rain (New York: Morrow, 1975);

Possession (New York: Morrow, 1977);

Sherbrookes (New York: Morrow, 1978);

Stillness (New York: Morrow, 1980);

Group Portrait: Joseph Conrad, Stephen Crane, Ford Madox Ford, Henry James, and H. G. Wells (New York: Morrow, 1982; London: Faber & Faber, 1982);

About My Table and Other Stories (New York: Morrow, 1983);

The Beaux Arts Trio (New York: Morrow, 1985; London: Gollancz, 1985);

Running in Place: Scenes from the South of France (New York: Atlantic Monthly, 1989);

The Writers' Trade and Other Stories (New York: Morrow, 1990);

In the Name of Mercy (New York: Warner, 1995);

Old Scores (New York: Warner, 1997);

The Lost Suitcase: Reflections on the Literary Life (New York: Columbia University Press, 2000);

What Remains (New York: Warner, 2000).

OTHER: John Gardner, *Stillness and Shadows*, edited, with an introduction, by Delbanco (New York: Knopf, 1986; London: Secker & Warburg, 1987);

Speaking of Writing: Selected Hopwood Lectures, edited, with an introduction, by Delbanco (Ann Arbor: University of Michigan Press, 1990);

Writers and Their Craft: Short Stories and Essays on the Narrative, edited by Delbanco and Laurence Goldstein (Detroit: Wayne State University Press, 1991);

Talking Horse: Bernard Malamud on Life and Work, edited by Delbanco and Alan Cheuse (New York: Columbia University Press, 1996);

The Writing Life: Hopwood Lectures, Fifth Series, edited, with an introduction, by Delbanco (Ann Arbor: University of Michigan Press, 2000).

Nicholas Delbanco, best known for his novels, enjoys a reputation for being a writer's writer. As this designation indicates, Delbanco concerns himself most intensely with the craft of writing fiction; he is a writer who seriously and consciously labors over the sound and structure of his work, who insists just as emphatically upon the practice as upon the gift of art. While this sense of craftsmanship is apparent in Delbanco's novels, it is particularly and dramatically present in his short stories, where compression and concision draw the reader's attention to the author's artfulness.

Delbanco's stylistic rigor and precision have a certain Old World quality, as befits his familial history. Both his parents came from families of substance. His mother's family were bankers in Berlin; his father's family were in the import-export business, and the Delbanco name could be traced to Venice, where the Delbancos were bankers and moneylenders. Both Delbanco's father, Kurt, and his mother, Barbara, were German-born and Jewish and lived in Berlin until Adolf Hitler's rise to power. They fled Germany separately for England, where they married in 1938.

Nicholas Franklin Delbanco was born in London on 27 August 1942. He lived in England until 1948, when the family immigrated to the United States and settled in Larchmont, New York. As a youngster Delbanco attended Fieldston School and acquired both an intellectual and a social education that distinguished him at an early age. In 1959 Delbanco entered Harvard University, studying literature and eventually graduating magna cum laude in 1963. Two events of especial note occurred while Delbanco was at Harvard: in the summer of 1960 he met and fell in love with singer and songwriter Carly Simon, with whom he enjoyed a sustained relationship and to whom he dedicated his first novel, *The Martlet's Tale,* published in 1966. (Simon is also featured on the cover of his 1968 novel, *Grasse,*

Nicholas Delbanco (photograph by Stephen Rose)

3/23/66.) Also, in the summer of 1962 Delbanco attended a fiction workshop at Harvard taught by novelist John Updike, who influenced Delbanco in his writing of *The Martlet's Tale*.

From Harvard, Delbanco proceeded to Columbia University and graduate study in international relations; while at Columbia he was awarded a Woodrow Wilson Fellowship. Eventually, however, he wrote his master's thesis in English and comparative literature and graduated with his M.A. in 1966. That same year, while still a student at Columbia, Delbanco published his first novel at age twenty-three, enjoying the kind of youthful success that later informed many of his short stories. Also in 1966 Delbanco took a position on the literature faculty of Bennington College, temporarily replacing Bernard Malamud while he was on sabbatical; Delbanco ended up staying at Bennington for nearly the next twenty years.

On 12 December 1970 Delbanco married Elena Greenhouse, whose father, Bernard Greenhouse, was the founding cellist of the Beaux Arts Trio. From that marriage has come two daughters: Francesca Barbara, born in 1974 (whose middle name came from her pater-

nal grandmother, who died before Francesca's birth the same year), and Andrea Katherine, born in 1978. Throughout the decades of the 1970s and 1980s Delbanco contributed to the growth of the writing program at Bennington; in 1977, with novelist and close friend John Gardner he initiated the Bennington Writing Workshop, and in 1983 he was named director of the M.F.A. program in writing. Despite his long association with Bennington—in *Contemporary Authors Autobiography Series* he referred to it as "the locus of his adult life"—Delbanco eventually made the decision to leave the school and to resettle, in 1985, with his family in Ann Arbor, Michigan. He has since directed the M.F.A. program in creative writing at the University of Michigan.

Delbanco has turned to the short story in his career somewhat as a diversion. In his autobiographical sketch in *Contemporary Authors Autobiography Series* he writes that the 1983 collection, *About My Table and Other Stories,* "takes as its topic the domestic life." The domestic realm, with its sense of family and of generational connection—or disconnection—centers the first story in the collection, "What You Carry." Kenneth Perrera is a man especially "family-proud," born (like Delbanco) into distinguished Italian and German lineages. Particularly important in Perrera's world is his mother, Elizabeth, who exerts a beneficent maternal and imaginative power over her son. When Elizabeth suffers a first heart attack and lies recuperating in a hospital, she asks her recently married son to give her a grandchild before she dies; Kenneth, pressed by her desire, urgently engenders a child with his wife, Susan.

The birth comes too late, however. Perrera's mother dies after a second attack; the baby is born—a girl, named Elizabeth after her grandmother, who grows into a precocious child. Perrera finds himself increasingly concerned with her knowledge of her past—her Jewish heritage, her familial history, and the life of her namesake. Now a parent, Perrera wants his daughter to understand "how the past pertains"; he wants his child to establish a belated but necessary connection with the woman who now can only be part of a story, captured in memories, words, and photographs.

The images that most dominate Robert Lewin's mind in "The Consolation of Philosophy" are those inflected with desire. Like many of Delbanco's protagonists, Lewin is a middle-aged man among women—wives, daughters, lovers, and particularly in Lewin's case, former lovers. Situated in an uneasy marriage, the father of an adolescent daughter, Lewin finds himself veering more and more into dreams "of escape." More specifically, Lewin—an architect—spends his imaginative capital constructing an alternative life, a what-might-have-been existence with his first lover, Sally, an actress. Much of the story consists of Lewin's constructions, interspersed with recollections of actual history from the relationship. Suspecting his wife's infidelity, he imagines another kind of relationship for himself, one that liberates him through the possibilities of change. Yet, the power and responsibility of being a father pull Lewin back into the familiar orbit of family. Afflicted with conflicting desires, he must reconcile his several masculine roles.

The main character in the third story in this collection, "The Executor," also wrestles with problems of the past, in the form of the papers of an artist and long-time family friend and dependent, Jason Simpson. Edward is a recently divorced, thirty-five-year-old museum curator, a man whose lack of imaginative vision led him finally to deal in art rather than to create it. As he pores over Simpson's letters, he pores also over his common past with Simpson and his wife and recalls the lessons taught him by the artist: lessons in sight, perception, and invention. Edward comes to worry over his own "translucence" and lack of substance. Like other Delbanco protagonists, Edward must learn to practice the patient arts of appreciation and valuation.

Thus, his decision to abandon Simpson's papers to the elements is an authentic act of imaginative art.

In "Traction" Alexander Cullinan is another father of daughters who finds himself having to deal with a family crisis. His youngest daughter, Gillian, undergoes surgery to correct a severely dislocated hip, and in recovering she must spend extended time in a cast and in traction. Cullinan and his wife, an alcoholic, struggle with each other and with their helplessness as parents to eliminate or assuage their daughter's suffering. A lawyer, Cullinan is stranded in the Midwest by bad weather during a business trip, and the rest of the story follows his slow progress in returning to his home and family. The competing impulses of motion and stasis, mobility and immobility provide the story with its central motif.

Separation and distance also inform Delbanco's "Ostinato," in which the central character—a concert pianist named Richard Bentham—travels to avoid the tensions of his marriage and of the past, particularly his relationship with Mishiko, a young Japanese woman who several years previously had been brought into the Bentham household as a housekeeper and who eventually became Richard's mistress. When Mishiko attempts by letter to reestablish contact with the Benthams, the pain and "nastiness" of Richard's marriage to Helen is exacerbated. While on a concert tour of Canada, Richard meets Mishiko and her new boyfriend; although they do not rekindle their relationship, Mishiko sends an insinuating letter to Helen. Richard and Helen begin the halting process of resolving the tensions between them, but Mishiko is given the last word, declaring her happiness in a third letter and hinting at a possible re-entry into the Benthams' world.

Where Richard Bentham travels northward, George Allison in "Marching through Georgia" journeys south. Allison, a thirty-eight-year-old history professor at Skidmore College, makes a professional pilgrimage to Georgia and Louisiana to lecture on his specialty—the American Civil War. Though he "liked travel," Allison feels all the time his alienness: the Northern academic carpetbagger claiming to know the history of a place though ignorant of the place itself. Allison acknowledges his inauthenticity: "He was a fake."

Allison receives word of an auto accident involving his students, one of whom is especially close to him. When he returns home he visits the girl in the hospital, and her openness leads him to feel a strange mixture of parental and sexual love for her, a desire to "eradicate distance." On the way home from the hospital, while reflecting on his role as a father to two daughters, Allison himself is involved in a traffic accident. The shock

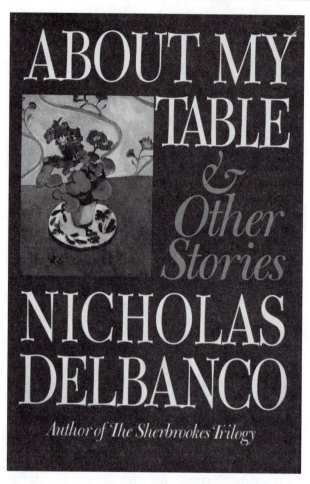

Dust jacket for Delbanco's 1983 collection of stories about domestic life and generational relationships

brings Allison up short and recalls to him the lessons of mortality.

A similar motif of passage shapes Delbanco's story "Some in Their Body's Force," in which Peter Danto wrestles with assorted images of travel and travail. Ensconced in domestic life, Danto maintains his present life while casting back sporadically into the narrative of his masculine past. As Danto notes near the end of his story: "He had been a ladies' man and now was a family man." The narrative of that present life focuses particularly on Danto's teenaged daughter Lucinda, who is emerging into young womanhood, into sexual being. It is an emergence with which Danto is especially nervous, for he recalls his own encounters with women. One of the accomplishments of this story is the way in which Delbanco delineates the several images of women from Danto's past; in recalling these women—most, but not all, of them former lovers—he examines the several stages of womanhood and considers the likely course his own daughter's experience will take. Danto knows the impressive "force" of the body

and its long arc of memory: "The memory of sex, he thought, can be as powerful as its expectation."

With "Northiam Hall," Delbanco suggests the direction of the stories in his second collection, *The Writers' Trade and Other Stories* (1990). The protagonist, Martin Rother, is a thirty-nine-year-old writer, though one who writes books about other writers' books. Rother is moderately successful but alone and perplexed by the trajectory of his life; he has lost, he senses, his "sense of urgency." When he is offered the chance to write a biography of the American expatriate poet Harold Emmett, a Stephen Crane-like figure, Rother takes up the task, leaving for England in "quest of an elusive character." At the same time, he seeks answers to his own dilemma.

In England, Rother finds the burned-out ruin of Emmett's onetime home, Northiam Hall, and a sense of Emmett's temporariness in this place. He also visits the house in which Emmett died, now inhabited by the poet's granddaughter, who labors to maintain his memory. Paintings of the poet hang on the walls; his hairbrush—with his supposed hairs—lies undisturbed on the dresser. The evidences of his life are meager and of limited meaning. Rother discovers that Emmet was not known well, even by his daughter and his granddaughter, and is "better left alone."

A similar gloominess hangs over the final story of the collection, "About My Table," a story—in its tone and its focus—appropriately dedicated to the memory of John Gardner, Delbanco's close friend and colleague, who died in 1982. The central character is a thirty-eight-year-old journalist, Daniel, who finds himself besieged by death in his daily round of domestic and professional life. Within the span of one week three of his acquaintances are struck down suddenly. At the same time, Daniel and his wife celebrate the fourth birthday of their daughter, a ritual that competes with the series of funerals. The birthday party affirms Daniel's place in his domestic universe, while it reminds him also of the instability and impermanence of youth. In the end he realizes that his response to the deaths illuminates his own self-absorption and acknowledges that marriage and family are the only stays against accident and loss.

With the stories in Delbanco's second collection, *The Writers' Trade and Other Stories,* Delbanco thematizes his vocation even more strongly. All nine stories in this collection feature writer-protagonists and, together, furnish a biography of the writing self, describing and examining the stages in a writer's development. The writers in these stories are likely to have been plagued by early success, evoking Delbanco's own experience of being published young and to moderate critical acclaim. Many of the elements in these stories hint of autobiography; for example, the details of Delbanco's own first novel, *The Martlet's Tale*—the cover art, the story and its conception, and the author's photograph—all make their way directly into the fictional fabric of the stories.

Certainly, the doubts Mark Fusco acknowledges in "The Writers' Trade" are doubts familiar to Delbanco. Having "sold his novel when he was twenty-two," Fusco finds himself initiated into the life of the prematurely successful writer and ensnared by the attractive rituals of acclaim and publicity: publication parties, praiseful reviews, lunches with editors, and renewed sexual connections with the former lover of a good friend. At the same time, the novice craftsman struggles with his craft. When a fatal train accident interrupts the rich flow of Fusco's life, the delicate artifices of his writing seem suddenly inconsequential in the face of a tragic reality.

Delbanco's study of the apprentice process continues in the next story, "And with Advantages," the protagonist of which is Ben, a twenty-six-year-old, once-published novelist. Having achieved some recognition for that first novel, Ben is now at work on his second, a fictive autobiography—a detail that evokes Delbanco's own fictive autobiography, *In the Middle Distance* (1971). He is confident in his youth, looking to "supplant" the old men who precede him in the writers' trade. Yet, precocity seems to carry with it an inherent paradox: the need for validation by an older voice, the very voice the young writer seeks to supplant.

The opportunity for such validation presents itself when Ben takes a job as caretaker for Slote, an older, well-known and well-established writer. In his seventy-seven years Slote has accumulated, it seems to Ben, the kinds of critical and experiential weight that lend the writer's life ratification. Slote's younger wife, Gretchen, complicates matters for Ben, as does Ben's lover, Jane, who was also involved with Slote. When Slote suddenly dies, Ben emerges confused and disillusioned from the experience of his apprenticeship. What he has learned from this particular "Master" remains unclear.

The third story in this collection, "You Can Use My Name," veers slightly from a concern with the writer as early success to look more closely at a writer in crisis. The story provides a history, both of the individual writer and of the relationship among writers. Adam Frieberg, a thirtyish writer, discovers himself "adrift"—unpublished, unconfident, unconnected; his writing, he laments, is "unearned." Frieberg's failure stands in stark contrast to the meteoric, glitzy success of his longtime friend, Richard, who has entered the world of the best-selling novelist, replete with Hollywood deals, designer drugs, and empty-hearted relationships. Adam and Richard's friendship dates back to their

graduate days in the Iowa Writers' Workshop and their triangular relationship with another writer, Marian.

One of Delbanco's clear concerns in this story is with the often troubled variations played upon the writerly friendship as these three figures move through the courses of their lives. Adam passes through two brief, beleaguered marriages and enters upon a period of pilgrimage and "rootlessness," indulging himself in a "traveler's oblivion." Richard begins to collapse and calls upon Adam to take over his life. Marian also finds herself back in Adam's world, though he seems to desire escape from that connection. Disconnection, in fact, seems to be the guiding motif of this story, as Adam struggles with keeping his past at bay even as he works to quicken his own present life as a writer.

A similar labor is performed by the protagonist of "His Masquerade"—a poet and professor, Clint, who feels, near middle age, the loss of his once "large ambition." He is a writer in search of a story, looking for "something to write for. About." He is also trying to maintain a marriage; like so many of Delbanco's male protagonists, Clint finds the mechanics of marriage difficult and seems subtly out of rhythm with his wife, Kathryn.

When his campus and home are visited by another poet, Samuel Tench Hazeltine, Clint is cast into the role of "acolyte"; Hazeltine comes avowing his admiration for Clint's work and declaring his intent to "save" and instruct him: "I'm here to teach you everything you don't already know." Hazeltine is another model of the successful writer, who has become wrapped up in his own reputation and has lost his compelling vision and voice. Repeatedly in this collection Delbanco's writers agonize over the problem of fraudulence and the loss of imaginative vitality. In the end Clint recovers some of his vitality within the arms of his wife and in the energizing, affirming physical act of love.

Delbanco's writers are, in fact, haunted by this consciousness of the fraudulent self, of the impersonating voice. David Lewin, in the longest, most fully developed story of the collection, "The Day's Catch," contemplates the variety of voice and the implications of its failure. The first part details the life of the young writer—David Lewin at twenty-two—and his early attempts at constructing stories: "He believed, that season, in a return to ancient techniques. He wrote fables, parables." This first part also recalls David's early history with his lover, Alice, the woman who eventually becomes his wife. Indeed, part 1 of "The Day's Catch" consists mostly of Alice's history: her life, her family, and her coming-of-age in the pressurized times of the 1960s. Familiarly for Delbanco's readers, David and

⑨

Hair sprouted from his nostrils also; capillaries marked the delta of his cheeks.

men
One night he stayed for dinner with three men. They were old and honored, long-time friends: a
painter, a theatrical producer and a judge. The painter kept an unlit pipe clamped between his
teeth; he had thick tufts of hair in his ears. The theatrical producer wore a turtleneck and
tweeds, the judge a leisure suit. Slote stammered; the others seemed deaf. There was Boccherini
in the background, or perhaps the wine was strong, but the men shouted and pounded the table
and laughed great rumbling laughs. They spat; they shook with glee. They told stories about
women, other friends, themselves when young; they sputtered with shared pleasure when they told

men   the chandelier
the one about the green room and pink ceiling and   glass poker with that blonde. "You filled the
inside straight," the judge said to the painter; "Remember, you sonofabitch."
The painter——Quentin Wallace——took a red and black pentel from the marmalade jar by the phone.
He took an envelope also and sketched a naked woman with pendulous breasts, long red hair. He did
this rapidly, frowning. Then he drew the four of them, all naked and erect, their penises engorged
and ruby-tipped. A deck of cards emerged from her spread legs   on their knees

Remembered
        "Remember Gretchen," asked the judge
        Slote laughed. "Remembered her memory right to the doctor.."
        "What a night," said Wallace. "What a night!"
        They talked in this manner at length. Alan hoped waited for the spark of wit, the proof of
                                        bit-size
eminence earned. They swallowed cashews and celery sticks; they told ephenat jokes. "How do you
fit five elephants in a Volkswagen?" asked the Judge. "Two in the front and three in the back,"
Slote answered. They chortled and drank. nodded and drank.
        "What of the larger life?" he asked himself, pouring; what of the impersonal issues of politics
and art/, the impersonal issues of state? ; why do I dance attention on old age? The very echo,
in this phrase, of Yeats would strike the men as laughable——a boy pursued by lust and rage, that
young girl standing there.   They spat into their handkerchiefs; they laughed and shook and spat. blew.

        "You sonofabitch," said Alfred Lydenberg. "You cocksucking sonofabitch."
        "An inside straight," said Slote.
        "Come off it,"Allie," Wallace said. "You never took her home."
        "And then when I was carrying that ladder up in Bleeker Street. Where I slipped on the porch
and sprained my ankle wrecked my back, remember? in the loft
        "What happened to her anyhow? She married, I remember that, some lawyer from Atlanta."
        "Coke, I think."
        "He means Coca-cola," said Slote. "The Coca-cola fortune, twice removed."
        "Can't be too careful these days." This struck them as uproarious; they "Like Cunard, remember?
"Like little Nancy Cunard..."
                                                                        might
        They could tell him how careers are made, how their careers were fashioned; they could speak
an easy   of the late great. They could describe Manhattan when it was a pioneering place, when Harlem
        was a welcome place to visit after dark; they had known Thomas Hart Benton, Josephine Baker,
                                        Ava
        Frank O'Hara, Chaplin, Gardner, Ruth. They could, if they elected to, demonstrate to Alan the
        secrets of longevity and growth, the proper measure of ambition and mete modesty, the usages
        of smoke-filled rooms and satin sheets on waterbeds, the way that
        Roosevelt got round the congress, Fiorellos's handshake, the Masonic Temple rites the fix was
        in, they'd tell him, for Katharine Anne Porter and Norman Mailer and all the pretty little horses
        in the Whitney stable; they would explain the wheel of fortune and how it's rigged.. The spinning
        wheel, they would explain, was Gretchen's little counterweight, and even she rolled her hips when
        when she rolled her hips the fix was in. They had watched the rise and fall of fortunes,
        hemlines, tidelines, hula hoops and wigs; the map of Africa and Asia, the map of the
        planets and Central America, the moon——all had been altered since they began to study
        maps, the age of the computer was a fantasy, and missiles and the laser beam; they could tell
        him, if they chose to, they could make him welcome in the world.
        "Can't drink like I used to," said the Judge.
        "No, nor nothing else," said Slote.
        "A civil tongue You never with," said Wallace. They laughed.

Page from the author's revised typescript for "And with Advantages," included in his 1990 collection,
The Writers' Trade and Other Stories *(Collection of Nicholas Delbanco)*

Alice retreat into sexual desire, finding at least temporary solace and integrity in their physical love.

At the beginning of the story's second part fifteen years have passed. David and Alice have married and borne a son; David has published three novels, has known some success, yet feels "himself a mouthpiece"— "not so much a writer as someone being written." The authorial voice has turned ventriloquistic, inauthentic, cheaply manufactured. His marriage has also gone sour. A trip to the island of Tortola for a second honeymoon and a test of their love's endurance provides a landscape for story and storytelling, as Alice, David, and a mutual old friend swap tales of marital and familial wreckage. David comes to recognize his failure as a husband, a failure linked to his writing life: "He had fashioned a career. He had written three books and was completing a fourth. He had used up their story. He was nothing on his own." Having exhausted the material in his life, in his wife's life, and in their lives together, David stands on the edge of crisis, unsure of how to proceed.

Crisis—artistic and personal—is also at the heart of the next story, "Panic." Robert Patton, forty-three years old and divorced for two years, finds himself amid a welter of rituals: weddings, christenings, burials, and reunions fill his days and remind him of the dull passage of time. Like many of the other writers in this collection, Patton's marriage seemed to consist of talk and tired, formulaic sex, and his relationship with his one child—a son—sometimes seems too much of a struggle.

More troubling, perhaps, is Patton's circumstance as a writer. He describes the condition of his career and reputation in terms that might well have been applied at one time to Delbanco himself:

> His skill was a surveyor's skill, his habit that of witness. He could identify snippets of speech, the overheard fragment, the volitional veiled glance. He knew, in a room, who was sleeping with whom, or wanted to; his talent was control. Reviewers praised his tact, his chilly noticing eye. They did so, however, in terms as measured as his own—and this had come to worry Robert; his work had been at best a moderate success. . . . He dreamed of a great summons, an immoderate subject, the panic that is Pan's penetrating entry, a cry. Meantime, he built his small books. They were shapely and succinct. He was neither stupid nor lazy, and he wanted once to write a story or a novel that was larger than its author, that would demonstrate craft anchored, not adrift. With increasing bitterness, he doubted that he would.

Desiring the large emotion, the oversized subject, the frightening rush of the physical and visceral wave, Patton finds himself a master of the modest moment. The terms of his talent and of his success are not the terms

Dust jacket for Delbanco's 1990 collection of stories featuring authors as protagonists

on which he had begun his writing career. Like many of the preceding stories, "Panic" concludes on a desolate note. Patton, in bed with a married lover, also embraces the sadness that envelops him: "he was married to silence, wedded to failure forever."

In "Palinurus" Delbanco creates a pair of writers and focuses on the relationship between them. George Chapman is a successful, forty-nine-year-old writer best known for his novel *Virgil*, a loose retelling of the *Aeneid*. Five years Chapman's junior, Enoch still seeks recognition and achievement—"His career had little of the reach and bright trajectory of Chapman's nor the success"—while teaching at Middlebury College and struggling with a recent divorce. He is also another of Delbanco's acolyte figures (Chapman calls him "my pal Palinurus," a reference to Aeneas's faithful crewman), who settles for mere "proximity to greatness" rather than the true article itself. Enoch's friendship is extended further when Chapman asks him to serve as his literary executor (this story has echoes of Delbanco's own relationship with John Gardner, for whom Delbanco functioned as literary executor upon Gardner's death) and then dies unexpectedly in an automobile accident.

Enoch inherits a literary ghost whose life is of obsessive interest to biographers, agents, publicists, and late-claiming friends. He has to deal with the dismal aftermath of the writer's life, the shaping of the writer into a figure of literary history. Enoch discovers that no one wants the same story of that life, that each survivor desires his or her own narrative of that life; as Chapman's Palinurus, Enoch must "keep track" not only of his own fragmented existence, but also of a reputation that is not his own.

A different kind of guardianship serves as a motif in the next story in the collection, "The Brass Ring," in which the relationship is fraternal rather than artistic. Frederick Hasenclever is a writer who has "settled into middle age" and whose reputation, "if small, felt nonetheless secure." At fifty-six years old Hasenclever has been twice married and has experienced the loss of both parents. In his last book—a novel titled *The Brass Ring*—he took up the matter of Jewish identity. Like Delbanco, Hasenclever knows the meaning—and savors the use—of the word *vastation,* which is part of the moral and spiritual vocabulary of both men: "It's the absolute absence of God."

Frederick shares the point of view in the story with his younger brother, Arnold, an actor, who collapses suddenly with a debilitating illness and is tended during his recovery by his brother. Thrust into the role of guardian, Frederick comes to reassess the nature of familial relations and, like other of Delbanco's protagonists, tests his writerly life against the demands of felt experience. Delbanco emphasizes Hasenclever's loss of his sense of identity as a writer by objectifying his protagonist, periodically referring to him simply as "the writer." As a consequence, Hasenclever becomes a character in his own story, sacrificing his artistic identity to the demands of being a brother. Familial membership, Delbanco suggests, necessarily involves obligation. Family bonds exert a palpable force; for Hasenclever, they are "a tactile presence, a part of him inalienably." Filling the gap left by death's intrusions, they are, perhaps, the last best argument against nothingness.

With the final story of the collection, "Everything," Delbanco brings the reader to the endpoint of his narrative and structural arc. Where *The Writers' Trade* begins with an ascendant young writer, it ends with an aged writer in decline. Martin Peterson, in his seventies and in the care of a housekeeper, engages his days in remembering the details of others' lives. At the same time Peterson drifts across the surface of his own past, casting back over his life, trying to figure the logic that has brought him to the present pass.

Peterson discovers a personal history made up of women who loved him for his scope of vision for a time but abandoned him, exhausted with his neediness, his infidelities, and his cruel wit. Peterson also wonders over his own career's passage ("Martin Peterson, the novelist, had been 'promising' and then was 'accomplished' and now was 'distinguished'") and the ways in which language now serves him only in reflection and recollection; he writes only within his head or by way of dictation.

In the end, what Peterson observes in his backward glance is the hard fact of his own regret. The writing life, he concludes, has been mere diversion, a labor of ultimate inconsequence. Delbanco, by closing his collection with this story, seems to echo Peterson's sentiment; an examination of "the writer's trade," he ruefully admits, reveals the severe and unpromising limits of that trade. And yet, as Delbanco demonstrates, the trade endures.

Interviews:

Gregory L. Morris, "An Interview with Nicholas Delbanco," *Contemporary Literature,* 25 (Winter 1984): 386–396;

Robert Buckeye, "An Interview with Nicholas Delbanco," in his *In the Middle Distance, Nicholas Delbanco* (Middlebury, Vt.: Abernethy Library, 1992), pp. 7–16.

References:

Robert Buckeye, *In the Middle Distance, Nicholas Delbanco* (Middlebury, Vt.: Abernethy Library, 1992);

Nancy Mairs, "What's a Poor Writer to Do?" *New York Times Book Review,* 18 March 1990, p. 12.

Papers:

The Nicholas Delbanco Collection is part of the Special Collections, Middlebury College Libraries, Middlebury, Vermont.

Gail Godwin

(18 June 1937 –)

Jane Hill
State University of West Georgia

See also the Godwin entry in *DLB 6: American Novelists Since World War II, Second Series.*

BOOKS: *The Perfectionists* (New York: Harper & Row, 1970; London: Cape, 1971);

Glass People (New York: Knopf, 1972);

The Odd Woman (New York: Knopf, 1974; London: Cape, 1975);

Dream Children (New York: Knopf, 1976; London: Gollancz, 1977);

Violet Clay (New York: Knopf, 1978; London: Gollancz, 1978);

A Mother and Two Daughters (New York: Viking, 1982; London: Heinemann, 1982);

Mr. Bedford and the Muses (New York: Viking, 1983; London: Heinemann, 1984);

The Finishing School (Franklin Center, Pa.: Franklin Library, 1984; New York: Viking, 1985; London: Heinemann, 1985);

A Southern Family (New York: Morrow, 1987; London: Heinemann, 1987);

Father Melancholy's Daughter (New York: Morrow, 1991; London: Deutsch, 1991);

The Good Husband (New York: Ballantine, 1994; London: Deutsch, 1994);

Evensong (New York: Ballantine, 1999).

RECORDING: *Gail Godwin Reads "Dream Children,"* Columbia, Mo., American Audio Prose Library, 1986.

Gail Godwin (courtesy of the author)

Gail Godwin became a nationally prominent literary figure when her fifth novel, *A Mother and Two Daughters* (1982), became a best-seller. Critics have often focused on Godwin's portrayal of female characters, often a protagonist torn between the demands of convention and expectation and the longings of her strong, independent spirit. Godwin's work is also often analyzed for those elements that connect it to the tradition of Southern fiction. Predominant among these elements is a concern with family and those ghosts of the past that inhabit present lives, but racial issues are also significant in several works. Because Godwin writes from a strong historical sense of the novel in English, her work provides avenues of exploration for critics and readers interested in intertextuality. Finally, matters of the spirit and faith have become even more central in the later novels.

Although Godwin's reputation rests so strongly on her novels that she has been introduced as "the author of twelve novels," she is, in fact, the author of ten novels and two collections of short stories: *Dream Children* (1976) and *Mr. Bedford and the Muses* (1983). Both collections were well received upon publication, and both provide significant insights into Godwin's development as a writer, her theories of fiction, and the novels that overshadow them. Both collections are full of references, characters, settings, and scenes that recall one or more of the novels. All but one of the stories in the second collection deal specifically with the profession and development of the protagonist, a writer; and seven of the fifteen stories in *Dream Children* also feature writers as central characters.

Godwin's short fiction thus provides an indication of her sense of the writer's life. Because the short stories also reflect and echo the novels, these collections might be read primarily as footnotes to Godwin's more significant work. But the individual stories are full of their own insights, perspectives, surprises, and moments of recognition. Also, to a greater extent than many contemporary story collections, Godwin's two volumes have a unity of theme and a crafted structure as collections that make them more than simply addenda to her longer fiction.

Gail Kathleen Godwin was born in Birmingham, Alabama, on 18 June 1937, the daughter of Mose Winston Godwin and Kathleen Krahenbuhl Godwin. When she was two, her parents separated, and she and her mother moved to North Carolina, living at first with her maternal grandparents. After Thomas Krahenbuhl's death in 1939, Godwin, her mother, and grandmother became a small, unconventional family, with Kathleen Godwin as primary breadwinner. Both the North Carolina setting and the female household of these years appear frequently in Godwin's fiction. In 1948 Kathleen Godwin married Frank Cole; the resulting stepfamily dynamic has also provided material for Godwin's work.

In 1955, the same year she entered Peace Junior College in Raleigh, North Carolina, Godwin was reunited with her father. Three years later, when she was a student at the University of North Carolina at Chapel Hill, Mose Godwin committed suicide. After graduating from UNC, Godwin became a reporter for the *Miami Herald* and married Douglas Kennedy, a photographer for the paper. Divorced in 1961, Godwin moved to London, where she worked in the Travel Service at the U.S. Embassy. While in England, she married and divorced Ian Marshall, a British physician and psychotherapist. Returning to the United States in 1966, Godwin entered graduate school at the University of Iowa, receiving a master's degree in 1968 and a Ph.D. in English in 1971.

The publication of her first novel, *The Perfectionists* (1970), took place while she was still a student at Iowa.

Like much of her fiction, it has a strong autobiographical element, tracing the courtship and tumultuous marriage of a young American woman to a British psychotherapist. In fact, the briefest Godwin biographical summary can be read as an outline for many of the settings, plots, and themes of her fiction.

Since she began her publishing career, Godwin has supported herself primarily by her writing, although she has done some teaching. She has made her home primarily in the state of New York, but her ties to Asheville and the South have remained strong. For many years Godwin's companion and sometimes collaborator has been the composer and author Robert Starer, whom she met at an artist's colony. Their collaborations include the chamber operas *The Last Lover* (1975), *Anna Margarita's Will* (1976), and *Remembering Felix* (1987), and the compositions *Magdalen at the Tomb* (1999) and *Abraham Remembers* (2000).

In many ways *Dream Children* and *Mr. Bedford and the Muses* represent two different but equally important facets of Godwin's sensibilities and tendencies as a writer. The stories in *Dream Children* began appearing in magazines in 1971. It is the younger writer's book, and its controlling theme is the exploration and testing of limits. The characters are people who have all gone beyond limits of some kind; the resolutions are often beyond the boundaries of physical reality. *Mr. Bedford and the Muses,* on the other hand, includes stories that first appeared in magazines beginning in 1976, and the novella and five stories that make up the later collection are about learning to live within limits. The characters come to accept security and accomplishment or to accommodate lesser lives with a modicum of grace and dignity. Once a reader grasps the unity and coherence of each collection, this dichotomy in the themes and characters of the two books—a difference also reflected in the narrative style of each—serves as a good introduction to the conflicts and paradoxes that dominate all of Godwin's characters.

To understand better the relationship between the short stories in *Dream Children* and the other writing that Godwin was doing simultaneously—that is, her novels—one might explore the central conceit of one of the stories, "The Legacy of the Motes." Its protagonist, an American Ph.D. student doing research at the British Museum, finds himself on the verge of completing his dissertation, "A Catalogue of Metaphysical Conceits," when he is suddenly plagued by vision trouble. The condition, diagnosed as muscae volitantes, causes the young man to see tiny wings floating within his realm of vision as he ponders his manuscript. Eventually, the stress of the condition causes him to return to the United States without completing his project. Some years later, a friendly museum employee who has read the manuscript tells him in a letter that the condition might have been a psychological manifestation of his inadvertent omission of one of the most important of the metaphysical conceits: the wings from George Herbert's poem "Easter Wings" (1633).

Godwin's use of Herbert's famous image invites consideration not only of the metaphysical poets and their aesthetic but also of the Christian allegory inherent in Herbert's use of the image. Godwin also complicates the image beyond Herbert's rather straightforward message. The failed student's wings are her conceit for the writer's condition: his or her obsessions, arrogance, and limitations. The inability of established structures or systems to help the student deal with this problem is another layer of Godwin's commentary on the writer's fate in the contemporary world.

The tone and atmosphere of the other stories in *Dream Children* are closely connected to the writer's condition as embodied in the wings of "The Legacy of the Motes." Even when the characters are not writers themselves, they share the feelings of obsession and arrogance that define the student in this story—feelings that generally grow out of the hyperordinary, passive, constrained existence that the almost-realized scholar typifies. The characters in the collection often share the student's inevitable confrontation with personal limits and the limits of reality.

While the three novels that preceded *Dream Children* employ traditional narrative strategies, the structures of several stories in the collection suggest Godwin's interest in narrative experimentation during this period. "Death in Puerto Vallarta" consists of thirty-four numbered sections, most no more than a paragraph in length, some only a sentence. "Notes for a Story," as its title suggests, is presented as an unfinished story, one its "author" has presumably been unable to complete for a variety of reasons. To construct the narrative in "False Lights," Godwin employs an exchange of letters between two women who have never met. "My Lover, His Summer Vacation," told as if it were daily journal entries, with hour and minute notations, is also highly unusual in terms of point of view. The only use of first-person in the story is the title; the journal-like entries of the woman to whose lover the title refers are in third-person, and the lover also has third-person entries from his point of view, as does his wife. "Why Does a Great Man Love?" is told in three separate sections (their information and details often overlapping) headed "Facts," "Rumors," and "Conjectures." Another story with a suggestive title, "Interstices," although not so experimental as some of the stories, is a modernist narrative with several viewpoints intercutting and contradicting one another in a seemingly random fashion. None of these various narrative

Dust jacket for Godwin's 1976 collection of stories, focusing on obsessive protagonists

strategies appears in the novels that are contemporary to them in time of composition.

One way Godwin underscores the testing of limits in *Dream Children* is through characters linked to the occult, the mystical, the supernatural, or the spiritual. This link can be rather conventional, as with the Anglican priest in "An Intermediate Stop." He has a visionary experience in which God reveals Himself and communicates with the priest. This experience is highly personal, profoundly felt, and quite real for the character, and he eventually shares it in a small book he writes. Religious mysticism also plays a role in the experience of Adriana Trachey, the protagonist of "Indulgences," though her experience is less conventional. Raised by an uncle, once a would-be priest, Adriana grows up immersed in the lives of the saints and draws on their inspiration in her career as a costume designer. But Adriana also draws from this background a particular sense of the undercurrent of sexual tension and repression as manifested in the religious life. Her uncle, a nervous mentor in this arena, creates in his young ward a confusion of real and spiritual, mystical and psychological that results in the adult Adriana's inability to perceive limits that "normal" women perceive in regard to sexual behavior. Yet, this failure is also the source of her genius as a designer.

Lucy, a character in "Interstices," has a similar inability to understand limits, but the visions that lead her beyond the boundaries of mundane life result not in a successful artistic career but in institutionalization and shock therapy. When her husband's best friend becomes her lover after he drives Lucy home from treatment, Godwin again suggests a direct link between certain failures to perceive limits and sexuality.

In the final piece, "Notes for a Story," Nora, the main character, believes that she has the ability to project herself into different rooms of her house; but that is not the only example of altered consciousness in the story. Nora's childhood friend Catherine, who comes to visit, seeks meaning and truth through use of hallucinogens as well as through occult and metaphysical means. In Catherine's seeking, Godwin portrays a desperate neediness that calls into question the less directly judged excesses of characters in the earlier stories. Comparing the feeling in this story to the tone of the opening title story is to read the collection as moving from sympathetic recognition of characters' needs for something beyond reality to what is almost impatience with such characters (even those for whom the narrator continues to feel sympathy) for their failure to progress beyond such needs.

Mrs. McNair, the protagonist of "Dream Children," is a woman who has suffered a wrenching loss. Her child dies at birth, but the next morning she is mistakenly presented a healthy baby as her own. This experience sends her to the world of the occult, as she searches for ways to maintain her connection to that other baby, the "dream" child she has lost but who still lives somewhere, with other parents. The narrator allows, in the sympathetic rendering of this woman and her situation, the possibility that her "solution" within the world beyond the boundaries of reality is a viable alternative to the harsh facts of her life.

In Gretchen, the protagonist of "Some Side Effects of Time Travel," Godwin creates the closest approximation in this collection to a "typical" Godwin female seeking her best life. Gretchen, a writer exhausted with the effort to observe and record her real experience, enters into a pact with a friend. They imagine that they can somehow merge their separate selves to create a third woman. Because Gretchen is a writer, the focus of the supernatural activity is linked to the effort to draw or to erase the line between reality and fiction.

Godwin provides an emphasis on the sexuality of these characters that is notably more intense than is her rendering of such subject matter in the early novels. There is a raw, uninhibited quality to the treatment of sex that is rare in literary fiction of the time, perhaps especially in that written by women. Certainly, the influence of D. H. Lawrence on Godwin's work–an influence that is perhaps too obvious in the first two novels and that continues to be significant in later work–is one source of the vivid sexual treatment in these stories. Other probable influences on this distinctive element of the fiction are classical myths, the pressurized eroticism of the lives of the saints and other religious stories, and the psychosexual theories of Carl Gustav Jung and Sigmund Freud.

The religious and classical influence can be seen in Adriana's encounters with the saints as a child in "Indulgences" and in Gretchen's adolescent crush on a nun at her parochial school in "Some Side Effects of Time Travel." In both "Dream Children" and "A Sorrowful Woman" the asexuality of the characters has the religious feel of chastity as a great purifying and healing force. In a different way, the sad, lonely chastity of Mrs. Wakeley's life in "Nobody's Home" (as well as the chaste widowhood of her alter ego, Clara Jones) and the young student's life in "The Legacy of the Motes" suggest that, for humans, the absence of sexuality is too great a denial of their essential nature and, therefore, a guarantee of distortions and terrors every bit as "real" as the indulgence of Adriana, whose list of lovers, composed to answer the question of her most recent partner, is more than seventy names long.

The suggestion of Jungian archetypal images of sexuality is also clearly a part of Gretchen's experience in "Some Side Effects of Time Travel." But her testing of sexual boundaries remains the stuff of imagination and dreams, of her mental sex life. These are not realized sex scenes, but *Dream Children* has those, too. There are the memories of past sex that Adriana's list-making generates in "Indulgences" and the almost-orgy of "Notes for a Story." A great poet and his giantess wife make passionate love on a mountaintop in "The Woman Who Kept Her Poet." In "Interstices" two couples have gritty "real" sex in juxtaposition to the "angelic" sex between protagonist Lucy and her lover. Of course, Lucy is the character who is insane and who, Godwin seems to suggest here, can therefore hold onto the naive notion of ethereal sex. For the most part, *Dream Children* denies the possibility that sex can be a viable way to transcend the limitations of self in a positive, meaningful way, a possibility that does become reality in a later novel, *A Mother and Two Daughters*. In

2/crackup at Chipmunk Lake

little chipmunk running behind that tree. ~~They were a bright-eyed~~ *Its their mating season, you know*
~~and busily skittered across away to see their mating season~~

Miles sat down on ~~the~~ a mushroom-festered stump ~~afoxxterrand~~
and ~~howled~~ *bawled*. His sobs echoed over the lake, drowning out the
motorboat pulling skiers over the sparkling lake. "Miles...
Miles! Pull yourself together." Selma Lee was getting frightened
now. The men in her novels never cried. ~~They were extremely and~~
~~silent with dark eyebrows that knit together in intense attention~~
~~business~~ Three hours later, they had put him, doped with valium *tranquilizers*
and Scotch, on a rented Cessna to Boston, from there to be transferred by jet to Miami, where his wife would be waiting with a
psychiatrist. The last thing he saw as the little twin-engine
lifted him away from the small airport that looked like a hunting
lodge, ~~was Selma,~~ her thin hair lifting like a thistle away from
her head, waving her handkerchief/at him. *bravely* There was someone else
standing there, too, also seeing him off. But gradually afterwards
he had been able to excise this figure from succeeding drafts of
~~his memory.~~ One of the few comforts of ~~being an aging writer, was.~~
~~you had~~
~~the license to alter the facts.~~

a writer of any age, was, you had the license to alter the facts.

Miles was a nervous believer in signs and portents. Things
had not been going well for him that year, the year that culmina-
ted in the Crackup at Chipmunk Lake, and even as he drove to the
Conference---one of the newer ones, only in its second year, still
idealistic about "Literature," and run by an efficient young
associate professor who was something of a poet herself--- he kept
seeing/his life in the signs he passed, driving northward in his *commentaries on*
old Buick on the Adirondack Highway. BUMP AHEAD...FALLING ROCK

They had taken up a collection of tranquilizers & whisky

Page from the revised typescript for Godwin's unpublished story "Crackup at Chipmunk Lake" (Collection of Gail Godwin)

that narrative all three of the title characters find a transcendent, apparently lasting sexual relationship.

"Why Does a Great Man Love?" introduces a paradox that grows out of Jungian concepts as well. The great man of the title dreams of an ideal nymphet, age nine, who happens to be forty feet tall. This baby giant would love and nurture the great man beyond all reasonable expectations. Here Godwin establishes the concept of the male as one who manipulates the female, seeks to shape real women to an image, an ideal, that is far beyond his power to control or manipulate, who is a giant to his mere, mortal self. The young woman who marries the "great" man in "The Woman Who Kept Her Poet" is literally a giant; coupled with her youth, her stature makes her the living embodiment of the other great man's fantasy of a baby giant.

By far the most extreme sexual scenario in *Dream Children* occurs in "Layover" (even the title is suggestive), in which the mythic largeness of woman is forced to its most extreme conclusion. A female air traveler purposely misses a connection and finds herself in a private room in an airport. There she services man after man, expanding, stretching to fulfill the unending male need that dominates the atmosphere. When she finally decides to resume her travels, airline officials prevent her boarding. They say her ticket is out of date, but she knows that it is her now overwhelming size that prevents her from resuming her normal life. Instead, she continues to expand and to find ordinary human experience less and less satisfying.

Ultimately, the statement on sex in *Dream Children* is one of dissatisfaction and terror. The sexual territory explored is situated at the outer limits of experience, even in the 1970s heyday of the sexual revolution when the stories were composed and are presumably set. By the end of the collection, in "Notes for a Story," the main character has found shelter within a more traditional, committed relationship. She feels nervous about having settled for security, for the ordinary, an old Godwin nemesis; but the story reaffirms her decision as Nora and her lover, Rudy, reject the group sex scene proposed by her visiting friend and even fight violently to preserve their commitment and security.

The various theories of and attitudes toward writing espoused in the stories also unify *Dream Children* as a collection. In "Some Side Effects of Time Travel" Gretchen embraces one approach to fiction, vowing to strive for a more natural, less self-conscious narrative that predates Jamesian self-consciousness and the expectations of clever readers. As Julia Richardson does in *A Southern Family* (1987), Gretchen seeks a narrative that stops short of interpretation and ironic complexity. Yet, she still links fiction to the personal. Karl Bandema, on the other hand, argues in "False Lights" for a fiction of

the future that focuses on elements purer than the personal. He hopes artists of the future will be receivers for the universe's messages, not recorders of their own experience. For Karl, art has been a trickster, robbing him of his life as he struggled to record and interpret his past experience. Gretchen also wonders if her effort to observe and record her experience does not somehow ultimately separate her from the actuality of living.

Esther, a poet in "Interstices," thinks of the poem she will write about a sexual encounter as she is having the experience; furthermore, she is certain that the sex, as she will render it in the poem, will be superior to the actual event. The priest who turns author in "An Intermediate Stop" believes his encounter with God to be far more satisfying in reality than it is in his written account of that event, but even for him the writing somehow diminishes the lived experience. Audiences seem as interested in his descriptions of English country life as they are in his epiphany.

Despite the ambiguities inherent in the artistic life, *Dream Children* suggests that the powers of the writer are finally the most useful available. Mrs. Wakeley, the main character in "Nobody's Home," is the least artistic, the most mundane character in the entire collection. Yet, she too recognizes that the imaginative abilities associated with art are equally necessary to the nonartist, the mundane person merely trying to live a life. She attributes the collapse of her marriage to her own and her husband's inability to imagine the other separate from the relationship that binds them. Mrs. Wakeley, in fact, comes to define the mundane marriage as the loss of one's ability to see beyond the details, which is another way of saying the loss of the creative vision that transforms the mere mortal into the lovable approximation of the ideal that one holds in one's mind and so inevitably cherishes against all reason. Without the transforming power of artistic vision, one can no longer see anything except the details, the too horribly real.

The tone and subject matter of the six stories in *Mr. Bedford and the Muses* make clear that Godwin is working much closer to the "real" world than she was in *Dream Children*. The "Author's Note" at the end of the book serves to reinforce and emphasize that difference. In the note Godwin explains the "muses" that inspired each of the stories; that is, she connects things that have occurred in the real world to the events and characters in the stories. She acknowledges the influence of Henry James, from whom she has taken her motto as a writer. Like James, she believes that "the air around us is thick with . . . 'the virus of suggestion.'" Out of that belief, she has chosen his admonition to "Try to be one of those people on whom nothing is lost!" as her motto.

Because these stories are so grounded in closely observed "real" life, they are naturally more contained by the limits of the natural world than are the stories in the earlier collection. In each of the six, the main character accepts rather than challenges those boundaries, a tendency suggested by Nora and Rudy's rejection of Catherine's challenge to their safe, secure, traditional lives in "Notes for a Story."

Mr. Bedford and the Muses also returns to the motif of the writer's craft that informs several of the stories in *Dream Children*. Again, Godwin's "Author's Note" underscores the importance of that theme. The novella "Mr. Bedford," named for a pet turtle, fills almost half the book, and it is also the primary focus of Godwin's note. She explains that Mr. Bedford, both the turtle and the story that bears his name, served to cure a bout with writer's block. After realizing the hundred pages of a novel she had earnestly been producing were going nowhere, Godwin had a dream and then rummaged around in her journals from the period the dream called forth. That rummaging produced memories of Mr. Bedford and the people who owned him, a couple Godwin had known while living in London in the early 1960s.

She began writing about Mr. Bedford and the time, place, and people associated with him "not because I felt I ought to be writing" but "in order to recapture and understand. . . . but with the perspective that time and distance *and imagination* can bestow." The turtle became her "official Writing Mascot," and from his image she was able to draw good advice for any writer: "Go slowly . . . this is a quest, not a race or a contest." Indeed, the stories in this book follow the advice of these mentors and mottoes, for their pace is leisurely. Their structures are straightforward; there is none of the modernist experimentation that dominates many of the stories in the earlier collection. The tone is far more reflective than insistent.

"Mr. Bedford" concerns the struggle of Carrie Ames, an American woman living in England, to become a writer. Carrie's biography is, in essence, the author's. Godwin explains her meddling with reality or "truth" this way: "For obvious reasons, I'll change all the names, including my own. Also, made-up names make it easier to invent when you come to memory gaps. And this sometimes leads to bonuses. In the middle of 'inventing,' you discover you are remembering. Or, even better, you discover the real truth that lay buried beneath the literal happenings." In this story the conflict between fiction-making and lived experience is presented in a relatively pragmatic way, without the angst of the writers in *Dream Children*. Yet, Godwin's portrait of Carrie yields its own angst.

A typical Godwin protagonist—one might even say archetypal—Carrie finds herself torn between the sense of security she feels with her landlords, the East-

ons, in the eclectic "family" they create in their boarding house, and the longing to be independent, which she sees as necessary to her art. The paradox is that a genuinely independent person lacks the connectedness out of which fiction springs. The lesson Carrie must learn in her time in England is how to balance the involvement that produces material with the independence that allows that material to be shaped into art.

The Eastons, who are represented as fallen American elites struggling to maintain appearances on the meager resources generated by their boarders, serve as a caution to Carrie. If she fails to become a successful writer, theirs is the life she might find herself living. But they also serve as models to her, for the Eastons are supreme fiction-makers themselves. They can persuade an astute observer such as Carrie to buy into their self-generated version of reality, even after she knows it to be a fiction. That is precisely the power that a successful writer must possess, of course, and thus the Eastons become guides as well as cautions for Godwin's protagonist. By watching them stage-manage others to fit the narrative they must perpetuate, Carrie learns to manage characters and plots. By observing the power that the Eastons obtain by being able to enter into the consciousness of others and provide what those others need (for example, Mrs. Easton's uncanny accuracy in decorating Carrie's second room in their house), Carrie learns the lessons of point of view necessary to the writer.

The turtle, Mr. Bedford, is for the Eastons a symbol of a time and a place to which they can never return. From the turtle's role in their lives, Carrie (and by extension, Godwin) learns that a writer must discover and cling to such deposits of the past, mining them thoroughly for their richness, if she is to succeed at the craft. She learns an equally important lesson about entering into another's point of view. Mrs. Easton's rendition of the story of Mr. Bedford is at first off-putting to Carrie, for the tale casts her landlords as less than her initial, romantic image of them. But something about the story and her former landlady's way of telling it persuades Carrie not only to resume her position in the Easton household but also to reconsider her view of the Eastons. She says, "So often, especially when we are younger, we see other people only in relation to what they are to us; we freeze them into what they are *now*. But her story had broken the ice, or at least made a crack in it . . . and . . . I could glimpse them as fluid creatures still moving in the auras of their colorful pasts."

In the five short stories that follow the novella, the main characters find themselves working toward the same sort of recognition and expansion of perspective that Carrie experiences as she listens to Mrs. Easton's

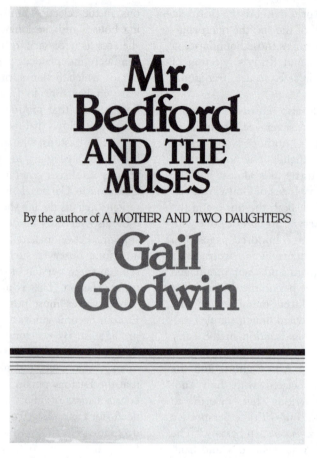

Dust jacket for Godwin's 1983 collection of stories, including "Mr. Bedford," in which a young woman gains insights about writing
from the tale of her landlords' pet turtle

story. This insight comes from acknowledging limitations in oneself and others; thus, the romanticism that pervades the initial state of each of these protagonists is altered or transformed, leaving each of them in a final state that is both more realistic and more intense because of the initial romanticism.

In "A Father's Pleasures" Rudolf Geber, a world-renowned pianist, finally finds romantic inspiration in his marriage to a woman young enough to be his daughter. When she leaves him for the son of his first marriage, instead of collapsing into failure, he moves to Japan, marries a Japanese woman, and produces his greatest art and two more children, one a musical prodigy. In a millennial performance of Franz Liszt's "Mephisto Waltz," Geber experiences an ecstatic insight that incorporates the totality of his experience—reality known and transformed by his art. Thus, his prevailing vision survives and prospers.

Constance LeFevre, the successful novelist who is the protagonist of "Amanuensis," lives a relatively straightforward life, taking lovers whose limitations are entirely recognized. But when a bitter former lover tries to embarrass her by planting a young woman as her amanuensis in order to gather material for a tell-all roman à clef about the woman who rejected him, the plan backfires. Constance and the girl develop an intense, true relationship that transcends the scorned lover's limited agenda. When the book comes out, at the moment that Constance is confronted by the reality behind her relationship with the young woman, with what should be the destruction of her romantic vision of that bond, she is able to see beyond the destruction to a more complete truth. For her, the young woman can remain her "angel of release."

Rudolf and Constance need to be released from the limitations of a romanticized view of self and others; Charles St. John, the protagonist of "St. John," needs to be released from his self-imposed repression of his romantic impulses. This release is accomplished through a sojourn in the country, where he works on his second novel. While there, he enters into a strange and unpredictable relationship with an eccentric older woman who shares his name, St. John. This temporary deviation from his fixed course alters him as a man and as a writer.

Clearly, the madness and romance of Charles's sojourn in the country is a positive experience that feeds his art. But it is also a temporary experience, as his conventional life at the end of the story attests. That he continues to write successfully within the confines of his more traditional life testifies to the lasting power of such transforming experiences and to the necessity, for the artist, of realizing the limits of such experience. The acknowledgment of this necessity most clearly separates the characters in *Mr. Bedford and the Muses* from those in *Dream Children*.

In both "The Angry-Year" and "A Cultural Exchange" the female protagonist is, like Carrie Ames in "Mr. Bedford," a young woman who shares Godwin's biography. In "The Angry-Year" her name is Janie Lewis, and she is a college student at a large state university in the late 1950s. In "A Cultural Exchange" she becomes Amanda Sloane, and she spends time in Denmark, seeking to develop herself as a writer. In "The Angry-Year" her antagonist appears to be a fraternity-president boyfriend, the epitome of conventionality and social acceptance; in "A Cultural Exchange" the foe is an aging landlord who seeks to guide the young woman into a traditional female role. But Janie and Amanda eventually come to recognize that the true adversary lies within. Janie sees her real culprit as "the crass conformist who'd been harboring inside the rebel all along," and she leaves this crucial year of her life with a "deep, abiding, central anger" that becomes a protection against too easily succumbing to the temptations of a limited life, too limited if one wishes to be a writer, at least.

When Amanda returns to Denmark years after the bitter rupturing of her relationship with her land-lord, Mr. Engelgard, she learns from his son that the old man died still bitter, glad that Amanda, in their power struggle, had refused his offer to introduce her to Isak Dinesen, one of her idols. Engelgard dies glad that Dinesen died before Amanda could meet her. But Amanda is not paralyzed by their struggle. She can hear the son's story with fondness, can remember the struggle with his father as an important step in her evolving sense of herself, and can genuinely wish that Engelgard were alive to hear her apology. Rather than giving in too completely to romanticism, Amanda, like Carrie and Janie and many Godwin women from the novels, finds herself transformed and strengthened by her testing of the limits and her ability to shape and control those experiences through art.

Although at this stage in Godwin's career it is unlikely that her reputation as a novelist will be eclipsed by her work as a short-story writer, *Dream Children* and *Mr. Bedford and the Muses* represent a substantial accomplishment in the genre of short fiction and deserve attention on that ground alone. Beyond that claim, however, is the perhaps even more substantial contribution these collections can make to understanding Godwin as a fiction-maker and as a chronicler of the lives of women in the second half of the twentieth century.

References:

Jane Hill, *Gail Godwin* (New York: Twayne, 1992);

Deborah Kuhlmann, "Mothering Our 'Dream' Children from Gail Godwin," *Short Story* (1993): 61–73;

Lihong Xie, *The Evolving Self in the Novels of Gail Godwin* (Baton Rouge: Louisiana State University Press, 1995).

Richard Grayson

(4 June 1951 –   )

Tom Whalen
Tulane University

BOOKS: *Disjointed Fictions* (Harrisburg, Pa.: Cumberland, 1978);

With Hitler in New York and Other Stories (New York: Taplinger, 1979);

Lincoln's Doctor's Dog & Other Stories (Adelphi, Md.: White Ewe, 1982);

Eating at Arby's: The South Florida Stories (Brooklyn, N.Y.: Grinning Idiot, 1982);

I Brake for Delmore Schwartz: Stories (Somerville, Mass.: Zephyr, 1983);

The Greatest Short Story that Absolutely Ever Was (New Orleans: Lowlands, 1989);

Narcissism and Me (New York: Mule & Mule, 1989);

I Survived Caracas Traffic: Stories from the Me Decades (Greensboro, N.C.: Avisson, 1996);

The Silicon Valley Diet and Other Stories (Los Angeles: Red Hen, 2000).

Richard Grayson, 1981 (from the dust jacket of Lincoln's Doctor's Dog & Other Stories, *1982)*

Critics have classified Richard Grayson as a postmodern metafictionist, an experimentalist, a compulsive autobiographer, social critic, satirist, parodist, and stand-up comedian. For the past three decades, he has also been one of the most prolific and inventive practitioners of the short-story form, although only followers of the little-magazine scene know it. Grayson's fictional concerns include, but are not limited to, the project of fiction-making itself and the attendant commercial difficulties in an era when it is possible to ask the question that was the focus of a conference at Brooklyn College that Grayson coordinated: "Can publishing and literature co-exist?" The titles of Grayson's story collections reflect his preoccupation with self-reflexivity and the American pop culture of celebrities, fads, bumper stickers, and T-shirt slogans. Picking through the junk heap of American culture (television, teen magazines, *Soap Opera Digest*) for his subjects, Grayson registers the effect of this commercial bombardment on the individual. The light, comic, sometimes flat and seemingly superficial quality of his fiction belies the seriousness of his critique.

Richard Grayson was born on 4 June 1951 in Brooklyn, New York, the son of Daniel Grayson, a clothing manufacturer and salesman, and Marilyn Grayson, a homemaker. He was educated in the public schools of Brooklyn and graduated from Midwood High School in 1968. After a year in which the panic attacks he suffered grew into full-fledged agoraphobia, Grayson entered Brooklyn College, where he was a student activist and from which he graduated with a bachelor's degree in political science (Phi Beta Kappa) in June 1973. Intending to become a writer, Grayson enrolled in a master's program in English at Richmond College (now the College of Staten Island) and then in the fledgling Master of Fine Arts program in creative writing at Brooklyn College, where he studied fiction writing with Susan Fromberg Schaeffer and metafictionists Jonathan Baumbach and Peter Spielberg, two of the founding members of the Fiction Collective. As a graduate student Grayson's goal was to produce one story each week and submit his work not only to his fiction-writing workshop classes but also to the scores of literary and "little" magazines being published in the mid to late 1970s.

In 1975 Grayson began his long college teaching career as an adjunct and temporary full-time instructor of English and other subjects at Long Island University. In the same year he started working as an editorial assistant at the Fiction Collective and published his first story in a literary magazine, *New Writers*. Within five years, Grayson had published more than one hundred stories in little magazines. With the exception of his first hardcover collection, *With Hitler in New York and Other Stories* (1979), and his articles and essays in *People, The New York Times*, and other periodicals, Grayson's career has taken place totally in the world of small presses, little magazines, and later, online magazines.

Grayson's first book was a collection of six stories, *Disjointed Fictions*, published first in 1978 as a special issue of the magazine *X, A Journal of the Arts*. In his introduction to a 1981 edition of the book, Richard Kostelanetz called Grayson "a compulsive fictioner who . . . has a penchant for transforming everything he can into fiction." As Kostelanetz noted, a principal character in Grayson's work is named "Richard Grayson," making it difficult for some critics to separate the author from the character. In *Disjointed Fictions* Grayson evinced many elements found in his later work: revealing details, often of an embarrassing nature, that purport to be from the author's own life and those of his relatives; pop culture references and celebrities used as characters; puns, silly jokes, and odd references to obscure scientific or historical facts; an attempt to get the reader to believe that the story is being improvised on the spot; and a concern with the purpose and uses of fiction.

The first story in *Disjointed Fictions* is "A Disjointed Fiction," five seemingly unrelated fragments, the first of which is an acknowledged (within the fragment) steal from Jorge Luis Borges. Grayson states that the anarchist's bomb that killed Czar Alexander II in St. Petersburg in 1881 led directly to the anti-Semitism that resulted in the migration of Russian Jews to the United States and thus to "the entrance of the noun 'chutzpah' into The Random House Dictionary of the English Language; Al Jolson's rendition of 'Mammy' in blackface; seven gold medals won by the United States Olympic swimming team at Munich in 1972; the Ziegfeld Follies; a certain kind of suburban vulgarity typified by the town of Woodmere, Long Island," and indirectly to Grayson's birth in the United States, his becoming a fiction writer, and finally to "the writing of this story, and ultimately to your reading of it." Grayson then suggests readers who have complaints about his work should address them to the anarchist whose bomb snuffed out the life of the czar, as the author would take no responsibility whatsoever for his fiction. Other fragments of the story include a humorous account of a dinner at the home of the daughter of sportscaster Howard Cosell; a thumbnail biography of Theodore Roosevelt that manages to turn every detail of Roosevelt's biography into a detail from the writer's own life; and a final segment that apologizes for "the mess" Grayson has created in the story.

Other stories in *Disjointed Fictions* deal with concerns to which Grayson returned in later fiction. "Inside Barbara Walters" features "the famous TV personality" in a series of absurd adventures, each of them dealing with the difficulty of being a reader in a world where the visual image is king. "Progress" prefigures Grayson's later, more overtly gay-themed fiction in its depiction of a trio of loquacious, muddleheaded adolescents whose identities are conflated. "Escape from the Planet of the Humanoids" directly addresses the reader in a series of commands ("Look:"; "Listen:"; "Pay attention:"), ending with Grayson taking the manuscript of a story (presumably this one) to the photocopier, sending out multiple copies to little magazines, and promptly getting rejected.

With Hitler in New York and Other Stories was brought out by Taplinger, a commercial publisher in New York City. Grayson's editor, Wesley Strick, divided the collection into six parts: "Introduction," "Objects," "Families," "Women," "Subjects," and "Artifacts." The front jacket flap of the book presents the paragraph about the assassination of Czar Alexander II leading to "my writing of this book, and ultimately, to your reading of it."

In the title story a backpacking Adolf Hitler in blue jeans arrives in New York on Laker Airlines to spend time with his Jewish girlfriend. The story opens with the narrator waiting at Kennedy Airport with his friend Ellen for her boyfriend. Hitler, Ellen, and the narrator watch television, eat ice cream, and smoke a joint. The narrator admires Hitler's wit and grace, even when the dictator is jet-lagged and worn out by an oppressive New York heat wave. As the story progresses, Hitler and his American friends eat at McDonald's, stroll in Greenwich Village, sip egg creams, and go to the Brighton Beach boardwalk, where a band of Russian Jews entertain themselves by singing Yiddish folk songs. Hitler listens intently, understands the slightly bawdy lyrics (unlike his American pals), and walks off before the old Jews recognize who he is.

The friendship between Hitler and the narrator, who is Jewish, deepens as they pass the dog days of summer. As an expression of his affection, Hitler gives the narrator a volume of Rainer Maria Rilke's poems. The narrator's grandfather dies in Florida, but since the narrator does not want to dampen Hitler's going-away party, he tells no one about the death. Hitler is a success at the party, holding his beer well and charming all the guests who have come to meet him. The narrator's admiration has by now turned to love. Drunk, the narrator and Hitler talk about winning Nobel Prizes—the narrator for literature and Hitler for peace. At the conclusion of the story, the narrator confides to Hitler that his grandfather has died. To stop the narrator from crying, Hitler tells funny stories, and the narrator drives Hitler home, feeling somewhat less mournful.

As Alvin H. Rosenfeld noted in his 1985 study *Imagining Hitler,* "Substitute almost anyone else for Hitler and the story would fail. With Hitler in it, though it is a fictional tour de force, it is the furthest extension to date of the neutralization of the historical Hitler and the normalization of a new image of the man." By removing Hitler's murderous anti-Semitism and imbuing him with positive qualities, Rosenfeld argued, "the story is designed to bring about an alignment of the reader's feelings with the narrator's," so that by the end of the story the reader hates to see Hitler go. Free of all references to World War II and the Holocaust, the story has de-Nazified Hitler and made him a friend of Jewish people. Rosenfeld noted that Grayson has removed Hitler from history and "made him safe. . . . There are no ironies here, weak or strong, only erasures so complete as to disarm the historical sense altogether." Jack Saunders suggested in the *Delray Beach News Journal* that in portraying Hitler as a hail-fellow-well-met, Grayson was attempting to demonstrate Hannah Arendt's concept of "the banality of evil" in regard to the Nazis. In an interview in *Gargoyle* conducted by Gretchen Johnsen and Richard Peabody, Grayson said that one of his aims was to show just how much is lost when the name "Hitler" gives up its force and no longer evokes anything of consequence from the past. In that respect at least, "With Hitler in New York" is about the power of a word, a name.

Other pieces in the volume, such as a collection of not-all-that-bizarre personal ads, seem more authentic than funny, while a piece such as "Chief Justice Burger, Teen Idol," mixing the style of a teenage girl's fan mag-

azine with the stiff judicial conservative, seems closer to pure satire out of *Mad Magazine* than fiction. On the other hand, by employing the style of trashy pop culture and capturing it so closely, Grayson manages to make its junkiness show. As with Donald Barthelme, Grayson has found new ways to recycle "the trash phenomena" of American culture.

The "Family" section features what Stuart Schoffman in the *Los Angeles Times* called Grayson's "parade of Jewish relatives." Some of the stories, such as "On the Boardwalk" or "Slowly, Slowly in the Wind" are slice-of-life set pieces about eccentric grandparents—such as Great-Grandma Chaikah, who cannot understand why Jews never make strikes on the television show *Bowling for Dollars.* These stories are related from the point of view of a narrator who seems somewhere between thirteen and an unworldly twenty-one. In "Wednesday Night at Our House" Grayson employs a question-and-answer format to depict the dreary, immobilized lives of a Brooklyn family of five that presumably resembles his own tightly knit family of two parents and three male children.

In what several critics called the most reflexive piece in the volume, "But in a Thousand Other Worlds," the character Richard Grayson writes a story titled "But in a Thousand Other Worlds" that comes to life. A touchy creature on a low-cholesterol diet, the story is sent out first to slick magazines such as *The New Yorker, Harper's,* and *The Atlantic Monthly,* getting summarily rejected (*The New Yorker* compares it unfavorably to the work of Barthelme) and becoming more bitter. At the Bread Loaf Writers Conference (where Grayson held a scholarship in 1977), the novelist John Gardner, author of *On Moral Fiction* (1978), calls the story "immoral," whereupon it bites him on the leg, embarrassing the author, who flees back home to Brooklyn and sends the story out to "a little mag that pays in copies." Returning with a coffee stain and its pages stapled together, "But in a Thousand Other Worlds" collapses. At Coney Island Hospital a doctor tells Richard that the story is unpublishable, that perhaps a major rewrite could have saved it once, but it is now too late. The character Richard cries at the death of his story while his friend Nina merely notes that the title always seemed unwieldy to her.

In a review titled "How Bad Are These Stories?" for the *Minneapolis Tribune,* D. G. Wnek suggested that this story epitomized Grayson's laziness and failure to lavish any care on his slapdash fictions. Agreeing, *Kirkus Reviews* suggested that Grayson's lack of patience and follow-through leads him to flounder once he has thought up an outrageous premise or a few jokes; not knowing what else to do, Grayson merely repeats his shticks, hoping for laughs of recognition. Similarly, Page Edwards in *Library Journal* found the stories in *With Hitler in New York and Other Stories* "little more than cleverly linked scenes . . . quick, conscious attempts to dazzle." Many critics noted Grayson's willingness to take fictional risks but found that many of his stories deflated at their conclusions. James R. Frakes in *The Plain Dealer* found Grayson's Jewish family stories—"almost traditional, never sentimental"—his most effective pieces.

The mixed critical notices of *With Hitler in New York and Other Stories* also compared Grayson to a wide variety of writers and performers: Kurt Vonnegut, Woody Allen, Erma Bombeck, Fran Lebowitz, Steve Martin, Gilbert Sorrentino, Monty Python, Nathanael West, Franz Kafka, Bob Hope, William Saroyan, and the Marx Brothers. Greil Marcus, in *Rolling Stone,* commented that the work was "where avant-garde fiction goes when it turns into stand-up comedy." *Publishers Weekly* treated the book as mostly humor, "poking fun at American life" with a "staccato style" in "sharp, witty stories." Kathleen Krog noted in the *Hollywood (Florida) Sun-Tattler* that unlike most metafictionists, Grayson has a persistent sentimental streak, shown in stories such as "Peninsular People," with its rather sweet collection of characters that anyone would like as neighbors. Daniel Curzon remarked in the *San Francisco Voice* on the persistent gay undercurrent running through *With Hitler in New York and Other Stories* and urged the young writer to write more explicitly on gay themes. Mark VanDine wrote in the *Penn State Collegian* that Grayson's stories seemed to be closer to plot outlines, introducing a situation and characters and having them interact to no great effect.

The book ends with a specious "Note on the Type," a parody of Knopf's end-of-the-volume notes, featuring spurious facts about real type fonts and the preferences of authors: "John Updike, an American author of Dutch descent, insists that all his novels be set in Janson. John Cheever's novels are set in Monticello, although he too prefers Janson. But Cheever is a reticent man and does not like to make an issue of it." We also learn what James M. Cain and Wallace Stevens have in common: "both are set in Electra." This hilarious send up should have alerted reviewers to Grayson's eagerness to puncture the balloon of American literary pretensions even if it meant playing the nebbish in order to do it.

The title of Grayson's third book, *Lincoln's Doctor's Dog & Other Stories* (1982), is based on an old publishing joke. Books about Lincoln always seemed to sell well; so did books about doctors and books about dogs. Thus, if an author were to write a book about Lincoln's doctor's dog, he would have a sure-fire best-seller. The title story is the account of a rather obnoxious mid-

Dust jacket for Grayson's 1979 collection, which includes stories of the author's extended family as well as farcical treatments of historical figures such as Adolf Hitler and Warren Burger

dle-aged man who is attempting to write a story about Lincoln's doctor's dog. The absurd doings of the title character, a pup named Sparky who eventually becomes minister to Nicaragua and a successful nineteenth-century entrepreneur, are comic background and nearly irrelevant to the doings of the narrator, who watches soap operas to get ideas and watches teenage basketball players to get his sexual gratification. So clueless is the narrator as to what makes a story that after he has finished the putative "Lincoln's Doctor's Dog," he calls up editor Theodore Solotaroff, then an influential figure in the publishing world, only to get Mrs. Solotaroff, who clearly thinks she is dealing with a deranged man who informs her that her husband will publish his "masterpiece."

Other stories in the volume offer what seem to be representations of rather ordinary lives, through the author's typically skewed perspective. Grayson uses conjunctive adverbs (*however, moreover, therefore*) as titles of the sections of "Douglas, Apropos of Nothing," to describe moments in the hero's life. The sections in the Oedipal magic-realism story "Appearance House" are headed by three simple sentences, starting with one word (*There*) and ending with "There was a house. I was a boy there. I had to leave." And in the creepily unpleasant "The Second Person" Grayson employs *you* as the narrator. In "Why Van Johnson Believes in ESP"–its title apparently taken from a supermarket tabloid headline–Grayson uses second-rate Hollywood actors and other semicelebrities to comment on the longing and loneliness that lies behind the public's insatiable appetite for mass media.

Grayson moved to South Florida in 1981, but continued to live in New York for at least several months out of the year. In 1982 he published *Eating at Arby's: The South Florida Stories* as a result of a $3,000 Florida Arts Council fellowship in literature; on his application, Grayson had proposed to write a collection of stories about South Florida. The result was a chapbook of one- and two-page "stories" told in the repetitive, inane style of Dick and Jane reading primers.

Grayson's Dick and Jane are Manny and Zelda, a pair of apparently retired South Florida condo dwellers who are unutterably stupid about the world around them. Although they are retirees, Zelda has living grandparents, Grandma and Grandpa, who reside in Century Village, a well-known senior citizens' community, and "who drive each other crazy all day." Grayson presents a world of shopping malls offering meretricious consumer goods, refugees escaping Caribbean political and economic oppression (Manny mistakes a group of Haitian boat people for tourists lured by the attractions of Miami Beach), violent crime (Manny and Zelda's friend Jose, a Miami store owner, teaches them how to use a gun but in the last story becomes the fatality of a robbery), and drugs (after standing in a bank next to "boys who had just taken a trip to Colombia" and were "depositing a lot of money," Manny notes that he has heard many Floridians say they would like to make just one trip to Colombia and wonders "what there is to do in that place").

Grayson also looks at other early 1980s aspects of life in South Florida: hurricanes, race riots (their black chiropractor in the African American Liberty City neighborhood informs the couple that "some people felt they were treated unfairly"), ugly architecture, an automobile-centered society (missing an exit on I-95, Manny notes that careless elderly drivers and teenagers on Quaaludes are equally likely to cause car accidents), intellectual poverty (seeing a bookstore in the mall, Zelda says wistfully, "I read a book once"), and the presumably nonnutritious food at the Arby's restaurant where Zelda and Manny go out to eat. Grayson also

takes on such specific South Florida targets as the "condo commando," the long winter visits by unwanted relatives (Zelda gets a headache that lasts the entire stay of her sister-in-law, Norma), restaurant early-bird specials catering to senior citizens who steal rolls and condiments, and resentment toward bilingualism (Manny brags that he is bilingual because he can ask Jose "Como esta Usted?").

Eating at Arby's is an angry satire about a vacuous region, but the simplistic prose and the fact that even the most doltish South Florida resident can feel superior to Manny, Zelda, and their friends made the book quite popular with locals after Grayson publicized it in the media. The only objections came from the arts community and civic boosters. However, even the Florida Arts Council apparently recognized Grayson's contribution to the state of cultural affairs in Florida and awarded him two more Individual Artist Fellowship grants.

While an English professor at Broward Community College and a computer education instructor at Florida International University, Grayson began a series of what he called "publicity art" stunts, the purpose of which was to get media coverage for absurd or nonexistent events. Running for the town council in Davie, Florida, in 1982, Grayson garnered 26 percent of the vote while advocating giving horses the right to vote. (He pledged to vote "neigh" on every issue until that happened.) As a candidate for president in 1984, Grayson got his photo in *People, USA Today,* and many newspapers because of his whimsical platform: advocating immediate nuclear war and the moving of the nation's capital to Davenport, Iowa; making El Salvador the fifty-first state; and asking Jane Wyman to run as his vice presidential candidate because of the actress's prior experience in "dumping Ronald Reagan." In 1989 *Business Week* and the *New York Post* featured photos of Grayson in front of the New York Stock Exchange panhandling for $27 billion so that he could join in the bidding to take over the RJR Nabisco corporation. In recessionary 1990, Grayson appeared on the Cable News Network (CNN) twice: as the publisher of a magazine called *Pauper,* dedicated to glamorizing the poor, and then as head of the Save Donald Trump campaign, supposedly to rescue the billionaire real-estate developer from financial ruin. To protest a Florida federal judge's ruling that a rap album by the group 2 Live Crew was obscene, Grayson began an organization called Radio Free Florida to send copies of the banned music from his summer home in Manhattan, where the record was freely available. Grayson also wrote a humor column for the *Hollywood (Florida) Sun-Tattler.*

I Brake for Delmore Schwartz: Stories (1983), Grayson's most popular book, includes some of his most skillful tours de force. "Y/Me" is a meditation on the letter *Y* and its place in history and the narrator's life: "In junior high I learned to swim at the YMCA. I did quadratic equations, solving for X and for Y. Y. A. Tittle gave me his autograph. I got stung by a yellowjacket. In Spanish we read *Platero y Yo*. Yuri Gagarin became the first man to orbit the earth." The story ends with an exhortation to the reader to "worship Y; pray to it; make your body into a Y and give thanks for this remarkable letter." The energy and inventiveness of Grayson's language makes "Y/Me" one of his best fictions.

"The Autobiography of William Henry Harrison's Cold" takes the point of view of the cold virus that ended the life and the one-month administration of the nineteenth-century president who caught a chill after giving a "dull, pompous" inaugural address lasting for hours on a frigid day in Washington. The cold denies that he was part of a plot by Harrison's enemies or his vice president, John Tyler, and believes he did the country a service "in taking the life of a man so ill-equipped for leadership."

"Nice Weather, Aren't We?"–the title phrase a seemingly nonsensical but comprehensible bit of small talk by a stranger in an elevator–shows the narrator, an M.F.A. student, struggling to write a story that will outdo those of his graduate workshop rival, Bruce. But during the course of the "story," Bruce comes in and discovers that the narrator has used him as an unsavory character. Enraged, Bruce punches the narrator, who wonders how he will finish the story while in pain from a black eye. Almost immediately, however, the narrator announces he has made up the assault by Bruce and the story will go on–somehow. After recounting his dismay over rejections of his work and the lies he tells, not only on the page but to friends, the narrator explains that he writes only because he is so unhappy and urges the reader not to judge him: "All I do really is manipulate reality. Is that so bad? I don't know how else to live? End of story."

Only the title story in *I Brake for Delmore Schwartz*, as Ivan Gold noted in *The New York Times Book Review*, "threatens to become a well-made story." The narrator–a young writer, part-time cab driver, and adjunct college instructor living in a Brooklyn apartment with bars on his windows–has to come to terms with the fact that his girlfriend, Alix, has left him for his best friend, Tom, a struggling painter. He also must decide whether to join Tom in giving up his dreams of an artistic career in favor of going to New York University to learn computer programming. The narrator identifies with the poet Delmore Schwartz, whom he resembles both physically and in his incipient paranoia, and has made up the bumper sticker of the title to put on his car. Although neighborhood vandals have ripped it so that

the slogan is now unreadable, it conveys the narrator's desire not to hurt anyone like the mad, disheveled poet who ended his days wandering the streets of New York in a stupor. Ultimately the narrator decides to "call up Tom and leave a message on his machine," and the book ends with a renunciation of the writing life that Grayson himself contemplated many times without truly going through with it.

The Greatest Short Story That Absolutely Ever Was (1989) features a title piece in which Grayson again mocks both the blockbuster ethos of the 1980s book publishing business and the inconsequential nature of his own fictional efforts, largely published in obscure literary magazines or small-press books. The story is a compilation of gossip column items à la Larry King or Liz Smith, each ending with the requisite ellipses. These items concern Richard Grayson, an "ultra-talented" "super-writer," who, it is rumored, is at work on "another one of his short-story masterpieces." Breathlessly, the gossip columnist reveals details of the plot ("based on his own adventures on the psychiatrist's couch and in graduate school"), the secrecy surrounding work on the story (the author's eighty-two-year-old grandmother was said to be interviewing "all the candidates for the honor of typist . . . in the back booth of the Bagel Whole Restaurant in Plantation, Florida"), and a possible movie deal involving superstar actors (Tom Cruise reportedly gets down on his hands and knees to grovel before Grayson, who demands that the actor "put on fifty pounds and a dirty blond wig and glasses to play the main character, said to be based on Richie himself").

After pages of this hype-filled buildup, the author/character angrily denies to *USA Today* that "his much ballyhooed masterpiece doesn't even exist," but finally the "dynamic young superwriter who's shaken up America with his fantastic innovations in short fiction" announces at a closed-circuit press conference that he is abandoning his story but will begin a new story, "an experimental piece about all the furor writing the first story caused." As the always-limited public taste for the metafictional experiments of the late 1960s and early 1970s faded, Grayson seemed to have a clear-eyed view that his work would be ignored, but instead of retreating into bitter grousing, the author preferred to look at the absurdity of what the last sentence of the story calls "the public's resistance to fiction that they can't understand."

By titling another work in the volume "There Are Eight Million Stories in New York; This Is One of the Stupidest," Grayson again engages in self-deprecating criticism while continuing to subvert the short-story form. The tale begins: "Mark Schickler–no, let's call him Alan Moskowitz. Alan Moskowitz is a law student

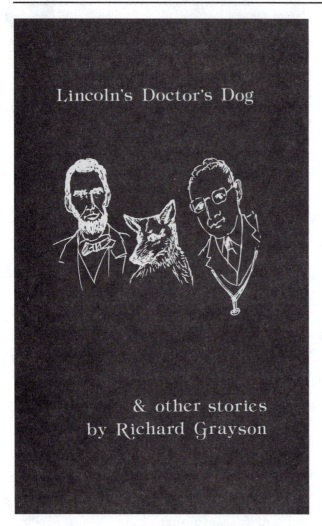

Dust jacket for Grayson's 1982 collection inspired by such varied sources as publishing in-jokes and tabloid headlines

exhorts readers to "move into an old 'I Love Lucy' rerun and get out of this damn city. And for God's sake, no more stories."

Other stories in *The Greatest Short Story That Absolutely Ever Was* similarly deconstruct themselves. The characters in "Let the Reader Beware" come to the realization that they are characters in a story; one realizes she is blind because the author has made no mention of her having eyes. "Myself Redux" mixes supposed autobiography and warped history around a final complex pun on the phrase "it's just a story." And "This Way to the Egress" ends with the narrator's apologies for the piece: "I just call it a story because I don't know what else to call it. It's just some things I'm writing down on a rainy night."

Grayson's next chapbook, *Narcissism and Me* (1989), presents the author in a similar mode. All of the stories are comic satires or parodies featuring relentless wordplay, authorial asides, solipsistic narrators who invite deliberate confusion with the author, false confessions (often of an embarrassing nature), and corny jokes.

"I Saw Mommy Kissing Citicorp" is a look at New York City at the height of the Yuppified Reagan years. The story opens with the Chairman of the Federal Reserve Board, a large, cigar-smoking man who clearly is former chairman Paul Volcker, unsuccessfully trying to get a cash advance at an automatic teller machine on the Upper West Side of Manhattan. Unable to get his money, the Fed Chairman refuses to leave the lobby of the Chase Manhattan Bank, causing a fiscal crisis and a major story for the news media. This media event allows Grayson to satirize the junk journalism practiced by the tabloids and network news, the financial machinations of Wall Street (another major crisis occurs when, because of a typo, a *Wall Street Journal* columnist touts "punk bands" instead of "junk bonds"), soaring real-estate prices, the commodification of everything, government bureaucracy, and the impersonalization and dissociation caused by technological devices such as the videocassette recorder and the ATM.

On MTV, Xerox Sankabrand, lead singer of The Vomit Seekers, croons: "I pay my Visa bill with my MasterCard / So what's the commotion? / Money's just information in motion." Grayson's story comments on the waning importance of the physical foundations of society in favor of intangible assets such as knowledge, organizational structures, and intellectual property. The Controller of the Currency lectures the Korean ambassador, a transvestite who shops at Benetton, under the misapprehension that the man is the ambassador from Japan. At the end of the story, a physical manifestation triumphs as the Fed Chairman's elderly mother floats out of her window

in New York City, just like his grandfather never was." Seemingly improvising like one of the *toomlers* in a Borscht Belt hotel (at one time Grayson's parents owned a hotel in the Catskills), the author maniacally grabs onto anything that might get his audience to guffaw or at least to pay attention. The Pynchonesque events careen on, relating everything from the plot of an *I Love Lucy* episode to 1970s scenes of child prostitutes in Greenwich Village to the story of a Chinese Armenian breakfast-cereal mogul, all the while undercut by the author's repeated assertion that these digressions have nothing to do with the story. In the end readers find that the "author" has died and somewhere in the middle a new "author" has had to come in and finish the job, racing haphazardly in and out of the minds of various passersby in Washington Square Park, one of whom says, "So what kind of story is this that began so unpromisingly and has degenerated further into pure gibberish?" The second author finally runs out of energy and

at Trump Tower over to the Citicorp building, on whose sloping roof she bestows a holy kiss. Seeing his mother, the Fed Chairman, beaten by the recalcitrant ATM machine, experiences an epiphany of relief: "It's the float, he thinks. It's the float," a reference to the "float" time between the deposit of a check and when it clears, and an acknowledgment that in an information society, the "float" is a throwback to a simpler world where real space and distance were crucial. The postscript of the story states that the malfunctioning ATM has been replaced by a newer model with a computer-generated voice, and the Fed Chairman has been replaced by the punk rocker Xerox Sankabrand, who tells the nation, "The business of America is show business."

"Innovations" satirizes the metafictionists themselves, as a hapless M.F.A. student writes a story about D.L., his creative writing professor and mentor, who is constantly humiliated publicly by senior citizens and welfare recipients when he tells them he is "an innovative fiction writer." Noting that creative-writing workshops could not take place without the use of the word "resonant," the narrator tries to please D.L. by writing a story called "Resonance," only to have the professor reject it as lacking in the title quality. Grayson's satire is directed toward his own metafiction in parenthetical asides to the reader, such as "Somehow these days most of my stories seem to be the fictional equivalents of all those recordings of 'I've Got to Be Me'" and "Look, this story might not be very interesting to read, but then, is your own life really much more interesting? So don't blame me. Blame D.L. if you must blame someone. Because I said so, that's why." In the end the author/narrator places his creative-writing professor in 1950s Miami Beach "with its uninhibited monuments to lavish and pretentious ignorance," feeling no triumph that D.L. will never write an innovative story again—because "neither will I. But then I never got the hang of it anyway."

The title story of *Narcissism and Me* begins: "I am reading a story by Richard Grayson. I am reading the first line of the story. The first line is, 'I am reading a story by Richard Grayson.'" The story gets increasingly self-reflexive and recursive, with detours discussing "Richard's" therapist, Dr. Gentile, and his Uncle Moe, as well as Christopher Lasch's *The Culture of Narcissism* (1978) and Norman Podhoretz's *Making It* (1967)—until finally the story self-destructs: "You can't read any more of this story because it is over. Grayson's a bore. . . . and the rest of us—you, me, Uncle Moe, Dr. Gentile, Christopher Lasch—are tired of this sort of self-indulgence masquerading as art."

In 1991, frustrated by the literary scene—fewer publishing outlets in a time of deep cuts in arts funding and a sense of futility, given his small audience—and spurred by his experiences attending a series of obscenity trials involving 2 Live Crew, Grayson entered the University of Florida College of Law in Gainesville. After graduating with high honors and various academic awards, Grayson joined the faculty as a staff attorney in social policy at the law school think tank, the Center for Governmental Responsibility. Drawing on his earlier interests in computer education, Grayson produced two volumes of legal memoranda on issues involving the use of computers in education for the state of Florida. He worked on projects involving public interest law, intellectual property, affirmative action, the environment, and biotechnology; he also began to publish serious op-ed pieces on various issues and emerged as a local gay-rights activist. However, he also renewed his interest in writing fiction, though he viewed himself primarily as a "hobbyist."

New stories led to another book-length collection in 1996. *I Survived Caracas Traffic* bears the subtitle *Stories from the Me Decades* and features pieces set in the mid 1970s to late 1980s. Grayson is presented in both his satiric, experimental mode and his more representational stories.

The whimsical "Twelve Step Barbie" takes the world's most popular doll through a midlife crisis. Barbie, no longer young, is a recovering alcoholic and wracked with pain from an autoimmune disease she believes she acquired from breast implants—Grayson's explanation for her oft-discussed improbable proportions. Now fortyish and weather-beaten, Barbie goes to the bank for a loan for her asbestos-removal business and is no longer surprised that the handsome young loan officer does not give her a second glance. Barbie's glamour has been replaced by the wisdom that comes with age and its inevitable disappointments. A plaintiff in a class-action suit against the breast implant manufacturer, Barbie is reunited with her former boyfriend Ken, who is now Kendra, having undergone a sex-change operation (though it is noted that even as a male, Ken had been lacking a penis) and also having been made ill by breast implants. The story ends on a sweet note, as the pair recall their past and contemplate their future friendship.

In "The Man Who Gave Away Millions" Grayson narrates a story based on a news event from the late 1960s in which a young hippie manipulated the media into thinking he had inherited a fortune and was planning to give it all away to people in need. The drugged-out protagonist, Sam Jellicoe, is a total phony, yet he manages to hoodwink both the needy and the greedy, as well as Ed Sullivan, who has Jellicoe perform a guitar solo on his television show. The story illustrates Grayson's concern with the media-driven infatuation with celebrity and its unhealthy effects as civic life is replaced by a insidiously seductive pop culture based on the commodification of everything.

Other stories find Grayson in familiar territory, portraying the isolating entropy of depression among baby boomers unwilling to grow up in "Where the Glacier Stops" and "My Plan to Kill Henry Kissinger." Satirical, bizarre stories with labored jokes and puns are also included, as in "A Man, A Plan, A Canal, Panama." In "A Clumsy Story" Grayson artfully diagrams and parodies M.F.A. workshop fiction.

After returning to fiction writing as a resident at artists' colonies in Illinois, California, and Wyoming, Grayson went back to South Florida in 1998. Grayson's more-recent fiction has not received consistently favorable reviews. Jaimy Gordon said in *American Book Review*, "Grayson is not a graceful stylist, and as soon as the expression of a personality (or the illusion of this) disappears from them, his inventions and satires move on leaden feet." Grayson's later work, having shed the cloak of reflexivity and satire, is more realistic but paradoxically less real. The world is not rendered but reported. In his earlier fiction the lack of sensory content becomes part of the linguistic texture of the work; in his recent, more realistic fiction it reveals limits to Grayson's prose style.

Grayson's stories in *The Silicon Valley Diet and Other Stories* (2000) deal with gay relationships in the 1990s against the backdrop of a culture defined by cyberspace, mass media, a consumer-driven society, immigration, and racial conflicts. Though these stories utilize many of Grayson's techniques, such as loose associations around a central motif—frequently the computer world or food—they are nonetheless more straightforward. Overall, the book received good reviews. *Publishers Weekly* (15 May 2000) called the stories "compulsively talky and engagingly disjunctive flash snapshots of gay men in their twenties, thirties and forties . . . and lighter and funnier than much gay fiction." Pat MacEnulty, in his review for *The Fort Lauderdale Sun-Sentinel* (28 May 2000), found Grayson's "italicized passages that serve as a counterpoint to the narrative . . . superfluous," yet praised the stories overall as "funny, intelligently written and original" and declared that the stories of gay relationships "serve up slices of life as we know it right here and now with hate crimes, weight worries and easy money for Internet whizzes."

Certainly Grayson is a marginal figure in contemporary American fiction, and he and his fictional persona seem quite aware of this fact. But by obsessively focusing his lens on the life of one "Richard Grayson," Richard Grayson reveals more about American society and the role of the writer within it than do some better-known or "polished" authors. Taken as a body of work, Grayson's short fiction ultimately appears to be one ongoing, career-long writing project, focused always on the effects of contemporary culture on the self.

Reference:

Alvin H. Rosenfeld, *Imagining Hitler* (Bloomington: Indiana University Press, 1985).

Barry Hannah

(23 April 1942 –   )

Richard E. Lee
State University of New York College at Oneonta

See also the Hannah entry in *DLB 6: American Novelists Since World War II, Second Series.*

BOOKS: *Geronimo Rex* (New York: Viking, 1972);
Nightwatchmen (New York: Viking, 1973);
Airships (New York: Knopf, 1978);
Ray (New York: Knopf, 1980; Harmondsworth, U.K.: Penguin, 1981);
Two Stories (Jackson, Miss.: Nouveau Press for the Mississippi Civil Liberties Union, 1982);
Black Butterfly (Winston-Salem, N.C.: Palaemon, 1982);
Power and Light: A Novella for the Screen from an Idea by Robert Altman (Winston-Salem, N.C.: Palaemon, 1983);
The Tennis Handsome (New York: Knopf, 1983);
Captain Maximus: Stories (New York: Knopf, 1985);
Hey Jack! (New York: Dutton/Seymour Lawrence, 1987);
In Honor of Oxford at One Hundred and Fifty (Grenada, Miss.: Salt-works Press, 1987);
Boomerang (Boston: Houghton Mifflin/Seymour Lawrence, 1989);
Never Die (Boston: Houghton Mifflin/Seymour Lawrence, 1991);
Airships; and Ray (London: Vintage, 1991);
Bats out of Hell (Boston: Houghton Mifflin/Seymour Lawrence, 1993);
High Lonesome (New York: Atlantic Monthly Press, 1996).

OTHER: *Men without Ties,* edited, with contributions, by Hannah (New York: Abbeville Press, 1997).

As is probably the case with all twentieth-century writers of the American South who deal in quirky narratives replete with violence, Barry Hannah has had his share of encounters with critics and readers who reduce him to an update of William Faulkner, Eudora Welty, or Flannery O'Connor. Hannah's present employment at the University of Mississippi ("Ole Miss") allows him to shrug at what he has

Barry Hannah *(photograph © by Susan Lippman; from the dust jacket for* High Lonesome, *1996)*

dubbed "the Faulkner industry," by virtue of his presence at its center. In fact, Hannah lives in the shadow of the Compson House, where Faulkner had Benjy look out at the world. This detachment from within the storm is a pattern for him, as he places himself at a distance from the currents of what pass for mainstream literary considerations. His engaged disengagement is one of the few mainstays in a vigorous career that recalls more of the experimental fire of Charlie Parker or Frank Zappa and less of the pedantry of those writers in residence safely seated in the humanities departments of the American academy. Although he is the first to acknowledge his debts to the writers who have gone before him, Hannah's catalogue of influences is too eclectic to suggest a scope or focus for the common reader. He acknowledges the influence of Ernest Hemingway, Faulkner, James Joyce, Henry Miller, and Joseph Conrad and cites the Southern Gothic tradition as integral to his development as a writer. He is equally quick to mention his most influential editor, Gordon Lish (first at *Esquire,* later at

Dust jacket for Hannah's first collection, featuring stories later expanded into the novels Ray *(1980) and* The Tennis Handsome *(1983)*

profound awareness of human nature, often captured in lyrical and startling phrasing. He is challenging, engaging, and ultimately frightening in his portrayals of the paradoxically passionate, yet soulless interactions of people in the American twentieth century. Scatology, physical violations of every imaginable—and unimaginable—sort, warfare, heedless and senseless violence, and other expressions of the carnal world pepper his explorations of the rhythms of life each person seeks in his or her trudge through mortality. Reminiscent of Walt Whitman's insistence that contradiction is devoutly to be desired, Hannah is also a proponent of true love, dogged determination, and grace under pressure. In two other ways is he like Whitman: he insists that a certain rugged kind of masculinity is to be savored, and he sees time as an incongruous chain in which the future is the past—what has been once will always be. He is a joyful exponent of living life largely and of never letting facts get in the way of a good story as he warps the events of his life to the needs of his art.

Barry Hannah was born on 23 April 1942, in Meridian, Mississippi. His parents, William and Elizabeth (née King), were staunchly middle class both socially and economically; his father made his living as an insurance salesman, and the family moved with him through the Deep South, living in Mississippi, Alabama, and Louisiana. His father attended Ole Miss, rooming with James Eastland (later a long-standing U.S. senator from the state), so Hannah's return to his father's alma mater provides a first proof of the notion that what has happened secures what will happen. Hannah married his first wife, the former Meridith Johnson (to whom he dedicated *Geronimo Rex,* 1972), while still completing graduate school. Their marriage resulted in three children, on whom Hannah dotes: two sons, Barry Jr. and Ted, and a daughter, Lee.

Hannah attended Mississippi College, graduating with a B.A. (with a premed concentration) in 1964. He received an M.A. in 1966 and an M.F.A. in creative writing in 1967 from the University of Arkansas, where he met three professors who were to have a profound influence on his life and writing: Bill Harrison, Ben Kimpel, and Jim Whitehead. Mark Charney, in his 1992 book-length treatment of Hannah, says that "Harrison introduced Hannah to his first agent; Kimpel introduced him to European literature; and Whitehead, the poet from Mississippi, taught Hannah that a love of poetry and fiction does not lessen one's masculinity." Whitehead's contribution to Hannah's literary output is particularly important due to Hannah's insistent return to what might be termed themes of masculine alienation in his fiction. The title of his M.F.A. thesis, *Habitats of the Meatblossom,* prefigures a concern with the familiar places people choose to

Knopf); writer and friend Thomas McGuane; and an acquaintance, poet Richard Brautigan. Additionally, many other individuals, including Walker Percy, John Berryman, the Beat Generation writers Allen Ginsberg and Jack Kerouac, and Jimi Hendrix, deserve mention as influences.

Hannah insists, in interview after interview, that writing should always be fresh and never pedestrian and that there must be a rhythm and a love for the words themselves. This love of language recalls Ezra Pound's injunctions to "make it new" and to write always in mind of music. Indeed, Hannah's strength, acknowledged even by those who bemoan his overall narrative strategies, lies in his ability to locate precisely the right word or phrase. The quick magic he displays in his viscerally visual prose is an apt metaphor for Hannah's place within any literary tradition: he acknowledges stylistic conventions of a sort, then veers and wheels with sharp, biting, and always tuneful phrases that sum up and dispense with whole lives in a single sentence. The best of his short stories display a haunt and a turn of phrase for carnal imagery that tromp throughout his work.

Presently ensconced in the English department of the University of Mississippi at Oxford since the mid 1980s (with brief stints elsewhere, including at the Iowa Writers' Workshop), Hannah has had a well-traveled career. He was a teacher of literature and fiction at Clemson University in South Carolina from 1967 to 1973; writer-in-residence at Middlebury College in Vermont in 1974–1975; faculty member of the English department at the University of Alabama at Tuscaloosa from 1975 to 1980; a screenwriter for Robert Altman in Hollywood in 1980; writer-in-residence at the University of Iowa at Iowa City in 1981; writer-in-residence at the University of Montana at Missoula in 1982–1983; and twice writer-in-residence at his present campus of the University of Mississippi in 1982 and 1984–1985. All of this moving about, combined with regular bouts of heavy drinking and assorted forms of hedonism, took its toll on Hannah's personal life. By 1980, the time of his brief and unsuccessful foray into Hollywood screenwriting, Hannah had divorced his second wife, Patricia Busch, the "blue-eyed Nebraska lady" referred to in the dedication to *Airships* (1978), and had come to recognize that he needed to abandon his alcoholic ways, regardless of how romantic it might be to crash and burn at an early age. Hannah is now married to Susan Varas Hannah, to whom he dedicated *Hey Jack!* in 1987. In an often-quoted interview with Robert vanArsdall in 1983, Hannah mentions that he had dried out while in California, suggesting that his wild days were behind him. In an interview with Randy Kennedy for the 9 July 1998 *New York Times,* however, Hannah recounts that he had not had a drink in "over seven years."

Hannah has been the recipient of many awards throughout his career, beginning with his acceptance of the Bellaman Foundation Award in Fiction in 1970. He was granted the Bread Loaf Fellowship for Writing in 1971. *Geronimo Rex* was nominated for the National Book Award in 1972; it won the William Faulkner Prize for Writing that same year. His first short-story collection, *Airships,* was granted the Arnold Gingrich Short Fiction Award (from *Esquire* magazine) in 1978. He received a special award for his literary accomplishments from the American Institute of Arts and Letters in 1979. He was granted the Guggenheim Award in 1983. More recently, he was honored with the Mississippi Governor's Award in the Arts in 1986, and the Mississippi Institute of Arts and Letters granted him its Award in Fiction in 1994.

Hannah has published seven novels and either six or seven collections of short stories, depending upon whether one chooses to view *Power and Light: A Novella for the Screen from an Idea by Robert Altman* (1983) as a "long" short story, a novella, or a screenplay; has edited a book on fashion designer Gianni Versace, *Men without Ties* (1997); and has been a consistent contributor to many of the most prestigious literary journals—especially in the South. He has written unproduced screenplays in Hollywood, where writers get to "make money and sleep with movie stars." As far back as 1983, though, he saw himself primarily as "a novelist, a short-story writer, and whatever happens is gravy on that side," as he told vanArsdall. Although he has had considerable success as a novelist, his strengths, and certainly his interests, seem exceptionally well suited for the short-story form. In fact, several of his novels grew out of either individual stories–such as his first novel, *Geronimo Rex,* which developed from a story he wrote while still a student in Arkansas–or from a combination of initially unconnected stories. *The Tennis Handsome* (1983), for example, derived from two tales from *Airships.* He sees "too much rationalization in the novel" form, as he remarked to Rob Trucks in 1998: "its power to lift and shock and to reveal unknown territory has been given over."

Inevitably, however, an understanding of Hannah's novels is crucial to any careful analysis of his stories. So many of his themes are rehearsed in the shorter form and then expanded into novels that it is useful to look at the more overt statements in the longer works, where there is "too much rationalization." Many of his critics would agree that he is best in the shorter form, and Hannah himself finds that it is "physically and emotionally . . . more satisfying to write a short story." Whatever overview of his astonishing range of narratives one might choose, however, one must treat all of his works to arrive at a sense of what the short fiction is doing, because Hannah never wastes any research or any preparatory work.

Hannah's first novel, *Geronimo Rex,* was based upon his short story "The Crowd Punk Season Drew," originally published in the student anthology, *Intro.* Harry Monroe, a callow Louisiana youth, moves self-indulgently through this coming-of-age novel to end up newly married and about to enter the graduate program in English at the University of Arkansas. In both *Geronimo Rex* and Hannah's second novel, *Nightwatchmen* (1973)–in which Harry appears as a secondary character–he draws upon the facts of his own life, shaping and structuring a fictional response to what would otherwise be mere autobiographical detail. Giving a glimpse of future Hannah stylistics, the author has Harry embrace violence as perhaps the only legitimate avenue of expression (the close of the novel and his embarkation upon a writing career suggest that writing is merely aggression of another sort); locates the action entirely within an American South bound up in its own struggle with the past; consistently uses music as an apt metaphor for a purer form of creation; and fragments the linearity of the narrative—in this case, by having the reader view Harry almost exclusively through the eyes of the eccentric characters with whom he interacts. The mythic figure of Geronimo is more than just an idol: his choral voice, barking approval when violence seems likely, serves Harry well, helping to speed his development as a person both by giving advice and by providing a moral yardstick for a universe that is, to Harry, an undeniably dangerous place.

In this first work Hannah also displays a flair for paradoxical presentation that underlies much of his later work. For example, Harry's penchant for violence—including senselessly slaughtering a peacock when in the second grade and erupting into violence at Peter Lepoyster's mansion and later at his cabin—is all the more startling because of the evenhanded delivery of the detail. David Madden's analysis of *Geronimo Rex,* from the aesthetic distance of the tenth anniversary of its publication, addresses this central theme: "Hannah suggests a mandate to violence in his description of what boredom and inner void do to adolescents the summer after graduation in towns like Dream of Pines [Harry's hometown, and the site of the first third of the novel]: 'I have red welts all over me from standing nude with my air rifle and firing it against the wall almost pointblank, willfully suffering the ricochets when they come back.'"

Guns abound throughout *Geronimo Rex* and much of Hannah's other work, an indication of the author's own enthusiastic appreciation of firearms. It is difficult not to see Harry Monroe's attachment to the pistol he keeps next to his leg throughout much of *Geronimo Rex* in the same light as Hannah has at times treated weapons himself. A possibly apocryphal story that first surfaced in an *Esquire* magazine account in 1988 and was repeated in *The New York Times* mentions an incident at the University of Alabama in which Hannah waved a reportedly unloaded pistol at a class of students who were unwilling to listen to him play the trumpet. At other times, he told Kennedy, "when he needed to make holes in the walls of an apartment for stereo wires, he would use a shotgun. When his car once filled with water during a rainstorm, he riddled the floor-board with bullets to drain it." Hannah's response to such stories focuses on the tendency of "middle-class minds" to turn actions such as these "into a cowboy thing." Whether such self-perpetuating tales are true is an interesting point, and one that Hannah seems uninterested in settling. Regardless, there is no denying that such tales enhance his reputation for living life romantically.

This willingness to freely play with fact, romanticized and mythologized for the purposes of a personal fiction, is also perhaps the distinction between truth and lying or between the authentic and the imagined. It is also the basis for printed fictions, which are more easily accepted. As Mark Charney puts it, quoting Hannah, he has "cited his innovative and controversial use of autobiography as a primary factor distinguishing his work from that of other Southern writers: 'They remain obsessed by autobiography, but I use it as a mode to get to the real stuff, which is almost always lying.'" Charney believes that Hannah, in his first two novels, "uses autobiographical incident as a catalyst to encourage an imaginative response rather than as a means to convey or relive personal history." In the powerful and provocative short story "Water Liars," the issue of acceptable personal fictions and the harsh and unwelcome glare of real truth (what Hannah described in 1998 as "what you think of yourself at three AM") is again at work. Hannah's concern with what it means to be true to self and others is at the core of his fiction. Rob Trucks, interviewing Hannah in 1998, observed that there were many "Hannah elements in that story . . . I see 'Water Liars' as an almost prototypical Barry Hannah work . . . the poignancy, the hit and hurt of the ending line, 'We were both crucified by the truth.'"

Harry in *Geronimo Rex,* like Hannah, is hard to dismiss, precisely because the scathing judgments of all in his orbit are tempered and consistently offset by this tendency to introspection and critical evaluation. The ribaldry of the novel is opposed to the disdain and disregard Geronimo visits upon Harry when he mistreats women. Additionally, the obstinate permanence of the past—positively presented in the cross-cultural interactions of Harry, Geronimo, and a mulatto named Harley Butte—is disturbingly and jarringly represented in Lepoyster, the nightmarish bigot with a penchant for incest and pornography (at one point, he writes a highly charged pornographic letter to his own wife). Harry despises Lepoyster, yet Lepoyster helps him realize that violence romanticized is violence nonetheless.

In his prescient review of *Geronimo Rex* for *The New Yorker* (9 September 1972), John Updike wrote that "Mr. Hannah can seize a person and hurl him into print. . . . The author does not shy from pushing an image into absurdity, and pulling it out on the other side. . . . Some of the metaphors carry the shock of real poetry." Updike detailed in his generally positive review the attitudes that have become the elements of most subsequent serious reviews of Hannah's work: acknowledgment of a magnificent prose style that sometimes becomes self-conscious wordplay, underlining the weaknesses of narrative form and style that plague his novels.

His second novel, *Nightwatchmen,* was something of a disappointment to reviewers and to Hannah himself. He admits that he "wrote that book in a hurry, some of it in New York, which wasn't very good for me"; he also acknowledges that he "delivered it more quickly than I should have in order to capitalize on the success of *Geronimo Rex.*" Although Harry Monroe and his seventeen-year-old bride, Prissy, are involved in the plot, the story centers around a series of brutal campus murders. A serial killer named the Knocker is stalking the Southern Mississippi University community, and the reader is treated to the Faulkneresque narrative technique of having information passed to the reader by way of taped recitations of the murders by those who knew the victims. The arrival of Hurricane Camille both increases the carnage and scours clean the site of the novel. Water, in all its symbolic potentialities, excites Hannah. The novel ends with the murderer found by the eccentric detectives—found, murdered, and then buried.

Hannah's first collection of short stories, *Airships,* was published in 1978 after a five-year hiatus. The negative tone that informed most of the reviews of *Nightwatchmen* returned Hannah to his early focus on the integrity of the event itself as evidenced in the less expansive short form. The collection begins with "Water Liars," dealing with the difference between surface appearances and real things deceptively hidden from the casual view. Like its companion pieces, "All the Hearkening Faces at the Rail"—also from *Airships*—and "High-Water Railers," the opening story in the 1993 collection *Bats out of Hell,* the setting is a seemingly placid pier at a small southern lake, on Farte Cove. Reminiscence and scathing banter draw truth from the characters just as patience and baited hooks draw surprising fish from the lake.

The narrator of "Water Liars" is, as Rob Trucks has observed, of a Christlike and contemplative age, the same age as the narrator of *Ray* (1980): "Last year I turned thirty-three years old and, raised a Baptist, I had a sense of being Jesus and coming to something decided in my life." The importance of water as a cleansing symbol of renewal is reinforced by Hannah's choice of a Baptist community setting. The narrator has come to Farte Cove to fish, wishing to clear his mind of the uncomfortable revelation by his wife of ten years that she had had a sexual history prior to having met him: "For ten years she'd sworn I was the first. I could not believe her history was exactly equal with mine. It hurt me to think that in the era when there were supposed to be virgins she had allowed anyone but *me,* and so on." The egotism of his self-delusion is highlighted by his

comment at the end of the story, spurred by a story of wild high-schoolers partying—"drunken children . . . smokin' dope and two-thirds of them nekid swimmin." The narrator's reminiscences of his own behavior as a teenager are typical for a Hannah protagonist: "But I was the worst. . . . In the mad days back then, I dragged the panties off girls and talked badly about them in the morning." As he thinks of his wife, however, his illogical double standard envisions her as a writhing, nubile, "nekid" high-school student: "I could see my wife in 1960 in the group of high-schoolers she must have had. I could not bear the roving carelessness of teenagers, their judgeless tangling of wanting and bodies."

Hannah then performs a signature turn of thought to go with his turns of phrase, adding to this cocktail of past and present by skipping forward a year and shifting the perspective to "a new younger man, maybe sixty but with the face of a man who had surrendered." This unnamed speaker tells a shocking but apocryphal story (for "Water Liars" is about "true" tales, all of which happened, unverifiably, to "other folks") that happened to him; he was witness to his then-young daughter writhing in a "tangle of wanting" with an older, mustached man. Hannah's portrait, brief as it is, of this man with his "distressed pride," who "had never recovered from the thing he'd told about," is the same picture of a young/old, defeated man Hannah presents eighteen years later in "Get Some Young," the opening story of his collection *High Lonesome* (1996). In "Water Liars" the reader can intimate that the narrator, too, will never get over the epiphany that his wife had a life before his gaze created her, because he ignores the outrage of those on the pier who insist that "This ain't the place" for such stories. "Truth," in this story, is a private revelation. The narrator brings the sad, "surrendered" younger man back to his cabin, and the two men, both lost in their own skins, are yoked in the reader's mind: "He was out there away from his wife the same as me. . . . Just an older guy with a big, hurting bosom. He wore a suit and the only way you'd know he was on vacation was he'd removed his tie. . . . And we were kindred. We were both crucified by the truth."

Many jarring and disturbing narratives are included among the twenty stories in *Airships* (nine of which had been previously published in *Esquire* under the influential tutelage of Gordon Lish). One of these, "Testimony of Pilot," introduces the character of Quadberry, who resurfaces in *Ray.* "Dragged Fighting from His Tomb" begins a preoccupation, running throughout Hannah's fiction (including "Knowing He Was Not My Kind Yet I Followed" in *Airships*), with the complex figure of Confederate general J. E. B. Stuart. In "Dragged Fighting from His Tomb" a Confederate soldier hero-

Dust jacket for Hannah's 1993 collection of stories linked by themes of war and aging

ically avoids an ambush while bemoaning his conclusion that "we are all overbrained and overemotioned . . . we are all a dizzy and smelly farce." Captain Howard kills many Union soldiers, dares ask Stuart why they are killing men in the North, is arrested, escapes, deserts to the Union side, tracks and kills Stuart, and recounts the tale from the distance of 1901, when his "lusts surpass his frame."

The plots of many of the stories in this collection are astounding. In "Quo Vadis, Smut" a flying squad of perversion police finesse a pornographer—who has tied his "supposed sweetheart underneath a bull, all naked"—into swallowing ground glass, after which the narrator returns to the ritualized sexual abuse of his fifth wife. "Eating Wife and Friends" begins in another of Hannah's boardinghouses (as does "Mother Rooney Unscrolls the Hurt" later in the collection). Set in a postapocalyptic future, Hannah here gets a chance to visit more of the land he seems to share with another erstwhile enfant terrible, Harlan Ellison. (Ellison's "A Boy and His Dog" deals with a similar theme, and another Ellison story, "Strawberry Spring," covers, superficially, the same thematic ground as *Nightwatchmen*.) Cannibalism and a decidedly dark vision of human nature are placed in the foreground as a hus-

band and father contemplates life and what constitutes really living when a famine takes hold: "The thing of it was that you could stay alive a phenomenal length of time on almost nothing, counting talking and singing. Which sent communication and melody back into the crapper"—an observation that perhaps says something of how Hannah views Art, and specifically writing, in the grand and shaggy scheme of things.

In "Coming Close to Donna" an unpopular and unsuccessful twenty-year-old version of Harry Monroe returns from his failure at junior college to "wear smart clothes and walk up and down Sunset Strip. That will show them." His inability to write—he has failed at English composition—forces him back to his hometown, where "everybody thinks I'm a fag." In a cemetery he watches a fistfight between two contenders for a sexual encounter with Donna, an eighteen-year-old "whose feet are red and not handsome around the toes." As Donna strips for the narrator, he realizes that the two battling boys have become too serious in their struggle. Both are dead, and Donna "goes to the two bodies, and is absorbed in a tender, unnatural act over the blue jeans of Hank and Ken." Sex, death, and music combine here, as in so many other Hannah narratives, as Vince, the narrator, loses his virginity at the cemetery in the presence of the two corpses "who had sung a pretty fine duet in their rock band." Six months later, Donna is strung out on heroin and begs Vince to "screw me" so she can "get back to my old neighborhood"; for Donna, sex is the only way home. Vince obligingly takes her back to the cemetery and crushes her skull with a tombstone, saying, "some of us are made to live for a long time. Others for a short time. Donna wanted what she wanted. I gave it to her."

Among the stories in *Airships,* one other stands out as a beacon of Hannah's concerns with memory, the middle-class pretensions of pseudo-intellectuals, the secret lives of women, and the dreamy and salacious presence of all things past in all moments of the present. In the short piece "Deaf and Dumb," Minny dreams away the afternoon, unable to push away her swarming memories of Harold, the man "who had taken her virginity." She also remembers her more recent submissions to the camera for her husband, who recalls the leering Peter Lepoyster of *Geronimo Rex.* As Minny's reverie continues, she becomes concerned that the babysitter is not watching the children: "She's paid to stay. They're my responsibility. The teenagers come by our street so fast in their cars . . . they use it as a blasting alley. One boy I met with before college liked to speed that way. We raced everywhere." Memories, as in "High-Water Railers," are "like things thrown up by eutrophic lakes." Always, sex is there as a lightning rod, to reassure the reader that regularly reinforced carnality is a safe haven: "there's nothing like that hot blowing out in you when you are coming yourself," thinks Minny; "I, good Lord, thank You for that. It keeps a body going through the trash in daylight. Good intercourse is a work of art. Minny was asleep."

Back in the narrative flow, the reader is about to witness Minny's son whack her in the mouth with a hammer, around the handle of which is a none-too-subtly present king snake. Hannah's matter-of-fact reportorial detachment was apparent in his shocking description of a woman tied to a bull's belly in "Quo Vadis, Smut" and again features in the ending of "Deaf and Dumb": Minny's youngest boy "knew it was a sin to be asleep in the daytime, the babysitter gone. He looked at her awhile. Then he hit her in the mouth with the hammer . . . she thought she was still in a dream and she felt very guilty for her sleep." Minny is not unaware of having traded sex for middle-class torpor, mixing memory with desire and cash money: "Lucky for me Daryl is good looking. I couldn't stand phonying-up to one with hair on his knees. They once tried to hire me as an interior decorator. . . . They offered me a salary of $5700 a year. Daryl got on the phone . . . 'You got to raise the ante . . . Let us know if you can get it up over nigger wages'. . . . I guess I'm lucky how much I love Daryl,

who's a silly ass by any judgment." Fleeting self-awareness often gives way in Hannah to an embrace of more comforting fictions.

Reviewing *Airships,* Richard Locke wrote in *The New York Times Book Review* (21 May 1978) what has become a consensual critical observation with respect to Hannah's fiction: that the author's consistent use of first-person narrative perspective, coupled to the violent and anarchic actions of many of his characters, creates a certain sameness that works against his deft touch with the lyricism of the language he displays. "The speaker is always the same: he comes on as the voice of the New South, a Country-and-Western *homme moyen sensuel,* your average horny s.o.b. just trying to get along in this crazy violent American world." Locke also identifies Hannah with both the Southern Gothic tradition and regionally distant contemporaries such as John Irving. The vast array of writers with whom he has been compared calls to mind the panoply of influences—scattered, eclectic, tangentially connected at best—Hannah himself admits to when questioned. But if any writer who has an "offhanded way with plot and structure" is apt fodder for comparison, perhaps the distinctiveness of Hannah's voice is the only constant and the critics' wheeling attempts at linkage with someone more familiar are less useful than usual in Hannah's case. "So Barry Hannah often sounds like a sour-mash William Saroyan. He is nothing if not charming, but he is also sloppy, self-indulgent, and writes as if a loose colloquiality were all there is to Vonnegut or Brautigan. What makes his stories unusual is that they have none of the creepy Spanish-moss effect of most 'literary' Southern writing."

Also in review of *Airships,* Michael Malone in *The Nation* (10 June 1978) registers a similar criticism: "Hannah's tools (technical and thematic) come out of a Southern kit: the 'Gothic' humor that is like sculpting gargoyles on Piggly-Wiggly stores, the lush rhythmic, almost incantational prose, the vocal quality of the writing. Point of view is almost always from a first person narrator, or more precisely, a raconteur." Malone, too, locates Hannah within a tradition that inevitably includes Faulkner, Welty, and O'Connor, not least because Hannah consistently circles chronological events, often interrogating and investigating the present through the eyes of the past: "Like Faulkner, Hannah is compelled by the past." For example, the Civil War becomes the lens through which to view the Vietnam conflict in stories such as "Dragged Fighting from His Tomb." In a more developed way, a short story detailing the generational conflicts between a young athlete and his admiring mentor ("Return to Return" in *Airships*) becomes material for a later novel, *The Tennis Handsome.*

For *Ray,* his third novel–published in 1980–Hannah chose to treat the Vietnam War directly, continuing strands begun in several stories in *Airships.* Using the experiences of his real-life friend Quisenberry as background for his treatment of jet pilots, Hannah fashioned the character of Quadberry, who appears in both the second story in *Airships,* "Testimony of Pilot," and this longer work. The novel follows the haunted narrative of Ray, a seemingly immortal doctor returned from Vietnam who recalls the gruesome horror of his time there while recounting and reliving his similar experiences in Virginia during the Civil War. Although the downbeat nature of the theme seems pessimistic, Hannah's triumph in this work is his paradoxical ability to instill in Ray a desire to jump out of bed each day to do his job and indulge himself in the pursuit of sex, violence, and over-the-top excitement.

In his next novel, *The Tennis Handsome,* Hannah was able to salvage some of an unpublished nonfiction book on the professional tennis tour (specifically focusing on Bob Lutz). He incorporated the reportorial work he had done for this book (ultimately rejected by Lippincott) with the texts of two unrelated short stories from *Airships.* The first story, "Return to Return," introduces three of the primary characters in the novel: Baby Levaster, a decadent from the South, now a medical man; Dr. Word, an ardent devotee of the purity of athleticism (especially in young boys) who enters into an affair with the title character's mother; and French Edward, a natural athlete–all beauty, grace, speed, and unpredictable imbecility off the court. "Midnight and I'm Not Famous Yet," the second of the seed stories from *Airships* that became *The Tennis Handsome,* concerns Bob Smith, like French Edward and Baby Levaster a product of the Vicksburg, Mississippi, vicinity, and his return from Vietnam after a harrowing tour of duty. Among the more memorable scenes in the novel are French's attempted murder of Dr. Word using his tennis stroke as a weapon and the rape of a woman by a walrus. As in *Ray,* the reader is immersed in war, sex, and violence: increasingly familiar Hannah territory.

In 1985 Hannah published *Captain Maximus,* a mixed bag that includes a screenplay (more like a treatment), *Power and Light,* which had already been published two years previously. Overall, this volume is a scattershot group of stories that lean even more toward minimalism than does some of the leaner, sharper pieces in *Airships.* Hannah suggested to Trucks that the volume "was an example of what I could do for about three years. It was almost like a cripple taking his first steps back into what he loves." That he had yet to become comfortable with being forty years old might account for the biting tone that many of the strongest stories (for example "Idaho" and "Even

Greenland") display. "There's something you can't duplicate about being twenty-eight," said Hannah; "You know things that a forty-year-old doesn't know anymore, or has lost."

Hannah's endings often signal possibilities and options, but not everyone is willing to grant credit to material that seems to slip away from his control. For example, in his examination of "Idaho," a spare tribute to recently deceased poet Richard Hugo, Terrence Rafferty asked: "is this story not about a poet's natural death but about the narrator's veering back and forth between suicide and murder? . . . Is it significant that Hannah, Hugo, Hemingway, and Hendrix share an initial?" In "Even Greenland" a pilot engaged in a war of words, crafting new metaphors for snow, refuses to eject from his doomed jet. Yet, Captain Ned Maximus, who, unlike Hendrix, makes it to middle age, says in "Ride, Fly, Penetrate, Loiter" that, "at forty, I am at a certain peace." As is the case in so many of Hannah's character studies, there is often an underlying irony to what characters unwittingly reveal about themselves.

In 1987 Dutton published Hannah's fifth novel, *Hey Jack!,* in which the author returns to the Mississippi university setting first seen in *Geronimo Rex* and *Nightwatchmen.* Another war veteran–this time from the Korean War–with the allusive name of Homer serves as the centerpiece of a narrative in which all the oddball eccentrics in the universe swirl around him. Readers do not discover that the antiheroic Homer is the narrator until the last page because he speaks of himself always in the third person: a distancing maneuver in keeping with recurring issues of self-awareness related to Hannah's short stories.

A strictly autobiographical novel, *Boomerang* was published in 1989. The karmic principle of repayment surfaces throughout the work, as three boomerang-throwing sessions structure Hannah's meditations on manliness, violence, sex, the impossibility of surviving marriage, drinking, dogs, and celebrity. It is worth recalling that Hannah sees himself as a sort of a "peacetime war correspondent," a journalist not necessarily bound by the data he collects, as he told Robin Street in 1990: "Journalists are bound by the facts. They must work with the facts given. A writer can go to art to make a statement. It doesn't depend on a set of data. . . . sometimes life will give you a perfect story. But usually you have to lie. You have to shape and form the story."

Hannah's 1991 novel, *Never Die,* is set outside of the author's usual matrix of the Deep South, the university community, Vietnam, and communal living arrangements such as Mother Rooney's boardinghouse. The setting is still the South, but it is Nitburg, Texas, in 1910, and the sweep of the Old West as it draws to a technologically driven close is the unreal context Hannah has chosen.

Other published works include limited editions such as a poetry collection, *In Honor of Oxford at One Hundred and Fifty* (1987), and the short stories re-presented as in *Black Butterfly* (1982) and *Two Stories* (1982)– including "Ride, Fly, Penetrate, Loiter," which found its way into *Captain Maximus* in 1985. In this last story Hannah was again able to salvage at least a title and a thematic treatment. Unable to find a publisher for a book-length treatment, "Maximum Ned," Hannah grants the title to the protagonist of "Ride, Fly, Penetrate, Loiter," which is about fighter pilots. Like Whitman's narrator in *Leaves of Grass* (1855)–and like Jimi Hendrix, whom Hannah idolized–these fighter-jocks sound their "barbaric yawps" across the landscape as they live beyond the edge of experience. Maximum Ned voices this Hannahesque truism: "The Deep South might be wretched, but it can howl." In 1983 Hannah published a screen treatment as a novella in *Power and Light,* about a group of female electric company employees in Seattle, which also found its way into *Captain Maximus* two years later.

Hannah's next collection of stories, arguably his best, is *Bats out of Hell*. Mature, startling, too varied for easy linkage, the contents include titles of a sort readers have come to expect from Hannah: "Upstairs, Mona Bayed for Dong," "Death of a Bitch," "Rat-faced Auntie," "Evening of the Yarp: A Report by Roonswent Dover," "Nicodemus Bluff," "Mother Mouth," "Bats out of Hell Division." These stories, and the others that make up the collection, while vaguely linked by the themes of war and aging, resist plot summary. More powerful than the incongruous plots, perhaps, are the sounds of the words themselves and the chilling clarity of the insights.

A random selection of sentences that Hannah tosses at his readers reveals the author as secure in his choices of words and images: "Mr. Pool was beating my father on the neck with a hard pepperoni sausage" ("Nicodemus Bluff"); "we imagine he required so many women because he never got it right, he fouls it up time after time–the Uzi of sex" ("That Was Close, Ma"); "He has had a secret life not many know about, and those who knew wish they didn't. . . . In one book even the space aliens are Communists, led by a nude queen who stitched the hammer and sickle on the backs of helpless nude American men with a giant atomic sewing machine" ("Dental"); "Wretched hesitation, Harold said, is what embalms our lives, and that was what age demanded of you more and more, to get less and less life" ("Scandale d'Estime").

In "High-Water Railers" Hannah allows his readers to glimpse adolescent male hormonal ragings from the calmer shore of old men recalling the urgencies of their youths with detachment, if not aplomb. As if to underline the presence of the past in all things "new" and present, this story makes a metaphor of a geologic term: human memory in this story functions like a eutrophic lake, one that has many aquatic and avian rarities because of regular floods from the "great continental river." The main character here is as surprised by his memories as he is "intrigued by what the lake gave up." The lake's regurgitation of deep, true things stands in for the revelations that rewrite the past and sour all notions of history, as the widow of a highly regarded former college president offhandedly reveals that her husband had become a pederast in his dotage. Like fish from the lake, memories turn rancid quickly if exposed to too much sunlight. As the old men sit at the end of the pier at Farte Cove, the reader is told that "the world was in such a sorry state, it made a man lie sometimes to be sane."

In his 1996 short-story collection, *High Lonesome,* Hannah continues to provide vivid narratives and a seemingly endless supply of eccentric characterizations. Lending weight to the notion that what is past is present, Hannah's incisive ability to summarize (and dismiss) whole lives in a phrase reaches its finest form in this collection: "Since he had returned from Korea he and his wife lived in mutual disregard, which turned three times a month into animal passion then diminished on the sharp incline to hatred, at last collecting in time into silent fatigue."

This opening from the highly regarded first story, "Get Some Young," leads the reader into the depths of passion, adultery, and the deep waters of knowledge as five boys go to a camp house in the woods. One of them, Swanly, is a disturbingly beautiful teenage boy. He is struck dumb by love, though he fancies himself aware beyond his years: "Swanly was a prescient boy. He hated that their youth might end. He saw the foul gloom of job and woman ahead, all the toting and fetching, all the counting of diminished joys like sheep with plague; the arrival of beard hair, headaches, the numerous hospital trips, the taxes owed and further debts, the mean and ungrateful children, the washed and waxen dead grown thin and like bad fish heaved into the outer dark." Hannah evokes an ominous sense of tragedy, one like Sophocles' *Oedipus Rex,* where foreknowledge leads not to any avoidance of dark destiny but to an arrogance that creates the disaster. The reader is never told how Swanly comes by his knowledge, but he is no more immune from tragedy than is Oedipus. The swan is, of course, symbolic of immortality, so his name provides an ironic foreshadowing of his fate; like many adolescents, he thinks he will live forever. He may, but it will not be pleasant.

Dust jacket for Hannah's 1996 collection of stories, nominated for a Pulitzer Prize in fiction

In typical Hannah fashion, there are various forms of misogyny, shotguns, and grotesques, like the hermit Sunballs, whose eyes are plucked out by Tuck, the old-before-his-time, cuckolded storekeeper: "Sunballs moved his hands and the boys viewed the eyes bruised like a swollen burglar's mask, the red grief of pounded meat in the sockets. The fingers of both Tuck's hands were mud red and fresher around the knife handle." Prior knowledge, foresight, must be punished in both Greek and southern traditions. Knowledge must be bought with hard currency. Swanly becomes a gibbering outcast, and his mother, his initiator into the ways of woman, who was "refractory until this change in her son, withdrew into silent lesbian despair with another of her spirit then next into a church and out of this world, where her husband continued to make his inardent struggles." Hannah's own thoughts on age notwithstanding, twenty-eight-year-olds who possess this kind of sweeping gaze run

the risk of ending up like Oedipus and Swanly, and for the same reasons.

All the stories in *High Lonesome* share a scathing insight into the paradoxical realities of human living. "Carriba" tells of a writer who has researched the lives of "Mississippi criminal Irish" and found that if you "take away the harassment and dogged persecution of the police . . . the folks had little cause to exist." He attempts to salvage the younger members of the family by helping them to avoid the trap of place and paternity that had led the older boy to kill his father. The narrator is soul-sick, a "geezer": "Around age forty-five there might be a pop and a hiss in your heart, and you are already on your way, a geezer. Nothing is good or like it used to be, not even nookie. A great gabby sadness swarms over you. You are an ancient mariner yanking on the arms of the young. See here, see here." He initiates a bizarre therapy group for Modock—the instrument of his hideous father's "suicide-by-son"—and a matricide in the town. Hannah's prose here is typically vivid and surprising: "she was currently over in Hattiesburg failing at something menial"; "Some say depression among the poor shows up instantly as fat. The boy was not only neckless but nigh to growing another face across."

The concentrated style Hannah has honed over three decades as a working writer continues throughout *High Lonesome*. It is not music, but something specific to the way words work when they are worked with well; "people who try to make a direct connection between prose lines and music are fools," he told Trucks in 1998. "You can't write music. Those who try to get it on the page are idiots. It's a whole different thing, but the motive is much the same." In these stories he continues to help his readers discover things about being human by warping his own life and experience to his needs. Readers do not have to decide if Hannah's characters' statements are autobiographical. They can hear the "truth" of a life behind the weight of his comments about sex, women, ambition, and the troubling realities of existence in the midst of other people in samplings such as: "In his late forties the lifetime monster of lust had released him, first time since he was eleven, just as the lifetime monster of drink had released him four years ago" ("Ned Maxy, He Watching You"); "Lovers are the most hideously selfish aberrations in any given territory. They are not nice, and careless to the degree of blind metal-hided rhinoceroses run amok" ("Through Sunset into the Raccoon Night"). Hannah, ever fresh, is often problematic for critics since they are never sure what surprises he may have in store for them.

Even though he was widely praised upon the publication of *Geronimo Rex* in 1972, and even more heralded by critics when Knopf released *Airships* in 1978, Hannah's work has tended to generate mixed reviews. As a general rule, critics and reviewers have tended to favor Hannah's short-story work over his efforts in the novel form. Few, though, have gone quite so far as Terrence Rafferty in *The Nation,* saying that the novel form is inappropriate for the explorations in narrative style that characterize Hannah's writings. Looking back over his publications in 1985, Rafferty accused Hannah of "an almost mystical belief in his own easy manipulation of language—as if the exact combination of words and images will induce visions, like a prayer. This is a feeling that's probably more common in poets and musicians than in novelists . . . in the work he's produced since *Airships,* Hannah is barely a novelist at all." Even those who disparage the novels, however, inevitably mention his ability to work with images, to use contrast to throw visual potential on mere words. In a review of *The Tennis Handsome* for *New York* (16 May 1983), Carolyn Clay summarizes the ambivalence so often voiced regarding Hannah's novelistic tendencies: "Hannah's talent . . . is undeniable, even frightening, but in the end, it tumbles down on us . . . The gonzo approach, in which he is well versed, may be best suited to short fiction."

Critical reception of the later novels, *Hey Jack!,* *Boomerang,* and *Never Die,* has tended to repeat the concerns of earlier reviewers, with an expected mixture of acceptance and disdain for what are alternately seen as caricatures and insightfully drawn characters. Increasingly, however, awareness of Hannah's use of violence had come to dominate reviews, especially the later collections of short stories. Once other writers began to also bring gore to the page, a stylistic difference began to be drawn between, for example, Hannah and Bret Easton Ellis, as Alex Raksin did in the *Los Angeles Times* (28 February 1993), reviewing *Bats out of Hell.* Raksin argues that Hannah does something different from "and far more difficult" than Ellis's technique: "He shows why his characters have come to need their nihilistic anger . . . in order to survive." As Hannah experiments both with content and with structure, it is inevitable that he will encounter critics prepared to read in a certain way and to dismiss his attempts at new kinds of narrative order in his texts.

In an extended analysis of Hannah's tendency to marry the historical, the autobiographical, the fictional, and the grotesque, Ruth D. Weston, in her 1991 essay "'The Whole Lying Opera of It': Dreams, Lies, and Confessions in the Fiction of Barry Hannah," observes that "Hannah's protagonists indulge in secular rituals of confession that alternate with dreams and lies in a vicious circle that provides coherent narrative structure to a fiction which appears on its surface to be the epitome of postmodern fragmentation." Weston, using the rigorous discourse analysis of narratology, sees Hannah as an important example of a certain kind of narrative structure, one that relies upon the reader's expectations of form to fill in the narrative gaps and provide a "cognitive strategy" for unification. Weston's analysis makes a strong case for Hannah as the exponent of a certain kind of fiction unlikely to find its way onto the shelves of grocery stores: "although Hannah's plots are not conventional, they constitute a significant postmodern 'chaos' of mini-plots designed to appeal to the narrative desires of writer, hero, and reader to find meaning in the gap between dreams, lies, and confessions."

Hannah certainly agrees that popular literary tastes, and writing itself, is too pedestrian, that it should embrace challenge and experimentation. Interviewer Randy Kennedy reports that Hannah sees himself as a "bulwark against a creeping homogenization in American fiction . . . 'blandness has taken over everywhere, or just idiot low sensation' . . . he also bemoans a generation of young writers afraid to take risks."

The first book-length treatment of Hannah's work through *Boomerang* provides a strong overview of his movement from "a preoccupation with unconventional narrative form" and a "shift from violence and isolation to peaceful alternatives and community acceptance." Mark Charney makes compelling points throughout his book and is particularly strong in his analysis of *Airships* and the overarching connections between and among the twenty stories in the collection: "The inability to face 'truth' about themselves and those around them is the characteristic that binds together most of the narrators." But while some of the stories in the later collections, *Bats out of Hell* and *High Lonesome,* are easily viewed in the light in which Charney analyzes *Captain Maximus,* highlighting "Hannah's characters' need for peaceful alternatives to replace the violence of the past and present," this observation seems difficult to relate to Hannah's overall literary vision. For example, in the pensive, if frenzied, tales from *High Lonesome* that share the "peaceful alternatives" Charney refers to—stories such as "Snerd and Niggero," "Ned Maxy, He Watching You," and "Through Sunset into the Raccoon Night"—any "community acceptance" of the tacitly more mature characters is lessened by the gore and hormones of the opening story, "Get Some Young," and the closing lines of "Uncle High Lonesome," which caps the collection by recounting a murder that is cynically left unpunished. Readers are told offhandedly of "the victim sentenced to remain dead . . . For years now I have dreamed I killed somebody. The body has been hidden, but certain people know I am guilty, and they show up and I know, deep within, what they are wanting, what this is all about." Although regret is the mature alternative to violence visited upon others, the fact of the violence remains.

It seems certain that interest in Hannah will increase as time passes. The first Ph.D. dissertation on Hannah was completed at the University of North Carolina at Chapel Hill in 1990. Ruth Weston of Oral Roberts University, arguably Hannah's most acute critic, published the second book-length treatment of Hannah, *Barry Hannah, Postmodern Romantic,* in 1998. A reviewer of *Ray* put it well in 1980: "Mr. Hannah's novel . . . doesn't go down easily. . . . One has to admire Mr. Hannah's originality and jagged unpredictability. One has to admire his willingness to look at 'God's especially ugly creatures' without sentimentalizing or blinking." His verve and style, his way with the language alone, will ensure that he will continue to be a writer to contend with in years to come. Although his novels may allow him to paint on a broader canvas, his short-story work is what sustains his readers, and it is in this genre that he most confidently displays the stylistics that have come to mark him as an important writer.

Interviews:

Robert vanArsdall, "The Spirits Will Win Through: An Interview with Barry Hannah," *Southern Review,* 19, 2 (Spring 1983): 317–341;

Robin Street, "Shut Up and Watch and Listen," *Writer's Digest* (September 1990): 39;

Rob Trucks, "A Conversation with Barry Hannah," *Black Warrior Review,* 24, 2 (Spring/Summer 1998): 13–40;

Randy Kennedy, "At Home with Barry Hannah: Mellowing Out but Unbowed," *New York Times,* 9 July 1998, pp. F1, F9.

References:

Mark Charney, *Barry Hannah* (New York: Twayne, 1992);

Owen W. Gilman, "Barry Hannah," in *Contemporary Fiction Writers of the South: A Bio-Bibliographic Sourcebook,* edited by Joseph M. Flora and Robert Bain (Westport, Conn.: Greenwood Press, 1993), pp. 213–221;

David Madden, "Barry Hannah's *Geronimo Rex* in Retrospect," *Southern Review,* 19 (Spring 1983): 309–316;

Terrence Rafferty, "Gunsmoke and Voodoo," *Nation,* 240 (1 June 1985): 677–679;

Kenneth Seib, "'Sabers, gentlemen, sabers': The J. E. B. Stuart Stories of Barry Hannah," *Mississippi Quarterly,* 45 (Winter 1991): 41–53;

Michael P. Spikes, "What's in a Name? A Reading of Barry Hannah's *Ray,*" *Mississippi Quarterly,* 42 (Winter 1988–1989): 69–82;

John Updike, "From Dyna Domes to Turkey-Pressing," *New Yorker,* 48 (9 September 1972): 121–124;

Ruth D. Weston, *Barry Hannah, Postmodern Romantic* (Baton Rouge: Louisiana State University Press, 1998);

Weston, "Debunking the Unitary Self and Story in the War Stories of Barry Hannah," *Southern Literary Review,* 27 (Spring 1995): 96–106;

Weston, "'The Whole Lying Opera of It': Dreams, Lies, and Confessions in the Fiction of Barry Hannah," *Mississippi Quarterly,* 44 (Fall 1991): 411–428.

William Harrison

(29 October 1933 –   )

Sharon L. Jones
Earlham College

BOOKS: *The Theologian* (New York: Harper & Row, 1965; London: Gollancz, 1966);
In a Wild Sanctuary (New York: Morrow, 1969; London: Gollancz, 1970);
Lessons in Paradise (New York: Morrow, 1971);
Roller Ball Murder (New York: Morrow, 1974); republished as *Rollerball: 13 Selected Stories* (London: Futura, 1975);
Africana (New York: Morrow, 1977; London: Hamilton, 1977);
Savannah Blue (New York: Richard Marek, 1981; Feltham, U.K.: Hamlyn, 1981);
Burton and Speke (New York: St. Martin's Press, 1982; London: W. H. Allen, 1984);
Three Hunters (New York: Random House, 1989);
The Buddha in Malibu: New and Selected Stories (Columbia: University of Missouri Press, 1998);
The Blood Latitudes: A Novel (Denver, Colo.: MacMurray & Beck, 2000).

PRODUCED SCRIPTS: *Rollerball,* motion picture, United Artists, 1975;
A Shining Season, based on William Buchanan's book, television, Columbia Pictures Television, CBS, 1979;
Mountains of the Moon, by Harrison and Bob Rafelson, motion picture, TriStar Pictures, 1990.

Although William Harrison may be best known as the author of the 1974 short story "Roller Ball Murder," which was made into a critically acclaimed 1975 movie starring James Caan, he has written many well-received novels and short stories. His work features a wide variety of characters and settings that transcend time and place. His short stories, like his novels, center on nonconformist individuals who challenge the customs and beliefs of their society. He has written two short-story collections, *Roller Ball Murder* (1974) and *The Buddha in Malibu: New and Selected Stories* (1998), which Paula Friedman of *The New York Times* (12 July 1998) referred to as a

William Harrison (photograph by Mort Gitelman; from the dust jacket for Savannah Blue, *1981)*

work of "spare, understated prose" that "heightens our sense of horror at the flagrantly decaying lives" of the characters. This assessment reflects the essential elements of Harrison's short fiction. He employs straightforward, concise language to document the harsh realities of modern life as he focuses on how individuals handle conflicts with themselves, other people, and the external environment. His characters, often lonely and alienated, seek comfort in temporal, sensual pleasures such as sex, eating, shopping, drinking alcohol, assuming false identities, experimenting with mysticism and astrology, and playing competitive sports as a means to stave off the emptiness and inadequacy of their lives.

Born in Dallas, Texas, on 29 October 1933 to Samuel Scott Harrison and Mary Etta (née Cook) Harrison, William Neal Harrison earned a B.A. from Texas Christian University in 1955 and an M.A. from Vanderbilt University in 1959. He married Merlee Kimsey on 2 February 1957, and they have three children: Laurie, Quentin, and Sean. Harrison attended graduate school at the University of Iowa in 1962 and later began teaching in the department of English at the University of Arkansas, Fayetteville, from 1964 to 1998. He cofounded the creative writing program at that university in 1965. He is now a professor emeritus residing in Fayetteville. Harrison has won a variety of prestigious awards, including a Guggenheim fellowship in 1973–1974, a National Endowment for the Arts grant in 1977, and the Christopher Award, which is given for high achievement in television, for *A Shining Season* (1979). He has written several novels, including *The Theologian* (1965), *In a Wild Sanctuary* (1969), *Lessons in Paradise* (1971), *Africana* (1977), *Savannah Blue* (1981), *Burton and Speke* (1982), *Three Hunters* (1989), and *The Blood Latitudes: A Novel* (2000).

Harrison explores the tragedies and triumphs that individuals face in coping with daily life, often using first-person narrators to show the perspectives of people from a variety of backgrounds and beliefs. The stories become thoughtful examinations of how both internal and external factors shape people's perceptions of themselves and the world around them. At other times he employs third-person narrators as a means of providing a broader and more distanced rendering of human life and experience. In his preface to *Roller Ball Murder* Harrison addresses the role of the short-story writer. He notes, "Most of life, though, is lived and understood at a less public frequency—filled with small griefs, joys, ironies, absurdities, and pains. And that's how the story testifies."

The stories in the volume illustrate the points Harrison makes in the preface. In "The Warrior," Harrison examines the theme of alienation through his portrayal of a mercenary (the first-person narrator) who lives at the port of Javea, within sight of the African coastline. A modern warrior, he feels marginalized because of his occupation, but still needed by society because of the prevalence of violence and war. Bothered by the presence of tourists attending a film festival nearby, he desires to kill them all because he thinks movies promote an artificial reality devoid of truth.

Harrison's penchant for characters that live on the margins of society continues in "The Hermit," a story featuring a third-person narrator. The main character, Ossinger, lives in isolation in Montana. A man with a troubled past, Ossinger served time in jail for killing his wife and her lover. Cone, a storekeeper who has groceries delivered to Ossinger, seeks contact with the isolated man by sending him gifts as a means of drawing him back into society. Cone views the hermit as symbolic of the plight of modern man: "And isn't that, he wondered, what a man is: the reticent creature, a thing born to be tucked into itself, an inscrutable beast, too, taught by every society to endure pain and anxiety in a silence which could be interpreted as strength." Eventually, Ossinger tires of his isolation and seeks communion with Cone by going to his store. The story represents the alienation and isolation in modern life, yet also posits the possibility of reintegration through friendship and understanding.

The sense of alienation that marks "The Hermit" reappears in "Down the Blue Hole," a story told by a mystic named Homer Bogardus who perfects the art of vanishing by disappearing into a blue hole in two different places simultaneously, a situation that suggests Harrison's interest in magic realism. Homer's desire to escape and disappear stems from the sense of disconnected emptiness he feels for the modern world. He notes, "Some days, like today, I dream beyond my powers—what if I can do almost anything?—to the Blue Hole where it might not be so bad to live forever." He succeeds in vanishing into the blue hole, where he can be free from the stress, uncertainty, and strains of daily living.

While the narrator of "Down the Blue Hole" uses his mystic powers to cope with the demands of daily life, the first-person narrator of "Eating It" uses eating as a form of escapism. The young male narrator lives with his Auntie Drew, an earthy woman who does not understand the meaning of moderation. She delights in the pleasures of pornography and eating, two temporary ways of feeding the emotional and physical emptiness she experiences as a human being. Her nephew views hers as "a true sensualist" despite the fact that she is seventy years old. In a scene reminiscent of a Franz Kafka story, Auntie Drew and her nephew give in to their shared gluttony by eating their home. The narrator muses, "Eat it all, we were saying in harmony, eat everything; choking, gagging, we stuffed it all in, and a happy nausea was overtaking me, a bliss of gluttony, the joy of the gorge." Harrison's "Eating It" surrealistically suggests the desperation of humans in the modern world who seek to fill the void in their lives with suicidal insatiability.

Deprivation versus excessive consumption marks "The Pinball Machines." The first-person narrator, the son of a barber in the Midwest during the Depression, recounts his father's resistance of a get-rich-quick scheme. His father rejects the opportunity to accept some pinball machines from a wealthy man in town to generate quick income. He feels that they promote greed and the illusion of wealth without hard work. This morality tale illustrates that those who refuse to be seduced by crass materialism can find spiritual fulfillment and contentment.

In contrast, "Roller Ball Murder" chronicles the life of a man who falls prey to greed and materialism, with fatal consequences. The first-person narrator, Jonathan E., feels a sense of loneliness and alienation despite his superstar status as an athlete. As Elizabeth Ann Hull notes, "The world depicted in the short story is one in which Jonathan can place full trust in no one, not even those he's closest to." The story and the subsequent motion picture (for which Harrison wrote the screenplay) center on a sports competition that is subsidized by big business. A popular spectator sport, roller ball reflects the obsession with violence and money on the part of the fans and the companies that fund the activity. According to David L. Vanderwerken, "The world of 'Roller Ball Murder' is one we are familiar with, overpopulated and over-organized, rich in consumer goods but poor in spirit." Jonathan's fame, money, and the temporary thrill of winning fail to provide him with a sense of fulfillment and happiness. The only winners are the corporations that make money from the competitions. Jonathan states, "The most powerful men in the world are the executives. They run the major corporations which fix prices, wages, and the general economy, and we all know they're crooked, that they have almost unlimited power and money, but I have considerable power and money myself and I'm still anxious." The story ends with Jonathan preparing for an all-star game with stakes so high that no one can survive. The ending of "Roller Ball Murder" suggests that alienation, violence, greed, and materialism lead inevitably to both spiritual and physical death.

In "The Blurb King" the narrator, Harry Neal, views everything as a commodity, including one's own identity. He works for an ad company that creates blurbs, and his success rests in the desperation of individuals to find or add meaning to their lives by willfully accepting contrived, false endorsements. He notes how a blurb "dispels life's bitterness" so

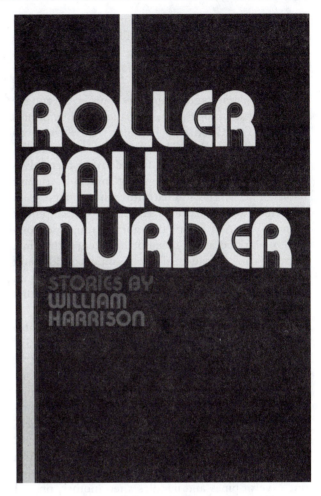

Dust jacket for Harrison's 1974 collection, featuring the title story about a warlike sport in a dystopian future

that people feel more optimistic and hopeful about themselves and the future. The story, a satire, critiques capitalistic commodification.

Like "Eating It," consumption as a method of coping is a major theme in "A Cook's Tale." The cook, a Swede, works for a university hospital cafeteria, where he befriends coworker Emma Bryant, the wife of a college student. At a party thrown by Emma, he feels alienated because of his lack of education, and he uses alcohol to fill his emptiness. He leaves the party and goes back to the kitchen at the university hospital to prepare some food for the partygoers. But in his drunken condition, he returns to the party without food because it takes the bread too long to bake. After a brief sexual encounter with Emma, he returns to the kitchen, retrieves his bread, and heads home, where he feeds his physical appetite. However, both eating and sex represent only a temporary fulfillment.

The negative consequences of uncontrollable desires resurface in "The Arsons of Desire," a story in which the narrator, an arsonist and firefighter, receives pleasure, joy, and fulfillment from setting fires. He ponders if the source of his illness stems from the alienation and isolation of contemporary life. He notes, "I'm kissed by a strange and awful god. My dread and desire are one." An equally intense sense of loneliness, alienation, and emptiness propels "The Good Ship Erasmus," in which, even though health and well-being become commodities, individuals have a difficult time denying themselves the sensual pleasure of engaging in self-destructive habits. The first-person narrator, who smuggles and sells cigarettes onboard the ship, views contemporary times as a period when "the moral distinctions completely blur" because human beings seem "adrift in a sensual sea." Because of their conflicted ideas of what constitutes genuine morality, the individuals on the ship cannot abstain from the very behavior that can ruin their health and even kill them.

The brainless pursuit of sensual pleasure is also the subject of "Under the House." Told in the third person, the story chronicles the life of Johnny Breck, a plumber with a penchant for bedding his clients. His irrational fear of going under the house is a metaphor for his fear of the unknown. In one of his sexual escapades, he pursues women in an apartment house and finds himself heading down underneath the house, where he successfully faces this fear. As a consequence, Breck "keeps moving along, through one cave of pipes and puddles after another, on and on, and he becomes contented, settled into his duty and contented, because now he is mending the world and loving its women as they said they wanted love." He seeks metaphorical fulfillment in repairing their plumbing and conquering the fear of the unknown rather than the sensual pleasures of sexually satisfying women for a temporary thrill.

The quest for happiness constitutes the central theme of "Nirvana, Gotterdammerung, and the Shot Put." This story also focuses on a marginalized character in the world of competitive sports. Toby Grogan is an athlete who uses sports and Zen to find fulfillment and meaning in his life. When he practices shot put, he retreats inside himself and excludes the rest of the world. At the Munich Olympics he positions himself away from the rest of the competitors on the day the games begin. After a fracas with the police for not competing within the boundaries of the track, which reflects his nonconformity, he runs across the countryside practicing shot put by himself: "At last he was alone, his followers gone, arching that iron ball into the thin mountain air, mostly staying up in the high country away from the cities, pausing, crouching, putting the shot from his deep trance,

passing on." His pursuit of his game isolates and estranges him from humankind.

Isolation also marks "Weatherman: A Theological Narrative," a tale about a meteorologist who deludes himself into thinking he can control the weather and the environment. His delusion of being God stems from the solitary nature of his job. Although he has memories of family and a past sense of communion with others, his present life reveals his lack of connection with the rest of humanity. His sense of dissociation and madness causes him to quit his job and kill himself to end the pain he feels. Like several other stories in the collection, "Weatherman: A Theological Narrative" ends with the death or the disappearance of the main character, which suggests that these two alternatives function as an antidote to the alienation and isolation of humans in the emptiness of the contemporary world.

Many of the stories in *Roller Ball Murder* were also included in *The Buddha in Malibu: New and Selected Stories*. Divided into three sections, the stories again focus on marginalized figures who struggle against societal constraints as they seek elusive physical, spiritual, sexual, and emotional fulfillment. Physical settings in these tales amplify the central themes as landscape becomes a metaphor for the human condition. In part 1, "The Movies and Malibu," Harrison presents characters associated with the motion picture and television industries. These deluded individuals live in a world of artificiality, illusion, and falsehoods. As Friedman noted, "Magnetized by movie glamour and greed, these men and women have been drawn from all over the country, willing to scheme, lie and cheat and failing to see that they have become their own victims. What Harrison so aptly renders is the way their soul hunger is displaced, converted into unfulfillable appetites of the body."

In "The Rocky Hills of Trancas" Harrison presents a teenage narrator who lives in Malibu, but on the wrong side of the proverbial tracks because of his father's failure as a screenwriter. His parents, unhappily married, separate as a result of his father's womanizing, which includes a romp with his own son's girlfriend. As a means of revenge against his father's transgressive behavior, the son steals his scripts, rewrites one, wins a competition, and tries to succeed in the movie industry.

A perceptive youth, the narrator notes the correlation between the human condition and the physical landscape. He muses, "The climate is warm and sunny; everyone hears success stories, gets glimpses of celebrities, and it's a palm-tree world, a halter-top world, where phrases like Malibu or development

Promotional poster for the 1975 United Artists movie version of Harrison's most famous story, with a screenplay by the author

deal roll off the tongue, but one lives on a personal fault line where everything is shaky and terrifying." Each section of the story begins with a term associated with moviemaking: Setting, Backstory, Storyline, Close Up, Panning Left, Racking Focus, Jump Cut, Quick Take, Wide Angle, Plot Point, Wild Tracking, Slow Fade, and Trailer. The list reinforces the commentary on the artificiality of the world of make-believe and the real world.

In "Yes, I've Bought a Couple of Options Myself" Harrison furthers the motifs of greed and materialism. Told from the third-person perspective, the story documents the life of Cappy, an escort-service employee who accompanies a real-estate agent named Hazen Wilson to a meeting with a wealthy couple who plan to purchase an expensive home and possibly produce movies in California. Claiming to

be a movie producer, Cappy convinces the couple to hire him as a production executive. The story suggests that in Hollywood anything can be bought, sold, or invented, including identity, occupation, and credentials.

Similarly, "The Buddha in Malibu" focuses on the deceptiveness and dishonesty of the motion picture industry and on characters whose sense of emptiness drives them to fill that void with wealth, material goods, and fame. As a consequence, any sense of spiritual or moral grounding seems virtually impossible to attain. The protagonist, Brock, works as a bodyguard for Ennis, a movie producer. Out of his paranoia and general malice Ennis shoots his own bodyguard, but this act actually helps Ennis's faltering career because of the publicity he receives. While Brock is in the hospital recovering from his injuries, his girlfriend, Luanne, presents him with a miniature Buddha. She notes that Buddha would have a hard time surviving in Malibu because there is no "middle path" that lies "between sensuality and ascetic mortification" there. Individuals such as Ennis follow their compulsions without thinking of the consequences, and they have no self-restraint. Ultimately, Brock rejects Buddhism and ideas of moderation in favor of materialism and a hefty raise from Ennis. The story illustrates the conflict between greed and moderation in contemporary life.

Lack of moderation is also the subject of "The Cockatoo Tower," which focuses on Corey, a construction contractor who services clients in Malibu. This tale critiques the alienation of individuals wealthy enough to have disposable income. Corey, a complete materialist, has sex with one of his female clients in a cockatoo tower he constructs for her, because he wants to dominate and possess her and persuade her to abandon relationships that she is having with the husbands of other female clients. A pragmatist, he fears that marital discord among his clients might result in divorce and a cancellation of their remodeling plans. Harrison's story addresses the artificiality of romantic relationships fraught with infidelity, dishonesty, materialism, and the banal pursuit of sensual pleasures.

The emphasis on artificiality and the lack of identity individuals feel in the world of moviemaking reverberate throughout "Stuntman." The main character earns a living by impersonating actors who cannot perform their own stunts in pictures. The story presents Hollywood as a world of illusion, where distinctions between reality and fantasy constantly blur. The stuntman has no name and no true identity. His life and death are manufactured by the movie industry. He uses his occupation and his nurse's fascination with his bruises to seduce her. In the end, the stuntman's life seems meaningless and empty because he lacks real identity and real action.

The pursuit of hedonistic pleasures is the topic of "Pretty Girl and Fat Friend." The narrator tries to seduce two young women in an airport bar. He uses a false name and identity, claiming to be the owner of a photo laboratory in Malibu. He does not realize, however, that the two women also lie about their identities when they claim to be a medical doctor and a trainer. When he heads to a hotel with the women, they beat him up and rob him of his credit cards. Failing to learn a lesson from his experiences, he lies to an attendant on his flight back home after his stay in the hospital, telling her he is a travel-magazine photographer. His lack of fulfillment and his overweening desire for bodily pleasures give him pause at the end of the story: "Would serenity and peace never come to me?" The story focuses on how the pursuit of carnal pleasures without honesty and moderation can have serious physical, emotional, and psychological repercussions.

Lies, deceit, and manipulation also appear in "The Big Bang Theory of Love." Told in third person, the story focuses on Paco, a movie producer, who asks an astrologer named Letti to read the chart of Tom, a man with whom he wants to produce a movie. Letti meets Tom, who tells her he thinks Paco paid someone to pose as a scriptwriter to close a movie deal. Letti's experiences with Paco and Tom and her readings of Stephen Hawking's *A Brief History of Time* (1988) bring her to the conclusion that humans represent "lost matter in the seas of the big bang" in relation to the rest of the universe. In her quest to make meaning out of life and experience, she decides that astrology, like physics, might hold some answers to the eternal question about human destiny.

The section titled "Africa and Anarchy" includes "The Magician of Soweto," "The Warrior," "On Location," and "Sun City." Five of Harrison's novels, including *Africana* and *The Blood Latitudes,* have African settings, and his travels on the continent have been extensive. Despite the transition in setting from Western to non-Western world, these stories rearticulate the themes of alienated, disaffected individuals seeking fulfillment, often through lies, cheating, and deception. "The Magician of Soweto," a frequently anthologized story, chronicles the experiences of Tommy, a white American who colludes with a black South African, Moses Kawanda, to steal goods for his shop. Thrillseekers, Tommy and Moses attend a card game at the home of Mr. Rashi, an Indian merchant who is aware of the source of goods for Moses's shop. Tommy expertly manipulates his cards to win the game, and Mr. Rashi demands part of the money Tommy wins. Mr. Rashi threatens to drop them off in White City after the card game, where he knows that a black and white man seen together will be viciously attacked. However, before he can follow through with his plan, a black mob surrounds the car during a riot, and the police intervene. Tommy manages somehow to escape South Africa, although he is a thief who should be jailed, while Moses is imprisoned. When Moses cites the injustice, Tommy replies that "it's the way of the world."

"On Location" returns to the artificiality of moviemaking and details the life of a technical adviser. The adviser's job is to blur the lines between fantasy and reality, but it creates a sense of alienation, dislocation, and loneliness in him. Pondering the meaning of his experiences, he accidentally shoots himself while on location. The story records his meaningless death in an equally meaningless world.

Manipulation, exploitation, greed, and sensuality are subjects treated by "Sun City," which chronicles the life of Denna Wilson, a white American singer performing in South Africa. Despite her feelings about apartheid, her desire for fame and fortune win out over her "politics," and she decides to sing in "the Las Vegas of Africa." The story presents Sun City as a place of excess, wealth, glitz, and glamour that belies the danger, despair, and blatant racial oppression in South Africa. Denna's hedonistic desire for a romantic relationship involves her with Becker, a journalist who desires to become famous by exposing the racism and abuse against blacks in South Africa. He convinces Denna to record the experiences of Toppy, a horn player in the band that backs her. As a consequence of telling his story, Toppy is arrested by the authorities, and Becker becomes a famous journalist who gets a high-profile job in England, leaving Denna behind, lonely and unfulfilled. The story functions as a cautionary tale about the consequences of exploiting others for personal gain.

The section titled "The Future and Forever" features "Roller Ball Murder," "The Arsons of Desire," "Down the Blue Hole," "The Makeup Man," "The Good Ship Erasmus," and "Weatherman: A Theological Narrative." Artificiality, superficiality, and identity construction form the basis of "The Makeup Man," a darkly humorous tale about a fad in plastic surgery in which ugliness is seen as desirable. When ugliness becomes a hotly sought commodity by the motion picture industry, Sylvia, an actress, has the makeup man reshape her into a monster figure to cash in on the vogue, but she soon tires of the fad and wants to be recast into a beautiful person. However, her quest for the transformation of her identity becomes problematic because the makeup man cannot reverse his work. The story is an indictment of appearance as a commodity. Sylvia dies when the makeup man tries to undo his work, peeling back layers of skin down to her skull. The makeup man, then, becomes a god-like figure who can create or destroy. The story, like others in the collection, bitterly condemns American consumerism.

Harrison's short-story collections include a provocative array of selections that differ in setting, time period, and narrative perspective, yet center around his astute analysis of the human condition. Through deft characterizations and his straightforward prose style, Harrison captures the complexities of marginalized individuals in an objective manner.

References:

Elizabeth Ann Hull, "Merging Madness: Roller Ball as a Cautionary Tale," in *Clockwork Worlds: Mechanized Environments in Science Fiction,* edited by Richard D. Erlich and Thomas P. Dunn (Westport, Conn.: Greenwood Press, 1983), pp. 163–180;

David L. Vanderwerken, "Roller Ball: Sport and Society in the Future," *Arete: The Journal of Sport Literature,* 11 (Spring 1985): 39–45.

William Hoffman

(16 May 1925 –   )

William L. Frank
Longwood College

BOOKS: *The Trumpet Unblown* (Garden City, N.Y.: Doubleday, 1955);

Days in the Yellow Leaf (Garden City, N.Y.: Doubleday, 1958);

A Place for My Head (Garden City, N.Y.: Doubleday, 1960);

The Dark Mountains (Garden City, N.Y.: Doubleday, 1963);

Yancey's War (Garden City, N.Y.: Doubleday, 1966);

A Walk to the River (Garden City, N.Y.: Doubleday, 1970; London: Hale, 1972);

A Death of Dreams (Garden City, N.Y.: Doubleday, 1973; London: Hale, 1975);

Virginia Reels (Urbana: University of Illinois Press, 1978);

The Land That Drank the Rain (Baton Rouge: Louisiana State University Press, 1982);

Godfires (New York: Viking, 1985);

By Land, by Sea (Baton Rouge: Louisiana State University Press, 1988);

Furors Die (Baton Rouge: Louisiana State University Press, 1990);

Follow Me Home (Baton Rouge: Louisiana State University Press, 1994);

Tidewater Blood (Chapel Hill, N.C.: Algonquin, 1998; London: Hale, 1999);

Doors (Columbia: University of Missouri Press, 1999);

Blood and Guile (New York: HarperCollins, 2000).

PLAY PRODUCTION: *The Love Touch,* Abingdon, Virginia, Barter Theatre, 22 August 1964.

William Hoffman (photograph by Kent Moody; from the dust jacket for Follow Me Home, *1994)*

While William Hoffman has set his fiction almost exclusively in the mountainous coalfields of Virginia and the Tidewater region surrounding the Chesapeake Bay, "his themes," as Jeanne Nostrandt wrote in her essay on William Hoffman for *Contemporary Fiction Writers of the South* (1993), "delve into the complexities of the human condition and the plight of the human spirit in any place and at any time." Although some reviewers have called Hoffman a regional writer, focusing on his concern for the Southern values of family, community, and religious faith, they fail to see that the so-called regional aspects of his stories are equally applicable to the human condition everywhere, much like the regional stories of William Faulkner have long been considered descriptive of humanity across the globe. Hoffman's stories in particular deal with the age-old questions of faith and disbelief, doubt and certainty, relationships, commitment, love and hate, and the loneliness of the individual, even when surrounded by friends and family.

Hoffman's fictional voice has been steady and consistent for more than fifty years. He has published twelve novels and four collections of short stories and written another thirty or more stories, most of them also published. Hoffman is known to several writers—Fred Chappell, George Garrett, Tom Wolfe—as a writer's writer, and his work is generally eagerly awaited and enthusiastically received (and reviewed) by his readers, but he has never achieved the universal recognition that critics such as George Core and Ron Carter argue he and his work deserve.

Henry William Hoffman was born in Charleston, West Virginia, on 16 May 1925. His mother, Julie Beckley Hoffman, and his father, Henry William Hoffman, divorced soon after Hoffman was born, and he was reared in Charleston by his mother and maternal grandmother. Although Hoffman grew up in Charleston during the Depression years, he never knew poverty; during his formative years the family of four—Hoffman, his grandmother, his mother, and his sister, Janet—regularly vacationed in Florida and lived in one of the more prominent sections of Charleston. He also attended summer camps and sailing camps on the Chesapeake Bay, and sailing has remained an influence and a passion with Hoffman throughout his life. Hoffman graduated from Kentucky Military Institute in 1943 and immediately tried to enlist in the Air Corps but was turned down because he was color-blind. Drafted soon thereafter into the army, he was assigned to the medical corps and was part of the Normandy invasion force of June 1944. The war left emotional and psychological scars on Hoffman that have never faded, and his four war novels are among the most powerful he has written.

Two days after his discharge Hoffman entered Hampden-Sydney College in Virginia. Its strong Presbyterian ties coupled with his own strict Presbyterian upbringing constitute a second major influence on his life and his fiction. He received his B.A. from Hampden-Sydney in 1949, spent one year in law school at Washington and Lee University in Lexington, Virginia—Tom Wolfe was a fellow classmate—and after the journal *Shenandoah* accepted a short story for publication, Hoffman went off to the Writers' Workshop at the University of Iowa for an additional year (1950–1951). He worked briefly for the Chase National Bank in New York City before he received a call from Hampden-Sydney College, inviting him to return to the English department to teach. While there he met and married Alice Sue Richardson of Bluefield, West Virginia, on 17 April 1957. The Hoffmans have two daughters: Ruth Beckley Hoffman and Margaret Kay Hoffman.

Hoffman taught at Hampden-Sydney until 1959, living a few miles away in Farmville, Virginia, the locale—under the name "Tobaccoton"—for much of his fiction. The family moved to a farm in Charlotte Court House in Virginia in 1964, where they raised horses;

riding was another of Hoffman's favorite hobbies. Hoffman returned to Hampden-Sydney in the mid 1960s as writer in residence and remained there until the early 1970s. Since then he has taught only one writing course, in the fall of 1978, a course he calls "a gift to Hampden-Sydney." Hoffman continues to live and write on his fifty-acre Charlotte County farm.

Beginning in the late 1980s, Hoffman has received increasing recognition for his short fiction. In 1988 "Sweet Armageddon" was chosen by the *Virginia Quarterly Review* as the best story published in the journal that year; in 1989 he was awarded for the second time the Andrew Nelson Lytle Prize by the *Sewanee Review;* in 1990 he won the Jeanne Charpiot Goodheart Prize for Fiction, sponsored by *Shenandoah;* in 1993 Longwood College bestowed upon him the John Dos Passos Prize for Excellence in Literature; and in 1995 he was given the Hillsdale Prize for Fiction by the Fellowship of Southern Writers. In 1996 Hoffman was inducted into the Fellowship of Southern Writers at a ceremony in Chattanooga, Tennessee. In addition, Hoffman holds honorary doctorates from Hampden-Sydney College, Washington and Lee University, and Sewanee.

Hoffman's first short-story collection, *Virginia Reels,* was published by the University of Illinois Press in 1978. It comprises nine stories that were earlier published in six periodicals over a period of eleven years, from 1966 through 1977. The stories anticipate the setting for the vast majority of Hoffman's stories and novels: Tidewater Virginia, including the Chesapeake Bay area; Richmond, the state capital; rural Southside Virginia; and the mountains and coal mining regions of West Virginia, where Hoffman grew up.

George Core, editor of the *Sewanee Review,* in which four of these stories first appeared (according to Core, *Sewanee Review* has published more stories by Hoffman than by any other writer, living or dead), notes on the jacket of the book that "William Hoffman is one of the finest American short-story writers of our time. His stories are beautifully paced and cleanly written: nothing is wasted, everything counts. Here is an author who is a master of the enlivening detail, the casual aside, the necessary idiom. Hoffman's fiction ranges from hilarity to pathos to terror; his humorous response to man's folly is as memorable as his profound vision of man's depravity."

The first story in the collection, "The Spirit in Me," which originally appeared in the *Sewanee Review* in 1974, is narrated by its protagonist, a self-appointed minister named Gormer. A snake-handling preacher, Gormer's father had once been arrested for using snakes in his rituals. After Gormer is seriously injured in a methane explosion in a coal mine, he interprets the

Dust jacket for Hoffman's 1978 collection of stories set primarily in Tidewater Virginia and West Virginia mining country

explosion as a sign from God and a calling from the Holy Spirit: "That summer I go into the mountain. . . . The first days as I worked setting locust props to hold the roof, a blue light flashes before me and cracks like a thousand whips. . . . The whips crack through the mine, and a voice says, 'You are my instrument!' . . . Fire damp they call it—methane—but I know Whose terrible power has rent the darkness."

Following in his father's footsteps, Gormer assumes the position of lay minister for a rural church located on land belonging to the descendants of the patriarch who first mined coal from the neighboring mountains. He runs into conflict with the man's granddaughter, who has returned to repair and repaint the long-neglected family mansion. As his father before him, Gormer handles snakes, which he has come to see as his children, during his services: "Now I have children of my own, not from a wife, but from the Spirit. I feed and treat them tenderly. . . . My children know me, the heat of my hand, and they raise their heads when I lower meals to them. . . . I hold them as gently as wafers." When the woman learns about the practice,

she locks him out of the church and hires another preacher. Gormer goes into town to protest but is warned by the deputy sheriff that the woman has the law on her side.

Gormer conceives what he considers an appropriately biblical revenge against the granddaughter. He observes her entertaining a suitor on the terrace of the mansion, on the nearby lake, and in her private bathhouse. After the couple goes for a late-night swim, Gormer acts:

> He lifts and carries her into the bathhouse. A click causes light to die. I slip to the door and hear them inside. . . . I shut off power by screwing out fuses. Kneeling on the wooden steps, I lovingly feed my children through the doorway. They flow off my palms into darkness. I pull the door closed and drop the heavy padlock into the hasp. She and her man hear and try to switch on lights. They rattle the door. . . . The switch keeps clicking. As I walk toward the forest I hear her gasp. I do not even turn at the first scream.

The poet and critic Fred Chappell, in his essay "Taking Measure: Violent Intruders in William Hoffman's Short Fiction" for *The Fictional World of William Hoffman* (2000), highly praises both Hoffman and "The Spirit in Me": "Figures like Gormer are hardly uncommon in Southern literature and have been limned with wonderful skill by Davis Grubb, Harry Crews, Madison Jones and other writers. But I think no one has done the job so deadly and with such deft economy as William Hoffman. 'The Spirit in Me' is a nightmare as deep and dark as they come, but it finishes in fourteen pages."

The second story in the collection, "Sea Tides," originally published in the September 1966 issue of *McCall's* magazine, takes the reader to one of Hoffman's favorite locales, the ocean. In the course of the story Rufus, the lonely survivor of a failed marriage, and his unnamed sister, fearing that they may lose their mother's inheritance should she marry again, hire a private detective to gather information on their mother's latest suitor, Leonard Dementi. They learn enough about Dementi's past for Rufus to threaten to expose him to their mother if he should follow through on a planned visit. When Dementi fails to show up for a dinner at which Rufus's mother intended to announce their engagement, she is brokenhearted, and by the end of the story Rufus and his sister realize that their selfishness has deprived their mother of what was possibly her last chance at a meaningful relationship.

"The Darkened Room," first published in the *Sewanee Review* in 1975, evokes the grotesque characterizations of Sherwood Anderson and Flannery O'Connor. Richard, a high-school boy trying to get enough money to run away to California, has observed and timed the comings and goings of a young, prosperous couple and enters their home one evening, confident of having several hours to uncover their cash and jewelry. Upon entering "the last room, the one at the dark end of the house," Richard "believed he'd come to judgment. On a throne at the center of the room was massed a dark figure with phosphorescent eyes. Richard tasted vomit and almost fouled himself."

The woman, the mother of the man of the house, Billyboy, is so grotesque to behold that the couple has hidden her away so she will not embarrass them in front of their society friends. Partly because she does not want Richard to be arrested, and partly because she feels like the two are coconspirators against her son and his wife, she helps Richard to escape when the couple returns home earlier than expected. Read as a metaphor, "The Darkened Room" seems to say that every family has its dark, hideous secrets and that often there is little connection between appearance and reality.

Although Hoffman says he has never turned a short story into a novel or started out with a short story and ended up with a novel, *A Death of Dreams* is a fully developed version of "Your Hand, Your Hand," the next story in *Virginia Reels*. Originally published in the fall/winter 1971–1972 issue of the *Carleton Miscellany,* it is the story of Buzz Dyer, a young and successful Richmond, Virginia businessman, recently divorced, who is in a private hospital for alcoholics. Thinking he is about to be discharged, Buzz is accompanied by a nurse to a meeting with the director of the hospital, Dr. Bodine. Instead the nurse escorts him to a surrealistic cabaret setting within the hospital itself, and Buzz soon finds himself seated before a fully stocked bar and next to a flirtatious and pretty young woman. It is, of course, a test, and Buzz flunks badly; after succumbing to the girl's invitation to join her in a drink he becomes violently ill and is carried off by orderlies with instruction from Dr. Bodine to "clean him and take him to his room," to which the girl adds "and hurry. . . . We have another one." If it is cruel out there in the real world, Hoffman says, it can be just as cruel and unforgiving in the antiseptic confines of the hospital.

"Amazing Grace," initially published in the *Sewanee Review* in 1977, is a first-person-narrated story of a grandmother, Nana, and one of her children who has grown up and away from his rural and religious roots. Nana, whose extended family treasures her homemade biscuits, rolls, and salt-rising bread loaves, deserts her kitchen and pouts until her prodigal son, known to the boy narrator as Uncle Henry, agrees to Nana's wishes to be baptized in the local river by Nana's rural pastor, along with Uncle Henry's wife and teenage son. After-

ward, Nana returns to her kitchen and resumes her baking for the family.

Although the plotline is slight, the characters are multidimensional, and Hoffman's treatment has its brighter and more humorous moments. His use of language is deft and memorable, as his description of Nana indicates: "Over the years she'd grown shorter and thicker, not fat because she'd never stayed still long enough to gather fat, but stout the way an oak tree is stout." In a sentence worthy of Mark Twain's Huck Finn, the narrator reports: "I'd seen her hit a mule so hard with a hoe handle that he was cross-eyed for ten minutes."

"A Darkness on the Mountain" first appeared in the February 1969 issue of *Cosmopolitan*. It narrates the story of Anna Mae and her two suitors, Roy and the town's bully, Buster Beard. Roy first notices Anna Mae at church and shortly begins courting her in the tradition of mountain folk, calling at her home with a box of candy in hand and spending as much time talking with her parents as he does with her. When Buster moves in on Roy and consumes more than half the box of chocolate-covered cherries Roy has brought for Anna Mae, the two boys engage in a long and violent knife fight, during which Roy is cut badly by a lucky thrust from Buster.

Laid up for a week with his wounds, Roy has time to plan a cold and dark revenge. One night he ambushes Buster as he returns from a visit to see Anna Mae and takes him to a deserted coal mine at the Kentucky border. There he binds Buster with wire to a rotting prop, so that if he pulls too hard to free himself he will pull out the prop and bring the mountain down upon him. Roy leaves Buster in the abandoned mine for three full days, returning after midnight on the third night to find a whimpering and repentant young man pleading with him not to leave him again with the rats and the dark. Roy takes Buster to his mother's grave and has him swear "before God and on this grave" that if he ever reveals what happened the devils will drag his mother's soul to hell and "burn her forever." In the last scene of the story Roy is again courting Anna Mae, with no Buster Beard to come between them.

"A Southern Sojourn," earlier published in the summer 1974 issue of the *Transatlantic Review,* brings together a lonely engineer from Minnesota and a black waitress from Virginia. Orson, sent to Virginia by his company to supervise the installation of a boiler in a new knitting mill, is increasingly drawn to Eunice, a young woman who comes to cook and waitress at the ten-unit Dixie Motel, Orson's home away from home. They commence an affair, with her coming to his room almost every night from early July through mid September, when he is scheduled to return to Minnesota. They

Dust jacket for Hoffman's 1988 collection of stories depicting the everyday crises of characters in Virginia

part without saying goodbye–he to return to his wife and family and "the land of sky-blue," as she calls it, she to continue in her dead-end job. There can be no satisfactory ending to their relationship. She has filled his temporary loneliness, and he has given a few dollars to one who deserves a better hand than fate has dealt her.

"A Walk by the River," originally titled "The Gorge" when it was published in the summer 1978 *Sewanee Review,* is the story of Shep, recently divorced from his wife, Katie, who appears throughout the story in several flashback scenes; a young, nameless runaway; and her most recent sex partner, also unnamed. After the man steals his car keys, billfold, and hiking boots, Shep and the girl are left alone: "She was the first woman since Katie. For a long time he hadn't wanted anyone, and then he'd become uncertain he could handle a woman ever again, but with this slight girl he was repaired. He kissed her face and hair, wanting to forget, and almost able to, that she was hippie trash." What Shep receives from the encounter on the river's walk is certainly not redemption or salvation, but it does renew

his confidence in himself as a man, rescued from what has been a dull existence as credit manager of a local department store.

The final story in *Virginia Reels,* "Sea Treader," first published in the fall 1971 issue of *The Saturday Evening Post,* evinces Hoffman's long love affair with sailing. The story is set on the Bromanni River, which, Hoffman writes, "emptied into the Chesapeake a few miles below the landing." The story is an initiation story both for its narrator, Billy Benson, a high-school student who works on boats part time, and its protagonist, E. B. Freestone, a sixty-year-old candy-factory worker. Freestone has had an unfulfilled dream for all of his adult life to own a sailboat and sail it to the ocean. Under the boy's tutoring Freestone masters all of the details of handling a boat by himself, and in the final scene of the story he is seen heading downriver toward Chesapeake Bay on what the attentive reader realizes will be his final sail. Freestone gradually wins first acceptance and then admiration and loyalty from Billy, and Billy comes to realize the wrongness of stereotyping people based on appearance and speech habits.

Of the twelve stories in Hoffman's second collection, *By Land, by Sea* (1988), eight take place in rural Southside Virginia, Danville, Richmond, and adjacent towns and counties; four are set on or near the Atlantic Ocean and Chesapeake Bay. Regardless of setting, Hoffman's characters and the daily conflicts they confront are, as always, the essence of his fiction.

In "Fathers and Daughters," a partly autobiographical story, a wealthy lumberman worries that his daughter, well educated, physically attractive, and "groomed for William and Mary" and high society beyond college, will run off with one of the local lower-class "rowdydowdies." In "Indian Gift" a dirt-poor but honest and hardworking farmer, trying to save enough money to send his son to the University of Virginia at Charlottesville, is a victim of the weather and a con man, Dip Cooley. Cooley unloads a hot tractor on the unsuspecting farmer and disappears, leaving him to face the law and depriving him of his pride and dignity as well as his livelihood. In "Smoke" a young boy on the verge of manhood discovers the real meaning of courage when his terminally ill uncle makes the county bully back down during a life-and-death confrontation.

Hoffman has much to say about growing old as well as about growing up in these stories. In "Moon Lady" a soon-to-be forty-year-old "boy" discovers beauty, mysticism, ritual, and liturgy in an old woman whose "lavender eyes were like wild, confederate violets that grew along the churchyard wall." In "Lover," a plaintive hymn to youth and innocence, a sixty-four-year-old widower, who has forgotten what it is to love and enjoy life, attempts to turn back time and reenter his earlier life: "I assume that for me love is dead. I live for the company, the increase of business. . . . When, therefore, I experience a surge of love, I am shocked." Gail, the young girl he desires, "doesn't look at all like Helen except for her body's petiteness and a certain narrowness of face. . . . I wake during the night thinking of her." When the two finally meet and he invites her to his home, first for a game of tennis and then for a tour of his house, he can no longer distinguish between the real and the unreal, nor between love and lust: "I must live it one last time—the youth and Helen, the hope, the promise of glory, the soaring. Gail struggles but finds I am indeed strong. She'll no longer think of me as old. . . . I ride the wind."

"Lover" is not the strongest love story of the several in the collection; however, "Landfall," "Altarpiece," and "Faces at the Window" vie for this designation. "Landfall" opens with Chris and his terminally ill wife, Belle, already two days into a sea voyage aboard their wooden sloop, *Wyndor* (a name Hoffman has given both to his Charlotte Court House farm and to his Mathews, Virginia, home on Chesapeake Bay). The story opens with the line "Chris's wife was not immediately suspicious"; Chris has not told her that the voyage is to be not only their last voyage together, but also the last voyage for each: "He couldn't tell her he'd be unable to endure seeing her among those gaunt, terrified bodies connected to tubes and plastic bags, people who smelled of urine and fear, all living horrors, some hairless, others with great bites taken out of them by surgeons. The sea was the clean way." United throughout their married life, they will go united into death. In "Altarpiece," another story of a bereft and lonely widower, Peck, the protagonist, discovers renewal with one of the least likely of social castoffs: Jenny, a thrice-married, thrice-divorced dreamer. While initially Peck is drawn to Jenny because they share "great sadness: the fellowship of grief," ultimately he reaches out to her, both literally and figuratively, because of their mutual need for communion and compassion.

The third of this trio, "Faces at the Window," is the most triumphant of the three. Again Hoffman's basic theme is one of renewal, this time between the aristocratic young Robenna and the recently widowed new minister in Tobaccoton, Dave Carson. Dave's preaching initially attracts Robenna to him, but his rugged masculinity gradually brings her to accept the failure of her first marriage and to realize that life is not yet nearly over for her: "She was still a pretty woman in the classic manner. Like porcelain she considered herself, fine imported china." After a brief courtship consisting largely of golf dates and sedate afternoon teas, Robenna invites Dave to the annual Fall Cotillion, and in her home that same night their love is consummated: "She thought of this man who had again brought her alive, this combination of the spiritual and the earthy. Might she be a minister's wife? . . . She wondered whether the pain and humiliation of her marriage to Whitt had been a way of molding and preparing her for this moment. God, the master potter, at work." Hoffman, a devout Presbyterian since his youth, has always made religion and belief central elements of his fiction. Unsurprisingly, he locates the direct hand of God in the coming union of Robenna and Dave.

"Cuttings" is about Asbury, a Richmond stockbroker challenged by his family and his own fear to cut down an aging oak tree that, after a severe winter storm, is leaning toward Asbury's summer cottage on Chesapeake Bay: "He circled the tree as one might a serpent." Determined to prove to himself that he is still capable of felling properly his dying tree, Asbury fashions both a brace and a four-by-four to tilt the tree away from the house, and with a chainsaw bought especially for the occasion he succeeds in cutting the tree down, "its length lying exactly where he wished." As he leaves the following morning, "A gentle, aching sadness entwined with a descending peace. Like the tree, time was sawing at him; and like the oak, too, he would endure until fallen, he hoped with a portion of its dignity, will, and strength." The story is based on an actual incident involving Hoffman, when he, too, had to fell a tree left by a storm leaning toward his home in Mathews. The story involves both the routine challenges and obstacles one faces every day, as well as the reverence one feels for so graceful a creation as the aged oak.

"Moorings" is also set on the Chesapeake Bay and is the story of two couples, Jess and Josie, born on and to the bay, and Claire and Freddie, a much younger couple whose new wealth and party-giving lifestyle corrupt Jess and trouble Josie, the narrator of the story. Gradually, Claire and Freddie unintentionally drive a wedge between Jess and Josie. The young couple hires Jess to undertake more and more handyman jobs for them, and Jess is seduced by the easy money he makes. By the end of the story Jess and Josie are practically estranged; Josie's concern that no good would come from Jess's increasingly intimate relationship with the younger couple proves to be prophetic.

"Patriot," one of the most moving and elegiac stories Hoffman has written, can be read biographically as a tribute to his father and maternal grandfather, the latter the founder of a coal mining dynasty, the former a coal miner himself. The story can also be read metaphorically as a tribute to the strong, determined, God-fearing coal miners of West Virginia and Kentucky who are depicted working hard under impossible conditions, caring for their families, and living free and independent lives in good times and bad. Narrated by the son of the unnamed and unsung protagonist, the story is set in the mining region of West Virginia and covers the years from the early 1940s into the early 1970s. The reader, through the eyes of the son, follows the father from the flush times when coal was king to the days when he is no longer able to mine coal, work for the highway department, or even do occasional odd jobs for the local power company. Through a lifetime of honest toil on the part of his father, the son learns lessons of endurance, love, dignity, compassion, and patriotism. The story evokes Hoffman's relationship with his own father, from whom he was estranged until the two reunited in the late 1970s.

The final story in *By Land, by Sea,* "The Question of Rain," is a story of doubt, faith, and belief. The towns in the southeastern part of Virginia and the surrounding region have been for weeks in the grip of a deadly drought, and the well-educated, well-intentioned but perhaps overly theological minister, Wayland, is visited by several delegations of his congregation requesting that he hold a "Special Prayer Day for Rain."

Resistant at first, he succumbs reluctantly to their wishes after he drives to Richmond to seek advice from his former seminary teacher. He is worried about the effect on members of his congregation if he does hold a special prayer service for rain and nothing happens. That night, after holding a packed service pleading for God's intercession, the drenching rains come, bringing new life to the community and a different kind of faith and belief to Wayland.

All eleven of the stories in Hoffman's third collection, *Follow Me Home* (1994), had been previously published: "Dancer," "Abide with Me," "Points," and "Expiation" in the *Sewanee Review;* "Tides" in the *Southern Review;* "Coals," "Boy up a Tree," and "Business Trip" in *Shenandoah;* "Sweet Armageddon" and "The Secret Garden" in the *Virginia Quarterly;* and "Night Sport" in *The Atlantic Monthly.* The first story in the collection is "Dancer," an exquisite, finely chiseled portrait of Lizzie, called to dance with her long-deceased husband, Oliver, by the mysterious music that she alone can hear: "As she was fixing to listen to the news, she heard the music a second time that night. Despite the wind, the music sounded just beyond the door. All right, she said, and danced a little, a fox-trot, her arms held to Oliver. Because her eyes were closed, she failed to see the car's splayed headlights. Wind music masked the engine." Rescued by her well-intentioned but insensitive sister, Mary Belle, and taken to Richmond, Lizzie becomes a virtual prisoner of Mary Belle and her husband, Chester. Overhearing a conversation between them that clearly indicates they intend to put Lizzie in a convalescent home so they can travel to Spain, Lizzie again hears the music: "Toward the end of the week music drifted in on the smell of mowed grass. . . . The men had been painting eaves at the rear of the house and left the ladder standing. She didn't seem to be climbing as much as growing lighter. . . . She'd never minded heights. She felt weightless and as if drifting among treetops. . . . feeling lighter than air lifted her arms and stepped into the swirl of a flowing waltz."

The second story of the collection, "Tides," takes the reader to Hoffman's home away from home, the Chesapeake Bay area, the setting for an increasing number of his short stories. "Tides" begins with a father and son on a sailing and fishing trip, "a ritual celebrating the official end of fun in my life," the son, Dave, remarks, for he has just graduated from college and will soon enter a management training program at a North Carolina bank. The trip takes a chilling turn, however, when they are kidnapped by a gun-wielding drug runner who commandeers their boat to take him to Baltimore. During the tension-packed odyssey that follows, father and son separately try to buoy up one another's confidence and courage. Unable to communicate because the drug runner keeps them physically separated, they plot independently to protect and rescue the other. "Tides" is another fine example of one of Hoffman's favorite (and most moving) themes in his fiction: the relationship between a father and the son he loves.

"Coals" is the lightest story in the collection, although it is not slight. It is a story rich in human relationships, in which a black housekeeper-cook gets the better of her aging, mean-spirited mistress. The cook, Celeste, learned long ago how to read well the mind and spirit of her white employers. When her husband, Jim, corrects her grammar and word choice, Celeste giggles and replies: "They like it when I dumb. . . . Make them feel smarter. Feel smarter, they treat me better. Everybody happy."

"Coals" is rich in dialogue and dialect and, as always with Hoffman, full of minor but highly realistic characters recognizable to every inhabitant of Southside Virginia, such as the small-town banker, Banker John, or Raincoat, the elderly black man who keeps the matronly ladies of the town supplied with their medicinal liquor: "Raincoat got extra pockets in his raincoat. Sometime he carry so many tonics for ladies in Tobaccoton be clink like a china cabinet during thunder. They 'fraid preacher see them in the tonic store. . . . He come to Miss Alice Louella's every Tuesday, Thursday, and Saturday, and when he leaving he clink not as much as he coming."

"Sweet Armageddon" is set in Richmond but could have been essentially the same story set in any other town, city, or crossroads in Virginia. It is the story of the last, sad days of a minister, Amos, and his wife, whose lifework has been rejected by those they sought to save and seemingly overlooked by the Lord Himself. Amos, who runs into a former college classmate at the post office where he has gone to pick up his pittance of a retirement check, "wouldn't even attempt to explain he's been to the mountains, runty towns, the muddied Amazon, to Philistines everywhere, that he'd been mocked and rejected and was not only awaiting the end but praying for it. . . . In a sick, facile society that had forgotten its roots, he carried spiritual contagion."

"Night Sport," one of Hoffman's most chilling stories, is the only one that could be called a war story, although more specifically it deals with the lingering effects of war on an individual. "Night Sport" is such a disturbing story that many readers of *The Atlantic Monthly* wrote in to cancel their subscriptions to protest its publication. As critic Gordon Van Ness wrote in the essay "*Follow Me Home* and the Ethics of Redemption," "'Night Sport' . . . is the oldest story in *Follow Me Home,* and its darkly pessimistic narrative and black tone link the collection to Hoffman's earlier stories." The protagonist of the story, Chip, a Vietnam War veteran who

Dust jacket for Hoffman's 1994 collection, featuring such characters as an embittered Vietnam War veteran, an aging minister, a bootlegger, and a sly housekeeper

lost his legs in the war and now lives by himself in a rural area of Southside Virginia, has grown increasingly bitter about what the war and society have done to his life. He rejects his family, his former girlfriend, and his mother's well-intentioned but overly sanctimonious minister and "baits" his house to invite a break-in.

His victim-to-be is Tommy Walker, a student at a nearby prep school who is required to do something daring for initiation into one of the clubs at St. Johns. Tommy's surname subconsciously deepens Chip's hatred of society and all those whose lives have not been affected by the war. In an eye-for-an-eye reenactment from the Old Testament, Chip attains a measure of revenge by firing both barrels of his shotgun into the right and left calves of Tommy's legs. He then calls the sheriff's office to report a break-in and attempt on his life and removes the evidence—mail and papers he has allowed to accumulate on the porch—of his bait. Chip's actions are cruel, senseless, and sadistic, but perhaps no more so than actions he witnessed during the Vietnam War.

"Boy up a Tree" is a marvelous first-person point of view story about growing up, lost opportunities, class disparities, and relationships that seem plausible and possible until the cold reality of circumstance takes over. Hoffman's language, always stimulating and appropriate, carries the force of the story as when he writes descriptively of Senator Lamar Bristow, "who resembled a slit-eyed possum wearing a polka-dot bow tie." The story infuses the clash of two cultures with a sense of nostalgia.

"Abide With Me" is the most humorous story of the collection, although the humor is mixed with a great deal of pathos. The plot has to do with Harmon's erection on a mountain of a grotesque statue of Jesus to fulfill a promise he made to the Lord. The statue soon becomes the laughingstock of the valley, however, and Harmon's pastor, the Reverend Amos Stillwater, calls on Harmon to ask him to remove the offensive statue: "He opened the door for Reverend Amos, who moved slow as lard flowing across a skillet. 'That man could eat the legs off an elephant and ask for the ears. . . . If Reverend Amos was a hog, we'd had him 'fore now.'" Soon the Reverend Amos is joined by others, and Harmon has to decide whether he is serving his Lord by keeping the statue he has built on public display or by removing what is perceived more and more as a laughable symbol of misplaced faith.

The last story in the collection, "Expiation," is one of Hoffman's strongest. It involves his protagonist's coming to grips with his early life; his acceptance of the parents and past he has always been ashamed of, or at least hidden from others; his kinship with others just like him, white and black; and his ultimate decision to undo the lie he had lived so long and hope that his wife, Anne, will be able to accept the truth that only now, late in life, he is willing to lay claim to. "Expiation" has been expanded by Hoffman into an as-yet-unpublished novel, tentatively titled "Lies."

"Points," a hunting story set in Charlottesville, handles well two of Hoffman's favorite themes: the father-son relationship between Beau and Alfred (which also includes the conflict between the two generations) and the moral and ethical dilemma between winning at all costs and playing by the rules of the game; "Business Trip" involves a trio of businessmen on their annual hunt in the Big Allegheny Mountains of West Virginia, with the city slicker, Clarence, getting the last laugh over his hunting companions and adversaries. "The Secret Garden," set in Richmond, is a hauntingly beautiful but emotionally wrenching story about the passionate Rachel—a mother, wife, daughter, and lover—and the failed attempts on the part of various family members to control her. Rachel's story is told from multiple points of view with compassion, sensitivity, and understanding.

Another collection of Hoffman's short fiction, *Doors,* was published in 1999. Once again all ten stories that appear in it were previously published: "Doors," Stones," and "Place" in *Shenandoah;* "Roll Call" and "Blood" in the *Virginia Quarterly Review;* and half the stories—"Landings," "Winter Wheat," "Prodigal," "Humility," and "Tenant"—in the *Sewanee Review.* In an interview with Hoffman that appeared in the 4 June 1999 *Farmville Herald* shortly after *Doors* was published, Hoffman was asked about the title of the collection: "I wanted to start this collection with a story most readers would probably like. I didn't want to scare readers off with a story that might startle too much. Also, in every one of these stories doors occur. So the reader is looking through ten different doors and at the people who live inside that particular structure. . . . I wanted readers to see these places as a series of doors and a series of people living beyond the threshold."

In the title story the unnamed narrator, an aging widow, hires the local handyman, Horace Puckett, to rebuild the ancient furnace in her house. But when Horace knocks at the front door to enter and inspect the furnace, she sends him "around back to the outside basement entrance because I wasn't in the habit of letting laborers come through the front door or the kitchen one either if it could be avoided. I assumed he didn't know better." By the end of the story Horace is teaching the once haughty and proud widow about acceptance, dignity, humility, and expiation. "Windy Belle, the ageless flame-headed proprietress at the Little Ritz Hair Salon" is a minor character in "Doors" but a major character and the victim of a murder-suicide in "Tenant," in which a Washington, D.C., couple buys a farmhouse and acreage in rural Southside Virginia and makes the mistake of hiring an insanely jealous man, Dexter Barrow, to help run the farm.

As Ron Carter has pointed out in his review of *Doors* for the 27 June 1999 *Richmond Times-Dispatch,* the story "Stones," which received an O. Henry Prize in 1966, "delineates the curious combination of social progress and cultural stasis that permeates the rural south." The story is told from the point of view of a high-school boy, Chip, who agrees to work for A. I. Benjamin, a mysterious black man from New York who plans to destroy the plantation home he has bought.

In "Blood" the setting shifts from Tobaccoton to the mining country of West Virginia. The story has much autobiographical material in it. Its protagonist, Les, like Hoffman growing up, lives with his mother and grandmother. Les is told that his father walked out on his family, and his domineering grandmother forbids anyone in the home to mention his name. Les is determined to find out more about his father, and after surprising his Aunt Clara while she is having sex on a fire trail with a married member of their church congregation, he forces her to tell him all that she knows about the circumstances of his father's leaving. Later, caught drinking beer at a party on the river, Les is sent to a military school in Georgia. He uses the opportunity of a long spring break to detour to West Virginia in search of his father. Hoffman seems to say that blood ties are really the ties that bind. Many of Hoffman's stories and several of his novels involve a son's search for his father, a literal search or an emotional-psychological one.

Of the remaining six stories in *Doors,* three are set in rural Southside Virginia: "Prodigal," "Place," and "Winter Wheat." All three are narrated in the first person and depend on dramatic irony: the reader reaches the moment of truth long before the characters come to realize it. In "Prodigal" a young man who had left home as a boy returns to see his father, a former uneducated, redneck country preacher in a brand new "Jeffersonian structure of major proportions, classic, columned, porticoed, the mortar gleaming white between cardinal bricks newly laid." The boy knows that the father has lied, cheated, and stolen to obtain the money to build the church, however. In "Place," Mimi, a well-educated, horse-loving young woman, learns that her idol, Gaston Farley, is a user of people as well as of horses: Gaston, in explaining why he has used a shotgun to destroy Mimi's favorite horse, Midnight Baron, replies offhandedly, "Not breeding stock and can't again be safely ridden." When Mimi asks Gaston if he had ever thought that Baron "wouldn't still love the sunshine, the grass, the company of mares," he replies, "Better cool off with a swim." Days later, after waiting in vain for a call from Gaston, Mimi rides over to his house on a cold Saturday night only to see it warmly lighted and glittering. She, too, has been replaced.

Although Hoffman has declined to name a favorite story in *Doors,* telling the interviewer for the *Farmville Herald* that "my stories are all my children and I always try to treat my children equally," George Core, in his review of *Doors* for the spring 2000 issue of *Sewanee Review,* asserts that "Winter Wheat" is the best story in the collection in terms of characterization, plot, and use of language, idiom, and dialect. The narrator, Matthew, marries late in life to Jessie Hamlett—"Truth is Miss Jessie don't have much chance except me. That withered left calf of hers." They are satisfied with their lives until Jessie begins spending too much time with the new principal at Red Oak Lower School, Philip Sauers, who also sings in the church choir. Telling Matthew that she is going to Atlanta for her brother's birthday, Jessie

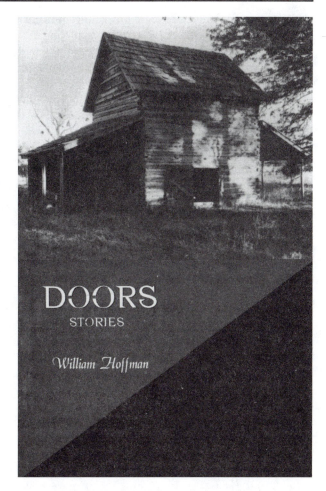

Dust jacket for Hoffman's 1999 collection of stories linked by a motif of doors

instead spends the weekend with Sauers. Caught in her lie when Matthew calls Atlanta, Jessie hurts her husband even more when she tells him that the only reason she stays with him is that "I'm too old for him."

Biding his time, Matthew catches Philip fishing on the river, pretends to befriend him, and then drowns him: "He thrashes, but he's not much man. Whatever does Jessie see in him? 'Won't take long,' I tell bubbles of his silent screaming face. Like drowning a cat." Matthew buries the body where he intends to sow a new crop of winter wheat and that Thanksgiving invites Jessie to "come stand on our porch . . . I have her look out over the wheat. . . . 'Let us give the good Lord thanks for an abundant crop,' I tell her."

Compared to "Winter Wheat," the remaining three stories are slight. Only one is light, almost a comedy. "Humility" is in the rich tradition of a Lee Smith story, the story of a local hometown football hero who marries a rich girl from the big city and brings her home to help him in his dream to turn Shawnee Valley into a luxurious vacation spa. "Roll Call," set in Richmond, is an initiation story for the young, unnamed narrator, who learns that family pride is not enough to sustain in life a good-hearted ne'er-do-well. And "Landings," set on the Chesapeake Bay, brings together at the end of the story two social outcasts, a severely burned former military pilot who has lost the will to live and a self-anointed caretaker who pities the man and tries to rescue him from the path he is taking to self-destruction. Later, the man must save his caretaker's life when a strong current and panic threaten her with drowning. The incident is another instance of the weak reaching out to help the weaker and a further comment on one of Hoffman's favorite subjects, the separation between appearance and reality.

Hoffman's twelve published novels complement his stories, addressing many of the same issues at greater length. Thematically, the novels fall into three groups: the first comprises *The Trumpet Unblown* (1955), *Days in the Yellow Leaf* (1958), and *Yancey's War* (1966), which all show the effects of war both on the novels' protagonists and on all those with whom he comes in contact following his wartime experiences; the second group, made up of *A Place for My Head* (1960), *The Dark Mountains* (1963), *A Walk to the River* (1970), *A Death of Dreams* (1973), and *Tidewater Blood* (1998), focus on the importance of place, the fragility of human relationships, the influence of the past upon the present, and the emptiness of material success; and the third group—comprising *The Land That Drank the Rain* (1982), *Godfires* (1985), and *Furors Die* (1990)—consists of more philosophical novels, in which both the central characters and the author struggle with questions of spiritual disillusionment, the possibility of redemption, the enormous power of love to suffocate or bring about renewal, and the apparent failure of religion to provide the means for acceptance or salvation. Since the publication of *Doors* in 1999, Hoffman has published two additional short stories in the *Sewanee Review*—"Pursuit" (Fall 1999) and "Black Swan" (Winter 1999)—and another novel, *Blood and Guile* (2000).

Taken as a whole, Hoffman's short stories introduce his readers to characters as real and as believable as any in twentieth-century American literature, many of them as memorable as Eudora Welty's or William Faulkner's Mississippi characters, from Gormer, the snake-handling minister in "The Spirit in Me" to Matthew, the avenging farmer in "Winter Wheat," and Chip, the psychotic Vietnam veteran of "Night Sport." Apart from brilliant and searing characterization, Hoffman gives the reader of his short fiction a strong sense of place. He has done for Southside Virginia, the mountains of Virginia and West Virginia, and the Tidewater-Chesapeake Bay area what Faulkner did for the Mississippi delta and the hills of Oxford—one can almost smell the sea breezes of "Sea Tides," "Sea Treader," and "Moorings" or feel the red clay of "A Southern Sojourn" or "Winter Wheat." As with all gifted writers, however, the themes of Hoffman's stories are what remain with his readers: courage, honor, pride, humility, self-sacrifice, loneliness, and love for land, for family, and for the forgotten, abused, and ill-used. Fred Chappell's comment on Hoffman's short fiction offers a refreshing insight: "His relish for accessible story lines, thematic clarity, informative detail, strong characterization, and satisfying structure is unmistakable. Almost any page shows his enjoyment of these customary elements of fiction composition as well as his quiet proficiency in their application. He rarely writes what we would call an 'experimental' story; he probably feels no need, being so expert in the art of straightforward narrative."

References:

William L. Frank, ed., *The Fictional World of William Hoffman* (Columbia: University of Missouri Press, 2000).

Jeanne Nostrandt, "William Hoffman," in *Contemporary Fiction Writers of the South,* edited by Joseph M. Flora and Robert Bain (Westport, Conn.: Greenwood Press, 1993), pp. 222–233.

Mary Hood

(16 September 1946 –   )

Dede Yow
Kennesaw State University

BOOKS: *How Far She Went: Stories* (Athens: University
of Georgia Press, 1984);
And Venus Is Blue: Stories (New York: Ticknor & Fields,
1986);
Familiar Heat (New York: Knopf, 1995).

OTHER: Raymond Andrews, *Rosiebelle Lee Wildcat
Tennessee,* foreword by Hood (Athens: University
of Georgia Press, 1988);
"Tropic of Conscience," in *The New Georgia Guide,*
edited by Thomas G. Dyer and Stanley W. Lindberg (Athens: University of Georgia Press, 1996),
pp. 105–135;
"The Essential Clue and Connection," in *Eudora Welty:
Writers' Reflections upon First Reading Welty,* edited
by Pearl Amelia McHaney (Athens, Ga.: Hill
Street Press, 1999), pp. 55–57.

SELECTED PERIODICAL PUBLICATIONS–
UNCOLLECTED: "A Stubborn Sense of Place: Writers and Writing on the South," by Hood and others, *Harper's Magazine* (August 1986): 35–45;
"Alligators and White Mules," *Art & Antiques* (January
1988): 67–73.

Mary Hood (photograph © by Allen Phillips Jr.)

Mary Hood began publishing her short stories in
the early 1980s when writers such as Raymond
Carver, Bobbie Ann Mason, and Ann Beattie were
writing fiction called minimalist, characterized by a
detached first-person narrator whose story had no resolution. At the same time the second Southern Rena-
scence was flourishing, dominated by the voices of
strong women whose themes echo the traditional
regional concern with family and community, but
whose demographics shift beyond local setting and
character. While Hood breaks ranks with the minimal-
ists–her third-person narrator allows no distance from
the characters, and the stories have conclusions–she
joins Eudora Welty, Lee Smith, Alice Walker, Anne
Tyler, Doris Betts, Tina McElroy Ansa, and Ellen Douglas in writing stories of men and women who struggle

with the bonds of love, family, and place. Published
originally in such prestigious magazines as *The Georgia
Review, The Kenyon Review,* and *Harper's,* the stories in
How Far She Went (1984) and *And Venus Is Blue* (1986)
have been chosen for twenty-two anthologies in the
"best and new" categories as well as reprinted in text-
books. Hood's novel, *Familiar Heat* (1995), translated
into several languages, is set on the Florida coast, but
Hood locates her short fiction in her native Georgia.

Mary Elizabeth Hood was born on 16 September 1946 in the Golden Isles off the southern coast in Brunswick, Georgia. Her father, William Charles Hood, was an aircraft worker; her mother, Mary Adella Katherine Rogers Hood, was a teacher of Latin. Their love of nature and of the spoken and written word had a great influence on Hood, who earned her A.B. in Spanish in 1967 from Georgia State University and whose intimate familiarity with the natural world infuses the settings of her stories with realism and immediacy. Her family settled in 1970 in Woodstock, a small community in the foothills of the Appalachians, north of Atlanta. Hood has not married, and she and her mother still live in the family home with cats, a Labrador retriever, various hens, roosters, chicks, and seasonal blooming and herbal gardens.

In "A Stubborn Sense of Place: Writers and Writing on the South" (1986) Hood wrote: "I cannot think of a single more important influence on my writing, and certainly upon my life, than my parentage." The marriage between her Georgian mother and her New Yorker father is reflected in her fiction by her "decision to try to sound like the Southern talkers I had heard tell such wonderful things" censored by the "Northern conscience . . . that stands ready, tapping its foot, jingling the car keys, rustling the map, wanting me to *get on with it,* asking with every turn and delay of plot, 'So?'" Hood claims that she "thought of myself as American, blooming where planted—which happens to be with a Southern exposure."

Growing up, Hood saw the landscape of her home state from the family's 1939 Mercury. Perched in the "quaint rear jump seats," she and her brother traveled the blue highways of the state, and she wrote in "Alligators and White Mules" (1988) that "Sunday drive by Sunday drive our family learned its place—the Georgia landscape was our TV, and we never tired of the channel." This terrain and its seasons set the stage for her stories. The rural characters depend upon the land for physical and spiritual sustenance, and when the relationship is broken, their world edges toward destruction, whether it is a marriage doomed, as in "Solomon's Seal," or trees razed for development, as in "Moths." A Southern writer in location and subject, Hood is an American writer in her belief in the land as Eden.

The speech of Hood's characters derives from the voices she has heard on the bus, in the church choir (where for years she sang alto or soprano depending on where the biggest talkers were), in the polling places where she worked as an officer, or in the little craft stores where she sold her handpainted saws. Like Flannery O'Connor, Hood has a sharp eye and a tone-sensitive ear. The literary heritage of her characters'

language is rooted in the local-color writing of the nineteenth-century South, and while she retains the integrity of the dialect and diction of northwest Georgia, she takes equal care with the diction of her omniscient narrator. Her goal—never to condescend to her characters—is reflected in the apparent seamless connections between narrative voice and characters. David Baker, in *The Kenyon Review* (1987), finds Hood's choosing to tell her stories from a third-person point of view remarkable in a literary period of "first-person confessionalism." Her third-person narrator "appears gracious and unselfish," while her characters "seem cared for, listened to, 'loved,' as Welty would say." Welty, even more than O'Connor, was a "revelation and continues to be so," Hood wrote in *Eudora Welty: Writers' Reflections upon First Reading Eudora Welty* (1999): "What I owe her and what I will never forget, is that I saw and heard—from her first words—my own world with kittens drinking raw milk from hubcaps, sixth graders singing 'Paper of Pins,' the convict catching the tossed pack of Marlboros from the drive-by stranger, the mailbox balloons shot with BB's, beautiful quick fools and the heart-breaking dead—my own world rendered visible."

While Hood's diction, character, and situation are created from careful attention to the life around her, wide reading and research complete the grounding of her fiction in the real world. Her library reflects her eclectic tastes. She has a wall of short fiction, a wall of natural history and field guides, and a wall of language—history of language, theory of language, and dictionaries of foreign languages. She has one whole specialty bookcase on bookbinding, printing, and manuscripts, and as the first writer in residence at Berry College (1997–1998), she even taught a course in bookmaking. The natural world is also her study; she is familiar with all birds and plants of her region and beyond.

From first publication, Hood's fiction has garnered awards. Her debut collection, *How Far She Went,* won the Flannery O'Connor Award for Short Fiction and the *Southern Review* Louisiana State University Short Fiction Award. Hood renders with perfect detail the everyday life of her fictional world. Isolation is the plight of the characters in the nine stories of this volume. For some, the distance can be spanned by love, but others are entrapped by situation or temperament. Set in a small area of rural northwest Georgia, these stories transcend place as the characters struggle in and out of marriage, nourished by the bonds of family and damned by the sins that persist through generations.

In three of the stories in *How Far She Went* the sins are generational, ending only when an act arrests the cycle, breaking down the barrier of old hurts. The title story is about a grandmother and her fifteen-year-old

Hood

How Far She Went

How Far
She Went
Stories by
Mary Hood

Mary Hood

ISBN 0-8203-0733-8

Georgia

Winner of the
Flannery O'Connor Award for Short Fiction

Dust jacket for Hood's 1984 collection of stories linked by their characters' isolation

granddaughter who are forced to live together by the death of the girl's mother and her father's abandonment. The grandmother, shamed and deserted years ago by her baby's father, had borne her own daughter alone and had watched her run wild and die early, leaving this child who would "be just like her, would carry the hurting on into another generation." The girl flashes against the constant cold anger of the grandmother, who despises her small acts of rebellion, her tight jeans and loud music. But when the girl flirts with some mean drunks on motorcycles, she puts their lives in jeopardy, and the grandmother chooses to sacrifice her little dog–the only creature, it appears, that she loves. The act is an epiphany for both. When they walk down the dirt path home, with the old woman bearing her lifeless dog, the girl "walked close behind her, exactly where *she* walked, matching her pace, matching her stride, close enough to put her hand forth (if the need arose) and touch her granny's back where the faded voile was clinging damp, the merest gauze between their wounds."

In "A Man Among Men" Thomas, a hardworking law officer, was rejected by his father in favor of his profligate brother, whose untimely death the old

man would not acknowledge. As though by legacy, Thomas enforces his emotional isolation by refusing to love his own rebellious son, Dean. Following the rules keeps Thomas's pain in check until he is called to the scene of a drug overdose of a boy that looks eerily like his own son. Carrying out his duty to inform the mother, he is unprepared for the truth he hears in her keening: "You don't love them for it, but you love them. There's good in between the bad times. . . . the Lloyd Jesus knows I love all my boys!" Each of the three sections of the story opens with a different view of Thomas's father lying in the casket, the inevitable burial ahead. At the end of the story, Thomas stands with Dean at the gravesite, and there they reach across the emotional divide.

A legacy of temper forms a specious bond between the father and son in "Manly Conclusions." Carpenter, the father, has a "tree-topping temper"; his bumper sticker vaunts, "I don't get mad. I get even." His wife has dealt with the repercussions of his rage for years, but when Dennis, their teenage son, has disappeared to seek revenge on the weekender neighbors who have shot the family collie, they discover that Carpenter's gun is missing. A "new specter rose between them, unspeakable, contagious." Paralyzed by insight, Carpenter cannot answer the phone ringing at the end of the story.

Solitary women live isolated by place, circumstances, and choice in the stories "Inexorable Progress," "Solomon's Seal," and "Lonesome Road Blues." "Inexorable Progress," which first appeared in *The Georgia Review,* was selected by John Updike and Shannon Ravenel for inclusion in *The Best American Short Stories, 1984.* Angelina, the protagonist, isolates herself emotionally and psychologically; she is like a "tree stripped to the natural bone, soul-naked in the emptying wind." She dreams about her stillborn child, mourns her husband's Sunday absences on hunting trips, and binges on brandy. When the lump in her breast proves benign, giving her a second chance, she renounces cigarettes and alcohol, runs four miles a day, crochets, and canvasses door-to-door against the ERA until her "streak of pure happiness" ends: "Sometime during the week of Easter, Angelina made up her mind." Her attempt to kill herself with a pistol is abortive, and she lies in her hospital bed, "clawing at the IV's in her wrists that tethered her to life . . . small and sharpeyed and at bay somehow, vulnerable but valiant, like a little beast who would gnaw off its own foot to escape the trap." From her bedside her husband tells their daughter that Angelina has "another chance."

Like Angelina, the mountain woman in "Solomon's Seal" refuses love. She lives on an isolated half acre in a patched cabin with a husband who pays more attention to his hunting dogs. Her barren marriage yields both a lush garden of fruits and vegetables and her decision "after a time to give as good as she got, which wasn't much." She seethes for forty years: the "madder she got, the greener everything grew"—everything but the plant, Solomon's seal. They divorce; he gets the house; and she keeps the lot. Alone, finally, she breaks one by one the plates never taken out of her hope chest. She covers her seedlings with the hand-sewn coverlet, now yellowed, and checks her dying Solomon's seal. She cannot coax this flower, a six-pointed star used as an amulet in love, to grow for her: "'You'd think I could learn,' she said. But she never did."

The wife in "Lonesome Road Blues," the opening story of the volume, is yet another solitary woman. Freed from her husband's sickroom, she has had "more than a nodding acquaintance with Duty." She goes out in the hot, dry summer to the state fair with the purpose of inviting a musician, Lovingood of the Grape Arbor Pickers, to come home with her to be nourished and refreshed: "There were olive smudges under his eyes, hollows in his cheeks." He takes a long nap, alone, on her clean, cool sheets, dried on the line in the

sun. He showers, eats the home cooking, and goes back for his evening gig, after which she sees him dialing a number from a little scrap of paper a girl had handed him that afternoon. Alone, the woman "drives home over the same dark empty roads, in the same ruts, the same dust rising and falling behind her." A country woman, she is sustained by resting her eyes on the "blue green mountains beyond and beyond."

Two years after the publication of *How Far She Went* by the University of Georgia Press, Ticknor and Fields published Hood's second collection, *And Venus Is Blue.* In 1987 this volume won the Lillian Smith Award, and in 1988 Hood was voted Georgia Author of the Year by the Dixie Council of Authors and Journalists. She was also given the 1988 Townsend Award for Fiction. The acclaim of these two collections afforded her opportunities she had waited for through twelve years of rejection slips. In 1992 she was given a residency at the Hambidge Center in Rabun Gap, Georgia. The following year she went to the MacDowell Colony in Peterborough, New Hampshire, and returned to the University of Georgia as visiting writer from April through June. The critical reception of *And Venus Is Blue* was impressive. Alice McDermott, in *The New York Times Book Review* (17 August 1986), called it a "marvelous collection" and Hood a writer who is "consummately honest. She does not fear the bleak conclusions of some lives or the quiet fleeting triumphs of others." In *The Georgia Review* (1987) Judith Kitchen wrote, "Once she has drawn us into her stories, Mary Hood keeps us there—dead center, all ears."

The theme of isolation Hood developed in *How Far She Went* is deepened in the second volume by the attenuation of another form of connection—to the family's past and to the land where that past is rooted. Her belief that connection to the land gives spiritual sustenance is reflected in the dedication of her first collection of stories to a place, the community she lives in: "LITTLE VICTORIA, big enough." But even as she was writing, Cherokee County was fast becoming an exurb of Atlanta, transformed by Sunbelt sprawl. Hood wrote in *The New Georgia Guide* that for rural people, home and work are no longer "centralized around the family farm. Today, they work in the paper mill or in the carpet factory or sewing or cleaning houses for the subdivision builders, or building the houses themselves."

Routed by land clearing for subdivisions and golf courses, the humans and animals in *And Venus Is Blue* struggle to survive their dying world. The gradual destruction of Hood's own neighborhood is mirrored in these stories, in which new shopping centers, trailers, rental homes, and junkyards take over the countryside. The old folk were disappearing, being taxed off the land, and Hood wanted to honor these people who worked with their hands. As an artist, she was struggling with the language of her characters. She recounted in a roundtable discussion transcribed in the *Kennesaw Review* (Fall 1988):

> I write about people that will never read my stories. I went through a tremendous crisis with diction. . . . I didn't write anything until I decided who it was that I wanted to be able to read it. . . . The story I wrote called 'Moths' is about a pulpwood cutter. . . . He was the man I wanted to write that story for, and it meant I had to consider how to tell everything . . . without condescension in any way and yet have it accessible. Access is one way that we can overcome prejudice even if it remains academic.

"Moths," placed in the middle of this second volume, is a story about Cheney, a middle-aged day-laborer whose work is to cut pulpwood for a development like any of those down the road from Hood's Little Victoria. He finds a bug in the woods, a beautiful moth with "silver-green wings like two dogwood leaves," but it has been damaged by the truck and is dying. Fascinated by its beauty, he goes to look up the name in the library, a place he has never been. But the librarian "came and stood between him and the books. 'And you want?' She was as clean as Sunday. Her hands were white enough to make bread." Cheney's undershirt is stained with blood from a coworker's accident: "He wished he didn't have so much of Ward's blood on his undershirt. He wished he didn't have so much rosin on his jeans. He wished that he had washed his hands. He put his hat back on. 'I come in the wrong store,' he said. 'Reckon I just didn't notice where I was.' He went out." The story closes with Cheney and his family in the warm spring air, the baby asleep. His consolation is only momentary, because when the trees are gone, he will be without work, forced like the moth out of his world.

Hood complements the quiet, elegiac mood of "Moths" with a story about generations finding connection in the old homeplace. "Finding the Chain" is the story of a modern blended household whose members must relinquish individual ties in order to become one family. The adoption papers have come through on two of the children, and Cliffie and her husband, Ben, have a new baby of their own. Cliffie takes them all back to her Grandma's old cabin in the woods so they will know her roots. When they try to clean the flue so they can start a fire, the search for a chain that can handle the job gives rise to the central image: the chains of the front porch "courting swing" that Cliffie's grandfather hung on her sixteenth birthday. Drew, the angry and rebellious child who calls his stepfather "Mister," has lost one of the chains while playing with it in the field.

Dust jacket for Hood's 1986 collection of stories set primarily in the increasingly urbanized landscape of her native Georgia

Cliffie marshals them all to find it; they sweep the field searching as the first snow the children and Ben have ever seen starts to fall: "They closed ranks against the coming dark, against the soft, random flurries, against the idea of giving up." In this story a return to the land, to the elements, offers the possibility of a union.

Hood dedicated this second collection of stories, "For my family, where I learned." But some of her characters have never had any family to anchor them. Rhonda in "After Moore" was fifteen when she met Moore, a manufacturer's rep, in a suburban bar. She is thirty now, her story told by a wry, omniscient narrator from the marriage counselor's office: "her mother had dropped out of sight two marriages ago. With no family, and no diploma, she had chosen the best she could, and made the most of her chances." As for Moore's family, his father sold their home when his wife died and lives in a trailer on a hill in a junkyard. Moore flaunts his infidelity on weeklong trips to Vegas and the Bahamas. When Rhonda finally leaves, Moore lures her back by building the family their first house; they had shuffled from one rental property to the next. Rhonda thinks maybe she will put roots down for the first time.

Candy in "Desire Call of the Wild Hen" is a child of wealth "who perfected her skiing and her tan when she was fifteen, the year her parents died in the crash of her father's Lear jet." She lived with the relative closest to water and at nineteen married Phil, who was established in construction in Atlanta and flew her to discos, the steeplechase, and the Braves games in his Cessna. Before the pool for their suburban home is finished, Phil leaves Candy and their daughter, Melanie, for other women. By age ten, Melanie has learned enough about loss to save an empty box from the trash to bury her turtle in when he dies. Candy sits in the empty pool at night and screams, her future as empty as her past.

Hawk Hawkins in "The Goodwife Hawkins" had no past; his only connections were business, and his family was a convenience. He owned three business supply yards for contractors; suburban sprawl had made him rich, and he "was always spreading his money around to make himself feel good." He donated the acreage, the steel, and the concrete for the new baseball field; he was a former mayor, a Shriner, a Legionnaire. Vinnie had been the model wife, keeping his payroll, raising his sons, cooking huge fish and game suppers. They were grandparents when Hawk ran them into a cattle truck after too many mint juleps, injuring Vinnie's back and his brain. The abuse began with Hawk blacking Vinnie's eye with his cane. On Wednesday night before Thanksgiving, he let her relax every hour to baste the bird; the rest of the time "Hawk taped her mouth shut with two-inch-wide adhesive and stood her against the refrigerator door, at attention, while he sat at the dinette table, pouring whiskey into his coffee and aiming the pistol at her good heart." Home is transformed into hell: when Vinnie leans over to pick up Hawk's TV remote, he kicks her; when she throws him a surprise birthday party, after his cronies leave he slits her arm with the serving knife. All three sons had not been home at the same time in five years, and when Hawk is finally unable to keep the business, they want the money up front. The story opens with Hawk's death and Vinnie's "first free acts" when she opens doors and windows and steps outside, "shivering in the surprise of being alive in the tender sun while acorns fell . . . . A pair of flickers whirred up as the dog threaded through the sparkling hedge." Nature has the power to heal in Hood's world.

Spiritual degeneration that occurs once connections to family and land are broken is embodied in the character of Ginnie, a teenage girl, whom Judith Kitchen describes as "possibly the most unnerving character in recent literature—amoral, supremely spoiled, deliberately manipulative." For the story "Something Good for Ginnie" Hood won a Pushcart Prize in 1986 and a $30,000 Whiting Award for fiction. Ginnie's parents are defeated by circumstances and finally by Ginnie. When Ginnie was thirteen, her mother fell out of a tree trying to get Ginnie a bird's nest and broke her back on a "Posted" sign. She had to be detoxed before surgery. Ginnie's father, Doc Daniels, struggles with a failing family business, a pharmacy patronized only by old-timers who did not want to drive to the mall and tourists asking directions back to the interstate. As for their alienated daughter, she sexually torments a mentally handicapped boy and burns his trailer down. She teases Jordan, the young boy who tutors her in math, and lures him into her father's dark pharmacy to be shot as an intruder by Doc Daniels when he hears a noise as he patrols the property. Splattered with the boy's blood, Ginnie laments about her clothing, "This was a Laura Ashley." As Ginnie and her father leave the emergency room—Jordan dies three days later—Ginnie says, "I guess this cooks it about the Datsun for graduation, doesn't it?" The narrator passes no judgment, and neither does Ginnie's mother, who "turned her mind's channel to another station, just like she did the TV." As for Doc, "he didn't really believe in evil, born in, unchangeable. People could change."

The characters in these stories do change as their world dies, and their struggle to adapt also changes those they love. In the complex and lyrical novella "And Venus Is Blue," the suicide of James, Delia's father, resonates through her past, leaving her angry and lost in the present. James was a carpenter with a love of his craft whose dream was to buy up and rebuild the vacant mill houses of the community as they should have been built. Instead he had to build new houses for a developer. Toni, Delia's mother, has a pattern of leaving and returning that, despite James's complete love, plants in Delia a fear of separation and loss. Her dread is made a reality by her father's suicide when she is eighteen, herself a wife and mother. The epigraph to the story prefigures Delia's torment: "Imagine a photograph album, with a bullet fired pointblank through it, every page with its scar. Murder attacks the future; suicide aims at the past." The narrative moves from daybreak to midnight, spanning the day when Delia is notified of James's suicide and reviewing the lifetime she spent fearing it.

Every intense moment Delia recalls in her life is permeated with her father's death. In each of the sections, her memory selects, transforms, edits, and telescopes her foreknowledge represented by her physical surroundings and her psychic torment. In the second section, "Dawn: Delia, Age Two," she is a baby playing in spilled red paint that becomes her father's spilled red blood. In "Morning: Delia, Age Four," left by the hateful woman who keeps her while James works, she has drawn a baby robin alone, like herself, in a nest with lightning and thick rain all around it. In "Forenoon: Delia, Age Nine," the bird in her drawing has become a live rabbit taken from a hutch to be dressed and sold, and the rabbit becomes Delia with her mother claiming her head, her father her body, and her squealing in her sleep. In the closing section, "Midnight," she comes back home to the funeral to face the loss of her father. The story opens with a picture of Delia: "She rested in the doorway now, all black and white, like her own picture crooked in a frame." She asks who did it; whom should she shoot? The answer goes farther back than any of her memories to the past that was lost to the steelyard and the cotton mill.

Mary Hood continues to be acknowledged as one of the best writers of fiction today. She held the John and Renee Grisham Chair of Visiting Southern Writer at the University of Mississippi in 1996. She was visiting writer at Centre College in Danville, Kentucky, in the winter term of 1999, and she was also named Writer of the Decade in honor of the tenth anniversary of the Contemporary Literature and Writing Conference at Kennesaw State University. The terrain of her fiction is changing, but Hood is discovering new landscapes and new characters to tell her stories. She set her novel, *Familiar Heat*, in a small Florida fishing village.

The structure is complex, interweaving the lives and fates of her characters, a diverse cast that includes Cubans, Greeks, and black and white Americans. Like the characters in her short stories, some have the chance to connect and survive; others are less fortunate or less wise. In whatever form it might take, her fiction is likely to continue to illuminate an elemental truth of the heart: to be whole, people need a place, a past, and other people. Without these, life is as precarious as forest land in the suburbs.

References:

David Aiken, "Mary Hood: The Dark Side of the Moon," in *Southern Writers at Century's End,* edited by Jeffrey J. Folks and James Perkins (Lexington: University of Kentucky Press, 1997), pp. 21–31;

David Baker, "Time and Time Again," *Kenyon Review* (Winter 1987): 137–142;

Judith Kitchen, "The Moments That Matter," *Georgia Review,* 41 (Spring 1987): 209–214;

Dan Pope, "The Post-Minimalist American Story or What Comes After Carver?" *Gettysburg Review,* 1, no. 2 (1988): 331–342;

George R. Scott, "Fields of Praise: A Woman's Harvest," *Kennesaw Review,* 2 (Fall 1988): 82–101.

Papers:

Some of Mary Hood's manuscripts are in the Watkins Collection at Robert W. Woodruff Library, Emory University.

William Humphrey

(18 June 1924 – 20 August 1997)

Ashby Bland Crowder
Hendrix College

See also the Humphrey entries in *DLB 6: American Novelists Since World War II, Second Series* and *DLB 212: Twentieth-Century American Western Writers, Second Series.*

BOOKS: *The Last Husband and Other Stories* (New York: Morrow, 1953; London: Chatto & Windus, 1953);

Home from the Hill (New York: Knopf, 1958; London: Chatto & Windus, 1958);

The Ordways (New York: Knopf, 1965; London: Chatto & Windus, 1965);

A Time and a Place (New York: Knopf, 1968); republished as *A Time and a Place: Stories of the Red River Country* (London: Chatto & Windus, 1969);

The Spawning Run (New York: Knopf, 1970; London: Chatto & Windus, 1970);

Proud Flesh (New York: Knopf, 1973; London: Chatto & Windus, 1973);

Farther Off from Heaven (New York: Knopf, 1977; London: Chatto & Windus, 1977);

Ah, Wilderness! The Frontier in American Literature (El Paso: Texas Western Press, 1977);

My Moby Dick (Garden City, N.Y.: Doubleday, 1978; London: Chatto & Windus, 1979);

Hostages to Fortune (New York: Delacorte/Seymour Lawrence, 1984; London: Secker & Warburg, 1985);

The Collected Stories of William Humphrey (New York: Delacorte/Seymour Lawrence, 1985; London: Secker & Warburg, 1986);

Open Season: Sporting Adventures of William Humphrey (New York: Delacorte/Seymour Lawrence, 1986);

No Resting Place (New York: Delacorte/Seymour Lawrence, 1989; London: Alison, 1989);

September Song (Boston: Houghton Mifflin/Seymour Lawrence, 1992).

SELECTED PERIODICAL PUBLICATION–
UNCOLLECTED: "The Mountain of Miracles," *New Yorker,* 36 (29 October 1960): 120, 122, 124, 127–128, 130–132, 135–144.

William Humphrey (photograph © 1985 by Stan Wayman; from the dust jacket for The Collected Stories of William Humphrey, *1985)*

Although William Humphrey's reputation mainly rests upon his five novels, he began his career with a book of short stories, *The Last Husband and Other Stories* (1953), and he continued to write short stories throughout his life. Following the publication of his first two novels, *Home from the Hill* (1958) and *The Ordways* (1965), he produced a second volume of short stories: *A Time and a Place* (1968). His stories to that point, together with two until then unpublished, were published in *Collected Stories* in 1985. Reviewing this volume in *The St. Petersburg Times* (18 August 1985), Robert Atwan

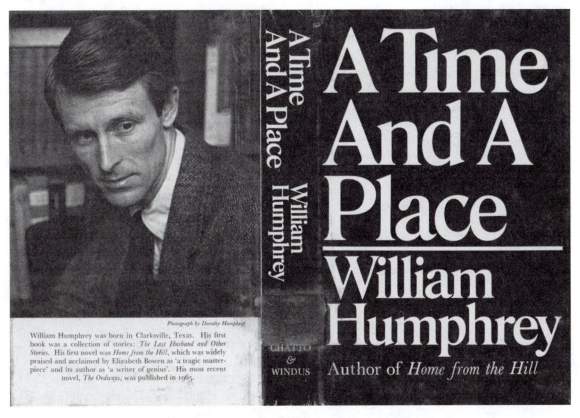

Dust jacket for the first British edition (1969) of Humphrey's 1968 collection of stories about the effects of economic hardship

acknowledged Humphrey as a traditional storyteller: "Pride, shame and loyalty motivate the characters in these stories, not ego, guilt and group affiliations. At times, Humphrey's world view seems closer to Homer, Virgil and Sophocles than it does to any modern thinker. Fate and fortune seem far more important than their modern replacements—self-determination and success. The gods are jealous and ill-tempered; human purpose is often futile." The two previously unpublished stories in this volume, "Dolce Far' Niente" and "The Patience of a Saint," look toward the subject of Humphrey's final short-story volume, *September Song* (1992), a collection of stories about the losses attendant upon old age.

William Joseph Humphrey was born in Clarksville, Texas, on 18 June 1924, the only son of Clarence and Nell Varley Humphries. His father, the son of a part-Indian sharecropper, had left home to make a living as an automobile mechanic. Nell Humphries altered the name to Humphrey to obscure the connection with her husband's less-than-respectable family and because she thought the name "Humphrey" possessed a higher elegance quotient. *Farther Off from Heaven* (1977), Humphrey's memoir, dwells upon the most significant event of his childhood: the death of his father in a car acci-

dent on 4 July 1937. Immediately after the death he and his mother moved to Dallas, where she could find a job to support them.

In addition to attending high school, Humphrey enrolled in the Dallas Institute of Fine Arts, having won a scholarship based upon the drawings he submitted. He aspired to be a painter, but he gave up the idea when his doubts about his abilities were enhanced by his learning that he was color blind. In 1941 he enrolled at Southern Methodist University; the following year he transferred to the University of Texas at Austin, joined the Young Communist League, and then returned the next year to SMU, where he remained until an abrupt departure in 1944. After working in a Chicago defense factory for a few months, he returned to Dallas to work on *The Southern Weekly* before moving to New York City in 1945. In Woodstock, New York, he met Dorothy Cantine, who was married and had a baby daughter; she left her husband for Humphrey, and they were married in Brooklyn four years later. Humphrey found a job first at the Merchant Marine Hospital on Staten Island and then at the Gotham Book Mart in Manhattan, but only after he and his wife and stepchild moved in 1947 to Brewster, New York, was he able to devote time to writing fiction.

Manuscript page and revised typescript page for "The Ballad of Jesse Neighbours," the first story in A Time and a Place
(Estate of William Humphrey; courtesy of Ashby Bland Crowder)

9

All night long it fell like a freshet spring ~~rain~~ on the noisy sheet-
iron roof, and the smell grew hellish; but Bull lay unsleeping
in his bed, smacking his old woman's bony flat behind whenever
he suspected her of dozing off, listening to the patter overhead, and crooning, "Oh, keep it up,
sweet Lord. Oh, pour it down. Don't never stop till I tell you."

Towards daybreak the next morning the crew succeeded in
capping the well, and they went out to have a look around. The
The ~~ground~~ looked as if it had paved overnight with asphalt
earth was black, as if it had been burned over, smelled as if
it had been burnt, and from the eaves of buildings, from the
handles of tools long abandoned in the yard, from the leaves of
trees and plants, from fence wires, the black liquid ~~hung~~ looped in
thick unfalling ~~drops~~ slow stringy. Dying songbirds staggered about the
greasy yard, their wings heavy and tired, and upon the black
pools lay grasshoppers and crickets in thick still swarms.

"Won't nothing ever grow here again," Mrs. Childress whined,
seeing her dead jonquils and the black ened oil-soaked earth they
stood in.

"I hope to God it won't!" cried Bull. "I've done raised all the
crops I ever aim to off of it!"

Breakfast (oily biscuits, coffee that seemed to have have
been drained from a crankcase) was hardly over when Bull said,
"All right, gals, fix your faces. We're heading for the city.
Don't bother packing nothing. We won't want none of this trash--
the sweep of his arm comprehended the sum of their previous lives--
never no more."

So they piled in the cab of the truck (a pick-up, cut down from
a La Salle sedan) and took off. Finding her shoes (which were
old anyway, and the heels all run ~~turned~~ over) black and gummy after
crossing the yard, Naomi slipped them off and as they pulled

Left margin, handwritten (vertical): haul him so out to with over the iron workout. (and otherwise expose only vestige to his previous life).

Humphrey's first short story, "In Sickness and Health," was published in the Winter 1949 issue of *Accent*. His second, "Man with a Family," which portrays death as an ordinary surprise, appeared in *Accent* the following summer and is the less important of the two. Inspired by Katherine Anne Porter's "A Day's Work" (1940), "In Sickness and Health" is the first of several Humphrey stories that probe marital relationships. Mr. and Mrs. Emmett Grogan are miserably married, seemingly bound together only in a perverse tug-of-war contest involving the subversion of each other's will. Mr. Grogan is seriously ill, and his wife likes to emphasize that fact to him and everybody else; therefore, he does everything he can to contradict her view of his condition. After trying to enjoy an afternoon at the neighborhood pub, he barely makes it home, finally admitting to his wife that he is dying. The story reveals the deep current of Mrs. Grogan's intentional cruelty. Her response to her husband's plight is to drain her tea, pick "a leaf off her tongue," and assume a contrary position, jeering vindictively: "You're well enough to swill with the pigs at McLeary's, you're well enough to bring me up a scuttle of coal from the cellar."

On the basis of this publication, Vassar College in Poughkeepsie invited Humphrey to give a reading of his fiction. Charles Shattuck, an editor of *Accent,* was so impressed by his performance that he wrote to Theodore Weiss, head of the English department at Bard College, to recommend Humphrey for a faculty position. The outcome was that Humphrey taught at Bard in Annandale-on-Hudson from 1949 until 1958.

During his fourth year at Bard, Humphrey published *The Last Husband and Other Stories*. The ten stories more or less alternate between ones set in the rural and small-town South where he was born and the big-city northeast commuter environment where he had gone to live. Perhaps there is a thematic motive in this design, but more importantly it points to Humphrey's desire from the beginning to be more than a regional Southern writer. Still, the stories belonging to both settings focus on common subjects: marriage, parenthood, and the problems of adolescents.

The title story, "The Last Husband," depicts one man's extraordinary effort to achieve an authentic life in the midst of meaninglessness. Edward Gavin is married to a woman who is incapable of love, yet he will not give up on the ideal of a marriage based upon mutual love. To achieve this goal, he engages in an extensive campaign of philandering in hopes of making Alice jealous. When Gavin finally gives up on his emotionally dead wife and creates an ideal home with a woman named Katherine, Alice refuses to give him a divorce. She has suddenly experienced a "climacteric" and realizes that her professional life as a magazine

advertising artist is a failure and that life is generally a sad disappointment. Her motivation for holding on to her husband is that she needs him to share in her disappointment; she cannot bear to see him happy. The story derives special richness from its point of view: the narrator, Charlie, observes Gavin with various degrees of incomprehension. Charlie rather sadly takes a cynical view of Gavin's exuberant efforts to embrace the best in life and is blind to the fact that his own marriage is disintegrating because of his neglect.

"The Hardys," first published in *The Sewanee Review* (April 1949), is the last story in the volume and is the other one devoted solely to the examination of a marriage. The Hardys, like the Grogans, are an old couple. Unlike the Grogans, however, the Hardys love each other a great deal, yet the action of the story demonstrates that love in itself is not enough to head off misery. The story takes place on the day that the couple are preparing to give up the house they have lived in for fifty years; they are marking their belongings for sale, a process that stimulates memories. Humphrey alternates the center of consciousness of the third-person narrative several times between the husband and the wife. This technique reveals that Clara Hardy has for a lifetime made much of little things and all along has been mistaken about her husband's motives and feelings. For fifty years she has been miserably jealous of Mr. Hardy's first wife, who had died in childbirth. Mr. Hardy has lived in the present, while his wife's present moments have been ruined by a perverse attention to the past—a primary theme in two other stories in the volume and of Humphrey's first three novels.

One other story in this volume, "The Fauve," concerns a marital relationship, though its main focus is the effect of failure upon a painter. James Ruggles is either an unrecognized genius or a painter who is unsuccessful for good reason; the objective third-person narrator is of little help in resolving this crucial issue, and the details of the story straddle the line. Whatever standing as an artist Ruggles is supposed to have, as a human being he is sorely wanting. His treatment of his wife is appalling; yet, the story includes a great deal of humor that inclines the reader to sympathize with Ruggles's efforts to cope with his lack of recognition as an artist.

Apart from the title story, the most significant stories in *The Last Husband and Other Stories* are "The Shell" and "Quail for Mr. Forester," both of which are based on the author's early life in Clarksville, Texas. These two stories, even more than "The Hardys," embody the central theme of Humphrey's first three novels—the chilling effect that the dead hand of the past has upon the present. In "The Shell" the sixteen-year-old Joe–like his literary predecessors, Ernest Hemingway's Nick

Adams and William Faulkner's Ike McCaslin–has an experience that prepares him for manhood. His father has been dead for four years, and Joe seeks to define himself as a man by measuring himself against the memory of his father's expertise as a hunter. The boy has an unexploded shotgun shell that had belonged to his father; his plan is to take this shell on a quail hunt and fire it so effectively that he will simultaneously extend his father's life and define his own. His effort leads to utter paralysis of the will, until he discovers that his father's shell–an emblem of the past–is a dud. Instantly he is freed from his attachment to a dead father and can fulfill himself in the present.

The achieving of sexual maturity is another aspect of Joe's growth. Through diction that at first only hints at sexual matters, Humphrey takes Joe past his oedipal relationship with his mother to a figurative climax in which he overcomes impotence. "The Shell" includes some outstanding lyrical passages. This story, like all of his novels, is influenced by the death of Humphrey's father (the novels offer variations on the separation of father and son).

"Quail for Mr. Forester," first published in *The New Yorker* (11 October 1952), is based on a festive quail dinner held by Humphrey's parents for the remnant of Clarksville antebellum aristocracy. The narrator is an adult looking back at himself and his family when he was a boy. In this story, as in the later novel *Proud Flesh* (1973), the family symbolizes the South. The story is set in the 1930s, when hard times emphasized the extent to which the shining glory of the Old South had faded. As John M. Grammer notes, the first-person narrator perceives that his parents view Mr. Forester as a "living monument" to a lost past. Emphasizing the vanity of those who attempt to revive the past, the story reveals that Mr. Forester has actually accommodated himself to the changes that occurred in the South following the Civil War, and he horrifies the family of backward-lookers by expressing pleasure in various modern conveniences and modes of entertainment. He thus fails to meet the expectations of his hosts, who sought to use him to bolster their dissatisfaction with every aspect of the present. However, Mr. Forester is Humphrey's hero, because he has shed the pretense that the past can be a substitute for the present. "Quail for Mr. Forester" effectively undermines the Southern cult of memory.

"A Fresh Snow" seems at first to clarify the difference between the corrupt nostalgia of the family in "Quail for Mr. Forester" and a reasonable and proper nostalgia. The root meaning of nostalgia is evoked, the longing for a homeland: a young Southern woman who has married a Northerner and moved to the North indulges in remembrance of the fellowship associated with graveyard-cleaning day (an activity common to several of Humphrey's books) and front-porch conviviality on summer evenings. When the woman's son comes in from the snow after school, she seeks to warm the alien coldness with "the slow warm liquid flow" of a Southern voice, and by making cocoa, putting her son on her lap, and telling him "all about the South, where he was born." The reader is momentarily lulled by the attractive tableaux with which this sweet story ends, but then remembers that the mother has had to forbid her son from playing in the snow with his friends, and a familiar pattern emerges: present activity is sacrificed by a devotion to a lost past. The reader has misgivings over the mother's shutting out the present, even if it is cold and uninviting, in order to replace it with a memory, even if it is warm.

Two other stories in the volume are the least successful. "Sister," first published in *Harper's Bazaar* (May 1950), is an account of how a neglected daughter makes her presence felt in her family; and "Report Card" conveys the importance of education to the lower classes.

Five years after his first book of short stories, Humphrey published his first novel, *Home from the Hill* (1958), which develops at least three of the themes from the short stories–an adolescent's advance to manhood through hunting, the relationship between a boy and his parents, and the killing effect of the past on the present. The success of this novel and the financial rewards from the Metro-Goldwyn-Mayer movie based on it enabled Humphrey to quit teaching. He and his wife spent most of the next four years in England, France, and Italy. During this time he started his second novel, *The Ordways;* his third novel, *Proud Flesh;* and all ten of the stories that made up his second book of short stories, *A Time and a Place*. None of these projects was finished when, in September 1963, Humphrey assumed the Visiting Glasgow Professorship at Washington and Lee University, Lexington, Virginia. *The Ordways* (1965) was not completed until April 1964.

After a semester in Virginia the Humphreys returned to England and settled in an ivy-covered fourteenth-century cottage in Telscombe near his English publisher, Ian Parsons, and Leonard Woolf, with whom Humphrey became lasting friends. Humphrey got about two-thirds of *Proud Flesh* written by the end of summer 1964; but, reaching an impasse with the novel, he moved on to Italy in the autumn and resumed work on the group of short stories. The Humphreys became weary of their roaming life and in June of 1965 bought an antique house outside of Hudson, New York. Almost simultaneously Humphrey accepted a yearlong appointment to teach at Massachusetts Institute of Technology. Moving and commuting delayed the appearance of *A Time and a Place* until 1968.

This second volume of short stories was quite different from the first. Instead of a mix of stories with Southern and Northern settings, all of the stories, as the title suggests, are set in one place and at one time: the Red River Valley, which includes East Texas and southeastern Oklahoma, during the Depression and drought in the 1930s. The stories expose the shortcomings of capitalism and emphasize both the gullibility of victims of economic and natural disaster and the depravity of those who take advantage of the gullible. The cast of characters includes gangsters, overnight oil millionaires, a rainmaker, a human fly, a luckless plowman of hardscrabble, a cheated Indian, and other types belonging to Depression and dust-bowl Texas and Oklahoma. Although John Steinbeck found some loveliness in the midst of the deprivations of this region, Humphrey takes a hard, unsentimental look at the simple reality of the grimmest prospects of life. In a measured way, however, he relieves his grim gaze with humor. In a 21 February 1968 letter to his friend Weiss, he wrote of *A Time and a Place:* "I think I'm more pleased to have written it than either of the two novels."

"The Ballad of Jesse Neighbours," the first story in the volume, is a prose approximation of a traditional ballad, a form that in itself makes the narrative voice sympathetic to the downtrodden protagonist. The subject matter is balladlike—"the old story: poor boy, heiress, and her father"—and so are the techniques: repetition of musical chords, repetition of details, and abrupt transitions. Jesse is in fact a ballad singer, and several well-known ballads appear in the story to mark the progress of the tale. At the outset Jesse hopes to marry Naomi Childress, but when her father strikes oil she advances socially beyond his reach; when neighbors also begin to strike oil, the increase in land values extinguishes his hope of owning his own small farm. Humphrey provides the perfect symbolic picture of Jesse's helplessness in the midst of forces stronger than he: "From every blade of grass, like a viscous black dew, hung a single unfalling drop. A dying songbird staggered about the yard, his wings heavy and useless." When Jesse elects to join the ranks of the outlaw heroes of popular ballads—the likes of Pretty Boy Floyd—and is captured, tried, and electrocuted, the story concludes on a strong ballad note. On the long train trip back from Texas with his body, his parents keep Jesse's guitar on their laps: "it happened now and again that one or the other would brush the strings, drawing from them a low chord like a sob."

While Jesse Neighbours is luckless, Dobbs in "A Job of the Plains" appears to have all the luck anybody could want: after years of trying to eke out a living on the poorest of land, he strikes oil and becomes a millionaire. But Dobbs is unable to enjoy any of the benefits belonging to a rich man, and his family disintegrates because of the riches. This story, which is a parody of the Book of Job, ends with a telling variation on the biblical text: "So Dobbs died, being old before his time, and having had his fill of days." Humphrey's version of the biblical story makes God out to be a trickster; for what seems to be good fortune at the end of a hard time is really just a worse time. The story conveys Humphrey's profound unbelief in a good God. By making his story of Dobbs dependent upon a biblical text, Humphrey sacrifices a sense of reality even more than he does in "The Ballad of Jesse Neighbours" with its dependence on the ballad tradition. Perhaps this departure from realism accounts for the author's difficulty in placing these stories: both were turned down by three magazines before "The Ballad of Jesse Neighbours" was published in *Esquire* (September 1963) and "A Job of the Plains" in the twentieth-anniversary issue of *Quarterly Review of Literature* (Fall 1965).

A Time and a Place includes three additional stories about oil-drilling and its effects—"The Pump," published in *Esquire* (January 1964), "A Home Away from Home," and "A Good Indian." The latter, the best of these three, is the first-person narrative of a car salesman who despises Indians and considers them deserving of every injustice done to them—an attitude he feels justifies his fleecing of an Indian who had already been tricked out of his oil-rich land. The narrator's childhood sympathy with the plight of the Indians, which he recalls in order to illustrate the maturity of his present views, only condemns his grown-up inhumanity in the eyes of the reader. The story suggests that the car salesman has merely jumped on the capitalist bandwagon; the Indians, after all, were nothing but socialists (they traditionally held land in common), according to the narrator. The title "A Good Indian" refers to the racist quip "The only good Indian is a dead Indian"; the story was originally published in *The Saturday Evening Post* (28 August 1965) under the title "The Gaudiest Thing on Wheels," an allusion to the Cadillac in which the unfortunate Indian killed himself on the day that he bought it.

"The Rainmaker" (*The Saturday Evening Post*, 2 December 1967) is about a "scientific" version of the traditional folk rainmaker: Professor Orville Simms operates a mechanical device fitted with gauges, vacuum tubes, and coils. This complicated-looking contraption inspires desperate dust-bowl dwellers to have confidence in his services; however, his victims tar and feather him upon discovering that he is a fraud. Although the story is marked by broad caricature and unsophisticated humor, the drought-stricken land where even weeds will not grow is effectively limned through the imagery of illness (for example, stock ponds are "dry white scabs"). Still, the story does little more than provide a rather extreme example of a dust-bowl swindler.

"The Human Fly" (*Esquire,* September 1968) is a further indication of how desperate people in Texas became during the worst of the Depression and dust storms. Set in 1935, the story is about a daredevil who attempts to scale a high building for a fee. Stan Reynolds, a resident in New Jerusalem (one of the names Humphrey uses for Clarksville), undertakes to climb the Gothic courthouse for $1,000 so that he can move to California, the place of hope for many. The chamber of commerce finances this enterprise in the expectation that the crowds to be attracted will boost business in the town. Humphrey's story demonstrates that everybody is a loser when the sole basis for a relationship is monetary gain: Stan falls and becomes an invalid and ward of the town for life.

"Mouth of Brass," the most moving piece in the volume, is the story of a white boy's friendship with a black man, Finus Watson, a tamale vendor with a "proud and mighty" bass voice. On a day when the boy accompanies Finus on his rounds, Finus teaches the boy to see his surroundings in a new way, to penetrate with understanding eyes, and to grasp the relationship between localities; the boy is astonished by the new sense of his town that Finus gives him. But Finus has one more lesson for his young friend, which he teaches through his own death. When a redneck murders Finus in full view of the townspeople, the boy sees mirrored in the pool of Finus's blood the racism at the heart of his town. Humphrey's decision to employ an adult first-person narrator recalling a memory from childhood has several advantages, such as the fact that an adult has a developed ability with language and can manipulate sound and image to evoke the presence and meaning of Finus; and some of the insights of the narrator are dependent upon his maturity. Yet, the experience that he recounts is so indelibly printed on his consciousness that it retains its original immediacy.

"A Voice from the Woods" (*Atlantic Monthly,* October 1963) is another retrospective piece. Although the story involves a son's remembrance, the most significant memory belongs to his mother, who is prompted by the cooing of a dove to recall a wild young man who courted her in their youth and later died in a bank robbery. She associates the dove with her former lover because a dove was cooing when he met her in a graveyard to receive her refusal to marry him. When the memory of a ghost from her past presents itself, the woman has a sudden realization of how important that memory is to her. "A Voice from the Woods"—unlike the other stories concerned with the 1930s—reveals something about the years-later present, and it reminds the

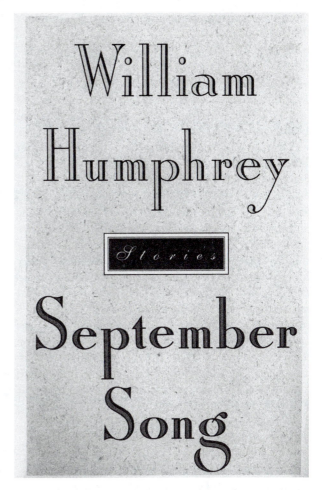

Dust jacket for Humphrey's 1992 collection of stories drawn from his and his wife's experiences of aging

reader that the sudden discovery of an almost-forgotten memory can produce a powerful emotional effect.

The tenth story in *A Time and a Place* is "The Last of the Caddoes," a title that plays on James Fenimore Cooper's *The Last of the Mohicans* (1826); the story first appeared in *Esquire* (October 1968). It produces a powerful sense of the terror that can lurk in ordinary human relationships, although it lacks the poignancy of some of the other stories in the volume. While the subject matter is not like that of Edgar Allan Poe, the way in which communication between the living and the dead is presented as a matter of fact does remind one of Poe. Jimmy Hawkins learns as a boy that he is part Indian. At first his mother withholds this information, but in a moment of anger with her son she divulges his Indian heritage. Jimmy develops his Indian identity assiduously; and when, in a ritual on his thirteenth birthday, he acquires the name Snake-in-His-Mother's-Bosom, he seems destined to kill his mother. Humphrey develops the story along the lines of Indian myth, but then he clearly overlays the theme and imagery of Aeschylus's *The Libation Bearers*. "The Last of the Caddoes" does in fact turn into a version of the ancient story of Orestes and his mother. Jimmy Hawkins tries to avoid his fate by running away from home, but when his mother pursues him, he seems in the end to be awaiting the birth of fate. By encouraging the reader to see his Texas boy as a modern-day Orestes, Humphrey lends his story universality, gives the story stature, and keeps the reader from easily concluding that the protagonist is merely a deranged teenager.

"The Last of the Caddoes" anticipates Humphrey's third novel, *Proud Flesh,* which is a full retelling of *The Orestia,* and so this story seems to step away from the dominant concerns of *A Time and a Place.* The other stories, however, adhere remarkably, although Larry King exaggerated when he said in *The New York Times Book Review* (3 November 1968) that *A Time and a Place* reads like a novel. Many of the stories do possess a remarkable collective unity of effect as one after another they portray the effect that hard times have on the poor and insist that all promises of relief are chimerical. The saddest perception in the volume is that hard times foster a meanness of spirit and a desire in people to look out for themselves first.

Before turning to fiction again, Humphrey supplemented his first fishing book, *The Spawning Run* (1970), with *My Moby Dick* (1978), about his encounter with an enormous one-eyed trout, and his autobiographical *Farther Off from Heaven.* Then he published two more novels, *Hostages to Fortune* (1984), the story of a man's reaction to his son's suicide, and *No Resting Place* (1989), a dramatic account of the Trail of Tears and the subsequent expulsion of the Indians from Texas.

Humphrey's final book was a return to the genre with which he had begun: *September Song* (1992) is a series of twenty short stories based mainly upon his and his wife's experiences of growing old. Several stories dramatize the isolation caused by deafness. "The Dead Languages," for example, grew out of Humphrey's attending a local murder trial that he had hoped to base a novel on; the main character finds that the proceedings elude him: his deafness leaves him "marooned alone on a desert island watching his ship sail off without him into the infinite ocean." The story concludes with an expression of desperation: "he would have dashed himself against the rocks to have heard the sirens sing."

Humphrey's stories seem to argue that even family members cannot provide solace for those shipwrecked in old age. A daughter's self-serving desire to get her mother into a nursing home in "Be It Ever So Humble," a sister's manipulation of her brother in "A Labor of Love," and several other such instances suggest that family is just one of the problems that the aged must face.

If ever humor was called for to make a grim view of life tolerable, it is in *September Song,* and Humphrey fulfills that expectation in some instances. The first story, "A Portrait of the Artist as an Old Man," is a thinly disguised account of a reporter's visit to Humphrey in order to gather facts for the author's obituary. When the writer realizes that "Here was death in the guise of a young woman," he then recovers from his sad realization by concocting a bizarre life story that reaches far beyond his own experience. This invention, the reader understands, is an aspect of what motivates the fiction writer in the first place: he cheats death by imaginatively taking on lives other than his own. The old writer's behavior also indicates that he wants to be remembered for the stories he invents (his work); let them be my obituary, he means.

The longest story in the volume is "The Apple of Discord," first published in *American Short Fiction* (1991). Seth Bennett's own disintegration is explored via the disintegration of the little world that he lives in: the apple farm that has been in his family for generations is sold, destined to be divided up as a site for a housing development–and Seth's own daughters have abetted the transformation. Humphrey weaves literary parallels that enrich this rather ordinary event: the Greek story of the apple of discord, the biblical story of the Fall of man, and Anton Chekhov's *The Cherry Orchard* (1904), William Shakespeare's *King Lear* (1606). The amalgam makes for a somewhat mock heroic tone; yet, as in much of Humphrey's work, the tone straddles the line between parody and seriousness. The basic conflict of "The Apple of Discord" is between Seth, who holds to the status quo, and his three daughters, who embrace change and thus perversely represent progress. In the end the old man botches his suicide and reluctantly vouchsafes to remain in a changed world.

The title story, "September Song," is a new version of James Joyce's "Eveline" (1914) in which Virginia Tyler, a seventy-six-year-old great-grandmother, plans to leave her doddering husband of forty-nine years to run off with a former illicit lover whose wife has died. Like Joyce's pathetic aspirant to fulfillment, Virginia makes plans to leave her empty life; but, also like Eveline, she begins to ruminate on the promises that tie her to her present condition. When the moment to act arrives, she fails to find the will, and the reader sadly concludes that she feels too old to really live. Humphrey prevents the reader from thinking that she has taken the noble course when he writes: "Around her neck she felt a collar tighten." Indeed, Maxwell Anderson's song from *Knickerbocker Holiday* (1938) is appropriate background music to this story: the "few precious days" that Virginia might have had with her lover will instead be a "plentiful waste of time" with a husband who has lost interest in her.

The volume also includes two stories about old hunters whose proximity to death puts them in a changed relationship to the hunted. In "Buck Fever" an aged hunter anticipates his final chance to kill a deer that he has stalked for years. Humphrey builds up the man's excitement over the encounter, but when he has the animal in his sight, he spares its life. Then a sudden snowstorm overwhelms the hunter, and he is the one who meets his death on the hunt. The theme seems in part a Bruegelian one: men and their doings have little significance in the context of natural processes. In another story, "Mortal Enemies," the "hunter" actually kills his prey but feels sorry afterward. The old man in this story hates woodchucks because they have devoured his gardens for years. When he kills one on the edge of his lawn, however, he is surprised to find that awareness of his own impending death has broadened his sympathies: "He wanted everything to go on living. What they had in common had made peace between him and his old enemy."

Some of the stories in *September Song* fail to fit the main concept of the volume—one even seems a leftover from *A Time and a Place,* and some are so brief they barely qualify as stories. "Last Words" is merely a suicide letter written by a divorced woman to her husband upon the occasion of his remarriage. At the same time, "A Heart in Hiding," one of the briefest pieces—a little more than three pages—is nonetheless quite moving. It concerns a couple that has been married for many years; after the wife dies in a moment of anticipated happiness, the details of the story represent effectively the husband's feeling of emptiness, but he is bewildered by an absence of grief. When that emotion finally hits, however, it does so with a great reserve of force. A bamboo backscratcher that the man notices in a drugstore triggers his grief, and the gates of stopped-up emotion open. In this brief story Humphrey convinces the reader that old age is no protection from the deepest sorrow.

Reviewers gave *September Song* a mixed reception: though they acknowledged Humphrey's skill as a storyteller, several also judged the volume as uneven and not as good as his best. Molly Giles said in *The New York Times Book Review* (23 August 1992): "Many of these pieces seem no more than thinly spun conceits that fizzle and fade, and while there are flashes of humor and insight, they are too often flawed by sentimentality and lack of energy." A critic for the *Virginia Quarterly Review* (Winter 1993) said that Humphrey had once again achieved "impressive results" and that "*September Song* (like Humphrey's previous story collection, *A Time and a*

Place) is a gathering of tales on a common theme—here that of advancing age, lost powers, encroaching death. It sounds gloomy, and at times it is, for Humphrey's has always been a grim vision, like that of his great model Thomas Hardy." Jonathan Yardley, though he considered this volume a minor Humphrey effort, nonetheless recognized *September Song* as the capstone to the career of a serious writer who "has dedicated his life to his writing with a fidelity all too rare in a culture that encourages facile success and empty honor" (*Washington Post Book World,* 5 July 1992).

Humphrey died at his home in Hudson, New York, on 20 August 1997 of esophageal cancer. His bed was littered with books and pages of stories that he was trying to write at the last. His ashes were buried on 25 October 1997 in the churchyard of St. Paul's Episcopal Church in Tivole, New York. For half a century Humphrey explored in his fiction, long and short, the depths of loss and pain with a high seriousness rare in contemporary literature.

Interviews:

Lon Tinkle, "For Bill Humphrey a Degree at Last," *Dallas Morning News,* 1 June 1969, p. 7C;

Carl R. Sherman, "A Novelist Finds Teaching Gratifying . . . ," *Northhampton Daily Hampshire Gazette* (Mass.), 30 December 1976, p. 7;

Geoffrey Stokes, "Literature Is Hell: The Strange Success of William Humphrey," *Village Voice* (September 1984): 1, 21;

Herbert Mitgang, "His Main Crop Is Words," *New York Times Book Review,* 18 August 1985, p. 3;

Robert Compton, "On Becoming a Writer," *Dallas Morning News,* 8 February 1987, p. 8C;

Jennifer Fortenbaugh, "William Humphrey: The Writer as Witness," *The Paper,* 7 May–3 June 1987, pp. 5–7;

Ashby Bland Crowder, "History, Family, and William Humphrey," *Southern Review,* 24 (Autumn 1988): 825–839;

Crowder, "William Humphrey: Defining Southern Literature," *Mississippi Quarterly,* 41 (Fall 1988): 529–540;

Gérard Guégan, "A Table avec William Humphrey," *Passages,* no. 14 (February 1989): 86;

Jose Yglesias, "William Humphrey," edited by Sybil Steinberg, *Publishers Weekly,* 235 (2 June 1989): 64–65;

Crowder, *Writing in the Southern Tradition: Interviews with Five Contemporary Authors* (Amsterdam & Atlanta: Rodopi, 1990), pp. 3–34, 183–189;

Edward K. Shanahan, "A Journey into the World of Writing," *Daily Hampshire Gazette,* 27 June 1992.

References:

Bert Almon, *William Humphrey: Destroyer of Myths* (Denton: University of North Texas Press, 1998);

L. Dwight Chaney, "William Humphrey, Regionalist: Southern or Southwestern?" *Journal of the American Studies Association of Texas,* 19 (October 1988): 91–98;

Gary Davenport, "The Desertion of William Humphrey's Circus Animals," *Southern Review,* 23 (April 1987): 494–503;

John M. Grammer, "Where the South Draws Up to a Stop: The Fiction of William Humphrey," *Mississippi Quarterly,* 44 (Winter 1990–1991): 5–21;

Sylvia Grider and Elizabeth Tebeaux, "Blessings into Curses: Sardonic Humor and Irony in 'A Job of the Plains,'" *Studies in Short Fiction,* 23 (Summer 1986): 297–306;

James W. Lee, *William Humphrey,* Southern Writers Series (Austin: Steck-Vaughn, 1967);

Elizabeth Tebeaux, "Irony as Art: The Short Fiction of William Humphrey," *Studies in Short Fiction,* 26 (Summer 1989): 323–334;

Mark Royden Winchell, "Beyond Regionalism: The Growth of William Humphrey," *Sewanee Review,* 96 (Spring 1988): 287–292;

Winchell, *William Humphrey,* Western Writers Series (Boise, Idaho: Boise State University Press, 1992).

Papers:

The major collection of William Humphrey's correspondence, manuscripts, and notebooks is at the Harry Ransom Humanities Research Center, University of Texas at Austin (William Humphrey and A. A. Knopf Collections). Letters are also at Princeton University (Theodore and Renée Weiss Collection); the University of Reading in England (Chatto and Windus Collection); the University of Sussex in England (Leonard Woolf Collection); the University of Mississippi (Seymour Lawrence Collection); University of Maryland at College Park (Katherine Anne Porter Collection); Southern Methodist University (William Humphrey Collection); Columbia University (Anne Laurie Williams and F. W. Dupee Collections); and Editions Gallimard, Paris, France (William Humphrey files). Jean Lambert of Souvigny, France, has a large collection of letters from the Humphreys.

Charles Jackson

(6 April 1903 – 21 September 1968)

Curt Meanor
Cleveland State University

BOOKS: *The Lost Weekend* (New York: Farrar & Rinehart, 1944; London: John Lane, 1945);

The Fall of Valor (New York & Toronto: Rinehart, 1946);

The Outer Edges (New York: Rinehart, 1948; London: Nevill, 1950);

The Sunnier Side: Twelve Arcadian Tales (New York: Farrar, Straus, 1950; London: Nevill, 1950); republished as *The Sunnier Side: Arcadian Tales* (Syracuse: Syracuse University Press, 1996);

Earthly Creatures: Ten Stories (New York: Farrar, Straus & Young, 1953; London: Nevill, 1954);

A Second-Hand Life (New York: Macmillan, 1967; London: W. H. Allen, 1967).

Charles Jackson in 1944 (photograph © Bettmann/CORBIS)

With the publication of his best-known work, *The Lost Weekend*, on 27 January 1944, Charles Jackson reached the pinnacle of commercial and critical fame. The novel was acclaimed as a "masterpiece of psychological precision" by Phillip Wylie in *The New York Times Book Review* (30 January 1944) for its realistic depiction of alcoholism as displayed through the protagonist of the novel, Don Birnam. Indeed, the portrayal in the novel of the alcoholic with his attendant self-destruction, delusion, and moral decay shocked its readers with "the impact of a sledge-hammer." In *The White Logic: Alcoholism and Gender in American Modernist Fiction* (1994), one of the few critical studies to consider the novel in detail, John W. Crowley observes that it marks "a major shift in the representation of alcoholism in American literature , . . it neither denies the alcoholism of the protagonist nor elevates him into a culture hero," as did the novels of some of Jackson's more famous contemporaries such as F. Scott Fitzgerald and Ernest Hemingway. The success of *The Lost Weekend* not only made Jackson famous but also gave him a period of financial and artistic independence. He continued his examinations of controversial topics with the publication of *The Fall of Valor* (1946), which deals with homosexuality, and *The Outer Edges* (1948), the story of a murder in a small town and its deleterious effects upon the community.

The popular success of *The Lost Weekend* has overshadowed Jackson's short fiction. In the genre of the short story, however—which he describes in the "Note to the Reader" that begins *Earthly Creatures: Ten Stories* (1953) as "the form I love"—the reader can more completely experience Jackson's realistic depiction of human behavior and the sad, yet fondly reminiscent tone he takes toward humanity. The characters who populate his stories represent early-twentieth-century American society, which he experienced both as a child in small-town, upstate New York and as a struggling writer and family man in New York City. His protagonists are usually boys, young men, fathers, or husbands who undergo disturbing epiphanies regarding the seemingly ordered world in which they live.

In an attempt to define fiction, Jackson observed in *The Sunnier Side: Twelve Arcadian Tales* (1950) that "it is all but impossible to define the difference between life and 'life' . . . one is concerned with what is true, the other with truth." To bridge this gap between "what is true" and "truth" Jackson creates his settings and characters in vividly realistic detail—an effective verisimilitude that he uses to discover a deeper reality concerning mankind. Jackson believed that the purpose of literature was to help the reader experience what was beyond his capability as a social being: "In real life our perceptions and sympathies are circumscribed by personal prejudices, indifference, familiarity, lack of time, preoccupations and so on; in literature they are released, become limitless, larger than life—larger than we are capable of on our own." The topics he explores are often provocative queries into social and personal issues such as homelessness, sexual abuse, homosexuality, self-hatred, voyeurism, and social intolerance.

Although Jackson's first collection of short stories, *The Sunnier Side,* is not strictly autobiographical, he states clearly in the introduction that the ideas for his stories are based on his own experience: "In a small town it's practically impossible not to know practically everything about practically everybody else . . . and this, plus the fact that one's childhood impressions are the deepest and most lasting, the purest and probably the most universal, makes for a never-failing source of fiction." The small town he writes of is his childhood home of Newark, New York, the "Arcadia" that is the setting for all of the stories. Born 6 April 1903 in Summit, New Jersey, the third of five children to Frederick George and Sarah (Williams) Jackson, Charles Reginald Jackson experienced early in life the pain of loss that is reflected in some of his most memorable and effective stories. In 1915 his father abandoned the family, leaving Charles and his siblings to be raised by his mother. The following year an even greater tragedy struck the family with the deaths of his oldest sister and youngest brother in an automobile accident. Both of these events find their way into Jackson's fiction. Eight of the twelve stories in the collection concern either a fatherless youth or a family in which the father is absent. The last, "Rachel's Summer," is centered on the accidental death of the narrator's sister and how her death resulted from the intolerant and destructive social mores of their town.

Jackson writes in the realistic tradition of Sherwood Anderson's *Winesburg, Ohio* (1919), a collection with obvious similarities to *The Sunnier Side*. Both collections have a recurring protagonist and present a modern version of the bildungsroman or coming-of-age story. Like Anderson, Jackson examines the effects of social hypocrisy and sexual repression on the inhabitants of small-town, postagricultural America.

Jackson alludes to another, larger tradition by labeling his stories "Arcadian tales." Although the subtitle refers to the actual Arcadia Township, in which Newark, New York, is located, it also harks back to the pastoral tradition, which emphasizes the idealization of rustic beauty, innocence, and harmony through the depiction of the simple lives of shepherds. As the tradition developed in the Eclogues of Virgil, the Latin epic poet, the shepherds also experienced the disappointment of unfulfilled love and the grief of death. Jackson's Arcadian tales are also set in a harmonious, natural world beneath which lies disappointment and suffering. It is a world where the individual, in his Edenic natural surroundings, is beset, betrayed, and violated by his fellow human beings. Through the personal and social conflicts of Arcadia's residents, the reader witnesses the death of innocence and youth from the encroachment of society upon the individual in his natural environment. In his introduction to the collection Jackson explains how this dualistic world influenced his narrative style: "One doesn't write for the sunnier side alone; its best use is by way of contrast. Or if you do restrict yourself to the sunnier side, you're sure to be using only half." This statement might also explain the tone of Jackson's protagonist Don Birnam, who never denies his soul-wrenching experiences, yet maintains a fond reminiscence for his past.

The collection begins with a story, also called "The Sunnier Side," in which Jackson uses an unusual, self-reflexive narration. The structure of the story, a dialogue in the form of fictional letters exchanged between Jackson and Dorothy Brenner, a former Arcadian, creates a sense of reality upon which the rest of the stories are based. Jackson recalls Dorothy and her three friends "coming down Dalton street with linked arms . . . ready to sweep everything before" them. He tells the story of Dorothy's three friends, all of whom were raised in the idyllic surroundings of Arcadia. Each comes to a tragic end, however; two of them meet unnatural deaths, and one suffers from chronic alcoholism.

The story "Palm Sunday" exemplifies Jackson's characteristic nostalgic voice, which is based on memory as a vehicle for his storytelling as well as the recurring theme of small-town hypocrisy and its harmful

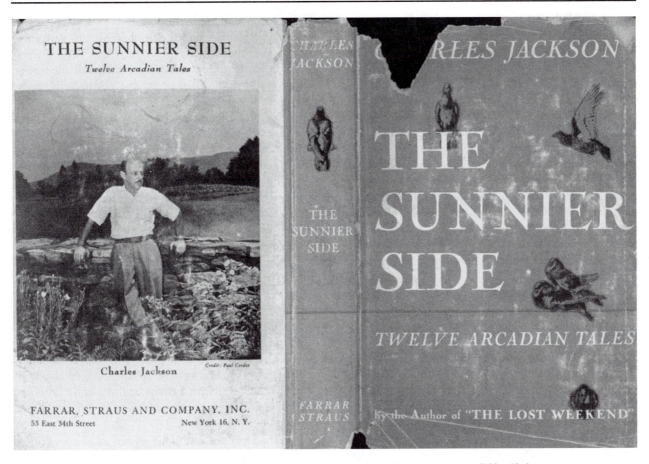

Title page for Jackson's 1950 collection, which depicts the inner lives of the citizens in a small New York town

effects upon Arcadia's inhabitants. The narrative proceeds from a young man's recollection of his sexual abuse as a child by a local choir director, Ray Verne. The narrator, Don Birnam, has never talked about the incident with anyone, but which is suddenly brought back to his consciousness when he hears an old church hymn on the radio. The hymn, "The Palms," was taught to him years before by the abusive choir director. Jackson develops a nostalgic voice in the story by weaving it episodically within a framing incident–Don's visit to an acquaintance's house to see a boat that the man's son has made. While the neighbor is proudly showing his son's work, Don overhears the church hymn playing on the radio somewhere in the house and his consciousness drifts between past and present. This narrative technique shows how Jackson keeps the theme of memory in the forefront of his stories. Memory is not only a source for his stories; it also plays a vital role as a purgative influence upon his protagonist. Don discovers that in "back of the music, the particular music of 'The Palms', was a realer connection, something that I could only now, for the first time in my life, willingly explore."

"Palm Sunday" is also an example of how Jackson uses many of his stories to condemn the hypocritical acquiescence of society toward its members' moral and ethical deviance. Jackson deliberately locates the sexual abuse of the narrator in the two churches of Arcadia, ostensibly the foundation of its moral and spiritual values. The town silently condones Verne's corrupting predilections because he is perceived as a "man of real talent . . . active in all the school and church affairs . . . in demand where a good singer was needed." Although suspicion of his desires lies not far beneath the townspeople's admiration for Verne, Arcadia directs its intolerance toward the children. After the young narrator begins taking music lessons from Verne, he is informed by his girlfriend that her mother has forbidden her to associate with him if he is "a friend . . . Ray Verne." Even his own mother reproaches him in an accusing manner, asking "What's Ray Verne calling you up for?" and then berating him when he claims not to know the purpose of the call. Jackson uncovers the hypocrisy of Arcadia in its refusal to confront Ray Verne, thus giving his misdeeds a silent stamp of approval.

Like "Palm Sunday," many of the other Arcadian tales reveal a disturbing hidden truth that lies just beneath the facade of respectable, small-town America. In "The Break," however, the reader perceives a disillusionment and betrayal that originates from within the character of Don Birnam. The story recounts the experience of an idealistic youth as he wanders the fields and forests surrounding Arcadia. He sets out on this romanticized journey each Saturday, giving his vivid imagination free rein to conjure up scenarios involving the vanished American frontier of Kit Carson, Father Jacques Marquette, lone outposts, and bison. He seeks out these adventures in a pastoral setting of forests, fields, and pastures. This setting also contains a women's mental institution and the railroad leading into town, however—stark evidence of man's intrusion upon nature.

On this particular Saturday young Don's excursion is interrupted by a real-life adventure. As he crawls through a culvert running underneath the train tracks, he sees a man sitting inside it and infers that he must be the escaped convict whom the town had heard about the previous week. Thinking quickly, the boy feigns friendliness toward the convict and offers to help him hitch a ride by getting the conductor to slow down the next train. Once on board the train, however, Don informs the conductor of the dangerous situation, and the police capture the convict as the train pulls into Arcadia.

As his adventure unfolds Don realizes "this encounter might well turn into the great moment of his life." After the convict is recaptured, however, young Don gradually loses the sense of fulfillment he relished. Instead, he begins "unaccountably, to feel funny inside, almost sorry" for his betrayal of the convict. The reader realizes that the title refers not to the attempted escape of the prisoner but to the boy's "break with all he had ever been or believed before" in his romanticized world. The convict represents the boy's romantic heroes; like them, he is an individual overcoming great obstacles put in his way by an adversarial world. Jackson does not allow the boy to be enlightened with an epiphany, however. Although he admits vague feelings of guilt over betraying the convict, there is no heartfelt vow to purge himself of his pride. Instead, he reasons in a realistically human fashion that he will learn to live by the bourgeois standards of the masses rather than his own high ideals: "Everybody thought it was great, and maybe, in time, he'd think so, too. Given a little more time, maybe he'd look at it like the others." The last sentence of the story leaves little doubt of the corruption of young Don's ideals as "dim feelings of pride began to stir in his breast, and he began to look forward to the papers."

Spiritual pride is also the topic of "How War Came to Arcadia," which describes Arcadia's preparation for and reaction to the U.S. entry into World War I. Jackson's satirical tone scathingly condemns the townspeople's naive attitudes and nationalistic pride. There is a subtle but effective foreshadowing of the theme that Arcadia fails to acknowledge the darker aspects of world events as Don remembers the "thrill of the charge of the Ku Klux Klan . . . in *The Birth of a Nation*." Such details document Jackson's theory that a writer must reveal the "truth" that lies beneath his characters' perceptions and which are suppressed by the "prejudices . . . indifference . . . and preoccupations" of life. The truth that he reveals in this story is that Arcadia is completely unaware of the actual suffering and horror occurring an ocean away in Europe. For example, Jackson satirizes the shallow activities of Mrs. Kirtle, a woman active in many of the local social clubs. The letters she writes to soldiers overseas consist of descriptions of her garden, "a witty story . . . about a mouse named Claude," and her experience in light opera. The inane and self-centered nature of her letters is heightened by her obviously feigned empathy as she ludicrously relates, "I wish I could be there in the trenches with you now . . . and help cheer you by singing 'Three Little Maids from School.'"

Mrs. Kirtle is not alone in her misdirected pride, however. Don observes that in the town "the festival was really on now. Arcadia broke out in a rash of flags. . . . The Red Cross headquarters on South Main Street was like a continual garden party" as the women volunteers stage tableaux in the front window of the newspaper office and knitting becomes a craze. There are, however, some individuals who recognize the shameful behavior of the town. Don's brother, Gerald, who has joined the Student's Army Training Corps at the local university, becomes enraged when he discovers that his mother has hung a service flag in the front window for him. He tears it down, shouting, "You're not going to make a fool out of me," evidently believing that the flags should be reserved for the soldiers who are doing the actual fighting.

The war finally comes to Arcadia in the form of a corpse. A local family, the Hamiltons, receive news that their son has been killed in France. After the war ends the body is sent home. The family does not know how to react to the situation and the body remains on the porch of the Hamiltons' house for two days before it is buried without ceremony. The incident reveals that the townspeople are willing, even eager, to participate in the war from their insular, distant vantage point, but when the true effects of the conflict reach home they are incapable of reacting in an honorable manner even when it comes to burying one of their own sons.

Jackson's rendering of small-town dysfunction against the background of the U.S. entry into World War I develops his continuing theme of the destruction of idealistic notions by the violent tendencies of mankind. The Great War is, of course, the quintessential vehicle for displaying these human tendencies, and Jackson masterfully understates the horror and inhumanity of the conflict in order to emphasize the townspeople's failure to respond to it in an honorable and humane manner.

The influence of Anderson's *Winesburg, Ohio* upon Jackson's Arcadian tales is evident throughout the collection. The unity of the stories through a common setting and the development of the coming-of-age motif through the use of a recurrent narrator certainly owe a debt to Anderson's experimental form. The themes of small-town intolerance and the destruction of the social and moral fabric of rural America at the start of the twentieth century underlie both collections. Perhaps the story in *The Sunnier Side* that possesses the clearest parallels to Anderson's Winesburg tales is "Sophistication." Like Anderson's story of the same name, Jackson's tale features an adolescent narrator who works for the town paper as preparation for a career in writing. Both stories also add a modern twist to the tradition of the bildungsroman in order to show the effects of an industrialized world upon a vanishing agricultural one. Despite these similarities in character and societal conflict, the two stories differ greatly in tone and theme. Anderson's character, George Willard, rises above the fetters of his small-town life and takes "hold of the thing that makes the mature life of men and women in the modern world possible," whereas Don Birnam becomes evermore entangled by the stultifying influences of Arcadia. Even so, there seems little doubt that Jackson directly alludes to Anderson's story and invites the reader to compare the similarities and differences.

Jackson's tale concerns a rumored affair between Don's boss, Marvin Tyndall, the editor of the town newspaper, and his assistant, Arlene Arthur. Stirred by his awakening impulses for love and self-expression and his close proximity to the couple, Don idealizes the alleged relationship of his coworkers in his writing by comparing the couple to the Arthurian lovers, Lancelot and Guinevere. In fact, this romanticizing develops into a strangely overpowering preoccupation, causing him to identify, too closely perhaps, with their emotions. Don sees himself as a sort of human amalgamation of their forbidden love: "In him alone, he felt, their love came into its fullest understanding, perhaps more, even, than it ever did in each other, since lovers are selfish and see only themselves even in their lover's eyes." The fact that the relationship is an adulterous one supports Don's ideal-

ized worldview in which he employs a modern version of Arthurian courtly love. Marvin is "Lancelot wroth with himself, the adulterer guilt-ridden."

In the course of a conversation with the young narrator, Marvin reveals that he is indeed something of a modern Lancelot. He confesses to Don that, despite having three children, he has never seen his wife nude because he believes there is no reason to "turn marriage into . . . just plain pleasure." Jackson suggests that Marvin and Don are kindred spirits in terms of their idealized conception of love and that Marvin is having the affair nobly in order to preserve the sanctity of his marriage. But it must be kept in mind that if the readers accept the interpretation, they succumb to the power of the town's gossip and are therefore as guilty. As in many of his stories, Jackson's subtle attention to detail effectively engages the reader, in keeping with his writerly goal of making "us realize something about ourselves which, under the circumstances in real life, would not have occurred to us."

Of all the Arcadian tales the last story in *The Sunnier Side,* "Rachel's Summer," most poignantly demonstrates the malicious nature of small-town narrow-mindedness. In the introduction to the 1995 edition of the collection, Crowley observes that the story reveals how the "confusion of denial with tolerance could have dire consequences" for Arcadia. An adult Don Birnam, now living in New York City, recounts the untimely death of his sister, Rachel, whom he remembers as "the most vivid and alive creature I had ever seen." During one of Don's visits home, many years after his sister's death, his mother confides to him the circumstances of the tragedy. A rumor that Rachel had become pregnant had been circulating through the town and found its way to her mother by way of Mrs. Kirtle, the elitist busybody who also appears in "How War Came to Arcadia." Although Rachel's mother believes the rumor is untrue, she forbids her from making her customary summer trip to her grandmother's farm because the townspeople would assume that her absence means she had gone away to get an abortion. More disappointing to Don than the recollection of Rachel's death is the fact that even after thirty years, his mother's concern is still centered on the small-town opinions of Arcadia: she tells Don that Rachel died "too soon," meaning not that her life ended before it was fulfilled but that she died before the rumor of her pregnancy could be disproved.

Although *The Sunnier Side* did not sell well, Jackson was generally praised for his consistently skillful narrative style. The reviewer for *The Atlantic* (May 1950) called the stories "trivial and unpleasant," but

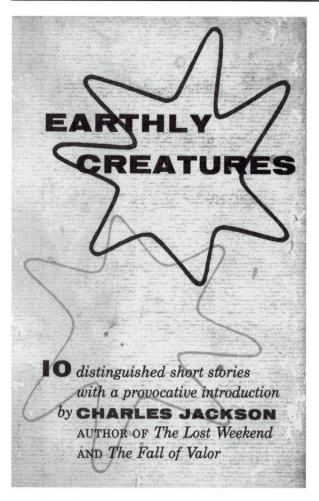

Cover for the paperback publication of Jackson's 1953 collection of psychological studies

Kelsey Guilfoil, writing in *The Chicago Tribune* (16 April 1950), commended Jackson for the realism of the collection and for effectively expressing "that small-town life—any life for that matter—is a mixture of beauty and ugliness."

Jackson's second collection of short stories, *Earthly Creatures,* is an assemblage of previously published works and stories that were appearing in print for the first time. It features none of the binding structural techniques, such as the recurring narrator or common setting, that are present in *The Sunnier Side.* Jackson's characteristic striving to reveal the life that lies underneath the surface of his characters and the homes, apartments, restaurants, and sanatoriums they occupy is evident, however. Although Jackson retains the tendency to use "the sunnier side" of his characters' lives to illuminate their darker, hidden nature, some of these stories also express a faith in the ability of human nature to reaffirm and redeem itself. The collection received mixed reviews, such as short-story scholar William Peden's critique in *The Saturday Review* (10 October 1953): "He is concerned with important subjects—man's loneliness, his capacity for self-destruction, his need for understanding. These stories are good enough to make us want them to be a little better. They make us wish that Mr. Jackson weren't quite so glib or facile in tossing off a character or disposing of a situation. His treatment, in other words, does not always measure up to the demands of his subject matter." In his introduction to the collection Jackson expresses his own doubts concerning the quality of the stories "Romeo" and "Money," confessing that they "are examples of the kind of story which, in the telling, did not come off as planned (that old fallibility again)." He also observes that the story "A Sunday Drive" has "lost . . . the immediacy of the situation" that has "vitiated with the passing years."

The first story in the collection, "The Boy Who Ran Away," is similar to *The Lost Weekend* in its psychological study of its protagonist, Henry Price. Henry's problem, however, is not alcoholism but a self-loathing that manifests itself in his feelings toward his physically and socially awkward young nephew, Danny. When he sees Danny, he remembers "his own childhood and his constant burning, baffling childish fears." Rather than feeling sympathy for the child, Henry is only capable of directing an intense animosity toward him. Although Henry's projection does not possess the social stigmas or the extremes of aberrant behavior of Don Birnam's alcoholism, it proves to be a destructive force in Henry's life, affecting his family as well as his spirit.

Henry's troubles begin on New Year's Eve when his wife, Barbara, offers to have the maid watch their two nephews, John and Danny, as well as their own two daughters, Mary and Barbie, while the parents attend a party at a nearby home. The level of Henry's antipathy toward Danny is equal only to the affection he showers upon his eldest daughter, Mary, and therein lies the catalyst for conflict in the story. When Danny breaks Henry's new prized possession, a model of a 1909 Stanley Steamer given to him by Mary, Henry flies into a rage, cancels the New Year's plans, and sends the children to bed. On the surface his actions are those of a husband and father merely having a bad holiday with his relatives. But by revealing Henry's thoughts to the reader, Jackson takes a much darker, angst-filled view of his character's existence. Henry admits that he has a deep-seated hatred of Danny and that he will "never, never, never forgive him." He willingly perpetuates the hatred and isolation he experienced as a child. Danny flees back to his parents' home, and both he and Henry bring in the New Year in dark isolation. Henry also realizes there is "nothing in life more unbearable than to hate one-self." Henry's life of existential misery grows out of a childhood with which he has failed to come to terms.

Jackson does not limit himself to revealing the hidden lives of male characters. Several of the stories have female protagonists to whom Jackson gives an equal amount of space and individuality as well as a sincere and realistic voice. In "Romeo," the first of these stories, Jackson returns to the theme of mankind's idealized vision of the world, which was central to *Arcadian Tales*. However, in "Romeo" the world of experience does not subvert his character's longings. Instead, Jackson shows how one's faith in perfection can reaffirm life through the interplay of idealized and actual love. Alice Harvey is a middle-aged housewife who is satisfied with her life, loves her husband, and has accepted the fact that she has never experienced the love she dreamed of as an adolescent. She gets a chance to revisit those past dreams when her son brings home a dinner guest, Gavin Douglas, an actor with whom he works at the local theater and who was also the object of Alice's young infatuation. As a young girl Alice "had fallen in love at sight of the handsome actor and through him . . . with Smith Harvey," her husband. The suspense of the story hinges on the question of whether Gavin will live up to Alice's idealized memories of him. Even as a young girl watching Gavin play Romeo in William Shakespeare's play, she "would not have dreamed of marrying Gavin Douglas. You did not marry Romeo." To her, the "other" love continues to be "a romantic abstract, impossible of realization, something to possess in secret and to cherish all her life." When Gavin arrives she finds that she is at peace with the decisions she has made. Gavin lives up to the charming yet unreachable figure of her memory and in so doing reaffirms her love for her husband. The story is a subtle tribute to love's ability to validate and enrich life. Jackson's low-key conflict and static character development break with narrative tradition, but he manages to create a tale that is universally relevant.

"A Sunday Drive" continues with the theme of renewal as a young writer struggles with his identity in a chain of events that leads him to the graves of his unknown relatives and provides him with a vision of his own significance. Like "Romeo," it finds the poignancy in one of life's routine moments that might otherwise be overlooked. The young writer, known only as Mr. Stevens, and his pregnant wife experience the unsettling changes faced by all young families expecting a child. The circumstances erupt in a conflict between the couple when she holds him to his promise to take her on a Sunday afternoon drive. Trying to break through a bout of writer's block, he barely contains his resentments toward her, which are both overt (concerning the

interruption of his writing) and unconscious (concerning his transformation into a parent). As he grudgingly gives in to her wish, his mood threatens to ruin the event until they stumble upon the cemetery where his paternal grandparents are buried and he is suddenly thrust back in time when, as a boy, he wept over his dead grandmother, whom he hardly knew. He finds the graves of his ancestors and, in so doing, realizes that the birth of his own child, not his writing, is the true creative act that will define him. His child, like he and his ancestors, are links in a chain of immortality. Jackson interweaves aspects of the act of writing with life and death imagery to create a profound tale of the loss of perspective, the act of creation, and the renewal of the human spirit.

In opposition to "A Sunday Drive," "The Cheat" presents a less-than-hopeful view of marital relations. Fran Brown takes a vacation, literally, from her husband and two daughters. She alternately appreciates her husband for allowing her the respite and finds "relief that he wouldn't be underfoot for awhile . . . that she wouldn't have to put up with him and the children evening after endless evening." While staying at the Tall Pines Inn, she meets Arthur Davis and decides that he is "going to be the one" with whom she will have a fling. Her determination to have the affair is tinged with guilt and a sense that Arthur must see her as less than respectable if he believes she will follow through with her halfhearted flirtations. Her conflicting emotions sustain the plot until the reality of her situation deflates her fantasy. After rebuffing his advances the previous evening, Fran finds Arthur in the morning writing to his children, an activity she had been engaged in when she first saw him. Arthur had not mentioned his children to her before, and Fran is enraged and humiliated because of her naiveté. She discovers that reality will forever intrude upon her fantasies of true and unhindered love, and she walks angrily away from Arthur knowing that "most certainly . . . she didn't want to see him again or say good-bye."

Fran Brown is an example of Jackson's occasional use of a character with whom the reader can find little or no sympathy. Unlike the protagonists of *The Sunnier Side,* who were mostly victims of society, some of the characters in *Earthly Creatures* are self-centered, unfeeling products of the world they live in. Some, such as Henry Price in "The Boy Who Ran Away," will never experience a life-changing realization but will continue to live in misery and self-delusion, while for others, such as Mr. Stevens in "A Sunday Drive," there is hope for renewal or reaffirmation.

Mildred, in "The Sleeper Awakened," falls somewhere in between victim and victimizer. Her awakening is not a hopeful sign of renewal but a nightmarish existential realization. She lives with her sister and brother-in-law, Alice and Sam, as well as a quiet boarder, Mr. Menzies, who rents the room next to hers, though he spends little time there. Mildred maintains her lonely existence working at a packing company and helping her sister keep house on the weekends. She has no desire to make any friends, feeling that Alice and Sam are the only company she needs. Her attitude toward Mr. Menzies at first seems to be one of indifferent annoyance. She finds cleaning his room a distasteful chore and wishes he would come home at a decent hour. His late hours, in fact, bother her so much that she is unable to sleep until he comes home. Her habit develops into a vigil that includes listening through the thin walls as he goes through his nightly routines. She complains several times to her sister of her sleepless nights until the innocent boarder is finally evicted. At the conclusion of the story Mildred realizes that her annoyance with Mr. Menzies has become an obsession, and she resigns herself to endless nights of "utter sleeplessness."

Mildred's obsession with her neighbor is an abnormal variation of Jackson's need to show the truth hidden beneath the events of his characters' lives, to discover the motivations and frustrated desires of human beings. Although Mildred claims to be content with the life she leads, her nightly vigils have tapped into her nurturing instincts, which she is unable to control. As a result, she continues to lose sleep even though she knows that Mr. Menzies will no longer be coming home. In this respect Jackson returns to the literary tradition of Anderson. Mildred fits Anderson's definition of the "grotesque"—a person who attempts to live by one "truth" or principle and, in so doing, distorts it and ends up living a lonely, dispossessed life. Mildred's unconscious need for companionship and nurturing keeps her awake at night waiting for Mr. Menzies.

After the publication of *Earthly Creatures,* Jackson's writing career declined sharply. For years he battled addictions to alcohol and the prescription drug Secanol,

and tuberculosis eventually left him with only one lung. Periodic stays in hospitals and sanatoriums and treatment by psychiatrists as well as membership in Alcoholics Anonymous helped him regain his health for brief periods. He also suffered from extended periods of writer's block and believed that they could only be relieved through the use of drugs and alcohol. What resulted was a continual cycle of relapses and periods of partial abstinence that did not increase his literary production. His wife, Rhoda, astutely remarked in the introduction to *The Sunnier Side,* "he has done his best writing, most of it, in a period of sobriety—i.e., *The Lost Weekend,* 'Palm Sunday,' 'Rachel's Summer.' He doesn't see that pills change his sense of values and that his writing, under pills, hasn't the same fundamental honesty." He attempted several projects between the years of 1951 and 1968, but little was published except for a review, a few short stories, and his last novel, *A Second-Hand Life,* in 1967. In 1968 Charles Jackson died of an overdose of sleeping pills.

Charles Jackson's contribution to American short fiction must be found in his rendering of small-town America in the tradition of Sherwood Anderson and the regionalist tradition of other writers such as Sarah Orne Jewett and Mark Twain. Although his stories may not possess the stylistic achievements of these writers, Jackson's talent resided in his ability to re-create the intolerance and oppression of small-town life while maintaining a compassionate tone for the settings, which defined his characters and ultimately himself. His writing rarely condemns society without interjecting a sense of acceptance for a world built as much on human fallibility as it is on compassion and the resilience of the human spirit.

References:

John W. Crowley, *The White Logic: Alcoholism and Gender in American Modernist Fiction* (Amherst: University of Massachusetts Press, 1994), pp. 135–157;

Crowley, Introduction to *The Sunnier Side: Arcadian Tales* (Syracuse: Syracuse University Press, 1996).

Shirley Jackson
(14 December 1916 – 8 August 1965)

Dale Hrebik
Xavier University

See also the Jackson entry in *DLB 6: American Novelists Since World War II, Second Series.*

BOOKS: *The Road Through the Wall* (New York: Farrar, Straus, 1948);

The Lottery, or, The Adventures of James Harris (New York: Farrar, Straus, 1949; London: Gollancz, 1950); republished as *The Lottery and Other Stories* (Farrar, Straus & Giroux, 1982);

Hangsaman (New York: Farrar, Straus & Young, 1951; London: Gollancz, 1951);

Life Among the Savages (New York: Farrar, Straus & Young, 1953; London: Joseph, 1954);

The Bird's Nest (New York: Farrar, Straus & Young, 1954; London: Joseph, 1955);

The Witchcraft of Salem Village (New York: Random House, 1956);

Raising Demons (New York: Farrar, Straus & Cudahy, 1957; London: Joseph, 1957);

The Sundial (New York: Farrar, Straus & Cudahy, 1958; London: Joseph, 1958);

The Haunting of Hill House (New York: Viking, 1959; London: Joseph, 1960);

We Have Always Lived in the Castle (New York: Viking, 1962; London: Joseph, 1963);

9 Magic Wishes (New York: Crowell-Collier, 1963);

Famous Sally (New York: Harlin Quist, 1966);

Come Along With Me: Part of a Novel, Sixteen Stories, and Three Lectures, edited by Stanley Edgar Hyman (New York: Viking, 1968);

One Ordinary Day, with Peanuts (Mankato, Minn.: Creative Education, 1990);

Just An Ordinary Day, edited, with an introduction, by Laurence Jackson Hyman and Sarah Hyman Stewart (New York: Bantam, 1997).

Collection: *The Magic of Shirley Jackson,* edited by Stanley Edgar Hyman (New York: Farrar, Straus & Giroux, 1966).

RECORDING: *The Daemon Lover and The Lottery,* read by Jackson, Folkways Records, FL 79728, 1963.

Shirley Jackson (photograph © by Laurence J. Hyman; from the dust jacket for Just An Ordinary Day, *1997)*

OTHER: *The Bad Children: A Musical in One Act for Bad Children,* book and lyrics by Jackson, music by Allan Jay Friedman (Chicago: Dramatic Publishing, 1959).

Shirley Jackson is most often associated with the chilling short story "The Lottery." First published in *The New Yorker* in 1948, it immediately met with an unprecedented public reaction, generating a tremendous amount of mail, almost all of it negative. The story has since been anthologized frequently as well as adapted for the stage and screen. It is now considered an American classic. "The Lottery" did much to generate Jackson's reputation for mastery of the bizarre and the haunting–in *The Magic of Shirley Jackson* (1966) her husband, Stanley Edgar Hyman, quotes one description of his wife as the "Virginia Werewolf of séance-fiction"– a reputation that she did not always appreciate and that may have contributed to a lack of critical attention to her work. The reputation "The Lottery" established for her, fair or not, never really faded, despite her remarkably varied output: in addition to short stories, she also wrote novels, plays, television scripts, children's books, and humorous family memoirs.

Shirley Hardie Jackson was born in San Francisco on 14 December 1916 to Leslie Hardie Jackson and Geraldine Bugbee Jackson. She spent her early childhood in Burlingame, California. She started writing poetry and keeping a journal at an early age; entries date as far back as 1932. Shortly after that first entry, the Jacksons moved to Rochester, New York, where Jackson enrolled in the University of Rochester in 1934. She withdrew after two years to spend a year pursuing her career as a writer, producing a self-imposed quota of a thousand words a day. Later, she returned to school and attended Syracuse University for two years (from 1938 to 1940), during which time she published several pieces of fiction and nonfiction in campus magazines. At Syracuse she met Hyman, whom she married in 1940; together they founded one of the campus magazines, *The Spectre*.

After graduation and marriage, Jackson moved to New York City. Her first national publication came in 1941 when *The New Republic* printed "My Life with R. H. Macy," a short story based on her experiences working at Macy's Department Store. She continued to publish short stories regularly over the next few years and also gave birth to a son, Laurence, and a daughter, Joanne.

In 1945 Jackson and her family left New York City for Bennington, Vermont, where Hyman had a teaching position. She published more short stories, including "The Lottery" in 1948. That same year, Jackson's first novel, *The Road Through the Wall,* was published, followed a year later by a collection of short stories, *The Lottery, or, The Adventures of James Harris* (1949). Two more children were born: Sarah in 1948 and Barry in 1951.

The Lottery, or, The Adventures of James Harris was the only one of Jackson's short-story collections to be published during her lifetime. The name James Harris is taken from an old ballad that Jackson excerpts in her book. In the ballad, a young man named James Harris seduces a young woman into taking a journey by ship.

Once the voyage has begun, the young woman sees Harris's cloven hoof and realizes he is a devil. He tells her that he is taking her to Hell and then breaks the ship apart and drowns her in the sea. A character named James Harris (or something similar, such as Jim or Jimmy) is integral to six stories–"The Daemon Lover," "Like Mother Used to Make," "The Villager," "Elizabeth," "Seven Types of Ambiguity," and "Of Course"–and crops up in a secondary capacity in a few others, always in a threatening or outright evil capacity.

Jackson's depictions of her James Harris character never stray too far from the ballad original, an evil seducer. In addition to the named characters, unnamed characters bear physical descriptions that echo the one of Harris from "The Daemon Lover": a tall, fair man in a blue suit. In "The Intoxicated," for example, an unidentified man who matches that description appears at a party; he does nothing but engage the hostess in conversation, but because of his identification with Harris, he adds a menacing air to the story. Many of the references to Harris were new to the book, accomplished by adding new material or by changing the names and attributes of characters from previously published stories. For instance, Joan Wylie Hall notes in *Shirley Jackson: A Study of the Short Fiction* (1993) that the original drafts of "The Intoxicated" read, "a heavy red-faced man in a grey suit"; only when the story appeared in the collection did the description change to match Harris. Such changes are obviously meant to strengthen the structural coherence of the collection.

The critics differ on whether James Harris is an effective device or not. Some critics feel his reoccurrences were a weak attempt at unifying the collection– in *Shirley Jackson* (1975), Lenemaja Friedman said, "none of the in-name-only Harris characters has any relationship or likeness to the others, and he is often only a minor character." Certainly, Harris is not a consistent single character; instead his persona takes on many ages and occupies several locations as well as professions (though he is most often a writer). Jackson's use of the Harris character in such widely different circumstances caused Donald Barr, in his 19 April 1949 review in *The New York Times,* to complain that it serves to "give a false unity to the book and confuse the meaning of individual stories." Hall, on the other hand, saw it as purposeful and credited it to "the devil's own shape-shifting nature." The inconsistency of the Harris character suggests that he is not a single person so much as a symbol or representation of something larger; Jackson seems to be using Harris as a way to personify the evil and irrational forces that influence people's lives in ways beyond their control. The casting of Harris as a writer supports this argument in a sense, since writers can be considered the ultimate cause of all the evil and irrational things that befall their characters.

The second story in the collection, "The Daemon Lover," most directly reflects the characterization of Harris from the ballad. The plots are essentially parallel; the primary difference is that instead of the sea voyage, Jackson's Harris seduces a young woman into an engagement, though both turn out to be hellish. In the story, Harris (never actually seen by the reader) leaves a woman on their wedding day for no apparent reason other than to satisfy his own perverse pleasure. Like many of Jackson's stories, this one depicts a lonely single woman living rather unsuccessfully in the city. The unnamed protagonist wakes on the day of her wedding after having "not slept well . . . remembering over and over, slipping again into a feverish dream." With "sudden horror" she realizes she needs to change the sheets, though whether out of guilt or anticipation is unclear. (Jackson is never direct with regards to sex, and this story is one of the few in which she alludes to it at all.) While awaiting the scheduled arrival of her fiancé, the protagonist drinks too much coffee to combat a headache; changes the bathroom towels three times; starts to write a letter to her sister and stops; hesitates over what dress to wear and, disliking both options, tears one and repairs it; accuses herself of trying to look prettier and younger than she is; and "cruelly" reminds herself that she is thirty-four, though her marriage license says thirty.

When Harris fails to arrive, she resolves to search for him throughout the city, trying to trace his steps. Along the way, everyone who gives her information seems to laugh at her or make cutting remarks, until finally a sarcastic youth directs her to an apartment in a run-down building. Nobody answers her knock, though she thinks she hears voices inside or "something that might have been laughter far away." She returns to the apartment repeatedly but there is still no answer, only the voices and laughter.

Hall remarked that the protagonist in this story, like most of Jackson's, "loses her customary equilibrium when a totally unexpected counterforce destroys the hard-won balance." In this instance the disturbing force is embodied specifically by Harris, though in other stories he seems only to be connected to it. All of Jackson's stories concern the intrusion of the unfamiliar on the familiar and the disturbance of the delicate balancing act of life, whether the unfamiliar is symbolized by Harris, some other external threat, or, occasionally, something familiar revealing heretofore unknown aspects.

The protagonist of "The Daemon Lover," realizing how ridiculous she would look—"Yes, it looks silly, doesn't it, me all dressed up and trying to find the young man who promised to marry me, but . . . I have

Jackson at work in the study of her husband, critic Stanley Edgar Hyman, in Bennington, Vermont, circa 1947 (from Judy Oppenheimer, Private Demons: The Life of Shirley Jackson, *1988)*

more than this, more than you can see"—does not report Harris's disappearance to the police. By vanishing on her wedding day, Harris strikes where the protagonist is most vulnerable, her dignity and sense of self. In addition, the reader is never truly sure of Harris's reality because he is never seen. Considering the vague description the protagonist gives to other characters in the story while searching for Harris—"He's rather tall, and fair. He wears a blue suit very often"—the reader cannot be sure other characters have seen Harris either. Given his ability to apparently disappear at will, and the incorporeal laughter that the protagonist hears, Harris does not seem to be entirely human and may well be the "daemon" of the title.

Perhaps capitalizing on the effectiveness of this story, Jackson uses Harris to represent the forces that tear at other characters' sanity and well-being throughout the rest of the book. Once the character is established, the reader is on the lookout for other references, which affect the way different stories are interpreted. Jackson uses the name throughout the collection to add an air of menace to what would otherwise be anonymous or neutral. For instance, in "A Fine Old Firm," Mrs. Friedman is assured by the anti-Semitic Mrs. Concord that her son, Charles, does not need an introduction to the law firm of Mr. Friedman since Charles is to join the WASPish firm of "Satterthwaite and Harris." Even if the reader misses the prejudice implied in the names, he or she still knows to distrust, if not actively dislike, anyone associated with the name Harris.

The inscrutable nature of the Harris character combined with the advertising and packaging of the book (quotations from a treatise on witches are interspersed throughout the stories) no doubt cemented Jackson's reputation as a writer of supernatural horror, despite the fact that only rarely does something truly unexplainable happen in the stories; much more often the cause of all the trouble is simply ignorant human cruelty. In his introduction to *The Magic of Shirley Jackson,* Hyman lamented this reputation, feeling that it led critics to misunderstand Jackson: "Her fierce visions of dissociations and madness, of alienation and withdrawal, of cruelty and terror, have been taken to be personal, even neurotic fantasies. Quite the reverse: They are a sensitive and faithful anatomy of our times, fitting symbols for our distressing world of the concentration camp and The Bomb."

Whatever the critical method applied to it, Jackson's world remains a bleak, malicious one, and the people populating it are cruel, treacherous, and deceitful, often lacking even the self-awareness to realize how terrible they are. The few who hope for or exhibit a little human kindness or warmth often end up victims.

The evil that lies within everyone, hiding behind the seemingly ordinary and normal, is a prevalent idea in Jackson's short fiction. Jackson suggests that evil lies in all people and that only with the greatest of efforts can human beings overcome their baser instincts. James Harris himself, for instance, appears exceptionally ordinary, and only in the context of the collection does his name and vague description become the embodiment of evil. Jackson seems to enjoy turning the readers' assumptions of who is innocent upside-down, as if to convince them that, in fact, no one is.

For instance, two parallel stories, "The Witch" and "The Renegade," both feature children who unexpectedly reveal their evil sides to their mothers. In "The Witch," a young mother takes her two children, a boy and a baby girl, on a train ride. A man, unnamed and older than the usual portrayal of Harris, though wearing a blue suit, sits down next to them. He engages the boy in conversation, and the mother eventually relaxes. As soon as she does, though, the man starts telling the boy about what he supposedly did to his baby sister: "I cut off her head and her hands and her feet and her

hair and her nose . . . and I hit her with a stick and I killed her." The boy is delighted and laughs with the man, while the mother is horrified. When the mother demands the man leave, the boy sides with the man even further by threatening his mother: "We'll chop her head off." The man agrees, adding, "And little sister's head, too." Once he is gone, the mother seems to regain her son, offering him a lollipop and getting him to agree that the man was "prob'ly" teasing. The story remains disturbing, however, possibly because of the ease with which the man introduces the boy to evil and how delighted the boy is with it. This seductive ease, particularly with children, seems to be one of Jackson's characteristic motifs, and one she returned to in other stories, including "The Lottery."

"The Renegade" also presents a mother confronted with the cruelty of strangers being reflected in her own children. In this instance, the Walpole family has recently moved from the city to the country (the tension between city folk and country folk, particularly the resentment of country people to newly arrived outsiders from the city, is another common motif in Jackson's fiction). Mrs. Walpole gets an early morning phone call from a neighbor, Mrs. Harris, who informs her that the Walpoles' dog, Lady, has killed some of the Harrises' chickens. Mrs. Harris demands that Mrs. Walpole "do something about the dog." As Mrs. Walpole proceeds through her day, she discovers that word has traveled around town, and everyone she meets has a recommendation as to what should be done. The most humane of these increasingly sadistic suggestions is simply chaining or shooting Lady; others include tying a dead chicken around her neck and letting a mother hen scratch her eyes out. But the worst is waiting for Mrs. Walpole when she returns home. The children enthusiastically relate the suggestion of "genial" Mr. Sheperd, which entails putting a rope and collar with inward-pointing spikes on Lady. The dog would then be induced to run at chickens; the rope would be pulled tight; and, as one child says, "The spikes cut her head off." As in "The Witch," children gleefully enjoy sadistic cruelty toward loved ones, especially when it involves lopping off heads. The children, however innocent of the real consequences of what they are saying—they pet and kiss the dog while happily explaining the spikes—express the latent cruelty that Jackson believes lies in all people and that adults display with unconscious ease, especially toward those in a weaker position, such as children, animals, and occasionally minorities.

Unlike "The Witch," however, in "The Renegade" the mother does not win the children back from evil. The situation is left unresolved (Lady's fate is never determined), and the children are apparently abandoned to their emerging evil inclinations. In fact, Mrs. Walpole leaves the children and goes outside; closing her eyes to the now unfriendly country, she feels "the sharp points closing in on her throat." This image strongly emphasizes the identification between Lady and Mrs. Walpole (both outsiders, both betrayed by their nearest loved ones) and hints at the inevitability of the evil that is to occur. As Friedman said, "The situation is presented; and the lesson, if any, comes from the reader's exposure to the evil and from the insights he gains therefrom."

Mothers, however, are not always a repository of goodness. Jackson follows "The Witch" and "The Renegade" with "After You, My Dear Alphonse," which depicts the prejudice of a mother. The plot is extremely simple—it depicts the events of a single afternoon in which a little boy, Johnny, brings his friend Boyd home for lunch. As often happens in Jackson's fiction, a stranger or outsider invades a character's home; however, in an inversion of Jackson's usual treatment of the situation, this time the invader is harmless and the invaded becomes the oppressor. At the same time, the story is typically Jacksonian in revealing the evil beneath an apparently benign exterior. However it is read, the power of the story lies in its characterization of the mother.

Mrs. Wilson is the epitome of a capable country woman (in the first sentence she is taking gingerbread out of the oven), who tells Johnny to invite Boyd in for lunch but then realizes her son's friend is African American. Outwardly charitable and polite, Mrs. Wilson reveals her prejudice in the assumptions she makes about Boyd and her inability to treat him as an individual. First, she assumes Johnny is making Boyd carry some wood, but Johnny explains the wood belongs to Boyd; that is why he is carrying it. While the boys eat, all of Mrs. Wilson's attempts to find differences between the boys are frustrated: Boyd is not any hungrier than Johnny; his father is not a laborer but instead a foreman; his mother does not work; and he does not have a large number of siblings. Revealing one last assumption, Mrs. Wilson tries to offer Boyd some used clothes that Boyd, in confusion, refuses since "we buy about everything we need." Increasingly annoyed, she takes the one thing Boyd actually wants—as he reaches for more gingerbread, she snatches the plate away.

Mrs. Wilson blames her annoyance on Boyd's ingratitude for not taking the secondhand clothes, though her discomfort actually stems from the failure of her assumptions, the revelation of her prejudice, and her inability to find significant differences between her boy and an African American child. The similarity between the two boys is underlined in the final exchange of the story: when Boyd asks Johnny if his mother is still mad, Johnny says, "She's screwy sometimes," to which Boyd replies, "So's mine."

Not all of Jackson's stories were explorations of evil, however; she wrote several stories she termed "pot-boilers," which were essentially slightly fictionalized versions of her domestic life. (She often did not even bother to change the names of her family members.) Centering on family squabbles, they were published regularly in women's magazines such as *Good Housekeeping* and *Woman's Home Companion*. Jackson herself did not put much value on these stories, distinguishing them from her serious fiction. She claimed in a 9 November 1949 letter to her parents that she wrote these stories "simply for money." Many of these stories were later collected into the books *Life Among the Savages* (1953) and *Raising Demons* (1957). One such piece, "Charles," first published in *Mademoiselle* in July 1948 and anthologized almost as frequently as "The Lottery," does provide a bridge between Jackson's domestic stories and what she perceived as her more literary work. While it is a realistic and humorous family story, it also provides another instance of Jackson's interest in the evil within everyone, even the most familiar.

The story begins with the narrator sending her young son, Laurie, off to his first day of kindergarten. Thereafter, Laurie returns home each day to tell stories of a classmate, Charles. Like most children in Jackson's work, Laurie exults in relaying acts of violence and mayhem and gleefully informs his worried parents about how Charles hits the teacher, kicks the teacher's friend, and punches another little boy. The mother becomes determined to attend a PTA meeting in order to find out who might be the mother of this terror, though once there she decides that of the assembled mothers, "None of them looked to me haggard enough." She approaches Laurie's teacher and sympathizes with her, mentioning that she must be quite busy keeping Charles in line, to which the teacher replies, "'We don't have any Charles in the kindergarten.'" Like many of Jackson's narrators, this one learns the truth a little too late, though the humiliation she experiences is not as painful as the fate that awaits many of Jackson's other characters. When this narrator realizes that Laurie is actually the terrible Charles, she is forced to confront the fact that everyone harbors some evil, even a seemingly innocent child, even her own.

"The Lottery" also exemplifies this theme and touches on nearly all of Jackson's other themes, while leaving the story open enough to imply multiple and equally justified readings. It is, in short, her masterpiece, and it has garnered a considerable amount of attention. As soon as it was published, literally hundreds of letters deluged the offices of *The New Yorker*, more than any other story had generated before. The

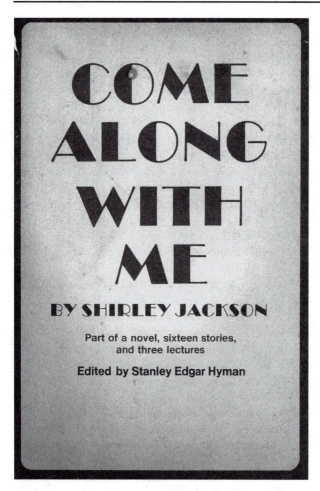

Dust jacket for the 1968 collection of Jackson's work edited by her husband, who wanted to expand her reputation beyond that of a supernatural-horror writer

letters were overwhelmingly negative—expressing, as Jackson said in "Biography of a Story," published in *Come Along With Me* (1968), "bewilderment, speculation and plain old-fashioned abuse." Jackson also noted tellingly, "People at first were not so much concerned with what the story meant; what they wanted to know was where these lotteries were held, and whether they could go there and watch."

Eventually, however, critics did concern themselves with the meaning of the story. "The Lottery" has been interpreted in several ways. Its symbolism, for instance, has been carefully scrutinized for its religious meanings. The story has been read as attacking a classist, capitalistic society; or as a feminist assault on an inherently patriarchal system. Often it is interpreted as showing the victimization of humanity by unchanging traditions and attitudes and, of course, as revealing the essentially primitive and evil nature of people. One of the wonders of "The Lottery" is that it can sustain so

many interpretations and still retain, decades after its original publication, the power to shock, enlighten, and entertain.

"The Lottery" employs the usual Jackson tone, a straightforward and matter-of-fact narration that serves to heighten the horror. The plot, like most of Jackson's, is deceptively simple: all the action takes place on a sunny afternoon in an average little American town. Tessie Hutchinson arrives late for the annual town lottery, which at first appears to be a rather festive event complete with children playing and adults chatting amicably. The true horror of the rite is gradually exposed through the villagers' nervousness and reluctance until, in the end, Tessie, terrified and desperately defiant, stands revealed as the lottery winner and is summarily stoned to death by the populace.

Many critics have noted a strong connection between Jackson's story and ancient scapegoat rites— ceremonies in which one person is sacrificed for the good of the whole, to expiate sins and ensure good fortune. Examples range from gifts to gods in return for a good harvest in ancient cultures, to the story of Christ's crucifixion. Much of the power of the story arises from the juxtaposition of the ancient death ritual with the modern village. Jackson credited two sources of inspiration: a Syracuse University professor's Introduction to Folklore course and Sir James Frazer's *The Golden Bough* (12 volumes, 1890–1915), a highly significant collection of folk tales and myths that profoundly influenced modern American literature.

As discussed by Barbara Allen in the *Tennessee Folklore Society Bulletin* (1980), Jackson's lottery conforms to the four aspects of a scapegoat ritual laid out by Frazer. First, the scapegoat itself serves as the individual, tangible representation of the entire community's less tangible evils—Tessie is sacrificed for the good of the community. Second, a regular time period is established between rituals, often a year, usually coinciding with the changing of the seasons—the lottery takes place on the same day every year near the summer solstice. Third, a period of license or lessening of moral restrictions precedes the ritual—the village children play at the beginning of the story, and normal work is suspended. Fourth, the scapegoat is seen as divine in nature, and the sacrifice is seen as redemptive. When a girl of the village voices her hope that the winner is not a friend, Old Man Warner gripes, "People ain't the way they used to be," implying that the winner used to be honored or at least respected.

At the same time, Jackson emphasizes the fact that the lottery ritual is devolving in the village; its original meaning and purpose has been lost: "There had been a recital of some sort," though this element is now forgotten, along with a ceremonial addressing of each lottery participant. Additionally, the physical tools are also deteriorating; wood chips have been replaced with paper, and the box is in disrepair. By separating the stoning from its justification, Jackson heightens the horror of the lottery and underlines her point that, as Allen puts it, "blind adherence to traditional forms of behavior that have lost their original meanings and acquired no new, positive ones, can be destructive." Furthermore, the empty continuation of the lottery becomes self-perpetuating: the unthinking and unjustified reenactment of the purging of evil from the community is itself evil and reinforces the need for further purging.

Helen E. Nebeker, in *American Literature* (1974), wrote the most complete treatment of the symbolic aspects of the story. She argues that the story does not just question the blind adherence to a scapegoat ritual but rather, on a larger scale, the blind adherence to religious traditions. Nebeker reads the symbols of the story as indicating an evolution of the lottery from a pagan ritual to a Hebraic and then a Christian tradition. The unquestioning acceptance of these traditions leads to Tessie Hutchinson's downfall, and by extension all of humankind's.

While there is some resistance to the lottery, it is only voiced indirectly and never acted upon. Mr. Adams says, "over in the north village they're talking of giving up the lottery." Old Man Warner speaks as the voice of tradition, calling all who question the lottery either a "Pack of crazy fools" or a "Pack of young fools," implying there is little, if any, difference between the two. The fact that "There's *always* been a lottery" is all the reason Old Man Warner needs to continue it. When the time for the stoning arrives, Adams leads the effort. Even Tessie, who perhaps displays an unspoken resistance to the lottery by showing up late, tells her husband to "Get up there," and only protests when her family is chosen. Even then, she wants her married daughter to draw with the family to lessen her own risk and, right up until the end, claims it "isn't fair." Tessie never protests the lottery itself, only that she was chosen.

Peter Kosenko, in the *New Orleans Review* (1985), maintains that the lottery is "no mere 'irrational' tradition," but rather "an ideological mechanism." Kosenko believes the lottery serves to reinforce the social order by instilling fear as well as perpetuating the ideology necessary to maintain the social order—an ideology and social order he finds essentially capitalist. The lottery, for instance, is controlled by the symbolically named Mr. Summers, who is both the most successful businessman and the mayor since he has "more time and energy," that is, money and leisure. His helpers are Mr. Graves, who wields power as the postmaster, and Mr. Martin, economically advantaged as the successful

town grocer. Who does the actual choosing in the lottery is also revealing: men draw for their households and families, while daughters get absorbed into their husbands' families once they are married, and had best have children quickly to lessen their own chances of getting picked. The village is a strict patriarchy, enforced by capitalist gender roles: men participate, through work, in the economy of the village as a whole, while women are relegated to the home.

Many of Jackson's themes culminate in "The Lottery." Old Man Warner's unthinking acceptance of the lottery mirrors Mrs. Wilson's unthinking acceptance of cultural stereotypes in "After You, My Dear Alphonse." Similarly, parallels may be drawn between Tessie Hutchinson and Mrs. Walpole from "The Renegade," both set upon by the apparently naive evil of their neighbors. The way a family can hide evil within itself—as seen in "The Renegade," "The Witch," "After You, My Dear Alphonse," and many others—is displayed when Tessie would willingly sacrifice her married daughter to better her chances, and again when Tessie's children both "beamed and laughed" after learning their mother was to die instead of them. The older generation passes on the evil to the younger, as seen in the placing of stones into little Davey's hands in "The Lottery" and the talk of decapitating baby sisters in "The Witch." "The Lottery," in distilling, concentrating, and exemplifying these themes, is a fitting title story and end to Jackson's first collection.

After persistent questioning from readers, Jackson finally addressed the meaning of the story in the 22 July 1948 issue of the *San Francisco Chronicle*: "Explaining just what I had hoped the story to say is very difficult. I suppose, I hoped, by setting a particularly brutal ancient rite in the present and in my own village, to shock the story's readers with a graphic dramatization of the pointless violence and general inhumanity in their own lives." No matter the interpretation, there is no denying her unqualified success.

After *The Lottery, or, The Adventures of James Harris*, Jackson continued to publish short stories in magazines, but never assembled another collection, instead publishing several novels. For many years during this period Jackson was treated by a psychiatrist because she suffered from depression and anxiety exacerbated by feelings of isolation and alienation. It is impossible not to see a connection between Jackson's own psychological difficulties and the terrors to which her characters are subjected. Jackson's characters are often alone with the rest of their world arrayed against them. In "Pillar of Salt," perhaps the most directly autobiographical representation of Jackson's own anxieties, a woman visiting New York City is so overcome by agoraphobia that she cannot even manage to cross a street, and her attempts to leave the block her hotel is on end in failure. Also, Jackson, who battled her own sense of being an outsider, always identifies with the outsider in her stories. Jackson repeatedly attacks the prejudice displayed by any group for those excluded from their midst, whether that prejudice is motivated by race, religion, or just geography and social snobbery. Jackson remained in Bennington, writing continuously for the rest of her life. When she died of heart failure in her sleep on 8 August 1965, she left an unfinished novel and many unpublished short stories.

A new collection of Jackson's stories did not appear until *The Magic of Shirley Jackson* was released after her death. This book, however, reprinted only stories already collected in *The Lottery, or, The Adventures of James Harris;* new Jackson short stories were not published in book form until the appearance of *Come Along With Me* in 1968. Edited by Hyman, *Come Along With Me* includes the beginning of the novel Jackson was working on when she died, as well as fourteen short stories and three lectures. While a few of the stories that were written early in her career are quite different from the stories in her first collection, many of the later pieces resemble those in *The Lottery, or, The Adventures of James Harris* both in content and tone.

As Hall noted in her analysis of Jackson's work, a James Harris-like character turns up in several stories, reflecting Jackson's continued interest in unhappy women and the men that prey on them emotionally. Three stories, "The Beautiful Stranger," "A Visit," and "The Rock," particularly echo the Harris stories from the first collection in portraying men with some supernatural powers bringing on the damnation of female protagonists. For instance, the unhappy housewife in "The Beautiful Stranger" is first surprised and then secretly delighted that a near-perfect duplicate has apparently replaced her husband. While Friedman concluded that the housewife has "lost touch with reality," Hall maintained that the apparent stranger is supernatural in nature, noting that Jackson removed a few scenes that appeared in earlier drafts and seemed to suggest insanity. Whether crazy or under the influence of a Harris-type evil entity, the housewife comes to a characteristically bad end; she arrives in her neighborhood one evening and realizes she cannot tell which house is hers.

Not all the stories in *Come Along With Me* parallel the fantastical ones in *The Lottery, or, The Adventures of James Harris,* however. The first, "Janice," was written while Jackson was in college and is, as Hyman relates in his preface, the story that so impressed him that it led to their meeting. Made up almost entirely of dialogue, the story is only about a page in length and consists of the narrator's friend Janice talking nonchalantly of her sui-

cide attempt. In an "almost whimsical, indifferent" tone, Janice tells first the narrator and then various friends how she almost killed herself that afternoon because she could not go back to school. Hyman said of this story, "In its economy and power it is surely prophetic of her later mastery." While lacking the clear menace of her later stories, "Janice" certainly has horrific elements and demonstrates that Jackson already had the ability to relate the extremes of human behavior in an almost offhand manner, a talent she later used to increase the shock value of some of her best stories.

As in many of Jackson's stories, a young woman is at the center of "Tootie in Peonage." While more cheerful and less polished than her later work, "Tootie in Peonage" does presage some of Jackson's themes. The older narrator of the story makes no secret of her scorn for the uncultured Tootie, who has come to work as a nanny and maid for the narrator's friend. Tootie is compared to an ape, and the narrator speaks with derision of her "complicated coiffure of curls," pinned-together dress, and bright red fingernails. Only when Tootie is pregnant and leaving can the narrator feel any "real sympathy" for her. More humorous than most of Jackson's work, "Tootie in Peonage" also resolves its conflict in an uncharacteristically harmless manner: Tootie quits and moves back home. The revelation of prejudice, in this case classism, through dialogue is a device that Jackson returns to later in both "After You, My Dear Alphonse" and "A Fine Old Firm." The undertones of class conflict in this story are elaborated on later, often in the form of differences between rural dwellers and their urban counterparts, in such stories as "The Summer People," "The Little House," and "Home."

"A Cauliflower in Her Hair" also entails conflict between a teenager and an older woman. Virginia Garland's friend Millie, like Tootie, wears too much makeup for Mrs. Garland. Additionally, she interrupts the Garlands' dinner. A flirtatious atmosphere is established between Mr. Garland and Millie: she assures Mr. Garland that he is not old, and he offers her a cigarette. Mrs. Garland makes it clear she disapproves of this flirtation, referring to Millie several times as a "child." The object of the satire is suburban mores, a subject Jackson seldom revisited in her later stories. The callousness of Mr. Garland, however, is not unusual for Jackson's husbands and male lovers; it plants the seeds for the marital discord that reaps so much havoc in such stories as "Got a Letter from Jimmy," "The Good Wife," and "What a Thought."

Jackson's next collection of short fiction, *Just An Ordinary Day,* did not appear until 1997, when previously unpublished and uncollected stories were interwoven and edited by her children, Laurence Jackson Hyman and Sarah Hyman Stewart. In their introduction to the book, they relate how, by going through Jackson's papers at the Library of Congress, they were able to assemble more than 130 stories, many unpublished. Also, they found many pieces that had appeared in various magazines but were never again published. Choosing fifty-four stories they felt were up to Jackson's standards, they produced *Just An Ordinary Day* in an effort to show the evolution of her craft over the course of her career as well as demonstrate her versatility to a new generation of readers. The stories cover the same themes as those in her other collections, running the gamut from humorous domestic pieces to tales of twisted psyches and supernatural horror.

Two stories in particular display Jackson's range—the events of an unpublished story, "Nightmare," were rewritten and absorbed into a published story, "The Omen." While "Nightmare" is an example of Jackson's psychological horror fiction, "The Omen" is much more complex. In the first version, a truck loudly advertising a contest in which the winner is the one who finds a "Ms. X" apparently follows a young woman, Miss Morgan. Ms. X is consistently described as matching Miss Morgan in appearance; in fact, the description of Ms. X changes throughout the story as Miss Morgan attempts to change her appearance. The story ends when Miss Morgan gives in and accepts her identity as Ms. X. Jackson displays her range by taking this fairly straightforward tale and making something entirely different from the same material.

The published version of this story, "The Omen," is more lighthearted—it begins with an old Granny who sets off to buy presents for her family, all written down on a list. The story shifts to Edith, a young woman who, faced with a choice between the man she wants to marry and the mother who refuses to let her, wishes for an omen to tell her what to do. It arrives in the form of Granny's list, which was left on a bus. The list leads Edith through an adventure similar to the one in "Nightmare"—this time the contestants need to find a Miss Murrain to win free groceries—and eventually causes her to call her fiancé and declare that she will marry him. In "Nightmare," no one spots Miss Morgan as Ms. X, and the feeling of the story is one of rising paranoia, accentuated by her inability to get away from the announcements of the contest and increasingly irrational thinking: "Could they sue her, take her into court, put her in jail for dressing like Miss X?" On the other hand, in "The Omen," Edith is spotted and dragged off, protesting all the way, by a woman who screams at everyone on the street that she has caught "the girl with the groceries." When the woman discovers her mistake, she blames Edith for not telling her. While "Nightmare" is disorienting and sinister, "The

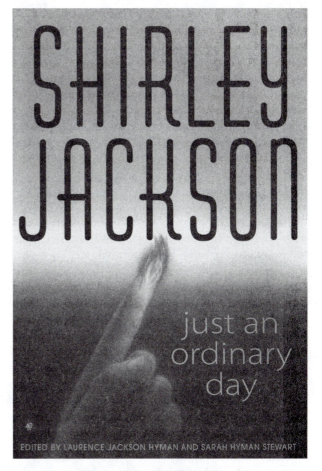

Dust jacket for the posthumous collection edited by Jackson's children. It includes "The Possibility of Evil," about a woman who destroys her neighbors' sense of security by constantly warning them of her suspicions.

Omen" achieves a rather absurdist humor. In Jackson's fiction, humor often is the flip side of horror, and the juxtaposition of these two stories reinforces the connection between the two.

Another instance of the connection between the horrific and the comic is one of Jackson's more famous stories included in this collection. "One Ordinary Day, with Peanuts" was included in *The Best American Short Stories, 1956* and published separately in 1990. In the story John Philip Johnson spends his day distributing peanuts, candy, money, and advice to various strangers he meets. During each encounter, his sincerity is stressed; at the beginning of the story, he believes the day to be the "best of all days" and the world "a wonderful place." Later, when offering to give a woman money to make up for causing her to be late for work, his "flat statement, obviously innocent of irony, could not be . . . anything but the statement of a responsible and truthful and respectable man." After spending his whole day performing good deeds, Mr. Johnson returns home to his wife and inquires politely about her day. Mrs. Johnson has spent the day purposefully making everyone she encountered miserable. The story ends with this exchange:

> "Fine," said Mr. Johnson. "But you do look tired. Want to change over tomorrow?"
> "I *would* like to," she said. "I could do with a change."
> "Right," said Mr. Johnson. "What's for dinner?"
> "Veal cutlet."
> "Had it for lunch," said Mr. Johnson.

With those five lines of dialogue, Jackson inverts what the reader had believed about the character and turns what had seemed good into something sinister. The Johnsons play at being good and evil, and their real enjoyment does not come from doing good deeds, but rather from the power that comes with affecting other people's lives arbitrarily. The ease and immediacy with which Mr. Johnson slips into his new role signals just how frivolously he takes the rest of humanity.

While many critics have written about "The Possibility of Evil," it was not collected until *Just An Ordinary Day*. Originally published a few months after Jackson's death, the story features much of what is familiar to Jackson's fiction. In *Studies in Short Fiction* (1978) John G. Parks declared this story a "key" because it includes "many of the elements basic to her work, including a sensitive but narrow female protagonist, a gothic house, economy of language, intimations of something 'other' or 'more,' a free-floating sense of depravity, experiences of disassociation, and a final turn about in events or a judgment." It is also, perhaps, one of her most direct treatments of the idea of the evil within human nature.

Miss Adele Strangeworth is obsessed with the possibility of evil and sees herself as a guardian of the good and right. She is typical of the older women often encountered in Jackson's fiction: she is much concerned with propriety, awash with a feeling of entitlement, and remarkably proud of the signs of her status (in this case, Strangeworth's prized rosebushes). As the last member of the most important family in the town, she feels it "belonged to her." Partly for that reason, she sends anonymous letters to the inhabitants of the town, warning not of facts or real dangers but instead of "the more negotiable stuff of suspicion," about what people might be doing or what could be true. Strangeworth is constantly on guard against "the possible evil lurking nearby," feeling that "as long as evil existed unchecked in the world, it was Miss Strangeworth's duty to keep her town alert to it." Unlike most of Jackson's characters, Strangeworth does understand that all people har-

bor evil within themselves; what causes her downfall is her inability to understand that truth about herself.

In trying to fight the evil within everyone, Strangeworth exhibits her own evil side. She destroys the peace of mind of her fellow townspeople and undermines the sense of trust necessary to build a community; in effect, she causes the very dissolution of her town that she means to prevent. One evening, she drops one of her letters on the way to the post office. The letter is delivered, however, by a couple of teenagers who saw her drop it. When Strangeworth wakes the next morning, she finds a letter much like her own in her mailbox: "She began to cry silently for the wickedness of the world when she read the words: Look Out at What Used to Be Your Roses." By destroying Strangeworth's prized rosebushes, the townspeople have exacted revenge for the evil she has done in the name of good.

While Strangeworth sees evil within everyone, she still imagines it as something external to somehow be fought and defeated, rather than as a part of everyone, conquered only by understanding and accepting it. If one has to find a moral center to Jackson's works, perhaps this story is it. In *Private Demons: The Life of Shirley Jackson* (1988), Judy Oppenheimer read this story as reflective of Jackson's image of herself and her desire to seem a "proper lady" while writing her own "terrible messages to the world."

Jackson's enduring popularity can be seen as a function of her two major genres, comedy and horror, but her impact is not limited to her mastery of the elements of these genres. Rather, her gift for storytelling and talent for portraying the subtleties of character—abilities that cut across genre lines—are what create the continuing interest in and enjoyment of her stories.

While the idea of evil is central to Jackson's work, her attribution of that evil to a human source, as an aspect of human nature, is what shapes the critical response to her work. Her psychological dissections of the darkness in human souls—the fear, loneliness, and hatred of the other that both cause and are the result of human evil—demand to be understood. While often bleak and pessimistic, Jackson ultimately is a moralist, holding up a mirror to show humanity its inhumanity. In a world of conflict, alienation, and hatred, where new instances of genocide, terror, and war appear in the news every year, Jackson will continue to have relevance and impact and will be guaranteed a place in the canon of contemporary authors.

Interviews:

John K. Hutchens, "On the Books," *New York Herald Tribune Book Review,* 8 May 1949, p. 17;

Harvey Breit, "Talk with Miss Jackson," *New York Times Book Review,* 26 June 1949, p. 15;

Lewis Nichols, "Demonologist," *New York Times Book Review,* 5 July 1953, p. 8;

"On an Author," *New York Herald Tribune Book Review,* 5 July 1953, p. 2;

Stanley J. Kunitz, ed., "Shirley Jackson," in *Twentieth Century Authors,* First Supplement (New York: Wilson, 1955), pp. 483–484;

Cathy Ciccolella, "Jackson Credits SU with Writing Start," *Daily Orange* (Syracuse University), 28 April 1965, pp. 1, 5.

Bibliographies:

Robert S. Phillips, "Shirley Jackson: A Checklist," *Papers of the Bibliographical Society of America,* 56 (January–March 1962): 110–113;

Phillips, "Shirley Jackson: A Chronology and a Supplementary Checklist," *Papers of the Bibliographical Society of America,* 60 (April–June 1966): 203–213;

Casey Herrick, "Shirley Jackson's 'The Lottery,'" *Bulletin of Bibliography,* 46 (June 1989): 120–121.

Biography:

Judy Oppenheimer, *Private Demons: The Life of Shirley Jackson* (New York: Putnam, 1988).

References:

Barbara Allen, "A Folkloristic Look at Shirley Jackson's 'The Lottery,'" *Tennessee Folklore Society Bulletin,* 46 (December 1980): 119–124;

Lenemaja Friedman, *Shirley Jackson* (Boston: Twayne, 1975);

Joan Wylie Hall, *Shirley Jackson: A Study of the Short Fiction* (New York: Twayne, 1993);

Peter Kosenko, "A Marxist/Feminist Reading of Shirley Jackson's 'The Lottery,'" *New Orleans Review,* 12 (Spring 1985): 27–32;

Helen E. Nebeker, "'The Lottery': Symbolic Tour de Force," *American Literature,* 46 (March 1974): 100–107;

Fritz Oehlschlaeger, "The Stoning of Mistress Hutchinson: Meaning and Context in 'The Lottery,'" *Essays in Literature,* 15 (Fall 1988): 259–265;

John G. Parks, "The Possibility of Evil: A Key to Shirley Jackson's Fiction," *Studies in Short Fiction,* 15 (Summer 1978): 320–323.

Papers:

The Library of Congress holds the Shirley Jackson Papers, which include manuscripts of published and unpublished stories as well as personal and business correspondence.

Greg Johnson

(13 July 1953 –   )

Michael Upchurch

BOOKS: *Emily Dickinson: Perception and the Poet's Quest* (University: University of Alabama Press, 1985);

Understanding Joyce Carol Oates (Columbia: University of South Carolina Press, 1987);

Distant Friends (Princeton, N.J.: Ontario Review, 1990);

A Friendly Deceit (Baltimore & London: Johns Hopkins University Press, 1992);

Pagan Babies (New York: Dutton, 1993);

Aid and Comfort (Gainesville: University Press of Florida, 1993);

Joyce Carol Oates: A Study of the Short Fiction (New York: Twayne, 1994; Oxford: Maxwell Macmillan, 1994);

I Am Dangerous (Baltimore & London: Johns Hopkins University Press, 1996);

Invisible Writer: A Biography of Joyce Carol Oates (New York & London: Dutton, 1998).

SELECTED PERIODICAL PUBLICATION–
UNCOLLECTED: "Marina," *Virginia Quarterly Review,* 67 (Spring 1991): 310–319.

Greg Johnson is a Southern writer who seems, in several important ways, not to have sprung from the Southern literary tradition. More urbane than parochial in outlook, more subdued than gothic in tone (at least in his most successful stories), he is a meticulous observer of human foibles and isolation. Although he sometimes is drawn to depicting extreme situations and personalities, he is at his best when he keeps his work understated and focuses on the drama of the ordinary. While his works include critical studies, biography, and a novel, his specialty–and strength–is the short story. He has published roughly seventy stories, thirty-seven of which have been published in three collections: *Distant Friends* (1990), *A Friendly Deceit* (1992), and *I Am Dangerous* (1996). Some of Johnson's stories have appeared in *Prize Stories: The O. Henry Awards* and *New Stories from the South: The Year's Best,* and Georgia Writers, Inc., has twice named him Georgia Author of the Year, in 1991 and 1997.

Greg Johnson (photograph by Billy Howard; from the dust jacket for Distant Friends, *1990)*

Johnson was born 13 July 1953, in San Francisco, where his father, Raymond, was stationed with the U.S. Air Force. Soon afterward the family was transferred to a military base near Liverpool, England, for three years. When Raymond Johnson's tour of duty came to an end, the family moved to Tyler, Texas–roughly one hundred miles east of Dallas–where Raymond had grown up. In Tyler, Raymond worked first in the police force and then at an oil refinery. In the 1960s he started a construction company with his wife that eventually allowed him to quit his oil-refinery job. In an unpublished interview Johnson described his early years as "working class" and his teen and college years as more affluent–"a spectrum that has helped in my writing," he asserted.

For his primary education Johnson attended a small Catholic school, similar to the one depicted in his novel *Pagan Babies* (1993). He earned his B.A. and M.A. degrees in English at Southern Methodist University in Dallas before moving to Emory University in Atlanta to earn his Ph.D. His dissertation, on Emily Dickinson, later became his first book. Thereafter he embarked on an academic career that included visiting appointments at Emory and tenure-track positions at Widener University in Chester, Pennsylvania (1980–1981) and the University of Mississippi in Oxford (1988–1989). In 1989, homesick for Atlanta, he took a position at Kennesaw State University in the northwest suburbs of the city, teaching courses in the graduate writing program as well as some undergraduate literature courses.

Johnson belongs to the generation that witnessed the suburbanization of the South and was saturated with a heavy dose of media exposure that, arguably, diluted the local color of the region. (Johnson's tale about compulsive shopping, "Scene of the Crime" from the 1996 collection *I Am Dangerous,* has the distinction of evoking a South virtually devoid of local color.) These changes in regional milieu are reflected in much of the writer's fiction, which, instead of being steeped in the past and the intricate algebra of small-town manners, is somewhat estranged from them. In Johnson's world it has become the rule rather than the exception for the younger people to move away from small towns, whether to Philadelphia, New York, or, most often, Atlanta. Once there, they find a chasm widening between their increasingly urban sensibilities and their semirural backgrounds.

That chasm is evident in such stories as "Leavings" (from *Distant Friends,* 1990), where a death in the family brings the protagonist, Claire, home to her native Georgia for the first time in years only to make a definitive break from it, and "Private Jokes" (from *A Friendly Deceit,* 1992) where Atlanta architect Chloe, with "conscious rudeness," puts off a visit from a "maiden aunt," in part because she simply would not fit into Chloe's world, where lust, career ambition, and the in-jokes alluded to in the title have become peculiarly conflated and confused.

The distance between countrified past and urban present is, in part, an ineluctable result of physical remove or years passing. Aesthetic tastes are involved as well, however. Indeed, the description of the protagonist in the title story from *Distant Friends* implicitly rejects the Southern gothic tradition: "His parents were dead, his memories of other relatives still in Georgia resembled cartoon figures from some grotesque Southern novel he might have read, but would never read again."

Dust jacket for Johnson's 1990 collection, focusing on such topics as marital discord, homosexuality, and Catholicism

While Johnson does occasionally stray into gothic territory, it is often with a twist, as he deliberately burlesques the gothic furnishings he uses. In "Alliances of Youth," from *I Am Dangerous,* the narrator, home in Georgia for the first time in twenty years, for the funeral of her beloved cousin, gives a "mock shudder" in anticipation of the scene she will find—a scene which, upon arrival, offers

> all the trappings of Southern gothicism. Shading the sinuous front drive (full of potholes, and threatened on both sides by thick crabgrass and kudzu) were a number of stately, decayed-looking trees; there was an imposing front veranda, complete with white columns and a creaking swing; from the third story, turrets jutted out like gaping, disconsolate eyes. There was even, dear God, a tight-lipped housekeeper, her black hair parted severely down the middle and plastered against her skull, whose every gesture seemed distinct with menace.

The story matches this setting description in eliciting unsettling effect from wry pastiche. In addition to mosly eschewing the gothic flourishes of his Southern literary forebears, Johnson brings other differences to his fiction: a Catholic background and a gay sensibility. These are most evident in *Pagan Babies,* about the life-long friendship between two Catholic school friends, Janice, who is straight, and Clifford, who is gay. In an 11 February 1993 interview with Rebecca Ranson of *The Southern Voice,* Johnson explained the role his personal background played in the book:

> It's not autobiographical exactly. I don't think in those terms while I'm writing. When the book was finished, I thought about Janice and Clifford . . . and thought that I had split myself apart. Each of them has characteristics that I have. I'm not like either, not as extreme. The characters had an energy in their lives that kept me going. I live a pretty quiet writer's life. It appealed to me to see what they were going to do to each other next. Growing up Catholic was first-hand experience.

In his short fiction, however, overt references to religious persuasion and sexual predilection are less commonly found and sometimes less directly addressed. Instead, his experience of "difference" is more subtle in its influence on his writing. Often the narrator of a Johnson story is an observer, extremely guarded in what he reveals about himself. Johnson's younger narrators usually are male, although his adult narrators can sometimes be women. In many cases in which the narrator is a young boy, however, his attention is focused on the female protagonist of the story. He also frequently tries his best to hold back from active participation in the conflicts confronting him, but his efforts just as frequently prove untenable.

In addressing Catholicism in his fictional world, Johnson makes clear he is somewhat removed from his childhood beliefs. In "The Burning," from *Distant Friends,* the adult narrator, looking back to his boyhood years, dispassionately characterizes "the Catholicism of the provincial South, of the working people" as "a religion vaguely insecure in its consciousness of that loud, Bible-thumping fundamentalism encroaching on all sides." In "Passion Play," from the same collection, the protagonist goes so far as to find his Catholic childhood "restrictive, monotonous, and somehow passionless despite the blood-hued imagery of that religion and its Gothic, wildly improbable beliefs." In one of Johnson's strongest stories, "Sanctity" from *I Am Dangerous,* the narrator bears witness to a showdown between a Catholic school nun and one of her pupils, a religious fanatic. The narrator himself has little stake in the theological particulars under question; instead he is more fascinated by their warping effect on the embattled protagonists before him. One senses that Johnson, as a "Catholic" writer, abandoned his faith without much struggle, while retaining a lingering interest in it as a subject, specifically the role it plays as a source of torment and/or comfort in the believer's mind.

Johnson's portrayal of gay life in his short fiction is in marked contrast to that in *Pagan Babies.* Often Johnson introduces gay characters as puzzles for outsiders to figure out. Sometimes the gay man in question is a family member, as in (by the merest hint) "Getting Through" from *A Friendly Deceit* or (by the most gradual disclosure) "Alliances of Youth." He can also be a tenant ("The Boarder" from *A Friendly Deceit*), a colleague ("Primordia" from *I Am Dangerous*), or a performer ("The Metamorphosis" from *Distant Friends*). In most instances Johnson reveals less about the character in question and more than about the people who are trying to decipher him. Johnson is interested in what happens on the cusp of things: the borderland where the private becomes public and inchoate feeling transforms—or fails to transform—into comprehensible behavior.

Johnson's writing influences have been various. After boyhood enthusiasms for Edgar Allan Poe and the television series *Alfred Hitchcock Presents,* Johnson read and emulated F. Scott Fitzgerald, John Steinbeck, Pearl S. Buck, and Truman Capote during his teenage years, patterning an attempt at a novella after Capote's *Breakfast at Tiffany's* (1958). Later came exposure to Jane Austen, Henry James, and the Brontës, along with Southern writers Eudora Welty, Flannery O'Connor, and Carson McCullers.

Another significant influence is Joyce Carol Oates, the subject of three books by Johnson, including a fine, insightful biography, *Invisible Writer* (1998). Oates published two of Johnson's earliest stories in *Ontario Review,* the magazine that she and her husband, Raymond Smith, edit, and later steered Johnson's first collection, *Distant Friends,* toward publication by Ontario Review Press. Oates's influence, however, has not consistently resulted in Johnson's best work. Like Oates, he sometimes makes literary excursions into realms of the morbid and psychotic, with erratic results.

Johnson's best stories deliver a kind of meticulous melancholy, balanced between sympathy and chill—a balance as unpredictable as it is quiet in outcome. In the precision of his character observation, Johnson has an affinity with some of James's short fiction and Welty's as represented by "A Memory" or "No Place for You, My Love"—although every now and then the rollicking high spirits of her "Why I Live at the P.O." will infiltrate his writing, too.

Repeatedly he studies people who are going through some shock that pushes them out of themselves and into painful perception of realities that loom behind everyday social exchanges. That shock can be pleasurable, as in "Him"–a shadowy gem from *A Friendly Deceit*–in which it takes the form of a sexual infatuation so distracting that it virtually dismantles the personality of its female protagonist. Or it can be traumatizing, as in "Intensive Care" (from the same collection), in which the protagonist, confronted with the death from AIDS of his younger brother, feels similarly "shoved out" of his normal personality, "the bluff good-natured daytime self that he'd evolved since boyhood days."

Johnson's gift in this story and others is not only for exposing the hard truths lurking beneath the veneer of conventional social manner, but also for depicting how people instinctively cover up those truths, once revealed. In "Leavetaking," from *I Am Dangerous,* a young husband inexplicably abandons his wife and infant son and then, upon returning home, promises never to leave his family again. Johnson complicates the seemingly happy ending by revealing that the husband's urge to flee, while now effectively suppressed, will nevertheless be a permanent part of the marriage: he makes his promise to stay "feeling that he was lying, knowing he wasn't."

Other stories similarly focus on troublesome or even criminal truths that are by general consensus suppressed or glossed over. In "Crazy Ladies," from *Distant Friends,* the eleven-year-old narrator is utterly thrown by how unchanged everything is when his parents' marital crisis, after being pushed toward a brink of no return, simply blows over. "Violence had failed to erupt," he complains, "and I became uneasy, tense, and vaguely suspicious." In "A House of Trees," from *I Am Dangerous,* family hostilities reach the point of violence and injury, but the cover-up is complete. There is no recrimination, no "unsightly heap of delayed, hysterical remorse . . . By the time I entered high school," the narrator remarks, "I knew that we were home free."

Johnson's sense of the drama in what fails to happen is just as acute. In "Wildfires," from *Distant Friends,* a woman coping with "a job that demanded skill but not art, a marriage that required more tact than love," teeters briefly at the brink of adultery with her husband's brother. Little is said and still less done, but the tension between husband, wife, and brother-in-law provides all the narrative momentum needed. In "Wildfires" and other stories Johnson is particularly shrewd in portraying the compromises people make in life.

Johnson's short fiction can be divided roughly into two categories: the first, which includes most–and most of his best–stories, focuses on family or marital conflict, with Johnson giving equal weight to two, three, or more characters; and the second focuses on self-contained figures who dominate the story as they

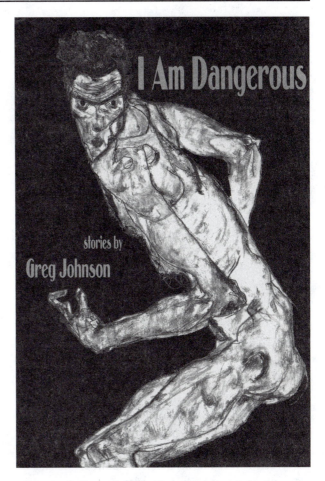

Dust jacket for Johnson's 1996 collection of stories exploring the extreme emotional states of their protagonists

undergo some crisis of their own (even if their crisis is "filtered" by means of a narrator who brings a cool or wry perspective to the drama in question). In either category, Johnson's approach can range from somber to humorous.

In portraying tensions within families Johnson is especially adept at rendering children trying to puzzle out adult realities from clues that are incomplete and inconsistent. In "Crazy Ladies," for example, Jamie attempts to deal with his philandering father's "sudden, nervous gaiety," his mother's consequent "new brusqueness," and his tomboyish sister's precipitate turn toward femininity as she enters her teens: "For a long while I stayed bewildered, feeling that the others had received a new set of instructions on how to live, but had forgotten to pass them along to me." The influence of Carson McCullers is apparent in the story.

"El Paso" and "The Burning," from *Distant Friends,* cover similar ground with even greater acuity. The first portrays a fourteen-year-old narrator, Steven, on his last summer visit to his Aunt Carolyn, Uncle

Hugh, and cousins Ted, Roger, and Henry in the West Texas city eponymous. The story, one of Johnson's best, never spells anything out even as it makes clear that Hugh's likely marital infidelity and Ted's sexual awakening are sending Steven's aunt into a tailspin. The emotional fallout ends with the punishment of the wrong party–the family's Mexican maid, Yolanda–and then a sweeping aside of the whole business "as if nothing had happened." The events of the summer leave a bad taste in Steven's mouth long afterward. Even as an adult, he finds himself occasionally fantasizing of somehow rescuing Yolanda from the Mexican "hovel" that he assumes is her lot in life. "And when I do," he says in the line that closes the story, "I don't take her to El Paso." Reviewer Gail Regier, in her winter 1993 *Southern Humanities Review* essay on *Distant Friends,* complains that the narrator of "El Paso" is "an outsider who can too easily dissociate himself (and thus, emotionally, the reader) from the philistine vulgarity he records." Such an approach is exactly Johnson's strength, however: the layering of tone that dissociation and the long view of retrospect allow. Despite such a remove, the narrator is undeniably haunted by the events he recalls.

In "The Burning" the ten-year-old narrator is left in one-on-one intimacy with his mother, with dismal results, after his father abandons the family. In one passage Johnson deftly describes the nature of children's observations of adult behavior. "Children," the narrator comments (again from a later adult perspective), "are extremely sensitive to psychological fluctuations in their parents–the subtle changes of mood, the buried tensions, the attempts to mask unlovely, primal emotions–but their perceptions, no matter how intense, fail to grasp the larger patterns in adult behavior, the complex causes and effects that often work themselves out very slowly, over a period of months or years. They have a dazzling moment of insight, but then the moment passes. Then they are children again."

In several instances Johnson's youthful observers try strenuously to hold themselves aloof from the conflicts that surround them. In fact, this difficult-to-sustain trick of observing and not participating is the animating dynamic behind several of Johnson's stories. In "Uncle Vic" (a semicomical tale from *I Am Dangerous*), for example, the narrator, Jimmy, asserts: "About Uncle Vic as on most touchy subjects in the family, I stay neutral." The turning point in the tale–in which Jimmy's mentally ill uncle comes to live with his sister (Jimmy's mother) over the vociferous objections of Jimmy's irascible dad and thuggish brother–comes when Jimmy begins to worry that he's "losing" his neutrality, "though I don't think anybody noticed." When his family does notice, mayhem ensues.

Similar testings of neutrality are more soberly treated in "A House of Trees" and "In the Deep Woods," also from *I Am Dangerous*. The latter is a perfect story about a jobless father trying to run away from failure. On a hunting trip with his quiet, watchful son (again the youngster is the narrator), he is observed to be "tracking some wilderness inside himself, paying scant attention to the outside world. And that world," the boy acknowledges, "included me." In both stories the youthful narrator is "cursed"–as he puts it in "A House of Trees"–with the ability "to view any situation from another person's point of view."

In still other stories, such as "Getting Through" (from *A Friendly Deceit*), marital discord is analyzed directly in a third-person narrative:

> Ruth did not seem to notice her husband's grim, aggressive handling of the car, and this pleased him. It meant she would not give him the indifferent stare that implied she was seeing through Graham, finding him once again dishonest, or frivolous, or obtuse; somehow worthy of contempt. This mild disgust sat strangely upon her petite, blond features, and it had chilled him often, throughout their long and placid marriage, to think that some lack of his could so decisively mar her still-girlish beauty, even for a moment. Now, in his knowledge that he might never suffer that look again–that his wife had lost something, irrevocably–Graham had a guilty thrill of satisfaction. The thrill eased his anger, his sense of strain. The guilt made him turn toward Ruth, smiling hopefully. She had fallen silent, not from anything he did but in response to some new turn in the pained, ill-lit labyrinth of her thinking.

The contorted animus underlying this "long and placid" union provides a satisfyingly complex backdrop to the main event of the story: the couple's response to the suicide of their only son, a piano "genius" whose life they have never understood, despite their efforts to do so.

Not all of the marriages Johnson describes are miserable, however. In "Evening at Home," from *I Am Dangerous,* he delivers quite the opposite: a marriage in which the husband, more through mere tone of voice rather than anything he says, helps lead his wife through the "predictable but bearable awkwardness" of a visit from her parents, who serve as reminders of her unhappy, perhaps even blighted girlhood and who disapprove of her marriage. (She is seven years older than her construction foreman husband and earns considerably more than him.) The story, along with hinting at how the entwining of contrasting temperaments can lend a marriage a tensile strength, is a masterful study of depression and emotional breakdown, in this case alleviated by the "kind and virile certainty" of that husbandly voice.

[in dialogue : Roy means King]

3-19-92   "Evening at Home"

parents driving over from Ft. Worth —

When the accident happened, June
Stood on her island was standing in the middle of
her garden kitchen thinking that
she looked like one of those newspaper ads the subdiv'is'in had
been running. A happy homemaker
at Windriver Estates, about the
caption might read, never mind
that she had a full-time job —
she made more money than Roy —
and never mind that their
sparkling beige stucco four-bedroom,
with its sleek surfaces of
cool white tile and gleaming
chrome, still felt nothing
like home. Arriving after work
she sometimes felt she too that she'd
stumbled into a TV set;
that Bill Cosby might appear
suddenly appear in a doorframe,
in one of his ugly expensive
sweaters. Nonetheless here
she stood, at her convenience

Two of Johnson's best stories, "A Dry Season" (from *A Friendly Deceit*) and "Alliances of Youth," instead of addressing crisis directly, examine its aftermath with a subtlety and poignancy that approaches perfection. "A Dry Season" portrays two women, former college roommates now in their thirties. Eleanor is restless in a stale yet still companionable marriage, while Nora is reeling from a seemingly happy relationship cut short by the suicide of her boyfriend. Eleanor's husband, Neil, has frustrations at work and, it is made clear, would desire a sexual relationship with Nora, under different circumstances. As this trio tries to make the best of things in a tranquil lakeside setting, teasing questions of possible betrayal arise, with sexual attraction and corresponding caution being layered, in imbricate fashion, over one another. Johnson dissects the yearning, the thwarted ambition, and the loneliness that threaten the balance of this three-way friendship. Little is said, but everything is suggested. "A Dry Season" is another marvelously precise story about something that fails to happen. It also coolly limns the gulf between what is said and what is left unsaid.

"Alliances of Youth," which was published in the *Kansas Quarterly* in 1987, almost ten years before appearing in *I Am Dangerous,* is about the secrets and conflicting memories that charismatic young Barrie leaves behind following his death in a small Southern town that has been both his prison and his sanctuary. The mix of comedy and tragedy in the power struggle that goes on among Barrie's survivors is perfectly balanced. The pixieish subtleties and treacheries that underlie Barrie's charms make him one of Johnson's most memorable characters, despite the fact that he spends the entire story, aside from a few flashbacks, in his coffin.

Barrie, openly gay to some, closeted to his mother and "long-time fiancée," is a consummate role-player, and a focus on the transition point between role-playing and "real" behavior occurs frequently in Johnson's fiction. In "Marina," an uncollected story published in the spring 1991 issue of *Virginia Quarterly Review,* another of Johnson's "carefully expressionless" young witnesses to adult marital troubles is self-conscious in the extreme about the role he plays in his family: "I withdrew my hands and splayed them and began flapping them at my sides, senseless as any 12-year-old. Though I was much older, mentally, I often found myself impersonating a child of exactly my age."

In the tricky title story of *A Friendly Deceit* a tender but tough single mother, her all-too-knowing son, and a ditzy, sentimental aunt construct, with varying degrees of success, a fiction around the notion of who, exactly, the child's father is and what became of him. Role-playing here is a matter of "tacit agreement," and yet the double consciousness it creates imposes a barrier between candor and consideration. This barrier allows for still more deceptions on the son's part, once he grows up–deceptions decidedly less friendly than those underlying his boyhood.

In the title story from *I Am Dangerous,* the role-playing becomes still more convoluted. The narrator, a floundering history student from a broken home, clings to his actress girlfriend as "the one safe haven in a world I sensed increasingly as fraught with peril." There are complications, however. His feelings for her come most strongly into focus when she is onstage: "Never did I love her more passionately, more recklessly, than when she was playing someone else." When she dumps him, he escapes to the movies, where during a showing of *The Heiress* (1949) he has a brief encounter with the attractive young woman in the seat next to him, the only other person in the theater. The narrator fantasizes about intimidating the young woman, play-acting at being "dangerous."

By the time the lights come up, however, he has reversed himself on several scores: he is eager to apologize to the weeping stranger next to him–it is unclear whether the movie or his unwanted presence has reduced her to tears–and he is fervently identifying with the star of the movie, Olivia de Havilland: "It didn't matter, of course, that she was a woman: we were going through the same thing, we were both romantic fools, we both deserved our fate." He never sees the weeping woman again but marries, has children, and becomes "reasonably happy teaching history to bored middle-schoolers," even though he now knows "the history books are nothing but lies and I can't teach the kids anything worth knowing. I'll never know their private histories and they'll never know mine, and what other kind of history is there?" His long-ago movie-theater encounter becomes a secret touchstone that renders the rest of his life into something of a performance: "We're playing our parts, that girl and I, struggling through our own lines as well as anybody." (Although by this point in the story the phrase "that girl" actually refers to three women: the narrator's wife, his former girlfriend, and the enigmatic movie-theater stranger.) The narrator's vacillations are played out with a verve both comic and forlorn, and Johnson's eye for the role of play-acting in genuine emotional trajectories is supple and sharp.

In stories focusing on solitary characters in extremis, Johnson produces more mixed results. He is at his best when he introduces some gallows humor to the situation, as in "The Boarder," in which a lonely, chatty landlady is at a loss to decipher the peculiar behavior of the exquisitely mannered young professor who recently has become her tenant. "I'm not a snoop," she protests, "it's just that it's so hard, not being able to know people."

22

Dad's shoulders had become hunched like an old man's, though he was still in his thirties. ~~Evidently he'd gotten a~~ *But his new job was a good one,* ~~good job, though,~~ *evidently,* for ~~by~~ *in* August he ~~was able to~~ move us into a better neighborhood, a *bigger* ~~better~~ house. My mother ~~seemed~~ relieved *was* *she said,* that she no longer had to keep all the rear blinds drawn, to avoid any glimpses of that mimosa tree. *After that,* ~~Among the three of us,~~ *we never* ~~we never~~ referred to what had happened, *again.* not in any of the weeks or months or years that followed. There were fond references to Cody's life, recollections of things he'd said or done, but never a word about his death. Eventually the story my parents had told to the doctors and the police, and to our relatives and neighbors—the story of his tragic accident—became so real in our minds that ~~after a while~~ *as time passed* it seemed an authentic memory, as good a version of what had happened as any other. *But I never felt very comfortable in our new head.* ~~I hadn't minded our move. It was just another house.~~ I slept in one room, bathed in another, ate in another, ~~It was all the same~~ *but all my actions* *my routine felt mechanical & strange.* ~~to me.~~ I was adrift in a vacuous loneliness and anxious for school to begin. I was only twelve, just starting junior high, but already I knew that I would study hard and graduate ~~near the top of my high~~ *with honors,* ~~school class,~~ that I would go to college and law school, that I would be successful and get married and have a family of my own someday. And I knew that occasionally, when one of my sons asked about ~~how things were when I was a young,~~ *my childhood* or about ~~his~~ *the* grandparents *they'd never met (they died six months apart, shortly after* ~~(who've been dead for several years),~~ or about that uncle who ~~died~~ *in my mother.* when he was just a kid, I wouldn't really mind telling them. *I got mine)* It would just be a story, *well,* after all, ~~but a story~~ as solid and *unshakable* real as the roof above our heads. ~~a story~~

The astute reader, meanwhile, has figured out that the genteel but elusive Professor Coates is a gay man who has let his tastes for late nights and rough trade get entirely out of hand. The mix in the story of downward spiral and screwball farce proves seductive.

"Primordia," from *I Am Dangerous,* is Johnson at his most experimental, putting an intriguing (and still comical) twist on another character headed toward meltdown. Its hallucinating and possibly gay college professor winds up deciding that his own nervous breakdown is "relatively unimportant . . . A waste of time, simply." He thus rejects any catharsis, epiphanies, or self-knowledge. "Sanctity," from the same collection, is a more sobering little masterpiece, pitting the will of a Catholic school nun against a religious-fanatic schoolboy engaged in "sudden, aberrant pursuit of his own doom." In positing the consequences of an "insatiable appetite for suffering" on the part of nun and schoolboy alike, Johnson pulls the reader into disturbing territory.

In other stories, the extremes that Johnson portrays are less plausible. "A Summer Romance," a story from *Distant Friends* written in the vein of Joyce Carol Oates, comes across as too rigged in its depiction of its teenage heroine in the company of a possible psychotic. "Hemingway's Cats" (from *I Am Dangerous*)–about a honeymoon couple threatened by the bride's tabloid-headline-worthy past–is equally difficult to believe. "Escalators," from *A Friendly Deceit,* again piles on the losses and tragedies to an improbable degree, although Elizabeth Ferber, in *The New York Times Book Review* (9 August 1992), found it to be "by far the collection's most powerful story." Occasionally Johnson also strains credulity by trying to put too much social message into a story, whether it concerns class antagonism ("Child of My Dreams," from *A Friendly Deceit*), homelessness ("Nickels and Dimes," also from *A Friendly Deceit*), or second-trimester abortions ("Little Death," from *I Am Dangerous*).

Other stories, while building to a plausibly frenzied or destructive climax, still fail to haunt the reader. Examples of these good, but not great, stories include "Wintering" from *Distant Friends,* about a widower shuttling like King Lear between his children's households; "Commitment" from *A Friendly Deceit,* about a suspicious wife who

succumbs to mental breakdown; and "Last Night" from *I Am Dangerous,* in which a man tries to pull out of a relationship with a suicidal woman. (Suicide, as backdrop or harrowing climax, is addressed in at least half a dozen stories.) Finally, there are some tales that feel more like curiosities than full-fledged stories, notably "The Metamorphosis" from *Distant Friends,* which reads like a highly compressed, transvestite variation on Nathanael West's *Day of the Locust* (1939), Tennessee Williams's *Suddenly Last Summer* (1958), and Robert Altman's *Nashville* (1975). "A&P Revisited" from *A Friendly Deceit,* a parody of John Updike's "A&P" in which a store clerk is only too glad to be robbed by a lesbian gang, is also something of an anomaly. Both of these stories have considerable verbal energy, but neither of them are terribly deep.

Johnson's fiction, at its best, is intricate without being ornate, distinguished by its finely distilled density of detail and its eye for inward conflict that never entirely surfaces into daylight reality. Such conflicts may occur within one troubled individual or within families, with outsiders catching only a fragmentary glimpse. In either instance Johnson is less interested in judging his characters than in examining the mechanics and caprice with which their actions give rise either to high drama or, just as often, no quantifiable consequence at all beyond an often suppressed memory. Johnson's pellucid prose does dependable justice to the subtleties and vagaries of the human behavior he observes, and his finest stories– including "El Paso," "The Burning," "Wildfires," "The Boarder," "Private Jokes," "Him," "A Dry Season," "Uncle Vic," "Evening at Home," "In the Deep Woods," "Sanctity," "I Am Dangerous," and "Alliances of Youth"–establish him as one of the leading practitioners of his art.

Interview:

Rebecca Ranson, "Writer's Profile," *Southern Voice,* 11 February 1993, p. 21.

Reference:

Gail Regier, "Distant Friends," *Southern Humanities Review,* 27 (Winter 1993): 81–83.

Rachel Maddux

(15 December 1912 – 19 November 1983)

Nancy A. Walker
Vanderbilt University

See also the Maddux entry in *DLB Yearbook: 1993.*

BOOKS: *The Green Kingdom* (New York: Simon & Schuster, 1957);

Abel's Daughter (New York: Harper, 1960);

A Walk in the Spring Rain (Garden City, N.J.: Doubleday, 1966; London: Sphere, 1970);

Fiction into Film: A Walk in the Spring Rain, by Maddux, Stirling Silliphant, and Neil D. Isaacs (Knoxville: University of Tennessee Press, 1970);

The Orchard Children (New York: Harper & Row, 1977);

Communication: The Autobiography of Rachel Maddux, and Her Novella, Turnip's Blood, edited, with an introduction, by Nancy A. Walker (Knoxville: University of Tennessee Press, 1991);

The Way Things Are: The Stories of Rachel Maddux, edited, with an introduction, by Walker (Knoxville: University of Tennessee Press, 1992).

SELECTED PERIODICAL PUBLICATIONS–
UNCOLLECTED: "Thoughts from a Country Orchard," by Maddux as "Apple Annie," *Buffalo River Review* (Linden, Tenn.), 1 October 1982 – 19 October 1983;

"A Princess in Oz," *Santa Barbara Review,* 1 (Fall/Winter 1993): 64–79.

Rachel Maddux (photograph by Mary Ellen Breyer; courtesy of Nancy A. Walker)

The short fiction of Rachel Maddux, most of it published posthumously in 1992, is difficult to categorize. In part she is a realist, depicting the lives of ordinary people and frequently evoking the texture and atmosphere of American life during the Depression and World War II. In her autobiography, *Communication: The Autobiography of Rachel Maddux, and Her Novella, Turnip's Blood* (1991), in fact, Maddux recalls her joy at discovering the fiction of Sherwood Anderson: "Those stories about people JUST LIKE THE ONES I KNEW, those very simple stories, where the words coming out of people's mouths sounded just like the words coming out of people's mouths–not going through the author's head first." Yet, just as Anderson's stories are not really simple, so Maddux's stories are suffused with elements of magic, the surreal, and the supernatural, incorporated so matter-of-factly as to seem all of a piece with the experiences of shop clerks, bus passengers, the wives of servicemen, and a good many children that are also represented. If there is a pervasive theme in Maddux's stories, it is the power of the human imagination to erase the boundary between fantasy and actuality–a power usually associated with children and one that contributes a note of whimsy to many of her stories.

Juanita Rachel Maddux was born on 15 December 1912 in Wichita, Kansas, the third child of Harry Maddux, a city employee, and Malisa (née Morison)

Maddux, who had grown up in a sod house on the Kansas prairie. In *Communication* Maddux portrays her father as subject to erratic mood swings and her mother as stoic and inattentive. Neither parent was equipped to recognize the precocity of their youngest child, and Maddux led an isolated childhood, adoring her much older sister, Erma, and seeking the larger world in books. After attending Wichita public schools, she studied at Wichita State University from 1930 to 1933 and then transferred to the University of Kansas, from which she was graduated in 1934 with a bachelor's degree in zoology. Although Maddux had written her first novel (now lost) at the age of nine, her ambition was to be a doctor, and she entered the University of Kansas Medical School in 1934. When health problems forced her to abandon her medical studies two years later, she settled in Kansas City, where between 1936 and 1941 she held a variety of jobs while beginning to write seriously. By the late 1930s Maddux was at the center of an informal salon of young writers, journalists, and artists who met at her apartment at 16 West Forty-third Street. Journalist Martin Quigley, in *Mr. Blood's Last Night: End of an Era in Journalism* (1980), recalls this group as "the only Bohemia in town" and describes Maddux as a "beautiful Junoesque young woman," a "reclusive mystic" who was "wise and gifted."

Maddux's career began on an auspicious note when her novella-length story "Turnip's Blood" was published in the prestigious *Story* magazine in 1936, followed by the short stories "Mother of a Child" and "We Are Each Other's Children." In 1938 "Turnip's Blood" was collected with novellas by Eric Knight, Helen Hull, Albert Maltz, and I. J. Kapstein—all originally published in *Story*—in the anthology *The Flying Yorkshireman*. The brief biographical statement that Maddux wrote for this volume suggests a lifelong commitment to writing and also indicates that she drew on her own experiences in her fiction:

> I began writing when I was six, due, I am sure, to the encouragement of my sister, Erma, who is indeed a joy, and "Turnip's Blood" is the first thing to come of it. There was a novel before "Turnip's Blood," written on brightly colored paper when I was seventeen, working nights in a newspaper office, but my pet white rat chewed it into small bits and built a house out of it for her family of six. It was a much better house than a novel. . . . "Rameses" in "Turnip's Blood" is my own dog who in real life sometimes answers to the name of Phaedeau.

The pet white rat figures in Maddux's story "The Little Woman," which is set in Depression-era Kansas City, as are the stories "No Smoking, No Spitting" and "They're Laughing." Maddux's stories of the Depression feature young people conscious of being survivors in a difficult time. They have little money but a great deal of spirit and optimism.

Maddux later claimed that rather than setting out deliberately to write "Turnip's Blood," she began hearing the words of the story in her head and finally wrote them down; she sent the story to her sister, who in turn sent it to *Story*. The novella has dreamlike qualities and, like other stories in Maddux's canon, deals with the anguish involved in moving from childhood to adulthood and losing one's sense of wonder and infinite possibility. Eve, a young woman in her twenties, has attended college but has chosen not to get a degree and supports herself cleaning offices at night. Her contentment with her simple life with her dog, Rameses, intrigues David Lawrence, a forty-year-old surgeon. Lawrence designs an intricate brace to satisfy Eve's dearest wish: to have Rameses sit at the table and eat with her. Shortly thereafter, Eve leaves to join a circus, but a fall from a horse confines her to a wheelchair, and her ensuing marriage to David signals the beginning of her adult life, marked by both fulfillment and loss.

The whimsy and originality of "Turnip's Blood" caught the attention of a Hollywood radio producer, Savington Crampton, who detoured to Kansas City to meet Maddux while on his way from the East Coast to California. The meeting began a lifelong friendship, and Maddux visited California several times in the late 1930s, apparently flirting with the idea of writing movie scripts, as did so many American writers during the 1930s and 1940s. Although she later scripted some of her own short fiction for stage performance and radio, Maddux continued to live and write in Kansas City.

By the time Maddux began to publish short fiction in *Story,* she had begun to envision her first and most ambitious novel, *The Green Kingdom,* which was not published until 1957. A comparison of *The Green Kingdom* and Maddux's short stories reveals how different she conceived the form and purpose of the two genres to be at this point in her career. *The Green Kingdom* is an elaborately plotted novel, its four sections corresponding to the four movements of the symphony that one of the central characters is composing. Although part of the inspiration for the novel, about a small group of people who find and for a time inhabit a mysterious green world beneath a mountain in the western United States, was undoubtedly the drought that exacerbated the Depression in the Midwest, the narrative has a visionary, utopian quality that lifts it from the realm of ordinary reality that anchors her short stories. *The Green Kingdom* deals with no less an issue than human survival—not merely physical, but also psychic and artistic. At the same time, however, Maddux's first novel insists, as do her stories, on the importance of the smallest moments of everyday existence; early in the narrative, two of the central characters are engaged in the ambitious—and essentially populist—project of creating a "Human Record" by encouraging ordinary people to write down the details of their everyday lives. And despite the precise details that locate most of the short stories on a map of reality rather than fantasy, the same imagination that could conceive of a completely green world gives many of the stories a fanciful or mysterious quality.

It is impossible to accurately date the stories that remained unpublished during Maddux's lifetime—twenty-four of the twenty-eight in *The Way Things Are: The Stories of Rachel Maddux* (1992)—but the inspiration for many of them can be traced to episodes in her life and places where she lived. "They're Laughing" captures the spirit of life in an American city during the Depression, not, as in the fiction of other writers of the period, by focusing on the most unfortunate victims of economic adversity but instead by depicting a group of young store clerks who participate in a barter economy and who hope to earn enough money for a real Christmas dinner by decorating their neighbor's store window for the season. The contrast between the resilience of the young clerks and the pomposity of the next-door store owner sounds a recurring theme in Maddux's fiction: a championing of individual human dignity against the forces of pride, greed, prejudice, and hypocrisy. Determined to keep up appearances rather than cope with reality, Mr. Wexler, Maddux writes, "hinted to the rest of us that if only we would walk briskly and wear white collars and make out invoices in triplicate and not call one another by our first names, the depression would simply go away." The unnamed narrator of "The Little Woman" seems to inhabit the same world, living from one paycheck to the next but taking comfort from such simple things as her pet white rat and a row of glass milk bottles to be redeemed for three cents apiece.

By 1941, when Maddux wrote her revealing autobiography in the form of a letter to a man she had met in California, she was engaged to marry King Baker, who had been studying engineering when military service interrupted his plans. The experiences of visiting Baker at Fort Leonard Wood, Missouri; moving with him to Occoquan, Virginia, following their December 1941 marriage; and waiting out the war in California while he was overseas are reflected in several of her stories as well as in her 1960 novel, *Abel's Daughter*. The stories set during the war years share some of the fanciful qualities of the Depression-era stories, but in most of them a sense of anxiety lurks just beneath the surface, and Maddux's letters and journals of the

Dust jacket for the posthumous collection (1992) of twenty-eight stories, twenty-four of which remained unpublished during Maddux's lifetime

period reveal that the war was not the only source of concern. Although she considered herself a professional writer by this time, she was painfully aware that she had given up a medical career and that her two years of medical school did not qualify her to be a nurse for the war effort. She was also preoccupied with the desire to have a child—children figure largely in her fiction—but fearful that her history of back problems and petit mal epilepsy made motherhood inadvisable. The themes of war and children converge in "Change," in which a pregnant young Navy wife goes to visit a friend's family for the weekend. Her adult fears about her husband, from whom she has not heard for three months, find an echo in a child's fear of passing the first grade and having to leave the teacher he loves.

More whimsical are the stories "Guaranteed" and "The House in the Woods." The former is narrated by a young woman on a long bus ride to visit her soldier-husband for a day. While the woman's anxieties about the war and her husband's fate are not part of the foreground of the story, they are subtly suggested by the comfort she derives from a fellow passenger, whom she secretly nicknames "Russet Eyes." Although she is initially amused by the simple terms in which he sees the world, she is ultimately reassured by his kindness and good manners and concludes that if circumstances required it, "he would have accepted the full responsibility for all of us, right up to the very last minute." "The House in the Woods" similarly deals with the yearning for stability during the uncertainty of wartime. When a young soldier is confined to an army hospital with a mysterious jaundice, he and his visiting wife construct a makeshift house in the nearby woods in order to give their brief times together a sense of domestic continuity. The female perspective in these stories casts World War II as a distant reality that nonetheless has the power to deeply unsettle American lives, and the publication of "The House in the Woods" in the February 1945 issue of Collier's suggests that the story had resonance with many couples for whom long bus rides and uncertainty had been daily realities for several years.

Maddux's years in Southern California are reflected in the lighthearted story "My Mexican Wife." The language barrier between the Americans and the Mexicans who work harvesting dates causes a series of comic misunderstandings, especially between the female narrator and a Mexican man who declares his love for her and announces in broken English that he wants to be her wife.

During the war years and into the early 1950s Maddux devoted much of her energy to completing The Green Kingdom, while King Baker returned from military service and began work in the electronics industry. A story that is simultaneously humorous and chilling, "Final Clearance" was inspired by the difficulty that Baker encountered in obtaining security clearance for a job as the Cold War gathered force. A recently widowed woman is shocked by the reappearance of her husband, who cannot be cleared for death until he can identify the county in which his mother-in-law was born. The couple drinks coffee and chats about the persistence of bureaucratic red tape, all the while aware that he is neither alive nor dead but instead captive in "Uncertainty."

A mixture of everyday detail and surreal elements also characterizes stories that explore the relationship between the individual and abstract concepts that loom so large they become personified. "No Special Hurry" derives its title from the epigraph quotation from Ernest Hemingway's A Farewell to Arms: the world kills "the very good and the very gentle and the very brave impartially. If you are none of these you can be sure it will kill you too but there will be no special hurry." The female protagonist is one of those for whom there is no special hurry, so when she is visited by Trouble, a familiar acquaintance, she briefly considers suicide but decides to face whatever Trouble has brought her this time. More whimsical is the story "My Walks with Confidence," in which Confidence is personified as a dapper little man with the annoying habit of disappearing just when he is needed. The first paragraph of the story locates it in the period immediately following World War II, although the theme is timeless: "Last week I read that President Truman had spoken with Confidence and that General Eisenhower had exuded Confidence in Paris, but how could Confidence have been in Washington and Paris last week when all the time I've had him right here locked in the cellar, where I hope he starves to death. I have put up with his eccentricities all I'm going to."

One of the most persistent and striking elements of Maddux's short fiction is her ability to imagine life from the perspective of a child. Eve, in "Turnip's Blood," weeps when she realizes that she is finally becoming an adult because she mourns the loss of childlike imagination. Although Maddux could understand the pain of such a loss, she apparently never really experienced it, and her child protagonists are utterly convincing. In an undated talk, published as "A Princess in Oz" in The Santa Barbara Review (Fall/Winter 1993), she defines imagination as "the re-capturing of one's childhood," when "there is a continual teeter-totter of the real and the imaginary, the subconscious and the conscious mind." The little girl in "Mother of a Child" comes to understand that "there is a difference between a real thing and something you pretend," but even this realization, which follows the girl's nine-month fantasy of being pregnant, is rendered precisely as a child would experience it. The fascination of a child with a celebrity is the subject of "You Nominate Yours; I'll Nominate Mine," in which the initial excitement of meeting an idol is replaced by painful shyness in her presence. For Paul, in "The Wonderful Rich Billboard of Kingston," the relative affluence of a neighborhood is measured by the quality of its billboards, so when he is taken to visit his wealthy aunt in a part of the city with no billboards at all, he concludes that the people there are very poor indeed. A few of Maddux's stories even seem to have been written with young readers in mind. "Loopus," for example, concerns a dog whose abnormally long tail is initially an embarrassment, but Loopus becomes a hero when his tail serves as a bridge during a flood.

By the time that Maddux's novel *Abel's Daughter,* a sensitive story of interracial understanding, was published in 1960, Maddux and her husband had left California to settle in rural Houston County, Tennessee, where they started an apple orchard and began to raise goats. The contrast between life in Los Angeles and the different values of the Tennessee countryside were embodied in her 1966 novel, *A Walk in the Spring Rain,* which was filmed in 1970 with Ingrid Bergman and Anthony Quinn. Although Maddux continued to write short stories, few of these were inspired by life in Tennessee, which tended to be the subject of her longer works, including the nonfiction *The Orchard Children* (1977), an account of Maddux and Baker's attempt to adopt two small children who had been abandoned by their parents. The only exception in the collection *The Way Things Are* is the story "Night's Comin', Miss Alice," which depicts the struggles of an elderly woman to keep up her small farm as her health fails.

Alice's determination is representative of Maddux's dedication to writing. During the last two years of her life she wrote a weekly column called "Thoughts from a Country Orchard" for the *Buffalo River Review,* a newspaper published in nearby Linden, Tennessee. Never able to earn a reliable living from her writing, she was nonetheless compelled to share her words with others. Years earlier, in the talk published posthumously as "A Princess in Oz," Maddux asserted that being a real writer has little to do with one's source of income: "If you are on the road toward great writing, if you even think you're on the road, then it will not matter if you do housework in Kansas, because you will know that you're a princess in Oz."

References:

Nancy Bradford, "Nature Spawns Novel for Rachel," *Nashville Tennessean,* 23 January 1966, pp. 3A, 6A;

Mary Ann Gibson, "A Look at Rachel Maddux: A Talented and Successful Author," *Tennessee Magazine* (August 1980): 10–11.

Papers:

Rachel Maddux's papers are housed in the special collections department of the Mugar Memorial Library at Boston University. The fourteen boxes of material contain correspondence, manuscripts, portions of her journal, and miscellaneous papers.

Jill McCorkle
(7 July 1958 –)

Robert A. Beuka
Louisiana State University

See also the McCorkle entry in *DLB Yearbook: 1987.*

BOOKS: *The Cheer Leader* (Chapel Hill, N.C.: Algonquin, 1984);

July 7th: A Novel (Chapel Hill, N.C.: Algonquin, 1984);

Tending to Virginia (Chapel Hill, N.C.: Algonquin, 1987; London: Cape, 1989);

Ferris Beach: A Novel (Chapel Hill, N.C.: Algonquin, 1990);

Crash Diet: Stories (Chapel Hill, N.C.: Algonquin, 1992);

Carolina Moon: A Novel (Chapel Hill, N.C.: Algonquin, 1996);

Final Vinyl Days and Other Stories (Chapel Hill, N.C.: Algonquin, 1998).

OTHER: "Dear Is a Greeting, Love Is A Closing," in *New Stories by Southern Women,* edited by Mary Ellis Gibson (Columbia: University of South Carolina Press, 1989), pp. 203–212;

"Secret Places," in *A Place Called Home: Twenty Writing Women Remember,* edited by Mickey Pearlman (New York: St. Martin's Press, 1996), pp. 86–97;

"The Snipe Hunt," in *Off the Beaten Path: Stories of Place,* edited by Joseph Barbato and Lisa Weinerman Horak (New York: North Point, 1988), pp. 59–74.

SELECTED PERIODICAL PUBLICATIONS–
UNCOLLECTED: "The Spell of Her Beautiful Garden," *Seventeen,* 43 (October 1984): 136–137;

"Our Summer Vacations," *Southern Living,* 25 (January 1990): 110–111;

"Blacktop Carnival," *Southern Living,* 25 (October 1990): 172;

"Listening to Flannery," *Flannery O'Connor Bulletin,* 24 (1995–1996): 127–128;

"Sidewise," *American Scholar,* 61 (Winter 2000): 160.

Jill McCorkle

Jill McCorkle is often hailed as a leading voice in the fiction of the "New South," a chronicler of the lives of everyday people whose strong connections to family and place help them to persevere through relationship woes and the travails of their seemingly prosaic, yet emotionally complicated lives. McCorkle's writing is characterized by her adeptness at catching the voice of the common person and her keen eye for detail as she precisely captures the trappings of working-class and middle-class life. Her work is often set in the small towns of what has come to be called the "New South," locales where generationally rooted sense of place is

186

slowly giving way to the interchangeable landmarks of late-twentieth-century America: strip malls, chain restaurants and hotels, and faceless apartment complexes. Against this bland backdrop McCorkle maps her characters' lives, imbuing what might otherwise be considered a mundane existence with vitality and depth through her balanced use of caustic wit and compassion for her characters. Noted from the outset of her career as an accomplished novelist, McCorkle has, with the publication of two short-story sequences in recent years, also established herself as a highly skilled short-story writer.

Jill Collins McCorkle was born in Lumberton, North Carolina, on 7 July 1958 to John Wesley McCorkle Jr., a postal worker, and Melba Ann (née Collins) McCorkle, a medical secretary. After graduating from Lumberton High School in 1976, McCorkle attended the University of North Carolina (UNC) at Chapel Hill, honing her writing skills under the tutelage of Max Steele and Louis Rubin and graduating with highest honors and a B.A. in creative writing in 1980. She went on to earn an M.A. in creative writing from Hollins College in Virginia in 1981. Already a promising talent in her university years, McCorkle published her first short story, "Mrs. Lela's Fig Tree," in the Fall 1979 issue of the UNC literary magazine *Cellar Door,* while her second published story, "Bare Facts," won her the Jesse Rehder Prize for fiction, the most prestigious writing award offered by UNC. Subsequently, while in the writing program at Hollins, McCorkle won the university's Andrew James Purdy Prize for fiction. After graduation she spent a brief period working as an office receptionist in New York City before relocating to Florida, where she was a teacher in the Brevard County public school system in 1982–1983. For a short time she held the position of acquisitions librarian at the Florida Institute of Technology Library in Melbourne, Florida, and in 1984 she returned to Chapel Hill, taking a job as a secretary at the medical school at UNC.

During the various moves and job changes in her postcollege years, McCorkle continued writing, completing her first novel, *The Cheer Leader* (1984), while in New York and her second, *July 7ʰ* (1984), during her years in Florida. Her return to native grounds coincided with McCorkle's explosion onto the literary scene; in 1984, the year she returned to Chapel Hill, the relatively young publishing house of Algonquin Books made the bold decision to publish both of McCorkle's "first" novels simultaneously. This unprecedented move garnered a good deal of attention for McCorkle, and the previously unknown author had suddenly arrived, to a good deal of critical acclaim. Her newfound status as successful author soon enabled

McCorkle to leave behind the world of the office receptionist, and in 1986 she accepted a lectureship in creative writing at UNC. Still, her years as a receptionist were not all for naught, for while working at the UNC medical school she met her future husband, medical student Dan Shapiro. The couple relocated to Boston in 1989, and McCorkle accepted a position teaching creative writing at Tufts University. After returning for a time to North Carolina in 1989, McCorkle and her husband moved again to Boston in 1992, and she accepted the position of Briggs-Copeland Lecturer at Harvard University. McCorkle continues to live in the Boston area with her husband and two children, where she serves on the creative-writing faculty at Bennington College, Bennington, Vermont.

McCorkle already had published four highly regarded novels and was a veteran short-story writer—having placed stories in such popular magazines as *Atlantic Monthly, The Southern Review, Cosmopolitan,* and *Seventeen*—when she published her first short-story collection, *Crash Diet,* in 1992. A collection of eleven stories that portray the relationship troubles and consequent identity crises of a series of female protagonists, *Crash Diet* garnered wide critical acclaim, winning the New England Bookseller's Award in 1993. In 1992 Brad Hooper, reviewer for *Booklist,* praised the "remarkable sensibility" McCorkle demonstrates in the collection, and in the same year Pam Houston, reviewer for *The Los Angeles Times,* called *Crash Diet* a "generous, warm and honest book." In these eleven short stories—nine of which are told in the first person—McCorkle presents several women who are struggling but undefeated, generating a sense of empathy for each through the same balance of hard-earned humor and pathos recognizable to fans of her previous novels.

The title story, which opens *Crash Diet,* offers what might be an apt metaphor for the collection as a whole: the story of a perpetually overweight, recently separated woman whose dwindling sense of self-worth is measured in the lost inches of her own shrinking body, as she embarks upon a "crash diet" in the wake of her separation and discovery of the "other woman" in her husband's life. Sandra, the first-person narrator, shows the tenacity that characterizes so many of the women in this collection with her opening words of the story, in which she handles her husband's departure with defiant nonchalance: "Kenneth left me on a Monday morning before I'd even had the chance to mousse my hair," she announces. Ultimately a survivor, like all of the women in *Crash Diet,* Sandra nonetheless struggles to find herself after the dissolution of her relationship; indeed, she is literally "losing" herself over the course of the story, as her largely unconscious yet obsessional avoidance of food causes her to

Dust jacket for McCorkle's 1992 collection, comprising mostly first-person accounts of optimistic women struggling with relationship problems and identity crises

lose so much weight that she eventually ends up in the hospital.

The turning point of the story comes after Sandra's release from the hospital, when the selfish Kenneth comes to visit only, it turns out, to have her sign the divorce papers. As her despondent husband informs Sandra that his relationship with the other woman has ended, Sandra signs the papers in what she refers to as "the script of a fat person." Thus liberated by her own signature, Sandra shows a newfound acceptance of herself in an observation that is characteristic of McCorkle's biting sense of humor: "some things you just can't shake; part of me will always be a fat person and part of Kenneth will always be gutter slime." The story closes, appropriately enough, with a successful dinner party thrown by Sandra, whose acceptance of food is symbolic of her newfound sense of self. In both literal and figurative terms, Sandra has learned to emphasize "growth" over "loss," finding that what remains at the end of her dissolved relationship is nothing less than herself.

The thematic concerns of "Crash Diet" resurface in several other stories as McCorkle shapes the collection around the dominant, recurring theme of women

surviving troubles with men. "Man Watcher" is a loosely plotted tale that chronicles the observations of the narrator, a divorced woman named Lucinda, on the various types of men she sees. Lucinda has so honed her precise—perhaps embittered—powers of observation that she proposes to write a "book about it all, all the different types of the species. You know it would sort of be like Audubon's bird book. I'd call it *Male Homo Sapiens: What You Need to Know to Identify Different Breeds*."

This categorizing approach also informs the stories "First Union Blues" and "Comparison Shopping," two more first-person narratives that find their protagonists immersed in unsatisfying relationships, longing for more passionate relationships from the past while facing an unrewarding present and uncertain future. In each of these stories McCorkle uses diametrically opposed male characters (the virile, romantic, reckless man of the past versus the conventionally successful, staid, unappealing man of the present) as foils to help express her narrator's longings and insecurities. Each of these tales also ends with a moment of sudden affirmation, as McCorkle's heroines offer variations on the concluding declaration of Maureen Dummer, narrator of "First Union Blues," who—after facing her relationship crises and determining to survive on her own—concludes simply, "I want to live."

The majority of the stories in this collection are also united by McCorkle's precisely realistic treatment of the New South landscape. Typically setting her tales in small southern towns, like that of her native Lumberton, where the once time-honored sense of community identity is rapidly eroding, McCorkle explores the emotional crises of her female protagonists against the background of what is becoming an indistinguishable and often alienating terrain. Amid denizens of condo "communities" and interchangeable subdivisions, McCorkle's heroines often struggle in discovering their own identity within a homogeneous environment.

In this regard the reader senses the irony in statements such as Maureen's in "First Union Blues": "before I knew it, I was . . . living in a condo with a wreath on every wall and a big hooked rug that I bought at the outlet mall over near the airport. That place has got everything you might want and then some. Everything." When McCorkle's narrators work toward defining themselves against such an uninspiring backdrop, the effort is not always successful. As Norlinda, the narrator of "Comparison Shopping," comments, noting the similarity of behavior and identity in her subdivision, "That's how it is here in Windhaven Estates; we all do the same things. . . . I'm starting to get the hang of it now, though it hasn't been easy."

McCorkle's precise brand of realism, most prominently featured in her attention to the details of the contemporary New South landscape, puts her in the company of such other masters of contemporary realism as Randall Jarrell and Bobbie Ann Mason. For many critics this facet of McCorkle's writing is what makes her stories so effective. Jack Butler, for example, in his 1992 review of *Crash Diet* in *The New York Times*, praised McCorkle's convincing, acute depiction of the New South while noting the centrality of place in the struggles of McCorkle's characters: "It is their milieu that these women seek to escape. Jill McCorkle renders it brilliantly, again and again delivering the shock of recognition. 'That's just how it *is*,' readers across the country will say to themselves in repeated delight." Others disagree, arguing that McCorkle's attention to the minutiae of contemporary existence can at times be overwhelming, undercutting the force of the story itself. Even Butler, in the same review, goes on to argue that the "repetition of similar locales and tacky detail becomes numbing after a time. It begins to seem an easy trick, relied on too often. Sometimes you feel as though you were *in* Wal Mart, not just enjoying a wickedly comic vision of the place."

Ultimately, however, McCorkle's close scrutiny of the trappings of late-twentieth-century existence serves as more than a means toward exhibiting her keen sense of humor—though in a fictional world where residents live on subdivision streets named after brands of liquor, and "Mr. Coffee" machines become symbols of life's greater concerns, her stories certainly accomplish that aim. The bulk of the stories here and in her subsequent collection, *Final Vinyl Days* (1998), demonstrate that McCorkle is profoundly concerned with the dynamics of place. Particularly for an author who grew up in a small, traditional southern town, the evolution of the small-town southern landscape in recent decades poses not only physical, but also emotional and psychological concerns. And while McCorkle traced the suburbanization of the small-town South in her 1990 novel, *Ferris Beach*, in her short fiction the landscapes of the past are for the most part already gone.

McCorkle acknowledged the importance of geography to her work in a personal interview in 1999, noting that the "sense of place" exhibited in her stories is the primary autobiographical element she sees in her fiction as a whole. Her childhood in Lumberton coincided with a profound change in the landscape of the small-town South, a period the author refers to as a "time of transition." Feeling that she grew up on the "cusp between the Old South and the New South," McCorkle sees the yearning for connection to past landscapes as a factor in much of her fiction. Indeed, as she wrote in her essay "Secret Places," included in the volume *A Place Called Home: Twenty Writing Women Remember* (1996), this need to inhabit vanished but remembered landscapes is a central facet of her fictional endeavor to begin with: "My wish would be that every scene from our lives is preserved on a neat little stage and all we have to do is step in," the author writes, concluding that her own indelible connection to the landscape of her youth is what fuels much of her writing: "It's not the place so much as what I have taken away from it; the images and smells and sounds. There is a feeling, like having a secret; it's powerful and wonderful and it's what keeps people and places alive. It's why people have the urge to go back and why they tell stories."

McCorkle's keen interest in capturing the dynamics of landscape and creating a sense of place illuminate a number of stories in *Crash Diet*, none more so than the haunting "Migration of the Love Bugs," a story that uses the seemingly aimless, never ending migratory patterns of the southern insect known as the "love bug" as a metaphor for the plight of the narrator, Alice, a woman who finds herself dislocated from her home of forty years, an apartment near Boston Common, and now living in what she describes as a "tin can" of a mobile home in a Florida retirement village. While her husband, Frank, remains incredulous to her sense of

MAD DOG   *use Marilyn Poem*

Well tuned instrument that begins to snap

If I were a dog I'dve been put down by now. Mad Dog. I dated a boy once who loved fine wines/ drank mogen David md 20 20-- maddog. I am of the frightened aggressive. I will bite you before you bite me. I am one the dog shrinks can't cure. They try prozac/ etc.

I am the liberal survivalist. I have everything but a gun. Don't believe in guns. I tell you what I do believ ein though. Dogs and baseball bats. come in here uninvited and I'm likely to brain you good and tell the dogs to haul you out to the woods.

When I am old I want to live with Scottie girl men I'll shell peas

pets are a good way to keep others away. Dogs/ cats/ birds who fly around and shit through the house. All of that is a positive thing if you don't want visitors. Cats hauling in half of a bird or mouse. That's what I told Woody. I said when you leave I'll replace you pound for pound with DOG. I got myself a Newfoundland and a Great Dane/ I call them ? and Bjorn. They weight the bed just right. I got a little papillion named ? to account for that five pound fluctuation he gets around the weekend. she likes to sleep on top of the newfie and rests on his great big neck like a little hood ornament.

my ? said why don't you grow up? Well i have. i have had my period a few times and everything. I'm so grown up I now have what I call the major period and the minor period. It just so happens that what I always wanted in life was dogs/ all sizes and shapes and colors. A whole universe that i could teach to get along with one another, share, be family. I've done that. If only the world could take note.

But it's not a grown up thing, they say.

And I say and men walking around a pasture swinging sticks after little balls is grown up? Racing cars around a track? Some women grow up to have their boobs enlarged and some to ?? Now why is a hobby in pet management any different?

Marissa clicks through hallways like a poodle all coifed and painted up.. What a bitch. I think if Marilyn Monroe had been a bitch she'd have been a lab. They'd have dressed her up like a poodle again and again but deep down a lab and who better for a lab to hook up with than a man with balls. *Where have you gone Joe D dead. Everybody*

Feminists are called Rabid

I don't have a whole lot of people friends. Go figure. I tell them to stop their goddamned yapping and get a life. I tell them that their longwinded tales of depression and neurosis bore the hell out of me. I'd rather watch back to back Jerry lewis movies while getting my toenails removed. yeah yeah yeah, I hear you.

Get on with it.

Woody had me wearing a choke. The kind with spikes. Figuratively of course though if you could make a wife wear one legally without being called Mr. Sade, he'd have done that. Like he'd say we are going to do this and we are not going to do that.

Disgruntled

When I feel good I write myself letters

Like Do NOT cuss out strangers Do NOT Rip off the ...

Page from the working-draft typescript for McCorkle's uncollected story "Mad Dog" (Collection of the author)

longing for the home they have left behind (he thinks of their new setting, where every mobile home has a "view of the driving range," as the Promised Land), Alice sees things differently: "I was thinking that if this was the Promised Land, Moses sure dealt me a bad hand," she muses. McCorkle credits the inspiration for this story to personal experience, noting that during her first period in Boston, when she and her husband lived off Boston Common, she had further occasion to reflect on the importance of home and a sense of place. For though the locales are reversed, again in "Migration of the Love Bugs," the author contrasts a richly depicted vision of the power of home with the desultory experience of life in a prefabricated landscape.

If such concerns over the alienating nature of the contemporary landscape, coupled with the problematic romantic relationships of her protagonists and their often humorous sense of perseverance, are the characteristics that define the typical story in *Crash Diet*, worth noting as well are those stories in which McCorkle breaks out of this mold. Two such efforts are the first-person narratives "Words Gone Bad" and "Waiting for Hard Times to End"; in each of these stories McCorkle experiments with her heroines' voices, offering narrators who stand in counterpoint to the majority of others in the collection.

In "Words Gone Bad" McCorkle tells the story of Mary, an aging African American janitor at a southern university whose dissatisfaction with the pace of social reform, and larger sense of spiritual longing, are captured in the image of the wasted words she must erase daily from the classroom blackboards. After contrasting the harsh realities of her own life with the idealism and dignity represented by the resonant words and phrases of the Civil Rights movement, McCorkle's narrator concludes that the hollowness of words themselves is tied to the larger social dilemma she faces: "there's always more words on the board, words and words and more words in their dusty slanted lines of white and yellow, erasers filled with words gone old or bad or both." Through Mary, McCorkle offers another angle of vision—her most explicitly political in the collection—on life in the New South.

"Waiting for Hard Times to End" is told by Bunny, an adolescent girl whose own coming-of-age drama is played out against her interest in the affairs of her sister, Rhonda, whom she idolizes. Rhonda has left home and, unbeknownst to the naive Bunny, is leading an increasingly desperate life of bad jobs and abusive relationships, one that will eventually end with her murder in a sleazy hotel. Enamored of what she imagines to be her sister's "glamorous" lifestyle, Bunny daily awaits the mail for another postcard from Rhonda describing her most recent adventures.

Perfectly capturing Bunny's naiveté, McCorkle builds the dramatic irony of the story, creating empathy for her narrator while suggesting the inevitability of both Rhonda's demise and Bunny's painful but necessary emergence into self-awareness and womanhood. Eventually coming to understand the painful reality behind the facade of her sister's words, Bunny determines at the end of the story to forge her own path, in a closing affirmation that is one of the most honest in the collection. Like "Words Gone Bad," "Waiting for Hard Times to End" questions the veracity of language itself, a telling gesture in a collection of primarily first-person narratives. With these two stories McCorkle further suggests the vulnerability that lies behind the spunky facade of the majority of her narrators.

Despite her success with the first-person form, perhaps the strongest stories in this collection are the two third-person narratives, "Gold Mine" and "Departures." In each of these moving, lyrical stories, one can sense the liberating influence of the third-person perspective: freed from the necessity of creating another narrative voice, McCorkle is able to imbue her characters with a newfound depth, using the third-person form to maximum effect in portraying the sort of vulnerability that is only hinted at in the first-person narratives of the collection.

"Gold Mine" tells the story of Ruthie Kates, a mother of two who, along with her now-estranged husband, Jim, had years ago opened and lovingly restored an old motel along the main highway of a seaside town in South Carolina. The inevitable ruin of this endeavor is foretold in the first line of the story: "The day the interstate opened was the day Highway 301 and Petrie, South Carolina, died." Another rumination on the parallels between place and experience, this story offers the now nearly defunct motel as a symbol of the dissolution of the romantic relationship between Ruthie and Jim. For just as Ruthie's Goodnight Inn has been replaced by one of the generic chain hotels that have sprouted up along the new interstate, I-95, Ruthie herself has been replaced by a younger woman named Barbara: "Barbara is like I-95. She is fast and lively and young, and Ruthie is 301, miles of tread stains and no longer the place to go."

McCorkle shapes the narrative as a series of recollections Ruthie experiences over the course of a single afternoon, as she stands watch over her two young children by the pool of the nearly abandoned hotel. Contrasting the youthful optimism that had Ruthie and Jim believing their hotel—and their relationship—to be a "gold mine" with the painful experience of abandonment, McCorkle paves the way for the return of Jim that evening, a moment captured in breathtaking imagery that belies the fact that Ruthie's optimism remains

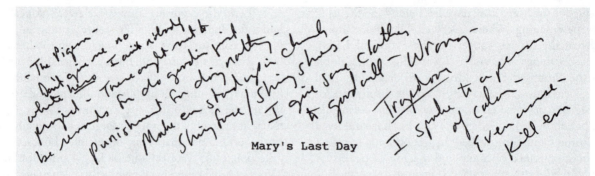

Mary's Last Day

At ten am the temperature has already hit 100 and the
weather station says it will keep rising. Mary squints out at
the thin red line, the glare from the tin roof of her porch
making everything in the yard wavy. The big oak tree that was
big when she was only seven and climbing up its rough trunk, nose
pressed between chunks of bark as she grabbed and pulled herself
up, quivers overhead. Now she is seventy one and it is the
hottest summer that she can ever recall, every summer of her life
spent here in this very house, the corner of an old black
neighborhood that has slowly been taken over by young college
students within walking distance of the campus where Mary spent
the last forty years of her life working, sweeping and mopping
and cleaning up somebody else's garbage, somebody that knows
better or ought to given what their folks pay for them to sit and
straddle their long legs out, toes of dirty sneakers marking up
the walls. Retirement. Shit.

She has worked every day of her grown life. She has
drycleaned, breathing steam and chemicals, she could feel the
folds of her lungs starching and stiffening. She has kept other
peoples babies, changed their stinking diapers and whispered the
love words when young mama is out somewheres looking like she
might be somebody in a business suit. They say oh Mary, how we

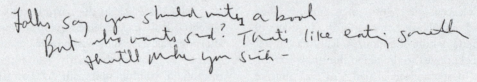

Page from the working-draft typescript for McCorkle's story "Mary's Last Day" (Collection of the author)

tempered by pain. The use of third-person mode in this story allows McCorkle to avoid the sometimes cloying tendency in her first-person narratives toward strident self-affirmations, allowing her to create instead a tale that is at once personal and universal. As reviewer Pam Houston notes, "Taking the biggest risk in the book, 'Gold Mine' allows the abandoned Ruthie to find her strength not through determination and independence, but through acceptance and forgiveness."

Certainly the most widely praised story in *Crash Diet* is "Departures," an elegiac story of an aging woman's ongoing attempt to come to terms with her husband's death. Three years after the passing of her husband, Walter, Anna Craven continues to mourn his departure, attempting to stave off loneliness by spending the majority of her time in crowded shopping malls and airports, "any place where she can be surrounded by people without having to interact with any of them." The story shifts between scenes of Anna alone in crowed places, where she takes solace in the people who surround her, to passages that find her recalling moments of her life with Walter. Anna's recurring recollection of youthful summers at a seaside cottage with Walter and their growing family provides a yearning, lyrical counterpoint to her life now, which despite her tendency to immerse herself in crowds, is defined by her isolation.

Critical reaction to "Departures" has been overwhelmingly positive, with the majority of reviewers noting this story as the finest one in the collection. Characteristic of the critical response is the assessment of Greg Johnson, who reviewed the story for *The Georgia Review* in 1992. Johnson sees the story as a turning point of sorts for McCorkle as a short-story writer: "Fully and compassionately imagined, 'Departures' has the force of a miniature novel, and it suggests the author's possible development out of her more facile and superficial first-person approach." Indeed, McCorkle herself has noted "Departures" as one of her favorite stories of the collection, saying that it marked a significant change for her as a writer. With its depth of emotion, its nuanced narrative voice, and its sophisticated yet understated play with narrative time frames and recurring imagery, this story does suggest McCorkle's development as a short-story writer, presaging in both its themes and its technique stories that appear in her next story collection, *Final Vinyl Days.*

While one can certainly find thematic links between *Crash Diet* and McCorkle's 1998 collection, *Final Vinyl Days,* the latter collection also reveals new directions in both form and content, developments related to changes in McCorkle's life in the intervening years. In 1992, the year *Crash Diet* was published, the author and her husband again relocated to Boston, and

McCorkle left behind the southern milieu that featured so prominently in many of her earlier stories. Tending to a growing family while continuing her career in the classroom, McCorkle nonetheless in these years saw her writing career flourish; in 1993 she received the New England Booksellers' Association award for her body of work, while in 1996 her novel *Carolina Moon* was published to wide critical acclaim. *Final Vinyl Days* cemented her reputation as a short-story writer. This collection of nine stories reveals a maturing artist whose increasing mastery of the short-story form is paralleled by a heightened thematic interest in mortality, vulnerability, and the uncertainty of life.

If the title story of her previous collection suggests the dominant themes of *Crash Diet* as a whole, much the same can be said of the title story of *Final Vinyl Days.* This first-person narrative is told by a post-collegiate record store employee and college-town hanger-on—one of three male protagonists in the collection—who laments the passing of what he considers the golden age of rock and roll, as evidenced by the advent of the compact disc and the increasing irrelevance of his store and his role—seller of "classic" used vinyl albums. The story is, among other things, a miniature compendium of rock and roll history, as the narrator's mounting identity crisis and increasing string of unsatisfactory one-night stands are set to a soundtrack of classic rock references to Roy Orbison, The Beatles, and The Byrds. This characteristic alone makes the story emblematic of the collection as a whole, in that all of the stories in *Final Vinyl Days* make references to popular songs, a technique that suggests McCorkle's shaping of the collection—consciously or otherwise—in the form of a record album.

McCorkle's recurring musical references are more than a gimmicky narrative trick, however; in "Final Vinyl Days" the author makes the link between the pop music of bygone days and her protagonist's growing awareness of his mortality and the passing of time, as well as his mounting sense of alienation from the world in which he lives. And in this sense, "Final Vinyl Days" uses the musical metaphor in a way that reverberates throughout the collection, as the majority of the stories here feature characters who, often in reaction to the loss of a loved one, confront the uncertainty of a finite existence in an often confounding world. For the narrator of "Final Vinyl Days," this uncertainty takes the form of his stubborn rejection of everything new in the music world. Shaken by the deaths of his musical idols Marvin Gaye and Del Shannon, the narrator redoubles his efforts to live his life in the past; at the close of the story he fantasizes about his college sweetheart and their "perfect 1970 romance," even as he relates his increasing penchant for one-night stands

Dust jacket for McCorkle's 1998 collection of stories set mostly in the recently urbanized New South

with a "series of younger and younger women," who leave a "mountain of CD covers dumped on my floor." With this telling final image, McCorkle suggests her narrator's emotional imprisonment, and this theme is one that recurs in the stories that follow "Final Vinyl Days" in the collection.

A particularly noteworthy story is "A Blinking, Spinning, Breathtaking World," which chronicles a recently divorced young mother's emotional break-down. In the face of an impending snowstorm, the protagonist, Charlotte, takes her son to an indoor amusement/theme park called Wonderland, and both the threatening winter weather and the carnivalesque setting of the action become metaphors for Charlotte's emotional turmoil. Though at one point Charlotte had been on the point of "begging" her husband to "start all over," even willing to "pretend that he had never cheated on her," by the end of the story it becomes apparent that Charlotte's sense of isolation is as all-encompassing as it is debilitating. After suffering a panic attack at the amusement park, Charlotte hurries her son back to their car, and McCorkle closes the story by chronicling Charlotte's thoughts in the car, using the carnival metaphor once again to emphasize the uncer-

tainty that leaves her entrapped: "There was no magic potion; no incantation to make the world stop blinking, stop spinning. She could only hope that her body would keep moving–slow step by slow step–to the lines for the rest of the breathtaking rides. But for now, she was scared frozen, scared to death."

The cold, haunting closing of this story signals a larger change of perspective in the collection as a whole; for while in *Crash Diet* McCorkle chose to conclude almost all of the stories with declarations of defiant, optimistic perseverance, in *Final Vinyl Days* the prevailing tone is less self-assured, more cognizant of the fragility of life. Part of this shift had to do with her own change of perspective; in particular, McCorkle has noted that the responsibilities of motherhood influenced her writerly perspective. Less inclined to identify with the unfettered optimism of some of her earlier protagonists, McCorkle notes that in the years preceding *Final Vinyl Days* she found herself becoming increasingly interested in offering more nuanced portrayals of vulnerable characters and their relationships. This change in perspective can be seen in such efforts as "Last Request" and "Dysfunction 101," two stories whose female characters, even as adults, suffer emotionally from their parents' legacies of infidelity and abandonment. While both protagonists vow to go on with their lives, the prevailing mood at the close of both of these stories is one of acceptance rather than defiant survival, a feeling captured by the narrator of "Dysfunction 101": "First, you recognize what was wrong . . . and then you *accept* it. This does not mean that you *agree* with it, just that you say, yes, that is what happened. And then you walk off and leave it there; it is not your mess to clean up."

Despite McCorkle's more reflective tone in *Final Vinyl Days,* the collection as a whole is still spiked by the author's trademark wit, and several stories recall the sensibility of *Crash Diet.* Among these is "Paradise," the opening story of the collection, which tells the story of the blossoming romance between a couple named Adam and Eve. Setting their initial meeting at the wedding of mutual friends in small-town North Carolina, McCorkle uses her keen eye for kitschy detail in constructing a hilariously precise rendering of the trappings of a southern wedding. The couple manage to escape this dubious Eden and—uncharacteristically for McCorkle—the story's end finds them presumably embarked on a happy life together.

Another platform for McCorkle's biting humor can be found in "Your Husband is Cheating On Us," an imaginative piece structured as a monologue from a spurned mistress directed toward her lover's wife. Now that a third woman has entered the picture, the mistress—who refers to herself as "Big Foot"—senses a sisterhood of sorts with the wife and counsels her on what she should do about her philandering husband. After deriding the new, second mistress ("she works at Blockbuster Video and wears way too much eye makeup"), Big Foot concludes, "Tell him he better shape his butt up or you are out of here, sister. Make him sweat." Although perhaps not the most successful story in the collection, "Your Husband is Cheating On Us" manages to generate an idiosyncratic sense of compassion for the brassy Big Foot and her would-be friend.

But the most adventurous stories in the collection—and ultimately the most powerful—are those in which McCorkle confronts the pain of the loss of loved ones, a recurring theme in *Final Vinyl Days* that resonates with the author's life experience. In the years that followed the publication of her previous story collection she saw the passing of several relatives and old family friends. The author notes the dislocating effect of this kind of loss, explaining that she found herself "suddenly in a place in life where a lot of those people weren't around anymore." Particularly painful was the loss of her father, and McCorkle says that the grief she

experienced at his passing found its way into her subsequent fictional work.

"Life Prerecorded," one of the finest stories in the collection, centers on the emotional struggles of a young mother-to-be whose anxiety over impending childbirth manifests itself in a series of dreams she has about now-departed loved ones. Autobiographical in nature—the author describes it as the story in the collection "closest to me"—"Life Prerecorded" recalls in both its complex structure and its often elegiac tone the gem of her first collection, "Departures." Evidencing McCorkle's increasing confidence with narrative structure, the story shifts time frames and moods rapidly, in a narrative rhythm that mirrors the emotional state of its narrator, who describes her feelings as "discombobulated."

Yet, despite her frenetic play with narrative structure, McCorkle manages to imbue the story with a lyrical tone, as the narrator's recurring memories of loved ones from her past—particularly her now-departed grandmother—coupled with her newfound friendship with an elderly widower from her apartment building, mark the story as another concerned with the importance of the past and her characters' connections to it. And while the narrator's imagined conversations with her grandmother and conjured images of her neighbor's wife may be illusions, they serve to quell her emotional turmoil, and with that perhaps McCorkle suggests that these are the necessary illusions. "What we don't know is enormous," the narrator at one point opines, a fitting comment in a story that revolves around the mystery of love and loss and the yearning for permanence.

The final two stories in the collection share some of the thematic concerns of "Life Prerecorded." The first of these, "It's a Funeral! RSVP," stands as the collection's most straightforward attempt to confront the pain and mystery of death. The story of a woman who plans "early funerals," celebrations of life for those who are about to die, "It's a Funeral" plays a cathartic role in a collection haunted throughout by the loss of loved ones. While some townspeople have taken to referring to the protagonist derisively as the "Mistress of Death," she sees her funeral catering business differently, considering the parties she throws to be offering a model of hope for the living as well as the dying. In a passage that recalls McCorkle's own life experiences in the 1990s, the narrator offers the rationale behind her new business: "I was about to turn forty and already many of my very favorite people were dead. I had children, and I wanted them to grow up with a clear vision of hope. A sense of nature and art and all that has walked this earth before them." And this adventurous story, part linear narrative and part philosophical essay, works toward establishing such a vision of hope, providing a redemptive, healing moment in the collection.

The final story, "The Anatomy of Man," extends McCorkle's philosophical excursion, closing the collection on an experimental, spiritually questing note. This inventive third-person narrative is focalized through the perceptions of a young pastor who, after closing up his church for the night, immerses himself in the baptismal pool, in what has become a ritualistic event for him. The narrative takes the form of an interior monologue, as the pastor attempts to come to grips with his spiritual uncertainty, frustrated sexuality, and longing for a renewed sense of purpose in life. Finding the greatest solace in memories of his deceased great-uncle, a man whose visionary qualities had him eventually branded insane and sent to an institution, the pastor works through these memories in an effort to understand his own fading spiritual vision. As he contemplates leaving the church, a voice comes from the darkness, advising the pastor to "Do things. . . . Keep the doors open." Fittingly, McCorkle's deus ex machina, appearing on the last page of the collection, does not provide neat closure for this story or for the collection, instead emphasizing openness.

In his 1990 review for the *Atlanta Journal* of McCorkle's novel *Ferris Beach* (1990), critic S. Keith Graham remarked that by that point, six years after her stunning literary debut, "everyone this side of Richmond recognizes Ms. McCorkle as one of the best in the new generation of Southern writers." After the success of *Ferris Beach,* with not only another novel but also two compelling short-story sequences to her credit since that time, Jill McCorkle's literary reputation has spread. A wickedly funny writer who has become more than a humorist, and a precise chronicler of the landscape of the New South whose finest work nevertheless easily transcends regional labels, McCorkle has proven herself to be nothing less than a first-rate novelist and short-story writer. Currently, McCorkle is working on a novel and another short-story collection, which is sure to be good news for fans of McCorkle's increasingly inventive and searching brand of realism.

Interviews:

Bob Summer, "Jill McCorkle," *Publishers Weekly* (12 October 1990): 44–45;

Ellen Lesser, "Voices with Stories to Tell: A Conversation with Jill McCorkle," *Southern Review,* 26 (Winter 1990): 53–64;

Janice O'Leary, "Interview with Jill McCorkle," *Agni,* 45 (1997): 194–200;

Charline R. McCord, "'I Still See With a Southern Eye': An Interview with Jill McCorkle," *Southern Quarterly,* 36 (Spring 1998): 103–112.

References:

Barbara Bennett, "'Reality Burst Forth': Truth, Lies, and Secrets in the Novels of Jill McCorkle," *Southern Quarterly,* 36 (Fall 1997): 107–122;

Bennett, *Understanding Jill McCorkle* (Columbia: University of South Carolina Press, 2000);

Lynn Z. Bloom, "Jill McCorkle," in *Contemporary Fiction Writers of the South: A Bio-Bibliographical Sourcebook,* edited by Joseph M. Flora and Robert Bain (Westport, Conn.: Greenwood Press, 1993), pp. 295–302;

Patricia Kane, "When Women Tell Stories: Jill McCorkle's Tending to Virginia," *Notes on Contemporary Literature,* 19 (May 1989): 7;

Todd Pierce, "Jill McCorkle: The Emergence of the New South," *Southern Studies,* 5 (Fall–Winter 1994): 19–30;

Elinor Ann Walker, "Celebrating Voice and Self in Jill McCorkle's *Crash Diet,*" *Notes on Contemporary Literature,* 23 (1993): 11–12;

Walker, "Dizzying Possibilities, Plots, and Endings: Girlhood in Jill McCorkle's Ferris Beach," in *The Girl: Construction of the Girl in Contemporary Fiction by Women,* edited by Ruth O. Saxton (New York: St. Martin's Press, 1998), pp. 79–94.

Reginald McKnight
(26 February 1956 –)

Karl Zuelke
University of Cincinnati

BOOKS: *Moustapha's Eclipse* (Pittsburgh: University of Pittsburgh Press, 1988);
I Get on the Bus (Boston: Little, Brown, 1990);
The Kind of Light That Shines on Texas (Boston: Little, Brown, 1992);
White Boys: Stories (New York: Holt, 1998).

OTHER: *African-American Wisdom,* selected, with an introduction, by McKnight (San Rafael, Cal.: New World Library, 1994);
Wisdom of the African World, selected, with an introduction, by McKnight (Novato, Cal.: New World Library, 1996).

Reginald McKnight's stories chronicle the experience of African Americans struggling to establish, and understand, their cultural identity within the context of a racially divided society. Often the stories involve black adolescent characters trying, with varying degrees of success, to cope with the personal pain that results from a confrontation with broader societal forces bearing down upon them. At times racially situated alienation is countered by an enhanced awareness of the value of the African American experience; at other times characters are left victimized. Occasionally the racial stereotyping and discrimination of the dominant white culture compels black characters to turn against themselves. In a brief interview for *Contemporary Authors,* regarding his work, McKnight said: "I think very generally my work deals with the deracinated African-Americans who came of age after the civil rights struggle. These are people who are at the front lines of the struggle for *human* rights. They're part of the struggle whether they want to be or not, for they are in the thick of the white world, daily being judged by their employers, peers, et cetera as to the depths of their intellects and souls."

All of his three critically acclaimed story collections and his novel are characterized by remarkably vivid voices (the bulk of McKnight's work is written in the first-person voice) who give utterance to the strug-

Reginald McKnight (photograph © UCIR/Kimberly Pasko; from the dust jacket for Moustapha's Eclipse, *1988)*

gle. While many of his stories involve adolescent African American males, McKnight's superb ear can extend as well to female, white, elderly, and African characters, all rendered with careful attention to the rhythm and diction of a wide variety of speech patterns. For example, McKnight's deeply moving story "Into Night" records with an almost hallucinatory intensity the impressions of an uneducated, elderly African American woman who listens to her daughter severely beating her young son. "Rebirth" is told in the equally convincing voice of a white racist "who had not seen a lynching for many years." In contrast to the unflinching look at racially generated distress, McKnight's voices can also be quite funny, as in "Who Big Bob?" where a "Professor Longwind" tells a wonderful tall tale straight out of the American comic tradition pioneered by Mark Twain.

Some of McKnight's most acclaimed stories are set in Africa and involve young African American intellectuals forced to integrate a mystical, folk-centered tradition into their empiricist Western training, almost always with intensely disorienting results. The characters are forced into a recognition of an inherent duality in African American experience; yet, the traditions of Africa that are part of that experience are found to be so far in the past as to seem alien and impossible to assimilate, and the traditions of contemporary America do not include them because of their African ancestry. The resultant disorientation is reminiscent of a larger postmodernist dislocation, and critics have gone so far as to dub McKnight a worthy successor to Ralph Ellison.

Reginald McKnight was born in Fürstenfeldbrück, Germany, on 26 February 1956, the son of Pearl (née Anderson) McKnight, a dietician, and Frank McKnight, a cook stationed in Germany with the U.S. Air Force. After his retirement from the air force he became a contractor. Frank McKnight's military career resulted in frequent relocation of his family. In an interview with William Walsh (*Kenyon Review,* Spring 1994), Reginald McKnight said that his family moved "from Germany to New York, briefly, then to California, Colorado, Texas, Alabama, Louisiana, all over the place. But mainly I grew up in Colorado, and I consider Colorado my home."

McKnight served with the U.S. Marine Corps, was honorably discharged in 1976, then continued his education at Pikes Peak Community College, where he received an A.A. degree in 1978. He graduated with honors from Colorado College in 1981 with a B.A. and went on to receive an M.A. from the University of Denver in 1987.

McKnight has taught at several American universities, and his career has also taken him to Africa. In 1981 he received a Thomas J. Watson Fellowship that provided him with the opportunity to spend an entire year in Senegal, and in 1981–1982 he taught English as a foreign language at the American Cultural Center in the capital, Dakar—experience that has provided a rich source of inspiration for his writing. Jerome Klinkowitz (*North American Review,* March 1989) credits these "poles of experience," American and African, for providing a "powerful generative technique" for McKnight's stories, and indeed McKnight was quoted in *Essence* (March

1991) as saying, "I didn't consider myself a writer until I went to Africa." McKnight's African experience often directly inspires his writing. While in Africa, McKnight contracted malaria, and during his recovery the woman who nursed him through the illness told him stories in her native language, which McKnight did not understand. McKnight has the protagonist of *I Get on the Bus* experience a similar situation. Carolyn E. Megan, in her article "New Perceptions on Rhythm in Reginald McKnight's Fiction" (*Kenyon Review,* Spring 1994), reports that "McKnight said he drew upon the comforting rhythms and sounds he remembers the nurse having made" to write the scene.

In the United States, McKnight has taught English at a language school in Colorado Springs; he was a lecturer at Arapahoe Community College in Littleton, Colorado; an instructor in English at Metropolitan State University in Denver; associate professor of English at the University of Pittsburgh; and he briefly taught at Carnegie-Mellon University and served as a visiting professor at Western Michigan University.

McKnight is currently professor of English at the University of Maryland. He serves as fiction editor for *African-American Review* and as advisory editor for *Callaloo.* In 1985 he married Michele Davis; they were divorced in 1991. McKnight has two daughters, Rachael and Muriel Rose. He lives in Baltimore, Maryland.

An incident at the University of Pittsburgh prompted McKnight eventually to leave the university. He heard of a party where several of his colleagues had spent an evening telling racist jokes. In the Walsh interview McKnight discussed his dismay at having discovered such attitudes among his colleagues. "The more I thought about it, the more difficult it became to spend time with these people, comport myself like a typical colleague would. I began to despise them more and more; then I just decided to go ahead and look for work elsewhere."

McKnight often writes with a first-person voice because "the first-person stories, whether they are autobiographical or not, are more personal, much more intimate." In reaction to the incident at Pittsburgh, McKnight claims, "my pain isn't necessarily instructive for people," but it is difficult not to read his stories, especially in light of the Pittsburgh incident, as drawing in a personal way on the universal pain of the African American experience.

McKnight's first collection of stories, *Moustapha's Eclipse,* was the 1988 winner of the Drue Heinz Literature Prize from the University of Pittsburgh Press and won the 1989 Ernest Hemingway Foundation Award from PEN American Center. The reception of the Drue Heinz Prize was a milestone in McKnight's career, coming during a period of frequent story rejections. "All of a sudden I'd gone from considering giving up writing [to] very soon after [having] a contract to do *I Get on the Bus* with Little, Brown. It was just this weird position where I felt like the floodgates of fortune had opened up."

Critical reception of *Moustapha's Eclipse* was generally favorable. Greg Johnson wrote in *Georgia Review* (Summer 1989): "Surely the most striking feature of this brief collection is its ambitious scope: we sense McKnight attempting to define modern black consciousness by allowing each story to articulate fully a significant feature of black suffering, rebellion, or assimilation." In service to his articulation of black experience, McKnight's technique here appropriates an especially wide variety of voices, both white and black, African and American, as a way of approaching the questions of race, racism, and cultural identity from many angles.

At their best the voices can take on a remarkable power, as in "Peaches," described by Klinkowitz as a "genuine masterpiece." Rita, the narrator, is involved with Marc, a young white man, "but there was always something fleeting about him. Something just out the corner of my eye." The quality reveals itself as the specter of racism when, in a moment of lovelorn strain, he uses a racial slur against her, which she describes as "the word. The beast-incubus word." In sorrow over his own callousness, Marc leaves the United States for Liberia, vowing not to come back "till he really, really understood what blackness was." The story generates its compelling momentum when Rita's father, trying to soothe her, takes her outside to gather peaches. He begins a verbal, jazzlike riff, a fanciful celebration of peaches, saying how he "never would have looked twice at Momma had she never stuffed peaches under her sweater back in '47," how "peaches at one time contained an explosive substance instead of sugar." "He tells me," Rita says, "how Big Daddy used to push his cart around the streets of Alabaster, Alabama, hollering 'Waaaatermelon? Strawberries and Peeeachez! Cold, sweet Peeeachez!' Peaches and cream, peach ice cream, peacherinoes and peacherines, peach yogurt, peach popsicles, peach lipstick, peach pie, jam and jelly. 'Cold, sweet peeeeachez!'" When Rita offers her father one from the basket, he replies, "Shooot, naw, Baby Sister, I cain't eat them things." Their laughter triggers a release of Rita's grief, and her father further soothes her by methodically examining every peach in the basket until he finds the perfect one and offers it to his daughter—which she rejects as well. Peaches as such are not as important as the shared cultural and linguistic traditions that can give rise to such lavish celebration of them—the celebration of peaches, at its deepest level, is a celebra-

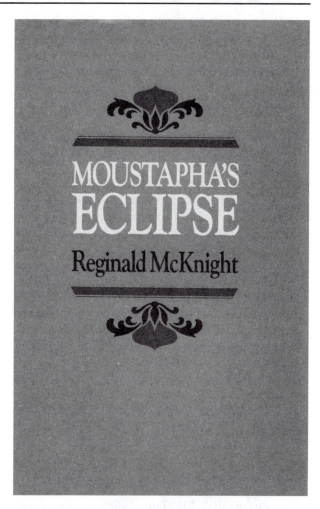

Dust jacket for McKnight's 1988 collection of stories that examine the African and American roots of African American culture

tion of the black heritage that Rita's boyfriend has insulted.

While the voices of McKnight's characters are often used, as in "Peaches," to serious effect, there is much potential for humor as well. "Who Big Bob?" is a marvelously funny story that recalls nothing so much as the comic tales of Mark Twain at his best—although without the "disgusting archness" a character in another story accuses Twain of. Several men, worn out from a day of picking cotton in brutal heat, relax with cards, guitars, and liquor, until Professor Longwind, "who tell a story like nobody's bidness," tells a tall one, about the hot day he spent in the "rooty-poot little town name of Quemado, along the Rio Grande." Big Bob is feared to have been drinking again, so the populace is laying low. Professor Longwind waits in the bar until "the hugest, pug ugliest man I ever seen, come through the doors. . . . Great googly-moogly, the boy was uglyyyyy! 'How do?' I said, just as calm as I please. He looked down at me with that one red eye and didn't said nothing back. He just picked up a whiskey bottle and bit off the top, sucked down all the booze in about two seconds, then ate the whole bottle, chewing it real slow." By the end of Professor Longwind's tale, one of the laborers narrates, "Merlie was dead sleep. But Walter, Calvin and me we was crying, laughing." As in "Peaches," the story takes on momentum as a tribute to the language and culture of its teller, and a tale as entertaining as this one needs no more serious context for its justification.

Three of the stories in *Moustapha's Eclipse* concern the conflict that arises when a black American educated in the Western, rational tradition confronts the mystical traditions of African folk consciousness. The story from which the collection takes its title, "Uncle Moustapha's Eclipse," is told to the American by Idi, the nephew of Moustapha, a prosperous village farmer. As in all of McKnight's stories, the voice of the narrator is vividly rendered. "You would not believe it, my friend. The sunshine is so heavy there that a man can reach his hand into the hot air and squeeze the sunshine like wet clay. The mosquito there can only walk and the baboons move like old men, in Sakaam." Uncle Moustapha is enamored with the "things" of white culture: chocolate, watches, books, and French bread. When he learns of an impending solar eclipse due on his sixtieth birthday, he allows an American scientist to monitor the event on his land, although Moustapha regards it not as a celestial phenomenon but as his "very special gift from Allah." In spite of the scientist's warning Moustapha stares for too long at the sun, imagining that he can see it better than through the scientist's telescope. He begins to experience black spots that fly through his vision—a precursor to his impending blindness. Moustapha personifies the black spot as Death, and in a show of bravado offers it a cigarette. "And you say it's true?" asks the American, to which Idi responds, "You must keep an eye on story-telling Africans." This final exchange suggests a profound difference in the orientation of speaker and listener: the American is concerned with truth as empirical fact, the African with the more elusive and poetic cultural truths embodied in the story.

Johnson maintains that "Uncle Moustapha's Eclipse" and the other African stories "suggest the concerns of much postmodernist fiction with the unreliability of narrative as a representational medium and with the essentially playful artifices of the storyteller divorced from a social or ethical function." Within the story Uncle Moustapha chooses to visit a Western doctor rather than the local marabou, as his wife insists, because, as she says, it was the "white magic that put him in this situation." His particular mixing of Western and folk traditions leads to blindness, an extreme manifestation of the dislocation experienced by the visiting American forced by circumstances to confront both cultures—a dislocation that is also characteristic of postmodernism in broader terms.

The other African stories in the collection reach similar conclusions regarding the cultural divide the main character faces. In "Mali Is Very Dangerous" the protagonist meets Moustapha Diole, who promptly bilks him out of all the money in his wallet and then tries to sell him a charmed "juju" belt that would protect him from knives and bullets. The narrator submits in exasperation to Moustapha's insistence that he stab him in the stomach, and to the narrator's surprise Moustapha remains unscratched, leading the narrator to think: "So there I was. I'd seen what M.D.'s miraculous belt could do, or more objectively, what his miraculous stomach could do, or what my eyes could not do, or whatever. I didn't know what to say. I vacillated between what was and what wasn't was." Caught between the miraculous and the rational, with neither explanation satisfactory, the narrator's language degenerates—a vivid illustration of his dilemma.

The third African story, "How I Met Idi at the Bassi Dakaru Restaurant," is narrated by an American anthropologist who is "lonely, dazed, and flat-brained. Couldn't conjure one reason to stay. Senegal, particularly Dakar, is the most discombobulating place I know." Unlike the other two African stories, the narrator enters the world of Idi "almost believing" his stories about how Idi magically overcomes the technology of a Western storekeeper. Helped by beer and kola nuts, his "anthropological objectivity flowed away." By the end of the day the narrator is too addled to make it home on his own. While alcohol and the narcotic effects of kola are ostensibly the cause of the narrator's intoxication, the implication is that Idi's stories, which lead the narrator into an unfamiliar world, are as much to blame.

One other story, "First I Look at the Purse," concerns the confrontation of an American character with an unfamiliar, mystical experience, though the story is set in an American city. Some reviewers have singled out "First I Look at the Purse" for its convincing rendering of an African American street voice, and the voice is compelling in its own right. The story opens, "I'll be honest with you. I didn't get my bone wet until I was seventeen or so. But I'll tell you one thing; I knew every way they was to make a hen unleash that mighty greenback." The narrator meets a new girl in school, Alicia, competes for her attention with the other boys, and wins. She is from a relatively wealthy background and spends money on him, but he admits, "I couldn't never bring myself to lay down with her, though. She was too good somehow." Alicia is interested in "things like auras and magnetism. All this metaphysical stuff." His relationship with her leads him to out-of-body experiences and a kind of peace that takes him far beyond what sex has brought to him. When his friends learn that he has not been sleeping with her, they tease him, causing him to suddenly end the relationship. When she slips a note into his pocket, he takes it home to read, and "Next thing you know them tiny stars was tingling through my Jello body. I was deep in space." As in the stories set in Africa, the narrator is drawn into a nonrational mode of experience that contradicts the ordinary American way of encountering the world. The fact that his paranormal experience brings him peace, coupled with the misogynistic, pecuniary attitudes of his "normal" self, is a commentary on the relative negative value of "normal" American attitudes, especially when viewed in context with other stories in the volume.

The negative side of American values becomes especially apparent in the stories with white narrators. These stories confront racism head on, at times facing the brutality with a frankness that can be disturbing. "Rebirth" opens with the observation that "Treadwell had not seen a lynching for many years. The souvenirs his father and uncles had deftly sliced from the charred bodies of those black men had long ago disintegrated in the jars of vinegar in which they had been stored. He thought they would last forever, but as he grew older he learned that nothing lasts forever." Another story, "Getting to Be Like the Studs," concerns a mixed race couple at a military base in the Deep South. While less horrific than "Rebirth," the story still ends with the white narrator betraying a racist streak: "I didn't hit him or call him nigger which woulda been really hard on him. He really would be better off with his own kind. Everybody is." Johnson criticizes these stories as lacking in the psychological subtlety that marks some of the others, although Ellen Lesser, in the *New England Review and Breadloaf Quarterly* (Autumn 1989), characterizes them as "hard hitting and important."

McKnight's next book, the novel *I Get on the Bus,* continues the exploration of fictional territory visited in *Moustapha's Eclipse,* with a disoriented American confronting Africa. Evan Norris leaves behind his girlfriend, Wanda, and travels to Senegal with the Peace Corps—a position that he resigns once he gets there, because "I must admit that the Peace Corps is not what I had hoped it would be. In fact, it is worthless. Or I am. I teach a little English here and there, but mainly I do nothing." Evan was described by McKnight in the *Essence* interview as "a passive but internally angry guy who usually shapes himself to a given situation and just slides by. But in Africa he can't do that. He has to confront and reach into himself in order to survive." On his own in Senegal, Evan embarks on a series of hallucinatory adventures, many of which take place in his imagination, and some of which may or may not be real. For example, he thinks that he kills an amputee begging in the street, and only later in the novel does he find out that he could not have done it—though the guilt associated with the murder haunts him.

In attempting to reject his American influences, Evan becomes seduced by Senegalese culture, especially as embodied by Aminata, the daughter of a village marabou who takes him in. Evan's sexual experience with her leads toward healing and a discovery of the influences that have been poisoning his mind, and this in turn leads him to a connection with her former lover, Lamont, a more intellectual embodiment of Senegalese culture. But Evan comes to finds the couple frightening, and the djinni, demms, and spirits he seems to encounter, associated with the Senegalese characters, are too disturbing for him to tolerate. The alternative to life in Senegal with Lamont and Aminata, proposed by Africa Ford, an expatriate American who lives hustling and selling T-shirts in Dakar, is no more viable. As Lamont tries a final time to scare Evan into an acceptance of Senegalese ways, Evan says: "sometimes, you know, sometimes I really hate being black"—a condition he cannot reject. Evan's rejection of his restrictive American heritage, though, and his refusal to assimilate into an African one, leaves him a free man, although in an ambivalent, existential way.

Stories of experience in Africa are left behind in McKnight's second collection, *The Kind of Light That Shines on Texas* (1992), but the vivid voices and the occasionally bleak view of race relations relieved by flashes of humor are still in evidence. Reception of the book was positive, and the title story was honored with a 1990 O. Henry Award. Joyce Reiser Kornblatt, writing in *The New York Times Book Review* (8 March 1992), described McKnight as "a writer who hears the complex symphony of daily talk, who functions as a kind of medium for his varied narrators' manic confessions, lyric incantations, heartbroken appeals and indictments. Each monologue in 'The Kind of Light That Shines on Texas' is verbal music." As is characteristic of McKnight's work, the panoply of voices serves to examine racial issues from a variety of angles, in ways that can sometimes be surprising.

In "Quitting Smoking" the author deftly turns a story about one kind of hatred into a surprising, different vein—and an African American becomes its victim. Scott, the black narrator, is writing a letter to a friend, describing life with Anna, his white girlfriend. She has been raped, and their discussions of her victimization and resultant anger take him back to an incident in his past when he saw a woman being attacked and did not offer assistance. He begins smoking again, symbolic of an impending breakup with Anna since he had quit to please her. In an attempt to save the relationship he flushes his cigarettes and cleans their apartment, but the tension between them, exacerbated by her rape, gives rise to a discussion about how much better the world would be if it were run by women. Scott gives voice to the suspicion that has been haunting him: "You know, babe, considering all that's happened to you, I wouldn't be surprised if you hated men." Her reply turns the story from a dramatization of male guilt to an even more disturbing revelation of racially situated anger that makes a victim of Scott because of his race. "I'm surprised I don't hate black men," she says. "The guy who raped me was black."

The title story concerns Clint, a black narrator looking back at a portion of his youth spent struggling to get along in a mostly white school in Texas. One of the two other black students is Marvin, a large, quiet boy, the object of school ridicule. Clint says to one of his classmates, regarding Marvin, "He's like a pig or something. Makes me sick." To which the classmate replies, "Does it make you ashamed to be colored?" Clint replies that it does not, "but I meant yes. Yes if you insist on thinking us all the same. Yes, if his faults are mine, his weaknesses inherent in me." The situation points to an insidious quality of racism that can lead a character to turn shame against himself on merely racial grounds. The story comes to a head when, in a game of "murder ball," Clint accidentally bloodies the nose of an intimidating school bully, Oakley. Oakley corners him in the locker room, and Clint, in terror, points at Marvin saying, "How come you're after *me* and not *him?*" If, as the story makes clear, Oakley is after him for racist causes, and, as Clint admits, the "colored weaknesses" he sees in himself are inherent in Marvin as well, then Marvin should make an equally inviting target. The story is resolved when Marvin saves Clint from the beating he has feared. Marvin's quiet strength in the face of adversity casts him in a new light, which also leads to Clint's enhanced appreciation for Marvin's blackness and thus his own. At the end of the story Clint notices Ah-so, the black girl in his class. "She had a very gen-

tle-looking face, really. That surprised me." Shame at his blackness has been turned to pride in blackness, which brings the girl to his attention in a way he would have been incapable of seeing before—the adult narrator, however, must still struggle with the memory of betrayal. The story rescues a black character from victimization at the hands of racist violence, as well as from a self-directed hatred that has its source in an overwhelmingly racist environment.

Another story in the collection approaches the disturbing situation of self-directed anger, though in the broader arena of family relations in the context of African American history. In "Into Night" a grandmother listens to the abusive beating of her rambunctious grandson at the hands of her daughter. The boy cries, "I love you, Mama" as he is whipped with a belt. The grandmother is helpless to stop the beating, remembering as she does the same beatings she gave to her daughter and that she received at the hands of her own mother. "I heard me too, my own screams, and my brothers and sisters, my mama, papa, aunts, uncles and on back, and on back. . . . I couldn't understand why it was only now I was hearing just how turrible it is. I heard burning crosses and natureless men, women split open like pigs' knuckles, heard the pain of vanishing blue jungles and dry red soil." The remarkable passage succinctly chronicles the history of Africans, reaching back finally into a distant, unimaginable past, "Then just black, so black I couldn't hear nothing no more, nor see, nor breathe, nor move. I wisht I coulda helped that boy, but I couldn't move." The passage is moved to a hallucinatory intensity by the shared history of pain, leading the grandmother, in Kornblatt's estimation, to become "the seer, the redemptive spirit for whom all the characters in the book seem to be yearning."

Other stories in *The Kind of Light That Shines on Texas* work to examine racial situations. "Roscoe in Hell" is told in the voice of a dead drug addict telling the story of his life from hell. A few stories in the collection tackle different issues, however. "The Homunculus: A Novel in One Chapter" is a fable about the fate of artists when their work devours them, and the final story in the collection, "Soul Food," is an experimental, surreal story told in the second person, which uses a yearning for cannibalism as a metaphor for human despair.

McKnight's 1998 collection, *White Boys,* continues to explore the specter of a society divided along racial lines, and two of the stories return to Africa, continuing an exploration of the disorienting results of an American in contact with the ways of African consciousness. In "He Sleeps" an American anthropologist in Senegal to collect folk stories is taken in by a village couple, Alaine and Kene. His experience leads him to have dreams for the first time in his life. While this development is a step toward reaching an understanding of the ways of his hosts, he is too analytically detached from his experience—in the Western academic tradition—to understand their culture or, ultimately, their expectations of him. His detachment leads to an unintended insult toward his hosts when, during a shouting match between Kene and the neighbors, he watches from a distance rather than making his presence in the household felt. He is forgiven eventually, and his dreams chronicle his growing assimilation into the culture of his new family. The final scene presents a dream in which, during an erotically charged moment with Kene, his personality fuses with hers and "we see our freedom everywhere we look, for everywhere we look, we see ourselves." He is too detached during the daytime, however, to understand the breakthrough his dreams symbolize, even though such was the purpose of his coming to Africa.

The other story set in Africa, "Palm Wine," concerns a young anthropoligist's romantic idealization of African culture, symbolized for him by palm wine. The main character, as he tells a group of Senegalese, is "trying to help all black people by recovering our forgot things." The group of Africans he meets, who introduce him to palm wine—an undrinkable beverage, it turns out—sense his condescending attitude and ask him to leave because he is "not a good man." Years later, as he retells the story, the narrator is still beset by remorse at his youthful inability to understand the culture he went to discover.

The remaining two stories, and the novella that gives the collection its title, examine race relations from the point of view of middle-class African Americans. "The More I Like Flies" presents a black cafeteria worker at the Air Force Academy engaged in long talks with a coworker. The conversation betrays a poorly hidden streak of racial condescension in the white worker. The chance landing of a fly on the narrator's hand and the coincidental resemblance of a female coworker to a friend from his school days spark the memory of a cruel racial insult the narrator had suffered. "One thing that's great about being white: The rest of my sophomore year I never could figure out words to hurt Dianna as much as she'd hurt me. . . . Six, seven years now, and I still don't think I could."

"White Boys," one of the few McKnight stories written in third-person voice, examines the lives of two families at a military base in Louisiana to show that the poisonous presence of racial hatred affects whites as well as blacks. Derrick Oates, the main char-

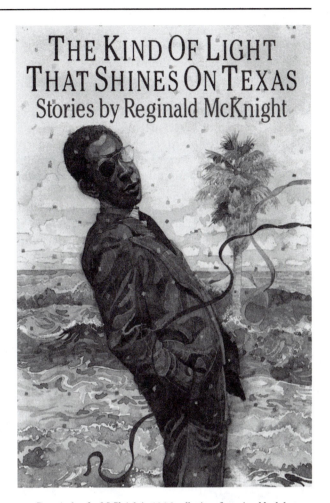

Dust jacket for McKnight's 1992 collection, featuring bleak but sometimes humorous stories of race relations

acter, innocently takes snow from the car of Sergeant Hooker, his white neighbor, who Derrick's father sees right away "got the look of a redneck peckerwood from top to bottom." Derrick incurs the wrath of his father and the neighbor for touching the white man's car. "And so it begins," says Sergeant Hooker to his wife, days of "speechifying and pacing and window gazing." Hooker's son, Garret, befriends Derrick and finds himself forced to choose between loyalty to his father and his friend when Sergeant Hooker tries to get his son to go along with a vicious prank—a "fishing trip" that would lead to a staged lynching, in order to "do something very strong to that boy, to teach him his lesson." Garret ends the friendship with a string of racial insults, but he does so out of kindness, in order to save his friend from the brutality of the staged lynching Garret knows is coming.

In its portrayal of racial hatred, "White Boys" concentrates most of its attention on the dynamic within and between both families. The parents in the black Oates family are mercilessly disciplinarian, and the implication is that the pressure of life in a racist milieu is at least partially responsible for the hard-edged treatment of their children. The peace of the family is shattered by beatings and belt-whippings, surely an attempt to recall the whipping victims receive at the hands of a lynch mob. The imbecilic hatred of Sergeant Hooker causes his wife to sneak into her son's room at night with whispered attempts to explain to him how his father is capable of such anger. The promise of human friendship between the boys is destroyed, and the attempt of Mrs. Hooker and Mrs. Oates to strike up a friendship is equally doomed. Every facet of the lives of both families is deformed by racism, underlining power to infiltrate even the bosom of love that the family ideally represents.

The novella is bleak in its unsparing revelation of the evils of racial hatred, but as in many of McKnight's stories the tortured kindness of Garret invokes a human potential for redemption. McKnight's fictional world—while unflinching in its indictment of the insidious, destructive power of racism on the human soul—is not a cynical world, and it is not a defeated one. McKnight is a writer with a great heart who can keep his eye on the values of kindness and understanding, even amid the storm of racial injustice he is compelled to examine. The high estimation in which critics have held his work is testament to his powers as a writer and as a chronicler of the African American experience with its poignant mixture of pain and celebration.

Interview:

William Walsh, "We Are, in Fact, a Civilization: An Interview with Reginald McKnight," *Kenyon Review,* 16 (1994): 27–43.

References:

Greg Johnson, "Wonderful Geographics," *Georgia Review,* 43 (Summer 1989): 412–414;

Jerome Klinkowitz, "Generating the Story," *North American Review,* 274 (March 1989): 69–72;

Ellen Lasser, "Telling Tales: In Search of the New Short Story," *New England Review and Bread Loaf Quarterly,* 12 (August 1989): 106–108;

Carolyn E. Megan, "New Perceptions on Rhythm in Reginald McKnight's Fiction," *Kenyon Review,* 16 (1994): 56–62.

Lorrie Moore

(13 January 1957 –   )

Robin A. Werner
Tulane University

BOOKS: *Self-Help* (New York: Knopf, 1985; London: Faber & Faber, 1985);

Anagrams (New York: Knopf, 1986; London: Faber & Faber, 1987);

The Forgotten Helper: A Story for Children (New York: Kipling, 1987); republished as *The Forgotten Helper: A Christmas Story* (New York: Delacorte, 2000);

Like Life (New York: Knopf, 1990; London: Faber & Faber, 1990);

Who Will Run the Frog Hospital? (New York: Knopf, 1994; London: Faber & Faber, 1994);

Birds of America (New York: Knopf, 1998; London: Faber & Faber, 1998).

OTHER: *I Know Some Things: Stories about Childhood by Contemporary Writers,* edited by Moore (Boston: Faber & Faber, 1992); republished as *The Faber Book of Contemporary Stories about Childhood* (Boston & London: Faber & Faber, 1997).

Lorrie Moore (photograph by Joyce Ravid; from the dust jacket for Birds of America, *1998)*

Lorrie Moore's artful short fiction plays upon hauntingly familiar pangs in its depiction of the pitfalls of modern existence. Throughout, a darkly witty sense of humor pervades the often desperate lives of her characters. Much of the criticism of Moore's work has focused on this humor, described variously as "wry" and "apt." However, as Ralph Sassone points out in his article "This Side of Parody: Lorrie Moore Gets Serious," her use of humor produces dramatic effects: "Although a cursory reading of her work might make it seem coolly satirical, its aftereffect is the memory of palpable pain. . . . Funniness is simultaneously a leavening agent for her wrenching narratives, a temporary paregoric for her characters, and a distancing device that perpetuates their alienation."

For all this wit and pain, Moore's reflections of life, seemingly confessional, appear as intimate views into the psyches of real people. This quality, perhaps, is what often leads critics to assume Moore's stories are autobiographical, an assumption Moore herself has strenuously denied. The major themes of Moore's work center around the trials of contemporary existence—love, loss, loneliness—and often reveal profound psychological implications. As Vince Passaro pointed out in *Mirabella* (February 1992): "Certain themes and situations recur: Moore tends toward heroines in their child bearing years, often enduring an erosion of physical health, loneliness, and an exasperation at men and men's stupid vanities." Often her characters operate in settings that isolate them, whether in an urban center or tucked away in a monotonous suburb. The vast majority of her protagonists are female, and thus her stories wrestle with issues that are particularly poignant for contemporary women: divorce, love affairs, motherhood, and illness. Throughout her work sadness exists in a tense duality with humor, each offsetting and intensifying the other. Her minimalist prose explodes with intensity; the empty spaces of the plot resonate with expression.

Lorrie Moore was born Marie Lorena Moore on 13 January 1957, in Glens Falls, New York. Both her father, Henry T. Moore Jr., an insurance company executive who came from a family of academics, and her mother, Jeanne (Day) Moore, a former nurse, were avid readers of nonfiction. Moore was the second of four children and, as Don Lee noted in *Ploughshares* (Fall 1998), "remembers her parents as rather strict Protestants, politically minded and culturally alert." Moore became interested in creative writing at an early age, but it was not until college that she began to focus on this vocation. She told Vince Passaro: "I was always writing a little bit but not in a serious way. . . . As far as reading, it was typical little girl stuff. I remember thinking there would be no reason to read a book if it wasn't a mystery." She was first published in 1976 at the age of nineteen, as the first-prize winner in a *Seventeen Magazine* writing contest, which she won with her story "Raspberries." After high school Moore went on to complete her undergraduate work, studying writing at St. Lawrence University in northern New York state. At St. Lawrence, Moore studied creative writing with critic and fiction writer Joe David Bellamy, was inducted into Phi Beta Kappa, and graduated summa cum laude in 1978. After graduating Moore moved to Manhattan, where she worked as a paralegal until 1980. Although she had loved writing in college, she told Passaro, she "had no sense of how you went from being a student and taking creative writing classes to being a real writer. It seemed impossible."

Then, in 1980, she was accepted into the M.F.A. program at Cornell University. At Cornell she studied with Alison Lurie, who was instrumental in getting Moore's first collection published. In 1982 she received her M.F.A. and became a member of the Associated Writing Programs and the Author's Guild. Moore worked as a lecturer at Cornell from 1982 to 1984 and taught there again in 1990 as a visiting associate professor. In 1983 Moore sold to Knopf her first collection, *Self-Help* (1985), comprised almost completely of stories from her master's thesis. In 1984 Moore became an assistant professor at the University of Wisconsin, where she subsequently became an associate professor in 1987 and finally a full professor of English in 1991. She has also served as a Sidney Harman Writer-in-Residence at Baruch College in the year 2000. She continues to teach at the University of Wisconsin, Madison.

A year after Moore moved to Wisconsin, her acclaimed debut short-story collection, *Self-Help,* was published. Throughout her career Moore has alternated genres, with novels generally following her collections of short stories. Both of her novels, *Anagrams* (1986) and *Who Will Run the Frog Hospital?* (1994), reflect her skill at the short story in the episodic nature of their narratives and their fragmentary style. Moore's novels are acclaimed, but she is best known for her short fiction. She has also published work in such magazines as *Fiction International, Ms, The New York Times Book Review, Paris Review, The New Yorker, The Yale Review,* and *Harper's.*

The nine stories that make up *Self-Help* reveal many of the traits that have come to distinguish Moore's more mature writing. One of her major strengths is her skill at creating characters. Despite the minimalism of these stories, the characters she depicts are vivid and familiar, humorous and poignant. Moore's dramatic use of character in her narratives can be seen from the first story of *Self-Help*, "How to Be an Other Woman." The principal character of this story, Charlene, is a frustrated woman who has not fulfilled her intellectual potential. Through the course of the affair that comprises the narrative of the story, Charlene's illusions about herself begin to break down.

"How to Be an Other Woman" narrates this breakdown of self in a fragmentary style, modeled on an instruction manual, filled with lists and snatches of witty dialogue. This style is repeated in five other stories in this collection, her distanced narration contrasting sharply with the emotional upheaval of the events being narrated. On the surface a tale of a woman having an affair, the story by its title reveals a word game typical of Moore's style, brought out later when the narrator instructs:

> Wonder if you are getting old, desperate. Believe that you have really turned into another woman:
>
> > your maiden aunt Phyllis;
> > some vaporish cocktail waitress;
>
> > a glittery transvestite who has wandered, lost, up from the Village.

This punning on the conventional connotations of the title in a list, like some likely suspects in a detective story, plays into the other principal theme of the story: the question of identity.

The instructions advising the reader on how to be an "other woman" presents the strain of Charlene's relationship through a breakdown of her identity. The tale begins by evoking spy thrillers as Charlene meets her married lover in "expensive beige raincoats," predatorily examining each other: "collars upturned and slowly razoring the cab and store-lit fog like sharkfins. You begin to circle, gauging each other in primordial sniffs." Moore never names this lover; he remains "he" throughout the story. This withholding of names is a device that appears periodically throughout Moore's short fiction. It is not till after the first sexual encounter that Charlene's lover reveals that he is married. The only information he provides about his wife is that her name is Patricia and that she makes lists. Almost immediately Charlene begins to make lists as well, changing her identity in response to this piece of information. Her lists begin to intersperse the plot, emphasizing the breakdown of the character's sense of self through their combination of work goals and distress over her fraught relationship. This interspersal of elements breaking up the flow of the narrative is characteristic of many of Moore's short stories. "How to Be an Other Woman" examines self-definition: the narrator comes to define herself as a mistress; yet, this identity remains something alien to her, not a part of who she wants to be. The words "Wonder who you are" appear a few pages into the story, isolated, alone on a single line of text after a paragraph detailing her married lover leaving in the middle of the night to go home so that Patricia will not suspect anything.

In breaking off his relationship with Charlene, the lover finally reveals the truth of his situation, that in fact he is only living with Patricia and is married to a third woman named Carrie. In an effort to comfort her he reveals a different perception of Charlene than her narrative has presented: "Charlene, what I've always admired about you, right from when I first met you, is your strength, your independence." This differs so completely from the impression left by the rest of the narrative that the reader is left unclear as to where the truth of this woman lies. In the end this story becomes about the way identity can be lost in a love relationship as well as revealing the masochism of the other woman's position and the duplicity of the man.

In "What Is Seized," Moore again examines a woman's identity—this time that of a wife losing her husband. The story adopts a more traditional narrative form but still employs the episodic shifts and interspersed elements that are characteristic of Moore's writing, particularly in *Self-Help*. "What Is Seized" also introduces another major theme in Moore's work, the relationship of mothers and daughters and how their roles are subject to reversal. Moore uses photographs and letters throughout the tale to weave together past, present, and future timelines documenting the early life

Dust jacket for Moore's 1985 collection, featuring several stories parodying self-help manuals

of Lynnie's mother as Lynnie narrates more recent events. The mother's past identity is revealed through spirited and vibrant photographs of her from early childhood through young womanhood, pictures that Lynnie and her foster brother, James, love to look at. The mother of later years, whose letters to Lynnie at college are eloquent pleas for understanding, is a broken woman, very different from the one in the old photographs. These letters appear throughout the story, foretelling the future, and Lynnie's cold, terse responses contrast sharply with her mother's pain. Moore plays upon the title through the mother's repeated statement "What is beautiful is seized," while the significance of the missing word *beautiful* in the title is left up to the reader's imagination.

Physical breakdowns that parallel inner turmoil frequently occur in Moore's work, physicalizing the emotional pain and compounding the trauma. In "What Is Seized" bodily and emotional loss are viciously combined in the mother's life as she loses her husband to divorce and her breasts to cancer. Lynnie emphasizes this combination in her narration: "I was fifteen when my father left us and my mother had her mastectomy. Both things happened suddenly, quietly, without announcement. As if some strange wind rushed in and swept things up into it, then quickly rushed out again; it simply left what it left."

Disease and the pain and potential role reversals they bring are common themes in these early stories. The physical breakdown often becomes an embodiment of emotional trauma. After the father's departure the divisions between the interspersed photos and letters and the timeline become less clearly defined, and the reader is instead presented with "a series of pictures here of mothers and daughters switching places—women switching places to take care of one another." The title "What Is Seized" reflects both the things that Lynnie observes her mother losing but also the loss of her mother, whose funeral is depicted in the final moments of the story. In this story abandonment becomes a theme of Lynnie's mother's life, but such loneliness and neediness are not reserved only for women in Moore's fiction.

In some ways the story "How" seems to be an inversion of the relationship patterns of "What Is Seized." In this story, another parody of self-help books, the woman pulls back from the stifling intimacy of the relationship and the man experiences loss and disease, although with his disease, as with much of the romantic relationship, "there is never anything conclusive." The characters are never named, nor is the mysterious kidney ailment that the man begins to suffer from identified. Mimicking an instruction manual, the entire story is told in direct address, using the word *you* repeatedly in a way that makes the reader complicit in the events of the narrative. The signs of discomfort are mingled with affection almost from the beginning in this relationship, as illustrated in the second paragraph when the instructions state: "Feel discovered, comforted, needed, loved, and start sometimes, somehow, to feel bored."

As "How" progresses the moments of love grow briefer and the instructions increasingly reflect the female character's dissatisfaction, leading to a mounting sense of claustrophobic tension. Escape is both longed for and feared as romantic gestures degenerate into neediness. In contrast to "What Is Seized," "How" depicts a woman being stifled by the emotional needs of her lover, but the woman is still distanced from herself by this relationship. At one point, after the man has become ill and the woman has begun to have an affair, the narrative asserts bluntly: "You will horrify yourself." The phrases "There will be an endless series of tests" and "There is never anything conclusive" are repeated like mantras, taking on varying significances

each time. Initially they refer only to the man's mysterious illness, but later they come to have a deeper resonance for the relationship as a whole. Finally, the woman leaves, but despite her freedom she is alone and regretful. The story concludes in an overwhelming sense of loss with the words: "One of those endings."

Read together, the effects of the stories in the volume tend to intensify each other. The man's kidney problems and the female narrator's need for escape stand in contrast to preceding stories such as "How to Be an Other Woman" and "What Is Seized," in which women need support that men cannot or will not provide. As variations on the themes surface again and again, each retelling is colored by those that came before, through related plot elements and the themes of loss, frustration, and longing. Wit and trauma exist side by side throughout this collection, and even the minor details poignantly recall the realism of these frustrated lives. The repeated stylistic device of aping instruction manuals or self-help books both alienates the characters and makes the reader complicit in the events of the narratives. Although sometimes lacking in depth, the themes of loneliness, isolation, and frustration, so much a part of all of Moore's work, are vividly portrayed in *Self-Help*. Crisp and episodic, the collection exhibits an ironic sense of humor as it examines the futility and desperation of contemporary existence.

Much of the criticism focuses on Moore's use of humor, occasionally suggesting that because her works are funny they do not merit serious examination. In an interview with Dwight Garner for the on-line magazine *Salon* (27 October 1998), Moore defends her use of humor by pointing out that the world is funny and that individuals spend much of their time attempting to be humorous: "If you're going to ignore that, what are you doing? You're just saying that part of the world . . . doesn't exist. And of course it exists." Throughout Lorrie Moore's work it is apparent that this dark humor, and the pain it masks, are part of her intense contemplation of contemporary existence. Beginning in *Self-Help*, Moore presents characters that become typical in her work—individuals who are sarcastic, witty, and secretly vulnerable. These characters, usually women, populate all three of Moore's collections of short stories.

The reviews of *Self-Help* were largely laudatory. The reviewer for *Library Journal* (15 March 1985) characterizes Moore's wit as "quicksilver" and "self-protective." Michiko Kakutani, writing in *The New York Times* (6 March 1985), describes the collection as possessing "some fine, funny and very moving pictures of contemporary life." At the same time reviewers sometimes criticized the collection for its stylistic devices and the resulting lack of coherence and depth. Kakutani also criticizes Moore's dialogue: the conversations "sputter out in gasps of non sequiturs or clichés." These are faults that Moore gradually resolves throughout the course of her next two collections of short stories.

After *Self-Help,* Moore published in other genres. In 1986 she published her first novel, *Anagrams.* Then, in 1987 she published *The Forgotten Helper,* a story for children. During this period she was splitting her time between Madison and Manhattan, resisting the loneliness she experienced when in the Midwest and not wanting to completely give up her life in New York. In 1989 Moore was awarded a Rockefeller Fellowship and received a National Endowment for the Arts award. In 1990 Moore received the first of six Best American Short Story awards (she was also a recipient in 1991, 1992, 1993, 1998, and 1999). Also in 1990, Moore published her second collection of short stories, *Like Life.*

In *Like Life* Moore's writing style is more subdued. While the general themes in these eight stories are much the same as in *Self-Help,* the narratives of her second collection show greater range of emotion and have less of a satiric edge. Moving away from the stylistic devices of the self-help parodies and fragmentary narratives, Moore's objects of study in *Like Life* range from a woman having simultaneous affairs with two men ("Two Boys") to an examination of relationships in an unnamed, pestilential urban hell that seems to be a dark reflection of New York City ("Like Life"). As in *Self-Help,* many of these stories focus on protagonists who are middle-class white women, but two of the eight stories, "Vissi d'Arte" and "Starving Again," present male narrators and the female protagonist of the title story, "Like Life," exists in extreme poverty. Once more the interspersed humor intensifies the frustration and pain, but in *Like Life* there is more depth, some mingled notes of compassion, and occasionally even moments of tenderness appearing through the isolation. The characters in *Like Life* also seem to have a greater sense of self-awareness. In *Like Life,* even more than in *Self-Help,* the focus is on relationships and missed connections, mainly romantic. The theme of romance flows throughout the collection as the romances of one story speak to the flirtations of the next in a dialogue covering many different levels of pain and irony. The style is more straightforward, but Moore still employs the juxtaposition of different textual elements to intensify the emotion of the story, such as the student evaluations that appear in "You're Ugly, Too."

In the first story, "Two Boys," a story in some ways strikingly similar to "How to Be an Other Woman," which opened *Self-Help,* the reader follows Mary as her simultaneous love affairs with two very different men lead her into a breakdown. Issues of innocence and purity become growing obsessions for Mary as the color white and the cleanliness of her apartment are contrasted sharply with the blood on the street outside the butcher's shop above which she lives. Such visual details allegorize her feelings of pollution as her entanglements with the two men deepen. The two men in the story are referred to only by the dehumanized appellations "Number One" and "Number Two." Mary's deepening identity crisis seems a more traumatic version of the one that formed the basis of "How to Be the Other Woman" and is punctuated by encounters with a strange little girl.

The unnamed girl, prepubescent and bold, seems to be trying on the trappings of experience, only intensifying the reader's impression of her youth. Meanwhile the troubled Mary alters her clothing and surroundings, struggling to regress back into the innocence and purity the child seemingly rejects: "In the park, an eleven-year-old girl loped back and forth in front of her. Mary looked up. The girl was skinny, flat-chested, lipsticked. She wore a halter top that left her bare-backed, shoulder blades jutting like wings. She spat once, loud and fierce, and it landed by Mary's feet." The girl offers the ambiguous epiphany of the narrative, pointing at a row of sausages in the butcher shop and announcing: "Look! . . . There they are. All our old boyfriends." These phallic pieces of dead meat somehow speak of more experience than Mary is completely able to grasp, and she asks herself after wondering what grade the girl is in: "Could there be a grade for what this girl knew in her bulleted heart? What she knew was the sort of thing that grew in you like a tree, unfurling in your brain, pushing out into your fingers against the nails." The story ends as Mary teeters on the brink of reassembling her life after the dissolution of her affair with "Number One" and the suicide of "Number Two."

Later in the collection, the story "You're Ugly, Too" examines the damaging effects of solitude on a woman in her thirties. "You're Ugly, Too," like "Two Boys," follows a slightly disturbed female character's search for self-awareness. In a way the narrative is an examination of the life of the terminally lonely and a study of modern courtship rituals. Negative course evaluations flash in and out of a narrative that delineates Zoë's failed relationships in the Midwest town where she teaches. The focus of the story is Zoë's sister's attempt at matchmaking, trying to set up a meeting between Zoë and a friend named Earl. The students' evaluations of her courses link the personal and professional, connecting various aspects of Zoë's existence. The description of her empty house, for which she purchases furniture only to return it due to paranoid fantasies, deepens this portrait of emptiness. In addition, Moore brings in another recurring motif in her fiction— a mysterious ailment, a growth in Zoë's abdomen, which she keeps secret but which hangs morbidly over the final party scene.

Zoë's failure to connect with people is made vividly clear at her sister's Halloween party. Earl, the prospective suitor, appears embarrassingly attired as a naked woman in a costume that often becomes the focus of the narrative as it shifts and deteriorates throughout the evening. As Zoë and Earl talk, her thoughts reflect another of Moore's realistic insights into contemporary psychology:

> She had to learn not to be afraid of a man, the way, in your childhood, you learned not to be afraid of an earthworm or a bug. Often, when she spoke to men at parties, she rushed things in her mind. As the man politely blathered on, she would fall in love, marry, then find herself in a bitter custody battle with him for the kids and hoping for a reconciliation, so that despite all his betrayals she might no longer despise him, and in the few minutes remaining, learn, perhaps what his last name was and what he did for a living, though probably there was already too much history between them.

The hurried syntax of the last sentence, running through phrases punctuated only by commas, reflects the thoughts of the lonely narrator in a way that is both disturbingly familiar and yet strangely humorous.

In an odd final gesture that shows the extent to which her instincts of attraction and repulsion have been distorted, Zoë tries to push Earl off the balcony. This "joke" recalls her earlier thoughts of "gorillas, how when they had been kept too long alone in cages, they would smack each other in the head instead of mating." Earl, now angry rather than needy, turns on her, and the story concludes with Zoë flirting, "She smiled at him, and wondered how she looked." Earl's response to this sudden switch to flirtation is left up to the reader's imagination.

Moore's contemporary, realistic take on dysfunctional relationships is also the theme of "The Jewish Hunter." Odette, a New York poet supporting herself with a fellowship in the Midwest, starts a relationship with a farm lawyer named Pinky. Despite depicting a relationship that is clearly doomed to failure, this story does feature some poignant moments. The stickily sweet tenderness of passages from their first sexual encounter ("He was a kisser, and he kissed and kissed. It seemed the kindest thing that had ever happened to her") are ironically interspersed with examples of failed communication, as when Pinky needs to view Holocaust documentaries after sex–sex for Pinky is somehow inexorably connected with his parents' death in a concentration camp. Unlike the love scenes in most of Moore's work, this story is at times quite tender:

> At night he began to hold her in a way that stirred her deeply. He slept with one hand against her head, as if to protect her from bad thoughts. Or, perhaps thoughts at all. How quickly bodies came to love each other, promise themselves to each other always, without asking permission. From the mind! If only she could give up her mind, let her heart swell, inflamed, her brain stepping out for whole days, whole seasons, her work shrinking to limericks.

The theme of the mind-body split in this story, which focuses on the female character's mind and lingers over the details of the male character's body, reverses traditional gender assumptions. It is clear to the reader from the beginning of the story that Odette will have to leave to return to New York when her fellowship is over and that Pinky, a farm lawyer, would never make it in New York. In this, as in most of Moore's work, the two fail to really connect; communication breaks down between them and they move on with their lives, alone.

In the title story, which concludes the collection, Moore moves to an entirely different setting to explore romantic relationships between men and women. Most of Moore's stories take place in middle- or upper-middle-class settings, whether urban or rural. "Like Life," in contrast, is set in a familiar, yet alien, poverty-stricken urban area. In a dreamlike slum that seems to echo the dystopia of George Orwell's *Nineteen Eighty-four* and where the heroine's response to a diagnosis of pre-cancer is "Isn't that . . . like *life?*," Moore once more probes the issues that arise in a failing relationship. The narrative explores Mamie's doomed attempts to leave Rudy, an artist rebelling against the yuppie art world. At times Rudy's presence seems to be holding Mamie back, embarrassing and stifling her, but in the end their relationship becomes a comfort in the midst of their chronic illness and poverty. The title of the story resurfaces throughout like a musical variation on a theme, and in the end, unlike many of the relationships Moore examines, the two main characters are reunited, at least for the moment.

Several critics reversed their earlier stance and praised *Like Life* for its continued use of dark humor. In this collection, Sassone claims, "she proves that although her natural gift is for kinetic prose about the bright and wired, she can also write understated stories in which the mood is closer to a hush." Other critics found in the collection a broader thematic range and deeper emotional engagement than in *Self-Help*. John Casey's review in *The Chicago Tribune* (20 May 1990) described Moore's writing in *Like Life* as a mix of "comedy and sadness, wisecracks and poignancy." This collection is more self-reflexive and probes more deeply into the problematic conditions of life. The humor and language games serve to intensify the dark elements of the tales rather than existing for their own sake, as some critics felt they did in her earlier collection.

In her review for *The New York Times* (8 June 1990), Kakutani also compared *Like Life* with *Self-Help:* "Although the stories in 'Like Life' are as funny and archly observant as those in Ms. Moore's earlier collection ('Self-Help'), they are also softer, wiser, more minor-key." Kakutani went on to say that *Like Life* is superior largely due to the addition of "lyrical meditation" and the ability of these characters "to examine–however gingerly–their hurts and missed connections." Again, Moore was praised for her ability to delineate fictional characters that seem somehow familiar, as if they were autobiographical. The reviews also praise Moore's ability to depict varying types of human pain in her exploration of contemporary existence.

After publishing *Like Life,* Moore edited an anthology, *I Know Some Things: Stories about Childhood by Contemporary Writers* (1992). In 1993 she received her first O. Henry Award (which she was also awarded in 1998), for her story "Charades," and in 1994 published her second novel, *Who Will Run the Frog Hospital?.* In 1998 Moore received the National Magazine Award–an achievement she repeated in 1999–and published another collection of short stories, *Birds of America.*

Birds of America continues Moore's exploration of the enigmatic breakdown of connections between people. A further refinement and intensification of this theme, the collection still includes elements of dark humor, but the subject matter examines more serious crises in even greater depth. Stories such as "Charades" depict family relationships both strained and evolving. Throughout this collection of twelve stories, familial relationships and families in crisis are portrayed with Moore's typical wit and pathos. In the six stories that are not directly focused on familial relationships, such as "Willing," "Agnes of Iowa," "Beautiful Grade," and "What You Want to Do Fine," characters are often lost and looking for homes, and even in these six stories familial relationships surface intermittently. Children also form an important thread, linking the stories in *Birds of America* like a recurring theme, often depicted in various kinds of danger, both emotional and physical.

In "Charades" Moore examines the relationships between parents and their adult children through the role-playing game of the title. The narrator, Therese, one of the ten female narrators in *Birds of America,* is in many ways a typical Moore protagonist: a woman in her thirties, well educated, white, middle-class, and slightly uneasy about her existence. Therese's siblings have assembled at their parents' house for the Christmas holidays with their spouses, and the story presents their evolving relationships as the family plays a

Dust jacket for Moore's 1998 collection of darkly comic stories about families in crisis

game of charades. The theatricality of their relationships is emphasized through such descriptions as "Usually, no one in Therese's family expresses much genuine feeling anyway; everyone aims instead–though gamely!–for enactments." Therese observes the changes her family has undergone, the marriages, births, and inevitable aging.

Her thoughts reveal that somehow, on this holiday, her family has become alien, different, older. Her father, for example, has always been witty, competitive, tense; games have usually brought out the best and worst in him. Now, however, he seems anxious and elderly. Her response to her mother is equally layered with positive and negative thoughts: when Therese kisses her, "Her mother smiles exuberantly, her face in a kind of burst; she loves affection, is hungry and grateful for it. When she was younger, she was a frustrated, mean mother, and so she is pleased when her children act as if they don't remember." Moore shows a family coming together despite the fact that the siblings seem to be divided against each other. Ultimately, the various divisions in the family group are overcome through the presence of Therese's infant niece, Winnie, who sits "calm and observant in her mother's arms, a pink incontinent Buddha who knows all her letters" and "seems like the sanest person in the room." The realistic combination of joy, confusion, and despair ends with goodbyes, which to Therese's mind "sounds like *could cry.*"

Perhaps the most acclaimed story from *Birds of America* is "People Like That Are the Only People Here: Canonical Babbling from Peed Onk," about a woman dealing with her infant son's cancer. Once again, Moore's writing seems autobiographical, but she claims that all her work is entirely fictionalized and refuses to discuss her and her husband's experiences with their child's cancer. As Moore told Dwight Garner, the story "was fiction . . . I re-imagined everything. . . . Fiction can come from real-life events and still be fiction. It can still have that connection, that germ." Moore strenuously resists autobiographical interpretations of any of her stories or novels. In fact, she claims that when she reads publicly she intentionally selects stories with male protagonists to avoid being identified with the narrator. The issue of correspondence between details from Moore's life and from her stories notwithstanding, "People Like That Are the Only People Here" certainly provides an intimate look at modern-day tragedy.

The visual quality of certain moments in the story, such as when the mother finds a blood clot in her baby's diaper, are vivid. The blood clot is described as "a tiny mouse heart packed in snow"–anything except what it actually is. Such descriptions present not only Moore's skill with language, but also illustrate the mother's attempts throughout this story to mentally deflect the child's illness into and onto other things. As the story follows the family through the traumatic series of events to the uncertain ending, Moore's gift for mixing tenderness, wit, sadness, and realism is apparent. Familiar themes, regarding social roles, a woman questioning her identity, a relationship breaking down, and strained communication, are present in the story but overshadowed by the trauma the characters are undergoing. The failing relationship is not a cause but merely a symptom of the pain.

"People Like That Are the Only People Here" emphasizes a new theme, which, in turn, comments on Moore's work in general: the difficulty of actually expressing pain. The narrator, referred to only as "the mother," confronts this insufficiency of language whenever her husband suggests she write about their experiences, but it becomes most prominent in the discussions of the child. Failed communication plays a prominent role in all of Moore's writing, but in this story the surgeon's suggestion that the infant's inability to put his pain into words lessens its severity leads the mother to philosophize on the nature of pain in language. What begins as an attempt at comforting a grieving mother turns into a testament to the lack of understanding surrounding the parents: "Who can say what babies do with their agony and shock? Not they themselves. (Baby talk: isn't it a stitch?) They put it all no place anyone can really see. They are like a different race, a different species: they seem not to experience pain the way *we* do. Yeah, that's it: their nervous systems are not as fully formed, *and they just don't experience pain the way we do.*"

"Terrific Mother" follows "People Like That Are the Only People Here" to conclude *Birds of America.* Although slightly anticlimactic after the intensity of the penultimate story, "Terrific Mother," with its examination of two people finding themselves and each other, is also one of the finest in this collection. Adrienne has "entered a puritanical decade, a demographic moment– whatever it was–when the best compliment you could get was, 'You would make a terrific mother.' The wolf whistle of the nineties." Adrienne accidentally kills a friend's infant in a fall from a picnic bench and then retreats into solitude for seven months, after which she finally agrees to marry her boyfriend, Martin, and travel with him to a European scholars' retreat. The rest of the story details her healing process and mocks the pretensions of the academics surrounding her. These scholars from various disciplines are described as being overeducated to the point that they "can no longer converse with their own mothers. . . . They have literally lost their mother tongue."

Adrienne's self-discovery is aided by a visit to a masseuse, who leads her toward physical and emotional well-being: "With these hands upon her, she felt a little forgiven, and began to think generally of forgiveness, how much it was required in life: to forgive everyone, yourself, the people you loved, and then wait to be forgiven by them." Although the conclusion does not resolve all of the relationship's communication and intimacy problems, the focus on forgiveness and healing makes the story stand out among Moore's generally less optimistic tales of dysfunctional individuals, such as "How," "You're Ugly, Too," "Beautiful Grade," and "Willing."

Criticism of *Birds of America* has centered on the increasing intensity of Moore's fiction in both plot and language, the greater depth and complexity of her characters, and her use of searing, dark humor. James McManus, in his 20 September 1998 review for *The New York Times,* "The Unbearable Lightness of Being," called Moore's writing "fluid, cracked, mordant, colloquial." Her sentences can "hold, even startle, us as they glide beneath the radar of ideological theories of behavior to evoke the messy, god-awful behavior itself." McManus observed that in a few instances–in "Charades," for example–the dialogue seems to degenerate into wisecracking but overall praised the collection for articulating the pain and humor of contemporary existence: "it will stand by itself as one of our funniest, most telling anatomies of human love and vulnerability." In her review for *The Washington Post* (25 September 1998) Carolyn See criticizes the fact that so much of Moore's work reflects the unhinged perceptions of upper-middle-class, well-educated women. She praises *Birds of America,* however, for taking on deeper issues such as cancer and death rather than limiting her scope to that of failed relationships.

At their best, Moore's short stories are poignant reflections of the human spirit on trial. Alternately hilarious and distressing, Moore's short fiction generally presents a sharp and cynical view of modern existence that often seems like autobiographical reflections on the world of a middle-class woman, exhibiting a kind of self-reflection of which her characters, such as Zoë in "You're Ugly, Too," Mary in "Two Boys," and Charlene in "How to Be an Other Woman," are usually incapable. Moore's fiction has much in common with other writers of her generation, such as Amy Hempel and Deborah Eisenberg. As Passaro observed, her writing offers "immediacy and intelligence, an unassailable skepticism about our public culture and our private habits, and a narrative efficiency and humor that is sharp enough to cut the bone." Throughout her work a dark humor pervades, lightening the painful plots and charming the reader with wit and irony. As her work in short fiction evolves, it has moved away from the gimmicky, yet highly amusing, stylistic devices of *Self-Help* and toward a more profound exploration of the psychology of the characters she creates. Certain themes, however, have remained constant: failing relationships and communication breakdowns, the pain of loss compounded by the physical pain of disease, the frustration and guilt of feeling trapped in a relationship, loneliness and the human need–yet resistance to–real intimacy. Moore's witty, painful, and believable reflections of contemporary existence have gained her a rightful place among writers of the late-twentieth and early-twenty-first centuries.

Interviews:

Vince Passaro, "Books," *Mirabella* (February 1992): 46, 48, 51;

Dwight Garner, "Moore's Better Blues: Lorrie Moore Finds the Lighter Side of Ordinary Madness in 'Birds of America,'" *Salon.com,* 27 October 1998 <www.salon.com/books/int/1998/10/cov_27int.html>.

References:

Don Lee, "About Lorrie Moore," *Ploughshares,* 24 (Fall 1998): 224–229;

Michael Schumacher, *Reasons to Believe* (New York: St. Martin's Press, 1988).

Kent Nelson
(21 April 1943 –   )

Teresa Winterhalter
Armstrong Atlantic State University

BOOKS: *The Tennis Player and Other Stories* (Urbana: University of Illinois Press, 1977);

Cold Wind River (New York: Dodd, Mead, 1981);

All Around Me Peaceful (New York: Dell, 1989);

The Middle of Nowhere (Salt Lake City: Peregrine Smith, 1991);

Language in the Blood (Salt Lake City: Peregrine Smith, 1991);

Discoveries: Stories of the San Juan Mountains (Ouray, Colo.: Western Reflections, 1998);

Toward the Sun: The Collected Sports Stories of Kent Nelson (New York: Breakaway, 1998).

SELECTED PERIODICAL PUBLICATIONS–
UNCOLLECTED: "Crossing," *Sewanee Review,* 55 (1978): 157–175;

"The Orange Grove Book of Dreams," *New Virginia Review,* 8 (1991): 68–75;

"Dakota Rose," *Witness,* 8 (1991): 76–81;

"A World of Unnamed Things," *Nimrod,* 38 (1994): 145–160;

"The Dark Ages," *Southern Review,* 32 (Winter 1997): 114–123;

"Rituals of Sleep," *Chicago Tribune Literary Supplement,* 28 September 1997, p. 14.

Kent Nelson (photograph © by Miriam Berkley)

In his short fiction, written mostly in the last quarter of the twentieth century, Kent Nelson exhibits an extraordinary beauty and fluency of narrative voice. His uncomplicated plotlines unfold with elegance, even in the most rustic settings. Frequently set in the American West and Southwest, his stories also reflect a naturalist's knowledge of bird, plant, and animal life. Yet, as his language swells at key moments into highly lyrical description, Nelson moves well beyond nature writing, creating a poetics of perception through which to rediscover an already inhabited land. So doing, he renders the everyday world oddly strange, yet–in his descriptive precision–hauntingly familiar. This quality of his prose is in part what led W. D. Wetherell to proclaim on the dust jacket of *Toward the Sun: The Collected Sports Sto-* *ries of Kent Nelson* (1998) that "Kent Nelson has written . . . as accomplished a body of short fiction as anyone writing today."

Although he has received little critical attention, his command of language casts a powerful spell. More importantly, the overarching effect of his narrative voice is that his stories appear deceptively simple. For Nelson, style is not merely a question of fashioning words upon the page; rather, his considerable lyricism allows him to render seemingly unutterable aspects of his characters' inner lives. His four collections of short stories, *The Tennis Player and Other Stories* (1977), *The Middle of Nowhere* (1991), *Discoveries: Stories of the San Juan Mountains* (1998), and *Toward the Sun,* plus the steady stream of fiction he has published in the intervening years (some ninety-six stories in various literary and mass-market venues and three novels), all distinguish Nelson as one of the finest short-story writers of the post–World War II years. Within each work his narrative poetics cannot be separated from his discursive landscapes of human emotion.

Much like poems, in fact, Nelson's stories include an undercurrent of suggested meanings. Stressing both erotic splendor and sexual emptiness, he traces the theme of male-female love as if trying to discover imaginatively just what the unremitting search for connection means. At the same time he focuses on the intricacies of the natural world, implying that the outdoors are a sanctuary of counsel and redemption for his characters. In this dual emphasis on the insufferable ache and solace of solitude he suggests that the quest for self-realization is as essential as the quest for communion. Indeed, because many of his main characters are either athletes or artists, defined by their struggles to reach their marks, he reveals how the search for love may be inextricable from a contrary need for an autonomous identity.

Although Nelson's thematic concerns are marked by such sentiment, his delivery of them defies romantic accounting. While the physical world mirrors his characters' inner lives, his story lines often center upon things that are missing, on people who are leaving or are absent, or upon words his characters cannot quite say. Through this governing metaphor of absence—which also structures his three novels, *Cold Wind River* (1981), *All Around Me Peaceful* (1989), and *Language in the Blood* (1991)—he achieves a delicate balance between telling all and not telling enough. Leading readers to the edge of understanding, Nelson's omissions become intrinsic to his themes. In these gaps he intimates resolutions that defy expression but are, nevertheless, things readers already consciously, subconsciously, or intuitively know. Thereby resisting pat conclusions, he creates a narrative indeterminacy to engage readers in their own processes of interpretation. Like poems, then, his stories appear in carefully measured forms, inviting rereading and opening multiple passageways to discovery.

Kent Sadlier Nelson was born in Cincinnati, Ohio, on 21 April 1943 to Jane and Albert Nelson. In 1948 his family moved to Colorado Springs, Colorado, where he grew up and from an early age nurtured his fascination with birds and the wilderness. His father was less than successful as an attorney but was a fairly good amateur actor and photographer who demanded a great deal from his three children. Because Nelson's father changed jobs frequently and money was a problem, his mother taught elementary school. In an interview with Susan Emerick Robertson for *The Missouri Review* (March 1988) he recalled, with a note of apparent distaste, how his father "drove around town in a yellow Cadillac convertible," posturing hale and hearty, although the family was not well-to-do. In the same interview he said his father "was a kind person, but he did things for me because of what he wanted, not because of what I might have wanted." Perhaps more telling, he adds that from his father he was "taught independence," but "not taught to love." Similarly, he describes his mother as a repressed, unaffectionate person who "took little interest in her own grandchildren."

Yet, despite his painful memories of his parents, Nelson often renders sympathetic portraits of fathers and mothers. And his adolescent years with them in Colorado nevertheless gave him two other lifelong influences—nature and sports. As a youth he published a nature newspaper, and his first attempt at a novel, at age ten, was about children who witness a hunter shoot an egret. He was also highly successful in high-school athletics, winning varsity letters in six sports. Even in these early years, however, he felt some discordance between his allegiance to the natural world and the demands of competition. He recounts sitting on his rooftop watching birds, wondering why later that afternoon he would endure the violence of a football game.

The emotional ambivalence embedded in this memory echoes throughout much of Nelson's early life. Following his brother's lead, he attended Yale University on a full academic scholarship, majored in political science (which he later recalled was a waste of time), played varsity ice hockey and tennis, and graduated in 1965 with academic distinction. Still, he was unsure of his future. He attended Harvard University Law School, concentrating on environmental law, graduated in 1968, and passed the bar exam in Colorado; yet, he has never practiced law. His ambivalence toward pursuing law as a profession, however, might be linked in part to the creative-writing class he took at Yale. In this class he won the Wallace Short Story Prize and published a story in the *Yale Daily News,* which led him to consider the possibility of writing fiction as a career. Then, in his first year of law school, he suffered a spinal tumor, which made the abstract notion of his own death seem real and caused him to evaluate his priorities. After marrying Judith Ann Hunter in 1968, he sequestered himself in a crumbling castle in Northern Bavaria that had been in his mother's family since the 1600s. During a three-year sojourn there, he read three hun-

Dust jacket for Nelson's 1991 collection of stories that explore male-female relationships from both points of view

taught tennis lessons), and then in Charleston, South Carolina, where in 1974 their daughter, Dylan, was born. Two years later, the family moved to the San Juan Mountains in Colorado, where a son, Taylor, was born in 1977. This marriage, however, ended in 1985; throughout the difficult period of the dissolution of the marriage, Nelson continued to write and publish. In 1986 he married Laurie Anna Barker, and, until they divorced in 1992, they lived primarily in Exeter, New Hampshire, at Exeter Academy, where she taught. Two daughters, Lanier and Anna Leonie, were born to them in 1988 and 1989, respectively. Throughout his last two marriages, Nelson traveled alone and with his wives to Alaska, South Texas, Arizona, Maine, and the Pacific Northwest in search of rare birds. In addition, his enthusiasm for sports has never waned; in 1980 he took up squash and in 1989 played in the A-League in Boston and was ranked sixth in his age group nationally.

The Tennis Player and Other Stories, Nelson's first volume of short stories, is dedicated to his second wife, Nona. This dedication seems particularly appropriate because the collection focuses on the vague forms of dependency the male protagonists feel with respect to the women in their lives. In this focus Nelson suggests that human ties are crucial, even as his protagonists desire separation from or create distances between themselves and others. The title story, for example, focuses on Nicky, a semiprofessional tennis player who is trying to return to his old life after an unnamed illness or injury. His internal replay of the voices that surrounded him as he lay comatose in the hospital, resounding with echoes of Nelson's own recovery from his spinal tumor, structures the central motif of isolation in the story.

Even as Nicky is attempting a "comeback" to human connectedness, the inward space he inhabits offers him flight outside the mundane world of involvement with others. Therefore, while his day-to-day involvements return him to a promising tennis career, he makes love to his girlfriend, Caroline, only to forestall connection—because he does "not want to think about what it might be she had to tell him." Through his struggle to love Caroline, who is carrying his child, and to act responsibly by pursuing tennis, Nicky expresses his inarticulate sadness. His decision to withdraw from her is portrayed sympathetically; although he becomes "deeply tanned" by practicing in the sun, there is something pale and intangible in his spirit. The woman who helps him reenter the country-club world never fully completes his inner quest, as he reflects: "Caroline was my only respite, and yet I knew it was she I could never come back to." Nicky has been defeated by accepting his own situation: his resignation seems painfully complete when "later, sometime during

dred novels (supplementing the one hundred he read his last year of law school) and began writing in a conscious effort to train for the writer's life.

In many ways the years between Yale and Europe defined Nelson's life; yet, his personal relationships, especially those with women, also have hugely influenced his career as a writer. These relationships (ranging from marriages to profound platonic friendships), like the central idea in much of his fiction, have been defined by moments of distance and absence as much as by closeness. Perhaps the importance of women in his artistic life is best summarized by his reply to Roberton's observation in *The Missouri Review* interview that "your men characters look longingly to women for definition, as if women were somehow gateways to self-knowledge and self-realization"; Nelson added "especially if they're not there."

After three years in Europe he divorced, returned to the United States, and in 1973 met his second wife, Nona Hastie, who encouraged him to continue writing. They lived in Montana, again in Europe (where Nelson

their lovemaking, he had told her that he loved her"; "he knew he had to say it," although "he could not stand the dishonesty."

These parallels between "The Tennis Player" and Nelson's own experience with illness invite autobiographical associations between Nicky and the author, but they also preview how Nelson's evolution as a writer took him beyond those associations. No simple transposition of his life onto the scenes in his fiction is adequate to the task of charting the stylistic nuances that distinguish his writing. Indeed, as similar as Nicky may appear to Nelson himself, the development of his character also adumbrates explicitly literary concerns that draw Nelson's reflections well beyond his personal circumstances. In his thoughts, for example, Nicky casts himself beyond the stars through the shadow patterns of the leaves, and Nelson weights these descriptive moments to increase the poignancy of his internal questioning. Thus, early in his literary career Nelson draws upon his lifelong fascination with the environment to establish the natural world as an entryway to the unspeakable parts of one's existence. Although this emphasis is muted (even at times more ornamental than germane) in the early work, it nevertheless foreshadows the difficult task he sets for himself–to make the intangible, even abstract, process of searching for meaning materialize in concrete language.

"The Humpbacked Bird" (winner of the Emily Clark Balch Prize for fiction in 1975) is another accomplished early attempt to render the inexpressible in narrative. Two men, Tom and Schafer, scour the land around the wild Sierra del Carmen in West Texas in search of a missing boy. During their climb through formidable terrain, Tom recalls how he was in a similar setting at the time his own father abandoned him. He also reveals he has discovered (and left) the boy's dead body–he was killed by a rattlesnake–behind a cairn. He uses this information as a lever into Schafer's confidence, for, at some point, he must tell why he knows Schafer's girlfriend, Alene, who has suddenly left, will never return. Tom has been Alene's confidant in her decision to leave, and Nelson counterbalances his expressions of emotion with scenes of vultures and coyotes scavenging in the desert spaces. With his keen eye for the habits of carrion feeders, Nelson draws readers into the death-in-life emptiness the men feel. Tom reveals that sexual experiences in the men's pasts have left indelible memories and psychological scars on their present lives. The story closes, however, with Schafer "climbing high into the darkness," riding on the back of a bird "across some gulf" and into an inexplicable emotional awareness. Within its descriptive detail this story presages Nelson's future stylistic mastery; he captures the illusory stillness of an ever-changing landscape, using it to vivify the soaring experience of living.

In addition to foreshadowing Nelson's stylistic development, however, *The Tennis Player and Other Stories* also immediately reveals a strong thematic chain of connection among its stories. Throughout, Nelson elicits sympathetic responses to his male characters by re-creating their experiences of living through the vagaries of emotion. Indeed, this approach establishes the trajectory of his thematic arc as he traces characters caught between the solid demands of physical realities and ill-defined internal desires for something more. In their mute sufferings, Nelson establishes a continuity of focus that suggests that these stories are best understood as a sequence. Each story discerns various contours of the gap between the circumstances of his characters and the things they privately feel.

"The Man Who Paid to Sleep," for example, relates a brief exchange between an insomniac, Mr. Ashe, and his dowdy, "severe" female analyst. He has come to her because he wants to be able to sleep. Yet, even in his expressed need, communication fails. Impulsively cutting short their session, he wildly treks cross-country to see a woman (his first sexual encounter) that his analyst forced him to recall. Once he locates this woman, his quest is complete, even though she never recognizes him. Nelson suggests, however, that the object of Ashe's search defies translation into explicit language: he cannot tell his analyst why merely catching sight of this woman relieves his sleeplessness. Just as he reflects that "being lost in strange places is becoming familiar," he knows resolution comes to him from a source that necessarily eludes direct forms of communication. Moreover, through this indeterminancy, it becomes clear that Mr. Ashe is no screwball at large on the West Coast; rather, he is Nelson's embodiment of those vague forms of understanding that direct people's lives.

Two other significant stories in this collection further explore these near misses in communication, which, Nelson suggests, reveal underlying emotional connections. Both "Looking into Nothing" (included in *Best American Short Stories 1976*) and "Every Day a Promise" follow the internal voices of male protagonists who think much more than they say. Barry, in "Looking into Nothing," spends an entire night talking to himself, miles from the ranch on which he works. Alone in a wide-open space, Barry is one of Nelson's earliest romantic heroes–a lonely outsider who reappears in many settings throughout his work. Perceiving himself as on the lookout for (or providing comfort to) a missing hired hand, in his bivouac Barry recounts the events of an impossible love affair to no one but "the blackness behind the stars." His monologue makes clear that he can recount the story only to that blackness, and "it hurt him to look at the sky like that." His life is defined by a rugged, masculine reality unalloyed by his need to be held in intimate conversation and closeness.

Similarly, McCallum, the high-jump champion of "Every Day a Promise"–who shares a domestic arrangement with a woman, Hillary, and her two children–also possesses an inner life that is concealed from those closest to him, symbolized by the basement apartment he keeps as a secret retreat. Even though he feels "resurrected" by clearing the bar at an important track meet, his fulfillment is "a resurrection without joy." Thus, unable to articulate the motions of his heart, McCallum reveals the "gap in his spirit" that ultimately leaves him "helpless." Quite possibly, McCallum is the most helpless of all the male characters in this volume, because his isolation is thoroughly self-imposed. He cannot enfold those around him, but neither can he exit the lie of devotion and commitment his presence among them implies. He can no more articulate what his spirit is seeking than the reader can infer what it lacks. The sense of incompleteness in the story leaves the reader not knowing if McCallum will resign from his struggle to dissemble–if he will continue to take the initiative of flinging his body over the high bar and by extension commit himself to actions propelled by his own volition–or if he will quietly accept the limitations of his immediate situation and come to equate comfort with love.

Nelson's insight into the psychological and emotional states of his male characters suggests that, for him, verisimilitude of character relies upon faithfully rendering the internal heft of emotional ambivalence. This understanding threads throughout *The Tennis Player and Other Stories,* but perhaps "To Go Unknowing" best encapsulates the resultant inner torment his male characters suffer. In this story Marcos, the protagonist, literally is trapped by circumstance. Having been chosen to play Jesus in the Easter pageant of a small town in the foothills of the Sangre de Cristo Mountains of New Mexico, Marcos is ceremonially sacrificed in a reenactment of the Passion. Although he dreams of "flying free of the world," he "says nothing" to alter the events that transpire. In the dramatic conclusion, when his mother holds him after he is finally taken down and weeps, Marcos's reflections reveal that he believes no one knows what he has felt. Marcos's martyrdom symbolically represents the knowledge shared by many of Nelson's early male protagonists: they know their plight is in their own hands, but because they feel powerless to alter their lives, they face sacrificing their dreams of deeper human connection.

Yet, in his next volume of stories, Nelson moves beyond the internal exploration he hones through these heroes to expand his frame of reference and consequently the inner lives of other, heretofore minor characters. In his first two novels, *Cold Wind River* and *All Around Me Peaceful,* he brings his shadowy female characters into clearer focus, and many of the stories in *The Middle of Nowhere* (published simultaneously with his highly acclaimed novel *Language in the Blood,* winner of the Edward Abbey Award for Ecofiction in 1992) are told from a woman's point of view. More importantly, these stories stress the simultaneous perceptions that men and women must define, defer to, and even compromise in their relationships with one another. By broadening his range of narrative perspective he avoids becoming trapped (as he has said he fears) in writing the same story repeatedly. Indeed, Nelson's increasing command over point of view becomes instrumental in developing his larger stylistic enterprise of wresting meaning from incoherence.

In some ways this shift in focus is intimated in the outlines of Nelson's own life. The years between 1973 and 1992 are, in fact, bracketed by his second and third marriages. Indeed, a sense of his characters' enmeshment in one another's lives runs throughout his later work. Yet, at the same time, his stories often center on the struggle to connect and the sense of restlessness often accompanies feeling bound to the conditions of sharing a life. Drawing from his own feelings, Nelson verifies and expands the idea of being held captive to wanderlust.

Nelson was restless and frequently had little money during this period. At certain points, while working under the auspices of prestigious grants, he was able to concentrate primarily on writing. In 1978 and 1991 he won fellowships from the National Endowment for the Arts; in 1986 he received an Ingram-Merrill Fellowship; and in 1988 and 1990 grants from the New Hampshire Council for the Arts. After separating from his second wife he returned to another love, the West, working as a hired man for $7 an hour on an alfalfa ranch in South Dakota. In 1991 he accepted a yearlong fellowship to the Writers' Film Project, financed by Steven Spielberg. Then, his growing list of publications enabled him to secure non-tenure-track teaching positions. In 1992 he was the Distinguished Visiting Writer at Wichita State University; in 1995 he was the Coal Royalty Chairman at the University of Alabama; and in 1996 he was visiting professor in creative writing at the University of Tennessee.

As the narrative emphasis in *The Middle of Nowhere* reflects, Nelson understood his needs were never wholly disentangled from those around him. In fact, ever mindful of his responsibilities, throughout the years he has maintained a close relationship with each of his four children. No doubt because many of the stories in *The Middle of Nowhere* focus on wives and children in their own rights or in their relationships to one another, the reader sees not only Nelson's restlessness, but also the importance of marriage and children that has seeped into his life. Such connections also help to determine the courses he takes on his excursions through multiplicities in narrative perspective, the emotional worlds of women and children becoming the pivot points and narrative fulcrums of his stories. It is fitting that he dedicated *The Middle of Nowhere* to his two oldest children, Dylan and Taylor, for in it he explores the concentric circles of influence that surround any given life.

This collection is perhaps Nelson's most powerful, if not his most important, volume of stories. The lyrical and visionary qualities of the earlier fiction emerge through the preceding stories and filter into the inner quests and interpersonal desires that dominate these narratives. As John Jay Osborn Jr., author of *The Paper Chase* (1971), notes on the dust jacket of the collection, "these stories activate feelings you've forgotten you had, for the people you love, and the country around you." Throughout the collection Nelson demonstrates the extent to which he has mastered conveying grace through language. In each story some strange mystery unravels in a familiar setting, and through the reverberations of Nelson's precise rendering of mood and place, ineffable aspects of human emotion materialize. Moreover, the stories also discern multiple levels of feeling, as increasingly Nelson's characters are understood through their relationships to one another. In one form or another each character endures some disconnection. Because Nelson layers perspectives, however, no one character emerges as the misunderstood hero. Even at the unresolved, sometimes abrupt conclusion of a story, Nelson engages sensory descriptions of the natural world, letting poetry imply what remains unsaid between the characters. This swerve in narrative focus paradoxically leads the reader to feel closer to his characters' inner worlds.

Much of the force of *The Middle of Nowhere* depends upon a central analogy for human existence stressed by the title. In story after story Nelson's characters are lost in emotionally confusing landscapes. They are not so much confounded by their external situations as by the contours of their inward longings, however. The title story, which received the Pushcart Prize in 1990 and has been reprinted several times, focuses on Stephen, a pensive, working-class, bookish seventeen-year-old. Stephen's divorced mother has recently died, and he has gone to live with his father in

a trailer purposefully situated in the desolate outskirts of Tucson. The father parades a series of women past Stephen, finally bringing home Goldie, an Irish woman, to live with them. To please Goldie, the father works long hours, and in his absence Stephen also falls in love with her. After a sexual encounter with Goldie, Stephen departs suddenly early the next morning. His departure leaves many of the events of the plot unresolved, but in this refusal to answer all the questions the story raises, Nelson gains greater resolution. Stephen sets out for the Pacific coast to look for a place like the ones Goldie told him of in Ireland, "where it snows into the sea." Describing his subsequent life in hindsight, he says, "I wasn't certain of anything. It was the beginning for me of a sadness which, I suppose, had to come to me sometime, an aching that lasted for years." In this closing image Stephen escapes not only the present, but also reaches for the promise of meaning that forever may be beyond his grasp. He frees himself, as he must, but he also suffers the pain that many suffer when freedom means letting go of what they long to embrace.

In this description and in other small ways, "The Middle of Nowhere" pays homage to James Joyce, as Nelson bows to Joyce's insights into the nexus of paralyzed lives within the citizens of Dublin and shows his own increased perceptions into the interrelatedness of the emotional states of his characters. Indeed, this story is not only the tale of a lonely adolescent. With a stunning economy of metaphor Nelson reveals that Stephen's father and Goldie, also, are trapped in an endless search for connection. On their nighttime rides together through the desert back roads in search of a mountain lion, Stephen's father finally "wears out," because he feels inadequate to the task of giving Goldie what she wants. Goldie, however, is unique among his lovers precisely because she wants to find what cannot be seen. She wants that essential knowledge of love—an essence hauntingly symbolized by the mountain lion that eludes them. By tethering the reader to each of the characters' struggle for fulfillment, Nelson suspends judgment about their needs or failures. He suggests that lived realities can never be singular in perspective; rather, multiple feelings and personalities create the uneven terrain of life.

By sustaining a loose, comprehensive relationship among the stories in the volume, Nelson draws readers further into this lived complexity, creating a richer landscape of emotions to which his earlier work has only alluded. In "Invisible Life" (included in *Best American Short Stories 1986*), "I Had to Do Something," and "The Mine from Nicaragua" (included in *Prize Stories, O. Henry Awards Anthology,* 1992), Nelson's themes encompass the world of middle-aged romance. He descries—at least sotto voce—the inner and outer realities of mature people as they share space and time. Each of these stories explores a different aspect of marriage, marital separation, or the attendant impact of both on children's needs and perceptions. "Invisible Life" and "I Had to Do Something," for example, examine the everyday patterns of married couples who juggle the demands of careers and children with their search for love. Both focus on husbands and wives who cannot outreach the emotional gulfs that divide them.

In "Invisible Life" Allison tries to "live her life" by going back to graduate school after twelve years defined by marriage and three children, the youngest of whom is a baby. She reasons she is not trying to "be liberated at all," and as she tends children and fixes meals she clearly is not so much rejecting her present situation as expressing her need for other means of fulfillment. Her husband, the narrator of the story, sees the situation differently, however. In fact, his description of his mother, who has come to visit, reveals more about him than it does about her. Noting that it is "as though the news Allison had given her had made her suddenly and irrevocably old," he projects himself into her reflection on the windowpane. He feels outworn, displaced, and left out, and even imagines his mother and his wife are in collusion against him. This sense of being excluded ultimately causes his childhood fears of vulnerability and isolation in the dark to resurface. Thus, Nelson's overarching focus reveals how two discrete realities simultaneously depend upon and conflict with one another. In this convoluted landscape Nelson cuts to the quick of the inner lives of two people trying to share one world.

An additional perspective in this story, however, shows that despite their separate realities the husband and wife remain connected through their children. Especially as Nelson's language crests in the last few lines, the reader recognizes that the children are not just expected members of the cast. They are, rather, conduits through which judgment of either parent is suspended. Recalling a discussion with his daughter Tricia about the protozoan life in a drop of water, the narrator goes out alone to watch "the slow current curl among the rocks, wondering what did happen to the invisible creatures in the water, and waiting for Tricia to come to me." By the end of the story he knows the gaps in his marriage cannot be filled by the mere presence of his wife–he sees they both have invisible lives. Yet, the children occupy a separate space in their relationship, a space the narrative thrust aligns with the inscrutable, invisible forces of nature; they become a source of insight for those undone by the mystery of disconnection.

"I Had to Do Something" is a similar story, but here the inquiry into the effects of marital distance comes from the woman's point of view. In this story the couple shares an upscale and comfortable life. The husband, Larry, is so successful at law, in fact, that the family spends an entire summer at a vacation cottage in the Adirondacks. Slow disclosures during their time there, however, reveal that Larry is involved with another woman, and after a weekend punctuated by silences he announces that he intends to spend the rest of his vacation with her. In Larry's shadowiness and taciturn walks, however, Nelson creates an obvious disjuncture between the wife's emotional response to the news and Larry's sense of himself. Again, Nelson constructs a world of multiple perspectives that refuses easy moral conclusions.

Readers align, however, most closely with the narrator's sense of abandonment as she spends the day after Larry leaves working out her private suffering by cutting and splitting firewood. As she battles blackflies and oils chainsaws, she attempts to manage the pain of Larry's leaving and the strength she requires to endure it before her children. This powerful metaphor, however, also introduces an element of the plot that snags Nelson's otherwise flawless female perspective. The narrator recognizes that Rennie, the handyman who serves as the proprietor of the place, is solicitous of her, and she refers to him as "a man who could fix things," an innuendo of romantic potential that suggests a too-quick resolution to the narrator's crisis. While this story reverberates with multiple perspectives, the reader finds Nelson auditioning voices that are, at certain moments, still circumscribed by his own consciousness.

Nelson regains his fluid narrative stride by focusing on the magical intervention of children. Coming upon her mother enveloped in sadness, Astrid, the couple's youngest daughter, holds out her swimming snorkel to her and says, "Breathe." Then, at the close of the story she climbs into bed with her mother, as if drawn by an intuitive awareness of her despair. When her mother tells her "we'll be stronger in the broken place" and suggests their pain is like a bone that must knit, Astrid's role in the story becomes clear. Astrid embodies Nelson's wager that the deepest connections occur beneath the surface of spoken words. Under the bedcovers the narrator and her child weave the blessing of human comfort as the lyrical descriptions again build. In the last lines the narrator reflects: "Lightning flashed farther away and left us in its wake the darkness and a soft drizzle which fell around us like music through the leaves." As in "Invisible Life" the child is the catalyst for the adult's moment of peace; perhaps only children know the way back to the spiritual grace of the natural world.

"The Mine from Nicaragua," however, presents no such consolation, although it explores another important aspect of Nelson's concerns for the strains within marital relationships, although without the consoling presence of children. In this story a large object has washed ashore on a private stretch of beach on the eastern seaboard. Amid his neighbors' speculations about what the object might be, Barkley, the protagonist, jibes that it might be an old war mine, foreshadowing the dangerous, unspoken desires about to make landfall in his own life. He has a comfortable marriage to Muriel, but during the impromptu beach party that follows the discovery of the object, he is introduced to a beautiful cellist visiting her cousin at the beach. Barkley lingers at the party because he sees in this woman a spirit that promises to fulfill his unnamed needs. He senses this rapport, however, only because they share an interest in birds, the landscape, and art, marking his dream of her with a conspicuous romanticism. He is transfixed at the end of the evening by strains of her music drifting across the sand.

Nelson does not, however, leave him in the limbo of nameless ambivalence, as were similarly situated earlier heroes; rather, at this moment, Barkley comes to a peaceful realization. As he watches "the sea's long reach, churn up from its depth its new harvest of shells, while all around him in the dunes ornamented with sea oats were hundreds of sleeping plovers," his fulfillment becomes evident. Recognizing his desires are naturally restless beneath their slumbering surface, Barkley faults no one that his marriage delivers him into romantic dreams of other women. Nor does he conclude that his dream-speckled connection to the cellist means Muriel is insufficient. For the first time a male character finds comfort, even while knowing that the complexities and contradictions of his life may never be resolved or diminished.

Most clearly, two other significant stories in the volume, "Yellow Flowers" and "A Country of My Own Making," reveal the thematic possibilities of Nelson's multiplication of point of view. "Yellow Flowers" probes the secret life of an eight-year-old boy as he retreats from the objective world and shuts himself into a world of illusions. Through Nelson's command of perspective, the boy's story, as well as his parents' attempts to understand the private life of their child, reveals the emotional realities of all three. Similarly, "A Country of My Own Making" constructs perspectives from various points along the course of a life. The story traces events that cause the female narrator to revisit the deaths of her parents, the disappearance of old loves, and her final choice to return to her hometown as the person she is, not as the girl she was. Although she sees in the stories of an old friend "a life not unusual, a slow dissimulation not unlike my own," her present narrative lens is far more complex, and through

it she sees that too much has intervened for them ever to reconnect.

Accumulating among these perspectives, however, the final vision in both stories discerns the passage of the natural world to speechless lands within inner consciousness. The father watches his son, at the close of "Yellow Flowers," "pause in a game and stare into the woods or maybe at the clouds sliding across the early autumn sky." At that moment he knows his son wants "to disappear again." In "A Country of My Own Making" the narrator reflects that "there were stories there . . . new worlds I intended to make of the passing seasons. In the far distance—miles away still—the solitary light of my own house appeared beyond the low hills. . . . trembling, it seemed, in the clear air, like a comet moving away from me even as I rushed toward it along the highway through the dark air." Both central figures find the natural world integrates perspectives in their fields of inner vision. In these moments Nelson demonstrates why he places such a premium on lyrical description. These scenes suggest that language never really captures all of the complexities of consciousness; yet, he brings the reader closer to those elusive parts through his command of connotations. In focusing the reader's attention outward Nelson employs what T. S. Eliot termed "the objective correlative" and makes those inner understandings, which refuse to be captured in words, somehow legible.

The title "A Country of My Own Making," then, summarizes how Nelson's diction yields equivalencies for the inarticulate aspects of self. It implies that people make their own countries—their inner worlds—through the stories they tell themselves about themselves. In Nelson's case, and his narrator's, this context shaping is precisely the enterprise of the fiction writer. And because both want their words to touch upon what cannot be expressed, they seek a language that extends beyond surface delineations. This search is also central to "A World of Unnamed Things" (published in *Nimrod* in 1994) and "The Dark Ages" (published in the Winter 1997 issue of *The Southern Review*), later stories in which the protagonists question how words not only reflect, but also construct, realities. It is also the metaphysical core of *Language in the Blood* (for which the working title was "A Vocabulary of Love"), in which Nelson explores how language, at best, approximates the indescribable knowledge that one is in love. All of these narratives embody why Nelson has characterized writing as the most difficult undertaking possible for him. They demonstrate that the tactile experience of living not only seems to defy translation into language, it also gathers meaning through the fictions created about it. The writer, then, carries the enormous charge of taking what cannot be expressed, pressing it into

Dust jacket photo of Nelson during a cross-country marathon,
an experience he draws on for the title story
in Toward the Sun *(1998)*

words, and acknowledging that the visions rendered exert exegetical pressure back onto life itself.

In all of the stories in this volume, by a movement away from the singular point of view, Nelson manifests the unifying thrust of his larger current of thought—that no life, even in its quest for self-realization, can ever be wholly independent of the lives with which it is connected, nor can it be distilled from the land that supports it. As Nelson developed this understanding throughout the 1980s, many of his stories took on an increasingly political and social focus. "Crossing" (published in *Sewanee Review* in 1978 and selected for inclusion in *100 Best Stories, The Pushcart Prize* in 1982), "The Orange Grove Book of Dreams" (published in *The New Virginia Review* in 1991), and "Dakota Rose" (first published in *Witness* in 1991; winner in the PEN Syndicated Fiction Project in 1991 and broadcast on National Public Radio in 1993) relate the struggles of immigrants, immigration patrol workers, and Native Americans to break the chains of culture and cultural bias to admit the possibility of a different future.

This augmented social focus also increases the scope of Nelson's persistent faith in the grandeur of the

natural world. The lives of his characters shimmer under the genuine insights in his language, but increasingly (as he revises several of his earlier stories) these characters also become avatars of the wilderness itself. Making them embody the forces that the contemporary world seems bent on destroying, he suggests that nature is not only a balm for troubled hearts; it is also the fire in the veins that modern existence threatens to extinguish. As civilization slithers closer to those last hiding places of solace and energy, he explores the consequences this encroachment can have on his characters' souls.

Because Nelson emphasizes the vital force of the natural world, he is often aligned with other nature and environmentalist writers such as Alison Hawthorne Deming, Jim Harrison, and Rick Bass. Among these writers is a common argument that the loss of the cultural soul results from the destruction of the natural environment. Nelson distinguishes himself among them, however, through the narrative technique he refines in his third collection, *Discoveries: Stories of the San Juan Mountains*. In it his words are meticulously chosen; several of the stories are revisions of earlier stories, and they provide evidence that questions of style are inextricable from those of theme. Refashioning his language to resist romanticizing the worlds of his characters, he lays out a nearly neutral position in regard to the traditional elegy for the loss of nature. No amount of lyricism clouds his sense of the daunting, even violent, potential of the physical world. Yet, for Nelson even the most hostile world must turn upon a poetics beyond the capacities of human comprehension. Thus, writing with apparent detachment about the places to which his characters are resolutely attached, he demonstrates his abiding respect for the places he loves. To a certain extent the authorial detachment is an illusion of his simple, rich phrasing, for in the years since his third divorce he has spent countless hours writing, hiking, running, birding, and being in those places that bring him (and his fiction) closest to the shared forms of human and wild existence.

Indeed, each of the stories in *Discoveries* bears the imprint of Nelson's maturing watchfulness. Notably, the title story, which first appeared in *The Southern Review* in 1986, was reprinted in *The Middle of Nowhere* in 1993 and was revised again for *Discoveries*, demonstrates his refined narrative acuity. Jack, the protagonist, who is drawn to discover the secret his wife, Arliss, keeps in her journal, increasingly must turn his search for understanding back toward himself. In the most recent version of the story his need to fish the Animas River outside Ouray, Colorado, is inextricably bound up in his need to navigate uncharted places. As the story progresses these unknown regions come to include not only the secrets of the woman to whom he is married but also hidden places within himself.

In the earlier versions of the story Jack's obsession with his wife's journal primarily reveals his frustration with things he cannot control. In the version in *Discoveries,* however, Nelson redesigns descriptive passages to accentuate Jack's symbiosis with the world around him. In the version in *The Middle of Nowhere,* when Jack finally picks up Arliss's journal to read it, Nelson describes the strain of his action but leaves his agency separate from the influence of the environment. When Jack rushes to find the journal, his adrenaline-laced search is narrated in one paragraph, and the narrator's impressions of the river and the sunlight are described in a subsequent one. In the later version, however, Nelson integrates Jack's movements with the sway of the river's surface. As he picks up the journal, in "the riffles downstream was a brilliant flash without color or depth, as if the light had its source not in the sun, but in the river itself." In this fluid simultaneity Nelson refashions the swollen emotions that have absorbed Jack throughout the story. His fears move beyond inflammations requiring the salve of natural surroundings and align with the forces of nature itself. His hunt for the unknown aspects of his wife's desires becomes an instinctual search, bearing him along with a drive as inscrutable as the source of the light in the river. Nelson's seamless narrative technique thus re-creates Jack's insight as a moment unmediated by the filter of authorial perspective. His descriptive fidelity to one's simultaneous inward and outward existence allows readers to participate in the actual sensory and meditative processes that constitute Jack's moments of perception and understanding.

Each of the stories in this collection recounts such a defining moment of discovery. No matter where in the mountains the story is set—in the hermitage of a gold prospector in "A Way of Dying" or in a Telluride ski resort in "The Actress"—each centers on a moment of realization that is as undeniable as it is difficult to pin down. Whether depicting a young man's first scent of death in "Wind Shift," the fallibility of a strong-willed parent in "One Turned Wild," a woman's silent communion with a herd of elk in "The Spirits of Animals," or a mother's newly formed sense of herself in "Encounters," Nelson shows the crucial interaction between environment and personality in bringing his characters to new levels of awareness. In his control over narrative technique he eludes the trap of romanticized excursions to the wilderness to reclaim lost glory; because he refuses to misread the effects of nature, no essential wholeness is restored by the mere increase in his characters' perceptions. Instead, as does Jack in "Discoveries," his characters realize the forces that

drive them exceed their potential to slip the tug of instinct. Nelson pays his deepest tribute to the power of the wilderness by stressing that nature is always in flux; his characters become most vital when they accept their lives as part of an ongoing natural process.

From this initial understanding, Nelson's prose never loses its restlessness. In particular, in "One Turned Wild" and "Light and Rain" he explores the signature of the animal within human nature. A wild dog in a middle-class family's backyard in "One Turned Wild" negates their belief in their tame existence. A woman who catches fish with her bare hands in "Light and Rain" supplies transcendence beyond futile, self-defeating attempts to cleave to memory and forestall the evolution of time. In both stories the natural world presses upon characters who are making a pretense of normalcy—a trip to the supermarket or a day's hike up a mountain trail—forcing them to admit that routine cannot keep nature's unpredictability at bay. Marshall, the father in "One Turned Wild," wearies under the demands of his everyday world. The appearance of a wild Chesapeake Bay retriever in his garden one morning, however, promises to reunite him with elemental forces his daily existence denies. Yet, when the dog lunges upon Marshall's young son, he is forced to shoot him, even though his "muscles worked smoothly," its "legs bent, body low to the ground," even though "he was beautiful flying through the meadow." In "Light and Rain" Chaney, a young man who struggles with haunting memories of a woman he once loved, hikes mountain trails to find forgetfulness in the ache of his muscles and a flask of whiskey. Instead, in the abundance of another woman's affinity with the natural world, he learns love itself may be as cyclical as the weather. Taking off his clothes as well as the resistance they symbolize, he wades "naked into the pool" to join her at the end of the story, "and the rain fell over them."

No doubt Nelson's lifetime love affair with birding—an obsession that has led him to compile a life list of more than seven hundred species of birds and that has also led him into some of the most remote spaces on the American continent—determines the vivid rendering of these scenes and his unerring sense of place. Or, as he commented in an unpublished interview in March 1998, "In the process of looking for birds, you learn to look at everything." In stories such as these Nelson communicates a political imperative. In underscoring that his characters' lives are merely segments of a larger reality, he stresses that his readers also must recognize the divinity in their environment. *Discoveries* courses with the sincerity of a writer who is committed to the preservation of the natural world.

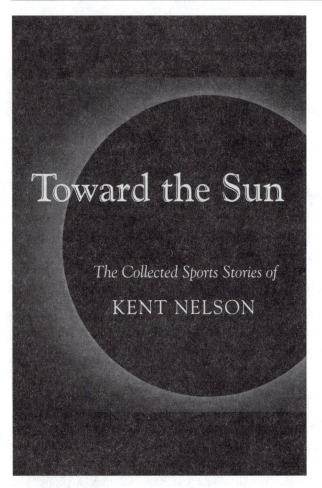

Dust jacket for the 1998 collection focusing on Nelson's lifetime interest in the psychology of athletes

Perhaps "Toward the Sun," also the title story in his 1998 collection of sports stories, is most charged with the sense of urgency that accompanies this commitment. In this story, which is more about responding to elemental drives than about the training of a long-distance runner, Nieman runs to deny a domesticated life. Unlike that of earlier male characters, his flight is not from a woman at home (a profile painfully rendered from a woman's point of view in the 1990 story "On the Way to California"). Rather, it is an embrace of the wild urge he has felt to run throughout his life. It is interesting to note that, in the years just prior to the publication of this volume, Nelson himself had run two marathons in the same mountains in which Nieman trains. Just as Nelson claimed he only ran the races to see if he could, Nieman refuses scholarships and competitions, running purely to satisfy impulse. For readers, however, deeply unsettling images enter, taking the story well beyond the markers of any road race. During his last run Nieman smears himself with elk urine in order to mask his scent and chases a herd of elk. His

victory becomes evident when he flees the traps of social expectation. Any moral judgment of him because of the woman he leaves on the trail, even though the story is narrated from her point of view, is marginal and slight. She, too, reflects that "to cage an animal destroys its essence," asking what it becomes "when it cannot hunt and run free?" Nelson's message is completely convincing, because, like the narrator in this story, the reader fully believes his vision of Nieman's success.

Indeed, throughout his work Nelson verifies that the act of reading is most powerful when it is the journey of the individual, the self who is after some sort of answer, some corroboration of the sensations of existing, thinking, and feeling. He relies upon the reader's identification with the text to transmit his environmental message, to fortify the political impact of his work. His most recent stories increase the intensity of this identification, in fact, because they increase the perspectives from which understanding accrues. The irresolution of the stories insists that readers' interpretive faculties bristle to attention.

Several of the stories in *Toward the Sun* are revisions of earlier versions, but Nelson's more clearly formulated compositional principle—to raise readers above their limited angles of perspective—is reflected in them. This reach upward is embodied in the title of the collection, from a line in Stephen Spender's "I Think Continually of Those Who Are Truly Great," and suggests that athletes are "born of the sun," compelled to "travel a short while" beyond their own limitations. Throughout the collection, sports are driving obsessions for the central characters, but athletic accomplishment is not their strongest motivation. These stories move from squash courts to hockey arenas and track meets, but they also take the reader close to the sources of fire in their protagonists' personal histories. In "A False Encounter" a grief-stricken son traces his father's suicide back to a moment when he got up from a knockout punch to face certain defeat. In "Projections" a man with a promising career in the National Hockey League loses his edge and declines so far that he finally causes the death of his own son. In "Floating" a recently divorced father takes his basketball-dribbling son camping in order to bring them closer, only to discover his profound fear of losing him.

Other stories, such as "The Tennis Player," "Every Day a Promise," and "The Squash Player," were revised by Nelson for this volume; he tempers his earlier perspectives on his heroes' isolated lives with a discerning narrative distance. He is less apologetic for their shortcomings, more candid about their circumstances, and more psychologically probing. Also, as he redraws these protagonists he is increasingly concerned with the processes of aging. His heroes are, at moments, no longer physically dominant. Sports, then, are a crucible that shapes, transforms, and even deforms his characters' lives. But in all their contests, Nelson re-creates the unruly, incendiary struggles within the hearts and minds of his protagonists.

Throughout *Toward the Sun* Nelson's male characters (including those from earlier stories) become more substantial and varied, even more intellectual, charming, and vital. Such is the case especially with the most recent story in the collection, "Alton's Keeper." In this story Tom Pritchett, a Charleston real-estate agent, finds that playing squash breaks down the barriers of his background and breeding. Alton, a photographer and Pritchett's elusive friend who engineers a connection between Pritchett and Yolanda, a young black woman from an inner-city neighborhood, appears and disappears, as if to prompt tensions latent in the biases of class and culture to moments of crisis. Circling around each other, these characters emphasize that squash is the occasion through which Nelson demonstrates how societal prejudice attempts to predetermine personal outcomes.

Through Alton, who functions as a synthesizing agent to blend otherwise divided lives, Nelson suggests that people are born and die alone but are here to connect. At the close of the story, "as the high white spire of St. Michael's ran its shadow down onto the sidewalk" and Pritchett "crosses into the sun," Nelson underscores this imperative. Contemplating Alton's ability to see things in cluttered fields of vision that other people miss, Pritchett apprehends how Alton's visionary powers drew him to Yolanda. Because he can find coherence in the random surface of things, he can calibrate gradations and stopgaps to admit light into others' lives. In an instant again made vibrant by the relationship of Nelson's authorial voice to the natural world, Pritchett leaves the shadows, crossing into the sun with the sensation of Alton's foreknowledge.

Moreover, as is characteristic of much of Nelson's late work, the author's growing contentment with his solitary life in Ouray is reflected in the deepening humanity of his characters. The process of becoming more human means for Pritchett recognizing within himself the push to become more than he already is. Throughout, Alton compels others to negotiate the accidents of birth that create such vexed and difficult worlds. He suggests the inequitable configurations of society may be changed if human beings allow their innate senses, not their learned biases, to guide them. Alton is not only Pritchett's secret sharer and alter ego, but also Nelson's. In fact, he is a character who accomplishes in fiction the enlightening effect Nelson hopes his writing will have upon his actual readers.

In addition to "Alton's Keeper," two other late stories widen the scope of Nelson's quickening powers of observation. "Rituals of Sleep," which won a Nelson Algren Award in 1997, and "Voice" extend his discourse on love, demonstrating that his persistent search for understanding supersedes any didacticism on his part. In both stories his narrative technique is more experimental than it has been before. For the first time he balances and blends male and female narrative voices, establishing distance in order to maintain the integrity of each narrator's persona and also to shatter certain collective myths about gender and the unions of men and women. In particular, the women in his later stories (women who stand in tandem with Mattie, the protagonist of his unpublished novel "Land that Moves, Land that Stands Still") are not flimsy or vulnerable. Yet, neither are they the popularized images of self-righteousness that sometimes pass as feminism. The female protagonist in "Rituals of Sleep," who is closely modeled on Nelson's former wife Laurie, is a woman with an inner life as deep as the man's with whom she conarrates her story. Thus, her side of the story is part of an unfolding dialogue on love, a dialogue Nelson has been rehearsing his characters to enter throughout his work, which becomes, finally, a conversation between two voices committed to making themselves known and understood.

Moreover, in "Voice"—where part of the challenge of the story is to figure out exactly who is speaking—the initial ambiguity about the gender of the first-person (female) narrator formalizes Nelson's interest in how gender influences perspective in a story. Although he has narrated from a woman's point of view before, in this story (because the female narrator is an artist and a birder, who witnesses the death of her father and struggles to live independently) Nelson explicitly transposes the outlines of his own life onto a female narrator. While his interest in the female perspective has been present throughout, here he experiments not only with seeing events from another's point of view, but also with actually crossing expected boundaries for identity. In so doing, he literalizes his thematic concern for tearing down barriers in human understanding in his deployment of style.

In "Voice" Nelson's narrative montage between a first-person female and a third-person male speaker relates a brief encounter between a married man, Rick, and a single woman, the narrator. Both characters struggle with individual pain: Rick with a withering marriage, and the female narrator with her isolation as a pianist in a middle-class world. Nelson establishes a connection between their private realities that is stronger than the quotidian events that place them together at Rick's son's birthday party and displays the interdependency of their separate lives. At the same time a motif of silence threads throughout the story in the form of the blank spaces that separate the narrative voices. Herein, he transforms silence from his earlier expression of loss and self-absorption into an affirmation of love. In these alternating perspectives his narrative disjuncture makes audible the understanding that words are superfluous to what the narrators know in their hearts: that one narrator's presence necessarily bears the traces of the other's absence, their perspectives blending and overlapping as much as they stand in contrast to one another. In effect, this overlay of narrative voices allows him to re-create the seemingly inexpressible process through which human beings arrive at understandings of one another.

Clearly, as was noted by a reviewer in *Kirkus Reviews* (15 September 1998), Nelson is "a prodigiously talented, but still too-little-known writer." He is also a writer who, despite his relative lack of recognition, produces short fiction, as Speer Morgan notes in his preface to the 1991 volume of *The Best of the Missouri Review: Fiction, 1978–1990,* that is destined to be "classic." "It will be in print a hundred years from now," he adds, and asserts that he feels prickles along the back of his neck while reading Nelson's short prose.

Beyond predictions about durability, however, Kent Nelson's work shows his reverence for and knowledge of the natural world—a devotion that enables him to conduct forays into the inarticulate wilderness within the human soul. Taking the reader there, he stresses that the actual wilderness must be preserved for the spiritual, as well as the physical, ecosystems it supplies. Nelson's work also shows how the search for love and the journey toward individual identity exist side by side. For both his male and female characters these searches necessarily occur in the physical world, making them elemental and dynamic, while they are also often possessive and even indifferent to others. Within this emphasis Nelson insists that the self must be preserved, even if simultaneously it must be relinquished in order to achieve love. His rendering of this paradox is at the heart of what makes his vision powerful. Still, the abiding truth behind his concern for nature's plenitude and for the dishevelment and naked exposure of the self is that love is crucial. Even at the risk of immersion in death, his later characters see love as the rescue from it. Nelson's work, then, will be remembered far beyond the parallels that may be drawn to place him among his contemporaries—because, finally, in the courage of his vision and the benediction of his eloquence, he leaves his readers burning to push onward.

Interview:

Susan Emerick Robertson, "An Interview with Kent Nelson," *Missouri Review,* 11 (March 1988): 109–132.

Lewis Nordan

(23 August 1939 –)

Tom Noyes
Concordia College

BOOKS: *Welcome to the Arrow-Catcher Fair: Stories* (Baton Rouge: Louisiana State University Press, 1983);

The All-Girl Football Team: Stories (Baton Rouge: Louisiana State University Press, 1986);

Music of the Swamp (Chapel Hill, N.C.: Algonquin Books, 1991);

Wolf Whistle: A Novel (Chapel Hill, N.C.: Algonquin Books, 1993);

The Sharpshooter Blues: A Novel (Chapel Hill, N.C.: Algonquin Books, 1995);

Lightning Song (Chapel Hill, N.C.: Algonquin Books, 1997);

Boy with Loaded Gun: A Memoir (Chapel Hill, N.C.: Algonquin Books, 2000).

Collection: *Sugar Among the Freaks: Selected Stories,* introduction by Richard Howarth (Chapel Hill, N.C.: Algonquin Books, 1996).

Lewis Nordan at the time his 1997 novel, Lightning Song, *was published*

In a 1997 interview with Russell Ingram and Mark Ledbetter, Lewis Nordan discussed the relevance of one particular figurative image—lake water as a black mirror—that appears repeatedly throughout his fiction. "When I was a boy," Nordan said,

> I would look down into the water and know its depths held scary things, like those big ol' alligator gar as long as our fishing boats. The water held beautiful things as well, bluegills and crappie, but none of it was visible. When you looked into that water, all you saw was yourself and whatever was behind you, like the trees or the clouds. What I am doing in the elemental story I mean to tell is to have each character face the mirrored water, and before the end of the story be beneath its surface to confront all of its joys and all of its terrors.

Lewis Alonzo Nordan was born 23 August 1939 in Jackson, Mississippi, to Lemuel Alonzo Nordan and Sara Hightower Nordan. When Nordan was still an infant, his father died. His mother eventually remarried. Nordan characterizes his stepfather, Gilbert Russell Bayles, as a man who was periodically kind and attentive; but his struggle with alcoholism was a burden to his family and he was frequently emotionally and physically absent from his wife and stepson's life.

Nordan's fiction is deeply rooted in autobiography. His stories are set in the Mississippi Delta—Nordan grew up in the small Mississippi Delta town of Itta Bena—and much of his work depicts the plight of a fatherless boyhood and the effects of alcoholism on a family. Rather than serving to limit his fictional imagination, however, Nordan's adherence to memory fuels his creative powers. What is perhaps most notable and innovative about Nordan's fiction is not the moral and dramatic significance of a writer wading through his past—although this aspect of his work is certainly palpable and relevant—but rather the ways in which Nordan's unprivileged, emotionally spent narrators resist sentimentality and self-pity by putting their faith in both humor and the redemptive potential of language and story. While comparisons of Nordan to other Southern writers are often well-founded, it is just as legitimate to note his artistic individuality. Nordan's links to Flannery O'Connor and William Faulkner, for example, are evident in his allegiance to his Southern roots and his penchant for writing about freaks, grotesques, and complicated, idiosyncratic families; but Nordan's rich, nitty-gritty brand of lyricism, his impeccable comic timing, and his awareness of the complex powers and phenomena of memory combine to offer readers a truly original sensibility and a peculiarly resonant fictional vision.

After graduating from high school, Nordan served in the U.S. Navy from 1958 to 1960. He attended Millsaps College in Jackson, Mississippi, receiving his B.A. degree in 1963. On 28 April 1962 he married Mary Mitman; the couple had three sons: Russell Ammon, John Robert, and Lewis Eric. Nordan taught in public schools in Titusville, Florida, between 1963 and 1965, and then returned to Mississippi, where he entered the M.A. program of Mississippi State University. After receiving his M.A. in English in 1966, Nordan went on to Auburn University in Alabama, where he pursued a doctorate in Shakespeare Studies and was an instructor in the English department until 1971. He subsequently was an English instructor at the University of Georgia, Athens, until 1974.

Nordan became serious about writing fiction only after he was unable to land a tenured university teaching job in Shakespeare Studies with the Ph.D. he received from Auburn University in 1973. After a few years of working odd jobs to help support his wife and their three sons, Nordan entered the M.F.A. program in fiction at the University of Arkansas. Although he did not complete the program, his exposure to fellow writers there, such as William Harrison, Ellen Gilchrist, and Lee K. Abbott, helped him to focus his talent. Early in his tenure at Arkansas, in a lunch conversation with Harrison, Nordan figured out and articulated for the first time what it was he wanted to write about. In his introduction to *Sugar Among the Freaks: Selected Stories* (1996), Richard Howarth quotes Nordan as saying, "I told [Harrison], 'I think I want to write about love and death in a comic way.' I said this without knowing exactly what that meant."

After a three-year stint teaching as an associate professor at the University of Arkansas, Nordan published his first book, a collection of stories titled *Welcome to the Arrow-Catcher Fair* (1983). That same year he became a professor of creative writing at the University of Pittsburgh, and, in January, his troubled first marriage ended in divorce; he married his second wife, Alicia Blessing, on 3 July 1986. His sec-

ond collection, *The All-Girl Football Team,* was published in 1986. Although *The All-Girl Football Team* was republished in 1989 in a Vintage Books paperback edition, both collections went out of print relatively soon after they were published. Following publication of Nordan's critically acclaimed third book of fiction, *Music of the Swamp* (1991), and two successful novels, *Wolf Whistle* (1993) and *The Sharpshooter Blues* (1995), Nordan's current publisher, Algonquin Books of Chapel Hill, bought the rights for the first two books from Louisiana State University Press and republished most of the nineteen stories from the two collections in one volume, titled *Sugar Among the Freaks* (1996).

Arrow-Catcher, Mississippi, serves as the setting for most of the fifteen stories in *Sugar Among the Freaks*. In creating Arrow-Catcher, Nordan relies heavily on childhood memories of his real-life hometown, Itta Bena, and its inhabitants. Through the eyes and voices of colorful, tragicomic characters such as Robert McIntyre from "The Sin Eater," Golden Rondelle from "Welcome to the Arrow-Catcher Fair," two stories from *Welcome to the Arrow-Catcher Fair,* and Sugar Mecklin, who appears in several stories in *Sugar Among the Freaks* and is revisited in *Music of the Swamp,* Nordan introduces his readers to a world where childhood and adulthood blur, where conflicts and events of the past are constantly being reimagined, reevaluated, and reexperienced. In this way there is a mythic quality to many of the stories in *Sugar Among the Freaks*. As Nordan's characters reinvent themselves in stories of the past, they come to better understand their present lives and more clearly and creatively imagine their futures. Of course, in moving so freely back and forth in time, the notions of past, present, and future often become problematic for Nordan's characters; while the act of remembering can afford them insight into their present predicaments, it can also trap them in cycles of self-destruction. In this way Nordan's stories are starkly true and profound meditations on the dual powers of memory and its role in the construction of the self. In a 1998 essay published in *Southern Literary Journal,* Edward J. Dupuy writes, "Nordan tells stories of Sugar Mecklin who tells stories of himself, and in the telling also tells a story, one could say, about the telling of stories about one's self." Living in the past sometimes comforts and nurtures Nordan's characters, and it sometimes opens wounds and retards emotional growth. Building an image of the present self through memory of the past self is, of course, necessary and inevitable; Nordan's stories remind the reader that it is also potentially painful.

In "The Sears and Roebuck Catalog Game," originally collected as the fourth story in *The All-Girl Football Team,* an unnamed narrator–the experienced reader of Nordan can deduce from details of the story that the narrator is Sugar Mecklin–revisits his fourteenth summer to relive a stranger's drowning, his mother's attempted suicide, and his father's tragic discovery of the power of imagination. As Sugar recounts the summer's events, several themes emerge. The story explores the connections between memory and imagination and imagination and mortality, and in its depictions of Sugar's troubled parents it considers both the healing power and the destructive potential of reimagining the past.

The first death in "The Sears and Roebuck Catalog Game" is that of a stranger. Sugar spends his fourteenth summer working for his father, Gilbert, on a painting job at the county high school. There Sugar witnesses the drowning of "a gangly retarded girl with long arms and stringy hair" in the outdoor pool. He says, "I watched her rise up out of the water, far up, so that half her body showed above the surface, then she sank out of sight. Once more she came back up, and then she sank again. . . . After a while the child's body was retrieved, slick and terrible."

This girl's death triggers in Sugar both recollection and foreshadowing. First, it reminds Sugar of a game he and his mother had played when he was younger. In the game mother and son would leaf through the Sears and Roebuck catalogue and imagine lives for the models. "My mother was wonderful at this game," Sugar says. "She made up elaborate dossiers on each of the characters I asked her to invent. She found names and occupations and addresses and proper mates for each. Sears and Roebuck was a real world to me, with lakes and cities and operas and noisy streets and farmlands and neighborhoods." The girl's drowning death reminds Sugar of one particular day when the game took a dark turn. His mother informed him there had been a death in Sears and Roebuck; one of the Sporting Goods models, she told him, had committed suicide.

Upon returning home on the afternoon of the girl's drowning, Sugar's father immediately drinks himself to sleep, not out of sorrow or shock, Sugar says, but to "prepare himself for whatever drama was certain to develop now that [my mother] knew of the death." Sugar's mother reacts as predicted. As her husband sleeps, she delivers to Sugar a disturbing and semicoherent lecture on the nature of death that ends with her posing a chilling question to her son: "'If I asked you to–oh, let me see now, what could I ask my young man to do for me?–if I asked you to,

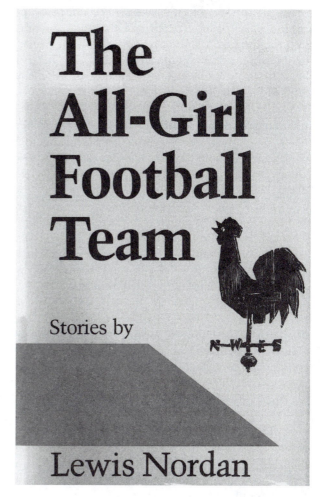

Dust jacket for Nordan's 1986 collection of short stories, mostly set in the fictional rural Mississippi town of Arrow-Catcher

well, to *kill me . . .* if I asked you to do that, honey, would you do it?'" When Sugar is too frightened to answer, his mother launches into a bizarre pseudo-autobiography, telling Sugar things about her childhood and parents he knows to be false. "It was exactly like a story she might make up about the Sears and Roebuck people," Sugar says. Later that summer Sugar's mother attempts suicide by slicing her arm with a razor blade. Sugar saves her life.

The central tension of "The Sears and Roebuck Catalog Game" is the incompatibility of Sugar's parents: his mother's penchant for melodrama and reimagining her life, and his father's attempts to avoid both phenomena through alcohol. This contrast is dramatized and complicated when, during the mother's recovery in the hospital, Sugar and Gilbert play the Sears and Roebuck catalogue game without her. While they fail at first–"My father and I were incapable of inventing a world together," Sugar says– Gilbert, in a determined second attempt, opens the catalogue to the women's clothing section, faces the picture of a model "standing in the wind, looking into the distance," and he is moved. "She sees me," he says. This realization marks a turn in Gilbert's life. "It was in this moment," Sugar says, "that my father's imagination was born."

The birth of Gilbert's imagination is not a positive thing for either himself or for his family. While his wife eventually recovers from her suicide attempt by learning to quiet and control her dark fantasies, Gilbert's condition worsens. Previously a quiet drunk, Gilbert becomes a storyteller after playing the Sears and Roebuck catalogue game for the first time, and the tales he tells wreak emotional havoc on him. Through his stories Gilbert reminds himself of lost youth, former lovers, and his experiences in the war, and, as a result of indulging these memories, he spends the remainder of his life in misery.

For a writer such as Nordan who relies so heavily on melding imagination with memory, the dynamics of "The Sears and Roebuck Catalog Game" are curious; one character saves her life by learning to rein in her imagination, and another character loses his already shaky grip on emotional stability when he yields to his imagination. In one sense, the story serves as a cautionary tale, citing the dangers of remembering and imagining even as the narrator practices both. This apparent contradiction is palpable in much of Nordan's fiction. His narrators know they tread on dangerous ground, yet somehow they cannot help themselves.

In the title story from Nordan's second collection, also republished in *Sugar Among the Freaks,* "The All-Girl Football Team," Gilbert's immersion in imagination is cast in a more positive light. In one of Nordan's most humorous and most profound stories the teenage narrator—again, the reader can assume that the unnamed narrator is Sugar Mecklin—deals with questions of sexual identity and desire in the face of his father's occasional cross-dressing and his own participation in a high school fund-raising event, an all-girl football game.

Sugar's attraction-repulsion to the gender switching makes for an equally entertaining and enlightening story. From the beginning Sugar is infatuated with the transformation of his female classmates into football players. "They were beautiful," he says. "Hulda Raby had long legs and boyish hips and large breasts, and when she was dressed in our school colors and was wearing pads and cleats and a rubber mouthpiece, I thought no one on earth had ever had such a good idea as the all-girl football team." When Sugar is elected head cheerleader for the game, however, his enthusiasm wanes, and he is

prepared to boycott the event. Gilbert encourages his son to go through with the role-playing, though. Gilbert himself dresses in drag twice a year—on Halloween and for the town's annual fund-raising production of the "Womanless Wedding"—and he tells his son that he will guide him through the experience. "I will dress you in a skirt and a sweater and nice underwear," Gilbert tells his startled son, "and you will feel beautiful."

Sugar relents, and the events that night have a profound effect on him. Initially, he is elated with his new femininity. He allows himself to be swept away by the excitement of the game, the energy and rhythm of the cheers he performs, and the pageantry of the halftime homecoming festivities—every couple consists of a girl in cleats and pads and a boy in heels and a skirt—and as he begins to feel comfortable in his costume, his imagination forces him to reevaluate and reenvision himself. He says, "My arms were woman-arms, my feet woman-feet, my voice, my lips, my fingers. I stood on the sweet sad brink of womanhood. . . ."

At one point, however, Sugar's imagination strays too far for his own comfort. He realizes during the halftime ceremony that the person on the field to whom he is most attracted is not one of the girls dressed as a boy, but one of the boys dressed as a girl. "Tony Pirelli, the kid who coached the team . . . I had never seen anyone so beautiful as Tony Pirelli. He never smiled, and now his sadness called out to me, it made me want to hold him and protect him from all harm, to kiss his lips and neck, to close his brown eyes with my kisses. . . ." Sugar confesses, "I believed I was a lesbian," and this belief is upsetting enough to literally chase him away from the game. Frightened by the power of his imagination and the unpredictability of his own desires, Sugar runs scared through the dark streets of Arrow-Catcher, toward home. Just as suddenly as his attraction for Tony Pirelli had descended upon him, though, another realization stops him. Sugar says,

> And then something happened. . . . The southern sky seemed to fill with light—no, not light, but with something like light, with meaning, I want to say. . . . I began walking back toward the football field. I was not a woman. I did not feel like a woman. I was not in love with a boy. I was a boy in costume for one night of the year, and I was my father's child and the child of this strange southern geography. I was beautiful, and also wise and sad and somehow doomed with joy.

While this sudden and vague epiphany truncates the story somewhat awkwardly and perhaps spares Sugar from having to investigate more fully his conflicting instincts and identities, it also reflects his desire and his ability to control his imagination. Unlike the parents in "The Sears and Roebuck Catalog Game," the narrator of "The All-Girl Football Team" is able to temper his imagination. Sugar's return to the football game, and, later, his attendance at the homecoming dance where everyone has returned to traditional dress, suggests that he has achieved a measure of balance and perspective. He is not willing to abandon reality, nor is he willing to ignore his fantasies. While he does not validate as real his feelings and desires from earlier in the evening–he recognizes that the phenomenon of the all-girl football game was imaginary and illusionary– neither does he discount the experience and realizations his sharp imagination has afforded him. As he dances with a female partner, Sugar again exercises his imagination. "I imagined that I would marry . . . some beautiful woman . . . and that together we would have sons and that we would love them and teach them to be gentle and to love the music we were dancing to and to wear dresses and that, in doing this, we would somehow never grow old and that love would last forever."

Published in 1991, *Music of the Swamp* has been considered a novel but it is really a series of interconnected short stories, many of which were published seperately earlier–Nordan calls it a "novel-in-stories" in his foreword to *Sugar Among the Freaks*. In this book Nordan continues his exploration of the themes of imagination and memory, focusing especially on the ramifications of these phenomena in the father-son relationship of Gilbert and Sugar. The stories in *Music of the Swamp* are richer and more ambitious than their predecessors collected in *Sugar Among the Freaks*, and they more fully illustrate Nordan's range as a storyteller and also the range of emotions inherent to Gilbert and Sugar's relationship. From the bluesy, lyrical somberness of the title story to the earthy, profound humor of "Porpoises and Romance," *Music of the Swamp* offers full-bodied depictions of one child's struggles with his parents' doomed marriage, suicidal tendencies, and alcoholism. What is perhaps most relevant for Sugar, however, even more than the moral failings and emotional ineptitude of his tragically flawed family, is the realization that, despite the pain and frustration they cause one another, his parents will always continue to reach out for one another and for him–even after death, through his reimagination of their lives together–and he will always, perhaps despite his better judgment, reciprocate.

Cover for the 1996 collection of Nordan's short stories, many of which feature Sugar Mecklin, Nordan's alter ego

This knowledge proves both comforting and discouraging for Sugar. The last story in the collection, "Owls," ends on a decidedly hopeful note, though, as the now middle-aged Sugar has been able to find love and intimacy with the person to whom he is telling his stories. As Sugar shares his painful childhood with his lover, he is affirmed by her attentiveness and her declaration of love for him, and this intimacy, in a once-removed, retroactive manner, allows Sugar to finally connect with his father. Through memory and imagination Sugar's stories connect past and present and, momentarily anyway, do so in a way that provides him with a potentially optimistic future. The facts of Sugar's past life with his father do not matter in this healing process as much as does the narrative act of reimagining this past life.

Recognizing the workings and importance of this aspect of Nordan's fiction, James F. Nicosia places *Music of the Swamp* in what he claims to be the distinctly Southern literary tradition of writers who not only marry elements of the past and present, but do so by revising the past in the present. Nicosia writes, "The events in and of themselves . . . do not intrinsically hold the answers to [Sugar's] questions. The narrator of these stories knows what he is setting out to find, and by reconstructing the past in a way that gives him answers, he will find success." At the end of "Owls," Sugar describes what has been achieved through his sharing of the stories with his lover: "Every good thing that I had expected, longed to feel with my father, I felt with her. And I also felt it with my father, and I heard his voice speak those words of love, though he was already a long time dead. He was with me in a way he could not be in life." One way to describe Nordan's project in *Music of the Swamp* is as a narrative-induced reunion. Through reconstructing and reseeing the past through imaginative storytelling, Sugar and Gilbert Mecklin are able to find one another after the fact of their relationship in ways they were unable to during the fact.

The nature of Gilbert and Sugar's relationship is suggested in their early morning exchange at the beginning of the title story in *Music of the Swamp*. "Sugar Mecklin astonished his father at the breakfast table by grabbing him suddenly and holding onto him for all he was worth. . . . he said . . . , 'I love you, Daddy!' in a bright voice, and his father struggled and finally muttered, 'Good luck on your travels through life.'" Two elements of the story work particularly well in illuminating this theme of emotional estrangement and disconnection: Nordan's use of music, specifically Elvis Presley's 1956 hit single, *Heartbreak Hotel,* and blues singer Bessie Smith's brand of what the characters refer to as "wrist-cutting music," and his manipulation of the roving third-person narrator.

At the beginning of "Music of the Swamp" young Sugar wakes up to a music-filled Sunday morning. The mice who live in his mattress are "singing," and Presley, whom Sugar has never heard before, is "in full uh-huh complaint on Sugar's Philco radio." All this music and the dreams that Sugar has had during the night about a mermaidlike creature who would foretell his future, or endow him with power and knowledge, convince Sugar that this day is somehow special, that "something new and completely different from anything he had ever known was about to jump out at him from somewhere unexpected."

Sugar leaves his house and heads toward Roebuck Lake in search of the mermaid. Instead of finding her, however, Sugar witnesses a baptism service—the hymns the people sing are reminiscent of *Heartbreak Hotel* in that they are "about loneliness, and the defeat of loneliness, and the heartbreak if it could not

be defeated, as it probably never could"—and runs into his friend, Sweet Austin, who tells Sugar that he has found a dead body in the water.

As is the case in "The Sears and Roebuck Catalog Game," the drowning ultimately leads to Sugar's consideration of a parent's suicide attempt—in this story, his father's rather than his mother's—and when Sugar and Sweet return to Sugar's home in need of comfort and help in understanding what they have encountered, they are instead faced with a drunken Gilbert who silences them when they try to tell him about the body. Sugar says, "Me and Sweet Austin found a dead man, Daddy," and Gilbert answers, "Hush, hush up, Sugar. Listen to this song." While Gilbert's answer to his son would seem to point to an uncaring, self-consumed father, the intermittent third-person narrator alters this perception by suggesting that Gilbert's shortcomings as a parent are not rooted in selfishness, but rather in an inability to communicate. Of Gilbert's hushing Sugar, the narrator says, "The last thing in the world he meant to do was to tell his boy to hush up. What he meant to say was that there was just so much death in the Delta, it was everywhere, he didn't know how a child could stand all of it." By telling Sugar and Sweet to be quiet and to listen to Bessie Smith's song—in her singing Gilbert hears her message that "the Delta was bad . . . and it was magic, it hypnotized you, you couldn't resist it even if you tried"—he is making an effort, albeit a weak one, to address and contextualize for the boys their experience with the dead body. Of course, the boys do not realize this is the case. Rather, they associate Bessie Smith and her "wrist-cutting" music with Gilbert's previous suicide attempts, so rather than providing them with any clarification or understanding, the song actually deepens their confusion and fear.

In an interesting shift at the end of the story, Sugar's optimistic anticipations from earlier that morning are satisfied, albeit in a skewed manner. When Sweet Austin breaks down during the Bessie Smith song because he associates the dead body in the lake with his father, whom he believes is dead—Gilbert knows that Curtis Austin is actually alive, but he is glad for the boy's sake that Curtis is absent from Sweet's life—Sugar's mother comforts Sweet by taking him in her arms. "Me and Gilbert love you," she says. "We love you like you was our own boy." Although these words chase Gilbert into the kitchen for another shot of whiskey, Sugar is buoyed by them. In watching his friend receive love and assurance from his mother, Sugar realizes his parents' love for him. The reader may not respond so optimistically to the scene, given Gilbert's retreat to the whiskey bottle, but Sugar "believed he was part of a family, and this filled him with love. The world was not the way Sugar Mecklin wanted it to be, but he had to admit, this particular day had turned out even better than he had expected when he woke up. . . ."

This same type of fragile, questionable hope is what is offered at the end of "Porpoises and Romance," a more humorous and earthy story than "Music of the Swamp." Narrated exclusively by Sugar, the story recounts Gilbert's desperate, last-ditch effort to save his marriage by taking his wife on a second honeymoon. Against his wishes and according to hers, they are accompanied by Sugar. Gilbert's well-intentioned but wrong-headed actions on the trip are, inevitably, unsuccessful, but in his failures Sugar comes to know Gilbert and understand the nature of his parents' relationship more fully.

Ironically, Gilbert gets most of his ideas for revitalizing his marriage from a publication entitled *Connections*. Although most of the advice in the magazine deals in sexual fantasies, *Connections* also offers tips for other methods of rekindling marital romance. One piece of advice in particular catches Gilbert's eye. *Connections* advises its reader to "Find a metaphor for romance, and pursue it with all your heart." After sunrises do not work, Gilbert eventually settles on dolphins.

The family's beach trip to the Gulf of Mexico—they arrive on the tails of a hurricane—affords them access to porpoises, and despite the storm-ravaged, carcass-littered beach, they decide to stay. When porpoises finally appear to the family, what is supposed to be a magical and graceful moment is instead frightening and grotesque. A school of bluefish attracts a horde of dolphins close to shore, and a bloodbath ensues. "There were too many to count," says Sugar of the porpoises. "They were crazed. Maybe still psychotic from the effects of the hurricane. . . . The carnage was spectacular." Sugar's parents are just as astonished and, because of the metaphorical significance they have already invested in the porpoises, distraught. Rather than inspiring renewed intimacy, the porpoises' presence instigates confessions from both husband and wife that they are no longer sure of the love they once shared, and this conversation seems to signal their impending separation.

While this is, of course, a disappointing development and memory for Sugar, he refuses to end his story with the image of the savage porpoises: "It's not the end," he tells the reader. "There is one more thing to tell." The final scene in the story takes place later that month when the three characters take a car

ride along the coast, across the border from Mississippi into Florida. The conversation between husband and wife is easygoing, not heavy or intentionally and falsely intimate as was the case during the honeymoon, and Sugar is able to join in. Topics vary from Sugar's precocious questions about sexual intimacy, to the reproductive habits of animals, to Gilbert's pretending that he is John Dillinger driving a getaway car. The family is able to relax and share laughter. While neither the narrator nor the reader can completely forget the porpoises and the imminent dissolution of the parents' marriage, there is offered in this scene, through the characters' enjoyment of each other, a glimmer of positivity. Despite the family's shortcomings, this scene suggests that recovery is possible, especially for Sugar, because there are moments like these that he can cling to in his memory and use to make stories.

While many fiction writers bristle at the suggestion that their work is autobiographical, Nordan is open to discussing the ways in which his own personal history influences his characters. What he does take issue with, however, is the tendency of some critics and reviewers to too readily associate Nordan with Sugar the son and not with Gilbert the father. In a 1995 interview with Blake Maher, Nordan spoke of what he believes to be the dual author-character sympathy that exists in his work. Nordan said,

> People always have asked, "Are you Sugar?" But nobody's ever asked, "Are you Gilbert?". . . . I feel very much a part of the life of Gilbert as well. . . . it would be very pleasing for me to be Sugar and not Gilbert. But, in fact, the mistakes that Gilbert makes are the very mistakes that I also made, and so I identify with his pain quite as thoroughly as I do with Sugar's. . . . Sugar's life is yet to be lived and he still has choices available to him. . . . Gilbert's life is not ruined and not wrecked, [but] it is pretty far along the line of bad choices and mistakes that he is going to have to live with . . . and I feel very deeply for him.

The tension between Sugar and Gilbert is only one of the tensions that propel Nordan's short fiction. Every character and every situation, no matter how desperate or flawed, is rendered sympathetically, but also unflinchingly. The book received awards from the Mississippi Institute of Arts and Letters and the American Library Institute of Arts and Letters.

Published in 1993, Nordan's novel *Wolf Whistle* is a fictionalization of the 1955 Emmet Till lynching, which occurred near Nordan's hometown. His next novel, *The Sharpshooter Blues,* followed two years later. Featuring Hydro Raney, an encephalitic boy who lives in the swamp just outside of Arrow Catcher, it won the Notable Book Award of the American Library Association, and the Best Fiction Award of the Mississippi Institute of Arts and Letters. Of *Lightning Song* (1997), Nordan's coming-of-age novel about a twelve-year-old boy's discovery of romance and sexuality, reviewer Valerie Sayers declared in *The New York Times* (25 May 1997) that "Mr. Nordan won't settle for a single sexual stereotype, and when he juxtaposes the ordinary and the Southern surreal, he evokes pity and sadness and affection and hope." *Boy with Loaded Gun: A Memoir* (2000), Nordan's first nonfiction book, is a frank but funny autobiographical account of his boyhood on the Delta, the alcoholism and infidelities that doomed his first marriage, the death of his second son in infancy and his eldest son's suicide, and the impulses to storytelling that made him an author.

Nordan's characters are exposed as both vulnerable and brutal, funny and sad, selfless and selfish; the relationships they forge are at once intimate and distant, nurturing and alienating, permanent and temporary. Death and life coexist in these stories, as do elements of comic and tragic, sublime and grotesque, and past and present. Lewis Nordan's short fiction is distinctively resonant in its capacity to accommodate these dichotomies, in its ability to remind readers of life's simplicity as well as its complexity, of love's fragility as well as its resilience.

Interviews:

Blake Maher, "An Interview with Lewis Nordan," *Southern Quarterly,* 34 (Fall 1995): 113–123;

Russell Ingram and Mark Ledbetter, "An Interview with Lewis Nordan," *Missouri Review,* 20 (1997): 75–89.

References:

Edward J. Dupuy, "Memory, Death, the Delta, and St. Augustine: Autobiography in Lewis Nordan's *The Music of the Swamp*," *Southern Literary Journal,* 30 (1998): 97–108;

James F. Nicosia, "'Still I Am Not Sure What Was Real and What My Mind Invented': The Southern Tradition of (Re)Creating the Past in Lewis Nordan's *Music of the Swamp*," *Southern Studies,* 4 (Spring 1993): 67–79.

William Peden
(22 March 1913 – 23 July 1999)

Meg Watson
Louisiana State University

BOOKS: *The American Short Story: Front Line in the National Defense of Literature* (Boston: Houghton Mifflin, 1964); revised and enlarged as *The American Short Story: Continuity and Change, 1940–1975* (Boston: Houghton Mifflin, 1975);

Night in Funland and Other Stories (Baton Rouge: Louisiana State University Press, 1968);

Twilight at Monticello (Boston: Houghton Mifflin, 1973);

Fragments and Fictions: Workbooks of an Obscure Writer (Wichita, Kans.: Watermark, 1990).

OTHER: *The Life and Selected Writings of Thomas Jefferson,* edited by Peden and Adrienne Koch (New York: Modern Library, 1944);

The Selected Writings of John and John Quincy Adams, edited by Peden and Koch (New York: Knopf, 1946);

Increase Mather, *Testimony Against Prophane Customs,* edited by Peden (Charlottesville: University Press of Virginia, 1953);

Thomas Jefferson, *Notes on the State of Virginia,* edited by Peden (Chapel Hill: University of North Carolina Press, 1955);

Stories: Jean Stafford, John Cheever, Daniel Fuchs, William Maxwell, introduction by Peden (New York: Farrar, Straus & Cudahy, 1956);

Modern Short Stories from Story Magazine, introduction by Peden (New York: Grosset & Dunlap, 1960);

Twenty-Nine Stories, edited by Peden (Boston: Houghton Mifflin, 1960);

The Golden Shore: Great Short Stories Selected for Young Readers, compiled by Peden (New York: Platt & Munk, 1967);

New Writing in South Carolina, edited by Peden and George Garrett (Columbia: University of South Carolina Press, 1971);

Short Fiction: Shape and Substance, edited by Peden (Boston: Houghton Mifflin, 1971).

William Peden is representative of the rare literary mind that can successfully assume the diverse roles of editor, critic, teacher, and creative writer. In addition

William Peden (courtesy of Dr. Margaret Sayers Peden)

to distinguishing himself as a professor of literature and director of university writing programs, he wrote histories and short stories, compiled anthologies and critical surveys, and served as editor of magazines, presses, and reviews. Through all of these endeavors Peden remained particularly devoted to the genre of the short story, always working to secure for short fiction a well-respected place in the world of literary studies. At a time when short fiction was perhaps read but little taught or studied by teachers of American literature, he published a critical survey of the genre, *The American Short Story: Front Line in the National Defense of Literature* (1964). In this highly influential work, Peden examines the history, form, and contemporary practice of short-story writing, attending to the aesthetic merits of the genre with a regard rarely seen from within the American academy. With this volume Peden galvanized the study of the contemporary short story as a legitimate artistic form; he even argued that "it seems increasingly possible that future generations of historians of American literature will find in the short story, rather than the novel or the drama and poetry, the major literary contribution of recent years."

Substantiating this claim were his many illustrations of how the short story was the most suitable genre for capturing the accelerated tempo and fragmented character of the twentieth century. This assertion certainly held true for his own creative work, for though he enjoyed some success with a late novel, his short stories enabled him to depict most compellingly the peculiar character of midcentury America. In the tradition of Sherwood Anderson, John Cheever, and John Updike, Peden renders the brokenness and confusion of everyday families with a delicate poignancy that is made possible, in part, by the brisk nature of the form itself. He frequently writes of middle-class individuals affiliated with Midwestern or East Coast universities, protagonists who struggle to find emotional or spiritual fulfillment in a world where successes are often "academic" in all senses of the word. Nevertheless, this context of the university also allows Peden to refract powerful moments of love and compassion, small triumphs that emerge from the hard times of modern revolutions in politics, economics, ethics, and intellectual thought. Again, these moments are delivered with a force that is intensified by the brevity of the form and the age in which Peden situates them. His fiction, then, displays the same regard for the potential of the genre that is underscored in much of his critical work. This regard was essential to improving and validating the work of midcentury short-story writers, and it has led many literary historians to agree with Eugene Current-Garcia, who asserted in the October 1968 *Southern Review* that Peden "redefined the artistic standards of modern short fiction."

William Harwood Peden was born on 22 March 1913 to Horatio and Catherine (Hanna) Peden in Long Island, New York. His childhood was essentially a quiet and happy one. The family home was near the sound in Freeport, Long Island, which allowed Peden access to local boating and shellfishing. His father, a banker, and his mother, a homemaker, were both active community members. Catherine Peden was often involved with local library projects, and as an avid reader she encouraged young William to develop his love of books. He was consistently a good student as well as a member of his high-school track team. Although Peden did not have the violent, turbulent childhood that frequently surfaces in the work of creative writers, elements of his time on the Eastern seaboard certainly yielded plenty of meaningful experiences from which he later drew in his fiction. From the white shells of the coast to cross-country running, many images from these early years in New York appear in his writing.

From Long Island, Peden left for college, earning his B.S. in 1934, M.S. in 1936, and Ph.D. in 1942 at the University of Virginia. While finishing his doctorate Peden held an instructorship at the University of Maryland, and upon completion of the degree he returned to Charlottesville, this time as a faculty member of the extension division of the U.S. Armed Forces Institute. Steeped in the strong historical, intellectual, and cultural traditions of the Mid-Atlantic, Peden developed a familiarity with the region and its residents that rivaled his connection to his childhood residence; ultimately Charlottesville even surpassed Long Island as a backdrop for much of his fiction.

Peden's close ties to the university, both as student and as faculty member, also provided much material for his creative writing. Yet, during these years it was not fiction so much as history and biography that captured Peden's attention. He wrote his doctoral dissertation on Thomas Jefferson (one of Peden's boyhood heroes), examining Jefferson "as an intellectual, not as a politician." He also edited several books and research aids, including biographies, bibliographies, and collections of selected writings, on figures such as Jefferson, John Adams, and John Quincy Adams. Through all of this work that might be characterized as "pure history," however, Peden displayed a strong interest in the more "literary" questions of stories and storytelling. Drawn to the human dramas of thinkers and their ideas, he demonstrated even in this early writing a thorough appreciation for the nature of narrative and its construction.

Despite his attachment to the East Coast, Peden accepted a teaching position in the English department of the University of Missouri in 1946. In the three decades following his arrival in Columbia, in addition to serving as professor of English and director of the university writing program, Peden made substantial contributions to the editing and publication of contemporary fiction, both within and beyond Missouri. In 1958 he helped found the University of Missouri Press, which has grown to publish more than fifty titles per year. While serving as director of the press from 1958 to 1962, Peden also served as editor of *Story* magazine from 1959 to 1962. In addition, he was influential in the founding of the *Missouri Review,* which now awards an annual Peden Prize for short fiction. Greg Michalson, current managing editor of the *Review,* commented in the *Columbia Missourian* (26 July 1999) that Peden's commitment to supporting and distributing quality short fiction helped the *Review* survive its inevitably difficult founding years: "Bill even lent us his office before we had an office of our own. . . . He was one of the guiding forces–particularly in the magazine's fiction, the area *Missouri Review* has built its reputation on."

Peden's efforts toward expanding the circulation and popularity of the short story were not confined to work at magazines and presses. In a period of a little more than ten years he also edited or helped compile four impressive anthologies: *Stories: Jean Stafford, John Cheever, Daniel Fuchs, William Maxwell* (1956); *Modern Short Stories from Story Magazine* (1960); *Twenty-Nine Stories* (1960); and *The Golden Shore: Great Short Stories Selected for Young Readers* (1967). With each collection, as the titles indicate, Peden sought a different set of readers, from avid followers of the latest names in contemporary fiction to young adults new to the genre. This range of targeted audiences further attests to Peden's commitment to building a nationwide readership and appreciation of short fiction.

In addition to seeing that quality writing was published, he also reasserted the artistic merits of the genre itself. To this end, much of his scholarship during the 1960s and 1970s worked toward rescuing the modern short story from its position as the neglected child of literary studies, granting it a rightful place among the older, more established genres. The single most influential piece of such scholarship was *The American Short Story,* much of which he wrote during 1961 and 1962 with the support of a Guggenheim Fellowship. In this relatively brief and highly readable volume Peden undertakes several tasks, from outlining the lineage of the short story to cataloguing its contemporary practitioners. In the first chapter, "Background and Antecedents," he offers a brief history of the genre and argues that "it is the only major literary form of essentially American origin." In the second chapter Peden surveys recent trends in publishing and production. He traces the popularity of the short story from its earliest appearances in mass-circulation (or "mediocre") magazines to its growing prevalence in "good quality" weeklies and monthlies, new literary journals, and university press publications. With his own involvement in the publishing industry allowing him particular insight into the trends of the periodical market, Peden supplements this summary of publishing history with commentary as to how these trends might have affected short-story writers and the substance of their work.

The third chapter treats "The Period in Retrospect," referring to the interval 1940–1963, on which Peden focuses throughout the remainder of the book. In this chapter he first addresses questions of form, commending contemporary advances in technical skill and mechanical adroitness. With this commendation, however, he also issues a warning: virtuosity of technique in itself, unaccompanied by a "largeness of vision," will never give rise to a memorable short story. Instead, he argues, "The indispensable element in a short story . . . is the presence of a consciousness larger than that of any of the characters of a particular story, an illumination above and beyond plot, setting, theme, and incident." In the second portion of the chapter Peden documents the overarching themes and popular modes of recent short fiction. He suggests that "the War and the Bomb" have been the pervading influences on the twenty-five years of fiction he surveys; he also notes the rise in "everyday" fiction, in which ordinary "non-heroes" struggle with the realization that "somehow, somewhere along the line, the American dream of progress, decency, and order has gone awry."

With the rest of the volume, Peden divides mid-century short fiction into three primary categories: the "short fiction of manners"; the "grotesque, the abnormal, and the bizarre"; and postwar fiction, which he further divides into war-related, Jewish, African American, regional, and science fiction. By presenting the stories and the authors most representative of each of these categories, he quickly inventories much of the best and most popular modern short fiction. Surveyed authors include Cheever, Updike, James Purdy, Katherine Anne Porter, and Flannery O'Connor. In fact, some of the more stringent critics of the book have suggested that because of the wide scope of this inventory, Peden fails to offer in-depth critical evaluation of any of the works he presents. A reviewer for the 1 November 1964 issue of *Choice,* for instance, asserted that Peden "races madly" through his assessments; and Richard Kostelanetz commented in the *Chicago Review* (1966) that "Peden discusses short stories as though they were newspaper feature articles, giving us their plots, locales and summary descriptions of the major characters."

It is true that the bulk of Peden's work in this volume is more catalogue than analysis; he even includes an appendix titled "One Hundred Notable American Short Story Writers, 1940–1963: A Checklist." Superficial as any such extensive catalogue must be, however, many other critics agree with Alfred P. Klausler's argument in the *Christian Century* (30 September 1964) that this inventory in itself "makes the book a valuable handbook and guide." Because Peden so successfully captures the range and reach of work that had been done in the short-story genre, a large portion of the literary community has agreed with L. W. Griffin's statement in *Library Journal* (August 1964) that with this book "Peden has done a considerable service to American letters."

While this period was clearly a momentous one in terms of Peden's scholarly career, it was equally important in a more personal sense. In the year following the publication of *The American Short Story* Peden was introduced to Margaret Sayers, who had come to the University of Missouri as a transfer student in 1946. A notable teacher and scholar, Sayers went on to become a professor emeritus in the department of Romance languages as well as a prolific writer and translator. Sayers and Peden were married on 18 September 1965. Each had two children from previous marriages: Peden had two daughters, Sally and Eliza, and Sayers had one daughter, Kerry, and one son, Kyle. Described in the *Columbia Missourian* (26 July 1999) by a family friend as "idyllic," the marriage remained strong until Peden's death thirty-four years later.

The evolution of this new family was accompanied by the emergence of Peden's fiction, for in addition to generating scholarship and editing publications, Peden was also writing stories of his own. After placing pieces in magazines such as *New Mexico Quarterly, Story,* and *Denver Quarterly,* he published his first and only full short-story collection, *Night in Funland and Other Stories* (1968). A collection that fits within Peden's self-described subgenre of "the grotesque, the abnormal, and the bizarre," this set of ten stories features a cast of characters both literally and figuratively marked by disease, debility, and dismemberment. Through these unlikely heroes, Peden explores the broken and feeble quality of midcentury, middle-class life, frequently in the context of the American university. Eight of the ten stories are either set on a university campus (often the University of Virginia) or feature professors, students, and their families as protagonists.

Peden's treatment of the academy and its constituents is unshrinking, yet sympathetic. More solemn than the Kingsley Amis tradition of academic fiction, the collection abounds with faculty members so engrossed in the "work of the mind" that they often fail to establish and maintain meaningful relationships with those people closest to them. However weak and ineffective these characters prove to be in their searches for interpersonal healing and reconciliation, they continue to search nonetheless. Finally, this image of the search prevents the collection from becoming simply a narrow study of academe and makes it a broader exploration of more universal hopes and failures.

The title story, "Night in Funland," arguably one of the best in the collection, displays many of the char-

acteristic strengths and prevalent thematic concerns of Peden's creative work. This story of a father's struggle to reestablish a meaningful relationship with his young, convalescent daughter opens as the two drive to a night of diversion at a rural carnival. The "Funland" that Peden creates, however, is a nightmarish inversion of expectations. Located in an unnamed town in the West, the amusement park is a dark and otherworldly departure from the typical, neon-lit fairground of piping organ music and laughing children. Peden consistently uses a subtle irony that disconcerts the reader as it fails to disconcert the characters: Amanda gleefully cheers for Rollo, the sad, caged chimpanzee who "enjoys himself" as he obediently performs pathetic roller-skating routines; and her father twice affirms that "this is the nicest park there is," even while obsessively fretting about the germs that Amanda might encounter. All pretenses of happiness fade, however, when Amanda somehow vanishes from atop a preternatural Ferris wheel, literally disappearing into thin air. Her father is then forced to concede to the dark, depressed quality of the night.

Whether one reads this inverted Funland as an elaborate metaphor for the father's experience of his child's death, or simply as a bizarre landscape indicative of "the new American Gothic," the final images of the story are no less moving in their rendering of the father's horror. He screams into the empty night, while the surrounding carnivalgoers with their "blank paper faces" hardly acknowledge, much less empathize with, his loss. The only true recognition of the father's anguish comes from the captive chimpanzee, who "pressed his tan face against the bars and gazed with comprehending eyes at the dark figure with uplifted head outlined like a corpse against the spokes of the great wheel blazing in the night." The creature most capable of understanding the entrapment of human loneliness is not even human at all.

The use of animals to magnify the pathos of human characters' predicaments is a familiar device in this collection. Eight of the ten stories display almost Orwellian symbols of wild, mutilated, lame, or deformed beasts to echo the failings and foibles of their human counterparts. Some critics, including Current-Garcia, have argued that many of these creatures are "employed obtrusively but ineffectively." In "The White Shell Road," for instance, in which a graphic depiction of a dog being hit by a car is intended to mirror the anguish of two separating lovers, the poignant slips into the melodramatic. Similarly overdrawn is the old, impotent dachshund, "all musket and no gunpowder," of "Wherefore Art Thou, Romeo?" In that story the absurdity of the feeble dog virtually parodies rather than deepens the exploration of the waning relationship between an aging professor and his alcoholic wife.

No less obtrusive, but certainly more effective, is Peden's canine symbolism in "Pilgrims," in which an old, lame, stump-tailed dog named Penrod and a bantam rooster named Roderick Usher are awarded to the three human protagonists as door prizes at a late-night party with the Kiwanians. As the story opens on "the morning after," Penrod befriends Horatio, a university instructor who alternates between passing out and being sick through the course of the entire story. The alliance between these two ailing creatures proves fitting, as each displays a touching yet pitiful loyalty to an indifferent master: Penrod to Horatio, and Horatio to his wife, LeeAnna, who carries on a none-too-secret affair with their friend, Theo. Like "Wherefore Art Thou, Romeo?" and the similar story "Goodnight, Ladies; Goodnight, Sweet Ladies," "Pilgrims" is a study of impotence, deceit, and failed relationships. Yet, in this case Peden displays a certain playfulness in his rendering of the sad creatures and the trio's inept handling of them. The very placement of barnyard animals in the context of cramped faculty housing is comically odd, and the humor of the unlikely predicament is heightened by some deadpan dialogue: "You'd be surprised how much a chicken eats and evacuates," Theo explains to LeeAnna. This aspect of the comic lends a charming vitality to the characters' ineptness and failure, thereby rescuing the story from sheer sentimentality.

A similar mixture of the pathetic and the quixotic is displayed in "Easter Sunday," in which a group of drunken medical students empties a huge, mounted water buffalo in order to play a cruel collegiate prank on their class president. The gutted beast, like the crippled hound and bantam rooster, is somehow laughable, even while suggesting the emptiness of human relationships.

More successful still is "The Cross Country Dog," narrated by Bill, a young assistant professor of English charged with entertaining a distinguished guest lecturer at his university. As the two drive to a reception honoring the speaker, Bill tells the story of a stray dog who became the mascot of a cross-country team Bill had coached years ago. Through the course of the story Peden frequently draws attention to the professor's position as narrator and to the act of narration itself, as Bill often stops to be reassured by his guest that the story is interesting enough to continue. After informing his listener of the dog's slow transition from weak, mangy mutt to strong, healthy mascot, Bill tells of the day that the dog completed a grueling three-mile course with the rest of the team, only to continue sprinting around the track when the race was over, finally

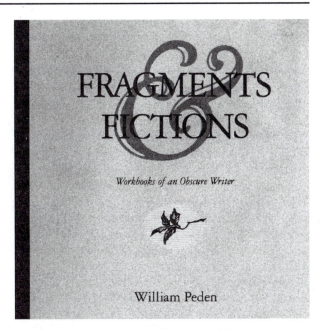

Dust jacket for Peden's 1990 collection of "mini-fictions" and excerpts from his notebooks, including ideas for scenes and comments on meetings with other writers

jumping maniacally into a reflection pool after his last lap. Touching in its own right, the tale takes on even greater significance when considered as an illustration of the "manic" narrative drive to tell stories, a parallel suggested not only by the highly self-conscious narrative framework but also by the narrator's sharing a name with the author. The story ends with Bill's refusal to tell his guest whether the dog eventually drowned in the pool; "that's another story," he says. This resistance to narrative closure not only mirrors the dog's attempt to sustain his ecstatic run but also suggests the human attempt to sustain the storytelling moment and the interpersonal connection it brings.

This thematic concern with issues of narrative also manifests itself in Peden's experimentation with form. Though Walter Sullivan, in the *Sewanee Review* (Summer 1970), characterized the collection as "being traditional in concept and construction," Peden does deviate from the strictly linear, realist form in several stories. With "The Gunner and the Apeman," for instance, a story that illustrates two graduate students' barroom lesson in the "philosophy of materialism," Peden plays with the chronology of events so as to heighten the reader's expectations and to comment on the bulk of the action before it ever takes place. Even more experimental is the melancholy dream sequence of "Requiem," which significantly challenges the "tyranny of realism" that has governed much of twentieth-century American fiction. Narrated in the first person by an unnamed protagonist, the son of a professor, the story unfolds not as a successive series of cause-and-effect plot points but as a sequence of dense descriptions of a dreamer's journey through a dark, Gotham-like city. Admirable as Peden's attempt at experiment is, however, the story ultimately fails to engage the reader's involvement or empathy; dreams are rarely as interesting to others as they are to the dreamer. With little dialogue or true action to propel the reader forward, the narrative finally becomes mired in Peden's thick descriptions, poetic and poignant though they may be.

Similar in tone, but more captivating in effect, is "The Boy on the Bed," another story that treats the father/child relationship. The protagonist is David, a young boy uprooted from his home in Virginia when his family moves to the dry climate of New Mexico for the benefit of his consumptive mother. Ignored by his mother and disregarded by his father, who is preoccupied with his university teaching and forthcoming novel, the boy has only housekeepers and library books as companions. The story turns on the boy's discovery of his psychological double in an empty apartment near the public library: a beautiful, sleeping boy chained to the foot of an iron bed. When David returns the next day, determined to free the boy from his prison, he finds that the boy has disappeared.

Crushed, David returns home and curls up on his own bed, wanting to run to his father for comfort but finding himself as isolated as his doppelgänger. When his father does attempt to console him, David can only say "I hate you, I hate you very much" and hope "that his father would leave him alone or go up to the University and peck away on his typewriter at a dirty novel that nobody would ever want to read." Like the otherworldly Ferris wheel of the title story, the "reality" of the boy's vision remains uncertain, but this uncertainty lends the story psychological depth and intrigue. Such psychological complexity, focalized through images bordering on grotesque, seem to justify the observation made in *Choice* (September 1968) that some of Peden's stories "take on the nuances of such masters as Poe, Hemingway, and Anderson."

Following the publication of *Night in Funland and Other Stories* Peden returned briefly to his East Coast origins when he became a visiting professor at the University of Maryland in 1971. That same year, Peden edited the collection *New Writing in South Carolina* with longtime colleague and friend George Garrett. Published for the South Carolina Tricentennial Commission by the University of South Carolina Press, the volume compiled the best prose and poetry of contemporary South Carolina authors in order to celebrate the first three hundred years of state history. As the editors note in the introduction, neither Peden nor Garrett was, in fact, a South Carolinian, though they both had relatives living there. The

fact that Peden was invited to evaluate work from a state to which he was, in effect, "an outsider" stands as a mark of the high esteem in which his critical judgment was held by this time. Further testament of this esteem was the invitation to serve as a judge for a National Book Award competition, as well as hundreds of book review requests from publications such as *The New York Times* and *Saturday Review*.

A second work published in 1971 was *Short Fiction: Shape and Substance,* a volume that combines Peden's talents as critic and editor. *Short Fiction* includes selected pieces from some of Peden's most-admired authors, including Porter, Anderson, Katherine Mansfield, and James Joyce. Peden's opening remarks in this volume serve as an introduction to the short story, offered in terms basic enough for newcomers to the genre, yet mixed with observations profound and insightful enough for scholars. In this introduction he outlines the history of the genre, offers a basic working definition of "short story," and includes several pages of quotations from well-known short-story authors expressing their views on the most essential elements of short fiction. He also reiterates his central assumption that the short story is particularly well-suited to the temper of the twentieth century:

> Revolutions in personal ethics and geo-political morality, undreamed-of confrontations ranging from bloodshed on American college campuses to massacres on the streets of world capitals, racial crises at home and abroad, the war in Vietnam and the less publicized wars in a dozen other theaters of operations—in a world of such enormous problems, the quick, unresolved, and fragmented short story seems to be more at home than the older literary forms.

He then outlines the primary formal elements of the genre, integrating his commentary with exemplary passages from successful stories, many of which are included in the volume. Concluding Peden's exposition is his reaffirmation of the possibilities of the form, in which he strikes his characteristic balance between a belief in "literary standards" and the importance of personal taste and interpretation.

Two years later Peden took a brief departure from his extensive work with the short story to publish his first and only novel, *Twilight at Monticello* (1973). Like much of his short fiction, this longer work draws heavily on Peden's experiences within the university, leading at least one reviewer for *The New York Times Book Review* (3 June 1973) to conclude that "Mr. Peden paints a recognizable (and depressing) picture of the liberal-arts Establishment." Set in Charlottesville, the novel recounts the reunion of a group of Jefferson scholars. The long weekend is an unusually eventful one, with a remarkably high incidence of sex and death among the academics. Adding to the drama are the stories that surface about Jefferson himself: intermingled with the rumors of plagiarism, adultery, murder, and suicide among the Jeffersonians are similar rumors of the incest and infidelity of the man they all study. Despite Peden's extensive firsthand knowledge of both Jeffersonian scholarship and academic infighting, parts of the novel remain slight and undeveloped, almost certainly because of Peden's greater familiarity and comfort with prose of shorter length. Thus, while the novel stands as an inventive integration of his interests, most critics have agreed with the assessment in the *Virginia Quarterly Review* (Summer 1973) that Peden "seems little at ease" with writing in this genre.

Peden soon returned to the form with which he was at ease, releasing a revised and expanded version of *The American Short Story,* retitled *The American Short Story: Continuity and Change, 1940–1975* (1975). In addition to covering a greater period of time in the later edition, Peden also expands his discussion of Jewish, African American, regional, and experimental authors. As with the reception of the original volume, critical response to the updated version was somewhat mixed. Some critics, such as the reviewer for *Choice* (April 1976), remained unsatisfied with the cursory nature of Peden's criticism, calling his style "tedious to the point of distraction." Others, however, continued to find Peden's work invaluable in the study of short fiction, both in terms of its bibliographic resources and its critical analyses.

Peden's second and final collection of original pieces appeared fifteen years later, titled *Fragments and Fictions: Workbooks of an Obscure Writer* (1990). As the title suggests, this volume includes no full-length, complete stories, as such. Instead, the book is divided into two parts. The first is a selection of miscellanies from the notebooks that Peden had kept throughout his career. Some of these "fragments" are notes from Peden's own travels, experiences, and encounters with other writers: breakfast with Jorge Luis Borges; drinks with Cheever; and gossip with James Baldwin. Allen Weakland, in *Booklist* (15 January 1991), characterized these fragments as "interesting thumbnail vignettes of the U.S. literati," and concluded that they are "not unlike F. Scott Fitzgerald's notebooks—in other words, well worth reading."

Other "fragments" in this section include the author's jottings of images, scenes, or themes that might later be developed into full-length stories. Most of these Peden did not expand, leaving the reader with the pleasant task of inventing his or her own surrounding story for such scenes as: "An elderly woman, in an old but well-taken-care-of limousine, liveried chauffeur; and in the back seat beside her, a goat." A few of the segments are recognizable as foundations for later stories, such as

this obvious origin of "Easter Sunday": "The morning I awakened to look directly into the snarling face of a stuffed leopard one of my fraternity brothers had temporarily 'borrowed' from the zoological museum." Enjoyable in their own right, these bits of stories also provide insight into the creative writing process, serving as examples of how autobiographical material can be transformed into successful fiction. On the whole, Peden's collection of fragments, alternately gripping and comical, is engaging.

The second portion of the volume consists of fifteen "mini-fictions," many of which had been previously published in various journals and reviews. Though written in complete prose form and spanning several pages, these fictions are in many ways as compact as the fragments of the first section; as William A. Donovan noted in *Library Journal* (15 November 1990), they "work best as mood pieces or intriguing sketches, story line playing a minor role." Even with the absence of fully developed narrative lines, however, these sketches offer a condensed sampling of Peden at his best. They reveal his Edgar Allan Poe-like penchant for the uncanny, as a numinous house-shoe materializes from a dream in "The Blue Slipper"; his acute rendering of the spousal relationship, as Jasper and Anna struggle to revive a time-worn marriage in "Husband and Wife"; and his awareness of the poignant, if humorous, connection between man and beast, as the first-person narrator of "The Polar Bear in the Ozarks" discovers that a wild, wayward polar bear is wearing his shoes. Most critics and readers have agreed with Genevieve Stuttaford's comment in *Publishers Weekly* (26 October 1990) that "the book offers no conclusions; the author's satisfactions, disappointments and conjectures about human verities are enough."

Peden died in Jefferson City, Missouri, on 23 July 1999, following a long battle with Alzheimer's disease. Although he will likely occupy only a minor position among the short-story writers of his era, as vital practitioner, critic, and editor, his legacy is secure. The combination of his assiduous efforts in writing, publishing, and theorizing the genre marks Peden as one of the primary contributors to the development of the short story in the twentieth century.

References:

Eugene Current-Garcia, "Night in Funland," *Southern Review,* 4 (October 1968): 1073–1076;

Walter Sullivan, "'Where Have All the Flowers Gone?': The Short Story in Search of Itself," *Sewanee Review,* 78 (Summer 1970): 531–542.

Papers:

Peden's papers are located at the University of Missouri at Columbia.

C. E. Poverman

(8 November 1944 –   )

Victoria Nelson

BOOKS: *The Black Velvet Girl* (Iowa City: University of
Iowa Press, 1976);
Susan (New York: Viking, 1977);
Solomon's Daughter (New York: Viking, 1981; Harmonds-
worth, U.K. & New York: Penguin, 1983);
My Father in Dreams (New York: Scribners, 1988);
Skin: Stories (Princeton: Ontario Review Press, 1992);
On the Edge (Princeton: Ontario Review Press, 1997).

SELECTED PERIODICAL PUBLICATIONS–
UNCOLLECTED: "With the Opposite Hand," *Wit-
ness,* 9 (Spring/Summer 1995): 173–178;
"Landlocked," *Santa Monica Review,* 7 (Spring/Summer
1995): 111–136;
"Deer Season," *Ontario Review,* 44 (Spring 1996): 27–43;
"Washington Crossing the Delaware," *Gettysburg
Review,* 10 (Winter 1997): 571–584.

C. E. Poverman (courtesy of the author)

Having begun writing in a period that emphasized the sociopolitical novel, the female bildungsroman, and works defined by their ethnic voice, C. E.
Poverman has, in his short-story collections and novels, created a distinct body of work in late-twentieth-century American literature. His fiction, which
chronicles the journey of the individual human consciousness through the world, is notable for its
nuanced mimesis of the dense texture of the interior
life and personal relationships, erotic and familial.
"Fiction is the transformation and invention of feelings
and images," he said in an interview with Christopher
J. Patyk for *The Arizona Daily Wildcat* (18 April 1989),
"Nothing is as fascinating as what goes on between
people." Even when he inhabits the consciousness of a
down-and-outer, a working-class female, or a nonwhite
character, Poverman remains the ultimate maverick,
unlinkable to any easy discussion of larger issues oth-
ern than the simply human.

In Poverman's hands the domestic novel, traditionally the provenance of women writers, becomes a
device for exploring, most typically, the separation of a
male "outlaw" from his respectable family of origin and
the tortuous path back, through marriage and children,
to the settled and circumscribed world of "inlaws," sig-
nifying, in the old sense of the word, those individuals
who reside within convention and ordinary social
boundaries. He uses the short-story medium, on the
other hand, to focus more intently, though not exclusively, on the "outlaw" motif–the liminal territory outside the core experience of the nuclear family that
receives the fullest representation in his autobiographi-

cally grounded novels. Many of his stories—nine of which have been included in *The Best American Short Stories,* O. Henry Award, and Pushcart Prize anthologies—explore an expanded notion of gender, its postures and impostures.

The stubbornly trend-defying originality of Poverman's work is closely linked to the trajectory of his personal life, in which can be traced a multileveled rejection of, then qualified reconciliation with, his origins—geographic, class, and ethnic. Charles Everit Poverman was born on 8 November 1944 in New Haven, Connecticut, the only son of A. David Poverman, a successful surgeon educated at the University of Vermont. Poverman commented to Victoria Nelson, in an unpublished 10 October 1999 interview, that his upbringing "lacked the succor of a deep mainstream connection to Judaism"; religion was not emphasized by his parents, whose forebears included Jewish immigrants from Russia, Lithuania, and Germany. His mother, Helen Goldberg Poverman, was a Smith College graduate and at one time an aspiring playwright who had attended Yale Drama School. A sister, Judith, preceded him by four years. Nicknamed "Buzz" in childhood for his speedy behavior, Poverman grew up in a sheltered environment of privilege that included sailing—his father's passion—and all the other appurtenances available to a Jewish middle-class professional family living in a gentrified and Gentile East Coast suburb.

On Labor Day 1955, at age eleven, Poverman contracted polio during the last major epidemic before Jonas Salk's polio vaccine was released. After months of hospitalization undergoing painful physiotherapy, he was the only child in the ward who neither died nor ended up permanently paralyzed. In a twist of fate, his sister endured an adulthood of paralysis after a motorcycle accident in her early twenties, an incident that Poverman cites as a watershed in his own life and his understanding of family dynamics, and one that turns up repeatedly in his fiction. Both events doubtlessly contributed to the prominence in Poverman's work—also markedly atypical for late-twentieth-century American literature—of the body and the life of the senses: male and female beauty, sexuality, and athletic prowess on the one hand, and injury, disability (both mental and physical), and unexpected violence on the other hand. Later episodes in his life and fiction display a deliberate effort to seek out and record those marginal, unpredictable, and often violent experiences of the world not contained in what a character in the uncollected story "Landlocked" (1995) describes as the "dark, constricting, airless" atmosphere of New England.

Poverman attended Hopkins, a venerable private school in New Haven, where he swam competitively

and graduated in 1962. His semiautobiographical novel *My Father in Dreams* (1988) vividly chronicles the experience of a suburban boy forced to discover his own Jewishness, through the only other Jew in school, in such an atmosphere of constrained WASP gentility. At Yale—which the main character in *My Father in Dreams,* Jed Hartwick, refers to only as the "Great Grey," the object of his scattered, futile acts of rebellion—Poverman continued to swim competitively, earning a letter his sophomore year. He also studied writing under Robert Penn Warren, was a Senior Scholar of the House and president of his senior society, *Elihu,* and graduated with "Exceptional Distinction" in 1966.

Six days after graduation, Poverman went to India on a Fulbright teaching fellowship, an event he has termed an "awakening" from the bubble of upper-middle-class privilege—and a challenge to every moral assumption he had ever held. After nine months of teaching and a short stint as a famine relief worker in India, he lived briefly in Thailand before returning to the United States. In 1969, he earned an M.F.A. with honors from the University of Iowa Writing Program. After earning his degree Poverman lived four years in Hawaii, where he was briefly an instructor at the University of Hawaii, surfer, ambulance driver, bartender, and crisis center counselor. Out of these experiences came many of the stories in his first collection of stories, *The Black Velvet Girl* (1976), and his first novel, *Susan* (1977), the story of a young Asian American woman living in Hawaii.

In a personal correspondence to Nelson dated 1 November 1999, Poverman remarked that "I rarely write about something I haven't touched or tasted. Like a baby, I have to put it in my mouth to know it." Out of direct sensory experience, however, he has crafted a highly sophisticated aesthetic that might best be described—in the words of a character in a story included in *Skin: Stories* (1992), "Children's Law"—as a "pointillism of the spirit in metamorphosis." The effect of this verbal pointillism is both vivid and exact, a total synaesthetic immersion in a musical prose rhythm that is associative but never loose, that repeats its own refrains and, often eschewing quotation marks to demarcate dialogue, conflates boundaries between subject and object so that the reader seems to swim back and forth from inner to outer reality, from one character's consciousness to another's. The steady accumulation of seemingly disparate but carefully selected sensory detail and emotional association is the critical mass that gives the stories their final, definitive push to resolution. Poverman's art is such that he tricks his readers into believing they are experiencing, or living, a natural process, not a highly controlled construction.

Dust jacket for Poverman's 1992 collection of stories about modern relationships

Of *The Black Velvet Girl,* which won the Iowa School of Letters Short Fiction Award in 1976, competition judge Donald Barthelme wrote: "Poverman takes us to new places, new cities of the imagination. He is adept, surprising, sometimes harsh, and frequently very funny—a real discovery." The daring exuberance of these mostly first-person stories, which Poverman wrote between the ages of twenty-two and thirty, is displayed in "Deathmasks of Xo." In this gender-bending tale, an American hippie is kidnapped by Indian bandits because of his beauty and forced to perform as a dancing "girl" at wedding parties as cover for an elaborate extortion devised by the bandit leader, Ram Lal, who also takes him as a lover. Inspired by dreams of a mysterious woman known only as Xo, the hippie frees himself from his not-altogether unpleasant slavery in a fireball-eating contest that proves fatal to Ram Lal. For all its outrageous surface plot, the story is a perfect and subtle parable of a masculine rite of passage in which

the inchoate yearning for the female mate (as yet only a negative, unrealized "deathmask") overturns a powerful father's seductive dominance.

"The Gift: Bihar, India" expresses the foundational tenet of Poverman's work: that real knowledge comes through deep instinct and the senses, not the mind. The young missionary woman whom David, the main character, has come to help in a village devastated by disease describes how, as a child, she only "really knew" her father was dead when she touched his body in the funeral home. In a flash of empathic merging that is the hallmark trait of many of Poverman's male and female characters, David "suddenly felt a chill and imagined himself, eyes closed, hands folded across his chest, lying in the casket." Later, after a village baby has died, the missionary touches David's hand, but after the initial warmth his fingers are "chilled." Without any conscious understanding of his own reaction, David has sensed an emotional deadness at the center of this woman that repels contact even as she reaches out for it.

"Tooth," a comic fairytale about a dentist obsessed both with whitening the narrator's blackened tooth and fixing him up with his daughter, includes the recurring theme of capitulation to the intrusive father. In his quest to beautify a passive young male, Dr. Goldman and his bevy of female assistants are not unlike Ram Lal and his bandit gang in "Deathmasks of Xo." Eventually the offending tooth, the narrator's only weapon against the forces of conformity, marriage, and respectability, is metamorphosed, and so is his attitude. Wearing a ring made from gold culled from teeth the dentist has pulled, Goldman's daughter looks enticing now—but the real marriage, the reader understands, would be with her father.

The title tale of the collection, a farcical chronicle of a young man's problems in staying faithful to his Hawaiian-Chinese girlfriend, expresses the basic dilemma of many subsequent stories, that one part of the male protagonist wants "Out" once he is "In" a relationship, and vice versa: "the process of getting from Out to In and In to Out is wearing, it is hard on the body, hard on the feet, hard on the hide, everyone only sees you In-Between, which is an inexplicable state, you become a bastard, target for invectives of all kinds." The slapstick resolution of this story, in which he joins forces with Hawaiian gangsters to escape the wrath of women and the local authorities, keeps the hapless hero firmly on the side of the Outs.

This ongoing identification of the main character with the outlaws against the inlaws, together with a sometimes cruel descriptive acuity, informs many of the other stories in this collection: in "Resurrection at Hanauma Bay," the story of an intellectual whose relationships are real to him only when they fit into the elaborate mythic schemes he spins in his mind, a female character is described as having the look of one "waiting for a piece of meat to fall from the table." In the climax of "In the Remains of Her Speech," about a young man who returns to Connecticut to assist his parents in caring for his paralyzed sister, the sister soils her bed and exposes herself to her brother; then, as he bends to take her to the bathroom, she bites his hand. Reacting instinctively, he slaps her. Over this yawning interpersonal chasm only the shakiest bridge of denial and hypocrisy can be erected. In this story—as in the fuller exposition of the sister's tragedy in the novel *Solomon's Daughter* (1981)—the family is presented as a battleground of emotional manipulation and clinging dependency verging on incest.

The story "Retour Du Sahara" expertly distills the main themes of this collection. In the opening scene, a bravura display of Poverman's verbal pointillism, the narrator, Jack, sees his mother approaching on an Eastern street in midwinter. By the time mother and son finally meet, after two pages of description, the two have traversed only half a city block, but the reader has traversed the length and breadth of Jack's mind. The intensely rich and varied stream of associations—from a therapist carving turtle-shell jewelry to reflections on carbon in human bodies and the stars—proves integral in every detail to the central concern of the story: "the problem of closeness and why it should be a problem in the first place and how some people could take only so much closeness even though they wanted more and some wanted closeness but it made them miserable at the same time it made them happy and so on." The title of the story—literally, "Return to the Sahara"—refers to an obscure logo on a T-shirt worn by Jack's lover, for whom he has abandoned his wife. In his endless obsessive ruminations on this phrase—was it a song? a French movie?—it is clear that Jack is displacing his need to find a reason for having left the woman he deeply loves. His lover's easy pronouncement, at the climax of the story—that he likes her because she is a "bitch" and his wife is not—convinces neither him nor the reader.

A pivotal period, one that marks the beginning of the pendulum swing from outlaw back to inlaw in Poverman's life and work alike, began when he returned permanently to the U.S. mainland in 1973. Short teaching stints at Yale University and the Connecticut Continuing Education Center gained him his first footing in the American professional mainstream, then once again allowed him to escape to a landscape radically different from that of his Connecticut childhood—this time to the American Southwest. In 1977 Poverman took a position at the University of Arizona at Tucson, where he has taught in the writing program ever since. In 1980, he married the photographer Linda Fry. Their son, Dana, was born in 1983 and their daughter, Marisa, in 1987.

In Tucson, with his first collection of stories and his first novel already published, Poverman began the major work of his writing career. His novel *Solomon's Daughter,* a study of an East Coast dysfunctional family told from the point of view of the father, appeared in 1981 and was republished in the Penguin Contemporary American Fiction Series in 1983. By 1988, the long road of emotional maturation from outlaw to inlaw, from rebel son to joyous father, had become the overarching subject of his major novel, *My Father in Dreams*. Subsequent fiction has foregrounded Arizona, where Poverman continued his lifelong work in crisis centers (which, he told interviewer Suzanne Crawford in 1989, has helped him understand "the degree to which a family and its ongoing relationships form people"), and the San Francisco Bay area, where he spent several summers in the early 1990s working as a private investigator for a friend from Tucson, an experience he drew on in his novel *On the Edge* (1997).

Published in 1992, Poverman's second collection, *Skin,* was favorably received, with reviewers demonstrating more awareness of the special qualities of his writing. In the Winter 1992 issue of *The Georgia Review,* Greg Johnson noted that *Skin* "powerfully dramatizes the stress and confusion of people who try, quixotically and sometimes nobly, to get inside the skin of another person." Commenting on the way the title story seemed to emulate the real-life process of finding a story among many disparate threads, David L. Ulin observed in *The Village Voice Literary Review* (November 1992) that these "quiet mechanics" grant access to the main character's essence "in a way that a more linear, controlled approach to storytelling would never allow," opening up a sense of expanding possibilities. "Poverman," Ulin wrote, "is unafraid to let his writing take its own course, no matter where that course may lead. Thus, even when some stories in *Skin* seem on the verge of rambling, he does not rein them in—a risky decision, but one that imbues the entire collection with a vast sense of depth and breadth, of messy, unkempt life where loose ends proliferate and not everything is neatly resolved." In his review of *Skin* in the Fall 1993 issue of *Studies in Short Fiction,* Daniel Frick gave a blanket description of the characters in Poverman's stories as "spiritual exiles" drifting through "a world

6/11   ①

He was going deer hunting in the morning...
They'd been arguing on and off about his
hunting for days — it seemed unbelievable to
Kurt that he'd actually gone on talking,
explaining this with her — and now, tonight, they'd
argued one more time, ~~or perhaps had~~ and then
~~they'd dropped it~~ They'd dropped it, or both
had given up with nothing ~~at~~ resolved or
resolvable with a tight, angry silence (between
and instead) driven ~~to a bar~~ from her place
to a bar, just to get out, be out, ~~our own place.~~ Now, as
~~they~~ Kurt pulled ~~up~~ in to the parking lot, ~~as~~ she fell
~~reached down~~ felt for something on the floor of
the truck, reached down, and pulled ~~up~~
something up into the light...

"Oh, my god, what is this," she turned the
sheath ~~test~~ knife over in the silvery light from the
mercury-vapor lamp. "What is this?"
~~"Should I take you~~ Do you want to go home, fellow? ~~I'll drop you at~~ your place."
~~It what~~ He He reached for the knife...
~~that~~ "What is this..." Her voice had a cutting
edge. ~~He~~ He started the truck and put it into
gear. "Let me just take you home..."
She reached over and handed him the knife.
"Well, you can leave me here... I'm getting a
drink — I want to dance, ~~has some~~ hear some ~~music~~..." She handed
it to him.

Manuscript for the short story "Deer Season," published in the Spring 1996 issue of The Ontario Review *(Collection of the author)*

in which supposedly clear distinctions—such as the difference between male and female, the line between sanity and madness—are not absolute."

As did Ulin and Johnson, Frick chose to focus on the cross-dressers and self-mutilators in *Skin* rather than the broader range of human experience these stories encompass. This somewhat distorted perspective has been a recurring feature in critical assessment of Poverman's work (including a brief and dismissive review of *My Father in Dreams,* his most artistically successful and ambitious work, in the 23 July 1989 *New York Times* that castigated its "unsympathetic characters" and "dubious motives and themes"). Reviewers have often not seemed familiar with the full range of his work, have overlooked its ironic honesty, or have simply emphasized sensational content over deliberately understated representation. In *Skin,* for example, side by side with stories that boast a new cast of outlaw characters, there are an equal number of inlaw domestic stories as well as transitional stories that carry through the familiar theme of displaced adult children still overshadowed by parental power and groping to find their way in life—yet who now are offered the promise of transformation. In "Children's Law," two highly educated lost souls bemoan the fact they suffer from "the famous father disease," whose primary symptom is "whatever you do . . . it doesn't matter, not *really,* the life led by your father is more real than any life you can possibly live." Their personal limbo is a dreary commune that the narrator dubs the "*One Step Back, One Step Sideways* House," where everyone "used to be married to someone else or used to do something else." The only way out of this womblike existence for the narrator proves to be through his woman friend's neglected son, the one they both call "the kid," who has never been quite real to either of these child-adults: finally, on an outing to a park, the narrator is able to say the boy's name and touch him—and suddenly the world opens up.

In "Fathers' Weekend," another transitional story of an "In-Between" that is also a rare and unclichéd rendering of a man's "biological clock," thirty-year-old Jack travels from his adopted home in the Southwest to stand in as substitute father for his disabled sister's two boys at an East Coast summer camp. At the "father and son swim," this unmarried uncle is struck first by the gross fact of physical duplication between parent and child, then is deeply moved by the spectacle of "these fathers, gentle, swimming with their sons in the July heat, gleaming with water, each son so aware of and aching toward his father." In negotiating his uneasy relationship with the older of his two nephews, Jack remembers his own childhood emotional crisis at camp and a counselor who comforted him just by spending time with him. Through the story run dual themes: the many kinds of fathering that can pass between generations and the contrast between the desert, a place outside time, and the East with its strongly demarcated seasons, which by extension are also the passing seasons of manhood that only seem to stand still to the childless person. To his mother's judgment that he "looks different," Jack protests defensively that he "weighs the same," though the concluding passage of the story suggests that beneath his conscious awareness he is already identifying with the law of the seasons and his own need for fatherhood, which are the same thing: "I gaze up at the elms towering in the dark. I look down at my body. I weigh just the same. I take a deep breath, let it out slowly, and stare up into the thick motionless leaves."

Like "Retour Du Sahara," the highly accomplished "Africa"—the multilayered, deceptively anecdotal tale of a photography curator who has lost his unerring sense of what is beautiful—boasts a title that seems to stand off to the side of the main events of the story but that, as in the former story, proves to be the key that unlocks its secrets. Dismissed from his work on a museum show called *The Faces of Love* and sent to France on a low-level mission to catalogue the works of a French photographer, the curator and his wife are drawn into the small drama of the Russian countess in whose house they are boarding and Zoeller, her German sculptor-turned-chauffeur. When Zoeller casually mentions "You can smell Africa from here," the curator, electrified, finds his senses suddenly reawakened. And when he glimpses the secret love the countess and chauffeur share for each other, he regains his sense of beauty a second time. By the end of the story, Zoeller has gone to Africa, the curator's wife is pregnant, and the countess, her last link to love broken, is dead. Poverman carries the reader indirectly but inexorably to the conclusion that the life of the senses, and by extension life itself, perception and procreation, draws its energy from the presence of love—and withers in the absence of love.

"Intervention" considers shifting perceptions of what is right and wrong in relationships, their everlasting emotional murkiness. When a wife persuades her husband's friends to confront him in a therapist's office about his alcohol and drug abuse, the central question quickly becomes: Who is conning whom—the feckless husband with his deals, lies, and evasions, or the long-suffering wife, who has used the intervention as a way to find out about his infidelities and ultimately dump him? In this version Poverman tips the reader's sympathies more heavily toward the outmaneuvered husband—by giving the wife her own secret lover—than he does in the novel *On the Edge,* in which the same incident is reimagined in a key chapter.

"Cutter" takes up a favorite theme of Poverman's, the erosion of gender boundaries, and spins it into a masked ball of multiple identities in which distinguishing the false from the true, reality from pretense, is virtually impossible. In the crisis center where Jorge works, the voices on the phone may be who they say they are—people in desperate need, or, as the story opens, a declared serial killer about to dispatch his next victim—or they may be only impersonators, sick people faking other kinds of sickness. There is also Miguel, a boy Jorge helped save from sexual assault, now a grown man making his living as a female impersonator in bars. The revelation of the serial killer's true identity is less important than the sense the reader receives—in this convincing fictional demonstration of a postmodern moral—that there is no such thing as the unitary consciousness, that consciousness is composed of many people, male and female.

The centerpiece title story of the collection presents a disturbing variation on this theme. A self-possessed, determined young woman who wants to make something of herself becomes involved—against her better judgment—with a young Marine who frequents the bar where she waitresses. Lewis is a man Kim instantly perceives as "very strong and very weak at the same time. Almost like there was a hole in him." But, seduced by his golden skin, "the tightest skin she had ever seen," she is drawn into an unnerving symbiosis in which what she believes is shared "knowledge" passes wordlessly between them, through their skins. Kim lives vicariously what she thinks are Lewis's memories of Vietnam: "jungle treetops a solid green floor, someone down there, I was being lowered through the clouds, treetops coming up beneath my feet. . . ." The only problem, as she discovers, is that Lewis has never been to Vietnam, and the violent attacks that hospitalize him each time she tries to leave are—as in "Cutter"—self-inflicted. Yet, she knows that his nightmares of war are, in the deepest sense, real. Now, in hiding at her parents' house in another town, Kim understands that in some completely insidious way he has infected her and gotten under her skin: "There used to be a place in me where things hit," she reflects. "Now there is silence; things fall through an opening in me." She also knows that Lewis wants to kill her, though he loves her, because their mysterious symbiotic exchange, sexual and emotional, has produced a single merged being, within which Kim is now—Poverman allows his readers to draw the startling, implicit conclusion for themselves—the shared self, hence shared target, of Lewis's need to inflict violence.

"Desert Light" features Gracie, a character who appears in tandem with her husband (named variously Jed, Michael, and Jack) in several of Poverman's inlaw fictions, and her disturbed sister, who comes to house-sit in Tucson and is soon trapped in an abusive marriage. This tale prefigures the concluding and consummate inlaw story of the volume, "We All Share the Sun and Moon," in which Jed and Gracie are now visiting her family in California, when an unstable sister, Jan, becomes pregnant. In the ongoing saga of the rebel who finds his way back from the edge to the center via the humanizing experience of marriage and children, Jed is now a committed husband and father, even though he still carries a seed of his former alienation within him when he occasionally feels "that sense of surprise and amazement at seeing his children, as though they were someone else's, that it was someone else's life, that his realer self must always be alone."

When Jed's sense of responsibility moves him to try to convince his wife that they should adopt Jan's baby, Gracie points out that doing so means permanently incorporating this sister and her disruptive energy into their own nuclear family. Jed, fueled by memories of the anxiety and anger he had felt when their son Teddy was temporarily lost during a family vacation in the Pacific Northwest, presses his case. Finally, Teddy's own extreme reaction brings resolution. Unconsciously aping the emblem of nature turned on its head, the boy hangs upside down in a fig tree, refusing to climb down until his father assures him they are not going to adopt the baby. In the vexing determination of moral responsibility, the child's instinctive wisdom has saved his father from a catastrophic mistake. Even as the story emphasizes the deep physical and communal bonds of family—Gracie's older sister instinctively nurses Gracie's baby when it cries—it also draws fine discriminations: a good deed is not always synonymous with what is natural and truly healthy.

Published in *The Gettysburg Review* in 1997, the uncollected story "Washington Crosses the Delaware," besides expressing the deeply humane tenor of his later work, closes the circle on a central event in Poverman's life and fiction. Here, in a moving resolution to mend the psychic wounds given and received in the family of origin, the main character journeys back East for a last visit with his dying disabled sister. Even as his earlier terror and rage are dissipated by the realization of her impending death, Michael has a dream in which he sees an image of his father, upside down, that is also somehow his sister.

In an intuitive epiphany he understands for the first time his sister's early vehement rejection (by means of a nose job, name change, and marriage to a Connecticut blue blood) of her Jewishness:

> Joan was her father's other self, he a second generation Jew rising from the streets out of poverty, professional, with a God-like ego, she had silently gotten his message exactly, but upside down . . . and like a lightning rod grounding his repressed fury, Joan had lived out his unrealized rage and ambivalence, her accident the culmination of that anger.

Sitting at a child's desk in the elementary school they had both attended, gazing at the figure of George Washington in the hallway mural, Michael realizes to his enormous sorrow that "he loved her and it was too late." Yet, he also experiences a redemptive vision of peace and closure. In death Joan becomes his big sister again, come to fetch him from school: "He saw her appear in the doorway in her plaid dress and long braids, and then take his hand and slip her arm around him, and he heard her say, it's okay, Michael, let's go home now."

In his *Walden; or, Life in the Woods* (1854), Henry David Thoreau maintains that "all sensuality is one, though it takes many forms; all purity is one." This statement might serve as an epigram for C. E. Poverman's fiction. Never wavering from a focus on what is most serious about life, it displays an abiding sensuousness that is at the same time deeply moral, thoughtfully rendering what Poverman identified in a 1989 interview with J. C. Martin as the central experience of being human—"transcendence and self-acceptance as an endless process."

Interviews:

J. C. Martin, "Author Translates Life into Fiction," *Arizona Star,* 1 April 1989;

Christopher J. Patyk, "Professor Discovers Himself in Fiction," *Arizona Daily Wildcat,* 18 April 1989, p. 10;

Suzanne Crawford, "Family, Craft, and Telling a Story," *Tucson Guide* (Fall 1989): 138–140;

Charlotte Lowe, "Literary Survivor," *Tucson Citizen,* 16 March 1993, p. B1.

Reference:

Tim Vanderpool, "Gumshoe Gestalt," *Tucson Weekly,* 22–28 January 1998, pp. 14–16.

Padgett Powell
(25 April 1952 –   )

Brad Vice
University of Cincinnati

BOOKS: *Edisto* (New York: Farrar, Straus & Giroux, 1984; London: Secker & Warburg, 1984);

A Woman Named Drown (New York: Farrar, Straus & Giroux, 1987);

Typical (New York: Farrar, Straus & Giroux, 1991);

Edisto Revisited (New York: Holt, 1996);

Aliens of Affection (New York: Holt, 1998);

Mrs. Hollingsworth's Men (Boston: Houghton Mifflin, 2000).

SELECTED PERIODICAL PUBLICATIONS–UNCOLLECTED: "On Coming Late to Faulkner," *Oxford American*, no. 18 (Fall 1997): 26–29;

"Whupped Before Kilt," *Oxford American*, no. 23 (Summer 1998): TK.

Padgett Powell (photograph © by Marion Ettlinger; from the dust jacket for Aliens of Affection, *1998)*

Padgett Powell is one of the most linguistically inventive American authors and one of the fiction writers of the contemporary South who follows the tracks laid by William Faulkner, the man Flannery O'Connor once described as the "big train." "The first thing I ever wrote was bad Faulkner," admits Powell in his contributor's note in a 1997 issue of *The Oxford American* magazine, which featured his autobiographical essay "On Coming Late to Faulkner." In the article Powell addresses his former self, the unpublished neophyte, in relation to Faulkner: "[You] with your two-cylinder syntax are a mule and cart being borne down by the Dixie Limited. Fond mocking is, actually, all that you can do, given the roar of the train that blasts you from the track." One might say the same of the mature and successful Powell, whose "fond mocking" is not always easy to digest, with his goofy, white-trash sensibility mixed with an ornate, almost Latinate syntax. Since finding Faulkner, Powell has, in his own words, "made" six books of fiction: four novels, *Edisto* (1984), *A Woman Named Drown* (1987), *Edisto Revisited* (1996), and *Mrs. Hollingsworth's Men* (2000); and two collections of short stories, *Typical* (1991) and *Aliens of Affection* (1998). *Typical* comprises twenty-two short stories, most of them thematically connected vignettes scattered among a few

longer, more traditional short stories. *Aliens of Affection* comprises two novellas, "Wayne" and "All Along the Watchtower," and five full-length short stories. Powell is also a prolific nonfiction essayist; his articles and book reviews have appeared in many literary magazines and newspapers, including *The New York Times Book Review* and *Esquire.*

Powell was born in Gainesville, Florida, on 25 April 1952. His father, Albine Batts Powell, was a brewmaster, and his mother, Bettyre Palmer Powell, taught school. The family relocated to South Carolina when Powell was a young boy. His first love was not literature but science, and in 1975 he graduated from the College of Charleston, in Charleston, South Carolina, with a

B.A. in chemistry. His scientific training may be responsible for the precision of his prose. Soon after graduation Powell became a graduate student at the University of Tennessee in Knoxville to work toward a master's degree in chemistry, but he soon found himself spending more time reading than studying chemistry. Having lost interest in school, he spent a few years drifting around the Southeast and working as a freight handler, household mover, and orthodontic technician.

Powell worked for almost six years as a roofer in Texas, writing in his spare time, before he eventually entered the prestigious M.F.A. program at the University of Houston, where he studied with the legendary fiction writer Donald Barthelme. In an interview Powell described his former teacher as a kind, caring man who took Powell under his wing because he saw something of himself in his student's determination. Powell recalls that "We had similar tastes. We liked the same things, the same bars, the same books, the same women. The only thing we differed on was music. I only like rock and roll. He always wanted to talk about jazz. He really wasn't so much a writer as a jazz painter on the page." Powell received his master's degree in 1982. During his time in Houston, Powell met his future wife, the poet Sidney Wade, whom he married on 22 May 1984. Both Powell and Wade are now professors at the University of Florida in Powell's hometown of Gainesville. They have two daughters, Amanda Dahl and Elena, both born in the same hospital as their father and grandfather.

Powell burst onto the literary scene with the publication in 1984 of *Edisto,* a book Walker Percy praised as "a truly remarkable first novel, both as a narrative and in its extraordinary use of language. It reminds one of *Catcher in the Rye,* but it's better—sharper, funnier, more poignant." Named for a largely undeveloped strip of South Carolina coast, "too small for the Arabs to bother to take," *Edisto* is narrated by a precocious twelve-year-old boy, Simons Manigault. Simons's mother, separated from his father and called "the Duchess" by Edisto's native black population because of her status as a displaced member of the local gentry, desperately wants her son to grow up to be a writer. Because of the Duchess's lofty aspirations for him, Simons's narration is one of the most unusual voices in recent literary history. Similar to Mark Twain's Huckleberry Finn, Simons is a wild creature, fond of skipping school, fishing, and hanging out at the Baby Grand, a local juke joint where the patrons, largely black, slip him beer. For the most part, he is as completely "unsivilized" as Twain's protagonist describes himself to be, except for the heavy doses of Greek and Latin classics Simons's mother force-feeds him daily. As long as Simons continues his literary

pursuits, the Duchess turns a blind eye to his truant behavior and allows him to do as he pleases. Simons's mixture of puerile freedom and erudition leads to a literary style that is both philosophically penetrating and winsomely charming.

By the end of the novel Simons's parents have reconciled and his family moves to the plastic world of Hilton Head, South Carolina, a resort island full of condominiums, golf courses, and, worst of all, prep schools. Forced to leave the wildness of his former existence behind, Simons finds himself in a hollow new world where he no longer feels like an individual. *Edisto* is a bildungsroman, not only of one boy, but of a whole way of life in the South. As the sleepy agrarian past disappears in favor of a new commercial landscape, there is no room for sentimentality or regret. "It's the modern world. I have to accept it," Simons declares in the final chapter of the novel. "I'm a pioneer."

In 1984 *Edisto* was nominated for a National Book Award and was selected for inclusion in *Time* magazine's list of the year's best fiction, along with works by Norman Mailer, Saul Bellow, John Updike, and Milan Kundera. These honors helped Powell to return to his hometown of Gainesville as a professor of creative writing. He proved to be a dynamic teacher both in and out of class. Not only did Powell show his students how to construct well-made stories, but he would also throw wild parties where the former chemist would instruct his students on how to make homemade bombs out of bottles of Aqua Velva and balloons filled with hydrogen. In 1986, shortly before the publication of his second novel, *A Woman Named Drown,* Powell received the Whiting Foundation Writers' Award.

Like Powell's first novel, *A Woman Named Drown* fared well with critics, using the same combination of ordinary circumstances mixed with extraordinary prose. The protagonist, Al, is a Ph.D. student of inorganic chemistry who, like Simons in *Edisto,* is desperate to avoid responsibility. Al studies chemistry not because he is a "true scientist" like his friend Tom, another student in the same doctoral program, but a "scientist by default." Al sees science as a dodge, an excuse to keep from taking over his millionaire father's pipe business. As the novel opens, Al receives a Dear John letter from his longtime girlfriend, who has left him for a "famous crystallographer." Depressed, he drops out of the doctoral program and, on the rebound, moves in with an older woman he hardly knows, a down-and-out actress named Mary Constance Baker whose last role was in a play titled *A Woman Named Drown.* After the tumultuous affair ends, Al decides to visit Tom in Alabama, where he has taken a new job. Al finds that his friend has become disappointingly middle-class. Since Tom has abandoned "true" science for

T Y P I C A L

P A D G E T T
P O W E L L

*Dust jacket for Powell's 1991 short-story collection, featuring
"Mr. Irony," a metafictional depiction of Powell's mentor,
Donald Barthelme*

growth. According to Powell, *Edisto* is based on a real person, while *A Woman Named Drown* is "pure fiction." His second novel began as a dream he had while enrolled in a writing workshop taught by Barthelme at the University of Houston. The dream was so vivid that Powell wrote it down quickly and read it to the class. "They thought it was horrible," he recalled, "But you always feel embarrassed with a story at first." Powell added, "the story goes through a gestation period in your mind and you know you have to write it. So you do, and then you really embarrass yourself." This insight into the writing process referred not only to his previous work but also to a new book he was in the middle of writing, tentatively titled "Mr. Irony." At the time of the interview, Powell described the book as being about two women from Texas who take an incredibly cheap world tour with two gentlemen, one of whom is the title character. "I'm not sure what I've got here," he said about the manuscript, "except that it's supposed to be humorous, and it needs work."

"Mr. Irony" underwent significant revision over the next three years. Some of this time Powell spent traveling. In 1989 he was a Fulbright fellow in Turkey. Upon his return "Mr. Irony" was published, not as a novel but as a densely packed short story, in *The Paris Review*. It was a landmark story for Powell's career, for it marked a complete departure from his previously realistic fiction and served as a sort of *ars poetica*. "Mr. Irony" is a dazzling piece of metafiction.

Even in Powell's first two novels, one can easily see that he was attempting to adopt the humor and linguistic playfulness that Barthelme engineered in short-story collections such as *Come Back, Dr. Caligari* (1964) and novels such as *The Dead Father* (1975). But neither *Edisto* nor *A Woman Named Drown* pushed the boundaries of fiction as much as Powell's next work, the 1991 short-story collection *Typical*, in which "Mr. Irony" was republished. With this book he proved that he was approaching the kind of postmodern assault on form that had made his mentor famous.

The arch-absurdist Barthelme is thinly disguised as the title character in "Mr. Irony," the longest story and the centerpiece of the collection. Powell himself appears in the story as Mr. Irony's "student of low-affected living edged with self-deprecating irony." Teacher and student embark on the "Man-at-His-Best World Tour," via "unspecified variable means of transport," with two Texas women found at the International Hostelry for Available Traveling Women. The two couples dive from the cliffs in Acapulco, ride elephants in Lanxang (Laos) and join a Rocky Mountain goat safari. Toward the end of the tour, Mr. Irony's student narrator decides to withdraw himself from the narrative in hopes of making the story better: "I had in fact picked up my

money, Al gives in as well and returns to school to complete his degree, knowing that the upcoming year will be his last before he is forced to become the custodian of his father's pipe empire.

In a review of *A Woman Named Drown* published in the 7 June 1987 issue of *The New York Times Book Review*, T. Coraghessan Boyle writes that "All of these adventures are enlivened by the distinctive, understated humor that is Mr. Powell's signature. He presents a terrific, hyper-real dialogue in quick bludgeoned pieces, and his narrator's phrasing and dialect are always surprising and inventive."

In an interview published with Boyle's review of *A Woman Named Drown*, Powell discussed his work thus far and his plans for the future with journalist Alex Ward. "I don't want to be thought of as a six-bout fighter," said Powell, who, like his character Al, is fond of boxing metaphors. "I'd rather be considered for what I do over the long haul." Being valued for the long haul means showing a certain amount of variance and

self-deprecating ironic ways from Mr. Irony, whose student I allegedly was. . . . I could serve the tale best, I thought, and finally not without considerable self-deprecation and irony, by removing myself from it, and deciding thereupon to do so, and hereby pronounce myself expunged from this affair as teller—." The narration is saved by Mr. Irony himself, who assures his student that he should not make himself "scarce" because he has the ability and talent to finish the tale. Powell's statement concerning the nature of art is clear. Irony, self-doubt, and self-deprecation are tools the writer must use to prevent his ego from getting ahead of the work, but these should never be used as an excuse for quitting. "Things need you, son," Mr. Irony tells his protégé near the end of the story.

Typical begins with an epigraph from Barthelme asserting that the virtue of desire is greater than the virtue of honesty: "Truth is greatly overrated, volition where it exists must be protected, wanting itself can be obliterated, some people have forgotten how to want." Of the characters that populate the stories of *Typical,* some are more honest than others, but all somehow deal with a reduced capacity to want; most of them have become emotionally paralyzed by their dreary, everyday lives.

The metafictional "Mr. Irony" spawned a series of "Mister" stories that are featured in *Typical,* including "Mr. Nefarious," "Miss Resignation," "Dr. Ordinary," "General Rancidity," and "Mr. Irony Renounces Irony." They are mostly amusing, lyrical vignettes, one- or two-page portraits of characters whose personalities seem to be wholly dependent on the habits or emotional states indicated by their names. Many of these stories seem as if they could have been written by Barthelme himself. Like his mentor, Powell appears to prefer short fiction that explores the limits of language rather than stories that rehash tired plots and draw their power from a simple conflict. In this way the series of "Mister" stories that occupy much of *Typical* are anything but typical.

In other stories from the collection, such as "The Winnowing of Mrs. Schuping" and "Letter from a Dogfighter's Aunt, Deceased," Powell melds his postmodern training with his Southern gothic upbringing to forge a style that is completely his own. Reminiscent of Carson McCullers's work, "The Winnowing of Mrs. Schuping" is a portrait of a feisty spinster who has decided to simplify her life by divesting herself of responsibilities and possessions. The occupation of winnowing away her life requires a new name, and she arbitrarily renames herself Mrs. Schuping. Unlike Mr. Irony, who loves to travel and wax philosophical about the nature of narrative, Mrs. Schuping gives up travel and reading altogether. She has come to distrust reality completely, and this distrust immobilizes her. She is content to preside serenely over the deterioration of her house, until her winnowing plans are interrupted by a local sheriff, a fat, amorous man who, "in the river of life's winnowing," acts as a "big boulder in the bed of the dwindling stream."

"Letter from a Dogfighter's Aunt, Deceased" is a ghost story told from the perspective of the ghost, an unusual narrative point of view that is both first person and omniscient. This meditative perspective comes from one long dead, but not too long. Aunt Humpy, formerly a stuck-up librarian maniacally intent on correcting her family's grammar, now lovingly watches over Brody, a nephew she helped run away from home so that he could become a breeder of fighting dogs. From her vantage point in Heaven she looks kindly on her fierce nephew, who is now a non-churchgoer and career criminal. Brody lives on the margins of society, a rogue white male determined to be free of middle-class mores. Aunt Humpy is proud of her nephew because she is now free of the "myriad prejudices and passions and myopias that made us the human being we mortally became." She appreciates the purity of Brody's lawless existence in the same way that he appreciates the purity of the thoroughbred dogs he conditions "to a point suggesting piano wires and marble, reduced by another sculpted cat to a soft red lump resembling bloody terry cloth." In a sense Aunt Humpy is an apologist for the Southerners about whom Powell writes best: tough, mean, yet often sweet boys and men such as Simons and Al, whose self-determined sense of right and wrong often comes into conflict with those in the mainstream.

In the title story, "Typical," Powell proves that he has not lost his ear for the way white, blue-collar Southern males talk and carry themselves. "Typical" is a loosely structured interior monologue filtered through the consciousness of an unemployed steel-mill worker, John Payne. Payne's observations concerning the nature of money, sex, marriage, and race are both comic and narrow-minded, yet his insights into his own limitations and shortcomings are nothing short of remarkable: "I'm not nice, not too smart, don't see too much point in pretending to be either. Why I am telling anyone this trash is a good question. . . . There are many mysteries in this world. I should be a better person, I know I should, but I don't see that finally being up to choice. If it were, I would not stop at being a better person. Who would?" Payne is a "typical" white male, frustrated by his lot in life. Depressed by his inability to control his life, Payne has lost the desire to do anything but drink. As Barthelme warned in the epigraph to the book, Payne has "forgotten how to want." Now he is merely another victim of social and eco-

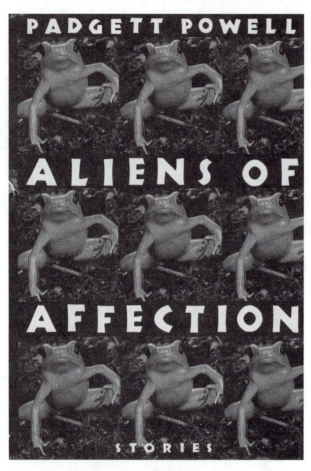

Dust jacket for Powell's second collection of short fiction, which was published in 1998 and depicts several mentally unbalanced protagonists

nomic forces beyond his control, and rather than continue to combat these indiscriminately, he has given in to a sort of blue-collar fatalism.

"Typical" was selected for inclusion in the 1990 edition of *The Best American Short Stories* and also won a Pushcart Prize that year. Several other pieces from *Typical* were selected for inclusion in other prize-winning anthologies. "Letter from a Dogfighter's Aunt, Deceased" was selected for inclusion in the anthology *The Literary Ghost: Great Contemporary Ghost Stories* (1991) under the title "Voice from the Grave." "The Winnowing of Mrs. Schuping" was anthologized in the 1992 edition of *New Stories From the South* and was later selected by novelist Anne Tyler for inclusion in *Best of the South: From Ten Years of New Stories from the South* (1996).

In 1996 Powell returned to the novel genre as well as to his most popular character, Simons Manigault, with *Edisto Revisited*. The narrative begins just after Simons has graduated from architecture school. No longer is he a wild creature of the Carolina coast. His education has caused him, like many of the characters

in *Typical*, to give up hope. Profoundly depressed, Simons finds that he has no desire to do anything but consume alcohol. He is momentarily saved by a passionate love affair with his cousin Patricia. The novel wastes little time in laying the foundations of an incestuous romance in the Faulknerian tradition. But even this relationship becomes too much responsibility for Simons to handle, and eventually he flees back to Edisto to find his old friends. Although *Edisto Revisited* did not draw the lavish praise that *Edisto* did, reviewers still found much to like in the book, calling it a tour de force of style. Near the end of *Edisto Revisited* Simons, determined to grow up, renounces the self-defeating indulgences of alcohol, just as Powell himself decided around this time to stop drinking.

There is always a hint in Powell's writing that his fiction is really just autobiography cast into a multitude of masks and personae. Powell has indicated in interviews that Simons is based on a "real person," while the chemistry-student protagonist of *A Woman Named Drown* pursues Powell's abandoned study of science. "Typical" and "Mr. Irony" reflect two different aspects of Powell's personality. The unemployed Payne is a realistic character reminiscent of the kind of men that Powell would have worked with closely as a day laborer in Texas, while "Mr. Irony" depicts Powell's relationship with his teacher Barthelme and employs the artful fictional techniques that Barthelme practiced.

The fictive positions in "Typical" and "Mr. Irony" seem to be mixed in "Wayne's Fate," another of the stories in *Typical*. Wayne is a half-intoxicated roofer who loses his balance atop a high building and is decapitated during the fall. His severed head lands in a five-gallon bucket of mastic. The story concludes with the reattachment of his head and the semiresurrection of his corpse. At the end the reader discovers that Wayne is not fully functional but is capable of making lewd comments. He convinces the narrator of the story, a fellow roofer, to make a few lewd comments to the owner of the home they are repairing while they await the paramedics.

Several other Wayne stories were published in Powell's 1998 short-story collection, *Aliens of Affection*. These stories display a further renovation of Powell's style and an intensification of his linguistic playfulness. He uses extravagant language as a tool to create further ironic space between author and characters as well as between characters and readers. Unlike Powell's previous writings, in which he seemed rather intimate with his characters, in the aptly titled *Aliens of Affection* he holds his characters at arm's length. Not only are they emotionally alienated from the reader, they are alienated from themselves. Few characters in these stories speak with the clarity or coherence of Payne in "Typical." Most of them are psychotic, drug-addled, and even brain-damaged. In essence, Powell has abandoned realism for a fictional world filtered through a myriad of unusual psychological states.

In the other Wayne stories in *Aliens of Affection* Wayne has not prospered since his decapitation in *Typical*. He is now out of work, and his teeth are falling out. His wife, Felicia (Wayne refers to her simply as "Ugly"), kicks him out of their home for being selfish. As it turns out in the course of the Wayne stories, he is a harmless, irresponsible drunk who drifts from one episode to the next, pointlessly rotating among women, bars, and menial jobs. The last section of "Wayne" is told by an intrusive narrator who explains that Wayne's lack of psychological depth is worthy of study: "Wayne isn't afraid of anything because he knows he is afraid. I, by contrast, think myself fearless, and when something scares me, *it scares the shit out of me*." These moments of fear force the narrator to "undergo a little private analysis the likes of which have never troubled Wayne." Wayne's cowardice, meanness, low intelligence, and lack of motivating psychology are actually assets. The narrator editorializes the ending of the sequence by again comparing Wayne to himself, lamenting, "For all my teeth! Muscles! College!" The narrator is plagued by a sense of self-doubt that never hinders Wayne: "Wayne may be roofing, but I am afraid."

A trilogy of stories in *Aliens of Affection* appears under the title "All Along the Watchtower." The stories feature a nameless pseudohero resembling Wayne—perhaps the same protagonist in all three stories, perhaps not—who negotiates the indistinct boundaries of personality. In "Chihuahua" the narrator, a former mental patient, sets off on an arbitrary quest to locate a fifty-pound Chihuahua. This takes him south of the border to Mexico, where he finds not only the freakish dog but also a local nurse who supplies the narrator with pills, sex, and the illusion that life can be simple and even pastoral. The narrator of "Stroke" also seems to have diminished mental capacity. The narrative unfolds with all the unimpeded honesty of a stroke victim who cannot edit his thoughts. In the forty-page title story, "Aliens of Affection," the last in the trilogy, the narrator inhabits yet another haze of delusion in which metaphors become literal and the actual world is lost in a fog of language. But readers are still sure they are in the South, or at least the literary South, because of the presence of a devil-may-care Southern belle, Dale Mae.

The departure from traditional narrative and plot in *Typical* is extended to a radical reinvention of the concept of characters in *Aliens of Affection*. Many readers might accuse Powell's later characters of flatness, but what they lack in depth they make up for in originality. Because several of the characters in *Aliens of Affection* are

mentally deficient and are incapable of articulating the futility of their own lives as perceptively as Payne in "Typical," or as eloquently as Simons in *Edisto* and *Edisto Revisited* and Al in *A Woman Named Drown*, they are more content to let the absurdity of the world they live in speak for itself. When commentary is needed, the author must make it directly himself, as he does at the end of the Wayne stories.

Another of Powell's schizoid characters, Rod, takes on the persona of Scarliotti in "Scarliotti and the Sinkhole," also from *Aliens of Affection*. Rod is a trailer-park resident who has been struck in the head by the side mirror of a moving truck. Because he refuses to take his medication, he develops a split personality disorder and creates a new persona to act out his more heroic side. Rod names this more heroic and dangerous alter ego Scarliotti. As Scarliotti, Rod manages to seduce a gas station attendant who really only sleeps with him in order to drink his beer and take his medication. The story ends with a sinkhole threatening to swallow up Rod's trailer. It is difficult to determine whether this sinkhole is a literal danger or an absurdist metaphor for Rod's increasingly dismal existence. He cannot combat the sinkhole as Scarliotti, nor even escape from it as Rod. The story ends with a babbling monologue that shifts between a meditation on dog-fighting and an analysis of the Confederate general J. E. B. Stuart.

It is difficult to decide whether Powell's Southern absurdism is a tool for social commentary or simply a tool to poke fun at his characters. To some extent, the radical assault on character in the stories of *Aliens of Affection* seems to be another attempt to comment upon the changing nature of the South, which is described as a "vale of dry tears" in the story "Trick or Treat." In contrast to colorful, realistic characters such as Simons and Al, who follow in a long line of disaffected Southerners mourning the loss of the old, aristocratic South, Powell's more recent characters are simply incapable of fitting in. They are victims of insanity, stroke, and brain damage, failing to adjust to contemporary life but still clinging to fragmented memories of the old South, to such things as dogfights and Civil War heroes. In an essay titled "Whupped Before Kilt," originally appearing in a 1998 issue of *The Oxford American* magazine and later republished as the preface to the 1998 edition of *New Stories From the South*, Powell points out that since the South lost the Civil War, Southern literature has been a literature focused on failure. Quoting Faulkner's Wash Jones in *Absalom, Absalom!* (1936)–"Well, Kernel, they mought have kilt us, but they ain't whipped us yit, air they?"–Powell asserts that the "literature of the South is full of people running around admitting or denying their whippedness." In contrast to the state of "whippedness," he sees integrity to be "the denial of whippedness." The various figures that populate Powell's later short stories display the unusual characteristic of being "whupped," but because they do not know they are whipped they retain a certain amount of integrity. The reader knows that characters such as Wayne and Rod are victims of circumstance. As victims they will inevitably be bested in their personal dogfights with the world at large. Wayne and Rod, however, do not know that they are underdogs. Their ignorance to their plight causes them to be fearless, and in this fearlessness readers may find a small but deep reservoir of integrity. As with *Typical,* the stories in *Aliens of Affection* brought Powell awards for the power and insight of his writing. "Aliens of Affection," the final story in the trilogy "All Along the Watchtower," was selected for the 1998 edition of *New Stories from the South.* That same year, "Wayne in Love" was selected by Garrison Keillor for inclusion in *The Best American Short Stories.*

Throughout his career, Powell has attempted to reinvent the literature of the old South by paying particular attention to the aspects of the Southern literary tradition that make it unique, primarily the language of the region. From *Edisto* to *Aliens of Affection,* Powell's adept use of inventive syntax, coupled with his finely tuned ear for dialect, has drawn favorable comparisons with such masters of regionalism as Twain and Faulkner. Powell is not, however, a writer lost in the past; his subject matter is that of the contemporary South, a new urban landscape that threatens to erase the identity of the old South as the region gives in to commercial forces from beyond its borders. The traditional theme of defeated Southerner is consistent throughout Powell's body of work. The author's nonconformist "whupped" characters, from Simons to Wayne, are used to critique a culture that has given itself over to the vapid worship of success.

As a writer of short fiction, Powell is one of the few writers who have successfully managed to combine postmodern absurdism with the gothic and grotesque traditions of Southern regionalism. In this sense, his short stories appear to be the direct heir to the work of Barthelme and O'Connor. Like his teacher Barthelme, Powell frequently abandons traditional narrative for fictions that seem to exist in a pure realm of language. Much of his work is unencumbered by realistic plots, and even in his more straightforward stories the settings and characters can only be described as odd or idiosyncratic. Like O'Connor, Powell endeavors to create memorable misfits, his most notable creations being the meditative Mrs. Schuping and the crazed roofer Wayne. Many of Powell's characters seem to be allegorical in nature, with personalities invented to question conventional notions of individuality or even philosophical notions of free will; others are just plain funny.

Interview:

Alex Ward, "A Better Class of Fools," *New York Times,* 7 June 1987, sec. 7, p. 9.

Francine Prose
(1 April 1947 –)

Troy L. Thibodeaux
New York University

BOOKS: *Judah the Pious* (New York: Atheneum, 1973; London: Chatto & Windus, 1973);

The Glorious Ones (New York: Atheneum, 1974);

Stories from Our Living Past, edited by Jules Harlow and Seymour Rossel; illustrated by Erika Weihs (New York: Behrman, 1974);

Marie Laveau (New York: Berkley, 1977);

Animal Magnetism (New York: Putnam, 1978);

Household Saints (New York: St. Martin's Press, 1981; London: Virago, 1994);

Hungry Hearts (New York: Pantheon, 1983);

Bigfoot Dreams (New York: Pantheon, 1986; London: Futura, 1989);

Women and Children First: Stories (New York: Pantheon, 1988);

Primitive People (New York: Farrar, Straus & Giroux, 1992);

The Peaceable Kingdom: Stories (New York: Farrar, Straus & Giroux, 1993);

Hunters and Gatherers (New York: Farrar, Straus & Giroux, 1995);

Dybbuk: A Story Made in Heaven (New York: Greenwillow, 1996);

Guided Tours of Hell: Novellas (New York: Metropolitan/ Holt, 1997)—comprises *Guided Tours of Hell* and *Three Pigs in Five Days;*

The Angel's Mistake: Stories of Chelm, illustrated by Mark Podwal (New York: Greenwillow Books, 1997);

You Never Know: A Legend of the Lamed-Vavniks, illustrated by Podwal (New York: Greenwillow, 1998);

Blue Angel (New York: HarperCollins, 2000);

The Demon's Mistake: A Story from Chelm, illustrated by Podwal (New York: Greenwillow Books, 2000).

PRODUCED SCRIPT: *Janis,* motion picture, by Prose and Nancy Savoca, Redeemable Features, 1999.

OTHER: "The Arrival of Eve," in *Gates to the New City: A Treasury of Modern Jewish Tales,* edited by

Francine Prose (photograph © 1993 by Judy Linn; from the dust jacket for The Peaceable Kingdom*)*

Howard Schwartz (New York: Avon, 1983), pp. 118–119;

Ida Fink, *A Scrap of Time and Other Stories,* translated by Prose and Madeleine Levine (New York: Pantheon, 1988; London: Penguin, 1989);

Fink, *The Journey,* translated by Prose and Johanna Weschler (New York: Farrar, Straus & Giroux, 1992);

"The Seven Month Home," in *A Place Called Home: Twenty Writing Women Remember,* edited by Mickey Pearlman (New York: St. Martin's Press, 1996), pp. 59–67;

Fink, *Traces: Stories,* translated by Prose and Philip Boehm (New York: Metropolitan, 1997);

Melissa Harris, ed., *Master Breasts: Objectified, Aestheticized, Fantasized, Eroticized, Feminized by Photography's Most Titillating Masters,* introduction by Prose (New York: Aperture, 1998);

"What Makes a Short Story?" in *On Writing Short Stories,* edited by Tom Bailey (New York: Oxford University Press, 2000).

SELECTED PERIODICAL PUBLICATIONS– UNCOLLECTED: "Learning from Chekhov," *Western Humanities Review,* 41 (Spring 1987): 1–14;

"Good Guy, Bad Guy," *Antioch Review,* 49 (Fall 1991): 538–550;

"Small Miracles," *Redbook,* 180 (December 1992): 70;

"She and I . . . and Someone Else," *Antaeus,* 73/74 (Spring 1994): 51–53;

"In the Back Seat for Seven Years," *New York Times,* 12 March 1995, pp. 41–42;

"Outer City Blues," *New York Times Magazine* (21 April 1996): 68;

"The Old Morgue," *Threepenny Review,* 71 (Fall 1997);

"The Lunatic, the Lover, and the Poet," *Atlantic Monthly,* 281 (March 1998): 64–80;

"Hawks and Sparrows," *GQ: Gentlemen's Quarterly,* 68 (April 1998): 152–160;

"Scent of a Woman's Ink," *Harper's* (June 1998): 61–70;

"I Know Why the Caged Bird Cannot Read," *Harper's,* 299 (September 1999): 76–84.

Francine Prose has been praised for the imaginative breadth of her narratives, and her gifts as a traditional storyteller have earned comparisons with such great fabulists as Geoffrey Chaucer and Isak Dinesen (Karen Blixen). But Prose has also received praise for her incisive observations of contemporary behavior and for the funny, frequently biting social satire that these observations occasion. This range of subject matter and technique gives some indication of the versatility of Prose's abilities: versatility that has produced novels, short-story collections, children's books, and many uncollected stories and articles published in major newspapers and in magazines as different as *Hudson Review* and *People, The New Yorker* and *Redbook, Antaeus* and *Atlantic Monthly.* But the two poles of Prose's narrative strategies–at one end, the traditional folklorist's methods that employ a ranging historical and fantastic imagination, and at the other end the satirist's propensity to cast an uncompromising eye on the follies and disappointments of contemporary life–reflect more than

the scope of Prose's career; they also indicate the path her writing has taken.

From her early novels, with their complex weaving of legend, history, and the fabulous, Prose has moved increasingly into more-realist modes engaged with her own time and place. Prose's fiction demonstrates an almost linear progression from the imaginary to the realistic, and her work in the short-story form, her period of greatest activity in which falls almost at the exact center of this thematic and stylistic progression, seems to have played a central role in this shift of focus.

Born in Brooklyn, New York, on 1 April 1947 to Philip Prose and Jessie Rubin Prose, Francine Prose makes light of what she considers an unremarkable upbringing: "It was a Brooklyn childhood," she told Mickey Pearlman in an interview published in 1990, "On the weekends I'd just go to the city and hang out. . . . It's not a novel." While her early experience may not have merited novel-length treatment, it has played a significant role in many of her short stories. In particular, the experience of being the child of two physicians seems to have affected not only the subject matter of her work but her understanding of her role as a writer as well. Exposure to her father's work as a Bellevue pathologist may have influenced Prose's developing capacity for acute observation, but of even greater importance, according to Prose in her autobiographical essay "The Old Morgue," published in *The Threepenny Review* (Fall 1997), was the community of storytelling among the pathologists: "what engaged me more than the painstakingly thorough postmortems were the stories I was hearing about the morgue's most notorious cases: the tumor discovered, unexpectedly, on a routine chest X ray." Just as observing her father's work as a physician may have fostered her interest in storytelling, watching her mother so successfully combine her family and professional roles may have contributed to Prose's confidence in pursuing her own vocation. She told Pearlman that "It never occurred to me that you couldn't do what you wanted to do. Only when I went to college and women started to say 'How was it growing up with this kind of a mother,' did it suddenly seem odd to me." Along the path of doing what she wanted to do, Prose received her B.A. degree in English summa cum laude from Radcliffe College in 1968 and her M.A. degree, also in English, from Harvard University in 1969.

In 1971, living in Cambridge, Massachusetts, and ostensibly working on an autobiographical novel, Prose decided to make a profound break from what had become a stultifying routine in her

life. She convinced the man with whom she was living to use his graduate mathematics fellowship to
pay for a year in a Bombay mathematics institute.
For ten months in Bombay, Prose immersed herself
in the classic novels contained in the rather dated
collection of the University of Bombay Library. In
place of her typical fare of postmodern novels, Prose
recalls, she found herself reading "Proust, Dosto-
evsky, Turgennev–they were all the library had,"
and she also discovered the master storytelling of
the Danish writer Dinesen.

Under these combined new literary and environmental influences Prose began drafting what
became her first published novel–*Judah the Pious*
(1973). Far from the autobiographical novel Prose
had been planning (and that might have been
expected from a first-time novelist), *Judah the Pious* is
an elaborate, imaginative tale in the tradition of
Hasidic folklore. Set in the seventeenth- or eighteenth-century court of the king of Poland, the novel
recounts the efforts of Rabbi Eliezer of Rimanov to
convince the king of Poland to reinstate Jewish
burial rituals. The rabbi's argument soon evolves
into an elaborate inner narrative, and distinctions
between reality and myth, story and teller begin to
blur.

Prose returned to the United States with a full
draft of the novel in hand and taught creative writing at Harvard University through 1972. With the
assistance of one of Prose's former professors, *Judah
the Pious* was published in 1973. It was widely
acclaimed by critics and received the Jewish Book
Council Award for that year. Moreover, in the process of producing this first novel, Prose found a pattern that worked for her in later books: travel for
inspiration, fantasy as motivation, and the intersection of the mythical and the real as her characteristic
fictional realm. Although she eventually made her
home in New York City, Prose traveled extensively
in the United States and Mexico, producing in four
years' time three novels (each set in the past and
revolving around the possibility of supernatural
occurrences) and *Stories from Our Living Past* (1974), a
book of retellings of Jewish morality tales for children. Although not all as warmly received as *Judah
the Pious* had been, Prose's novels of the late 1970s
continued to receive critical praise and to expand
her reputation. She was named a *Mademoiselle* magazine Mlle Award winner in 1975 and was profiled as
one of "Twelve Women Working to Make Things
Better" in the article accompanying the announcement.

On 24 September 1976 Prose married painter
and sculptor Howard "Howie" Michels, and in the

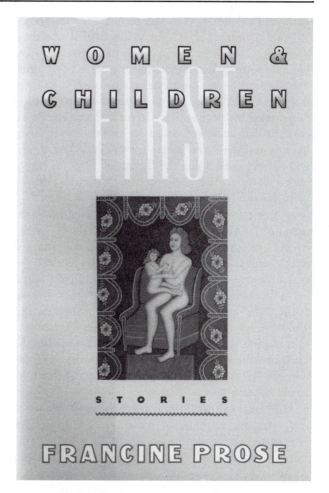

*Dust jacket for Prose's 1988 collection, focusing on the bond
between women and their children*

fall of 1977, Prose and Michels left their Manhattan
loft for Prose's second Indian tour, which she
describes in the "The Seven Month Home" (1996)
as a "strenuous and almost nonstop marathon journey from the mountains and lakes of Kashmir down
to the ancient temples on the beaches south of
Madras." On their return to the United States, Prose
and Michels moved to upstate New York, eventually
settling in a farmhouse near Woodstock, which they
called home for nearly a decade. Their first son,
Bruno, was born in 1978, and their second son,
Leon, in 1982.

Shortly after Leon's birth, Prose accepted a
position as visiting lecturer in fiction at the University of Arizona. This post was the first in a series of
teaching positions that she held from 1982 until
1989, when she decided not to teach full-time any
more. During this period, Prose taught at some of
the most prestigious writing programs and writers'
conferences in the country, including the Iowa Writers' Workshop, Sarah Lawrence College, Warren

Wilson College, and the Breadloaf and Sewanee Writers' Conferences. Occasionally at first and then as a rule, Prose's family joined in her scholar-gypsy life, temporarily leaving behind the New York farmhouse and driving, sometimes cross-country, to their interim home. Even after she had begun to turn down teaching positions at distant institutions, Prose continued to have a passion for travel. She has frequently written travel pieces for *The New York Times,* and she received a Fulbright grant in 1989 for travel in Yugoslavia. She also received National Endowment for the Arts grants in 1979 and in 1985.

Prose's novels during this period continue to include fantastic events, but increasingly these events are cast as mysterious eruptions in ordinary lives, and the settings of the novels move ever closer, both geographically and temporally, toward Prose's own world. For example, *Bigfoot Dreams* (1986), the last of Prose's novels published in the 1980s, involves the sordid world of newspaper tabloid writing, but Prose allows a hint of wonder into even this disreputable environment, as she explores the possibility that a tabloid writer's fabrications begin to come true.

From 1986 to 1992, Prose published short stories exclusively, many of which were collected in *Women and Children First: Stories* (1988). In these stories, some first published in *The New Yorker, Antaeus, Atlantic, Commentary,* and *Ploughshares,* Prose has almost completely abandoned the more traditional storytelling modes, the fantastic events, and the distant settings of much of her earlier work. Nearly every piece in the collection is firmly grounded in the present (frequently even the tense is present), and the great majority of events are positively mundane in comparison to her earlier fantasies. Even within this restricted sphere of possibilities, however, there are important links to the more capacious realms of Prose's imagination. As Michiko Kakutani noted in a 5 March 1988 *New York Times* review of the collection, a recurring theme in many of these stories is the search for an alternative faith that will provide meaning in the characters' lives. Whereas many of Prose's earlier narratives explore the implications of living by faith, the short stories more frequently dwell on the outskirts of faith, depicting the leap itself as sometimes comic, sometimes bewilderingly foreign to other characters, yet still somehow vaguely desirable.

The opening line of "Tibetan Time," the first story in the collection, is indicative of the ambivalence toward faith evident in many of these stories: "Most of the Buddhists were therapists from the Upper West Side." While the nonchalance of the

voice in this opening avoids outright hostility, the surprising assemblage of elements does create an air in which, not only Buddhists, but therapists and Upper West Siders in general are opened for scrutiny. Such ambivalence is in tune with the insecurity of the protagonist of the story, Ceci, a kindergarten teacher who, in response to a newspaper ad, has found herself in attendance at an all-day meditation retreat at a mountaintop Buddhist monastery. She has also paid an extra $50 for a private interview during the retreat with a Tibetan lama visiting the United States.

Ceci has been drawn to the mountaintop by a welter of motivations: curiosity, a simple desire to escape the city for a while, and a more complex desire to make sense of her own suffering. In one of the more poignant revelations in this collection, Ceci tells the lama, "My husband broke up with me at a sushi bar. We were sitting side by side. The sushi chef wasn't watching exactly, but he was there. My husband told me that he was moving to Arizona; then he ordered another cucumber salmon-skin roll." What Ceci seeks, like so many of the characters in this collection, is some compensation, justification, or explanation for the emotional peril that lurks just beneath the surface of her life. In some sense, then, the impending chaos that haunts Prose's characters in *Women and Children First* represents the darker side of the multifarious imagination evinced in her earlier work. Here, as in the more-fantastic novels, anything can happen, but in these more realistic settings that possibility is as much cause for fear as for hope.

In "Creature Comforts," for example, the spiritual quest is itself evidence that almost anything can happen in Prose's world. The story is told from the perspective of Kate, a woman who becomes fascinated by the strange spiritual experiment her brother-in-law Rice is undertaking. Kate is a wary observer of Rice from the beginning of the story: he has a history of drug use, drinking problems, legal infractions, and unpredictable behavior; and he has just moved into her guest house for a month, during which time Kate's husband, Nicky, will be out of town. Kate's initial reaction upon learning of Rice's intention to do some "spiritual homework" is particularly telling: "Well, really: Rice and Pammy [Rice's wife] are just the type for some major religious conversion." Yet, throughout the story there is a consistent note of near desperation in Kate's reflections, the sense that her own life is in need of some kind of renewal, spiritual or at least emotional. Her frantic efforts to remain occupied by housework while Nicky is out of town have ceased to offer their narcotic effect: "It always feels as if she is showing someone: Look what I've done, at the hours I've passed, how much less time is left until he comes home."

In effect, Kate is able to distract herself from her own need for renewal by her increasingly invasive scrutiny of Rice's life. She peruses his reading material, titles such as *Diet and Spiritual Health, Food for This World and the Next,* and *Rational Fasting.* She discovers, by reading his diary, that Rice is attempting an ascetic purification through weaning himself from protein. And he has decided to enlist his cat in this spiritual-nutritional experiment, seeking to "liberate" the cat from protein as well. The unsettling ending of the story, a passage that is both lyrical and disturbing, further serves to reinforce the anxious sense of unpredictability that haunts the story from its beginning.

It is no surprise, then, that the disaster-movie cliché title, *Women and Children First,* should resonate with renewed meaning throughout these stories of lives in distress. Moreover, as these characters cast about for some steady point amid the turmoil of their lives, frequently the only bonds that seem to hold are those between women and children. As Stephen McCauley pointed out in his 27 March 1988 *New York Times Book Review* article, in these stories "Women find themselves psychically and physically more connected to their children than to the men with whom they conceived them. It's as if, while these people were dutifully playing the hands they were dealt, someone came along and raised the stakes, changed the rules and switched players. And how could they not have noticed?"

Two stories in particular bear out this division in poignant detail: "Women and Children First" and "Tomatoes." In the title story a mother and son have developed such an uncanny psychical bond that the mother decides that they should be tested for ESP. As she gives the ESP researcher an account of one example of this mysterious connection, the mother, Janet, reveals the sort of inverse proportion, so prevalent in these stories, that obtains between the bond of mother to child and the bond between the parents. She says that in response to these moments of extrasensory communication, her former husband "used to say he felt like an actor in one of those disaster movies with the Titanic sinking and everyone yelling, 'Women and children first!' except that his wife and kid had already gone and left him standing on deck, watching their lifeboat float off."

This same image reappears in "Tomatoes," but here the point of view has been reversed, and the reader sees the impending disaster from the perspective of the husband and father. As the story opens, the protagonist, Vincent, is visiting his dying father. Struggling to make conversation, Vincent considers relating a bit of news that reveals the widening division in his family: "What news could he give him? Marianne and the kids have taken up fishing; at least twice a week they paddle a friend's boat out onto the reservoir and sit there, casting. As far as Vincent knows, they haven't caught anything. Vincent has never gone with them, though they always ask." Here Prose has made literal the lifeboat image from "Women and Children First," and the physical distance between Vincent and his family parallels the emotional rift that is at least in part attributable to the trauma of Vincent's father's terminal illness.

Vincent's response to this widening gap between himself and his family is to become infatuated with his father's physical therapist, Lauren. The bulk of the story describes Vincent's awkward, hapless flirtation with Lauren as he drives her to her next therapy appointment. The story ends with one of the few fantastic events in this collection: a giant bird of prey drops a large freshwater bass near the road as Vincent and Lauren drive past. The site of this rather unpromising flirtation is thus mysteriously aligned with the site of Vincent's wife and children on their fruitless fishing expedition. Yet, Prose is far too subtle to allow any easy resolution of the emotional difficulties of this situation–despite the almost miraculous summons back to his normal life, Vincent remains unresolved at the close of the story, as he tentatively offers the fish to Lauren.

Perhaps the most striking of the tales of family division in the collection is "Electricity," which weaves the plot of family disintegration together with a tale of spiritual searching. Anita, the protagonist, has returned to her parents' house with her newborn baby in tow. Anita's husband, Jamie, has announced that he is in love with another woman– choosing his hospital visit following Anita's delivery as the appropriate time to reveal this news. Her parents' home proves hardly less predictable than her own, however, as she discovers that her father, Sam, a man who "never went to *shul* in [his] life," has become "a born again Hasid." The sudden conversion has completely unsteadied Anita's mother, who, in a sense, is left standing on the shore of their old life while her husband drifts away into his newfound faith. She suddenly finds herself required, after thirty-three years of marriage, to begin keeping a kosher household and to follow the particular restrictions of her husband's sect–to keep two sets of dishes, to have sex with her husband only through a hole in a sheet. The strain in the relationship between Anita's parents thus parallels the rift in Anita's own marriage, and Anita concludes that "what's hurting her family . . . is the unpredictability, the shaky sense that everyone is finally unreliable." Anita thus comes to the realization that seems to underlie the entire collection of stories.

The conversion experience of Anita's father is itself in many ways a response to this profound unpredictability. "Dad, what's the story?" Anita asks him, and her father launches into the tale of his conversion: "Once upon a time, a jeweler was taking the subway home to East Flatbush from his shop in Forty-sixth Street." His conversion narrative is the tale of his apparently miraculous rescue from being robbed at knife point on the subway. The agent of his rescue is a young Hasid who seems to be able to exert mysterious control over electrical currents, in this case causing the subway lights to blink an SOS signal. The young man attributes this power—the power that frightens away the potential muggers and that thus saves Sam—to his rebbe. Sam's newfound faith therefore stems, at least in part, from his desire to exert control over a dangerously unpredictable world. Moreover, the form of Sam's story marks storytelling itself as a similar attempt to gain control. As Victoria Aarons points out in a 1997 essay, "Sam tries to stand outside of the experience, to deflect it. He creates a story in which he becomes his own character, and thus as the 'writer' of the story, Sam maintains seeming control over the cultural and historical dissonance that has apparently become his life." The fairy-tale structure of this small inner narrative may, in addition, serve as an indication of the shift in Prose's narrative strategies. Here Prose has allowed the jagged narrative of Anita's domestic disaster to subsume her father's carefully patterned tale, a narrative that seeks fairy-tale control over the disorder of daily life. In addition, by allowing Anita's mother to voice her dissent in the larger narrative, Prose calls into question the tidiness of the conversion tale. The situational irony of this story is, however, everywhere unstable—as Anita is introduced to the strangeness, and eventually to the power of her father's faith, the conversion narrative seems to grow beyond its certain boundaries within Sam's framed narrative, complicating the ironic edge of the story.

"Electricity" is just one of the many stories in *Women and Children First* that manipulates in self-conscious fashion the structural richness that accompanies moments of storytelling within the stories. Characters frequently become self-conscious about their own narrative moments, as in "Other Lives," a story in which a woman saves up a story, harboring it from beginning to near end of the narrative, withholding it from her husband and a friend, so that she can tell it to the man with whom she has become infatuated. Other stories in the collection give storytelling the effect of ritual, and still others depict characters in the act of framing a narrative life through which they attempt to escape their own. In both "Everyday Disorders" and "Everyone Had a Lobster" characters use moments of narrative construction as a means to escape their own lives and to entrap other characters. In the latter story a group of people watch their entire day on videotape, in the process making a joke of the near drowning of one of their group. The story ends with a character's reflection that "it amazed her that what you'd hoped was the start of your life could turn out to be a scene in someone else's porno movie." As in "Electricity," the weaving of a story within a story takes on significance as an effort to gain control, power over the powerlessness or meaninglessness of the characters' lives, but in each of these stories the power dynamic of narrative also reveals ethical questions. In "Everyday Disorders" a character steals details from the lives of those she meets, weaving them into the narrative of her own marvelously eventful life. In "Everyone Had a Lobster" the characters create narrative frames that dehumanize the people around them, allowing them to see others as mere props in a play of their own construction. Just as the unpredictability of Prose's characters' lives is at once full of fantasy and full of peril, the effort to master the chaos of living through storytelling can be a momentary salvation for some characters, a ruthless means of manipulation for others.

In 1992 Prose published *Primitive People,* a scathing depiction of contemporary life that seems to grow directly out of some of the bitterest elements of the stories in *Women and Children First.* Commenting on this novel in a 1992 interview with John F. Baker, Prose claimed, "As I look at the world I find it's getting ever more brutal. . . . I'm astonished at the way people who supposedly like each other talk to each other these days, and I was trying to get that tone into the book." The novel depicts in harsh detail the meanly violent lives of exurbanites in Hudson Landing, Maryland, as seen through the eyes of Simone, a Haitian au pair who has fled the violence of her own country. At once funny and terrible, this novel extends Prose's realist capacities even farther into the realm of social criticism.

In 1993 Prose's work was introduced to a new audience when her novel *Household Saints* (1981) was made into a movie directed by Nancy Savoca and starring Tracey Ullman. Savoca and Prose later collaborated on the screenplay for *Janis,* a 1999 movie about the singer Janis Joplin. Also in 1993 Prose published *The Peaceable Kingdom,* her second volume of original short stories. This second collection serves in great part as a crystallization and extension of many of the themes and devices developed in *Women and Children First.* As in the earlier volume, the stories here are rooted in the realistic yet retain a sense of extraordinary possibility, and many of the narratives in the later volume continue the self-conscious reflections on storytelling that Prose has used so effectively. In addition, several of the stories further the social satire that was nascent in much of *Women and Children First* and that reached its fullest expression in *Primitive People.* For the most part, however, the stories look with compassion and wit at the scenes of domestic disorders. Both the compassion and the wit, though, stem from the close scrutiny that Prose applies to these situations, and it is this aspect of the stories that Roz Spafford, writing in a 10 October 1993 *San Francisco Chronicle* review, recognized as "the taxidermic quality of these lives, the cataloging of disasters."

"Talking Dog," the first story in the volume, exemplifies the ways in which Prose further develops the themes of unpredictability and the imminent threat of catastrophe that bind so many of her stories. The narrator, examining the moment of her adolescence in which the story is set, reflects, "That year it came as a great surprise how many sad things could happen at once. At first you might think the odds are that one grief might exempt you, but that year I learned the odds are that nothing can keep you safe." The awkwardness and uncertainty of her eighth-grade year is compounded and refracted through family grief: her father is going blind, diagnosed with a disease of the retina, and her sister has just received news that her boyfriend, Jimmy Kowalchuk, on whom the narrator has her own significant crush, has been killed in Vietnam. As in much of Prose's work, however, this tragic but unrealistic unpredictability is countered by a fantastic sense of the unpredictable, as Prose invokes the fabulist's device of talking animals. "One night at dinner my sister told us that every culture but ours believed that ordinary household pets were the messengers of the dead"—and so the sister begins talking to animals—a white dog, a pet iguana—seeking a message from Jimmy Kowalchuk.

As the story reveals, one may not even find certainty in grief: the narrator's father has been misdiagnosed, his blindness caused not by a disease of the retina but by a terminal brain tumor; and Jimmy

Dust jacket for Prose's 1993 collection of stories about the lapses of communication within romantic relationships

Kowalchuk has been counted a casualty by a clerical error. In this disastrous reversal of disasters—the sister has married another man before Jimmy's return—the realistic and fabulous realms of the story merge: the sister claims that the white dog had "personally guaranteed" that Jimmy was still alive and had offered to lead her to Florida, where Jimmy had always dreamed of living. Even more fantastically, when the sister and Jimmy do move to Florida, a white dog shows up on the first day and runs directly to the sister as if it knows her.

One of the strengths of this story and of several of the stories in the collection is the narrative distance through which Prose mediates between the event and reflections upon the event. As Ron Carlson pointed out in *The New York Times Book Review* (10 October 1993), Prose makes ample use of the distance between the time of narration and the time of the story, creating an additional resonance that raises the stories "above the busy surface of Ms. Prose's witty and dark observations." The narrative of "Talking Dog" exists somewhere between the reflective moment the narrator inhabits and the distraught adolescence she reflects upon; through this device, Prose is able to engage both the raw emotional power of the experience and the difficult wisdom that experience brings.

This same narrative distance is at work in "Ghirlandaio," a story of an eleven-year-old girl's first love and of her parents' impending (but as yet unacknowledged) divorce, a presence that haunts the story and colors the girl's experience. Between its assortment of apt details and its incisive observations, Prose's narrative manages both to participate fully in the childhood world and to retain enough detachment to render that world doubly meaningful upon reflection:

> We were at that age when much is secret, much is embarrassing, when certain questions—what to do with our shoulders and knees, and whether people like us—assume an intensity they will never have again. At that age, everyone and everything is love object, mirror and judge, and we go around frantically wasting ourselves on whatever is nearby.

The narrator is frantically wasting herself worrying about her teacher's apparent dislike for her and trying to find a way to be alone with the boy she has decided she likes. All of these elements—the childhood romance, the parental divorce, the schoolroom drama—converge around a Dominico Ghirlandaio double portrait of a boy and his grandfather, who suffers from a disease that disfigures his nose. The narrator has discovered the painting on a museum visit with her father, a doctor whose taste in art reflects his medical training: "paintings of saints curing lepers; Van Gogh with his digitalis-distorted color sense; Monet, whose retinal degeneration my father pronounced to have influenced his later works; and most of all astigmatic El Greco. . . ." Both the narrator's museum visits with her father and the medical interest that guides their viewing are elements drawn directly from Prose's own life, a fact that reflects again the importance of the short stories in Prose's movement toward realism.

Perhaps an even more sophisticated use of narrative distance is at work in "Hansel and Gretel," a story set in the early weeks of a young woman's doomed first marriage but narrated from a twenty-year distance. Polly, the narrator, suffers through a torturous weekend at the home of a woman, the mother of her new husband's former girlfriend. The inherent tension of the situation is exacerbated by the eccentricity of the woman they are visiting (a famous conceptual artist whose latest project involves a series of photographs depicting the artist having sex with her cat) and the instability of her husband, Nelson (a man prone to "episodes" who commits a series of subtle betrayals over the course of the weekend). As the story winds to a close, however, Prose manages to evoke even greater resonance from her narrative distance by allowing the two time periods to cross in the recent past. Polly recounts a return to the rural Vermont area where she had spent the painful weekend. Secure in her new life, accompanied by her second husband and their children, Polly meditates upon the signs of her new life that lie hidden around the old—her two selves separated by an unbridgeable gap of time yet brought together in coincidences of proximity.

Polly's relationship with Nelson is characteristic of many of the relationships in *The Peaceable Kingdom*. Many of the stories share a concern with the lapses of communication and the gaps between expectations and reality, that undermine this and nearly every other romance in the collection. The cumulative effect of such failed communication creates the sense that it is an inescapable aspect of the cultural situation Prose describes. In stories such as "Cauliflower Heads" and "Amazing" Prose manages to conflate contemporary social concerns with her characters' domestic troubles: discussion of toxic waste serves to block real communication between newlyweds; technological information-overload masks the discontent of an entire family. Prose maintains a peculiar "flair for depicting our cultural fallout," as Jill Neimark noted, reviewing the collection in October 1993 for *Chicago Tribune Books*. This ability is evident throughout *The Peaceable Kingdom*, and it frequently serves a dual purpose—at once excoriating the cultural vacuity that infects these lives and eliciting compassion for the characters who thus contribute to the forces that alienate them from one another.

In 1996 Prose and her husband moved back to New York City, seeking better educational opportunities for their sons and the thrill of living in Manhattan again. As Prose explains in "Outer City Blues," an April 1996 *New York Times* piece describing the decision, "Living in the country required an active inner life and the energy to make things happen; here in the city that world thrums around us with an energizing momentum independent of our inner resources." Prose has continued her prolific output of editorials and journalism, frequently provoking heated responses to her thought-provoking pieces on issues such as the status of women's fiction and the criteria and methods for selecting and teaching literature in the high schools. She has also served as contributing editor for *Doubletake* magazine, and she writes regular art reviews, travel pieces, and book reviews for several major periodicals, including *The Wall Street Journal* and *The New York Times Magazine*. Prose continues to teach at major writers' conferences and teaches regularly in the creative-writing program of the New School for Social Research.

Although she has not published a collection of short stories since *The Peaceable Kingdom* appeared, Prose has published several uncollected stories since that time. Her adaptation of a Jewish folk story, *You Never Know: A Legend of the Lamed-Vavniks* (1998) received both the Sydney Taylor Award for books for younger children and the National Jewish Book Award. In addition to these awards Prose has received four Pushcart Prizes, has been named a Fellow of the New York Institute for the Humanities and, in 1999, was designated a Director's Fellow at the New York Public Library's Center for Scholars and Writers. A novel, *Blue Angel,* was published in April 2000 by HarperCollins.

Interviews:

Mickey Pearlman, "Francine Prose," in *Inter/View: Talks with America's Writing Women,* edited by Pearlman and Katherine Usher Henderson (Lexington: University of Kentucky Press, 1990);

John F. Baker, "Francine Prose," *Publishers Weekly,* 239 (13 April 1992): 38–39;

Deborah Eisenberg, "Francine Prose," *Bomb,* 45 (Fall 1993).

Biography:

Rena Potok, "Francine Prose," in *Jewish American Women Writers: A Bio-Bibliographical and Critical Sourcebook,* edited by Sara R. Horowitz (Westport, Conn.: Greenwood Press, 1994), pp. 302–313.

Reference:

Victoria Aarons, "Responding to an Old Story: Susan Fromberg, Leslea Newman, and Francine Prose," in *Daughters of Valor: Contemporary Jewish American Women Writers,* edited by Jay L. Halio and Ben Siegel (Newark: University of Delaware Press, 1997).

Mark Richard

(1955 –   )

Adam Sol
University of Cincinnati

BOOKS: *The Ice at the Bottom of the World: Stories* (New York: Knopf, 1989; London: Cape, 1990);
Charity: Stories (London: Cape, 1992; New York: Nan A. Talese, 1998);
Fishboy: A Ghost's Story (New York: Nan A. Talese, 1993; London: Hodder-Stoughton, 1994).

PRODUCED SCRIPTS: "Rings of Saturn," television, *Party of Five,* Fox, 13 January 1999;
"White Rabbit," television, *Chicago Hope,* CBS, 11 November 1999.

OTHER: "Who Is That Man Tied to the Mast?" in *Why I Write,* edited by Will Blythe (Boston: Little, Brown, 1998).

SELECTED PERIODICAL PUBLICATIONS– UNCOLLECTED: "Twenty-One Days Back," *Shenandoah* (Fall 1980);
"Just Name Some Place," *The Quarterly* (Spring 1989): 98–101;
"Checkmate," *Esquire* (August 1998): 144.

Mark Richard (photograph © Robert Yage; from the dust jacket for Charity, *1998)*

Mark Richard's two collections of stories and one novel have already earned him a reputation as one of the most talented writers of fiction in America. His stories are a rich banquet of dynamic storytelling and linguistic prowess. Compared variously to William Faulkner, Mark Twain, and Flannery O'Connor, Richard writes in a genre that was referred to as "Maritime Gothic" by Margot Mifflin, in *The New York Times Book Review* (1993). Richard's fiction resists the categories in which reviewers and critics attempt to place it, however. Darker in outlook than Twain, funnier than Faulkner, and with more interest in the surreal than most writers of so-called trailer-park fiction, Richard's work offers a range of pleasures for readers of the short story.

Mark Richard (pronounced ri-SHARD) grew up in the Virginia Beach town of Franklin, the son of William Edgar Richard Jr. and Clara (née Sonnier) Richard, both originally from Louisiana. Richard's first recognition came at age thirteen, as the youngest radio announcer in the United States, at WYSR-AM in Franklin. Most important in Richard's development as a person and a writer was his stint as a commercial fisherman, working on oceangoing trawlers and coastal steamers from Nova Scotia to the Caribbean. As he told Amy Hempel in *Esquire* in May 1993, Richard began this part of his life partially as a result of "a swaggering macho overcompensation" for bad hips, which had kept him in casts for many years as a boy. He signed on with some friends from Washington and Lee University, but when his friends returned to school, Richard stayed aboard the trawlers, temporarily leaving Washington and Lee. In an interview published in the 10 February 2000 issue of *Bold Type,* Richard called the experience

the most exhilarating, terrifying, important work stint that I did . . . I don't think there are a lot of opportunities for young people to have defining experiences, things that really push you to the edge of your abilities. . . . I was eager to overachieve, to push myself, and see what the limits of my new physical self were. I did a lot of different things that served their own purposes. All of them were great places to get material for stories. I didn't know it at the time; I thought I was misspending my youth, that I had wasted my college education and that I was a loser, all of which may be true.

Richard returned to Washington and Lee three years later, where he completed a degree with a double major in English and journalism. By then he had already begun writing stories and had successfully published one, "Twenty-one Days Back," in the literary journal *Shenandoah.* Subsequent jobs as a real-estate salesman, aerial photographer, advertising copywriter, and editor for the journal *Military Business Review* followed, taking Richard from Washington, D.C., to Richmond, Virginia, and eventually back to Virginia Beach. With the encouragement of *Esquire* editor Tom Jenks, Richard moved to New York, where he worked in a variety of fields—as a bartender, legal proofreader, private investigator, and teacher—while continuing to write. He published stories in *Esquire, The Quarterly,* and *Shenandoah.* Richard was a student at Gordon Lish's well-known writers' workshop, though he admits that after the second class he unsuccessfully asked for his money back. New York is also where Richard met his future wife, Jennifer Allen, whose first book, *Better Get Your Angel On: Stories* (1989), was edited by Lish at Alfred A. Knopf.

Richard's first collection of stories, *The Ice at the Bottom of the World* (1989), won both the Whiting Award and the PEN/Hemingway Award for best first book of fiction in 1990. The stories in this collection are a rare combination of powerful storytelling, sensitive character portrayal, and linguistic grace. Many of the stories focus on impoverished Southerners in the coastal areas of Virginia. This milieu, coupled with Richard's rich and complicated language and imagery, has led some critics to compare Richard and other Southern writers such as William Faulkner. But Richard's sense of the surreal, and the resilient humor of his characters, limits the comparison.

What Richard does inherit and develop from Faulkner is a sense of the music of language and dialogue. As he has admitted in an on-line interview with *Bold Type,* "A lot of my work begins with sounds, and then the visual world comes second." Most of Richard's stories are written in first person, and the sense of the story being told pervades the narration. The language of Richard's characters—their rhythms and idioms, neologisms and poetry—form an essential element to the stories. "Happiness of the Garden Variety," for instance, from *The Ice at the Bottom of the World,* includes a three-hundred-word sentence, in which the narrator tries to explain, in an awkward, embarrassed, switchback, wandering way, why killing his employer's horse "was all the worse" because of the circumstances surrounding his affection for the horse. Some critics have compared Richard to Mark Twain, but the use of rural speech patterns in Richard's fiction has little in common with Twain's efforts at authenticity. Characters' accents and phrasing do not only serve the story, they are part of the story itself.

Richard's work tells a variety of tales about characters on the margins, but the author has a particularly deft hand when portraying children, especially the matter-of-fact way that children deal with trauma and loss. His stories "Strays" and "This Is Us, Excellent," from *The Ice at the Bottom of the World,* as well as "*The Birds* for Christmas," "Gentleman's Agreement," "Charity," and "Memorial Day," from *Charity* (1998), each revolve around boys' attempts to understand the difficult and often brutal world they inhabit. "This Is Us, Excellent," for instance, opens with two brothers racing around their neighborhood pretending to be their favorite television heroes and entering their house to witness the aftermath of their father beating their mother: "What we've missed here is our dad helping our mom up for another blap across the mouth." The narrator's response to the situation, though, is not what one would expect from this scene: "This is excellent," because the event means that their guilt-ridden father will give their mother enough money to take the family out for pizza. "So much sports on makes it less the chance for our dad to have an interest in coming down the hall to beat our asses. It's just our mom this time. This really is excellent. Now we get to go snag a 'za at Psycho Za". The matter-of-fact, even upbeat way in which the boys in "This Is Us, Excellent" respond to the violence in their home compounds the impact of Richard's brutal description of the scene. Much of Richard's fiction demonstrates a similar sensitivity to how shame, pain, and violence feed off each other.

Richard's stories travel in cycles—cycles of violence, cycles of community. Often his stories do not resolve, but rather confirm a cycle that will continue for

Dust jacket for Richard's 1989 collection, comprising sometimes darkly comic accounts of characters trapped in cycles of poverty, violence, and emotional conflict

their central characters. For some, as for the narrator of "Her Favorite Story," these cycles can be nourishing. After the death of his lover in a violent hurricane, the central character becomes, for a time, a loner bordering on madness, "the haint the kids come to try to spook out at night with their lights." But he gradually returns to the life he had known before he met his lover, joining with friends who regularly get into fights with truckers passing through their small town: "I figure I'll come down out of these woods swinging, putting in together with my friends, getting a fair knock of human life, taking a tall walk back into this town." In this case even the violence of these fights helps return the central character to a sense of equilibrium and community, which he had lost during the storm.

In other stories the cycles in which the characters find themselves are more destructive. "Strays" begins and ends with the mother of a poor family running away through the field of corn next door. In between, the two boys who have been left behind when their father goes in search of their mother are to be taken care of by their Uncle Trash. When Uncle Trash instead cheats the boys out of their meager savings and leaves them alone to go drinking in town, the older boy

demonstrates the ripple effect that bullying has had on his family: "I am burning hot at Uncle Trash. Then I am burning hot at our father for leaving us with him to look for our mother. Then I am burning hot at my mother for running off. . . . There is only one thing left to do, and that is to take all we still have left that we own and throw it at my brother—and I do." The obvious humor of the scene nevertheless reveals the disturbing lessons the boys have learned. Despite their uncle's admonitions not to "burn down the house," the boys manage to do just that, and when their returning parents see the destruction of their home, their mother is once again sent "flat-footed running rustle through the corn all burned up by the summer sun." The cycle of the story is set in motion once again.

Many of the characters in the collection live a precarious existence, cornered by poverty, violence, and emotional distress. Richard's stories are not exercises in condescending pity, however. His characters exhibit a resilient humor, strength, and strangeness that circumvents sentimentality. In the title story of *The Ice at the Bottom of the World,* a woman shoots her ailing husband after years of living "half-married," since he worked at sea for months at a time. When asked why she used nine bullets instead of one, Louise answers, "the first one was for love, and the other eight were for something Bill said to me over dinner in front of company in nineteen sixty-six." Louise's explanation is in keeping with the bizarre logic that dominated the family's life, leading them, for example, to celebrate a belated Christmas in July. If Richard's characters often follow a train of thought that is strange or comical, they nevertheless possess a tangible humanity that makes them vivid and believable, even if their surroundings or circumstances are beyond immediate comprehension.

In the story that closes the collection, "Feast of the Earth, Ransom of the Clay," a vagrant of questionable sanity demonstrates a sense of occasion and insight that makes him more than just a town eccentric. The clay-eating Mr. Leon, wearing a vest made from the skins of dead cats, arrives at the funeral service of a local "bird-calling biddy," who had been kind to him during her life. Mr. Leon—who acts as a kind of dark subconscious of the town in which he lives—offers a tribute to the woman by repeating the birdcalls her husband had recorded years before and which the woman played constantly on a record player until she died. Mr. Leon's recitation feels much more appropriate a eulogy for the woman than the priest's offering of "There are many mansions in the house of the Lord." He then proceeds to eat a mouthful of clay "from the lip of the grave."

"Feast of the Earth, Ransom of the Clay," is further evidence of Richard's tendency to use surrealist imagery, what Mifflin called a "malevolent magic realism." Another example is "On the Rope," which describes a flood so horrific that "all you could hear was the sound of the floodwaters boiling all around, boiling away everything from the face of the earth." The narrator's uncle, while trying to help in the rescue, witnesses a series of horrors, including the "diamond-shining eyes" of snakes attempting to survive the flood by climbing to the tops of trees and a baby tied to a rope that, when pulled upon by the uncle "from where it went deep into the water, . . . did not feel like it gave as much as it felt like it was being let go of." "On the Rope" is more imagistic than narrative—a tendency that has led some readers to criticize Richard's work—but the mythical power of the imagery and the attention to linguistic detail make this story one of the most powerful in the collection. Richard's use of surreal imagery is far from an intellectual game, as some reviewers—for example, Mark Kamine in *The New Leader* (4 September 1989)—have seen it: "Fishboy" and "On the Rope" are stories with mythical rather than realistic aims. As Richard stated in the interview with Mifflin, "I don't think you can talk about the mechanics of fiction without touching on what it means to be a citizen of the world,"

and this quasi-religious sense in his fiction overwhelms the need to portray the world in realistic terms. If the destruction in "On the Rope" attains biblical proportions, or if "Fishboy" becomes a creature out of Ovid's *Metamorphosis,* the power of the stories lies within their ability to conjure these myths and mine their insights within a new, original context.

If there is one dominant theme to the collection, it is in the inextricability of beauty, humor, violence, and pain. The collection is rife with images of beauty and terror unevenly mingling—a burning dog in "Strays," a couple making love in the midst of a lightning storm in "Her Favorite Story"—and Richard's work seems to assert that these qualities are frequently linked. In the world that Richard portrays, beauty and danger are never far from each other, and the precariousness of happiness makes it all the more valuable. The fact that many of the characters in Richard's work live near water and are at risk from floods and storms contributes to the precariousness of their lives and happiness. Even when the chaos in the characters' lives is fairly benevolent, as in "Happiness of the Garden Variety," the chaos and the benevolence are impossible to differentiate. More often, happiness and love are gained in small bursts between tragedies or in the midst of them.

"Fishboy" is the strangest of the stories in *The Ice at the Bottom of the World* and also, perhaps, the least successful. Here, finally, the music of the language and the voice of the narrator-hero obscure any story beyond the hints of what can later be found in the novel of the same name that Richard published in 1993. The success of *The Ice at the Bottom of the World* earned Richard fellowships from the National Endowment for the Arts and the New York Foundation for the Arts. These fellowships helped him to return temporarily to Virginia Beach to complete *Fishboy,* which develops the imagistic short story of the boy with the wandering eye into what Amy Hempel, writing in *Esquire,* called "an eloquent fever dream, a tale told headlong in the language of incantation." The novel draws significantly from Richard's own experiences aboard fishing trawlers but includes a variety of characters more likely to be met in fiction than at sea. One has tattooed a map of the world on his skin and is in constant search of a mermaid who saved his life; one tells fortunes by playing cat's cradle; a third has a body turned inside out so that his muscles and veins are visible. These men make up part of the crew for the craft on which the young Fishboy has escaped his earlier life on the shore, which was almost as bizarre and threatening. The novel draws on the Bible, on Herman Melville's *Moby-Dick* (1851) and Homer's *The Odyssey,* and a range of styles from children's tale to dark surrealism to trace the brief life of

*Dust jacket for the first U.S. edition (1998) of Richard's 1992
collection, focusing on "homemade" gestures of kindness
and justice along the margins of society*

the University of Mississippi (1994–1995), and finally
at Arizona State University in Tempe (1997–1998).
Richard also has an interest in writing for movies and
television–even as an undergraduate at Washington
and Lee he had written screenplays–and has contributed scripts to the television series *Party of Five* and *Chicago Hope,* as well as adapted stories by himself and
Eudora Welty for television and movie production.

In the meantime, Richard was writing and publishing the stories that would comprise his collection
Charity, which also tells tales of characters living on
the fringes of society–hospitalized children,
small-time criminals, unemployed longshoremen. But
Charity shows Richard's increasing power and control
as a writer–the stories cohere more tightly as a collection than do those in *The Ice at the Bottom of the
World* and simultaneously offer a wider range of characters and situations.

The front cover of *Charity* shows a homemade
"angel" made from electrical tape, which possesses one
gold wing attached with string. Homemade forms of
charity, justice, and tenderness are the uniting themes of
the collection. Because the characters in these stories
cannot expect the pure forms of these abstractions, the
imperfect forms that they can access take on more
meaning. When, in "*The Birds* for Christmas," a
drunken former hospital patient brings a portable television to convalescent boys at a hospital so that they
can watch Alfred Hitchcock's *The Birds,* even the fear
evoked by the movie becomes an aspect of the man's
charity by providing a respite from the relentless boredom and depression the boys continually confront. In
"Gentleman's Agreement," when a threatening father
uses a pair of scissors to remove stitches from his son's
head, this rough, awkward act seems tender, an expression of love. In another story, "Where Blue Is Blue,"
down-and-out denizens of a tourist beach find their own
way to solve the murder of a carnival contortionist.

These "homemade" forms of justice extend
beyond the world of the rural South where Richard
again draws most of the settings for his stories. The
brief story "Charming 1 br, fr. dr. wndws, quiet, safe.
Fee.," which appeared in the 1996 anthology *The Literary Insomniac: Stories and Essays for Sleepless Nights*–Richard
has acknowledged suffering from insomnia himself–
takes place in an anonymous city populated by gangsters and "riffraff." It is told in second person, which
adds to the late-night strangeness of the piece. The central character lives in the apartment of the title, "which
you will never be able to afford," and takes it on himself
to enact a kind of justice on the "drunken gangster
patrons of the pasta place diagonally under your apartment," bombing them with a latex condom filled with
water. Intended as a form of poetic justice against the

this strange creature who "began as a boy, a
human-being boy."

Fishboy received critical praise from a variety of
sources and brought Richard to a wider audience.
Some critics found difficulty with the density of Richard's language; Suzanne MacNeille, for example, writing for *The New York Times Book Review* in 1989, called
it "self-conscious and contrived." The novel brought
Richard wide respect, particularly among academic
circles. Richard was also the focus of a two-part special
article in *The New York Times Book Review* by Michael
Norman titled "A Book in Search of a Buzz: The Marketing of a First Novel." The article traced Richard's
efforts to promote his book from his relationship with
his editor through an extended tour in a 1979 Cadillac
borrowed from a friend.

Following the publication of *Fishboy* and his extensive 1993 book tour, Richard held several teaching positions at the university level: as the first Tennessee
Williams fellow at the University of the South (1994),
the second recipient of the John Grisham Fellowship at

crass gangsters, the act also indicates just how desperate the insomniac is to distract himself from sleep, and even after the gangsters leave, "you sit and wait on the corner of the bed, playing with the pistol, waiting for the trash truck, the bakery, a robbery, the dawn." In the world of this insomniac there is no difference between a robbery or the bakery opening–either serves only to give the night some shape beyond the blank boredom and quiet frustration of his inability to sleep.

For all their threat of violence and darkness, Richard's stories are often comic, and his touch of rough humor brings sympathy and life to his characters. In "Where Blue Is Blue," a police detective tries to solve the contortionist's murder by distributing homemade paintings of his clues to his suspects, who are ordered to "nail up on the walls of our rat-holes and sewer pipes the piece he was going to give each of us." "Fun at the Beach" establishes a comic tone with its opening: "Got a letter from a girl said we ought to get together before her husband gets parole." In "Plymouth Rock," a cruel sibling rivalry is summed up humorously: "I have seen the future of law enforcement in this country and it is my brother Douglas." It is the combination of humor, language of extreme tightness and craft, and a profound sympathy for his cornered and often damaged characters that makes the stories in *Charity* so accomplished.

Richard also continues in the stories of *Charity* to work beyond realism and strive for the mythic and mystical. In the more recent collection, though, Richard's touch is more assured and the mythic elements are no longer wildly bizarre but instead are poignant and strange. Witness the opening sentence from "Memorial Day": "The boy mistook death for one of the landlady's sons come to collect the rent." "Death" is characterized as charming and pleasant–a figure the boy can be interested in and then frustrated by: "The boy was beginning to tire of death hanging around so much and talking talking talking." As the reader senses, death ultimately intends to claim the boy, and this circumstance adds an element of foreboding to their generally pleasant conversations. Death here is nearby, neighborly, and polite; and Richard's rework-

ing of the archetypal figure remakes the very character of death in a way that makes it seem more familiar and yet more strange and terrifying.

Similarly, the narrator of "Never in This World" attempts to seduce a young woman using ghost stories. When he sees the real ghost of his friend, Guy, however, he sees "no need to summon Guy's ghost for the girl." The narrator does not explain specifically why Guy's ghost is so much more disturbing than the others he has described to the girl, but his reticence is enough to explain that even the temptations of sex are far outweighed by his fear. This sense of the otherworldly within the everyday is stronger in this collection than in *The Ice at the Bottom of the World,* where often the otherworldly exists beside the natural but rarely mingles with it as smoothly as it does in "Never in This World" and "Memorial Day."

Stories from Richard's two collections have appeared in a variety of venues, including *Esquire, Harper's,* and *The New Yorker.* They have also been selected for inclusion in the anthologies *New Stories from the South, The Pushcart Prize Stories,* and *Best American Short Stories.*

The job writing for *Party of Five* brought Richard to Los Angeles, where he lives with his wife, writer Jennifer Allen, and their two children. He is also a writer for *Chicago Hope* and has adapted Eudora Welty's *Delta Wedding* (1946) for a television production to air in 2001.

Interview:

"An Interview with Mark Richard," *Bold Type* (online magazine), 10 February 2000 <www.randomhouse.com/boldtype/0898/richard/interview.html>.

References:

Amy Hempel, "*Fishboy*," *Esquire,* 119 (May 1993): 35;

Suzanne MacNeille, "In Short: Fiction," *New York Times Book Review* (28 May 1989);

Michael Norman, "A Book in Search of a Buzz: The Marketing of a First Novel," *New York Times Book Review* (30 January 1994, 6 February 1994).

Jane Smiley

(26 September 1949 –)

Thom Conroy
Ohio University

See also the Smiley entry in *DLB 227: American Novelists Since World War II, Sixth Series.*

BOOKS: *Barn Blind* (New York: Harper & Row, 1980; London: Flamingo, 1994);

At Paradise Gate: A Novel (New York: Simon & Schuster, 1981; London: Flamingo, 1995);

Duplicate Keys (New York: Knopf, 1984; London: Cape, 1984);

The Age of Grief: Stories and a Novella (New York: Knopf, 1987; London: Collins, 1988);

Catskill Crafts: Artisans of the Catskill Mountains (New York: Crown, 1988);

The Greenlanders (New York: Knopf, 1988; London: Collins, 1988);

Ordinary Love and Good Will: Two Novellas (New York: Knopf, 1989); republished as *Ordinary Love: Two Novellas* (London: Collins, 1990);

The Life of the Body: A Story (Minneapolis: Coffee House, 1990);

A Thousand Acres (New York: Knopf, 1991; London: Collins, 1991);

Moo (New York: Knopf, 1995; London: Flamingo, 1995);

The All-True Travels and Adventures of Lidie Newton: A Novel (New York: Knopf, 1998; London: HarperCollins, 1998);

Horse Heaven (New York: Knopf, 2000).

Jane Smiley (photograph by Stephen Mortensen; from the dust jacket for Ordinary Love and Good Will, *1989)*

OTHER: "Turnpike," in *Voices Louder Than Words: A Second Collection,* edited by William Shore (New York: Vintage, 1991), pp. 97–113;

"Can Mothers Think?" in *The True Subject: Writers on Life and Craft,* edited by Kurt Brown (St. Paul, Minn.: Graywolf, 1993), pp. 3–15;

Untitled commentary on "Lily," in *American Voices: Best Short Fiction by Contemporary Authors,* edited by Sally Arteseros (New York: Hyperion, 1993), pp. 213–214;

"Can Writers Have Friends?" in *Between Friends: Writing Women Celebrate Friendship,* edited by Mickey Pearl-man (New York: Houghton Mifflin, 1994), pp. 44–55;

"The Bathroom," in *Home: American Writers Remember Rooms of Their Own,* edited by Sharon Sloan Fiffer and Steve Fiffer (New York: Pantheon, 1995), pp. 106–115;

"Full Cry," in *Women on Hunting,* edited by Pam Houston (Hopewell, N.J.: Ecco, 1995), pp. 186–198;

The Best American Short Stories 1995, edited by Smiley and Katrina Kennison, with an introduction by Smiley (Boston & New York: Houghton Mifflin, 1995);

"Afterword: Gen-Narration," in *Family: American Writers Remember Their Own,* edited by Sharon Sloan Fiffer and Steve Fiffer (New York: Pantheon, 1996), pp. 241–247;

"Two Plates, Fifteen Screws," in *The Healing Circle: Authors Writing of Recovery,* edited by Patricia Foster and Mary Swander (New York: Plume, 1998), pp. 99–106;

Thomas Hardy, *The Return of the Native,* introduction by Smiley (New York: Signet, 1999);

"What Stories Teach Their Writers: The Purpose and Practice of Revision," in *Creating Fiction: Instruction and Insights from Teachers of the Associated Writing Programs,* edited by Julie Checkoway (Cincinnati: Story, 1999), pp. 244–255;

"You Can Never Have Too Many," in *The Barbie Chronicles: A Living Doll Turns Forty,* edited by Yona Zeldis McDonough (New York: Touchstone, 1999), pp. 189–192.

SELECTED PERIODICAL PUBLICATIONS–UNCOLLECTED:

FICTION

"All-American Garden," *House and Garden,* 164 (June 1992): 122–129, 156;

"Wisconsin: Three Visions Attained," *New York Times Magazine,* 7 March 1993, II: 28–29, 42, 44, 46, 48;

"So Shall We Reap," *Sierra,* 79 (March/April 1994): 74–80, 82, 140–141;

"The Call of the Hunt," *Outside,* 19 (November 1994): 114–122;

"Puissance," *Flyway: A Literary Review,* 1 (Spring 1995): 23–32;

"North Carolina's Equestrian Heaven," *New York Times Magazine,* 17 September 1995, II: 55–57, 60, 64;

"The Big Soak," *Vogue,* 185 (October 1995): 256, 258, 260;

"My Gelding Myself," *Outside,* 20 (November 1995): 112–118, 159;

"Say It Ain't So, Huck: Second Thoughts on Mark Twain's 'Masterpiece,'" *Harper's,* 292 (January 1996): 61–67;

"Dream House," *Architectural Digest,* 54 (November 1997): 46, 48, 52;

"Oaxaca: Baroque Jewel in a Pre-Hispanic Setting," *New York Times Magazine,* 14 May 2000, II: 24–25, 40, 42, 44–45.

A Pulitzer Prize–winning novelist, Jane Smiley has also won acclaim for her work as an author of short fiction. In *The Age of Grief: Stories and a Novella* (1987), *Ordinary Love and Good Will: Two Novellas* (1989), *The Life of the Body: A Story* (1990), and numerous uncollected short stories, Smiley writes about the com-

plex, often secret, emotional dynamics that underlie ordinary human relationships. Often passive and usually sympathetic, Smiley's characters salvage self-knowledge out of the intricate histories and traumas of their inner lives. Smiley is adept at exploring the subtle exchanges of intimacy that commonly lead her characters to a condition of understanding. At the heart of Smiley's fiction is her belief that there are answers–sometimes bitter, even grievous–to the questions that afflict human beings.

Jane Graves Smiley was born on 26 September 1949 to James La Verne Smiley and Frances (née Graves) Smiley, a writer, in Los Angeles. By the time Smiley was four years old, her parents had divorced, and Smiley moved with her mother to St. Louis, where she lived in close contact with a large extended family. In 1960, Smiley's mother married William J. Nuelle, who had two children of his own. After graduating from high school, Smiley enrolled in Vassar College in New York. During the summer of 1970, Smiley lived with John B. Whiston in a commune in New Haven, Connecticut. In September of that year the two were married.

After their marriage Smiley and Whiston moved to Iowa City, where Whiston pursued graduate work in history and Smiley worked in a factory. In December of 1972, Smiley was accepted into the doctoral program at the University of Iowa. In 1974 she began participating in the Iowa Writers' Workshop, continuing work on her M.A., which she completed the following year. In 1975 she and Whiston divorced. With the aid of a Fulbright-Hays grant, Smiley spent the academic year of 1976–1977 in Iceland, researching Icelandic sagas for her doctoral dissertation. During this same year she also received her M.F.A. from the Iowa Writers' Workshop. In 1978, Smiley completed her Ph.D. and married editor William Silag.

In the years leading up to her position with Iowa State University, where she taught literature and creative-writing courses from 1982 to 1997, Smiley began publishing short fiction in various journals, and finished two novels, *Barn Blind* (1980) and *At Paradise Gate* (1981), which won the Friends of American Writers Prize that year. *Barn Blind* chronicles the life of Kate Karlson, a domineering mother of four teenage children. In this first novel Smiley begins the exploration of family dynamics that she continues to refine throughout much of her work. In *At Paradise Gate* the impending death of Ike Robinson provides an opportunity for Anna Robinson and her three daughters to revisit the family's shared regrets, sorrows, and personal victories. Both novels demonstrate Smiley's capacity for creating characters who are not afraid to

Dust jacket for Smiley's 1987 collection, in which the title novella
deals with the marital problems of a pair of dentists

delve into the convolutions of family history in the quest for self-knowledge.

Smiley's skill as an author of short fiction first became evident in 1982, when she was awarded an O. Henry Award for "The Pleasure of Her Company," originally published in *Mademoiselle* (1981). "The Pleasure of Her Company," which would eventually be collected in *The Age of Grief*, tells the story of Florence, a woman whose lack of emotional understanding allows her to mistake acquaintanceship for genuine intimacy. When Francine and Philip move into the Victorian house in Florence's neighborhood–"the one lovely place on her otherwise undistinguished block"– Florence cultivates what she believes to be a deep friendship with Francine. Within a few months, Philip and Francine have separated for an unspecified reason, and Francine has moved into an apartment. Bryan, a man whom Florence is dating, tells her that he saw Francine having lunch with another woman. Eventually, Florence must face the fact that Francine has been hiding her romantic relationship with Helen

during the whole period of her friendship with Florence. The story concludes when Philip, still living in the Victorian home, reveals the truth about Florence's friendship with Frances and him. He says, "We needed you, Florence; it was nice to have you fall in love with us, and admire us. It was a relief to talk about something else besides the central issue."

Florence's revelation is rendered particularly poignant by Smiley's narrative seduction of the reader. Like Florence, the reader is inclined to believe in the sincerity of the friendship with Francine, despite the absence of any evidence of genuine emotional attachment. In this way Smiley uses readerly expectations to heighten the impact of the conclusion of the story. In a 1994 interview with Alexander Neubauer, Smiley discusses how she teaches her creative-writing students to exploit these kinds of "negotiations" between author and reader. Smiley explains, "The student writer's responsibility is not to fulfill the reader's expectations, but to understand them, and to use that understanding to manipulate them."

Smiley's third novel, a Manhattan murder-mystery titled *Duplicate Keys* (1984), marked Smiley's first turn from a rural or suburban setting to an urban one. The story centers around Alice Ellis, a woman who is drawn into a mystery when two of her close friends are found murdered in the apartment that she is supposed to be house-sitting.

In the summer of 1984, Smiley traveled to England, Denmark, and Greenland, and began work on her fourth novel, *The Greenlanders* (1988). The following year, Smiley's status as an author of short fiction was solidified when "Lily" (1984) co-won first prize in *Prize Stories 1985: The O. Henry Awards.*

In "Lily," originally published in *The Atlantic* and later collected in *The Age of Grief,* Smiley introduces a character whose naiveté and compulsion for order prevent her from comprehending the inexplicable complexities of intimacy. The story opens when Kevin and Nancy Humboldt, two friends from college with a shaky marriage, come to Columbus to spend a weekend with Lily. While there Kevin confesses to Lily that Nancy intends to end their marriage for "a dumb cowboy" named Hobbs Nolan. On the final evening of their visit Kevin presses Lily to tell him whether she thinks Nancy loves him. Lily, who has no knowledge of the dynamics of marriage, answers, "No." In the final scene of the story Nancy and Kevin's lovemaking awakens Lily in the middle of the night. After the knocking on the wall subsides, Lily hears Nancy screaming in fear, and she runs to investigate. When Lily enters their room, she sees that Kevin has chopped off half of Nancy's waist-length hair. The story ends when Nancy lashes out at Lily, admonishing her for judging what she does not understand.

Like Florence, Lily suffers from a lack of understanding about the true complexities of human intimacy. In her compulsion to bring a distinct order to life's emotional crises, Lily underestimates the diverse, often contradictory, impulses underlying motivation and desire. In Smiley's fiction human emotions are riddled with secrets, founded on opposition and mystery, and no character is entitled to neglect the truth of the heart's complexity. In her essay "Can Writers Have Friends?" (1994), Smiley proposes that the "key feature" of "serious fiction" is its engagement with the most difficult predicaments of the human condition. "After laying out the ramifications of the dilemma," Smiley continues, "the serious fiction writer, with the aid of the culturally given tools of plot and language, proposes a solution to the dilemma, which the reader may accept or reject . . . ." Smiley's insistence on proposing a solution to her characters' dilemmas highlights the fundamentally moral nature of Smiley's approach to fiction.

In February 1986, Smiley and Silag were divorced. In July of the following year Smiley married the screenwriter Stephen Mortensen. During the same year Smiley published *The Age of Grief,* which received a Book Critics Circle Award nomination. The title novella, composed during Smiley's breakup with Silag, provides an intimate portrait of marriage, parenthood, and the emotional trauma of infidelity. In this first-person novella, the narrator is a dentist named Dave Hurst who shares an office with his wife, Dana, also a dentist. When the narrator begins to suspect that Dana is having an affair with the musical director of her choral group, the ordinary life that the Hursts share with their three daughters appears to be in jeopardy. At about the same time that Dave begins to doubt Dana's fidelity, the youngest child, Leah, starts to favor Dave over Dana, demanding her father's exclusive love and attention.

In response to the troubles at home Dave cherishes the "meditative" quality of his job. His feelings about teeth reflect his admiration for their stability, their absoluteness, their consistency—qualities he feels are absent from his own emotional life:

> Teeth outlast everything. Death is nothing to a tooth. Hundreds of years in acidic soil just keeps a tooth clean. A fire that burns away hair and flesh and even bone leaves teeth dazzling like daisies in the ashes. Life is what destroys teeth. Undiluted apple juice in a baby bottle, sourballs, the pH balance of drinking water, tetracycline, sand in your bread if you were in the Roman army, biting seal-gut thread if you are an Eskimo woman, playing the trumpet, pulling your own teeth with pliers.

In an emotional turn, Dave discovers that Dana's affair has not been with the choral director as he suspected but with a dental hygienist named Delilah. In the last scene of *The Age of Grief,* Dana decides to end her affair with Delilah and stay with Dave and the family. Dave's final wisdom reveals the true fragility and scope of marital intimacy when he says, "It seems to me that marriage is a small container, after all, barely large enough to hold some children. Two inner lives, two lifelong meditations of whatever complexity, burst out of it, cracking it, deforming it. Or maybe it is not a thing at all, nothing, something not present." That Smiley ends her novella without offering any further insight into the situation speaks to the inescapable complexity of human emotion. Emotions, unlike teeth, are never stable, never consistent, never predictable. It is, in fact, their capacity to startle, to unhinge, and to ravage lives, that endows human emotions with potency and consequence.

In 1988, "Long Distance" became Smiley's third story to win an O. Henry Award for short fiction. Also collected in *The Age of Grief,* "Long Distance" tells the story of Kirby Christianson, a man recently returned from teaching English in Japan. At the beginning of the story Kirby receives a call from Mieko, a Japanese woman. Mieko informs him that her father's lung cancer will prevent her from coming to the United States to visit him. Though Kirby recognizes that "in his whole life he has never given up a pleasure that he cherished as much as Mieko cherished this one," he offers her no consolation on the subject. On the way to his brother Harold's home in Minneapolis to visit his family for Christmas, Kirby calls up pleasant images of his stay in Japan in order to divert his mind from a treacherous snowstorm, but he does not give a second thought to Mieko's emotional state. At Harold's house, Kirby must endure the presence of his brother Eric, a Ph.D. in American history who specializes in "the family." On the second day of the visit Kirby feels so sorry for himself that he starts drinking bourbon at nine in the morning and manages to get drunk enough to argue child rearing with Eric. Though Kirby tries to sleep that night, he wakes up after only an hour or two. Leanne, Harold's wife, is also awake, and Kirby confesses to her that he had an affair with Mieko. Leanne says that the one thing she can bear about Eric is that, "He never tries to get something for nothing."

In "Long Distance," Kirby emerges as one of Smiley's least sympathetic characters. Unlike Florence, in "The Pleasure of Her Company," his emotional trauma is not brought on by naiveté, but by indifference. Unlike Dave in *The Age of Grief,* he does not deny the wrong done by another against him but rather the hurt he inflicts on another. Leanne's comment at the closing of the story reveals the pernicious nature of Kirby's shortcoming. Though Kirby's brother Eric may be overbearing and narrow-minded, he does not value his own pleasure over the feelings of others. To do so, as Kirby does, is to knowingly betray the sanctity of intimacy, and in Smiley's fiction there is no injury more ignominious than that.

In 1988 Smiley published *Greenlanders,* her fourth novel, and a volume comprising her two novellas, *Ordinary Love & Good Will.* In "Ordinary Love," the narrator, Rachel Kinsella, comes to terms with the marital affair that broke up her family many years before the story begins. In placing the most significant dramatic event of the story prior to its opening, Smiley challenges the reader's expectation of linear plot. In *Understanding Jane Smiley* (1999), Neil Nakadate maintains that the narrative structure of "Ordinary Love" was a purposeful departure from convention. "'Ordi-

nary Love,'" he writes, "was a conscious attempt at nontraditional plotting, in which family conversation and its revelations replaced climax and epiphany as the crucial focus." Smiley's decision to write a novella in which the present dramatic action takes place in dialogue—Rachel's confession of her affair to her children, and her son Michael's revelation of his girlfriend Lucie's recent abortion—generates a mood of familial intimacy that turns out to be more significant than the events of the narrative. Though Smiley is successful in exploring the emotional depths of a family's history, the attention she devotes to dialogue and the narrator's psychology sometimes undermines the advance of the story.

"Good Will," a more traditionally structured narrative, tells of the downfall of Bob Miller, a homesteader, who lives with his wife, Liz, and his ten-year-old son, Tommy, in a house that he built outside of Moreton, Pennsylvania. Bob, Liz, and Tommy enjoy a secluded and completely self-sufficient lifestyle, spinning their own clothing, growing their own food, and raising lambs to slaughter. Problems begin in October, when Tommy destroys the dolls of Annabel Harris, the only African American child in his class at school. Bob repays Dr. Lydia Harris, Annabel's mother, by stripping and refinishing her floors. The two form a relationship, Bob reflects, "that is not friendship or business or romance, but speculation, fascination." Though it is not clear that Tommy's violent outbursts against Annabel are the direct result of Bob's attitude of racial "fascination," Smiley presents a deft rendering of the subtleties of race relations.

Tensions build within the Miller's home, until Tommy accidentally burns down the Harris house while trying to set fire to their satellite dish. Months later, as a result of the incident the Millers are living in an apartment in Moreton. Bob and Liz are employed in menial positions at the local university, and in order to maintain custody of Tommy, they have had to agree to allow him to be counseled "until the counselor dismisses him." Dr. Harris's insurance company is suing the Millers for their property, on the grounds that Bob and Liz's negligent lifestyle contributed to Tommy's arson. By the end of "Good Will" there is no trace left of the life that the Millers once lived. They now own a telephone, clocks, a television, and a car. Moreover, there is some indication that Liz will no longer defer to Bob's judgment the way she did in the past. During one argument, for instance, she calls her husband a "megalomaniac."

Unwilling or unable to accept the changes to his circumstance, Bob clings to the conflicts embodied in his previous life: "Let us have fragments," he declares. "Let the racial hatred that has been expressed through

Dust jacket for Smiley's 1989 collection of novellas about dysfunctional families

us lie next to the longing that I feel for Lydia Harris; let Tom's innocence lie next to his envious fury; let Liz's grief for the farm lie next to her blossoming in town; let my urge to govern and supply every element of my son's being lie next to our tenuous custody; let the poverty the welfare department sees lie next to the wealth I know was mine." His closing monologue indicates that, though he may not renounce his shortcomings, he has come to understand them; and, in Smiley's fiction, understanding is always worth the cost at which it comes.

In 1990 Smiley published *The Life of the Body: A Story,* a limited edition volume. After being reprinted in *Antaeus,* the story won Smiley her fourth O. Henry Award in 1996. "The Life of the Body," perhaps Smiley's most emotionally poignant short story, centers around Sarah, a narrator who is in "the worst trouble I have ever heard of anyone being in." Five months before the opening of the story, Sarah's youngest child, Dory, fell down the steps and died. In her grief Sarah began an extramarital affair with Jonathan, a neighbor. In his grief Sarah's husband, Jake, fell into a state of deep emotional isolation that has only intensified with each passing month. When "The Life of the Body" begins, Sarah is pregnant with Jonathan's child. Though she wants to tell her sister, Rhonda, about the pregnancy, Sarah fears the complicated emotional repercussions of that confession.

"Begun as a tribute to sadness," Sarah's relationship with Jonathan is founded on a kind of complete physical abandonment, a sensuousness with room for both the physical ravages of grief and the intense pleasures of a sexual passion. Aside from her relationship with Jonathan, Sarah's only other physical outlet is the modern-dance class she takes with her sister. As she dances, Sarah begins to forget the people who populate her thoughts during the rest of the day. One by one, they "vanish," until even Jonathan himself disappears in the movement of the dance. In the final scene of the story, Sarah confesses her pregnancy to Rhonda and then rushes in to dance. As she dances, she realizes that it is only in the moment of physical sensation, in "the feeling of life running through the tissues," that she will ever truly know the grief and passion that sustain her.

In the "Biographies" section of *Prize Stories: The O. Henry Awards* (1996), Smiley comments on the powerful emotion she explored in "The Life of the Body." She writes, "This story makes me feel exposed and a little fragmented. I'm glad I was capable of such raw emotion once, but I'm also glad that I don't do this sort of thing all the time." Though it may expose more "raw emotion" than any of Smiley's short fiction, "The Life of the Body" also speaks to the complexities of intimacy, the secrets that bind families together, and the mysterious potency of people's inner lives, themes that are consistent throughout her work.

In 1991 Smiley published *A Thousand Acres,* a feminist reimagining of William Shakespeare's *King Lear,* which won her the Pulitzer Prize, the National Book Critics Circle Award, and the Heartland Award. *A Thousand Acres* tells the story of the Cooks, a Midwestern farming family, dually devastated by incest and a technological revolution in American agriculture. When Ginny Cook, the eldest daughter, remembers the sexual abuse she suffered at her father's hands, she begins to question the familial and communal foundations of her reality. In *A Thousand Acres* Smiley exposes the irreconcilable violence, self-hatred, and deception that lie just under the surface of the American dream.

In 1995 Smiley published her sixth novel, *Moo,* which received a Book Critics Circle Award nomination. In *Moo,* a comedy set in a college in a small Midwesterntown, Smiley tries her hand at satire. The book takes aim at the petty politics and the weave of competing rhetoric that underlie the contemporary academy.

In 1998 Smiley published *The All-True Travels and Adventures of Lidie Newton,* an historical novel set in the mid nineteenth century in America's Midwest territory, a region divided by the issue of abolition. Smiley tells the gripping story of Lidia Harkness, later Lidie Newton, a woman thrust into the adventures of the unsettled Kansas Territory.

In a 1993 interview with Mickey Pearlman, Smiley confirms the "conservative" view implicit in her fiction. She says, "The goal of my characters is a sort of acceptance and what follows in one's self and one's cohorts and one's friends. My characters never die screaming in rage." Though never didactic, Smiley's stories serve to instruct her readers in the subtle, often secret, truths of human intimacy. As fiction that refuses to let its characters "die screaming in rage," Smiley's stories are inherently moral. If her characters continue to plumb the depths of the human heart for understanding, it is because Smiley believes enduring truth can never be found anywhere else. They must face the consequences of their own familial histories, but through this path they come to a new understanding, both of themselves and of their place in the community at large.

Interviews:

Mickey Pearlman, "Jane Smiley," in his *Listen to Their Voices: Twenty Interviews with Women Who Write* (New York: Norton, 1993);

Alexander Neubauer, "Jane Smiley," in his *Conversations on Writing Fiction: Interviews with Thirteen Distinguished Teachers of Fiction Writing in America* (New York: HarperCollins, 1994).

Reference:

Neil Nakadate, *Understanding Jane Smiley* (Columbia: University of South Carolina Press, 1999).

Michael Stephens

(4 March 1946 –   )

Eamonn Wall
University of Missouri–St. Louis

BOOKS: *Season at Coole,* as Michael Gregory Stephens (New York: Dutton, 1972);
Alcohol Poems, as Michael Gregory Stephens (Binghamton, N.Y.: Loose Change Press, 1973);
Paragraphs (Amherst, Mass.: Mulch Press, 1974);
Tangun Legend: Korean Bear Myth (Iowa City, Iowa: Seamark Press, 1977);
Still Life (New York: Kroesen Books, 1978);
Shipping Out: A Novel (Cambridge, Mass.: Apple-wood Press, 1979);
Circles End (New York: Spuyten Duyvil, 1982);
Translations (Bronx, N.Y.: Red Hanrahan, 1984);
The Dramaturgy of Style: Voice in Short Fiction (Carbondale: Southern Illinois University Press, 1986);
Horse (New York: Kairos, 1989);
Lost in Seoul: And Other Discoveries on the Korean Peninsula (New York: Random House, 1990);
Jigs and Reels: Short Prose (Brooklyn, N.Y.: Hanging Loose, 1992);
After Asia: Poems (New York: Spuyten Duyvil, 1993);
The Brooklyn Book of the Dead: A Novel (Normal, Ill.: Dalkey Archive, 1994);
Green Dreams: Essays Under the Influence of the Irish (Athens: University of Georgia Press, 1994);
Our Father: A Play (New York: Spuyten Duyvil, 1997);
Going Thoreau, as M. G. Stephens (New York: Poetry New York, 1998);
Where the Sky Ends: A Memoir of Alcohol and Family, as M. G. Stephens (Center City, Minn.: Hazelden Information and Educational Services, 1999).

PLAY PRODUCTIONS: *A Splendid Occasion in Spring,* New York, West End Bar, 9 February 1974;
Off-Season Rates, Yale Playwrights Projects, 1978;
Cloud Dream, Yale Playwrights Projects, 1979;
Our Father, New York, 1980;
R & R, New York, October 1984.

Michael Stephens (photograph © by Lori Wolan)

Michael Stephens's work is difficult to categorize; for almost three decades he has excelled in a variety of literary genres. His 1980 play, *Our Father,* ran off-Broadway on weekends for five years. In addition, he has published another play, four volumes of poetry, five books of nonfiction, four novels, and three collections of short fiction. He is best known for his novels and nonfiction, particularly the Coole family novels—*Season at Coole* (1972) and *The Brooklyn Book of the Dead* (1994)—and the memoir *Green Dreams: Essays Under the Influence of the Irish* (1994), which received the Associated Writing Programs Award for creative nonfiction in 1994. In these three works the focus is on the Irish American world and the individuals who comprise it. Writing of the dysfunctional Cooles in Brooklyn and on Long Island, Stephens reveals himself as a notable literary stylist with a true comic spirit.

The essays in *Green Dreams* serve as an ideal complement to the novels. In this volume Stephens writes of the close world of East New York, where he spent his early years and from which he has drawn many of the characters and the places of his fiction. In the final section of *Green Dreams* Stephens also details his ongoing recovery from alcoholism, a disease that runs rampant through the lives of many of his fictional characters. In addition, the essays he includes on writing and writers point to those literary figures who have impressed and influenced him most: James Joyce, Flann O'Brien, Samuel Beckett, W. B. Yeats, James Stephens, Thomas Bernhard, and Italo Calvino.

Stephens's work has not received much critical recognition; for the most part, he remains "a writer's writer," praised by fellow authors such as Stephen Dixon, Robert Creeley, and Hubert Selby Jr. One reason why his work is not better known is a result of his unpredictable publishing history: his books have been published by a variety of presses, many of them small with little access to major centers of distribution, and several of these books are out of print.

Michael Gregory Stephens was born in Washington, D.C., on 4 March 1946 into the large family of James Stewart Stephens and Rose Frances Drew Stephens. He was one of sixteen children, though seven did not survive infancy. James Stephens was a customs inspector on Pier 90 in the Hell's Kitchen section of Manhattan, an area that is important in the Irish American mythology of New York, as it was controlled by Irish gangsters. Stephens spent his first four years living in the East New York section of Brooklyn before his family moved to Long Island, settling in Williston Park. Although he spent just a brief part of his early life in East New York, he returns to it often in his work; it is a significant spur to his imagination. Even after his family had migrated to Long Island, Stephens often returned to Brooklyn for extended periods to stay with his aunts and his father's stepmother, who was an Irish speaker from County Roscommon. In this household, he developed an interest in Irish and Irish American culture and was exposed to the Irish oral tradition, the influence of which is important in his work. Stephens attended St. Aidan's Grammar School, Chaminade Prep in Mineola, and Herrick's High School before going on to attend the State Uni-

versity of New York, College at Cortland, for three years.

Stephens received B.A. (1975) and M.A. (1976) degrees in English and writing from the City College of New York, and an M.F.A. in playwriting from Yale University in 1979. Since 1975 he has taught writing at many colleges and universities, including Fordham University, New York University, Columbia University, Alfred University (where he was Gertz Professor of Writing) Princeton University, SUNY at Purchase, and Montclair State College. In 1986 he taught at the University of Hawaii at Manoa. In addition to teaching, Stephens has worked as an editor and writer in the City of New York Comptroller's Office and as a public relations specialist for The Asia Society. Stephens lived in Korea for a time, and in addition to the collection of essays *Lost in Seoul: And Other Discoveries on the Korean Peninsula* (1990), he has contributed articles on Korea to such publications as the *Los Angeles Times* and *Discovery Channel Magazine*. From 1994 to 1996 he was a senior editor and writer for *Flatiron News*. Of all the jobs Stephens has had over the years, perhaps the most remarkable was his stint as a semiprofessional boxer taking part in illegal prizefights, or "smokers," in Upstate New York between 1963 and 1965. He has also written on boxing for *The New York Times, The Washington Post,* and *Boxing Illustrated.*

The stories in *Paragraphs* (1974), Stephens's first collection, defy traditional notions of the genre. Just as *The Brooklyn Book of the Dead* could be construed as a group of interlinked stories that form a novel, so too could the stories in *Paragraphs* be seen as a novel—or even, given their intense brevity, as a series of prose poems. Furthermore, the listing of literary influences in "Love," the final story in the volume, blurs the distinction between fiction and nonfiction: Stephens mentions Jorge Luis Borges, Frank O'Connor, James Stephens, and Andrei Codrescu as being important influences on his work as a short-story writer. In *Paragraphs,* despite Stephens's stated reverence for Irish short-story writers, it is clear that in form and material he is writing against the classic Irish conception of the short story, particularly as it is articulated by O'Connor in *The Lonely Voice, A Study of the Short Story* (1963). These stories, like Borges's, are brief and unstable. As Donald Barthelme, Robert Coover, and John Barth were attempting in their fictions at the time, Stephens also seeks to subvert the genre.

In "Study with Nudes" a man awakens in a room in a house near the sea and wanders naked through the day to the beach, bookstores, and parties. Everyone he meets is also nude, so nudity is not an issue in the story; instead, the focus is on perception, and what people will reveal of themselves when clothing, which they use to hide their inner selves, is removed. *Paragraphs* also includes drawings by Fritz Bultman that complement the stories, and in "Study with Nudes" Stephens argues that the short story, like the drawing, is "the simple process of one man's hand moving the muscles of his body thru the dictates of his imagination—supple, reclining, pouring all his sexual energy into the finite space of the drawing." According to Stephens's narrator, in the novel or in longer pieces of short fiction, the nude "is a prelude for a pornographic stunt" rather than something true and artistic. Stephens's desire is to maintain a closeness to the object being described; he does not want to be carried away by the torrential narrative of the novel as it takes on a life and energy of its own. The collaboration between Stephens and Bultman evokes the avant-garde work of the New York School of poets.

"Mooney's 'Bartleby'" is an homage to Herman Melville's 1853 story "Bartleby the Scrivener" and an exploration of people and place that anticipates Stephens's novels. The narrator, in prison for robbing a liquor store (though he professes innocence), relates the story of a man named O'Dwyer who was incarcerated for the murder of his father. The narrator has heard this particular story from his jailer, a man named Mooney, whose father and grandfather had worked as jailers in the Tombs Prison in New York. Because of the narrator's intense interest in the work of Melville, Mooney shares the information that his grandfather was Bartleby's jailer and that Bartleby shared a cell with O'Dwyer, a "large, ugly, pimply psychotic" who "suffered auditory hallucinations due to a chemical imbalance in his diet." As a result of a fall from a ladder while he was a teenager, O'Dwyer is perpetually in pain. Bartleby is repelled by O'Dwyer's smell and bad manners and refuses the sexual encounters that his cellmate proposes. The loneliness, the fact that O'Dwyer has no one to visit him from the outside with gifts, and Bartleby's rebuffs combine to drive O'Dwyer into rages: he pummels Bartleby and curses at everyone and everything. The story is an exploration of the deranged mind that can easily confuse the actual and fictional worlds.

For the most part, in *Paragraphs* Stephens is concerned with what moves people to love and be loved. The subject is explored with physical directness, as in "Pig" and "Jesus of Penis," though the more indirect and tangential approach of "Pastoral" and "Yo Soy Beans"—in which the worlds of nature, the imagination, and the body are brought freely into play—is

Cover for Stephens's 1992 collection of pieces that focus on New York City, its Irish American inhabitants, and questions of artistic form

more successful. The latter two stories are written with a deep sensuousness. At the same time, Stephens never leaves the designated space of the form or loses touch with the physical phenomena in which the writing is grounded. In terms of Stephens's writing as a whole, *Paragraphs* points more in the direction of his poetry than his fiction, particularly in its gentleness, though the experiments with form certainly point the way forward to what he has attempted in his novels.

Published in 1982, *Circles End,* Stephens's second "collection" of short fiction, is also a transgressive work. The single story in the volume is divided into fifteen parts, with most separated by brief poems or prose poems that are both a part of the narrative and a gloss on it. This Cheeveresque story traces a copywriter's journey home from the city to the suburbs. The endless train rides to and from the city, allied with the drudgery of work, have taken their

draft 2   5/14/00

TRANSPARENCY

His boss~~es~~ [were old man] a Korean ~~guy~~ who dressed like a cowboy. ~~He~~ wore ~~a~~

cowboy shirt ~~with cowboy-style~~ jeans, lizard-skin boots, and a

snakeskin belt with a huge turquoise buckle. The rumor was that

Mr. Kim was an old intelligence operative. For ~~keeping the~~

~~silence, he was given this~~ factory upstate on the Hudson in

Rivertown, right at the edge of the water.

The Kid did ~~all the~~ grunt work, none of the brain stuff, for

Mr. Kim and his wife.

Mr. Kim called The Kid, "The Shlepper."

Before coming to Rivertown, Kim had a hat factory in

Brooklyn, and he used ~~a lot of~~ Yiddish words that he must have

picked up from that New York City borough.

Revised typescript page for an unpublished story by Stephens (Collection of Michael Stephens)

toll on this unnamed commuter. He surmises as he waits to exit the train: "If one gets younger traveling at the speed of light, think of how much he ages traveling at the speed of the commuter train. Already another lifetime has fled him on this journey homeward." In psychological and emotional terms, the purpose of the journey home is to escape from the city and work, an enterprise built on delusion and illusion, according to the narrator. When one ventures into the city, one loses track of who one is; therefore, in order to know oneself again, it is necessary to return to the suburb, as is clearly indicated in the last lines of the final poem:

As though on your wrist
Let moon set and the Pleiades
Here I know you
At this point called circles end

When the train stops, his wife is waiting on the platform, ready to drive him home in the station wagon for a surprise birthday party, and the fiction ends with a strong sense of affirmation.

On the surface, as far as the theme goes, *Circles End* is not typical of Stephens's work. Almost without exception, the vision of suburbia and family life that he presents is a dark and destructive one. In suburbia, families are cut off from their ethnic roots, which they had left behind in the city; and they, like the houses they inhabit, fall into various forms of despair that are manifested in addictions (to alcohol and drugs, in particular) and that lead to rage against other family members and neighbors. Almost habitually, Stephens's lost suburbanites end up on the margins of society. Many of his characters get in trouble with the authorities. *Circles End* is quite the opposite in terms of the vision it espouses: in this book the city and the world of work represent a place and an enterprise built on fantasy from which one must escape. The wholesome world of suburbia is where the human spirit is re-energized after battling the world of the marketplace. The suburb is imbued with the sense of being timeless, whereas the city is governed by mechanized time.

Two related themes that are explored in some detail in *Circles End* are time and delusion. As a result of the endless commuting on the train, the narrator loses track of real time, which is represented by the time spent at home with his family, and becomes absorbed with it as an abstract concept. He ruminates on different methods of timekeeping, from watches to the notions presented by such theorists as Galileo and the train conductor, and, as he is drawn into this mode of thinking, he is drawn into fantasy. He imagines himself flirting with a young woman in the seat next to his, and he is drawn into a reverie with the engineer as he strives to bring together the mechanics of the train's operation with his own notions of how time moves. In the end, he is rescued from both by his arrival at his home station. The function of the short poems is to provide a bridge between real and imaginary time, a strategy that is most effective.

Published in 1992, *Jigs and Reels* is Stephens's best and most sustained work in the genre of short fiction. The volume includes seventy-three brief pieces, the shortest no more than a paragraph, the longest a mere three pages. The brevity and concentration are reminiscent of Beckett's later short fiction. *Jigs and Reels* is full of Stephens's familiar concerns. Primarily, Stephens is an urban writer; and in this collection New York and its ordinary and subterranean people are again at the forefront. In a 1994 interview, explaining his motives for writing *The Brooklyn Book of the Dead,* Stephens noted that "the compulsion to write this novel comes in part from knowing people, academicians, writers, people who have had these vaguely middle-class backgrounds, and knowing that these people just assumed I'd had the same experiences . . . I thought, man, if only they knew." Because he feels that the second-generation Irish American urban ghetto he experienced no longer exists, Stephens has made a point of recording it so that the lives and stories of the men and women who lived there are not forgotten.

One of the most memorable figures in Stephens's family background was his father's Irish-speaking stepmother, a woman who is remembered in "Grandmothers," a wicked and brilliant piece of portraiture. On the one hand, she is a truly beautiful woman who has taken great pains to keep her hair and skin in good condition (after she passes away, the mourners look at her face and note the absence of wrinkles). On the other hand, she is a foul-mouthed monster who directs a racist diatribe at a terrified vendor, and she drinks too much. In this respect, she is an example of a shanty Irish stereotype. Stephens has often worked with such people in his portraits of down-at-the-heel Irish Americans. He noted in the 1994 interview: "You think about stereotypes, but the thing is that sometimes truths can be revealed through them. In the end, I guess you just have to write what you know. The strange thing is that you can take these people and put them in Brooklyn or Long Island and they just don't change that much. They might as well be back in Dublin." Part of the complex nature of the Irish in America, something Stephens understands, is that it is capable of both embracing and rejecting stereotypical notions of its own identity. In this same vein, other stories depict the lives of Irish Americans as they drink and talk. A notable example is "War," which is set in a sleazy Manhattan bar and combines echoes of the Irish oral tradition with the world of the U.S. military.

Many of the stories exist primarily to celebrate the city itself. In "Walking the Bronx," the narrator is waiting on a subway platform for the train to take him back into Manhattan. From the elevated platform, he casts his gaze on the physical, literary, and historical Bronx he inhabits during his working day. He observes toughs with pit bulls and German shepherds, an elderly priest exiting a bar, and the general flotsam and jetsam who inhabit the gritty urban streets. He recalls hearing Seamus Heaney read his poems at Fordham University and remembers how much this experience evoked his childhood on Long

Island, where he grew up among rich truck farms. In many of the urban stories, the city is not merely observed but also absorbed through the senses. In this respect, given their impressionism and brevity, the stories in *Jigs and Reels* blur the distinction between fiction and poetry.

Stephens's third collection, like *Paragraphs* and *Circles End,* is interspersed with many linking stories that slow the pace of the narrative and celebrate the habitual and the momentary. In "Still Life with Anjou Pear," the most complex of these stories, the experience of holding a pear is the inspiration for several ruminations on the pear itself and its value to the artist as a central part of a still life. The pear is a starting point for imaginative flights of fancy that take the speaker to various warm countries such as Mexico and Morocco, involve him in the natural world, and allow him the possibility of asking questions concerning the nature of artistic experience and creativity. The pear is also compared, with great sensuality, to the breasts of a woman, in stark contrast to somewhat grotesque representations of women's body parts in other stories. In "The Skating Pond," a story in the same vein, the focus is on light as much

as it is on the movement of the skaters. Similarly, in "The Iris (ii)," a woman is captured in a moment of abandon, though the emphasis is as much on the notion of seeing as it is on the perceived woman. In the stories that comprise this collection, Stephens once again engages in a dialogue with artistic form and vision on both a theoretical and a practical level.

Michael Stephens's work, across a variety of genres, exhibits a sense of daring, a striving for originality, a single-mindedness, an engaging comic vision that contributes to his dark vision, and a fearless disregard for the fashionable. In his short fiction, he writes beyond the pale of the classic American short story; though, by writing as he does in the tradition of Beckett and Borges, he shows that his work can only be properly evaluated if it is considered in a wider international context. However, just as Joyce is a quintessentially Irish writer, so too is Stephens quintessentially American.

Interview:

Mike Hudson, "Dead On: Author Michael Stephens Strives Against the Odds," *Irish Echo* [New York], 9–15 March 1994, p. 41.

W. D. Wetherell

(5 October 1948 –   )

Carol-Lynn Marrazzo
Lebanon College

BOOKS: *Souvenirs* (New York: Random House, 1981);

Vermont River (Piscataway, N.J.: Nick Lyons/Winchester, 1984);

The Man Who Loved Levittown (Pittsburgh: University of Pittsburgh Press, 1985);

Hyannis Boat and Other Stories (Boston: Little, Brown, 1989);

Chekhov's Sister (Boston: Little, Brown, 1990);

Upland Stream: Notes on the Fishing Passion (Boston: Little, Brown, 1991);

The Smithsonian Guides to Natural America: Northern New England (Washington, D.C.: Smithsonian Books / New York: Random House, 1995);

The Wisest Man in America (Hanover, N.H.: University Press of New England, 1995);

Wherever That Great Heart May Be (Hanover, N.H.: University Press of New England, 1996);

North of Now: A Celebration of Country and the Soon to be Gone (New York: Lyons, 1998);

One River More (New York: Lyons, 1998).

RECORDING: "North of Peace," read by Wetherell, in *Patricia McConnel, Joyce Carol Oates, and W. D. Wetherell, Authors of Three of the "Ten Best" Short Stories in the PEN Syndicated Fiction Project, Read Their Stories,* Washington, D.C., Library of Congress, 1985.

W. D. Wetherell (photograph by News and Publications, University of Pittsburgh; from the dust jacket for The Man Who Loved Levittown, *1985)*

The young W. D. Wetherell spent his school vacations reading. He found that the authors who meant the most to him were Herman Melville and Henry David Thoreau, not J. D. Salinger; Fyodor Dostoyevsky, Nathaniel Hawthorne, Leo Tolstoy, Anton Chekhov, Joseph Conrad, Willa Cather, Franz Kafka, and Marcel Proust, not John Updike. These were his contemporaries in spirit and style, if not in time. Their works have affinities with Wetherell's writing, which Rick Bass has characterized as "an uncommon mix of orthodoxical storytelling."

Wetherell's best short stories are unflinching and compassionate accounts of ordinary people faced with bewildering incongruities that test the human heart. His themes include disconnection, desire, and remembrance. His settings include countryside, lakes, suburban tract houses, and ballparks. The characters in Wetherell's stories, many of whom are disillusioned and even broken, embody the particularly American conviction that everything matters—that with courage, people can do better and be better, not only as individuals but also as a society. This vein of informed optimism running through the work has led some reviewers to label Wetherell's less successfully realized stories didactic or sentimental. It may be more helpful, however, to regard them as American stories by a writer predisposed to traditional modes of fiction.

Walter David Wetherell was born in Mineola, New York, on 5 October 1948, the son of Walter J. and Elizabeth Hale Wetherell. His parents met during World War II in England, where both were serving in the armed forces, his mother as a nurse, his father as an officer in charge of a camp holding German prisoners of war. The couple married and raised their family in Hempstead and later Garden City, New York. Wetherell's father sold insurance to young families moving from the city to the subdivisions that blossomed on Long Island after the war because of the cheap mortgages available to veterans through the GI Bill. Wetherell attended school not far from Roosevelt Field, where Charles Lindbergh's *Spirit of Saint Louis* lifted off for Paris in 1927. A student of history, a voracious reader, and an autodidact by disposition and choice, Wetherell attended college only briefly. He found time to write while working variously as a magazine editor, salesman, tour guide, and teacher.

The breakthrough year for Wetherell as a writer was 1981. His first book, the novel *Souvenirs,* was published by Random House. He also received a National Education Association Writing Fellowship that year, the first of two, and his short story "The Man Who Loved Levittown" brought him an O. Henry Award. Two years later he received another O. Henry Award, for the story "If a Woodchuck Could Chuck Wood." ("Watching Girls Play" earned him a third O. Henry Award in 1999.) Wetherell's second book was *Vermont River* (1984), a collection of personal essays about "a year in the life of a writer and a fisherman." Edward Hoagland called *Vermont River* "a bold little gleeful book . . . astute and lyric," and the book established Wetherell's reputation as a first-rate nonfiction writer.

Wetherell's first collection of stories, *The Man Who Loved Levittown* (1985), earned him the reputation of a talented short-story writer as well. In a review of the collection in *The New York Times Book Review* (5 January 1986), Robert Ward described four of the stories as "unforgettable . . . They are so strong, so well executed, that I can see why the University of Pittsburgh Press chose to give its 1985 Drue Heinz Literature Prize for short fiction to W. D. Wetherell." Many of the stories feature political themes; Ward, however, thought that some of these stories were heavy-handed and found the characters in them underdeveloped. He also accused Wetherell of "standing on the soapbox."

Such is not the case with the title story of the collection, which Ward described as "brilliantly realized." In "The Man Who Loved Levittown" widower Tommy DiMaria witnesses the disintegration of a community as longtime friends, other "cowboys . . . pio-

neers," retire to Florida and young couples move in. At the opening of the story DiMaria says, "You realize what I had to do to get this place? It was thirty-odd years ago come July. I'm just out of the Army. Two kids, twins on their way, a wife who's younger than I am, just as naive, just as crazy hopeful." He heads to Long Island, where, through a bit of luck, he runs into Bill Levitt, the builder of the well-known subdivision Levittown. DiMaria explains that "Thanks to Big Bill Levitt we all had a chance. You talk about dreams. Hell, we had ours. We had ours like nobody before or since ever had theirs. SEVEN THOUSAND BUCKS! ONE HUNDRED DOLLARS DOWN!" The strength of the story resides in Wetherell's vision and craft, his mastery of working-class language, and his creation of DiMaria, a complex character. DiMaria belongs to a generation of builders: he worked on the lunar landing module, strove to create a community, and tried to make his family's life better. He also stole lumber for remodeling from a construction project on the turnpike and helped himself to "some surplus voltage," figuring "it was the land of milk and honey . . . all we had to do was plug in and help ourselves." When DiMaria's dog is run over, he blames a Jewish neighbor, and under cover of darkness he vengefully paints a giant red swastika on another neighbor's home, intending for it to be visible from the Jewish man's window. The story ends with DiMaria sprinkling gasoline from one end of his own house to the other, arson in mind, a displaced veteran's incendiary "Kilroy Was Here."

The next story in the collection, "If a Woodchuck Could Chuck Wood," is a dark Thanksgiving tale that begins with a holiday dinner of burned, meatless lasagna and a woodstove that goes cold. This holiday gathering of three generations sours when the family patriarch, school custodian Mike Senior, tries to put the best face on things. His optimism irritates Mike, his son, who is an out-of-work veteran. After dinner, father, son, and young grandson, Shawn, go outside to bring in wood for the stove, a trip that ends disastrously when a splintered ax injures Mike. Young Shawn realizes that "he always would be, too, forever trying to catch up, unable to escape a future consisting entirely of heavier logs, even thicker, more acrid smoke." When Mike Senior tells the boy that things will get better, Shawn calls him a liar, in effect denying his grandfather his dream, confirming his father's bitter pessimism, and shutting the door to hope for all three.

"Volpi's Farewell" explores another father-son relationship, but at the opposite end of the social and cultural spectrum. Volpi, a famous retired opera singer, visits his son's school to help with an amateur production of *La Bohème*. Although professionally accomplished, Volpi is a quite ordinary man: a collector of young girlfriends and only a part-time father, he bullies Ricky, his son, at the rehearsal and calls him an idiot. Ricky only smiles at this treatment, seemingly seeing right through his father. During the performance, however, when Ricky freezes on stage, Volpi sings out "Coraggio!" (Courage!) His booming voice—"like a benediction"—hushes the audience and "rings without diminishing as if by its compassion and force it can somehow outlast all the heartbreak . . . pain and disappointment. . . ." Wetherell is an opera buff and a believer in "the truth of art." But Volpi's benediction is a dramatic grand gesture from a man who only a few hours earlier publicly humiliated his son.

"The Bass, the River, and Sheila Mant" is a charming story about first loves. The story opens with the narrator reminiscing that "There was a summer in my life when the only creature that seemed lovelier to me than a largemouth bass was Sheila Mant." He tells the story of their single date, when, as he rowed Sheila upriver to a dance, he snagged a spectacular bass with a lure he had let down in the water and forgotten; "torn apart between longings, split in half," he chose to cut the line and lose the bass rather than appear foolish in Sheila's eyes. The closing paragraph, if not purely autobiographical, certainly speaks to Wetherell's love of fishing and his personality, as the narrator muses about himself: "Funny. Different. Dreamy. Odd. How many times was I to hear that in the years to come. . . ."

"Nickel a Throw" and "Why I Love America" are dark, warning stories. Gooden, in "Nickel a Throw," sits on a platform over a dunking pool at a country fair in order to raise money. Initially timid, Gooden grows vicious, goading passersby until the line at the dunking booth is the longest at the fair. At the close of this allegorical story, Gooden, drunk with success and power, feels as if he is held underwater by invisible hands and then released, "Alive, gasping, whimpering, warned." In "Why I Love America" Rufus, an illiterate man grieving over the death of his son in Vietnam, is by an odd twist of fate appointed to teach English to two Vietnamese immigrants. Kim-cha and Kim-choo come enthusiastically to Rufus for their lessons, and he acculturates them with the bitter vocabulary of the marginalized: "porter, unemployment, dishwasher, heartbreak, welfare, pain. . . ." In his review Ward complained that this story's "thematic exposition . . . overpowers the characters."

"North of Peace" places an antinuclear activist in a dingy laundromat where he proselytizes to the tired young mother of a misbehaving son about making the world safe for future generations. Eventually, the exhausted woman requests one of his brochures, and he feels "a surge of joy." This story of a man with a political agenda ends with biting irony: the mother

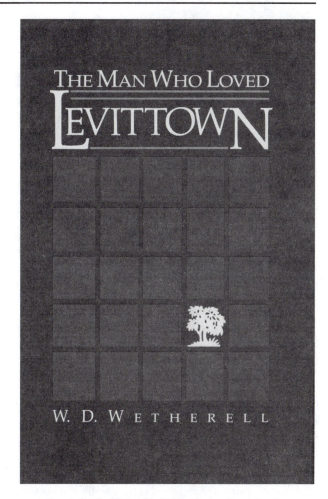

Dust jacket for Wetherell's 1985 collection of stories set in a working-class milieu

chooses a booklet, rolls it in her hands, and "with a gesture oiled by long practice," smacks her son's face.

Many of the stories in *The Man Who Loved Levittown* treat the plight of veterans, but in the closing story, "Spitfire Autumn," most of the action occurs during World War II, if only at its periphery. Through a series of flashbacks the narrator, Kay, conveys the heady life pulse of her generation, which reached maturity in Britain during rationing and the blitz. She tells the story of her friend, "The Angel of Piccadilly," a girl who seems to have possessed healing powers. When Angel invited injured and crippled soldiers to dance with her at a local canteen, they were miraculously healed. "Spitfire Autumn" is the only story in the collection in which war-related experiences include healing; this lends a somewhat hopeful tone to the concluding pages of the book.

In many ways *Hyannis Boat and Other Stories* (1989), Wetherell's second story collection, takes up where the first left off. It begins and ends with stories set in times of war and is concerned with remembrance and grace. The stories feature families, veterans, activists, dreamers, boys, and boats. Jodi Daynard, reviewing the book in *The New York Times Book Review* (18 June 1989), wrote that "Wetherell lifts these characters from their obscurity and makes them a living memorial to all those who've survived events beyond their control and comprehension."

Hyannis Boat and Other Stories displays Wetherell's growing mastery of the elements of his craft. Most striking is his increasingly effective use of place. His early nonfiction abounds with detailed descriptions of landscape; in contrast, the stories in *The Man Who Loved Levittown* have fairly spare descriptions—places exist as ideas, dreams, or destinations. In this second collection Wetherell brings to his fiction what Daynard calls "a naturalist's eye."

In "Hyannis Boat" the waters between Nantucket and Cape Cod are dense with fog that renders the physical world unreadable to the crew of a small ferry, which includes a teenager named Daniel. It is 8 May 1945, V-E Day, and the crew is eager to join the celebrations and begin new lives. Throughout the story the fog lifts and then falls again, like a theater scrim obscuring the view. On watch, Daniel discovers a linen-clad stowaway in the ferry's lifeboat, a ghostly figure who repeats an enigmatic "away, away" even when he escapes, with Daniel's complicity, and rows off into the fog. Rather than address the theme of the cultural decline of postwar America directly, as he did so successfully with DiMaria in "The Man Who Loved Levittown," Wetherell this time renders theme through landscape. Near the close of the story, just before the ferry begins to move again and the world is momentarily poised between the past and the future, Daniel looks at his surroundings. The ferry lies motionless in a thick black fog, but above it he sees,

> dead ahead over Hyannis, fireworks over Brewster and Falmouth and Orleans. They shot into the air in bundled columns of sparks . . . until the coast was covered with a dome of shimmering, parti-colored flakes . . . the light, as it lingered, seemed to become more garish and confused, so that at the last moments—as the final jubilant barrages were flung into the sky all at once—the horizon took on the molten, churning ugliness of overheated metal the instant before it cools into slag.

The passage displays a stunning shift in language: the fireworks are "shimmering, parti-colored" and "jubilant" but then become "garish and confused," with "molten, churning ugliness." The fireworks are a metaphor for V-E Day expectations—hopes and high spirits that, over time in postwar America, not only dimmed but grew corrupt.

Displaying an accuracy of mood and details gleaned from three summers Wetherell spent as a tour director, "Remembering Mr. C." follows a busload of older women visiting the Calvin Coolidge homestead in Vermont. Throughout the story the attention of the main character, Mrs. Cormier, alternates between memories of her marriage and the American history she sees on display. A contemporary of Coolidge, Lindbergh, and others whose pictures line the walls, she feels part of that time. While touring Coolidge's house, she admires an embroidered cushion; she slips a nail file from her purse and surreptitiously slices her initials into its underside: "'In reverence,' she whispers. 'Forever.'" Striking the familiar theme of remembrance, Wetherell depicts her as "a woman whose place in history is secure."

"Hundred Year War" is an emotionally lacerating story in which Wetherell displays his talent for creating true and haunting voices. Hickson is a wheelchair-bound taxi dispatcher whose vicious radio relays vividly underscore this story about Ngo Quang, a Washington, D.C., cabdriver. When Ngo Quang refuses customers because he hates "the kind that visited the [Vietnam Memorial] just to say they'd been there," Hickson's voice crackles bitterly: "Up to your old tricks, huh, No Dong? No pity for the historically inept, no rememberee no ridee, let them find a rickshaw." Ngo Quang, it turns out, accidentally killed an American soldier during the war and now feels driven to visit the wall so that the incident can become "something finished and real." Hickson, meanwhile, torments Ngo Quang with tales of an avenging veteran, Big Mac, an urban legend that turns out to be true. Before the grim close of the story, Hickson tells Ngo Quang that "You bring back the days when I still had a pair of legs. We were whole in those days." Hickson thus acknowledges history's timeless bond between them.

After offering a litany of everything wrong with modern shopping malls in the opening of "The Mall: A History," the history-teacher narrator sardonically cracks, "it's hard not to long for a surgically delivered nuclear strike." He goes on to tell the story of how he and his young buddies optimistically witnessed the construction of "the mall" thirty years earlier. Wetherell configures the narrator with conflicting yet balanced qualities, so that he is multidimensional and not just a clever bore: he possessed real innocence in his youth, mordant humor (the air in the mall is the "vaporization of greed"), personal insight, and a larger vision. He sadly admits that he is an associate professor of history at a third-rate college, and one of "our generation that is *all* sequel and anticlimax and nostalgia and regret." The idealism and optimism of this baby-boomer narrator are sadly tempered in his middle age by his lack of real achievement. His generation's accomplishments pale in comparison to those of the generation that preceded it. Wetherell's treatment of history and personal responsibility in "The Mall: A History," though still colored by anger, is more encompassing and complex than it is in "Why I Love America."

A former priest, congressman, husband, and possible "ex-believer in the human race," Thomas Beston is the "Antedeluvian Man" in the story of the same name. An antinuclear activist, the fifty-year-old Beston is suffering a midlife crisis, feeling antiquated in every way. Near the close of the story he discovers a fossilized bee in a diner's marble counter; this discovery triggers a sermon: "My dear friends. The extinct Coronus in its day was the most marvelous creature in a marvel-filled world." His sermon parallels his life and acts as a metaphor for mankind, which, in Beston's view, is "growing indifferent . . . doomed."

If Beston suffers from chronic introspection, professional baseball player Larry Poronto, pride of the Brooklyn Dodgers in "Brooklyn Wept," is a man just opening his eyes to his own weaknesses as a lackluster serviceman and shabby husband. Yet, he feels wonderfully alive to the world for the first time in his life. During a postgame news conference, Poronto explains the error he made that cost the Dodgers the World Series: "Larry 'Larrapin' Poronto, pride of the Dodgers, team captain for thirteen big seasons not counting the war," sees things now in a way he has never seen them before. There is beauty in the arc of a falling ball, the flight of a bird, and the fans in the bleachers. At the moment of the crucial play, with the game and his marriage at stake, he was astonished by the beauty he saw around him and faced a choice. Poronto explains that "the forty-year-old part [of me] I could feel being born right there and then, knows it's the last chance I'll ever have to take it all in, to rescue time from the glorious befores and the lousy afters. . . . I'm laughing from sheer joy, roaring in glee, and then . . . plunk. . . . The ball rolls to a stop on the grass." Poronto's epiphany is joyous, a brilliant contrast to Beston's growing self-absorption in "Antediluvian Man." The two stories illustrate Wetherell's deepening interest in the bittersweet surprises of middle age.

"Things to Come: Maine, 1951" is told using three points of view, breaking an old short-story rule and annoying some critics. The first character readers meet is Winston Grummer, a salesman who travels the countryside selling a car-tire inflating device, the MAP (Make Air Pay). From Grummer's point of view, the future is bright. Next is Roger, a Korean War veteran, small-garage owner, and mechanic,

Dust jacket for Wetherell's 1989 collection, examining the disillusionment of aging protagonists

blissfully at home and at peace in his small world in Maine. From Roger's point of view, his and his wife's future is safe and secure. Finally the reader meets Roger's wife, Laura, a lonely young bride who aches from wanting a baby, company, and nice things for the house. From her despondent point of view, the future holds nothing. Wetherell approaches the technical challenges of working with three points of view by assigning the characters their own agenda, distinctive syntax, vocabulary, and rhythm. He then tells their stories sequentially, the close of one tripping the beginning of the next, concluding with Laura's story and her lyric wanting, expressed in long sentences. When a box of small gifts for the house arrives for Laura courtesy of Grummer, her sad mood is immediately dispelled. Grummer has successfully read the conflict between Roger and Laura, and his gifts set in motion their questionable future together.

The closing story of *Hyannis Boat and Other Stories,* "What Peter Saw," is the longest and perhaps finest and could be considered the quintessential Wetherell story. Twelve-year-old Peter has two summer ambitions: to row a skiff to Martha's Vineyard and to see a girl naked. Relatives arrive bringing with them the young newlyweds Doreen and Danny. Danny is on a one-day leave before he is to be shipped overseas to Vietnam, and Peter is bewildered that anyone would travel so far to spend one day with a girl. He is also awestruck by Danny's shining, black combat boots. After lunch it is quietly arranged that Danny and Doreen will use Peter's room for a "nap" before they have to leave. Peter peeks in the bedroom window briefly–Wetherell does not reveal at this point what Peter sees–and not long afterward, the visiting relatives leave and the day winds down.

Specific details make this story vivid: the thick underbrush Peter navigates on his unsuccessful reconnaissance missions to a nearby girls' camp; the Hawaiian Punch and "gallon of antifreeze to pour on the water in case of sharks" he carefully stows aboard the skiff; the skiff itself, under Peter's guidance, tugged both home and away toward the horizon (an echo of Daniel's experience on the ferry in "Hyannis Boat"); the hydrangea and roses surrounding the family cottage; and the homemade potato salad in a big green bowl. The vividness of this summer world earns the reader's trust for the technically complicated close of the story. Later in the day, triggered by the sight of a swan, Peter's intuition takes a "sudden leap ahead," and he knows that "life would continue to present itself to him in that same shimmery, ungraspable way. . . ." Finally, in a carefully paced closing paragraph, Wetherell reveals that when Peter peeked in the window, he saw only Danny and Doreen crying as she tied "with inexpressible tenderness" the laces of Danny's combat boots. The boy who, at the opening of the story, hungers to master the world and his feelings glimpses the crying newlyweds and the black combat boots and begins to know that the truth is complex and there are no answers, "only these intertwined bewildering strands of beauty and sadness and mystery combined."

Four more of Wetherell's books were published before his next short-story collection appeared in 1996. His second novel, *Chekhov's Sister* (1990), was selected one of the Notable Books of 1990 by *The New York Times*. Janette Turner Hospital, reviewing the novel in *The New York Times Book Review* (25 March 1990), wrote that "this elegantly nuanced, subtly toned Chekhovian novel seems a startling direction for the writer who gave us such a slangy gallery of indomitable American oddballs in *The Man*

Who Loved Levittown." Hospital concluded by observing that Chekhov and Wetherell both stress the theme of human dignity in their work and that *Chekhov's Sister* succeeds at being "provocative, haunting, unsettling and, well, Chekhovian." In 1990 Wetherell was a resident scholar at the Rockefeller Foundation's Bellagio Conference Center in Italy. A second nonfiction collection, *Upland Stream: Notes on the Fishing Passion* (1991), was well received. In a review of the collection in *Library Journal* (15 March 1991) David Panciera wrote that "Wetherell is part of a tradition of articulate modern fly-fishing writers that includes John Gierach . . . William Humphrey, and Nick Lyons." In 1992 Wetherell received the National Magazine Award for fiction for his story "The Greatest Mayan Speller Extant," later included in his third short-story collection, *Wherever That Great Heart May Be* (1996). His third novel, *The Wisest Man in America,* was published in 1995. *Publishers Weekly* (2 January 1995) characterized the novel as "understated, resonantly thoughtful." But Noel Perrin, reviewing the book in *The New York Times Book Review* (23 April 1995), complained that "Every character and almost every scene is allegorical." A guidebook by Wetherell, *The Smithsonian Guides to Natural America: Northern New England,* was also published in 1995; it is part of a well-respected and widely available series.

Clearly, the years between the publication of *Hyannis Boat* and *Wherever That Great Heart May Be* were productive ones for Wetherell. During this period he also taught writing and traveled; his trips to Montana and Italy provided material for the stories in *Wherever That Great Heart May Be*. These years were busy years personally, too, as Wetherell and his wife, Celeste, started their family (they have two children). Among the most difficult experiences of this period of his life, however, may have been his mother's long illness and death.

The stories in *Wherever That Great Heart May Be* focus on families, loss, and the links between one generation and the next. It is a book of both real and metaphorical twilights, autumns, blizzards, and mountains to be climbed. Thematically consistent with Wetherell's previous story collections and novels, *Wherever That Great Heart May Be* is the work of a mature writer who commands enormous storytelling powers. In a review of the collection in the *Boston Book Review* (1 May 1996) Dan Cianfarini wrote of Wetherell that "There is a seductive, soothing ease in the best of his writing, a calm that allows a deftly turned phrase, an unexpected insight, or a singular image to startle like a trout breaking still water." The novelist Frederick Busch described *Wherever That*

Great Heart May Be as Wetherell's "most stirring work. . . . Here is why you read short fiction."

The collection opens with "Road to the City," the story of eight-year-old Donny, his dreamer of a father, and their journey one Fourth of July in a cement truck headed south. Regarding the landscape, Donny's father remarks, "all you see is good as gone, future's not in farming, I figured that out over there in Korea. You can wait for the city to come get you, or you can go and get the city." Donny's father is the classic Wetherell character, a good-hearted, blue-collar man who has fallen hard for the American dream. But the story is also about the need to be known and accepted by one's children. Recounting the turning point in their relationship, Donny recalls, "He looked at me like a man who wants his son to buy his illusions and see through them and forgive him for having them in the first place. . . ."

Themes of family and connection appear as well in "In a Maritime Province." A newly widowed photographer, Maslin, and his estranged daughter, Amy, take a trip to Nova Scotia. The story also explores a complex aftereffect of loss. Noticing a middle-aged woman's big belly, Amy happily concludes that the woman is pregnant; Maslin, on the other hand, believes she has a tumor and is dying. This response angers Amy, who says that her mother's death has gotten to Maslin "so deep you see with it now." At the close of the story Wetherell uses landscape as well as interior drama to reveal Maslin's emotional awakening as he painfully accepts the reality of death. He watches a "decrepit-looking trawler" making its way to sea, and "without any conscious effort he [is] there riding its bow, his face stung with saltiness, his heart rising up on each new swell, then shuddering back again, rising and shuddering back," a bruised but wiser, more complete, man.

At the opening of the title story of the collection, "Wherever That Great Heart May Be," the narrator says, "My grandfather Donald Buskirk deserves a footnote in America's literary history and this is it: he once offered a bribe to Herman Melville." It is set in the period after Melville had given up writing and was working as a customs inspector. Melville tells the young Buskirk a story when they meet. But Melville's role in "Wherever That Great Heart May Be" is brief. Wetherell's story grows to become a long, involved tale of adventure that closes with the narrator and his grandfather Buskirk sitting together on a bench holding hands, the grandfather serving as a medium linking the narrator to "the ordinary and famous, the heroes and villains, those whose hands had touched the hands of people

Dust jacket for Wetherell's 1996 collection of stories treating the importance of generational connections

who were alive two hundred years ago in the brave splendid exaggeration of America's start." Like a hand offered in love and friendship, stories link the grandson and grandfather and one generation to later ones. Stories connect people through the course of time and across cultures and boundaries; they are everywhere for the taking and telling. The narrator boldly states in the closing line, "Stories! Stories, stories, stories!" This affirmation is particularly poignant, in light of Wetherell's disclosure that his personal speculation regarding his grandfather's possible brush with Melville sparked the writing of "Wherever That Great Heart May Be."

A review in *Publishers Weekly* (29 January 1996) noted that Wetherell's stories "often combine a love of nature and of the conventional outdoor activities of boyhood with a darker and more mythic, almost magic-realist sensibility." "Snow" is about a young family living in an isolated section of Montana when a worldwide, cataclysmic snowstorm occurs. Echoing, perhaps, one of Wetherell's childhood favorites, Daphne du Maurier's short story "The Birds" (1952)–which was adapted for Alfred Hitchcock's popular motion picture *The Birds* (1963)–"Snow" depicts the natural world behaving unnaturally as cinnamon-smelling snow buries the Montana mountainside and everything everywhere, cities from Brazil to France. Keen descriptions of the family cabin, environs, and snow ground the story, which focuses on a mother in a panic over her sick baby; a father who helplessly explains that he is "just a surveyor" who does not "understand big things"; and Willem, their son, who monitors the shortwave radio. (Shortwave radios were a boyhood passion of Wetherell's.) Willem aspires to "understanding [the snow], seeing it and seeing it whole." The story ends heartbreakingly. Yet, there is a moment when the father takes Willem aside and tells him how he and his wife met, why they chose the life they chose and that they love one another. Love and family matter, the father is saying; his story becomes the vessel carrying his legacy to his son.

In contrast, the next story in the collection, "The Greatest Mayan Speller Extant," humorously presents the surreal world of marketing gurus and corporate endorsements. This story about the American addiction to winning centers on Daniel Patchen, a spin doctor, and his client, Placida Jones, a haughty Nicaraguan foster child, a Mormon, and a speller extraordinaire. The satire peaks at the national spelling bee, where Placida meets her match, a girl who is a spin doctor's worst nightmare and against whom a visibly rattled Placida does not have a chance: "The blind crippled dwarf with the blonde curls, voice box, hearing aids, seeing-eye dog, and crutches did her best to get to her feet, but the effort was too much for her." Wetherell, an admitted poor speller, once said that part of the pleasure of writing this story was choosing words for the bee, heart stoppers such as *tintinnabulation, schistosomiasis,* and *quinquennalia.*

"Natale's Hat" and "Mountain Wedding" employ a brush with death to explore the themes of grief, courage, and hope. "Second Sight" examines some of these same themes in a painful reunion between two war enemies who are now old men. Wulff, still healthy and active, is a German who escaped from an American prisoner-of-war camp in World War II. Frank Cooper, now crippled and mute from a stroke, was a guard at the camp who tracked the fleeing Wulff and let him escape. With Wulff targeted in his gunsight, Cooper experienced a rush of sympathy, not for Wulff himself but for his

desperate run toward the future. Wulff and Cooper consider the unforeseen consequences of this war incident as the story explores the themes of courage, duty, and desire. Wetherell's novel *The Wisest Man in America* features a similar scene of escape, in which an American soldier pursues a German prisoner of war up Mt. Washington in New Hampshire. Unlike Wulff, who hungers for life, the prisoner embraces death, hurling himself from a cliff "with a final plunging effort."

"Those Who Cross" is a fitting close to a collection concerned with parents, children, responsibility, and the natural rhythms and cycles of nature. Young Samuel becomes the boatman who ferries spirits from this world to the next, eventually ferrying his own mother who, one night, dies from the complications of childbirth. On this night, as Samuel rows with his mother on board, he observes

> Something remarkable . . . something he hadn't seen on any of his other crossings. The moonlight had attracted bass to the surface, young ones, little more than fingerlings, but these in the thousands, so the whole surface was broken apart in exuberant splashes, making it seem the bass were carrying the river on their backs. He rowed through their middle, the oars coated with a phosphorescence that was almost silver, and then, as if someone had drawn a border down the river with a pencil, the splashing stopped, the young bass were gone, the moon seemed to go in again, the river darkened and went still.

This passage is elegiac, American in flavor, and pure Wetherell in execution. The close of the story notes the riches of life and family, the brevity of one's time here, the pain of separation, and the membrane-thin line that separates the living from the dead; or, as young Peter glimpsed in "What Peter Saw," the "intertwined bewildering strands of beauty and sadness and mystery combined."

Wetherell's three short-story collections provide evidence of his maturation as a writer. *The Man Who Loved Levittown* can be characterized as a book by a passionate young writer who boldly and sometimes angrily explores the consequences of living in modern society. *Hyannis Boat* shows Wetherell capitalizing on his naturalist's eye, powers of description, and the skills honed in his nonfiction writing to explore the root causes of social dislocation. *Wherever That Great Heart May Be* is written with consummate artistry. Unflinching and unsentimental, the stories in the collection explore life's mysteries and offer no answers, only patterns and rhythms–frequently from

off his blazer, added it to the pile. Fine then. Their coats could make

friends, it would save him the bother--he took another swallow of Coke,

fought pleasantly the urge to belch.

"Ready?" Ms. Marston asked. "Five minutes--no, four and a half."

Trainee Bob rubbed his hands together, as if he were about to plunge

them into something difficult. "Ready Freddy," he said, still playing

it light, but Trainee Ian could tell from the way he kept licking his

lips and blinking that he was sweating bullets inside.

Ms. Marston borught them fast off the interstae onto the strip. It

was deserted, people home wathicng football or eating New Year's dinner,

adn the stoplights were urned off as if resting. The trainees knew the

holday was part of their test, so no one dared grumble. Only two kinds

of people worked New Year's, Ms. Marston had told them when they first

came to interview, the poor and the rich, and she left it hanging which

cateogry they chose to be in.

Trainee Ian, staring toward the mirror, could only see the blank

smoothness of Ms. Marston's forehead, adn he preferred concentraing on

the back of her hair instead. Even since leaving headquarers he'd been

trying to determine what color it was, and he was no closer to deciding

now than ever. It was reddish, but not red, blondish but not blonde--all

teh labels he kept comign up with were derived from metals. It seemed

poured form a mold, jsut as she herself seemed poured form a mold--a

pretty mold, a lithe mold, a perfect one, but a mold all the same, and

when he treid half-ehartedly to fantasie aout her, he didn't dream bout

taking her cloes off, but of finding a wya to chip at the vital part

of the mold, have it shater apart so he could see what, if anything,

lay beneath.

She seemed to sense this, his curiosity--she looked at him in

a contmous , sceptical way that was harder than the look she gave the others.

Page from the typescript, with revisions by the author, for Wetherell's unpublished story "The Motivational" (collection of the author)

nature—that do not explain love, grief, and beauty but illuminate them.

Two more nonfiction works by Wetherell were published in 1998: *One River More* and *North of Now: A Celebration of Country and the Soon to be Gone*. A review of *One River More* in *Kirkus Reviews* (1 July 1998) characterized Wetherell as "one of the best" writers on fly-fishing. John Rowen, reviewing the collection in *Booklist* (1 September 1998), wrote that "The essays are casual and congenial, reflecting both environmental concerns and strong family ties, and are sprinkled with a rich variety of literary allusions, from Tolstoy to Nelson Algren."

Readers familiar with the themes of disconnection, desire, and remembrance in Wetherell's fiction will find them explored in *North of Now*. Section titles include "Remembrance," "Village Life," "Old-Tim-ers," and "Continuance." Wetherell closes the book with a statement of personal belief, the tenets of which live in all his nonfiction, novels, and stories: "I place my faith on the truth of art, the beauty of the natural world, the consolation of human courage, and while I know it's old-fashioned of me, impossibly out-of-date, this is what I believe in and that's the way I was born."

In 1998 Wetherell received the Mildred and Harold Strauss Living Award from the American Academy of Arts and Letters, a prize of $50,000 annually for five years—a gift, in essence, of time to write. Past prize recipients include Cynthia Ozick, Raymond Carver, and John Casey. Thus, W. D. Wetherell, if not yet a household name, is now justly recognized by his peers as a major writer of his time.

Richard Yates
(3 February 1926 – 7 November 1992)

Blake Bailey
University of New Orleans

See also the Yates entry in *DLB 2: American Novelists Since World War II, DLB Yearbook: 1981,* and *DLB Yearbook 1992.*

BOOKS: *Revolutionary Road* (Boston & Toronto: Atlantic/Little, Brown, 1961);

Eleven Kinds of Loneliness: Short Stories (Boston & Toronto: Atlantic/Little, Brown, 1962);

A Special Providence (New York: Knopf, 1969);

Disturbing the Peace: A Novel (New York: Delacorte/Seymour Lawrence, 1975);

The Easter Parade: A Novel (New York: Delacorte/Seymour Lawrence, 1976);

A Good School: A Novel (New York: Delacorte/Seymour Lawrence, 1978);

Liars in Love: Stories (New York: Delacorte/Seymour Lawrence, 1981);

Young Hearts Crying (New York: Delacorte/Seymour Lawrence, 1984);

William Styron's Lie Down in Darkness: A Screenplay (Watertown, Mass.: Ploughshares, 1985);

Cold Springs Harbor (New York: Delacorte/Seymour Lawrence, 1986).

Collection: *The Collected Stories of Richard Yates,* introduction by Richard Russo (New York: Holt, forthcoming 2001).

OTHER: *Stories for the Sixties,* edited, with an introduction, by Yates (New York: Bantam, 1963).

For most of his career, Richard Yates seemed always on the brink of gaining the fame he so richly deserved. His first novel, *Revolutionary Road* (1961), was immediately hailed as a masterpiece of realism, a definitive portrait of postwar suburban malaise. William Styron called it "a deft, beautiful novel that deserves to be a classic," and Tennessee Williams said "if more is needed to make a masterpiece in modern American fiction, I am sure I don't know what it is." The novel was nominated for a National Book Award and sold ten thousand copies in hard-

Richard Yates (photograph © 1969 by John P. Lowens; from the dust jacket for A Special Providence, *1969)*

back, eminently respectable for a literary first novel, all the more so for a novel that many found almost unbearably depressing. "You see yourself here," wrote Fred Chappell in 1971. "When you have an argument with your wife, or with someone who is a bit less articulate than you . . . you begin to hear Frank Wheeler standing inside your voice, expostulating with false earnestness. A glib pompous fat voice with an undertone of hysteria, and it echoes hollow and ridiculous in the most comfortably furnished room."

Yates was also a master of the short story, and many believe that his first collection, *Eleven Kinds of Loneliness* (1962), is an even greater achievement than *Revolutionary Road*. Years after it was first published,

The New York Times Book Review (1 November 1981) declared it "almost the New York equivalent of *Dubliners,*" and pointed out that "the mere mention of its title is enough to produce quick, affirmative nods from a whole generation of readers." On the cover of the 1989 Vintage edition, the writer Ann Beattie called the book "sharply focused, beautifully written and powerfully moving. Deservedly it has become a classic."

But neither a "classic" novel nor a "classic" collection of short stories—and arguably there were more to come—was enough to elevate Yates's reputation among those of the greatest American writers, perhaps because it was only his fellow writers who recognized the magnitude of his achievement. Throughout Yates's career, his more-fortunate colleagues such as Kurt Vonnegut, Styron, Frank Conroy—and others, some of them former students of Yates—were tireless in their efforts to promote his work. With their help he received any number of prestigious grants and awards from the National Endowment of the Arts, the Rockefeller, Rosenthal and Guggenheim foundations, and the National Institute of Arts and Letters. Despite such consistent achievement and critical appreciation, however, Yates's books tended to sell a little more poorly each time they were published, while Yates himself continued to live in tiny furnished apartments in the cities where he happened to have jobs—New York, Washington, Iowa City, Boston, Los Angeles, Wichita, and finally Tuscaloosa. Sometimes the strain, financial and otherwise, became too much, and Yates would disappear into the alcoholism and mental illness that plagued him throughout his adult life, often resulting in long periods of institutional care. A few years before his death, the critic and novelist Carolyn See observed, "He's not going to get the recognition he deserves, because to read Yates is as painful as getting all your teeth filled down to the gum with no anesthetic."

An absolute realist both in terms of subject and style, what mattered most to Yates was what Hemingway liked to call "writing well and truly"—with extra emphasis, perhaps, on the second adverb. "Dick Yates never compromised with less than the perfect word or less than the whole truth," said his friend E. Barrett Prettyman Jr. The "whole truth" as Yates saw it, however, was hardly conducive to attracting a wide readership. His characters tend to be quietly desperate members of the middle class: attractive, well-educated people who cannot abide their mundane lives in prosperous, postwar America. Trapped in tedious, white-collar jobs, they try to escape from an oppressive sense of their own ano-

nymity by constructing romantic self-images; they convince themselves that they are more creative, intellectual, and sophisticated than most of their bourgeois counterparts, and thus deserve better things. Inevitably, such willful delusion leads to frustration and even disaster, as Yates's characters are made to face the awful truth of who they are and what they have allowed their lives to become.

Richard Walden Yates was born on 3 February 1926 in Yonkers, New York, the son of Vincent Matthew Yates and Ruth (née Maurer) Yates. Both parents were aspiring artists, the mother in particular, and would later serve as models for the manqué strivers who populate Yates's fiction. Vincent Yates studied to be a concert tenor, but was unable to make a living at it, and later became a salesman for General Electric in Schenectady, New York. Ruth Yates fancied herself a sculptor and cultivated her slender talent with what her son considered a foolish and irresponsible tenacity. After she divorced her husband in 1929, she continued to depend on him to subsidize her sculpting career, often at the expense of supporting her children. Yates's mother appears again and again in his fiction, portraits that reflect both his compassion and sometimes scathing bitterness. The importance of this relationship can hardly be overemphasized: it instilled in Yates an overwhelming impulse to expose not only the self-deceit of others, but of himself as well, forcing him to examine his motives, in life as in art, with pitiless objectivity.

Yates's mother insisted on sending her son to a proper New England boarding school, despite the fact that her former husband was hardly in a position to pay for such a wild extravagance. He finally relented when she was able to arrange a scholarship for Richard to Avon Old Farms School—a "funny little school" in Connecticut that was known for accepting misfits whom other schools would not take. Yates's school days are memorialized in his 1978 novel, *A Good School,* where he appears as the inept, disheveled, but somewhat resilient poor boy Bill Grove (a Yates persona who also appears in "Regards at Home" and the 1986 novel *Cold Springs Harbor*). Like Grove, Yates gradually gained a measure of social acceptance at Avon, and during his last two years he was editor of the school newspaper; this experience, he later claimed, was the beginning of his long apprenticeship as a writer.

After his graduation in 1944, Yates was drafted into the army along with most of his classmates. Like Robert Prentice in Yates's autobiographical novel, *A Special Providence* (1969), Yates got off to an awkward start as an eighteen-year-old infantry private in Belgium and France. Tall (six-foot-three inches), skinny, and clumsy, he tried to compensate for his physical shortcomings by flaunting his prep-school wisdom, which invariably provoked the ridicule of his older and less privileged comrades. Eventually Yates learned to keep silent and try to prove himself as a man of action rather than intellect. During the Battle of the Bulge he contracted pleurisy, but refused any immediate medical attention until he collapsed and was taken away by an ambulance. His weakened lungs left him a semi-invalid for the rest of his life.

On his return to New York in 1946, Yates took an apartment in the Village, where he planned to read as much as possible and live the life of a "knock-about intellectual," à la Frank Wheeler in *Revolutionary Road*. As he later reminisced in an article for *The New York Times Book Review* (19 April 1981), "At twenty . . . I embarked on a long binge of Ernest Hemingway that entailed embarrassingly frequent attempts to talk and act like characters in the early Hemingway books. And I was hooked on T. S. Eliot at the same time, which made for an uncomfortable set of mannerisms." In 1948 he met his first wife, Sheila Bryant, at a party in the Village. Sheila, like Frank Wheeler's wife April, had nursed modest acting ambitions prior to marriage, but was content to sacrifice this aspect of her Village identity for the pleasures of domesticity. But the marriage proved difficult from the start: Yates was soon fired from his job as a rewrite man for the United Press, and his pregnant wife was forced to take secretarial jobs to pay the bills.

Shortly after his daughter Sharon was born in 1950, Yates contracted tuberculosis and spent almost two years in veterans hospitals. As his friend and publisher Seymour Lawrence put it, Yates used the time "to read and read and read. Those hospitals were his Harvard, Yale, and Princeton." Yates's most important discovery was Flaubert: "*Madame Bovary*," he wrote in 1981, "seemed ideally suited to serve as a guide, if not a model, for the novel that was taking shape in my mind. I wanted that kind of balance and quiet resonance on every page, that kind of foreboding mixed with comedy, that kind of inexorable destiny in the heart of a lonely, romantic girl." The novel that was taking shape in Yates's mind, of course, was *Revolutionary Road,* though its slow gestation from draft to painstaking draft took many more years of exhausting, Flaubertian toil. Meanwhile, Yates benefited in another way from his long convalescence, as the experience provided material for two memorable short stories set in tuberculosis wards, "No Pain Whatsoever" and "Out with the Old," that later appeared in his collection, *Eleven Kinds of Loneliness.*

After he was discharged from the hospital, Yates received a veteran's disability pension that allowed him to quit his job and live abroad for two years. It was here that his artistic career began in earnest. As he later put it, "I had nothing to do but write short stories and try to make each one better than the last. I learned a lot." While in Europe, Yates wrote several drafts of at least two dozen stories, eight of which he managed to sell to magazines. The first of these, "Jody Rolled the Bones," was accepted in 1953 by the *Atlantic Monthly* and won the "Atlantic Firsts" award. More important, it attracted the attention of a young editor at the Atlantic Monthly Press, Seymour Lawrence, who encouraged Yates to put aside story-writing and start a novel. In 1956 Yates submitted 130 pages of a draft titled *The Getaway,* about a restless suburban couple who longs to escape to Europe and "discover themselves." Lawrence recommended a contract, but his associates at Atlantic/Little, Brown were less impressed, calling the novel "one of the many imitators of *The Man in the Gray Flannel Suit.*" Four years and several drafts later, the book, now titled *Revolutionary Road,* was finally accepted. It was immediately recognized as the work of a major talent, and Yates's life was forever changed. On the one hand, the strain of perfecting the novel–of making "every sentence right, every comma and semicolon in place," as Yates wrote to Lawrence–had taken a toll on his marriage, and he and Sheila were divorced in 1959; but his labors paid off, and in the years ahead Yates would be offered prestigious jobs, anthologies to edit, and the acclaim of his fellow writers.

Eleven Kinds of Loneliness was published the following year, and it consolidated Yates's reputation as a prose stylist and astute observer of postwar American society. As the title suggests, most of the stories are variations on Yates's lifelong themes of disillusionment and isolation–"exercises in the building up and tearing down of expectations," as Jerome Klinkowitz put it in 1986. The first two stories are early treatments of Yates's preoccupation with class differences. In "Doctor Jack-o'-lantern," a well-meaning young teacher tries to make a welfare child named Vincent Sabella feel at home in a suburban Long Island school. Her fourth-graders, however, are already adept at noting the indicators of class, and subject the squirming Vincent to a silent, withering appraisal of his "absurdly new corduroys, absurdly old sneakers and a yellow sweatshirt, much too small, with the shredded remains of a Mickey Mouse design stamped on his chest." When Vincent tries to win their approval by claiming to have seen a movie on everybody's lips, *Dr. Jekyll and Mr. Hyde,* he

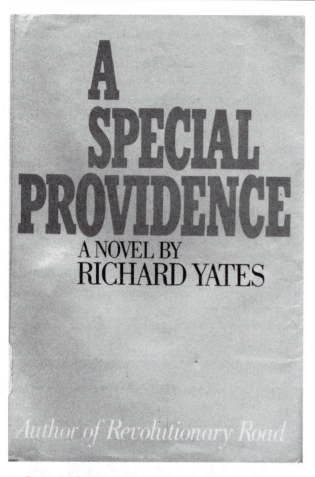

Dust jacket for Yates's 1969 novel, an autobiographical account of a World War II veteran and struggling writer

is ridiculed for his funny accent and obvious lying: "I sore that pitcha. Doctor Jack-o'-lantern and Mr. Hide." After Miss Price privately admonishes him about the importance of telling the truth, he vents his humiliation by scrawling obscenities in an alley behind the classroom. A prissy girl tells the teacher what Vincent has done, and the bewildered Miss Price wonders how to proceed—"sorting out half-remembered fragments of a book she had once read on the subject of seriously disturbed children. Perhaps, after all, she should never have undertaken the responsibility of Vincent Sabella's loneliness." She makes another attempt to reach the boy with a gentle speech about how much he has hurt her, and this seems to have the desired effect. Abjectly remorseful, Vincent leaves the classroom and is accosted by two popular boys, whom he tells with pathetic bravado that the teacher "din say nothin' . . . She let the ruler do her talkin' for her." The boys are duly impressed, until Miss Price discredits Vincent with a benignly cheerful greeting. This time the boys are unforgiving, and they run away jeering "So long,

Doctor Jack-o'-lantern!" Now hopelessly alienated from his more privileged peers, Vincent returns to the alley behind the classroom and draws a grotesque nude over the title "Miss Price."

"The Best of Everything" is another study of miscommunication between people of different social backgrounds. Grace is a sensitive office girl who has been educated in the ways of refined snobbery by her sophisticated roommate, Martha. When Grace is courted by a loutish young man of humble means named Ralph, the roommate dismisses him as the sort of guy who says "terlet" for "toilet" and whose mother keeps "those damn little china elephants on the mantelpiece." For a while Grace obediently tries to avoid him, but he persists, and one night at an American Legion dance she decides to marry him when he croons "Easter Parade" in her ear. (This song is a central motif in Yates's later novel of the same name, where it serves a similar purpose of evoking an ideal of romance that is inevitably shattered by reality.) When her roommate realizes that Grace's mind is made up, she tries to make amends for her earlier insensitivity by giving the couple a chance to be alone together in the apartment. Perhaps in homage to Martha's generosity, Grace decides to do the "sophisticated" thing by giving herself to Ralph before the wedding, and waits for him in a negligée. Ralph, however, has been out with the boys and can only "stay a minute" before he rejoins them. On his way out he says to his disappointed, but now quite resigned, bride-to-be, "I'm fulla beer. Mind if I use ya terlet?"

A more subtle handling of similar themes is found in "A Really Good Jazz Piano," a story Yates revised over the course of several years; it stands as one of the masterpieces of this collection. The protagonists, Carson Wyler and Ken Platt, are Yale graduates whiling away their early twenties in Europe. As with many of Yates's more-memorable characters, they are both nuanced individuals and utterly recognizable types—young men who seem to share the somewhat shallow, liberal-minded assumptions of their class and time, but who turn out to be almost as different on the inside as out: "Carson was the handsome one, the one with the slim, witty face and the English-sounding accent; Ken was the fat one who laughed all the time and tagged along." As the story opens, Ken calls his friend from Cannes, where he has spent a desperately lonely month while Carson has stayed in Paris to pursue a Swedish art student. Hoping to coax Carson into joining him, Ken announces that he has discovered a first-rate jazz pianist in one of the seaside bars: "He's a friend of mine," Ken says, and Carson assumes the man is black—"mostly from the slight edge of self-consciousness or pride" in Ken's voice when he calls the man "a friend."

Carson goes to Cannes and Ken introduces him to his discovery, Sid, who is indeed black and a superb musician. Carson (who has "the ability to find and convey an unashamed enjoyment in trivial things") sponsors the pianist for membership in the International Bar Flies, which involves a ritual of brushing each other's lapels and saying, "*Bzzz, bzzz!*" Ken, meanwhile, basks in Carson's approval for having made such a rare find—a black musician who possesses "*authentic* integrity," as Ken puts it, who practices his art in obscurity rather than "selling out" to the commercial shoddiness of America. As it happens, though, Sid is all too eager to sell out, and the two friends are appalled to find him truckling to a vulgar agent named Murray Diamond. When Sid pauses during his performance to give Carson the Bar Flies greeting, the latter humiliates him in front of the agent by sarcastically touching his shoulder and saying, "Buzz . . . Does that take care of it?" Ken is stunned by his friend's cruelty; on the verge of attacking him in the street, he is stopped by the look on Carson's face—"haunted and vulnerable and terribly dependent, trying to smile, a look that said Please don't leave me alone." One is left with the impression that the feckless Ken will benefit far more from his *Wanderjahr* in Europe than his worldly friend.

Perhaps Yates's favorite subject is the depths to which people can deceive themselves into thinking they are somehow special, set apart from the herd. In his later fiction he would usually reserve his scrutiny for the arty strivers of the middle class, but in "A Wrestler with Sharks" and "Builders" he focuses on working-class people whose humble lot in life makes them all the more susceptible to illusions of grandeur. In the first story, a former sheet-metal worker with writerly pretensions, Leon Sobel, takes a job with a dismal trade-union tabloid called *The Labor Leader.* Yates sketches this character with a few deft strokes: "He was . . . a very small, tense man with black hair that seemed to explode from his skull and a humorless thin-lipped face. . . . His eyebrows were always in motion when he talked, and his eyes, not so much piercing as anxious to pierce, never left the eyes of the listener." The narrator, a clever young man named McCabe who considers his employment on the *Leader* as strictly temporary, regards Sobel with a kind of polite condescension as the man confides that he is already the author of nine unpublished books: "Novels, philosophy, political theory— the entire gamut," Sobel explains. "The trouble with my books is, they tell the truth. And the truth is a

funny thing, McCabe. People wanna read it, but they only wanna read it when it comes from somebody they already know their name." Sobel is determined to make a name for himself by writing for the *Leader,* and after agonizing over paltry news items with such headlines as "PLUMBERS WIN 3¢ PAY HIKE," he is rewarded with an offer to write a column of his own on "labor gossip." His first (and last) effort, however, is laughably pretentious; titled "SOBEL SPEAKING," and attached to "a small portrait of himself in a cloth hat," the column proclaims its author to be "an 'ink-stained veteran' of many battles on the field of ideas, to be exact nine books have emanated from his pen." The editor rejects the piece amid much ridicule in front of the staff, and Sobel promptly quits. McCabe, sorry for his hapless former colleague, calls Sobel at home that night to suggest a possible opening at an even more dismal trade journal, but Sobel's wife answers and curtly refuses the offer. Taken aback by the woman's obvious, dignified devotion to her husband, the chastened McCabe is left "to climb guilty and sweating out of the phone booth."

In an interview for *Ploughshares* (December 1972) Yates described the last story of the collection, "Builders," as a "direct autobiographical blowout" that was sufficiently "objectified" to work as good fiction, and which emboldened him to make similar use of such material throughout his career. The protagonist, Robert Prentice (who also appears in a less successful work, *A Special Providence,* is a struggling writer who is "clearly and nakedly" a portrait of the artist as a rather callow young man. The story evokes Yates's early career in the Village, when he continued to pattern his life after Hemingway's—they both had been to war, skipped college, worked for a newspaper, and married young—though Yates's apprentice fiction showed little evidence of Hemingwayesque precocity. As Prentice/Yates remarks in the story, "it wasn't any 'Up in Michigan' that came out of my machine; it wasn't any 'Three Day Blow,' or 'The Killers'; very often, in fact, it wasn't really anything at all. . . ."

Prentice finally gets a break of sorts when he answers an ad placed by a middle-aged cabbie named Bernie Silver, who offers an "unusual freelance opportunity" to a writer with "imagination." The man proposes that Prentice ghostwrite a series of stories featuring a romanticized version of himself, Bernie Silver, as a heroic cabbie who changes the lives of his clients with bits of wise advice given in the nick of time. The "builders" metaphor reflects Bernie's approach to writing a well-made story; as he lectures Prentice, "Do you see where writing a story is building something too? Like building a house? . . . Before you build your walls you got to lay your foundation—and I mean all the way down the line." Finally, says Bernie, the most important aspect of the whole enterprise is the "windows": "Where does the light come in? . . . I mean the—the *philosophy* of your story; the *truth* of it. . . ." Prentice, desperate for money, conceals his disdain for the humbling assignment and becomes an earnest "builder" of Bernie's pathetically self-aggrandizing fictions. With a craftsmanship that surprises no one so much as himself, he writes about a delinquent who is saved from a life of crime by Bernie's folksy ruminations "about healthy, clean-living, milk-and-sunshine topics," as well as a story about "a small, fragile old gentleman" who almost succumbs to lonely, suicidal despair, until Bernie convinces him that he should go live with his daughter in Michigan. Bernie is delighted with these efforts, but, predictably enough, the project goes nowhere, and the two eventually fall out over money. At the end Prentice looks back over his story and wonders whether he has built it according to Bernie's rigorous specifications; he then adds the "chimney top"—the fact that he and his wife divorced shortly after the episode in question. "And where are the windows?" he wonders. "God knows, Bernie; God knows there certainly ought to be a window around here somewhere, for all of us."

On the strength of his first two books Yates was invited in 1964 to teach at the prestigious Writers' Workshop at the University of Iowa. By most accounts, he was an excellent teacher. He had "an instinctive and profound acuity when it came to seeing the heart of a story," as his student DeWitt Henry puts it, though some speak more ambivalently of Yates's almost obsessive "hectoring about the precision of language." In any case Yates took his teaching duties seriously, and his dedication—coupled with his heavy drinking—interfered with work on his second novel, *A Special Providence*. When it was finally published in 1969, it was a failure both critically and financially; the book was never reprinted, though Yates later came to regard it as a good learning experience in the writing of properly objectified fiction. As he said in the *Ploughshares* interview, he "never did achieve enough fictional distance on the character of Robert Prentice," and thus failed to avoid "both of the two terrible traps that lie in the path of autobiographical fiction—self-pity and self-aggrandizement."

Yates's third novel, *Disturbing the Peace* (1975), took almost as much time to finish as his second, and by the early 1970s his drinking was worse than ever. He was constantly short of money, and in 1971 he was denied tenure at Iowa. For the rest of his life

Yates would have a hard time finding new teaching appointments, as word of his alcoholism and precarious mental health was passed from one campus to the next. A manic-depressive, Yates tended to mix psychotropic drugs with alcohol during times of stress, which led to frequent breakdowns as he got older. His second marriage, to Martha Speer in 1968, was a casualty of his increasingly bizarre behavior, and in 1975 the couple divorced.

Always resilient in the practice of his craft, however, Yates's chaotic private life was ameliorated somewhat by several promising developments in his career. *Disturbing the Peace* was published the same year as his divorce, and helped to restore his reputation after the failure of his second novel. He was awarded a grant from the National Institute of Arts and Letters that enabled him to quit teaching for a few years and move back to New York, where he began work on what would prove to be one of his greatest novels, *The Easter Parade* (1976), which he finished in a miraculous (for Yates) eleven months. Reviews of the book were among the best Yates ever got: once again he was applauded as one of America's foremost realists, a true craftsman holding the line against the gathering tide of tricky postmodernism.

A Good School was published to respectful reviews in 1978, when Yates moved to Boston. He took a tiny, two-room apartment on Beacon Street, which his friend Andre Dubus remembers as a spartan testament to Yates's total devotion to his art: "It was a place that should be left intact when Dick moved, a place that young writers should go to, and sit in, and ask themselves whether or not their commitment to writing had enough heart to live, thirty years later, as Dick's did: with time as his only luxury, and absolute honesty one of his few rewards."

In 1981 Yates published his second story collection, *Liars in Love,* which was widely and admiringly reviewed amid somewhat meager sales. Most of the stories are unabashedly autobiographical; by the time they were written Yates's mother and sister had been dead for almost ten years, and he felt increasingly free to write candidly about his difficult family life as a child and young adult. Characters based on his mother had played prominent, rather unsympathetic roles in *A Special Providence* and *The Easter Parade,* but in the first and perhaps best story of this collection, "Oh, Joseph, I'm So Tired," she is portrayed with more compassion as Yates's resentment seems to have been tempered over time. (It is worth noting, however, that his final portrait of his mother in *Cold Springs Harbor* is unflattering as ever, perhaps reflecting Yates's ultimate verdict on the woman; in any case, his daughter Monica claims that Yates felt he had finally "gotten her right" in that last novel.)

"Oh, Joseph, I'm So Tired" is based on an actual incident wherein Yates's mother, in what would prove to be the biggest break of her dubious career, was given the opportunity to sculpt a bust of the newly elected Franklin D. Roosevelt in 1933. In the story Yates is quick to point out that she "wasn't a very good sculptor," and punctures the petty snobbery that lay behind her artistic aspirations: "Her idea was that any number of rich people, all of them gracious and aristocratic, would soon discover her: they would want her sculpture to decorate their landscaped gardens, and they would want to make her their friend for life." Meanwhile, the family lives in a gracious courtyard apartment, which they can scarcely afford, on Bedford Street in the Village, dominated by the mother's "high, wide, light-flooded studio."Her basic priorities are further suggested by "the roach-infested kitchen . . . barely big enough for a stove and sink that were never clean, and for a brown wooden icebox with its dark, ever-melting block of ice." The mother's best friend and pretentious alter ego is a woman named Sloane Cabot—a name she made up for herself "because it had a touch of class"—who works as a Wall Street secretary while she pursues her ambition of writing for the radio. Her meager talent and essential vulgarity are revealed by a mawkishly wishful script about an "enchanted circle of friends" who live around a courtyard in the Village, gamely enduring their genteel poverty as they await the artistic success that is just around the corner. The narrator remembers how he himself was described in the script as "a sad-eyed, seven-year-old philosopher" with a comical stutter, and reflects: "It was true that I stuttered badly . . . but I hadn't expected anyone to put it on the radio."

The mother withdraws her children from public school after they come home with lice in their hair, and arranges for them to be tutored at home by a poor Jewish violinist named Bart Kampen. The children are delighted: "Bart was probably our favorite among the adults around the courtyard. He was . . . young enough so that his ears could still turn red when he was teased by children; we had found that out in teasing him once or twice about such matters as that his socks didn't match." Kampen proves to be an excellent tutor, gentle and patient, but the arrangement comes to a disastrous end when the mother learns about an offhand remark he has made about "some rich, dumb, crazy woman" who has hired him to tutor her kids. The mother hears this gossip from a mutual acquaintance in Washington, D.C.,where she has just presented her bust to the

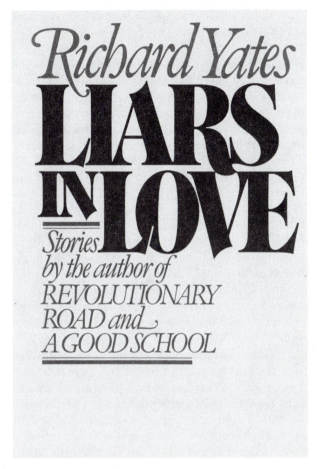

Dust jacket for Yates's 1981 collection, including autobiographical accounts of difficult family life

president amid a decided lack of fanfare; with insult added to the injury of an already crushing disappointment, the narrator imagines his mother's thoughts during the long train ride back to New York: "She was forty-one, an age when even romantics must admit that youth is gone, and she had nothing to show for the years but a studio crowded with green plaster statues that nobody would buy." The mother puts on a brave front for her children's benefit, pretending that her encounter with the president was a thrilling success, but then proceeds to nurse her grievance against Kampen with alcohol. Finally she confronts him with drunken bitterness: "All my life I've hated people who say 'Some of my best friends are Jews,'" she tells the startled Kampen. "Because *none* of my friends are Jews, or ever will be." The worst of his mother's nature thus revealed, the son lies in bed and ponders his family's entangled fate: "We would probably never see Bart again—or if we ever did, he would probably not want to see us. But our mother was ours; we were hers; and we lived with that knowledge as we lay listening for the faint, faint sound of millions."

"Regards at Home" is the story of how Yates eventually liberated himself from his mother some sixteen years later. Appearing as Bill Grove, he looks back at his postwar years in the Village, when his plans "to become a professional writer as soon as possible" were constantly waylaid by the obligation to care for his indigent, aging, hard-drinking mother. Though as a child Grove had "admired the way she made light of money troubles"–she stressed the romance of their poverty by reading Dickens to them in bed–he now begins to lose patience with the "childish and irresponsible" older woman who makes little effort to support herself and with whom he is forced to share his tiny apartment. After she threatens to complicate his life further by driving away the woman Grove intends to marry, he borrows some money from the bank and gives it to his mother: "I told her, in so many words, that she was on her own."

Grove's eagerness to free himself is contrasted with the filial piety of his friend and coworker, Dan Rosenthal, a talented artist who postpones his ambitions for the sake of a dependent family. For his part, Rosenthal envies the illusive freedom of Grove's life as a would-be writer living in the Village with a pretty wife–which in fact is anything but the idyllic "bohemian" affair that Rosenthal thinks it is: Grove's wife and he fight constantly, while the mother continues to be an obnoxious presence in their lives. Finally, when Grove wangles a veteran's pension to go abroad and pursue his writing career in earnest, he comes to realize his own good–if relatively selfish–fortune: "I had luck, time, opportunity, a young girl for a wife, and a child of my own." After a farewell party on the ship, Rosenthal advises him not to "piss it all away," and Grove hurries back to his cabin to "get my mother off the boat . . . and to take up the business of my life."

The title story of *Liars in Love* takes up where "Regards at Home" leaves off, with the Yates-like protagonist–here called Warren Mathews–living in London with his wife and two-year-old daughter. By now the daily ennui and cramped quarters of their tiny basement flat have combined to worsen the couple's differences until they can hardly even bring themselves to quarrel anymore; instead they pass the time in an atmosphere of tense civility as they try to avoid "getting in each other's way. 'Oh, sorry,' they would mutter after each clumsy little bump or jostle. 'Sorry. . . .'" Presently the wife decides to return to the States with their daughter, and Warren spends his first night alone in the flat pathetically winding

the crank of a cardboard music box that his daughter has left behind.

The story is one of Yates's most memorable studies of the effects of loneliness, the way it can warp a person's sense of reality. Warren's attempts to make some kind of human connection in London are forever thwarted by an inescapable feeling of alienation: "The very English language, as spoken by natives, bore so little relation to his own that there were far too many opportunities for missed points in every exchange. Nothing was clear." Desperate, Warren forces himself to pick up one of the prostitutes in Piccadilly Circus, and they return to the woman's shabby flat in northeast London; glad enough for the company, he tries "to keep an open mind" as the woman, Christine, tells well-practiced lies about her life as a prostitute and, later, about the baby whose crib occupies a conspicuous corner of the room.

Soon Warren's life is enmeshed with Christine's, which involves socializing with her fellow prostitutes as well as a jovial pimp named Alfred. At first, in true Yatesian fashion, he is able to accept the whole gloomy business with the help of some romantic self-flattery: "Nobody had to tell him what a triumph of masculinity it was to have a young whore offer herself to you free of charge. He didn't even need *From Here to Eternity* to tell him that. . . ." Ultimately, though, it occurs to Warren that the woman is maneuvering him into marriage, in the hope of giving her baby a father, and he tries to disentangle himself. She responds with an angry warning that her pimp is out to get him, but when Warren learns that this is a lie–indeed, that almost everything the woman says is a lie–he is no longer intimidated: "She was only a dumb little London streetwalker, after all." Free at last, Warren reconciles with his wife and prepares to return to New York, anxious to leave an alien world and his youthful naiveté behind.

"Saying Goodbye to Sally" returns to the theme of the title story and, to some extent, the entire collection–the lies that people tell themselves in the hope of escaping loneliness. This time the Yates surrogate is named Jack Fields, a writer whose first novel took five years to write and "left him feeling reasonably proud but exhausted almost to the point of illness." Fields's book is a critical success but sells poorly, and he is reduced to doing hackwork and drinking heavily. Before long, however, he is saved by an offer to go to Hollywood and write a screenplay based on a much-admired novel–just as Yates was in 1962, when he adapted Styron's 1951 novel *Lie Down in Darkness* for the director John Frankenheimer. The latter appears in the story as Carl

Oppenheimer, "a dramatic, explosive, determinedly tough-talking man of thirty-two," who bolsters his wunderkind status by acting the role of the blustery, hard-drinking "genius" while telling F. Scott Fitzgerald anecdotes for Fields's benefit.

Fields (who "had begun to see himself, not without a certain literary satisfaction, as a tragic figure") identifies strongly with Fitzgerald, all the more so when he begins to have an affair with a pretty Hollywood secretary in her mid thirties named Sally Baldwin. Fields views the woman as a Sheilah Graham substitute—the sort of throwaway romance that a great writer on the skids, à la Fitzgerald, might enjoy as he pulls himself together to write another masterpiece. Sally lives amid the garish opulence of a friend's house in Malibu, and soon Fields finds himself immersed in a nouveau-riche ménage only slightly more appealing than Warren Mathews's circle of prostitutes in "Liars in Love." Sally's housemate and fellow divorcée, Jill Jarvis, is a dim-witted vulgarian who neglects her young son while conducting a boozy affair with an oafish engineer named Cliff Myers. Finally, when Fields has seen enough, he determines to abandon Sally and her whole milieu in a way that leaves no hard feelings, taking her out for a last romantic dinner at a fancy restaurant. He tries to play the role of the gracious, worldly charmer, but Sally is not appeased by his patronizing compliments about her dress, and makes a remark that suggests she has seen through his pretensions from the start: The dress, she says, "might be useful in helping me trap the *next* counterfeit F. Scott Fitzgerald who comes stumbling out to Movieland." In the end the two seem equally relieved to relinquish their latest illusions and get on with their lives.

Following the critical success of *Liars in Love,* Yates spent the next three years working on his most ambitious novel since *Revolutionary Road.* Indeed, *Young Hearts Crying* (1984) resembled his first novel almost too closely: it, too, was the story of a promising young couple who are gradually chastened by the world, who try to transcend the sterility of their middle-class lives with artistic achievement that never quite materializes. Critics made much of the similarity between the two books, and tended to note the relative inferiority of *Young Hearts Crying* as evidence of Yates's faltering skills: some pointed out that the novel lacked the taut craftsmanship of *Revolutionary Road,* while its protagonists almost amounted to parodies of the brilliantly conceived Frank and April Wheeler. Yates was especially upset by Anatole Broyard's review in *The New York Times Book Review* (28 October 1984), the gist of which is suggested by its derisive headline, "Two-Fisted

Self-Pity." Yates and Broyard had been friends in the Village during the 1960s, and Yates saw the review as an act of betrayal.

By the mid 1980s Yates's financial situation was desperate: his books almost invariably failed to earn back their advances, a situation his publisher had been willing to tolerate because of the prestige of his name. But in recent years Yates had begun borrowing against future advances, until all parties concerned were thoroughly fed up. "Can you imagine how I feel," his agent Mitch Douglas wrote in an exasperated letter to Yates's publisher, Jackie Farber, "when Richard Yates tells me that he has lost fifteen pounds and looks like a concentration camp victim because he has had to survive the past few weeks on two eggs mixed in a glass of milk, and that he was going to have to go back in the hospital simply to have food to eat?" After the commercial failure of his last novel, *Cold Springs Harbor,* Yates moved to Los Angeles, where a former student, David Milch, offered him work writing treatments for television pilots. Though he affected to be grateful, Yates resented the flamboyant Milch, a successful television producer who apparently made little effort to conceal his role as patron and rescuer. For almost three years Yates failed to produce a salable treatment, and finally Milch ended their arrangement in 1989.

Yates's writing came to his rescue one last time. On the strength of his work in progress—a novel titled *Uncertain Times,* based on his experience as Robert Kennedy's speechwriter in 1963—his publisher offered Yates a two-book contract with an advance on signing and thirty-three equal monthly payments. The next year Yates accepted a one-year appointment to teach at the University of Alabama at Tuscaloosa. He tried heroically to attend to his teaching and get some writing done, but by then he had emphysema and could not breathe without an oxygen tank. He felt alert enough to write for only an hour or so a day, which was hardly enough for a man who typically took that long to adjust the wording of a single sentence. Finally, in November 1992, Yates traveled to the Birmingham VA hospital for minor surgery on a hernia, where he died of suffocation shortly after the operation.

"He drank too much, he smoked too much, he was accident-prone, he led an itinerant life, but as a writer he was all in place," said Seymour Lawrence, "He wrote the best dialogue since John O'Hara, and like O'Hara he was a master of realism, totally attuned to the nuances of American behavior and speech." This statement is an accurate assessment of Yates's achievement, and it is a pity that his excellent work is now in danger of being forgotten; one would like to remind the literate reading public that a body of superb books awaits their discovery, and that a singular man overcame drastic odds to write them. As Jayne Anne Phillips noted, perhaps a bit too hopefully, "Yates prevailed beyond his own lifetime, just as he intended. His work stands for him, essentially American, unassailable, triumphant."

Interviews:

DeWitt Henry and Geoffrey Clark, "An Interview with Richard Yates," *Ploughshares,* 1 (December 1972): 65–78;

Lee Grove, "Tales of Love, Talk of Lies," *Boston Magazine,* 73 (December 1981): 61–62, 64, 90, 92, 94, 96, 98, 100, 102.

References:

James Atlas, "A Sure Narrative Voice," *Atlantic Monthly,* 248 (November 1981): 84–85;

"The Books That Made Writers," *New York Times Book Review,* 25 November 1979, pp. 7, 80, 82, 84;

David Castronovo and Steven Goldleaf, *Richard Yates* (New York: Twayne, 1996);

Fred Chappell, "Revolutionary Road," in *Rediscoveries,* edited by David Madden (New York: Crown, 1971), pp. 245–255;

Andre Dubus, "A Salute to Mister Yates," *Black Warrior Review,* 15 (Spring 1989): 160–161;

Jerome Klinkowitz, "Richard Yates: The Wedding of Language and Incident," in his *The New American Novel of Manners: The Fiction of Richard Yates, Dan Wakefield, and Thomas McGuane* (Athens: University of Georgia Press, 1986), pp. 14–59;

Seymour Lawrence, "Richard Yates: A Requiem," *Poets and Writers Magazine* (September–October 1993): 12–17;

Ronald J. Nelson, "Richard Yates's Portrait of the Artist as a Young Thug: 'Doctor Jack-o'-lantern,'" *Studies in Short Fiction,* 32 (Winter 1995): 1–10;

Richard Yates: An American Writer (New York: Seymour Lawrence, 1993);

Elizabeth Venant, "A Fresh Twist in the Road: For Novelist Richard Yates, a Specialist in Grim Irony, Late Fame's a Wicked Return," *Los Angeles Times,* 9 July 1989, section 6, p. 1.

Papers:

The Mugar Memorial Library at Boston University has a collection of Richard Yates's papers.

John Yau
(5 June 1950 –   )

Garrett Caples
University of California at Berkeley

BOOKS: *Crossing Canal Street,* introduction by Robert Kelly (Binghamton, N.Y.: Bellevue, 1976);

Paul Kahn, John Yau, David Wilk, by Yau, Paul Kahn, and David Wilk (Carrboro, N.C.: Truck Press, 1976)–includes "Creation Story";

The Reading of an Ever-Changing Tale (Clinton, N.Y.: Nobodaddy, 1977);

Sometimes: Poems (New York: Sheep Meadow Press, 1979);

The Sleepless Night of Eugene Delacroix (Brooklyn, N.Y.: Release Press, 1980);

Broken Off by the Music (Providence, R.I.: Burning Deck, 1981);

Notarikon, by Yau and Jake Berthot (New York: Jordan Davies, 1981);

Corpse and Mirror (New York: Holt, Rinehart & Winston, 1983);

A. R. Penck (New York: Abrams, 1984);

Cities, photographs by Marsha Burns and Michael Burns, pastels by Randy Hayes (Seattle: Henry Art Gallery, University of Washington, 1987);

Poem Prints: Norman Bluhm and John Yau, by Yau and Norman Bluhm (New York: Cone Editions, 1987);

Radiant Silhouette: New and Selected Work, 1974–1988 (Santa Rosa, Cal.: Black Sparrow Press, 1989);

Big City Primer: Reading New York at the End of the Twentieth Century, photographs by Bill Barrette (New York: Timken, 1991);

Flee Advice, by Yau and Suzanne McClelland (Paris: Collectif Génération, 1991);

Giant Wall: Jürgen Partenheimer, Nineteen Etchings; John Yau, Poems and Prose, by Yau and Jürgen Partenheimer (San Francisco: Hine Editions, 1991);

Edificio Sayonara (Santa Rosa, Cal.: Black Sparrow Press, 1992);

In the Realm of Appearances: The Art of Andy Warhol (Hopewell, N.J.: Ecco, 1993);

Lowell Connector: Lines & Shots from Kerouac's Town, by Yau, Clark Coolidge, and Michael Gizzi; photographs by Barrette and Celia Coolidge (West Stockbridge, Mass.: Hard Press, 1993);

John Yau (photograph by Edith Massina)

Postcards from Trakl, poems by Yau, prints by Bill Jensen (West Islip, N.Y.: Universal Limited Art Editions, 1994);

Berlin Diptychon, photographs by Barrette (New York: Timken, 1995);

Hawaiian Cowboys (Santa Rosa, Cal.: Black Sparrow Press, 1995);

Piccadilly or Paradise: Poems, Drawings, by Yau and Trevor Winkfield (Santa Rosa, Cal.: Ferriss Editions, 1995);

Forbidden Entries (Santa Rosa, Cal.: Black Sparrow Press, 1996);

The United States of Jasper Johns (Cambridge, Mass.: Zoland, 1996);

My Symptoms (Santa Rosa, Cal.: Black Sparrow Press, 1998);

I Was a Poet in the House of Frankenstein, MEB/PNY Pamphlet Series, no. 36 (Brooklyn, N.Y.: MEB/PNY, 1999).

OTHER: John J. Moore, *John Moore: 30 March – 20 April, 1983, Hirschl and Adler Modern*, essay by Yau (New York: Hirschl & Adler Modern, 1983);

Robert Birmelin, *Harsh Truths*, with an essay by Yau (Toronto: Novak Graphics, 1985);

Fairfield Porter, *Fairfield Porter: The Collected Poems with Selected Drawings*, edited by Yau and David Kermani, introduction by John Ashbery (New York: Tibor de Nagy Editions / Promise of Learnings, 1985);

Miklos Pogany, *Miklos Pogany, Paintings and Works on Paper: The Phillips Collection, Washington, D.C., March 30 – May 26, 1985*, text by Yau (Washington, D.C.: The Collection, 1985);

Joan Thorne, *Joan Thorne: Recent Paintings, May 22 – June 21, 1985*, text by Yau (New York: Graham Modern, 1985);

Jane Freilicher, *Jane Freilicher: Paintings*, edited by Robert Doty, essays by Yau, John Ashbery, and Linda L. Cathcart (New York: Published for the Currier Gallery of Art by Taplinger, 1986);

Norbert Prangenberg, *Norbert Prangenberg*, introduction by Yau (New York: Hirschl & Adler Modern, 1986);

Guy Goodwin, *Guy Goodwin*, essay by Yau (Philadelphia: Dolan/Maxwell Gallery, 1986);

Norman Bluhm, *Norman Bluhm: Works on Paper 1947–1987: An Exhibition Organized by William Salzillo*, text by Yau (Clinton, N.Y.: Hamilton College, 1987);

"Roger Brown and Spectacle," in *Roger Brown*, introduction by Sidney Lawrence (New York: Braziller, in association with the Hirshhorn Museum & Sculpture Garden, 1987);

Forrest Bess, *Forrest Bess*, introduction by Yau (New York: Hirschl & Adler Modern, 1988);

Benjamin Péret, *Death to the Pigs and Other Writings*, translated by Rachel Stella, Yau, and others (Lincoln: University of Nebraska Press, 1988);

Martin Wong, *Martin Wong, November 5 – December 23, 1988: Curated by Jeanette Ingberman*, essay by Yau (New York: Exit Art, 1988);

"A Vision of the Unsayable," in *Brice Marden: Recent Paintings & Drawings* (London: Anthony d'Offay Gallery, 1988), pp. 5–17;

Air Lines: March 1 – April 16, 1989, Hillwood Art Gallery, Long Island University, C. W. Post Campus, Brookville,

New York: Curators, Carol Becker Davis, Judy Collischan Van Wagner, text by Yau (Brookville, N.Y.: Hillwood Art Gallery, Long Island University, 1989);

Four Painters: Michael Kessler, Archie Rand, Mark Schlesinger, Lynton Wells, curated, with an essay, by Yau (Flint, Mich.: Flint Institute of Arts, 1989);

Bruce Nauman, *Bruce Nauman, Prints 1970–89: A Catalogue Raisonne*, edited by Christopher Cordes and Debbie Taylor, essay by Yau (New York: Castelli Graphics / Lorence-Monk Gallery / Chicago: Donald Young Gallery, 1989);

Yuri Kuper, *Yuri Kuper: Recent Work, September 19 – October 14, 1989*, text by Yau (New York: Claude Bernard Gallery, 1989);

Joe Zucker, *Joe Zucker: September 28 – October 28, 1989, Hirschl & Adler Modern*, essay by Yau (New York: Hirschl & Adler Modern, 1989);

Jake Berthot, *Jake Berthot: Recent Work, 1988–89*, essay by Yau (New York: David McKee Gallery, 1989);

Dorothea Rockburne, *Dorothea Rockburne: New Work: Cut-Ins: December 2, 1989 to January 6, 1990*, introduction and text by Yau (New York: André Emmerich Gallery, 1989);

Neal Benezra, *Ed Paschke*, contributions by Yau, Dennis Adrian, and Carol Schreiber (New York: Hudson Hills Press / Chicago: Art Institute of Chicago, 1990);

Christopher Brown, *Christopher Brown, 1989–1990*, preface by Yau (San Francisco: Gallery Paule Anglim, 1990);

David Robilliard, *David Robilliard (1952–1988): September 13–October 6, 1990*, introduction by Yau (New York: Hirschl & Adler Modern, 1990);

Giulio Turcato, *Giulio Turcato*, text by Yau, Maurizio Calvesi, and Giovanna dalla Chiesa (Milan: Electa, 1990);

Anna Bialobroda, *Anna Bialobroda*, introduction by Yau (New York: Jason McCoy, 1991);

Dean Sobel, *Jackie Winsor*, essays by Yau and Peter Schjeldahl (Milwaukee, Wis.: Milwaukee Art Museum, 1991);

Bill Jacklin, *Bill Jacklin: Urban Portraits, New York 1986–1992*, text by Yau, David Elliott, and Nik Cohn (Oxford: Museum of Modern Art, 1992);

John Buck, *John Buck: Woodblock Prints*, essay by Yau (San Francisco: Fine Arts Museums of San Francisco, 1993);

Teresa Serrano, *Teresa Serrano: October–November 1994*, essay by Yau (New York: Annina Nosei Gallery, 1994);

Chuck Close, *Chuck Close: Recent Paintings*, essay by Yau (New York: PaceWildenstein, 1995);

Murder, Smart Art Press, 1, no. 4, curated by Yau (Santa Monica, Cal.: Smart Art Press, 1995);

Francisca Sutil, *Francisca Sutil: Cerebrations: October 18 – November 18, 1995,* text by Yau (New York: Nohra Haime Gallery, 1995);

Zucker, *Joe Zucker: A Decade of Paintings, 1983–1994: Track 16 Gallery and Mainspace, Bergamot Station Arts Center, February 3 – April 1, 1995,* edited by Yau (Santa Monica, Cal.: Smart Art Press, 1995);

In Pursuit of the Invisible: Selections from the Collection of Janice & Mickey Cartin: An Exhibition at the Loomis Chaffee School, edited by Yau, foreword by Mickey Cartin (West Stockbridge, Mass.: Hard Press, 1996);

Tom Levine, *Tom Levine: Paintings and Drawings, with an Essay by John Yau; Interview with Philip Yenawine; Galerie Wild, Frankfurt, February 16 – April 26, 1996; ID Galerie, Düsseldorf, April 19 – June 15, 1996,* essay by Yau (Frankfurt: Galerie Wild / Düsseldorf: ID Galerie, 1996);

Katharine Gates, ed., *Original Sin: The Visionary Art of Joe Coleman,* essays by Yau, Jim Jarmusch, and Harold Schechter (New York: HECK Editions, 1997);

An Anthology of Fetish Fiction, edited, with an introduction, by Yau (New York: Four Walls Eight Windows, 1998);

Anthony Sorce, *Anthony Sorce, Four Decades: Exhibition Curated by Stanley I. Grand,* essays by Yau and Stanley I. Grand (Wilkes-Barre, Pa.: Sordoni Art Gallery, Wilkes University, 1998);

Brenda Zlamany, *Brenda Zlamany,* essay by Yau (Los Angeles: Muse X Editions / New York: Stefan Stux Gallery, 1998);

Randy Hayes, *Randy Hayes, the World Reveiled,* text by Yau (Atlanta: Oglethorpe University Museum / Seattle: University of Washington Press, 1999);

Helmut M. Federle, *Helmut Federle,* text by Yau, Ferdinand Schmatz, and Elisabeth Samsonow (Cologne: König, 1999);

Laura Panno, *Tauriform,* text by Yau (Milan: Skira, 1999);

Sean Scully, *Sean Scully,* Reperes, no. 101, text by Yau (Paris: Galerie Lelong, 1999).

SELECTED PERIODICAL PUBLICATION–
UNCOLLECTED: "Neither Us Nor Them," *American Poetry Review,* 23 (March–April 1994): 45–54.

The fiction of Chinese American poet and art critic John Yau is best understood as the transformation of a personal dilemma into a formal imperative; that is, his experience of feeling outside both his own ancestry and the American culture into which he was born has led him to produce a body of work that resists easy categorization. As he told Brian Evenson in an interview in 1998, "my interest in hybridity, and what might come

after, may be due to that early realization that I wasn't quite this or that." Specifically, Yau's restlessness with fixed forms has resulted in his eroding the boundary between prose poem and short story, digging at it by turns from both sides until the distinction collapses. This attempt at fusion can be seen to its fullest extent in books such as *Forbidden Entries* (1996) and *My Symptoms* (1998). What these two books make evident, moreover, is the relation between his formal innovations and his second major thematic concern: the erotic. If the lack of an identifiable community is a problem that motivates his aesthetics, the erotic might be seen as a possible, if fitful or temporary, solution. Significantly, many of Yau's most successful unions of poem and narrative are love stories, though more often than not the depicted relationship fails. Yau is thus no sentimentalist but rather a dark optimist, his awareness of the obstacles to union being outweighed only by the insistence of his commitment to overcome them.

John Yau was born on 5 June 1950 in Lynn, Massachusetts, a dilapidated mill town. His father, Arthur Yau, had been born in New York City in 1921, son of an English mother and a Chinese father who had met in England during World War I. After briefly returning to England, the family moved to China, where Arthur Yau's parents eventually separated. Soon fending for himself, Arthur Yau survived by uncertain occupations, possibly as a gambler, prior to marrying Jane Chang and preceding her (as he was already a citizen) to the United States. Chang came from an influential Shanghai family; her father had been foreign ambassador to Belgium during the first Chinese Republic. Her family's objections to an interracial, economically insecure marriage hastened her own departure for the United States in 1949, setting sail on the last ship to leave Shanghai the evening it fell to the Communists. The mechanism for John Yau's cultural alienation was thus already in motion, as his half-white father had never assimilated to life in China, while his mother became an inadvertent exile, unable to return due to political sympathies. The couple reunited in Lynn, where Arthur Yau had secured a position as bookkeeper for a Chinese business, and shortly afterward their first son, John, was born. A second son, Arthur, followed ten years later, creating a peculiar distance even within Yau's sibling relationship.

By Yau's account, his father was a cruel, even sadistic parent. His mother, it appears, never quite adjusted to the change in status coming to America entailed, succumbing near the end of her life to what may have been bipolar episodes. Speaking the Mandarin of the educated classes and her local Shanghaiese, which isolated her from the predominantly Cantonese immigrant population, Jane Yau spent much of her time

Dust jacket for Yau's 1980 collection of stories that blend art and literary history with modern fictional events

reminiscing about a lost aristocracy. The linguistic isolation she felt replicated itself in the Yaus' family life, as she and her husband refused to teach their son Chinese, while continuing to speak it to each other. Growing up, Yau found himself at two removes from the Cantonese culture of Chinatown in Boston, even as he faced rejection from his white classmates in the U.S. schools he attended.

Following a move to Beacon Hill in Boston, the family once more relocated, to Brookline, where Yau attended junior high and high school. After two years at Boston University (1967–1969), he moved to Annandale-on-Hudson in Upstate New York, where he earned a B.A. degree at Bard College in 1972. At Bard he studied under Robert Kelly, who later wrote the introduction to Yau's first chapbook. During his junior year, Yau suffered severe injuries in a car accident after a night of bar hopping, as he related in 1990 to Edward Halsey Foster: "I convinced a man who had never driven a car

in his life but who was graduating the next day that he should have the pleasure of driving back onto the campus. . . . we hit the tree going about sixty or seventy miles an hour, and I went through the windshield and ended up under the car somehow." The sort of dark humor characterizing this account is best understood in light of the fact that Yau had just lost his deferment from military service and felt certain that he was about to be drafted and sent to Vietnam. In other words, the abandon he exhibited at this time in his life was not simply a matter of personal demons but also of his reaction to the paradox of facing military duty against a country whose inhabitants, in the eyes of white Americans, were virtually indistinguishable from himself. Whatever provoked the behavior that lead to the accident, the ensuing eight-month hospitalization, in traction, was clearly pivotal and traumatic.

By 1975 Yau had moved to New York City—where he has lived ever since—in order to study with John Ashbery at Brooklyn College. Ashbery was a significant influence on Yau, in terms of helping Yau decide to make his living by freelance art criticism and to find ways of incorporating identity into poetry while avoiding straight autobiography. While both poets are associated with the New York School inaugurated by Ashbery—along with Frank O'Hara, Barbara Guest, James Schuyler, Kenneth Koch, and, in fiction, Harry Mathews—neither author writes the sort of anecdotal poem usually but perhaps inaccurately associated with these poets. The resemblance of Yau's poetry to that of Ashbery is largely conceptual—both poets distrust the notion of a stable speaker or situation, for example—rather than stylistic; Yau eschews the loose rambling perfected by his teacher in favor of more overtly wrought verbal objects. In terms of his stories, however, the more direct influence on Yau is neither Ashbery nor Kelly (both of whom have written fiction) but rather Robert Creeley, from whom he took a summer class at Harvard University in 1972. Significantly, that year Creeley's *A Day Book* was published; Yau's fiction takes as its starting point this hybrid work of diaristic poetic prose rather than Creeley's more conventionally classifiable novels and stories.

While pursuing his M.F.A. degree under Ashbery, Yau published two chapbooks, *Crossing Canal Street* (1976) and *The Reading of an Ever-Changing Tale* (1977). Though none of the earlier booklet has ever been republished, most of the poems from the later one appear as the opening section of Yau's first full book, *Sometimes: Poems* (1979). The second section of *Sometimes*, "Marco Polo," includes Yau's first prose poems. While the pieces in this section are too fragmentary to be called short stories as such, "Marco Polo" contains several seeds of Yau's later fiction. The title of the section, ostensibly motivated by the travel depictions uniting these poems, also serves to announce what will be a recurring theme in Yau's subsequent prose, the appropriation of "the raw materials, goods, and culture of the *Other*" by the West, as he later termed it in his uncollected article "Neither Us Nor Them" (1994). While he acknowledged to Foster, in their 1990 interview, the importance of encountering Ezra Pound's translations of T'ang Dynasty poems in *Cathay* (1915)—they conveyed to him something "about being Chinese" at time when "There were no models [for Chinese authorship] among American poets"—in his 1994 article he criticizes the persistent attraction contemporary poets and critics have for Pound's paternalist appropriation.

Yau's response to such imperialism has largely consisted of a reappropriation of cultural material; in other words, he adapts the personae of various perpetrators and victims of imperialism to his own ends. Thus, the title piece of "Marco Polo" finds the returned adventurer hospitalized by an unknown speaker for his failure to decontextualize the intellectual booty of his voyage: "He claims he does not understand how windows can exist apart from their settings; or that buildings (this hospital, for example) are incidental to the narrative unfolding around them. It is necessary that I persuade him of the possibility. For aside from what could be brought back as cargo, he carried everything else in his mind." Clearly the speaker is bemused by Polo's perceived reluctance to support "the imperialistic notion that the work of other individuals, countries, and cultures belongs to whoever takes it," as Yau put it in "Neither Us Nor Them," to the point where such refusal is perceived as an illness. Other poems in "Marco Polo" echo the exploration in the title piece of the relationship between cultural materials and the contexts from which they are drawn. In "Nantucket," for example, a man finds the skeleton of a puppy abandoned in a bag on the side of the road and takes it home with him, seeing in it "the perfect memento of this island," established in the course of the bloody whaling industry of New England. "El Dorado" details a journey taken by unnamed "travelers" following a guidebook that seemingly predicts their every move. As they near their destination, however, their comfortable sense of having already digested the landscape begins to fade; "the sky jumps out of focus. . . . Memory was beginning to dwindle" as they lose mastery over a scene of proliferating and unexpected detail. In "The Motel Owner and His Wife," Yau gives the first indication of the relation of the erotic to the issue of identity in a vignette about Harold and Edith, proprietors of the Sun & Surf Motel. Significantly, the story opens with "It began on Columbus Day," joining this reminder of imperialism to this end-of-the-season opportunity the

couple have to vacation from their own lives. Harold leaves and returns as "Jonathan"; Edith dons a yellow gown abandoned by a guest, and the two enter one of the motel rooms, haunted by the lingering aura of countless other guests. In the end, however, Yau undercuts the couple's play, the scene dissolving not into sexual fantasy but, rather, indecision. "Now all that was needed was a story," as if to suggest a difference between adopting the trappings of another and actually inhabiting an identity toward some productive end.

While the prose poems of *Sometimes* remain poems, Yau's next book shows him already moving beyond the bounds of genre. *The Sleepless Night of Eugene Delacroix* (1980) might be considered the beginning of Yau's mature work, combining his increasing command of lyricism with his investigations into narrative and the history of art and literature. The French painter Eugène Delacroix, the French symbolist poet Stéphane Mallarmé ("The Clay Nursing Home"), and the nineteenth-century American painter Thomas Cole ("The Power of Suggestion") all appear, while a pair of characters named Siegfried and Sassoon (an allusion to the British World War I poet Siegfried Sassoon) drive cross-country to New York, initiating a series of oblique encounters in "A Different Prince." Most of these stories tie historical fact into modern fictional events, though the title story depicts the hypothetical sleepless night in question. In general, however, the art or artist in question becomes a vehicle for the narrator's or character's self-exploration, a technique Yau continued to refine in the years to come, although mainly in verse—for example, "Self-Portrait with Max Beckmann" in *Berlin Diptychon* (1995) and "Jack's Final Wire" in the tribute to Jack Kerouac on which Yau collaborated, *Lowell Connector: Lines & Shots from Kerouac's Town* (1993).

The opening story of *The Sleepless Night of Eugene Delacroix,* "Postcards from Nebraska," introduces a favorite device of Yau's, subsequently employed in both short stories and prose poems: the development of a work through a series of discreet paragraphs. One might view this device as a poet's solution to the problem of how to present fictional speakers or situations without linear narrative, though as likely as not Yau imported the idea from his study of painting (Jasper Johns and Andy Warhol, on each of whom Yau has written a monograph, tend to compose in series).

"Postcards from Nebraska" takes its title as a metaphor for its structure, each paragraph offering a brief facet of its writer's life, inconclusive in itself but accumulating into some sense of a particular person: "How do I get off on these trivial subjects? Only you are subject to them. Everyone else gets the major points in my life. You get the obscure subdivisions of subdivisions of minor points derived from other minor points which result from the major points everyone else knows about." This first postcard indicates the sensibility of the piece, implying a sense of intimacy based not on the "significant" events of life but rather on the seemingly incidental ones. Details accrue over the course of the series until the reader pieces together, if not a story, then at least a speaker (apparently a student of nutritional science) and a generalized situation (discontent with the Nebraskan scene of exile). Only in the second-to-last paragraph, however, does the reader learn the narrator is female, as Yau toys with assumptions about the relationship between author and narrator: "He kept insisting that I was the 'right girl.' . . . He then asked if I weren't the woman who ran every morning in mauve gym shorts. I couldn't deny that." Suddenly the very idea that the reader knows this speaker at all is called into question. In other words, these "postcards" may not actually be addressed to the reader but rather to some implied, invisible narrator, displaying previously-received correspondence. "Postcards from Nebraska" thus extends the themes of appropriation introduced in "Marco Polo" beyond the imperialist scenario to a general problem of human relations; how much can be learned about a person simply from a written record? How much shared context is needed in order to have an undistorted acquaintance with someone? The first "postcard" of the series invokes a recipient on a sufficiently undistorted level of intimacy even as it underscores the lack of identity between this fictional addressee and the literal reader of the text.

Aside from the technical innovation of discreet, yet cumulative paragraphs—further explored in "The Noise of Life," "The Discovery of Honey," and others—the expansion of the themes of "Marco Polo" evident in "Postcards from Nebraska" links several seemingly disparate stories in *The Sleepless Night of Eugene Delacroix*. The title piece might be considered Yau's own attempt at a reconstruction based on text, as a few suggestive details from Delacroix's journal entice the author to imagine his subject's interior, while "The Abandoned Observatory" follows a man who, unlike the travelers of "El Dorado," is only distanced from the civilization of his inquiry by textual and verbal accounts, until he comes to inhabit the space its people once did. But the most successful stories in *The Sleepless Night of Eugene Delacroix* are a suite of semi-autobiographical pieces—"Electric Drills," "The Telephone Call," and "Toy Trucks and Fried Rice"—in which Yau explores these issues from the other side, from the position of one whose social circumstances alienate him from self-knowledge.

This alienation is most explicitly formulated in "Toy Trucks and Fried Rice," which uses the memory of a Chinese Benevolent Association Christmas party to detail Yau's childhood experience of his ethnicity:

> He had been told ever since he could remember that he was Chinese. He had never lived in Chinatown and he couldn't speak Chinese. It was more complicated than that. His mother was from Shanghai and spoke the dialect common to that area. The people at the party . . . spoke Cantonese. . . . His mother reminded him that his grandfather was taller than anyone in this room, as were most people from Shanghai. His mother, however, was only a little over five feet tall, and in this way was indistinguishable from most of the women in the room.

Identity here only amounts to divisions instead of solidarity for a child already too aware of his difference from mainstream America. His mother's snobbery only proliferates the confusion, as her words clash with the visual information he receives. The story ends on no definitive note, refusing resolution to an unresolvable situation. The reader sees, however, some of the motives behind Yau's refusal, discussed during his interview with Evenson, to embrace the term "multiculturalism," since the traditional categories by which it aligns groups of people are an insufficient guarantee of community.

"Electric Drills" more or less offers its own summary: "I had been thinking of electric drills, and the part they played in my life—both in the psychological development and in the physical reconstruction of my body." The story juxtaposes two scenes eighteen years apart: the narrator's three-year-old self watching his father drill holes in a door "to scare me when I misbehaved" and his older self in a hospital after an automobile accident, seeing a doctor drill through his left leg. As the account begins, the narrator admits, "I used to have a fear of tools, largely because of my father," going on to describe the instruments as "red and shiny like a child's fire truck." The detail of color functions symbolically here, both in the sinister replacement of a toy appropriate to a three-year-old with an object of terror and in the stoplight effect his father's behavior has on part of his psychological development. In the hospital, "The drill was green, like the living room of [his parents'] apartment on Beacon Hill," so that while it recalls the scene of his psychological block, it also allows him to move on from it. Essentially the trauma is resolved through irony, the instrument of implied physical torture becoming the mechanism for bodily reconstruction. At the end, the narrator provides an incidental detail about bookshelves and furniture he later built "all with a gray electric drill," as if to suggest that the once-charged object, now drained of color, has returned to a neutral realm of things.

*Dust jacket for Yau's 1995 collection of stories, focusing mainly on the conflicted ethnic
identities of Asian American characters*

"Electric Drills" also offers examples of Yau's use of extended conceits: "For most of the time, when I was under morphine, I felt like America while a lot of riots were taking place in Canada. I knew it was going on, but I didn't particularly care." To a certain degree Yau employs such locutions as a vehicle for black humor, a way of distancing himself from the events he tells and thus avoiding self-pity or self-aggrandizement. Such a tone of half-amused self-observation is also important to "The Telephone Call," which focuses more closely on the grim details of his hospitalization, including the death of a roommate. By the time of *My Symptoms,* however, Yau's conceit-making became a crucial means of narrative advancement. Indeed, a story in that book, "Butcher, Baker, or Candlestick Maker"–in which a woman confesses her rationale for wanting to sleep with a fireman–could be said to be generated largely by such elaboration of metaphor.

Although, following *The Sleepless Night of Eugene Delacroix,* Yau did not publish another book of fictional prose until 1995, the ensuing years were by no means idle. During this time he made his reputation as an art critic, through articles and catalogues, as well as important monographs such as *In the Realm of Appearances: The Art of Andy Warhol* (1993). He also received several appointments teaching art and writing at various uni-

versities. Creatively, his chief occupation was poetry. After publishing *The Sleepless Night of Eugene Delacroix,* Yau collaborated with the artist Jake Berthot on *Notarikon* (1981), with poems by Yau and drawings by Berthot, followed by a collection of verse, *Broken Off By The Music* (1981). Yau's next book, *Corpse And Mirror,* was selected by Ashbery for the National Poetry Series and published by the firm of Holt, Rinehart, and Winston in 1983. The title sequence of prose poems–named after a series of Jasper Johns paintings–is crucial to the development of Yau's fiction, for here he begins to combine a denser surface texture with a more lyrical prose style of the type he observed in Creeley's work. *Cities,* with poems by Yau, photographs by Marsha Burns and Michael Burns, and pastels by Randy Hayes, was published in 1987. Another collaborative work was published that same year, *Poem Prints: Norman Bluhm and John Yau,* with poems by Yau and prints by Norman Bluhm. Subsequent volumes include *Radiant Silhouette: New and Selected Work, 1974–1988* (1989) and *Edificio Sayonara* (1992), both published by Black Sparrow Press, as well as *Big City Primer: Reading New York at the End of the Twentieth Century* (1991), a collaboration with sculptor and photographer Bill Barrette, published by Timken. Other collaborative works published in this period are *Flee Advice,* a limited edition book with black acrylic paintings by Suzanne McClelland and a poem by Yau, and another limited edition work, *Giant Wall: Jürgen Partenheimer, Nineteen Etchings; John Yau, Poems and Prose,* both published in 1991. During this period Yau also underwent a variety of significant personal events, some of which provide material for his later fiction. These include a seven-year relationship, beginning in 1980, with Rachel Stella—daughter of painter Frank Stella and art historian Barbara Rose—with whom he collaborated on several translations of the French surrealist Benjamin Péret; a brief marriage, from 1988 to 1990, to the painter Jane Hammond; the death of his mother in 1990, followed by that of his father the following year; and the beginning in 1992 of a relationship with the painter Jenny Scobel.

Published in 1993, *Lowell Connector,* a Kerouac tribute volume, includes poetry by Yau, Clark Coolidge, and Michael Gizzi, and photographs by Barrette and Celia Coolidge. *Postcards from Trakl,* a collaboration with the artist Bill Jensen, was published by Universal Limited Art Editions the following year, with poems by Yau and prints by Jensen. *Berlin Diptychon,* with poetry by Yau and photographs by Barrette, was published by Timken in 1995. Another collaboration, *Piccadilly or Paradise: Poems, Drawings,* with poems by Yau and drawings by Trevor Winkfield, was published by Ferriss Editions that same year.

Hawaiian Cowboys (1995) marked Yau's return to fiction writing and is, structurally, his only conventional short-story collection. In it he continues to explore issues of identity and unity, recontextualizing previously recorded incidents by situating them against new events. A cabdriver's string of insults over the narrator's inability to speak Chinese triggers a series of memories in "How to Become Chinese," beginning with the details of his father's half-English ancestry and his mother's Shanghaiese disdain for the Cantonese living in the United Sates. Blending fictional events with autobiographical details, Yau notes his mother's penchant for division constantly replaying itself as the narrator recalls: being mistaken for Japanese and spat at by a Chinese teenager; riding with a Pakistani cabdriver who is exasperated by the constant assumption he is an "Arab"; encountering a young Iranian woman and her father who pretend to be Iraqi during the 1980s. The memory that ultimately comes to dominate the story, however, concerns his former wife's dream that she became Chinese, which she believes indicates that the couple has grown close. Naturally, the narrator interprets the dream differently, given that the term "Chinese" has provided him with no stable sense of an identity; he feels distanced from his Connecticut Yankee wife as she exoticizes his ethnicity. She persists in dwelling on her dream until the narrator asks, bitingly,

whether she "made a mistake" and was "turning Japanese or Korean." This moment marks a downward turn in the relationship and, in the wake of their divorce, he doubts she still dwells on this fantasy.

"Topless" revisits Yau's car accident in the memory of a narrator who meets and begins a liaison with a dancer, Serena, whom he had briefly encountered during his hospitalization. Here the accident is explicitly linked to the possibility of being drafted into a war in which he feels community with neither side. His present bond with Serena, however, seems based on appreciation of her professional hybridity: she dances both in topless bars and at museums, while feeling connected to neither audience the locales imply. As she does with the outfits she wrests from her elegantly mismatched wardrobe, Serena attempts to fashion a coherent life, one which temporarily intersects with the narrator's own. For a time their early morning assignations provide a bond between them, but as the affair becomes mere routine, it peters out. Despite the refuge the erotic offers, neither character can relinquish or even acknowledge the extent of their self-protective solitude.

Like "Topless," "A Little Memento from the Boys" begins at Mike's Last Dive, a bar that, along with The Red Star, The Aerodrome, and The Doll Pit, furnishes the Manhattan backdrop for the core stories of *Hawaiian Cowboys.* While the setting and narrative voice suggest that the narrator of these and other stories may be the same person, Yau never makes the narrator's identity explicit, seeding his texts with similar but slightly inconsistent details. This vagueness seems deliberate, as Yau is less interested in creating an autobiographical character than he is in observing situations and possible responses to them. For all its vividness, Yau's Manhattan is a vast and anonymous place, where strangers achieve only passing union. Against this backdrop, "A Little Memento from the Boys" chronicles the juvenile high jinks of three Asians of mixed ancestry, who, between meditations on their common fate and nights of serious drinking, find employment refinishing apartments for the Yuppie invaders they despise. In the course of their work they meet Lila, who hires them for ten days while she flies to Los Angeles for business. As they work, they discover her gigantic dildo and her diary recounting her sexual fantasies. At the literal climax of the story, the three men use Lila's camera to take pictures of themselves masturbating into the last can of white paint, with which they add a final coat to her walls. There is no simple meaning to this act. Seemingly aggressive, it nonetheless indicates some fellow feeling; the "boys" find a reflection of their own estrangement in the isolated self-sufficiency of Lila's eroticism.

In the title story, a couple similar to, but not quite identifiable with, the one in "How to Become Chinese," vacation at a friend's house on the island of Hawaii. In a way "Hawaiian Cowboys" reverses the scenario of "How to Become Chinese," in that the couple's relationship deteriorates as the narrator cannot convey to his indifferent wife, Janet, the community he feels with the hybrid population of the island. The story opens with Janet's incomprehension over her husband's joy at being mistaken for an islander. The narrator finds comfort on this island where "all the creatures . . . came from somewhere else." On coming across a ranch town, the couple enters a diner in which the narrator is confronted with a scene that, for him, borders on surreality: "Most of the men are dressed like cowboys, and almost all of them are Asian or Hawaiian. Chinese, Japanese, Filipino, Polynesian, and Samoan. . . . I remember a photograph of me when I was a child, dressed up like Hopalong Cassidy, and the Davy Crockett hat I begged my mother to buy me for Christmas. This was before I realized I could never be Wyatt Earp, Jesse James, or Daniel Boone." The narrator here experiences a reversal of his estrangement from his 1950s American childhood by finding a context in which a Chinese cowboy suddenly makes sense. Unfortunately, he learns in Janet's inability to share his enthusiasm that they "have become strangers." As in "A Little Memento from the Boys," the narrator has yet to find the right balance in which his desire for community and for erotic union can comfortably coexist.

In *Hawaiian Cowboys* Yau shows further evidence of his resistance to simple narrative sequence. His conceit-making grows increasingly elaborate, one metaphor giving way to yet another, as in "A Little Memento from the Boys": "Virgo's glad he finally has friends who will knowingly roll each morsel and crumb of his offerings around on their tongues, lick their lips, and hoot and howl for more. We are ravenous dogs who gather in this noisy room each night, and tell more tales. No meat is too tough for us to tear from the bone. We're coyotes who've wandered into a ghost town." He goes beyond metaphor, however, in "Family Album," in which a play on words seemingly becomes the narrative motivation: "I like to watch a woman undress, while my brother likes to wear women's dresses." This tale, of a writer and his transvestite sibling, "is not something I made up, it is someone he makes up, someone in make-up." Yau here takes another step toward the fusion between prose poem and story, finding ways in which the narrative and its verbal surface become one. Accordingly, his next book, *Forbidden Entries*, explores this possibility through prose poems increasingly involved with his overall fictional project.

Aside from the prose-verse hybrid "Dream Hospital," *Forbidden Entries* comprises two major prose series: a group of five poems about character actor Peter Lorre and the seven-part title sequence. While neither are narratives per se, Yau experiments with maintaining an overall continuity even as he stresses the immediate surface of his prose. The Lorre poems, collected in a section called "Hollywood Asians" along with verses in his ongoing "Ghenghis Chan: Private Eye" series, constitute Yau's postmodernist inversion of Pound's poetics, one he has continued in a set of pieces about Boris Karloff, one of which was published as *I Was a Poet in the House of Frankenstein* (1999). Dipping into so-called low culture—the movies—Yau investigates the racial politics of the Golden Age of Hollywood, in which physically "flawed" white actors were assigned the roles of Asians and other ethnic characters. Lorre played Japanese detective Mr. Moto in a series of motion pictures based on John P. Marquand novels, while Karloff portrayed James Lee Wong, a Charlie Chan imitation, in another series. Surely it is no coincidence that the same actors often played "monstrous" parts: Karloff literally in dozens of Universal Pictures horror movies; Lorre figuratively, in such roles as the psychopathic child-killer in Fritz Lang's *M* (1931) and as the villainous Joel Cairo in *The Maltese Falcon* (1941), a character whose evident homosexuality was seen by contemporary audiences as perverse and unnatural. The Lorre prose poems are all monologues from the actor's point of view, presenting abstract but evocative situations in which the actor alternately revels and grovels: "I pull my kimono smoking gown tighter. . . . I was sure white oxen would come and break the screen separating me from the ones slumped in their plush velvet seats. . . . I was comic relief . . . You knew me by the slickness of my hair, the shriveled peanut I carried between my manicured teeth." In this piece, the provocatively titled "Peter Lorre Dreams He Is the Third Reincarnation of a Geisha," the scenario wavers dreamlike between the elaborately made-up, near-prostitute roles of actor and geisha. Through this analogy Lorre meditates on his ambiguous position as a Hollywood villain, in which commercial success depends on a large degree of self-abasement, a willingness to reinforce the intolerance of the U.S. public by fulfilling its ideas of perversion. Such a dilemma extends to minority actors themselves, in that their participation in moviemaking was (and often still is) dependent on their ability to portray stereotypes. In this sense the Lorre poems might be linked to another of Yau's ongoing critical projects, research into the life and work of Anna May Wong, the first Asian American movie star, whose career was continually beset by such difficulties.

Cover for Yau's 1998 collection of prose poems dealing with eroticism and questions of identity

While never offering anything like a straightforward narrative, the title sequence of *Forbidden Entries* seems to detail a disintegrating affair in a series of shifting scenes revolving around "I," "she," and "he." Significantly, the year the book was published–1996–also marked the stormy split between Yau and Scobel. Yau subsequently married the painter Eve Aschheim in 1997. The title is a triple pun, at once suggesting literal penetrating, figurative opening of usually closed areas of the psyche, and, of course, recording both sorts of information on paper. The role of narrator alternates among the three characters, though it is not always clear who is speaking. Freed from the constraint of literal narrative, Yau generates his text from the words themselves, through puns or more abstract, rhymed substitutions. "A fling sized bed" opens the second entry, suggestive of the uses to which it will be put. In the third, "Her hands divide the room into the potions he would have to drain if he was to levitate his shadow above her welcome. . . . The audience shifts in their

seats, unable to burn down the flights glancing at them from above their beds." As in James Joyce's *Finnegans Wake* (1939), the substitutions are built on recognizable phrases whose sense is suggested even as a new implication is grafted on it. While they yield no literal sense, the substitutions evoke a turbulent emotional register through associations with the resulting phrases ("burn down" replacing "turn down," for instance). Perhaps unsurprisingly, given the emphasis on suspicion, the technique here recalls the moody atmospherics of classic detective fiction, another so-called low genre that Yau admires.

In *My Symptoms,* published in 1998 by Black Sparrow Press, Yau most successfully achieves the integration between short story and prose poem toward which his fiction has always tended. The stories are, for the most part, shorter and tighter than those of *Hawaiian Cowboys;* indeed, of the thirty-five pieces in *My Symptoms,* only "Treasure Hunt," a quasi–detective story in which the narrator details his girlfriend's alleged attempt to kill him, would fit comfortably in the previous collection. Broadly speaking, the first section of the book concentrates on the erotic while the last returns to Yau's continuing exploration of identity. The thematic innovation of the first section resides in his increased use of female narrators who have their own highly particular erotic agendas. In "What She Told Him While They Pretended to Watch TV," for example, the narrator slides back and forth between the circumstances of two unsatisfying relationships. The distance provided by this nonautobiographical female persona allows Yau not only to examine different facets of male sexual betrayal in a way that would be difficult in a first-person male voice, but also seems to free him for even greater flights of invention in his conceits: a metaphor of the narrator's comparing herself to an airport somehow dissolves into a description of herself as a delicious but uneaten cake. However, it is the four intervening sections– "Lives of the Artists," "Lives of the Artists II," "Snow," and "Lives of the Poets"–that constitute the major formal innovation in the book. These sections are composed of between five and twenty-five prose paragraphs, each of which, taken separately, might be a freestanding prose poem but which, taken together, amount to a kind of narrative about two lovers. "Lives of the Artists," for example, details a disintegrating relationship over the course of eleven prose poems linked by recurring thematic increments–fish, water, hands, photographs, smells, closets–even as it displays the resistance of life to art, despite the persistent desire to discern such neat patterns. Is the female protagonist's obsessive painting of a fish related to a crass remark someone made about her genitalia? Is another woman's boyfriend good with his hands in bed because he plays piano? The answer to these questions is, inevitably, no, but the impulse toward artifice remains, and even photographs do not provide the characters with accurate information. As the relationship ends, the distortions of memory come to seem as inevitable as other artistic falsifications: "He knew that years from now he would remember this conversation but not what she smelled like. Or if she smelled like anything at all."

This issue of distortion is picked up in the last section of the book, in "The Story They Told Themselves," in which a vaguely identified "tribe" reinterprets material from a forgotten stage of its culture according to its present needs. Yau suggests a potentially liberating aspect of such distortion, as the tribe creates myths about itself useful to its continued existence. It is important to distinguish this self-mythologizing from the Poundian appropriation of cultural materials; though both are equally misleading—the tribe, for example, interprets a drawing of a man in a kayak as "a sled without runners or dogs"—the project of rereading one's own culture as a means of perpetuating it is quite different from simply absorbing the culture of another for one's own ideological justification. Hence, Yau's reappropriation of Hollywood Asia is an effort to determine his own place as an Asian in the United States. Yet, Yau maintains caution against mythologizing his own personal experiences. After returning once more to childhood materials—in "Incident," "Author as Paperweight," and others—Yau closes *My Symptoms* with an assessment of his own ongoing obsession with identity, "The Subject of the Story."

In "The Subject of the Story," Yau lays out an aesthetics that is in fact an ethics, as he contemplates the "difference between a story and the events upon which a story is built." In a distanced, third-person voice, he describes the attempt of another "he" to once more reiterate the facts in the case of his parents, of their coming to the United States, and of the childhood he endured as a result. The facts themselves seem paltry, or insufficient to amount to the story of a particular subject. By continually posing the question—what is the subject of a story?—Yau forces a realization of the gap between "subject" as a relatable event and as an actual person, and in so doing insists not on the identity but the difference between himself and the often first-person, autobiographical material he uses. He is aware of the constitutive aspect of language, but rather than assume it neutralizes an event's resistance to telling, he shows how the subtle distinctions between expressions constitute distinct events: "It was where his father began punishing him. Or, it is where

he first remembers his father punishing him. Or, it is where his father's punishments first came memorable." He also expresses the implicit distrust of event that has characterized his fiction since "Postcards from Nebraska." Wondering "whether or not this story"—the one his parents told him about themselves or the one he is telling now?—"is built upon an event," he suggests "a different question: What were the circumstances in which they told him their stories? Aren't the circumstances in which they spoke just as important as what they said?" Such an attitude not only explains the more situational, less-narrative approach of the later work, but also offers a rationale that is ultimately a defense of all otherness, racial or sexual. In other words, his stories in part seek to fill out the contexts of the information they contain: in "Tree Planting Ceremony" a woman's desire is to penetrate herself in front of her boyfriend with "a large polished acorn attached to a long yellow handle"; in "Come On" another woman wants to be hit during intercourse; and in "No More Monkey Business" one sibling is an emergency-room nurse while another is a maker of pornographic movies. The facts of any story might seem grotesque to someone whose view is distorted by lack of context.

But clearly, as Yau indicates both in "The Subject of the Story" and in the use of his own biographical facts, there are circumstances to every story that do not merely justify or excuse a protagonist's actions. Yau refuses to apologize for his characters' actions, however violent or perverse they may seem.

Interviews:

Edward Halsey Foster, "An Interview with John Yau," *Talisman*, 5 (Fall 1990): 31–50;

Brian Evenson, "Yau's Symptoms: A Conversation with John Yau," *Rain Taxi*, 3, no. 3 (1998): 16–18.

Bibliography:

"John Yau: A Selected Bibliography," *Talisman*, 5 (Fall 1990): 147–151.

References:

Edward Halsey Foster, ed., "A Symposium on John Yau: Commentary and Criticism," *Talisman*, 5 (Fall 1990): 113–134;

Patricia Wald, "'Chaos Goes Uncourted': John Yau's Dis(-)Orienting Poetics," in *Cohesion and Dissent in America*, edited by Carol Colatrella and Joseph Alkana (Albany: State University of New York Press, 1994), pp. 133–158.

Books for Further Reading

Allen, Frederick Lewis. *The Big Change: America Transforms Itself, 1900–1950*. New York: Harper, 1952.

Allen, Walter. *The Short Story in English*. Oxford: Clarendon Press / New York: Oxford University Press, 1981.

Aycock, Wendell M., ed. *The Teller and the Tale: Aspects of the Short Story*. Lubbock: Texas Tech University Press, 1982.

Barthes, Roland. *S/Z*, translated by Richard Miller. New York: Hill & Wang, 1974.

Bates, H. E. *The Modern Short Story: A Critical Survey*. Boston: The Writer, 1972.

Bayley, John. *The Short Story: Henry James to Elizabeth Bowen*. New York: St. Martin's Press, 1988.

Beachcroft, T. O. *The Modest Art: A Survey of the Short Story in English*. London & New York: Oxford University Press, 1968.

Boland, John. *Short Story Technique*. Crowborough, U.K.: Forest House Books, 1973.

Bonheim, Helmut. *The Narrative Modes: Techniques of the Short Story*. Cambridge, U.K.: D. S. Brewer, 1982.

Bruck, Peter, ed. *The Black American Short Story in the 20th Century: A Collection of Critical Essays*. Amsterdam: Grüner, 1977.

Chatman, Seymour. *Story and Discourse: Narrative Structure in Fiction and Film*. Ithaca, N.Y.: Cornell University Press, 1978.

Current-Garcia, Eugene, and Walton R. Patrick, eds. *What Is the Short Story?* Glenview, Ill.: Scott, Foresman, 1974.

Dijk, Teun A. van. *Macrostructures: An Interdisciplinary Study of Global Structures in Discourse, Interaction, and Cognition*. Hillsdale, N.J.: L. Erlbaum Associates, 1980.

Eikhenbaum, B. M. *O. Henry and the Theory of the Short Story,* translated by I. R. Titunik. Ann Arbor: University of Michigan Department of Slavic Languages and Literatures, 1968.

Friedman, Norman. *Form and Meaning in Fiction*. Athens: University of Georgia Press, 1975.

Gerlach, John. *Toward the End: Closure and Structure in the American Short Story*. University: University of Alabama Press, 1985.

Hanson, Clare. *Short Stories and Short Fictions, 1880–1980*. New York: St. Martin's Press, 1985.

Hendin, Josephine. *Vulnerable People: A View of American Fiction Since 1945*. New York & London: Oxford University Press, 1978.

Hooper, Brad. *Short-Story Writers and Their Work: A Guide to the Best*. Chicago: American Library Association, 1988.

Ingram, Forrest L. *Representative Short-Story Cycles of the Twentieth Century: Studies in a Literary Genre.* The Hague: Mouton, 1971.

Jameson, Frederic. *The Prison-House of Language: A Critical Account of Structuralism and Russian Formalism.* Princeton: Princeton University Press, 1972.

Kenner, Hugh. *A Homemade World: The American Modernist Writers.* New York: Knopf, 1974.

Klinkowitz, Jerome. *The Practice of Fiction in America: Writers from Hawthorne to the Present.* Ames: Iowa State University Press, 1980.

Klinkowitz. *The Self-Apparent Word: Fiction as Language/Language as Fiction.* Carbondale: Southern Illinois University Press, 1984.

Klinkowitz. *Structuring the Void: The Struggle for Subject in Contemporary American Fiction.* Durham, N.C.: Duke University Press, 1992.

Leitch, Thomas M. *What Stories Are: Narrative Theory and Interpretation.* University Park: Pennsylvania State University Press, 1986.

Levin, Gerald, ed. *The Short Story: An Inductive Approach.* New York: Harcourt, Brace & World, 1967.

Lohafer, Susan. *Coming to Terms with the Short Story.* Baton Rouge: Louisiana State University Press, 1983.

Lohafer and Jo Ellyn Clarey, eds. *Short Story Theory at a Crossroads.* Baton Rouge: Louisiana State University Press, 1989.

Magill, Frank N., ed. *Critical Survey of Short Fiction,* 7 volumes. Pasadena: Salem, 1993.

Mann, Susan Garland. *The Short-Story Cycle: A Genre Companion and Reference Guide.* New York: Greenwood Press, 1989.

May, Charles E. *The Short Story: The Reality of Artifice.* New York: Twayne, 1995.

May, ed. *Fiction's Many Worlds.* Lexington, Mass.: D. C. Heath, 1993.

May, ed. *The New Short Story Theories.* Athens: Ohio University Press, 1994.

May, ed. *Short Story Theories.* Athens: Ohio University Press, 1976.

O'Connor, Frank. *The Lonely Voice: A Study of the Short Story.* Cleveland: World, 1963.

O'Faolain, Sean. *The Short Story.* New York: Devin-Adair, 1951.

Peden, William. *The American Short Story: Continuity and Change, 1940–1975.* Boston: Houghton Mifflin, 1975.

Prince, Gerald. *A Grammar of Stories: An Introduction.* The Hague: Mouton, 1973.

Prince. *Narratology: The Form and Functioning of Narrative.* New York: Mouton, 1982.

Reid, Ian. *The Short Story.* New York: Routledge, 1991.

Rohrberger, Mary. *Hawthorne and the Modern Short Story: A Study in Genre.* The Hague: Mouton, 1966.

Rohrberger. *Story to Anti-Story.* Boston: Houghton Mifflin, 1979.

Ross, Danforth. *The American Short Story*. Minneapolis: University of Minnesota Press, 1961.

Scholes, Robert. *Structuralism in Literature: An Introduction*. New Haven: Yale University Press, 1974.

Shaw, Valerie. *The Short Story: A Critical Introduction*. New York & London: Longman, 1983.

Stephens, Michael. *The Dramaturgy of Style: Voice in Short Fiction*. Carbondale: Southern Illinois University Press, 1986.

Stummer, Peter O., ed. *The Story Must Be Told: Short Narrative Prose in the New English Literatures*. Würzburg: Königshausen & Neumann, 1986.

Summers, Hollis, ed. *Discussions of the Short Story*. Boston: D. C. Heath, 1963.

Todorov, Tzvetan. *The Poetics of Prose,* translated by Richard Howard. Ithaca, N.Y.: Cornell University Press, 1977.

Voss, Arthur. *The American Short Story: A Critical Survey*. Norman: University of Oklahoma Press, 1973.

Walker, Warren S. *Twentieth-Century Short-Story Explication, New Series*. Hamden, Conn.: Shoe String Press, 1993.

Weaver, Gordon, ed. *The American Short Story, 1945–1980: A Critical History*. Boston: Twayne, 1983.

Weixlmann, Joe. *American Short-Fiction Criticism and Scholarship, 1959–1977: A Checklist*. Chicago: Swallow Press, 1982.

West, Ray. *The Short Story in America, 1900–1950*. Chicago: Regnery, 1952.

Williams, Williams Carlos. *A Beginning on the Short Story: Notes*. Yonkers, N.Y.: Alicat Bookshop Press, 1950.

Contributors

Blake Bailey . . . . *University of New Orleans*

Robert A. Beuka . . . . *Louisiana State University*

Garrett Caples . . . . *University of California at Berkeley*

James Coan . . . . *State University of New York College at Oneonta*

Thom Conroy . . . . *Ohio University*

Gwen Crane . . . . *State University of New York at Oneonta*

Ashby Bland Crowder . . . . *Hendrix College*

Christine C. Ferguson . . . . *Tulane University*

William L. Frank . . . . *Longwood College*

Jane Hill . . . . *State University of West Georgia*

Dale Hrebik . . . . *Xavier University*

Sharon L. Jones . . . . *Earlham College*

Richard E. Lee . . . . *State University of New York, College at Oneonta*

Amy M. Lilly . . . . *University of Iowa*

Carol-Lynn Marrazzo . . . . *Lebanon College*

Curt Meanor . . . . *Cleveland State University*

Gregory L. Morris . . . . *Penn State University at Erie, Behrend College*

Victoria Nelson . . . . *Berkeley, California*

Tom Noyes . . . . *Concordia College*

Alexander McIlvaine Parsons . . . . *New Mexico State University*

Frederick Smock . . . . *Bellarmine College, Louisville*

Adam Sol . . . . *University of Cincinnati*

Troy L. Thibodeaux . . . . *New York University*

Michael Upchurch . . . .

Brad Vice . . . . *University of Cincinnati*

Nancy A. Walker . . . . *Vanderbilt University*

Eamonn Wall . . . . *University of Missouri–St. Louis*

Meg Watson . . . . *Louisiana State University*

Robin A. Werner . . . . *Tulane University*

Tom Whalen . . . . *Tulane University*

Teresa Winterhalter . . . . *Armstrong Atlantic State University*

Dede Yow . . . . *Kennesaw State University*

Karl Zuelke . . . . *University of Cincinnati*

Cumulative Index

Dictionary of Literary Biography, Volumes 1-234
Dictionary of Literary Biography Yearbook, 1980-1999
Dictionary of Literary Biography Documentary Series, Volumes 1-19

Cumulative Index

DLB before number: *Dictionary of Literary Biography,* Volumes 1-234
Y before number: *Dictionary of Literary Biography Yearbook,* 1980-1999
DS before number: *Dictionary of Literary Biography Documentary Series,* Volumes 1-19

A

Aakjær, Jeppe 1866-1930 . . . . .DLB-214

Abbey, Edwin Austin 1852-1911 . . . . . . .DLB-188

Abbey, Maj. J. R. 1894-1969 . . . . .DLB-201

Abbey Press DLB-49

The Abbey Theatre and Irish Drama,
1900-1945 . . . . .DLB-10

Abbot, Willis J. 1863-1934 . . . . .DLB-29

Abbott, Jacob 1803-1879 . . . . .DLB-1

Abbott, Lee K. 1947- DLB-130

Abbott, Lyman 1835-1922 . . . . .DLB-79

Abbott, Robert S. 1868-1940 . . . . .DLB-29, 91

Abe Kōbō 1924-1993 . . . . .DLB-182

Abelard, Peter circa 1079-1142? DLB-115, 208

Abelard-Schuman DLB-46

Abell, Arunah S. 1806-1888 . . . . .DLB-43

Abell, Kjeld 1901-1961 . . . . .DLB-214

Abercrombie, Lascelles 1881-1938 . . . . . . .DLB-19

Aberdeen University Press Limited DLB-106

Abish, Walter 1931- DLB-130, 227

Ablesimov, Aleksandr Onisimovich
1742-1783 . . . . .DLB-150

Abraham à Sancta Clara 1644-1709 . . . . . .DLB-168

Abrahams, Peter 1919- DLB-117, 225

Abrams, M. H. 1912- DLB-67

Abrogans circa 790-800 . . . . .DLB-148

Abschatz, Hans Aßmann von
1646-1699 . . . . .DLB-168

Abse, Dannie 1923- DLB-27

Abutsu-ni 1221-1283 . . . . .DLB-203

Academy Chicago Publishers DLB-46

Accius circa 170 B.C.-circa 80 B.C. DLB-211

Accrocca, Elio Filippo 1923- DLB-128

Ace Books DLB-46

Achebe, Chinua 1930- DLB-117

Achtenberg, Herbert 1938- DLB-124

Ackerman, Diane 1948- DLB-120

Ackroyd, Peter 1949- DLB-155, 231

Acorn, Milton 1923-1986 . . . . .DLB-53

Acosta, Oscar Zeta 1935?- DLB-82

Acosta Torres, José 1925- DLB-209

Actors Theatre of Louisville DLB-7

Adair, Gilbert 1944- DLB-194

Adair, James 1709?-1783? DLB-30

Adam, Graeme Mercer 1839-1912 . . . . . . .DLB-99

Adam, Robert Borthwick II 1863-1940 . . .DLB-187

Adame, Leonard 1947- DLB-82

Adameşteanu, Gabriel 1942- DLB-232

Adamic, Louis 1898-1951 . . . . .DLB-9

Adams, Abigail 1744-1818 . . . . .DLB-200

Adams, Alice 1926-1999 . . . . DLB-234, Y-86

Adams, Brooks 1848-1927 . . . . .DLB-47

Adams, Charles Francis, Jr. 1835-1915 . . . .DLB-47

Adams, Douglas 1952- Y-83

Adams, Franklin P. 1881-1960 . . . . .DLB-29

Adams, Hannah 1755-1832 . . . . .DLB-200

Adams, Henry 1838-1918 . . . . DLB-12, 47, 189

Adams, Herbert Baxter 1850-1901 . . . . . . .DLB-47

Adams, J. S. and C. [publishing house] DLB-49

Adams, James Truslow
1878-1949 . . . . DLB-17; DS-17

Adams, John 1735-1826 . . . . .DLB-31, 183

Adams, John 1735-1826 and
Adams, Abigail 1744-1818 . . . . .DLB-183

Adams, John Quincy 1767-1848 . . . . .DLB-37

Adams, Léonie 1899-1988 . . . . .DLB-48

Adams, Levi 1802-1832 . . . . .DLB-99

Adams, Samuel 1722-1803 . . . . .DLB-31, 43

Adams, Sarah Fuller Flower
1805-1848 . . . . .DLB-199

Adams, Thomas 1582 or 1583-1652 . . . . .DLB-151

Adams, William Taylor 1822-1897 . . . . . . .DLB-42

Adamson, Sir John 1867-1950 . . . . .DLB-98

Adcock, Arthur St. John 1864-1930 . . . . . .DLB-135

Adcock, Betty 1938- DLB-105

"Certain Gifts" DLB-105

Adcock, Fleur 1934- DLB-40

Addison, Joseph 1672-1719 . . . . .DLB-101

Ade, George 1866-1944 . . . . .DLB-11, 25

Adeler, Max (see Clark, Charles Heber)

Adonias Filho 1915-1990 . . . . .DLB-145

Advance Publishing Company DLB-49

Ady, Endre 1877-1919 . . . . .DLB-215

AE 1867-1935 . . . . .DLB-19

Ælfric circa 955-circa 1010 . . . . .DLB-146

Aeschines
circa 390 B.C.-circa 320 B.C. DLB-176

Aeschylus
525-524 B.C.-456-455 B.C. DLB-176

Afro-American Literary Critics:
An Introduction DLB-33

After Dinner Opera Company Y-92

Agassiz, Elizabeth Cary 1822-1907 . . . . . .DLB-189

Agassiz, Jean Louis Rodolphe
1807-1873 . . . . .DLB-1

Agee, James 1909-1955 . . . . .DLB-2, 26, 152

The Agee Legacy: A Conference at the University
of Tennessee at Knoxville Y-89

Aguilera Malta, Demetrio 1909-1981 . . . .DLB-145

Ai 1947- DLB-120

Aichinger, Ilse 1921- DLB-85

Aidoo, Ama Ata 1942- DLB-117

Aiken, Conrad 1889-1973 . . . . .DLB-9, 45, 102

Aiken, Joan 1924- DLB-161

Aikin, Lucy 1781-1864 . . . . .DLB-144, 163

Ainsworth, William Harrison 1805-1882 . .DLB-21

Aistis, Jonas 1904-1973 . . . . .DLB-220

Aitken, George A. 1860-1917 . . . . .DLB-149

Aitken, Robert [publishing house] DLB-49

Akenside, Mark 1721-1770 . . . . .DLB-109

Akins, Zoë 1886-1958 . . . . .DLB-26

Aksahov, Sergei Timofeevich
1791-1859 . . . . .DLB-198

Akutagawa, Ryūnsuke 1892-1927 . . . . . . .DLB-180

Alabaster, William 1568-1640 . . . . .DLB-132

Alain de Lille circa 1116-1202/1203 . . . . . .DLB-208

Alain-Fournier 1886-1914 . . . . .DLB-65

Alanus de Insulis (see Alain de Lille)

Alarcón, Francisco X. 1954- DLB-122

Alarcón, Justo S. 1930- DLB-209

Alba, Nanina 1915-1968 . . . . .DLB-41

Albee, Edward 1928- DLB-7

Albert the Great circa 1200-1280 . . . . .DLB-115

Albert, Octavia 1853-ca. 1889 . . . . .DLB-221

Alberti, Rafael 1902-1999 . . . . .DLB-108

Albertinus, Aegidius circa 1560-1620 . . . . .DLB-164

Alcaeus born circa 620 B.C. DLB-176

Alcott, Bronson 1799-1888 . . . . .DLB-1, 223

Alcott, Louisa May
1832-1888 . . . . DLB-1, 42, 79, 223; DS-14

Alcott, William Andrus 1798-1859 . . . . . . .DLB-1

Alcuin circa 732-804 . . . . .DLB-148

Alden, Beardsley and Company DLB-49

Alden, Henry Mills 1836-1919 . . . . DLB-79

Alden, Isabella 1841-1930 . . . . DLB-42

Alden, John B. [publishing house] DLB-49

Aldington, Richard
1892-1962 . . . . DLB-20, 36, 100, 149

Aldis, Dorothy 1896-1966 . . . . DLB-22

Aldis, H. G. 1863-1919 . . . . DLB-184

Aldiss, Brian W. 1925- DLB-14

Aldrich, Thomas Bailey
1836-1907 . . . . DLB-42, 71, 74, 79

Alegría, Ciro 1909-1967 . . . . DLB-113

Alegría, Claribel 1924- DLB-145

Aleixandre, Vicente 1898-1984 . . . . DLB-108

Aleksandravičius, Jonas (see Aistis, Jonas)

Aleksandrov, Aleksandr Andreevich
(see Durova, Nadezhda Andreevna)

Aleramo, Sibilla 1876-1960 . . . . DLB-114

Alexander, Cecil Frances 1818-1895 . . . . . DLB-199

Alexander, Charles 1868-1923 . . . . DLB-91

Alexander, Charles Wesley
[publishing house] DLB-49

Alexander, James 1691-1756 . . . . DLB-24

Alexander, Lloyd 1924- DLB-52

Alexander, Sir William, Earl of Stirling
1577?-1640 . . . . DLB-121

Alexie, Sherman 1966- DLB-175, 206

Alexis, Willibald 1798-1871 . . . . DLB-133

Alfred, King 849-899 . . . . DLB-146

Alger, Horatio, Jr. 1832-1899 . . . . DLB-42

Algonquin Books of Chapel Hill DLB-46

Algren, Nelson 1909-1981 . . . . . DLB-9; Y-81, Y-82

Allan, Andrew 1907-1974 . . . . DLB-88

Allan, Ted 1916- DLB-68

Allbeury, Ted 1917- DLB-87

Alldritt, Keith 1935- DLB-14

Allen, Ethan 1738-1789 . . . . DLB-31

Allen, Frederick Lewis 1890-1954 . . . . . . DLB-137

Allen, Gay Wilson 1903-1995 . . . . .DLB-103; Y-95

Allen, George 1808-1876 . . . . DLB-59

Allen, George [publishing house] DLB-106

Allen, George, and Unwin Limited DLB-112

Allen, Grant 1848-1899 . . . . .DLB-70, 92, 178

Allen, Henry W. 1912- Y-85

Allen, Hervey 1889-1949 . . . . DLB-9, 45

Allen, James 1739-1808 . . . . DLB-31

Allen, James Lane 1849-1925 . . . . DLB-71

Allen, Jay Presson 1922- DLB-26

Allen, John, and Company DLB-49

Allen, Paula Gunn 1939- DLB-175

Allen, Samuel W. 1917- DLB-41

Allen, Woody 1935- DLB-44

Allende, Isabel 1942- DLB-145

Alline, Henry 1748-1784 . . . . DLB-99

Allingham, Margery 1904-1966 . . . . DLB-77

Allingham, William 1824-1889 . . . . DLB-35

Allison, W. L. [publishing house] DLB-49

The *Alliterative Morte Arthure and the Stanzaic
Morte Arthur* circa 1350-1400 . . . . DLB-146

Allott, Kenneth 1912-1973 . . . . DLB-20

Allston, Washington 1779-1843 . . . . DLB-1

Almon, John [publishing house] DLB-154

Alonzo, Dámaso 1898-1990 . . . . DLB-108

Alsop, George 1636-post 1673 . . . . DLB-24

Alsop, Richard 1761-1815 . . . . DLB-37

Altemus, Henry, and Company DLB-49

Altenberg, Peter 1885-1919 . . . . DLB-81

Altolaguirre, Manuel 1905-1959 . . . . DLB-108

Aluko, T. M. 1918- DLB-117

Alurista 1947- DLB-82

Alvarez, A. 1929- DLB-14, 40

Alver, Betti 1906-1989 . . . . DLB-220

Amadi, Elechi 1934- DLB-117

Amado, Jorge 1912- DLB-113

Ambler, Eric 1909-1998 . . . . DLB-77

American Conservatory Theatre DLB-7

American Fiction and the 1930s DLB-9

American Humor: A Historical Survey
East and Northeast
South and Southwest
Midwest
West DLB-11

The American Library in Paris Y-93

American News Company DLB-49

The American Poets' Corner: The First
Three Years (1983-1986) Y-86

American Publishing Company DLB-49

American Stationers' Company DLB-49

American Sunday-School Union DLB-49

American Temperance Union DLB-49

American Tract Society DLB-49

The American Trust for the
British Library Y-96

The American Writers Congress
(9-12 October 1981) Y-81

The American Writers Congress: A Report
on Continuing Business Y-81

Ames, Fisher 1758-1808 . . . . DLB-37

Ames, Mary Clemmer 1831-1884 . . . . DLB-23

Amiel, Henri-Frédéric 1821-1881 . . . . DLB-217

Amini, Johari M. 1935- DLB-41

Amis, Kingsley
1922-1995 . . . . . . DLB-15, 27, 100, 139, Y-96

Amis, Martin 1949- DLB-194

Ammianus Marcellinus
circa A.D. 330-A.D. 395 . . . . DLB-211

Ammons, A. R. 1926- DLB-5, 165

Amory, Thomas 1691?-1788 . . . . DLB-39

Anania, Michael 1939- DLB-193

Anaya, Rudolfo A. 1937- DLB-82, 206

Ancrene Riwle circa 1200-1225 . . . . DLB-146

Andersch, Alfred 1914-1980 . . . . DLB-69

Andersen, Benny 1929- DLB-214

Anderson, Alexander 1775-1870 . . . . DLB-188

Anderson, Frederick Irving 1877-1947 . . . DLB-202

Anderson, Margaret 1886-1973 . . . . DLB-4, 91

Anderson, Maxwell 1888-1959 . . . . . . .DLB-7, 228

Anderson, Patrick 1915-1979 . . . . DLB-68

Anderson, Paul Y. 1893-1938 . . . . DLB-29

Anderson, Poul 1926- DLB-8

Anderson, Robert 1750-1830 . . . . DLB-142

Anderson, Robert 1917- DLB-7

Anderson, Sherwood
1876-1941 . . . . DLB-4, 9, 86; DS-1

Andreae, Johann Valentin 1586-1654 . . . . DLB-164

Andreas Capellanus
flourished circa 1185 . . . . DLB-208

Andreas-Salomé, Lou 1861-1937 . . . . DLB-66

Andres, Stefan 1906-1970 . . . . DLB-69

Andreu, Blanca 1959- DLB-134

Andrewes, Lancelot 1555-1626 . . . . .DLB-151, 172

Andrews, Charles M. 1863-1943 . . . . .DLB-17

Andrews, Miles Peter ?-1814 . . . . DLB-89

Andrian, Leopold von 1875-1951 . . . . DLB-81

Andrić, Ivo 1892-1975 . . . . .DLB-147

Andrieux, Louis (see Aragon, Louis)

Andrus, Silas, and Son DLB-49

Andrzejewski, Jerzy 1909-1983 . . . . DLB-215

Angell, James Burrill 1829-1916 . . . . DLB-64

Angell, Roger 1920- DLB-171, 185

Angelou, Maya 1928- DLB-38

Anger, Jane flourished 1589 . . . . DLB-136

Angers, Félicité (see Conan, Laure)

Anglo-Norman Literature in the Development
of Middle English Literature DLB-146

The Anglo-Saxon Chronicle circa 890-1154 . . DLB-146

The "Angry Young Men" DLB-15

Angus and Robertson (UK) Limited DLB-112

Anhalt, Edward 1914- DLB-26

Anners, Henry F. [publishing house] DLB-49

Annolied between 1077 and 1081 . . . . DLB-148

Annual Awards for *Dictionary of Literary Biography*
Editors and Contributors Y-98, Y-99

Anselm of Canterbury 1033-1109 . . . . . . DLB-115

Anstey, F. 1856-1934 . . . . .DLB-141, 178

Anthony, Michael 1932- DLB-125

Anthony, Piers 1934- DLB-8

Anthony, Susanna 1726-1791 . . . . DLB-200

Antin, David 1932- DLB-169

Antin, Mary 1881-1949 . . . . .DLB-221; Y-84

Anton Ulrich, Duke of Brunswick-Lüneburg
1633-1714 . . . . DLB-168

Antschel, Paul (see Celan, Paul)

Anyidoho, Kofi 1947- DLB-157

Anzaldúa, Gloria 1942- DLB-122

Anzengruber, Ludwig 1839-1889 . . . . DLB-129

Apess, William 1798-1839 . . . . .DLB-175

Apodaca, Rudy S. 1939- DLB-82

Apollonius Rhodius third century B.C. . . .DLB-176

Apple, Max 1941- DLB-130

Appleton, D., and Company DLB-49

Appleton-Century-Crofts. DLB-46

Applewhite, James 1935- DLB-105

Applewood Books DLB-46

Apuleius circa A.D. 125-post A.D. 164 . . .DLB-211

Aquin, Hubert 1929-1977 . . . . .DLB-53

Aquinas, Thomas 1224 or 1225-1274 . . . .DLB-115

Aragon, Louis 1897-1982. . . . . .DLB-72

Aralica, Ivan 1930- DLB-181

Aratus of Soli
     circa 315 B.C.-circa 239 B.C. DLB-176

Arbasino, Alberto 1930- DLB-196

Arbor House Publishing Company DLB-46

Arbuthnot, John 1667-1735 . . . . .DLB-101

Arcadia House DLB-46

Arce, Julio G. (see Ulica, Jorge)

Archer, William 1856-1924 . . . . .DLB-10

Archilochhus
     mid seventh century B.C.E. DLB-176

The Archpoet circa 1130?-? DLB-148

Archpriest Avvakum (Petrovich)
     1620?-1682 . . . . .DLB-150

Arden, John 1930- DLB-13

Arden of Faversham DLB-62

Ardis Publishers. Y-89

Ardizzone, Edward 1900-1979 . . . . .DLB-160

Arellano, Juan Estevan 1947- DLB-122

The Arena Publishing Company DLB-49

Arena Stage DLB-7

Arenas, Reinaldo 1943-1990 . . . . .DLB-145

Arensberg, Ann 1937- Y-82

Arghezi, Tudor 1880-1967. . . . . .DLB-220

Arguedas, José María 1911-1969 . . . . . . .DLB-113

Argueta, Manlio 1936- DLB-145

Arias, Ron 1941- DLB-82

Arishima, Takeo 1878-1923. . . . . .DLB-180

Aristophanes
     circa 446 B.C.-circa 386 B.C. DLB-176

Aristotle 384 B.C.-322 B.C. DLB-176

Ariyoshi Sawako 1931-1984 . . . . .DLB-182

Arland, Marcel 1899-1986. . . . . .DLB-72

Arlen, Michael 1895-1956 . . . . DLB-36, 77, 162

Armah, Ayi Kwei 1939- DLB-117

Armantrout, Rae 1947- DLB-193

Der arme Hartmann ?-after 1150. . . . . . . .DLB-148

Armed Services Editions DLB-46

Armstrong, Martin Donisthorpe
     1882-1974 . . . . .DLB-197

Armstrong, Richard 1903- DLB-160

Arndt, Ernst Moritz 1769-1860 . . . . .DLB-90

Arnim, Achim von 1781-1831 . . . . .DLB-90

Arnim, Bettina von 1785-1859 . . . . .DLB-90

Arnim, Elizabeth von
     (Countess Mary Annette Beauchamp Russell)
     1866-1941 . . . . .DLB-197

Arno Press DLB-46

Arnold, Edward [publishing house] DLB-112

Arnold, Edwin 1832-1904 . . . . .DLB-35

Arnold, Edwin L. 1857-1935 . . . . .DLB-178

Arnold, Matthew 1822-1888 . . . . .DLB-32, 57

     Preface to *Poems* (1853). DLB-32

Arnold, Thomas 1795-1842 . . . . .DLB-55

Arnott, Peter 1962- DLB-233

Arnow, Harriette Simpson 1908-1986 . . . . . .DLB-6

Arp, Bill (see Smith, Charles Henry)

Arpino, Giovanni 1927-1987 . . . . .DLB-177

Arreola, Juan José 1918- DLB-113

Arrian circa 89-circa 155 . . . . .DLB-176

Arrowsmith, J. W. [publishing house] DLB-106

The Art and Mystery of Publishing:
     Interviews Y-97

Arthur, Timothy Shay
     1809-1885 . . . . DLB-3, 42, 79; DS-13

The Arthurian Tradition and
     Its European Context DLB-138

Artmann, H. C. 1921- DLB-85

Arvin, Newton 1900-1963 . . . . .DLB-103

Asch, Nathan 1902-1964 . . . . .DLB-4, 28

Ash, John 1948- DLB-40

Ashbery, John 1927- DLB-5, 165; Y-81

Ashbridge, Elizabeth 1713-1755 . . . . .DLB-200

Ashburnham, Bertram Lord
     1797-1878 . . . . .DLB-184

Ashendene Press DLB-112

Asher, Sandy 1942- Y-83

Ashton, Winifred (see Dane, Clemence)

Asimov, Isaac 1920-1992 . . . . DLB-8; Y-92

Askew, Anne circa 1521-1546 . . . . .DLB-136

Aspazija 1865-1943 . . . . .DLB-220

Asselin, Olivar 1874-1937 . . . . .DLB-92

The Association of American Publishers Y-99

Astley, William (see Warung, Price)

Asturias, Miguel Angel 1899-1974 . . . . . . .DLB-113

Atheneum Publishers. DLB-46

Atherton, Gertrude 1857-1948. . . . . DLB-9, 78, 186

Athlone Press. DLB-112

Atkins, Josiah circa 1755-1781 . . . . .DLB-31

Atkins, Russell 1926- DLB-41

Atkinson, Louisa 1834-1872. . . . . .DLB-230

The Atlantic Monthly Press. DLB-46

Attaway, William 1911-1986 . . . . .DLB-76

Atwood, Margaret 1939- DLB-53

Aubert, Alvin 1930- DLB-41

Aubert de Gaspé, Phillipe-Ignace-François
     1814-1841 . . . . .DLB-99

Aubert de Gaspé, Phillipe-Joseph
     1786-1871 . . . . .DLB-99

Aubin, Napoléon 1812-1890 . . . . .DLB-99

Aubin, Penelope 1685-circa 1731 . . . . .DLB-39

     Preface to *The Life of Charlotta
     du Pont* (1723). DLB-39

Aubrey-Fletcher, Henry Lancelot (see Wade, Henry)

Auchincloss, Louis 1917- DLB-2; Y-80

Auden, W. H. 1907-1973 . . . . .DLB-10, 20

Audio Art in America: A Personal Memoir. . . Y-85

Audubon, John Woodhouse
     1812-1862 . . . . .DLB-183

Auerbach, Berthold 1812-1882 . . . . .DLB-133

Auernheimer, Raoul 1876-1948. . . . . .DLB-81

Augier, Emile 1820-1889 . . . . .DLB-192

Augustine 354-430. . . . . .DLB-115

Responses to Ken Auletta Y-97

Aulus Cellius
     circa A.D. 125-circa A.D. 180? DLB-211

Austen, Jane 1775-1817 . . . . .DLB-116

Auster, Paul 1947- DLB-227

Austin, Alfred 1835-1913. . . . . .DLB-35

Austin, Jane Goodwin 1831-1894 . . . . . . .DLB-202

Austin, Mary 1868-1934 . . . . . DLB-9, 78, 206, 221

Austin, William 1778-1841. . . . . .DLB-74

Australie (Emily Manning) 1845-1890. . . .DLB-230

Author-Printers, 1476-1599. . . . . .DLB-167

Author Websites Y-97

Authors and Newspapers Association DLB-46

Authors' Publishing Company DLB-49

Avallone, Michael 1924-1999. . . . . Y-99

Avalon Books DLB-46

Avancini, Nicolaus 1611-1686 . . . . .DLB-164

Avendaño, Fausto 1941- DLB-82

Averroëó 1126-1198. . . . . .DLB-115

Avery, Gillian 1926- DLB-161

Avicenna 980-1037. . . . . .DLB-115

Avison, Margaret 1918- DLB-53

Avon Books DLB-46

Avyžius, Jonas 1922-1999 . . . . .DLB-220

Awdry, Wilbert Vere 1911-1997 . . . . .DLB-160

Awoonor, Kofi 1935- DLB-117

Ayckbourn, Alan 1939- DLB-13

Aymé, Marcel 1902-1967. . . . . .DLB-72

Aytoun, Sir Robert 1570-1638 . . . . .DLB-121

Aytoun, William Edmondstoune
     1813-1865 . . . . .DLB-32, 159

B

B. V. (see Thomson, James)

Babbitt, Irving 1865-1933 . . . . .DLB-63

Babbitt, Natalie 1932- DLB-52

Babcock, John [publishing house] DLB-49

Babits, Mihály 1883-1941 . . . . .DLB-215

Babrius circa 150-200. . . . . .DLB-176

Baca, Jimmy Santiago 1952- DLB-122

Bache, Benjamin Franklin 1769-1798 . . . . .DLB-43

Bacheller, Irving 1859-1950. . . . . .DLB-202

Bachmann, Ingeborg 1926-1973 . . . . .DLB-85

Bačinskaitė-Bučienė, Salomėja (see Nėris, Salomėja)

Bacon, Delia 1811-1859. . . . . .DLB-1

Bacon, Francis 1561-1626 . . . . .DLB-151

Bacon, Sir Nicholas circa 1510-1579 . . . . . DLB-132

Bacon, Roger circa 1214/1220-1292 . . . . . DLB-115

Bacon, Thomas circa 1700-1768 . . . . DLB-31

Bacovia, George 1881-1957 . . . . DLB-220

Badger, Richard G., and Company DLB-49

Bage, Robert 1728-1801 . . . . DLB-39

Bagehot, Walter 1826-1877. . . . . DLB-55

Bagley, Desmond 1923-1983 . . . . DLB-87

Bagnold, Enid 1889-1981 . . . . . . DLB-13, 160, 191

Bagryana, Elisaveta 1893-1991. . . . . DLB-147

Bahr, Hermann 1863-1934. . . . . DLB-81, 118

Bailey, Abigail Abbot 1746-1815. . . . . . . DLB-200

Bailey, Alfred Goldsworthy 1905- DLB-68

Bailey, Francis [publishing house]. DLB-49

Bailey, H. C. 1878-1961 . . . . DLB-77

Bailey, Jacob 1731-1808 . . . . DLB-99

Bailey, Paul 1937- DLB-14

Bailey, Philip James 1816-1902. . . . . DLB-32

Baillargeon, Pierre 1916-1967. . . . . DLB-88

Baillie, Hugh 1890-1966. . . . . DLB-29

Baillie, Joanna 1762-1851 . . . . DLB-93

Bailyn, Bernard 1922- DLB-17

Bainbridge, Beryl 1933- DLB-14, 231

Baird, Irene 1901-1981 . . . . DLB-68

Baker, Augustine 1575-1641 . . . . DLB-151

Baker, Carlos 1909-1987 . . . . DLB-103

Baker, David 1954- DLB-120

Baker, Herschel C. 1914-1990 . . . . DLB-111

Baker, Houston A., Jr. 1943- DLB-67

Baker, Nicholson 1957- DLB-227

Baker, Samuel White 1821-1893 . . . . DLB-166

Baker, Thomas 1656-1740 . . . . DLB-213

Baker, Walter H., Company
    ("Baker's Plays") DLB-49

The Baker and Taylor Company. DLB-49

Balaban, John 1943- DLB-120

Bald, Wambly 1902- DLB-4

Balde, Jacob 1604-1668. . . . . DLB-164

Balderston, John 1889-1954 . . . . DLB-26

Baldwin, James 1924-1987 . . . . . DLB-2, 7, 33; Y-87

Baldwin, Joseph Glover 1815-1864. . . . . DLB-3, 11

Baldwin, Richard and Anne
    [publishing house] DLB-170

Baldwin, William circa 1515-1563 . . . . . . DLB-132

Bale, John 1495-1563 . . . . DLB-132

Balestrini, Nanni 1935- DLB-128, 196

Balfour, Sir Andrew 1630-1694 . . . . DLB-213

Balfour, Arthur James 1848-1930. . . . . . . DLB-190

Balfour, Sir James 1600-1657 . . . . DLB-213

Ballantine Books. DLB-46

Ballantyne, R. M. 1825-1894 . . . . DLB-163

Ballard, J. G. 1930- DLB-14, 207

Ballard, Martha Moore 1735-1812 . . . . . . DLB-200

Ballerini, Luigi 1940- DLB-128

Ballou, Maturin Murray
    1820-1895 . . . . .DLB-79, 189

Ballou, Robert O. [publishing house] DLB-46

Balzac, Honoré de 1799-1855. . . . . DLB-119

Bambara, Toni Cade 1939- DLB-38, 218

Bamford, Samuel 1788-1872 . . . . DLB-190

Bancroft, A. L., and Company. DLB-49

Bancroft, George 1800-1891. . . . . . DLB-1, 30, 59

Bancroft, Hubert Howe 1832-1918 . . .DLB-47, 140

Bandelier, Adolph F. 1840-1914 . . . . DLB-186

Bangs, John Kendrick 1862-1922. . . . .DLB-11, 79

Banim, John 1798-1842. . . . . . . .DLB-116, 158, 159

Banim, Michael 1796-1874 . . . . DLB-158, 159

Banks, Iain 1954- DLB-194

Banks, John circa 1653-1706. . . . . DLB-80

Banks, Russell 1940- DLB-130

Bannerman, Helen 1862-1946 . . . . DLB-141

Bantam Books DLB-46

Banti, Anna 1895-1985. . . . . .DLB-177

Banville, John 1945- DLB-14

Banville, Théodore de 1823-1891. . . . . . DLB-217

Baraka, Amiri 1934- DLB-5, 7, 16, 38; DS-8

Barańczak, Stanisław 1946- DLB-232

Baratynsky, Evgenii Abramovich
    1800-1844 . . . . DLB-205

Barbauld, Anna Laetitia
    1743-1825. . . . . DLB-107, 109, 142, 158

Barbeau, Marius 1883-1969 . . . . DLB-92

Barber, John Warner 1798-1885. . . . . DLB-30

Bàrberi Squarotti, Giorgio 1929- DLB-128

Barbey d'Aurevilly, Jules-Amédée
    1808-1889 . . . . DLB-119

Barbier, Auguste 1805-1882 . . . . DLB-217

Barbilian, Dan (see Barbu, Ion)

Barbour, John circa 1316-1395 . . . . DLB-146

Barbour, Ralph Henry 1870-1944 . . . . . . DLB-22

Barbu, Ion 1895-1961. . . . . DLB-220

Barbusse, Henri 1873-1935. . . . . DLB-65

Barclay, Alexander circa 1475-1552 . . . . . DLB-132

Barclay, E. E., and Company. DLB-49

Bardeen, C. W. [publishing house]. DLB-49

Barham, Richard Harris 1788-1845 . . . . . DLB-159

Barich, Bill 1943- DLB-185

Baring, Maurice 1874-1945. . . . . DLB-34

Baring-Gould, Sabine
    1834-1924 . . . . DLB-156, 190

Barker, A. L. 1918- DLB-14, 139

Barker, Arthur, Limited DLB-112

Barker, George 1913-1991 . . . . DLB-20

Barker, Harley Granville 1877-1946 . . . . . DLB-10

Barker, Howard 1946- DLB-13, 233

Barker, James Nelson 1784-1858 . . . . DLB-37

Barker, Jane 1652-1727. . . . . DLB-39, 131

Barker, Lady Mary Anne 1831-1911 . . . . DLB-166

Barker, William circa 1520-after 1576 . . . DLB-132

Barkov, Ivan Semenovich 1732-1768 . . . . DLB-150

Barks, Coleman 1937- DLB-5

Barlach, Ernst 1870-1938 . . . . DLB-56, 118

Barlow, Joel 1754-1812. . . . . DLB-37

The Prospect of Peace (1778) DLB-37

Barnard, John 1681-1770 . . . . DLB-24

Barne, Kitty (Mary Catherine Barne)
    1883-1957 . . . . DLB-160

Barnes, A. S., and Company DLB-49

Barnes, Barnabe 1571-1609 . . . . DLB-132

Barnes, Djuna 1892-1982 . . . . DLB-4, 9, 45

Barnes, Jim 1933- DLB-175

Barnes, Julian 1946- DLB-194; Y-93

Barnes, Margaret Ayer 1886-1967 . . . . . . DLB-9

Barnes, Peter 1931- DLB-13, 233

Barnes, William 1801-1886 . . . . DLB-32

Barnes and Noble Books DLB-46

Barnet, Miguel 1940- DLB-145

Barney, Natalie 1876-1972 . . . . DLB-4

Barnfield, Richard 1574-1627 . . . . .DLB-172

Baron, Richard W.,
    Publishing Company DLB-46

Barr, Amelia Edith Huddleston
    1831-1919 . . . . DLB-202, 221

Barr, Robert 1850-1912 . . . . .DLB-70, 92

Barral, Carlos 1928-1989 . . . . DLB-134

Barrax, Gerald William 1933- DLB-41, 120

Barrès, Maurice 1862-1923. . . . . DLB-123

Barrett, Eaton Stannard 1786-1820. . . . . . DLB-116

Barrie, J. M. 1860-1937. . . . . .DLB-10, 141, 156

Barrie and Jenkins DLB-112

Barrio, Raymond 1921- DLB-82

Barrios, Gregg 1945- DLB-122

Barry, Philip 1896-1949 . . . . .DLB-7, 228

Barry, Robertine (see Françoise)

Barse and Hopkins. DLB-46

Barstow, Stan 1928- DLB-14, 139

Barth, John 1930- DLB-2, 227

Barthelme, Donald
    1931-1989 . . . . .DLB-2, 234; Y-80, Y-89

Barthelme, Frederick 1943- Y-85

Bartholomew, Frank 1898-1985. . . . . . . .DLB-127

Bartlett, John 1820-1905. . . . . DLB-1

Bartol, Cyrus Augustus 1813-1900. . . . . . . DLB-1

Barton, Bernard 1784-1849. . . . . DLB-96

Barton, Thomas Pennant 1803-1869 . . . . DLB-140

Bartram, John 1699-1777 . . . . DLB-31

Bartram, William 1739-1823 . . . . DLB-37

Basic Books DLB-46

Basille, Theodore (see Becon, Thomas)

Bass, Rick 1958- DLB-212

Bass, T. J. 1932- Y-81

Bassani, Giorgio 1916- DLB-128, 177

Basse, William circa 1583-1653 . . . . DLB-121

Bassett, John Spencer 1867-1928. . . . . . . .DLB-17

Bassler, Thomas Joseph (see Bass, T. J.)

Bate, Walter Jackson 1918-1999 . . . . . DLB-67, 103

Bateman, Christopher
    [publishing house] DLB-170

Bateman, Stephen circa 1510-1584 . . . . . DLB-136

Bates, H. E. 1905-1974. . . . . DLB-162, 191

Bates, Katharine Lee 1859-1929 . . . . DLB-71

Batiushkov, Konstantin Nikolaevich
    1787-1855. . . . . DLB-205

Batsford, B. T. [publishing house] DLB-106

Battiscombe, Georgina 1905- DLB-155

The Battle of Maldon circa 1000 . . . . DLB-146

Baudelaire, Charles 1821-1867 . . . . DLB-217

Bauer, Bruno 1809-1882 . . . . DLB-133

Bauer, Wolfgang 1941- DLB-124

Baum, L. Frank 1856-1919 . . . . DLB-22

Baum, Vicki 1888-1960 . . . . DLB-85

Baumbach, Jonathan 1933- Y-80

Bausch, Richard 1945- DLB-130

Bausch, Robert 1945- DLB-218

Bawden, Nina 1925- DLB-14, 161, 207

Bax, Clifford 1886-1962 . . . . DLB-10, 100

Baxter, Charles 1947- DLB-130

Bayer, Eleanor (see Perry, Eleanor)

Bayer, Konrad 1932-1964 . . . . DLB-85

Baynes, Pauline 1922- DLB-160

Baynton, Barbara 1857-1929 . . . . DLB-230

Bazin, Hervé 1911-1996. . . . . DLB-83

Beach, Sylvia 1887-1962. . . . . DLB-4; DS-15

Beacon Press DLB-49

Beadle and Adams DLB-49

Beagle, Peter S. 1939- Y-80

Beal, M. F. 1937- Y-81

Beale, Howard K. 1899-1959. . . . . DLB-17

Beard, Charles A. 1874-1948 . . . . DLB-17

A Beat Chronology: The First Twenty-five
    Years, 1944-1969. . . . . DLB-16

Periodicals of the Beat Generation. DLB-16

Beattie, Ann 1947- DLB-218; Y-82

Beattie, James 1735-1803 . . . . DLB-109

Beatty, Chester 1875-1968 . . . . DLB-201

Beauchemin, Nérée 1850-1931 . . . . DLB-92

Beauchemin, Yves 1941- DLB-60

Beaugrand, Honoré 1848-1906 . . . . DLB-99

Beaulieu, Victor-Lévy 1945- DLB-53

Beaumont, Francis circa 1584-1616
    and Fletcher, John 1579-1625 . . . . DLB-58

Beaumont, Sir John 1583?-1627. . . . . DLB-121

Beaumont, Joseph 1616-1699. . . . . DLB-126

Beauvoir, Simone de 1908-1986 . . . . DLB-72; Y-86

Becher, Ulrich 1910- DLB-69

Becker, Carl 1873-1945 . . . . DLB-17

Becker, Jurek 1937-1997. . . . . DLB-75

Becker, Jurgen 1932- DLB-75

Beckett, Samuel
    1906-1989 . . . . DLB-13, 15, 233; Y-90

Beckford, William 1760-1844. . . . . DLB-39

Beckham, Barry 1944- DLB-33

Becon, Thomas circa 1512-1567 . . . . DLB-136

Becque, Henry 1837-1899 . . . . DLB-192

Beddoes, Thomas 1760-1808. . . . . DLB-158

Beddoes, Thomas Lovell 1803-1849 . . . . . . DLB-96

Bede circa 673-735 . . . . DLB-146

Beecher, Catharine Esther 1800-1878 . . . . . . DLB-1

Beecher, Henry Ward 1813-1887 . . . . . . DLB-3, 43

Beer, George L. 1872-1920 . . . . DLB-47

Beer, Johann 1655-1700 . . . . DLB-168

Beer, Patricia 1919-1999 . . . . DLB-40

Beerbohm, Max 1872-1956 . . . . DLB-34, 100

Beer-Hofmann, Richard 1866-1945 . . . . DLB-81

Beers, Henry A. 1847-1926 . . . . DLB-71

Beeton, S. O. [publishing house] DLB-106

Bégon, Elisabeth 1696-1755 . . . . DLB-99

Behan, Brendan 1923-1964 . . . . DLB-13, 233

Behn, Aphra 1640?-1689 . . . . DLB-39, 80, 131

Behn, Harry 1898-1973 . . . . DLB-61

Behrman, S. N. 1893-1973 . . . . DLB-7, 44

Belaney, Archibald Stansfeld (see Grey Owl)

Belasco, David 1853-1931 . . . . DLB-7

Belford, Clarke and Company. DLB-49

Belinksy, Vissarion Grigor'evich
    1811-1848 . . . . DLB-198

Belitt, Ben 1911- DLB-5

Belknap, Jeremy 1744-1798 . . . . DLB-30, 37

Bell, Adrian 1901-1980 . . . . DLB-191

Bell, Clive 1881-1964. . . . . DS-10

Bell, George, and Sons. DLB-106

Bell, Gertrude Margaret Lowthian
    1868-1926 . . . . DLB-174

Bell, James Madison 1826-1902. . . . . DLB-50

Bell, Madison Smartt 1957- DLB-218

Bell, Marvin 1937- DLB-5

Bell, Millicent 1919- DLB-111

Bell, Quentin 1910-1996 . . . . DLB-155

Bell, Robert [publishing house] DLB-49

Bell, Vanessa 1879-1961 . . . . DS-10

Bellamy, Edward 1850-1898 . . . . DLB-12

Bellamy, John [publishing house]. DLB-170

Bellamy, Joseph 1719-1790. . . . . DLB-31

La Belle Assemblée 1806-1837 . . . . DLB-110

Bellezza, Dario 1944-1996 . . . . DLB-128

Belloc, Hilaire 1870-1953 . . . . DLB-19, 100, 141, 174

Bellonci, Maria 1902-1986. . . . . DLB-196

Bellow, Saul 1915- DLB-2, 28; Y-82; DS-3

Belmont Productions DLB-46

Bels, Alberts 1938- DLB-232

Belševica, Vizma 1931- DLB-232

Bemelmans, Ludwig 1898-1962. . . . . DLB-22

Bemis, Samuel Flagg 1891-1973. . . . . DLB-17

Bemrose, William [publishing house] DLB-106

Ben no Naishi 1228?-1271? DLB-203

Benchley, Robert 1889-1945 . . . . DLB-11

Bencúr, Matej (see Kukučin, Martin)

Benedetti, Mario 1920- DLB-113

Benedictus, David 1938- DLB-14

Benedikt, Michael 1935- DLB-5

Benediktov, Vladimir Grigor'evich
    1807-1873 . . . . DLB-205

Benét, Stephen Vincent
    1898-1943 . . . . DLB-4, 48, 102

Benét, William Rose 1886-1950 . . . . DLB-45

Benford, Gregory 1941- Y-82

Benjamin, Park 1809-1864. . . . . DLB-3, 59, 73

Benjamin, S. G. W. 1837-1914. . . . . DLB-189

Benlowes, Edward 1602-1676 . . . . DLB-126

Benn Brothers Limited DLB-106

Benn, Gottfried 1886-1956 . . . . DLB-56

Bennett, Arnold 1867-1931 . . . DLB-10, 34, 98, 135

Bennett, Charles 1899-1995. . . . . DLB-44

Bennett, Emerson 1822-1905. . . . . DLB-202

Bennett, Gwendolyn 1902- DLB-51

Bennett, Hal 1930- DLB-33

Bennett, James Gordon 1795-1872. . . . . . . DLB-43

Bennett, James Gordon, Jr. 1841-1918. . . . DLB-23

Bennett, John 1865-1956 . . . . DLB-42

Bennett, Louise 1919- DLB-117

Benni, Stefano 1947- DLB-196

Benoit, Jacques 1941- DLB-60

Benson, A. C. 1862-1925. . . . . DLB-98

Benson, E. F. 1867-1940. . . . . DLB-135, 153

Benson, Jackson J. 1930- DLB-111

Benson, Robert Hugh 1871-1914. . . . . DLB-153

Benson, Stella 1892-1933. . . . . DLB-36, 162

Bent, James Theodore 1852-1897 . . . . . DLB-174

Bent, Mabel Virginia Anna ?-? DLB-174

Bentham, Jeremy 1748-1832 . . . . DLB-107, 158

Bentley, E. C. 1875-1956 . . . . DLB-70

Bentley, Phyllis 1894-1977. . . . . DLB-191

Bentley, Richard [publishing house] DLB-106

Benton, Robert 1932- and Newman,
    David 1937- DLB-44

Benziger Brothers DLB-49

Beowulf circa 900-1000 or 790-825 . . . . . . DLB-146

Berent, Wacław 1873-1940 . . . . DLB-215

Beresford, Anne 1929- DLB-40

Beresford, John Davys
    1873-1947 . . . . DLB-162, 178, 197

"Experiment in the Novel" (1929) DLB-36

Beresford-Howe, Constance 1922- DLB-88

Berford, R. G., Company DLB-49

Berg, Stephen 1934- DLB-5

Bergengruen, Werner 1892-1964 . . . . DLB-56

Berger, John 1926- DLB-14, 207

Berger, Meyer 1898-1959 . . . . DLB-29

Berger, Thomas 1924- DLB-2; Y-80

Berkeley, Anthony 1893-1971 . . . . DLB-77

Berkeley, George 1685-1753 . . . . DLB-31, 101

The Berkley Publishing Corporation DLB-46

Berlin, Lucia 1936- DLB-130

Bernal, Vicente J. 1888-1915 . . . . DLB-82

Bernanos, Georges 1888-1948 . . . . DLB-72

Bernard, Harry 1898-1979 . . . . DLB-92

Bernard, John 1756-1828 . . . . DLB-37

Bernard of Chartres circa 1060-1124? . . . DLB-115

Bernard of Clairvaux 1090-1153 . . . . DLB-208

Bernard Silvestris
    flourished circa 1130-1160 . . . . DLB-208

Bernari, Carlo 1909-1992 . . . . .DLB-177

Bernhard, Thomas 1931-1989 . . . . . . DLB-85, 124

Bernstein, Charles 1950- DLB-169

Berriault, Gina 1926-1999 . . . . DLB-130

Berrigan, Daniel 1921- DLB-5

Berrigan, Ted 1934-1983 . . . . DLB-5, 169

Berry, Wendell 1934- DLB-5, 6, 234

Berryman, John 1914-1972 . . . . DLB-48

Bersianik, Louky 1930- DLB-60

Berthelet, Thomas [publishing house] DLB-170

Berto, Giuseppe 1914-1978 . . . . .DLB-177

Bertolucci, Attilio 1911- DLB-128

Berton, Pierre 1920- DLB-68

Bertrand, Louis "Aloysius"
    1807-1841 . . . . DLB-217

Besant, Sir Walter 1836-1901 . . . . . . DLB-135, 190

Bessette, Gerard 1920- DLB-53

Bessie, Alvah 1904-1985 . . . . DLB-26

Bester, Alfred 1913-1987 . . . . DLB-8

Besterman, Theodore 1904-1976 . . . . DLB-201

The Bestseller Lists: An Assessment Y-84

Bestuzhev, Aleksandr Aleksandrovich
    (Marlinsky) 1797-1837 . . . . DLB-198

Bestuzhev, Nikolai Aleksandrovich
    1791-1855 . . . . DLB-198

Betham-Edwards, Matilda Barbara (see Edwards,
    Matilda Barbara Betham-)

Betjeman, John 1906-1984 . . . . DLB-20; Y-84

Betocchi, Carlo 1899-1986 . . . . DLB-128

Bettarini, Mariella 1942- DLB-128

Betts, Doris 1932- DLB-218; Y-82

Beùkoviù, Matija 1939- DLB-181

Beveridge, Albert J. 1862-1927 . . . . DLB-17

Beverley, Robert circa 1673-1722 . . . . . DLB-24, 30

Bevilacqua, Alberto 1934- DLB-196

Bevington, Louisa Sarah 1845-1895 . . . . . DLB-199

Beyle, Marie-Henri (see Stendhal)

Białoszewski, Miron 1922-1983 . . . . . . DLB-232

Bianco, Margery Williams 1881-1944 . . . DLB-160

Bibaud, Adèle 1854-1941 . . . . DLB-92

Bibaud, Michel 1782-1857 . . . . DLB-99

Bibliographical and Textual Scholarship
    Since World War II Y-89

Bichsel, Peter 1935- DLB-75

Bickerstaff, Isaac John 1733-circa 1808 . . . . DLB-89

Biddle, Drexel [publishing house] DLB-49

Bidermann, Jacob
    1577 or 1578-1639 . . . . DLB-164

Bidwell, Walter Hilliard 1798-1881 . . . . . . DLB-79

Bienek, Horst 1930- DLB-75

Bierbaum, Otto Julius 1865-1910 . . . . DLB-66

Bierce, Ambrose
    1842-1914? DLB-11, 12, 23, 71, 74, 186

Bigelow, William F. 1879-1966 . . . . DLB-91

Biggle, Lloyd, Jr. 1923- DLB-8

Bigiaretti, Libero 1905-1993 . . . . .DLB-177

Bigland, Eileen 1898-1970 . . . . DLB-195

Biglow, Hosea (see Lowell, James Russell)

Bigongiari, Piero 1914- DLB-128

Billinger, Richard 1890-1965 . . . . DLB-124

Billings, Hammatt 1818-1874 . . . . DLB-188

Billings, John Shaw 1898-1975 . . . . DLB-137

Billings, Josh (see Shaw, Henry Wheeler)

Binding, Rudolf G. 1867-1938 . . . . DLB-66

Bingham, Caleb 1757-1817 . . . . DLB-42

Bingham, George Barry 1906-1988 . . . . . DLB-127

Bingham, Sallie 1937- DLB-234

Bingley, William [publishing house] DLB-154

Binyon, Laurence 1869-1943 . . . . DLB-19

Biographia Brittanica DLB-142

Biographical Documents I Y-84

Biographical Documents II Y-85

Bioren, John [publishing house] DLB-49

Bioy Casares, Adolfo 1914- DLB-113

Bird, Isabella Lucy 1831-1904 . . . . DLB-166

Bird, Robert Montgomery 1806-1854 . . . DLB-202

Bird, William 1888-1963 . . . . DLB-4; DS-15

Birken, Sigmund von 1626-1681 . . . . DLB-164

Birney, Earle 1904- DLB-88

Birrell, Augustine 1850-1933 . . . . DLB-98

Bisher, Furman 1918- DLB-171

Bishop, Elizabeth 1911-1979 . . . . DLB-5, 169

Bishop, John Peale 1892-1944 . . . . . DLB-4, 9, 45

Bismarck, Otto von 1815-1898 . . . . DLB-129

Bisset, Robert 1759-1805 . . . . DLB-142

Bissett, Bill 1939- DLB-53

Bitzius, Albert (see Gotthelf, Jeremias)

Bjørnvig, Thorkild 1918- DLB-214

Black, David (D. M.) 1941- DLB-40

Black, Walter J. [publishing house] DLB-46

Black, Winifred 1863-1936 . . . . DLB-25

The Black Aesthetic: Background DS-8

Black Theaters and Theater Organizations in
    America, 1961-1982:
    A Research List DLB-38

Black Theatre: A Forum [excerpts] DLB-38

Blackamore, Arthur 1679-? DLB-24, 39

Blackburn, Alexander L. 1929- Y-85

Blackburn, Paul 1926-1971 . . . . .DLB-16; Y-81

Blackburn, Thomas 1916-1977 . . . . DLB-27

Blackmore, R. D. 1825-1900 . . . . DLB-18

Blackmore, Sir Richard 1654-1729 . . . . . . DLB-131

Blackmur, R. P. 1904-1965 . . . . DLB-63

Blackwell, Basil, Publisher DLB-106

Blackwood, Algernon Henry
    1869-1951 . . . . .DLB-153, 156, 178

Blackwood, Caroline 1931-1996 . . . . .DLB-14, 207

Blackwood, William, and Sons, Ltd. DLB-154

Blackwood's Edinburgh Magazine
    1817-1980 . . . . DLB-110

Blades, William 1824-1890 . . . . DLB-184

Blaga, Lucian 1895-1961 . . . . DLB-220

Blagden, Isabella 1817?-1873 . . . . DLB-199

Blair, Eric Arthur (see Orwell, George)

Blair, Francis Preston 1791-1876 . . . . DLB-43

Blair, James circa 1655-1743 . . . . DLB-24

Blair, John Durburrow 1759-1823 . . . . DLB-37

Blais, Marie-Claire 1939- DLB-53

Blaise, Clark 1940- DLB-53

Blake, George 1893-1961 . . . . DLB-191

Blake, Lillie Devereux 1833-1913 . . . DLB-202, 221

Blake, Nicholas 1904-1972 . . . . DLB-77
    (see Day Lewis, C.)

Blake, William 1757-1827 . . . . . .DLB-93, 154, 163

The Blakiston Company DLB-49

Blandiana, Ana 1942- DLB-232

Blanchot, Maurice 1907- DLB-72

Blanckenburg, Christian Friedrich von
    1744-1796 . . . . DLB-94

Blaser, Robin 1925- DLB-165

Blaumanis, Rudolfs 1863-1908 . . . . DLB-220

Bledsoe, Albert Taylor 1809-1877 . . . . . .DLB-3, 79

Bleecker, Ann Eliza 1752-1783 . . . . DLB-200

Blelock and Company DLB-49

Blennerhassett, Margaret Agnew
    1773-1842 . . . . DLB-99

Bles, Geoffrey [publishing house] DLB-112

Blessington, Marguerite, Countess of
    1789-1849 . . . . DLB-166

The Blickling Homilies circa 971 . . . . DLB-146

Blind, Mathilde 1841-1896 . . . . DLB-199

Blish, James 1921-1975 . . . . DLB-8

Bliss, E., and E. White
    [publishing house] DLB-49

Bliven, Bruce 1889-1977 . . . . .DLB-137

Blixen, Karen 1885-1962 . . . . DLB-214

Bloch, Robert 1917-1994 . . . . DLB-44

Block, Lawrence 1938- DLB-226

Block, Rudolph (see Lessing, Bruno)

Blondal, Patricia 1926-1959 . . . . DLB-88

Bloom, Harold 1930- DLB-67

Bloomer, Amelia 1818-1894 . . . . DLB-79

Bloomfield, Robert 1766-1823 . . . . DLB-93

Bloomsbury Group DS-10

Blotner, Joseph 1923- DLB-111

Bloy, Léon 1846-1917 . . . . DLB-123

Blume, Judy 1938- DLB-52

Blunck, Hans Friedrich 1888-1961 . . . . . . .DLB-66

Blunden, Edmund 1896-1974 . . .DLB-20, 100, 155

Blunt, Lady Anne Isabella Noel
1837-1917. . . . . .DLB-174

Blunt, Wilfrid Scawen 1840-1922 . . . .DLB-19, 174

Bly, Nellie (see Cochrane, Elizabeth)

Bly, Robert 1926- DLB-5

Blyton, Enid 1897-1968 . . . . .DLB-160

Boaden, James 1762-1839 . . . . .DLB-89

Boas, Frederick S. 1862-1957. . . . . .DLB-149

The Bobbs-Merrill Archive at the
Lilly Library, Indiana University Y-90

The Bobbs-Merrill Company. DLB-46

Bobrov, Semen Sergeevich
1763?-1810. . . . . .DLB-150

Bobrowski, Johannes 1917-1965. . . . . .DLB-75

The Elmer Holmes Bobst Awards in Arts
and Letters Y-87

Bodenheim, Maxwell 1892-1954 . . . . . .DLB-9, 45

Bodenstedt, Friedrich von 1819-1892 . . . .DLB-129

Bodini, Vittorio 1914-1970. . . . . .DLB-128

Bodkin, M. McDonnell 1850-1933 . . . . . . .DLB-70

Bodley, Sir Thomas 1545-1613 . . . . .DLB-213

Bodley Head DLB-112

Bodmer, Johann Jakob 1698-1783 . . . . . . .DLB-97

Bodmershof, Imma von 1895-1982 . . . . . .DLB-85

Bodsworth, Fred 1918- DLB-68

Boehm, Sydney 1908- DLB-44

Boer, Charles 1939- DLB-5

Boethius circa 480-circa 524 . . . . .DLB-115

Boethius of Dacia circa 1240-? DLB-115

Bogan, Louise 1897-1970 . . . . .DLB-45, 169

Bogarde, Dirk 1921- DLB-14

Bogdanovich, Ippolit Fedorovich
circa 1743-1803 . . . . .DLB-150

Bogue, David [publishing house] DLB-106

Böhme, Jakob 1575-1624 . . . . .DLB-164

Bohn, H. G. [publishing house] DLB-106

Bohse, August 1661-1742. . . . . .DLB-168

Boie, Heinrich Christian 1744-1806. . . . . . .DLB-94

Bok, Edward W. 1863-1930 . . . . .DLB-91; DS-16

Boland, Eavan 1944- DLB-40

Boldrewood, Rolf
(Thomas Alexander Browne)
1826?-1915 . . . . .DLB-230

Bolingbroke, Henry St. John, Viscount
1678-1751 . . . . .DLB-101

Böll, Heinrich 1917-1985 . . . . .DLB-69; Y-85

Bolling, Robert 1738-1775 . . . . .DLB-31

Bolotov, Andrei Timofeevich
1738-1833 . . . . .DLB-150

Bolt, Carol 1941- DLB-60

Bolt, Robert 1924-1995 . . . . .DLB-13, 233

Bolton, Herbert E. 1870-1953 . . . . .DLB-17

Bonaventura DLB-90

Bonaventure circa 1217-1274 . . . . .DLB-115

Bonaviri, Giuseppe 1924- DLB-177

Bond, Edward 1934- DLB-13

Bond, Michael 1926- DLB-161

Boni, Albert and Charles
[publishing house] DLB-46

Boni and Liveright. DLB-46

Bonner, Marita 1899-1971 . . . . .DLB-228

Bonner, Paul Hyde 1893-1968. . . . . DS-17

Bonner, Sherwood 1849-1883 . . . . .DLB-202

Robert Bonner's Sons DLB-49

Bonnin, Gertrude Simmons (see Zitkala-Ša)

Bonsanti, Alessandro 1904-1984 . . . . .DLB-177

Bontemps, Arna 1902-1973 . . . . .DLB-48, 51

The Book Arts Press at the University
of Virginia. Y-96

The Book League of America DLB-46

Book Publishing Accounting: Some Basic
Concepts Y-98

Book Reviewing in America: I. Y-87

Book Reviewing in America: II. Y-88

Book Reviewing in America: III Y-89

Book Reviewing in America: IV Y-90

Book Reviewing in America: V. Y-91

Book Reviewing in America: VI Y-92

Book Reviewing in America: VII Y-93

Book Reviewing in America: VIII. Y-94

Book Reviewing in America and the
Literary Scene Y-95

Book Reviewing and the
Literary Scene Y-96, Y-97

Book Supply Company DLB-49

The Book Trade History Group Y-93

The Booker Prize. Y-96

Address by Anthony Thwaite,
Chairman of the Booker Prize Judges
Comments from Former Booker
Prize Winners Y-86

Boorde, Andrew circa 1490-1549 . . . . . . .DLB-136

Boorstin, Daniel J. 1914- DLB-17

Booth, Franklin 1874-1948. . . . . .DLB-188

Booth, Mary L. 1831-1889 . . . . .DLB-79

Booth, Philip 1925- Y-82

Booth, Wayne C. 1921- DLB-67

Booth, William 1829-1912. . . . . .DLB-190

Borchardt, Rudolf 1877-1945. . . . . .DLB-66

Borchert, Wolfgang 1921-1947 . . . . . .DLB-69, 124

Borel, Pétrus 1809-1859. . . . . .DLB-119

Borges, Jorge Luis 1899-1986 . . . . .DLB-113; Y-86

Börne, Ludwig 1786-1837 . . . . .DLB-90

Bornstein, Miriam 1950- DLB-209

Borowski, Tadeusz 1922-1951. . . . . .DLB-215

Borrow, George 1803-1881 . . . . . .DLB-21, 55, 166

Bosch, Juan 1909- DLB-145

Bosco, Henri 1888-1976. . . . . .DLB-72

Bosco, Monique 1927- DLB-53

Bosman, Herman Charles 1905-1951 . . . .DLB-225

Boston, Lucy M. 1892-1990 . . . . .DLB-161

Boswell, James 1740-1795. . . . . .DLB-104, 142

Boswell, Robert 1953- DLB-234

Bote, Hermann
circa 1460-circa 1520. . . . . .DLB-179

Botev, Khristo 1847-1876. . . . . .DLB-147

Botta, Anne C. Lynch 1815-1891 . . . . .DLB-3

Botto, Ján (see Krasko, Ivan)

Bottome, Phyllis 1882-1963. . . . . .DLB-197

Bottomley, Gordon 1874-1948. . . . . .DLB-10

Bottoms, David 1949- DLB-120; Y-83

Bottrall, Ronald 1906- DLB-20

Bouchardy, Joseph 1810-1870 . . . . .DLB-192

Boucher, Anthony 1911-1968 . . . . .DLB-8

Boucher, Jonathan 1738-1804 . . . . .DLB-31

Boucher de Boucherville, George
1814-1894 . . . . .DLB-99

Boudreau, Daniel (see Coste, Donat)

Bourassa, Napoléon 1827-1916 . . . . .DLB-99

Bourget, Paul 1852-1935 . . . . .DLB-123

Bourinot, John George 1837-1902 . . . . . . .DLB-99

Bourjaily, Vance 1922- DLB-2, 143

Bourne, Edward Gaylord
1860-1908 . . . . .DLB-47

Bourne, Randolph 1886-1918 . . . . .DLB-63

Bousoño, Carlos 1923- DLB-108

Bousquet, Joë 1897-1950 . . . . .DLB-72

Bova, Ben 1932- Y-81

Bovard, Oliver K. 1872-1945. . . . . .DLB-25

Bove, Emmanuel 1898-1945 . . . . .DLB-72

Bowen, Elizabeth 1899-1973 . . . . . .DLB-15, 162

Bowen, Francis 1811-1890. . . . . .DLB-1, 59

Bowen, John 1924- DLB-13

Bowen, Marjorie 1886-1952 . . . . .DLB-153

Bowen-Merrill Company. DLB-49

Bowering, George 1935- DLB-53

Bowers, Bathsheba 1671-1718 . . . . .DLB-200

Bowers, Claude G. 1878-1958 . . . . .DLB-17

Bowers, Edgar 1924- DLB-5

Bowers, Fredson Thayer
1905-1991 . . . . .DLB-140; Y-91

Bowles, Paul 1910-1999. . . . . .DLB-5, 6, 218; Y-99

Bowles, Samuel III 1826-1878 . . . . .DLB-43

Bowles, William Lisles 1762-1850 . . . . . . .DLB-93

Bowman, Louise Morey 1882-1944. . . . . . .DLB-68

Boyd, James 1888-1944 . . . . .DLB-9; DS-16

Boyd, John 1919- DLB-8

Boyd, Thomas 1898-1935 . . . . .DLB-9; DS-16

Boyd, William 1952- DLB-231

Boyesen, Hjalmar Hjorth
1848-1895 . . . . .DLB-12, 71; DS-13

Boyle, Kay 1902-1992 . . . . .DLB-4, 9, 48, 86; Y-93

Boyle, Roger, Earl of Orrery 1621-1679 . . .DLB-80

Boyle, T. Coraghessan 1948- DLB-218; Y-86

Božić, Mirko 1919- DLB-181

Brackenbury, Alison 1953- DLB-40

Brackenridge, Hugh Henry
1748-1816 . . . . .DLB-11, 37

Brackett, Charles 1892-1969 . . . . DLB-26

Brackett, Leigh 1915-1978 . . . . DLB-8, 26

Bradburn, John [publishing house] DLB-49

Bradbury, Malcolm 1932- DLB-14, 207

Bradbury, Ray 1920- DLB-2, 8

Bradbury and Evans DLB-106

Braddon, Mary Elizabeth
    1835-1915 . . . . DLB-18, 70, 156

Bradford, Andrew 1686-1742 . . . . DLB-43, 73

Bradford, Gamaliel 1863-1932 . . . . DLB-17

Bradford, John 1749-1830 . . . . DLB-43

Bradford, Roark 1896-1948 . . . . DLB-86

Bradford, William 1590-1657 . . . . DLB-24, 30

Bradford, William III 1719-1791 . . . . . DLB-43, 73

Bradlaugh, Charles 1833-1891 . . . . DLB-57

Bradley, David 1950- DLB-33

Bradley, Ira, and Company DLB-49

Bradley, J. W., and Company DLB-49

Bradley, Marion Zimmer 1930-1999 . . . . . DLB-8

Bradley, William Aspenwall 1878-1939 . . . . DLB-4

Bradshaw, Henry 1831-1886 . . . . DLB-184

Bradstreet, Anne 1612 or 1613-1672 . . . . . DLB-24

Bradūnas, Kazys 1917- DLB-220

Bradwardine, Thomas circa
    1295-1349 . . . . DLB-115

Brady, Frank 1924-1986 . . . . DLB-111

Brady, Frederic A. [publishing house] DLB-49

Bragg, Melvyn 1939- DLB-14

Brainard, Charles H. [publishing house] . . . DLB-49

Braine, John 1922-1986 . . . . DLB-15; Y-86

Braithwait, Richard 1588-1673 . . . . DLB-151

Braithwaite, William Stanley
    1878-1962 . . . . DLB-50, 54

Braker, Ulrich 1735-1798 . . . . DLB-94

Bramah, Ernest 1868-1942 . . . . DLB-70

Branagan, Thomas 1774-1843 . . . . DLB-37

Branch, William Blackwell 1927- DLB-76

Branden Press DLB-46

Branner, H.C. 1903-1966 . . . . DLB-214

Brant, Sebastian 1457-1521 . . . . DLB-179

Brassey, Lady Annie (Allnutt)
    1839-1887 . . . . DLB-166

Brathwaite, Edward Kamau
    1930- DLB-125

Brault, Jacques 1933- DLB-53

Braun, Matt 1932- DLB-212

Braun, Volker 1939- DLB-75

Brautigan, Richard
    1935-1984 . . . . DLB-2, 5, 206; Y-80, Y-84

Braxton, Joanne M. 1950- DLB-41

Bray, Anne Eliza 1790-1883 . . . . DLB-116

Bray, Thomas 1656-1730 . . . . DLB-24

Brazdžionis, Bernardas 1907- DLB-220

Braziller, George [publishing house] DLB-46

The Bread Loaf Writers' Conference 1983 . . . Y-84

Breasted, James Henry 1865-1935 . . . . DLB-47

Brecht, Bertolt 1898-1956 . . . . DLB-56, 124

Bredel, Willi 1901-1964 . . . . DLB-56

Bregendahl, Marie 1867-1940 . . . . DLB-214

Breitinger, Johann Jakob 1701-1776 . . . . . . DLB-97

Bremser, Bonnie 1939- DLB-16

Bremser, Ray 1934- DLB-16

Brennan, Christopher 1870-1932 . . . . DLB-230

Brentano, Bernard von 1901-1964 . . . . . . DLB-56

Brentano, Clemens 1778-1842 . . . . DLB-90

Brentano's DLB-49

Brenton, Howard 1942- DLB-13

Breslin, Jimmy 1929-1996 . . . . DLB-185

Breton, André 1896-1966 . . . . DLB-65

Breton, Nicholas circa 1555-circa 1626 . . . DLB-136

The Breton Lays
    1300-early fifteenth century DLB-146

Brewer, Luther A. 1858-1933 . . . . DLB-187

Brewer, Warren and Putnam DLB-46

Brewster, Elizabeth 1922- DLB-60

Breytenbach, Breyten 1939- DLB-225

Bridge, Ann (Lady Mary Dolling Sanders
    O'Malley) 1889-1974 . . . . DLB-191

Bridge, Horatio 1806-1893 . . . . DLB-183

Bridgers, Sue Ellen 1942- DLB-52

Bridges, Robert 1844-1930 . . . . DLB-19, 98

The Bridgewater Library DLB-213

Bridie, James 1888-1951 . . . . DLB-10

Brieux, Eugene 1858-1932 . . . . DLB-192

Brigadere, Anna 1861-1933 . . . . DLB-220

Bright, Mary Chavelita Dunne (see Egerton, George)

Brimmer, B. J., Company DLB-46

Brines, Francisco 1932- DLB-134

Brink, André 1935- DLB-225

Brinley, George, Jr. 1817-1875 . . . . DLB-140

Brinnin, John Malcolm 1916-1998 . . . . . . DLB-48

Brisbane, Albert 1809-1890 . . . . DLB-3

Brisbane, Arthur 1864-1936 . . . . DLB-25

British Academy DLB-112

The British Critic 1793-1843 . . . . DLB-110

The British Library and the Regular
    Readers' Group Y-91

British Literary Prizes Y-98

*The British Review and London Critical
    Journal* 1811-1825 . . . . DLB-110

British Travel Writing, 1940-1997 . . . . . . DLB-204

Brito, Aristeo 1942- DLB-122

Brittain, Vera 1893-1970 . . . . DLB-191

Brizeux, Auguste 1803-1858 . . . . DLB-217

Broadway Publishing Company DLB-46

Broch, Hermann 1886-1951 . . . . DLB-85, 124

Brochu, André 1942- DLB-53

Brock, Edwin 1927- DLB-40

Brockes, Barthold Heinrich 1680-1747 . . . DLB-168

Brod, Max 1884-1968 . . . . DLB-81

Brodber, Erna 1940- DLB-157

Brodhead, John R. 1814-1873 . . . . DLB-30

Brodkey, Harold 1930-1996 . . . . DLB-130

Brodsky, Joseph 1940-1996 . . . . Y-87

Broeg, Bob 1918- DLB-171

Brøgger, Suzanne 1944- DLB-214

Brome, Richard circa 1590-1652 . . . . DLB-58

Brome, Vincent 1910- DLB-155

Bromfield, Louis 1896-1956 . . . . . . DLB-4, 9, 86

Bromige, David 1933- DLB-193

Broner, E. M. 1930- DLB-28

Bronk, William 1918-1999 . . . . DLB-165

Bronnen, Arnolt 1895-1959 . . . . DLB-124

Brontë, Anne 1820-1849 . . . . DLB-21, 199

Brontë, Charlotte 1816-1855 . . . . DLB-21, 159, 199

Brontë, Emily 1818-1848 . . . . DLB-21, 32, 199

Brook, Stephen 1947- DLB-204

Brook Farm 1841-1847 . . . . DLB-223

Brooke, Frances 1724-1789 . . . . DLB-39, 99

Brooke, Henry 1703?-1783 . . . . DLB-39

Brooke, L. Leslie 1862-1940 . . . . DLB-141

Brooke, Margaret, Ranee of Sarawak
    1849-1936 . . . . DLB-174

Brooke, Rupert 1887-1915 . . . . DLB-19, 216

Brooker, Bertram 1888-1955 . . . . DLB-88

Brooke-Rose, Christine 1923- DLB-14, 231

Brookner, Anita 1928- DLB-194; Y-87

Brooks, Charles Timothy 1813-1883 . . . . . . DLB-1

Brooks, Cleanth 1906-1994 . . . . DLB-63; Y-94

Brooks, Gwendolyn 1917- DLB-5, 76, 165

Brooks, Jeremy 1926- DLB-14

Brooks, Mel 1926- DLB-26

Brooks, Noah 1830-1903 . . . . DLB-42; DS-13

Brooks, Richard 1912-1992 . . . . DLB-44

Brooks, Van Wyck
    1886-1963 . . . . DLB-45, 63, 103

Brophy, Brigid 1929-1995 . . . . DLB-14

Brophy, John 1899-1965 . . . . DLB-191

Brossard, Chandler 1922-1993 . . . . DLB-16

Brossard, Nicole 1943- DLB-53

Broster, Dorothy Kathleen 1877-1950 . . . DLB-160

Brother Antoninus (see Everson, William)

Brotherton, Lord 1856-1930 . . . . DLB-184

Brougham and Vaux, Henry Peter Brougham,
    Baron 1778-1868 . . . . DLB-110, 158

Brougham, John 1810-1880 . . . . DLB-11

Broughton, James 1913-1999 . . . . DLB-5

Broughton, Rhoda 1840-1920 . . . . DLB-18

Broun, Heywood 1888-1939 . . . . DLB-29, 171

Brown, Alice 1856-1948 . . . . DLB-78

Brown, Bob 1886-1959 . . . . DLB-4, 45

Brown, Cecil 1943- DLB-33

Brown, Charles Brockden
    1771-1810 . . . . DLB-37, 59, 73

Brown, Christy 1932-1981 . . . . DLB-14

Brown, Dee 1908- Y-80

Brown, Frank London 1927-1962 . . . . .DLB-76

Brown, Fredric 1906-1972 . . . . .DLB-8

Brown, George Mackay
1921-1996 . . . . DLB-14, 27, 139

Brown, Harry 1917-1986 . . . . .DLB-26

Brown, Larry 1951- DLB-234

Brown, Marcia 1918- DLB-61

Brown, Margaret Wise 1910-1952 . . . . . . .DLB-22

Brown, Morna Doris (see Ferrars, Elizabeth)

Brown, Oliver Madox 1855-1874 . . . . .DLB-21

Brown, Sterling 1901-1989 . . . . . . .DLB-48, 51, 63

Brown, T. E. 1830-1897 . . . . .DLB-35

Brown, Thomas Alexander (see Boldrewood, Rolf)

Brown, William Hill 1765-1793 . . . . .DLB-37

Brown, William Wells
1814-1884 . . . . .DLB-3, 50, 183

Browne, Charles Farrar 1834-1867 . . . . . .DLB-11

Browne, Frances 1816-1879 . . . . .DLB-199

Browne, Francis Fisher 1843-1913 . . . . . . .DLB-79

Browne, Howard 1908-1999 . . . . .DLB-226

Browne, J. Ross 1821-1875 . . . . .DLB-202

Browne, Michael Dennis 1940- DLB-40

Browne, Sir Thomas 1605-1682 . . . . . . .DLB-151

Browne, William, of Tavistock
1590-1645 .DLB-121

Browne, Wynyard 1911-1964 . . . . . .DLB-13, 233

Browne and Nolan DLB-106

Brownell, W. C. 1851-1928 . . . . .DLB-71

Browning, Elizabeth Barrett
1806-1861 . . . . .DLB-32, 199

Browning, Robert 1812-1889 . . . . . . .DLB-32, 163

   Introductory Essay: *Letters of Percy
   Bysshe Shelley* (1852) DLB-32

Brownjohn, Allan 1931- DLB-40

Brownson, Orestes Augustus
1803-1876 . . . . DLB-1, 59, 73

Bruccoli, Matthew J. 1931- DLB-103

Bruce, Charles 1906-1971 . . . . .DLB-68

John Edward Bruce: Three Documents DLB-50

Bruce, Leo 1903-1979 . . . . .DLB-77

Bruce, Mary Grant 1878-1958 . . . . .DLB-230

Bruce, Philip Alexander 1856-1933 . . . . . .DLB-47

Bruce Humphries [publishing house] DLB-46

Bruce-Novoa, Juan 1944- DLB-82

Bruckman, Clyde 1894-1955 . . . . .DLB-26

Bruckner, Ferdinand 1891-1958 . . . . .DLB-118

Brundage, John Herbert (see Herbert, John)

Brutus, Dennis 1924- DLB-117, 225

Bryan, C. D. B. 1936- DLB-185

Bryant, Arthur 1899-1985 . . . . .DLB-149

Bryant, William Cullen
1794-1878 . . . . .DLB-3, 43, 59, 189

Bryce Echenique, Alfredo 1939- DLB-145

Bryce, James 1838-1922 . . . . .DLB-166, 190

Bryden, Bill 1942- DLB-233

Brydges, Sir Samuel Egerton 1762-1837 . . .DLB-107

Bryskett, Lodowick 1546?-1612 . . . . .DLB-167

Buchan, John 1875-1940 . . . . DLB-34, 70, 156

Buchanan, George 1506-1582 . . . . .DLB-132

Buchanan, Robert 1841-1901 . . . . . . .DLB-18, 35

   "The Fleshly School of Poetry and Other
   Phenomena of the Day" (1872), by
   Robert Buchanan DLB-35

   "The Fleshly School of Poetry: Mr. D. G.
   Rossetti" (1871), by Thomas Maitland
   (Robert Buchanan) DLB-35

Buchman, Sidney 1902-1975 . . . . .DLB-26

Buchner, Augustus 1591-1661 . . . . .DLB-164

Büchner, Georg 1813-1837 . . . . .DLB-133

Bucholtz, Andreas Heinrich 1607-1671 . . .DLB-168

Buck, Pearl S. 1892-1973 . . . . .DLB-9, 102

Bucke, Charles 1781-1846 . . . . .DLB-110

Bucke, Richard Maurice 1837-1902 . . . . . .DLB-99

Buckingham, Joseph Tinker 1779-1861 and
   Buckingham, Edwin 1810-1833 . . . . . .DLB-73

Buckler, Ernest 1908-1984 . . . . .DLB-68

Buckley, William F., Jr.
1925- DLB-137; Y-80

Buckminster, Joseph Stevens
1784-1812 . . . . .DLB-37

Buckner, Robert 1906- DLB-26

Budd, Thomas ?-1698 . . . . .DLB-24

Budrys, A. J. 1931- DLB-8

Buechner, Frederick 1926- Y-80

Buell, John 1927- DLB-53

Bufalino, Gesualdo 1920-1996 . . . . .DLB-196

Buffum, Job [publishing house] DLB-49

Bugnet, Georges 1879-1981 . . . . .DLB-92

Buies, Arthur 1840-1901 . . . . .DLB-99

Building the New British Library
   at St Pancras Y-94

Bukowski, Charles 1920-1994 . . . .DLB-5, 130, 169

Bulatović, Miodrag 1930-1991 . . . . .DLB-181

Bulgarin, Faddei Venediktovich
1789-1859 . . . . .DLB-198

Bulger, Bozeman 1877-1932 . . . . .DLB-171

Bullein, William
   between 1520 and 1530-1576 . . . . . . .DLB-167

Bullins, Ed 1935- DLB-7, 38

Bulwer-Lytton, Edward (also Edward Bulwer)
1803-1873 . . . . .DLB-21

   "On Art in Fiction "(1838) DLB-21

Bumpus, Jerry 1937- Y-81

Bunce and Brother DLB-49

Bunner, H. C. 1855-1896 . . . . .DLB-78, 79

Bunting, Basil 1900-1985 . . . . .DLB-20

Buntline, Ned (Edward Zane Carroll Judson)
1821-1886 . . . . .DLB-186

Bunyan, John 1628-1688 . . . . .DLB-39

Burch, Robert 1925- DLB-52

Burciaga, José Antonio 1940- DLB-82

Bürger, Gottfried August 1747-1794 . . . . . .DLB-94

Burgess, Anthony 1917-1993 . . . . .DLB-14, 194

The Anthony Burgess Archive at
   the Harry Ransom Humanities
   Research Center Y-98

Anthony Burgess's 99 Novels:
   An Opinion Poll Y-84

Burgess, Gelett 1866-1951 . . . . .DLB-11

Burgess, John W. 1844-1931 . . . . .DLB-47

Burgess, Thornton W. 1874-1965 . . . . . . .DLB-22

Burgess, Stringer and Company DLB-49

Burick, Si 1909-1986 . . . . .DLB-171

Burk, John Daly circa 1772-1808 . . . . .DLB-37

Burk, Ronnie 1955- DLB-209

Burke, Edmund 1729?-1797 . . . . .DLB-104

Burke, James Lee 1936- DLB-226

Burke, Kenneth 1897-1993 . . . . .DLB-45, 63

Burke, Thomas 1886-1945 . . . . .DLB-197

Burlingame, Edward Livermore
1848-1922 . . . . .DLB-79

Burnet, Gilbert 1643-1715 . . . . .DLB-101

Burnett, Frances Hodgson
1849-1924 . . . . DLB-42, 141; DS-13, 14

Burnett, W. R. 1899-1982 . . . . .DLB-9, 226

Burnett, Whit 1899-1973 and
   Martha Foley 1897-1977 . . . . .DLB-137

Burney, Fanny 1752-1840 . . . . .DLB-39

   Dedication, *The Wanderer* (1814) DLB-39

   Preface to *Evelina* (1778) DLB-39

Burns, Alan 1929- DLB-14, 194

Burns, John Horne 1916-1953 . . . . Y-85

Burns, Robert 1759-1796 . . . . .DLB-109

Burns and Oates .DLB-106

Burnshaw, Stanley 1906- DLB-48

Burr, C. Chauncey 1815?-1883 . . . . .DLB-79

Burr, Esther Edwards 1732-1758 . . . . .DLB-200

Burroughs, Edgar Rice 1875-1950 . . . . .DLB-8

Burroughs, John 1837-1921 . . . . .DLB-64

Burroughs, Margaret T. G. 1917- DLB-41

Burroughs, William S., Jr. 1947-1981 . . . . . .DLB-16

Burroughs, William Seward
1914-1997 . . . . . .DLB-2, 8, 16, 152; Y-81, Y-97

Burroway, Janet 1936- DLB-6

Burt, Maxwell Struthers
1882-1954 . . . . .DLB-86; DS-16

Burt, A. L., and Company DLB-49

Burton, Hester 1913- DLB-161

Burton, Isabel Arundell 1831-1896 . . . . . .DLB-166

Burton, Miles (see Rhode, John)

Burton, Richard Francis
1821-1890 . . . . DLB-55, 166, 184

Burton, Robert 1577-1640 . . . . .DLB-151

Burton, Virginia Lee 1909-1968 . . . . .DLB-22

Burton, William Evans 1804-1860 . . . . . . .DLB-73

Burwell, Adam Hood 1790-1849 . . . . .DLB-99

Bury, Lady Charlotte 1775-1861 . . . . .DLB-116

Busch, Frederick 1941- DLB-6, 218

Busch, Niven 1903-1991 . . . . .DLB-44

Bushnell, Horace 1802-1876 . . . . DS-13

Bussieres, Arthur de 1877-1913 . . . . DLB-92

Butler, Guy 1918- DLB-225

Butler, E. H., and Company DLB-49

Butler, Josephine Elizabeth 1828-1906 . . . DLB-190

Butler, Juan 1942-1981 . . . . DLB-53

Butler, Octavia E. 1947- DLB-33

Butler, Pierce 1884-1953 . . . . DLB-187

Butler, Robert Olen 1945- DLB-173

Butler, Samuel 1613-1680 . . . . DLB-101, 126

Butler, Samuel 1835-1902 . . . . DLB-18, 57, 174

Butler, William Francis 1838-1910 . . . . . . DLB-166

Butor, Michel 1926- DLB-83

Butter, Nathaniel [publishing house] DLB-170

Butterworth, Hezekiah 1839-1905 . . . . DLB-42

Buttitta, Ignazio 1899- DLB-114

Buzzati, Dino 1906-1972 . . . . .DLB-177

Byars, Betsy 1928- DLB-52

Byatt, A. S. 1936- DLB-14, 194

Byles, Mather 1707-1788 . . . . DLB-24

Bynneman, Henry
  [publishing house] DLB-170

Bynner, Witter 1881-1968 . . . . DLB-54

Byrd, William circa 1543-1623 . . . . .DLB-172

Byrd, William II 1674-1744 . . . . DLB-24, 140

Byrne, John Keyes (see Leonard, Hugh)

Byron, George Gordon, Lord
  1788-1824 . . . . DLB-96, 110

Byron, Robert 1905-1941 . . . . DLB-195

C

Caballero Bonald, José Manuel
  1926- DLB-108

Cabañero, Eladio 1930- DLB-134

Cabell, James Branch 1879-1958 . . . . DLB-9, 78

Cabeza de Baca, Manuel 1853-1915 . . . . . DLB-122

Cabeza de Baca Gilbert, Fabiola
  1898- DLB-122

Cable, George Washington
  1844-1925 . . . . .DLB-12, 74; DS-13

Cable, Mildred 1878-1952 . . . . DLB-195

Cabrera, Lydia 1900-1991 . . . . DLB-145

Cabrera Infante, Guillermo 1929- DLB-113

Cadell [publishing house] DLB-154

Cady, Edwin H. 1917- DLB-103

Caedmon flourished 658-680 . . . . DLB-146

Caedmon School circa 660-899 . . . . DLB-146

Cafés, Brasseries, and Bistros DS-15

Cage, John 1912-1992 . . . . DLB-193

Cahan, Abraham 1860-1951 . . . . DLB-9, 25, 28

Cain, George 1943- DLB-33

Cain, James M. 1892-1977 . . . . DLB-226

Caird, Mona 1854-1932 . . . . DLB-197

Čaks, Aleksandrs 1901-1950 . . . . DLB-220

Caldecott, Randolph 1846-1886 . . . . DLB-163

Calder, John (Publishers), Limited DLB-112

Calderón de la Barca, Fanny
  1804-1882 . . . . DLB-183

Caldwell, Ben 1937- DLB-38

Caldwell, Erskine 1903-1987 . . . . DLB-9, 86

Caldwell, H. M., Company DLB-49

Caldwell, Taylor 1900-1985 . . . . DS-17

Calhoun, John C. 1782-1850 . . . . DLB-3

Călinescu, George 1899-1965 . . . . DLB-220

Calisher, Hortense 1911- DLB-2, 218

A Call to Letters and an Invitation
  to the Electric Chair,
  by Siegfried Mandel DLB-75

Callaghan, Mary Rose 1944- DLB-207

Callaghan, Morley 1903-1990 . . . . DLB-68

Callahan, S. Alice 1868-1894 . . . . . . .DLB-175, 221

Callaloo Y-87

Callimachus circa 305 B.C.-240 B.C. DLB-176

Calmer, Edgar 1907- DLB-4

Calverley, C. S. 1831-1884 . . . . DLB-35

Calvert, George Henry 1803-1889 . . . . . DLB-1, 64

Calvino, Italo 1923-1985 . . . . DLB-196

Cambridge, Ada 1844-1926 . . . . DLB-230

Cambridge Press DLB-49

Cambridge Songs (Carmina Cantabrigensia)
  circa 1050 . . . . DLB-148

Cambridge University Press DLB-170

Camden, William 1551-1623 . . . . .DLB-172

Camden House: An Interview with
  James Hardin Y-92

Cameron, Eleanor 1912- DLB-52

Cameron, George Frederick
  1854-1885 . . . . DLB-99

Cameron, Lucy Lyttelton 1781-1858 . . . . DLB-163

Cameron, Peter 1959- DLB-234

Cameron, William Bleasdell 1862-1951 . . . DLB-99

Camm, John 1718-1778 . . . . DLB-31

Camon, Ferdinando 1935- DLB-196

Campana, Dino 1885-1932 . . . . DLB-114

Campbell, Bebe Moore 1950- DLB-227

Campbell, Gabrielle Margaret Vere
  (see Shearing, Joseph, and Bowen, Marjorie)

Campbell, James Dykes 1838-1895 . . . . . DLB-144

Campbell, James Edwin 1867-1896 . . . . . . DLB-50

Campbell, John 1653-1728 . . . . DLB-43

Campbell, John W., Jr. 1910-1971 . . . . DLB-8

Campbell, Roy 1901-1957 . . . . DLB-20, 225

Campbell, Thomas 1777-1844 . . . . . DLB-93, 144

Campbell, William Wilfred 1858-1918 . . . DLB-92

Campion, Edmund 1539-1581 . . . . DLB-167

Campion, Thomas 1567-1620 . . . . . .DLB-58, 172

Camus, Albert 1913-1960 . . . . DLB-72

The Canadian Publishers' Records
  Database Y-96

Canby, Henry Seidel 1878-1961 . . . . DLB-91

Candelaria, Cordelia 1943- DLB-82

Candelaria, Nash 1928- DLB-82

Canetti, Elias 1905-1994 . . . . DLB-85, 124

Canham, Erwin Dain 1904-1982 . . . . . . .DLB-127

Canitz, Friedrich Rudolph Ludwig von
  1654-1699 . . . . DLB-168

Cankar, Ivan 1876-1918 . . . . .DLB-147

Cannan, Gilbert 1884-1955 . . . . .DLB-10, 197

Cannan, Joanna 1896-1961 . . . . DLB-191

Cannell, Kathleen 1891-1974 . . . . DLB-4

Cannell, Skipwith 1887-1957 . . . . DLB-45

Canning, George 1770-1827 . . . . DLB-158

Cannon, Jimmy 1910-1973 . . . . .DLB-171

Cano, Daniel 1947- DLB-209

Cantú, Norma Elia 1947- DLB-209

Cantwell, Robert 1908-1978 . . . . DLB-9

Cape, Jonathan, and Harrison Smith
  [publishing house] DLB-46

Cape, Jonathan, Limited DLB-112

Čapek, Karel 1890-1938 . . . . DLB-215

Capen, Joseph 1658-1725 . . . . DLB-24

Capes, Bernard 1854-1918 . . . . DLB-156

Capote, Truman
  1924-1984 . . . . . . DLB-2, 185, 227; Y-80, Y-84

Caproni, Giorgio 1912-1990 . . . . DLB-128

Caragiale, Mateiu Ioan 1885-1936 . . . . . DLB-220

Cardarelli, Vincenzo 1887-1959 . . . . DLB-114

Cárdenas, Reyes 1948- DLB-122

Cardinal, Marie 1929- DLB-83

Carew, Jan 1920- DLB-157

Carew, Thomas 1594 or 1595-1640 . . . . DLB-126

Carey, Henry circa 1687-1689-1743 . . . . . DLB-84

Carey, M., and Company DLB-49

Carey, Mathew 1760-1839 . . . . .DLB-37, 73

Carey and Hart DLB-49

Carlell, Lodowick 1602-1675 . . . . DLB-58

Carleton, William 1794-1869 . . . . DLB-159

Carleton, G. W. [publishing house] DLB-49

Carlile, Richard 1790-1843 . . . . .DLB-110, 158

Carlyle, Jane Welsh 1801-1866 . . . . DLB-55

Carlyle, Thomas 1795-1881 . . . . DLB-55, 144

  "The Hero as Man of Letters: Johnson,
  Rousseau, Burns" (1841) [excerpt] DLB-57

  The Hero as Poet. Dante;
  Shakspeare (1841) DLB-32

Carman, Bliss 1861-1929 . . . . DLB-92

Carmina Burana circa 1230 . . . . DLB-138

Carnero, Guillermo 1947- DLB-108

Carossa, Hans 1878-1956 . . . . DLB-66

Carpenter, Humphrey 1946- DLB-155

  The Practice of Biography III: An Interview
  with Humphrey Carpenter Y-84

Carpenter, Stephen Cullen ?-1820? DLB-73

Carpentier, Alejo 1904-1980 . . . . DLB-113

Carrier, Roch 1937- DLB-53

Carrillo, Adolfo 1855-1926 . . . . DLB-122

Carroll, Gladys Hasty 1904- DLB-9

Carroll, John 1735-1815 . . . . DLB-37

Carroll, John 1809-1884 . . . . DLB-99

Carroll, Lewis 1832-1898 . . . . . . DLB-18, 163, 178

    The Lewis Carroll Centenary Y-98

Carroll, Paul 1927- DLB-16

Carroll, Paul Vincent 1900-1968 . . . . .DLB-10

Carroll and Graf Publishers DLB-46

Carruth, Hayden 1921- DLB-5, 165

Carryl, Charles E. 1841-1920 . . . . .DLB-42

Carson, Anne 1950- DLB-193

Carswell, Catherine 1879-1946 . . . . .DLB-36

Cărtărescu, Mirea 1956- DLB-232

Carter, Angela 1940-1992 . . . . .DLB-14, 207

Carter, Elizabeth 1717-1806 . . . . .DLB-109

Carter, Henry (see Leslie, Frank)

Carter, Hodding, Jr. 1907-1972 . . . . .DLB-127

Carter, John 1905-1975 . . . . .DLB-201

Carter, Landon 1710-1778 . . . . .DLB-31

Carter, Lin 1930- Y-81

Carter, Martin 1927-1997 . . . . .DLB-117

Carter, Robert, and Brothers DLB-49

Carter and Hendee DLB-49

Cartwright, John 1740-1824 . . . . .DLB-158

Cartwright, William circa 1611-1643 . . . . .DLB-126

Caruthers, William Alexander 1802-1846 . . .DLB-3

Carver, Jonathan 1710-1780 . . . . .DLB-31

Carver, Raymond
    1938-1988 . . . . DLB-130; Y-84, Y-88

    First Strauss "Livings" Awarded to Cynthia
      Ozick and Raymond Carver
      An Interview with Raymond Carver Y-83

Cary, Alice 1820-1871 . . . . .DLB-202

Cary, Joyce 1888-1957 . . . . .DLB-15, 100

Cary, Patrick 1623?-1657 . . . . .DLB-131

Casey, Juanita 1925- DLB-14

Casey, Michael 1947- DLB-5

Cassady, Carolyn 1923- DLB-16

Cassady, Neal 1926-1968 . . . . .DLB-16

Cassell and Company DLB-106

Cassell Publishing Company DLB-49

Cassill, R. V. 1919- DLB-6, 218

Cassity, Turner 1929- DLB-105

Cassius Dio circa 155/164-post 229 . . . . . .DLB-176

Cassola, Carlo 1917-1987 . . . . .DLB-177

The Castle of Perseverance circa 1400-1425 . .DLB-146

Castellano, Olivia 1944- DLB-122

Castellanos, Rosario 1925-1974 . . . . .DLB-113

Castillo, Ana 1953- DLB-122, 227

Castillo, Rafael C. 1950- DLB-209

Castlemon, Harry (see Fosdick, Charles Austin)

Čašule, Kole 1921- DLB-181

Caswall, Edward 1814-1878 . . . . .DLB-32

Catacalos, Rosemary 1944- DLB-122

Cather, Willa 1873-1947 . . . . . DLB-9, 54, 78; DS-1

Catherine II (Ekaterina Alekseevna), "The Great,"
    Empress of Russia 1729-1796 . . . . . . .DLB-150

Catherwood, Mary Hartwell 1847-1902 . . .DLB-78

Catledge, Turner 1901-1983 . . . . .DLB-127

Catlin, George 1796-1872 . . . . .DLB-186, 189

Cato the Elder 234 B.C.-149 B.C. DLB-211

Cattafi, Bartolo 1922-1979 . . . . .DLB-128

Catton, Bruce 1899-1978 . . . . .DLB-17

Catullus circa 84 B.C.-54 B.C. DLB-211

Causley, Charles 1917- DLB-27

Caute, David 1936- DLB-14, 231

Cavendish, Duchess of Newcastle,
    Margaret Lucas 1623-1673 . . . . .DLB-131

Cawein, Madison 1865-1914 . . . . .DLB-54

Caxton, William [publishing house] DLB-170

The Caxton Printers, Limited DLB-46

Cayrol, Jean 1911- DLB-83

Cecil, Lord David 1902-1986 . . . . .DLB-155

Cela, Camilo José 1916- Y-89

Celan, Paul 1920-1970 . . . . .DLB-69

Celati, Gianni 1937- DLB-196

Celaya, Gabriel 1911-1991 . . . . .DLB-108

A Celebration of Literary Biography Y-98

Céline, Louis-Ferdinand 1894-1961 . . . . . . .DLB-72

The Celtic Background to Medieval English
    Literature .DLB-146

Celtis, Conrad 1459-1508 . . . . .DLB-179

Center for Bibliographical Studies and
    Research at the University of
    California, Riverside Y-91

The Center for the Book in the Library
    of Congress Y-93

Center for the Book Research Y-84

Centlivre, Susanna 1669?-1723 . . . . .DLB-84

The Century Company DLB-49

Cernuda, Luis 1902-1963 . . . . .DLB-134

Cervantes, Lorna Dee 1954- DLB-82

Chaadaev, Petr Iakovlevich
    1794-1856 .DLB-198

Chacel, Rosa 1898- DLB-134

Chacón, Eusebio 1869-1948 . . . . .DLB-82

Chacón, Felipe Maximiliano 1873-? DLB-82

Chadwyck-Healey's Full-Text Literary Databases:
    Editing Commercial Databases of
    Primary Literary Texts Y-95

Challans, Eileen Mary (see Renault, Mary)

Chalmers, George 1742-1825 . . . . .DLB-30

Chaloner, Sir Thomas 1520-1565 . . . . . . .DLB-167

Chamberlain, Samuel S. 1851-1916 . . . . . . .DLB-25

Chamberland, Paul 1939- DLB-60

Chamberlin, William Henry 1897-1969 . . . .DLB-29

Chambers, Charles Haddon 1860-1921 . . .DLB-10

Chambers, María Cristina (see Mena, María Cristina)

Chambers, Robert W. 1865-1933 . . . . .DLB-202

Chambers, W. and R.
    [publishing house] DLB-106

Chamisso, Albert von 1781-1838 . . . . .DLB-90

Champfleury 1821-1889 . . . . .DLB-119

Chandler, Harry 1864-1944 . . . . .DLB-29

Chandler, Norman 1899-1973 . . . . .DLB-127

Chandler, Otis 1927- DLB-127

Chandler, Raymond 1888-1959 . . .DLB-226; DS-6

    Raymond Chandler Centenary Tributes
      from Michael Avallone, James Ellroy,
      Joe Gores, and William F. Nolan Y-88

Channing, Edward 1856-1931 . . . . .DLB-17

Channing, Edward Tyrrell 1790-1856 . . .DLB-1, 59

Channing, William Ellery 1780-1842 . . .DLB-1, 59

Channing, William Ellery II
    1817-1901 . . . . .DLB-1, 223

Channing, William Henry 1810-1884 . . .DLB-1, 59

Chaplin, Charlie 1889-1977 . . . . .DLB-44

Chapman, George
    1559 or 1560-1634 . . . . .DLB-62, 121

Chapman, John DLB-106

Chapman, Olive Murray 1892-1977 . . . . .DLB-195

Chapman, R. W. 1881-1960 . . . . .DLB-201

Chapman, William 1850-1917 . . . . .DLB-99

Chapman and Hall DLB-106

Chappell, Fred 1936- DLB-6, 105

    "A Detail in a Poem" DLB-105

Charbonneau, Jean 1875-1960 . . . . .DLB-92

Charbonneau, Robert 1911-1967 . . . . .DLB-68

Charles, Gerda 1914- DLB-14

Charles, William [publishing house] DLB-49

Charles d'Orléans 1394-1465 . . . . .DLB-208

Charley (see Mann, Charles)

Charteris, Leslie 1907-1993 . . . . .DLB-77

Chartier, Alain circa 1385-1430 . . . . .DLB-208

Charyn, Jerome 1937- Y-83

Chase, Borden 1900-1971 . . . . .DLB-26

Chase, Edna Woolman 1877-1957 . . . . . . .DLB-91

Chase, Mary Coyle 1907-1981 . . . . .DLB-228

Chase-Riboud, Barbara 1936- DLB-33

Chateaubriand, François-René de
    1768-1848 .DLB-119

Chatterton, Thomas 1752-1770 . . . . .DLB-109

    Essay on Chatterton (1842), by
      Robert Browning DLB-32

Chatto and Windus DLB-106

Chatwin, Bruce 1940-1989 . . . . .DLB-194, 204

Chaucer, Geoffrey 1340?-1400 . . . . .DLB-146

Chauncy, Charles 1705-1787 . . . . .DLB-24

Chauveau, Pierre-Joseph-Olivier
    1820-1890 . . . . .DLB-99

Chávez, Denise 1948- DLB-122

Chávez, Fray Angélico 1910- DLB-82

Chayefsky, Paddy 1923-1981 . . . . DLB-7, 44; Y-81

Cheesman, Evelyn 1881-1969 . . . . .DLB-195

Cheever, Ezekiel 1615-1708 . . . . .DLB-24

Cheever, George Barrell 1807-1890 . . . . . .DLB-59

Cheever, John
    1912-1982 . . . . . . .DLB-2, 102, 227; Y-80, Y-82

Cheever, Susan 1943- Y-82

Cheke, Sir John 1514-1557 . . . . .DLB-132

Chelsea House .DLB-46

Chênedollé, Charles de 1769-1833 . . . . . .DLB-217

Cheney, Ednah Dow 1824-1904 ..... DLB-1, 223

Cheney, Harriet Vaughn 1796-1889...... DLB-99

Chénier, Marie-Joseph 1764-1811....... DLB-192

Cherry, Kelly 1940...................... Y-83

Cherryh, C. J. 1942- Y-80

Chesebro', Caroline 1825-1873 .... DLB-202

Chesney, Sir George Tomkyns
   1830-1895 .... DLB-190

Chesnutt, Charles Waddell
   1858-1932 ....DLB-12, 50, 78

Chester, Alfred 1928-1971 .... DLB-130

Chester, George Randolph 1869-1924 ... DLB-78

The Chester Plays circa 1505-1532;
   revisions until 1575 .... DLB-146

Chesterfield, Philip Dormer Stanhope,
   Fourth Earl of 1694-1773 .... DLB-104

Chesterton, G. K.
   1874-1936.... DLB-10, 19, 34, 70, 98, 149, 178

Chettle, Henry circa 1560-circa 1607 .... DLB-136

Chew, Ada Nield 1870-1945........... DLB-135

Cheyney, Edward P. 1861-1947........ DLB-47

Chiara, Piero 1913-1986................DLB-177

Chicano History..................... DLB-82

Chicano Language DLB-82

Child, Francis James 1825-1896 ...... DLB-1, 64

Child, Lydia Maria 1802-1880........ DLB-1, 74

Child, Philip 1898-1978 .... DLB-68

Childers, Erskine 1870-1922........... DLB-70

Children's Book Awards and Prizes DLB-61

Children's Illustrators, 1800-1880 ..... DLB-163

Childress, Alice 1920-1994...........DLB-7, 38

Childs, George W. 1829-1894 .... DLB-23

Chilton Book Company............... DLB-46

Chin, Frank 1940- DLB-206

Chinweizu 1943- DLB-157

Chitham, Edward 1932- DLB-155

Chittenden, Hiram Martin 1858-1917 .... DLB-47

Chivers, Thomas Holley 1809-1858....... DLB-3

Cholmondeley, Mary 1859-1925 .... DLB-197

Chopin, Kate 1850-1904............. DLB-12, 78

Chopin, Rene 1885-1953 .... DLB-92

Choquette, Adrienne 1915-1973 .... DLB-68

Choquette, Robert 1905- DLB-68

Chrétien de Troyes
   circa 1140-circa 1190 .... DLB-208

Christensen, Inger 1935- DLB-214

The Christian Publishing Company...... DLB-49

Christie, Agatha 1890-1976......... DLB-13, 77

Christine de Pizan
   circa 1365-circa 1431 .... DLB-208

Christus und die Samariterin circa 950...... DLB-148

Christy, Howard Chandler 1873-1952 ... DLB-188

Chulkov, Mikhail Dmitrievich
   1743?-1792 .... DLB-150

Church, Benjamin 1734-1778 .... DLB-31

Church, Francis Pharcellus 1839-1906 .... DLB-79

Church, Peggy Pond 1903-1986........ DLB-212

Church, Richard 1893-1972 .... DLB-191

Church, William Conant 1836-1917 ..... DLB-79

Churchill, Caryl 1938- DLB-13

Churchill, Charles 1731-1764 .... DLB-109

Churchill, Winston 1871-1947 .... DLB-202

Churchill, Sir Winston
   1874-1965............... DLB-100; DS-16

Churchyard, Thomas 1520?-1604 ...... DLB-132

Churton, E., and Company DLB-106

Chute, Marchette 1909-1994 .... DLB-103

Ciardi, John 1916-1986............DLB-5; Y-86

Cibber, Colley 1671-1757 .... DLB-84

Cicero 106 B.C.-43 B.C............. DLB-211

Cima, Annalisa 1941- DLB-128

Čingo, Živko 1935-1987............. DLB-181

Cioran, E. M. 1911-1995 .... DLB-220

Čipkus, Alfonsas (see Nyka-Niliūnas, Alfonsas)

Cirese, Eugenio 1884-1955........... DLB-114

Cīrulis, Jānis (see Bels, Alberts)

Cisneros, Sandra 1954- DLB-122, 152

City Lights Books................... DLB-46

Cixous, Hélène 1937- DLB-83

Clampitt, Amy 1920-1994 .... DLB-105

Clancy, Tom 1947- DLB-227

Clapper, Raymond 1892-1944 .... DLB-29

Clare, John 1793-1864 .... DLB-55, 96

Clarendon, Edward Hyde, Earl of
   1609-1674..................... DLB-101

Clark, Alfred Alexander Gordon (see Hare, Cyril)

Clark, Ann Nolan 1896- DLB-52

Clark, C. E. Frazer Jr. 1925- DLB-187

Clark, C. M., Publishing Company DLB-46

Clark, Catherine Anthony 1892-1977..... DLB-68

Clark, Charles Heber 1841-1915 .... DLB-11

Clark, Davis Wasgatt 1812-1871 .... DLB-79

Clark, Eleanor 1913- DLB-6

Clark, J. P. 1935- DLB-117

Clark, Lewis Gaylord 1808-1873 ... DLB-3, 64, 73

Clark, Walter Van Tilburg
   1909-1971.................... DLB-9, 206

Clark, William (see Lewis, Meriwether)

Clark, William Andrews Jr. 1877-1934... DLB-187

Clarke, Austin 1896-1974 .... DLB-10, 20

Clarke, Austin C. 1934- DLB-53, 125

Clarke, Gillian 1937- DLB-40

Clarke, James Freeman 1810-1888 ..... DLB-1, 59

Clarke, Lindsay 1939- DLB-231

Clarke, Marcus 1846-1881 .... DLB-230

Clarke, Pauline 1921- DLB-161

Clarke, Rebecca Sophia 1833-1906 ...... DLB-42

Clarke, Robert, and Company......... DLB-49

Clarkson, Thomas 1760-1846.......... DLB-158

Claudel, Paul 1868-1955 .... DLB-192

Claudius, Matthias 1740-1815 .... DLB-97

Clausen, Andy 1943- DLB-16

Clawson, John L. 1865-1933 ....DLB-187

Claxton, Remsen and Haffelfinger....... DLB-49

Clay, Cassius Marcellus 1810-1903 ..... DLB-43

Cleage, Pearl 1948- DLB-228

Cleary, Beverly 1916- DLB-52

Cleary, Kate McPhelim 1863-1905..... DLB-221

Cleaver, Vera 1919- and
   Cleaver, Bill 1920-1981 .... DLB-52

Cleland, John 1710-1789............. DLB-39

Clemens, Samuel Langhorne (Mark Twain)
   1835-1910 ...DLB-11, 12, 23, 64, 74, 186, 189

   Mark Twain on Perpetual Copyright...... Y-92

Clement, Hal 1922- DLB-8

Clemo, Jack 1916- DLB-27

Clephane, Elizabeth Cecilia
   1830-1869 .... DLB-199

Cleveland, John 1613-1658 .... DLB-126

Cliff, Michelle 1946- DLB-157

Clifford, Lady Anne 1590-1676 .... DLB-151

Clifford, James L. 1901-1978 .... DLB-103

Clifford, Lucy 1853?-1929 .....DLB-135, 141, 197

Clifton, Lucille 1936- DLB-5, 41

Clines, Francis X. 1938- DLB-185

Clive, Caroline (V) 1801-1873 .... DLB-199

Clode, Edward J. [publishing house] DLB-46

Clough, Arthur Hugh 1819-1861........ DLB-32

Cloutier, Cécile 1930- DLB-60

Clouts, Sidney 1926-1982........... DLB-225

Clutton-Brock, Arthur 1868-1924 .... DLB-98

Coates, Robert M. 1897-1973 ......DLB-4, 9, 102

Coatsworth, Elizabeth 1893- DLB-22

Cobb, Charles E., Jr. 1943- DLB-41

Cobb, Frank I. 1869-1923 .... DLB-25

Cobb, Irvin S. 1876-1944 .... DLB-11, 25, 86

Cobbe, Frances Power 1822-1904 ...... DLB-190

Cobbett, William 1763-1835.........DLB-43, 107

Cobbledick, Gordon 1898-1969........DLB-171

Cochran, Thomas C. 1902- DLB-17

Cochrane, Elizabeth 1867-1922 ..... DLB-25, 189

Cockerell, Sir Sydney 1867-1962 .... DLB-201

Cockerill, John A. 1845-1896 .... DLB-23

Cocteau, Jean 1889-1963 .... DLB-65

Coderre, Emile (see Jean Narrache)

Coe, Jonathan 1961- DLB-231

Coetzee, J. M. 1940- DLB-225

Coffee, Lenore J. 1900?-1984........... DLB-44

Coffin, Robert P. Tristram 1892-1955 .... DLB-45

Cogswell, Fred 1917- DLB-60

Cogswell, Mason Fitch 1761-1830 .... DLB-37

Cohen, Arthur A. 1928-1986 .... DLB-28

Cohen, Leonard 1934- DLB-53

Cohen, Matt 1942- DLB-53

Colbeck, Norman 1903-1987 .... DLB-201

Colden, Cadwallader 1688-1776...... DLB-24, 30

Colden, Jane 1724-1766 .... DLB-200

Cole, Barry 1936- DLB-14

Cole, George Watson 1850-1939. . . . . . .DLB-140

Colegate, Isabel 1931- DLB-14, 231

Coleman, Emily Holmes 1899-1974 . . . . . . .DLB-4

Coleman, Wanda 1946- DLB-130

Coleridge, Hartley 1796-1849 . . . . .DLB-96

Coleridge, Mary 1861-1907 . . . . .DLB-19, 98

Coleridge, Samuel Taylor
    1772-1834 . . . . DLB-93, 107

Coleridge, Sara 1802-1852. . . . . .DLB-199

Colet, John 1467-1519 . . . . .DLB-132

Colette 1873-1954 .DLB-65

Colette, Sidonie Gabrielle (see Colette)

Colinas, Antonio 1946- DLB-134

Coll, Joseph Clement 1881-1921 . . . . . . .DLB-188

Collier, John 1901-1980. . . . . .DLB-77

Collier, John Payne 1789-1883. . . . . .DLB-184

Collier, Mary 1690-1762 . . . . .DLB-95

Collier, P. F. [publishing house] DLB-49

Collier, Robert J. 1876-1918. . . . . .DLB-91

Collin and Small DLB-49

Collingwood, W. G. 1854-1932. . . . . . . .DLB-149

Collins, An floruit circa 1653. . . . . .DLB-131

Collins, Isaac [publishing house] DLB-49

Collins, Merle 1950- DLB-157

Collins, Mortimer 1827-1876 . . . . .DLB-21, 35

Collins, Tom (see Furphy, Joseph)

Collins, Wilkie 1824-1889 . . . . . . .DLB-18, 70, 159

Collins, William 1721-1759 . . . . .DLB-109

Collins, William, Sons and Company DLB-154

Collis, Maurice 1889-1973 . . . . .DLB-195

Collyer, Mary 1716?-1763? DLB-39

Colman, Benjamin 1673-1747 . . . . .DLB-24

Colman, George, the Elder 1732-1794 . . . . .DLB-89

Colman, George, the Younger
    1762-1836 . . . . .DLB-89

Colman, S. [publishing house] DLB-49

Colombo, John Robert 1936- DLB-53

Colquhoun, Patrick 1745-1820 . . . . .DLB-158

Colter, Cyrus 1910- DLB-33

Colum, Padraic 1881-1972. . . . . .DLB-19

Columella fl. first century A.D. DLB-211

Colvin, Sir Sidney 1845-1927 . . . . .DLB-149

Colwin, Laurie 1944-1992 . . . . . . .DLB-218; Y-80

Comden, Betty 1919- and
    Green, Adolph 1918- DLB-44

Come to Papa Y-99

Comi, Girolamo 1890-1968. . . . . .DLB-114

The Comic Tradition Continued
    [in the British Novel]. DLB-15

Commager, Henry Steele 1902-1998. . . . . .DLB-17

The Commercialization of the Image of
    Revolt, by Kenneth Rexroth. DLB-16

Community and Commentators: Black
    Theatre and Its Critics DLB-38

Commynes, Philippe de
    circa 1447-1511 . . . . .DLB-208

Compton-Burnett, Ivy 1884?-1969 . . . . . . .DLB-36

Conan, Laure 1845-1924. . . . . .DLB-99

Concord History and Life DLB-223

Concord Literary History of a Town DLB-223

Conde, Carmen 1901- DLB-108

Conference on Modern Biography Y-85

Congreve, William 1670-1729 . . . . . . .DLB-39, 84

    Preface to *Incognita* (1692). DLB-39

Conkey, W. B., Company. DLB-49

Conn, Stewart 1936- DLB-233

Connell, Evan S., Jr. 1924- DLB-2; Y-81

Connelly, Marc 1890-1980 . . . . .DLB-7; Y-80

Connolly, Cyril 1903-1974 . . . . .DLB-98

Connolly, James B. 1868-1957. . . . . .DLB-78

Connor, Ralph 1860-1937 . . . . .DLB-92

Connor, Tony 1930- DLB-40

Conquest, Robert 1917- DLB-27

Conrad, John, and Company DLB-49

Conrad, Joseph 1857-1924. . . . DLB-10, 34, 98, 156

Conroy, Jack 1899-1990 . . . . Y-81

Conroy, Pat 1945- DLB-6

The Consolidation of Opinion: Critical
    Responses to the Modernists. DLB-36

Consolo, Vincenzo 1933- DLB-196

Constable, Archibald, and Company DLB-154

Constable, Henry 1562-1613. . . . . .DLB-136

Constable and Company Limited DLB-112

Constant, Benjamin 1767-1830. . . . . .DLB-119

Constant de Rebecque, Henri-Benjamin de
    (see Constant, Benjamin)

Constantine, David 1944- DLB-40

Constantin-Weyer, Maurice 1881-1964. . . .DLB-92

Contempo Caravan: Kites in a Windstorm. . . Y-85

A Contemporary Flourescence of Chicano
    Literature Y-84

The Continental Publishing Company DLB-49

Conversations with Editors Y-95

Conversations with Publishers I: An Interview
    with Patrick O'Connor Y-84

Conversations with Publishers II: An Interview
    with Charles Scribner III Y-94

Conversations with Publishers III: An Interview
    with Donald Lamm. Y-95

Conversations with Publishers IV: An Interview
    with James Laughlin Y-96

Conversations with Rare Book Dealers I: An
    Interview with Glenn Horowitz Y-90

Conversations with Rare Book Dealers II: An
    Interview with Ralph Sipper Y-94

Conversations with Rare Book Dealers
    (Publishers) III: An Interview with
    Otto Penzler Y-96

The Conversion of an Unpolitical Man,
    by W. H. Bruford DLB-66

Conway, Moncure Daniel
    1832-1907 . . . . .DLB-1, 223

Cook, David C., Publishing Company DLB-49

Cook, Ebenezer circa 1667-circa 1732 . . . . .DLB-24

Cook, Edward Tyas 1857-1919 . . . . .DLB-149

Cook, Eliza 1818-1889. . . . . .DLB-199

Cook, Michael 1933- DLB-53

Cooke, George Willis 1848-1923 . . . . .DLB-71

Cooke, Increase, and Company DLB-49

Cooke, John Esten 1830-1886 . . . . .DLB-3

Cooke, Philip Pendleton 1816-1850 . . . .DLB-3, 59

Cooke, Rose Terry 1827-1892 . . . . .DLB-12, 74

Cook-Lynn, Elizabeth 1930- DLB-175

Coolbrith, Ina 1841-1928 . . . . .DLB-54, 186

Cooley, Peter 1940- DLB-105

    "Into the Mirror" DLB-105

Coolidge, Clark 1939- DLB-193

Coolidge, George [publishing house]. DLB-49

Coolidge, Susan (see Woolsey, Sarah Chauncy)

Cooper, Anna Julia 1858-1964 . . . . .DLB-221

Cooper, Giles 1918-1966. . . . . .DLB-13

Cooper, J. California 19??- DLB-212

Cooper, James Fenimore 1789-1851 . . .DLB-3, 183

Cooper, Kent 1880-1965 . . . . .DLB-29

Cooper, Susan 1935- DLB-161

Cooper, William [publishing house] DLB-170

Coote, J. [publishing house]. DLB-154

Coover, Robert 1932- DLB-2, 227; Y-81

Copeland and Day. DLB-49

Ćopić, Branko 1915-1984 . . . . .DLB-181

Copland, Robert 1470?-1548. . . . . .DLB-136

Coppard, A. E. 1878-1957 . . . . .DLB-162

Coppée, François 1842-1908 . . . . .DLB-217

Coppel, Alfred 1921- Y-83

Coppola, Francis Ford 1939- DLB-44

Copway, George (Kah-ge-ga-gah-bowh)
    1818-1869 . . . . DLB-175, 183

Corazzini, Sergio 1886-1907 . . . . .DLB-114

Corbett, Richard 1582-1635 . . . . .DLB-121

Corbière, Tristan 1845-1875 . . . . .DLB-217

Corcoran, Barbara 1911- DLB-52

Cordelli, Franco 1943- DLB-196

Corelli, Marie 1855-1924. . . . . .DLB-34, 156

Corle, Edwin 1906-1956 . . . . Y-85

Corman, Cid 1924- DLB-5, 193

Cormier, Robert 1925- DLB-52

Corn, Alfred 1943- DLB-120; Y-80

Cornish, Sam 1935- DLB-41

Cornish, William circa 1465-circa 1524. . .DLB-132

Cornwall, Barry (see Procter, Bryan Waller)

Cornwallis, Sir William, the Younger
    circa 1579-1614 . . . . .DLB-151

Cornwell, David John Moore (see le Carré, John)

Corpi, Lucha 1945- DLB-82

Corrington, John William 1932- DLB-6

Corrothers, James D. 1869-1917 . . . . .DLB-50

Corso, Gregory 1930- DLB-5, 16

Cortázar, Julio 1914-1984 . . . . .DLB-113

Cortéz, Carlos 1923- DLB-209

Cortez, Jayne 1936- DLB-41

Corvinus, Gottlieb Siegmund
  1677-1746 . . . . DLB-168

Corvo, Baron (see Rolfe, Frederick William)

Cory, Annie Sophie (see Cross, Victoria)

Cory, William Johnson 1823-1892 . . . . . . DLB-35

Coryate, Thomas 1577?-1617 . . . . . . DLB-151, 172

Ćosić, Dobrica 1921- DLB-181

Cosin, John 1595-1672 . . . . DLB-151, 213

Cosmopolitan Book Corporation DLB-46

Costain, Thomas B. 1885-1965 . . . . DLB-9

Coste, Donat 1912-1957 . . . . DLB-88

Costello, Louisa Stuart 1799-1870 . . . . . . DLB-166

Cota-Cárdenas, Margarita 1941- DLB-122

Cotten, Bruce 1873-1954 . . . . DLB-187

Cotter, Joseph Seamon, Sr. 1861-1949 . . . . DLB-50

Cotter, Joseph Seamon, Jr. 1895-1919 . . . . DLB-50

Cottle, Joseph [publishing house] DLB-154

Cotton, Charles 1630-1687 . . . . DLB-131

Cotton, John 1584-1652 . . . . DLB-24

Cotton, Sir Robert Bruce 1571-1631 . . . . . DLB-213

Coulter, John 1888-1980 . . . . DLB-68

Cournos, John 1881-1966 . . . . DLB-54

Courteline, Georges 1858-1929 . . . . DLB-192

Cousins, Margaret 1905-1996 . . . . DLB-137

Cousins, Norman 1915-1990 . . . . DLB-137

Couvreur, Jessie (see Tasma)

Coventry, Francis 1725-1754 . . . . DLB-39

  Dedication, *The History of Pompey
    the Little* (1751) DLB-39

Coverdale, Miles 1487 or 1488-1569 . . . . DLB-167

Coverly, N. [publishing house] DLB-49

Covici-Friede DLB-46

Coward, Noel 1899-1973 . . . . DLB-10

Coward, McCann and Geoghegan DLB-46

Cowles, Gardner 1861-1946 . . . . DLB-29

Cowles, Gardner "Mike" Jr.
  1903-1985 . . . . DLB-127, 137

Cowley, Abraham 1618-1667 . . . . . . DLB-131, 151

Cowley, Hannah 1743-1809 . . . . DLB-89

Cowley, Malcolm
  1898-1989 . . . . DLB-4, 48; Y-81, Y-89

Cowper, William 1731-1800 . . . . . . DLB-104, 109

Cox, A. B. (see Berkeley, Anthony)

Cox, James McMahon 1903-1974 . . . . DLB-127

Cox, James Middleton 1870-1957 . . . . . . DLB-127

Cox, Palmer 1840-1924 . . . . DLB-42

Coxe, Louis 1918-1993 . . . . DLB-5

Coxe, Tench 1755-1824 . . . . DLB-37

Cozzens, Frederick S. 1818-1869 . . . . . . DLB-202

Cozzens, James Gould
  1903-1978 . . . . DLB-9; Y-84; DS-2

  James Gould Cozzens—A View from Afar . . Y-97

  James Gould Cozzens Case Re-opened Y-97

  James Gould Cozzens: How to Read Him . . Y-97

Cozzens's *Michael Scarlett* Y-97

Crabbe, George 1754-1832 . . . . DLB-93

Crace, Jim 1946- DLB-231

Crackanthorpe, Hubert 1870-1896 . . . . . DLB-135

Craddock, Charles Egbert (see Murfree, Mary N.)

Cradock, Thomas 1718-1770 . . . . DLB-31

Craig, Daniel H. 1811-1895 . . . . DLB-43

Craik, Dinah Maria 1826-1887 . . . . . . DLB-35, 136

Cramer, Richard Ben 1950- DLB-185

Cranch, Christopher Pearse 1813-1892 . DLB-1, 42

Crane, Hart 1899-1932 . . . . DLB-4, 48

Crane, R. S. 1886-1967 . . . . DLB-63

Crane, Stephen 1871-1900 . . . . DLB-12, 54, 78

Crane, Walter 1845-1915 . . . . DLB-163

Cranmer, Thomas 1489-1556 . . . . . DLB-132, 213

Crapsey, Adelaide 1878-1914 . . . . DLB-54

Crashaw, Richard 1612 or 1613-1649 . . . DLB-126

Craven, Avery 1885-1980 . . . . DLB-17

Crawford, Charles 1752-circa 1815 . . . . . DLB-31

Crawford, F. Marion 1854-1909 . . . . DLB-71

Crawford, Isabel Valancy 1850-1887 . . . . . DLB-92

Crawley, Alan 1887-1975 . . . . DLB-68

Crayon, Geoffrey (see Irving, Washington)

Creamer, Robert W. 1922- DLB-171

Creasey, John 1908-1973 . . . . DLB-77

Creative Age Press DLB-46

Creech, William [publishing house] DLB-154

Creede, Thomas [publishing house] DLB-170

Creel, George 1876-1953 . . . . DLB-25

Creeley, Robert 1926- DLB-5, 16, 169; DS-17

Creelman, James 1859-1915 . . . . DLB-23

Cregan, David 1931- DLB-13

Creighton, Donald Grant 1902-1979 . . . . . DLB-88

Cremazie, Octave 1827-1879 . . . . DLB-99

Crémer, Victoriano 1909?- DLB-108

Crescas, Hasdai circa 1340-1412? DLB-115

Crespo, Angel 1926- DLB-134

Cresset Press DLB-112

Cresswell, Helen 1934- DLB-161

Crèvecoeur, Michel Guillaume Jean de
  1735-1813 . . . . DLB-37

Crewe, Candida 1964- DLB-207

Crews, Harry 1935- DLB-6, 143, 185

Crichton, Michael 1942- Y-81

A Crisis of Culture: The Changing Role
  of Religion in the New Republic DLB-37

Crispin, Edmund 1921-1978 . . . . DLB-87

Cristofer, Michael 1946- DLB-7

Crnjanski, Miloš 1893-1977 . . . . DLB-147

Crocker, Hannah Mather 1752-1829 . . . . DLB-200

Crockett, David (Davy)
  1786-1836 . . . . DLB-3, 11, 183

Croft-Cooke, Rupert (see Bruce, Leo)

Crofts, Freeman Wills 1879-1957 . . . . DLB-77

Croker, John Wilson 1780-1857 . . . . DLB-110

Croly, George 1780-1860 . . . . DLB-159

Croly, Herbert 1869-1930 . . . . DLB-91

Croly, Jane Cunningham 1829-1901 . . . . . DLB-23

Crompton, Richmal 1890-1969 . . . . DLB-160

Cronin, A. J. 1896-1981 . . . . DLB-191

Cros, Charles 1842-1888 . . . . DLB-217

Crosby, Caresse 1892-1970 . . . . DLB-48

Crosby, Caresse 1892-1970 and Crosby,
  Harry 1898-1929 . . . . DLB-4; DS-15

Crosby, Harry 1898-1929 . . . . DLB-48

Cross, Gillian 1945- DLB-161

Cross, Victoria 1868-1952 . . . . DLB-135, 197

Crossley-Holland, Kevin 1941- DLB-40, 161

Crothers, Rachel 1878-1958 . . . . DLB-7

Crowell, Thomas Y., Company DLB-49

Crowley, John 1942- Y-82

Crowley, Mart 1935- DLB-7

Crown Publishers DLB-46

Crowne, John 1641-1712 . . . . DLB-80

Crowninshield, Edward Augustus
  1817-1859 . . . . DLB-140

Crowninshield, Frank 1872-1947 . . . . DLB-91

Croy, Homer 1883-1965 . . . . DLB-4

Crumley, James 1939- DLB-226; Y-84

Cruz, Victor Hernández 1949- DLB-41

Csokor, Franz Theodor 1885-1969 . . . . . . DLB-81

Csoóri, Sándor 1930- DLB-232

Cuala Press DLB-112

Cullen, Countee 1903-1946 . . . . DLB-4, 48, 51

Culler, Jonathan D. 1944- DLB-67

Cullinan, Elizabeth 1933- DLB-234

The Cult of Biography
  Excerpts from the Second Folio Debate:
  "Biographies are generally a disease of
  English Literature" – Germaine Greer,
  Victoria Glendinning, Auberon Waugh,
  and Richard Holmes Y-86

Cumberland, Richard 1732-1811 . . . . DLB-89

Cummings, Constance Gordon
  1837-1924 . . . . DLB-174

Cummings, E. E. 1894-1962 . . . . DLB-4, 48

Cummings, Ray 1887-1957 . . . . DLB-8

Cummings and Hilliard DLB-49

Cummins, Maria Susanna 1827-1866 . . . . . DLB-42

Cumpián, Carlos 1953- DLB-209

Cundall, Joseph [publishing house] DLB-106

Cuney, Waring 1906-1976 . . . . DLB-51

Cuney-Hare, Maude 1874-1936 . . . . DLB-52

Cunningham, Allan 1784-1842 . . . . . DLB-116, 144

Cunningham, J. V. 1911- DLB-5

Cunningham, Peter F.
  [publishing house] DLB-49

Cunquiero, Alvaro 1911-1981 . . . . DLB-134

Cuomo, George 1929- Y-80

Cupples, Upham and Company DLB-49

Cupples and Leon DLB-46

Cuppy, Will 1884-1949 . . . . DLB-11

Curiel, Barbara Brinson 1956- DLB-209

Curll, Edmund [publishing house]. DLB-154

Currie, James 1756-1805 . . . . .DLB-142

Currie, Mary Montgomerie Lamb Singleton,
 Lady Currie
 (see Fane, Violet)

Cursor Mundi circa 1300 . . . . .DLB-146

Curti, Merle E. 1897- DLB-17

Curtis, Anthony 1926- DLB-155

Curtis, Cyrus H. K. 1850-1933 . . . . .DLB-91

Curtis, George William
 1824-1892 . . . . .DLB-1, 43, 223

Curzon, Robert 1810-1873. . . . . .DLB-166

Curzon, Sarah Anne 1833-1898. . . . . . . .DLB-99

Cushing, Harvey 1869-1939 . . . . .DLB-187

Cynewulf circa 770-840 . . . . .DLB-146

Czepko, Daniel 1605-1660. . . . . .DLB-164

Czerniawski, Adam 1934- DLB-232

D

Dabit, Eugène 1898-1936. . . . . .DLB-65

Daborne, Robert circa 1580-1628 . . . . . . .DLB-58

Dąbrowska, Maria 1889-1965 . . . . .DLB-215

Dacey, Philip 1939- DLB-105

 "Eyes Across Centuries: Contemporary
 Poetry and 'That Vision Thing,'" DLB-105

Dach, Simon 1605-1659. . . . . .DLB-164

Daggett, Rollin M. 1831-1901 . . . . .DLB-79

D'Aguiar, Fred 1960- DLB-157

Dahl, Roald 1916-1990 . . . . .DLB-139

Dahlberg, Edward 1900-1977 . . . . .DLB-48

Dahn, Felix 1834-1912. . . . . .DLB-129

Dal', Vladimir Ivanovich (Kazak Vladimir
 Lugansky) 1801-1872 . . . . .DLB-198

Dale, Peter 1938- DLB-40

Daley, Arthur 1904-1974 . . . . .DLB-171

Dall, Caroline Wells (Healey) 1822-1912 . . .DLB-1

Dallas, E. S. 1828-1879. . . . . .DLB-55

 From *The Gay Science* (1866) DLB-21

The Dallas Theater Center DLB-7

D'Alton, Louis 1900-1951 . . . . .DLB-10

Daly, Carroll John 1889-1958 . . . . .DLB-226

Daly, T. A. 1871-1948 . . . . .DLB-11

Damon, S. Foster 1893-1971 . . . . .DLB-45

Damrell, William S. [publishing house] DLB-49

Dana, Charles A. 1819-1897 . . . . .DLB-3, 23

Dana, Richard Henry, Jr. 1815-1882 . . .DLB-1, 183

Dandridge, Ray Garfield DLB-51

Dane, Clemence 1887-1965 . . . . DLB-10, 197

Danforth, John 1660-1730 . . . . .DLB-24

Danforth, Samuel, I 1626-1674 . . . . .DLB-24

Danforth, Samuel, II 1666-1727. . . . . .DLB-24

Dangerous Years: London Theater,
 1939-1945 . . . . .DLB-10

Daniel, John M. 1825-1865 . . . . .DLB-43

Daniel, Samuel 1562 or 1563-1619 . . . . . . .DLB-62

Daniel Press. DLB-106

Daniells, Roy 1902-1979 . . . . .DLB-68

Daniels, Jim 1956- DLB-120

Daniels, Jonathan 1902-1981 . . . . .DLB-127

Daniels, Josephus 1862-1948 . . . . .DLB-29

Dannay, Frederic 1905-1982 and
 Manfred B. Lee 1905-1971 . . . . .DLB-137

Danner, Margaret Esse 1915- DLB-41

Danter, John [publishing house]. DLB-170

Dantin, Louis 1865-1945 . . . . .DLB-92

Danzig, Allison 1898-1987 . . . . .DLB-171

D'Arcy, Ella circa 1857-1937 . . . . .DLB-135

Darke, Nick 1948- DLB-233

Darley, Felix Octavious Carr 1822-1888 . .DLB-188

Darley, George 1795-1846 . . . . .DLB-96

Darwin, Charles 1809-1882. . . . . DLB-57, 166

Darwin, Erasmus 1731-1802 . . . . .DLB-93

Daryush, Elizabeth 1887-1977 . . . . .DLB-20

Dashkova, Ekaterina Romanovna
 (née Vorontsova) 1743-1810 . . . . .DLB-150

Dashwood, Edmée Elizabeth Monica de la Pasture
 (see Delafield, E. M.)

Daudet, Alphonse 1840-1897. . . . . .DLB-123

d'Aulaire, Edgar Parin 1898- and
 d'Aulaire, Ingri 1904- DLB-22

Davenant, Sir William 1606-1668 . . . .DLB-58, 126

Davenport, Guy 1927- DLB-130

Davenport, Marcia 1903-1996. . . . . DS-17

Davenport, Robert ?-? DLB-58

Daves, Delmer 1904-1977 . . . . .DLB-26

Davey, Frank 1940- DLB-53

Davidson, Avram 1923-1993 . . . . .DLB-8

Davidson, Donald 1893-1968 . . . . .DLB-45

Davidson, John 1857-1909 . . . . .DLB-19

Davidson, Lionel 1922- DLB-14

Davidson, Robyn 1950- DLB-204

Davidson, Sara 1943- DLB-185

Davie, Donald 1922- DLB-27

Davie, Elspeth 1919- DLB-139

Davies, Sir John 1569-1626 . . . . .DLB-172

Davies, John, of Hereford 1565?-1618. . . .DLB-121

Davies, Peter, Limited DLB-112

Davies, Rhys 1901-1978. . . . . .DLB-139, 191

Davies, Robertson 1913- DLB-68

Davies, Samuel 1723-1761 . . . . .DLB-31

Davies, Thomas 1712?-1785 . . . . . . .DLB-142, 154

Davies, W. H. 1871-1940. . . . . .DLB-19, 174

Daviot, Gordon 1896?-1952 . . . . .DLB-10
 (see also Tey, Josephine)

Davis, Arthur Hoey (see Rudd, Steele)

Davis, Charles A. 1795-1867 . . . . .DLB-11

Davis, Clyde Brion 1894-1962 . . . . .DLB-9

Davis, Dick 1945- DLB-40

Davis, Frank Marshall 1905-? DLB-51

Davis, H. L. 1894-1960 . . . . .DLB-9, 206

Davis, John 1774-1854 . . . . .DLB-37

Davis, Lydia 1947- DLB-130

Davis, Margaret Thomson 1926- DLB-14

Davis, Ossie 1917- DLB-7, 38

Davis, Paxton 1925-1994. . . . . Y-94

Davis, Rebecca Harding 1831-1910. . . . . . .DLB-74

Davis, Richard Harding 1864-1916
 . . . . DLB-12, 23, 78, 79, 189; DS-13

Davis, Samuel Cole 1764-1809 . . . . .DLB-37

Davis, Samuel Post 1850-1918. . . . . .DLB-202

Davison, Peter 1928- DLB-5

Davydov, Denis Vasil'evich
 1784-1839 . . . . .DLB-205

Davys, Mary 1674-1732. . . . . .DLB-39

 Preface to *The Works of
 Mrs. Davys* (1725). DLB-39

DAW Books. DLB-46

Dawson, Ernest 1882-1947 . . . . .DLB-140

Dawson, Fielding 1930- DLB-130

Dawson, William 1704-1752 . . . . .DLB-31

Day, Angel flourished 1586. . . . . .DLB-167

Day, Benjamin Henry 1810-1889 . . . . .DLB-43

Day, Clarence 1874-1935. . . . . .DLB-11

Day, Dorothy 1897-1980 . . . . .DLB-29

Day, Frank Parker 1881-1950 . . . . .DLB-92

Day, John circa 1574-circa 1640. . . . . .DLB-62

Day, John [publishing house]. DLB-170

Day, The John, Company DLB-46

Day Lewis, C. 1904-1972. . . . . .DLB-15, 20
 (see also Blake, Nicholas)

Day, Mahlon [publishing house] DLB-49

Day, Thomas 1748-1789 . . . . .DLB-39

Dazai Osamu 1909-1948 . . . . .DLB-182

Deacon, William Arthur 1890-1977. . . . . . .DLB-68

Deal, Borden 1922-1985 . . . . .DLB-6

de Angeli, Marguerite 1889-1987. . . . . . . .DLB-22

De Angelis, Milo 1951- DLB-128

De Bow, James Dunwoody Brownson
 1820-1867 . . . . .DLB-3, 79

de Bruyn, Günter 1926- DLB-75

de Camp, L. Sprague 1907- DLB-8

De Carlo, Andrea 1952- DLB-196

De Casas, Celso A. 1944- DLB-209

Dechert, Robert 1895-1975 . . . . .DLB-187

Dee, John 1527-1608 or 1609. . . . . . .DLB-136, 213

Deeping, George Warwick 1877-1950 . . . .DLB 153

Defoe, Daniel 1660-1731 . . . . .DLB-39, 95, 101

 Preface to *Colonel Jack* (1722) DLB-39

 Preface to *The Farther Adventures of
 Robinson Crusoe* (1719). DLB-39

 Preface to *Moll Flanders* (1722) DLB-39

 Preface to *Robinson Crusoe* (1719). DLB-39

 Preface to *Roxana* (1724). DLB-39

de Fontaine, Felix Gregory 1834-1896. . . . .DLB-43

De Forest, John William 1826-1906. . .DLB-12, 189

DeFrees, Madeline 1919- DLB-105

"The Poet's Kaleidoscope: The Element
of Surprise in the Making of
the Poem" DLB-105

DeGolyer, Everette Lee 1886-1956. . . . . . DLB-187

de Graff, Robert 1895-1981 . . . . Y-81

de Graft, Joe 1924-1978 . . . . DLB-117

De Heinrico circa 980? DLB-148

Deighton, Len 1929- DLB-87

DeJong, Meindert 1906-1991 . . . . DLB-52

Dekker, Thomas circa 1572-1632. . . . .DLB-62, 172

Delacorte, Jr., George T. 1894-1991. . . . . . DLB-91

Delafield, E. M. 1890-1943. . . . . DLB-34

Delahaye, Guy 1888-1969 . . . . DLB-92

de la Mare, Walter 1873-1956 . . DLB-19, 153, 162

Deland, Margaret 1857-1945 . . . . DLB-78

Delaney, Shelagh 1939- DLB-13

Delano, Amasa 1763-1823 . . . . DLB-183

Delany, Martin Robinson 1812-1885 . . . . . DLB-50

Delany, Samuel R. 1942- DLB-8, 33

de la Roche, Mazo 1879-1961 . . . . DLB-68

Delavigne, Jean François Casimir
1793-1843 . . . . DLB-192

Delbanco, Nicholas 1942- DLB-6, 234

Del Castillo, Ramón 1949- DLB-209

De León, Nephtal 1945- DLB-82

Delgado, Abelardo Barrientos 1931- DLB-82

Del Giudice, Daniele 1949- DLB-196

De Libero, Libero 1906-1981 . . . . DLB-114

DeLillo, Don 1936- DLB-6, 173

de Lisser H. G. 1878-1944 . . . . DLB-117

Dell, Floyd 1887-1969. . . . . DLB-9

Dell Publishing Company. DLB-46

delle Grazie, Marie Eugene 1864-1931. . . . DLB-81

Deloney, Thomas died 1600 . . . . DLB-167

Deloria, Ella C. 1889-1971 . . . . .DLB-175

Deloria, Vine, Jr. 1933- DLB-175

del Rey, Lester 1915-1993 . . . . DLB-8

Del Vecchio, John M. 1947- DS-9

Del'vig, Anton Antonovich 1798-1831 . . . DLB-205

de Man, Paul 1919-1983. . . . . DLB-67

DeMarinis, Rick 1934- DLB-218

Demby, William 1922- DLB-33

Deming, Philander 1829-1915 . . . . DLB-74

Deml, Jakub 1878-1961. . . . . DLB-215

Demorest, William Jennings 1822-1895 . . . DLB-79

De Morgan, William 1839-1917 . . . . DLB-153

Demosthenes 384 B.C.-322 B.C. DLB-176

Denham, Henry [publishing house] DLB-170

Denham, Sir John 1615-1669 . . . . DLB-58, 126

Denison, Merrill 1893-1975 . . . . DLB-92

Denison, T. S., and Company DLB-49

Dennery, Adolphe Philippe 1811-1899. . . DLB-192

Dennie, Joseph 1768-1812. . . . . .DLB-37, 43, 59, 73

Dennis, John 1658-1734 . . . . DLB-101

Dennis, Nigel 1912-1989 . . . . DLB-13, 15, 233

Denslow, W. W. 1856-1915. . . . . DLB-188

Dent, J. M., and Sons DLB-112

Dent, Tom 1932-1998 . . . . DLB-38

Denton, Daniel circa 1626-1703 . . . . DLB-24

DePaola, Tomie 1934- DLB-61

Department of Library, Archives, and Institutional
Research, American Bible Society Y-97

De Quille, Dan 1829-1898 . . . . DLB-186

De Quincey, Thomas 1785-1859 . . . .DLB-110, 144

"Rhetoric" (1828; revised, 1859)
[excerpt] DLB-57

Derby, George Horatio 1823-1861. . . . . . DLB-11

Derby, J. C., and Company DLB-49

Derby and Miller DLB-49

De Ricci, Seymour 1881-1942 . . . . DLB-201

Derleth, August 1909-1971 . . . . DLB-9; DS-17

The Derrydale Press. DLB-46

Derzhavin, Gavriil Romanovich
1743-1816. DLB-150

Desaulniers, Gonsalve 1863-1934. . . . . . . DLB-92

Desbordes-Valmore, Marceline
1786-1859. DLB-217

Deschamps, Emile 1791-1871 . . . . DLB-217

Deschamps, Eustache 1340?-1404 . . . . . . DLB-208

Desbiens, Jean-Paul 1927- DLB-53

des Forêts, Louis-Rene 1918- DLB-83

Desiato, Luca 1941- DLB-196

Desnica, Vladan 1905-1967 . . . . DLB-181

DesRochers, Alfred 1901-1978 . . . . DLB-68

Desrosiers, Léo-Paul 1896-1967 . . . . DLB-68

Dessì, Giuseppe 1909-1977 . . . . .DLB-177

Destouches, Louis-Ferdinand
(see Céline, Louis-Ferdinand)

De Tabley, Lord 1835-1895 . . . . DLB-35

Deutsch, André, Limited DLB-112

Deutsch, Babette 1895-1982 . . . . DLB-45

Deutsch, Niklaus Manuel (see Manuel, Niklaus)

Deveaux, Alexis 1948- DLB-38

The Development of the Author's Copyright
in Britain DLB-154

The Development of Lighting in the Staging
of Drama, 1900-1945 . . . . DLB-10

"The Development of Meiji Japan" DLB-180

De Vere, Aubrey 1814-1902. . . . . DLB-35

Devereux, second Earl of Essex, Robert
1565-1601 . . . . DLB-136

The Devin-Adair Company DLB-46

De Vinne, Theodore Low 1828-1914. . . . DLB-187

De Voto, Bernard 1897-1955 . . . . DLB-9

De Vries, Peter 1910-1993 . . . . .DLB-6; Y-82

Dewdney, Christopher 1951- DLB-60

Dewdney, Selwyn 1909-1979 . . . . DLB-68

Dewey, Thomas B. 1915-1981 . . . . DLB-226

DeWitt, Robert M., Publisher DLB-49

DeWolfe, Fiske and Company DLB-49

Dexter, Colin 1930- DLB-87

de Young, M. H. 1849-1925. . . . . DLB-25

Dhlomo, H. I. E. 1903-1956. . . . . . . .DLB-157, 225

Dhuoda circa 803-after 843 . . . . DLB-148

The Dial 1840-1844. . . . . DLB-223

The Dial Press DLB-46

Diamond, I. A. L. 1920-1988 . . . . DLB-26

Dibble, L. Grace 1902-1998 . . . . DLB-204

Dibdin, Thomas Frognall 1776-1847 . . . . DLB-184

Di Cicco, Pier Giorgio 1949- DLB-60

Dick, Philip K. 1928-1982 . . . . DLB-8

Dick and Fitzgerald. DLB-49

Dickens, Charles
1812-1870. . . . . .DLB-21, 55, 70, 159, 166

Dickey, James 1923-1997
. . . .DLB-5, 193; Y-82, Y-93, Y-96; DS-7, DS-19

James Dickey Tributes Y-97

The Life of James Dickey: A Lecture to
the Friends of the Emory Libraries,
by Henry Hart Y-98

Dickey, William 1928-1994 . . . . DLB-5

Dickinson, Emily 1830-1886 . . . . DLB-1

Dickinson, John 1732-1808. . . . . DLB-31

Dickinson, Jonathan 1688-1747 . . . . DLB-24

Dickinson, Patric 1914- DLB-27

Dickinson, Peter 1927- DLB-87, 161

Dicks, John [publishing house] DLB-106

Dickson, Gordon R. 1923- DLB-8

Dictionary of Literary Biography
Yearbook Awards . . .Y-92, Y-93, Y-97, Y-98, Y-99

The Dictionary of National Biography DLB-144

Didion, Joan 1934- . DLB-2, 173, 185; Y-81, Y-86

Di Donato, Pietro 1911- DLB-9

Die Fürstliche Bibliothek Corvey. Y-96

Diego, Gerardo 1896-1987 . . . . DLB-134

Digges, Thomas circa 1546-1595 . . . . DLB-136

The Digital Millennium Copyright Act:
Expanding Copyright Protection in
Cyberspace and Beyond Y-98

Dillard, Annie 1945- Y-80

Dillard, R. H. W. 1937- DLB-5

Dillingham, Charles T., Company DLB-49

The Dillingham, G. W., Company DLB-49

Dilly, Edward and Charles
[publishing house] DLB-154

Dilthey, Wilhelm 1833-1911 . . . . DLB-129

Dimitrova, Blaga 1922- DLB-181

Dimov, Dimitr 1909-1966 . . . . DLB-181

Dimsdale, Thomas J. 1831?-1866. . . . . . . DLB-186

Dinescu, Mircea 1950- DLB-232

Dinesen, Isak (see Blixen, Karen)

Dingelstedt, Franz von 1814-1881 . . . . . . DLB-133

Dintenfass, Mark 1941- Y-84

Diogenes, Jr. (see Brougham, John)

Diogenes Laertius circa 200 . . . . .DLB-176

DiPrima, Diane 1934- DLB-5, 16

Disch, Thomas M. 1940- DLB-8

Disney, Walt 1901-1966. . . . . DLB-22

Disraeli, Benjamin 1804-1881. . . . . . . DLB-21, 55

D'Israeli, Isaac 1766-1848 . . . . .DLB-107

Ditlevsen, Tove 1917-1976. . . . . .DLB-214

Ditzen, Rudolf (see Fallada, Hans)

Dix, Dorothea Lynde 1802-1887 . . . . .DLB-1

Dix, Dorothy (see Gilmer, Elizabeth Meriwether)

Dix, Edwards and Company DLB-49

Dix, Gertrude circa 1874-? DLB-197

Dixie, Florence Douglas 1857-1905 . . .DLB-174

Dixon, Ella Hepworth
    1855 or 1857-1932. . . . . .DLB-197

Dixon, Paige (see Corcoran, Barbara)

Dixon, Richard Watson 1833-1900 . . . . . .DLB-19

Dixon, Stephen 1936- DLB-130

Dmitriev, Ivan Ivanovich 1760-1837 . . . . .DLB-150

Dobell, Bertram 1842-1914 . . . . .DLB-184

Dobell, Sydney 1824-1874 . . . . .DLB-32

Dobie, J. Frank 1888-1964 . . . . .DLB-212

Döblin, Alfred 1878-1957 . . . . .DLB-66

Dobson, Austin 1840-1921 . . . . .DLB-35, 144

Doctorow, E. L. 1931- DLB-2, 28, 173; Y-80

Documents on Sixteenth-Century
    Literature. DLB-167, 172

Dodd, Anne [publishing house] DLB-154

Dodd, Mead and Company. DLB-49

Dodd, William E. 1869-1940. . . . . .DLB-17

Doderer, Heimito von 1896-1968 . . . . . . .DLB-85

Dodge, B. W., and Company DLB-46

Dodge, Mary Abigail 1833-1896 . . . . . . .DLB-221

Dodge, Mary Mapes
    1831?-1905 . . . . .DLB-42, 79; DS-13

Dodge Publishing Company DLB-49

Dodgson, Charles Lutwidge (see Carroll, Lewis)

Dodsley, R. [publishing house] DLB-154

Dodsley, Robert 1703-1764 . . . . .DLB-95

Dodson, Owen 1914-1983. . . . . .DLB-76

Dodwell, Christina 1951- DLB-204

Doesticks, Q. K. Philander, P. B.
    (see Thomson, Mortimer)

Doheny, Carrie Estelle 1875-1958 . . . . . . .DLB-140

Doherty, John 1798?-1854 . . . . .DLB-190

Doig, Ivan 1939- DLB-206

Doinaş, Ştefan Augustin 1922- DLB-232

Domínguez, Sylvia Maida 1935- DLB-122

Donahoe, Patrick [publishing house] DLB-49

Donald, David H. 1920- DLB-17

    The Practice of Biography VI: An
    Interview with David Herbert Donald . . . Y-87

Donaldson, Scott 1928- DLB-111

Doni, Rodolfo 1919- DLB-177

Donleavy, J. P. 1926- DLB-6, 173

Donnadieu, Marguerite (see Duras, Marguerite)

Donne, John 1572-1631 . . . . .DLB-121, 151

Donnelley, R. R., and Sons Company. DLB-49

Donnelly, Ignatius 1831-1901 . . . . .DLB-12

Donohue and Henneberry. DLB-49

Donoso, José 1924-1996 . . . . .DLB-113

Doolady, M. [publishing house]. DLB-49

Dooley, Ebon (see Ebon)

Doolittle, Hilda 1886-1961 . . . . .DLB-4, 45

Doplicher, Fabio 1938- DLB-128

Dor, Milo 1923- DLB-85

Doran, George H., Company DLB-46

Dorgelès, Roland 1886-1973 . . . . .DLB-65

Dorn, Edward 1929-1999 . . . . .DLB-5

Dorr, Rheta Childe 1866-1948 . . . . .DLB-25

Dorris, Michael 1945-1997 . . . . .DLB-175

Dorset and Middlesex, Charles Sackville,
    Lord Buckhurst, Earl of 1643-1706 . . . .DLB-131

Dorst, Tankred 1925- DLB-75, 124

Dos Passos, John
    1896-1970 . . . . .DLB-4, 9; DS-1, DS-15

    John Dos Passos: Artist Y-99

    John Dos Passos: A Centennial
    Commemoration. Y-96

Doubleday and Company DLB-49

Dougall, Lily 1858-1923 . . . . .DLB-92

Doughty, Charles M.
    1843-1926 . . . . .DLB-19, 57, 174

Douglas, Gavin 1476-1522. . . . . .DLB-132

Douglas, Keith 1920-1944 . . . . .DLB-27

Douglas, Norman 1868-1952. . . . . . .DLB-34, 195

Douglass, Frederick
    1817?-1895 . . . . .DLB-1, 43, 50, 79

Douglass, William circa 1691-1752 . . . . . .DLB-24

Dourado, Autran 1926- DLB-145

Dove, Arthur G. 1880-1946. . . . . .DLB-188

Dove, Rita 1952- DLB-120

Dover Publications DLB-46

Doves Press DLB-112

Dowden, Edward 1843-1913. . . . . . .DLB-35, 149

Dowell, Coleman 1925-1985 . . . . .DLB-130

Dowland, John 1563-1626. . . . . .DLB-172

Downes, Gwladys 1915- DLB-88

Downing, J., Major (see Davis, Charles A.)

Downing, Major Jack (see Smith, Seba)

Dowriche, Anne
    before 1560-after 1613 . . . . .DLB-172

Dowson, Ernest 1867-1900 . . . . .DLB-19, 135

Doxey, William [publishing house] DLB-49

Doyle, Sir Arthur Conan
    1859-1930 . . . . DLB-18, 70, 156, 178

Doyle, Kirby 1932- DLB-16

Doyle, Roddy 1958- DLB-194

Drabble, Margaret 1939- DLB-14, 155, 231

Drach, Albert 1902- DLB-85

Dragojević, Danijel 1934- DLB-181

Drake, Samuel Gardner 1798-1875 . . . . . .DLB-187

The Dramatic Publishing Company DLB-49

Dramatists Play Service DLB-46

Drant, Thomas early 1540s?-1578. . . . . . .DLB-167

Draper, John W. 1811-1882 . . . . .DLB-30

Draper, Lyman C. 1815-1891 . . . . .DLB-30

Drayton, Michael 1563-1631. . . . . .DLB-121

Dreiser, Theodore
    1871-1945 . . . . DLB-9, 12, 102, 137; DS-1

Dresser, Davis 1904-1977 . . . . .DLB-226

Drewitz, Ingeborg 1923-1986 . . . . .DLB-75

Drieu La Rochelle, Pierre 1893-1945. . . . .DLB-72

Drinker, Elizabeth 1735-1807. . . . . .DLB-200

Drinkwater, John
    1882-1937 . . . . .DLB-10, 19, 149

Droste-Hülshoff, Annette von
    1797-1848. . . . . .DLB-133

The Drue Heinz Literature Prize
    Excerpt from "Excerpts from a Report
    of the Commission," in David
    Bosworth's *The Death of Descartes*
    An Interview with David Bosworth Y-82

Drummond, William, of Hawthornden
    1585-1649 . . . . .DLB-121, 213

Drummond, William Henry
    1854-1907 . . . . .DLB-92

Dryden, Charles 1860?-1931. . . . . .DLB-171

Dryden, John 1631-1700 . . . . . . .DLB-80, 101, 131

Držić, Marin circa 1508-1567 . . . . .DLB-147

Duane, William 1760-1835 . . . . .DLB-43

Dubé, Marcel 1930- DLB-53

Dubé, Rodolphe (see Hertel, François)

Dubie, Norman 1945- DLB-120

Du Bois, W. E. B. 1868-1963 . . . . .DLB-47, 50, 91

Du Bois, William Pène 1916-1993. . . . . . .DLB-61

Dubus, Andre 1936-1999 . . . . .DLB-130

Ducange, Victor 1783-1833 . . . . .DLB-192

Du Chaillu, Paul Belloni 1831?-1903 . . . .DLB-189

Ducharme, Réjean 1941- DLB-60

Dučić, Jovan 1871-1943 . . . . .DLB-147

Duck, Stephen 1705?-1756 . . . . .DLB-95

Duckworth, Gerald, and Company
    Limited DLB-112

Dudek, Louis 1918- DLB-88

Duell, Sloan and Pearce. DLB-46

Duerer, Albrecht 1471-1528. . . . . .DLB-179

Duff Gordon, Lucie 1821-1869 . . . . .DLB-166

Dufferin, Helen Lady, Countess of Gifford
    1807-1867 . . . . .DLB-199

Duffield and Green DLB-46

Duffy, Maureen 1933- DLB-14

Dufief, Nicholas Gouin 1776-1834. . . . . . .DLB-187

Dugan, Alan 1923- DLB-5

Dugard, William [publishing house] DLB-170

Dugas, Marcel 1883-1947 . . . . .DLB-92

Dugdale, William [publishing house]. DLB-106

Duhamel, Georges 1884-1966 . . . . .DLB-65

Dujardin, Edouard 1861-1949. . . . . .DLB-123

Dukes, Ashley 1885-1959 . . . . .DLB-10

Dumas, Alexandre *père* 1802-1870 . . . . .DLB-119, 192

Dumas, Alexandre *fils* 1824-1895 . . . . . . .DLB-192

Dumas, Henry 1934-1968 . . . . .DLB-41

du Maurier, Daphne 1907-1989 . . . . .DLB-191

Du Maurier, George 1834-1896 . . . . DLB-153, 178

Dunbar, Paul Laurence
  1872-1906 . . . . DLB-50, 54, 78

Dunbar, William
  circa 1460-circa 1522 . . . . DLB-132, 146

Duncan, Norman 1871-1916 . . . . DLB-92

Duncan, Quince 1940- DLB-145

Duncan, Robert 1919-1988 . . . . . . DLB-5, 16, 193

Duncan, Ronald 1914-1982 . . . . DLB-13

Duncan, Sara Jeannette 1861-1922 . . . . . . DLB-92

Dunigan, Edward, and Brother DLB-49

Dunlap, John 1747-1812 . . . . DLB-43

Dunlap, William 1766-1839 . . . . . . DLB-30, 37, 59

Dunn, Douglas 1942- DLB-40

Dunn, Harvey Thomas 1884-1952 . . . . . . DLB-188

Dunn, Stephen 1939- DLB-105

  "The Good, The Not So Good" DLB-105

Dunne, Finley Peter 1867-1936 . . . . . . DLB-11, 23

Dunne, John Gregory 1932- Y-80

Dunne, Philip 1908-1992 . . . . DLB-26

Dunning, Ralph Cheever 1878-1930 . . . . . . DLB-4

Dunning, William A. 1857-1922 . . . . DLB-17

Dunsany, Lord (Edward John Moreton
  Drax Plunkett, Baron Dunsany)
  1878-1957 . . . . DLB-10, 77, 153, 156

Duns Scotus, John circa 1266-1308 . . . . . DLB-115

Dunton, John [publishing house] DLB-170

Dunton, W. Herbert 1878-1936 . . . . DLB-188

Dupin, Amantine-Aurore-Lucile (see Sand, George)

Durand, Lucile (see Bersianik, Louky)

Duranti, Francesca 1935- DLB-196

Duranty, Walter 1884-1957 . . . . DLB-29

Duras, Marguerite 1914-1996 . . . . DLB-83

Durfey, Thomas 1653-1723 . . . . DLB-80

Durova, Nadezhda Andreevna
  (Aleksandr Andreevich Aleksandrov)
  1783-1866 . . . . DLB-198

Durrell, Lawrence
  1912-1990 . . . . DLB-15, 27, 204; Y-90

Durrell, William [publishing house] DLB-49

Dürrenmatt, Friedrich 1921-1990 . . . . DLB-69, 124

Duston, Hannah 1657-1737 . . . . DLB-200

Dutton, E. P., and Company DLB-49

Duvoisin, Roger 1904-1980 . . . . DLB-61

Duyckinck, Evert Augustus
  1816-1878 . . . . DLB-3, 64

Duyckinck, George L. 1823-1863 . . . . DLB-3

Duyckinck and Company DLB-49

Dwight, John Sullivan 1813-1893 . . . . DLB-1

Dwight, Timothy 1752-1817 . . . . DLB-37

Dybek, Stuart 1942- DLB-130

Dyer, Charles 1928- DLB-13

Dyer, Sir Edward 1543-1607 . . . . DLB-136

Dyer, George 1755-1841 . . . . DLB-93

Dyer, John 1699-1757 . . . . DLB-95

Dyk, Viktor 1877-1931 . . . . DLB-215

Dylan, Bob 1941- DLB-16

E

Eager, Edward 1911-1964 . . . . DLB-22

Eames, Wilberforce 1855-1937 . . . . DLB-140

Earle, Alice Morse 1853-1911 . . . . DLB-221

Earle, James H., and Company DLB-49

Earle, John 1600 or 1601-1665 . . . . DLB-151

Early American Book Illustration,
  by Sinclair Hamilton DLB-49

Eastlake, William 1917-1997 . . . . DLB-6, 206

Eastman, Carol ?- DLB-44

Eastman, Charles A. (Ohiyesa)
  1858-1939 . . . . .DLB-175

Eastman, Max 1883-1969 . . . . DLB-91

Eaton, Daniel Isaac 1753-1814 . . . . DLB-158

Eaton, Edith Maude 1865-1914 . . . . DLB-221

Eaton, Winnifred 1875-1954 . . . . DLB-221

Eberhart, Richard 1904- DLB-48

Ebner, Jeannie 1918- DLB-85

Ebner-Eschenbach, Marie von
  1830-1916 . . . . DLB-81

Ebon 1942- DLB-41

E-Books Turn the Corner Y-98

Ecbasis Captivi circa 1045 . . . . DLB-148

Ecco Press DLB-46

Eckhart, Meister circa 1260-circa 1328 . . . DLB-115

The Eclectic Review 1805-1868 . . . . DLB-110

Eco, Umberto 1932- DLB-196

Edel, Leon 1907-1997 . . . . DLB-103

Edes, Benjamin 1732-1803 . . . . DLB-43

Edgar, David 1948- DLB-13, 233

Edgeworth, Maria 1768-1849 . . .DLB-116, 159, 163

The Edinburgh Review 1802-1929 . . . . DLB-110

Edinburgh University Press DLB-112

The Editor Publishing Company DLB-49

Editorial Statements DLB-137

Edmonds, Randolph 1900- DLB-51

Edmonds, Walter D. 1903-1998 . . . . DLB-9

Edschmid, Kasimir 1890-1966 . . . . DLB-56

Edwards, Amelia Anne Blandford
  1831-1892 . . . . .DLB-174

Edwards, Edward 1812-1886 . . . . DLB-184

Edwards, James [publishing house] DLB-154

Edwards, Jonathan 1703-1758 . . . . DLB-24

Edwards, Jonathan, Jr. 1745-1801 . . . . . . DLB-37

Edwards, Junius 1929- DLB-33

Edwards, Matilda Barbara Betham
  1836-1919 . . . . .DLB-174

Edwards, Richard 1524-1566 . . . . DLB-62

Edwards, Sarah Pierpont 1710-1758 . . . . . DLB-200

Effinger, George Alec 1947- DLB-8

Egerton, George 1859-1945 . . . . DLB-135

Eggleston, Edward 1837-1902 . . . . DLB-12

Eggleston, Wilfred 1901-1986 . . . . DLB-92

Eglītis, Anšlavs 1906-1993 . . . . DLB-220

Ehrenstein, Albert 1886-1950 . . . . DLB-81

Ehrhart, W. D. 1948- DS-9

Ehrlich, Gretel 1946- DLB-212

Eich, Günter 1907-1972 . . . . DLB-69, 124

Eichendorff, Joseph Freiherr von
  1788-1857 . . . . DLB-90

Eifukumon'in 1271-1342 . . . . DLB-203

1873 Publishers' Catalogues DLB-49

Eighteenth-Century Aesthetic Theories . . . DLB-31

Eighteenth-Century Philosophical
  Background DLB-31

Eigner, Larry 1926-1996 . . . . DLB-5, 193

Eikon Basilike 1649 . . . . DLB-151

Eilhart von Oberge
  circa 1140-circa 1195 . . . . DLB-148

Einhard circa 770-840 . . . . DLB-148

Eiseley, Loren 1907-1977 . . . . .DS-17

Eisenreich, Herbert 1925-1986 . . . . DLB-85

Eisner, Kurt 1867-1919 . . . . DLB-66

Eklund, Gordon 1945- Y-83

Ekwensi, Cyprian 1921- DLB-117

Eld, George [publishing house] DLB-170

Elder, Lonne III 1931- DLB-7, 38, 44

Elder, Paul, and Company DLB-49

The Electronic Text Center and the Electronic
  Archive of Early American Fiction at the
  University of Virginia Library Y-98

Eliade, Mircea 1907-1986 . . . . DLB-220

Elie, Robert 1915-1973 . . . . DLB-88

Elin Pelin 1877-1949 . . . . .DLB-147

Eliot, George 1819-1880 . . . . DLB-21, 35, 55

Eliot, John 1604-1690 . . . . DLB-24

Eliot, T. S. 1888-1965 . . . . .DLB-7, 10, 45, 63

  T. S. Eliot Centennial Y-88

Eliot's Court Press DLB-170

Elizabeth I 1533-1603 . . . . DLB-136

Elizabeth of Nassau-Saarbrücken
  after 1393-1456 . . . . .DLB-179

Elizondo, Salvador 1932- DLB-145

Elizondo, Sergio 1930- DLB-82

Elkin, Stanley 1930-1995 . . . .DLB-2, 28, 218; Y-80

Elles, Dora Amy (see Wentworth, Patricia)

Ellet, Elizabeth F. 1818?-1877 . . . . DLB-30

Elliot, Ebenezer 1781-1849 . . . . DLB-96, 190

Elliot, Frances Minto (Dickinson)
  1820-1898 . . . . DLB-166

Elliott, Charlotte 1789-1871 . . . . DLB-199

Elliott, George 1923- DLB-68

Elliott, Janice 1931- DLB-14

Elliott, Sarah Barnwell 1848-1928 . . . . . . DLB-221

Elliott, Thomes and Talbot DLB-49

Elliott, William 1788-1863 . . . . DLB-3

Ellis, Alice Thomas (Anna Margaret Haycraft)
  1932- DLB-194

Ellis, Edward S. 1840-1916 . . . . DLB-42

Ellis, Frederick Staridge
  [publishing house] DLB-106

The George H. Ellis Company DLB-49

Ellis, Havelock 1859-1939 . . . . .DLB-190

Ellison, Harlan 1934- DLB-8

Ellison, Ralph
1914-1994 . . . . DLB-2, 76, 227; Y-94

Ellmann, Richard 1918-1987 . . . . . DLB-103; Y-87

Ellroy, James 1948- DLB-226

Elyot, Thomas 1490?-1546 . . . . .DLB-136

Emanuel, James Andrew 1921- DLB-41

Emecheta, Buchi 1944- DLB-117

The Emergence of Black Women Writers DS-8

Emerson, Ralph Waldo
1803-1882 . . . . DLB-1, 59, 73, 183, 223

Ralph Waldo Emerson in 1982 . . . . Y-82

Emerson, William 1769-1811 . . . . .DLB-37

Emerson, William 1923-1997 . . . . Y-97

Emin, Fedor Aleksandrovich
circa 1735-1770 . . . . .DLB-150

Empedocles fifth century B.C. DLB-176

Empson, William 1906-1984 . . . . .DLB-20

Enchi Fumiko 1905-1986 . . . . .DLB-182

"Encounter with the West" DLB-180

The End of English Stage Censorship,
1945-1968 . . . . .DLB-13

Ende, Michael 1929-1995 . . . . .DLB-75

Endō Shūsaku 1923-1996 . . . . .DLB-182

Engel, Marian 1933-1985 . . . . .DLB-53

Engels, Friedrich 1820-1895 . . . . .DLB-129

Engle, Paul 1908- DLB-48

English, Thomas Dunn 1819-1902 . . . . . .DLB-202

English Composition and Rhetoric (1866),
by Alexander Bain [excerpt] DLB-57

The English Language: 410 to 1500 . . . . .DLB-146

Ennius 239 B.C.-169 B.C. DLB-211

Enright, D. J. 1920- DLB-27

Enright, Elizabeth 1909-1968 . . . . .DLB-22

Epic and Beast Epic DLB-208

Epictetus circa 55-circa 125-130 . . . . .DLB-176

Epicurus 342/341 B.C.-271/270 B.C. DLB-176

Epps, Bernard 1936- DLB-53

Epstein, Julius 1909- and
Epstein, Philip 1909-1952 . . . . .DLB-26

Equiano, Olaudah circa 1745-1797 . . . . .DLB-37, 50

Olaudah Equiano and Unfinished Journeys:
The Slave-Narrative Tradition and
Twentieth-Century Continuities, by
Paul Edwards and Pauline T.
Wangman DLB-117

Eragny Press DLB-112

Erasmus, Desiderius 1467-1536 . . . . .DLB-136

Erba, Luciano 1922- DLB-128

Erdrich, Louise 1954- DLB-152, 175, 206

Erichsen-Brown, Gwethalyn Graham
(see Graham, Gwethalyn)

Eriugena, John Scottus circa 810-877 . . . . .DLB-115

Ernst, Paul 1866-1933 . . . . .DLB-66, 118

Ershov, Petr Pavlovich 1815-1869 . . . . . . .DLB-205

Erskine, Albert 1911-1993 . . . . Y-93

Erskine, John 1879-1951 . . . . .DLB-9, 102

Erskine, Mrs. Steuart ?-1948 . . . . .DLB-195

Ervine, St. John Greer 1883-1971 . . . . . . .DLB-10

Eschenburg, Johann Joachim 1743-1820 . . .DLB-97

Escoto, Julio 1944- DLB-145

Esdaile, Arundell 1880-1956 . . . . .DLB-201

Eshleman, Clayton 1935- DLB-5

Espriu, Salvador 1913-1985 . . . . .DLB-134

Ess Ess Publishing Company DLB-49

Essex House Press DLB-112

Essop, Ahmed 1931- DLB-225

Esterházy, Péter 1950- DLB-232

Estes, Eleanor 1906-1988 . . . . .DLB-22

Estes and Lauriat DLB-49

Estleman, Loren D. 1952- DLB-226

Eszterhas, Joe 1944- DLB-185

Etherege, George 1636-circa 1692 . . . . .DLB-80

Ethridge, Mark, Sr. 1896-1981 . . . . .DLB-127

Ets, Marie Hall 1893- DLB-22

Etter, David 1928- DLB-105

Ettner, Johann Christoph 1654-1724 . . . . .DLB-168

Eupolemius flourished circa 1095 . . . . . . .DLB-148

Euripides circa 484 B.C.-407/406 B.C. . . . DLB-176

Evans, Caradoc 1878-1945 . . . . .DLB-162

Evans, Charles 1850-1935 . . . . .DLB-187

Evans, Donald 1884-1921 . . . . .DLB-54

Evans, George Henry 1805-1856 . . . . .DLB-43

Evans, Hubert 1892-1986 . . . . .DLB-92

Evans, M., and Company DLB-46

Evans, Mari 1923- DLB-41

Evans, Mary Ann (see Eliot, George)

Evans, Nathaniel 1742-1767 . . . . .DLB-31

Evans, Sebastian 1830-1909 . . . . .DLB-35

Evaristi, Marcella 1953- DLB-233

Everett, Alexander Hill 1790-1847 . . . . . . .DLB-59

Everett, Edward 1794-1865 . . . . .DLB-1, 59

Everson, R. G. 1903- DLB-88

Everson, William 1912-1994 . . . . . .DLB-5, 16, 212

Ewart, Gavin 1916-1995 . . . . .DLB-40

Ewing, Juliana Horatia 1841-1885 . . . .DLB-21, 163

The Examiner 1808-1881 . . . . .DLB-110

Exley, Frederick 1929-1992 . . . . . . .DLB-143; Y-81

von Eyb, Albrecht 1420-1475 . . . . .DLB-179

Eyre and Spottiswoode DLB-106

Ezera, Regīna 1930- DLB-232

Ezzo ?-after 1065 . . . . .DLB-148

F

Faber, Frederick William 1814-1863 . . . . . .DLB-32

Faber and Faber Limited DLB-112

Faccio, Rena (see Aleramo, Sibilla)

Fagundo, Ana María 1938- DLB-134

Fair, Ronald L. 1932- DLB-33

Fairfax, Beatrice (see Manning, Marie)

Fairlie, Gerard 1899-1983 . . . . .DLB-77

Fallada, Hans 1893-1947 . . . . .DLB-56

Fancher, Betsy 1928- Y-83

Fane, Violet 1843-1905 . . . . .DLB-35

Fanfrolico Press .DLB-112

Fanning, Katherine 1927 . . . . .DLB-127

Fanshawe, Sir Richard 1608-1666 . . . . . . .DLB-126

Fantasy Press Publishers DLB-46

Fante, John 1909-1983 . . . . DLB-130; Y-83

Al-Farabi circa 870-950 . . . . .DLB-115

Farabough, Laura 1949- DLB-228

Farah, Nuruddin 1945- DLB-125

Farber, Norma 1909-1984 . . . . .DLB-61

Farigoule, Louis (see Romains, Jules)

Farjeon, Eleanor 1881-1965 . . . . .DLB-160

Farley, Walter 1920-1989 . . . . .DLB-22

Farmborough, Florence 1887-1978 . . . . . .DLB-204

Farmer, Penelope 1939- DLB-161

Farmer, Philip José 1918- DLB-8

Farquhar, George circa 1677-1707 . . . . . . .DLB-84

Farquharson, Martha (see Finley, Martha)

Farrar, Frederic William 1831-1903 . . . . . .DLB-163

Farrar and Rinehart DLB-46

Farrar, Straus and Giroux DLB-46

Farrell, J. G. 1935-1979 . . . . .DLB-14

Farrell, James T. 1904-1979 . . . .DLB-4, 9, 86; DS-2

Fast, Howard 1914- DLB-9

Faulkner, George [publishing house] DLB-154

Faulkner, William
1897-1962 . . . . DLB-9, 11, 44, 102; DS-2; Y-86

William Faulkner Centenary Y-97

"Faulkner 100—Celebrating the Work,"
University of South Carolina, Columbia . .Y-97

Impressions of William Faulkner Y-97

Faulkner and Yoknapatawpha Conference,
Oxford, Mississippi Y-97

Faulks, Sebastian 1953- DLB-207

Fauset, Jessie Redmon 1882-1961 . . . . . . .DLB-51

Faust, Irvin 1924- DLB-2, 28, 218; Y-80

Fawcett, Edgar 1847-1904 . . . . .DLB-202

Fawcett, Millicent Garrett 1847-1929 . . . . .DLB-190

Fawcett Books DLB-46

Fay, Theodore Sedgwick 1807-1898 . . . . .DLB-202

Fearing, Kenneth 1902-1961 . . . . .DLB-9

Federal Writers' Project DLB-46

Federman, Raymond 1928- Y-80

Feiffer, Jules 1929- DLB-7, 44

Feinberg, Charles E. 1899-1988 . . . . DLB-187; Y-88

Feind, Barthold 1678-1721 . . . . .DLB-168

Feinstein, Elaine 1930- DLB-14, 40

Feiss, Paul Louis 1875-1952 . . . . .DLB-187

Feldman, Irving 1928- DLB-169

Felipe, Léon 1884-1968 . . . . .DLB-108

Fell, Frederick, Publishers DLB-46

Felltham, Owen 1602?-1668 . . . . . . .DLB-126, 151

Fels, Ludwig 1946- DLB-75

Felton, Cornelius Conway 1807-1862...... DLB-1

Fenn, Harry 1837-1911............. DLB-188

Fennario, David 1947- DLB-60

Fenno, Jenny 1765?-1803 .... DLB-200

Fenno, John 1751-1798 .... DLB-43

Fenno, R. F., and Company DLB-49

Fenoglio, Beppe 1922-1963............DLB-177

Fenton, Geoffrey 1539?-1608 .... DLB-136

Fenton, James 1949- DLB-40

Ferber, Edna 1885-1968 .... DLB-9, 28, 86´

Ferdinand, Vallery III (see Salaam, Kalamu ya)

Ferguson, Sir Samuel 1810-1886........ DLB-32

Ferguson, William Scott 1875-1954 ...... DLB-47

Fergusson, Robert 1750-1774 .... DLB-109

Ferland, Albert 1872-1943.............. DLB-92

Ferlinghetti, Lawrence 1919- DLB-5, 16

Fermor, Patrick Leigh 1915- DLB-204

Fern, Fanny (see Parton, Sara Payson Willis)

Ferrars, Elizabeth 1907- DLB-87

Ferré, Rosario 1942- DLB-145

Ferret, E., and Company DLB-49

Ferrier, Susan 1782-1854.............. DLB-116

Ferril, Thomas Hornsby 1896-1988 .... DLB-206

Ferrini, Vincent 1913- DLB-48

Ferron, Jacques 1921-1985 .... DLB-60

Ferron, Madeleine 1922- DLB-53

Ferrucci, Franco 1936- DLB-196

Fetridge and Company............... DLB-49

Feuchtersleben, Ernst Freiherr von
     1806-1849 .... DLB-133

Feuchtwanger, Lion 1884-1958......... DLB-66

Feuerbach, Ludwig 1804-1872 .... DLB-133

Feuillet, Octave 1821-1890 .... DLB-192

Feydeau, Georges 1862-1921 .... DLB-192

Fichte, Johann Gottlieb 1762-1814 .... DLB-90

Ficke, Arthur Davison 1883-1945........ DLB-54

Fiction Best-Sellers, 1910-1945 .... DLB-9

Fiction into Film, 1928-1975: A List of Movies
     Based on the Works of Authors in
     British Novelists, 1930-1959 .... DLB-15

Fiedler, Leslie A. 1917- DLB-28, 67

Field, Barron 1789-1846 .... DLB-230

Field, Edward 1924- DLB-105

"The Poetry File" DLB-105

Field, Eugene
     1850-1895 .... DLB-23, 42, 140; DS-13

Field, John 1545?-1588 .... DLB-167

Field, Marshall, III 1893-1956 .... DLB-127

Field, Marshall, IV 1916-1965 .... DLB-127

Field, Marshall, V 1941- DLB-127

Field, Nathan 1587-1619 or 1620 .... DLB-58

Field, Rachel 1894-1942 .... DLB-9, 22

A Field Guide to Recent Schools of American
     Poetry............................Y-86

Fielding, Helen 1958- DLB-231

Fielding, Henry 1707-1754...... DLB-39, 84, 101

"Defense of *Amelia*" (1752) DLB-39

From *The History of the Adventures of
     Joseph Andrews* (1742) DLB-39

Preface to *Joseph Andrews* (1742) DLB-39

Preface to Sarah Fielding's *The Adventures
     of David Simple* (1744) DLB-39

Preface to Sarah Fielding's *Familiar Letters*
     (1747) [excerpt]................ DLB-39

Fielding, Sarah 1710-1768 .... DLB-39

Preface to *The Cry* (1754)............ DLB-39

Fields, Annie Adams 1834-1915....... DLB-221

Fields, James Thomas 1817-1881 .... DLB-1

Fields, Julia 1938- DLB-41

Fields, Osgood and Company DLB-49

Fields, W. C. 1880-1946............. DLB-44

Fifty Penguin Years Y-85

Figes, Eva 1932- DLB-14

Figuera, Angela 1902-1984........... DLB-108

Filmer, Sir Robert 1586-1653 .... DLB-151

Filson, John circa 1753-1788 .... DLB-37

Finch, Anne, Countess of Winchilsea
     1661-1720...................... DLB-95

Finch, Robert 1900- DLB-88

Findley, Timothy 1930- DLB-53

Finlay, Ian Hamilton 1925- DLB-40

Finley, Martha 1828-1909 .... DLB-42

Finn, Elizabeth Anne (McCaul)
     1825-1921 .... DLB-166

Finney, Jack 1911-1995.............. DLB-8

Finney, Walter Braden (see Finney, Jack)

Firbank, Ronald 1886-1926 .... DLB-36

Firmin, Giles 1615-1697 .... DLB-24

First Edition Library/Collectors'
     Reprints, Inc..................Y-91

Fischart, Johann
     1546 or 1547-1590 or 1591 ....DLB-179

Fischer, Karoline Auguste Fernandine
     1764-1842...................... DLB-94

Fischer, Tibor 1959- DLB-231

Fish, Stanley 1938- DLB-67

Fishacre, Richard 1205-1248 .... DLB-115

Fisher, Clay (see Allen, Henry W.)

Fisher, Dorothy Canfield 1879-1958... DLB-9, 102

Fisher, Leonard Everett 1924- DLB-61

Fisher, Roy 1930- DLB-40

Fisher, Rudolph 1897-1934........ DLB-51, 102

Fisher, Steve 1913-1980 .... DLB-226

Fisher, Sydney George 1856-1927 .... DLB-47

Fisher, Vardis 1895-1968 .... DLB-9, 206

Fiske, John 1608-1677................ DLB-24

Fiske, John 1842-1901 ....DLB-47, 64

Fitch, Thomas circa 1700-1774 .... DLB-31

Fitch, William Clyde 1865-1909......... DLB-7

FitzGerald, Edward 1809-1883......... DLB-32

Fitzgerald, F. Scott 1896-1940
     ... DLB-4, 9, 86, 219; Y-81, Y-92; DS-1, 15, 16

F. Scott Fitzgerald Centenary
     Celebrations.......................Y-96

F. Scott Fitzgerald Inducted into the American
     Poets' Corner at St. John the Divine;
     Ezra Pound Banned.................Y-99

"F. Scott Fitzgerald: St. Paul's Native Son
     and Distinguished American Writer":
     University of Minnesota Conference,
     29-31 October 1982.................Y-82

First International F. Scott Fitzgerald
     Conference........................Y-92

Fitzgerald, Penelope 1916- DLB-14, 194

Fitzgerald, Robert 1910-1985 ....Y-80

Fitzgerald, Thomas 1819-1891 .... DLB-23

Fitzgerald, Zelda Sayre 1900-1948 ....Y-84

Fitzhugh, Louise 1928-1974 .... DLB-52

Fitzhugh, William circa 1651-1701 .... DLB-24

Flagg, James Montgomery 1877-1960.... DLB-188

Flanagan, Thomas 1923- Y-80

Flanner, Hildegarde 1899-1987 .... DLB-48

Flanner, Janet 1892-1978 .... DLB-4

Flannery, Peter 1951- DLB-233

Flaubert, Gustave 1821-1880 .... DLB-119

Flavin, Martin 1883-1967............. DLB-9

Fleck, Konrad
     (flourished circa 1220) DLB-138

Flecker, James Elroy 1884-1915 ......DLB-10, 19

Fleeson, Doris 1901-1970 .... DLB-29

Fleißer, Marieluise 1901-1974....... DLB-56, 124

Fleming, Ian 1908-1964 ....DLB-87, 201

Fleming, Paul 1609-1640 .... DLB-164

Fleming, Peter 1907-1971 .... DLB-195

Fletcher, Giles, the Elder 1546-1611..... DLB-136

Fletcher, Giles, the Younger
     1585 or 1586-1623................. DLB-121

Fletcher, J. S. 1863-1935.............. DLB-70

Fletcher, John (see Beaumont, Francis)

Fletcher, John Gould 1886-1950...... DLB-4, 45

Fletcher, Phineas 1582-1650........... DLB-121

Flieg, Helmut (see Heym, Stefan)

Flint, F. S. 1885-1960 .... DLB-19

Flint, Timothy 1780-1840...........DLB-73, 186

Flores-Williams, Jason 1969- DLB-209

Florio, John 1553?-1625...............DLB-172

Fo, Dario 1926- Y-97

Foix, J. V. 1893-1987 .... DLB-134

Foley, Martha (see Burnett, Whit, and Martha Foley)

Folger, Henry Clay 1857-1930 .... DLB-140

Folio Society DLB-112

Follen, Eliza Lee (Cabot) 1787-1860 .... DLB-1

Follett, Ken 1949- DLB-87; Y-81

Follett Publishing Company........... DLB-46

Folsom, John West [publishing house] DLB-49

Folz, Hans
     between 1435 and 1440-1513 ......DLB-179

Fontane, Theodor 1819-1898......... DLB-129

Fontes, Montserrat 1940- DLB-209

Fonvisin, Denis Ivanovich 1744 or 1745-1792 . . . . .DLB-150

Foote, Horton 1916- DLB-26

Foote, Mary Hallock 1847-1938 . . . . .DLB-186, 188, 202, 221

Foote, Samuel 1721-1777 . . . . .DLB-89

Foote, Shelby 1916- DLB-2, 17

Forbes, Calvin 1945- DLB-41

Forbes, Ester 1891-1967 . . . . .DLB-22

Forbes, Rosita 1893?-1967 . . . . .DLB-195

Forbes and Company DLB-49

Force, Peter 1790-1868 . . . . .DLB-30

Forché, Carolyn 1950- DLB-5, 193

Ford, Charles Henri 1913- DLB-4, 48

Ford, Corey 1902-1969 . . . . .DLB-11

Ford, Ford Madox 1873-1939 . . . .DLB-34, 98, 162

Ford, J. B., and Company DLB-49

Ford, Jesse Hill 1928-1996 . . . . .DLB-6

Ford, John 1586-? DLB-58

Ford, R. A. D. 1915- DLB-88

Ford, Richard 1944- DLB-227

Ford, Worthington C. 1858-1941 . . . . . . .DLB-47

Fords, Howard, and Hulbert DLB-49

Foreman, Carl 1914-1984 . . . . .DLB-26

Forester, C. S. 1899-1966 . . . . .DLB-191

Forester, Frank (see Herbert, Henry William)

Forman, Harry Buxton 1842-1917 . . . . . . .DLB-184

Fornés, María Irene 1930- DLB-7

Forrest, Leon 1937-1997 . . . . .DLB-33

Forster, E. M. 1879-1970 . . . . DLB-34, 98, 162, 178, 195; DS-10

Forster, Georg 1754-1794 . . . . .DLB-94

Forster, John 1812-1876 . . . . .DLB-144

Forster, Margaret 1938- DLB-155

Forsyth, Frederick 1938- DLB-87

Forten, Charlotte L. 1837-1914 . . . . .DLB-50

Charlotte Forten: Pages from her Diary .DLB-50

Fortini, Franco 1917- DLB-128

Fortune, Mary ca. 1833-ca. 1910 . . . . . . .DLB-230

Fortune, T. Thomas 1856-1928 . . . . .DLB-23

Fosdick, Charles Austin 1842-1915 . . . . . . .DLB-42

Foster, Genevieve 1893-1979 . . . . .DLB-61

Foster, Hannah Webster 1758-1840 . . DLB-37, 200

Foster, John 1648-1681 . . . . .DLB-24

Foster, Michael 1904-1956 . . . . .DLB-9

Foster, Myles Birket 1825-1899 . . . . .DLB-184

Foulis, Robert and Andrew / R. and A. [publishing house] DLB-154

Fouqué, Caroline de la Motte 1774-1831 .DLB-90

Fouqué, Friedrich de la Motte 1777-1843 .DLB-90

Four Seas Company DLB-46

Four Winds Press DLB-46

Fournier, Henri Alban (see Alain-Fournier)

Fowler and Wells Company DLB-49

Fowles, John 1926- DLB-14, 139, 207

Fox, John, Jr. 1862 or 1863-1919 . . . .DLB-9; DS-13

Fox, Paula 1923- DLB-52

Fox, Richard K. [publishing house] DLB-49

Fox, Richard Kyle 1846-1922 . . . . .DLB-79

Fox, William Price 1926- DLB-2; Y-81

Foxe, John 1517-1587 . . . . .DLB-132

Fraenkel, Michael 1896-1957 . . . . .DLB-4

France, Anatole 1844-1924 . . . . .DLB-123

France, Richard 1938- DLB-7

Francis, C. S. [publishing house] DLB-49

Francis, Convers 1795-1863 . . . . .DLB-1

Francis, Dick 1920- DLB-87

Francis, Sir Frank 1901-1988 . . . . .DLB-201

Francis, Jeffrey, Lord 1773-1850 . . . . .DLB-107

François 1863-1910 . . . . .DLB-92

François, Louise von 1817-1893 . . . . .DLB-129

Franck, Sebastian 1499-1542 . . . . .DLB-179

Francke, Kuno 1855-1930 . . . . .DLB-71

Frank, Bruno 1887-1945 . . . . .DLB-118

Frank, Leonhard 1882-1961 . . . . . . .DLB-56, 118

Frank, Melvin (see Panama, Norman)

Frank, Waldo 1889-1967 . . . . .DLB-9, 63

Franken, Rose 1895?-1988 . . . . . .DLB-228, Y-84

Franklin, Benjamin 1706-1790 . . . . DLB-24, 43, 73, 183

Franklin, James 1697-1735 . . . . .DLB-43

Franklin, Miles 1879-1954 . . . . .DLB-230

Franklin Library DLB-46

Frantz, Ralph Jules 1902-1979 . . . . .DLB-4

Franzos, Karl Emil 1848-1904 . . . . .DLB-129

Fraser, G. S. 1915-1980 . . . . .DLB-27

Fraser, Kathleen 1935- DLB-169

Frattini, Alberto 1922- DLB-128

Frau Ava ?-1127 . . . . .DLB-148

Frayn, Michael 1933- DLB-13, 14, 194

Frederic, Harold 1856-1898 . . . . .DLB-12, 23; DS-13

Freeling, Nicolas 1927- DLB-87

Freeman, Douglas Southall 1886-1953 . . . . DLB-17; DS-17

Freeman, Legh Richmond 1842-1915 . . . . .DLB-23

Freeman, Mary E. Wilkins 1852-1930 . . . . .DLB-12, 78, 221

Freeman, R. Austin 1862-1943 . . . . .DLB-70

Freidank circa 1170-circa 1233 . . . . .DLB-138

Freiligrath, Ferdinand 1810-1876 . . . . .DLB-133

Frémont, John Charles 1813-1890 . . . . . . .DLB-186

Frémont, John Charles 1813-1890 and Frémont, Jessie Benton 1834-1902 . . .DLB-183

French, Alice 1850-1934 . . . . .DLB-74; DS-13

French Arthurian Literature DLB-208

French, David 1939- DLB-53

French, Evangeline 1869-1960 . . . . .DLB-195

French, Francesca 1871-1960 . . . . .DLB-195

French, James [publishing house] DLB-49

French, Samuel [publishing house] DLB-49

Samuel French, Limited DLB-106

Freneau, Philip 1752-1832 . . . . DLB-37, 43

Freni, Melo 1934- DLB-128

Freshfield, Douglas W. 1845-1934 . . . . . .DLB-174

Freytag, Gustav 1816-1895 . . . . .DLB-129

Fried, Erich 1921-1988 . . . . .DLB-85

Friedman, Bruce Jay 1930- DLB-2, 28

Friedrich von Hausen circa 1171-1190 . . . .DLB-138

Friel, Brian 1929- DLB-13

Friend, Krebs 1895?-1967? DLB-4

Fries, Fritz Rudolf 1935- DLB-75

Fringe and Alternative Theater in Great Britain .DLB-13

Frisch, Max 1911-1991 . . . . .DLB-69, 124

Frischlin, Nicodemus 1547-1590 . . . . .DLB-179

Frischmuth, Barbara 1941- DLB-85

Fritz, Jean 1915- DLB-52

Froissart, Jean circa 1337-circa 1404 . . . . . .DLB-208

Fromentin, Eugene 1820-1876 . . . . .DLB-123

Frontinus circa A.D. 35-A.D. 103/104 . . . .DLB-211

Frost, A. B. 1851-1928 . . . . .DLB-188; DS-13

Frost, Robert 1874-1963 . . . . .DLB-54; DS-7

Frothingham, Octavius Brooks 1822-1895 . . . . .DLB-1

Froude, James Anthony 1818-1894 . . . . DLB-18, 57, 144

Fruitlands 1843-1844 . . . . .DLB-223

Fry, Christopher 1907- DLB-13

Fry, Roger 1866-1934 . . . . DS-10

Fry, Stephen 1957- DLB-207

Frye, Northrop 1912-1991 . . . . DLB-67, 68

Fuchs, Daniel 1909-1993 . . . . . DLB-9, 26, 28; Y-93

Fuentes, Carlos 1928- DLB-113

Fuertes, Gloria 1918- DLB-108

Fugard, Athol 1932- DLB-225

The Fugitives and the Agrarians: The First Exhibition Y-85

Fujiwara no Shunzei 1114-1204 . . . . .DLB-203

Fujiwara no Tameaki 1230s?-1290s? DLB-203

Fujiwara no Tameie 1198-1275 . . . . .DLB-203

Fujiwara no Teika 1162-1241 . . . . .DLB-203

Fulbecke, William 1560-1603? DLB-172

Fuller, Charles H., Jr. 1939- DLB-38

Fuller, Henry Blake 1857-1929 . . . . .DLB-12

Fuller, John 1937- DLB-40

Fuller, Margaret (see Fuller, Sarah Margaret, Marchesa D'Ossoli)

Fuller, Roy 1912-1991 . . . . .DLB-15, 20

Fuller, Samuel 1912- DLB-26

Fuller, Sarah Margaret, Marchesa D'Ossoli 1810-1850 . . . . DLB-1, 59, 73, 183, 223

Fuller, Thomas 1608-1661 . . . . .DLB-151

Fullerton, Hugh 1873-1945 . . . . .DLB-171

Fulton, Alice 1952- DLB-193

Fulton, Len 1934- Y-86

Fulton, Robin 1937- DLB-40

Furbank, P. N. 1920- DLB-155

Furman, Laura 1945- Y-86

Furness, Horace Howard 1833-1912 . . . . . DLB-64

Furness, William Henry 1802-1896 . . . . DLB-1

Furnivall, Frederick James 1825-1910 . . . . DLB-184

Furphy, Joseph
    (Tom Collins) 1843-1912 . . . . DLB-230

Furthman, Jules 1888-1966 . . . . DLB-26

Furui Yoshikichi 1937- DLB-182

Fushimi, Emperor 1265-1317 . . . . DLB-203

Futabatei, Shimei (Hasegawa Tatsunosuke)
    1864-1909 . . . . DLB-180

The Future of the Novel (1899), by
    Henry James. DLB-18

Fyleman, Rose 1877-1957 . . . . DLB-160

G

Gadda, Carlo Emilio 1893-1973 . . . . DLB-177

Gaddis, William 1922-1998 . . . . DLB-2, Y-99

Gág, Wanda 1893-1946 . . . . DLB-22

Gagarin, Ivan Sergeevich 1814-1882 . . . . DLB-198

Gagnon, Madeleine 1938- DLB-60

Gaine, Hugh 1726-1807 . . . . DLB-43

Gaine, Hugh [publishing house] DLB-49

Gaines, Ernest J. 1933- DLB-2, 33, 152; Y-80

Gaiser, Gerd 1908-1976 . . . . DLB-69

Galarza, Ernesto 1905-1984 . . . . DLB-122

Galaxy Science Fiction Novels DLB-46

Gale, Zona 1874-1938 . . . . DLB-9, 228, 78

Galen of Pergamon 129-after 210 . . . . DLB-176

Gales, Winifred Marshall 1761-1839 . . . . DLB-200

Gall, Louise von 1815-1855 . . . . DLB-133

Gallagher, Tess 1943- DLB-120, 212

Gallagher, Wes 1911- DLB-127

Gallagher, William Davis 1808-1894 . . . . . DLB-73

Gallant, Mavis 1922- DLB-53

Gallegos, María Magdalena 1935- DLB-209

Gallico, Paul 1897-1976 . . . . .DLB-9, 171

Galloway, Grace Growden 1727-1782 . . . . DLB-200

Gallup, Donald 1913- DLB-187

Galsworthy, John
    1867-1933 . . . . .DLB-10, 34, 98, 162; DS-16

Galt, John 1779-1839 . . . . DLB-99, 116

Galton, Sir Francis 1822-1911 . . . . DLB-166

Galvin, Brendan 1938- DLB-5

Gambit DLB-46

Gamboa, Reymundo 1948- DLB-122

Gammer Gurton's Needle. DLB-62

Gan, Elena Andreevna (Zeneida R-va)
    1814-1842. . . . . DLB-198

Gannett, Frank E. 1876-1957 . . . . DLB-29

Gaos, Vicente 1919-1980 . . . . DLB-134

García, Andrew 1854?-1943 . . . . DLB-209

García, Lionel G. 1935- DLB-82

García, Richard 1941- DLB-209

García-Camarillo, Cecilio 1943- DLB-209

García Lorca, Federico 1898-1936 . . . . . . DLB-108

García Márquez, Gabriel 1928- . . .DLB-113; Y-82

Gardam, Jane 1928- DLB-14, 161, 231

Garden, Alexander circa 1685-1756 . . . . . . DLB-31

Gardiner, Margaret Power Farmer
    (see Blessington, Marguerite, Countess of)

Gardner, John 1933-1982 . . . . .DLB-2; Y-82

Garfield, Leon 1921-1996. . . . . DLB-161

Garis, Howard R. 1873-1962 . . . . DLB-22

Garland, Hamlin 1860-1940 . . .DLB-12, 71, 78, 186

Garneau, Francis-Xavier 1809-1866 . . . . . . DLB-99

Garneau, Hector de Saint-Denys
    1912-1943 . . . . DLB-88

Garneau, Michel 1939- DLB-53

Garner, Alan 1934- DLB-161

Garner, Hugh 1913-1979 . . . . DLB-68

Garnett, David 1892-1981 . . . . DLB-34

Garnett, Eve 1900-1991 . . . . DLB-160

Garnett, Richard 1835-1906 . . . . DLB-184

Garrard, Lewis H. 1829-1887 . . . . DLB-186

Garraty, John A. 1920- DLB-17

Garrett, George
    1929- DLB-2, 5, 130, 152; Y-83

    Fellowship of Southern Writers Y-98

Garrett, John Work 1872-1942. . . . . DLB-187

Garrick, David 1717-1779 . . . . DLB-84, 213

Garrison, William Lloyd 1805-1879 . . . . DLB-1, 43

Garro, Elena 1920-1998 . . . . DLB-145

Garth, Samuel 1661-1719 . . . . DLB-95

Garve, Andrew 1908- DLB-87

Gary, Romain 1914-1980 . . . . DLB-83

Gascoigne, George 1539?-1577 . . . . DLB-136

Gascoyne, David 1916- DLB-20

Gaskell, Elizabeth Cleghorn
    1810-1865 . . . . DLB-21, 144, 159

Gaspey, Thomas 1788-1871 . . . . DLB-116

Gass, William H. 1924- DLB-2, 227

Gates, Doris 1901- DLB-22

Gates, Henry Louis, Jr. 1950- DLB-67

Gates, Lewis E. 1860-1924 . . . . DLB-71

Gatto, Alfonso 1909-1976 . . . . DLB-114

Gault, William Campbell 1910-1995 . . . . DLB-226

Gaunt, Mary 1861-1942 . . . . .DLB-174, 230

Gautier, Théophile 1811-1872 . . . . DLB-119

Gauvreau, Claude 1925-1971 . . . . DLB-88

The *Gawain*-Poet
    flourished circa 1350-1400 . . . . DLB-146

Gay, Ebenezer 1696-1787 . . . . DLB-24

Gay, John 1685-1732 . . . . DLB-84, 95

Gayarré, Charles E. A. 1805-1895 . . . . DLB-30

Gaylord, Charles [publishing house] DLB-49

Gaylord, Edward King 1873-1974 . . . . . DLB-127

Gaylord, Edward Lewis 1919- DLB-127

Geda, Sigitas 1943- DLB-232

Geddes, Gary 1940- DLB-60

Geddes, Virgil 1897- DLB-4

Gedeon (Georgii Andreevich Krinovsky)
    circa 1730-1763. . . . . DLB-150

Gee, Maggie 1948- DLB-207

Geßner, Salomon 1730-1788. . . . . DLB-97

Geibel, Emanuel 1815-1884 . . . . DLB-129

Geiogamah, Hanay 1945- DLB-175

Geis, Bernard, Associates DLB-46

Geisel, Theodor Seuss 1904-1991 . . .DLB-61; Y-91

Gelb, Arthur 1924- DLB-103

Gelb, Barbara 1926- DLB-103

Gelber, Jack 1932- DLB-7, 228

Gelinas, Gratien 1909- DLB-88

Gellert, Christian Füerchtegott
    1715-1769 . . . . DLB-97

Gellhorn, Martha 1908-1998 . . . . Y-82, Y-98

Gems, Pam 1925- DLB-13

Genet, Jean 1910-1986 . . . . .DLB-72; Y-86

Genevoix, Maurice 1890-1980 . . . . DLB-65

Genovese, Eugene D. 1930- DLB-17

Gent, Peter 1942- Y-82

Geoffrey of Monmouth
    circa 1100-1155 . . . . DLB-146

George, Henry 1839-1897 . . . . DLB-23

George, Jean Craighead 1919- DLB-52

George, W. L. 1882-1926. . . . . .DLB-197

George III, King of Great Britain and Ireland
    1738-1820. . . . . DLB-213

George V. Higgins to Julian Symons Y-99

Georgslied 896? DLB-148

Gerber, Merrill Joan 1938- DLB-218

Gerhardie, William 1895-1977 . . . . DLB-36

Gerhardt, Paul 1607-1676 . . . . DLB-164

Gérin, Winifred 1901-1981 . . . . DLB-155

Gérin-Lajoie, Antoine 1824-1882 . . . . DLB-99

German Drama 800-1280. . . . . DLB-138

German Drama from Naturalism
    to Fascism: 1889-1933 . . . . DLB-118

German Literature and Culture from Charlemagne
    to the Early Courtly Period DLB-148

German Radio Play, The DLB-124

German Transformation from the Baroque
    to the Enlightenment, The DLB-97

The Germanic Epic and Old English
    Heroic Poetry: *Widsith, Waldere,*
    and *The Fight at Finnsburg* DLB-146

Germanophilism, by Hans Kohn DLB-66

Gernsback, Hugo 1884-1967 . . . . .DLB-8, 137

Gerould, Katharine Fullerton
    1879-1944. . . . . DLB-78

Gerrish, Samuel [publishing house] DLB-49

Gerrold, David 1944- DLB-8

The Ira Gershwin Centenary Y-96

Gerson, Jean 1363-1429 . . . . DLB-208

Gersonides 1288-1344 . . . . DLB-115

Gerstäcker, Friedrich 1816-1872. . . . . . . DLB-129

Gerstenberg, Heinrich Wilhelm von
1737-1823 . . . . DLB-97

Gervinus, Georg Gottfried
1805-1871 . . . . DLB-133

Geston, Mark S. 1946- DLB-8

Al-Ghazali 1058-1111 . . . . DLB-115

Gibbings, Robert 1889-1958 . . . . DLB-195

Gibbon, Edward 1737-1794 . . . . DLB-104

Gibbon, John Murray 1875-1952 . . . . DLB-92

Gibbon, Lewis Grassic (see Mitchell, James Leslie)

Gibbons, Floyd 1887-1939 . . . . DLB-25

Gibbons, Reginald 1947- DLB-120

Gibbons, William ?-? DLB-73

Gibson, Charles Dana
1867-1944 . . . . DLB-188; DS-13

Gibson, Graeme 1934- DLB-53

Gibson, Margaret 1944- DLB-120

Gibson, Margaret Dunlop 1843-1920 . . . . DLB-174

Gibson, Wilfrid 1878-1962 . . . . DLB-19

Gibson, William 1914- DLB-7

Gide, André 1869-1951 . . . . DLB-65

Giguère, Diane 1937- DLB-53

Giguère, Roland 1929- DLB-60

Gil de Biedma, Jaime 1929-1990 . . . . DLB-108

Gil-Albert, Juan 1906- DLB-134

Gilbert, Anthony 1899-1973 . . . . DLB-77

Gilbert, Sir Humphrey 1537-1583 . . . . DLB-136

Gilbert, Michael 1912- DLB-87

Gilbert, Sandra M. 1936- DLB-120

Gilchrist, Alexander 1828-1861 . . . . DLB-144

Gilchrist, Ellen 1935- DLB-130

Gilder, Jeannette L. 1849-1916 . . . . DLB-79

Gilder, Richard Watson 1844-1909 . . . . DLB-64, 79

Gildersleeve, Basil 1831-1924 . . . . DLB-71

Giles of Rome circa 1243-1316 . . . . DLB-115

Giles, Henry 1809-1882 . . . . DLB-64

Gilfillan, George 1813-1878 . . . . DLB-144

Gill, Eric 1882-1940 . . . . DLB-98

Gill, Sarah Prince 1728-1771 . . . . DLB-200

Gill, William F., Company DLB-49

Gillespie, A. Lincoln, Jr. 1895-1950 . . . . DLB-4

Gilliam, Florence ?-? DLB-4

Gilliatt, Penelope 1932-1993 . . . . DLB-14

Gillott, Jacky 1939-1980 . . . . DLB-14

Gilman, Caroline H. 1794-1888 . . . . DLB-3, 73

Gilman, Charlotte Perkins 1860-1935 . . . . DLB-221

Gilman, W. and J. [publishing house] DLB-49

Gilmer, Elizabeth Meriwether 1861-1951 . . DLB-29

Gilmer, Francis Walker 1790-1826 . . . . DLB-37

Gilroy, Frank D. 1925- DLB-7

Gimferrer, Pere (Pedro) 1945- DLB-134

Gingrich, Arnold 1903-1976 . . . . DLB-137

Ginsberg, Allen 1926-1997 . . . . . . DLB-5, 16, 169

Ginzburg, Natalia 1916-1991 . . . . DLB-177

Ginzkey, Franz Karl 1871-1963 . . . . DLB-81

Gioia, Dana 1950- DLB-120

Giono, Jean 1895-1970 . . . . DLB-72

Giotti, Virgilio 1885-1957 . . . . DLB-114

Giovanni, Nikki 1943- DLB-5, 41

Gipson, Lawrence Henry 1880-1971 . . . . . DLB-17

Girard, Rodolphe 1879-1956 . . . . DLB-92

Giraudoux, Jean 1882-1944 . . . . DLB-65

Gissing, George 1857-1903 . . . . . DLB-18, 135, 184

The Place of Realism in Fiction (1895) . . DLB-18

Giudici, Giovanni 1924- DLB-128

Giuliani, Alfredo 1924- DLB-128

Glackens, William J. 1870-1938 . . . . DLB-188

Gladstone, William Ewart
1809-1898 . . . . DLB-57, 184

Glaeser, Ernst 1902-1963 . . . . DLB-69

Glancy, Diane 1941- DLB-175

Glanville, Brian 1931- DLB-15, 139

Glapthorne, Henry 1610-1643? DLB-58

Glasgow, Ellen 1873-1945 . . . . DLB-9, 12

Glasier, Katharine Bruce 1867-1950 . . . . . DLB-190

Glaspell, Susan 1876-1948 . . . . . . DLB-7, 9, 78, 228

Glass, Montague 1877-1934 . . . . DLB-11

Glassco, John 1909-1981 . . . . DLB-68

Glauser, Friedrich 1896-1938 . . . . DLB-56

F. Gleason's Publishing Hall DLB-49

Gleim, Johann Wilhelm Ludwig
1719-1803 . . . . DLB-97

Glendinning, Victoria 1937- DLB-155

The Cult of Biography
Excerpts from the Second Folio Debate:
"Biographies are generally a disease of
English Literature" Y-86

Glinka, Fedor Nikolaevich 1786-1880 . . . . DLB-205

Glover, Richard 1712-1785 . . . . DLB-95

Glück, Louise 1943- DLB-5

Glyn, Elinor 1864-1943 . . . . DLB-153

Gnedich, Nikolai Ivanovich 1784-1833 . . . DLB-205

Gobineau, Joseph-Arthur de
1816-1882 . . . . DLB-123

Godber, John 1956- DLB-233

Godbout, Jacques 1933- DLB-53

Goddard, Morrill 1865-1937 . . . . DLB-25

Goddard, William 1740-1817 . . . . DLB-43

Godden, Rumer 1907-1998 . . . . DLB-161

Godey, Louis A. 1804-1878 . . . . DLB-73

Godey and McMichael DLB-49

Godfrey, Dave 1938- DLB-60

Godfrey, Thomas 1736-1763 . . . . DLB-31

Godine, David R., Publisher DLB-46

Godkin, E. L. 1831-1902 . . . . DLB-79

Godolphin, Sidney 1610-1643 . . . . DLB-126

Godwin, Gail 1937- DLB-6, 234

Godwin, M. J., and Company DLB-154

Godwin, Mary Jane Clairmont
1766-1841 . . . . DLB-163

Godwin, Parke 1816-1904 . . . . DLB-3, 64

Godwin, William
1756-1836 . . . . DLB-39, 104, 142, 158, 163

Preface to *St. Leon* (1799) DLB-39

Goering, Reinhard 1887-1936 . . . . DLB-118

Goes, Albrecht 1908- DLB-69

Goethe, Johann Wolfgang von
1749-1832 . . . . DLB-94

Goetz, Curt 1888-1960 . . . . DLB-124

Goffe, Thomas circa 1592-1629 . . . . DLB-58

Goffstein, M. B. 1940- DLB-61

Gogarty, Oliver St. John 1878-1957 . . . . DLB-15, 19

Gogol, Nikolai Vasil'evich 1809-1852 . . . . DLB-198

Goines, Donald 1937-1974 . . . . DLB-33

Gold, Herbert 1924- DLB-2; Y-81

Gold, Michael 1893-1967 . . . . DLB-9, 28

Goldbarth, Albert 1948- DLB-120

Goldberg, Dick 1947- DLB-7

Golden Cockerel Press DLB-112

Golding, Arthur 1536-1606 . . . . DLB-136

Golding, Louis 1895-1958 . . . . DLB-195

Golding, William 1911-1993 . . . DLB-15, 100; Y-83

Goldman, Emma 1869-1940 . . . . DLB-221

Goldman, William 1931- DLB-44

Goldring, Douglas 1887-1960 . . . . DLB-197

Goldsmith, Oliver
1730?-1774 . . . . DLB-39, 89, 104, 109, 142

Goldsmith, Oliver 1794-1861 . . . . DLB-99

Goldsmith Publishing Company DLB-46

Goldstein, Richard 1944- DLB-185

Gollancz, Sir Israel 1864-1930 . . . . DLB-201

Gollancz, Victor, Limited DLB-112

Gombrowicz, Witold 1904-1969 . . . . DLB-215

Gómez-Quiñones, Juan 1942- DLB-122

Gomme, Laurence James
[publishing house] DLB-46

Goncourt, Edmond de 1822-1896 . . . . . . DLB-123

Goncourt, Jules de 1830-1870 . . . . DLB-123

Gonzales, Rodolfo "Corky" 1928- DLB-122

González, Angel 1925- DLB-108

Gonzalez, Genaro 1949- DLB-122

Gonzalez, Ray 1952- DLB-122

Gonzales-Berry, Erlinda 1942- DLB-209

"Chicano Language" DLB-82

González de Mireles, Jovita
1899-1983 . . . . DLB-122

González-T., César A. 1931- DLB-82

Goodbye, Gutenberg? A Lecture at the
New York Public Library,
18 April 1995, by Donald Lamm Y-95

Goodis, David 1917-1967 . . . . DLB-226

Goodison, Lorna 1947- DLB-157

Goodman, Paul 1911-1972 . . . . DLB-130

The Goodman Theatre DLB-7

Goodrich, Frances 1891-1984 and
Hackett, Albert 1900-1995 . . . . DLB-26

Goodrich, Samuel Griswold
1793-1860 . . . . DLB-1, 42, 73

Goodrich, S. G. [publishing house] DLB-49

Goodspeed, C. E., and Company. DLB-49

Goodwin, Stephen 1943- Y-82

Googe, Barnabe 1540-1594 . . . . DLB-132

Gookin, Daniel 1612-1687 . . . . DLB-24

Gordimer, Nadine 1923- DLB-225; Y-91

Gordon, Adam Lindsay 1833-1870. . . . . DLB-230

Gordon, Caroline
    1895-1981 . . . . . . .DLB-4, 9, 102; DS-17; Y-81

Gordon, Giles 1940- DLB-14, 139, 207

Gordon, Helen Cameron, Lady Russell
    1867-1949. . . . . DLB-195

Gordon, Lyndall 1941- DLB-155

Gordon, Mary 1949- DLB-6; Y-81

Gordone, Charles 1925-1995 . . . . DLB-7

Gore, Catherine 1800-1861 . . . . DLB-116

Gores, Joe 1931- DLB-226

Gorey, Edward 1925- DLB-61

Gorgias of Leontini
    circa 485 B.C.-376 B.C. DLB-176

Görres, Joseph 1776-1848 . . . . DLB-90

Gosse, Edmund 1849-1928. . . . . .DLB-57, 144, 184

Gosson, Stephen 1554-1624 . . . . .DLB-172

    The Schoole of Abuse (1579) DLB-172

Gotlieb, Phyllis 1926- DLB-88

Go-Toba 1180-1239 . . . . DLB-203

Gottfried von Straßburg
    died before 1230 . . . . DLB-138

Gotthelf, Jeremias 1797-1854. . . . . DLB-133

Gottschalk circa 804/808-869 . . . . DLB-148

Gottsched, Johann Christoph
    1700-1766 . . . . DLB-97

Götz, Johann Nikolaus 1721-1781. . . . . . . DLB-97

Goudge, Elizabeth 1900-1984. . . . . DLB-191

Gould, Wallace 1882-1940. . . . . DLB-54

Govoni, Corrado 1884-1965 . . . . DLB-114

Gower, John circa 1330-1408 . . . . DLB-146

Goyen, William 1915-1983. . . . .DLB-2, 218; Y-83

Goytisolo, José Augustín 1928- DLB-134

Gozzano, Guido 1883-1916 . . . . DLB-114

Grabbe, Christian Dietrich 1801-1836 . . . DLB-133

Gracq, Julien 1910- DLB-83

Grady, Henry W. 1850-1889 . . . . DLB-23

Graf, Oskar Maria 1894-1967. . . . . DLB-56

Graf Rudolf
    between circa 1170 and circa 1185. . . DLB-148

Grafton, Richard [publishing house]. DLB-170

Grafton, Sue 1940- DLB-226

Graham, George Rex 1813-1894 . . . . DLB-73

Graham, Gwethalyn 1913-1965 . . . . DLB-88

Graham, Jorie 1951- DLB-120

Graham, Katharine 1917- DLB-127

Graham, Lorenz 1902-1989 . . . . DLB-76

Graham, Philip 1915-1963 . . . . DLB-127

Graham, R. B. Cunninghame
    1852-1936 . . . . .DLB-98, 135, 174

Graham, Shirley 1896-1977 . . . . DLB-76

Graham, Stephen 1884-1975. . . . . DLB-195

Graham, W. S. 1918- DLB-20

Graham, William H. [publishing house]. . . DLB-49

Graham, Winston 1910- DLB-77

Grahame, Kenneth
    1859-1932 . . . . .DLB-34, 141, 178

Grainger, Martin Allerdale 1874-1941 . . . . DLB-92

Gramatky, Hardie 1907-1979 . . . . DLB-22

Grand, Sarah 1854-1943. . . . . .DLB-135, 197

Grandbois, Alain 1900-1975 . . . . DLB-92

Grandson, Oton de circa 1345-1397. . . . . DLB-208

Grange, John circa 1556-?. DLB-136

Granich, Irwin (see Gold, Michael)

Granovsky, Timofei Nikolaevich
    1813-1855 . . . . DLB-198

Grant, Anne MacVicar 1755-1838 . . . . . . DLB-200

Grant, Duncan 1885-1978 . . . . .DS-10

Grant, George 1918-1988. . . . . DLB-88

Grant, George Monro 1835-1902. . . . . DLB-99

Grant, Harry J. 1881-1963 . . . . DLB-29

Grant, James Edward 1905-1966 . . . . DLB-26

Grass, Günter 1927- DLB-75, 124

Grasty, Charles H. 1863-1924 . . . . DLB-25

Grau, Shirley Ann 1929- DLB-2, 218

Graves, John 1920- Y-83

Graves, Richard 1715-1804. . . . . DLB-39

Graves, Robert
    1895-1985 . . . .DLB-20, 100, 191; DS-18; Y-85

Gray, Alasdair 1934- DLB-194

Gray, Asa 1810-1888 . . . . DLB-1

Gray, David 1838-1861 . . . . DLB-32

Gray, Simon 1936- DLB-13

Gray, Thomas 1716-1771 . . . . DLB-109

Grayson, Richard 1951- DLB-234

Grayson, William J. 1788-1863. . . . . . . DLB-3, 64

The Great Bibliographers Series. Y-93

The Great Modern Library Scam. Y-98

The Great War and the Theater, 1914-1918
    [Great Britain] DLB-10

The Great War Exhibition and Symposium at
    the University of South Carolina. Y-97

Grech, Nikolai Ivanovich 1787-1867. . . . . DLB-198

Greeley, Horace 1811-1872 . . . . . . DLB-3, 43, 189

Green, Adolph (see Comden, Betty)

Green, Anna Katharine
    1846-1935 . . . . DLB-202, 221

Green, Duff 1791-1875 . . . . DLB-43

Green, Elizabeth Shippen 1871-1954 . . . . DLB-188

Green, Gerald 1922- DLB-28

Green, Henry 1905-1973 . . . . DLB-15

Green, Jonas 1712-1767. . . . . DLB-31

Green, Joseph 1706-1780. . . . . DLB-31

Green, Julien 1900-1998 . . . . DLB-4, 72

Green, Paul 1894-1981. . . . . .DLB-7, 9; Y-81

Green, T. and S. [publishing house] DLB-49

Green, Thomas Hill 1836-1882 . . . . DLB-190

Green, Timothy [publishing house] DLB-49

Greenaway, Kate 1846-1901 . . . . DLB-141

Greenberg: Publisher DLB-46

Green Tiger Press. DLB-46

Greene, Asa 1789-1838. . . . . DLB-11

Greene, Belle da Costa 1883-1950 . . . . . .DLB-187

Greene, Benjamin H.
    [publishing house] DLB-49

Greene, Graham 1904-1991
    . . DLB-13, 15, 77, 100, 162, 201, 204; Y-85, Y-91

Greene, Robert 1558-1592 . . . . .DLB-62, 167

Greene, Robert Bernard (Bob) Jr.
    1947- DLB-185

Greenhow, Robert 1800-1854 . . . . DLB-30

Greenlee, William B. 1872-1953. . . . . . . .DLB-187

Greenough, Horatio 1805-1852 . . . . DLB-1

Greenwell, Dora 1821-1882 . . . . DLB-35, 199

Greenwillow Books DLB-46

Greenwood, Grace (see Lippincott, Sara Jane Clarke)

Greenwood, Walter 1903-1974. . . . . .DLB-10, 191

Greer, Ben 1948- DLB-6

Greflinger, Georg 1620?-1677 . . . . DLB-164

Greg, W. R. 1809-1881 . . . . DLB-55

Greg, W. W. 1875-1959 . . . . DLB-201

Gregg, Josiah 1806-1850. . . . . DLB-183, 186

Gregg Press DLB-46

Gregory, Isabella Augusta Persse, Lady
    1852-1932 . . . . DLB-10

Gregory, Horace 1898-1982. . . . . DLB-48

Gregory of Rimini circa 1300-1358 . . . . . DLB-115

Gregynog Press DLB-112

Greiffenberg, Catharina Regina von
    1633-1694 . . . . DLB-168

Grenfell, Wilfred Thomason
    1865-1940. .DLB-92

Gress, Elsa 1919-1988 . . . . DLB-214

Greve, Felix Paul (see Grove, Frederick Philip)

Greville, Fulke, First Lord Brooke
    1554-1628 . . . . .DLB-62, 172

Grey, Sir George, K.C.B. 1812-1898 . . . . DLB-184

Grey, Lady Jane 1537-1554 . . . . DLB-132

Grey Owl 1888-1938 . . . . .DLB-92; DS-17

Grey, Zane 1872-1939 . . . . DLB-9, 212

Grey Walls Press DLB-112

Griboedov, Aleksandr Sergeevich
    1795?-1829. DLB-205

Grier, Eldon 1917- DLB-88

Grieve, C. M. (see MacDiarmid, Hugh)

Griffin, Bartholomew flourished 1596 . . . .DLB-172

Griffin, Gerald 1803-1840 . . . . DLB-159

Griffith, Elizabeth 1727?-1793. . . . . . . DLB-39, 89

    Preface to *The Delicate Distress* (1769) DLB-39

Griffith, George 1857-1906. . . . . .DLB-178

Griffiths, Ralph [publishing house]. DLB-154

Griffiths, Trevor 1935- DLB-13

Griggs, S. C., and Company DLB-49

Griggs, Sutton Elbert 1872-1930 . . . . .DLB-50

Grignon, Claude-Henri 1894-1976. . . . . . .DLB-68

Grigson, Geoffrey 1905- DLB-27

Grillparzer, Franz 1791-1872 . . . . .DLB-133

Grimald, Nicholas
circa 1519-circa 1562. . . . . .DLB-136

Grimké, Angelina Weld 1880-1958. . . .DLB-50, 54

Grimm, Hans 1875-1959 . . . . .DLB-66

Grimm, Jacob 1785-1863 . . . . .DLB-90

Grimm, Wilhelm 1786-1859 . . . . .DLB-90

Grimmelshausen, Johann Jacob Christoffel von
1621 or 1622-1676. . . . . .DLB-168

Grimshaw, Beatrice Ethel 1871-1953 . . . . .DLB-174

Grindal, Edmund 1519 or 1520-1583 . . . .DLB-132

Griswold, Rufus Wilmot 1815-1857 . . . .DLB-3, 59

Grosart, Alexander Balloch 1827-1899. . . .DLB-184

Gross, Milt 1895-1953 . . . . .DLB-11

Grosset and Dunlap. DLB-49

Grossman, Allen 1932- DLB-193

Grossman Publishers DLB-46

Grosseteste, Robert circa 1160-1253 . . . . .DLB-115

Grosvenor, Gilbert H. 1875-1966 . . . . . . .DLB-91

Groth, Klaus 1819-1899. . . . . .DLB-129

Groulx, Lionel 1878-1967 . . . . .DLB-68

Grove, Frederick Philip 1879-1949 . . . . . .DLB-92

Grove Press DLB-46

Grubb, Davis 1919-1980 . . . . .DLB-6

Gruelle, Johnny 1880-1938 . . . . .DLB-22

von Grumbach, Argula
1492-after 1563? DLB-179

Grymeston, Elizabeth
before 1563-before 1604 . . . . .DLB-136

Gryphius, Andreas 1616-1664 . . . . .DLB-164

Gryphius, Christian 1649-1706 . . . . .DLB-168

Guare, John 1938- DLB-7

Guerra, Tonino 1920- DLB-128

Guest, Barbara 1920- DLB-5, 193

Guèvremont, Germaine 1893-1968 . . . . . .DLB-68

Guidacci, Margherita 1921-1992 . . . . . . .DLB-128

Guide to the Archives of Publishers, Journals,
and Literary Agents in North American
Libraries Y-93

Guillén, Jorge 1893-1984 . . . . .DLB-108

Guilloux, Louis 1899-1980 . . . . .DLB-72

Guilpin, Everard
circa 1572-after 1608? DLB-136

Guiney, Louise Imogen 1861-1920 . . . . . .DLB-54

Guiterman, Arthur 1871-1943 . . . . .DLB-11

Günderrode, Caroline von 1780-1806 . . . .DLB-90

Gundulić, Ivan 1589-1638 . . . . .DLB-147

Gunn, Bill 1934-1989. . . . . .DLB-38

Gunn, James E. 1923- DLB-8

Gunn, Neil M. 1891-1973 . . . . .DLB-15

Gunn, Thom 1929- DLB-27

Gunnars, Kristjana 1948- DLB-60

Günther, Johann Christian
1695-1723 . . . . .DLB-168

Gurik, Robert 1932- DLB-60

Gustafson, Ralph 1909- DLB-88

Gütersloh, Albert Paris 1887-1973 . . . . . . .DLB-81

Guthrie, A. B., Jr. 1901-1991 . . . . .DLB-6, 212

Guthrie, Ramon 1896-1973 . . . . .DLB-4

The Guthrie Theater DLB-7

Guthrie, Thomas Anstey
(see Anstey, FC)

Gutzkow, Karl 1811-1878 . . . . .DLB-133

Guy, Ray 1939- DLB-60

Guy, Rosa 1925- DLB-33

Guyot, Arnold 1807-1884 . . . . DS-13

Gwynne, Erskine 1898-1948 . . . . .DLB-4

Gyles, John 1680-1755 . . . . .DLB-99

Gysin, Brion 1916- DLB-16

H

H.D. (see Doolittle, Hilda)

Habington, William 1605-1654 . . . . .DLB-126

Hacker, Marilyn 1942- DLB-120

Hackett, Albert (see Goodrich, Frances)

Hacks, Peter 1928- DLB-124

Hadas, Rachel 1948- DLB-120

Hadden, Briton 1898-1929 . . . . .DLB-91

Hagedorn, Friedrich von 1708-1754. . . . . .DLB-168

Hagelstange, Rudolf 1912-1984. . . . . .DLB-69

Haggard, H. Rider
1856-1925 . . . . .DLB-70, 156, 174, 178

Haggard, William 1907-1993 . . . . .Y-93

Hahn-Hahn, Ida Gräfin von
1805-1880 . . . . .DLB-133

Haig-Brown, Roderick 1908-1976 . . . . . . .DLB-88

Haight, Gordon S. 1901-1985 . . . . .DLB-103

Hailey, Arthur 1920- DLB-88; Y-82

Haines, John 1924- DLB-5, 212

Hake, Edward flourished 1566-1604 . . . . .DLB-136

Hake, Thomas Gordon 1809-1895 . . . . . . .DLB-32

Hakluyt, Richard 1552?-1616 . . . . .DLB-136

Halas, František 1901-1949 . . . . .DLB-215

Halbe, Max 1865-1944 . . . . .DLB-118

Haldane, J. B. S. 1892-1964 . . . . .DLB-160

Haldeman, Joe 1943- DLB-8

Haldeman-Julius Company DLB-46

Haldone, Charlotte 1894-1969 . . . . .DLB-191

Hale, E. J., and Son DLB-49

Hale, Edward Everett 1822-1909. . . .DLB-1, 42, 74

Hale, Janet Campbell 1946- DLB-175

Hale, Kathleen 1898- DLB-160

Hale, Leo Thomas (see Ebon)

Hale, Lucretia Peabody 1820-1900 . . . . . .DLB-42

Hale, Nancy
1908-1988 . . . . . . DLB-86; DS-17; Y-80, Y-88

Hale, Sarah Josepha (Buell)
1788-1879 . . . . .DLB-1, 42, 73

Hale, Susan 1833-1910 . . . . .DLB-221

Hales, John 1584-1656. . . . . .DLB-151

Halévy, Ludovic 1834-1908 . . . . .DLB-192

Haley, Alex 1921-1992 . . . . .DLB-38

Haliburton, Thomas Chandler
1796-1865 . . . . .DLB-11, 99

Hall, Anna Maria 1800-1881 . . . . .DLB-159

Hall, Donald 1928- DLB-5

Hall, Edward 1497-1547. . . . . .DLB-132

Hall, James 1793-1868 . . . . DLB-73, 74

Hall, Joseph 1574-1656 . . . . .DLB-121, 151

Hall, Radclyffe 1880-1943 . . . . .DLB-191

Hall, Samuel [publishing house]. DLB-49

Hall, Sarah Ewing 1761-1830. . . . . .DLB-200

Hallam, Arthur Henry 1811-1833 . . . . . . .DLB-32

On Some of the Characteristics of Modern
Poetry and On the Lyrical Poems of
Alfred Tennyson (1831) DLB-32

Halleck, Fitz-Greene 1790-1867 . . . . .DLB-3

Haller, Albrecht von 1708-1777 . . . . .DLB-168

Halliday, Brett (see Dresser, Davis)

Halliwell-Phillipps, James Orchard
1820-1889 . . . . .DLB-184

Hallmann, Johann Christian
1640-1704 or 1716? DLB-168

Hallmark Editions DLB-46

Halper, Albert 1904-1984 . . . . .DLB-9

Halperin, John William 1941- DLB-111

Halstead, Murat 1829-1908. . . . . .DLB-23

Hamann, Johann Georg 1730-1788 . . . . . .DLB-97

Hamburger, Michael 1924- DLB-27

Hamilton, Alexander 1712-1756. . . . . .DLB-31

Hamilton, Alexander 1755?-1804 . . . . . . .DLB-37

Hamilton, Cicely 1872-1952 . . . . DLB-10, 197

Hamilton, Edmond 1904-1977. . . . . .DLB-8

Hamilton, Elizabeth 1758-1816 . . . . .DLB-116, 158

Hamilton, Gail (see Corcoran, Barbara)

Hamilton, Gail (see Dodge, Mary Abigail)

Hamilton, Hamish, Limited. DLB-112

Hamilton, Ian 1938- DLB-40, 155

Hamilton, Janet 1795-1873. . . . . .DLB-199

Hamilton, Mary Agnes 1884-1962 . . . . . .DLB-197

Hamilton, Patrick 1904-1962. . . . . . .DLB-10, 191

Hamilton, Virginia 1936- DLB-33, 52

Hammett, Dashiell 1894-1961 . . . . .DLB-226; DS-6

The Glass Key and Other Dashiell Hammett
Mysteries Y-96

Dashiell Hammett: An Appeal in *TAC* Y-91

Hammon, Jupiter 1711-died between
1790 and 1806. . . . . .DLB-31, 50

Hammond, John ?-1663. . . . . .DLB-24

Hamner, Earl 1923- DLB-6

Hampson, John 1901-1955 . . . . .DLB-191

Hampton, Christopher 1946- DLB-13

Handel-Mazzetti, Enrica von 1871-1955 . . .DLB-81

Handke, Peter 1942- DLB-85, 124

Handlin, Oscar 1915- DLB-17

Hankin, St. John 1869-1909. . . . . .DLB-10

Hanley, Clifford 1922- DLB-14

Hanley, James 1901-1985 . . . . DLB-191

Hannah, Barry 1942- DLB-6, 234

Hannay, James 1827-1873 . . . . DLB-21

Hansberry, Lorraine 1930-1965 . . . . DLB-7, 38

Hansen, Martin A. 1909-1955 . . . . DLB-214

Hansen, Thorkild 1927-1989 . . . . DLB-214

Hanson, Elizabeth 1684-1737 . . . . DLB-200

Hapgood, Norman 1868-1937 . . . . DLB-91

Happel, Eberhard Werner 1647-1690. . . . DLB-168

The Harbinger 1845-1849 . . . . DLB-223

Harcourt Brace Jovanovich DLB-46

Hardenberg, Friedrich von (see Novalis)

Harding, Walter 1917- DLB-111

Hardwick, Elizabeth 1916- DLB-6

Hardy, Thomas 1840-1928 . . . . . DLB-18, 19, 135

"Candour in English Fiction" (1890) . . . DLB-18

Hare, Cyril 1900-1958 . . . . DLB-77

Hare, David 1947- DLB-13

Hargrove, Marion 1919- DLB-11

Häring, Georg Wilhelm Heinrich
(see Alexis, Willibald)

Harington, Donald 1935- DLB-152

Harington, Sir John 1560-1612 . . . . DLB-136

Harjo, Joy 1951- DLB-120, 175

Harkness, Margaret (John Law)
1854-1923 . . . . DLB-197

Harley, Edward, second Earl of Oxford
1689-1741 . . . . DLB-213

Harley, Robert, first Earl of Oxford
1661-1724 . . . . DLB-213

Harlow, Robert 1923- DLB-60

Harman, Thomas flourished 1566-1573 . . DLB-136

Harness, Charles L. 1915- DLB-8

Harnett, Cynthia 1893-1981 . . . . DLB-161

Harper, Fletcher 1806-1877 . . . . DLB-79

Harper, Frances Ellen Watkins
1825-1911 . . . . DLB-50, 221

Harper, Michael S. 1938- DLB-41

Harper and Brothers DLB-49

Harpur, Charles 1813-1868 . . . . DLB-230

Harraden, Beatrice 1864-1943 . . . . DLB-153

Harrap, George G., and Company
Limited DLB-112

Harriot, Thomas 1560-1621 . . . . DLB-136

Harris, Alexander 1805-1874 . . . . DLB-230

Harris, Benjamin ?-circa 1720 . . . . DLB-42, 43

Harris, Christie 1907- DLB-88

Harris, Frank 1856-1931 . . . . DLB-156, 197

Harris, George Washington
1814-1869 . . . . DLB-3, 11

Harris, Joel Chandler
1848-1908 . . . . DLB-11, 23, 42, 78, 91

Harris, Mark 1922- DLB-2; Y-80

Harris, Wilson 1921- DLB-117

Harrison, Mrs. Burton
(see Harrison, Constance Cary)

Harrison, Charles Yale 1898-1954 . . . . . . DLB-68

Harrison, Constance Cary 1843-1920 . . . DLB-221

Harrison, Frederic 1831-1923 . . . . DLB-57, 190

"On Style in English Prose" (1898) DLB-57

Harrison, Harry 1925- DLB-8

Harrison, James P., Company DLB-49

Harrison, Jim 1937- Y-82

Harrison, Mary St. Leger Kingsley
(see Malet, Lucas)

Harrison, Paul Carter 1936- DLB-38

Harrison, Susan Frances 1859-1935 . . . . . DLB-99

Harrison, Tony 1937- DLB-40

Harrison, William 1535-1593 . . . . DLB-136

Harrison, William 1933- DLB-234

Harrisse, Henry 1829-1910 . . . . DLB-47

Harryman, Carla 1952- DLB-193

Harsdörffer, Georg Philipp 1607-1658 . . . DLB-164

Harsent, David 1942- DLB-40

Hart, Albert Bushnell 1854-1943 . . . . . . DLB-17

Hart, Anne 1768-1834 . . . . DLB-200

Hart, Elizabeth 1771-1833 . . . . DLB-200

Hart, Julia Catherine 1796-1867 . . . . DLB-99

The Lorenz Hart Centenary Y-95

Hart, Moss 1904-1961 . . . . DLB-7

Hart, Oliver 1723-1795 . . . . DLB-31

Hart-Davis, Rupert, Limited DLB-112

Harte, Bret 1836-1902 . . . . DLB-12, 64, 74, 79, 186

Harte, Edward Holmead 1922- DLB-127

Harte, Houston Harriman 1927- DLB-127

Hartlaub, Felix 1913-1945 . . . . DLB-56

Hartlebon, Otto Erich 1864-1905 . . . . . . DLB-118

Hartley, L. P. 1895-1972 . . . . DLB-15, 139

Hartley, Marsden 1877-1943 . . . . DLB-54

Hartling, Peter 1933- DLB-75

Hartman, Geoffrey H. 1929- DLB-67

Hartmann, Sadakichi 1867-1944 . . . . DLB-54

Hartmann von Aue
circa 1160-circa 1205 . . . . DLB-138

Harvey, Gabriel 1550?-1631 . . . . DLB-167, 213

Harvey, Jean-Charles 1891-1967 . . . . . . DLB-88

Harvill Press Limited DLB-112

Harwood, Lee 1939- DLB-40

Harwood, Ronald 1934- DLB-13

Hašek, Jaroslav 1883-1923 . . . . DLB-215

Haskins, Charles Homer 1870-1937 . . . . . DLB-47

Haslam, Gerald 1937- DLB-212

Hass, Robert 1941- DLB-105, 206

Hastings, Michael 1938- DLB-233

Hatar, Győző 1914- DLB-215

The Hatch-Billops Collection DLB-76

Hathaway, William 1944- DLB-120

Hauff, Wilhelm 1802-1827 . . . . DLB-90

A Haughty and Proud Generation (1922),
by Ford Madox Hueffer DLB-36

Haugwitz, August Adolph von
1647-1706 . . . . DLB-168

Hauptmann, Carl 1858-1921 . . . . DLB-66, 118

Hauptmann, Gerhart 1862-1946 . . . . DLB-66, 118

Hauser, Marianne 1910- Y-83

Havel, Václav 1936- DLB-232

Havergal, Frances Ridley 1836-1879 . . . . DLB-199

Hawes, Stephen 1475?-before 1529 . . . . . DLB-132

Hawker, Robert Stephen 1803-1875 . . . . . DLB-32

Hawkes, John
1925-1998 . . . . DLB-2, 7, 227; Y-80, Y-98

John Hawkes: A Tribute Y-98

Hawkesworth, John 1720-1773 . . . . DLB-142

Hawkins, Sir Anthony Hope (see Hope, Anthony)

Hawkins, Sir John 1719-1789 . . . . DLB-104, 142

Hawkins, Walter Everette 1883-? DLB-50

Hawthorne, Nathaniel
1804-1864 . . . . DLB-1, 74, 183, 223

Hawthorne, Nathaniel 1804-1864 and
Hawthorne, Sophia Peabody
1809-1871 . . . . DLB-183

Hay, John 1835-1905 . . . . DLB-12, 47, 189

Hayashi, Fumiko 1903-1951 . . . . DLB-180

Haycox, Ernest 1899-1950 . . . . DLB-206

Haycraft, Anna Margaret (see Ellis, Alice Thomas)

Hayden, Robert 1913-1980 . . . . DLB-5, 76

Haydon, Benjamin Robert
1786-1846 . . . . DLB-110

Hayes, John Michael 1919- DLB-26

Hayley, William 1745-1820 . . . . DLB-93, 142

Haym, Rudolf 1821-1901 . . . . DLB-129

Hayman, Robert 1575-1629 . . . . DLB-99

Hayman, Ronald 1932- DLB-155

Hayne, Paul Hamilton 1830-1886 . . . DLB-3, 64, 79

Hays, Mary 1760-1843 . . . . DLB-142, 158

Hayward, John 1905-1965 . . . . DLB-201

Haywood, Eliza 1693?-1756 . . . . DLB-39

From the Dedication, *Lasselia* (1723) DLB-39

From *The Tea-Table* *DLB-39*

From the Preface to *The Disguis'd
Prince* (1723) DLB-39

Hazard, Willis P. [publishing house] DLB-49

Hazlitt, William 1778-1830 . . . . DLB-110, 158

Hazzard, Shirley 1931- Y-82

Head, Bessie 1937-1986 . . . . DLB-117, 225

Headley, Joel T. 1813-1897 . . DLB-30, 183; DS-13

Heaney, Seamus 1939- DLB-40; Y-95

Heard, Nathan C. 1936- DLB-33

Hearn, Lafcadio 1850-1904 . . . . . . DLB-12, 78, 189

Hearne, John 1926- DLB-117

Hearne, Samuel 1745-1792 . . . . DLB-99

Hearne, Thomas 1678?-1735 . . . . DLB-213

Hearst, William Randolph 1863-1951 . . . . DLB-25

Hearst, William Randolph, Jr.
1908-1993 . . . . DLB-127

Heartman, Charles Frederick
1883-1953 . . . . DLB-187

Heath, Catherine 1924- DLB-14

Heath, Roy A. K. 1926- DLB-117

Heath-Stubbs, John 1918- DLB-27

Heavysege, Charles 1816-1876 . . . . .DLB-99

Hebbel, Friedrich 1813-1863 . . . . .DLB-129

Hebel, Johann Peter 1760-1826 . . . . .DLB-90

Heber, Richard 1774-1833 . . . . .DLB-184

Hébert, Anne 1916- DLB-68

Hébert, Jacques 1923- DLB-53

Hecht, Anthony 1923- DLB-5, 169

Hecht, Ben 1894-1964 . . . DLB-7, 9, 25, 26, 28, 86

Hecker, Isaac Thomas 1819-1888 . . . . .DLB-1

Hedge, Frederic Henry 1805-1890 . . . . .DLB-1, 59

Hefner, Hugh M. 1926- DLB-137

Hegel, Georg Wilhelm Friedrich
    1770-1831 .DLB-90

Heidish, Marcy 1947- Y-82

Heißenbüttel, Helmut 1921-1996 . . . . .DLB-75

Heike monogatari DLB-203

Hein, Christoph 1944- DLB-124

Hein, Piet 1905-1996 . . . . .DLB-214

Heine, Heinrich 1797-1856 . . . . .DLB-90

Heinemann, Larry 1944- DS-9

Heinemann, William, Limited DLB-112

Heinesen, William 1900-1991 . . . . .DLB-214

Heinlein, Robert A. 1907-1988 . . . . .DLB-8

Heinrich Julius of Brunswick
    1564-1613 .DLB-164

Heinrich von dem Türlîn
    flourished circa 1230 . . . . .DLB-138

Heinrich von Melk
    flourished after 1160 . . . . .DLB-148

Heinrich von Veldeke
    circa 1145-circa 1190 . . . . .DLB-138

Heinrich, Willi 1920- DLB-75

Heinse, Wilhelm 1746-1803 . . . . .DLB-94

Heinz, W. C. 1915- DLB-171

Heiskell, John 1872-1972 . . . . .DLB-127

Hejinian, Lyn 1941- DLB-165

Heliand circa 850 . . . . .DLB-148

Heller, Joseph
    1923-1999 . . . . DLB-2, 28, 227; Y-80, Y-99

Heller, Michael 1937- DLB-165

Hellman, Lillian 1906-1984 . . . . . DLB-7, 228; Y-84

Hellwig, Johann 1609-1674 . . . . .DLB-164

Helprin, Mark 1947- Y-85

Helwig, David 1938- DLB-60

Hemans, Felicia 1793-1835 . . . . .DLB-96

Hemingway, Ernest 1899-1961 . . . DLB-4, 9, 102,
    210; Y-81, Y-87, Y-99; DS-1, DS-15, DS-16

The Hemingway Centenary Celebration at the
    JFK Library Y-99

Ernest Hemingway: A Centennial
    Celebration Y-99

The Ernest Hemingway Collection at the
    John F. Kennedy Library Y-99

Ernest Hemingway's Reaction to James Gould
    Cozzens Y-98

Ernest Hemingway's Toronto Journalism
    Revisited: With Three Previously
    Unrecorded Stories Y-92

Falsifying Hemingway Y-96

Hemingway: Twenty-Five Years Later Y-85

Not Immediately Discernible . . . but Eventually
    Quite Clear: The *First Light* and *Final Years*
    of Hemingway's Centenary Y-99

Second International Hemingway Colloquium:
    Cuba Y-98

Hémon, Louis 1880-1913 . . . . .DLB-92

Hempel, Amy 1951- DLB-218

Hemphill, Paul 1936- Y-87

Hénault, Gilles 1920- DLB-88

Henchman, Daniel 1689-1761 . . . . .DLB-24

Henderson, Alice Corbin 1881-1949 . . . . . .DLB-54

Henderson, Archibald 1877-1963 . . . . . . .DLB-103

Henderson, David 1942- DLB-41

Henderson, George Wylie 1904- DLB-51

Henderson, Zenna 1917-1983 . . . . .DLB-8

Henisch, Peter 1943- DLB-85

Henley, Beth 1952- Y-86

Henley, William Ernest 1849-1903 . . . . . .DLB-19

Henning, Rachel 1826-1914 . . . . .DLB-230

Henningsen, Agnes 1868-1962 . . . . .DLB-214

Henniker, Florence 1855-1923 . . . . .DLB-135

Henry, Alexander 1739-1824 . . . . .DLB-99

Henry, Buck 1930- DLB-26

Henry VIII of England 1491-1547 . . . . . .DLB-132

Henry of Ghent
    circa 1217-1229 - 1293 . . . . .DLB-115

Henry, Marguerite 1902-1997 . . . . .DLB-22

Henry, O. (see Porter, William Sydney)

Henry, Robert Selph 1889-1970 . . . . .DLB-17

Henry, Will (see Allen, Henry W.)

Henryson, Robert
    1420s or 1430s-circa 1505 . . . . .DLB-146

Henschke, Alfred (see Klabund)

Hensley, Sophie Almon 1866-1946 . . . . . . .DLB-99

Henson, Lance 1944- DLB-175

Henty, G. A. 1832?-1902 . . . . .DLB-18, 141

Hentz, Caroline Lee 1800-1856 . . . . .DLB-3

Heraclitus
    flourished circa 500 B.C. DLB-176

Herbert, Agnes circa 1880-1960 . . . . .DLB-174

Herbert, Alan Patrick 1890-1971 . . . . .DLB-10, 191

Herbert, Edward, Lord, of Cherbury
    1582-1648 . . . . .DLB-121, 151

Herbert, Frank 1920-1986 . . . . .DLB-8

Herbert, George 1593-1633 . . . . .DLB-126

Herbert, Henry William 1807-1858 . . . . .DLB-3, 73

Herbert, John 1926- DLB-53

Herbert, Mary Sidney, Countess of Pembroke
    (see Sidney, Mary)

Herbert, Zbigniew 1924-1998 . . . . .DLB-232

Herbst, Josephine 1892-1969 . . . . .DLB-9

Herburger, Gunter 1932- DLB-75, 124

Hercules, Frank E. M. 1917-1996 . . . . . . .DLB-33

Herder, Johann Gottfried 1744-1803 . . . . . .DLB-97

Herder, B., Book Company DLB-49

Heredia, José-María de 1842-1905 . . . . . . .DLB-217

Herford, Charles Harold 1853-1931 . . . . .DLB-149

Hergesheimer, Joseph 1880-1954 . . . . .DLB-9, 102

Heritage Press .DLB-46

Hermann the Lame 1013-1054 . . . . .DLB-148

Hermes, Johann Timotheus
    1738-1821 .DLB-97

Hermlin, Stephan 1915-1997? DLB-69

Hernández, Alfonso C. 1938- DLB-122

Hernández, Inés 1947- DLB-122

Hernández, Miguel 1910-1942 . . . . .DLB-134

Hernton, Calvin C. 1932- DLB-38

Herodotus
    circa 484 B.C.-circa 420 B.C. DLB-176

Heron, Robert 1764-1807 . . . . .DLB-142

Herr, Michael 1940- DLB-185

Herrera, Juan Felipe 1948- DLB-122

Herrick, E. R., and Company DLB-49

Herrick, Robert 1591-1674 . . . . .DLB-126

Herrick, Robert 1868-1938 . . . . DLB-9, 12, 78

Herrick, William 1915- Y-83

Herrmann, John 1900-1959 . . . . .DLB-4

Hersey, John 1914-1993 . . . . .DLB-6, 185

Hertel, François 1905-1985 . . . . .DLB-68

Hervé-Bazin, Jean Pierre Marie (see Bazin, Hervé)

Hervey, John, Lord 1696-1743 . . . . .DLB-101

Herwig, Georg 1817-1875 . . . . .DLB-133

Herzog, Emile Salomon Wilhelm
    (see Maurois, André)

Hesiod eighth century B.C. DLB-176

Hesse, Hermann 1877-1962 . . . . .DLB-66

Hessus, Helius Eobanus 1488-1540 . . . . . .DLB-179

Hewat, Alexander circa 1743-circa 1824 . . .DLB-30

Hewitt, John 1907- DLB-27

Hewlett, Maurice 1861-1923 . . . . DLB-34, 156

Heyen, William 1940- DLB-5

Heyer, Georgette 1902-1974 . . . . DLB-77, 191

Heym, Stefan 1913- DLB-69

Heyse, Paul 1830-1914 . . . . .DLB-129

Heytesbury, William
    circa 1310-1372 or 1373 . . . . .DLB-115

Heyward, Dorothy 1890-1961 . . . . .DLB-7

Heyward, DuBose 1885-1940 . . . . DLB-7, 9, 45

Heywood, John 1497?-1580? DLB-136

Heywood, Thomas
    1573 or 1574-1641 . . . . .DLB-62

Hibbs, Ben 1901-1975 . . . . .DLB-137

Hichens, Robert S. 1864-1950 . . . . .DLB-153

Hickey, Emily 1845-1924 . . . . .DLB-199

Hickman, William Albert 1877-1957 . . . . .DLB-92

Hidalgo, José Luis 1919-1947 . . . . .DLB-108

Hiebert, Paul 1892-1987 . . . . .DLB-68

Hieng, Andrej 1925- DLB-181

Hierro, José 1922- DLB-108

Higgins, Aidan 1927- DLB-14

Higgins, Colin 1941-1988. . . . . DLB-26

Higgins, George V.
1939-1999 . . . . DLB-2; Y-81, Y-98, Y-99

   George V. Higgins to Julian Symons Y-99

Higginson, Thomas Wentworth
1823-1911. DLB-1, 64

Highwater, Jamake 1942?- DLB-52; Y-85

Hijuelos, Oscar 1951- DLB-145

Hildegard von Bingen 1098-1179 . . . . DLB-148

Das Hildesbrandslied circa 820. . . . . DLB-148

Hildesheimer, Wolfgang
1916-1991. . . . . DLB-69, 124

Hildreth, Richard 1807-1865. . . . . . DLB-1, 30, 59

Hill, Aaron 1685-1750 . . . . DLB-84

Hill, Geoffrey 1932- DLB-40

Hill, George M., Company. DLB-49

Hill, "Sir" John 1714?-1775 . . . . DLB-39

Hill, Lawrence, and Company,
Publishers. DLB-46

Hill, Leslie 1880-1960. . . . . DLB-51

Hill, Susan 1942- DLB-14, 139

Hill, Walter 1942- DLB-44

Hill and Wang DLB-46

Hillberry, Conrad 1928- DLB-120

Hillerman, Tony 1925- DLB-206

Hilliard, Gray and Company DLB-49

Hills, Lee 1906- DLB-127

Hillyer, Robert 1895-1961 . . . . DLB-54

Hilton, James 1900-1954. . . . . DLB-34, 77

Hilton, Walter died 1396 . . . . DLB-146

Hilton and Company DLB-49

Himes, Chester 1909-1984 . . . .DLB-2, 76, 143, 226

Hindmarsh, Joseph [publishing house] DLB-170

Hine, Daryl 1936- DLB-60

Hingley, Ronald 1920- DLB-155

Hinojosa-Smith, Rolando 1929- DLB-82

Hippel, Theodor Gottlieb von
1741-1796 . . . . DLB-97

Hippocrates of Cos
flourished circa 425 B.C. DLB-176

Hirabayashi, Taiko 1905-1972 . . . . DLB-180

Hirsch, E. D., Jr. 1928- DLB-67

Hirsch, Edward 1950- DLB-120

Hoagland, Edward 1932- DLB-6

Hoagland, Everett H., III 1942- DLB-41

Hoban, Russell 1925- DLB-52

Hobbes, Thomas 1588-1679 . . . . DLB-151

Hobby, Oveta 1905- DLB-127

Hobby, William 1878-1964. . . . . DLB-127

Hobsbaum, Philip 1932- DLB-40

Hobson, Laura Z. 1900- DLB-28

Hobson, Sarah 1947- DLB-204

Hoby, Thomas 1530-1566 . . . . DLB-132

Hoccleve, Thomas
circa 1368-circa 1437 . . . . DLB-146

Hochhuth, Rolf 1931- DLB-124

Hochman, Sandra 1936- DLB-5

Hocken, Thomas Morland
1836-1910 . . . . DLB-184

Hodder and Stoughton, Limited. DLB-106

Hodgins, Jack 1938- DLB-60

Hodgman, Helen 1945- DLB-14

Hodgskin, Thomas 1787-1869 . . . . DLB-158

Hodgson, Ralph 1871-1962 . . . . DLB-19

Hodgson, William Hope
1877-1918 . . . . .DLB-70, 153, 156, 178

Hoe, Robert III 1839-1909. . . . . DLB-187

Hoeg, Peter 1957- DLB-214

Højholt, Per 1928- DLB-214

Hoffenstein, Samuel 1890-1947 . . . . DLB-11

Hoffman, Charles Fenno 1806-1884. . . . . . DLB-3

Hoffman, Daniel 1923- DLB-5

Hoffmann, E. T. A. 1776-1822 . . . . DLB-90

Hoffman, Frank B. 1888-1958 . . . . DLB-188

Hoffman, William 1925- DLB-234

Hoffmanswaldau, Christian Hoffman von
1616-1679. DLB-168

Hofmann, Michael 1957- DLB-40

Hofmannsthal, Hugo von
1874-1929. . . . . DLB-81, 118

Hofstadter, Richard 1916-1970. . . . . DLB-17

Hogan, Desmond 1950- DLB-14

Hogan, Linda 1947- DLB-175

Hogan and Thompson DLB-49

Hogarth Press. DLB-112

Hogg, James 1770-1835. . . . . . . .DLB-93, 116, 159

Hohberg, Wolfgang Helmhard Freiherr von
1612-1688 . . . . DLB-168

von Hohenheim, Philippus Aureolus
Theophrastus Bombastus (see Paracelsus)

Hohl, Ludwig 1904-1980 . . . . DLB-56

Holbrook, David 1923- DLB-14, 40

Holcroft, Thomas 1745-1809 . . . . DLB-39, 89, 158

   Preface to *Alwyn* (1780) DLB-39

Holden, Jonathan 1941- DLB-105

   "Contemporary Verse Story-telling". . . DLB-105

Holden, Molly 1927-1981. . . . . DLB-40

Hölderlin, Friedrich 1770-1843 . . . . DLB-90

Holiday House. DLB-46

Holinshed, Raphael died 1580 . . . . DLB-167

Holland, J. G. 1819-1881 . . . . .DS-13

Holland, Norman N. 1927- DLB-67

Hollander, John 1929- DLB-5

Holley, Marietta 1836-1926 . . . . DLB-11

Hollinghurst, Alan 1954- DLB-207

Hollingsworth, Margaret 1940- DLB-60

Hollo, Anselm 1934- DLB-40

Holloway, Emory 1885-1977 . . . . DLB-103

Holloway, John 1920- DLB-27

Holloway House Publishing Company . . . DLB-46

Holme, Constance 1880-1955 . . . . DLB-34

Holmes, Abraham S. 1821?-1908. . . . . . . DLB-99

Holmes, John Clellon 1926-1988 . . . . DLB-16

   "Four Essays on the Beat Generation" . . DLB-16

Holmes, Mary Jane 1825-1907 . . . . . DLB-202, 221

Holmes, Oliver Wendell 1809-1894. . . DLB-1, 189

Holmes, Richard 1945- DLB-155

   The Cult of Biography
   Excerpts from the Second Folio Debate:
   "Biographies are generally a disease of
   English Literature". Y-86

Holmes, Thomas James 1874-1959. . . . . .DLB-187

Holroyd, Michael 1935- DLB-155

Holst, Hermann E. von 1841-1904 . . . . . DLB-47

Holt, Henry, and Company DLB-49

Holt, John 1721-1784 . . . . DLB-43

Holt, Rinehart and Winston. DLB-46

Holtby, Winifred 1898-1935 . . . . DLB-191

Holthusen, Hans Egon 1913- DLB-69

Hölty, Ludwig Christoph Heinrich
1748-1776 . . . . DLB-94

Holub, Miroslav 1923-1998 . . . . DLB-232

Holz, Arno 1863-1929 . . . . DLB-118

Home, Henry, Lord Kames
(see Kames, Henry Home, Lord)

Home, John 1722-1808. . . . . DLB-84

Home, William Douglas 1912- DLB-13

Home Publishing Company DLB-49

Homer
circa eighth-seventh centuries B.C. . . .DLB-176

Homer, Winslow 1836-1910 . . . . DLB-188

Homes, Geoffrey (see Mainwaring, Daniel)

Honan, Park 1928- DLB-111

Hone, William 1780-1842. . . . . .DLB-110, 158

Hongo, Garrett Kaoru 1951- DLB-120

Honig, Edwin 1919- DLB-5

Hood, Hugh 1928- DLB-53

Hood, Mary 1946- DLB-234

Hood, Thomas 1799-1845 . . . . DLB-96

Hook, Theodore 1788-1841 . . . . DLB-116

Hooker, Jeremy 1941- DLB-40

Hooker, Richard 1554-1600. . . . . DLB-132

Hooker, Thomas 1586-1647. . . . . DLB-24

Hooper, Johnson Jones 1815-1862 . . . . . DLB-3, 11

Hope, Anthony 1863-1933 . . . . DLB-153, 156

Hope, Christopher 1944- DLB-225

Hopkins, Ellice 1836-1904 . . . . DLB-190

Hopkins, Gerard Manley
1844-1889 . . . . .DLB-35, 57

Hopkins, John (see Sternhold, Thomas)

Hopkins, John H., and Son DLB-46

Hopkins, Lemuel 1750-1801. . . . . DLB-37

Hopkins, Pauline Elizabeth 1859-1930. . . . DLB-50

Hopkins, Samuel 1721-1803 . . . . DLB-31

Hopkinson, Francis 1737-1791 . . . . DLB-31

Hoppin, Augustus 1828-1896 . . . . .DLB-188

Hora, Josef 1891-1945 . . . . .DLB-215

Horace 65 B.C.-8 B.C. DLB-211

Horgan, Paul 1903-1995 . . . . . DLB-102, 212; Y-85

Horizon Press DLB-46

Hornby, C. H. St. John 1867-1946. . . . . . .DLB-201

Hornby, Nick 1957- DLB-207

Horne, Frank 1899-1974 . . . . .DLB-51

Horne, Richard Henry (Hengist)
    1802 or 1803-1884 . . . . .DLB-32

Hornung, E. W. 1866-1921 . . . . .DLB-70

Horovitz, Israel 1939- DLB-7

Horton, George Moses 1797?-1883? DLB-50

Horváth, Ödön von 1901-1938 . . . . . .DLB-85, 124

Horwood, Harold 1923- DLB-60

Hosford, E. and E. [publishing house] DLB-49

Hoskens, Jane Fenn 1693-1770? DLB-200

Hoskyns, John 1566-1638 . . . . .DLB-121

Hosokawa Yūsai 1535-1610. . . . . .DLB-203

Hostovský, Egon 1908-1973 . . . . .DLB-215

Hotchkiss and Company DLB-49

Hough, Emerson 1857-1923. . . . . .DLB-9, 212

Houghton, Stanley 1881-1913 . . . . .DLB-10

Houghton Mifflin Company DLB-49

Household, Geoffrey 1900-1988 . . . . .DLB-87

Housman, A. E. 1859-1936 . . . . .DLB-19

Housman, Laurence 1865-1959 . . . . .DLB-10

Houwald, Ernst von 1778-1845 . . . . .DLB-90

Hovey, Richard 1864-1900 . . . . .DLB-54

Howard, Donald R. 1927-1987 . . . . .DLB-111

Howard, Maureen 1930- Y-83

Howard, Richard 1929- DLB-5

Howard, Roy W. 1883-1964. . . . . .DLB-29

Howard, Sidney 1891-1939 . . . . .DLB-7, 26

Howard, Thomas, second Earl of Arundel
    1585-1646 . . . . .DLB-213

Howe, E. W. 1853-1937 . . . . .DLB-12, 25

Howe, Henry 1816-1893 . . . . .DLB-30

Howe, Irving 1920-1993 . . . . .DLB-67

Howe, Joseph 1804-1873 . . . . .DLB-99

Howe, Julia Ward 1819-1910 . . . . . . .DLB-1, 189

Howe, Percival Presland 1886-1944 . . . . .DLB-149

Howe, Susan 1937- DLB-120

Howell, Clark, Sr. 1863-1936 . . . . .DLB-25

Howell, Evan P. 1839-1905 . . . . .DLB-23

Howell, James 1594?-1666. . . . . .DLB-151

Howell, Soskin and Company DLB-46

Howell, Warren Richardson
    1912-1984 . . . . .DLB-140

Howells, William Dean
    1837-1920 . . . . .DLB-12, 64, 74, 79, 189

    Introduction to Paul Laurence Dunbar,
    Lyrics of Lowly Life (1896). DLB-50

Howitt, Mary 1799-1888 . . . . .DLB-110, 199

Howitt, William 1792-1879 and
    Howitt, Mary 1799-1888 . . . . .DLB-110

Hoyem, Andrew 1935- DLB-5

Hoyers, Anna Ovena 1584-1655 . . . . . . .DLB-164

Hoyos, Angela de 1940- DLB-82

Hoyt, Henry [publishing house] DLB-49

Hoyt, Palmer 1897-1979. . . . . .DLB-127

Hrabal, Bohumil 1914-1997. . . . . .DLB-232

Hrabanus Maurus 776?-856. . . . . .DLB-148

Hronský, Josef Cíger 1896-1960 . . . . .DLB-215

Hrotsvit of Gandersheim
    circa 935-circa 1000. . . . . .DLB-148

Hubbard, Elbert 1856-1915 . . . . .DLB-91

Hubbard, Kin 1868-1930. . . . . .DLB-11

Hubbard, William circa 1621-1704 . . . . . .DLB-24

Huber, Therese 1764-1829 . . . . .DLB-90

Huch, Friedrich 1873-1913 . . . . .DLB-66

Huch, Ricarda 1864-1947 . . . . .DLB-66

Huck at 100: How Old Is
    Huckleberry Finn? Y-85

Huddle, David 1942- DLB-130

Hudgins, Andrew 1951- DLB-120

Hudson, Henry Norman 1814-1886 . . . . .DLB-64

Hudson, Stephen 1868?-1944 . . . . .DLB-197

Hudson, W. H. 1841-1922 . . . . .DLB-98, 153, 174

Hudson and Goodwin. DLB-49

Huebsch, B. W. [publishing house] DLB-46

    Oral History: B. W. Huebsch Y-99

Hueffer, Oliver Madox 1876-1931. . . . . . .DLB-197

Hugh of St. Victor circa 1096-1141 . . . . . .DLB-208

Hughes, David 1930- DLB-14

Hughes, Dusty 1947- DLB-233

Hughes, John 1677-1720. . . . . .DLB-84

Hughes, Langston
    1902-1967 . . . . DLB-4, 7, 48, 51, 86, 228

Hughes, Richard 1900-1976. . . . . .DLB-15, 161

Hughes, Ted 1930-1998 . . . . .DLB-40, 161

Hughes, Thomas 1822-1896 . . . . . . .DLB-18, 163

Hugo, Richard 1923-1982 . . . . .DLB-5, 206

Hugo, Victor 1802-1885 . . . . . .DLB-119, 192, 217

Hugo Awards and Nebula Awards DLB-8

Hull, Richard 1896-1973 . . . . .DLB-77

Hulme, T. E. 1883-1917 . . . . .DLB-19

Hulton, Anne ?-1779? DLB-200

Humboldt, Alexander von 1769-1859 . . . . .DLB-90

Humboldt, Wilhelm von 1767-1835. . . . . .DLB-90

Hume, David 1711-1776. . . . . .DLB-104

Hume, Fergus 1859-1932. . . . . .DLB-70

Hume, Sophia 1702-1774 . . . . .DLB-200

Humishuma (see Mourning Dove)

Hummer, T. R. 1950- DLB-120

Humorous Book Illustration DLB-11

Humphrey, Duke of Gloucester
    1391-1447 . . . . .DLB-213

Humphrey, William 1924-1997 . . .DLB-6, 212, 234

Humphreys, David 1752-1818. . . . . .DLB-37

Humphreys, Emyr 1919- DLB-15

Huncke, Herbert 1915-1996 . . . . .DLB-16

Huneker, James Gibbons 1857-1921 . . . . . .DLB-71

Hunold, Christian Friedrich
    1681-1721 . . . . .DLB-168

Hunt, Irene 1907- DLB-52

Hunt, Leigh 1784-1859 . . . . .DLB-96, 110, 144

Hunt, Violet 1862-1942 . . . . .DLB-162, 197

Hunt, William Gibbes 1791-1833 . . . . .DLB-73

Hunter, Evan 1926- Y-82

Hunter, Jim 1939- DLB-14

Hunter, Kristin 1931- DLB-33

Hunter, Mollie 1922- DLB-161

Hunter, N. C. 1908-1971 . . . . .DLB-10

Hunter-Duvar, John 1821-1899 . . . . .DLB-99

Huntington, Henry E. 1850-1927 . . . . . . .DLB-140

Huntington, Susan Mansfield
    1791-1823 . . . . .DLB-200

Hurd and Houghton DLB-49

Hurst, Fannie 1889-1968 . . . . .DLB-86

Hurst and Blackett. DLB-106

Hurst and Company DLB-49

Hurston, Zora Neale 1901?-1960 . . . . .DLB-51, 86

Husson, Jules-François-Félix (see Champfleury)

Huston, John 1906-1987 . . . . .DLB-26

Hutcheson, Francis 1694-1746. . . . . .DLB-31

Hutchinson, R. C. 1907-1975. . . . . .DLB-191

Hutchinson, Thomas 1711-1780 . . . . . .DLB-30, 31

Hutchinson and Company
    (Publishers) Limited DLB-112

Hutton, Richard Holt 1826-1897. . . . . . . .DLB-57

von Hutton, Ulrich 1488-1523 . . . . .DLB-179

Huxley, Aldous
    1894-1963 . . . . .DLB-36, 100, 162, 195

Huxley, Elspeth Josceline
    1907-1997 . . . . .DLB-77, 204

Huxley, T. H. 1825-1895 . . . . .DLB-57

Huyghue, Douglas Smith 1816-1891 . . . . . .DLB-99

Huysmans, Joris-Karl 1848-1907 . . . . .DLB-123

Hwang, David Henry 1957- DLB-212, 228

Hyde, Donald 1909-1966 and
    Hyde, Mary 1912- DLB-187

Hyman, Trina Schart 1939- DLB-61

I

Iavorsky, Stefan 1658-1722 . . . . .DLB-150

Iazykov, Nikolai Mikhailovich
    1803-1846 . . . . .DLB-205

Ibáñez, Armando P. 1949- DLB-209

Ibn Bajja circa 1077-1138 . . . . .DLB-115

Ibn Gabirol, Solomon
    circa 1021-circa 1058. . . . . .DLB-115

Ibuse, Masuji 1898-1993 . . . . .DLB-180

Ichijō Kanera
    (see Ichijō Kaneyoshi)

Ichijō Kaneyoshi (Ichijō Kanera)
    1402-1481 . . . . .DLB-203

The Iconography of Science-Fiction Art DLB-8

Iffland, August Wilhelm 1759-1814 . . . . . . DLB-94

Ignatow, David 1914-1997 . . . . DLB-5

Ike, Chukwuemeka 1931- DLB-157

Ikkyū Sōjun 1394-1481. . . . . DLB-203

Iles, Francis
   (see Berkeley, Anthony)

The Illustration of Early German Literar
   Manuscripts, circa 1150-circa 1300 . . DLB-148

Illyés, Gyula 1902-1983 . . . . DLB-215

Imbs, Bravig 1904-1946 . . . . DLB-4

Imbuga, Francis D. 1947- DLB-157

Immermann, Karl 1796-1840 . . . . DLB-133

Inchbald, Elizabeth 1753-1821 . . . . DLB-39, 89

Inge, William 1913-1973. . . . . DLB-7

Ingelow, Jean 1820-1897 . . . . DLB-35, 163

Ingersoll, Ralph 1900-1985. . . . . DLB-127

The Ingersoll Prizes Y-84

Ingoldsby, Thomas
   (see Barham, Richard Harris)

Ingraham, Joseph Holt 1809-1860 . . . . DLB-3

Inman, John 1805-1850 . . . . DLB-73

Innerhofer, Franz 1944- DLB-85

Innis, Harold Adams 1894-1952. . . . . DLB-88

Innis, Mary Quayle 1899-1972 . . . . DLB-88

Inō Sōgi 1421-1502. . . . . DLB-203

Inoue Yasushi 1907-1991 . . . . DLB-181

International Publishers Company DLB-46

Interviews:

   Anastas, Benjamin. Y-98

   Bank, Melissa Y-98

   Bernstein, Harriet Y-82

   Bosworth, David. Y-82

   Burnshaw, Stanley Y-97

   Carpenter, Humphrey Y-84, Y-99

   Carver, Raymond. Y-83

   Donald, David Herbert. Y-87

   Ellroy, James Y-91

   Greenfield, George Y-91

   Griffin, Bryan Y-81

   Guilds, John Caldwell. Y-92

   Higgins, George V. Y-98

   Hoban, Russell .Y-90

   Holroyd, Michael Y-99

   Horowitz, Glenn. Y-90

   Jenkinson, Edward B. Y-82

   Jenks, Tom Y-86

   Kaplan, Justin Y-86

   Krug, Judith Y-82

   Lamm, Donald .Y-95

   Laughlin, James Y-96

   Mailer, Norman Y-97

   Manchester, William. Y-85

   McCormack, Thomas. Y-98

   Mellen, Joan Y-94

   Mooneyham, Lamarr Y-82

   O'Connor, Patrick Y-84, Y-99

   Ozick, Cynthia .Y-83

   Penzler, Otto. Y-96

   Plimpton, George Y-99

   Potok, Chaim Y-84

   Prescott, Peter S. Y-86

   Rabe, David Y-91

   Reid, B. L. Y-83

   Reynolds, Michael Y-95, Y-99

   Schlafly, Phyllis. Y-82

   Schroeder, Patricia Y-99

   Scribner, Charles III. Y-94

   Sipper, Ralph Y-94

   Weintraub, Stanley. Y-82

   Editors, Conversations with Y-95

Irving, John 1942- DLB-6; Y-82

Irving, Washington 1783-1859
   . . . . DLB-3, 11, 30, 59, 73, 74, 183, 186

Irwin, Grace 1907- DLB-68

Irwin, Will 1873-1948. . . . . DLB-25

Isherwood, Christopher
   1904-1986 . . . . DLB-15, 195; Y-86

   The Christopher Isherwood Archive,
   The Huntington Library Y-99

Ishiguro, Kazuo 1954- DLB-194

Ishikawa Jun 1899-1987 . . . . DLB-182

The Island Trees Case: A Symposium on
   School Library Censorship
   An Interview with Judith Krug
   An Interview with Phyllis Schlafly
   An Interview with Edward B. Jenkinson
   An Interview with Lamarr Mooneyham
   An Interview with Harriet Bernstein Y-82

Islas, Arturo 1938-1991 . . . . DLB-122

Issit, Debbie 1966- DLB-233

Ivanišević, Drago 1907-1981. . . . . DLB-181

Ivaska, Astrīde 1926- DLB-232

Ivers, M. J., and Company DLB-49

Iwaniuk, Wacław 1915- DLB-215

Iwano, Hōmei 1873-1920 . . . . DLB-180

Iwaszkiewicz, Jarosław 1894-1980. . . . . . DLB-215

Iyayi, Festus 1947- DLB-157

Izumi, Kyōka 1873-1939. . . . . DLB-180

J

Jackmon, Marvin E. (see Marvin X)

Jacks, L. P. 1860-1955 . . . . DLB-135

Jackson, Angela 1951- DLB-41

Jackson, Charles 1903-1968 . . . . DLB-234

Jackson, Helen Hunt
   1830-1885 . . . . DLB-42, 47, 186, 189

Jackson, Holbrook 1874-1948. . . . . DLB-98

Jackson, Laura Riding 1901-1991. . . . . . . DLB-48

Jackson, Shirley 1916-1965 . . . . DLB-6, 234

Jacob, Naomi 1884?-1964. . . . . DLB-191

Jacob, Piers Anthony Dillingham
   (see Anthony, Piers)

Jacobi, Friedrich Heinrich 1743-1819 . . . . DLB-94

Jacobi, Johann Georg 1740-1841. . . . . DLB-97

Jacobs, George W., and Company. DLB-49

Jacobs, Joseph 1854-1916 . . . . DLB-141

Jacobs, W. W. 1863-1943. . . . . DLB-135

Jacobsen, Jørgen-Frantz 1900-1938. . . . . . DLB-214

Jacobson, Dan 1929- DLB-14, 207, 225

Jacobson, Howard 1942- DLB-207

Jacques de Vitry circa 1160/1170-1240. . . DLB-208

Jæger, Frank 1926-1977. . . . . DLB-214

Jaggard, William [publishing house]. DLB-170

Jahier, Piero 1884-1966 . . . . DLB-114

Jahnn, Hans Henny 1894-1959 . . . . . DLB-56, 124

Jakes, John 1932- Y-83

James, Alice 1848-1892. . . . . DLB-221

James, C. L. R. 1901-1989 . . . . DLB-125

James, George P. R. 1801-1860 . . . . DLB-116

James, Henry
   1843-1916 . . . . . . DLB-12, 71, 74, 189; DS-13

James, John circa 1633-1729 . . . . DLB-24

James, M. R. 1862-1936 . . . . DLB-156, 201

James, Naomi 1949- DLB-204

James, P. D. 1920- DLB-87; DS-17

James VI of Scotland, I of England
   1566-1625 . . . . .DLB-151, 172

*Ane Schort Treatise Conteining Some Reulis
and Cautelis to Be Obseruit and Eschewit
in Scottis Poesi (1584)* DLB-172

James, Thomas 1572?-1629 . . . . DLB-213

James, U. P. [publishing house] DLB-49

James, Will 1892-1942 . . . . .DS-16

Jameson, Anna 1794-1860 . . . . DLB-99, 166

Jameson, Fredric 1934- DLB-67

Jameson, J. Franklin 1859-1937 . . . . .DLB-17

Jameson, Storm 1891-1986. . . . . DLB-36

Jančar, Drago 1948- DLB-181

Janés, Clara 1940- DLB-134

Janevski, Slavko 1920- DLB-181

Janvier, Thomas 1849-1913 . . . . DLB-202

Jaramillo, Cleofas M. 1878-1956. . . . . . . DLB-122

Jarman, Mark 1952- DLB-120

Jarrell, Randall 1914-1965 . . . . DLB-48, 52

Jarrold and Sons. DLB-106

Jarry, Alfred 1873-1907. . . . . DLB-192

Jarves, James Jackson 1818-1888 . . . . DLB-189

Jasmin, Claude 1930- DLB-60

Jaunsudrabiņš, Jānis 1877-1962 . . . . DLB-220

Jay, John 1745-1829 . . . . DLB-31

Jean de Garlande (see John of Garland)

Jefferies, Richard 1848-1887 . . . . DLB-98, 141

Jeffers, Lance 1919-1985. . . . . DLB-41

Jeffers, Robinson 1887-1962 . . . . DLB-45, 212

Jefferson, Thomas 1743-1826 . . . . DLB-31, 183

Jégé 1866-1940 . . . . DLB-215

Jelinek, Elfriede 1946- DLB-85

Jellicoe, Ann 1927- DLB-13, 233

Jenkins, Elizabeth 1905- DLB-155

Jenkins, Robin 1912- DLB-14

Jenkins, William Fitzgerald (see Leinster, Murray)

Jenkins, Herbert, Limited. DLB-112

Jennings, Elizabeth 1926- DLB-27

Jens, Walter 1923- DLB-69

Jensen, Johannes V. 1873-1950 . . . . .DLB-214

Jensen, Merrill 1905-1980 . . . . .DLB-17

Jensen, Thit 1876-1957. . . . . .DLB-214

Jephson, Robert 1736-1803 . . . . .DLB-89

Jerome, Jerome K. 1859-1927 . . . .DLB-10, 34, 135

Jerome, Judson 1927-1991 . . . . .DLB-105

Jerrold, Douglas 1803-1857 . . . . .DLB-158, 159

Jesse, F. Tennyson 1888-1958 . . . . .DLB-77

Jewett, John P., and Company. DLB-49

Jewett, Sarah Orne 1849-1909 . . . .DLB-12, 74, 221

The Jewish Publication Society DLB-49

Jewitt, John Rodgers 1783-1821 . . . . .DLB-99

Jewsbury, Geraldine 1812-1880. . . . . .DLB-21

Jewsbury, Maria Jane 1800-1833 . . . . .DLB-199

Jhabvala, Ruth Prawer 1927- DLB-139, 194

Jiménez, Juan Ramón 1881-1958. . . . . . . .DLB-134

Joans, Ted 1928- DLB-16, 41

Jōha 1525-1602 . . . . .DLB-203

Johannis de Garlandia (see John of Garland)

John, Errol 1924-1988 . . . . .DLB-233

John, Eugenie (see Marlitt, E.)

John of Dumbleton
    circa 1310-circa 1349. . . . . .DLB-115

John of Garland (Jean de Garlande, Johannis de
    Garlandia) circa 1195-circa 1272 . . . . .DLB-208

Johns, Captain W. E. 1893-1968 . . . . . . .DLB-160

Johnson, Mrs. A. E. ca. 1858-1922 . . . . . .DLB-221

Johnson, Amelia (see Johnson, Mrs. A. E.)

Johnson, B. S. 1933-1973 . . . . .DLB-14, 40

Johnson, Benjamin [publishing house] DLB-49

Johnson, Benjamin, Jacob, and
    Robert [publishing house] DLB-49

Johnson, Charles 1679-1748 . . . . .DLB-84

Johnson, Charles R. 1948- DLB-33

Johnson, Charles S. 1893-1956 . . . . . . .DLB-51, 91

Johnson, Denis 1949- DLB-120

Johnson, Diane 1934- Y-80

Johnson, Dorothy M. 1905–1984 . . . . . .DLB-206

Johnson, E. Pauline (Tekahionwake)
    1861-1913 .DLB-175

Johnson, Edgar 1901-1995. . . . . .DLB-103

Johnson, Edward 1598-1672 . . . . .DLB-24

Johnson, Fenton 1888-1958 . . . . .DLB-45, 50

Johnson, Georgia Douglas 1886-1966 . . . . .DLB-51

Johnson, Gerald W. 1890-1980 . . . . .DLB-29

Johnson, Greg 1953- DLB-234

Johnson, Helene 1907-1995 . . . . .DLB-51

Johnson, Jacob, and Company. DLB-49

Johnson, James Weldon 1871-1938 . . . . . . .DLB-51

Johnson, John H. 1918- DLB-137

Johnson, Joseph [publishing house] DLB-154

Johnson, Linton Kwesi 1952- DLB-157

Johnson, Lionel 1867-1902. . . . . .DLB-19

Johnson, Nunnally 1897-1977 . . . . .DLB-26

Johnson, Owen 1878-1952. . . . . Y-87

Johnson, Pamela Hansford 1912- DLB-15

Johnson, Pauline 1861-1913. . . . . .DLB-92

Johnson, Ronald 1935-1998. . . . . .DLB-169

Johnson, Samuel 1696-1772 . . . . .DLB-24

Johnson, Samuel
    1709-1784 . . . . .DLB-39, 95, 104, 142, 213

Johnson, Samuel 1822-1882. . . . . .DLB-1

Johnson, Susanna 1730-1810 . . . . .DLB-200

Johnson, Terry 1955- DLB-233

Johnson, Uwe 1934-1984. . . . . .DLB-75

Johnston, Annie Fellows 1863-1931. . . . . . .DLB-42

Johnston, Basil H. 1929- DLB-60

Johnston, David Claypole 1798?-1865. . . . .DLB-188

Johnston, Denis 1901-1984 . . . . .DLB-10

Johnston, Ellen 1835-1873 . . . . .DLB-199

Johnston, George 1913- DLB-88

Johnston, Sir Harry 1858-1927 . . . . .DLB-174

Johnston, Jennifer 1930- DLB-14

Johnston, Mary 1870-1936. . . . . .DLB-9

Johnston, Richard Malcolm 1822-1898 . . . .DLB-74

Johnstone, Charles 1719?-1800? DLB-39

Johst, Hanns 1890-1978. . . . . .DLB-124

Jolas, Eugene 1894-1952 . . . . .DLB-4, 45

Jones, Alice C. 1853-1933 . . . . .DLB-92

Jones, Charles C., Jr. 1831-1893 . . . . .DLB-30

Jones, D. G. 1929- DLB-53

Jones, David 1895-1974 . . . . .DLB-20, 100

Jones, Diana Wynne 1934- DLB-161

Jones, Ebenezer 1820-1860 . . . . .DLB-32

Jones, Ernest 1819-1868. . . . . .DLB-32

Jones, Gayl 1949- DLB-33

Jones, George 1800-1870 . . . . .DLB-183

Jones, Glyn 1905- DLB-15

Jones, Gwyn 1907- DLB-15, 139

Jones, Henry Arthur 1851-1929 . . . . .DLB-10

Jones, Hugh circa 1692-1760 . . . . .DLB-24

Jones, James 1921-1977 . . . . . . .DLB-2, 143; DS-17

James Jones Papers in the Handy Writers'
    Colony Collection at the University of
    Illinois at Springfield Y-98

The James Jones Society Y-92

Jones, Jenkin Lloyd 1911- DLB-127

Jones, John Beauchamp 1810-1866 . . . . . .DLB-202

Jones, LeRoi (see Baraka, Amiri)

Jones, Lewis 1897-1939 . . . . .DLB-15

Jones, Madison 1925- DLB-152

Jones, Major Joseph
    (see Thompson, William Tappan)

Jones, Marie 1955- DLB-233

Jones, Preston 1936-1979. . . . . .DLB-7

Jones, Rodney 1950- DLB-120

Jones, Sir William 1746-1794 . . . . .DLB-109

Jones, William Alfred 1817-1900 . . . . .DLB-59

Jones's Publishing House. DLB-49

Jong, Erica 1942- DLB-2, 5, 28, 152

Jonke, Gert F. 1946- DLB-85

Jonson, Ben 1572?-1637. . . . . . . .DLB-62, 121

Jordan, June 1936- DLB-38

Joseph and George. Y-99

Joseph, Jenny 1932- DLB-40

Joseph, Michael, Limited DLB-112

Josephson, Matthew 1899-1978 . . . . .DLB-4

Josephus, Flavius 37-100. . . . . .DLB-176

Josiah Allen's Wife (see Holley, Marietta)

Josipovici, Gabriel 1940- DLB-14

Josselyn, John ?-1675 . . . . .DLB-24

Joudry, Patricia 1921- DLB-88

Jovine, Giuseppe 1922- DLB-128

Joyaux, Philippe (see Sollers, Philippe)

Joyce, Adrien (see Eastman, Carol)

Joyce, James 1882-1941 . . . . . .DLB-10, 19, 36, 162

    James Joyce Centenary: Dublin, 1982 . . . . . Y-82

    James Joyce Conference. Y-85

    A Joyce (Con)Text: Danis Rose and the
        Remaking of *Ulysses*. Y-97

    The New *Ulysses*. Y-84

Jozsef, Attila 1905-1937 . . . . .DLB-215

Judd, Orange, Publishing Company DLB-49

Judd, Sylvester 1813-1853 . . . . .DLB-1

Judith circa 930 . . . . .DLB-146

Julian of Norwich
    1342-circa 1420. . . . . .DLB-1146

Julius Caesar 100 B.C.-44 B.C. DLB-211

June, Jennie
    (see Croly, Jane Cunningham)

Jung, Franz 1888-1963. . . . . .DLB-118

Jünger, Ernst 1895- DLB-56

Der jüngere Titurel circa 1275 . . . . .DLB-138

Jung-Stilling, Johann Heinrich
    1740-1817 .DLB-94

Justice, Donald 1925- Y-83

Juvenal circa A.D. 60-circa A.D. 130 . . . . .DLB-211

The Juvenile Library
    (see Godwin, M. J., and Company)

K

Kacew, Romain (see Gary, Romain)

Kafka, Franz 1883-1924. . . . . .DLB-81

Kahn, Roger 1927- DLB-171

Kaikō Takeshi 1939-1989 . . . . .DLB-182

Kaiser, Georg 1878-1945 . . . . .DLB-124

Kaiserchronik circca 1147 . . . . .DLB-148

Kaleb, Vjekoslav 1905- DLB-181

Kalechofsky, Roberta 1931- DLB-28

Kaler, James Otis 1848-1912 . . . . .DLB-12

Kames, Henry Home, Lord
  1696-1782 . . . . DLB-31, 104

Kamo no Chōmei (Kamo no Nagaakira)
  1153 or 1155-1216 . . . . DLB-203

Kamo no Nagaakira (see Kamo no Chōmei)

Kampmann, Christian 1939-1988. . . . . . . DLB-214

Kandel, Lenore 1932- DLB-16

Kanin, Garson 1912-1999. . . . . DLB-7

Kant, Hermann 1926- DLB-75

Kant, Immanuel 1724-1804. . . . . DLB-94

Kantemir, Antiokh Dmitrievich
  1708-1744 . . . . DLB-150

Kantor, MacKinlay 1904-1977 . . . . DLB-9, 102

Kanze Kōjirō Nobumitsu 1435-1516 . . . . DLB-203

Kanze Motokiyo (see Zeimi)

Kaplan, Fred 1937- DLB-111

Kaplan, Johanna 1942- DLB-28

Kaplan, Justin 1925- DLB-111

  The Practice of Biography V:
    An Interview with Justin Kaplan Y-86

Kaplinski, Jaan 1941- DLB-232

Kapnist, Vasilii Vasilevich 1758?-1823 . . . DLB-150

Karadžić, Vuk Stefanović 1787-1864 . . . . . DLB-147

Karamzin, Nikolai Mikhailovich
  1766-1826. . . . . DLB-150

Karinthy, Frigyes 1887-1938. . . . . DLB-215

Karsch, Anna Louisa 1722-1791 . . . . DLB-97

Kasack, Hermann 1896-1966 . . . . DLB-69

Kasai, Zenzō 1887-1927 . . . . DLB-180

Kaschnitz, Marie Luise 1901-1974 . . . . . . DLB-69

Kassák, Lajos 1887-1967 . . . . DLB-215

Kaštelan, Jure 1919-1990 . . . . DLB-147

Kästner, Erich 1899-1974 . . . . DLB-56

Katenin, Pavel Aleksandrovich
  1792-1853. . . . . DLB-205

Kattan, Naim 1928- DLB-53

Katz, Steve 1935- Y-83

Kauffman, Janet 1945- DLB-218; Y-86

Kauffmann, Samuel 1898-1971 . . . . DLB-127

Kaufman, Bob 1925- DLB-16, 41

Kaufman, George S. 1889-1961 . . . . DLB-7

Kavanagh, P. J. 1931- DLB-40

Kavanagh, Patrick 1904-1967 . . . . DLB-15, 20

Kawabata, Yasunari 1899-1972. . . . . DLB-180

Kaye-Smith, Sheila 1887-1956. . . . . DLB-36

Kazin, Alfred 1915-1998 . . . . DLB-67

Keane, John B. 1928- DLB-13

Keary, Annie 1825-1879 . . . . DLB-163

Keating, H. R. F. 1926- DLB-87

Keats, Ezra Jack 1916-1983. . . . . DLB-61

Keats, John 1795-1821 . . . . DLB-96, 110

Keble, John 1792-1866 . . . . DLB-32, 55

Keeble, John 1944- Y-83

Keeffe, Barrie 1945- DLB-13

Keeley, James 1867-1934. . . . . DLB-25

W. B. Keen, Cooke and Company. DLB-49

Keillor, Garrison 1942- Y-87

Keith, Marian 1874?-1961 . . . . DLB-92

Keller, Gary D. 1943- DLB-82

Keller, Gottfried 1819-1890 . . . . DLB-129

Kelley, Edith Summers 1884-1956 . . . . DLB-9

Kelley, Emma Dunham ?-?. DLB-221

Kelley, William Melvin 1937- DLB-33

Kellogg, Ansel Nash 1832-1886 . . . . DLB-23

Kellogg, Steven 1941- DLB-61

Kelly, George 1887-1974. . . . . DLB-7

Kelly, Hugh 1739-1777 . . . . DLB-89

Kelly, Piet and Company DLB-49

Kelly, Robert 1935- DLB-5, 130, 165

Kelman, James 1946- DLB-194

Kelmscott Press DLB-112

Kemble, E. W. 1861-1933 . . . . DLB-188

Kemble, Fanny 1809-1893 . . . . DLB-32

Kemelman, Harry 1908- DLB-28

Kempe, Margery circa 1373-1438. . . . . . . DLB-146

Kempner, Friederike 1836-1904 . . . . DLB-129

Kempowski, Walter 1929- DLB-75

Kendall, Claude [publishing company]. . . . DLB-46

Kendall, Henry 1839-1882 . . . . DLB-230

Kendell, George 1809-1867 . . . . DLB-43

Kenedy, P. J., and Sons DLB-49

Kenkō circa 1283-circa 1352. . . . . DLB-203

Kennan, George 1845-1924 . . . . DLB-189

Kennedy, Adrienne 1931- DLB-38

Kennedy, John Pendleton 1795-1870 . . . . . . DLB-3

Kennedy, Leo 1907- DLB-88

Kennedy, Margaret 1896-1967 . . . . DLB-36

Kennedy, Patrick 1801-1873. . . . . DLB-159

Kennedy, Richard S. 1920- DLB-111

Kennedy, William 1928- DLB-143; Y-85

Kennedy, X. J. 1929- DLB-5

Kennelly, Brendan 1936- DLB-40

Kenner, Hugh 1923- DLB-67

Kennerley, Mitchell [publishing house] . . . DLB-46

Kenny, Maurice 1929- DLB-175

Kent, Frank R. 1877-1958 . . . . DLB-29

Kenyon, Jane 1947-1995 . . . . DLB-120

Keough, Hugh Edmund 1864-1912 . . . . .DLB-171

Keppler and Schwartzmann DLB-49

Ker, John, third Duke of Roxburghe
  1740-1804. . . . . DLB-213

Ker, N. R. 1908-1982 . . . . DLB-201

Kerlan, Irvin 1912-1963 . . . . DLB-187

Kern, Jerome 1885-1945. . . . . DLB-187

Kerner, Justinus 1776-1862. . . . . DLB-90

Kerouac, Jack 1922-1969 . . . . DLB-2, 16; DS-3

  The Jack Kerouac Revival Y-95

  "Re-meeting of Old Friends":
    The Jack Kerouac Conference Y-82

Kerouac, Jan 1952-1996 . . . . DLB-16

Kerr, Charles H., and Company DLB-49

Kerr, Orpheus C. (see Newell, Robert Henry)

Kesey, Ken 1935- DLB-2, 16, 206

Kessel, Joseph 1898-1979 . . . . DLB-72

Kessel, Martin 1901- DLB-56

Kesten, Hermann 1900- DLB-56

Keun, Irmgard 1905-1982 . . . . DLB-69

Key and Biddle. DLB-49

Keynes, Sir Geoffrey 1887-1982 . . . . DLB-201

Keynes, John Maynard 1883-1946 . . . . .DS-10

Keyserling, Eduard von 1855-1918 . . . . . . DLB-66

Khan, Ismith 1925- DLB-125

Khaytov, Nikolay 1919- DLB-181

Khemnitser, Ivan Ivanovich
  1745-1784 . . . . DLB-150

Kheraskov, Mikhail Matveevich
  1733-1807. . . . . DLB-150

Khomiakov, Aleksei Stepanovich
  1804-1860 . . . . DLB-205

Khristov, Boris 1945- DLB-181

Khvostov, Dmitrii Ivanovich
  1757-1835 . . . . DLB-150

Kidd, Adam 1802?-1831. . . . . DLB-99

Kidd, William [publishing house]. DLB-106

Kidder, Tracy 1945- DLB-185

Kiely, Benedict 1919- DLB-15

Kieran, John 1892-1981 . . . . .DLB-171

Kiggins and Kellogg DLB-49

Kiley, Jed 1889-1962 . . . . DLB-4

Kilgore, Bernard 1908-1967 . . . . .DLB-127

Killens, John Oliver 1916- DLB-33

Killigrew, Anne 1660-1685. . . . . DLB-131

Killigrew, Thomas 1612-1683 . . . . DLB-58

Kilmer, Joyce 1886-1918 . . . . DLB-45

Kilroy, Thomas 1934- DLB-233

Kilwardby, Robert circa 1215-1279 . . . . . DLB-115

Kimball, Richard Burleigh 1816-1892 . . . DLB-202

Kincaid, Jamaica 1949- DLB-157, 227

King, Charles 1844-1933 . . . . DLB-186

King, Clarence 1842-1901 . . . . DLB-12

King, Florence 1936 . . . . Y-85

King, Francis 1923- DLB-15, 139

King, Grace 1852-1932. . . . . .DLB-12, 78

King, Harriet Hamilton 1840-1920 . . . . . DLB-199

King, Henry 1592-1669 . . . . DLB-126

King, Solomon [publishing house] DLB-49

King, Stephen 1947- DLB-143; Y-80

King, Thomas 1943- DLB-175

King, Woodie, Jr. 1937- DLB-38

Kinglake, Alexander William
  1809-1891 . . . . DLB-55, 166

Kingsley, Charles
  1819-1875. . . . . .DLB-21, 32, 163, 178, 190

Kingsley, Henry 1830-1876 . . . . DLB-21, 230

Kingsley, Mary Henrietta 1862-1900 . . . . .DLB-174

Kingsley, Sidney 1906- DLB-7

Kingsmill, Hugh 1889-1949 . . . . DLB-149

Kingsolver, Barbara 1955- DLB-206

Kingston, Maxine Hong
1940- DLB-173, 212; Y-80

Kingston, William Henry Giles
1814-1880 . . . . .DLB-163

Kinnan, Mary Lewis 1763-1848. . . . . . . .DLB-200

Kinnell, Galway 1927- DLB-5; Y-87

Kinsella, Thomas 1928- DLB-27

Kipling, Rudyard
1865-1936 . . . . .DLB-19, 34, 141, 156

Kipphardt, Heinar 1922-1982 . . . . .DLB-124

Kirby, William 1817-1906 . . . . .DLB-99

Kircher, Athanasius 1602-1680 . . . . .DLB-164

Kireevsky, Ivan Vasil'evich 1806-1856 . . .DLB-198

Kireevsky, Petr Vasil'evich 1808-1856 . . .DLB-205

Kirk, Hans 1898-1962 . . . . .DLB-214

Kirk, John Foster 1824-1904 . . . . .DLB-79

Kirkconnell, Watson 1895-1977. . . . . .DLB-68

Kirkland, Caroline M.
1801-1864 . . . . DLB-3, 73, 74; DS-13

Kirkland, Joseph 1830-1893. . . . . .DLB-12

Kirkman, Francis [publishing house] DLB-170

Kirkpatrick, Clayton 1915- DLB-127

Kirkup, James 1918- DLB-27

Kirouac, Conrad (see Marie-Victorin, Frère)

Kirsch, Sarah 1935- DLB-75

Kirst, Hans Hellmut 1914-1989. . . . . .DLB-69

Kiš, Danilo 1935-1989 . . . . .DLB-181

Kita Morio 1927- DLB-182

Kitcat, Mabel Greenhow 1859-1922 . . . . .DLB-135

Kitchin, C. H. B. 1895-1967 . . . . .DLB-77

Kittredge, William 1932- DLB-212

Kiukhel'beker, Vil'gel'm Karlovich
1797-1846. . . . . .DLB-205

Kizer, Carolyn 1925- DLB-5, 169

Klabund 1890-1928 . . . . .DLB-66

Klaj, Johann 1616-1656 . . . . .DLB-164

Klappert, Peter 1942- DLB-5

Klass, Philip (see Tenn, William)

Klein, A. M. 1909-1972 . . . . .DLB-68

Kleist, Ewald von 1715-1759 . . . . .DLB-97

Kleist, Heinrich von 1777-1811 . . . . .DLB-90

Klinger, Friedrich Maximilian
1752-1831 . . . . .DLB-94

Klíma, Ivan 1931- DLB-232

Oral History Interview with Donald S.
Klopfer Y-97

Klopstock, Friedrich Gottlieb
1724-1803 . . . . .DLB-97

Klopstock, Meta 1728-1758 . . . . .DLB-97

Kluge, Alexander 1932- DLB-75

Knapp, Joseph Palmer 1864-1951 . . . . . . .DLB-91

Knapp, Samuel Lorenzo 1783-1838 . . . . . .DLB-59

Knapton, J. J. and P.
[publishing house] DLB-154

Kniazhnin, Iakov Borisovich
1740-1791. . . . . .DLB-150

Knickerbocker, Diedrich (see Irving, Washington)

Knigge, Adolph Franz Friedrich Ludwig,
Freiherr von 1752-1796 . . . . .DLB-94

Knight, Charles, and Company. DLB-106

Knight, Damon 1922- DLB-8

Knight, Etheridge 1931-1992. . . . . .DLB-41

Knight, John S. 1894-1981. . . . . .DLB-29

Knight, Sarah Kemble 1666-1727. . . . .DLB-24, 200

Knight-Bruce, G. W. H. 1852-1896. . . . . .DLB-174

Knister, Raymond 1899-1932 . . . . .DLB-68

Knoblock, Edward 1874-1945 . . . . .DLB-10

Knopf, Alfred A. 1892-1984 . . . . Y-84

Knopf, Alfred A. [publishing house] DLB-46

Knorr von Rosenroth, Christian
1636-1689 . . . . .DLB-168

"Knots into Webs: Some Autobiographical
Sources," by Dabney Stuart DLB-105

Knowles, John 1926- DLB-6

Knox, Frank 1874-1944 . . . . .DLB-29

Knox, John circa 1514-1572. . . . . .DLB-132

Knox, John Armoy 1850-1906. . . . . .DLB-23

Knox, Ronald Arbuthnott 1888-1957 . . . . .DLB-77

Knox, Thomas Wallace 1835-1896. . . . . . .DLB-189

Kobayashi Takiji 1903-1933 . . . . .DLB-180

Kober, Arthur 1900-1975. . . . . .DLB-11

Kocbek, Edvard 1904-1981. . . . . .DLB-147

Koch, Howard 1902- DLB-26

Koch, Kenneth 1925- DLB-5

Kōda, Rohan 1867-1947. . . . . .DLB-180

Koenigsberg, Moses 1879-1945 . . . . .DLB-25

Koeppen, Wolfgang 1906-1996. . . . . .DLB-69

Koertge, Ronald 1940- DLB-105

Koestler, Arthur 1905-1983 . . . . Y-83

Kohn, John S. Van E. 1906-1976 and
Papantonio, Michael 1907-1978. . . . . .DLB-187

Kokoschka, Oskar 1886-1980 . . . . .DLB-124

Kolb, Annette 1870-1967 . . . . .DLB-66

Kolbenheyer, Erwin Guido
1878-1962 . . . . .DLB-66, 124

Kolleritsch, Alfred 1931- DLB-85

Kolodny, Annette 1941- DLB-67

Kol'tsov, Aleksei Vasil'evich
1809-1842 . . . . .DLB-205

Komarov, Matvei circa 1730-1812. . . . . . .DLB-150

Komroff, Manuel 1890-1974 . . . . .DLB-4

Komunyakaa, Yusef 1947- DLB-120

Koneski, Blaže 1921-1993 . . . . .DLB-181

Konigsburg, E. L. 1930- DLB-52

Konparu Zenchiku 1405-1468?. DLB-203

Konrád, György 1933- DLB-232

Konrad von Würzburg
circa 1230-1287 . . . . .DLB-138

Konstantinov, Aleko 1863-1897. . . . . . . .DLB-147

Konwicki, Tadeusz 1926- DLB-232

Kooser, Ted 1939- DLB-105

Kopit, Arthur 1937- DLB-7

Kops, Bernard 1926?- DLB-13

Kornbluth, C. M. 1923-1958. . . . . .DLB-8

Körner, Theodor 1791-1813 . . . . .DLB-90

Kornfeld, Paul 1889-1942 . . . . .DLB-118

Kosinski, Jerzy 1933-1991 . . . . DLB-2; Y-82

Kosmač, Ciril 1910-1980 . . . . .DLB-181

Kosovel, Srečko 1904-1926 . . . . .DLB-147

Kostrov, Ermil Ivanovich 1755-1796 . . . . .DLB-150

Kotzebue, August von 1761-1819 . . . . . . .DLB-94

Kotzwinkle, William 1938- DLB-173

Kovačić, Ante 1854-1889. . . . . .DLB-147

Kovič, Kajetan 1931- DLB-181

Kozlov, Ivan Ivanovich 1779-1840. . . . . . .DLB-205

Kraf, Elaine 1946- Y-81

Kramer, Jane 1938- DLB-185

Kramer, Mark 1944- DLB-185

Kranjčević, Silvije Strahimir 1865-1908. . .DLB-147

Krasko, Ivan 1876-1958. . . . . .DLB-215

Krasna, Norman 1909-1984 . . . . .DLB-26

Kraus, Hans Peter 1907-1988. . . . . .DLB-187

Kraus, Karl 1874-1936. . . . . .DLB-118

Krauss, Ruth 1911-1993 . . . . .DLB-52

Kreisel, Henry 1922- DLB-88

Kreuder, Ernst 1903-1972 . . . . .DLB-69

Krėvė-Mickevičius, Vincas 1882-1954 . . .DLB-220

Kreymborg, Alfred 1883-1966. . . . . . . .DLB-4, 54

Krieger, Murray 1923- DLB-67

Krim, Seymour 1922-1989 . . . . .DLB-16

Kristensen, Tom 1893-1974. . . . . .DLB-214

Krleža, Miroslav 1893-1981. . . . . .DLB-147

Krock, Arthur 1886-1974. . . . . .DLB-29

Kroetsch, Robert 1927- DLB-53

Kross, Jaan 1920- DLB-232

Krúdy, Gyula 1878-1933 . . . . .DLB-215

Krutch, Joseph Wood 1893-1970. . . . .DLB-63, 206

Krylov, Ivan Andreevich 1769-1844 . . . . .DLB-150

Kubin, Alfred 1877-1959 . . . . .DLB-81

Kubrick, Stanley 1928-1999. . . . . .DLB-26

Kudrun circa 1230-1240 . . . . .DLB-138

Kuffstein, Hans Ludwig von
1582-1656 . . . . .DLB-164

Kuhlmann, Quirinus 1651-1689 . . . . .DLB-168

Kuhnau, Johann 1660-1722 . . . . .DLB-168

Kukol'nik, Nestor Vasil'evich
1809-1868 . . . . .DLB-205

Kukučín, Martin 1860-1928 . . . . .DLB-215

Kumin, Maxine 1925- DLB-5

Kuncewicz, Maria 1895-1989 . . . . .DLB-215

Kundera, Milan 1929- DLB-232

Kunene, Mazisi 1930- DLB-117

Kunikida, Doppo 1869-1908 . . . . .DLB-180

Kunitz, Stanley 1905- DLB-48

Kunjufu, Johari M. (see Amini, Johari M.)

Kunnert, Gunter 1929- DLB-75

Kunze, Reiner 1933- DLB-75

Kupferberg, Tuli 1923- DLB-16

Kurahashi Yumiko 1935- DLB-182

Kureishi, Hanif 1954- DLB-194

Kürnberger, Ferdinand 1821-1879 ...... DLB-129

Kurz, Isolde 1853-1944............... DLB-66

Kusenberg, Kurt 1904-1983 .... DLB-69

Kushner, Tony 1956- DLB-228

Kuttner, Henry 1915-1958 .... DLB-8

Kyd, Thomas 1558-1594 .... DLB-62

Kyffin, Maurice circa 1560?-1598.... DLB-136

Kyger, Joanne 1934- DLB-16

Kyne, Peter B. 1880-1957............. DLB-78

Kyōgoku Tamekane 1254-1332 .... DLB-203

L

L. E. L. (see Landon, Letitia Elizabeth)

Laberge, Albert 1871-1960 .... DLB-68

Laberge, Marie 1950- DLB-60

Labiche, Eugène 1815-1888 .... DLB-192

Labrunie, Gerard (see Nerval, Gerard de)

La Capria, Raffaele 1922- DLB-196

Lacombe, Patrice
        (see Trullier-Lacombe, Joseph Patrice)

Lacretelle, Jacques de 1888-1985 .... DLB-65

Lacy, Ed 1911-1968 .... DLB-226

Lacy, Sam 1903- DLB-171

Ladd, Joseph Brown 1764-1786 .... DLB-37

La Farge, Oliver 1901-1963 .... DLB-9

Lafferty, R. A. 1914- DLB-8

La Flesche, Francis 1857-1932.........DLB-175

Laforge, Jules 1860-1887............. DLB-217

Lagorio, Gina 1922- DLB-196

La Guma, Alex 1925-1985 ....DLB-117, 225

Lahaise, Guillaume (see Delahaye, Guy)

Lahontan, Louis-Armand de Lom d'Arce,
        Baron de 1666-1715? DLB-99

Laing, Kojo 1946- DLB-157

Laird, Carobeth 1895- Y-82

Laird and Lee..................... DLB-49

Lalić, Ivan V. 1931-1996 .... DLB-181

Lalić, Mihailo 1914-1992 .... DLB-181

Lalonde, Michèle 1937- DLB-60

Lamantia, Philip 1927- DLB-16

Lamartine, Alphonse de 1790-1869 ..... DLB-217

Lamb, Lady Caroline 1785-1828 .... DLB-116

Lamb, Charles 1775-1834......DLB-93, 107, 163

Lamb, Mary 1764-1874................ DLB-163

Lambert, Betty 1933-1983 .... DLB-60

Lamming, George 1927- DLB-125

L'Amour, Louis 1908-1988 ...... DLB-206; Y-80

Lampman, Archibald 1861-1899 .... DLB-92

Lamson, Wolffe and Company DLB-49

Lancer Books DLB-46

Landesman, Jay 1919- and
        Landesman, Fran 1927- DLB-16

Landolfi, Tommaso 1908-1979.........DLB-177

Landon, Letitia Elizabeth 1802-1838 ..... DLB-96

Landor, Walter Savage 1775-1864 ....DLB-93, 107

Landry, Napoléon-P. 1884-1956......... DLB-92

Lane, Charles 1800-1870 .... DLB-1, 223

Lane, John, Company DLB-49

Lane, Laurence W. 1890-1967 .... DLB-91

Lane, M. Travis 1934- DLB-60

Lane, Patrick 1939- DLB-53

Lane, Pinkie Gordon 1923- DLB-41

Laney, Al 1896-1988 ....DLB-4, 171

Lang, Andrew 1844-1912...... DLB-98, 141, 184

Langevin, André 1927- DLB-60

Langgässer, Elisabeth 1899-1950 .... DLB-69

Langhorne, John 1735-1779 .... DLB-109

Langland, William
        circa 1330-circa 1400 .... DLB-146

Langton, Anna 1804-1893 .... DLB-99

Lanham, Edwin 1904-1979............. DLB-4

Lanier, Sidney 1842-1881....... DLB-64; DS-13

Lanyer, Aemilia 1569-1645 .... DLB-121

Lapointe, Gatien 1931-1983 .... DLB-88

Lapointe, Paul-Marie 1929- DLB-88

Larcom, Lucy 1824-1893 .... DLB-221

Lardner, John 1912-1960 ....DLB-171

Lardner, Ring
        1885-1933 ....DLB-11, 25, 86, 171; DS-16

Lardner 100: Ring Lardner
        Centennial Symposium Y-85

Lardner, Ring, Jr. 1915- DLB-26

Larkin, Philip 1922-1985 .... DLB-27

La Roche, Sophie von 1730-1807 .... DLB-94

La Rocque, Gilbert 1943-1984 .... DLB-60

Laroque de Roquebrune, Robert
        (see Roquebrune, Robert de)

Larrick, Nancy 1910- DLB-61

Larsen, Nella 1893-1964.............. DLB-51

La Sale, Antoine de
        circa 1386-1460/1467 .... DLB-208

Lasker-Schüler, Else 1869-1945 ..... DLB-66, 124

Lasnier, Rina 1915- DLB-88

Lassalle, Ferdinand 1825-1864........ DLB-129

Latham, Robert 1912-1995........... DLB-201

Lathrop, Dorothy P. 1891-1980 .... DLB-22

Lathrop, George Parsons 1851-1898 ..... DLB-71

Lathrop, John, Jr. 1772-1820............ DLB-37

Latimer, Hugh 1492?-1555............. DLB-136

Latimore, Jewel Christine McLawler
        (see Amini, Johari M.)

Latymer, William 1498-1583 .... DLB-132

Laube, Heinrich 1806-1884 .... DLB-133

Laud, William 1573-1645............. DLB-213

Laughlin, James 1914-1997............. DLB-48

        James Laughlin Tributes................ Y-97

        Conversations with Publishers IV:
        An Interview with James Laughlin....... Y-96

Laumer, Keith 1925- DLB-8

Lauremberg, Johann 1590-1658........ DLB-164

Laurence, Margaret 1926-1987 .... DLB-53

Laurentius von Schnüffis 1633-1702..... DLB-168

Laurents, Arthur 1918- DLB-26

Laurie, Annie (see Black, Winifred)

Laut, Agnes Christiana 1871-1936 .... DLB-92

Lauterbach, Ann 1942- DLB-193

Lautreamont, Isidore Lucien Ducasse, Comte de
        1846-1870.....................DLB-217

Lavater, Johann Kaspar 1741-1801....... DLB-97

Lavin, Mary 1912-1996 .... DLB-15

Law, John (see Harkness, Margaret)

Lawes, Henry 1596-1662 .... DLB-126

Lawless, Anthony (see MacDonald, Philip)

Lawrence, D. H.
        1885-1930 ......DLB-10, 19, 36, 98, 162, 195

Lawrence, David 1888-1973............ DLB-29

Lawrence, Jerome 1915- and
        Lee, Robert E. 1918-1994 .... DLB-228

Lawrence, Seymour 1926-1994 .... Y-94

Lawrence, T. E. 1888-1935 .... DLB-195

Lawson, George 1598-1678 .... DLB-213

Lawson, Henry 1867-1922 .... DLB-230

Lawson, John ?-1711................. DLB-24

Lawson, John Howard 1894-1977 ...... DLB-228

Lawson, Louisa Albury 1848-1920..... DLB-230

Lawson, Robert 1892-1957............. DLB-22

Lawson, Victor F. 1850-1925 .... DLB-25

Layard, Sir Austen Henry
        1817-1894 .... DLB-166

Layton, Irving 1912- DLB-88

LaZamon flourished circa 1200 .... DLB-146

Lazarević, Laza K. 1851-1890 ....DLB-147

Lazarus, George 1904-1997 .... DLB-201

Lazhechnikov, Ivan Ivanovich
        1792-1869.................... DLB-198

Lea, Henry Charles 1825-1909 .... DLB-47

Lea, Sydney 1942- DLB-120

Lea, Tom 1907- DLB-6

Leacock, John 1729-1802 .... DLB-31

Leacock, Stephen 1869-1944 .... DLB-92

Lead, Jane Ward 1623-1704 .... DLB-131

Leadenhall Press.................... DLB-106

Leakey, Caroline Woolmer 1827-1881... DLB-230

Leapor, Mary 1722-1746.............. DLB-109

Lear, Edward 1812-1888 ....DLB-32, 163, 166

Leary, Timothy 1920-1996 .... DLB-16

Leary, W. A., and Company DLB-49

Léautaud, Paul 1872-1956 .... DLB-65

Leavitt, David 1961- DLB-130

Leavitt and Allen DLB-49

Le Blond, Mrs. Aubrey 1861-1934......DLB-174

le Carré, John 1931- DLB-87

Lécavelé, Roland (see Dorgeles, Roland)

Lechlitner, Ruth 1901- DLB-48

Leclerc, Félix 1914- DLB-60

Le Clézio, J. M. G. 1940- DLB-83

Lectures on Rhetoric and Belles Lettres (1783),
by Hugh Blair [excerpts] DLB-31

Leder, Rudolf (see Hermlin, Stephan)

Lederer, Charles 1910-1976............DLB-26

Ledwidge, Francis 1887-1917...........DLB-20

Lee, Dennis 1939- DLB-53

Lee, Don L. (see Madhubuti, Haki R.)

Lee, George W. 1894-1976.............DLB-51

Lee, Harper 1926- DLB-6

Lee, Harriet (1757-1851) and
Lee, Sophia (1750-1824) DLB-39

Lee, Laurie 1914-1997 ....DLB-27

Lee, Li-Young 1957- DLB-165

Lee, Manfred B. (see Dannay, Frederic, and
Manfred B. Lee)

Lee, Nathaniel circa 1645 - 1692 ....DLB-80

Lee, Sir Sidney 1859-1926........DLB-149, 184

Lee, Sir Sidney, "Principles of Biography," in
Elizabethan and Other Essays DLB-149

Lee, Vernon
1856-1935 ....DLB-57, 153, 156, 174, 178

Lee and Shepard DLB-49

Le Fanu, Joseph Sheridan
1814-1873 .... DLB-21, 70, 159, 178

Leffland, Ella 1931- Y-84

le Fort, Gertrud von 1876-1971 ....DLB-66

Le Gallienne, Richard 1866-1947.........DLB-4

Legaré, Hugh Swinton 1797-1843 ...DLB-3, 59, 73

Legaré, James M. 1823-1859 ....DLB-3

The Legends of the Saints and a Medieval
Christian Worldview DLB-148

Léger, Antoine-J. 1880-1950 ....DLB-88

Le Guin, Ursula K. 1929- DLB-8, 52

Lehman, Ernest 1920- DLB-44

Lehmann, John 1907- DLB-27, 100

Lehmann, John, Limited DLB-112

Lehmann, Rosamond 1901-1990 ....DLB-15

Lehmann, Wilhelm 1882-1968 ....DLB-56

Leiber, Fritz 1910-1992 ....DLB-8

Leibniz, Gottfried Wilhelm 1646-1716....DLB-168

Leicester University Press DLB-112

Leigh, W. R. 1866-1955 ....DLB-188

Leinster, Murray 1896-1975............DLB-8

Leisewitz, Johann Anton 1752-1806.......DLB-94

Leitch, Maurice 1933- DLB-14

Leithauser, Brad 1943- DLB-120

Leland, Charles G. 1824-1903..........DLB-11

Leland, John 1503?-1552............DLB-136 .

Lemay, Pamphile 1837-1918 ....DLB-99

Lemelin, Roger 1919- DLB-88

Lemercier, Louis-Jean-Népomucène
1771-1840 ....DLB-192

Le Moine, James MacPherson
1825-1912 ....DLB-99

Lemon, Mark 1809-1870...........DLB-163

Le Moyne, Jean 1913- DLB-88

Lemperly, Paul 1858-1939............DLB-187

L'Engle, Madeleine 1918- DLB-52

Lennart, Isobel 1915-1971 ....DLB-44

Lennox, Charlotte
1729 or 1730-1804................DLB-39

Lenox, James 1800-1880 ....DLB-140

Lenski, Lois 1893-1974 ....DLB-22

Lenz, Hermann 1913-1998 ....DLB-69

Lenz, J. M. R. 1751-1792 ....DLB-94

Lenz, Siegfried 1926- DLB-75

Leonard, Elmore 1925- DLB-173, 226

Leonard, Hugh 1926- DLB-13

Leonard, William Ellery 1876-1944......DLB-54

Leonowens, Anna 1834-1914 ......DLB-99, 166

LePan, Douglas 1914- DLB-88

Lepik, Kalju 1920-1999 ....DLB-232

Leprohon, Rosanna Eleanor 1829-1879....DLB-99

Le Queux, William 1864-1927 ....DLB-70

Lermontov, Mikhail Iur'evich
1814-1841 ....DLB-205

Lerner, Max 1902-1992...............DLB-29

Lernet-Holenia, Alexander 1897-1976.....DLB-85

Le Rossignol, James 1866-1969 ....DLB-92

Lescarbot, Marc circa 1570-1642 ....DLB-99

LeSeur, William Dawson 1840-1917 ......DLB-92

LeSieg, Theo. (see Geisel, Theodor Seuss)

Leslie, Doris before 1902-1982 ....DLB-191

Leslie, Eliza 1787-1858 ....DLB-202

Leslie, Frank 1821-1880.............DLB-43, 79

Leslie, Frank, Publishing House DLB-49

Leśmian, Bolesław 1878-1937 ....DLB-215

Lesperance, John 1835?-1891 ....DLB-99

Lessing, Bruno 1870-1940 ....DLB-28

Lessing, Doris 1919- DLB-15, 139; Y-85

Lessing, Gotthold Ephraim 1729-1781.....DLB-97

Lettau, Reinhard 1929- DLB-75

Letter from Japan...................Y-94, Y-98

Letter from London Y-96

Letter to [Samuel] Richardson on *Clarissa*
(1748), by Henry Fielding DLB-39

A Letter to the Editor of *The Irish Times*......Y-97

Lever, Charles 1806-1872 ....DLB-21

Leverson, Ada 1862-1933 ....DLB-153

Levertov, Denise 1923-1997 ....DLB-5, 165

Levi, Peter 1931- DLB-40

Levi, Primo 1919-1987 ....DLB-177

Levien, Sonya 1888-1960..............DLB-44

Levin, Meyer 1905-1981 ....DLB-9, 28; Y-81

Levine, Norman 1923- DLB-88

Levine, Philip 1928- DLB-5

Levis, Larry 1946- DLB-120

Levy, Amy 1861-1889 ....DLB-156

Levy, Benn Wolfe 1900-1973 ......DLB-13; Y-81

Lewald, Fanny 1811-1889 ....DLB-129

Lewes, George Henry 1817-1878.....DLB-55, 144

"Criticism In Relation To
Novels" (1863) DLB-21

The Principles of Success in Literature
(1865) [excerpt]..................DLB-57

Lewis, Agnes Smith 1843-1926 ....DLB-174

Lewis, Alfred H. 1857-1914 ....DLB-25, 186

Lewis, Alun 1915-1944 ....DLB-20, 162

Lewis, C. Day (see Day Lewis, C.)

Lewis, C. S. 1898-1963 .... DLB-15, 100, 160

Lewis, Charles B. 1842-1924...........DLB-11

Lewis, Henry Clay 1825-1850...........DLB-3

Lewis, Janet 1899-1999 ....Y-87

Lewis, Matthew Gregory
1775-1818 .... DLB-39, 158, 178

Lewis, Meriwether 1774-1809 and
Clark, William 1770-1838......DLB-183, 186

Lewis, Norman 1908- DLB-204

Lewis, R. W. B. 1917- DLB-111

Lewis, Richard circa 1700-1734 ....DLB-24

Lewis, Sinclair 1885-1951 ......DLB-9, 102; DS-1

Sinclair Lewis Centennial Conference Y-85

Lewis, Wilmarth Sheldon 1895-1979.....DLB-140

Lewis, Wyndham 1882-1957............DLB-15

Lewisohn, Ludwig 1882-1955 ...DLB-4, 9, 28, 102

Leyendecker, J. C. 1874-1951 ....DLB-188

Lezama Lima, José 1910-1976 ....DLB-113

Libbey, Laura Jean 1862-1924.........DLB-221

The Library of America................DLB-46

The Licensing Act of 1737 ....DLB-84

Lichfield, Leonard I [publishing house]...DLB-170

Lichtenberg, Georg Christoph 1742-1799 ..DLB-94

The Liddle Collection Y-97

Lieb, Fred 1888-1980................DLB-171

Liebling, A. J. 1904-1963............. DLB-4, 171

Lieutenant Murray (see Ballou, Maturin Murray)

Lighthall, William Douw 1857-1954 ......DLB-92

Lilar, Françoise (see Mallet-Joris, Françoise)

Lili'uokalani, Queen 1838-1917........DLB-221

Lillo, George 1691-1739..............DLB-84

Lilly, J. K., Jr. 1893-1966.............DLB-140

Lilly, Wait and Company DLB-49

Lily, William circa 1468-1522 ....DLB-132

Limited Editions Club DLB-46

Limón, Graciela 1938- DLB-209

Lincoln and Edmands DLB-49

Lindesay, Ethel Forence
(see Richardson, Henry Handel)

Lindsay, Alexander William, Twenty-fifth Earl
of Crawford 1812-1880.............DLB-184

Lindsay, Sir David circa 1485-1555......DLB-132

Lindsay, Jack 1900- Y-84

Lindsay, Lady (Caroline Blanche Elizabeth Fitzroy
Lindsay) 1844-1912...............DLB-199

Lindsay, Vachel 1879-1931 ....DLB-54

Linebarger, Paul Myron Anthony
(see Smith, Cordwainer)

Link, Arthur S. 1920-1998 . . . . DLB-17

Linn, John Blair 1777-1804 . . . . DLB-37

Lins, Osman 1924-1978 . . . . DLB-145

Linton, Eliza Lynn 1822-1898 . . . . DLB-18

Linton, William James 1812-1897 . . . . DLB-32

Lintot, Barnaby Bernard
  [publishing house] DLB-170

Lion Books DLB-46

Lionni, Leo 1910-1999 . . . . DLB-61

Lippard, George 1822-1854 . . . . DLB-202

Lippincott, J. B., Company DLB-49

Lippincott, Sara Jane Clarke 1823-1904 . . . DLB-43

Lippmann, Walter 1889-1974 . . . . DLB-29

Lipton, Lawrence 1898-1975 . . . . DLB-16

Liscow, Christian Ludwig 1701-1760 . . . . . DLB-97

Lish, Gordon 1934- DLB-130

Lisle, Charles-Marie-René Leconte de
  1818-1894. . . . . DLB-217

Lispector, Clarice 1925-1977. . . . . DLB-113

A Literary Archaelogist Digs On: A Brief
  Interview with Michael Reynolds by
  Michael Rogers Y-99

The Literary Chronicle and Weekly Review
  1819-1828 . . . . DLB-110

Literary Documents: William Faulkner
  and the People-to-People Program Y-86

Literary Documents II: *Library Journal*
  Statements and Questionnaires from
  First Novelists. Y-87

Literary Effects of World War II
  [British novel] DLB-15

Literary Prizes [British] DLB-15

Literary Research Archives: The Humanities
  Research Center, University of Texas Y-82

Literary Research Archives II: Berg Collection
  of English and American Literature of
  the New York Public Library Y-83

Literary Research Archives III:
  The Lilly Library Y-84

Literary Research Archives IV:
  The John Carter Brown Library Y-85

Literary Research Archives V:
  Kent State Special Collections Y-86

Literary Research Archives VI: The Modern
  Literary Manuscripts Collection in the
  Special Collections of the Washington
  University Libraries Y-87

Literary Research Archives VII:
  The University of Virginia Libraries Y-91

Literary Research Archives VIII:
  The Henry E. Huntington Library Y-92

Literary Research Archives IX:
  Special Collections at Boston University . . Y-99

The Literary Scene and Situation and . . . Who
  (Besides Oprah) Really Runs American
  Literature? Y-99

Literary Societies Y-98, Y-99

"Literary Style" (1857), by William
  Forsyth [excerpt]. DLB-57

Literatura Chicanesca: The View From
  Without DLB-82

Literature at Nurse, or Circulating Morals (1885),
  by George Moore DLB-18

Littell, Eliakim 1797-1870 . . . . DLB-79

Littell, Robert S. 1831-1896 . . . . DLB-79

Little, Brown and Company DLB-49

Little Magazines and Newspapers DS-15

The Little Review 1914-1929 . . . . DS-15

Littlewood, Joan 1914- DLB-13

Lively, Penelope 1933- DLB-14, 161, 207

Liverpool University Press DLB-112

The Lives of the Poets DLB-142

Livesay, Dorothy 1909- DLB-68

Livesay, Florence Randal 1874-1953 . . . . . DLB-92

"Living in Ruin," by Gerald Stern DLB-105

Livings, Henry 1929-1998 . . . . DLB-13

Livingston, Anne Howe 1763-1841 . . . DLB-37, 200

Livingston, Myra Cohn 1926-1996 . . . . . . DLB-61

Livingston, William 1723-1790 . . . . DLB-31

Livingstone, David 1813-1873 . . . . DLB-166

Livingstone, Douglas 1932-1996 . . . . DLB-225

Livy 59 B.C.-A.D. 17 . . . . DLB-211

Liyong, Taban lo (see Taban lo Liyong)

Lizárraga, Sylvia S. 1925- DLB-82

Llewellyn, Richard 1906-1983 . . . . DLB-15

Lloyd, Edward [publishing house] DLB-106

Lobel, Arnold 1933- DLB-61

Lochridge, Betsy Hopkins (see Fancher, Betsy)

Locke, David Ross 1833-1888 . . . . DLB-11, 23

Locke, John 1632-1704 . . . . DLB-31, 101, 213

Locke, Richard Adams 1800-1871 . . . . DLB-43

Locker-Lampson, Frederick
  1821-1895 . . . . DLB-35, 184

Lockhart, John Gibson
  1794-1854. . . . . DLB-110, 116 144

Lockridge, Ross, Jr. 1914-1948 . . . . . DLB-143; Y-80

Locrine and Selimus DLB-62

Lodge, David 1935- DLB-14, 194

Lodge, George Cabot 1873-1909 . . . . DLB-54

Lodge, Henry Cabot 1850-1924 . . . . DLB-47

Lodge, Thomas 1558-1625 . . . . DLB-172

  From *Defence of Poetry* (1579) DLB-172

Loeb, Harold 1891-1974 . . . . DLB-4

Loeb, William 1905-1981 . . . . DLB-127

Lofting, Hugh 1886-1947 . . . . DLB-160

Logan, Deborah Norris 1761-1839 . . . . . . DLB-200

Logan, James 1674-1751 . . . . DLB-24, 140

Logan, John 1923- DLB-5

Logan, Martha Daniell 1704?-1779 . . . . . . DLB-200

Logan, William 1950- DLB-120

Logau, Friedrich von 1605-1655 . . . . DLB-164

Logue, Christopher 1926- DLB-27

Lohenstein, Daniel Casper von
  1635-1683 . . . . DLB-168

Lomonosov, Mikhail Vasil'evich
  1711-1765 . . . . DLB-150

London, Jack 1876-1916 . . . . . . DLB-8, 12, 78, 212

The London Magazine 1820-1829 . . . . DLB-110

Long, H., and Brother DLB-49

Long, Haniel 1888-1956 . . . . DLB-45

Long, Ray 1878-1935 . . . . DLB-137

Longfellow, Henry Wadsworth
  1807-1882 . . . . DLB-1, 59

Longfellow, Samuel 1819-1892 . . . . DLB-1

Longford, Elizabeth 1906- DLB-155

Longinus circa first century DLB-176

Longley, Michael 1939- DLB-40

Longman, T. [publishing house] DLB-154

Longmans, Green and Company DLB-49

Longmore, George 1793?-1867 . . . . DLB-99

Longstreet, Augustus Baldwin
  1790-1870 . . . . DLB-3, 11, 74

Longworth, D. [publishing house] DLB-49

Lonsdale, Frederick 1881-1954 . . . . DLB-10

A Look at the Contemporary Black Theatre
  Movement DLB-38

Loos, Anita 1893-1981 . . . . . DLB-11, 26, 228; Y-81

Lopate, Phillip 1943- Y-80

López, Diana
  (see Isabella, Ríos)

López, Josefina 1969- DLB-209

Loranger, Jean-Aubert 1896-1942 . . . . DLB-92

Lorca, Federico García 1898-1936 . . . . . . DLB-108

Lord, John Keast 1818-1872 . . . . DLB-99

The Lord Chamberlain's Office and Stage
  Censorship in England DLB-10

Lorde, Audre 1934-1992 . . . . DLB-41

Lorimer, George Horace 1867-1939 . . . . . . DLB-91

Loring, A. K. [publishing house] DLB-49

Loring and Mussey. DLB-46

Lorris, Guillaume de (see *Roman de la Rose*)

Lossing, Benson J. 1813-1891 . . . . DLB-30

Lothar, Ernst 1890-1974 . . . . DLB-81

Lothrop, D., and Company DLB-49

Lothrop, Harriet M. 1844-1924 . . . . DLB-42

Loti, Pierre 1850-1923 . . . . DLB-123

Lotichius Secundus, Petrus 1528-1560 . . . DLB-179

Lott, Emeline ?-? DLB-166

Louisiana State University Press Y-97

The Lounger, no. 20 (1785), by Henry
  Mackenzie DLB-39

Lounsbury, Thomas R. 1838-1915 . . . . . . DLB-71

Louÿs, Pierre 1870-1925 . . . . DLB-123

Lovelace, Earl 1935- DLB-125

Lovelace, Richard 1618-1657? DLB-131

Lovell, Coryell and Company DLB-49

Lovell, John W., Company DLB-49

Lover, Samuel 1797-1868 . . . . DLB-159, 190

Lovesey, Peter 1936- DLB-87

Lovinescu, Eugen 1881-1943 . . . . DLB-220

Lovingood, Sut
  (see Harris, George Washington)

Low, Samuel 1765-? DLB-37

Lowell, Amy 1874-1925 . . . . DLB-54, 140

Lowell, James Russell
  1819-1891 . . . . DLB-1, 11, 64, 79, 189

Lowell, Robert 1917-1977. . . . . .DLB-5, 169

Lowenfels, Walter 1897-1976. . . . . .DLB-4

Lowndes, Marie Belloc 1868-1947. . . . . . .DLB-70

Lowndes, William Thomas 1798-1843 . . .DLB-184

Lownes, Humphrey [publishing house]. . .DLB-170

Lowry, Lois 1937- DLB-52

Lowry, Malcolm 1909-1957. . . . . .DLB-15

Lowther, Pat 1935-1975. . . . . .DLB-53

Loy, Mina 1882-1966. . . . . .DLB-4, 54

Lozeau, Albert 1878-1924 . . . . .DLB-92

Lubbock, Percy 1879-1965. . . . . .DLB-149

Lucan A.D. 39-A.D. 65 . . . . .DLB-211

Lucas, E. V. 1868-1938 . . . . .DLB-98, 149, 153

Lucas, Fielding, Jr. [publishing house] DLB-49

Luce, Clare Booth 1903-1987 . . . . .DLB-228

Luce, Henry R. 1898-1967. . . . . .DLB-91

Luce, John W., and Company. DLB-46

Lucian circa 120-180 . . . . DLB-176

Lucie-Smith, Edward 1933- DLB-40

Lucilius circa 180 B.C.-102/101 B.C. DLB-211

Lucini, Gian Pietro 1867-1914 . . . . .DLB-114

Lucretius circa 94 B.C.-circa 49 B.C. DLB-211

Luder, Peter circa 1415-1472 . . . . .DLB-179

Ludlum, Robert 1927- Y-82

Ludus de Antichristo circa 1160 . . . . .DLB-148

Ludvigson, Susan 1942- DLB-120

Ludwig, Jack 1922- DLB-60

Ludwig, Otto 1813-1865 . . . . .DLB-129

Ludwigslied 881 or 882 . . . . .DLB-148

Luera, Yolanda 1953- DLB-122

Luft, Lya 1938- DLB-145

Lugansky, Kazak Vladimir
  (see Dal', Vladimir Ivanovich)

Lukács, György 1885-1971 . . . . .DLB-215

Luke, Peter 1919- DLB-13

Lummis, Charles F. 1859-1928 . . . . .DLB-186

Lupton, F. M., Company. DLB-49

Lupus of Ferrières
  circa 805-circa 862. . . . . .DLB-148

Lurie, Alison 1926- DLB-2

Lustig, Arnošt 1926- DLB-232

Luther, Martin 1483-1546 . . . . .DLB-179

Luzi, Mario 1914- DLB-128

L'vov, Nikolai Aleksandrovich
  1751-1803 . . . . .DLB-150

Lyall, Gavin 1932- DLB-87

Lydgate, John circa 1370-1450. . . . . .DLB-146

Lyly, John circa 1554-1606 . . . . .DLB-62, 167

Lynch, Patricia 1898-1972 . . . . .DLB-160

Lynch, Richard flourished 1596-1601 . . . .DLB-172

Lynd, Robert 1879-1949 . . . . .DLB-98

Lyon, Matthew 1749-1822. . . . . .DLB-43

Lysias circa 459 B.C.-circa 380 B.C. DLB-176

Lytle, Andrew 1902-1995 . . . . .DLB-6; Y-95

Lytton, Edward
  (see Bulwer-Lytton, Edward)

Lytton, Edward Robert Bulwer
  1831-1891 .DLB-32

M

Maass, Joachim 1901-1972. . . . . .DLB-69

Mabie, Hamilton Wright 1845-1916 . . . . . .DLB-71

Mac A'Ghobhainn, Iain (see Smith, Iain Crichton)

MacArthur, Charles 1895-1956. . . . .DLB-7, 25, 44

Macaulay, Catherine 1731-1791. . . . . . . .DLB-104

Macaulay, David 1945- DLB-61

Macaulay, Rose 1881-1958 . . . . .DLB-36

Macaulay, Thomas Babington
  1800-1859 . . . . .DLB-32, 55

Macaulay Company DLB-46

MacBeth, George 1932- DLB-40

Macbeth, Madge 1880-1965 . . . . .DLB-92

MacCaig, Norman 1910-1996 . . . . .DLB-27

MacDiarmid, Hugh 1892-1978 . . . . .DLB-20

MacDonald, Cynthia 1928- DLB-105

MacDonald, George 1824-1905. . . .DLB-18, 163, 178

MacDonald, John D. 1916-1986 . . . . .DLB-8; Y-86

MacDonald, Philip 1899?-1980 . . . . .DLB-77

Macdonald, Ross (see Millar, Kenneth)

MacDonald, Wilson 1880-1967. . . . . .DLB-92

Macdonald and Company (Publishers) . . .DLB-112

MacEwen, Gwendolyn 1941- DLB-53

Macfadden, Bernarr 1868-1955. . . . . .DLB-25, 91

MacGregor, John 1825-1892 . . . . .DLB-166

MacGregor, Mary Esther (see Keith, Marian)

Machado, Antonio 1875-1939 . . . . .DLB-108

Machado, Manuel 1874-1947 . . . . .DLB-108

Machar, Agnes Maule 1837-1927. . . . . . . .DLB-92

Machaut, Guillaume de
  circa 1300-1377 . . . . .DLB-208

Machen, Arthur Llewelyn Jones
  1863-1947 . . . . .DLB-36, 156, 178

MacInnes, Colin 1914-1976 . . . . .DLB-14

MacInnes, Helen 1907-1985. . . . . .DLB-87

Mačiulis, Jonas (see Maironis, Jonas)

Mack, Maynard 1909- DLB-111

Mackall, Leonard L. 1879-1937 . . . . .DLB-140

MacKaye, Percy 1875-1956 . . . . .DLB-54

Macken, Walter 1915-1967 . . . . .DLB-13

Mackenzie, Alexander 1763-1820 . . . . . . .DLB-99

Mackenzie, Alexander Slidell
  1803-1848 .DLB-183

Mackenzie, Compton 1883-1972 . . . . .DLB-34, 100

Mackenzie, Henry 1745-1831 . . . . .DLB-39

Mackenzie, William 1758-1828 . . . . .DLB-187

Mackey, Nathaniel 1947- DLB-169

Mackey, Shena 1944- DLB-231

Mackey, William Wellington
  1937- DLB-38

Mackintosh, Elizabeth (see Tey, Josephine)

Mackintosh, Sir James 1765-1832 . . . . . .DLB-158

Maclaren, Ian (see Watson, John)

Macklin, Charles 1699-1797. . . . . .DLB-89

MacLean, Katherine Anne 1925- DLB-8

Maclean, Norman 1902-1990 . . . . .DLB-206

MacLeish, Archibald
  1892-1982 . . . . .DLB-4, 7, 45, 228; Y-82

MacLennan, Hugh 1907-1990 . . . . .DLB-68

MacLeod, Alistair 1936- DLB-60

Macleod, Fiona (see Sharp, William)

Macleod, Norman 1906-1985 . . . . .DLB-4

Mac Low, Jackson 1922- DLB-193

Macmillan and Company DLB-106

The Macmillan Company DLB-49

Macmillan's English Men of Letters,
  First Series (1878-1892) DLB-144

MacNamara, Brinsley 1890-1963 . . . . . . .DLB-10

MacNeice, Louis 1907-1963. . . . . .DLB-10, 20

MacPhail, Andrew 1864-1938 . . . . .DLB-92

Macpherson, James 1736-1796 . . . . .DLB-109

Macpherson, Jay 1931- DLB-53

Macpherson, Jeanie 1884-1946 . . . . .DLB-44

Macrae Smith Company DLB-46

Macrone, John [publishing house] DLB-106

MacShane, Frank 1927-1999 . . . . .DLB-111

Macy-Masius .DLB-46

Madden, David 1933- DLB-6

Madden, Sir Frederic 1801-1873 . . . . . . .DLB-184

Maddow, Ben 1909-1992. . . . . .DLB-44

Maddux, Rachel 1912-1983. . . . . . .DLB-234; Y-93

Madgett, Naomi Long 1923- DLB-76

Madhubuti, Haki R. 1942- DLB-5, 41; DS-8

Madison, James 1751-1836 . . . . .DLB-37

Madsen, Svend Åge 1939- DLB-214

Maeterlinck, Maurice 1862-1949. . . . . . .DLB-192

Mafūz, Najīb 1911- Y-88

Magee, David 1905-1977 . . . . .DLB-187

Maginn, William 1794-1842 . . . . . .DLB-110, 159

Mahan, Alfred Thayer 1840-1914 . . . . . . .DLB-47

Maheux-Forcier, Louise 1929- DLB-60

Mahin, John Lee 1902-1984 . . . . .DLB-44

Mahon, Derek 1941- DLB-40

Maikov, Vasilii Ivanovich 1728-1778. . . . .DLB-150

Mailer, Norman 1923-
  . . . . . . DLB-2, 16, 28, 185; Y-80, Y-83; DS-3

Maillart, Ella 1903-1997. . . . . .DLB-195

Maillet, Adrienne 1885-1963 . . . . .DLB-68

Maillet, Antonine 1929- DLB-60

Maillu, David G. 1939- DLB-157

Maimonides, Moses 1138-1204 . . . . .DLB-115

Main Selections of the Book-of-the-Month
  Club, 1926-1945 . . . . .DLB-9

Main Trends in Twentieth-Century Book
  Clubs. DLB-46

Mainwaring, Daniel 1902-1977 . . . . .DLB-44

Mair, Charles 1838-1927 . . . . DLB-99

Maironis, Jonas 1862-1932 . . . . DLB-220

Mais, Roger 1905-1955 . . . . DLB-125

Major, Andre 1942- DLB-60

Major, Charles 1856-1913 . . . . DLB-202

Major, Clarence 1936- DLB-33

Major, Kevin 1949- DLB-60

Major Books DLB-46

Makemie, Francis circa 1658-1708 . . . . DLB-24

The Making of Americans Contract Y-98

The Making of a People, by
 J. M. Ritchie DLB-66

Maksimović, Desanka 1898-1993 . . . . DLB-147

Malamud, Bernard
 1914-1986 . . . . DLB-2, 28, 152; Y-80, Y-86

Mălăncioiu, Ileana 1940- DLB-232

Malerba, Luigi 1927- DLB-196

Malet, Lucas 1852-1931 . . . . DLB-153

Mallarmé, Stéphane 1842-1898 . . . . DLB-217

Malleson, Lucy Beatrice (see Gilbert, Anthony)

Mallet-Joris, Françoise 1930- DLB-83

Mallock, W. H. 1849-1923 . . . . DLB-18, 57

"Every Man His Own Poet; or,
 The Inspired Singer's Recipe
 Book" (1877) DLB-35

Malone, Dumas 1892-1986 . . . . DLB-17

Malone, Edmond 1741-1812 . . . . DLB-142

Malory, Sir Thomas
 circa 1400-1410 - 1471 . . . . DLB-146

Malraux, André 1901-1976 . . . . DLB-72

Malthus, Thomas Robert
 1766-1834 . . . . DLB-107, 158

Maltz, Albert 1908-1985 . . . . DLB-102

Malzberg, Barry N. 1939- DLB-8

Mamet, David 1947- DLB-7

Manaka, Matsemela 1956- DLB-157

Manchester University Press DLB-112

Mandel, Eli 1922- DLB-53

Mandeville, Bernard 1670-1733 . . . . DLB-101

Mandeville, Sir John
 mid fourteenth century DLB-146

Mandiargues, André Pieyre de 1909- . . DLB-83

Manea, Morman 1936- DLB-232

Manfred, Frederick 1912-1994 . . . . DLB-6, 212, 227

Manfredi, Gianfranco 1948- DLB-196

Mangan, Sherry 1904-1961 . . . . DLB-4

Manganelli, Giorgio 1922-1990 . . . . DLB-196

Manilius fl. first century A.D. DLB-211

Mankiewicz, Herman 1897-1953 . . . . DLB-26

Mankiewicz, Joseph L. 1909-1993 . . . . DLB-44

Mankowitz, Wolf 1924-1998 . . . . DLB-15

Manley, Delarivière 1672?-1724 . . . . . . DLB-39, 80

Preface to *The Secret History, of Queen Zarah,
 and the Zarazians* (1705) DLB-39

Mann, Abby 1927- DLB-44

Mann, Charles 1929-1998 . . . . Y-98

Mann, Heinrich 1871-1950 . . . . DLB-66, 118

Mann, Horace 1796-1859 . . . . DLB-1

Mann, Klaus 1906-1949 . . . . DLB-56

Mann, Thomas 1875-1955 . . . . DLB-66

Mann, William D'Alton 1839-1920 . . . . . DLB-137

Mannin, Ethel 1900-1984 . . . . DLB-191, 195

Manning, Emily (see Australie)

Manning, Marie 1873?-1945 . . . . DLB-29

Manning and Loring DLB-49

Mannyng, Robert
 flourished 1303-1338 . . . . DLB-146

Mano, D. Keith 1942- DLB-6

Manor Books DLB-46

Mansfield, Katherine 1888-1923 . . . . DLB-162

Manuel, Niklaus circa 1484-1530 . . . . . . DLB-179

Manzini, Gianna 1896-1974 . . . . DLB-177

Mapanje, Jack 1944- DLB-157

Maraini, Dacia 1936- DLB-196

March, William 1893-1954 . . . . DLB-9, 86

Marchand, Leslie A. 1900-1999 . . . . DLB-103

Marchant, Bessie 1862-1941 . . . . DLB-160

Marchessault, Jovette 1938- DLB-60

Marcinkevičius, Justinas 1930- DLB-232

Marcus, Frank 1928- DLB-13

Marden, Orison Swett 1850-1924 . . . . . . DLB-137

Marechera, Dambudzo 1952-1987 . . . . . . DLB-157

Marek, Richard, Books DLB-46

Mares, E. A. 1938- DLB-122

Margulies, Donald 1954- DLB-228

Mariani, Paul 1940- DLB-111

Marie de France flourished 1160-1178 . . . DLB-208

Marie-Victorin, Frère 1885-1944 . . . . DLB-92

Marin, Biagio 1891-1985 . . . . DLB-128

Marincovič, Ranko 1913- DLB-147

Marinetti, Filippo Tommaso
 1876-1944 . . . . DLB-114

Marion, Frances 1886-1973 . . . . DLB-44

Marius, Richard C. 1933-1999 . . . . Y-85

Markfield, Wallace 1926- DLB-2, 28

Markham, Edwin 1852-1940 . . . . DLB-54, 186

Markle, Fletcher 1921-1991 . . . . DLB-68; Y-91

Marlatt, Daphne 1942- DLB-60

Marlitt, E. 1825-1887 . . . . DLB-129

Marlowe, Christopher 1564-1593 . . . . DLB-62

Marlyn, John 1912- DLB-88

Marmion, Shakerley 1603-1639 . . . . DLB-58

Der Marner before 1230-circa 1287 . . . . DLB-138

Marnham, Patrick 1943- DLB-204

The *Marprelate Tracts* 1588-1589 . . . . DLB-132

Marquand, John P. 1893-1960 . . . . DLB-9, 102

Marqués, René 1919-1979 . . . . DLB-113

Marquis, Don 1878-1937 . . . . DLB-11, 25

Marriott, Anne 1913- DLB-68

Marryat, Frederick 1792-1848 . . . . . . DLB-21, 163

Marsh, Capen, Lyon and Webb DLB-49

Marsh, George Perkins 1801-1882 . . . . . DLB-1, 64

Marsh, James 1794-1842 . . . . DLB-1, 59

Marsh, Narcissus 1638-1713 . . . . DLB-213

Marsh, Ngaio 1899-1982 . . . . DLB-77

Marshall, Edison 1894-1967 . . . . DLB-102

Marshall, Edward 1932- DLB-16

Marshall, Emma 1828-1899 . . . . DLB-163

Marshall, James 1942-1992 . . . . DLB-61

Marshall, Joyce 1913- DLB-88

Marshall, Paule 1929- DLB-33, 157, 227

Marshall, Tom 1938- DLB-60

Marsilius of Padua
 circa 1275-circa 1342 . . . . DLB-115

Mars-Jones, Adam 1954- DLB-207

Marson, Una 1905-1965 . . . . DLB-157

Marston, John 1576-1634 . . . . DLB-58, 172

Marston, Philip Bourke 1850-1887 . . . . . . DLB-35

Martens, Kurt 1870-1945 . . . . DLB-66

Martial circa A.D. 40-circa A.D. 103 . . . . DLB-211

Martien, William S. [publishing house] . . . DLB-49

Martin, Abe (see Hubbard, Kin)

Martin, Catherine ca. 1847-1937 . . . . DLB-230

Martin, Charles 1942- DLB-120

Martin, Claire 1914- DLB-60

Martin, Jay 1935- DLB-111

Martin, Johann (see Laurentius von Schnüffis)

Martin, Thomas 1696-1771 . . . . DLB-213

Martin, Violet Florence (see Ross, Martin)

Martin du Gard, Roger 1881-1958 . . . . . . DLB-65

Martineau, Harriet
 1802-1876 . . . . . DLB-21, 55, 159, 163, 166, 190

Martínez, Demetria 1960- DLB-209

Martínez, Eliud 1935- DLB-122

Martínez, Max 1943- DLB-82

Martínez, Rubén 1962- DLB-209

Martone, Michael 1955- DLB-218

Martyn, Edward 1859-1923 . . . . DLB-10

Marvell, Andrew 1621-1678 . . . . DLB-131

Marvin X 1944- DLB-38

Marx, Karl 1818-1883 . . . . DLB-129

Marzials, Theo 1850-1920 . . . . DLB-35

Masefield, John
 1878-1967 . . . . DLB-10, 19, 153, 160

Mason, A. E. W. 1865-1948 . . . . DLB-70

Mason, Bobbie Ann 1940- DLB-173; Y-87

Mason, William 1725-1797 . . . . DLB-142

Mason Brothers DLB-49

Massey, Gerald 1828-1907 . . . . DLB-32

Massey, Linton R. 1900-1974 . . . . DLB-187

Massinger, Philip 1583-1640 . . . . DLB-58

Masson, David 1822-1907 . . . . DLB-144

Masters, Edgar Lee 1868-1950 . . . . DLB-54

Mastronardi, Lucio 1930-1979 . . . . DLB-177

Matevski, Mateja 1929- DLB-181

Mather, Cotton 1663-1728 . . . . . DLB-24, 30, 140

Mather, Increase 1639-1723 . . . . DLB-24

Mather, Richard 1596-1669. . . . . .DLB-24

Matheson, Richard 1926- DLB-8, 44

Matheus, John F. 1887- DLB-51

Mathews, Cornelius 1817?-1889 . . . . . . .DLB-3, 64

Mathews, Elkin [publishing house] DLB-112

Mathews, John Joseph 1894-1979 . . . . . . .DLB-175

Mathias, Roland 1915- DLB-27

Mathis, June 1892-1927 . . . . .DLB-44

Mathis, Sharon Bell 1937- DLB-33

Matković, Marijan 1915-1985 . . . . .DLB-181

Matoš, Antun Gustav 1873-1914 . . . . . . .DLB-147

Matsumoto Seichō 1909-1992 . . . . .DLB-182

The Matter of England 1240-1400. . . . . . .DLB-146

The Matter of Rome early twelfth to late
    fifteenth century DLB-146

Matthew of Vendôme
    circa 1130-circa 1200. . . . . .DLB-208

Matthews, Brander
    1852-1929 . . . . DLB-71, 78; DS-13

Matthews, Jack 1925- DLB-6

Matthews, Victoria Earle 1861-1907 . . . . .DLB-221

Matthews, William 1942-1997 . . . . .DLB-5

Matthiessen, F. O. 1902-1950 . . . . .DLB-63

Matthiessen, Peter 1927- DLB-6, 173

Maturin, Charles Robert 1780-1824 . . . . .DLB-178

Maugham, W. Somerset
    1874-1965 . . . . . .DLB-10, 36, 77, 100, 162, 195

Maupassant, Guy de 1850-1893 . . . . .DLB-123

Mauriac, Claude 1914-1996. . . . . .DLB-83

Mauriac, François 1885-1970 . . . . .DLB-65

Maurice, Frederick Denison
    1805-1872 . . . . .DLB-55

Maurois, André 1885-1967 . . . . .DLB-65

Maury, James 1718-1769 . . . . .DLB-31

Mavor, Elizabeth 1927- DLB-14

Mavor, Osborne Henry (see Bridie, James)

Maxwell, Gavin 1914-1969 . . . . .DLB-204

Maxwell, H. [publishing house] DLB-49

Maxwell, John [publishing house] DLB-106

Maxwell, William 1908- DLB-218; Y-80

May, Elaine 1932- DLB-44

May, Karl 1842-1912 . . . . .DLB-129

May, Thomas 1595 or 1596-1650 . . . . . . .DLB-58

Mayer, Bernadette 1945- DLB-165

Mayer, Mercer 1943- DLB-61

Mayer, O. B. 1818-1891 . . . . .DLB-3

Mayes, Herbert R. 1900-1987 . . . . .DLB-137

Mayes, Wendell 1919-1992 . . . . .DLB-26

Mayfield, Julian 1928-1984 . . . . .DLB-33; Y-84

Mayhew, Henry 1812-1887 . . . . . .DLB-18, 55, 190

Mayhew, Jonathan 1720-1766 . . . . .DLB-31

Mayne, Ethel Colburn 1865-1941 . . . . . . .DLB-197

Mayne, Jasper 1604-1672. . . . . .DLB-126

Mayne, Seymour 1944- DLB-60

Mayor, Flora Macdonald 1872-1932 . . . . .DLB-36

Mayrocker, Friederike 1924- DLB-85

Mazrui, Ali A. 1933- DLB-125

Mažuranić, Ivan 1814-1890 . . . . .DLB-147

Mazursky, Paul 1930- DLB-44

McAlmon, Robert
    1896-1956 . . . . .DLB-4, 45; DS-15

McArthur, Peter 1866-1924. . . . . .DLB-92

McBride, Robert M., and Company DLB-46

McCabe, Patrick 1955- DLB-194

McCaffrey, Anne 1926- DLB-8

McCarthy, Cormac 1933- DLB-6, 143

McCarthy, Mary 1912-1989 . . . . . . .DLB-2; Y-81

McCay, Winsor 1871-1934 . . . . .DLB-22

McClane, Albert Jules 1922-1991 . . . . . . .DLB-171

McClatchy, C. K. 1858-1936. . . . . .DLB-25

McClellan, George Marion 1860-1934 . . . .DLB-50

McCloskey, Robert 1914- DLB-22

McClung, Nellie Letitia 1873-1951 . . . . . .DLB-92

McClure, Joanna 1930- DLB-16

McClure, Michael 1932- DLB-16

McClure, Phillips and Company DLB-46

McClure, S. S. 1857-1949. . . . . .DLB-91

McClurg, A. C., and Company DLB-49

McCluskey, John A., Jr. 1944- DLB-33

McCollum, Michael A. 1946 . . . . Y-87

McConnell, William C. 1917- DLB-88

McCord, David 1897-1997. . . . . .DLB-61

McCorkle, Jill 1958- DLB-234; Y-87

McCorkle, Samuel Eusebius
    1746-1811 . . . . .DLB-37

McCormick, Anne O'Hare 1880-1954 . . . .DLB-29

Kenneth Dale McCormick Tributes Y-97

McCormick, Robert R. 1880-1955 . . . . . . .DLB-29

McCourt, Edward 1907-1972. . . . . .DLB-88

McCoy, Horace 1897-1955 . . . . .DLB-9

McCrae, John 1872-1918. . . . . .DLB-92

McCullagh, Joseph B. 1842-1896. . . . . . . .DLB-23

McCullers, Carson
    1917-1967 . . . . .DLB-2, 7, 173, 228

McCulloch, Thomas 1776-1843. . . . . .DLB-99

McDonald, Forrest 1927- DLB-17

McDonald, Walter 1934- DLB-105, DS-9

    "Getting Started: Accepting the Regions
    You Own–or Which Own You," DLB-105

McDougall, Colin 1917-1984 . . . . .DLB-68

McDowell, Obolensky. DLB-46

McEwan, Ian 1948- DLB-14, 194

McFadden, David 1940- DLB-60

McFall, Frances Elizabeth Clarke
    (see Grand, Sarah)

McFarlane, Leslie 1902-1977 . . . . .DLB-88

McFee, William 1881-1966 . . . . .DLB-153

McGahern, John 1934- DLB-14, 231

McGee, Thomas D'Arcy 1825-1868 . . . . . .DLB-99

McGeehan, W. O. 1879-1933 . . . . . .DLB-25, 171

McGill, Ralph 1898-1969. . . . . .DLB-29

McGinley, Phyllis 1905-1978 . . . . .DLB-11, 48

McGinniss, Joe 1942- DLB-185

McGirt, James E. 1874-1930 . . . . .DLB-50

McGlashan and Gill. DLB-106

McGough, Roger 1937- DLB-40

McGrath, John 1935- DLB-233

McGrath, Patrick 1950- DLB-231

McGraw-Hill DLB-46

McGuane, Thomas 1939- DLB-2, 212; Y-80

McGuckian, Medbh 1950- DLB-40

McGuffey, William Holmes 1800-1873 . . . .DLB-42

McHenry, James 1785-1845. . . . . .DLB-202

McIlvanney, William 1936- DLB-14, 207

McIlwraith, Jean Newton 1859-1938. . . . . .DLB-92

McIntyre, James 1827-1906 . . . . .DLB-99

McIntyre, O. O. 1884-1938 . . . . .DLB-25

McKay, Claude 1889-1948 . . . . DLB-4, 45, 51, 117

The David McKay Company DLB-49

McKean, William V. 1820-1903 . . . . .DLB-23

McKenna, Stephen 1888-1967. . . . . .DLB-197

The McKenzie Trust Y-96

McKerrow, R. B. 1872-1940 . . . . .DLB-201

McKinley, Robin 1952- DLB-52

McKnight, Reginald 1956- DLB-234

McLachlan, Alexander 1818-1896. . . . . . . .DLB-99

McLaren, Floris Clark 1904-1978 . . . . .DLB-68

McLaverty, Michael 1907- DLB-15

McLean, John R. 1848-1916 . . . . .DLB-23

McLean, William L. 1852-1931. . . . . .DLB-25

McLennan, William 1856-1904. . . . . .DLB-92

McLoughlin Brothers DLB-49

McLuhan, Marshall 1911-1980 . . . . .DLB-88

McMaster, John Bach 1852-1932. . . . . . . .DLB-47

McMurtry, Larry
    1936- DLB-2, 143; Y-80, Y-87

McNally, Terrence 1939- DLB-7

McNeil, Florence 1937- DLB-60

McNeile, Herman Cyril 1888-1937 . . . . . . .DLB-77

McNickle, D'Arcy 1904-1977 . . . . . .DLB-175, 212

McPhee, John 1931- DLB-185

McPherson, James Alan 1943- DLB-38

McPherson, Sandra 1943- Y-86

McWhirter, George 1939- DLB-60

McWilliams, Carey 1905-1980 . . . . .DLB-137

Mda, Zakes 1948- DLB-225

Mead, L. T. 1844-1914 . . . . .DLB-141

Mead, Matthew 1924- DLB-40

Mead, Taylor ?- DLB-16

Meany, Tom 1903-1964 . . . . .DLB-171

Mechthild von Magdeburg
    circa 1207-circa 1282. . . . . .DLB-138

Medieval French Drama DLB-208

Medieval Travel Diaries DLB-203

Medill, Joseph 1823-1899 . . . . .DLB-43

Medoff, Mark 1940- DLB-7

Meek, Alexander Beaufort 1814-1865 . . . . . .DLB-3

Meeke, Mary ?-1816?.............. DLB-116

Meinke, Peter 1932- DLB-5

Mejia Vallejo, Manuel 1923- DLB-113

Melanchthon, Philipp 1497-1560 .... DLB-179

Melançon, Robert 1947- DLB-60

Mell, Max 1882-1971 .... DLB-81, 124

Mellow, James R. 1926-1997 .... DLB-111

Meltzer, David 1937- DLB-16

Meltzer, Milton 1915- DLB-61

Melville, Elizabeth, Lady Culross
circa 1585-1640 ....DLB-172

Melville, Herman 1819-1891 .... DLB-3, 74

Memoirs of Life and Literature (1920),
by W. H. Mallock [excerpt]......... DLB-57

Mena, María Cristina 1893-1965 ... DLB-209, 221

Menander
342-341 B.C.-circa 292-291 B.C......DLB-176

Menantes (see Hunold, Christian Friedrich)

Mencke, Johann Burckhard
1674-1732.................... DLB-168

Mencken, H. L.
1880-1956 .... DLB-11, 29, 63, 137, 222

Mencken and Nietzsche: An Unpublished
Excerpt from H. L. Mencken's My Life
as Author and Editor Y-93

Mendelssohn, Moses 1729-1786 .... DLB-97

Mendes, Catulle 1841-1909 .... DLB-217

Méndez M., Miguel 1930- DLB-82

Mens Rea (or Something)................. Y-97

The Mercantile Library of New York Y-96

Mercer, Cecil William (see Yates, Dornford)

Mercer, David 1928-1980............. DLB-13

Mercer, John 1704-1768 .... DLB-31

Meredith, George
1828-1909 ....DLB-18, 35, 57, 159

Meredith, Louisa Anne 1812-1895 .. DLB-166, 230

Meredith, Owen
(see Lytton, Edward Robert Bulwer)

Meredith, William 1919- DLB-5

Mergerle, Johann Ulrich
(see Abraham ä Sancta Clara)

Mérimée, Prosper 1803-1870 ...... DLB-119, 192

Merivale, John Herman 1779-1844....... DLB-96

Meriwether, Louise 1923- DLB-33

Merlin Press DLB-112

Merriam, Eve 1916-1992 .... DLB-61

The Merriam Company............. DLB-49

Merrill, James 1926-1995 ....DLB-5, 165; Y-85

Merrill and Baker................. DLB-49

The Mershon Company.............. DLB-49

Merton, Thomas 1915-1968........ DLB-48; Y-81

Merwin, W. S. 1927- DLB-5, 169

Messner, Julian [publishing house] DLB-46

Mészöly, Miklós 1921- DLB-232

Metcalf, J. [publishing house] DLB-49

Metcalf, John 1938- DLB-60

The Methodist Book Concern DLB-49

Methuen and Company DLB-112

Meun, Jean de (see Roman de la Rose)

Mew, Charlotte 1869-1928........ DLB-19, 135

Mewshaw, Michael 1943- Y-80

Meyer, Conrad Ferdinand 1825-1898 ... DLB-129

Meyer, E. Y. 1946- DLB-75

Meyer, Eugene 1875-1959 .... DLB-29

Meyer, Michael 1921- DLB-155

Meyers, Jeffrey 1939- DLB-111

Meynell, Alice 1847-1922 .... DLB-19, 98

Meynell, Viola 1885-1956 .... DLB-153

Meyrink, Gustav 1868-1932........... DLB-81

Mézières, Philipe de circa 1327-1405 .... DLB-208

Michael, Ib 1945- DLB-214

Michaëlis, Karen 1872-1950 .... DLB-214

Michaels, Leonard 1933- DLB-130

Micheaux, Oscar 1884-1951........... DLB-50

Michel of Northgate, Dan
circa 1265-circa 1340 .... DLB-146

Micheline, Jack 1929-1998 .... DLB-16

Michener, James A. 1907?-1997 .... DLB-6

Micklejohn, George
circa 1717-1818 .... DLB-31

Middle English Literature:
An Introduction DLB-146

The Middle English Lyric DLB-146

Middle Hill Press DLB-106

Middleton, Christopher 1926- DLB-40

Middleton, Richard 1882-1911........ DLB-156

Middleton, Stanley 1919- DLB-14

Middleton, Thomas 1580-1627 .... DLB-58

Miegel, Agnes 1879-1964 .... DLB-56

Mieželaitis, Eduardas 1919-1997 ..... DLB-220

Mihailović, Dragoslav 1930- DLB-181

Mihalić, Slavko 1928- DLB-181

Miles, Josephine 1911-1985 .... DLB-48

Miliković, Branko 1934-1961......... DLB-181

Milius, John 1944- DLB-44

Mill, James 1773-1836............DLB-107, 158

Mill, John Stuart 1806-1873 .... DLB-55, 190

Millar, Andrew [publishing house]...... DLB-154

Millar, Kenneth
1915-1983 ....DLB-2, 226; Y-83; DS-6

Millay, Edna St. Vincent 1892-1950..... DLB-45

Millen, Sarah Gertrude 1888-1968...... DLB-225

Miller, Arthur 1915- DLB-7

Miller, Caroline 1903-1992.......... DLB-9

Miller, Eugene Ethelbert 1950- DLB-41

Miller, Heather Ross 1939- DLB-120

Miller, Henry 1891-1980 ....DLB-4, 9; Y-80

Miller, Hugh 1802-1856............. DLB-190

Miller, J. Hillis 1928- DLB-67

Miller, James [publishing house]........ DLB-49

Miller, Jason 1939- DLB-7

Miller, Joaquin 1839-1913 .... DLB-186

Miller, May 1899- DLB-41

Miller, Paul 1906-1991 ....DLB-127

Miller, Perry 1905-1963 ....DLB-17, 63

Miller, Sue 1943- DLB-143

Miller, Vassar 1924-1998............ DLB-105

Miller, Walter M., Jr. 1923- DLB-8

Miller, Webb 1892-1940 .... DLB-29

Millhauser, Steven 1943- DLB-2

Millican, Arthenia J. Bates 1920- DLB-38

Mills and Boon.................... DLB-112

Milman, Henry Hart 1796-1868........ DLB-96

Milne, A. A. 1882-1956 ..... DLB-10, 77, 100, 160

Milner, Ron 1938- DLB-38

Milner, William [publishing house] DLB-106

Milnes, Richard Monckton (Lord Houghton)
1809-1885 .... DLB-32, 184

Milton, John 1608-1674 .... DLB-131, 151

Miłosz, Czesław 1911- DLB-215

Minakami Tsutomu 1919- DLB-182

Minamoto no Sanetomo 1192-1219 ..... DLB-203

The Minerva Press.................. DLB-154

Minnesang circa 1150-1280........... DLB-138

Minns, Susan 1839-1938 .... DLB-140

Minor Illustrators, 1880-1914......... DLB-141

Minor Poets of the Earlier Seventeenth
Century...................... DLB-121

Minton, Balch and Company.......... DLB-46

Mirbeau, Octave 1848-1917 .... DLB-123, 192

Mirk, John died after 1414? DLB-146

Miron, Gaston 1928- DLB-60

A Mirror for Magistrates............... DLB-167

Mishima Yukio 1925-1970 .... DLB-182

Mitchel, Jonathan 1624-1668 .... DLB-24

Mitchell, Adrian 1932- DLB-40

Mitchell, Donald Grant
1822-1908 .... DLB-1; DS-13

Mitchell, Gladys 1901-1983 .... DLB-77

Mitchell, James Leslie 1901-1935 .... DLB-15

Mitchell, John (see Slater, Patrick)

Mitchell, John Ames 1845-1918 .... DLB-79

Mitchell, Joseph 1908-1996 ....DLB-185; Y-96

Mitchell, Julian 1935- DLB-14

Mitchell, Ken 1940- DLB-60

Mitchell, Langdon 1862-1935.......... DLB-7

Mitchell, Loften 1919- DLB-38

Mitchell, Margaret 1900-1949 .... DLB-9

Mitchell, S. Weir 1829-1914.......... DLB-202

Mitchell, W. O. 1914- DLB-88

Mitchison, Naomi Margaret (Haldane)
1897-1999................... DLB-160, 191

Mitford, Mary Russell 1787-1855 ....DLB-110, 116

Mitford, Nancy 1904-1973 .... DLB-191

Mittelholzer, Edgar 1909-1965.........DLB-117

Mitterer, Erika 1906- DLB-85

Mitterer, Felix 1948- DLB-124

Mitternacht, Johann Sebastian
1613-1679 . . . . .DLB-168

Miyamoto, Yuriko 1899-1951 . . . . .DLB-180

Mizener, Arthur 1907-1988 . . . . .DLB-103

Mo, Timothy 1950- DLB-194

Modern Age Books DLB-46

"Modern English Prose" (1876),
by George Saintsbury DLB-57

The Modern Language Association of America
Celebrates Its Centennial Y-84

The Modern Library DLB-46

"Modern Novelists – Great and Small" (1855),
by Margaret Oliphant DLB-21

"Modern Style" (1857), by Cockburn
Thomson [excerpt] DLB-57

The Modernists (1932),
by Joseph Warren Beach. DLB-36

Modiano, Patrick 1945- DLB-83

Moffat, Yard and Company DLB-46

Moffet, Thomas 1553-1604 . . . . .DLB-136

Mohr, Nicholasa 1938- DLB-145

Moix, Ana María 1947- DLB-134

Molesworth, Louisa 1839-1921 . . . . .DLB-135

Möllhausen, Balduin 1825-1905 . . . . . . .DLB-129

Molnár, Ferenc 1878-1952 . . . . .DLB-215

Molnár, Miklós (see Mészöly, Miklós)

Momaday, N. Scott 1934- DLB-143, 175

Monkhouse, Allan 1858-1936 . . . . .DLB-10

Monro, Harold 1879-1932 . . . . .DLB-19

Monroe, Harriet 1860-1936. . . . . .DLB-54, 91

Monsarrat, Nicholas 1910-1979 . . . . .DLB-15

Montagu, Lady Mary Wortley
1689-1762 . . . . .DLB-95, 101

Montague, C. E. 1867-1928 . . . . .DLB-197

Montague, John 1929- DLB-40

Montale, Eugenio 1896-1981. . . . . .DLB-114

Montalvo, José 1946-1994 . . . . .DLB-209

Monterroso, Augusto 1921- DLB-145

Montesquiou, Robert de 1855-1921 . . . . .DLB-217

Montgomerie, Alexander
circa 1550?-1598 . . . . .DLB-167

Montgomery, James 1771-1854 . . . . . .DLB-93, 158

Montgomery, John 1919- DLB-16

Montgomery, Lucy Maud
1874-1942 . . . . .DLB-92; DS-14

Montgomery, Marion 1925- DLB-6

Montgomery, Robert Bruce (see Crispin, Edmund)

Montherlant, Henry de 1896-1972. . . . . . .DLB-72

The Monthly Review 1749-1844 . . . . .DLB-110

Montigny, Louvigny de 1876-1955 . . . . . .DLB-92

Montoya, José 1932- DLB-122

Moodie, John Wedderburn Dunbar
1797-1869. . . . . .DLB-99

Moodie, Susanna 1803-1885 . . . . .DLB-99

Moody, Joshua circa 1633-1697. . . . . .DLB-24

Moody, William Vaughn 1869-1910. . . . DLB-7, 54

Moorcock, Michael 1939- DLB-14, 231

Moore, Catherine L. 1911- DLB-8

Moore, Clement Clarke 1779-1863 . . . . . .DLB-42

Moore, Dora Mavor 1888-1979. . . . . .DLB-92

Moore, George 1852-1933. . . . DLB-10, 18, 57, 135

Moore, Lorrie 1957- DLB-234

Moore, Marianne 1887-1972 . . . . . . .DLB-45; DS-7

Moore, Mavor 1919- DLB-88

Moore, Richard 1927- DLB-105

Moore, T. Sturge 1870-1944 . . . . .DLB-19

Moore, Thomas 1779-1852 . . . . .DLB-96, 144

Moore, Ward 1903-1978 . . . . .DLB-8

Moore, Wilstach, Keys and Company DLB-49

Moorehead, Alan 1901-1983 . . . . .DLB-204

Moorhouse, Geoffrey 1931- DLB-204

The Moorland-Spingarn Research
Center DLB-76

Moorman, Mary C. 1905-1994 . . . . .DLB-155

Mora, Pat 1942- DLB-209

Moraga, Cherríe 1952- DLB-82

Morales, Alejandro 1944- DLB-82

Morales, Mario Roberto 1947- DLB-145

Morales, Rafael 1919- DLB-108

Morality Plays: *Mankind* circa 1450-1500 and
Everyman circa 1500 . . . . .DLB-146

Morante, Elsa 1912-1985. . . . . DLB-177

Morata, Olympia Fulvia 1526-1555. . . . . .DLB-179

Moravia, Alberto 1907-1990 . . . . .DLB-177

Mordaunt, Elinor 1872-1942 . . . . .DLB-174

More, Hannah
1745-1833 . . . . .DLB-107, 109, 116, 158

More, Henry 1614-1687 . . . . .DLB-126

More, Sir Thomas
1477 or 1478-1535 . . . . .DLB-136

Moreno, Dorinda 1939- DLB-122

Morency, Pierre 1942- DLB-60

Moretti, Marino 1885-1979 . . . . .DLB-114

Morgan, Berry 1919- DLB-6

Morgan, Charles 1894-1958 . . . . .DLB-34, 100

Morgan, Edmund S. 1916- DLB-17

Morgan, Edwin 1920- DLB-27

Morgan, John Pierpont 1837-1913 . . . . . .DLB-140

Morgan, John Pierpont, Jr. 1867-1943 . . . .DLB-140

Morgan, Robert 1944- DLB-120

Morgan, Sydney Owenson, Lady
1776?-1859. . . . . .DLB-116, 158

Morgner, Irmtraud 1933- DLB-75

Morhof, Daniel Georg 1639-1691 . . . . . . .DLB-164

Mori, Ōgai 1862-1922 . . . . .DLB-180

Móricz, Zsigmond 1879-1942 . . . . .DLB-215

Morier, James Justinian
1782 or 1783?-1849 . . . . .DLB-116

Mörike, Eduard 1804-1875 . . . . .DLB-133

Morin, Paul 1889-1963 . . . . .DLB-92

Morison, Richard 1514?-1556 . . . . .DLB-136

Morison, Samuel Eliot 1887-1976. . . . . . . .DLB-17

Morison, Stanley 1889-1967 . . . . .DLB-201

Moritz, Karl Philipp 1756-1793 . . . . .DLB-94

Moriz von Craûn circa 1220-1230. . . . . . . .DLB-138

Morley, Christopher 1890-1957 . . . . .DLB-9

Morley, John 1838-1923 . . . . DLB-57, 144, 190

Morris, George Pope 1802-1864 . . . . .DLB-73

Morris, James Humphrey (see Morris, Jan)

Morris, Jan 1926- DLB-204

Morris, Lewis 1833-1907 . . . . .DLB-35

Morris, Margaret 1737-1816. . . . . .DLB-200

Morris, Richard B. 1904-1989 . . . . .DLB-17

Morris, William
1834-1896 . . . . . .DLB-18, 35, 57, 156, 178, 184

Morris, Willie 1934-1999. . . . . Y-80

Morris, Wright
1910-1998 . . . . .DLB-2, 206, 218; Y-81

Morrison, Arthur 1863-1945 . . . . DLB-70, 135, 197

Morrison, Charles Clayton 1874-1966 . . . .DLB-91

Morrison, Toni
1931- DLB-6, 33, 143; Y-81, Y-93

Morrow, William, and Company DLB-46

Morse, James Herbert 1841-1923 . . . . .DLB-71

Morse, Jedidiah 1761-1826. . . . . .DLB-37

Morse, John T., Jr. 1840-1937 . . . . .DLB-47

Morselli, Guido 1912-1973 . . . . .DLB-177

Mortimer, Favell Lee 1802-1878 . . . . .DLB-163

Mortimer, John 1923- DLB-13

Morton, Carlos 1942- DLB-122

Morton, H. V. 1892-1979 . . . . .DLB-195

Morton, John P., and Company DLB-49

Morton, Nathaniel 1613-1685 . . . . .DLB-24

Morton, Sarah Wentworth 1759-1846. . . . .DLB-37

Morton, Thomas circa 1579-circa 1647 . . . .DLB-24

Moscherosch, Johann Michael
1601-1669 . . . . .DLB-164

Moseley, Humphrey
[publishing house] DLB-170

Möser, Justus 1720-1794 . . . . .DLB-97

Mosley, Nicholas 1923- DLB-14, 207

Moss, Arthur 1889-1969 . . . . .DLB-4

Moss, Howard 1922-1987 . . . . .DLB-5

Moss, Thylias 1954- DLB-120

The Most Powerful Book Review in America
[*New York Times Book Review*] Y-82

Motion, Andrew 1952- DLB-40

Motley, John Lothrop 1814-1877. . . .DLB-1, 30, 59

Motley, Willard 1909-1965 . . . . .DLB-76, 143

Motte, Benjamin Jr. [publishing house] . . .DLB-154

Motteux, Peter Anthony 1663-1718. . . . . .DLB-80

Mottram, R. H. 1883-1971. . . . . .DLB-36

Mount, Ferdinand 1939- DLB-231

Mouré, Erin 1955- DLB-60

Mourning Dove (Humishuma) between
1882 and 1888?-1936 . . . . DLB-175, 221

Movies from Books, 1920-1974 . . . . .DLB-9

Mowat, Farley 1921- DLB-68

Mowbray, A. R., and Company,
Limited DLB-106

Mowrer, Edgar Ansel 1892-1977 . . . . DLB-29

Mowrer, Paul Scott 1887-1971 . . . . DLB-29

Moxon, Edward [publishing house] DLB-106

Moxon, Joseph [publishing house] DLB-170

Mphahlele, Es'kia (Ezekiel) 1919- DLB-125

Mrożek, Sławomir 1930- DLB-232

Mtshali, Oswald Mbuyiseni 1940- DLB-125

Mucedorus DLB-62

Mudford, William 1782-1848 . . . . DLB-159

Mueller, Lisel 1924- DLB-105

Muhajir, El (see Marvin X)

Muhajir, Nazzam Al Fitnah (see Marvin X)

Mühlbach, Luise 1814-1873 . . . . DLB-133

Muir, Edwin 1887-1959 . . . . . . .DLB-20, 100, 191

Muir, Helen 1937- DLB-14

Muir, John 1838-1914. . . . . DLB-186

Muir, Percy 1894-1979 . . . . DLB-201

Mujū Ichien 1226-1312. . . . . DLB-203

Mukherjee, Bharati 1940- DLB-60, 218

Mulcaster, Richard
    1531 or 1532-1611 . . . . 'DLB-167

Muldoon, Paul 1951- DLB-40

Müller, Friedrich (see Müller, Maler)

Müller, Heiner 1929-1995 . . . . DLB-124

Müller, Maler 1749-1825 . . . . DLB-94

Muller, Marcia 1944- DLB-226

Müller, Wilhelm 1794-1827 . . . . DLB-90

Mumford, Lewis 1895-1990 . . . . DLB-63

Munby, A. N. L. 1913-1974 . . . . DLB-201

Munby, Arthur Joseph 1828-1910 . . . . DLB-35

Munday, Anthony 1560-1633 . . . . . .DLB-62, 172

Mundt, Clara (see Mühlbach, Luise)

Mundt, Theodore 1808-1861 . . . . DLB-133

Munford, Robert circa 1737-1783 . . . . DLB-31

Mungoshi, Charles 1947- DLB-157

Munk, Kaj 1898-1944. . . . . DLB-214

Munonye, John 1929- DLB-117

Munro, Alice 1931- DLB-53

Munro, George [publishing house] DLB-49

Munro, H. H. 1870-1916 . . . . DLB-34, 162

Munro, Neil 1864-1930 . . . . DLB-156

Munro, Norman L. [publishing house] DLB-49

Munroe, James, and Company. DLB-49

Munroe, Kirk 1850-1930 . . . . DLB-42

Munroe and Francis DLB-49

Munsell, Joel [publishing house] DLB-49

Munsey, Frank A. 1854-1925 . . . . DLB-25, 91

Munsey, Frank A., and Company DLB-49

Murakami Haruki 1949- DLB-182

Murav'ev, Mikhail Nikitich 1757-1807 . . . DLB-150

Murdoch, Iris 1919-1999 . . . . . . DLB-14, 194, 233

Murdoch, Rupert 1931- DLB-127

Murfree, Mary N. 1850-1922 . . . . DLB-12, 74

Murger, Henry 1822-1861 . . . . DLB-119

Murger, Louis-Henri (see Murger, Henry)

Murner, Thomas 1475-1537 . . . . .DLB-179

Muro, Amado 1915-1971 . . . . DLB-82

Murphy, Arthur 1727-1805 . . . . DLB-89, 142

Murphy, Beatrice M. 1908- DLB-76

Murphy, Dervla 1931- DLB-204

Murphy, Emily 1868-1933 . . . . DLB-99

Murphy, John, and Company DLB-49

Murphy, John H., III 1916- DLB-127

Murphy, Richard 1927-1993 . . . . DLB-40

Murray, Albert L. 1916- DLB-38

Murray, Gilbert 1866-1957 . . . . DLB-10

Murray, John [publishing house] DLB-154

Murry, John Middleton 1889-1957 . . . . . DLB-149

    "The Break-Up of the Novel" (1922) . . . DLB-36

Murray, Judith Sargent 1751-1820 . . . .DLB-37, 200

Murray, Pauli 1910-1985 . . . . DLB-41

Musäus, Johann Karl August 1735-1787 . . . DLB-97

Muschg, Adolf 1934- DLB-75

The Music of *Minnesang* DLB-138

Musil, Robert 1880-1942 . . . . DLB-81, 124

Muspilli circa 790-circa 850 . . . . DLB-148

Musset, Alfred de 1810-1857 . . . . . . .DLB-192, 217

Mussey, Benjamin B., and Company DLB-49

Mutafchieva, Vera 1929- DLB-181

Mwangi, Meja 1948- DLB-125

Myers, Frederic W. H. 1843-1901 . . . . . . DLB-190

Myers, Gustavus 1872-1942 . . . . DLB-47

Myers, L. H. 1881-1944 . . . . DLB-15

Myers, Walter Dean 1937- DLB-33

Mykolaitis-Putinas, Vincas 1893-1967 . . . DLB-220

Myles, Eileen 1949- DLB-193

N

Na Prous Boneta circa 1296-1328 . . . . . . DLB-208

Nabl, Franz 1883-1974 . . . . DLB-81

Nabokov, Vladimir
    1899-1977 . . . . .DLB-2; Y-80, Y-91; DS-3

    The Vladimir Nabokov Archive
    in the Berg Collection Y-91

    Nabokov Festival at Cornell Y-83

Nádaši, Ladislav (see Jégé)

Naden, Constance 1858-1889 . . . . DLB-199

Nadezhdin, Nikolai Ivanovich
    1804-1856 . . . . DLB-198

Naevius circa 265 B.C.-201 B.C. DLB-211

Nafis and Cornish DLB-49

Nagai, Kafū 1879-1959 . . . . DLB-180

Naipaul, Shiva 1945-1985 . . . . .DLB-157; Y-85

Naipaul, V. S. 1932- *. . .DLB-125, 204, 207; Y-85

Nakagami Kenji 1946-1992 . . . . DLB-182

Nakano-in Masatada no Musume (see Nijō, Lady)

Nałkowska, Zofia 1884-1954 . . . . DLB-215

Nancrede, Joseph [publishing house] DLB-49

Naranjo, Carmen 1930- DLB-145

Narezhny, Vasilii Trofimovich
    1780-1825. . . . . DLB-198

Narrache, Jean 1893-1970. . . . . DLB-92

Nasby, Petroleum Vesuvius (see Locke, David Ross)

Nash, Eveleigh [publishing house] DLB-112

Nash, Ogden 1902-1971 . . . . DLB-11

Nashe, Thomas 1567-1601? DLB-167

Nast, Conde 1873-1942 . . . . DLB-91

Nast, Thomas 1840-1902 . . . . DLB-188

Nastasijević, Momčilo 1894-1938 . . . . . . .DLB-147

Nathan, George Jean 1882-1958. . . . . . . .DLB-137

Nathan, Robert 1894-1985 . . . . DLB-9

The National Jewish Book Awards. Y-85

The National Theatre and the Royal
    Shakespeare Company: The
    National Companies DLB-13

Natsume, Sōseki 1867-1916 . . . . DLB-180

Naughton, Bill 1910- DLB-13

Navarro, Joe 1953- DLB-209

Naylor, Gloria 1950- DLB-173

Nazor, Vladimir 1876-1949 . . . . .DLB-147

Ndebele, Njabulo 1948- DLB-157

Neagoe, Peter 1881-1960 . . . . DLB-4

Neal, John 1793-1876 . . . . DLB-1, 59

Neal, Joseph C. 1807-1847 . . . . DLB-11

Neal, Larry 1937-1981 . . . . DLB-38

The Neale Publishing Company DLB-49

Nebel, Frederick 1903-1967 . . . . DLB-226

Neely, F. Tennyson [publishing house] . . . DLB-49

Negoiţescu, Ion 1921-1993 . . . . DLB-220

Negri, Ada 1870-1945 . . . . DLB-114

"The Negro as a Writer," by
    G. M. McClellan DLB-50

"Negro Poets and Their Poetry," by
    Wallace Thurman DLB-50

Neidhart von Reuental
    circa 1185-circa 1240 . . . . DLB-138

Neihardt, John G. 1881-1973 . . . . DLB-9, 54

Neilson, John Shaw 1872-1942 . . . . DLB-230

Neledinsky-Meletsky, Iurii Aleksandrovich
    1752-1828. . . . . DLB-150

Nelligan, Emile 1879-1941 . . . . DLB-92

Nelson, Alice Moore Dunbar 1875-1935 . . DLB-50

Nelson, Kent 1943- DLB-234

Nelson, Thomas, and Sons [U.K.] DLB-106

Nelson, Thomas, and Sons [U.S.]. DLB-49

Nelson, William 1908-1978 . . . . DLB-103

Nelson, William Rockhill 1841-1915 . . . . . DLB-23

Nemerov, Howard 1920-1991 . . . . .DLB-5, 6; Y-83

Németh, László 1901-1975 . . . . DLB-215

Nepos circa 100 B.C.-post 27 B.C. DLB-211

Nèris, Salomèja 1904-1945 . . . . DLB-220

Nerval, Gerard de 1808-1855 . . . . .DLB-217

Nesbit, E. 1858-1924 . . . . .DLB-141, 153, 178

Ness, Evaline 1911-1986 . . . . DLB-61

Nestroy, Johann 1801-1862 . . . . DLB-133

Neugeboren, Jay 1938- DLB-28

Neukirch, Benjamin 1655-1729 ....DLB-168

Neumann, Alfred 1895-1952 ....DLB-56

Neumann, Ferenc (see Molnár, Ferenc)

Neumark, Georg 1621-1681 ....DLB-164

Neumeister, Erdmann 1671-1756.......DLB-168

Nevins, Allan 1890-1971 ....DLB-17; DS-17

Nevinson, Henry Woodd 1856-1941 ....DLB-135

The New American Library DLB-46

New Approaches to Biography: Challenges from Critical Theory, USC Conference on Literary Studies, 1990 .... Y-90

New Directions Publishing Corporation ...DLB-46

A New Edition of *Huck Finn*............... Y-85

New Forces at Work in the American Theatre: 1915-1925 ....DLB-7

New Literary Periodicals: A Report for 1987...................Y-87

New Literary Periodicals: A Report for 1988...................Y-88

New Literary Periodicals: A Report for 1989...................Y-89

New Literary Periodicals: A Report for 1990...................Y-90

New Literary Periodicals: A Report for 1991...................Y-91

New Literary Periodicals: A Report for 1992...................Y-92

New Literary Periodicals: A Report for 1993...................Y-93

The New Monthly Magazine 1814-1884 ....DLB-110

The New Variorum Shakespeare........... Y-85

A New Voice: The Center for the Book's First Five Years Y-83

The New Wave [Science Fiction].........DLB-8

New York City Bookshops in the 1930s and 1940s: The Recollections of Walter Goldwater .. Y-93

Newbery, John [publishing house].......DLB-154

Newbolt, Henry 1862-1938.............DLB-19

Newbound, Bernard Slade (see Slade, Bernard)

Newby, Eric 1919- DLB-204

Newby, P. H. 1918- DLB-15

Newby, Thomas Cautley [publishing house] DLB-106

Newcomb, Charles King 1820-1894 ...DLB-1, 223

Newell, Peter 1862-1924 ....DLB-42

Newell, Robert Henry 1836-1901 ....DLB-11

Newhouse, Samuel I. 1895-1979 ....DLB-127

Newman, Cecil Earl 1903-1976 ....DLB-127

Newman, David (see Benton, Robert)

Newman, Frances 1883-1928............. Y-80

Newman, Francis William 1805-1897 ....DLB-190

Newman, John Henry 1801-1890 ....DLB-18, 32, 55

Newman, Mark [publishing house] DLB-49

Newnes, George, Limited DLB-112

Newsome, Effie Lee 1885-1979 ....DLB-76

Newspaper Syndication of American Humor DLB-11

Newton, A. Edward 1864-1940........DLB-140

Nexø, Martin Andersen 1869-1954.....DLB-214

Nezval, Vítěslav 1900-1958...........DLB-215

Ngugi wa Thiong'o 1938- DLB-125

Niatum, Duane 1938- DLB-175

The *Nibelungenlied* and the *Klage* circa 1200 ....DLB-138

Nichol, B. P. 1944- DLB-53

Nicholas of Cusa 1401-1464 ....DLB-115

Nichols, Beverly 1898-1983...........DLB-191

Nichols, Dudley 1895-1960 ....DLB-26

Nichols, Grace 1950- DLB-157

Nichols, John 1940- Y-82

Nichols, Mary Sargeant (Neal) Gove 1810-1884 ....DLB-1

Nichols, Peter 1927- DLB-13

Nichols, Roy F. 1896-1973...........DLB-17

Nichols, Ruth 1948- DLB-60

Nicholson, Edward Williams Byron 1849-1912 ....DLB-184

Nicholson, Norman 1914- DLB-27

Nicholson, William 1872-1949........DLB-141

Ní Chuilleanáin, Eiléan 1942- DLB-40

Nicol, Eric 1919- DLB-68

Nicolai, Friedrich 1733-1811 ....DLB-97

Nicolas de Clamanges circa 1363-1437 ...DLB-208

Nicolay, John G. 1832-1901 and Hay, John 1838-1905 ....DLB-47

Nicolson, Harold 1886-1968 ....DLB-100, 149

Nicolson, Nigel 1917- DLB-155

Niebuhr, Reinhold 1892-1971 ..... DLB-17; DS-17

Niedecker, Lorine 1903-1970...........DLB-48

Nieman, Lucius W. 1857-1935..........DLB-25

Nietzsche, Friedrich 1844-1900 ....DLB-129

Nievo, Stanislao 1928- DLB-196

Niggli, Josefina 1910- Y-80

Nightingale, Florence 1820-1910 ....DLB-166

Nijō, Lady (Nakano-in Masatada no Musume) 1258-after 1306 ....DLB-203

Nijō Yoshimoto 1320-1388 ....DLB-203

Nikolev, Nikolai Petrovich 1758-1815 ....DLB-150

Niles, Hezekiah 1777-1839 ....DLB-43

Nims, John Frederick 1913-1999 ....DLB-5

Nin, Anaïs 1903-1977............DLB-2, 4, 152

1985: The Year of the Mystery: A Symposium Y-85

The 1997 Booker Prize Y-97

The 1998 Booker Prize Y-98

Niño, Raúl 1961- DLB-209

Nissenson, Hugh 1933- DLB-28

Niven, Frederick John 1878-1944........DLB-92

Niven, Larry 1938- DLB-8

Nixon, Howard M. 1909-1983 ....DLB-201

Nizan, Paul 1905-1940.................DLB-72

Njegoš, Petar II Petrović 1813-1851 .....DLB-147

Nkosi, Lewis 1936- DLB-157

"The No Self, the Little Self, and the Poets," by Richard Moore...............DLB-105

Nobel Peace Prize

The 1986 Nobel Peace Prize: Elie Wiesel Y-86

The Nobel Prize and Literary Politics Y-86

Nobel Prize in Literature

The 1982 Nobel Prize in Literature: Gabriel García Márquez Y-82

The 1983 Nobel Prize in Literature: William Golding Y-83

The 1984 Nobel Prize in Literature: Jaroslav Seifert.................... Y-84

The 1985 Nobel Prize in Literature: Claude Simon Y-85

The 1986 Nobel Prize in Literature: Wole Soyinka Y-86

The 1987 Nobel Prize in Literature: Joseph Brodsky...................Y-87

The 1988 Nobel Prize in Literature: Najīb Mahfūz Y-88

The 1989 Nobel Prize in Literature: Camilo José Cela.................. Y-89

The 1990 Nobel Prize in Literature: Octavio Paz..................... Y-90

The 1991 Nobel Prize in Literature: Nadine Gordimer Y-91

The 1992 Nobel Prize in Literature: Derek Walcott................... Y-92

The 1993 Nobel Prize in Literature: Toni Morrison Y-93

The 1994 Nobel Prize in Literature: Kenzaburō Ōe Y-94

The 1995 Nobel Prize in Literature: Seamus Heaney................... Y-95

The 1996 Nobel Prize in Literature: Wisława Szymborsha Y-96

The 1997 Nobel Prize in Literature: Dario Fo Y-97

The 1998 Nobel Prize in Literature: José Saramago Y-98

The 1999 Nobel Prize in Literature: Günter Grass.................... Y-99

Nodier, Charles 1780-1844 ....DLB-119

Noel, Roden 1834-1894...............DLB-35

Nogami, Yaeko 1885-1985 ....DLB-180

Nogo, Rajko Petrov 1945- DLB-181

Nolan, William F. 1928- DLB-8

Noland, C. F. M. 1810?-1858 ....DLB-11

Noma Hiroshi 1915-1991 ....DLB-182

Nonesuch Press DLB-112

Noonan, Robert Phillipe (see Tressell, Robert)

Noonday Press.....................DLB-46

Noone, John 1936- DLB-14

Nora, Eugenio de 1923- DLB-134

Nordan, Lewis 1939- DLB-234

Nordbrandt, Henrik 1945- DLB-214

Nordhoff, Charles 1887-1947...........DLB-9

Norman, Charles 1904-1996 ....DLB-111

Norman, Marsha 1947- Y-84

Norris, Charles G. 1881-1945. . . . . DLB-9

Norris, Frank 1870-1902 . . . . .DLB-12, 71, 186

Norris, Leslie 1921- DLB-27

Norse, Harold 1916- DLB-16

Norte, Marisela 1955- DLB-209

North, Marianne 1830-1890 . . . . .DLB-174

North Point Press DLB-46

Nortje, Arthur 1942-1970 . . . . DLB-125

Norton, Alice Mary (see Norton, Andre)

Norton, Andre 1912- DLB-8, 52

Norton, Andrews 1786-1853. . . . . DLB-1

Norton, Caroline 1808-1877 . . . DLB-21, 159, 199

Norton, Charles Eliot 1827-1908 . . . . . DLB-1, 64

Norton, John 1606-1663. . . . . DLB-24

Norton, Mary 1903-1992 . . . . DLB-160

Norton, Thomas (see Sackville, Thomas)

Norton, W. W., and Company DLB-46

Norwood, Robert 1874-1932 . . . . DLB-92

Nosaka Akiyuki 1930- DLB-182

Nossack, Hans Erich 1901-1977 . . . . DLB-69

Not Immediately Discernible . . . but Eventually
    Quite Clear: The First Light and Final Years
    of Hemingway's Centenary Y-99

A Note on Technique (1926), by
    Elizabeth A. Drew [excerpts] DLB-36

Notker Balbulus circa 840-912 . . . . DLB-148

Notker III of Saint Gall circa 950-1022 . . DLB-148

Notker von Zweifalten ?-1095 . . . . DLB-148

Nourse, Alan E. 1928- DLB-8

Novak, Slobodan 1924- DLB-181

Novak, Vjenceslav 1859-1905 . . . . DLB-147

Novalis 1772-1801. . . . . DLB-90

Novaro, Mario 1868-1944 . . . . DLB-114

Novás Calvo, Lino 1903-1983 . . . . DLB-145

"The Novel in [Robert Browning's] 'The Ring and
    the Book'" (1912), by Henry James . . . DLB-32

The Novel of Impressionism,
    by Jethro Bithell DLB-66

Novel-Reading: The Works of Charles Dickens,
    The Works of W. Makepeace Thackeray
    (1879), by Anthony Trollope DLB-21

Novels for Grown-Ups Y-97

The Novels of Dorothy Richardson (1918),
    by May Sinclair. DLB-36

Novels with a Purpose (1864), by
    Justin M'Carthy DLB-21

Noventa, Giacomo 1898-1960 . . . . DLB-114

Novikov, Nikolai
    Ivanovich 1744-1818 . . . . DLB-150

Novomeský, Laco 1904-1976 . . . . DLB-215

Nowlan, Alden 1933-1983 . . . . DLB-53

Noyes, Alfred 1880-1958 . . . . DLB-20

Noyes, Crosby S. 1825-1908 . . . . DLB-23

Noyes, Nicholas 1647-1717 . . . . DLB-24

Noyes, Theodore W. 1858-1946 . . . . DLB-29

N-Town Plays circa 1468 to early
    sixteenth century. DLB-146

Nugent, Frank 1908-1965. . . . . DLB-44

Nugent, Richard Bruce 1906- DLB-151

Nušić, Branislav 1864-1938 . . . . DLB-147

Nutt, David [publishing house]. DLB-106

Nwapa, Flora 1931-1993 . . . . DLB-125

Nye, Bill 1850-1896 . . . . DLB-186

Nye, Edgar Wilson (Bill) 1850-1896 . . DLB-11, 23

Nye, Naomi Shihab 1952- DLB-120

Nye, Robert 1939- DLB-14

Nyka-Niliūnas, Alfonsas 1919- DLB-220

O

Oakes, Urian circa 1631-1681 . . . . DLB-24

Oakley, Violet 1874-1961 . . . . DLB-188

Oates, Joyce Carol 1938- . . .DLB-2, 5, 130; Y-81

Ōba Minako 1930- DLB-182

Ober, Frederick Albion 1849-1913 . . . . . DLB-189

Ober, William 1920-1993 . . . . Y-93

Oberholtzer, Ellis Paxson 1868-1936 . . . . DLB-47

Obradović, Dositej 1740?-1811. . . . . DLB-147

O'Brien, Edna 1932- DLB-14, 231

O'Brien, Fitz-James 1828-1862 . . . . DLB-74

O'Brien, Flann (see O'Nolan, Brian)

O'Brien, Kate 1897-1974 . . . . DLB-15

O'Brien, Tim 1946- DLB-152; Y-80; DS-9

O'Casey, Sean 1880-1964. . . . . DLB-10

Occom, Samson 1723-1792. . . . . .DLB-175

Ochs, Adolph S. 1858-1935 . . . . DLB-25

Ochs-Oakes, George Washington
    1861-1931 . . . . DLB-137

O'Connor, Flannery
    1925-1964 . . . . .DLB-2, 152; Y-80; DS-12

O'Connor, Frank 1903-1966 . . . . DLB-162

Octopus Publishing Group. DLB-112

Oda Sakunosuke 1913-1947 . . . . DLB-182

Odell, Jonathan 1737-1818 . . . . DLB-31, 99

O'Dell, Scott 1903-1989 . . . . DLB-52

Odets, Clifford 1906-1963 . . . . .DLB-7, 26

Odhams Press Limited DLB-112

Odoevsky, Aleksandr Ivanovich
    1802-1839 . . . . DLB-205

Odoevsky, Vladimir Fedorovich
    1804 or 1803-1869. . . . . DLB-198

O'Donnell, Peter 1920- DLB-87

O'Donovan, Michael (see O'Connor, Frank)

O'Dowd, Bernard 1866-1953 . . . . DLB-230

Ōe Kenzaburō 1935- DLB-182; Y-94

O'Faolain, Julia 1932- DLB-14, 231

O'Faolain, Sean 1900- DLB-15, 162

Off Broadway and Off-Off Broadway DLB-7

Off-Loop Theatres DLB-7

Offord, Carl Ruthven 1910- DLB-76

O'Flaherty, Liam 1896-1984. . . .DLB-36, 162; Y-84

Ogilvie, J. S., and Company DLB-49

Ogilvy, Eliza 1822-1912 . . . . DLB-199

Ogot, Grace 1930- DLB-125

O'Grady, Desmond 1935- DLB-40

Ogunyemi, Wale 1939- DLB-157

O'Hagan, Howard 1902-1982 . . . . DLB-68

O'Hara, Frank 1926-1966 . . . . . . .DLB-5, 16, 193

O'Hara, John 1905-1970. . . . . . . DLB-9, 86; DS-2

    John O'Hara's Pottsville Journalism Y-88

O'Hegarty, P. S. 1879-1955 . . . . DLB-201

Okara, Gabriel 1921- DLB-125

O'Keeffe, John 1747-1833 . . . . DLB-89

Okes, Nicholas [publishing house] DLB-170

Okigbo, Christopher 1930-1967 . . . . DLB-125

Okot p'Bitek 1931-1982 . . . . DLB-125

Okpewho, Isidore 1941- DLB-157

Okri, Ben 1959- DLB-157, 231

Olaudah Equiano and Unfinished Journeys:
    The Slave-Narrative Tradition and
    Twentieth-Century Continuities, by
    Paul Edwards and Pauline T.
    Wangman .DLB-117

Old English Literature:
    An Introduction DLB-146

Old English Riddles
    eighth to tenth centuries. DLB-146

Old Franklin Publishing House DLB-49

Old German Genesis and Old German Exodus
    circa 1050-circa 1130 . . . . DLB-148

Old High German Charms and
    Blessings. DLB-148

The Old High German Isidor
    circa 790-800 . . . . DLB-148

The Old Manse DLB-223

Older, Fremont 1856-1935. . . . . DLB-25

Oldham, John 1653-1683 . . . . DLB-131

Oldman, C. B. 1894-1969 . . . . DLB-201

Olds, Sharon 1942- DLB-120

Olearius, Adam 1599-1671. . . . . DLB-164

Oliphant, Laurence 1829?-1888 . . . . . DLB-18, 166

Oliphant, Margaret 1828-1897 . . . . . . DLB-18, 190

Oliver, Chad 1928- DLB-8

Oliver, Mary 1935- DLB-5, 193

Ollier, Claude 1922- DLB-83

Olsen, Tillie 1912 or 1913- . . .DLB-28, 206; Y-80

Olson, Charles 1910-1970. . . . . . . .DLB-5, 16, 193

Olson, Elder 1909- DLB-48, 63

Omotoso, Kole 1943- DLB-125

On Learning to Write. Y-88

Ondaatje, Michael 1943- DLB-60

O'Neill, Eugene 1888-1953 . . . . DLB-7

    Eugene O'Neill Memorial Theater
        Center DLB-7

    Eugene O'Neill's Letters: A Review Y-88

Onetti, Juan Carlos 1909-1994 . . . . DLB-113

Onions, George Oliver 1872-1961 . . . . . . DLB-153

Onofri, Arturo 1885-1928 . . . . DLB-114

O'Nolan, Brian 1911-1966 . . . . DLB-231

Opie, Amelia 1769-1853 . . . . .DLB-116, 159

Opitz, Martin 1597-1639 . . . . .DLB-164

Oppen, George 1908-1984. . . . . .DLB-5, 165

Oppenheim, E. Phillips 1866-1946 . . . . . . .DLB-70

Oppenheim, James 1882-1932 . . . . .DLB-28

Oppenheimer, Joel 1930-1988 . . . . . . .DLB-5, 193

Optic, Oliver (see Adams, William Taylor)

Oral History: B. W. Huebsch Y-99

Oral History Interview with Donald S.
    Klopfer Y-97

Orczy, Emma, Baroness 1865-1947 . . . . . . .DLB-70

Origo, Iris 1902-1988. . . . . .DLB-155

Orlovitz, Gil 1918-1973 . . . . .DLB-2, 5

Orlovsky, Peter 1933- DLB-16

Ormond, John 1923- DLB-27

Ornitz, Samuel 1890-1957 . . . . . . .DLB-28, 44

O'Rourke, P. J. 1947- DLB-185

Orten, Jiří 1919-1941 . . . . .DLB-215

Ortese, Anna Maria 1914- DLB-177

Ortiz, Simon J. 1941- DLB-120, 175

Ortnit and *Wolfdietrich* circa 1225-1250 . . . .DLB-138

Orton, Joe 1933-1967. . . . . .DLB-13

Orwell, George 1903-1950. . . . . . .DLB-15, 98, 195

    The Orwell Year Y-84

    (Re-)Publishing Orwell. Y-86

Ory, Carlos Edmundo de 1923- DLB-134

Osbey, Brenda Marie 1957- DLB-120

Osbon, B. S. 1827-1912 . . . . .DLB-43

Osborn, Sarah 1714-1796 . . . . .DLB-200

Osborne, John 1929-1994 . . . . .DLB-13

Osgood, Herbert L. 1855-1918 . . . . .DLB-47

Osgood, James R., and Company DLB-49

Osgood, McIlvaine and Company. DLB-112

O'Shaughnessy, Arthur 1844-1881 . . . . . .DLB-35

O'Shea, Patrick [publishing house] DLB-49

Osipov, Nikolai Petrovich
    1751-1799. . . . . .DLB-150

Oskison, John Milton 1879-1947 . . . . . . .DLB-175

Osler, Sir William 1849-1919 . . . . .DLB-184

Osofisan, Femi 1946- DLB-125

Ostenso, Martha 1900-1963. . . . . .DLB-92

Ostrauskas, Kostas 1926- DLB-232

Ostriker, Alicia 1937- DLB-120

Osundare, Niyi 1947- DLB-157

Oswald, Eleazer 1755-1795. . . . . .DLB-43

Oswald von Wolkenstein
    1376 or 1377-1445 . . . . .DLB-179

Otero, Blas de 1916-1979 . . . . .DLB-134

Otero, Miguel Antonio 1859-1944. . . . . . .DLB-82

Otero, Nina 1881-1965 . . . . .DLB-209

Otero Silva, Miguel 1908-1985 . . . . .DLB-145

Otfried von Weißenburg
    circa 800-circa 875? DLB-148

Otis, Broaders and Company DLB-49

Otis, James (see Kaler, James Otis)

Otis, James, Jr. 1725-1783. . . . . .DLB-31

Ottaway, James 1911- DLB-127

Ottendorfer, Oswald 1826-1900 . . . . .DLB-23

Ottieri, Ottiero 1924- DLB-177

Otto-Peters, Louise 1819-1895. . . . . .DLB-129

Otway, Thomas 1652-1685 . . . . .DLB-80

Ouellette, Fernand 1930- DLB-60

Ouida 1839-1908. . . . . .DLB-18, 156

Outing Publishing Company. DLB-46

Outlaw Days, by Joyce Johnson DLB-16

Overbury, Sir Thomas
    circa 1581-1613 . . . . .DLB-151

The Overlook Press. DLB-46

Overview of U.S. Book Publishing,
    1910-1945 . . . . .DLB-9

Ovid 43 B.C.-A.D. 17 . . . . .DLB-211

Owen, Guy 1925- DLB-5

Owen, John 1564-1622 . . . . .DLB-121

Owen, John [publishing house] DLB-49

Owen, Peter, Limited. DLB-112

Owen, Robert 1771-1858 . . . . DLB-107, 158

Owen, Wilfred 1893-1918 . . . . .DLB-20; DS-18

The Owl and the Nightingale
    circa 1189-1199 . . . . .DLB-146

Owsley, Frank L. 1890-1956 . . . . .DLB-17

Oxford, Seventeenth Earl of, Edward
    de Vere 1550-1604 . . . . .DLB-172

Ozerov, Vladislav Aleksandrovich
    1769-1816 . . . . .DLB-150

Ozick, Cynthia 1928- DLB-28, 152; Y-82

    First Strauss "Livings" Awarded to Cynthia
    Ozick and Raymond Carver
    An Interview with Cynthia Ozick Y-83

P

Pace, Richard 1482?-1536 . . . . .DLB-167

Pacey, Desmond 1917-1975 . . . . .DLB-88

Pack, Robert 1929- DLB-5

Packaging Papa: *The Garden of Eden* Y-86

Padell Publishing Company. DLB-46

Padgett, Ron 1942- DLB-5

Padilla, Ernesto Chávez 1944- DLB-122

Page, L. C., and Company DLB-49

Page, Louise 1955- DLB-233

Page, P. K. 1916- DLB-68

Page, Thomas Nelson
    1853-1922 . . . . DLB-12, 78; DS-13

Page, Walter Hines 1855-1918 . . . . . . .DLB-71, 91

Paget, Francis Edward 1806-1882 . . . . . . .DLB-163

Paget, Violet (see Lee, Vernon)

Pagliarani, Elio 1927- DLB-128

Pain, Barry 1864-1928. . . . . DLB-135, 197

Pain, Philip ?-circa 1666. . . . . .DLB-24

Paine, Robert Treat, Jr. 1773-1811. . . . . . .DLB-37

Paine, Thomas 1737-1809 . . . . DLB-31, 43, 73, 158

Painter, George D. 1914- DLB-155

Painter, William 1540?-1594 . . . . .DLB-136

Palazzeschi, Aldo 1885-1974 . . . . .DLB-114

Paley, Grace 1922- DLB-28, 218

Palfrey, John Gorham 1796-1881. . . . . . .DLB-1, 30

Palgrave, Francis Turner 1824-1897 . . . . . .DLB-35

Palmer, Joe H. 1904-1952 . . . . .DLB-171

Palmer, Michael 1943- DLB-169

Paltock, Robert 1697-1767 . . . . .DLB-39

Paludan, Jacob 1896-1975 . . . . .DLB-214

Pan Books Limited DLB-112

Panama, Norman 1914- and
    Frank, Melvin 1913-1988 . . . . .DLB-26

Panaev, Ivan Ivanovich 1812-1862 . . . . . .DLB-198

Pancake, Breece D'J 1952-1979 . . . . .DLB-130

Panduro, Leif 1923-1977 . . . . .DLB-214

Panero, Leopoldo 1909-1962. . . . . .DLB-108

Pangborn, Edgar 1909-1976. . . . . .DLB-8

"Panic Among the Philistines": A Postscript,
    An Interview with Bryan Griffin. Y-81

Panizzi, Sir Anthony 1797-1879 . . . . . . .DLB-184

Panneton, Philippe (see Ringuet)

Panshin, Alexei 1940- DLB-8

Pansy (see Alden, Isabella)

Pantheon Books. DLB-46

Papadat-Bengescu, Hortensia
    1876-1955 . . . . .DLB-220

Papantonio, Michael (see Kohn, John S. Van E.)

Paperback Library. DLB-46

Paperback Science Fiction DLB-8

Paquet, Alfons 1881-1944 . . . . .DLB-66

Paracelsus 1493-1541. . . . . .DLB-179

Paradis, Suzanne 1936- DLB-53

Páral, Vladimír, 1932- DLB-232

Pardoe, Julia 1804-1862. . . . . .DLB-166

Paredes, Américo 1915-1999 . . . . .DLB-209

Pareja Diezcanseco, Alfredo 1908-1993 . . .DLB-145

Parents' Magazine Press DLB-46

Parise, Goffredo 1929-1986. . . . . .DLB-177

Parisian Theater, Fall 1984: Toward
    A New Baroque Y-85

Parizeau, Alice 1930- DLB-60

Parke, John 1754-1789 . . . . .DLB-31

Parker, Dorothy 1893-1967 . . . . . . .DLB-11, 45, 86

Parker, Gilbert 1860-1932 . . . . .DLB-99

Parker, J. H. [publishing house] DLB-106

Parker, James 1714-1770. . . . . .DLB-43

Parker, John [publishing house] DLB-106

Parker, Matthew 1504-1575. . . . . .DLB-213

Parker, Theodore 1810-1860. . . . . .DLB-1

Parker, William Riley 1906-1968 . . . . . . .DLB-103

Parkman, Francis, Jr.
    1823-1893 . . . . DLB-1, 30, 183, 186

Parks, Gordon 1912- DLB-33

Parks, Tim 1954- DLB-231

Parks, William 1698-1750 . . . . .DLB-43

Parks, William [publishing house] DLB-49

Parley, Peter (see Goodrich, Samuel Griswold)

369

Parmenides
        late sixth-fifth century B.C. DLB-176

Parnell, Thomas 1679-1718. . . . . DLB-95

Parnicki, Teodor 1908-1988. . . . . DLB-215

Parr, Catherine 1513?-1548 . . . . DLB-136

Parrington, Vernon L. 1871-1929. . . . .DLB-17, 63

Parrish, Maxfield 1870-1966. . . . . DLB-188

Parronchi, Alessandro 1914- DLB-128

Parton, James 1822-1891 . . . . DLB-30

Parton, Sara Payson Willis
        1811-1872. . . . . DLB-43, 74

Partridge, S. W., and Company DLB-106

Parun, Vesna 1922- DLB-181

Pasinetti, Pier Maria 1913- DLB-177

Pasolini, Pier Paolo 1922- DLB-128, 177

Pastan, Linda 1932- DLB-5

Paston, George (Emily Morse Symonds)
        1860-1936 . . . . .DLB-149, 197

The Paston Letters 1422-1509 . . . . DLB-146

Pastorius, Francis Daniel
        1651-circa 1720 . . . . DLB-24

Patchen, Kenneth 1911-1972 . . . . DLB-16, 48

Pater, Walter 1839-1894. . . . . .DLB-57, 156

        Aesthetic Poetry (1873) DLB-35

Paterson, A. B. "Banjo" 1864-1941. . . . . . DLB-230

Paterson, Katherine 1932- DLB-52

Patmore, Coventry 1823-1896 . . . . DLB-35, 98

Paton, Alan 1903-1988 . . . . .DS-17

Paton, Joseph Noel 1821-1901 . . . . DLB-35

Paton Walsh, Jill 1937- DLB-161

Patrick, Edwin Hill ("Ted") 1901-1964 . . DLB-137

Patrick, John 1906-1995 . . . . DLB-7

Pattee, Fred Lewis 1863-1950. . . . . DLB-71

Pattern and Paradigm: History as
        Design, by Judith Ryan DLB-75

Patterson, Alicia 1906-1963 . . . . DLB-127

Patterson, Eleanor Medill 1881-1948 . . . . . DLB-29

Patterson, Eugene 1923- DLB-127

Patterson, Joseph Medill 1879-1946 . . . . . . DLB-29

Pattillo, Henry 1726-1801. . . . . DLB-37

Paul, Elliot 1891-1958. . . . . DLB-4

Paul, Jean (see Richter, Johann Paul Friedrich)

Paul, Kegan, Trench, Trubner and
        Company Limited DLB-106

Paul, Peter, Book Company DLB-49

Paul, Stanley, and Company Limited. . . . DLB-112

Paulding, James Kirke 1778-1860 . . . DLB-3, 59, 74

Paulin, Tom 1949- DLB-40

Pauper, Peter, Press DLB-46

Pavese, Cesare 1908-1950 . . . . .DLB-128, 177

Pavić, Milorad 1929- DLB-181

Pavlov, Konstantin 1933- DLB-181

Pavlov, Nikolai Filippovich 1803-1864 . . . . DLB-198

Pavlova, Karolina Karlovna 1807-1893 . . . . DLB-205

Pavlović, Miodrag 1928- DLB-181

Paxton, John 1911-1985 . . . . DLB-44

Payn, James 1830-1898. . . . . DLB-18

Payne, John 1842-1916. . . . . DLB-35

Payne, John Howard 1791-1852. . . . . DLB-37

Payson and Clarke DLB-46

Paz, Octavio 1914-1998 . . . . Y-90, Y-98

Pazzi, Roberto 1946- DLB-196

Peabody, Elizabeth Palmer 1804-1894 . DLB-1, 223

Peabody, Elizabeth Palmer
        [publishing house] DLB-49

Peabody, Oliver William Bourn
        1799-1848. . . . . DLB-59

Peace, Roger 1899-1968 . . . . DLB-127

Peacham, Henry 1578-1644? DLB-151

Peacham, Henry, the Elder 1547-1634 . . .DLB-172

Peachtree Publishers, Limited. DLB-46

Peacock, Molly 1947- DLB-120

Peacock, Thomas Love 1785-1866 . . . DLB-96, 116

Pead, Deuel ?-1727 . . . . DLB-24

Peake, Mervyn 1911-1968 . . . . DLB-15, 160

Peale, Rembrandt 1778-1860 . . . . DLB-183

Pear Tree Press. DLB-112

Pearce, Philippa 1920- DLB-161

Pearson, H. B. [publishing house]. DLB-49

Pearson, Hesketh 1887-1964. . . . . DLB-149

Peck, George W. 1840-1916. . . . . DLB-23, 42

Peck, H. C., and Theo. Bliss
        [publishing house] DLB-49

Peck, Harry Thurston 1856-1914. . . . . DLB-71, 91

Peden, William 1913-1999 . . . . DLB-234

Peele, George 1556-1596 . . . . DLB-62, 167

Pegler, Westbrook 1894-1969 . . . . .DLB-171

Pekić, Borislav 1930-1992 . . . . DLB-181

Pellegrini and Cudahy DLB-46

Pelletier, Aimé (see Vac, Bertrand)

Pemberton, Sir Max 1863-1950 . . . . DLB-70

de la Peña, Terri 1947- DLB-209

Penfield, Edward 1866-1925. . . . . DLB-188

Penguin Books [U.K.]. DLB-112

Penguin Books [U.S.] DLB-46

Penn Publishing Company DLB-49

Penn, William 1644-1718 . . . . DLB-24

Penna, Sandro 1906-1977 . . . . DLB-114

Pennell, Joseph 1857-1926 . . . . DLB-188

Penner, Jonathan 1940- Y-83

Pennington, Lee 1939- Y-82

Pepys, Samuel 1633-1703 . . . . DLB-101, 213

Percy, Thomas 1729-1811 . . . . DLB-104

Percy, Walker 1916-1990 . . . . . .DLB-2; Y-80, Y-90

Percy, William 1575-1648. . . . . .DLB-172

Perec, Georges 1936-1982 . . . . DLB-83

Perelman, Bob 1947- DLB-193

Perelman, S. J. 1904-1979 . . . . DLB-11, 44

Perez, Raymundo "Tigre" 1946- DLB-122

Peri Rossi, Cristina 1941- DLB-145

Perkins, Eugene 1932- DLB-41

Perkoff, Stuart Z. 1930-1974. . . . . DLB-16

Perley, Moses Henry 1804-1862 . . . . DLB-99

Permabooks DLB-46

Perovsky, Aleksei Alekseevich
        (Antonii Pogorel'sky) 1787-1836 . . . . DLB-198

Perrin, Alice 1867-1934. . . . . DLB-156

Perry, Bliss 1860-1954 . . . . DLB-71

Perry, Eleanor 1915-1981. . . . . DLB-44

Perry, Matthew 1794-1858 . . . . DLB-183

Perry, Sampson 1747-1823 . . . . DLB-158

Persius A.D. 34-A.D. 62 . . . . DLB-211

Perutz, Leo 1882-1957 . . . . DLB-81

Pesetsky, Bette 1932- DLB-130

Pestalozzi, Johann Heinrich 1746-1827 . . . . DLB-94

Peter, Laurence J. 1919-1990 . . . . DLB-53

Peter of Spain circa 1205-1277 . . . . DLB-115

Peterkin, Julia 1880-1961 . . . . DLB-9

Peters, Lenrie 1932- DLB-117

Peters, Robert 1924- DLB-105

        "Foreword to *Ludwig of Bavaria*" DLB-105

Petersham, Maud 1889-1971 and
        Petersham, Miska 1888-1960. . . . . . . DLB-22

Peterson, Charles Jacobs 1819-1887 . . . . . . DLB-79

Peterson, Len 1917- DLB-88

Peterson, Levi S. 1933- DLB-206

Peterson, Louis 1922-1998 . . . . DLB-76

Peterson, T. B., and Brothers DLB-49

Petitclair, Pierre 1813-1860. . . . . DLB-99

Petrescu, Camil 1894-1957 . . . . DLB-220

Petronius circa A.D. 20-A.D. 66. . . . . DLB-211

Petrov, Aleksandar 1938- DLB-181

Petrov, Gavriil 1730-1801. . . . . DLB-150

Petrov, Valeri 1920- DLB-181

Petrov, Vasilii Petrovich 1736-1799 . . . . . DLB-150

Petrović, Rastko 1898-1949 . . . . .DLB-147

Petruslied circa 854?. DLB-148

Petry, Ann 1908-1997. . . . . DLB-76

Pettie, George circa 1548-1589. . . . . DLB-136

Peyton, K. M. 1929- DLB-161

Pfaffe Konrad flourished circa 1172 . . . . . DLB-148

Pfaffe Lamprecht flourished circa 1150 . . DLB-148

Pfeiffer, Emily 1827-1890 . . . . DLB-199

Pforzheimer, Carl H. 1879-1957 . . . . DLB-140

Phaedrus circa 18 B.C.-circa A.D. 50 . . . . DLB-211

Phaer, Thomas 1510?-1560 . . . . DLB-167

Phaidon Press Limited DLB-112

Pharr, Robert Deane 1916-1992. . . . . DLB-33

Phelps, Elizabeth Stuart 1815-1852. . . . . . DLB-202

Phelps, Elizabeth Stuart 1844-1911. . . .DLB-74, 221

Philander von der Linde
        (see Mencke, Johann Burckhard)

Philby, H. St. John B. 1885-1960 . . . . . . DLB-195

Philip, Marlene Nourbese 1947- DLB-157

Philippe, Charles-Louis 1874-1909 . . . . . . DLB-65

Philips, John 1676-1708. . . . . DLB-95

Philips, Katherine 1632-1664 . . . . DLB-131

Phillipps, Sir Thomas 1792-1872 . . . . .DLB-184

Phillips, Caryl 1958- DLB-157

Phillips, David Graham 1867-1911 . . . . .DLB-9, 12

Phillips, Jayne Anne 1952- Y-80

Phillips, Robert 1938- DLB-105

  "Finding, Losing, Reclaiming: A Note
    on My Poems" DLB-105

Phillips, Sampson and Company DLB-49

Phillips, Stephen 1864-1915 . . . . .DLB-10

Phillips, Ulrich B. 1877-1934 . . . . .DLB-17

Phillips, Willard 1784-1873 . . . . .DLB-59

Phillips, William 1907- DLB-137

Phillpotts, Adelaide Eden (Adelaide Ross)
  1896-1993 . . . . .DLB-191

Phillpotts, Eden 1862-1960 . . DLB-10, 70, 135, 153

Philo circa 20-15 B.C.-circa A.D. 50 . . . . . DLB-176

Philosophical Library DLB-46

Phinney, Elihu [publishing house] DLB-49

Phoenix, John (see Derby, George Horatio)

PHYLON (Fourth Quarter, 1950),
  The Negro in Literature:
  The Current Scene DLB-76

Physiologus circa 1070-circa 1150 . . . . .DLB-148

Piccolo, Lucio 1903-1969 . . . . .DLB-114

Pickard, Tom 1946- DLB-40

Pickering, William [publishing house] DLB-106

Pickthall, Marjorie 1883-1922 . . . . .DLB-92

Pictorial Printing Company DLB-49

Piercy, Marge 1936- DLB-120, 227

Pierro, Albino 1916- DLB-128

Pignotti, Lamberto 1926- DLB-128

Pike, Albert 1809-1891 . . . . .DLB-74

Pike, Zebulon Montgomery
  1779-1813 . . . . .DLB-183

Pillat, Ion 1891-1945 . . . . .DLB-220

Pilon, Jean-Guy 1930- DLB-60

Pinckney, Eliza Lucas 1722-1793 . . . . . . .DLB-200

Pinckney, Josephine 1895-1957 . . . . .DLB-6

Pindar circa 518 B.C.-circa 438 B.C. DLB-176

Pindar, Peter (see Wolcot, John)

Pineda, Cecile 1942- DLB-209

Pinero, Arthur Wing 1855-1934 . . . . .DLB-10

Pinget, Robert 1919-1997 . . . . .DLB-83

Pinnacle Books .DLB-46

Piñon, Nélida 1935- DLB-145

Pinsky, Robert 1940- Y-82

  Robert Pinsky Reappointed Poet Laureate . Y-98

Pinter, Harold 1930- DLB-13

Piontek, Heinz 1925- DLB-75

Piozzi, Hester Lynch [Thrale]
  1741-1821 . . . . .DLB-104, 142

Piper, H. Beam 1904-1964 . . . . .DLB-8

Piper, Watty DLB-22

Pirckheimer, Caritas 1467-1532 . . . . .DLB-179

Pirckheimer, Willibald 1470-1530 . . . . . . .DLB-179

Pisar, Samuel 1929- Y-83

Pitkin, Timothy 1766-1847 . . . . .DLB-30

The Pitt Poetry Series: Poetry Publishing
  Today Y-85

Pitter, Ruth 1897- DLB-20

Pix, Mary 1666-1709 . . . . .DLB-80

Pixerécourt, René Charles Guilbert de
  1773-1844 . . . . .DLB-192

Plaatje, Sol T. 1876-1932 . . . . .DLB-125, 225

Plante, David 1940- Y-83

Platen, August von 1796-1835 . . . . .DLB-90

Plath, Sylvia 1932-1963 . . . . .DLB-5, 6, 152

Plato circa 428 B.C.-348-347 B.C. DLB-176

Platon 1737-1812 . . . . .DLB-150

Platt and Munk Company DLB-46

Plautus circa 254 B.C.-184 B.C. DLB-211

Playboy Press DLB-46

Playford, John [publishing house] DLB-170

Plays, Playwrights, and Playgoers DLB-84

Playwrights on the Theater DLB-80

Der Pleier flourished circa 1250 . . . . .DLB-138

Plenzdorf, Ulrich 1934- DLB-75

Plessen, Elizabeth 1944- DLB-75

Pletnev, Petr Aleksandrovich
  1792-1865 . . . . .DLB-205

Pliekšāne, Elza Rozenberga (see Aspazija)

Pliekšāns, Jānis (see Rainis, Jānis)

Plievier, Theodor 1892-1955 . . . . .DLB-69

Plimpton, George 1927- DLB-185

Pliny the Elder A.D. 23/24-A.D. 79 . . . . . .DLB-211

Pliny the Younger
  circa A.D. 61-A.D. 112 . . . . .DLB-211

Plomer, William
  1903-1973 . . . . .DLB-20, 162, 191, 225

Plotinus 204-270 . . . . DLB-176

Plume, Thomas 1630-1704 . . . . .DLB-213

Plumly, Stanley 1939- DLB-5, 193

Plumpp, Sterling D. 1940- DLB-41

Plunkett, James 1920- DLB-14

Plutarch circa 46-circa 120 . . . . .DLB-176

Plymell, Charles 1935- DLB-16

Pocket Books DLB-46

Poe, Edgar Allan 1809-1849 . . . . DLB-3, 59, 73, 74

Poe, James 1921-1980 . . . . .DLB-44

The Poet Laureate of the United States
  Statements from Former Consultants
  in Poetry Y-86

Pogodin, Mikhail Petrovich
  1800-1875 . . . . .DLB-198

Pogorel'sky, Antonii
  (see Perovsky, Aleksei Alekseevich)

Pohl, Frederik 1919- DLB-8

Poirier, Louis (see Gracq, Julien)

Poláček, Karel 1892-1945 . . . . .DLB-215

Polanyi, Michael 1891-1976 . . . . .DLB-100

Pole, Reginald 1500-1558 . . . . .DLB-132

Polevoi, Nikolai Alekseevich
  1796-1846 . . . . .DLB-198

Polezhaev, Aleksandr Ivanovich
  1804-1838 . . . . .DLB-205

Poliakoff, Stephen 1952- DLB-13

Polidori, John William 1795-1821 . . . . . . .DLB-116

Polite, Carlene Hatcher 1932- DLB-33

Pollard, Alfred W. 1859-1944 . . . . .DLB-201

Pollard, Edward A. 1832-1872 . . . . .DLB-30

Pollard, Graham 1903-1976 . . . . .DLB-201

Pollard, Percival 1869-1911 . . . . .DLB-71

Pollard and Moss DLB-49

Pollock, Sharon 1936- DLB-60

Polonsky, Abraham 1910-1999 . . . . .DLB-26

Polotsky, Simeon 1629-1680 . . . . .DLB-150

Polybius circa 200 B.C.-118 B.C. DLB-176

Pomilio, Mario 1921-1990 . . . . .DLB-177

Ponce, Mary Helen 1938- DLB-122

Ponce-Montoya, Juanita 1949- DLB-122

Ponet, John 1516?-1556 . . . . .DLB-132

Poniatowski, Elena 1933- DLB-113

Ponsard, François 1814-1867 . . . . .DLB-192

Ponsonby, William [publishing house] . . . DLB-170

Pontiggia, Giuseppe 1934- DLB-196

Pony Stories DLB-160

Poole, Ernest 1880-1950 . . . . .DLB-9

Poole, Sophia 1804-1891 . . . . .DLB-166

Poore, Benjamin Perley 1820-1887 . . . . . . .DLB-23

Popa, Vasko 1922-1991 . . . . .DLB-181

Pope, Abbie Hanscom 1858-1894 . . . . . . .DLB-140

Pope, Alexander 1688-1744 . . . . . DLB-95, 101, 213

Popov, Mikhail Ivanovich
  1742-circa 1790 . . . . .DLB-150

Popović, Aleksandar 1929-1996 . . . . .DLB-181

Popular Library .DLB-46

Porete, Marguerite ?-1310 . . . . .DLB-208

Porlock, Martin (see MacDonald, Philip)

Porpoise Press .DLB-112

Porta, Antonio 1935-1989 . . . . .DLB-128

Porter, Anna Maria 1780-1832 . . . . .DLB-116, 159

Porter, David 1780-1843 . . . . .DLB-183

Porter, Eleanor H. 1868-1920 . . . . .DLB-9

Porter, Gene Stratton (see Stratton-Porter, Gene)

Porter, Henry ?-? DLB-62

Porter, Jane 1776-1850 . . . . DLB-116, 159

Porter, Katherine Anne
  1890-1980 . . . . DLB-4, 9, 102; Y-80; DS-12

Porter, Peter 1929- DLB-40

Porter, William Sydney
  1862-1910 . . . . DLB-12, 78, 79

Porter, William T. 1809-1858 . . . . .DLB-3, 43

Porter and Coates DLB-49

Portillo Trambley, Estela 1927-1998 . . . . .DLB-209

Portis, Charles 1933- DLB-6

Posey, Alexander 1873-1908 . . . . .DLB-175

Postans, Marianne circa 1810-1865 . . . . . .DLB-166

Postl, Carl (see Sealsfield, Carl)

Poston, Ted 1906-1974 . . . . DLB-51

Potok, Chaim 1929- DLB-28, 152

   A Conversation with Chaim Potok Y-84

Potter, Beatrix 1866-1943 . . . . DLB-141

Potter, David M. 1910-1971 . . . . DLB-17

Potter, Dennis 1935-1994 . . . . DLB-233

The Harry Potter Phenomenon Y-99

Potter, John E., and Company DLB-49

Pottle, Frederick A. 1897-1987 . . . . . DLB-103; Y-87

Poulin, Jacques 1937- DLB-60

Pound, Ezra 1885-1972 . . . . . DLB-4, 45, 63; DS-15

Poverman, C. E. 1944- DLB-234

Povich, Shirley 1905-1998 . . . . .DLB-171

Powell, Anthony 1905- DLB-15

Dawn Powell, Where Have You Been All
   Our Lives? Y-97

Powell, John Wesley 1834-1902 . . . . DLB-186

Powell, Padgett 1952- DLB-234

Powers, J. F. 1917-1999 . . . . DLB-130

Pownall, David 1938- DLB-14

Powys, John Cowper 1872-1963 . . . . DLB-15

Powys, Llewelyn 1884-1939 . . . . DLB-98

Powys, T. F. 1875-1953 . . . . DLB-36, 162

Poynter, Nelson 1903-1978 . . . . DLB-127

The Practice of Biography: An Interview
   with Stanley Weintraub Y-82

The Practice of Biography II: An Interview
   with B. L. Reid Y-83

The Practice of Biography III: An Interview
   with Humphrey Carpenter Y-84

The Practice of Biography IV: An Interview with
   William Manchester Y-85

The Practice of Biography VI: An Interview with
   David Herbert Donald Y-87

The Practice of Biography VII: An Interview with
   John Caldwell Guilds Y-92

The Practice of Biography VIII: An Interview
   with Joan Mellen Y-94

The Practice of Biography IX: An Interview
   with Michael Reynolds Y-95

Prados, Emilio 1899-1962 . . . . DLB-134

Praed, Mrs. Caroline (see Praed, Rosa)

Praed, Rosa (Mrs. Caroline Praed)
   1851-1935 . . . . DLB-230

Praed, Winthrop Mackworth 1802-1839 . . DLB-96

Praeger Publishers DLB-46

Praetorius, Johannes 1630-1680 . . . . DLB-168

Pratolini, Vasco 1913-1991 . . . . .DLB-177

Pratt, E. J. 1882-1964 . . . . DLB-92

Pratt, Samuel Jackson 1749-1814 . . . . DLB-39

Preciado Martin, Patricia 1939- DLB-209

Preface to *The History of Romances* (1715), by
   Pierre Daniel Huet [excerpts] DLB-39

Préfontaine, Yves 1937- DLB-53

Prelutsky, Jack 1940- DLB-61

Premisses, by Michael Hamburger DLB-66

Prentice, George D. 1802-1870 . . . . DLB-43

Prentice-Hall DLB-46

Prescott, Orville 1906-1996 . . . . Y-96

Prescott, William Hickling
   1796-1859 . . . . DLB-1, 30, 59

The Present State of the English Novel (1892),
   by George Saintsbury DLB-18

Prešeren, Francn 1800-1849 . . . . DLB-147

Preston, May Wilson 1873-1949 . . . . . . DLB-188

Preston, Thomas 1537-1598 . . . . DLB-62

Price, Reynolds 1933- DLB-2, 218

Price, Richard 1723-1791 . . . . DLB-158

Price, Richard 1949- Y-81

Priest, Christopher 1943- DLB-14, 207

Priestley, J. B.
   1894-1984 . . . . DLB-10, 34, 77, 100, 139; Y-84

Primary Bibliography: A Retrospective Y-95

Prime, Benjamin Young 1733-1791 . . . . DLB-31

Primrose, Diana floruit circa 1630 . . . . . . DLB-126

Prince, F. T. 1912- DLB-20

Prince, Thomas 1687-1758 . . . . DLB-24, 140

Pringle, Thomas 1789-1834 . . . . DLB-225

Printz, Wolfgang Casper 1641-1717 . . . . . DLB-168

Prior, Matthew 1664-1721 . . . . DLB-95

Prisco, Michele 1920- DLB-177

Pritchard, William H. 1932- DLB-111

Pritchett, V. S. 1900-1997 . . . . DLB-15, 139

Probyn, May 1856 or 1857-1909 . . . . DLB-199

Procter, Adelaide Anne 1825-1864 . . . DLB-32, 199

Procter, Bryan Waller 1787-1874 . . . . DLB-96, 144

Proctor, Robert 1868-1903 . . . . DLB-184

*Producing Dear Bunny, Dear Volodya: The Friendship
   and the Feud* Y-97

The Profession of Authorship:
   Scribblers for Bread Y-89

Prokopovich, Feofan 1681?-1736 . . . . DLB-150

Prokosch, Frederic 1906-1989 . . . . DLB-48

The Proletarian Novel DLB-9

Pronzini, Bill 1943- DLB-226

Propertius circa 50 B.C.-post 16 B.C. DLB-211

Propper, Dan 1937- DLB-16

Prose, Francine 1947- DLB-234

Protagoras circa 490 B.C.-420 B.C. DLB-176

Proud, Robert 1728-1813 . . . . DLB-30

Proust, Marcel 1871-1922 . . . . DLB-65

Prynne, J. H. 1936- DLB-40

Przybyszewski, Stanislaw 1868-1927 . . . . DLB-66

Pseudo-Dionysius the Areopagite floruit
   circa 500 . . . . DLB-115

Public Domain and the Violation of Texts Y-97

The Public Lending Right in America Statement by
   Sen. Charles McC. Mathias, Jr. PLR and the
   Meaning of Literary Property Statements on
   PLR by American Writers Y-83

The Public Lending Right in the United Kingdom
   Public Lending Right: The First Year in the
   United Kingdom Y-83

The Publication of English
   Renaissance Plays DLB-62

Publications and Social Movements
   [Transcendentalism] DLB-1

Publishers and Agents: The Columbia
   Connection Y-87

Publishing Fiction at LSU Press Y-87

The Publishing Industry in 1998:
   Sturm-und-drang.com Y-98

The Publishing Industry in 1999 . . . . .Y-99

Pückler-Muskau, Hermann von
   1785-1871 . . . . .DLB-133

Pufendorf, Samuel von 1632-1694 . . . . . . DLB-168

Pugh, Edwin William 1874-1930 . . . . DLB-135

Pugin, A. Welby 1812-1852 . . . . DLB-55

Puig, Manuel 1932-1990 . . . . DLB-113

Pulitzer, Joseph 1847-1911 . . . . DLB-23

Pulitzer, Joseph, Jr. 1885-1955 . . . . DLB-29

Pulitzer Prizes for the Novel, 1917-1945 . . . . DLB-9

Pulliam, Eugene 1889-1975 . . . . .DLB-127

Purchas, Samuel 1577?-1626 . . . . DLB-151

Purdy, Al 1918- DLB-88

Purdy, James 1923- DLB-2, 218

Purdy, Ken W. 1913-1972 . . . . .DLB-137

Pusey, Edward Bouverie 1800-1882 . . . . . . DLB-55

Pushkin, Aleksandr Sergeevich
   1799-1837 . . . . DLB-205

Pushkin, Vasilii L'vovich 1766-1830 . . . . DLB-205

Putnam, George Palmer 1814-1872 . . . . .DLB-3, 79

Putnam, Samuel 1892-1950 . . . . DLB-4

G. P. Putnam's Sons [U.K.] DLB-106

G. P. Putnam's Sons [U.S.] DLB-49

   A Publisher's Archives: G. P. Putnam Y-92

Puzo, Mario 1920-1999 . . . . DLB-6

Pyle, Ernie 1900-1945 . . . . DLB-29

Pyle, Howard 1853-1911 . . . . DLB-42, 188; DS-13

Pym, Barbara 1913-1980 . . . . . . DLB-14, 207; Y-87

Pynchon, Thomas 1937- DLB-2, 173

Pyramid Books DLB-46

Pyrnelle, Louise-Clarke 1850-1907 . . . . DLB-42

Pythagoras circa 570 B.C.-? DLB-176

Q

Quad, M. (see Lewis, Charles B.)

Quaritch, Bernard 1819-1899 . . . . DLB-184

Quarles, Francis 1592-1644 . . . . DLB-126

The Quarterly Review 1809-1967 . . . . . . DLB-110

Quasimodo, Salvatore 1901-1968 . . . . DLB-114

Queen, Ellery (see Dannay, Frederic, and
   Manfred B. Lee)

The Queen City Publishing House DLB-49

Queneau, Raymond 1903-1976 . . . . DLB-72

Quennell, Sir Peter 1905-1993 . . . . . DLB-155, 195

Quesnel, Joseph 1746-1809 . . . . DLB-99

The Question of American Copyright
   in the Nineteenth Century
      Preface, by George Haven Putnam
      The Evolution of Copyright, by
        Brander Matthews
      Summary of Copyright Legislation in

the United States, by R. R. Bowker
Analysis of the Provisions of the
Copyright Law of 1891, by
George Haven Putnam
The Contest for International Copyright,
by George Haven Putnam
Cheap Books and Good Books,
by Brander Matthews DLB-49

Quiller-Couch, Sir Arthur Thomas
1863-1944 . . . . DLB-135, 153, 190

Quin, Ann 1936-1973 . . . . .DLB-14, 231

Quincy, Samuel, of Georgia ?-? DLB-31

Quincy, Samuel, of Massachusetts
1734-1789 . . . . .DLB-31

Quinn, Anthony 1915- DLB-122

Quinn, John 1870-1924 . . . . .DLB-187

Quiñónez, Naomi 1951- DLB-209

Quintana, Leroy V. 1944- DLB-82

Quintana, Miguel de 1671-1748
A Forerunner of Chicano Literature . .DLB-122

Quintillian circa A.D. 40-circa A.D. 96 . . .DLB-211

Quintus Curtius Rufus fl. A.D. 35 . . . . . .DLB-211

Quist, Harlin, Books DLB-46

Quoirez, Françoise (see Sagan, Françoise)

R

R-va, Zeneida (see Gan, Elena Andreevna)

Raabe, Wilhelm 1831-1910 . . . . .DLB-129

Raban, Jonathan 1942- DLB-204

Rabe, David 1940- DLB-7, 228

Raboni, Giovanni 1932- DLB-128

Rachilde 1860-1953 . . . . .DLB-123, 192

Racin, Kočo 1908-1943 . . . . .DLB-147

Rackham, Arthur 1867-1939 . . . . .DLB-141

Radauskas, Henrikas 1910-1970 . . . . . . .DLB-220

Radcliffe, Ann 1764-1823 . . . . DLB-39, 178

Raddall, Thomas 1903- DLB-68

Radichkov, Yordan 1929- DLB-181

Radiguet, Raymond 1903-1923 . . . . .DLB-65

Radishchev, Aleksandr Nikolaevich
1749-1802 . . . . .DLB-150

Radnóti, Miklós 1909-1944 . . . . .DLB-215

Radványi, Netty Reiling (see Seghers, Anna)

Rahv, Philip 1908-1973 . . . . .DLB-137

Raich, Semen Egorovich 1792-1855 . . . . . .DLB-205

Raičković, Stevan 1928- DLB-181

Raimund, Ferdinand Jakob 1790-1836 . . . . .DLB-90

Raine, Craig 1944- DLB-40

Raine, Kathleen 1908- DLB-20

Rainis, Jānis 1865-1929 . . . . .DLB-220

Rainolde, Richard
circa 1530-1606 . . . . .DLB-136

Rakić, Milan 1876-1938 . . . . .DLB-147

Rakosi, Carl 1903- DLB-193

Ralegh, Sir Walter 1554?-1618 . . . . .DLB-172

Ralin, Radoy 1923- DLB-181

Ralph, Julian 1853-1903 . . . . .DLB-23

Ramat, Silvio 1939- DLB-128

Rambler, no. 4 (1750), by Samuel Johnson
[excerpt] DLB-39

Ramée, Marie Louise de la (see Ouida)

Ramírez, Sergío 1942- DLB-145

Ramke, Bin 1947- DLB-120

Ramler, Karl Wilhelm 1725-1798 . . . . . . .DLB-97

Ramon Ribeyro, Julio 1929- DLB-145

Ramos, Manuel 1948- DLB-209

Ramous, Mario 1924- DLB-128

Rampersad, Arnold 1941- DLB-111

Ramsay, Allan 1684 or 1685-1758 . . . . . . .DLB-95

Ramsay, David 1749-1815 . . . . .DLB-30

Ramsay, Martha Laurens 1759-1811 . . . . .DLB-200

Ranck, Katherine Quintana 1942- DLB-122

Rand, Avery and Company DLB-49

Rand, Ayn 1905-1982 . . . . .DLB-227

Rand McNally and Company DLB-49

Randall, David Anton 1905-1975 . . . . . . .DLB-140

Randall, Dudley 1914- DLB-41

Randall, Henry S. 1811-1876 . . . . .DLB-30

Randall, James G. 1881-1953 . . . . .DLB-17

The Randall Jarrell Symposium:
A Small Collection of Randall Jarrells
Excerpts From Papers Delivered at the
Randall Jarrel Symposium Y-86

Randolph, A. Philip 1889-1979 . . . . .DLB-91

Randolph, Anson D. F.
[publishing house] DLB-49

Randolph, Thomas 1605-1635 . . . . . .DLB-58, 126

Random House DLB-46

Ranlet, Henry [publishing house] DLB-49

Ransom, Harry 1908-1976 . . . . .DLB-187

Ransom, John Crowe 1888-1974 . . . . .DLB-45, 63

Ransome, Arthur 1884-1967 . . . . .DLB-160

Raphael, Frederic 1931- DLB-14

Raphaelson, Samson 1896-1983 . . . . .DLB-44

Rashi circa 1040-1105 . . . . .DLB-208

Raskin, Ellen 1928-1984 . . . . .DLB-52

Rastell, John 1475?-1536 . . . . DLB-136, 170

Rattigan, Terence 1911-1977 . . . . .DLB-13

Rawlings, Marjorie Kinnan
1896-1953 . . . . DLB-9, 22, 102; DS-17

Rawlinson, Richard 1690-1755 . . . . .DLB-213

Rawlinson, Thomas 1681-1725 . . . . .DLB-213

Raworth, Tom 1938- DLB-40

Ray, David 1932- DLB-5

Ray, Gordon Norton 1915-1986 . . . .DLB-103, 140

Ray, Henrietta Cordelia 1849-1916 . . . . . .DLB-50

Raymond, Ernest 1888-1974 . . . . .DLB-191

Raymond, Henry J. 1820-1869 . . . . . . .DLB-43, 79

Michael M. Rea and the Rea Award for the
Short Story Y-97

Reach, Angus 1821-1856 . . . . .DLB-70

Read, Herbert 1893-1968 . . . . .DLB-20, 149

Read, Herbert, "The Practice of Biography," in
*The English Sense of Humour and
Other Essays* .DLB-149

Read, Martha Meredith DLB-200

Read, Opie 1852-1939 . . . . .DLB-23

Read, Piers Paul 1941- DLB-14

Reade, Charles 1814-1884 . . . . .DLB-21

Reader's Digest Condensed Books DLB-46

Readers Ulysses Symposium Y-97

Reading, Peter 1946- DLB-40

Reading Series in New York City Y-96

The Reality of One Woman's Dream:
The de Grummond Children's
Literature Collection Y-99

Reaney, James 1926- DLB-68

Rebhun, Paul 1500?-1546 . . . . DLB-179

Rèbora, Clemente 1885-1957 . . . . .DLB-114

Rebreanu, Liviu 1885-1944 . . . . .DLB-220

Rechy, John 1934- DLB-122; Y-82

The Recovery of Literature:
Criticism in the 1990s: A Symposium Y-91

Redding, J. Saunders 1906-1988 . . . . . .DLB-63, 76

Redfield, J. S. [publishing house] DLB-49

Redgrove, Peter 1932- DLB-40

Redmon, Anne 1943- Y-86

Redmond, Eugene B. 1937- DLB-41

Redpath, James [publishing house] DLB-49

Reed, Henry 1808-1854 . . . . .DLB-59

Reed, Henry 1914- DLB-27

Reed, Ishmael
1938- DLB-2, 5, 33, 169, 227; DS-8

Reed, Rex 1938- DLB-185

Reed, Sampson 1800-1880 . . . . .DLB-1

Reed, Talbot Baines 1852-1893 . . . . .DLB-141

Reedy, William Marion 1862-1920 . . . . . . .DLB-91

Reese, Lizette Woodworth 1856-1935 . . . . .DLB-54

Reese, Thomas 1742-1796 . . . . .DLB-37

Reeve, Clara 1729-1807 . . . . .DLB-39

Preface to *The Old English Baron* (1778) . . .DLB-39

The Progress of Romance (1785) [excerpt] . . .DLB-39

Reeves, James 1909-1978 . . . . .DLB-161

Reeves, John 1926- DLB-88

"Reflections: After a Tornado,"
by Judson Jerome DLB-105

Regnery, Henry, Company DLB-46

Rehberg, Hans 1901-1963 . . . . .DLB-124

Rehfisch, Hans José 1891-1960 . . . . .DLB-124

Reich, Ebbe Kløvedal 1940- DLB-214

Reid, Alastair 1926- DLB-27

Reid, B. L. 1918-1990 . . . . .DLB-111

The Practice of Biography II:
An Interview with B. L. Reid Y-83

Reid, Christopher 1949- DLB-40

Reid, Forrest 1875-1947 . . . . .DLB-153

Reid, Helen Rogers 1882-1970 . . . . .DLB-29

Reid, James ?-? .DLB-31

Reid, Mayne 1818-1883 . . . . .DLB-21, 163

Reid, Thomas 1710-1796 . . . . .DLB-31

Reid, V. S. (Vic) 1913-1987 . . . . .DLB-125

Reid, Whitelaw 1837-1912 . . . . DLB-23

Reilly and Lee Publishing Company DLB-46

Reimann, Brigitte 1933-1973 . . . . DLB-75

Reinmar der Alte
circa 1165-circa 1205 . . . . DLB-138

Reinmar von Zweter
circa 1200-circa 1250 . . . . DLB-138

Reisch, Walter 1903-1983 . . . . DLB-44

Reizei Family DLB-203

Remarks at the Opening of "The Biographical
Part of Literature" Exhibition, by
William R. Cagle Y-98

Remarque, Erich Maria 1898-1970 . . . . . . DLB-56

Remington, Frederic
1861-1909 . . . . DLB-12, 186, 188

Reminiscences, by Charles Scribner Jr. DS-17

Renaud, Jacques 1943- DLB-60

Renault, Mary 1905-1983. . . . . Y-83

Rendell, Ruth 1930- DLB-87

Rensselaer, Maria van Cortlandt van
1645-1689 . . . . DLB-200

Repplier, Agnes 1855-1950. . . . . DLB-221

Representative Men and Women: A Historical
Perspective on the British Novel,
1930-1960 . . . . DLB-15

Research in the American Antiquarian Book
Trade. Y-97

Rettenbacher, Simon 1634-1706 . . . . DLB-168

Reuchlin, Johannes 1455-1522 . . . . .DLB-179

Reuter, Christian 1665-after 1712. . . . . . DLB-168

Revell, Fleming H., Company DLB-49

Reuter, Fritz 1810-1874. . . . . DLB-129

Reuter, Gabriele 1859-1941 . . . . DLB-66

Reventlow, Franziska Gräfin zu
1871-1918. . . . . DLB-66

Review of Reviews Office. DLB-112

Review of [Samuel Richardson's] *Clarissa* (1748),
by Henry Fielding DLB-39

The Revolt (1937), by Mary Colum
[excerpts] DLB-36

Rexroth, Kenneth
1905-1982 . . . . . . .DLB-16, 48, 165, 212; Y-82

Rey, H. A. 1898-1977 . . . . DLB-22

Reynal and Hitchcock DLB-46

Reynolds, G. W. M. 1814-1879 . . . . DLB-21

Reynolds, John Hamilton 1794-1852 . . . . . DLB-96

Reynolds, Sir Joshua 1723-1792 . . . . DLB-104

Reynolds, Mack 1917- DLB-8

A Literary Archaelogist Digs On: A Brief
Interview with Michael Reynolds by
Michael Rogers .Y-99

Reznikoff, Charles 1894-1976. . . . . . . DLB-28, 45

Rhett, Robert Barnwell 1800-1876 . . . . . . DLB-43

Rhode, John 1884-1964 . . . . DLB-77

Rhodes, James Ford 1848-1927. . . . . DLB-47

Rhodes, Richard 1937- DLB-185

Rhys, Jean 1890-1979 . . . . .DLB-36, 117, 162

Ricardo, David 1772-1823 . . . . .DLB-107, 158

Ricardou, Jean 1932- DLB-83

Rice, Elmer 1892-1967 . . . . DLB-4, 7

Rice, Grantland 1880-1954. . . . . .DLB-29, 171

Rich, Adrienne 1929- DLB-5, 67

Richard de Fournival
1201-1259 or 1260. . . . . DLB-208

Richard, Mark 1955- DLB-234

Richards, David Adams 1950- DLB-53

Richards, George circa 1760-1814 . . . . DLB-37

Richards, Grant [publishing house] DLB-112

Richards, I. A. 1893-1979 . . . . DLB-27

Richards, Laura E. 1850-1943 . . . . DLB-42

Richards, William Carey 1818-1892 . . . . . DLB-73

Richardson, Charles F. 1851-1913 . . . . DLB-71

Richardson, Dorothy M. 1873-1957 . . . . . . DLB-36

Richardson, Henry Handel
(Ethel Florence Lindesay
Robertson) 1870-1946 . . . . .DLB-197, 230

Richardson, Jack 1935- DLB-7

Richardson, John 1796-1852. . . . . DLB-99

Richardson, Samuel 1689-1761. . . . . DLB-39, 154

Introductory Letters from the Second
Edition of *Pamela* (1741) DLB-39

Postscript to [the Third Edition of]
Clarissa (1751) DLB-39

Preface to the First Edition of
Pamela (1740) DLB-39

Preface to the Third Edition of
Clarissa (1751) [excerpt]. DLB-39

Preface to Volume 1 of *Clarissa* (1747). . . DLB-39

Preface to Volume 3 of *Clarissa* (1748) . . DLB-39

Richardson, Willis 1889-1977. . . . . DLB-51

Riche, Barnabe 1542-1617 . . . . DLB-136

Richepin, Jean 1849-1926. . . . . DLB-192

Richler, Mordecai 1931- DLB-53

Richter, Conrad 1890-1968 . . . . DLB-9, 212

Richter, Hans Werner 1908- DLB-69

Richter, Johann Paul Friedrich
1763-1825. . . . . DLB-94

Rickerby, Joseph [publishing house]. DLB-106

Rickword, Edgell 1898-1982 . . . . DLB-20

Riddell, Charlotte 1832-1906 . . . . DLB-156

Riddell, John (see Ford, Corey)

Ridge, John Rollin 1827-1867 . . . . .DLB-175

Ridge, Lola 1873-1941 . . . . DLB-54

Ridge, William Pett 1859-1930. . . . . DLB-135

Riding, Laura (see Jackson, Laura Riding)

Ridler, Anne 1912- DLB-27

Ridruego, Dionisio 1912-1975 . . . . DLB-108

Riel, Louis 1844-1885. . . . . DLB-99

Riemer, Johannes 1648-1714. . . . . DLB-168

Rifbjerg, Klaus 1931- DLB-214

Riffaterre, Michael 1924- DLB-67

Riggs, Lynn 1899-1954. . . . . .DLB-175

Riis, Jacob 1849-1914 . . . . DLB-23

Riker, John C. [publishing house]. DLB-49

Riley, James 1777-1840 . . . . DLB-183

Riley, John 1938-1978. . . . . DLB-40

Rilke, Rainer Maria 1875-1926. . . . . DLB-81

Rimanelli, Giose 1926- DLB-177

Rimbaud, Jean-Nicolas-Arthur
1854-1891 . . . . .DLB-217

Rinehart and Company DLB-46

Ringuet 1895-1960. . . . . DLB-68

Ringwood, Gwen Pharis 1910-1984 . . . . . . DLB-88

Rinser, Luise 1911- DLB-69

Ríos, Alberto 1952- DLB-122

Ríos, Isabella 1948- DLB-82

Ripley, Arthur 1895-1961. . . . . DLB-44

Ripley, George 1802-1880 . . . . .DLB-1, 64, 73

The Rising Glory of America:
Three Poems DLB-37

The Rising Glory of America:
Written in 1771 (1786),
by Hugh Henry Brackenridge and
Philip Freneau DLB-37

Riskin, Robert 1897-1955 . . . . DLB-26

Risse, Heinz 1898- DLB-69

Rist, Johann 1607-1667 . . . . DLB-164

Ristikivi, Karl 1912-1977 . . . . DLB-220

Ritchie, Anna Mowatt 1819-1870 . . . . DLB-3

Ritchie, Anne Thackeray 1837-1919. . . . . DLB-18

Ritchie, Thomas 1778-1854 . . . . DLB-43

Rites of Passage [on William Saroyan]. Y-83

The Ritz Paris Hemingway Award. Y-85

Rivard, Adjutor 1868-1945. . . . . DLB-92

Rive, Richard 1931-1989 . . . . DLB-125, 225

Rivera, Marina 1942- DLB-122

Rivera, Tomás 1935-1984 . . . . DLB-82

Rivers, Conrad Kent 1933-1968. . . . . DLB-41

Riverside Press. DLB-49

Rivington, Charles [publishing house] . . . DLB-154

Rivington, James circa 1724-1802. . . . . . . DLB-43

Rivkin, Allen 1903-1990. . . . . DLB-26

Roa Bastos, Augusto 1917- DLB-113

Robbe-Grillet, Alain 1922- DLB-83

Robbins, Tom 1936- Y-80

Roberts, Charles G. D. 1860-1943 . . . . DLB-92

Roberts, Dorothy 1906-1993 . . . . DLB-88

Roberts, Elizabeth Madox
1881-1941 . . . . .DLB-9, 54, 102

Roberts, James [publishing house] DLB-154

Roberts, Kenneth 1885-1957 . . . . DLB-9

Roberts, Michèle 1949- DLB-231

Roberts, William 1767-1849 . . . . DLB-142

Roberts Brothers DLB-49

Robertson, A. M., and Company. DLB-49

Robertson, Ethel Florence Lindesay
(see Richardson, Henry Handel)

Robertson, William 1721-1793 . . . . DLB-104

Robins, Elizabeth 1862-1952 . . . . .DLB-197

Robinson, Casey 1903-1979. . . . . DLB-44

Robinson, Edwin Arlington 1869-1935 . . . DLB-54

Robinson, Henry Crabb 1775-1867 . . . . . .DLB-107

Robinson, James Harvey 1863-1936 . . . . . .DLB-47

Robinson, Lennox 1886-1958 . . . . .DLB-10

Robinson, Mabel Louise 1874-1962. . . . . .DLB-22

Robinson, Marilynne 1943- DLB-206

Robinson, Mary 1758-1800 . . . . .DLB-158

Robinson, Richard circa 1545-1607. . . . . .DLB-167

Robinson, Therese 1797-1870. . . . . . .DLB-59, 133

Robison, Mary 1949- DLB-130

Roblès, Emmanuel 1914-1995 . . . . .DLB-83

Roccatagliata Ceccardi, Ceccardo
    1871-1919 . . . . .DLB-114

Roche, Billy 1949- DLB-233

Rochester, John Wilmot, Earl of
    1647-1680 .DLB-131

Rock, Howard 1911-1976 . . . . .DLB-127

Rockwell, Norman Perceval 1894-1978 . . .DLB-188

Rodgers, Carolyn M. 1945- DLB-41

Rodgers, W. R. 1909-1969 . . . . .DLB-20

Rodríguez, Claudio 1934-1999 . . . . .DLB-134

Rodríguez, Joe D. 1943- DLB-209

Rodríguez, Luis J. 1954- DLB-209

Rodriguez, Richard 1944- DLB-82

Rodríguez Julia, Edgardo 1946- DLB-145

Roe, E. P. 1838-1888 . . . . .DLB-202

Roethke, Theodore 1908-1963 . . . . . .DLB-5, 206

Rogers, Jane 1952- DLB-194

Rogers, Pattiann 1940- DLB-105

Rogers, Samuel 1763-1855. . . . . .DLB-93

Rogers, Will 1879-1935 . . . . .DLB-11

Rohmer, Sax 1883-1959 . . . . .DLB-70

Roiphe, Anne 1935- Y-80

Rojas, Arnold R. 1896-1988 . . . . .DLB-82

Rolfe, Frederick William
    1860-1913 . . . . .DLB-34, 156

Rolland, Romain 1866-1944 . . . . .DLB-65

Rolle, Richard circa 1290-1300 - 1340. . . .DLB-146

Rölvaag, O. E. 1876-1931 . . . . .DLB-9, 212

Romains, Jules 1885-1972 . . . . .DLB-65

Roman, A., and Company. DLB-49

Roman de la Rose: Guillaume de Lorris
    1200 to 1205-circa 1230, Jean de Meun
    1235-1240-circa 1305 . . . . .DLB-208

Romano, Lalla 1906- DLB-177

Romano, Octavio 1923- DLB-122

Romero, Leo 1950- DLB-122

Romero, Lin 1947- DLB-122

Romero, Orlando 1945- DLB-82

Rook, Clarence 1863-1915 . . . . .DLB-135

Roosevelt, Theodore 1858-1919 . . . . . DLB-47, 186

Root, Waverley 1903-1982 . . . . .DLB-4

Root, William Pitt 1941- DLB-120

Roquebrune, Robert de 1889-1978 . . . . . . .DLB-68

Rosa, João Guimarães 1908-1967. . . . . .DLB-113

Rosales, Luis 1910-1992 . . . . .DLB-134

Roscoe, William 1753-1831 . . . . .DLB-163

Danis Rose and the Rendering of *Ulysses* Y-97

Rose, Reginald 1920- DLB-26

Rose, Wendy 1948- DLB-175

Rosegger, Peter 1843-1918 . . . . .DLB-129

Rosei, Peter 1946- DLB-85

Rosen, Norma 1925- DLB-28

Rosenbach, A. S. W. 1876-1952. . . . . . . .DLB-140

Rosenbaum, Ron 1946- DLB-185

Rosenberg, Isaac 1890-1918 . . . . . . .DLB-20, 216

Rosenfeld, Isaac 1918-1956 . . . . .DLB-28

Rosenthal, M. L. 1917-1996. . . . . .DLB-5

Rosenwald, Lessing J. 1891-1979. . . . . . .DLB-187

Ross, Alexander 1591-1654 . . . . .DLB-151

Ross, Harold 1892-1951 . . . . .DLB-137

Ross, Leonard Q. (see Rosten, Leo)

Ross, Lillian 1927- DLB-185

Ross, Martin 1862-1915. . . . . .DLB-135

Ross, Sinclair 1908- DLB-88

Ross, W. W. E. 1894-1966 . . . . .DLB-88

Rosselli, Amelia 1930-1996 . . . . .DLB-128

Rossen, Robert 1908-1966. . . . . .DLB-26

Rossetti, Christina Georgina
    1830-1894 . . . . .DLB-35, 163

Rossetti, Dante Gabriel 1828-1882 . . .DLB-35

Rossner, Judith 1935- DLB-6

Rostand, Edmond 1868-1918 . . . . .DLB-192

Rosten, Leo 1908-1997 . . . . .DLB-11

Rostenberg, Leona 1908- DLB-140

Rostopchina, Evdokiia Petrovna
    1811-1858 .DLB-205

Rostovsky, Dimitrii 1651-1709 . . . . .DLB-150

Rota, Bertram 1903-1966. . . . . .DLB-201

    Bertram Rota and His Bookshop. Y-91

Roth, Gerhard 1942- DLB-85, 124

Roth, Henry 1906?-1995 . . . . .DLB-28

Roth, Joseph 1894-1939. . . . . .DLB-85

Roth, Philip 1933- DLB-2, 28, 173; Y-82

Rothenberg, Jerome 1931- DLB-5, 193

Rothschild Family DLB-184

Rotimi, Ola 1938- DLB-125

Routhier, Adolphe-Basile 1839-1920 . . . . .DLB-99

Routier, Simone 1901-1987 . . . . .DLB-88

Routledge, George, and Sons. DLB-106

Roversi, Roberto 1923- DLB-128

Rowe, Elizabeth Singer 1674-1737 . . . . .DLB-39, 95

Rowe, Nicholas 1674-1718. . . . . .DLB-84

Rowlands, Samuel circa 1570-1630 . . . . . .DLB-121

Rowlandson, Mary
    circa 1637-circa 1711 . . . . .DLB-24, 200

Rowley, William circa 1585-1626 . . . . . . .DLB-58

Rowse, A. L. 1903-1997. . . . . .DLB-155

Rowson, Susanna Haswell
    circa 1762-1824 . . . . DLB-37, 200

Roy, Camille 1870-1943. . . . . .DLB-92

Roy, Gabrielle 1909-1983 . . . . .DLB-68

Roy, Jules 1907- DLB-83

The G. Ross Roy Scottish Poetry Collection
    at the University of South Carolina Y-89

The Royal Court Theatre and the English
    Stage Company. DLB-13

The Royal Court Theatre and the New
    Drama. DLB-10

The Royal Shakespeare Company
    at the Swan Y-88

Royall, Anne 1769-1854. . . . . .DLB-43

The Roycroft Printing Shop DLB-49

Royde-Smith, Naomi 1875-1964 . . . . . . .DLB-191

Royster, Vermont 1914- DLB-127

Royston, Richard [publishing house]. DLB-170

Różewicz, Tadeusz 1921- DLB-232

Ruark, Gibbons 1941- DLB-120

Ruban, Vasilii Grigorevich 1742-1795 . . . .DLB-150

Rubens, Bernice 1928- DLB-14, 207

Rudd and Carleton DLB-49

Rudd, Steele (Arthur Hoey Davis) DLB-230

Rudkin, David 1936- DLB-13

Rudolf von Ems circa 1200-circa 1254 . . .DLB-138

Ruffin, Josephine St. Pierre
    1842-1924 . . . . .DLB-79

Ruganda, John 1941- DLB-157

Ruggles, Henry Joseph 1813-1906. . . . . . .DLB-64

Ruiz de Burton, María Amparo
    1832-1895 . . . . DLB-209, 221

Rukeyser, Muriel 1913-1980 . . . . .DLB-48

Rule, Jane 1931- DLB-60

Rulfo, Juan 1918-1986. . . . . .DLB-113

Rumaker, Michael 1932- DLB-16

Rumens, Carol 1944- DLB-40

Rummo, Paul-Eerik 1942- DLB-232

Runyon, Damon 1880-1946 . . . . . DLB-11, 86, 171

Ruodlieb circa 1050-1075 . . . . .DLB-148

Rush, Benjamin 1746-1813 . . . . .DLB-37

Rush, Rebecca 1779-?. DLB-200

Rushdie, Salman 1947- DLB-194

Rusk, Ralph L. 1888-1962. . . . . .DLB-103

Ruskin, John 1819-1900. . . . . . .DLB-55, 163, 190

Russ, Joanna 1937- DLB-8

Russell, B. B., and Company. DLB-49

Russell, Benjamin 1761-1845 . . . . .DLB-43

Russell, Bertrand 1872-1970. . . . . .DLB-100

Russell, Charles Edward 1860-1941 . . . . . .DLB-25

Russell, Charles M. 1864-1926 . . . . .DLB-188

Russell, George William (see AE)

Russell, Countess Mary Annette Beauchamp
    (see Arnim, Elizabeth von)

Russell, R. H., and Son DLB-49

Russell, Willy 1947- DLB-233

Rutebeuf flourished 1249-1277 . . . . .DLB-208

Rutherford, Mark 1831-1913. . . . . .DLB-18

Ruxton, George Frederick 1821-1848 . . . .DLB-186

Ryan, Michael 1946- Y-82

Ryan, Oscar 1904- DLB-68

Ryga, George 1932- DLB-60

Rylands, Enriqueta Augustina Tennant
  1843-1908 .... DLB-184

Rylands, John 1801-1888 .... DLB-184

Ryleev, Kondratii Fedorovich
  1795-1826................. DLB-205

Rymer, Thomas 1643?-1713........ DLB-101

Ryskind, Morrie 1895-1985 .... DLB-26

Rzhevsky, Aleksei Andreevich
  1737-1804 .... DLB-150

S

The Saalfield Publishing Company DLB-46

Saba, Umberto 1883-1957 .... DLB-114

Sábato, Ernesto 1911- DLB-145

Saberhagen, Fred 1930- DLB-8

Sabin, Joseph 1821-1881............. DLB-187

Sacer, Gottfried Wilhelm 1635-1699 .... DLB-168

Sachs, Hans 1494-1576................DLB-179

Sack, John 1930- DLB-185

Sackler, Howard 1929-1982 .... DLB-7

Sackville, Thomas 1536-1608.......... DLB-132

Sackville, Thomas 1536-1608
  and Norton, Thomas 1532-1584 ..... DLB-62

Sackville-West, Edward 1901-1965...... DLB-191

Sackville-West, V. 1892-1962 .... DLB-34, 195

Sadlier, D. and J., and Company DLB-49

Sadlier, Mary Anne 1820-1903.......... DLB-99

Sadoff, Ira 1945- DLB-120

Sadoveanu, Mihail 1880-1961 .... DLB-220

Sáenz, Benjamin Alire 1954- DLB-209

Saenz, Jaime 1921-1986 .... DLB-145

Saffin, John circa 1626-1710 .... DLB-24

Sagan, Françoise 1935- DLB-83

Sage, Robert 1899-1962 .... DLB-4

Sagel, Jim 1947- DLB-82

Sagendorph, Robb Hansell 1900-1970 ... DLB-137

Sahagún, Carlos 1938- DLB-108

Sahkomaapii, Piitai (see Highwater, Jamake)

Sahl, Hans 1902- DLB-69

Said, Edward W. 1935- DLB-67

Saigyō 1118-1190 .... DLB-203

Saiko, George 1892-1962 .... DLB-85

St. Dominic's Press................ DLB-112

Saint-Exupéry, Antoine de 1900-1944 .... DLB-72

St. John, J. Allen 1872-1957....... DLB-188

St. Johns, Adela Rogers 1894-1988....... DLB-29

The St. John's College Robert Graves Trust . . Y-96

St. Martin's Press DLB-46

St. Omer, Garth 1931- DLB-117

Saint Pierre, Michel de 1916-1987 ...... DLB-83

Sainte-Beuve, Charles-Augustin
  1804-1869 .... DLB-217

Saints' Lives DLB-208

Saintsbury, George 1845-1933 ....DLB-57, 149

Saiokuken Sōchō 1448-1532 .... DLB-203

Saki (see Munro, H. H.)

Salaam, Kalamu ya 1947- DLB-38

Šalamun, Tomaž 1941- DLB-181

Salas, Floyd 1931- DLB-82

Sálaz-Marquez, Rubén 1935- DLB-122

Salemson, Harold J. 1910-1988.......... DLB-4

Salinas, Luis Omar 1937- DLB-82

Salinas, Pedro 1891-1951 .... DLB-134

Salinger, J. D. 1919- DLB-2, 102, 173

Salkey, Andrew 1928- DLB-125

Sallust circa 86 B.C.-35 B.C......... DLB-211

Salt, Waldo 1914- DLB-44

Salter, James 1925- DLB-130

Salter, Mary Jo 1954- DLB-120

Saltus, Edgar 1855-1921............ DLB-202

Salustri, Carlo Alberto (see Trilussa)

Samain, Albert 1858-1900............ DLB-217

Sampson, Richard Henry (see Hull, Richard)

Samuels, Ernest 1903-1996........... DLB-111

Sanborn, Franklin Benjamin
  1831-1917.................... DLB-1, 223

Sánchez, Luis Rafael 1936- DLB-145

Sánchez, Philomeno "Phil" 1917- DLB-122

Sánchez, Ricardo 1941-1995........... DLB-82

Sánchez, Saúl 1943- DLB-209

Sanchez, Sonia 1934- DLB-41; DS-8

Sand, George 1804-1876......... DLB-119, 192

Sandburg, Carl 1878-1967 ....DLB-17, 54

Sanders, Ed 1939- DLB-16

Sandoz, Mari 1896-1966.......... DLB-9, 212

Sandwell, B. K. 1876-1954 .... DLB-92

Sandy, Stephen 1934- DLB-165

Sandys, George 1578-1644 .... DLB-24, 121

Sangster, Charles 1822-1893 .... DLB-99

Sanguineti, Edoardo 1930- DLB-128

Sanjōnishi Sanetaka 1455-1537 .... DLB-203

Sansay, Leonora ?-after 1823 .... DLB-200

Sansom, William 1912-1976 .... DLB-139

Santayana, George
  1863-1952 ....DLB-54, 71; DS-13

Santiago, Danny 1911-1988 .... DLB-122

Santmyer, Helen Hooven 1895-1986........ Y-84

Sanvitale, Francesca 1928- DLB-196

Sapidus, Joannes 1490-1561 ....DLB-179

Sapir, Edward 1884-1939............. DLB-92

Sapper (see McNeile, Herman Cyril)

Sappho circa 620 B.C.-circa 550 B.C. DLB-176

Saramago, José 1922- Y-98

Sardou, Victorien 1831-1908 .... DLB-192

Sarduy, Severo 1937- DLB-113

Sargent, Pamela 1948- DLB-8

Saro-Wiwa, Ken 1941- DLB-157

Saroyan, William 1908-1981 ...DLB-7, 9, 86; Y-81

Sarraute, Nathalie 1900-1999 .... DLB-83

Sarrazin, Albertine 1937-1967 .... DLB-83

Sarris, Greg 1952- DLB-175

Sarton, May 1912-1995 ....DLB-48; Y-81

Sartre, Jean-Paul 1905-1980 .... DLB-72

Sassoon, Siegfried
  1886-1967 .... DLB-20, 191; DS-18

Siegfried Loraine Sassoon:
  A Centenary Essay
  Tributes from Vivien F. Clarke and
  Michael Thorpe Y-86

Sata, Ineko 1904- DLB-180

Saturday Review Press................ DLB-46

Saunders, James 1925- DLB-13

Saunders, John Monk 1897-1940 .... DLB-26

Saunders, Margaret Marshall
  1861-1947 .... DLB-92

Saunders and Otley DLB-106

Savage, James 1784-1873............. DLB-30

Savage, Marmion W. 1803?-1872........ DLB-21

Savage, Richard 1697?-1743 .... DLB-95

Savard, Félix-Antoine 1896-1982 .... DLB-68

Savery, Henry 1791-1842............. DLB-230

Saville, (Leonard) Malcolm 1901-1982... DLB-160

Sawyer, Ruth 1880-1970.............. DLB-22

Sayers, Dorothy L.
  1893-1957 ....DLB-10, 36, 77, 100

Sayle, Charles Edward 1864-1924 ...... DLB-184

Sayles, John Thomas 1950- DLB-44

Sbarbaro, Camillo 1888-1967.......... DLB-114

Scalapino, Leslie 1947- DLB-193

Scannell, Vernon 1922- DLB-27

Scarry, Richard 1919-1994............ DLB-61

Schaefer, Jack 1907-1991............. DLB-212

Schaeffer, Albrecht 1885-1950 .... DLB-66

Schaeffer, Susan Fromberg 1941- DLB-28

Schaff, Philip 1819-1893................DS-13

Schaper, Edzard 1908-1984 .... DLB-69

Scharf, J. Thomas 1843-1898 .... DLB-47

Schede, Paul Melissus 1539-1602........DLB-179

Scheffel, Joseph Viktor von 1826-1886... DLB-129

Scheffler, Johann 1624-1677 .... DLB-164

Schelling, Friedrich Wilhelm Joseph von
  1775-1854.................... DLB-90

Scherer, Wilhelm 1841-1886 .... DLB-129

Scherfig, Hans 1905-1979............. DLB-214

Schickele, René 1883-1940 .... DLB-66

Schiff, Dorothy 1903-1989 ....DLB-127

Schiller, Friedrich 1759-1805 .... DLB-94

Schirmer, David 1623-1687 .... DLB-164

Schlaf, Johannes 1862-1941 .... DLB-118

Schlegel, August Wilhelm 1767-1845 ..... DLB-94

Schlegel, Dorothea 1763-1839.......... DLB-90

Schlegel, Friedrich 1772-1829 .... DLB-90

Schleiermacher, Friedrich 1768-1834 ..... DLB-90

Schlesinger, Arthur M., Jr. 1917- DLB-17

Schlumberger, Jean 1877-1968 .... DLB-65

Cumulative Index

Schmid, Eduard Hermann Wilhelm
(see Edschmid, Kasimir)

Schmidt, Arno 1914-1979 . . . . .DLB-69

Schmidt, Johann Kaspar (see Stirner, Max)

Schmidt, Michael 1947- DLB-40

Schmidtbonn, Wilhelm August
1876-1952 . . . . .DLB-118

Schmitz, James H. 1911- DLB-8

Schnabel, Johann Gottfried
1692-1760 . . . . .DLB-168

Schnackenberg, Gjertrud 1953- DLB-120

Schnitzler, Arthur 1862-1931 . . . . . . .DLB-81, 118

Schnurre, Wolfdietrich 1920-1989 . . . . . . .DLB-69

Schocken Books .DLB-46

Scholartis Press DLB-112

Scholderer, Victor 1880-1971 . . . . .DLB-201

The Schomburg Center for Research
in Black Culture DLB-76

Schönbeck, Virgilio (see Giotti, Virgilio)

Schönherr, Karl 1867-1943 . . . . .DLB-118

Schoolcraft, Jane Johnston 1800-1841 . . . .DLB-175

School Stories, 1914-1960 . . . . .DLB-160

Schopenhauer, Arthur 1788-1860 . . . . . . .DLB-90

Schopenhauer, Johanna 1766-1838 . . . . . . .DLB-90

Schorer, Mark 1908-1977 . . . . .DLB-103

Schottelius, Justus Georg 1612-1676 . . . . .DLB-164

Schouler, James 1839-1920 . . . . .DLB-47

Schrader, Paul 1946- DLB-44

Schreiner, Olive
1855-1920 . . . . .DLB-18, 156, 190, 225

Schroeder, Andreas 1946- DLB-53

Schubart, Christian Friedrich Daniel
1739-1791 . . . . .DLB-97

Schubert, Gotthilf Heinrich 1780-1860 . . . .DLB-90

Schücking, Levin 1814-1883 . . . . .DLB-133

Schulberg, Budd 1914- DLB-6, 26, 28; Y-81

Schulte, F. J., and Company DLB-49

Schulz, Bruno 1892-1942 . . . . .DLB-215

Schulze, Hans (see Praetorius, Johannes)

Schupp, Johann Balthasar 1610-1661 . . . . .DLB-164

Schurz, Carl 1829-1906 . . . . .DLB-23

Schuyler, George S. 1895-1977 . . . . . . .DLB-29, 51

Schuyler, James 1923-1991 . . . . .DLB-5, 169

Schwartz, Delmore 1913-1966 . . . . . . .DLB-28, 48

Schwartz, Jonathan 1938- Y-82

Schwartz, Lynne Sharon 1939- DLB-218

Schwarz, Sibylle 1621-1638 . . . . .DLB-164

Schwerner, Armand 1927-1999 . . . . .DLB-165

Schwob, Marcel 1867-1905 . . . . .DLB-123

Sciascia, Leonardo 1921-1989 . . . . .DLB-177

Science Fantasy .DLB-8

Science-Fiction Fandom and Conventions . . .DLB-8

Science-Fiction Fanzines: The Time
Binders DLB-8

Science-Fiction Films DLB-8

Science Fiction Writers of America and the
Nebula Awards DLB-8

Scot, Reginald circa 1538-1599 . . . . .DLB-136

Scotellaro, Rocco 1923-1953 . . . . .DLB-128

Scott, Dennis 1939-1991 . . . . .DLB-125

Scott, Dixon 1881-1915 . . . . .DLB-98

Scott, Duncan Campbell 1862-1947 . . . . . .DLB-92

Scott, Evelyn 1893-1963 . . . . .DLB-9, 48

Scott, F. R. 1899-1985 . . . . .DLB-88

Scott, Frederick George 1861-1944 . . . . . .DLB-92

Scott, Geoffrey 1884-1929 . . . . .DLB-149

Scott, Harvey W. 1838-1910 . . . . .DLB-23

Scott, Paul 1920-1978 . . . . .DLB-14, 207

Scott, Sarah 1723-1795 . . . . .DLB-39

Scott, Tom 1918- DLB-27

Scott, Sir Walter
1771-1832 . . . . . . .DLB-93, 107, 116, 144, 159

Scott, Walter, Publishing
Company Limited DLB-112

Scott, William Bell 1811-1890 . . . . .DLB-32

Scott, William R. [publishing house] DLB-46

Scott-Heron, Gil 1949- DLB-41

Scribe, Eugene 1791-1861 . . . . .DLB-192

Scribner, Arthur Hawley 1859-1932 . . . . DS-13, 16

Scribner, Charles 1854-1930 . . . . DS-13, 16

Scribner, Charles, Jr. 1921-1995 . . . . .Y-95

    Reminiscences DS-17

Charles Scribner's Sons DLB-49; DS-13, 16, 17

Scripps, E. W. 1854-1926 . . . . .DLB-25

Scudder, Horace Elisha 1838-1902 . . . .DLB-42, 71

Scudder, Vida Dutton 1861-1954 . . . . .DLB-71

Scupham, Peter 1933- DLB-40

Seabrook, William 1886-1945 . . . . .DLB-4

Seabury, Samuel 1729-1796 . . . . .DLB-31

Seacole, Mary Jane Grant 1805-1881 . . . . .DLB-166

The Seafarer circa 970 . . . . .DLB-146

Sealsfield, Charles (Carl Postl)
1793-1864 . . . . .DLB-133, 186

Sears, Edward I. 1819?-1876 . . . . .DLB-79

Sears Publishing Company DLB-46

Seaton, George 1911-1979 . . . . .DLB-44

Seaton, William Winston 1785-1866 . . . . . .DLB-43

Secker, Martin [publishing house] DLB-112

Secker, Martin, and Warburg Limited DLB-112

Second-Generation Minor Poets of the
Seventeenth Century DLB-126

Sedgwick, Arthur George 1844-1915 . . . . . .DLB-64

Sedgwick, Catharine Maria
1789-1867 . . . . .DLB-1, 74, 183

Sedgwick, Ellery 1872-1930 . . . . .DLB-91

Sedley, Sir Charles 1639-1701 . . . . .DLB-131

Seeberg, Peter 1925-1999 . . . . .DLB-214

Seeger, Alan 1888-1916 . . . . .DLB-45

Seers, Eugene (see Dantin, Louis)

Segal, Erich 1937- Y-86

Šegedin, Petar 1909- DLB-181

Seghers, Anna 1900-1983 . . . . .DLB-69

Seid, Ruth (see Sinclair, Jo)

Seidel, Frederick Lewis 1936- Y-84

Seidel, Ina 1885-1974 . . . . .DLB-56

Seifert, Jaroslav 1901-1986 . . . . DLB-215; Y-84

Seigenthaler, John 1927- DLB-127

Seizin Press DLB-112

Séjour, Victor 1817-1874 . . . . .DLB-50

Séjour Marcou et Ferrand, Juan Victor
(see Séjour, Victor)

Sekowski, Jósef-Julian, Baron Brambeus
(see Senkovsky, Osip Ivanovich)

Selby, Bettina 1934- DLB-204

Selby, Hubert, Jr. 1928- DLB-2, 227

Selden, George 1929-1989 . . . . .DLB-52

Selden, John 1584-1654 . . . . .DLB-213

Selected English-Language Little Magazines
and Newspapers [France, 1920-1939] . . .DLB-4

Selected Humorous Magazines
(1820-1950) DLB-11

Selected Science-Fiction Magazines and
Anthologies DLB-8

Selenić, Slobodan 1933-1995 . . . . .DLB-181

Self, Edwin F. 1920- DLB-137

Self, Will 1961- DLB-207

Seligman, Edwin R. A. 1861-1939 . . . . . . .DLB-47

Selimović, Meša 1910-1982 . . . . .DLB-181

Selous, Frederick Courteney
1851-1917 . . . . .DLB-174

Seltzer, Chester E. (see Muro, Amado)

Seltzer, Thomas [publishing house] DLB-46

Selvon, Sam 1923-1994 . . . . .DLB-125

Semmes, Raphael 1809-1877 . . . . .DLB-189

Senancour, Etienne de 1770-1846 . . . . . . .DLB-119

Sendak, Maurice 1928- DLB-61

Seneca the Elder
circa 54 B.C.-circa A.D. 40 . . . . .DLB-211

Seneca the Younger
circa 1 B.C.-A.D. 65 . . . . .DLB-211

Senécal, Eva 1905- DLB-92

Sengstacke, John 1912- DLB-127

Senior, Olive 1941- DLB-157

Senkovsky, Osip Ivanovich
(Jósef-Julian Sekowski, Baron Brambeus)
1800-1858 . . . . .DLB-198

Šenoa, August 1838-1881 . . . . .DLB-147

"Sensation Novels" (1863), by
H. L. Manse DLB-21

Sepamla, Sipho 1932- DLB-157, 225

Seredy, Kate 1899-1975 . . . . .DLB-22

Sereni, Vittorio 1913-1983 . . . . .DLB-128

Seres, William [publishing house] DLB-170

Serling, Rod 1924-1975 . . . . .DLB-26

Serote, Mongane Wally 1944- DLB-125, 225

Serraillier, Ian 1912-1994 . . . . .DLB-161

Serrano, Nina 1934- DLB-122

Service, Robert 1874-1958 . . . . .DLB-92

Sessler, Charles 1854-1935 . . . . .DLB-187

Seth, Vikram 1952- DLB-120

Seton, Elizabeth Ann 1774-1821 . . . . .DLB-200

Seton, Ernest Thompson
1860-1942 .... DLB-92; DS-13

Setouchi Harumi 1922- DLB-182

Settle, Mary Lee 1918- DLB-6

Seume, Johann Gottfried 1763-1810 ...... DLB-94

Seuse, Heinrich 1295?-1366 ....DLB-179

Seuss, Dr. (see Geisel, Theodor Seuss)

The Seventy-fifth Anniversary of the Armistice:
The Wilfred Owen Centenary and
the Great War Exhibit
at the University of Virginia Y-93

Severin, Timothy 1940- DLB-204

Sewall, Joseph 1688-1769 .... DLB-24

Sewall, Richard B. 1908- DLB-111

Sewell, Anna 1820-1878 .... DLB-163

Sewell, Samuel 1652-1730 .... DLB-24

Sex, Class, Politics, and Religion [in the
British Novel, 1930-1959] DLB-15

Sexton, Anne 1928-1974 .... DLB-5, 169

Seymour-Smith, Martin 1928-1998...... DLB-155

Sgorlon, Carlo 1930- DLB-196

Shaara, Michael 1929-1988............ Y-83

Shadwell, Thomas 1641?-1692 .... DLB-80

Shaffer, Anthony 1926- DLB-13

Shaffer, Peter 1926- DLB-13, 233

Shaftesbury, Anthony Ashley Cooper,
Third Earl of 1671-1713 .... DLB-101

Shairp, Mordaunt 1887-1939 .... DLB-10

Shakespeare, Nicholas 1957- DLB-231

Shakespeare, William 1564-1616 .....DLB-62, 172

The Shakespeare Globe Trust Y-93

Shakespeare Head Press DLB-112

Shakhovskoi, Aleksandr Aleksandrovich
1777-1846 .... DLB-150

Shange, Ntozake 1948- DLB-38

Shapiro, Karl 1913- DLB-48

Sharon Publications DLB-46

Sharp, Margery 1905-1991........... DLB-161

Sharp, William 1855-1905 .... DLB-156

Sharpe, Tom 1928- DLB-14, 231

Shaw, Albert 1857-1947 .... DLB-91

Shaw, George Bernard
1856-1950 ....DLB-10, 57, 190

Shaw, Henry Wheeler 1818-1885....... DLB-11

Shaw, Joseph T. 1874-1952............ DLB-137

Shaw, Irwin 1913-1984........DLB-6, 102; Y-84

Shaw, Mary 1854-1929............ DLB-228

Shaw, Robert 1927-1978 .... DLB-13, 14

Shaw, Robert B. 1947- DLB-120

Shawn, William 1907-1992........... DLB-137

Shay, Frank [publishing house]......... DLB-46

Shea, John Gilmary 1824-1892......... DLB-30

Sheaffer, Louis 1912-1993 .... DLB-103

Shearing, Joseph 1886-1952 .... DLB-70

Shebbeare, John 1709-1788 .... DLB-39

Sheckley, Robert 1928- DLB-8

Shedd, William G. T. 1820-1894 .... DLB-64

Sheed, Wilfred 1930- DLB-6

Sheed and Ward [U.S.]............... DLB-46

Sheed and Ward Limited [U.K.] DLB-112

Sheldon, Alice B. (see Tiptree, James, Jr.)

Sheldon, Edward 1886-1946............ DLB-7

Sheldon and Company................ DLB-49

Shelley, Mary Wollstonecraft
1797-1851 .... DLB-110, 116, 159, 178

Shelley, Percy Bysshe
1792-1822................DLB-96, 110, 158

Shelnutt, Eve 1941- DLB-130

Shenstone, William 1714-1763 .... DLB-95

Shepard, Clark and Brown............ DLB-49

Shepard, Ernest Howard 1879-1976 ..... DLB-160

Shepard, Sam 1943- DLB-7, 212

Shepard, Thomas I, 1604 or 1605-1649... DLB-24

Shepard, Thomas II, 1635-1677 .... DLB-24

Shepherd, Luke
flourished 1547-1554 .... DLB-136

Sherburne, Edward 1616-1702 .... DLB-131

Sheridan, Frances 1724-1766........ DLB-39, 84

Sheridan, Richard Brinsley 1751-1816 .... DLB-89

Sherman, Francis 1871-1926 .... DLB-92

Sherman, Martin 1938- DLB-228

Sherriff, R. C. 1896-1975 ......DLB-10, 191, 233

Sherry, Norman 1935- DLB-155

Sherwood, Mary Martha 1775-1851..... DLB-163

Sherwood, Robert 1896-1955.........DLB-7, 26

Shevyrev, Stepan Petrovich
1806-1864 .... DLB-205

Shiel, M. P. 1865-1947 .... DLB-153

Shiels, George 1886-1949............. DLB-10

Shiga, Naoya 1883-1971 .... DLB-180

Shiina Rinzō 1911-1973 .... DLB-182

Shikishi Naishinnō 1153?-1201........ DLB-203

Shillaber, B.[enjamin] P.[enhallow]
1814-1890 .... DLB-1, 11

Shimao Toshio 1917-1986 .... DLB-182

Shimazaki, Tōson 1872-1943 .... DLB-180

Shine, Ted 1931- DLB-38

Shinkei 1406-1475................... DLB-203

Ship, Reuben 1915-1975 .... DLB-88

Shirer, William L. 1904-1993............ DLB-4

Shirinsky-Shikhmatov, Sergii Aleksandrovich
1783-1837..................... DLB-150

Shirley, James 1596-1666 .... DLB-58

Shishkov, Aleksandr Semenovich
1753-1841...................... DLB-150

Shockley, Ann Allen 1927- DLB-33

Shōno Junzō 1921- DLB-182

Shore, Arabella 1820?-1901 and
Shore, Louisa 1824-1895 .... DLB-199

Short, Peter [publishing house].........DLB-170

Shorthouse, Joseph Henry 1834-1903 .... DLB-18

Shōtetsu 1381-1459 .... DLB-203

Showalter, Elaine 1941- DLB-67

Shulevitz, Uri 1935- DLB-61

Shulman, Max 1919-1988............. DLB-11

Shute, Henry A. 1856-1943 .... DLB-9

Shuttle, Penelope 1947- DLB-14, 40

Sibbes, Richard 1577-1635 .... DLB-151

Siddal, Elizabeth Eleanor 1829-1862 .... DLB-199

Sidgwick, Ethel 1877-1970............DLB-197

Sidgwick and Jackson Limited DLB-112

Sidney, Margaret (see Lothrop, Harriet M.)

Sidney, Mary 1561-1621 .... DLB-167

Sidney, Sir Philip 1554-1586........... DLB-167

An Apologie for Poetrie (the Olney
edition, 1595, of Defence of Poesie) DLB-167

Sidney's Press...................... DLB-49

Sierra, Rubén 1946- DLB-122

Sierra Club Books DLB-49

Siger of Brabant circa 1240-circa 1284 ... DLB-115

Sigourney, Lydia Howard (Huntley)
1791-1865.............DLB-1, 42, 73, 183

Silkin, Jon 1930- DLB-27

Silko, Leslie Marmon 1948- DLB-143, 175

Silliman, Benjamin 1779-1864.......... DLB-183

Silliman, Ron 1946- DLB-169

Silliphant, Stirling 1918- DLB-26

Sillitoe, Alan 1928- DLB-14, 139

Silman, Roberta 1934- DLB-28

Silva, Beverly 1930- DLB-122

Silverberg, Robert 1935- DLB-8

Silverman, Kenneth 1936- DLB-111

Simak, Clifford D. 1904-1988........... DLB-8

Simcoe, Elizabeth 1762-1850........... DLB-99

Simcox, Edith Jemima 1844-1901....... DLB-190

Simcox, George Augustus 1841-1905..... DLB-35

Sime, Jessie Georgina 1868-1958 .... DLB-92

Simenon, Georges 1903-1989......DLB-72; Y-89

Simic, Charles 1938- DLB-105

"Images and 'Images,'" DLB-105

Simionescu, Mircea Horia 1928- DLB-232

Simmel, Johannes Mario 1924- DLB-69

Simmes, Valentine [publishing house] DLB-170

Simmons, Ernest J. 1903-1972 .... DLB-103

Simmons, Herbert Alfred 1930- DLB-33

Simmons, James 1933- DLB-40

Simms, William Gilmore
1806-1870.............DLB-3, 30, 59, 73

Simms and M'Intyre................ DLB-106

Simon, Claude 1913- DLB-83; Y-85

Simon, Neil 1927- DLB-7

Simon and Schuster DLB-46

Simons, Katherine Drayton Mayrant
1890-1969 .... Y-83

Simović, Ljubomir 1935- DLB-181

Simpkin and Marshall
[publishing house] DLB-154

Simpson, Helen 1897-1940 .... DLB-77

Simpson, Louis 1923- DLB-5

Simpson, N. F. 1919- DLB-13

Sims, George 1923- DLB-87; Y-99

Sims, George Robert 1847-1922. . . DLB-35, 70, 135

Sinán, Rogelio 1904- DLB-145

Sinclair, Andrew 1935- DLB-14

Sinclair, Bertrand William 1881-1972 . . . . .DLB-92

Sinclair, Catherine 1800-1864 . . . . .DLB-163

Sinclair, Jo 1913-1995 . . . . .DLB-28

Sinclair, Lister 1921- DLB-88

Sinclair, May 1863-1946 . . . . .DLB-36, 135

Sinclair, Upton 1878-1968 . . . . .DLB-9

Sinclair, Upton [publishing house] DLB-46

Singer, Isaac Bashevis
    1904-1991 . . . . DLB-6, 28, 52; Y-91

Singer, Mark 1950- DLB-185

Singmaster, Elsie 1879-1958. . . . . .DLB-9

Sinisgalli, Leonardo 1908-1981 . . . . .DLB-114

Siodmak, Curt 1902- DLB-44

Sîrbu, Ion D. 1919-1989. . . . . .DLB-232

Siringo, Charles A. 1855-1928 . . . . .DLB-186

Sissman, L. E. 1928-1976 . . . . .DLB-5

Sisson, C. H. 1914- DLB-27

Sitwell, Edith 1887-1964. . . . . .DLB-20

Sitwell, Osbert 1892-1969 . . . . .DLB-100, 195

Skácel, Jan 1922-1989 . . . . .DLB-232

Skalbe, Kārlis 1879-1945 . . . . .DLB-220

Skármeta, Antonio 1940- DLB-145

Skeat, Walter W. 1835-1912 . . . . .DLB-184

Skeffington, William
    [publishing house] DLB-106

Skelton, John 1463-1529 . . . . .DLB-136

Skelton, Robin 1925- DLB-27, 53

Škéma, Antanas 1910-1961 . . . . .DLB-220

Skinner, Constance Lindsay
    1877-1939 . . . . .DLB-92

Skinner, John Stuart 1788-1851 . . . . .DLB-73

Skipsey, Joseph 1832-1903. . . . . .DLB-35

Skou-Hansen, Tage 1925- DLB-214

Škvorecký, Josef 1924- DLB-232

Slade, Bernard 1930- DLB-53

Slamnig, Ivan 1930- DLB-181

Slančeková, Božena (see Timrava)

Slater, Patrick 1880-1951 . . . . .DLB-68

Slaveykov, Pencho 1866-1912 . . . . .DLB-147

Slaviček, Milivoj 1929- DLB-181

Slavitt, David 1935- DLB-5, 6

Sleigh, Burrows Willcocks Arthur
    1821-1869 . . . . .DLB-99

A Slender Thread of Hope:
    The Kennedy Center Black
    Theatre Project DLB-38

Slesinger, Tess 1905-1945 . . . . .DLB-102

Slick, Sam (see Haliburton, Thomas Chandler)

Sloan, John 1871-1951 . . . . .DLB-188

Sloane, William, Associates DLB-46

Small, Maynard and Company DLB-49

Small Presses in Great Britain and Ireland,
    1960-1985 . . . . .DLB-40

Small Presses I: Jargon Society. Y-84

Small Presses II: The Spirit That Moves
    Us Press Y-85

Small Presses III: Pushcart Press Y-87

Smart, Christopher 1722-1771 . . . . .DLB-109

Smart, David A. 1892-1957 . . . . .DLB-137

Smart, Elizabeth 1913-1986 . . . . .DLB-88

Smedley, Menella Bute 1820?-1877 . . . . . .DLB-199

Smellie, William [publishing house]. DLB-154

Smiles, Samuel 1812-1904 . . . . .DLB-55

Smiley, Jane 1949- DLB-227, 234

Smith, A. J. M. 1902-1980 . . . . .DLB-88

Smith, Adam 1723-1790 . . . . .DLB-104

Smith, Adam (George Jerome Waldo Goodman)
    1930- DLB-185

Smith, Alexander 1829-1867 . . . . . . .DLB-32, 55

    "On the Writing of Essays" (1862) DLB-57

Smith, Amanda 1837-1915 . . . . .DLB-221

Smith, Betty 1896-1972 . . . . Y-82

Smith, Carol Sturm 1938- Y-81

Smith, Charles Henry 1826-1903 . . . . .DLB-11

Smith, Charlotte 1749-1806 . . . . .DLB-39, 109

Smith, Chet 1899-1973. . . . . .DLB-171

Smith, Cordwainer 1913-1966. . . . . .DLB-8

Smith, Dave 1942- DLB-5

Smith, Dodie 1896- DLB-10

Smith, Doris Buchanan 1934- DLB-52

Smith, E. E. 1890-1965 . . . . .DLB-8

Smith, Elder and Company DLB-154

Smith, Elihu Hubbard 1771-1798 . . . . .DLB-37

Smith, Elizabeth Oakes (Prince)
    1806-1893 .DLB-1

Smith, Eunice 1757-1823 . . . . .DLB-200

Smith, F. Hopkinson 1838-1915 . . . . DS-13

Smith, George D. 1870-1920 . . . . .DLB-140

Smith, George O. 1911-1981 . . . . .DLB-8

Smith, Goldwin 1823-1910 . . . . .DLB-99

Smith, H. Allen 1907-1976 . . . . .DLB-11, 29

Smith, Harrison, and Robert Haas
    [publishing house] DLB-46

Smith, Harry B. 1860-1936 . . . . .DLB-187

Smith, Hazel Brannon 1914- DLB-127

Smith, Henry circa 1560-circa 1591. . . . . .DLB-136

Smith, Horatio (Horace) 1779-1849 . . . . . .DLB-116

Smith, Horatio (Horace) 1779-1849 and
    James Smith 1775-1839 . . . . .DLB-96

Smith, Iain Crichton 1928- DLB-40, 139

Smith, J. Allen 1860-1924 . . . . .DLB-47

Smith, J. Stilman, and Company DLB-49

Smith, Jessie Willcox 1863-1935 . . . . . . .DLB-188

Smith, John 1580-1631. . . . . .DLB-24, 30

Smith, Josiah 1704-1781 . . . . .DLB-24

Smith, Ken 1938- DLB-40

Smith, Lee 1944- DLB-143; Y-83

Smith, Logan Pearsall 1865-1946 . . . . . . .DLB-98

Smith, Mark 1935- Y-82

Smith, Michael 1698-circa 1771 . . . . .DLB-31

Smith, Pauline 1882-1959 . . . . .DLB-225

Smith, Red 1905-1982 . . . . DLB-29, 171

Smith, Roswell 1829-1892 . . . . .DLB-79

Smith, Samuel Harrison 1772-1845 . . . . . .DLB-43

Smith, Samuel Stanhope 1751-1819 . . . . . .DLB-37

Smith, Sarah (see Stretton, Hesba)

Smith, Sarah Pogson 1774-1870 . . . . .DLB-200

Smith, Seba 1792-1868. . . . . .DLB-1, 11

Smith, Stevie 1902-1971 . . . . .DLB-20

Smith, Sydney 1771-1845. . . . . .DLB-107

Smith, Sydney Goodsir 1915-1975. . . . . . .DLB-27

Smith, Sir Thomas 1513-1577 . . . . .DLB-132

Smith, W. B., and Company DLB-49

Smith, W. H., and Son DLB-106

Smith, Wendell 1914-1972. . . . . .DLB-171

Smith, William flourished 1595-1597 . . . .DLB-136

Smith, William 1727-1803 . . . . .DLB-31

    A General Idea of the College of Mirania
    (1753) [excerpts] DLB-31

Smith, William 1728-1793 . . . . .DLB-30

Smith, William Gardner 1927-1974 . . . . . .DLB-76

Smith, William Henry 1808-1872 . . . . . . .DLB-159

Smith, William Jay 1918- DLB-5

Smithers, Leonard [publishing house] DLB-112

Smollett, Tobias 1721-1771 . . . . .DLB-39, 104

    Dedication, Ferdinand Count
    Fathom (1753) DLB-39

    Preface to Ferdinand Count Fathom (1753) . .DLB-39

    Preface to Roderick Random (1748) DLB-39

Smythe, Francis Sydney 1900-1949 . . . . . .DLB-195

Snelling, William Joseph 1804-1848 . . . . .DLB-202

Snellings, Rolland (see Touré, Askia Muhammad)

Snodgrass, W. D. 1926- DLB-5

Snow, C. P. 1905-1980 . . . . DLB-15, 77; DS-17

Snyder, Gary 1930- DLB-5, 16, 165, 212

Sobiloff, Hy 1912-1970. . . . . .DLB-48

The Society for Textual Scholarship and
    TEXT Y-87

The Society for the History of Authorship,
    Reading and Publishing Y-92

Soffici, Ardengo 1879-1964 . . . . .DLB-114

Sofola, 'Zulu 1938- DLB-157

Solano, Solita 1888-1975 . . . . .DLB-4

Soldati, Mario 1906-1999 . . . . .DLB-177

Šoljan, Antun 1932-1993 . . . . .DLB-181

Sollers, Philippe 1936- DLB-83

Sollogub, Vladimir Aleksandrovich
    1813-1882 . . . . .DLB-198

Solmi, Sergio 1899-1981 . . . . .DLB-114

Solomon, Carl 1928- DLB-16

Solway, David 1941- DLB-53

Solzhenitsyn and America Y-85

Somerville, Edith Œnone 1858-1949 . . . . .DLB-135

Somov, Orest Mikhailovich
    1793-1833 . . . . DLB-198

Sønderby, Knud 1909-1966 . . . . DLB-214

Song, Cathy 1955- DLB-169

Sono Ayako 1931- DLB-182

Sontag, Susan 1933- DLB-2, 67

Sophocles 497/496 B.C.-406/405 B.C. DLB-176

Šopov, Aco 1923-1982 . . . . DLB-181

Sørensen, Villy 1929- DLB-214

Sorensen, Virginia 1912-1991 . . . . DLB-206

Sorge, Reinhard Johannes 1892-1916 . . . . DLB-118

Sorrentino, Gilbert 1929- DLB-5, 173; Y-80

Sotheby, James 1682-1742 . . . . DLB-213

Sotheby, John 1740-1807 . . . . DLB-213

Sotheby, Samuel 1771-1842 . . . . DLB-213

Sotheby, Samuel Leigh 1805-1861 . . . . . . DLB-213

Sotheby, William 1757-1833 . . . . DLB-93, 213

Soto, Gary 1952- DLB-82

Sources for the Study of Tudor and Stuart
    Drama DLB-62

Souster, Raymond 1921- DLB-88

The *South English Legendary circa thirteenth-fifteenth
    centuries* DLB-146

Southerland, Ellease 1943- DLB-33

Southern, Terry 1924-1995 . . . . DLB-2

Southern Illinois University Press Y-95

Southern Writers Between the Wars DLB-9

Southerne, Thomas 1659-1746 . . . . DLB-80

Southey, Caroline Anne Bowles
    1786-1854 . . . . DLB-116

Southey, Robert 1774-1843 . . . . . .DLB-93, 107, 142

Southwell, Robert 1561?-1595 . . . . DLB-167

Sowande, Bode 1948- DLB-157

Sowle, Tace [publishing house] DLB-170

Soyfer, Jura 1912-1939 . . . . DLB-124

Soyinka, Wole 1934- DLB-125; Y-86, Y-87

Spacks, Barry 1931- DLB-105

Spalding, Frances 1950- DLB-155

Spark, Muriel 1918- DLB-15, 139

Sparke, Michael [publishing house] DLB-170

Sparks, Jared 1789-1866 . . . . DLB-1, 30

Sparshott, Francis 1926- DLB-60

Späth, Gerold 1939- DLB-75

Spatola, Adriano 1941-1988 . . . . DLB-128

Spaziani, Maria Luisa 1924- DLB-128

Special Collections at the University of Colorado
    at Boulder Y-98

The Spectator 1828- DLB-110

Spedding, James 1808-1881 . . . . DLB-144

Spee von Langenfeld, Friedrich
    1591-1635 . . . . DLB-164

Speght, Rachel 1597-after 1630 . . . . DLB-126

Speke, John Hanning 1827-1864 . . . . DLB-166

Spellman, A. B. 1935- DLB-41

Spence, Catherine Helen 1825-1910 . . . . . DLB-230

Spence, Thomas 1750-1814 . . . . DLB-158

Spencer, Anne 1882-1975 . . . . DLB-51, 54

Spencer, Charles, third Earl of Sunderland
    1674-1722 . . . . DLB-213

Spencer, Elizabeth 1921- DLB-6, 218

Spencer, George John, Second Earl Spencer
    1758-1834 . . . . DLB-184

Spencer, Herbert 1820-1903 . . . . DLB-57

    "The Philosophy of Style" (1852) DLB-57

Spencer, Scott 1945- Y-86

Spender, J. A. 1862-1942 . . . . DLB-98

Spender, Stephen 1909-1995 . . . . DLB-20

Spener, Philipp Jakob 1635-1705 . . . . DLB-164

Spenser, Edmund circa 1552-1599 . . . . . . DLB-167

    Envoy from The Shepheardes Calender . . . DLB-167

    "The Generall Argument of the
    Whole Booke," from
    The Shepheardes Calender DLB-167

    "A Letter of the Authors Expounding
    His Whole Intention in the Course
    of this Worke: Which for that It Giueth
    Great Light to the Reader, for the Better
    Vnderstanding Is Hereunto Annexed,"
    from The Faerie Queene (1590) DLB-167

    "To His Booke," from
    The Shepheardes Calender (1579) DLB-167

    "To the Most Excellent and Learned Both
    Orator and Poete, Mayster Gabriell Haruey,
    His Verie Special and Singular Good Frend
    E. K. Commendeth the Good Lyking of
    This His Labour, and the Patronage of
    the New Poete," from
    The Shepheardes Calender DLB-167

Sperr, Martin 1944- DLB-124

Spicer, Jack 1925-1965 . . . . DLB-5, 16, 193

Spielberg, Peter 1929- Y-81

Spielhagen, Friedrich 1829-1911 . . . . DLB-129

"Spielmannsepen" (circa 1152-circa 1500) . . DLB-148

Spier, Peter 1927- DLB-61

Spillane, Mickey 1918- DLB-226

Spinrad, Norman 1940- DLB-8

Spires, Elizabeth 1952- DLB-120

Spitteler, Carl 1845-1924 . . . . DLB-129

Spivak, Lawrence E. 1900- DLB-137

Spofford, Harriet Prescott
    1835-1921 . . . . DLB-74, 221

Spring, Howard 1889-1965 . . . . DLB-191

Squibob (see Derby, George Horatio)

Squier, E. G. 1821-1888 . . . . DLB-189

Stacpoole, H. de Vere 1863-1951 . . . . DLB-153

Staël, Germaine de 1766-1817 . . . . . . DLB-119, 192

Staël-Holstein, Anne-Louise Germaine de
    (see Staël, Germaine de)

Stafford, Jean 1915-1979 . . . . .DLB-2, 173

Stafford, William 1914-1993 . . . . DLB-5, 206

Stage Censorship: "The Rejected Statement"
    (1911), by Bernard Shaw [excerpts] . . . DLB-10

Stallings, Laurence 1894-1968 . . . . .DLB-7, 44

Stallworthy, Jon 1935- DLB-40

Stampp, Kenneth M. 1912- DLB-17

Stănescu, Nichita 1933-1983 . . . . DLB-232

Stanev, Emiliyan 1907-1979 . . . . DLB-181

Stanford, Ann 1916- DLB-5

Stangerup, Henrik 1937-1998 . . . . DLB-214

Stankevich, Nikolai Vladimirovich
    1813-1840 . . . . DLB-198

Stanković, Borisav ("Bora")
    1876-1927 . . . . .DLB-147

Stanley, Henry M. 1841-1904 . . . DLB-189; DS-13

Stanley, Thomas 1625-1678 . . . . DLB-131

Stannard, Martin 1947- DLB-155

Stansby, William [publishing house] DLB-170

Stanton, Elizabeth Cady 1815-1902 . . . . . . DLB-79

Stanton, Frank L. 1857-1927 . . . . DLB-25

Stanton, Maura 1946- DLB-120

Stapledon, Olaf 1886-1950 . . . . DLB-15

Star Spangled Banner Office DLB-49

Stark, Freya 1893-1993 . . . . DLB-195

Starkey, Thomas circa 1499-1538 . . . . . . DLB-132

Starkie, Walter 1894-1976 . . . . DLB-195

Starkweather, David 1935- DLB-7

Starrett, Vincent 1886-1974 . . . . .DLB-187

The State of Publishing Y-97

Statements on the Art of Poetry DLB-54

Stationers' Company of London, The DLB-170

Statius circa A.D. 45-A.D. 96 . . . . DLB-211

Stead, Robert J. C. 1880-1959 . . . . DLB-92

Steadman, Mark 1930- DLB-6

The Stealthy School of Criticism (1871), by
    Dante Gabriel Rossetti DLB-35

Stearns, Harold E. 1891-1943 . . . . DLB-4

Stedman, Edmund Clarence 1833-1908 . . . DLB-64

Steegmuller, Francis 1906-1994 . . . . DLB-111

Steel, Flora Annie 1847-1929 . . . . . . DLB-153, 156

Steele, Max 1922- Y-80

Steele, Richard 1672-1729 . . . . DLB-84, 101

Steele, Timothy 1948- DLB-120

Steele, Wilbur Daniel 1886-1970 . . . . DLB-86

Steere, Richard circa 1643-1721 . . . . DLB-24

Stefanovski, Goran 1952- DLB-181

Stegner, Wallace 1909-1993 . . . . .DLB-9, 206; Y-93

Stehr, Hermann 1864-1940 . . . . DLB-66

Steig, William 1907- DLB-61

Stein, Gertrude
    1874-1946 . . . . .DLB-4, 54, 86, 228; DS-15

Stein, Leo 1872-1947 . . . . DLB-4

Stein and Day Publishers DLB-46

Steinbeck, John 1902-1968 . . . .DLB-7, 9, 212; DS-2

    John Steinbeck Research Center Y-85

Steiner, George 1929- DLB-67

Steinhoewel, Heinrich 1411/1412-1479 . . . .DLB-179

Steloff, Ida Frances 1887-1989 . . . . .DLB-187

Stendhal 1783-1842 . . . . DLB-119

Stephen Crane: A Revaluation Virginia
    Tech Conference, 1989 . . . . Y-89

Stephen, Leslie 1832-1904 . . . . . .DLB-57, 144, 190

Stephen Vincent Benét Centenary Y-97

Stephens, A. G. 1865-1933. . . . . .DLB-230

Stephens, Alexander H. 1812-1883 . . . . . . .DLB-47

Stephens, Alice Barber 1858-1932 . . . . . .DLB-188

Stephens, Ann 1810-1886 . . . . .DLB-3, 73

Stephens, Charles Asbury 1844?-1931. . . . .DLB-42

Stephens, James 1882?-1950 . . . .DLB-19, 153, 162

Stephens, John Lloyd 1805-1852 . . . . . . .DLB-183

Stephens, Michael 1946- DLB-234

Sterling, George 1869-1926 . . . . .DLB-54

Sterling, James 1701-1763. . . . . .DLB-24

Sterling, John 1806-1844 . . . . .DLB-116

Stern, Gerald 1925- DLB-105

Stern, Gladys B. 1890-1973 . . . . .DLB-197

Stern, Madeleine B. 1912- DLB-111, 140

Stern, Richard 1928- DLB-218; Y-87

Stern, Stewart 1922- DLB-26

Sterne, Laurence 1713-1768 . . . . .DLB-39

Sternheim, Carl 1878-1942. . . . . . . .DLB-56, 118

Sternhold, Thomas ?-1549 and
　　John Hopkins ?-1570 . . . . .DLB-132

Steuart, David 1747-1824 . . . . .DLB-213

Stevens, Henry 1819-1886. . . . . .DLB-140

Stevens, Wallace 1879-1955. . . . . .DLB-54

Stevenson, Anne 1933- DLB-40

Stevenson, D. E. 1892-1973 . . . . .DLB-191

Stevenson, Lionel 1902-1973 . . . . .DLB-155

Stevenson, Robert Louis 1850-1894
　　. . . . . .DLB-18, 57, 141, 156, 174; DS-13

　"On Style in Literature:
　　Its Technical Elements" (1885) DLB-57

Stewart, Donald Ogden
　　1894-1980 . . . . .DLB-4, 11, 26

Stewart, Dugald 1753-1828 . . . . .DLB-31

Stewart, George, Jr. 1848-1906 . . . . .DLB-99

Stewart, George R. 1895-1980. . . . . .DLB-8

Stewart, Randall 1896-1964. . . . . .DLB-103

Stewart and Kidd Company DLB-46

Stickney, Trumbull 1874-1904. . . . . .DLB-54

Stieler, Caspar 1632-1707. . . . . .DLB-164

Stifter, Adalbert 1805-1868 . . . . .DLB-133

Stiles, Ezra 1727-1795 . . . . .DLB-31

Still, James 1906- DLB-9

Stirner, Max 1806-1856. . . . . .DLB-129

Stith, William 1707-1755. . . . . .DLB-31

Stock, Elliot [publishing house] DLB-106

Stockton, Frank R.
　　1834-1902 . . . . .DLB-42, 74; DS-13

Stoddard, Ashbel [publishing house] DLB-49

Stoddard, Charles Warren
　　1843-1909 . . . . .DLB-186

Stoddard, Elizabeth 1823-1902 . . . . .DLB-202

Stoddard, Richard Henry
　　1825-1903. . . . . .DLB-3, 64; DS-13

Stoddard, Solomon 1643-1729. . . . . .DLB-24

Stoker, Bram 1847-1912. . . . . . . .DLB-36, 70, 178

Stokes, Frederick A., Company DLB-49

Stokes, Thomas L. 1898-1958 . . . . .DLB-29

Stokesbury, Leon 1945- DLB-120

Stolberg, Christian Graf zu 1748-1821. . . . .DLB-94

Stolberg, Friedrich Leopold Graf zu
　　1750-1819 .DLB-94

Stone, Herbert S., and Company. DLB-49

Stone, Lucy 1818-1893 . . . . .DLB-79

Stone, Melville 1848-1929 . . . . .DLB-25

Stone, Robert 1937- DLB-152

Stone, Ruth 1915- DLB-105

Stone, Samuel 1602-1663. . . . . .DLB-24

Stone, William Leete 1792-1844 . . . . .DLB-202

Stone and Kimball DLB-49

Stoppard, Tom 1937- DLB-13, 233; Y-85

　Playwrights and Professors DLB-13

Storey, Anthony 1928- DLB-14

Storey, David 1933- DLB-13, 14, 207

Storm, Theodor 1817-1888 . . . . .DLB-129

Story, Thomas circa 1670-1742 . . . . .DLB-31

Story, William Wetmore 1819-1895 . . . . . . .DLB-1

Storytelling: A Contemporary Renaissance . . . Y-84

Stoughton, William 1631-1701. . . . . .DLB-24

Stow, John 1525-1605 . . . . .DLB-132

Stowe, Harriet Beecher
　　1811-1896 . . . . .DLB-1, 12, 42, 74, 189

Stowe, Leland 1899- DLB-29

Stoyanov, Dimitr Ivanov (see Elin Pelin)

Strabo 64 or 63 B.C.-circa A.D. 25 . . . . . .DLB-176

Strachey, Lytton 1880-1932. . . . . .DLB-149; DS-10

Strachey, Lytton, Preface to Eminent
　　Victorians .DLB-149

Strahan, William [publishing house] DLB-154

Strahan and Company. DLB-106

Strand, Mark 1934- DLB-5

The Strasbourg Oaths 842. . . . . .DLB-148

Stratemeyer, Edward 1862-1930 . . . . .DLB-42

Strati, Saverio 1924- DLB-177

Stratton and Barnard DLB-49

Stratton-Porter, Gene
　　1863-1924 . . . . .DLB-221; DS-14

Straub, Peter 1943- Y-84

Strauß, Botho 1944- DLB-124

Strauß, David Friedrich 1808-1874 . . . . . .DLB-133

The Strawberry Hill Press DLB-154

Streatfeild, Noel 1895-1986 . . . . .DLB-160

Street, Cecil John Charles (see Rhode, John)

Street, G. S. 1867-1936. . . . . .DLB-135

Street and Smith. DLB-49

Streeter, Edward 1891-1976. . . . . .DLB-11

Streeter, Thomas Winthrop 1883-1965. . .DLB-140

Stretton, Hesba 1832-1911. . . . . . . .DLB-163, 190

Stribling, T. S. 1881-1965 . . . . .DLB-9

Der Stricker circa 1190-circa 1250 . . . . . . .DLB-138

Strickland, Samuel 1804-1867 . . . . .DLB-99

Stringer, Arthur 1874-1950 . . . . .DLB-92

Stringer and Townsend DLB-49

Strittmatter, Erwin 1912- DLB-69

Strniša, Gregor 1930-1987 . . . . .DLB-181

Strode, William 1630-1645 . . . . .DLB-126

Strong, L. A. G. 1896-1958 . . . . .DLB-191

Strother, David Hunter 1816-1888 . . . . .DLB-3

Strouse, Jean 1945- DLB-111

Stuart, Dabney 1937- DLB-105

Stuart, Jesse 1906-1984 . . . . .DLB-9, 48, 102; Y-84

Stuart, Lyle [publishing house] DLB-46

Stuart, Ruth McEnery 1849?-1917 . . . . . .DLB-202

Stubbs, Harry Clement (see Clement, Hal)

Stubenberg, Johann Wilhelm von
　　1619-1663 . . . . .DLB-164

Studio. DLB-112

The Study of Poetry (1880), by
　　Matthew Arnold DLB-35

Sturgeon, Theodore 1918-1985. . . . .DLB-8; Y-85

Sturges, Preston 1898-1959 . . . . .DLB-26

"Style" (1840; revised, 1859), by
　　Thomas de Quincey [excerpt]. DLB-57

"Style" (1888), by Walter Pater. DLB-57

Style (1897), by Walter Raleigh
　　[excerpt] DLB-57

"Style" (1877), by T. H. Wright
　　[excerpt] DLB-57

"Le Style c'est l'homme" (1892), by
　　W. H. Mallock DLB-57

Styron, William 1925- DLB-2, 143; Y-80

Suárez, Mario 1925- DLB-82

Such, Peter 1939- DLB-60

Suckling, Sir John 1609-1641?. DLB-58, 126

Suckow, Ruth 1892-1960. . . . . .DLB-9, 102

Sudermann, Hermann 1857-1928 . . . . . . .DLB-118

Sue, Eugène 1804-1857 . . . . .DLB-119

Sue, Marie-Joseph (see Sue, Eugène)

Suetonius circa A.D. 69-post A.D. 122 . . .DLB-211

Suggs, Simon (see Hooper, Johnson Jones)

Sui Sin Far (see Eaton, Edith Maude)

Suits, Gustav 1883-1956 . . . . .DLB-220

Sukenick, Ronald 1932- DLB-173; Y-81

Suknaski, Andrew 1942- DLB-53

Sullivan, Alan 1868-1947 . . . . .DLB-92

Sullivan, C. Gardner 1886-1965 . . . . .DLB-26

Sullivan, Frank 1892-1976 . . . . .DLB-11

Sulte, Benjamin 1841-1923 . . . . .DLB-99

Sulzberger, Arthur Hays 1891-1968 . . . . .DLB-127

Sulzberger, Arthur Ochs 1926- DLB-127

Sulzer, Johann Georg 1720-1779 . . . . .DLB-97

Sumarokov, Aleksandr Petrovich
　　1717-1777 . . . . .DLB-150

Summers, Hollis 1916- DLB-6

A Summing Up at Century's End Y-99

Sumner, Henry A. [publishing house] DLB-49

Surtees, Robert Smith 1803-1864 . . . . . . .DLB-21

A Survey of Poetry Anthologies,
　　1879-1960 .DLB-54

Surveys: Japanese Literature, 1987-1995 . . . . DLB-182

Sutherland, Efua Theodora 1924-1996 . . . . DLB-117

Sutherland, John 1919-1956 . . . . DLB-68

Sutro, Alfred 1863-1933 . . . . DLB-10

Svendsen, Hanne Marie 1933- DLB-214

Swados, Harvey 1920-1972 . . . . DLB-2

Swain, Charles 1801-1874. . . . . DLB-32

Swallow Press DLB-46

Swan Sonnenschein Limited DLB-106

Swanberg, W. A. 1907- DLB-103

Swenson, May 1919-1989. . . . . DLB-5

Swerling, Jo 1897- DLB-44

Swift, Graham 1949- DLB-194

Swift, Jonathan 1667-1745 . . . . DLB-39, 95, 101

Swinburne, A. C. 1837-1909 . . . . DLB-35, 57

Swineshead, Richard floruit circa 1350 . . . . DLB-115

Swinnerton, Frank 1884-1982. . . . . DLB-34

Swisshelm, Jane Grey 1815-1884 . . . . DLB-43

Swope, Herbert Bayard 1882-1958. . . . . . . DLB-25

Swords, T. and J., and Company DLB-49

Swords, Thomas 1763-1843 and Swords, James ?-1844. . . . . DLB-73

Sykes, Ella C. ?-1939 . . . . .DLB-174

Sylvester, Josuah 1562 or 1563-1618 . . . . DLB-121

Symonds, Emily Morse (see Paston, George)

Symonds, John Addington 1840-1893 .DLB-57, 144

"Personal Style" (1890). DLB-57

Symons, A. J. A. 1900-1941 . . . . DLB-149

Symons, Arthur 1865-1945. . . . . . .DLB-19, 57, 149

Symons, Julian 1912-1994 . . . . . DLB-87, 155; Y-92

Julian Symons at Eighty Y-92

Symons, Scott 1933- DLB-53

A Symposium on *The Columbia History of the Novel* Y-92

Synge, John Millington 1871-1909 . . . . DLB-10, 19

Synge Summer School: J. M. Synge and the Irish Theater, Rathdrum, County Wiclow, Ireland Y-93

Syrett, Netta 1865-1943 . . . . .DLB-135, 197

Szabó, Lőrinc 1900-1957 . . . . DLB-215

Szabó, Magda 1917- DLB-215

Szymborska, Wisława 1923- DLB-232, Y-96

T

Taban lo Liyong 1939?- DLB-125

Tabucchi, Antonio 1943- DLB-196

Taché, Joseph-Charles 1820-1894 . . . . . . DLB-99

Tachihara Masaaki 1926-1980 . . . . DLB-182

Tacitus circa A.D. 55-circa A.D. 117 . . . . DLB-211

Tadijanović, Dragutin 1905- DLB-181

Tafdrup, Pia 1952- DLB-214

Tafolla, Carmen 1951- DLB-82

Taggard, Genevieve 1894-1948 . . . . DLB-45

Taggart, John 1942- DLB-193

Tagger, Theodor (see Bruckner, Ferdinand)

Taiheiki late fourteenth century DLB-203

Tait, J. Selwin, and Sons DLB-49

Tait's Edinburgh Magazine 1832-1861 . . . . . DLB-110

The Takarazaka Revue Company Y-91

Talander (see Bohse, August)

Talese, Gay 1932- DLB-185

Talev, Dimitr 1898-1966 . . . . DLB-181

Taliaferro, H. E. 1811-1875 . . . . DLB-202

Tallent, Elizabeth 1954- DLB-130

TallMountain, Mary 1918-1994 . . . . DLB-193

Talvj 1797-1870 . . . . DLB-59, 133

Tamási, Áron 1897-1966 . . . . DLB-215

Tammsaare, A. H. 1878-1940. . . . . DLB-220

Tan, Amy 1952- DLB-173

Tandori, Dezső 1938- DLB-232

Tanner, Thomas 1673/1674-1735 . . . . . . DLB-213

Tanizaki Jun'ichirō 1886-1965 . . . . DLB-180

Tapahonso, Luci 1953- DLB-175

The Mark Taper Forum DLB-7

Taradash, Daniel 1913- DLB-44

Tarbell, Ida M. 1857-1944 . . . . DLB-47

Tardivel, Jules-Paul 1851-1905 . . . . DLB-99

Targan, Barry 1932- DLB-130

Tarkington, Booth 1869-1946 . . . . DLB-9, 102

Tashlin, Frank 1913-1972 . . . . DLB-44

Tasma (Jessie Couvreur) 1848-1897 . . . . DLB-230

Tate, Allen 1899-1979 . . . . . .DLB-4, 45, 63; DS-17

Tate, James 1943- DLB-5, 169

Tate, Nahum circa 1652-1715 . . . . DLB-80

Tatian circa 830 . . . . DLB-148

Taufer, Veno 1933- DLB-181

Tauler, Johannes circa 1300-1361 . . . . . . .DLB-179

Tavčar, Ivan 1851-1923 . . . . DLB-147

Taylor, Ann 1782-1866. . . . . DLB-163

Taylor, Bayard 1825-1878 . . . . DLB-3, 189

Taylor, Bert Leston 1866-1921. . . . . DLB-25

Taylor, Charles H. 1846-1921 . . . . DLB-25

Taylor, Edward circa 1642-1729 . . . . DLB-24

Taylor, Elizabeth 1912-1975 . . . . DLB-139

Taylor, Henry 1942- DLB-5

Taylor, Sir Henry 1800-1886 . . . . DLB-32

Taylor, Jane 1783-1824. . . . . DLB-163

Taylor, Jeremy circa 1613-1667 . . . . DLB-151

Taylor, John 1577 or 1578 - 1653 . . . . . . DLB-121

Taylor, Mildred D. ?- DLB-52

Taylor, Peter 1917-1994 . . . . .DLB-218; Y-81, Y-94

Taylor, Susie King 1848-1912 . . . . DLB-221

Taylor, William, and Company DLB-49

Taylor-Made Shakespeare? Or Is "Shall I Die?" the Long-Lost Text of Bottom's Dream? Y-85

Teasdale, Sara 1884-1933 . . . . DLB-45

Telles, Lygia Fagundes 1924- DLB-113

Temple, Sir William 1628-1699 . . . . DLB-101

Tench, Watkin ca. 1758-1833. . . . . DLB-230

Tenn, William 1919- DLB-8

Tennant, Emma 1937- DLB-14

Tenney, Tabitha Gilman 1762-1837 . . . . .DLB-37, 200

Tennyson, Alfred 1809-1892 . . . . DLB-32

Tennyson, Frederick 1807-1898 . . . . DLB-32

Tenorio, Arthur 1924- DLB-209

Tepliakov, Viktor Grigor'evich 1804-1842 . . . . DLB-205

Terence circa 184 B.C.-159 B.C. or after. DLB-211

Terhune, Albert Payson 1872-1942 . . . . . . DLB-9

Terhune, Mary Virginia 1830-1922 . . . . DS-13, DS-16

Terry, Megan 1932- DLB-7

Terson, Peter 1932- DLB-13

Tesich, Steve 1943-1996. . . . . .Y-83

Tessa, Delio 1886-1939 . . . . DLB-114

Testori, Giovanni 1923-1993 . . . . . .DLB-128, 177

Tey, Josephine 1896?-1952. . . . . DLB-77

Thacher, James 1754-1844 . . . . DLB-37

Thackeray, William Makepeace 1811-1863 . . . . .DLB-21, 55, 159, 163

Thames and Hudson Limited DLB-112

Thanet, Octave (see French, Alice)

Thatcher, John Boyd 1847-1909 . . . . .DLB-187

Thayer, Caroline Matilda Warren 1785-1844. . . . . DLB-200

The Theatre Guild DLB-7

The Theater in Shakespeare's Time DLB-62

Thegan and the Astronomer flourished circa 850 . . . . DLB-148

Thelwall, John 1764-1834. . . . . DLB-93, 158

Theocritus circa 300 B.C.-260 B.C. DLB-176

Theodorescu, Ion N. (see Arghezi, Tudor)

Theodulf circa 760-circa 821 . . . . DLB-148

Theophrastus circa 371 B.C.-287 B.C. DLB-176

Theriault, Yves 1915-1983 . . . . DLB-88

Thério, Adrien 1925- DLB-53

Theroux, Paul 1941- DLB-2, 218

Thesiger, Wilfred 1910- DLB-204

They All Came to Paris DS-16

Thibaudeau, Colleen 1925- DLB-88

Thielen, Benedict 1903-1965 . . . . DLB-102

Thiong'o Ngugi wa (see Ngugi wa Thiong'o)

Third-Generation Minor Poets of the Seventeenth Century DLB-131

This Quarter 1925-1927, 1929-1932 . . . . .DS-15

Thoma, Ludwig 1867-1921 . . . . DLB-66

Thoma, Richard 1902- DLB-4

Thomas, Audrey 1935- DLB-60

Thomas, D. M. 1935- DLB-40, 207

D. M. Thomas: The Plagiarism Controversy. Y-82

Thomas, Dylan 1914-1953 . . . . . .DLB-13, 20, 139

The Dylan Thomas Celebration Y-99

Thomas, Edward
1878-1917 . . . . DLB-19, 98, 156, 216

Thomas, Frederick William 1806-1866 . . . DLB-202

Thomas, Gwyn 1913-1981 . . . . DLB-15

Thomas, Isaiah 1750-1831 . . . . DLB-43, 73, 187

Thomas, Isaiah [publishing house]. DLB-49

Thomas, Johann 1624-1679 . . . . DLB-168

Thomas, John 1900-1932. . . . . .DLB-4

Thomas, Joyce Carol 1938- DLB-33

Thomas, Lorenzo 1944- DLB-41

Thomas, R. S. 1915- DLB-27

Thomasîn von Zerclære
circa 1186-circa 1259. . . . . .DLB-138

Thomasius, Christian 1655-1728 . . . . .DLB-168

Thompson, Daniel Pierce 1795-1868 . . . . .DLB-202

Thompson, David 1770-1857. . . . . .DLB-99

Thompson, Dorothy 1893-1961 . . . . .DLB-29

Thompson, Francis 1859-1907. . . . . .DLB-19

Thompson, George Selden (see Selden, George)

Thompson, Henry Yates 1838-1928 . . . . .DLB-184

Thompson, Hunter S. 1939- DLB-185

Thompson, Jim 1906-1977. . . . . .DLB-226

Thompson, John 1938-1976. . . . . .DLB-60

Thompson, John R. 1823-1873 . . . . . . .DLB-3, 73

Thompson, Lawrance 1906-1973. . . . . . . .DLB-103

Thompson, Maurice 1844-1901. . . . . . . DLB-71, 74

Thompson, Ruth Plumly 1891-1976 . . . . . .DLB-22

Thompson, Thomas Phillips 1843-1933 . . .DLB-99

Thompson, William 1775-1833 . . . . .DLB-158

Thompson, William Tappan
1812-1882 .DLB-3, 11

Thomson, Edward William 1849-1924 . . . .DLB-92

Thomson, James 1700-1748 . . . . .DLB-95

Thomson, James 1834-1882 . . . . .DLB-35

Thomson, Joseph 1858-1895 . . . . .DLB-174

Thomson, Mortimer 1831-1875. . . . . .DLB-11

Thoreau, Henry David
1817-1862 . . . . .DLB-1, 183, 223

The Thoreauvian Pilgrimage: The Structure of an
American Cult. DLB-223

Thorpe, Adam 1956- DLB-231

Thorpe, Thomas Bangs 1815-1878 . . . . .DLB-3, 11

Thorup, Kirsten 1942- DLB-214

Thoughts on Poetry and Its Varieties (1833),
by John Stuart Mill DLB-32

Thrale, Hester Lynch
(see Piozzi, Hester Lynch [Thrale])

Thubron, Colin 1939- DLB-204, 231

Thucydides
circa 455 B.C.-circa 395 B.C. DLB-176

Thulstrup, Thure de 1848-1930 . . . . . . .DLB-188

Thümmel, Moritz August von
1738-1817 . . . . .DLB-97

Thurber, James 1894-1961 . . . . DLB-4, 11, 22, 102

Thurman, Wallace 1902-1934. . . . . .DLB-51

Thwaite, Anthony 1930- DLB-40

The Booker Prize
Address by Anthony Thwaite,
Chairman of the Booker Prize Judges
Comments from Former Booker
Prize Winners Y-86

Thwaites, Reuben Gold 1853-1913 . . . . . .DLB-47

Tibullus circa 54 B.C.-circa 19 B.C. DLB-211

Ticknor, George 1791-1871 . . . . . . .DLB-1, 59, 140

Ticknor and Fields. DLB-49

Ticknor and Fields (revived) DLB-46

Tieck, Ludwig 1773-1853. . . . . .DLB-90

Tietjens, Eunice 1884-1944 . . . . .DLB-54

Tilney, Edmund circa 1536-1610. . . . . . .DLB-136

Tilt, Charles [publishing house]. DLB-106

Tilton, J. E., and Company DLB-49

Time and Western Man (1927), by Wyndham
Lewis [excerpts]. DLB-36

Time-Life Books .DLB-46

Times Books DLB-46

Timothy, Peter circa 1725-1782 . . . . .DLB-43

Timrava 1867-1951 . . . . .DLB-215

Timrod, Henry 1828-1867. . . . . .DLB-3

Tindal, Henrietta 1818?-1879 . . . . .DLB-199

Tinker, Chauncey Brewster 1876-1963 . . .DLB-140

Tinsley Brothers DLB-106

Tiptree, James, Jr. 1915-1987. . . . . .DLB-8

Tišma, Aleksandar 1924- DLB-181

Titus, Edward William
1870-1952 . . . . .DLB-4; DS-15

Tiutchev, Fedor Ivanovich 1803-1873 . . . .DLB-205

Tlali, Miriam 1933- DLB-157, 225

Todd, Barbara Euphan 1890-1976. . . . . . .DLB-160

Tofte, Robert
1561 or 1562-1619 or 1620. . . . . DLB-172

Toklas, Alice B. 1877-1967. . . . . .DLB-4

Tokuda, Shūsei 1872-1943. . . . . .DLB-180

Tolkien, J. R. R. 1892-1973 . . . . DLB-15, 160

Toller, Ernst 1893-1939. . . . . .DLB-124

Tollet, Elizabeth 1694-1754 . . . . .DLB-95

Tolson, Melvin B. 1898-1966 . . . . . . .DLB-48, 76

Tom Jones (1749), by Henry Fielding
[excerpt]. DLB-39

Tomalin, Claire 1933- DLB-155

Tomasi di Lampedusa, Giuseppe
1896-1957 . . . . .DLB-177

Tomlinson, Charles 1927- DLB-40

Tomlinson, H. M. 1873-1958 . . . DLB-36, 100, 195

Tompkins, Abel [publishing house]. DLB-49

Tompson, Benjamin 1642-1714 . . . . .DLB-24

Ton'a 1289-1372 . . . . .DLB-203

Tondelli, Pier Vittorio 1955-1991 . . . . . . .DLB-196

Tonks, Rosemary 1932- DLB-14, 207

Tonna, Charlotte Elizabeth 1790-1846 . . .DLB-163

Tonson, Jacob the Elder
[publishing house] DLB-170

Toole, John Kennedy 1937-1969 . . . . Y-81

Toomer, Jean 1894-1967 . . . . .DLB-45, 51

Tor Books DLB-46

Torberg, Friedrich 1908-1979 . . . . .DLB-85

Torrence, Ridgely 1874-1950. . . . . .DLB-54

Torres-Metzger, Joseph V. 1933- DLB-122

Toth, Susan Allen 1940- Y-86

Tottell, Richard [publishing house] DLB-170

"The Printer to the Reader," (1557)
by Richard Tottell. DLB-167

Tough-Guy Literature. DLB-9

Touré, Askia Muhammad 1938- DLB-41

Tourgée, Albion W. 1838-1905. . . . . .DLB-79

Tourneur, Cyril circa 1580-1626. . . . . . . .DLB-58

Tournier, Michel 1924- DLB-83

Tousey, Frank [publishing house] DLB-49

Tower Publications DLB-46

Towne, Benjamin circa 1740-1793 . . . . . . .DLB-43

Towne, Robert 1936- DLB-44

The Townely Plays fifteenth and sixteenth
centuries DLB-146

Townshend, Aurelian
by 1583-circa 1651 . . . . .DLB-121

Toy, Barbara 1908- DLB-204

Tracy, Honor 1913- DLB-15

Traherne, Thomas 1637?-1674 . . . . .DLB-131

Traill, Catharine Parr 1802-1899 . . . . .DLB-99

Train, Arthur 1875-1945 . . . . .DLB-86; DS-16

The Transatlantic Publishing Company . . .DLB-49

The Transatlantic Review 1924-1925 . . . . DS-15

The Transcendental Club 1836-1840 . . . .DLB-223

Transcendentalism. DLB-223

Transcendentalists, American DS-5

A Transit of Poets and Others: American
Biography in 1982. . . . . Y-82

transition 1927-1938. . . . . DS-15

Translators of the Twelfth Century: Literary Issues
Raised and Impact Created. DLB-115

Travel Writing, 1837-1875 . . . . .DLB-166

Travel Writing, 1876-1909 . . . . .DLB-174

Travel Writing, 1910-1939 . . . . .DLB-195

Traven, B. 1882? or 1890?-1969? DLB-9, 56

Travers, Ben 1886-1980 . . . . .DLB-10, 233

Travers, P. L. (Pamela Lyndon)
1899-1996 . . . . .DLB-160

Trediakovsky, Vasilii Kirillovich
1703-1769 . . . . .DLB-150

Treece, Henry 1911-1966 . . . . .DLB-160

Trejo, Ernesto 1950- DLB-122

Trelawny, Edward John
1792-1881 . . . . DLB-110, 116, 144

Tremain, Rose 1943- DLB-14

Tremblay, Michel 1942- DLB-60

Trends in Twentieth-Century
Mass Market Publishing DLB-46

Trent, William P. 1862-1939. . . . . .DLB-47

Trescot, William Henry 1822-1898. . . . . . .DLB-30

Tressell, Robert (Robert Phillipe Noonan)
1870-1911 . . . . .DLB-197

Trevelyan, Sir George Otto
1838-1928 . . . . DLB-144

Trevisa, John circa 1342-circa 1402 . . . . . DLB-146

Trevor, William 1928- DLB-14, 139

Trierer Floyris circa 1170-1180 . . . . DLB-138

Trillin, Calvin 1935- DLB-185

Trilling, Lionel 1905-1975 . . . . DLB-28, 63

Trilussa 1871-1950 . . . . DLB-114

Trimmer, Sarah 1741-1810 . . . . DLB-158

Triolet, Elsa 1896-1970 . . . . DLB-72

Tripp, John 1927- DLB-40

Trocchi, Alexander 1925- DLB-15

Troisi, Dante 1920-1989 . . . . DLB-196

Trollope, Anthony 1815-1882 . . . . DLB-21, 57, 159

Trollope, Frances 1779-1863 . . . . DLB-21, 166

Trollope, Joanna 1943- DLB-207

Troop, Elizabeth 1931- DLB-14

Trotter, Catharine 1679-1749 . . . . DLB-84

Trotti, Lamar 1898-1952 . . . . DLB-44

Trottier, Pierre 1925- DLB-60

Troubadours, *Trobaíritz,* and Trouvères . . DLB-208

Troupe, Quincy Thomas, Jr. 1943- DLB-41

Trow, John F., and Company DLB-49

Trowbridge, John Townsend 1827-1916 . DLB-202

Truillier-Lacombe, Joseph-Patrice
1807-1863 . . . . DLB-99

Trumbo, Dalton 1905-1976 . . . . DLB-26

Trumbull, Benjamin 1735-1820 . . . . DLB-30

Trumbull, John 1750-1831 . . . . DLB-31

Trumbull, John 1756-1843 . . . . DLB-183

Tscherning, Andreas 1611-1659 . . . . DLB-164

Tsubouchi, Shōyō 1859-1935 . . . . DLB-180

Tucholsky, Kurt 1890-1935 . . . . DLB-56

Tucker, Charlotte Maria
1821-1893 . . . . DLB-163, 190

Tucker, George 1775-1861 . . . . DLB-3, 30

Tucker, James 1808?-1866? DLB-230

Tucker, Nathaniel Beverley 1784-1851 . . . . . DLB-3

Tucker, St. George 1752-1827 . . . . DLB-37

Tuckerman, Henry Theodore 1813-1871 . . DLB-64

Tumas, Juozas (see Vaižgantas)

Tunis, John R. 1889-1975 . . . . .DLB-22, 171

Tunstall, Cuthbert 1474-1559 . . . . DLB-132

Tuohy, Frank 1925- DLB-14, 139

Tupper, Martin F. 1810-1889 . . . . DLB-32

Turbyfill, Mark 1896- DLB-45

Turco, Lewis 1934- Y-84

Turgenev, Aleksandr Ivanovich
1784-1845 . . . . DLB-198

Turnball, Alexander H. 1868-1918 . . . . . . DLB-184

Turnbull, Andrew 1921-1970 . . . . DLB-103

Turnbull, Gael 1928- DLB-40

Turner, Arlin 1909-1980 . . . . DLB-103

Turner, Charles (Tennyson) 1808-1879 . . . DLB-32

Turner, Ethel 1872-1958 . . . . DLB-230

Turner, Frederick 1943- DLB-40

Turner, Frederick Jackson
1861-1932 . . . . .DLB-17, 186

Turner, Joseph Addison 1826-1868 . . . . DLB-79

Turpin, Waters Edward 1910-1968 . . . . . . DLB-51

Turrini, Peter 1944- DLB-124

Tutuola, Amos 1920-1997 . . . . DLB-125

Twain, Mark (see Clemens, Samuel Langhorne)

Tweedie, Ethel Brilliana
circa 1860-1940 . . . . DLB-174

The 'Twenties and Berlin, by Alex Natan . DLB-66

Twysden, Sir Roger 1597-1672 . . . . DLB-213

Tyler, Anne 1941- DLB-6, 143; Y-82

Tyler, Mary Palmer 1775-1866 . . . . DLB-200

Tyler, Moses Coit 1835-1900 . . . . .DLB-47, 64

Tyler, Royall 1757-1826 . . . . DLB-37

Tylor, Edward Burnett 1832-1917 . . . . DLB-57

Tynan, Katharine 1861-1931 . . . . DLB-153

Tyndale, William circa 1494-1536 . . . . . DLB-132

U

Udall, Nicholas 1504-1556 . . . . DLB-62

Ugrêsić, Dubravka 1949- DLB-181

Uhland, Ludwig 1787-1862 . . . . DLB-90

Uhse, Bodo 1904-1963 . . . . DLB-69

Ujević, Augustin ("Tin") 1891-1955 . . . . . DLB-147

Ulenhart, Niclas flourished circa 1600 . . . DLB-164

Ulibarrí, Sabine R. 1919- DLB-82

Ulica, Jorge 1870-1926 . . . . DLB-82

Ulivi, Ferruccio 1912- DLB-196

Ulizio, B. George 1889-1969 . . . . DLB-140

Ulrich von Liechtenstein
circa 1200-circa 1275 . . . . DLB-138

Ulrich von Zatzikhoven
before 1194-after 1214 . . . . DLB-138

Ulysses, Reader's Edition Y-97

Unaipon, David 1872-1967 . . . . DLB-230

Unamuno, Miguel de 1864-1936 . . . . DLB-108

Under, Marie 1883-1980 . . . . DLB-220

Under the Microscope (1872), by
A. C. Swinburne DLB-35

Ungaretti, Giuseppe 1888-1970 . . . . DLB-114

Unger, Friederike Helene 1741-1813 . . . . . DLB-94

United States Book Company DLB-49

Universal Publishing and Distributing
Corporation DLB-46

The University of Iowa Writers' Workshop
Golden Jubilee Y-86

The University of South Carolina Press Y-94

University of Wales Press DLB-112

University Press of Kansas Y-98

University Press of Mississippi Y-99

"The Unknown Public" (1858), by
Wilkie Collins [excerpt] DLB-57

Uno, Chiyo 1897-1996 . . . . DLB-180

Unruh, Fritz von 1885-1970 . . . . DLB-56, 118

Unspeakable Practices II: The Festival of Vanguard
Narrative at Brown University Y-93

Unsworth, Barry 1930- DLB-194

Unt, Mati 1944- DLB-232

The Unterberg Poetry Center of the
92nd Street Y Y-98

Unwin, T. Fisher [publishing house] DLB-106

Upchurch, Boyd B. (see Boyd, John)

Updike, John 1932-
. . . . DLB-2, 5, 143, 218, 227; Y-80, Y-82; DS-3

John Updike on the Internet Y-97

Upīts, Andrejs 1877-1970 . . . . DLB-220

Upton, Bertha 1849-1912 . . . . DLB-141

Upton, Charles 1948- DLB-16

Upton, Florence K. 1873-1922 . . . . DLB-141

Upward, Allen 1863-1926 . . . . DLB-36

Urban, Milo 1904-1982 . . . . DLB-215

Urista, Alberto Baltazar (see Alurista)

Urquhart, Fred 1912- DLB-139

Urrea, Luis Alberto 1955- DLB-209

Urzidil, Johannes 1896-1976 . . . . DLB-85

The Uses of Facsimile Y-90

Usk, Thomas died 1388 . . . . DLB-146

Uslar Pietri, Arturo 1906- DLB-113

Ussher, James 1581-1656 . . . . DLB-213

Ustinov, Peter 1921- DLB-13

Uttley, Alison 1884-1976 . . . . DLB-160

Uz, Johann Peter 1720-1796 . . . . DLB-97

V

Vac, Bertrand 1914- DLB-88

Vācietis, Ojārs 1933-1983 . . . . DLB-232

Vaičiulaitis, Antanas 1906-1992 . . . . DLB-220

Vaculík, Ludvík 1926- DLB-232

Vaičiūnaite, Judita 1937- DLB-232

Vail, Laurence 1891-1968 . . . . DLB-4

Vailland, Roger 1907-1965 . . . . DLB-83

Vaižgantas 1869-1933 . . . . DLB-220

Vajda, Ernest 1887-1954 . . . . DLB-44

Valdés, Gina 1943- DLB-122

Valdez, Luis Miguel 1940- DLB-122

Valduga, Patrizia 1953- DLB-128

Valente, José Angel 1929- DLB-108

Valenzuela, Luisa 1938- DLB-113

Valeri, Diego 1887-1976 . . . . DLB-128

Valerius Flaccus fl. circa A.D. 92 . . . . DLB-211

Valerius Maximus fl. circa A.D. 31 . . . . . DLB-211

Valesio, Paolo 1939- DLB-196

Valgardson, W. D. 1939- DLB-60

Valle, Víctor Manuel 1950- DLB-122

Valle-Inclán, Ramón del 1866-1936 . . . . . DLB-134

Vallejo, Armando 1949- DLB-122

Vallès, Jules 1832-1885 . . . . DLB-123

Vallette, Marguerite Eymery (see Rachilde)

Valverde, José María 1926-1996 . . . . DLB-108

Van Allsburg, Chris 1949- DLB-61
Van Anda, Carr 1864-1945 ....DLB-25
van der Post, Laurens 1906-1996 ....DLB-204
Van Dine, S. S. (see Wright, Williard Huntington)
Van Doren, Mark 1894-1972............DLB-45
van Druten, John 1901-1957 ....DLB-10
Van Duyn, Mona 1921- DLB-5
Van Dyke, Henry 1852-1933 .....DLB-71; DS-13
Van Dyke, Henry 1928- DLB-33
Van Dyke, John C. 1856-1932 ....DLB-186
van Gulik, Robert Hans 1910-1967 .... DS-17
van Itallie, Jean-Claude 1936- DLB-7
Van Loan, Charles E. 1876-1919.......DLB-171
Van Rensselaer, Mariana Griswold 1851-1934 ....DLB-47
Van Rensselaer, Mrs. Schuyler (see Van Rensselaer, Mariana Griswold)
Van Vechten, Carl 1880-1964.........DLB-4, 9
van Vogt, A. E. 1912- DLB-8
Vanbrugh, Sir John 1664-1726...........DLB-80
Vance, Jack 1916?- DLB-8
Vančura, Vladislav 1891-1942 ....DLB-215
Vane, Sutton 1888-1963 ....DLB-10
Vanguard Press DLB-46
Vann, Robert L. 1879-1940 ....DLB-29
Vargas, Llosa, Mario 1936- DLB-145
Varley, John 1947- Y-81
Varnhagen von Ense, Karl August 1785-1858 ....DLB-90
Varnhagen von Ense, Rahel 1771-1833 ....DLB-90
Varro 116 B.C.-27 B.C................DLB-211
Vasiliu, George (see Bacovia, George)
Vásquez, Richard 1928- DLB-209
Vásquez Montalbán, Manuel 1939- DLB-134
Vassa, Gustavus (see Equiano, Olaudah)
Vassalli, Sebastiano 1941- DLB-128, 196
Vaughan, Henry 1621-1695 ....DLB-131
Vaughan, Thomas 1621-1666 ....DLB-131
Vaughn, Robert 1592?-1667 ....DLB-213
Vaux, Thomas, Lord 1509-1556 ....DLB-132
Vazov, Ivan 1850-1921 ....DLB-147
Véa Jr., Alfredo 1950- DLB-209
Vega, Janine Pommy 1942- DLB-16
Veiller, Anthony 1903-1965 ....DLB-44
Velásquez-Trevino, Gloria 1949- DLB-122
Veley, Margaret 1843-1887 ....DLB-199
Velleius Paterculus circa 20 B.C.-circa A.D. 30 ....DLB-211
Veloz Maggiolo, Marcio 1936- DLB-145
Vel'tman Aleksandr Fomich 1800-1870 ....DLB-198
Venegas, Daniel ?-? DLB-82
Venevitinov, Dmitrii Vladimirovich 1805-1827 ....DLB-205
Vergil, Polydore circa 1470-1555.......DLB-132

Veríssimo, Erico 1905-1975 ....DLB-145
Verlaine, Paul 1844-1896.............DLB-217
Verne, Jules 1828-1905 ....DLB-123
Verplanck, Gulian C. 1786-1870 ....DLB-59
Very, Jones 1813-1880.................DLB-1
Vian, Boris 1920-1959.................DLB-72
Viazemsky, Petr Andreevich 1792-1878 ....DLB-205
Vickers, Roy 1888?-1965..............DLB-77
Vickery, Sukey 1779-1821 ....DLB-200
Victoria 1819-1901 ....DLB-55
Victoria Press.....................DLB-106
Vidal, Gore 1925- DLB-6, 152
Vidal, Mary Theresa 1815-1873 ....DLB-230
Viebig, Clara 1860-1952 ....DLB-66
Viereck, George Sylvester 1884-1962 ....DLB-54
Viereck, Peter 1916- DLB-5
Viets, Roger 1738-1811 ....DLB-99
Viewpoint: Politics and Performance, by David Edgar DLB-13
Vigil-Piñon, Evangelina 1949- DLB-122
Vigneault, Gilles 1928- DLB-60
Vigny, Alfred de 1797-1863.............. DLB-119, 192, 217
Vigolo, Giorgio 1894-1983 ....DLB-114
The Viking Press.....................DLB-46
Vilde, Eduard 1865-1933...........DLB-220
Villanueva, Alma Luz 1944- DLB-122
Villanueva, Tino 1941- DLB-82
Villard, Henry 1835-1900 ....DLB-23
Villard, Oswald Garrison 1872-1949 ....DLB-25, 91
Villarreal, Edit 1944- DLB-209
Villarreal, José Antonio 1924- DLB-82
Villaseñor, Victor 1940- DLB-209
Villegas de Magnón, Leonor 1876-1955 ....DLB-122
Villehardouin, Geoffroi de circa 1150-1215 ....DLB-208
Villemaire, Yolande 1949- DLB-60
Villena, Luis Antonio de 1951- DLB-134
Villiers, George, Second Duke of Buckingham 1628-1687..........DLB-80
Villiers de l'Isle-Adam, Jean-Marie Mathias Philippe-Auguste, Comte de 1838-1889 ....DLB-123, 192
Villon, François 1431-circa 1463? DLB-208
Vine Press DLB-112
Viorst, Judith ?- DLB-52
Vipont, Elfrida (Elfrida Vipont Foulds, Charles Vipont) 1902-1992........DLB-160
Viramontes, Helena María 1954- DLB-122
Virgil 70 B.C.-19 B.C. DLB-211
Vischer, Friedrich Theodor 1807-1887 ...DLB-133
Vitruvius circa 85 B.C.-circa 15 B.C......DLB-211
Vitry, Philippe de 1291-1361..........DLB-208
Vivanco, Luis Felipe 1907-1975 ....DLB-108

Viviani, Cesare 1947- DLB-128
Vivien, Renée 1877-1909 ....DLB-217
Vizenor, Gerald 1934- DLB-175, 227
Vizetelly and Company...............DLB-106
Voaden, Herman 1903- DLB-88
Voß, Johann Heinrich 1751-1826 ....DLB-90
Voigt, Ellen Bryant 1943- DLB-120
Vojnović, Ivo 1857-1929 ....DLB-147
Volkoff, Vladimir 1932- DLB-83
Volland, P. F., Company...............DLB-46
Vollbehr, Otto H. F. 1872?-1945 or 1946. ....DLB-187
Volponi, Paolo 1924- DLB-177
von der Grün, Max 1926- DLB-75
Vonnegut, Kurt 1922- DLB-2, 8, 152; Y-80; DS-3
Voranc, Prežihov 1893-1950...........DLB-147
Voynich, E. L. 1864-1960 ....DLB-197
Vroman, Mary Elizabeth circa 1924-1967 ....DLB-33

W

Wace, Robert ("Maistre") circa 1100-circa 1175 ....DLB-146
Wackenroder, Wilhelm Heinrich 1773-1798. ....DLB-90
Wackernagel, Wilhelm 1806-1869 ......DLB-133
Waddington, Miriam 1917- DLB-68
Wade, Henry 1887-1969 ....DLB-77
Wagenknecht, Edward 1900- DLB-103
Wagner, Heinrich Leopold 1747-1779 .....DLB-94
Wagner, Henry R. 1862-1957 ....DLB-140
Wagner, Richard 1813-1883 ....DLB-129
Wagoner, David 1926- DLB-5
Wah, Fred 1939- DLB-60
Waiblinger, Wilhelm 1804-1830 ....DLB-90
Wain, John 1925-1994...... DLB-15, 27, 139, 155
Wainwright, Jeffrey 1944- DLB-40
Waite, Peirce and Company DLB-49
Wakeman, Stephen H. 1859-1924......DLB-187
Wakoski, Diane 1937- DLB-5
Walahfrid Strabo circa 808-849.........DLB-148
Walck, Henry Z......................DLB-46
Walcott, Derek 1930- DLB-117; Y-81, Y-92
Waldegrave, Robert [publishing house]. . . DLB-170
Waldman, Anne 1945- DLB-16
Waldrop, Rosmarie 1935- DLB-169
Walker, Alice 1900-1982 ....DLB-201
Walker, Alice 1944- DLB-6, 33, 143
Walker, George F. 1947- DLB-60
Walker, John Brisben 1847-1931 ....DLB-79
Walker, Joseph A. 1935- DLB-38
Walker, Margaret 1915- DLB-76, 152
Walker, Ted 1934- DLB-40
Walker and Company.................DLB-49
Walker, Evans and Cogswell Company ...DLB-49

Wallace, Alfred Russel 1823-1913 ...... DLB-190

Wallace, Dewitt 1889-1981 and
    Lila Acheson Wallace 1889-1984.... DLB-137

Wallace, Edgar 1875-1932 .... DLB-70

Wallace, Lew 1827-1905.............. DLB-202

Wallace, Lila Acheson
    (see Wallace, Dewitt, and Lila Acheson Wallace)

Wallant, Edward Lewis
    1926-1962 .... DLB-2, 28, 143

Waller, Edmund 1606-1687 .... DLB-126

Walpole, Horace 1717-1797..... DLB-39, 104, 213

    Preface to the First Edition of
    The Castle of Otranto (1764).......... DLB-39

    Preface to the Second Edition of
    The Castle of Otranto (1765).......... DLB-39

Walpole, Hugh 1884-1941 .... DLB-34

Walrond, Eric 1898-1966............. DLB-51

Walser, Martin 1927- DLB-75, 124

Walser, Robert 1878-1956 .... DLB-66

Walsh, Ernest 1895-1926 .... DLB-4, 45

Walsh, Robert 1784-1859 .... DLB-59

Walters, Henry 1848-1931 .... DLB-140

Waltharius circa 825................ DLB-148

Walther von der Vogelweide
    circa 1170-circa 1230 .... DLB-138

Walton, Izaak 1593-1683 .... DLB-151, 213

Wambaugh, Joseph 1937- DLB-6; Y-83

Wand, Alfred Rudolph 1828-1891...... DLB-188

Waniek, Marilyn Nelson 1946- DLB-120

Wanley, Humphrey 1672-1726........ DLB-213

Warburton, William 1698-1779 .... DLB-104

Ward, Aileen 1919- DLB-111

Ward, Artemus (see Browne, Charles Farrar)

Ward, Arthur Henry Sarsfield (see Rohmer, Sax)

Ward, Douglas Turner 1930- DLB-7, 38

Ward, Mrs. Humphry 1851-1920 .... DLB-18

Ward, Lynd 1905-1985 .... DLB-22

Ward, Lock and Company DLB-106

Ward, Nathaniel circa 1578-1652 .... DLB-24

Ward, Theodore 1902-1983............ DLB-76

Wardle, Ralph 1909-1988 .... DLB-103

Ware, William 1797-1852 .... DLB-1

Warne, Frederick, and Company [U.K.]... DLB-106

Warne, Frederick, and Company [U.S.] ... DLB-49

Warner, Anne 1869-1913............. DLB-202

Warner, Charles Dudley 1829-1900...... DLB-64

Warner, Marina 1946- DLB-194

Warner, Rex 1905- DLB-15

Warner, Susan Bogert 1819-1885...... DLB-3, 42

Warner, Sylvia Townsend
    1893-1978.................. DLB-34, 139

Warner, William 1558-1609............DLB-172

Warner Books DLB-46

Warr, Bertram 1917-1943 .... DLB-88

Warren, John Byrne Leicester (see De Tabley, Lord)

Warren, Lella 1899-1982 .... Y-83

Warren, Mercy Otis 1728-1814 ..... DLB-31, 200

Warren, Robert Penn
    1905-1989 ....DLB-2, 48, 152; Y-80, Y-89

Warren, Samuel 1807-1877........... DLB-190

Die Wartburgkrieg circa 1230-circa 1280... DLB-138

Warton, Joseph 1722-1800 ....DLB-104, 109

Warton, Thomas 1728-1790.......DLB-104, 109

Warung, Price (William Astley)
    1855-1911 .... DLB-230

Washington, George 1732-1799 .... DLB-31

Wassermann, Jakob 1873-1934 .... DLB-66

Wasserstein, Wendy 1950- DLB-228

Wasson, David Atwood 1823-1887 ... DLB-1, 223

Watanna, Onoto (see Eaton, Winnifred)

Waterhouse, Keith 1929- DLB-13, 15

Waterman, Andrew 1940- DLB-40

Waters, Frank 1902-1995........DLB-212; Y-86

Waters, Michael 1949- DLB-120

Watkins, Tobias 1780-1855 .... DLB-73

Watkins, Vernon 1906-1967 .... DLB-20

Watmough, David 1926- DLB-53

Watson, James Wreford (see Wreford, James)

Watson, John 1850-1907 .... DLB-156

Watson, Sheila 1909- DLB-60

Watson, Thomas 1545?-1592.......... DLB-132

Watson, Wilfred 1911- DLB-60

Watt, W. J., and Company DLB-46

Watten, Barrett 1948- DLB-193

Watterson, Henry 1840-1921.......... DLB-25

Watts, Alan 1915-1973 .... DLB-16

Watts, Franklin [publishing house]....... DLB-46

Watts, Isaac 1674-1748 .... DLB-95

Waugh, Alec 1898-1981 .... DLB-191

Waugh, Auberon 1939- DLB-14, 194

    The Cult of Biography
    Excerpts from the Second Folio Debate:
    "Biographies are generally a disease of
    English Literature".................. Y-86

Waugh, Evelyn 1903-1966.....DLB-15, 162, 195

Way and Williams DLB-49

Wayman, Tom 1945- DLB-53

We See the Editor at Work Y-97

Weatherly, Tom 1942- DLB-41

Weaver, Gordon 1937- DLB-130

Weaver, Robert 1921- DLB-88

Webb, Beatrice 1858-1943 and
    Webb, Sidney 1859-1947 .... DLB-190

Webb, Frank J. ?-? DLB-50

Webb, James Watson 1802-1884 .... DLB-43

Webb, Mary 1881-1927 .... DLB-34

Webb, Phyllis 1927- DLB-53

Webb, Walter Prescott 1888-1963 .... DLB-17

Webbe, William ?-1591 .... DLB-132

Webber, Charles Wilkins 1819-1856? ... DLB-202

Webster, Augusta 1837-1894 .... DLB-35

Webster, Charles L., and Company...... DLB-49

Webster, John 1579 or 1580-1634? DLB-58

    John Webster: The Melbourne
    Manuscript....................... Y-86

Webster, Noah 1758-1843 ... DLB-1, 37, 42, 43, 73

Weckherlin, Georg Rodolf 1584-1653 ... DLB-164

Wedekind, Frank 1864-1918 .... DLB-118

Weeks, Edward Augustus, Jr.
    1898-1989 ....DLB-137

Weeks, Stephen B. 1865-1918 ....DLB-187

Weems, Mason Locke 1759-1825...DLB-30, 37, 42

Weerth, Georg 1822-1856 .... DLB-129

Weidenfeld and Nicolson............. DLB-112

Weidman, Jerome 1913-1998........... DLB-28

Weiß, Ernst 1882-1940............... DLB-81

Weigl, Bruce 1949- DLB-120

Weinbaum, Stanley Grauman 1902-1935 .. DLB-8

Weintraub, Stanley 1929- DLB-111

    The Practice of Biography: An Interview
    with Stanley Weintraub.............. Y-82

Weise, Christian 1642-1708 .... DLB-168

Weisenborn, Gunther 1902-1969.... DLB-69, 124

Weiss, John 1818-1879 .... DLB-1

Weiss, Peter 1916-1982 .... DLB-69, 124

Weiss, Theodore 1916- DLB-5

Weisse, Christian Felix 1726-1804 .... DLB-97

Weitling, Wilhelm 1808-1871.......... DLB-129

Welch, James 1940- DLB-175

Welch, Lew 1926-1971? DLB-16

Weldon, Fay 1931- DLB-14, 194

Wellek, René 1903-1995 .... DLB-63

Wells, Carolyn 1862-1942 .... DLB-11

Wells, Charles Jeremiah circa 1800-1879 .. DLB-32

Wells, Gabriel 1862-1946............. DLB-140

Wells, H. G. 1866-1946 .....DLB-34, 70, 156, 178

Wells, Helena 1758?-1824 .... DLB-200

Wells, Robert 1947- DLB-40

Wells-Barnett, Ida B. 1862-1931..... DLB-23, 221

Welty, Eudora
    1909- DLB-2, 102, 143; Y-87; DS-12

    Eudora Welty: Eye of the Storyteller Y-87

    Eudora Welty Newsletter................ Y-99

    Eudora Welty's Ninetieth Birthday Y-99

Wendell, Barrett 1855-1921 .... DLB-71

Wentworth, Patricia 1878-1961 .... DLB-77

Wentworth, William Charles
    1790-1872...................... DLB-230

Werder, Diederich von dem 1584-1657 .. DLB-164

Werfel, Franz 1890-1945 .... DLB-81, 124

Werner, Zacharias 1768-1823.......... DLB-94

The Werner Company................ DLB-49

Wersba, Barbara 1932- DLB-52

Wescott, Glenway 1901- DLB-4, 9, 102

Wesker, Arnold 1932- DLB-13

Wesley, Charles 1707-1788 .... DLB-95

Wesley, John 1703-1791 .... DLB-104

Wesley, Mary 1912- DLB-231

Wesley, Richard 1945- DLB-38

Wessels, A., and Company DLB-46

Wessobrunner Gebet circa 787-815 ....DLB-148

West, Anthony 1914-1988.............DLB-15

West, Dorothy 1907-1998 ....DLB-76

West, Jessamyn 1902-1984 ....DLB-6; Y-84

West, Mae 1892-1980 ....DLB-44

West, Nathanael 1903-1940........DLB-4, 9, 28

West, Paul 1930- DLB-14

West, Rebecca 1892-1983 ....DLB-36; Y-83

West, Richard 1941- DLB-185

West and Johnson DLB-49

Westcott, Edward Noyes 1846-1898.....DLB-202

The Western Messenger 1835-1841 ....DLB-223

Western Publishing Company..........DLB-46

Western Writers of America Y-99

The Westminster Review 1824-1914.......DLB-110

Weston, Elizabeth Jane circa 1582-1612 ..DLB-172

Wetherald, Agnes Ethelwyn 1857-1940....DLB-99

Wetherell, Elizabeth (see Warner, Susan Bogert)

Wetherell, W. D. 1948- DLB-234

Wetzel, Friedrich Gottlob 1779-1819 ......DLB-90

Weyman, Stanley J. 1855-1928 .....DLB-141, 156

Wezel, Johann Karl 1747-1819 ....DLB-94

Whalen, Philip 1923- DLB-16

Whalley, George 1915-1983 ....DLB-88

Wharton, Edith
  1862-1937 ...... DLB-4, 9, 12, 78, 189; DS-13

Wharton, William 1920s?- Y-80

"What You Lose on the Swings You Make Up
  on the Merry-Go-Round" Y-99

Whately, Mary Louisa 1824-1889......DLB-166

Whately, Richard 1787-1863 ....DLB-190

  From *Elements of Rhetoric* (1828;
    revised, 1846) DLB-57

What's Really Wrong With Bestseller Lists .. Y-84

Wheatley, Dennis Yates 1897-1977 ....DLB-77

Wheatley, Phillis circa 1754-1784.....DLB-31, 50

Wheeler, Anna Doyle 1785-1848?......DLB-158

Wheeler, Charles Stearns 1816-1843...DLB-1, 223

Wheeler, Monroe 1900-1988.............DLB-4

Wheelock, John Hall 1886-1978 ....DLB-45

Wheelwright, J. B. 1897-1940............DLB-45

Wheelwright, John circa 1592-1679......DLB-24

Whetstone, George 1550-1587.........DLB-136

Whetstone, Colonel Pete (see Noland, C. F. M.)

Whicher, Stephen E. 1915-1961 ....DLB-111

Whipple, Edwin Percy 1819-1886......DLB-1, 64

Whitaker, Alexander 1585-1617 ....DLB-24

Whitaker, Daniel K. 1801-1881........DLB-73

Whitcher, Frances Miriam
  1812-1852 ....DLB-11, 202

White, Andrew 1579-1656.............DLB-24

White, Andrew Dickson 1832-1918 ......DLB-47

White, E. B. 1899-1985 ....DLB-11, 22

White, Edgar B. 1947- DLB-38

White, Edmund 1940- DLB-227

White, Ethel Lina 1887-1944 ....DLB-77

White, Henry Kirke 1785-1806 ....DLB-96

White, Horace 1834-1916 ....DLB-23

White, Phyllis Dorothy James (see James, P. D.)

White, Richard Grant 1821-1885 ....DLB-64

White, T. H. 1906-1964 ....DLB-160

White, Walter 1893-1955 ....DLB-51

White, William, and Company DLB-49

White, William Allen 1868-1944.......DLB-9, 25

White, William Anthony Parker
  (see Boucher, Anthony)

White, William Hale (see Rutherford, Mark)

Whitechurch, Victor L. 1868-1933 ....DLB-70

Whitehead, Alfred North 1861-1947.....DLB-100

Whitehead, James 1936- Y-81

Whitehead, William 1715-1785 ......DLB-84, 109

Whitfield, James Monroe 1822-1871 .....DLB-50

Whitfield, Raoul 1898-1945............DLB-226

Whitgift, John circa 1533-1604 ....DLB-132

Whiting, John 1917-1963 ....DLB-13

Whiting, Samuel 1597-1679 ....DLB-24

Whitlock, Brand 1869-1934............DLB-12

Whitman, Albert, and Company........DLB-46

Whitman, Albery Allson 1851-1901 ......DLB-50

Whitman, Alden 1913-1990............. Y-91

Whitman, Sarah Helen (Power)
  1803-1878 ....DLB-1

Whitman, Walt 1819-1892 ....DLB-3, 64, 224

Whitman Publishing Company..........DLB-46

Whitney, Geoffrey 1548 or 1552?-1601 ..DLB-136

Whitney, Isabella flourished 1566-1573...DLB-136

Whitney, John Hay 1904-1982 ....DLB-127

Whittemore, Reed 1919-1995 ....DLB-5

Whittier, John Greenleaf 1807-1892........DLB-1

Whittlesey House DLB-46

Who Runs American Literature? Y-94

Whose *Ulysses?* The Function of Editing Y-97

Wicomb, Zoë 1948- DLB-225

Wideman, John Edgar 1941- DLB-33, 143

Widener, Harry Elkins 1885-1912.......DLB-140

Wiebe, Rudy 1934- DLB-60

Wiechert, Ernst 1887-1950.............DLB-56

Wied, Martina 1882-1957 ....DLB-85

Wiehe, Evelyn May Clowes (see Mordaunt, Elinor)

Wieland, Christoph Martin 1733-1813 ....DLB-97

Wienbarg, Ludolf 1802-1872...........DLB-133

Wieners, John 1934- DLB-16

Wier, Ester 1910- DLB-52

Wiesel, Elie 1928- DLB-83; Y-86, Y-87

Wiggin, Kate Douglas 1856-1923 ....DLB-42

Wigglesworth, Michael 1631-1705.......DLB-24

Wilberforce, William 1759-1833 ....DLB-158

Wilbrandt, Adolf 1837-1911...........DLB-129

Wilbur, Richard 1921- DLB-5, 169

Wild, Peter 1940- DLB-5

Wilde, Lady Jane Francesca Elgee
  1821?-1896 ....DLB-199

Wilde, Oscar
  1854-1900 ...DLB-10, 19, 34, 57, 141, 156, 190

  "The Critic as Artist" (1891) DLB-57

  From "The Decay of Lying" (1889).....DLB-18

  "The English Renaissance of
    Art" (1908) DLB-35

  "L'Envoi" (1882) DLB-35

Wilde, Richard Henry 1789-1847 ......DLB-3, 59

Wilde, W. A., Company DLB-49

Wilder, Billy 1906- DLB-26

Wilder, Laura Ingalls 1867-1957 ....DLB-22

Wilder, Thornton 1897-1975 ..... DLB-4, 7, 9, 228

  Thornton Wilder Centenary at Yale Y-97

Wildgans, Anton 1881-1932 ....DLB-118

Wiley, Bell Irvin 1906-1980.............DLB-17

Wiley, John, and Sons.................DLB-49

Wilhelm, Kate 1928- DLB-8

Wilkes, Charles 1798-1877.............DLB-183

Wilkes, George 1817-1885.............DLB-79

Wilkinson, Anne 1910-1961 ....DLB-88

Wilkinson, Eliza Yonge
  1757-circa 1813 ....DLB-200

Wilkinson, Sylvia 1940- Y-86

Wilkinson, William Cleaver 1833-1920 ...DLB-71

Willard, Barbara 1909-1994 ....DLB-161

Willard, Frances E. 1839-1898 ....DLB-221

Willard, L. [publishing house] DLB-49

Willard, Nancy 1936- DLB-5, 52

Willard, Samuel 1640-1707 ....DLB-24

Willeford, Charles 1919-1988 ....DLB-226

William of Auvergne 1190-1249 ....DLB-115

William of Conches
  circa 1090-circa 1154...............DLB-115

William of Ockham circa 1285-1347.....DLB-115

William of Sherwood
  1200/1205-1266/1271 ....DLB-115

The William Chavrat American Fiction Collection
  at the Ohio State University Libraries ... Y-92

Williams, A., and Company DLB-49

Williams, Ben Ames 1889-1953........DLB-102

Williams, C. K. 1936- DLB-5

Williams, Chancellor 1905- DLB-76

Williams, Charles 1886-1945....... DLB-100, 153

Williams, Denis 1923-1998 ....DLB-117

Williams, Emlyn 1905- DLB-10, 77

Williams, Garth 1912-1996 ....DLB-22

Williams, George Washington
  1849-1891 ....DLB-47

Williams, Heathcote 1941- DLB-13

Williams, Helen Maria 1761-1827 ....DLB-158

Williams, Hugo 1942- DLB-40

Williams, Isaac 1802-1865.............DLB-32

Williams, Joan 1928- DLB-6

Williams, John A. 1925- DLB-2, 33

Williams, John E. 1922-1994 .... DLB-6

Williams, Jonathan 1929- DLB-5

Williams, Miller 1930- DLB-105

Williams, Nigel 1948- DLB-231

Williams, Raymond 1921- DLB-14, 231

Williams, Roger circa 1603-1683 .... DLB-24

Williams, Rowland 1817-1870.......... DLB-184

Williams, Samm-Art 1946- DLB-38

Williams, Sherley Anne 1944-1999 ...... DLB-41

Williams, T. Harry 1909-1979 .... DLB-17

Williams, Tennessee
1911-1983............. DLB-7; Y-83; DS-4

Williams, Terry Tempest 1955- DLB-206

Williams, Ursula Moray 1911- DLB-160

Williams, Valentine 1883-1946 .... DLB-77

Williams, William Appleman 1921- DLB-17

Williams, William Carlos
1883-1963 .... DLB-4, 16, 54, 86

Williams, Wirt 1921- DLB-6

Williams Brothers................... DLB-49

Williamson, Henry 1895-1977 .... DLB-191

Williamson, Jack 1908- DLB-8

Willingham, Calder Baynard, Jr.
1922-1995 .... DLB-2, 44

Williram of Ebersberg circa 1020-1085 .. DLB-148

Willis, Nathaniel Parker
1806-1867......DLB-3, 59, 73, 74, 183; DS-13

Willkomm, Ernst 1810-1886 .... DLB-133

Willumsen, Dorrit 1940- DLB-214

Wilmer, Clive 1945- DLB-40

Wilson, A. N. 1950- DLB-14, 155, 194

Wilson, Angus 1913-1991 ..... DLB-15, 139, 155

Wilson, Arthur 1595-1652 .... DLB-58

Wilson, August 1945- DLB-228

Wilson, Augusta Jane Evans 1835-1909 ... DLB-42

Wilson, Colin 1931- DLB-14, 194

Wilson, Edmund 1895-1972............ DLB-63

Wilson, Effingham [publishing house] ... DLB-154

Wilson, Ethel 1888-1980 .... DLB-68

Wilson, F. P. 1889-1963 .... DLB-201

Wilson, Harriet E. Adams 1828?-1863?... DLB-50

Wilson, Harry Leon 1867-1939 .... DLB-9

Wilson, John 1588-1667 .... DLB-24

Wilson, John 1785-1854 .... DLB-110

Wilson, John Dover 1881-1969 .... DLB-201

Wilson, Lanford 1937- DLB-7

Wilson, Margaret 1882-1973 .... DLB-9

Wilson, Michael 1914-1978 .... DLB-44

Wilson, Mona 1872-1954 .... DLB-149

Wilson, Robley 1930- DLB-218

Wilson, Romer 1891-1930 .... DLB-191

Wilson, Thomas 1523 or 1524-1581 .... DLB-132

Wilson, Woodrow 1856-1924 .... DLB-47

Wimsatt, William K., Jr. 1907-1975 ..... DLB-63

Winchell, Walter 1897-1972 .... DLB-29

Winchester, J. [publishing house] DLB-49

Winckelmann, Johann Joachim
1717-1768 .... DLB-97

Winckler, Paul 1630-1686 .... DLB-164

Wind, Herbert Warren 1916- DLB-171

Windet, John [publishing house] DLB-170

Windham, Donald 1920- DLB-6

Wing, Donald Goddard 1904-1972 ..... DLB-187

Wing, John M. 1844-1917 .... DLB-187

Wingate, Allan [publishing house] DLB-112

Winnemucca, Sarah 1844-1921 ....DLB-175

Winnifrith, Tom 1938- DLB-155

Winning an Edgar Y-98

Winsloe, Christa 1888-1944........... DLB-124

Winslow, Anna Green 1759-1780....... DLB-200

Winsor, Justin 1831-1897 .... DLB-47

John C. Winston Company DLB-49

Winters, Yvor 1900-1968.............. DLB-48

Winterson, Jeanette 1959- DLB-207

Winthrop, John 1588-1649.......... DLB-24, 30

Winthrop, John, Jr. 1606-1676 .... DLB-24

Winthrop, Margaret Tyndal 1591-1647.. DLB-200

Winthrop, Theodore 1828-1861 .... DLB-202

Wirt, William 1772-1834 .... DLB-37

Wise, John 1652-1725................. DLB-24

Wise, Thomas James 1859-1937........ DLB-184

Wiseman, Adele 1928- DLB-88

Wishart and Company............... DLB-112

Wisner, George 1812-1849............. DLB-43

Wister, Owen 1860-1938 ....DLB-9, 78, 186

Wister, Sarah 1761-1804.............. DLB-200

Wither, George 1588-1667 .... DLB-121

Witherspoon, John 1723-1794.......... DLB-31

Withrow, William Henry 1839-1908..... DLB-99

Witkacy (see Witkiewicz, Stanisław Ignacy)

Witkiewicz, Stanisław Ignacy
1885-1939 .... DLB-215

Wittig, Monique 1935- DLB-83

Wodehouse, P. G. 1881-1975........ DLB-34, 162

Wohmann, Gabriele 1932- DLB-75

Woiwode, Larry 1941- DLB-6

Wolcot, John 1738-1819.............. DLB-109

Wolcott, Roger 1679-1767 .... DLB-24

Wolf, Christa 1929- DLB-75

Wolf, Friedrich 1888-1953 .... DLB-124

Wolfe, Gene 1931- DLB-8

Wolfe, John [publishing house]........DLB-170

Wolfe, Reyner (Reginald)
[publishing house] DLB-170

Wolfe, Thomas 1900-1938
........DLB-9, 102, 229; Y-85; DS-2, DS-16

The Thomas Wolfe Collection at the University
of North Carolina at Chapel Hill........ Y-97

Fire at Thomas Wolfe Memorial Y-98

The Thomas Wolfe Society Y-97

Wolfe, Tom 1931- DLB-152, 185

Wolfenstein, Martha 1869-1906........ DLB-221

Wolff, Helen 1906-1994................. Y-94

Wolff, Tobias 1945- DLB-130

Wolfram von Eschenbach
circa 1170-after 1220 .... DLB-138

Wolfram von Eschenbach's Parzival:
Prologue and Book 3 .... DLB-138

Wolker, Jiří 1900-1924............. DLB-215

Wollstonecraft, Mary
1759-1797 ....DLB-39, 104, 158

Wondratschek, Wolf 1943- DLB-75

Wood, Anthony à 1632-1695.......... DLB-213

Wood, Benjamin 1820-1900............ DLB-23

Wood, Charles 1932- DLB-13

Wood, Mrs. Henry 1814-1887 .... DLB-18

Wood, Joanna E. 1867-1927 .... DLB-92

Wood, Sally Sayward Barrell Keating
1759-1855.................... DLB-200

Wood, Samuel [publishing house] DLB-49

Wood, William ?-? DLB-24

The Charles Wood Affair:
A Playwright Revived................ Y-83

Woodberry, George Edward
1855-1930 ....DLB-71, 103

Woodbridge, Benjamin 1622-1684....... DLB-24

Woodcock, George 1912-1995.......... DLB-88

Woodhull, Victoria C. 1838-1927 .... DLB-79

Woodmason, Charles circa 1720-?....... DLB-31

Woodress, Jr., James Leslie 1916- DLB-111

Woodson, Carter G. 1875-1950.........DLB-17

Woodward, C. Vann 1908-1999 ....DLB-17

Woodward, Stanley 1895-1965 ....DLB-171

Wooler, Thomas 1785 or 1786-1853 .... DLB-158

Woolf, David (see Maddow, Ben)

Woolf, Leonard 1880-1969 ......DLB-100; DS-10

Woolf, Virginia
1882-1941 ....DLB-36, 100, 162; DS-10

Woolf, Virginia, "The New Biography," New York
Herald Tribune, 30 October 1927..... DLB-149

Woollcott, Alexander 1887-1943 .... DLB-29

Woolman, John 1720-1772 .... DLB-31

Woolner, Thomas 1825-1892 .... DLB-35

Woolrich, Cornell 1903-1968.......... DLB-226

Woolsey, Sarah Chauncy 1835-1905..... DLB-42

Woolson, Constance Fenimore
1840-1894 ....DLB-12, 74, 189, 221

Worcester, Joseph Emerson 1784-1865 .... DLB-1

Worde, Wynkyn de [publishing house]...DLB-170

Wordsworth, Christopher 1807-1885.... DLB-166

Wordsworth, Dorothy 1771-1855 ......DLB-107

Wordsworth, Elizabeth 1840-1932....... DLB-98

Wordsworth, William 1770-1850.....DLB-93, 107

Workman, Fanny Bullock 1859-1925 ... DLB-189

The Works of the Rev. John Witherspoon
(1800-1801) [excerpts] DLB-31

A World Chronology of Important Science
Fiction Works (1818-1979).......... DLB-8

World Publishing Company DLB-46

World War II Writers Symposium at the University
   of South Carolina, 12–14 April 1995 .... Y-95

Worthington, R., and Company DLB-49

Wotton, Sir Henry 1568-1639..........DLB-121

Wouk, Herman 1915- Y-82

Wreford, James 1915- DLB-88

Wren, Sir Christopher 1632-1723 ....DLB-213

Wren, Percival Christopher 1885-1941...DLB-153

Wrenn, John Henry 1841-1911........DLB-140

Wright, C. D. 1949- DLB-120

Wright, Charles 1935- DLB-165; Y-82

Wright, Charles Stevenson 1932- DLB-33

Wright, Frances 1795-1852 ....DLB-73

Wright, Harold Bell 1872-1944 ....DLB-9

Wright, James 1927-1980...........DLB-5, 169

Wright, Jay 1935- DLB-41

Wright, Louis B. 1899-1984 ....DLB-17

Wright, Richard 1908-1960.... DLB-76, 102; DS-2

Wright, Richard B. 1937- DLB-53

Wright, Sarah Elizabeth 1928- DLB-33

Wright, Willard Huntington ("S. S. Van Dine")
   1888-1939 ....DS-16

Writers and Politics: 1871-1918,
   by Ronald Gray DLB-66

Writers and their Copyright Holders:
   the WATCH Project................ Y-94

Writers' Forum Y-85

Writing for the Theatre,
   by Harold Pinter.................DLB-13

Wroth, Lawrence C. 1884-1970........DLB-187

Wroth, Lady Mary 1587-1653..........DLB-121

Wurlitzer, Rudolph 1937- DLB-173

Wyatt, Sir Thomas circa 1503-1542 .....DLB-132

Wycherley, William 1641-1715 ....DLB-80

Wyclif, John
   circa 1335-31 December 1384......DLB-146

Wyeth, N. C. 1882-1945 ....DLB-188; DS-16

Wylie, Elinor 1885-1928 ....DLB-9, 45

Wylie, Philip 1902-1971................DLB-9

Wyllie, John Cook 1908-1968..........DLB-140

Wyman, Lillie Buffum Chace
   1847-1929 ....DLB-202

Wymark, Olwen 1934- DLB-233

Wynne-Tyson, Esmé 1898-1972 ....DLB-191

X

Xenophon circa 430 B.C.-circa 356 B.C. DLB-176

Y

Yasuoka Shōtarō 1920- DLB-182

Yates, Dornford 1885-1960 .... DLB-77, 153

Yates, J. Michael 1938- DLB-60

Yates, Richard 1926-1992 . DLB-2, 234; Y-81, Y-92

Yau, John 1950- DLB-234

Yavorov, Peyo 1878-1914 ....DLB-147

The Year in Book Publishing............. Y-86

The Year in Book Reviewing and the Literary
   Situation Y-98

The Year in British Drama Y-99

The Year in British Fiction Y-99

The Year in Children's
   Books Y-92–Y-96, Y-98, Y-99

The Year in Children's Literature Y-97

The Year in Drama Y-82-Y-85, Y-87–Y-96

The Year in Fiction ...Y-84–Y-86, Y-89, Y-94–Y-99

The Year in Fiction: A Biased View Y-83

The Year in Literary Biography Y-83–Y-98

The Year in Literary Theory.........Y-92–Y-93

The Year in London Theatre Y-92

The Year in the Novel......Y-87, Y-88, Y-90–Y-93

The Year in Poetry Y-83–Y-92, Y-94–Y-99

The Year in Short Stories Y-87

The Year in the Short Story...... Y-88, Y-90–Y-93

The Year in Texas Literature Y-98

The Year's Work in American Poetry....... Y-82

The Year's Work in Fiction: A Survey Y-82

Yearsley, Ann 1753-1806.............DLB-109

Yeats, William Butler
   1865-1939 .... DLB-10, 19, 98, 156

Yep, Laurence 1948- DLB-52

Yerby, Frank 1916-1991 ....DLB-76

Yezierska, Anzia 1880-1970 ....DLB-28, 221

Yolen, Jane 1939- DLB-52

Yonge, Charlotte Mary
   1823-1901 ....DLB-18, 163

The York Cycle
   circa 1376-circa 1569.............DLB-146

A Yorkshire Tragedy DLB-58

Yoseloff, Thomas [publishing house]......DLB-46

Young, Al 1939- DLB-33

Young, Arthur 1741-1820 ....DLB-158

Young, Dick 1917 or 1918 - 1987 ...... DLB-171

Young, Edward 1683-1765 ....DLB-95

Young, Francis Brett 1884-1954 ....DLB-191

Young, Gavin 1928- DLB-204

Young, Stark 1881-1963 ...... DLB-9, 102; DS-16

Young, Waldeman 1880-1938..........DLB-26

Young, William
   publishing house] DLB-49

Young Bear, Ray A. 1950- DLB-175

Yourcenar, Marguerite
   1903-1987 .... DLB-72; Y-88

"You've Never Had It So Good," Gusted by
   "Winds of Change": British Fiction in the
   1950s, 1960s, and After............DLB-14

Yovkov, Yordan
   1880-1937 ....DLB-147

Z

Zachariä, Friedrich Wilhelm 1726-1777 ....DLB-97

Zagajewski, Adam 1945- DLB-232

Zagoskin, Mikhail Nikolaevich
   1789-1852 ....DLB-198

Zajc, Dane 1929- DLB-181

Zālīte, Māra 1952- DLB-232

Zamora, Bernice 1938- DLB-82

Zand, Herbert 1923-1970...............DLB-85

Zangwill, Israel 1864-1926...... DLB-10, 135, 197

Zanzotto, Andrea 1921- DLB-128

Zapata Olivella, Manuel 1920- DLB-113

Zebra Books DLB-46

Zebrowski, George 1945- DLB-8

Zech, Paul 1881-1946 ....DLB-56

Zeidner, Lisa 1955- DLB-120

Zeidonis, Imants 1933- DLB-232

Zeimi (Kanze Motokiyo) 1363-1443 .....DLB-203

Zelazny, Roger 1937-1995 ....DLB-8

Zenger, John Peter 1697-1746 ....DLB-24, 43

Zepheria.........................DLB-172

Zesen, Philipp von 1619-1689 ....DLB-164

Zhukovsky, Vasilii Andreevich
   1783-1852 ....DLB-205

Zieber, G. B., and Company DLB-49

Zieroth, Dale 1946- DLB-60

Zigler und Kliphausen, Heinrich
   Anshelm von 1663-1697 ....DLB-168

Zimmer, Paul 1934- DLB-5

Zinberg, Len
   (see Lacy, Ed)

Zindel, Paul 1936- DLB-7, 52

Zingref, Julius Wilhelm 1591-1635 ......DLB-164

Zinnes, Harriet 1919- DLB-193

Zinzendorf, Nikolaus Ludwig von
   1700-1760 ....DLB-168

Zitkala-Ša 1876-1938 ....DLB-175

Zīverts, Mārtiņš 1903-1990 ....DLB-220

Zola, Emile 1840-1902...............DLB-123

Zolla, Elémire 1926- DLB-196

Zolotow, Charlotte 1915- DLB-52

Zschokke, Heinrich 1771-1848...........DLB-94

Zubly, John Joachim 1724-1781 ....DLB-31

Zu-Bolton II, Ahmos 1936- DLB-41

Zuckmayer, Carl 1896-1977 ....DLB-56, 124

Zukofsky, Louis 1904-1978 ....DLB-5, 165

Zupan, Vitomil 1914-1987............DLB-181

Župančič, Oton 1878-1949.............DLB-147

zur Mühlen, Hermynia
   1883-1951 ....DLB-56

Zweig, Arnold 1887-1968..............DLB-66

Zweig, Stefan 1881-1942 ....DLB-81, 118

Cumulative Index